CHILDREN OF GOD IN THE WORLD

Paul O'Callaghan

CHILDREN OF GOD IN THE WORLD

An Introduction to Theological

Anthropology

The Catholic University of America Press

Washington, D.C.

Originally published in Italian as *Figli di Dio nel mondo: Trattato di antropologia teologica* (Rome: Edusc, 2013). Copyright © 2013 Paul O'Callaghan.

Library of Congress Cataloging-in-Publication Data

Names: O'Callaghan, Paul, 1956– author.

Title: Children of God in the world : an introduction to theological anthropology / Paul O'Callaghan.

Other titles: Figli di Dio nel mondo. English

Description: Washington, D.C. : The Catholic University of America Press, 2016. | Includes bibliographical references and index.

Identifiers: LCCN 2016036431 | ISBN 9780813229003 (pbk. : alk. paper)

Subjects: LCSH: Theological anthropology—Christianity.

Classification: LCC BT701.3 .O23 2016 | DDC 233—dc23

LC record available at https://lccn.loc.gov/2016036431

CONTENTS

PART 4. CHRISTIAN ANTHROPOLOGY

PRINCIPAL ABBREVIATIONS

BDAG	*A Greek-English Lexicon of the New Testament and Other Early Christian Literature* (ed. Bauer et al.)
CCC	*Catechism of the Catholic Church*
COH	*Christ Our Hope: An Introduction to Eschatology* (O'Callaghan)
DH	*Enchiridion symbolorum, definitionum et declarationum de rebus fidei et morum* (ed. Denzinger and Hünermann)
DISF	*Dizionario Interdisciplinare di Scienza e Fede* (ed. Tanzella-Nitti and Strumìa)
DPL	*Dictionary of Paul and His Letters* (ed. Hawthorne et al.)
DTC	*Dictionnaire de théologie catholique* (ed. Vacant et al.)
GS	*Gaudium et Spes* (Vatican Council II)
JDJ	*Joint Declaration on the Doctrine of Justification* (Lutheran World Federation and the Roman Catholic Church)
LG	*Lumen Gentium* (Vatican Council II)
LS	*Laudato Si'* (Pope Francis)
NIDNTTE	*New International Dictionary of New Testament Theology and Exegesis* (ed. Silva)
PG	*Patrologiae cursus completus, series graeca* (ed. Migne)
PL	*Patrologiae cursus completus, series latina* (ed. Migne)
SCG	*Summa contra Gentiles* (Thomas Aquinas)
S.Th.	*Summa Theologiae* (Thomas Aquinas)
TDNT	*Theological Dictionary of the New Testament* (ed. Kittel et al.)
TDOT	*Theological Dictionary of the Old Testament* (ed. Botterweck et al.)
WA	*Dr Martin Luthers Werke: Schriften* (M. Luther)
WBC	*Word Biblical Commentary* (ed. Metzger et al.)

CHILDREN OF GOD IN THE WORLD

INTRODUCTION

This treatise on theological anthropology works off of five presuppositions. The first is that *it is based on a search for unity and integrity*. As we inquire into human identity, we commonly experience a wearying sense of complexity and incertitude. However, this does not mean that our explanation of human nature and of the human person need be involved or complicated. In fact, anthropology seeks above all a once-off, simple, unitary, integrated explanation of human identity. The search for truth, in fact, is always a search for unity, for simplicity, for harmony, for coherence. In other words, in order to do anthropology it is not enough to gather a mass of disconnected "information" on what it means to be human. What we really seek is a single word that gives meaning to the whole. Cardinal Newman, speaking of academic life, spoke of the need for the intellect to be "trained and formed to have a connected view or grasp of things."[1] The modern period has made an enormous effort, to the point of exhaustion, in search of this unique response, this definitive, simple word, this integral explanation. The effort has not paid off generously. In 1929 the philosopher Martin Heidegger observed:

No other epoch has accumulated so great and so varied a store of knowledge concerning man as the present one. No other epoch has succeeded in presenting its knowledge of man so forcibly and so captivatingly as ours, and no other has succeeded in making this knowledge so quickly and so easily accessible. But also, no epoch is less sure of its knowledge of what man is than the present one. In no other epoch has man appeared so mysterious as in ours.[2]

Postmodern philosophy has only confirmed Heidegger's diagnosis.[3] Postmodernism is characterized, according to Jean-François Lyotard, by a generalized skepticism

---

1. J. H. Newman, *The Idea of a University, Defined and Illustrated* (London: Longmans, Green, 1925), xvii. The text, fruit of a series of conferences given by Newman at University College, Dublin, of which he was the first rector, was first published in 1852.

2. M. Heidegger, *Kant and the Problem of Metaphysics* (Bloomington: Indiana University Press, 1962), 216, citing an important work published a year earlier by M. Scheler, *Die Stellung des Menschen im Kosmos* (Darmstadt: Reichl, 1928), 13f. Scheler's work is considered the first work published, strictly speaking, on "philosophical anthropology" (see chapter 1, note 59). For an English translation, see *The Human Place in the Cosmos* (Evanston, Ill.: Northwestern University Press, 2009).

3. See I. Sanna, *L'antropologia cristiana tra modernità e postmodernità* (Brescia: Queriniana, 2001).

in respect of what he calls "metanarratives," that is, all-encompassing and integrating explanations of reality as a whole.[4] Jacques Derrida speaks of the phenomenon of "dissemination," that is, the dispersion and decomposition of human thought.[5] Meanwhile, Gianni Vattimo speaks of "weak thought" (*pensiero debole*), a new way of thinking about reality, one of decidedly modest pretensions.[6] In the same direction, Zygmunt Bauman uses the term "liquid modernity" to describe society and culture that is in a constant state of flux.[7] Yet we must admit that this impoverished and sterile approach is the "realistic" end product of the failure of modern anthropology. Philosophers and scientists, in spite of the extraordinary effort they have made to understand human nature, have been simply unable to provide a unitary explanation of a wide variety of unresolved human polarities (what Romano Guardini calls "polar oppositions").[8] Examples include the polarity between soul or spirit and body, between interiority and exteriority, between nature and history, between freedom and determinism, between sociality and individuality, and between woman and man, person and nature, mortality and immortality, mundaneness and transcendence—that is, in one way or another, between the aspiration to infinitude that is present in all humans and their concomitant experience of finitude (on these polarities, see the first chapter, second section).

Modern thought, in its varied and often rationalistic attempts to resolve these polarities, to overcome with definitive Cartesian clarity the discrepancies present in human life, has preferred for the most part to exclude or recalibrate one or other of the poles in question, considering it the product of a false or alienated view of life. Different anthropologies have developed over recent centuries, taking their cues from the thought of Plato, Aristotle, Spinoza, and Marx, from paleontologists, ethnologists, psychologists, sociologists, sociobiologists, and neurobiologists.[9] These anthropologies are typified more by what they do not say than by what they do, by what they exclude a priori than by what they affirm. Herbert Marcuse is emblematic of this regard in his 1960s work *One-Dimensional Man*.[10] Thus, from a naïve optimism that has marked the modern period, we have passed smoothly and unawares to the epistemological realism (or pessimism) of the postmodern. Postmodern thinkers realize that modern thought, in attempting to comprehend the entire human being starting from itself, has lost its bearings. In real terms they recognize that humans are living, mysterious, free, elusive beings, impossible to comprehend, inserted within a vast array of complex personal narratives and relationships, their behavior unforeseeable. Postmodern authors realize,

---

4. "Simplifying somewhat, we can consider 'postmodern' all human incredulousness before metanarratives. Doubtless this is an effect of scientific progress, which involves the need for incredulousness." J.-F. Lyotard, *The Postmodern Condition: A Report on Knowledge* (Minneapolis: University of Minnesota Press, 1999), 5.

5. See J. Derrida, *La dissémination* (Paris: Seuil, 1972). Translated into English as *Dissemination* (London: Athlone Press, 1997).

6. See G. Vattimo and P. A. Rovatti, eds., *Il pensiero debole*, 2nd ed. (Milan: Feltrinelli, 1984), translated into English as *Weak Thought* (Albany: State University of New York Press, 2012).

7. See Z. Bauman, *Liquid Modernity* (Cambridge: Polity Press, 2000).

8. On the question of "polar opposition" in Guardini, see A. Granados Temes, *Persona y experiencia religiosa en Romano Guardini* (Rome: Pontificia Università della Santa Croce, 1997), 53–75.

9. See chapter 2, notes 56ff. and corresponding text; chapter 19, notes 119ff. and corresponding text.

10. See H. Marcuse, *One-Dimensional Man: Studies in the Ideology of Advanced Industrial Society* (Boston: Beacon Press, 1968).

perhaps without admitting it, that humans, when they attempt to understand reality without having recourse to an exterior or transcendent perspective (as a child of God, made in the image and likeness of God, etc.), become a growing enigma to themselves.

According to the Christian view of reality, all the polarities that make up the richness of human life can and should be systematically accepted, incorporated, and integrated for the simple reason that all are wanted by God; all form part of his original and simple design.[11] Benedict XVI insisted on this point at the very inauguration of his pontificate.[12] Pope Francis, in his encyclical *Laudato Si'*, speaks repeatedly of an "integral ecology" that takes into account the entirety of human reality.[13] Because the human being is deeply unitary, anthropology would be a failure should it be incapable of offering a single, straightforward explanation of human life. This is the fundamental challenge a Christian anthropology must face. Pope Benedict taught that "the faith is not a parallel world of feelings that we can still afford to hold on to, rather it is the key that encompasses everything, gives it meaning, interprets it and also provides its inner ethical orientation: making clear that it is to be understood and lived as tending towards God and proceeding from God."[14] In this way, theological reflection is meant to provide a way toward unity and integration among the sciences, avoiding the trap of hyperspecialization.[15]

11. "No other, mythical or religio-philosophical, anthropology can attain a satisfactory idea of man, an idea that integrates all the elements, but the Christian one." Hans Urs von Balthasar, *Theo-Drama*, vol. 2, *Dramatis Personae: Man in God* (San Francisco: Ignatius, 1990), 343.

12. "If we let Christ into our lives, we lose nothing, nothing, absolutely nothing of what makes life free, beautiful and great. No! Only in this friendship are the doors of life opened wide. Only in this friendship is the great potential of human existence truly revealed. Only in this friendship do we experience beauty and liberation. And so, today, with great strength and great conviction, on the basis of long personal experience of life, I say to you, dear young people: Do not be afraid of Christ! He takes nothing away, and he gives you everything. When we give ourselves to him, we receive a hundredfold in return." Benedict XVI, *Discourse for the Beginning of the Petrine Ministry*, homily, St. Peter's Square, April 24, 2005. In Francis and Benedict XVI, *Lumen Fidei*, Encyclical Letter, June 29, 2013, it is observed that John Henry Newman "listed among the characteristic notes for distinguishing the continuity of doctrine over time its power to assimilate everything that it meets in the various settings in which it becomes present and in the diverse cultures which it encounters, purifying all things and bringing them to their finest expression" (par. 48).

13. See Francis, *Laudato Si*, Encyclical Letter, May 24, 2015 [hereafter "*LS*"], pars. 62, 124, and 137–62.

14. Pope Benedict XVI, discourse to seminarians in Freiburg, September 24, 2011 (full text provided on vatican.va). In the same discourse, Benedict had the following to say: "Our world today is a rationalist and thoroughly scientific world, albeit often somewhat pseudo-scientific. But this scientific spirit, this spirit of understanding, explaining, know-how, rejection of the irrational, is dominant in our time. There is a good side to this, even if it often conceals much arrogance and nonsense. *The faith is not a parallel world of feelings that we can still afford to hold on to, rather it is the key that encompasses everything, gives it meaning, interprets it and also provides its inner ethical orientation:* making clear that it is to be understood and lived as tending towards God and proceeding from God. Therefore it is important to be informed and to understand, to have an open mind, to learn. Naturally in twenty years' time, some quite different philosophical theories will be fashionable from those of today: when I think what counted as the highest, most modern philosophical fashion in our day, and how totally forgotten it is now.... Still, learning these things is not in vain, for there will be some enduring insights among them. And most of all, this is how we learn to judge, to think through an idea—and to do so critically—and to ensure that in this thinking the light of God will serve to enlighten us and will not be extinguished. Studying is essential: only thus can we stand firm in these times and proclaim within them the reason for our faith. And it is essential that we study critically—because we know that tomorrow someone else will have something else to say—while being alert, open and humble as we study, so that our studying is always with the Lord, before the Lord, and for him" (emphasis added).

15. Pope Francis observes that "dialogue among the various sciences is likewise needed, since each can

Still, two important observations need to be made with respect to this fundamental presupposition of *the search for unity and integrity*. First, of the extraordinary variety of elements that make up human life, one must be systematically excluded from the Christian view: sin, the willful exclusion of God from human life. Sin destroys humans in that it breaks up the relationships that bind them to God, to one another, to themselves, and to creation as a whole.[16] Thus the "sin factor" should be kept in mind at every stage throughout this study as a malignant power capable of destroying humans in every possible way, of dehumanizing them; at heart, in fact, the presence sin is capable of deforming all anthropological reflection.

The second observation is as follows. The philosopher Isaiah Berlin (in an essay on Tolstoy) suggested that intellectuals are like foxes or hedgehogs. His point of departure for this image is the poem of the Greek poet Archilochus, who stated that "the fox knows many things, but the hedgehog knows only one great thing."[17] By implication, Berlin observes, some philosophers and thinkers may be considered like hedgehogs because they have an ample and unitary vision within which they fit everything else. Others, however, are like foxes in that they are very erudite and smart and have a wide variety of interests, but they do not manage to combine all their knowledge into a single, simple, harmonic whole. Berlin suggests that Tolstoy had the boundless interests of the fox yet considered the hedgehogs superior beings. Looking upon the complexity of human life, therefore, the Russian novelist is afflicted, Berlin suggests, because "he has a pained faith that moves towards a complete and serene view of all things in which everything is resolved, all doubts are eliminated, peace and understanding is eventually obtained."[18]

This observation reminds us that, as Christian believers, in our search for an integral understanding of the world and human life, we are convinced that while on earth we will never obtain a complete, single, integral, simple, definitive understanding of things. That is so because humans themselves are pilgrims on the road to eschatological fullness.[19] As J.-B. Metz observed, "eschatological reserve" and the provisionality that derives from it is an essential mark of the Christian message and of theological reflection.[20]

The second presupposition is that *the human being is eccentric* in that he lives and exists, he understands and develops himself, always in the context of relationship, of the other.[21] The eccentric character of humans may be seen in the fact that we live and

tend to become enclosed in its own language, while specialization leads to a certain isolation and the absolutization of its own field of knowledge" (*LS*, par. 201). On this issue, see P. O'Callaghan, "The Role of Theology in the Promotion of a Pluralistic University," *PATH* 14 (2015): 69–93.

16. See *LS*, par. 66.

17. See I. Berlin, *The Hedgehog and the Fox: An Essay on Tolstoy's View of History* (New York: Simon and Schuster, 1953), 1.

18. Ibid., 79.

19. See note 21 below.

20. See J. B. Metz, *Zur Theologie der Welt* (Mainz: Grünewald, 1968), 99. Translated into English as *Theology of the World* (New York: Herder and Herder, 1971).

21. On the eccentric character of the human being, see, for example, W. Pannenberg, *Anthropology in a Theological Perspective* (Edinburgh: T. and T. Clark, 1985), esp. 56–70. In confirmation of the value of the "eccentric" in anthropology, we can observe that its opposite—the egocentric—has generally been considered pathological, as something obscure, sterile, and corruptible, something to be excluded. See also H. Plessner,

act within a wide variety of more or less demanding relationships with others (with God, with other humans, with nature) and in the fact that we express ourselves beyond ourselves, in friendship, in art, in music, in literary creation, in conversation. Yet humans are eccentric also because our desire to know ourselves—to do anthropology—is carried out principally in the context of the other, that is, on the basis of an external, transcendent perspective. The term "transcendent" here is not meant to be understood as equivalent to "divine" but rather refers to some reality that goes beyond our personal and immediate subjectivity and experience. In that sense, "eccentric" may be considered equivalent to "objective." As we shall see in the second chapter, every culture, every philosophy or religious vision, possesses a perspective (or various perspectives) of its own, external to humans, in the light of which we act, situate, and understand ourselves. In fact, what gives unity and integrity to any anthropological discourse (in reference to the first presupposition) is the perspective in question.

The presence of such a perspective is verified fully within Christian anthropology. As we shall see, the "transcendent perspective" typical of Christian theology is Jesus Christ in person, the Son of God made man, God's living Word, the one who reveals the eternal love of the Father, a topic we shall deal with in chapter 3. Christ is the living perspective for all anthropology; as John says, "he himself knew what was in man" (Jn 2:25).[22] Vatican Council II's constitution *Gaudium et Spes* says so openly, teaching that "Christ fully reveals man to himself and brings to light his most high calling" (no. 22). Besides, if on the one hand this perspective is offered to humans in Christ as the revelation of the unconditioned love of God for them, on the other hand it must be accepted by humans themselves in faith, a Christologically qualified faith. In this sense, Schönborn speaks of Jesus' "capacity to 'impose' himself."[23]

The third presupposition refers to a central aspect of anthropology, ethics and religion, which is always present at an implicit or explicit level in the life of humans. It is that *humans are beings searching for immortality*. In this treatise, humans are considered as finalized beings, directed toward a future meant to become stable and perpetual.[24] The term "immortality" is used here in the widest possible sense. In effect, the history of philosophy and religion has shown that immortality may be understood in different ways, both individual and collective, indicating at times physical survival; lasting personal reputation through one's family name, children, or works; a life of perpetual contemplation of God; immortality of the human spirit or soul, eternal life, resurrection from the dead; and so on. Humans, whatever they do, however they act, resist disappearance. They invest their best energies in life because they want to leave an ample trace of themselves (we might say of their "spiritual genes") in the world

---

Die Stufen des Organischen und der Mensch: Einleitung in die philosophische Anthropologie, 2nd ed. (Berlin: W. de Gruyter, 1965), 292.

22. Scriptural references are taken from the Revised Standard Version.

23. C. Schönborn, M. Konrad, and H. P. Weber, *God Sent His Son: A Contemporary Christology* (San Francisco: Ignatius Press, 2010), 60.

24. This book on theological anthropology is the second of a trilogy. The first deals with what comes at the end, that is, eschatology, the immortal destiny of humans: P. O'Callaghan, *Christ Our Hope: An Introduction to Eschatology* (Washington D.C.: The Catholic University of America Press, 2011) [hereafter "*COH*"]. Throughout this text it will frequently be seen that the treatise of anthropology must be eschatologically contextualized. The third volume of the trilogy will deal with the theology of creation.

they live in. In doing so they attempt in a way to overcome death, the ultimate enemy. To this may be added the fact that despair, that is, loss of the will to live, is considered in all cultures something pathological, anomalous, improper. Even when attempting to deny all immortality, humans in a sense hold on to it.

The presupposition of immortality is at the very heart of the Christian message (as at that of all religions). In effect, Christ promises humans salvation in God's name, in the most ample and total form possible, and therefore immortality: "I came that they may have life, and have it abundantly" (Jn 10:10). That is, Christ not only brings us to awareness of an already existent, consolidated human immortality (this could be a kind of Gnosticism) but also in person communicates immortality in fullness to believers, above all as God's gift, an eschatological gift: eternal life and the resurrection of the dead at the end of time. The immortality Christ gives humans who believe in him is precisely the immortality of those who share in his own life, those who are coheirs with him, that is, *children of God* by grace. This description is perhaps the one that best describes what a Christian believer becomes through God's grace, and is to be found in the title of this work. Besides, throughout the text we shall pay special attention to (1) the risen Christ (chapter 3), the source of immortal life because he himself is the Immortal One, (2) divine grace (chapters 5–12 and 14–17), the concrete origin of eternal life, (3) divine filiation, which the believer shares with Christ (chapter 13), and (4) the theological virtue of hope (chapter 15, section 4), with which humans obtain their ultimate eschatological end.

What I have just said serves to introduce the *fourth* presupposition: the *Christological priority of theological anthropology*. We have already mentioned Vatican II's statement that "Christ fully reveals man to himself," which will be considered in detail in chapter 3. And this presupposition helps us to appreciate the order in which the content of the work is presented (see the contents).

Classical theological anthropology was divided into two parts, which constituted in real terms two distinct treatises.[25] In the first, called *De Deo creante et elevante*, humans were considered, on the basis of God's act of creation, "made in the image and likeness of God" (Gn 1:26ff.), and therefore as persons composed of body and spirit, elevated to friendship with God, and then subsequently fallen into sin and in need of salvation. In the second part, usually called *De gratia*, humans were considered as receptors of justifying grace, which pardons sin and produces sanctification. That is, the first thing considered is the nature of human beings, which is looked upon in a preponderantly philosophical way while leaving a series of issues on the meaning and purpose of human life unresolved in the hope of a more complete response. This response comes, in effect, at a second stage completely centered on divine grace, in this way completing the picture of Christian theological anthropology.

This scheme has the advantage of a chronological clarity of exposition besides dis-

---

25. On the ordering of the treatise of theological anthropology, see G. Colombo, "Problematicità dell'antropologia teologica," *Vita e pensiero* 54 (1971): 586–95; G. Colzani, "Recenti manuali di Antropologia teologica in lingua italiana e tedesca," *Vivens homo* 3 (1992): 391–407; A. Scola, G. Marengo, and J. Prades López, *La persona umana: Antropologia teologica* (Milan: Jaca Book, 2000), 25–49; F. G. Brambilla, "Antropologia teologica," *Teologia*, edited by G. Barbaglio, G. Bof, and S. Dianich (Cinisello Balsamo: San Paolo, 2002), 72–108; F. G. Brambilla, *Antropologia teologica: Chi è l'uomo perché te ne curi?* (Brescia: Queriniana, 2005).

tinguishing clearly between the order of nature and that of grace. But despite these advantages, this way of focusing theological anthropology has at least two drawbacks. The first drawback consists of giving the impression that the life of grace is superimposed a posteriori on human nature, as if the latter was already more or less complete in its original constitution, leaving aside the presence of sin. In doing so, theological anthropology in the strict sense would provide an unsatisfactory, extrinsic way of understanding Christian life (see chapter 18), prejudicial from the spiritual and pastoral point of view, besides being out of keeping with the teaching of the New Testament (especially that of Paul and John, which will be considered in chapters 5–6) and many of the Church Fathers. The theology of the New Testament and of the Christians of the early centuries, in effect, includes creation, redemption, and eschatological consummation in a single eternal divine project that was, from the very beginning, a project of grace entirely directed to the Father through the Son in the Holy Spirit (chapter 12).

The second problem is that of the extrinsic character of the discourse on grace, this time from the epistemological point of view. The doctrine of grace, which constitutes the principal part of this treatise, is none other than the believer's reflection on the life of Christ in human beings and on their divine filiation, both of which are the fruit of the saving work of Christ lived out in the Church. And the Christian cannot understand humanity—the human being in its entirety—as if this new life was marginal; he can understand it only from the standpoint of Christ and of his life. Grace may not be considered as an epistemologically irrelevant "icing on the cake." Four-fifths of the history of Western philosophy has developed in dialogue with Christian revelation, whether implicit or explicit, whether in a positive or a negative way. The rest has developed in close relationship with other religions. To do philosophy as if Christianity and religion did not exist is unthinkable. Besides, Christ is not only the savior but also the creator of the world. Hence, our reflection on Christ should have precedence over that which concerns other aspects of human life, especially when the latter may be considered from the point of view of philosophy, of religion in general, and of science. This is so because Christ is the living perspective, the source and way of all being and all grace. As we shall see in the last part of this work (chapters 18–25), many aporias that arise in the area of philosophy and science (especially what I have called the "unresolved polarities") are brought out into the open, clarified, and determined only in the light of the project of grace that Christ reveals and carries out by making us children of God.

"In order to understand our hope," and therefore our destiny, Pope Leo the Great said, "we must reflect on what grace has conceded to our human nature."[26] Maximus the Confessor distinguishes among five fundamental polarities within the human constitution: man and woman, paradise and the earth inhabited, cosmic earth and heaven, the sensitive and the spiritual sphere, God and the creature. The one who solves and clarifies the multiple tensions between these different elements is Christ, the Logos who synthesizes them all.[27] Maximus "elaborates a grandiose vision in which Christ, through the efficacy of saving action, unifies and redeems in himself the human being, and through humans, the whole of the cosmos."[28] According to

---

26. Pope Leo the Great, *Sermo* 7, 6.
27. See Maximus the Confessor, *Ambigua*, 41; *Quaest. ad Thalass.*, 4.
28. Z. Grocholewski, "Cristo come principio di unificazione," *PATH* 11 (2012): 10.

John H. Newman, the life of grace "is necessary in order to synthesize the signs, without suggesting new content, but rather offering a vision of the whole, making the eye proportionate to what is seen."[29]

Pope Francis speaks of a certain moment of his adolescence when he discovered that God had thought about him, sought him out, and called him, taking the initiative before he even realized it. "From that moment onward God is the One who is 'ahead' of us," he said. "You are looking for him but he is the one to find you first. You wish to meet him, but he is the one who comes to find you."[30] It is no surprise, therefore, that Francis insists on the primacy of grace in the life of the Church and in theological reflection, as does Benedict XVI.[31]

We must insist on the epistemological relevance of the discourse of grace over the whole of anthropology, including that which is developed in the ambit of philosophy and science. Grace in effect reveals human life and existence to the core as a life that derives from a divine gift and is directed to perpetual communion with the Trinity. Grace comes first; anthropology blossoms as a result.

Summing up, we may say that the awareness of the presence of grace, that is, the divine life given to humans that flows from the saving work of Christ in the power of the Holy Spirit, is made present through the Church in the sacraments and the word. It impregnates the entire life of humans and of creation itself with light and intelligibility; it exerts "pressure," as it were, on the human intelligence, bringing all the contributions of philosophies, religions, and sciences to a unitary fullness. In doing so, the fact and dynamism of divine grace clarifies the aporias present in all three, integrating their specific contribution to the whole, discerning their validity and importance, pointing out their limits.[32] In this reflection, of course, we must keep in mind what was already said regarding the necessary "eschatological reserve": we cannot as yet say everything, we cannot provide a complete picture. Only in Mary, mother of God and of humans, the one who is full of grace, the prototype of the Christian and of humanity, is a balanced fullness to be found. She is the *Mater unitatis*, "the mother

---

29. According to A. E. McGrath, *The Open Secret: A New Vision for Natural Theology* (Malden, Mass.: Blackwell, 2008). See also *Lumen Fidei*, par. 48.

30. S. Rubin and F. Ambrogetti, *El Papa Francisco: Conversaciones con Jorge Bergoglio* (Barcelona: Vergara/ Grupo Zeta, 2013), 43. See P. O'Callaghan, *God Ahead of Us: The Story of Divine Grace* (Minneapolis, Minn.: Fortress, 2014), 2.

31. "The salvation which God offers us is the work of his mercy. No human efforts, however good they may be, can enable us to merit so great a gift. God, by his sheer grace, draws us to himself and makes us one with him.... He sends his Spirit into our hearts to make us his children, transforming us and enabling us to respond to his love by our lives. The Church is sent by Jesus Christ as the sacrament of the salvation offered by God.... Through her evangelizing activity, she cooperates as an instrument of that divine grace which works unceasingly and inscrutably. Benedict XVI put it nicely at the beginning of the Synod's reflections [the Synod on the Word of God]: 'It is important always to know that the first word, the true initiative, the true activity comes from God and only by inserting ourselves into the divine initiative, only begging for this divine initiative, shall we too be able to become—with him and in him—evangelizers.' This principle of the *primacy of grace* must be a beacon which constantly illuminates our reflections on evangelization." Francis, *Evangelii Gaudium*, Apostolic Exhortation, November 24, 2013, par. 112.

32. I developed the idea that Christian faith illumines and vivifies human reason and makes it grow in P. O'Callaghan, "L'incontro tra fede e ragione nella ricerca della verità," *Fede e ragione: L'incontro e il cammino; In occasione del decimo anniversario dell'enciclica Fides et ratio*, edited by G. Maspero and M. Pérez de Laborda (Siena: Cantagalli, 2011), 35–59.

of unity," as Augustine said.[33] As Josemaría Escrivá wrote: "'A great sign appeared in Heaven: a woman adorned with the sun, with the moon under her feet, and a crown of twelve stars about her head.' From this, you and I and everyone may be sure that nothing perfects our personality so much as correspondence with grace."[34]

The fifth and last presupposition is that *spiritual experience plays a role* in the development of anthropology. All dogmatic reflection is developed in three stages, inseparable from one another, which we might call authority, reasoning, and spiritual conviction. We speak of authority in the sense that theological reflection always begins with a series of texts, theses, or authoritative ideas that contain revelation ultimately deriving from God, who is the only Lord. This is especially the case of scripture, the witness of Church Fathers and liturgical life, the public and universal declarations of the Church (magisterium), and so on.[35] Then we pass on to the reasoning process, because on the basis of what we have accepted through faith we reflect, assimilate, confront, clarify, compare—that is, we reason. This involves a reflection both divine and human, a reasoning within the faith, that is complex and demanding, perhaps the most sublime intellectual challenge humans can carry out. Finally, a critical role is played by personal spiritual conviction. Each author has his own, and these convictions determine the points of inflection in the authors' thought, moments of discernment, and ways of organizing and ordering materials. Without recognizing these convictions, theological reflection would be necessarily partial, unbalanced, enigmatic, perhaps inhuman.[36]

In structuring this treatise I have given particular importance to two fundamental spiritual convictions drawn from the life, writings, and work of Josemaría Escrivá: *divine filiation* and *Christian secularity*. Both elements are profoundly present in scripture, in Christian tradition, and in the Church's teaching. Still, the founder of Opus Dei knew how to give them a new vitality because they were, for him, spiritual convictions, convictions consolidated within his spirit by the Spirit, convictions that influenced his thought, and even more his actions and Christian intuitions. In this text the two themes will be presented at specific points (we shall consider divine filiation in chapter 13 and Christian secularity in chapter 24). In real terms, however, they will be present in a transversal way throughout this text of theological anthropology, thus justifying its title: *Children of God in the World*.

There are four principal parts of this treatise. The first (chapters 1–3) is concerned with questions of a methodological kind. First we shall look into the deep bond that unites the scientific, the philosophical, and the theological aspects of anthropology while recognizing the autonomy and specificity of each of these three areas of knowledge. Then we shall consider anthropology from the historical point of view in an attempt to seek out and clarify a suitable perspective in our search for meaning in the wider context of human immortality. The last methodological chapter considers the

---

33. Augustine, *Sermo* 192, 2. See chapter 12, notes 134ff., and corresponding text.

34. Josemaría Escrivá, *Furrow* (Dublin: Four Courts, 1990), no. 443, citing Rv 12:1.

35. Authority expresses the otherness and transcendence of divine revelation. See P. O'Callaghan, "The Role of Theology in the Promotion of a Pluralistic University," *PATH* 14 (2015): 69–93, esp. 82–84.

36. On the role of the saints in theology, see F.-M. Léthel, *Théologie de l'amour de Jésus: Écrits sur la théologie des saints* (Venasque: Éditions du Carmel, 1996).

Christian perspective of anthropology as a living, personal perspective—Jesus Christ, the Son of God, creator, incarnate, dead and risen, the alpha and omega of the universe—on the basis of the well-known text of *Gaudium et Spes*, "Christ fully reveals man to himself" (no. 22).

The second part (chapters 4–11) offers a Biblical and historical study of the theology of grace in humans: the doctrine of the human being "made in the image and likeness of God," the doctrine of grace in Paul and John, and the different stages of the development of the dogma of grace, from the Church Fathers right up to the twentieth century.

In the third part (chapters 12–17) I attempt to provide a complete systematic study of the theology of Christian grace, of the new life that derives from Christ, dead and risen, in the power of the Holy Spirit. This may be considered the central part of this treatise. The fourth and final part (chapters 18–25), entitled "Christian Anthropology," draws a variety of conclusions from our study of Christian grace, providing a reflection on different aspects of human life in the light of faith.

I am very grateful to Professors Antonio Aranda, Antonio Ducay, José María Galván, Antonio Malo, Giulio Maspero, Vito Reale, Santiago Sanz, Giuseppe Tanzella-Nitti, and Robert Wielockx for their suggestions and contributions, which were often decisive, especially in the publication of the Italian version of the work, *Figli di Dio nel mondo*.[37] I also wish to thank Professor J. F. Keating of Providence College for his invaluable observations on the English translation, as well as James Kruggel, John Martino, Theresa Walker, Marylin Martin, Paul Higgins, and all the staff at the Catholic University of America Press for their customary professionalism and helpfulness.

37. P. O'Callaghan, *Figli di Dio nel mondo: Trattato di antropologia teologica* (Rome: Edusc, 2013).

PART 1   METHODOLOGICAL CONSIDERATIONS

1   SITUATING ANTHROPOLOGY AMONG SCIENCE, PHILOSOPHY, AND THEOLOGY

The philosopher does not know all things, but knows rather the "all" of things. ARISTOTLE[1]

We never really advance a step beyond ourselves. DAVID HUME[2]

Man will become better only when we have made him understand what he is. ANTON CHEKHOV[3]

Man, forever unsatisfied! CAMEROON PROVERB

A Phenomenological Preamble: Situating Man between Reality and Aspiration

Humans inevitably want to know themselves, they want to know about the meaning of their life, they want to know their identity, their inner truth, their destiny. On the basis of this knowledge they desire and attempt to achieve their ultimate identity, to realize themselves. I have used the terms "to know" and "to achieve" because all persons, as they know themselves and act, experience a discrepancy between the concrete situation they are in (their present identity or situation, concrete, finite, and mundane) and an ultimate ideal to which they aspire (a fullness of identity that is definitive, ideal, or, if you wish, eschatological). Humans would be unable to realize their potentialities if they did not have, besides the knowledge of their present and concrete situation, a certain knowledge of the nature and content of their final identity that is definitive and ultimate. In other words, humans possess a present identity that is not full, and, at the same time, they aspire to a full identity that is not present. The perception of this discrepancy becomes the immediate motive of their actions

1. Aristotle, *Metaphysics* I.2.982a.
2. David Hume, *A Treatise on Human Nature* 1.2.6.
3. Anton Chekhov, *Notebooks*, edited by S. S. Kotelansky, L. Woolf (New York: Ecco Press, 1987), 15.

as they strive to realize their perceived potentialities to the full. Of course this dynamic of a not yet realized human life that is at once temporal and finalized cannot be absent from any kind of anthropological inquiry. It would be impossible to do anthropology if we had no knowledge of the present, real, concrete, and finite situation of humans. And it would be meaningless to do anthropology if the ultimate identity to which we aspire was completely unknown to us. Robert Spaemann observes that, paradoxically, human nature "is defined through something that is not itself, through anticipation. Only if the structure of anticipation is written into the general structure of nature, is it possible to conceive the human being as one who is open to the absolute and at the same time is a natural being."[4] Still, the same author recognizes that the precise profile of the human being escapes us: "No anthropology can teach us how we are supposed to be: 'Be perfect as your heavenly Father is perfect.'"[5]

To Know the Human Being

Humans know themselves in two complementary ways: from within themselves, that is, their own resources (for example, through philosophical and scientific analysis, immediate perception, personal observation, introspection) or with the assistance and witness of other people and traditions (faith/religion, myth, poetic imagination, cultural traditions, social life). The two ways toward self-knowledge and self-realization are closely bound up with one another, although each has its own sphere of autonomy and fruitful tension with the other.

However, we may ask: what is the source of the presence in humans, by knowledge or intuition, of the ideal to which they aspire, over and above their direct perception of their own contingent situation, given the fact that their full self-realization has not yet taken place?

One possibility is that we obtain knowledge of our as yet unrealized ideal from other people (family, friends, society, traditions, religious faith). Their lives present us in a more or less attractive or imperative way with an ideal, a vision, that we have not yet achieved. Obviously this is a valid approach from many points of view, because the identity and self-realization of individuals are formed always on the basis of surrounding culture, in their relationship with other people (see chapter 22). "Our knowledge of ourselves must include how our concerns and priorities are influenced by the presence of others," observes the economist Amartya Sen.[6] And, in the words of the novelist and playwright Oscar Wilde, "Most people are other people. Their thoughts are someone else's opinions, their lives a mimicry, their passions a quotation." And essentially the same thing is said by the philosopher Charles Taylor: "We are always socially embedded."[7]

4. R. Spaemann, "Sulla nozione di natura umana," in *Natura e ragione: Saggi di antropologia* (Rome: Edusc, 2006), 19–39, 36.

5. Ibid., 39. The Biblical citation is from Mt 5:48.

6. See his study A. K. Sen, "Other People," *Proceedings of the British Academy* 111 (2001): 319.

7. C. Taylor, *A Secular Age* (Cambridge, Mass.: Belknap Press of Harvard University Press, 2007), 157. On this work of Taylor, see P. O'Callaghan, "The Eclipse of Worship: Theological Reflections on Charles Taylor's *A Secular Age*," *Euntes Docete* 62, no. 2 (2009): 89–123; J. Grondin, "Charles Taylor a-t-il des raisons de croire à proposer? Grandeur et limites d'une justification de l'option métaphysique de la croyance par des enjeux éthiques," *Science et Esprit* 64 (2012): 245–62.

Still, this does not as yet provide an exhaustive answer to our questions about unrealized human identity. We should still ask: what brings us to make our own the ideal we aspire to, the image of humanity others give us? Why should such an ideal be emulated? Why does it attract us? Why does it find a acute resonance within us? Why do humans feel the urge to imitate others, to make their own the other person's way of acting, what the Greeks called *mimesis*? In receiving and accepting the vision and understanding of others, do humans not run the risk of losing themselves, of acting gregariously, of living off the expectancies of the crowd, of losing all authenticity?[8]

Jean-Jacques Rousseau analyzed the opposite of gregariousness—individualism—during the eighteenth century. His understanding was that when humans strive to live by following the ideas or lifestyles of others, their natural *amour de soi*, "love of self," urged on by competitiveness, is transformed into *amour propre*, "self-love." Their effort to develop a social life becomes, therefore, a kind of self-mutilation. Rousseau exhorts his readers to throw off the weight of social expectancies and live according to their own nature and personal inclinations.[9] Marx and Freud, in turn, were of the opinion that the effort to unthinkingly imitate and follow others reveals a kind of "superstructure" that alienates humans and just consolidates their immaturity. Perhaps for this reason the philosopher Ralph W. Emerson considered the imitation that humans practice to be a kind of suicide.[10] In fact, it can easily happen that an ideal presented to humans as something worthwhile emulating turns out to be an artificial product that meets neither the needs of their nature nor the demands of their destiny. Perhaps the "ideal" they perceive in others should not be assimilated but rather identified and excluded. In effect, "ideals" that others present us with are not always meant to be accepted and absorbed.

Perhaps it might be suggested that, at the origin of the presence in humans of an inescapable aspiration toward an infinite ideal, strongly desired and not as yet reached, is to be found a germinal reality that is present within humans themselves—their interiority, their spiritual constitution, the "divine" that is within them. But of course a further question could be asked: where does this spiritual impulse come from, this aspiration toward transcendence, toward the infinite, toward the immortal? Later on we shall attempt to respond to this question when we consider that humans, one by one, have been made in the image and likeness of God, they are driven by a desire to see God, and are constituted as a union of body and soul.[11] In any case, it is clear that humans assimilate from others what finds resonance with themselves, what corresponds to their own spiritual makeup.[12] As Goethe put it (in *Faust*), "what you have received from your ancestors you must rediscover it yourself, in order to possess it truly."

---

8. On this issue, see R. R. Reno, "Fear of Redemption," *First Things* 144 (June-July 2004): 29–34.

9. See J.-J. Rousseau, *The Social Contract* (1762).

10. "Envy is ignorance. Imitation is suicide.... Insist on yourself; never imitate. Your own gift you can present every moment with the cumulative force of a whole life's cultivation; but of the adopted talent of another you have only an extemporaneous half possession. That which each can do best, none but his Maker can teach him." R. W. Emerson, *Self-Reliance and Other Essays* (New York: Dover, 1993), 101.

11. In chapters 3, 18, and 19, respectively.

12. On this dynamic, see *COH* 19–25.

Situating an Integral Anthropology between Science, Philosophy, and Theology

From the previous reflection we can make three observations. In the first place, the driving force behind the anthropological question—behind human action it-self—is to be found in the discrepancy, or nonidentity, between two elements well known to humans: on the one hand, the present, finite, and concrete situation that is directly perceived and in which one lives and, on the other hand, the ideal toward which one aspires, an ideal that is considered both future and possible. The latter is experienced less clearly and directly than the former, and is usually more or less in-fluenced by the expectancies of other people, by the culture in which we live, by our own "spiritual" life, by religious tradition, and, at heart, by God himself.

In the second place, the present, concrete situation of humans (the first element) is expressed and known principally through science and phenomenology, through which humans attempt to explain and describe their nature in general terms. Philos-ophy and religion, however, concentrate preferably on the human subject and on the aspiration and ideal toward which humans tend (the second element). These two ele-ments link closely with one another, without however ever fully merging. A material-istic thought system, such as Stoicism, considers the concrete and present situation of humans (the first element) as more real and more authentic, and therefore closer to the truth, closer to the human essence. Thus the discrepancy and tension between the two elements is resolved by marginalizing the second one, the ideal, declaring it unreachable or illusory. On the other hand, a more spiritualistic philosophy, such as Platonism, is centered preferably on the ideal to be obtained, on the totality already germinally present in the immortal soul that contemplates the divine essence, and tends to leave aside the concrete, actual, situation of humans (eliminating it sooner or later), for the latter is immersed in, blinded, or seriously conditioned by corrupt-ible matter. Thus Platonism has few scruples in considering philosophical and reli-gious research and scientific inquiry antithetical.[13]

The third observation is that the tension between the present, concrete situation, on the one hand, and the transcendent aspiration, on the other, may not be resolved or explained by a Christian believer with the simplistic ease of a Stoic or a Platonist. The believer cannot simply choose between concreteness and the ideal, between mat-ter and spirit, between now and then. In fact, the truth that comes from science (from spontaneous knowledge and phenomenology) cannot a priori contradict the truth that comes through faith (which deals with the origin and destiny of humans), and vice versa, because both have God as their ultimate source.[14] For this reason we can say that an anthropology worked out in the light of Christian faith is, or is meant to be, an integral anthropology.

---

13. See Plato, *Phaedo* 65–67.
14. See Pope John Paul II, *Fides et Ratio*, Encyclical Letter, September 14, 1998, pars. 9, 45, 61.

Anthropology and Anthropologies

The classical Greek term used to designate the human being is *anthrōpos*, from which of course is derived the term "anthropology."[15] Among the ancients, for example, the poet Homer, *anthrōpos* was often used to express the idea of the human as an intermediate being between gods and animals. Other times, for example, in the *Histories* of Herodotus, *anthrōpos* designates the slave as against the free man, who is *kyrios* (lord) and *eleutheros* (free). Frequently the term is used in an impersonal way to designate humans in general (the term *arsēn*, "man," refers to the male member of the human species). All in all, it may be said that *anthrōpos* is not a semantically rich term.

The term "anthropology," however, appeared for the first time in the sixteenth century, principally referring to the physiological, psychological, biological, and ethical aspects of human life. Today the term evokes this understanding preferentially. According to the *Oxford English Dictionary*, it refers to the study of the development of human societies and cultures, as well as human zoology, evolution, and ecology—that is, elements humans have in common with animals. Frequently, in fact, anthropology is closely associated with paleontology (which studies remains of fossil animals and plants) and ethnology (the study of the characteristics of various peoples and races and the differences and relationships between them). In the eighteenth century the discipline of "cultural anthropology" began to emerge: it refers to comparative studies of human cultures and their development.[16] All in all, the common usage of the term anthropology is marked (1) by special attention to the physical, nonspiritual, side of humanity; (2) by a consideration of the natural, common human condition, not so much that of the individual person; and (3) by a special interest in the past, especially with respect to the origins of living beings.

The phenomenologist philosopher Max Scheler was in all probability the first to use the term "philosophical anthropology" in 1928, even though the notion is already present in the writings of Kant and many others.[17] In the area of twentieth-century philosophy, Edmund Husserl studied humans with a phenomenological method and was followed in different ways by Maurice Merleau-Ponty, Martin Heidegger, Jean-Paul Sartre, and others. Gabriel Marcel employed transcendental reflection, Cornelio Fabro used an introspective method, and Claude Lévi-Strauss used a structural method in understanding human nature. Hans-Georg Gadamer and Paul Ricoeur applied a hermeneutic method, Martin Buber and Emmanuel Lévinas a dialogical method. Throughout the nineteenth century, different treatises of "theological anthropology" (or "supernatural anthropology") appeared, coinciding with the traditional treatise

---

15. See W. F. Arndt and F. W. Gringrich, *A Greek-English Lexicon of the New Testament and Other Early Christian Literature*, 3rd ed. (Chicago: University of Chicago Press, 1957) [hereafter "*BDAG*"], 81f., s.v. ἄνθρωπος; *The New International Dictionary of New Testament Theology*, edited by C. Brown (Exeter: Paternoster Press, 1980), 1:302–9, s.v. ἄνθρωπος.

16. By way of example, see C. Tullio-Altan, *Manuale di antropologia culturale: Storia e metodo*, 3rd ed. (Milan: Bompiani, 1998).

17. See M. Scheler, *Die Stellung des Menschen im Kosmos* (Munich: Nymphenburger, 1947), 9. The work was first published in 1928. It was translated into English as *The Human Place in the Cosmos*, edited by M. S. Frings (Evanston, Ill.: Northwestern University Press, 2009). See I. Kant, *Anthropology from a Pragmatic Point of View* (Cambridge: Cambridge University Press, 2006). The work was first published in 1798.

on grace. The term "theological anthropology" appears for the first time in a work of Josef Geiselmann and subsequently in several works of Karl Rahner.[18]

Though aware of the wide variety of different approaches to anthropology, we shall proceed in this phenomenological reflection by asking three fundamental questions:

- What is the human being?
- Who is the human being?
- Why do we do anthropology?

What Is the Human Being?

Anthropology considers principally human nature, what human beings are, what they have in common with one another. All the sciences contribute more or less to this knowledge. They begin with a process of observation of humans and their behavior, and this is followed by analysis and abstraction on the basis of the data obtained. We can think of the contributions made to anthropology by physics, chemistry, biochemistry, biology, neurobiology, zoology, physiology and anatomy, experimental psychology, paleontology, ethnology, psychology, sociology, political philosophy, and so on. All these sciences contribute to showing us what humans are, what their common characteristics are, how they act, how they normally behave. Besides, it might be said that scientific investigation operates according to a democratic criterion, a "majority vote," a kind of "normality," because science attempts to identify the average and common situation among humans, their "normal" characteristics: classes, aptitudes, principal races, common characteristics, and types of behavior. It is true that other sciences, such as medicine and psychiatry, deal with the exceptions, the pathologies. Still, indirectly they function within the criterion of normality because their ultimate purpose is to bring the exceptions back within the norm in so far as this is possible. The very plasticity of human nature, therefore, is not closed to rigorous scientific investigation, as can be seen in the study of cultural anthropology and neurobiology. All the different forms of scientific knowledge can be studied, described, documented, checked, corroborated, verified, corrected, and understood with ever greater perfection and depth. Besides, they have a common characteristic of special interest: they are easy to communicate among people because they may be expressed as clearly objectified information, in simple language forms. Thus they are sharable forms of knowledge that express, in their very communicability, common human nature.[19]

Christian doctrine confirms unhesitatingly the validity of this approach to the

18. See J. R. Geiselmann, *Die theologische Anthropologie Johann Adam Möhlers: Ihr geschichtlicher Wandel* (Freiburg: Herder, 1955). On this issue, see Scola, Marengo, and Prades López, *La persona umana*, 26f.

19. As regards the stages in which we know things, Berdjaev makes the following observation. "The unifying logos is indeed revealed in the acquisition of knowledge. But it is revealed by degrees, in dependence upon the spiritual condition of men and their spiritual community. The social logos is the objectivized logos. The paradox lies in the fact that the universally binding character of cognition is to be found in the highest degree in mathematics and the physical sciences. Here cognition depends less upon spiritual conditions and the spiritual community which people share. It produces the same results for men of different religious beliefs, different nationalities and different classes. On the other hand, knowledge in the historical and social sciences and in sciences of the spirit and of values, that is to say in philosophy, has a lower degree of universally binding character just because it presupposes a greater spiritual community in which people share. Least of all universally binding are truths of a religious character, because they presuppose the maximum of

knowledge of humans; the development of science from the eighteenth century on-ward has been inspired to an important degree by Christian philosophical and theo-logical reflection.[20] Given that the world has been made by God from nothing, that is, without presuppositions of any kind, the following may be said.

First, the intelligibility present in created reality cannot contradict what is com-municated to humans through revelation and faith.[21] Not only that, but because God created all that exists, the entire unitary intelligibility of the universe finds its ultimate source in God. Second, the transcendence of God with respect to the created world eliminates the fear that humans have always experienced before the cosmos and the unpredictable, competitive, envious, and irascible divinities that seem to inhabit and control it, often in an arbitrary way. Because God is completely distinct from the cre-ated world at an ontological level, there is no need to focus things in terms of coopera-tion or synergy between God and the world, as is typical of paganism.[22] For this rea-son, theology, the study of God, cannot be confused with empirical science, the study of the created world, and vice versa. They are simply different areas of study. In the third place, God has made humans from the beginning in his image and likeness, as his children, in such a way that they can dominate the earth as his ambassadors. Hu-mans exercise this dominion through knowledge, work, and activity of all kinds.

The Limits of a Purely Scientific Investigation of Human Nature

Is empirical science capable of saying all that can be said about humans? Does science have the last word? Or is there something else to say, something substantial-ly new? At the beginning of Charles Dickens's novel *Hard Times*, the schoolteacher Thomas Gradgrind insists with his young students that they should pay attention only to "the facts," that is, to certain, scientifically identifiable information on the world and humanity.[23] However, the narrative shows that in this way it is possible to express only a part, indeed a small part, of the richness of human life, as may be seen in the disconcerted reactions of the little protagonist Sissy Jupe, the daughter of cir-cus artists. Pure science, in fact, deals with reality as a dead thing, closed to novelty and to the mystery of life and the person. The philosopher Leszek Kolakowski has shown that natural sciences study reality simply as a dead object, with the danger of falling into a kind of necrophilia (or love of death), closed to the richness and unpre-dictability of human life and love and freedom.[24]

---

spiritual community. Within the religious body these truths are accepted as the most universally binding, but outside it they appear as the least universally binding, as the least 'objective' and the most 'subjective.'" N. A. Berdjaev, *Slavery and Freedom* (London: G. Bles, 1943), 115.

20. On this topic, see the works of Pierre Duhem, Stanley Jaki, and others. On Duhem, see F. J. López Ruiz, "Duhem, Pierre Maurice Marie," in G. Tanzella-Nitti and A. Strumìa, eds., *Dizionario Interdisciplinare di Scienza e Fede*, 2 vols. (Rome: Urbaniana University Press, 2002) [hereafter "*DISF*"], 2:1706–18. See also S. L. Jaki, *The Road of Science and the Ways to God* (Chicago: University of Chicago Press, 1978).

21. F. Ardusso, "Fede," in *DISF* 1:607–24.

22. See O'Callaghan, *La metafisica cristiana* (Rome: Pontificia Università della Santa Croce, 1997), 56–64, 70, 80f.

23. See C. Dickens, *Hard Times* (London: Longman, 1970). First published in 1854.

24. See L. Kolakowski, *The Presence of Myth* (Chicago: University of Chicago Press, 1989). In the religious

Anthropology taken in the fullest sense should not exclude systematically a series of questions that may not be dealt with satisfactorily by the empirical sciences, especially all that relates to human individuality, freedom, love, the origin of the human species, life, and destiny, questions that simply cannot be reduced to the natural, the typical, the emblematic. These aspects of human life, which are considered principally by philosophers and theologians, should not contradict the conclusions of science. In fact, they should be in a position to free science from the ideological slavery of attempting to say the last word about man. Pope Francis writes: "The gaze of science ... benefits from faith: faith encourages the scientist to remain constantly open to reality in all its inexhaustible richness."[25] Thus, philosophy and theology, when they attempt to give meaning to human existence in its entirety, when they ponder the chronological and spiritual extremes of human life, in real terms liberate science, avoiding the ideology that derives from attempting to say the last word. Besides, as the scientist and philosopher Karl Popper has shown, science is faithful to its proper purpose only when it accepts to work in the context of hypotheses, that is, accepting the rigorously provisional character of its own conclusions.[26]

For this reason, we can say that the primary purpose of philosophical and theological reflection is not one of contributing directly or competitively to our scientific knowledge of human nature. They pretend neither to place themselves on the same level as science nor to enter into competition with it. "The philosopher does not know all things, but knows the 'all' of things," said Aristotle.[27] Perhaps we may say the same thing about the one who believes; according to Benedict XVI, already cited, "faith is not a parallel world of feelings that we can still afford to hold on to, rather it is the key that encompasses everything, gives it meaning, interprets it and also provides its inner ethical orientation."[28] In effect, philosophy and especially theology offer science a living reminder to be faithful to its own finality, to avoid attempting to say more than it is capable of doing. Specifically, theological reflection, based on God's plan in Christ, (1) makes it clear that scientific research is just beginning to scratch the surface of the created world and of humanity; (2) invites humans not to limit themselves to a narcissistic contemplation of their own knowledge and ideas but rather to direct their gaze toward the creator to praise him for the sublimity and beauty of his great work; (3) offers a unitary vision of reality, ensuring that science does not become ideological, integrating different aspects of human life, placing each aspect of human knowledge in its proper, orderly, place; and (4) provides a reflection that goes

---

sphere, an approach of this kind may be found among Gnostic thinkers, who were influential during the early Christian centuries. By means of special revelation, Gnostic authors offered humans (or at least some of them, the chosen ones) esoteric information (*gnōsis*) to facilitate their own liberation and development. They consider faith (*pistis*), however, as a poor and insecure source of knowledge that is reserved for the masses, for those who are not chosen, for those who have no special knowledge and stand in need of receiving it from others. It should be kept in mind that Christian revelation involves much more than new knowledge, because it is directed toward establishing a communion of faith and love between God and man. On this issue, see G. Tanzella-Nitti, *Lezioni di teologia fondamentale* (Rome: Aracne, 2007), 140–49.

25. See Francis, *Lumen Fidei*, par. 34.

26. On the role of the "working hypothesis" in science, see K. R. Popper, *Conjectures and Refutations: The Growth of Scientific Knowledge*, 16th ed. (New York: Harper and Row, 1985).

27. Aristotle, *Metaphysics* I.2.982a.

28. The full text is cited in note 14 of the introduction.

beyond the results of science with regard to the origin (protology), end (teleology and eschatology), and meaning of human life and the created world.

In this sense we can understand that both theology and philosophy attempt to respond preferentially to the second question we asked: who is the human being?

Who Is the Human Being?

What is the human being? This question refers, as we saw earlier, to the essence or the nature of humans, to human "normality," to the common characteristics of humans in general. To this question, in principle it should be possible to give an ever more perfect response. Still, this kind of study does not provide the last word, as has been pointed out by the philosopher Hannah Arendt, in glossing Augustine's "Quaestio mihi factus sum" (I have become for myself a question).[29] And she says: "The moment we want to say *who* somebody is, our very vocabulary leads us astray into saying *what* he is; we get entangled in a description of qualities he necessarily shares with others like him; we begin to describe a type or a 'character' in the old meaning of the word, with the result that his specific uniqueness escapes us."[30] If it were possible to reduce anthropology to a mere description of human nature, each person would be no more than a mere exemplar of the human species.[31] Obviously each human being is that ... but is much more besides.

The Value of the Individual Human Being

When we come to know another person, we do not begin by asking: "What are you?" or "What is your nature?" because it is obvious and immediate to us that the other person belongs to the same species as ourselves. The fact of sharing a nature with another person is in fact what makes it possible for us to communicate with them. Common nature is the point of departure for further questions, because humans would be incapable of placing themselves in a meaningful way before others if they did not share the same nature. To know a person we do not ask, "What are you?" but rather "Who are you?" With this question we wish to obtain answers to other specific questions: (1) What are your peculiar and individual traits, especially your name? (2) What is your history and narrative? (3) Who are your parents, relatives, and friends, where were you born, and where do you live? That is to say, where and how do you situate yourself with respect to the rest of the world?

Arendt suggests, in fact, that the distinction between the two questions—what and who is the human being—is revealed not so much in terms of abstract knowledge but rather through love.[32] She adds that both language and human action belong

29. Augustine distinguishes the questions "Who am I?" and "What am I?," directing the former to humans as a question they ask themselves and the latter to God: see *Confessiones* X, 6, 17, and Arendt, *The Human Condition*, 2nd ed. (Chicago: University of Chicago Press, 1959), 10n2. On this issue, see also R. Spaemann, *Persons: The Difference between "Someone" and "Something"* (Oxford: Oxford University Press, 2006).

30. Arendt, *The Human Condition*, 181.

31. It may be noted that people are easily surprised and preoccupied by the disappearance of twenty species of animals or plants but hardly at all at the death of twenty human individuals. Still, Joseph Stalin said, "one death is a tragedy, a million deaths is a statistic."

32. Arendt, *The Human Condition*, 242.

principally to the order of the "who."[33] Already in the Middle Ages, Richard of St. Victor and Alexander of Hales noted that the question *Quis est?* (Who is man?) is directed to the person, whereas *Quid est?* (What is man?) is directed simply to the nature.[34] We shall return to this issue in the final chapter, on the human being as a person.

Unresolved Polarities: Determination and Liberty

As we saw, the term "what" refers to human nature and "who" to human individuals, to their history and relationships with others, that is, to the person. We can also say that the two elements—the what and the who—are not completely independent of one another, for between them there are nuances that derive from the presence in humans of what we already called unresolved polarities.

Let us take an example of this.[35] From the point of view of nature, of what man is, the human being is presented more or less as determined (this is what we are told by physiologists, psychologists, sociologists, and neuroscientists). From the point of view of being a person (who man is), we normally affirm that each human being is free; in fact, Christian faith openly insists on the ethical responsibility that accompanies human action.[36]

And we ask, how can these two affirmations be reconciled, that humans are at once determined and free? Is it more correct to say that humans are naturally free, or is it better to say they are determined? Or might we perhaps say that they are half free and half determined? Or maybe that theirs is a finite freedom, that they are not capable of acting freely before an infinite object (such as God)? Could we solve the dilemma in a dualistic way, as has happened frequently throughout history, by saying that according to their corporeity humans are determined, and according to their spirit or soul they are free? Or might we ask which of the two dimensions is more original and foundational and which is more apparent and conditioned, perhaps the result of alienation, in opposition to the other dimension, which is real and lasting. To the question of human liberty we shall return later on. But it remains an open one: is it possible to speak of humans as natural beings and as persons at one and the same time and on the same plane? Can this "polarity" be resolved? If so, how? Or when? In speaking of humans, is it possible to harmonize the two questions? Or are they simply irreconcilable?

33. "In acting and speaking, men show who they are, they reveal actively their unique personal identities and thus make their appearances in the human world, while their physical identities appear without any activity of their own in the unique shape of the body and the sound of the voice." Ibid., 179.

34. See F. Russo, *La persona umana: Questioni di antropologia filosofica* (Rome: Armando, 2000), 121.

35. Many other "unresolved polarities" may be mentioned, because contrast and opposition abound in every anthropology. The following pairs may be mentioned. Nature is known in terms of the abstract, whereas the person is real and concrete. Nature is functional and temporary, whereas the person is permanent. Before having or possessing, there is being. Before the unconscious knowableness of nature, we can situate the responsible fidelity of the person. Before the complete and detailed analysis of things, we can situate the unconditioned acceptance of persons. Before the collectivity, the individual. Before the complex and fragmentary within nature, the simplicity and unity of the concrete individual. Before death, life; before permanence, perishableness; before possession, reception; before the rational, the intuitive; before the corruptible, immortality; before the essentialism of abstract nature, the existential reality of the person; before pure reason, faith; before use and abuse, love and generous dedication; before dominating thought and action, suffering and contemplation; before pure law, gift; before the problem, the mystery; before the *in nobis*, the *extra nos*; before the *a se*, the *ab alio*; before the body, the spirit; and so on.

36. See chapters 16 and 20.

An exclusively "scientific" understanding of humanity would suggest that what is true and lasting and valuable is nature (in this case, determined),[37] while the other aspects of human life (such as freedom, love, individuality, etc.) belong to the realm of imagination, and therefore would be superstructural, sentimental, and poetic elements, extraneous to nature, artificially added on, that express escapism or conditioning.

Is Man Truly an Irreplaceable Being?

People frequently say that each human being is *unique*, absolute in a certain sense, and therefore unrepeatable, irreplaceable, worthy of being unconditionally respected on account of being a person. Still, looking at things more closely, this all seems to be a dream, an inordinate and unjustifiable pretext. The divergences between individuals are not that great, and, all in all, for most human activities it is not difficult to find someone who is in a position to take the place of another. In other words, from the functional point of view the human individual seems to be fully replaceable ... anything but singular and absolute. If one person gets sick or dies, someone else can generally take his place. So what does it mean to say that each human being is irreplaceable?

It is true that humans in their actions and relationships with others consider and present themselves as irreplaceable, for example, when someone says, "I am somebody," or "I am important," or "I am not being taken into account," or "My rights are not being respected." But this attitude might just as well be a form of camouflaged egotism. It would be more realistic and coherent to present oneself by saying, "I am one more exemplar of the human species, one of the 75 billion human individuals who, since the advent of *homo sapiens*, have inhabited and inhabit the earth; I do what I can in my circumstances, and that is enough."

From the point of view of Christian faith, besides, it might be more proper to say that the deep, existential questions of humans on the value of life and their possible irreplaceability derive at least in part from human sinfulness, from which Christ came to save us. Martin Luther spoke, in fact, of an incurable egotism that is present in every human action and thought, believing that the sinner at heart is a "cor incurvatum in seipsum" (a heart turned in on itself).[38] Some beliefs typical of Eastern religions (especially the Buddhist doctrine of *nirvāna* and the *advaita* of Hinduism, which involves a union with the divinity that overcomes every form of duality) consider that all emphasis on human individuality, which is considered to be typical of Western thought, is in fact a sign of a failed salvation, of alienating egotism, of an imperfection that must be overcome on the way to perfection. Perhaps the eighteenth-century philosopher Denis Diderot was right when he said: "There is only one great individual: the all."[39] Marxist humanism focuses things in a like way. The human individual should allow itself to sink into commonness and universality. Only

37. See the position of B. F. Skinner, *Beyond Freedom and Dignity* (New York: Bantam Books, 1972), on the irrelevance of human liberty.

38. M. Luther, *In ep. S. Pauli ad Galatas Comm.*, in *Dr Martin Luthers Werke: Schriften* (Weimar: H. Bohlaus Nachfolger, 1883–2000) [hereafter "WA"; translated and edited as *Luther's Works* by J. Pelikan and H. T. Lehmann (Saint Louis, Mo.: Concordia, 1961–2001)], 40.1:282.

39. D. Diderot, "Le rêve de d'Alembert," in *Oeuvres complètes* (Paris: Hermann, 1987), 17:98.

in that way will it realize its full potential. Perfection should consist of a seamless union with the divine, which surpasses all dispersion and individuality. Hence the question remains open: does our attachment to the value of individuality (a reflection of what we consider to be the irreplaceable character of humans) find its deepest roots in the being of humans, or should it be considered rather as a kind of sinful alienation to be overcome with God's help?

Still, the spontaneous and universal tendency for humans to affirm themselves as unique and irreplaceable is undeniable. All humans resist elimination, substitution, even though they may not always admit to doing so. Humans vigorously object to being put aside, and in a special way they reject death. This conviction is common among philosophers, writers, and thinkers, especially in the Christian world. The Italian poet Giacomo Leopardi says: "With the experience of life it is very true to say that those men whom the French call 'original,' are not only not rare, but are so common that I can say that the most strange thing in society is to find a man who is not truly original."[40] And François de la Rochefoucault observes that "it is easier to know man in general than to know one man in particular."[41] Against the collectivism of Hegel, the philosopher Søren Kierkegaard once wrote: "The individual [in Danish, *den Enkelt*]: with this category the cause of Christianity stands or falls.... For everyone I manage to draw to the category of the 'individual,' I ensure he will become a Christian. Or better, since nobody can make this happen for anybody else, I can guarantee that he soon will become one."[42]

However, is there any way we can justify this conviction philosophically?

Gabriel Marcel: Situating the Human Being between Problem and Mystery

The twentieth-century philosopher and playwright Gabriel Marcel reflected on the questions of life, of the person, of the consistency of human love and hope, and in particular of the value of individuals and their personal and intimate experiences within the human community. His reflection was clearly centered on the question "Who is man?" He suggests that it is possible to consider reality, and in particular human life, in two different ways: as a problem and as a mystery.[43]

When we consider reality as a "problem," we see it as something we come to know, to understand fully, to resolve, and to dominate once and for all. We could consider the Genome Project as an example of this approach: scientists attempt to fully map the DNA of humans. In effect, reality is looked upon as a problem to resolve, to un-

---

40. G. Leopardi, *Essays, Dialogues, and Thoughts*, edited by B. Dobell (Westport, Conn.: Hyperion Press, 1978), no. 97.

41. F. de la Rochefoucault, *Maximes et autres oeuvres morales*, edited by A. Borrot (Paris: Bordas, 1949), no. 436.

42. See S. Kierkegaard, "The Point of View, Supplement," in *Kierkegaard's Writings* 22 (Princeton, N.J.: Princeton University Press, 1998), 122f.; orig. *Samlede Vaerker* (Copenhagen: Gyldendal, 1930), 13:608f. On this topic, see also T. Melendo, *Las dimensiones de la persona: Biblioteca Palabra* (Madrid: Palabra, 1999), 97.

43. See especially G. Marcel, *Être et avoir* (Paris: Aubier-Montaigne, 1935); *Le mystère de l'être* (Paris: Aubier-Montaigne, 1963), translated into English as *Being and Having* (Westminster: Dacre Press, 1949); and *The Mystery of Being* (Lanham, Md.: University Press of America, 1983). On Marcel, see P. O'Callaghan, "La metafísica de la esperanza y del deseo en Gabriel Marcel," *Anuario Filosófico* 22 (1989): 55–92.

derstand down to the last detail; our knowledge of it would thus be instrumental, re-ferring to the functionality of things, to their measurable potentialities, to a clear and complete knowledge of their nature. This knowledge would provide us, in principle, with a definitive dominion over things.

According to Marcel, however, there is another way of knowing reality and being, which requires on the behalf of humans a disposition to look upon them as a mystery, that is, as something they can never comprehend or dominate perfectly, as a reality that simply exists and that will always be in some ways greater and deeper than the observer. Indeed it may be said that the knower becomes immersed in reality, as it were, just as a swimmer is immersed in the sea, knowing it while being supported by it. Only through "mysterious" reflection is it possible to "comprehend" things as they are, especially human persons in their intimacy and true reality. "Being is immedi-ately present to us," says Marcel, "but we are not immediately present to it."[44] Marcel's inquiry is undertaken in the context of a transcendental and religious philosophy, of dramatic and artistic expression, in which one must renounce any kind of scien-tific verification that pretends to be complete, closed, and definitive. The book Pietro Prini wrote on Marcel sums up this idea in the title: *The Science of the Unverifiable*.[45] According to Marcel himself, this describes his position excellently. Marcel is aware that it is simply impossible to explain everything about reality, especially with respect to humans, on the basis of a scientific-empirical, rationalistic, problematic inquiry, as if to be a "person" could be reduced to having a "personality," that is, a sum of gen-eral characteristics shared by many other individuals. Reality is mysterious, greater than our capacity to know it; personal reality is especially so.

The philosopher Ernst Cassirer concludes:

Religion never pretends to clarify the mystery of man. It confirms and deepens this mys-tery. The God of whom it speaks is a *Deus absconditus*, a hidden God. Hence even his image, man, cannot be other than mysterious. Man also remains a *homo absconditus*. Religion is no "theory" of God and man and of their mutual relation. The only answer that we receive from religion is that it is the will of God to conceal himself.[46]

In the final chapter of this treatise (25), we shall return again to the question of the human person, which constitutes the most definitive, complete description of the human being inspired by Christian faith.

Why Do We Do Anthropology?

In order to justify the study of any aspect of anthropology it is usually enough to establish its immediate efficacy, the concrete results it can produce. In that sense empirical science is frequently verified and justified by technology. That is to say, technology usually offers the true why of science: we study reality in order to use it

44. Cited by R. Troisfontaines, *De l'Existence a l'Etre: La philosophie de G. Marcel*, 2nd ed., 2 vols. (Paris: Nauwelaerts, 1953), 1:15; see also P. O'Callaghan, "La metafisica di Gabriel Marcel," *PATH* 5 (2006): 401–24.

45. P. Prini, *Gabriel Marcel e la metodologia dell'inverificabile* (Rome: Studium, 1950).

46. E. Cassirer, *An Essay on Man: An Introduction to a Philosophy of Human Culture* (Hamburg: F. Meiner, 2006), 17, commenting on the anthropology of Blaise Pascal.

to our benefit. In that sense our search for knowledge is inevitably interested, pragmatic. Still, because our inquiry into the nature of the human being goes beyond the empirical sciences, beyond pragmatic concerns, in the sense that its object belongs to the ambit of "mystery" and not only to that of "problem," we should ask ourselves why we undertake it. Why do humans reflect on their own life and existence and nature? What is the purpose of anthropology? Why do we wish to know our identity, when other living beings seem to take little or no interest in the matter? In effect, whereas humans wonder if primates belong in some way to their own race, primates seem to take very little interest in such questions.[47] Humans publish specialized periodicals on dolphins, but dolphins, as far as we know, do not pay us a similar compliment. This is so because nonhuman animals know themselves and act on the basis of a hard-wired instinct mechanism that brings them to satisfy their immediate, finite needs. Humans, of course, are capable of functional and finite knowledge, as animals are, but besides, and simultaneously, they are open to all things, to the infinite: as Aristotle said of humans, "anima est quodammodo omnia" (the human soul is capable of identifying itself with all existing things).[48] Humans wish to know themselves and all creatures, without exception, and they perceive that they are capable of doing so. And we ask again: why? To what purpose?

Returning to the binomials mentioned at the beginning of this chapter, "reality" and "aspiration," "concreteness" and "ideal," we can ask, In studying humans, are we motivated by a desire for pure knowledge, for clear contemplation? Or are we urged to do so by a desire to improve our lives, to change reality, perhaps to manipulate it, to make it what it is not? Affirmations made about humans often have wider implications of an ethical kind, they have a teleological or vectorial aspect, because they express an intention that goes further; they open out to an implicit declaration that goes beyond simple affirmations. In effect, the study of anthropology may have different real motivations, more or less recognized as such by humans themselves. Three may be mentioned.

The first and most obvious motivation is that humans want to know themselves in order to overcome the natural perplexities of life, and in that way, act in a freer and more responsible way in keeping with their nature and identity. This is the ethical motivation. Secondly, humans attempt to know themselves with a view to contemplating, admiring, and discovering their own lives as creatures of God, made in his image and likeness, and, as a result, to love other people and communicate to them their own treasures and talents. This is because the true purpose of human life is one of "giving glory to God" and loving one's neighbor.[49] This motivation may be called doxological. It is, or should be, fundamental for a believer. Third, people may attempt to know humans at large with a view to dominating and controlling them. Let us consider the latter explanation, which may be called the dominating motivation.

---

47. On the convergence and stronger divergence between humans and primates, see K. Pollard, "What Makes us Human?," *Scientific American* (May 2009): 44–49.

48. Aristotle, *De anima* III.8.431b21.

49. On the meaning of the expression "to give glory to God," see *COH* 149–88; P. O'Callaghan, "Gloria de Dios," in *Diccionario de San Josemaría Escrivá de Balaguer*, edited by J. L. Illanes (Burgos: Monte Carmelo, 2013), 565–71.

Knowledge and Dominion

The following adage is well known: *Abstrahe et impera!* ("Know to foresee, foresee to dominate"). Francis Bacon was probably the first one to say, "Knowledge is power." The seventeenth-century English philosopher Thomas Hobbes spoke of "what we can do with [knowledge] when we have it."[50] According to Friedrich Nietzsche, the "will to knowledge" is simply a specific part of the deepest human impulse, which is "the will to power." In the same direction may be understood the famous book of Dale Carnegie, *How to Win Friends and Influence People.* At a more philosophical level, the work of Jürgen Habermas on hermeneutics, *Knowledge and Human Interests,* considers the question openly.[51] Humans, he explains, know and attempt to know things that have a special interest for them, an ulterior purpose.[52] Hans Jonas and others have shown that the object of scientific knowledge, especially the life sciences, tends to be a mechanized and reduced conception of nature, which humans use and manipulate for their own purposes.[53]

Within the process of knowledge three stages may be described. *First,* a spontaneous interest arises toward a particular object, even though it is as yet almost completely unknown to us. This encounter provokes a sense of awe and serves as a reminder of human finitude. Philosophy begins always, said Aristotle, with a sense of wonder. *Second,* once known, the object known becomes, as it were, "just one more thing" that after producing surprise and wonder then gives rise to respect, and perhaps fear, in ever-diminishing quantities. The thing known is just there; should it disappear, it would not matter much. Perhaps we can say that through knowledge the object known is "epistemologically dominated," or assimilated, by the knowing subject. It has lost for the knower its mysterious power; using Marcel's terminology, it is no longer considered as a "mystery" to be contemplated and respected, a mystery that always surpasses us, but rather as a "problem" that has been resolved and therefore dominated. *Third,* humans are often moved to know themselves (and other things) in a search of their own interest, in such a way that the known thing becomes an extension of their own will, their own power and dominion over reality. First of all, the unknown thing produces a challenge and a stimulus; once known, it becomes an object of conquest that leads to dominion, and also, perhaps, to boredom, to self-complacency, to indifference, to destruction.

Christians can recognize in a possessive or dominating search for self-knowledge a significant trace of sin present in their lives. And they can recognize the need to overcome it, in their quest to do anthropology putting in its place alternative motivations that we have called "ethical" and "doxological."

50. T. Hobbes, "Leviathan," in *The English Works,* edited by W. Molesworth (Aalen: Scientia, 1966), 3:13. It was first published in 1839.

51. See J. Habermas, *Knowledge and Human Interests* (London: Heinemann, 1972).

52. Napoleon once said: "I love power. But I love it as an artist. As a musician loves his violin, to obtain from it different sounds and chords and harmonies."

53. See H. Jonas, *Gnosis und spätantiker Geist* (Gottingen: Vandenhoeck & Ruprecht, 1934), and other works.

Agnosticisms and the Relative Value of Human Knowledge

When humans doubt the existence of things they do not manage to know and dominate, the result is the phenomenon of agnosticism. It is often the fruit of an impatient frustration of humans incapable of knowing and dominating reality with their own means. Agnosticism moves on three planes relating respectively to God, to humans, to the cosmos.

The first plane is agnosticism with respect to God. Here we can observe the attitude of considering as nonexistent what cannot be experienced and dominated directly, leading one to be unsure whether or not God exists; this is often followed up by atheism, in which the existence of a supreme being is openly denied. The phenomenon is well known.[54]

On the second plane, throughout recent centuries an enormous effort has been made to understand and explain scientifically what the human being is. Yet we are still far from obtaining a complete, definitive, and unitary explanation of what humans are that takes each and every aspect of their being into account. And not only that; the more we seek an explanation, the further it seems to move away from us. Many philosophers and writers in the modern period have reflected on this epistemological hurdle, this incapacity to describe humanity in a definitive way.

"Among all the natural sciences," wrote Nicholas Malebranche toward the end of the seventeenth century, "the science of man is the most noble. Still, this science is not the one most cultivated nor the most complete of those we have. Most humans just neglect it completely. And also among those who are interested in science, few are those who apply themselves to it and very few indeed those who do so successfully."[55] In the words of the early nineteenth-century playwright Friedrich M. von Klinger:

The physiologists, the psychologists, the anthropologists and the anatomists decipher, describe, explain, dissect man in order to tell us who he is, of what he is made. These experts however can only tell us what keeps man together, what makes man to be. In reality, the primitive peoples did the same thing searching for the music in the lute brought to them by the Europeans, breaking it up into small pieces.[56]

"Man is difficult to discover, and unto himself most difficult of all," Nietzsche wrote. "The spirit often lies concerning the soul. And this causes the spirit of gravity."[57] This situation is well diagnosed by Martin Heidegger in a text already cited in the introduction.[58] And the phenomenologist Max Scheler comes to the same conclusion:

We have a theological, a philosophical and a scientific anthropology before us, which, as it were, have no concern one with the other: yet we do not have one uniform idea of the

---

54. See C. Fabro, *Introduzione all'ateismo moderno* (Rome: Studium, 1964).

55. N. Malebranche, "Recherche de la vérité," books 1–3, in *Oeuvres complètes de Malebranche*, vol. 1, edited by G. Rodis-Lewis (Paris: Vrin, 1961); English translation: *The Search after Truth*, edited by T. M. Lennon and P. J. Olscamp (Cambridge: Cambridge University Press, 1997).

56. F. M. Klinger, *Betrachtungen und Gedanken über verschiedene Gegenstände der Welt und der Literatur* (1803).

57. F. W. Nietzsche, *Thus spake Zarathustra*, translated by T. Common, 4th ed. (Edinburgh, 1916), 178.

58. See Heidegger, *Kant and the Problem of Metaphysics*, introduction, no. 2.

human being. The ever-growing number of specialized disciplines which deal with the human being conceal, rather than reveal, his nature, no matter how valuable these disciplines may be.... Hence, one can say that in no historical era has the human being become so much of a problem to himself as in ours.[59]

Pope John Paul II in 1979 repeated this idea:

Perhaps one of the most obvious weaknesses of present-day civilization lies in an inadequate view of man. Without doubt, our age is the one in which man has been most written and spoken of, the age of the forms of humanism and the age of anthropocentrism. Nevertheless it is paradoxically also the age of man's deepest anxiety about his identity and his destiny, the age of man's abasement to previously unsuspected levels, the age of human values trampled on as never before.[60]

In our effort to know humanity, we find ourselves in the presence of an insuperable mystery, because in reality it is greater than we are. In effect there is something in humans that does not allow itself to be manipulated or objectified or fully understood: an unforeseen richness, an unfathomable depth, a spirit that does not perish. In this ambit, the believer would say, only God is present, only the one who created all things can have the last word. As Hannah Arendt said, "If we have a nature or essence, then surely only a god could know and define it."[61]

Finally, on the third plane, agnosticism with respect to God and humans leads us to attempt to understand fully all that is left about human beings: the reality within which they live—the cosmos, the earth, nature—what God has given them as an integral part of their life on earth. However, as the present ecological crisis has shown, the cosmos also resists all human attempts to comprehend and dominate it fully.[62] Faith invites us instead to contemplate the created world, to accept it gratefully as a gift that leads us to adore the creator, following the example of the heavens, "which are telling the glory of God" (Ps 19:1), of the stars that joyfully "shine with gladness for him who made them" (Bar 3:34). And in Francis's encyclical *Laudato Si'* we read: "Father, we praise you with all your creatures. They came forth from your all-powerful hand; they are yours, filled with your presence and your tender love. Praise be to you!"[63]

In effect, human existence is situated within an ample panorama of elements (God, humanity, the cosmos) that surpass the finite intelligence of humans. These elements are realities that they must learn to trust, in which they must "swim" as people do in the sea, allowing themselves be drawn along by its currents. Using the language of Gabriel Marcel again, we can say that the whole of reality, created and uncreated, spiritual and material, is not a mere problem to be understood and resolved and dominated once and for all, but a mystery in which we live, in which we are immersed, which can only be fully "known" through faith, humility, dedication, fidelity, and love.

One last point. In the area of physics, this presupposition likewise holds to a cer-

---

59. Scheler, *Die Stellung des Menschen im Kosmos*, 11f.

60. John Paul II, *Inaugural Address*, Third Conference of CELAM, Puebla, Mexico, *January 28, 1979*, I, 9. The Pope speaks of the daring of prophets and the evangelical prudence of pastors.

61. Arendt, *The Human Condition*, 10.

62. See *LS*, pars. 66f.

63. *LS*, final prayer.

tain degree. On the basis of the "principle of indetermination" the physicist Werner Heisenberg holds that humans, when they approach material things to measure and observe them, experience the phenomenon that reality itself seems to change due to the presence of the very instruments that are used to measure it.[64] Though this effect may be negligible at a macroscopic level, the presence of an observer at an atomic or subatomic level may change the perception of reality substantially. In other words, even in the area of the exact sciences, pure "objectivity" is impossible.

Conclusion: The Role of Theology in Understanding the Human Being

To conclude, we may make four observations that stem from Christian faith-reflection on the human being, that is, Christian anthropology.

The Created World and the Presence of Sin

Christian salvation and the very existence of humans and the created world are to be considered as a gift or grace of God, the free fruit of his love. To some degree, we are in a position to know the essence or nature of humans, yet the concrete individual existence of humans is not as easy to grasp. In that concreteness is rooted the individuality, unicity, and irreplaceableness of each person, as well as the very mystery of divine self-giving. In effect, our knowledge of the concrete existence of humans, especially that of the individual, does not lead us in the first place to a better knowledge of human nature, as if individuals were mere exemplars of a common human nature. It leads us rather to the creator who gave them existence, the savior who purifies human hearts stained by sin, one by one, the God who wants to lead them to glory.

In fact, we may say that the epistemological difficulties we experience in coming to know humans, which we have just described, especially with respect to their individuality, derive to an important degree from the presence in humans (and also in Christians) of sin. Sin induces humans to consider creation as if the creator did not exist, substituting a respectful and patient dominion under God with an independent, despotic, arbitrary, and even violent dominion. By means of reason humans are certainly in a position to know created things, their nature and inner workings, but at the same time they are tempted to dominate and manipulate them, not respecting their interior purpose, their concrete otherness and existence, their origin and end in God. Sin is the very thing that makes it arduous for humans to profoundly appreciate the singularity of humans, their being "persons," their irreplaceable character, their inherent dignity. We may say, therefore, that the human being who inquires into his own situation, who does anthropology, stands in need of a purification that frees them from sin, because the latter brings them inevitably toward an impoverished understanding of human dignity.[65]

64. W. Heisenberg, *The Physicist's Conception of Nature* (London: Hutchinson, 1958), esp. chap. 1.
65. See the reflection of Cassirer in *An Essay on Man*, 10–17, on Augustine, Thomas Aquinas, and Pascal.

The Limits of Human Understanding

Christian wisdom is not quite the same thing as human wisdom, because it is marked deeply by divine revelation culminating in the cross of Christ (1 Cor 1:18–25). Thus it tends to emphasize the "apophatic" (or negative) side of the path to knowledge of God and humans. While Stoicism offers a vision of human nature that was in principle complete and perfect, Christianity does the very opposite, teaching us that humans are made in the image and likeness of *God*, and God of course is unknown. Christian faith brings us to a greater knowledge of what it means to be human but to an even greater awareness of what we do not yet know about our race. Ernst Cassirer observes that "there always remains one point on which the antagonism between the Christian and the Stoic ideals proves irreconcilable. The asserted absolute independence of man, which in the Stoic theory was regarded as man's fundamental virtue, is turned in the Christian theory into his fundamental vice and error. As long as man perseveres in this error, there is no possible road to salvation."[66] Theology reminds humans to recognize the limits of the knowledge they have of themselves. Nicholas of Cusa in the thirteenth century spoke of the *docta ignorantia*, "wise ignorance"; Lutherans insist on the need to approach the mysteries of faith with a theology that is centered on the tragedy and apparent failure and contradiction of the cross (the *theologia crucis*).[67] Likewise, Thomas Aquinas teaches that the limit of human knowledge of God consists precisely in the conviction that we do not know him.[68] It is clear, therefore, that theological reflection does not depend on or find support in the mere accumulation of data that together end up providing a complete picture, but rather on a vision, a perspective, that gives unity and meaning to all this information. And humans cannot achieve this with their own powers.

The Circular Knowledge of God and Humans and Man's Fundamentally Relational Character

As we have seen, Christian theology places special emphasis on the question "Who is the human being?" while giving full weight to the other question, "What is the human being?" This is so because the theologian attempts to think about human beings from the standpoint of God, humanity's beginning and end. God is the one who, in creating humans, defines and gives them not only their essence or nature but also their concrete individual existence as persons, the means to live, to know themselves, and to realize their potentialities; God is the ultimate end of their lives.

It is fair to say that an ample range of thinkers have considered the "who" as a minor accident in comparison with the "what" of human existence (perhaps Plato, also idealism): first of all, humans are, and subsequently they proceed to establish relationships with others. In the Christian view of things, however, metaphysical pre-

---

66. Ibid., 12f.

67. See O'Callaghan, *Fides Christi*, 20f.

68. "Hoc est ultimum cognitionis humanae de Deo, quod sciat se Deum nescire." Aquinas, *De potentia* q. 7, a. 5, ad 14. See also Aquinas, *In Boeth. De Trinitate*, q. 1, a. 2, ad 1; q. 2, a. 1, ad 6. On this topic, see M. Pérez de Laborda, "La preesistenza delle perfezioni in Dio: L'apofatismo di San Tommaso," *Annales Theologici* 21 (2007): 279–98; "Il progresso nella conoscenza di Dio secondo san Tommaso," *Acta Philosophica* 18 (2009): 309–34.

cedence is given to the "who" over the "what." This is so because the concrete existence of humans as individuals with a specific nature rests on the founding relationship with the creator, who has thought about them, one by one, from all eternity (Eph 1:4), has given them existence, has taken care of them and saved them when they sinned, has given them his life, and will bring them to the fullness of glory in communion with himself. From the point of view of the origin of existence, we can say that the human being is, in the first place, a person, and then a nature; he is primarily a being *ab alio* (existing from another) and as a result a being *a se* (ontologically autonomous), even though subjective human perception may seem to suggest the opposite.[69] Therefore, the human capacity to relate—to God, to others, to oneself, to nature—is not simply a derived, secondary, or accidental feature of human life, something that develops during the personal history of the human being. It is rather something that is constitutive and original, based on the very act with which God communicates being at creation, making humans exist "in relation" to other beings. For this reason, they can realize their potentialities fully only in relationship with others and, fundamentally, in openness to the gifts of God, principally divine grace. Benedict XVI has the following to say in the encyclical *Caritas in Veritate:*

As a spiritual being, the human creature is defined through interpersonal relations. The more authentically he or she lives these relations, the more his or her own personal identity matures. It is not by isolation that man establishes his worth, but by placing himself in relation with others and with God. Hence these relations take on fundamental importance. The same holds true for peoples as well. A metaphysical understanding of the relations between persons is therefore of great benefit for their development. In this regard, reason finds inspiration and direction in Christian revelation, according to which the human community does not absorb the individual, annihilating his autonomy, as happens in the various forms of totalitarianism, but rather values him all the more because the relation between individual and community is a relation between one totality and another.[70]

In fact all the fundamental definitions given to humans by Christian theologians are of a relational kind: humans are made "in the image and likeness of God"; "Christ fully reveals man to himself"; the believer becomes a "child of God," etc. The same approach is taken by the Church Fathers. Irenaeus says: "Gloria Dei vivens homo, gloria hominis visio Dei" (The living man is God's glory; the vision of God is man's glory).[71] Minucius Felix, a third-century author, explains it as follows: "If you do not think seriously what is the divinity, you will never understand man."[72] And Augustine in his *Soliloquia* proclaims: "Animam et Deum scire cupio. Nihilne plus? Nihil omnino" (I desire to know God and the soul [for Augustine the true essence of the human being is the soul]. And anything else? Absolutely nothing else.)[73] The same idea may be found in his circular affirmation and prayer: "noverim me, noverim te" (I will know myself, I will know you).[74] Humans, in knowing themselves (their soul), know God as

---

69. According to Spaemann, "Person and nature are simply incommensurable with one another." *Sulla nozione di natura umana,* 29.

70. Pope Benedict XVI, *Caritas in Veritate,* Encyclical Letter, June 29, 2009, par. 53.

71. Irenaeus, *Adv. Haer.* III, 20, 2–3.

72. Minucius Felix, *Octavius* 17, 2.

73. Augustine, *Soliloquia* I, 7. This work is habitually but not always attributed to Augustine.

74. Ibid. II, 1.

well, though imperfectly, as the origin of their soul. And knowing God, they come to know themselves ever better. Thus, through a circular and ascending process, a true virtuous circle, humans know their own interior reality better and better as they immerse themselves more and more in God. Finally, we can mention Catherine of Siena, who says that we can direct our prayer to God, saying: "In your nature, O eternal Deity, I will know my nature."[75]

Hence, according to the Christian vision of things, the possibility of entering into a relationship with God is written into the depths of each human being. Humans can thus be defined as beings that pray, or at least, beings that can and should pray. "Prayer is not a need, it is an ontological necessity, an act which founds the very being of humans," the Jewish philosopher Abraham Heschel wrote. "The dignity of humans is not to be found in their capacity to fabricate utensils, machines, arms; it is in the first place in the fact of having received the capacity of directing themselves to God. This gift must be included in the definition of humans."[76]

In brief, the human being is not a being *a se*, with an aspiration or openness toward infinitude and a certain capacity to reach it; that is, he is not a nature, an exemplar of the species, who later on becomes a person. Rather the human being is entirely defined and determined by God, because God and only God gave him existence, personal existence, an existence that is expressed in calling and relationship; "only God," although God does use other creatures to communicate his gifts to humans.[77] In the coming chapter we shall consider in a more detailed way how anthropology, throughout history, has always been understood in a relational context, that is, on the basis of a perspective external to humans themselves.

The Place of Science within a Theological Discourse

We can make the following fourth and final observation. What has just been said on our knowledge of humanity from the point of view of God and revelation, on the priority of person over nature, could conceivably be read as a way of trivializing science and therefore the effort humans make to know created reality with their own powers. In the reflection just made, is there not the danger of falling into a kind of fideism with respect to humans? To this we should respond that the affirmation of the priority of person over nature, of God over man, of relationship over autonomy, should not turn the scientific discourse into something superficial or unimportant. It is more likely, in fact, that this approach would do science a good service by ensuring that it does not attempt to become all-encompassing or ideological. Bonaventure spoke of the need to bring all human disciplines under the guide of theology, what he called the "reductio artium in theologiam" (reduction of the arts to theology).[78] God gave the world its inner intelligibility, which reason attempts to discover through science. God is the one who created humans so that they can know and thus praise him for his gifts, dominating the earth, as his image (Gn 1:26–28), with intelligence, wisdom, and will (Sir 17:1–12).

---

75. Catherine of Siena, *Or.* 24.

76. A. J. Heschel, *Man's Quest for God: Studies in Prayer and Symbolism* (New York: Scribner, 1954), 77.

77. See chapter 16, notes 157ff., and corresponding text.

78. See Bonaventure, *De reductione artium ad theologiam notis illustrata.*

In a somewhat simplistic way we may make the following affirmations:

· Science, in its very different forms, inquires principally into human nature, into what humans are.[79] Theologians need to take science seriously because, in challenging human thought on the basis of an objective knowledge of created reality, it also challenges them to seek new solutions and explanations on the basis of revelation and theological reflections, though not simple reflex replicas of scientific findings.

· Philosophy and theology, without neglecting reflection on human nature, look primarily into who humans are, in the widest sense of the word; and whereas philosophy attempts to clarify what it means to say that humans are "persons," theology pays particular attention to their being called one by one by God, to their identity as children of God, made in the image and likeness of the creator, called to share in divine lordship over the earth and in God's own life; theological reflection, in other words, takes the treatise on divine grace as its point of departure, that is, theological anthropology in a strict sense, which we shall consider in the next two sections (chapters 4–17).

· Finally, there is a series of "mixed questions" through which we can attempt to establish a synthesis between the different elements that derive from science, philosophy, and theology, with themes such as human freedom, historicity, the social quality of humans, the understanding of human insertion and presence in the world through work, the constitution of humans in body and soul, the individuality of humans as "persons." These topics will be considered in the fourth and final section of the book, titled "Christian Anthropology."

---

79. As Hans Jonas and others have pointed out, science is driven to an important degree by a desire to use nature. In that sense, technology determines the dynamics of science. In the section headed "Why Do We Do Anthropology?," see notes 53ff. and the corresponding text.

2 HISTORICAL PERSPECTIVES ON HUMANITY IN SEARCH OF IMMORTALITY

What you are you do not see; what you see is but your shadow.
RABINDRANATH TAGORE[1]

If we have a nature or essence, then surely only a god could know and define it.
HANNAH ARENDT[2]

Everything which is not eternal is unendurable, everything of value in life
if it is not eternal, is of no value.   N. A. BERDJAEV[3]

In the first chapter we considered anthropology from a phenomenological angle, attempting to answer three questions. What is the human being? Who is the human being? Why do we do anthropology? In this chapter we shall consider human nature from the standpoint of history: what different philosophies and religions have said of the human being. G. K. Chesterton spoke in a vivid way of the "democracy of the dead," that is, of the contribution that epochs past can and should make to our understanding of the world and of history.[4] Likewise, the philosopher Wilhelm Dilthey declared that "it is only history that will show up what humans are."[5]

---

1. R. Tagore, "Stray Birds," v. 18.
2. Arendt, *The Human Condition*, 10.
3. Berdjaev, *Slavery and Freedom*, 267.
4. "Tradition means giving a vote to the most obscure of all classes, our ancestors. It is the democracy of the dead." Chesterton goes on to say: "Tradition refuses to submit to the small and arrogant oligarchy of those who merely happen to be walking about. All democrats object to men being disqualified by the accident of birth; tradition objects to their being disqualified by the accident of death. Democracy tells us not to neglect a good man's opinion, even if he is our groom; tradition asks us not to neglect a good man's opinion, even if he is our father." G. K. Chesterton, *Orthodoxy* (Garden City, N.Y.: Doubleday, 1959); quotation from chap. 4, "The Ethics of Elfland."
5. W. Dilthey, "Die drei Grundformen der Systeme in der ersten Hälfte des 19. Jahrhunderts," in *Gesammelte Schriften IV* (Gottingen: Vandenhoeck & Ruprecht, 1959), 529. On the topic of tradition, see also an essay of J. Ratzinger, "Anthropological Foundations of the Concept of Tradition," in *Principles of Catholic Theology: Building Stones for a Fundamental Theology* (San Francisco: Ignatius, 1987), 85–101.

Perspectives on Humanity

In both classic and modern thought anthropology is situated as far as possible from discourse on the gods. Besides, among the ancients anthropology was not considered a central philosophical discipline, even though it was always present at an implicit level in the study of epistemology, metaphysics, political philosophy, and ethics. In that sense, modern "anthropocentrism" (according to which humanity itself is the point of reference for understanding human beings, religion, and everything else) is probably an exception, an anomaly, in the history of thought. But it is clear that philosophers of whatever period, when they have spoken of God, of love, of ethical and civil behavior, of war, of celebration, of marriage, of family, of the future, of politics, of the law, when they explain their position on art, on music, on literature, on warfare, in real terms, have been speaking of themselves: they were doing anthropology. The apparent neglect of an explicit anthropology, therefore, did not mean disinterest in human beings but just went to show the difficulty the latter had in knowing themselves objectively as unitary and independent beings, distinguishable from their surroundings. With respect to the world and others, in fact, humans perceived themselves as having what Charles Taylor called "a porous identity."[6]

In this chapter, therefore, instead of studying humans from within human phenomenology, as we did in the previous chapter, we shall seek out external perspectives on humanity, which, in different moments of history, have thrown a light on anthropology. In other words, instead of an anthropocentric, analytic, introspective method, we shall follow an "eccentric," historical, method. This approach is to be found in the following expression of the Indian writer and philosopher Rabindranath Tagore: "What you are you do not see; what you see is but your shadow."[7] In other words, humans are not capable of knowing themselves directly; they must study the shadows that an external light, a different perspective, casts on the ground of their existence and actions in time and space. Lao Tzu, the Chinese "old master" of the sixth century B.C., understood this principle when he wrote: "Whoever looks at himself will not illuminate."[8] The philosopher Martin Buber observes that anthropology becomes problematic whenever humans lose the sense of their place within the world.[9] And the analytical philosopher Ludwig Wittgenstein observes: "The meaning of the world must be outside the world."[10] "A person who has no horizon," writes Hans-Georg Gadamer, "is a man who does not see far enough and hence overvalues what is nearest to him. Contrariwise, to have an horizon means not to be limited to what is nearest, but to be able to see beyond it."[11] Finally, the historian of religion Wilhelm Schmidt holds that there is "a parallel between the different types of religion and the different stages of cultural development. Each one of these types corresponds to a certain attitude of man toward the world which conditions his whole existence. The different

---

6. See Taylor, *A Secular Age*, 32ff.
7. See note 1.
8. Lao Tzu, *Tao te Ching*, edited by V. von Strauss (Zurich: Manesse Verlag, 1959), no. 24.
9. See M. Buber, *Das Problem des Menschen*, 4th ed. (Heidelberg: Lambert Schneider, 1971), 47.
10. L. Wittgenstein, *Tractatus logico-philosophicus*, 6.41 (New York: Routledge, 1961).
11. H.-G. Gadamer, *Truth and Method* (New York: Crossroad, 1986), 269.

divinities which he invokes reflect those aspects of reality upon which his well-being depends on the particular circumstances in which he finds himself."[12]

Throughout this chapter we shall consider five different historical perspectives on humans and their lives, all of them in the context of the human quest for immortality.

The Quest for Immortality

Humans experience a common and insuperable impulse toward permanence, conservation, survival, immortality. This impulse is present throughout all periods of human history, of philosophy and religions, though it is explained in many different ways.[13] This impulse toward immortality is what moves humans to tirelessly seek out the definitive meaning of life and strive to overcome the separation between their present, contingent situation, on the one hand, and their unachieved ideal, on the other, as we saw at the beginning of chapter 1. In all probability, it is fair to say that the impulse toward immortality is the basis of religion itself. It certainly is at the core of Christianity.

The desire for immortality, the desire to live on forever, is particularly present in the classic doctrine of the immortality of the human soul.[14] In the myth of Pandora, hope is presented as the last thing left in the "box" because it is present in the depths of the human spirit. Victor Hugo asked himself on one occasion: "Does the soul exist?" And he replied: "Immortality is the destiny of humans. Without immortality, the whole of creation becomes for humans an immense 'why.' Listen therefore to the dazzling affirmation that springs up from all consciences."[15] Gabriel Marcel expressed the same idea when he said that for him hope seemed to be the fabric out of which the soul is made.[16] His expression "'I love you,' means 'you should not die,'" is well known.[17] Abraham Heschel likewise says: "No soul exists that did not feel the impulse to know something that goes beyond this life, beyond conflict and agony."[18] And the novelist Ernst Jünger said that "man is a being animated by hope, by a shim-

---

12. Schmidt's position is summarized thus in L. Bouyer, *Rite and Man: Natural Sacredness and Christian Liturgy* (Notre Dame, Ind.: University of Notre Dame Press, 1963), 24.

13. Understandably, the bibliography on the topic of human immortality is vast. From the historical point of view, see for example L. R. Farnell, *Greek Hero Cults and Ideas of Immortality: The Gifford Lectures Delivered in the University of St. Andrews in the Year 1920* (Oxford: Clarendon Press, 1921); T. Chakungal, *The Concept of Immortality and the Principal Upanisads* (Rome, 1971); F. Ma'súmián, *Life after Death: A Study of the Afterlife in World Religions*, 2nd ed. (Oxford: Oneworld, 1996); J. Gevaert, "L'affermazione filosofica dell'immortalità," *Salesianum* 28 (1966): 95–129; J. Pieper, *Death and Immortality* (South Bend, Ind.: St. Augustine's Press, 2000); A. N. Flew, "Immortality," in *The Encyclopedia of Philosophy*, edited by P. Edwards (New York: MacMillan, 1972), 4:139–50; W. A. De Pater, *Immortality: Its History in the West* (Leuven: Acco, 1984); P. O'Callaghan, "La muerte y la inmortalidad," in *Philosophica: Enciclopedia filosófica on line*, edited by F. Fernández Labastida and J. A. Mercado (Rome, 2009), available at http://www.philosophica.info/archivo/2009/voces/muerte-inmortalidad/Muerte; COH 19–25.

14. On hermeneutical questions regarding the immortality of the soul, see *COH* 14–18.

15. V. Hugo, *William Shakespeare* (Paris: Hachette, 1880), I, 5:1.

16. Marcel, *Être et avoir*, 117.

17. G. Marcel, in his drama *La mort de demain*.

18. A. J. Heschel, "The Concept of Man in Jewish Thought," in *The Concept of Man: A Study in Comparative Philosophy*, edited by S. Radhakrishnan and P. T. Raju (New Delhi: HarperCollins, 1995), 108–57, 113.

mer of eternity. A ray of immortality has penetrated him. This distinguishes his way of loving from any other kind of love."[19] It is true that Christianity has confirmed and reinforced the common awareness of human immortality. As Nicholas Berdjaev puts it:

At one time in Egypt the dignity of immortality was attributed only to the king; all the rest of the people were mortal. In Greece to begin with only gods or demi-gods or heroes and supermen were regarded as immortal; the people were mortal. Christianity alone has recognized all men as worthy of immortality, that is to say it makes the idea of immortality absolutely democratic. But a process of putting the life of the people on a democratic basis which does not mechanically place men on a level, which does not deny quality, is to make an aristocracy. Every man ought to be recognized as an aristocrat.[20]

Perhaps the most surprising thing is that this desire for immortality is a stable feature of human life, in spite of the obvious fact that all must die. Amid the poverty, insecurity, and suffering of this fleeting and fragile life, there always remains—in apparent tension with all weakness and mortality—the impulse toward the definitive possession of the good, a thrust toward security and peace that last forever.[21] And this impulse is not to be found in other living beings with which humans share the planet earth.

Five Historical Perspectives in Which to Situate Anthropology

I have chosen five perspectives from different periods of history, mainly from within Western civilization, in which to situate anthropology historically. Many others might as well have been considered. They are the primitive or pagan perspective, centered on nature; the classical Greek perspective, centered on the cosmos; the Jewish perspective, based on God himself as the only Lord of the universe; the Christian perspective, founded on Jesus Christ, Son of God and redeemer of the world; and, finally, the modern perspective, which places humans themselves at the center of their own existence. These perspectives will be considered, as we said, starting from the way they focus the human impulse toward immortality, that is, the way in which different periods have given expression to hope of personal or collective survival after death and beyond this impermanent life.

Of these perspectives it may be said that in some cases they are more or less imposed by circumstances (for example, the first one, which I have called primitive or pagan, centered on nature); on other occasions they are chosen more or less freely by humans (this is the case of the Greek perspective, based on the cosmos, and the modern one, based on humans themselves); in other cases there is a combination of the two: the Jewish and Christian perspectives are "imposed" by God, that is, revealed by him, but they must be "chosen" by humans, that is, received through faith. Each perspective involves an epistemology; this, in turn, points to a specific understanding of

19. E. Jünger, *The Glass Bees* (New York: NYRB, 2000).

20. Berdjaev, *Slavery and Freedom*, 176f.

21. See P. O'Callaghan, "La muerte del cristiano como incorporación a la Pascua de Cristo," *Scripta Theologica* 33 (2001): 773–822.

immortality, a theology and an anthropology. As we shall see, the grandeur and poverty of the modern perspective derive principally from the fact that humans have chosen—somewhat narcissistically—a perspective that is none other than themselves. It is deeply anthropocentric.

The Primitive Perspective: The Power of Nature

First we shall consider, briefly, one of the most influential and diffuse implicit anthropologies, found in what might be called "primitive" cultures, which provide us with interesting and perennial elements for understanding the human search for meaning. It may be said that in this cultural setting, myth predominates over reason, collectivity over the individual.[22] In these cultures, humans are acutely aware their own weakness, fragility, and finitude when faced with the magnificence, the greatness, and the power of nature in all its manifestations. Human life is determined and motivated by the need to survive. And early humans did this principally through hunting, in which they developed their skills and defined their *modus vivendi* in a communitarian way. On the walls of the caves of Lascaux in France and Altamira in Spain (fifteenth century B.C.) are to be found exceptionally well-preserved paleolithic rock paintings that represent, among other things, bisons being hunted by humans. It is clear that the survival of the latter depended on suppression of the lives of the animals, as long as they managed to capture and kill them: the death of one living being made the survival of the other possible. The quality and elegance of the designs indicate, among other things, the admiration humans experienced before nature, of the latter's beauty and power. At the same time, the human beings, the hunters, were presented with simple black lines, without any decorative detailing. Man's attention was focused, therefore, on the external world, not on himself. He contemplated and represented artistically the living source of his own life and survival, that is, the animal, who was admired and respected as well as being hunted and killed. This perspective provides the very opposite of an anthropocentric vision of things: humans look outside themselves, toward the other, toward the powers incarnate in nature, in order to find in them the guarantee and future of their own lives.

On the basis of this perspective centered on nature, in natural, "pagan" religions the divinities are presented as forces hidden in different elements of nature: in the mountains, the stars, the sun, the sea, the forests, the lakes, the fields. Humans are meant to give homage to each element of nature in order to satisfy it; by offering part of their own earnings, the hunted animal, or their own lives, they obtain protection and therefore survival. In other words, this living exchange with the divine powers present in the natural world is what assures them of physical survival and thus a generic immortality. In effect, a personal or individual immortality is not envisaged—humans live in close communion with nature and understand their lives as corporeal, perishable, and mortal but rather the immortality of the tribe or family, of one's own name and pedigree, which is expressed, among other ways, in communion with the dead and ancestor cults. Berdjaev writes: "Lévy-Bruhl says with truth that in primi-

---

22. See the collection of essays by J. Ries, *Preistoria e immortalità: La vita dopo la morte nella preistoria e nelle civiltà orali*, edited by R. Nanini (Milan: Jaca Book, 2012).

tive communities, the consciousness of the individual depends upon the consciousness of the group. But this is not the final truth about man."[23]

It is probably fair to say that this vision was present to some degree among the tribes which, some fifteen hundred to two thousand years before Christ, began to constitute, around Abraham, the people of Israel, the people of the Covenant.[24]

The Greek Perspective: The Cosmos and the Logos

The fundamental intuitions and convictions present in Greek philosophy are shared to an important degree by other Eastern philosophies and religions, those of Persia (present-day Iran), of Egypt, of Mesopotamia (Iraq), and of India.[25] Still, the classical Greek vision, that of Pythagoras, Socrates, Plato, Aristotle, the Stoics, and others, is especially relevant in this study, first on account of its inner richness and coherence, then because of its insistence on the centrality of human reason and, because Christian theology developed in a close dialogue with it,[26] and finally because it provides us with the written works of the principal authors, which has allowed us to reflect rigorously on their thought.

The Greek vision also marks the end of the predominance of polytheistic mythology, of natural and primitive religions of the kind we have just described, the place of myth being taken by reason and by a more unitary, spiritual, and transcendent view of the divinity. The divinity is considered as *Logos*, reason, which molds and directs all things, unifies diversity, gives order (Greek, *kosmos*) to the whole, and impresses form (*morphē*) on prime matter.[27] Human activity par excellence shifts from physical, external, practical, and collective action (for example, hunting) to the spiritual, interior, and individual activity of thought with which humans, illuminated by God, come to know the Logos. Gradually reason begins to take the place of myth:[28] from a hard-won and collective survival of the tribe, there is movement toward an affirmation of the immortality of the soul; from the preponderance of matter, there is a shift toward the preeminence of spirit.

Among the reasons that this new vision consolidated in the Mediterranean world from the sixth century B.C. onward should be mentioned the established social dis-

---

23. Berdjaev, *Slavery and Freedom*, 103.

24. See the different positions in M. Tábet, *Introduzione al Pentateuco e ai libri storici dell'Antico Testamento* (Rome: Edusc, 2001), 37–51.

25. On Hindu anthropology, which has very remote origins, see P. T. Raju, "The Concept of Man in Indian Thought," in *The Concept of Man: A Study in Comparative Philosophy*, edited by S. Radhakrishnan and P. T. Raju (New Delhi: HarperCollins, 1995), 206–305. According to the *Taittiriya Upanishad*, there are five different ways of understanding the human being: on the basis of natural processes, from the actions of the gods, from the effects of sacrifices, from penance and incantations, and from cosmic processes and the creative processes of the Atman (or supreme divinity, identified with the consciousness or the universal "I"). Only the last of these processes, however, is in a position to surpass and include the others, according to Raju, 223f. Humans, in other words, are considered and understood properly in the light of the divine. The weakness of this explanation, however, is to be found in the fact that it is not always easy to distinguish between the Atman and humans themselves. Thus the theocentric approach can easily slide toward anthropocentrism.

26. See John Paul II, *Fides et Ratio*, pars. 37f.

27. On the development of the Greek and Christian understandings of the "Logos," see O'Callaghan, "L'incontro tra fede e ragione," 39–44.

28. On the role of myth in the process of acquiring knowledge, see P. O'Callaghan, "Il luogo del mito nell'incontro tra fede e ragione," *Nuntium* 12 (2008): 139–42.

tinction between slave and free man.[29] This critical element of social structure allowed a certain (small) number of individuals to live a life that was no longer precarious and enervating, without the obligation of performing manual work in order to survive, having at their disposal a multitude of slaves to carry out the harder and menial chores. It is interesting to note that the Greek word for "free," *eleutheros*, expresses above all a social condition: literally, the free man is a "member of a people," one who is politically free, capable of controlling his own life and that of others with the help of slaves (nonfree men).[30] For the Greeks it would have been unthinkable to say that all humans are free. They saw only a small minority as such. This situation offered the free the opportunity of living a restful life dedicated to thought, to the art of governance, to philosophy, to contemplation. In other words, humans began to situate what was real and lasting—and thus immortality—not so much in the ambit of external activity, physical work, and fatigue within nature, which expresses and produces a fleeting form of survival, but in that of thought, in being able to lift oneself above material things, their changeableness and corruptibility by means of reason, not only by physical strength. From this condition emerged civilization, ethics, law, the art of war, politics, and so on, which indelibly marked the classical Greek world and then the whole of Western civilization. In it humans discovered themselves as thinking beings.

In any case, humans began to consider nature surrounding them no longer as a mysterious, blind power but as *kosmos*, that is, unitary and ordered nature, because in it was present reason, the Logos. Martin Heidegger was the one who recently discovered the original understanding of the Greek Logos that had been aired by the philosopher Heraclitus, that is, as a bond, a connection and union between existent things (possibly the term Logos comes from *legō*, which means to "recollect," to "unite," to "pronounce").[31] To know, to think, in other words, means to "put together," to realize and contemplate the order and unity present in things. In the Greek world humans began to consider themselves and the world around them, to study the processes by which they knew things (epistemology) through abstraction, contemplation, and dialogue. They discovered themselves as thinking beings capable of going beyond ephemeral and passing things and began to inquire into the notion of a universal and permanent truth that is common to humans and gods alike. Let us consider two important ways in which the Greeks understood the process of knowing things, that is, epistemology, those of Plato and Aristotle.[32]

---

29. On this question, see C. E. Manning, "Stoicism and Slavery in the Roman Empire," *Aufstieg und Niedergang der römischen Welt* 36, no. 3 (1989): 1518–43.

30. See BDAG, 316f., s.v. ἐλεύθερος.

31. See M. Heidegger, *Heraklit, Martin Heidegger Gesamtausgabe*, vol. 2, Abteilung: Vorlesungen, 1923–1944 (Frankfurt: V. Klostermann, 1979). See also M. Heidegger, *Heraclitean Fragments: A Companion Volume to the Heidegger/Fink Seminar on Heraclitus*, edited by J. Sallis and K. Maly (Tuscaloosa: University of Alabama Press, 1980). On this question, see E. L. Miller, "The Logos of Heraclitus: Updating the Report," *Harvard Theological Review* 74, no. 2 (1981): 161–76. On the term "Logos," see BDAG, 598–601, s.v. λόγος.

32. The materialistic atomism of Democritus should also be mentioned. Democritus begins with the classic distinction between the four fundamental elements of which the universe is composed: earth, air, fire, and water. And he says that we know things because the fine atoms of which they are composed penetrate our senses directly. Thus fire is known to us through the penetration of fire into the human senses (Empedocles developed this idea), water by the penetration of water, and so on. Clearly it is a materialistic and elementary epistemology.

The spiritualistic epistemology and dualistic anthropology of Plato   Plato, taking up the doctrine of Socrates, "does not conceive of any philosophy, of any conception of the world and of life, if not through man who is part of it."[33] According to this great philosopher, man in the depth of his being is a spiritual soul (*psyche*) that exists incorruptibly, from all eternity and forever. In a previous, pre-corporeal existence, this soul gazed on the "world of ideas" in which it was able to contemplate all things. "The soul, being immortal and born many times, has effectively seen all things, those of above and those of below [Hades], in such a way that there is nothing that it has not learned."[34] Plato defines an idea as "a being that really is, without color, without shape and invisible, and which can be contemplated by the guide of the soul, that is the intellect, and around which is present true knowledge."[35] Plato explains that after the descent of the soul into matter as a result of a primitive fall, humans forgot all they had contemplated and now live imprisoned in a mortal body in the darkness of a deep cavern. "For whatever obscure reason," he says, "man became heavy, all full of forgetfulness and wickedness, and fell onto the earth."[36] Still, with the aid of the senses and a serious attempt at dialogue with others, human memory is stimulated and man—in contact with things and with the help of primitive myths that explain his formation and fall—begins to know again (or, better, to recognize) the things forgotten. Things are known, therefore, through a process of reminiscence, that is, recognizing what has already been seen and then fallen into oblivion.[37] To know is to remember. Because all humans, all souls, have contemplated at the beginning the world of ideas, in principle all are capable of understanding the same things, which is what makes dialogue, intellectual sharing, and common truth possible. The dialectic method used by Socrates to reach knowledge is well known.

Because truth and thought are perpetual in that they are incorruptible, and thought is the principal activity of the soul, Plato deduces that the soul itself must be immortal, destined to share in the fortunes of the gods.[38] Mortality, pain, conflict, and finitude, therefore, are all attributable to the body and to matter, which are temporal and perishable, destined to disappear, and not to the soul. Humans, therefore, are composed of two elements, body and soul, that are incompatible with and antagonistic to one another. The duality experienced by humans corresponds to an ontological dualism present from the very beginning of their existence: the soul is a kind of emanation of the superior divinity, and the body, as an organ of punishment, has a mate-

33. B. Groethuysen, *Anthropologie philosophique*, 2nd ed. (Paris: Gallimard, 1980), 17. First published in 1953.

34. Plato, *Meno* 81c.   35. Plato, *Phaedo* 247c.

36. Ibid., 248c.

37. Discussed especially in the *Meno* and the *Republic*. In the *Meno* Plato asks how we can encounter what is not already present in our mind. His answer is through remembering, anamnesis. However, anamnesis, Lévinas observes, reduces other people with whom we dialogue to the role of midwives and necessarily mitigates the otherness of the known person. Something of a kind may be found in Descartes's *Méditation* III and Augustine's *De Magistro*, which use the category of "recollection." To overcome the danger of anonymity in the process of knowing the other, therefore, Lévinas insists on Kierkegaard's doctrine of the relationship of the individual with God. On this question, see B. Treanor, "God and the Other Person: Levinas's Appropriation of Kierkegaard's Encounter with Otherness," *Proceedings of the American Catholic Philosophical Association* 75 (2002): 313–24.

38. See Plato, *Phaedo*, in *COH* 23–25.

rial and nondivine origin. Humans, therefore, are superior to the rest of the cosmos not only because they attempt to know and dominate it (as did Protagoras, precursor of Plato, who said that "man is the measure of all things") but because their true being is divine in character, though subordinate to God. In fact, Plato was openly opposed to Protagoras and said that "not man but God is the measure of all things."[39]

In substance, the thought of Plato involves the following logical stages: from an anthropological perspective (man is situated within a unitary and ordered cosmos and acts accordingly) emerges a specific epistemology (that of reminiscence), which implies a form of immortality (in this case, the individual and spiritual immortality of the soul), a theology (in principle, one that is monotheistic in character, in which the Logos and other spiritual beings emanate from God), and an anthropology (man is seen as composed of two opposing elements, body and soul).

Science and human identity in Aristotle   The epistemology of Aristotle, differently from the spiritual variety of Socrates and Plato, begins with empirical data perceived through the senses.[40] In humans there is an intrinsic union between body and soul (this is the so-called hylomorphic theory), and man is called a "rational animal." According to Aristotle, we know things through a process of abstraction from singular elements and sensible data. Humans at the beginning of their existence did not contemplate everything in the world of ideas and later fell on into oblivion, as Plato thought; rather, the human mind may be considered a clean slate without any "previous idea." Humans abstract intelligibility which things themselves contain, as the bee draws nectar from the flower. Thought can become common and universal (to be potentially shared by all humans) either because nature, which we all know, is unique and unitary (it is *kosmos*) or because, according to some commentators on Aristotle (Alexander of Aphrodisias and Averroes), the process of abstraction is attributed to a kind of intellect common to all humans (the "agent" or "possible" intellect).[41] From this many would suggest that human immortality is attributable to the common intellect that is shared and imper-

39. See Protagoras, *On the Truth* or *Subversive Discourses*. See also Plato, *Laws* 716.

40. On the philosophy of Aristotle, see, for example, E. Berti, *Profilo di Aristotele* (Rome: Studium, 1979); E. Berti and I. Yarza, *Struttura e significato della Metafisica di Aristotele: 10 lezioni* (Rome: Edusc, 2006). On Aristotle's work *De anima*, see R. M. Polansky, *Aristotle's De Anima* (New York: Cambridge University Press, 2007).

41. According to Aristotle, there are two intellects in humans, the passive and the active (also called, respectively, the "possible intellect" and the "agent intellect"). The agent intellect is the more noble and divine part of the intellect, whereas the possible intellect is receptive to the action of intelligible species and belongs fully to the soul. The possible intellect (*nous pathētikos*) "is separable, impassible and unmixed" (*De anima* III.5.430a17–18). It is corruptible and not immortal. The agent intellect (*nous poiētikos*), however, is immortal but distinct from the soul because it thinks and loves *through* the latter, in such a way that only "when it is separate it becomes that which it truly is" (ibid., a22–23). According to different commentators on Aristotle, among them Alexander of Aphrodisias and Averroes, the agent intellect is identified with God himself. The same position was maintained recently by M. Burnyeat, *Aristotle's Divine Intellect* (Milwaukee, Wis.: Marquette University Press, 2008), 41f. This is a God who contains in himself, who is in himself, the entire system of correct concepts that permit the intelligible forms to be present in the human intellect. Other authors, however, such as Themistius and Avicenna, insist on personal immortality of the agent intellect. See O. Hamelin, *La théorie de l'intellect d'après Aristotle et ses commentateurs* (Paris: Vrin, 1953); H. J. Blumenthal, *Aristotle and Neoplatonism in Late Antiquity: Interpretations of the De Anima* (London: Duckworth, 1996). On the agent intellect in Aristotle and Thomas Aquinas, see J. F. Sellés, ed., *El intelecto agente en la escolástica renacentista* (Pamplona: Eunsa, 2006). I am grateful to Professor I. Yarza for the information he provided me with on this debate.

sonal for all humans. God is presented as a cosmic divinity at the source of all movement (he is called "the unmoved mover") and has little involvement with the world and
its intelligibility. Prayer by humans would be meaningless.

The anthropological perspective of Aristotle is again the cosmos, known by humans through an epistemology of abstraction, with an understanding of immortality
of a collective kind (the common intellect), a theology in which God is the source of
movement within the universe, and a unitary anthropology (man as a unity of body
and soul). The advantage of Aristotle's system is that it gives value to empirical reality
and science and, therefore, to the material world that really exists. At the same time,
in holding to the essential materiality of humans and their autonomy before God, his
position has been interpreted by Platonists and Christians as countenancing atheism
and irreligion. He does not manage to provide a satisfactory explanation either of individual immortality or of God. For this reason the Church Fathers for the most part
preferred to use Plato in their theological and spiritual speculations.[42]

The Jewish Perspective: God, the Only
Lord of the Covenant

The origins of Israel go back some fifteen hundred to two thousand years before
Christ. Judaism from the beginning of its history took root in a variety of nomadic
and pagan peoples who were not particularly sophisticated from a cultural, intellectual, or religious standpoint.[43] The identity and unity of Israel, its extraordinary
history and singularity, are to be found not in its ethnic origins or cultural strength
but in the fact that, through the Covenant established by Yahweh with Abraham, its
people became the people of God under his special and perpetual guidance and protection. Many manifestations of this identity are to be found throughout the books
of the Old Testament.[44] Interestingly, Heschel calls Judaism "God's quest for man."[45]

God, the only Lord of the Covenant　For the people of Israel, the "perspective" from
which humans consider themselves has been neither chosen by them nor imposed by
the external world. Rather it has been given to them directly by God, who makes himself present in their life. In effect, God has established a lasting Covenant and shows
himself as the only Lord of every single aspect of the life of the people. Neither idols
nor alternative divinities are tolerated. Thus it is not a question of humans looking
for meaning in their lives, the human search for the Logos typical of the Greeks, but
rather a divine search for humans, "the anthropology of God who takes care of man,"
in the words of Heschel.[46] In effect, the perspective is that of God as Lord, the al-

42. The majority of the Church Fathers did not establish a significant dialogue with Aristotle. Many of
them considered him an atheist. There are exceptions, of course. On this question, see A.-J. Festugière, *L'idéal
religieux des grecs et l'Évangile*, 2nd ed. (Paris: Librairie V. Lecoffre J. Gabalda & C.ie, 1932). On this work, see
D. T. Runia, "Festugière Revisited: Aristotle in the Greek Patres," *Vigiliae christianae* 43 (1989): 1–34.

43. On the origins of Israel, see note 24 above.

44. On the topic of the Old Testament Covenant, see S. W. Hahn, *Kinship by Covenant: A Canonical Approach to the Fulfillment of God's Saving Promises* (New Haven, Conn.: Yale University Press, 2009).

45. A. J. Heschel, *God in Search of Man: A Philosophy of Judaism* (Cleveland, Ohio: World Publishing,
1963), 425.

46. A. J. Heschel, *Man Is Not Alone: A Philosophy of Religion* (New York: Jewish Publication Society,
1951), 134.

mighty, the only Lord of heaven and earth. Israel does not offer rational explanations to account for the situation of humanity, although to some degree this is to be found later on in Hebrew wisdom literature. The substantial message of the Old Testament is quite simple: God is Lord and faithfully takes care of "his" people, of all their needs, both material and spiritual. As a result, the children of the Covenant, made in the image and likeness of God, are meant to submit themselves entirely to him in faith, completely excluding attachment to any other "divinity."

In this way, any alternative "perspective" on humanity is thereby excluded. Humans understand and situate themselves solely before God. Israel, therefore, is not a people that develops on the basis of a rich and unitary culture, allowing itself to evolve over time like the faithful of any other religion. Rather it is God who, having created the entire universe and humans, and retaining an absolute sovereignty over them, has freely founded a people with whom he establishes a Covenant. For this reason Judaism is a deeply vital religion, one of pilgrimage, powerfully centered on God, who must be considered king, Lord, the only and ultimate horizon for the life of the chosen people. It is a religion in which the very possibility of rejecting God or his will—through blasphemy, rebellion, or idolatry—is a paradoxical sign of its authenticity (if the people had "invented" their own god, of course, it would make no sense for them to rebel against it or seek out alternative divinities). God is meant to be praised and recognized for what he is and for what he has done for his people, not so much (as in paganism) for the favors and protection he provides, because "the earth is the Lord's and everything it contains" (Ps 24:1). God must be praised and thanked; he must be obeyed and not "understood."

If the "primitive" perspective was centered on nature and the classical Greek perspective on ordered and unitary and knowable cosmos, in the Jewish perspective the role of nature or of the cosmos is assumed by the Covenant. God has established a Covenant with humans, and humans understand their lives not so much as one more part of the natural world or of the cosmos (the human being considered as a "microcosmos") but, in the face of the powerful action of God over the world, sharing in this power as one made in his image and likeness.[47] The point of reference for those called by God, their "organ of identity" as it were, is no longer physical strength or ability or intellect, but the heart (in Aramaic, *lēb*), with which they guard the memory of all the divine benefits they have received throughout their history. "Bless the Lord, my soul, and forget not all his benefits" (Ps 103:2). In the words of Heschel, "The essence of Jewish religious thinking does not lie in entertaining a concept of God but in the ability to articulate a memory of moments of illumination by his presence. Israel is not a people of definers but a people of witnesses."[48] Immortality belongs not so much to the individual but to the people within their history, insofar as they believe in a God who is always faithful to the Covenant. At the same time, death is considered to be a loss of the most precious gift the Old Testament speaks of, that is, life, because God is the God of the living, the God of Abraham, Isaac, and Jacob. The loss of life is closely connected with sin and is normally seen as a punishment for the primitive Fall.[49]

---

47. On man as a microcosm in Greek thought, see R. Allers, "Microcosmos from Anaximander to Paracelsus," *Traditio* 2 (1944): 319–407.

48. Heschel, *God in Search of Man*, 140.   49. See Gn 3:17–19; Wis 1:13–14, 2:23–24.

By way of synthesis we can say the following: a perspective (God as the only Lord, who establishes a Covenant and thus founds a people) opens the way to an epistemology (considering the whole of reality in the light of the Covenant), a kind of immortality (that of the people), a theology (God as almighty, merciful, faithful, etc.), and an anthropology that is clearly unitary, as we shall see presently.

The positive side of Old Testament anthropology lies in the fact that humans discover themselves throughout their everyday life of contact with God, with the earth and with matter as God's greatest work, superior to nature and the cosmos, the only creature to be made in his image and likeness (Ps 139:13–16):[50]

For you formed my inward parts, you knitted me together in my mother's womb. I praise you, for you are fearful and wonderful. Wonderful are your works! You know me well; my frame was not hidden from you, when I was being made in secret, intricately made in the depths of the earth. Your eyes beheld my unformed substance; in your book were written, every one of them, the days that were formed for me, when as yet there was none of them.

And again: "What is man that you are mindful of him, and the son of man that you care for him? Yet you made him little less than a God, and crowned him with glory and honor. You have given him dominion over the works of your hands; you have put all things under his feet" (Ps 8:4–6). In other words, humans come to know themselves, from the outset of the Old Testament, on the basis of what God, the Lord, does for them. From this fundamental perspective, more concrete elements of Jewish anthropology begin to develop.

Still, Old Testament anthropology is in many ways incomplete, fragile and unsure of itself. In spite of the promises of God and his professed fidelity, the people are doubtful and hesitant, at least in certain periods, and they fall into blasphemy and idolatry in others. These doubts may be expressed in four areas: individual immortality, the fidelity of God, the exclusion of other peoples, and the distance God maintains from his people.[51] All four have highly relevant implications for anthropology.

The first area of doubt is the question of individual immortality. The Old Testament attributes to the "dead," or *refa'im*, a kind of survival that is poor and ephemeral. In fact, the state of the *refa'im* who inhabit "hell" (*she'ol*) is one of indigence, obscurity, anonymity, undifferentiated existence. The dead are like shades of humans. It is understandable that the sacred writers would insist on this point once we take into account two facts: (1) that the cult of the dead is clearly opposed to the anti-idolatrous thrust of the prophetic books, and (2) that the Semitic cult was unrelated to any kind of human immortality that excluded corporeity and life in society.[52] Still, immortality as a complement to God's power and fidelity is a promise for the future: that of the people is guaranteed (Nm 23:19; 1 Sm 15:29; Rom 11:29); that of individuals, however, remains an open question.

The second area of doubt is the experience of God's fidelity. Throughout the his-

---

50. On Hebrew anthropology, see Heschel, "The Concept of Man in Jewish Thought"; *God in Search of Man*; and *Man Is Not Alone*. See also the useful text of H. W. Wolff, *Anthropology of the Old Testament*, 6th ed. (Philadelphia: Fortress, 1974).

51. This topic is developed in P. O'Callaghan, "La persona umana tra filosofia e teologia," *Annales Theologici* 13 (1999): 71–105.

52. See *COH* 76–78. See chapter 19, note 54 and corresponding text.

tory of the people of God we can observe a kind of spiritual struggle between Yahweh and his people on account of the vicissitudes of life, failures of different kinds, and the people's apparent abandonment by God. The ways of providence in the Old Testament show something of the definitive and unconditional love of God toward humans, but at the same time they hide it. And as believers wonder whether God is truly faithful to his promises, at the same time they ask about their own situation. The doubts they experience about God's fidelity have important anthropological consequences. These doubts are expressed by the Psalmist (Ps 77:7–12):

Will the Lord spurn for ever, and never again be favorable? Has his unwavering love for ever ceased? Are his promises at an end for all time? Has God forgotten to be gracious? Has he in anger shut up his compassion?" And I say, "It is my grief, that the right hand of the Most High has changed." I will call to mind the deeds of the Lord; I will remember your wonders of old. I will meditate on all your work, and muse on your mighty deeds.

Some of God's people, doubting divine omnipotence, are tempted by idolatry, seeking out alternative divinities capable of satisfying human needs that God seems to take no interest in, as in pagan religions. Others, doubting rather divine goodness, challenge God, who is three times Holy, with a sterile spirit of rebellion and blasphemy. In real terms, the same suspicion is present in both cases: the impression is given that the love of God is not definitive, or perhaps that humans (or at least the individual human being) are not willing to accept perpetual divine favor. Doubting God in his omnipotence, goodness, and fidelity brings them to cast a shadow over their own lives, dignity, and destiny. Nonetheless, it is fair to say that on the whole the Old Testament teaches that, in spite of the inconstancy of humans, God remains always faithful. The prophets insist on it repeatedly.

The third area in which the chosen people express doubt is the universality of God's love for humans. In the Old Testament it would seem that divine favor, as expressed in the Covenant, is directed exclusively, or almost exclusively, to the chosen people, that is, to a numerically limited group of persons. In fact, at times the love of God for "his" people seems to motivate the punishment or killing of other peoples not chosen by God (Nm 21:21–35, 31; 2 Sm 8, 10; etc.). It would seem that divine favor is directed only to some, the chosen people; others—members of other races, nonbelievers on the whole—do not enjoy the same privilege.[53] In the light of the Old Testament, then, what idea of humanity as a whole emerges? What is the situation of the rest of humans and, in particular, of those who do not belong to the people of God? It would seem that the love of God toward humans is not universal, and therefore there is no theological justification for single human "race"; in this context it seems to be impossible to speak of the equality of all humans before God.

The fourth area of doubt has to do with the question of universal prayer. The possibility of an intimate and direct relationship with God, face to face, seems to be reserved for some privileged individuals among the Israelites. Only a chosen few, normally in the context of special functions of government, of prophetic exhortation, and of cult over the people of God, are in a position to speak with God directly, to

---

53. See G. Tanzella-Nitti, "Una immagine credibile di Dio: La rilettura della violenza nella Bibbia alla luce dell'evento di Gesù di Nararet," *Annales Theologici* 28, no. 1 (2014): 85–121.

pray. This is the case, for example, of kings, of the great prophets (especially Moses), and occasionally of priests (Ex 19–20). The intimacy of humans with God is therefore limited and focused in a functional way, because it refers to the good of God's people as a whole and not to the individual situation of each one.

In brief, we can say that the Old Testament offers us a theology, an ample doctrine on the action and nature of God before humans, but not as yet a finished anthropology with a definitive profile. For such an anthropology true believers would have to wait for the fullness of time, the coming of the messiah, Jesus Christ. We shall consider this issue now, as well as in the next chapter and frequently throughout this treatise.

The Christian Perspective: Jesus Christ the Savior

The anthropological perspective typical of the New Testament does not change substantially with respect to that of the Old, as we have just described it. Humans continue reading their lives and nature in the light of the Covenant that God wished to establish with them. But the Christian perspective is made present in a new way: in the person of the Son of God made man, Jesus Christ, in this way intensifying and amplifying the Old Testament vision. The fundamental perspective of the sovereignty of God and of the Covenant he established with humans is not revised, but it is manifested in a clearly tangible, paternal, merciful, universal, and definitive way in Jesus Christ, who becomes, through the resurrection, "our Lord." In the Old Testament the saving acts of God are made present powerfully within the history of humanity, but in the New, primacy is taken by the living history of the person of the Son of God made man, Jesus Christ. Christians in that sense not only believe in God, they not only trust the one who has created them, but they become believers in a God who has sent his only Son in human flesh to save us. The proper profile of Christian faith, and the Christian perspective, therefore, is delineated and determined by the gift of the incarnation of the Word (see chapter 12). Before considering the Christological aspect of anthropology in the coming chapter, we shall address the four anthropological challenges that arose in the Old Testament, just listed, and see that in the context of the saving work of Christ, such challenges are substantially met.

First, Christian faith in individual immortality. From the moment of the resurrection of Christ from the dead, the point of departure for Christian preaching and for the Church's universal mission, immortality is offered to each and every human being, or person. Besides, the promise of the resurrection of the dead shows that immortality includes human corporeity to the fullest possible degree, and thus the entire human being.[54] Hannah Arendt speaks of the

Hebrew creed which stresses the potential immortality of the people, as distinguished from the pagan immortality of the world on one side and the Christian immortality of individual life, on the other. At any event this Christian immortality that is bestowed upon the person, who in his uniqueness begins life by birth on earth, resulted not only in the more obvious increase of other-worldliness, but also in an enormously increased importance of life on earth.[55]

---

54. On this issue, see P. O'Callaghan, "Risurrezione," in *DISF* 2:1218–31. A 2002 English translation of this article may be found at www.inters.org/resurrection. See also *COH* 74–114.

55. Arendt, *The Human Condition*, 315.

Second, we address the believer's experience of God's fidelity. The suspicion Jewish believers had regarding God's definitive "attitude" toward humans is completely overcome in the New Testament, at an objective level at least. This is so because it is God's own consubstantial Son who suffers maltreatment and death on account of human incredulousness and sin. Thus Christian believers, united with the head of the Church and believing in him, have no reason to complain about their pains and upsets, no motive for doubting the love and mercy of God. In a sense, through the incarnation God has incorporated himself into the sorrow, the bewilderment, and the suffering of humanity. Besides, the incarnate Word, rising up from the dead, ascending to the right hand of God and sending the Spirit, will remain always "to make intercession for" humans (Heb 7:25), as a tangible and unfailing guarantee of God's faithful commitment in favor of humanity. Christians may still experience the harshness of injustice, the rigor of pain, the cruelty of incomprehension, but on account of their union with Christ, dead and risen, faithful and obedient to the end, the Father through the Spirit infuses into their heart an unwavering hope.

Third, as for doubts about the universality of God's love, with the resurrection of Christ and the sending of the Holy Spirit begins the universal mission of the Church bringing the good news of salvation to all humans (Mt 28:18–20; Mk 16:15f.). In this mission we come to understand the ultimate reason for the Covenant between God and Israel, which is the salvation of humanity. As the prophet Isaiah tells us, "It is too light a thing that you should be my servant to raise up the tribes of Jacob and to restore the preserved of Israel? I will give you as a light to the nations, that my salvation may reach to the end of the earth" (Is 49:6). The fact that with the coming of Christ salvation is potentially destined to all human beings without exception gives us certainty that for God all humans are equal in dignity, all are equally worthy, as God's creatures, of receiving the divine gifts, of eschatological communion. "There is neither Jew nor Greek, there is neither slave nor free, there is neither male nor female; for you are all one in Christ Jesus," Paul concludes (Gal 3:28).

Fourth, regarding doubts about intimacy with God, in the New Testament divine intimacy is opened to all: "No longer do I call you servants, for the servant does not know what his master is doing; but I have called you friends, for all that I have heard from my Father I have made known to you" (Jn 15:15). With the revelation of our divine filiation in Christ, all without exception are invited and given the real possibility to direct their minds and hearts toward the creator of the universe with the simplicity and trust of children; in this, besides, we can perceive something of the irreplaceable dignity of each person before God. The reception of grace makes humans, all humans, capable of directing their minds and hearts to God in filial intimacy, and, at the same time, it allows them to perceive the value of the human person, of each person.

Still, in spite of these fundamental elements, it is also true that the New Testament does not contain an anthropology that is either fully developed or completely new. Certainly Paul and John, as we shall see, develop quite a complete reflection on the doctrine of grace, on the life of God in humans. Yet, from the time of the Church Fathers on, an ample and coherent Christian anthropology begins to consolidate, in close dialogue with philosophy, on the basis of a believing reflection on the person of the Word of God made man, savior of the world, to which we shall turn shortly.

The Modern Perspective: The Advent
of Anthropocentrism

From the sixteenth century onward a new style and perspective began to consolidate in the Western world. The interesting thing is that it does not offer a really new perspective on humanity but involves rather the negation of all perspectives, in the sense that philosophers attempt to understand humanity starting with humanity itself. Modernity is the anthropocentric period par excellence, which will be followed by a post-Christian and a postmodern period.

The Christian origin of modern anthropocentrism   It has sometimes been said that only in the late Middle Ages, the Renaissance, and the modern period have we come to discover the dignity, freedom, and intrinsic value of each and every person. It was commonly held, especially in the wake of the Thirty Years' war (1618–48), that religions had in fact hidden humans from themselves, covering over their true dignity, violently alienating them from their proper nature, not allowing them to live autonomous lives.[56] This classic (and simplistic) thesis was applied by the nineteenth-century historian Jacob Burckhardt to the Renaissance period, represented by Francis Petrarch and John Pico della Mirandola among others.[57]

More recently, Hans Blumenberg, in his 1966 work *The Legitimacy of the Modern Age*, admits, as Burckhardt did, that Christian faith has contributed decisively to the growth of the modern awareness of the dignity and freedom of each person.[58] He says, however, that once these truths have been discovered in a definitive way, modern anthropology should leave the Christianity that nurtured them behind once and for all and hold unhesitatingly to the autonomy and dignity of the human individual independent of Christian or any other revelation. In this sense, modernity is new, unique, or, as he says in the title of his work, "legitimate." Yet Blumenberg identifies modernity not with the triumph of reason but rather with an affirmation of the autonomy and self-affirming capacity of humans. For this reason he holds that the doc-

---

56. For different recent explanations of the origins of modernity, see M. Fazio, *Historia de las ideas contemporáneas: Una lectura del proceso de secularización*, 2nd ed. (Madrid: Rialp, 2007); Taylor, *A Secular Age*; M. Lilla, *The Stillborn God: Religion, Politics, and the Modern West* (New York: Knopf, 2007); M. A. Gillespie, *The Theological Origins of Modernity* (Chicago: University of Chicago Press, 2008); B. S. Gregory, *The Unintended Reformation: How a Religious Revolution Secularized Society* (Cambridge, Mass.: Belknap Press of Harvard University Press, 2012). On the question of modern anthropocentrism, see P. O'Callaghan, "L'Europa e la speranza: Tra promessa e ricordo; Riflessione intorno all'Ecclesia in Europa," *PATH* 4 (2005): 241–70; "The Eclipse of Worship"; and "La relación entre modernidad y evangelización," *Scripta Theologica* 45 (2013): 41–64.

57. See J. Burckhardt, *The Civilization of the Renaissance in Italy: An Essay* (Garden City, N.Y.: Phaidon, 1960). First published in 1860. On Petrarch, see M. A. Gillespie, "Petrarch and the Invention of the Individual," *The Theological Origins of Modernity*, 44–68. The thesis of Pico della Mirandola on the myth of the Renaissance is presented and criticized by L. Bakelants, "Les rapports de l'humanisme et de la Réforme," *Revue de l'Université de Bruxelles* 18 (1966): 264–82; H. de Lubac, *Pic de la Mirandole: Études et discussions* (Paris: Aubier-Éditions Montaigne, 1974).

58. See H. Blumenberg, *The Legitimacy of the Modern Age* (Cambridge, Mass.: MIT Press, 1985; originally published in 1966). See the bibliography on the discussion of Blumenberg's thesis in Scola, Marengo, and Prades López, *La persona umana*, 30n14. See also W. Pannenberg, "Christianity as the Legitimacy of the Modern Age: Thoughts on a Book by Hans Blumenberg," in *The Idea of God and Human Freedom* (Philadelphia: Westminster Press, 1973), 178–90; Gillespie, *The Theological Origins of Modernity*, 11f.

trine of Christian grace impedes the definitive shift to modernity: in effect, humans under divine grace will never achieve the full freedom that is their due because they will always be dominated by another—by God, or perhaps by the Church.

According to a recent study by Marcel Gauchet, the real reason for the consolidation of modernity over/after Christianity may be found in the fact that Christian theology took the freedom and responsibility of humans very seriously, seeing in them the true protagonists of the creative and ethical processes of history, that is, freedom. This represents, paradoxically, an exit from religion.[59] We shall return to the complex relationship between grace, freedom, and autonomy in chapter 20.

The eighteenth-century philosopher Immanuel Kant is one of those who most openly attempted to place man himself at the very center of anthropology while avoiding having any systematic recourse to God or religion.[60] The ambit of philosophy, he said, may be summed up in four questions. What can I think? What must I do? What can I hope for? What is man? According to Kant, in fact, the first three questions all lead to the fourth one: What is man? "At heart all this may be reduced to anthropology," he concludes.[61] To understand humanity and the world, he says, we should leave aside all fundamental Christian doctrines on the Trinity, the incarnation, and any ecclesiastical structure: "The decorations ... should be put away.... The cords of sacred tradition, with its accessories, statutes and observations, which provided excellent services in the past, will become bit by bit superfluous. In fact they will end up being a chain."[62] And Habermas observes that Kant "on the one hand considers religion [obviously, the Christian religion] as a source of a morality that satisfies the canons of reason, but on the other hand as a dark rock, which philosophy must purge from obscurantism and fanaticism."[63]

The nineteenth-century empiricist philosopher John Stuart Mill wrote in the following optimistic tone:

I grant that some of the precepts of Christ as exhibited by the Gospels—rising above the Paulism which is the foundation of ordinary Christianity—carry some kinds of moral goodness to a greater height than had ever been attained before, though much even of what is supposed to be peculiar to them is equaled in the *Meditations* of Marcus Antoninus, which we have no ground for believing to have been in any way indebted to Christianity. But this benefit, whatever it amounts to, has been gained. Mankind have entered into the possession of it. *It has become the property of humanity*, and cannot now be lost by anything short of a return to primeval barbarism."[64]

---

59. M. Gauchet, *La révolution moderne* (Paris: Gallimard, 2007).

60. See my critique of Kant's focus on the value of modernity: "Il compito della teologia: porre domande o elaborare risposte?" in *Theo-loghía: Risorsa della universitas scientiarum*, edited by M. Sodi (Rome: Lateran University Press, 2011), 37–55.

61. I. Kant, *Logic*, introduction, iii.

62. I. Kant, *Religion within the Limits of Reason Alone*, A170/B179.

63. J. Habermas, *Zwischen Naturalismus und Religion: Philosophische Aufsätze* (Frankfurt: Suhrkamp, 2005), 164. Translated into English as *Between Naturalism and Religion: Philosophical Essays* (Cambridge: Polity, 2008).

64. J. S. Mill, "The Utility of Religion," in *Three Essays on Religion*, 3rd ed. (London: Longmans, Green, Reader, and Dyer, 1874), 69–125, 97f.; emphasis added. The emperor and Stoic philosopher Marcus Aurelius, also called Antoninus, died in 180 A.D., once Christianity was well established. So there could have been quite some influence of the latter on the former.

Nonetheless, the thesis of Kant, Mill, Blumenberg, and others,[65] typical of modernity and tending toward secularization, has not been generally accepted by Catholic authors such as George Bernanos and Romano Guardini[66] or by Protestants such as Wolfhart Pannenberg.[67] Bernanos, reflecting on the emptying of the soul of our civilization, says: "A civilization does not collapse like a building; it would be more correct to say that it empties out of its substance stage by stage until nothing is left but the shell."[68] Guardini is realistic (and pessimistic) when he says, in his 1950 work *The End of the Modern World*, that without Christian faith,

when man fails to ground his personal perfection in divine Revelation, he still retains an awareness of the individual as a rounded, dignified and creative human being. He can have no consciousness, however, of the real person who is the absolute ground of each man, an absolute ground superior to every psychological or cultural advantage or achievement. The knowledge of what it means to be a person is inextricably bound up with the faith of Christianity. An affirmation and cultivation of the personal can endure for a time perhaps after faith has been extinguished, but gradually they too will be lost.[69]

Guardini goes on to speak of the "disloyalty" or "dishonesty" of the modern period, in the sense that modernity has not loyally recognized and treasured the true source of its most authentic and enduring thought forms.[70] Still, the humanistic product of lived Christianity is marked, as it were, by a kind of "cultural inertia" that, though present and influential, inevitably loses vigor and strength as time go by when it is not nourished by the living wisdom and divine sap that gave rise to it in the first place. Criticizing Blumenberg, Pannenberg finds the roots of Christian appreciation for humanity and the created world in the doctrine of the incarnation of the divine Word: "It was faith in the saving presence of the Incarnation that made it possible to demand a permanence of faith in creation."[71] In several chapters of the last section of this treatise, we shall consider various examples of this phenomenon.[72]

Besides, despite the common acceptance of gratuitous statements regarding medieval obscurantism, it is now well established that the birth of a clear awareness of the dignity of the human individual may be situated in the early Middle Ages and not in the Renaissance period, as Burckhardt thought.[73] The anthropology of the first

---

65. The following authors have been particularly influential during the twentieth century on the secularizing direction Christianity was taking: H. Cox, *The Secular City: Secularization and Urbanization in Theological Perspective*, 10th ed. (New York: Macmillan, 1966); F. Gogarten, *Verhängnis und Hoffnung der Neuzeit: Die Säkularisierung als theologisches Problem* (Munich: Siebenstern Taschenbuch, 1966), translated into English as *Despair and Hope for Our Time* (Philadelphia: Pilgrim Press, 1970).

66. R. Guardini, *The End of the Modern World* (Wilmington, Del.: ISI Books, 1998).

67. See Pannenberg, "Christianity as the Legitimacy of the Modern Age." Pannenberg considers the liberation that Protestantism offered in relation to Catholic ecclesiastical structures in positive terms.

68. G. Bernanos, *La France contre les robots* (Paris: Plon, 1970), cited in G. Ravasi, "Le anime d'Europa: Un saggio sulle radici del vecchio continente," *East* 3 (February 2005), 30–34, 32.

69. R. Guardini, *The End of the Modern World*, 98f.

70. See ibid., 99.

71. Pannenberg, "Christianity as the Legitimacy of the Modern Age," 174. Pannenberg criticized the position of Blumenberg on the basis of the inseparability of Christian faith in the incarnation and the affirmation of the value of creation.

72. See also O'Callaghan, "Il compito della teologia," 46–50.

73. See R. W. Southern, "Medieval Humanism," in *Medieval Humanism and Other Studies* (New York: Harper and Row, 1970), 29–60; C. Morris, *The Discovery of the Individual 1050–1200* (London: SPCK, 1972);

medieval philosophers, says Aron J. Gurevic, may be summed up in the formula *individuum est ineffabile*, "the individual is ineffable."[74] Goethe put it in another way: "The mother-tongue of Europe is Christianity."[75] And even Kant recognized that "the Gospel is the source from which our civilization has grown up."[76]

Similar positions are to be found in twentieth-century scholars such as Jacques Maritain, Karl Löwith, and Eric Voegelin.[77] Löwith writes:

The historical world in which it was possible for the "prejudice" that anyone who had a human face possessed for this reason the dignity and destiny of being human, is not originally the world ... of the Renaissance, but the world of Christianity, in which humans, through the God-man Christ, have found their position before themselves and their neighbor. The image which makes the European a human being, is substantially determined by the idea the Christian carries within himself, as image of God.... This historical reference ... is indirectly clarified by the fact that only with the weakening of Christianity has humanity become problematic for itself.[78]

The twentieth-century British poet and playwright T. S. Eliot said the following:

The dominant force in creating a common culture between peoples each of which has its distinct culture, is religion. Please do not, at this point, make a mistake in anticipating my meaning. This is not a religious talk, and I am not setting out to convert anybody. I am simply stating a fact. I am not so much concerned with the communion of Christian believers today; I am talking about the common tradition of Christianity which has made Europe what it is, and about the common cultural elements which this common Christianity has brought with it.... It is in Christianity that our arts have developed; it is in Christianity that the laws of Europe have—until recently—been rooted. It is against a background of Christianity that all our thought has significance. An individual European may not believe that the Christian Faith is true, and yet what he says, and makes, and does, will all spring out of his heritage of Christian culture and depend upon that culture for its meaning. Only a Christian culture could have produced a Voltaire or a Nietzsche. I do not believe that the culture of Europe could survive the complete disappearance of the Christian Faith. And I am convinced of that, not merely because I am a Christian myself, but as a student of social biology. If Christianity goes, the whole of our culture goes with it.[79]

The modern turn toward subjectivity   Lucien Goldmann characterized the modern period in the following terms: "the principal object of all philosophical thought is man, his conscience, his conduct. At heart, all philosophy is anthropology."[80] No mat-

---

R. W. Hanning, *The Individual in Twelfth-Century Romance* (New Haven, Conn.: Yale University Press, 1977); C. W. Bynum, "Did the Twelfth Century Discover the Individual?" *Journal of Ecclesiastical History* 31 (1980): 1–17; W. Ullmann, *The Individual and Society in the Middle Ages* (London: Methuen, 1967); Taylor, *A Secular Age*.

74. See A. J. Gurevich, *The Origins of European Individualism* (Oxford: Blackwell, 1995), 1–21

75. Cited by O'Callaghan, "L'Europa e la speranza," 252.

76. Cited by G. Ravasi, "Le anime d'Europa," 30.

77. See J. Maritain, *Religion and Culture* (London: Sheed and Ward, 1931); See K. Löwith, *Meaning in History: The Theological Implications of the Philosophy of History* (Chicago: University of Chicago Press, 1949); E. Voegelin, *The New Science of Politics: An Introduction* (Chicago: University of Chicago Press, 1987). First published in 1952. On the position of Löwith and Voegelin, see H. Syse, "Karl Löwith and Eric Voegelin on Christianity and History," *Modern Age* (Summer 2000): 253–62.

78. K. Löwith, *From Hegel to Nietzsche: the Revolution in Nineteenth-Century Thought* (London: Constable, 1965), 379.

79. T. S. Eliot, *Notes towards the Definition of Culture* (New York: Harcourt, Brace, 1949), 126.

80. L. Goldmann, *Le Dieu caché: Étude sur la vision tragique dans les Pensées de Pascal et dans le théâtre de*

ter how we resolve the question of the relationship between Christian faith and modern anthropology, this period is strongly marked by two features. On the one hand, there is a highly positive and optimistic vision of humanity and of its capacities and talents: human beings have value in themselves, are capable of realizing their potentialities, of improving their fortunes. Human dignity, talent, and capacity are localized, as it were, in the intellect and the will (in the mind, the spirit), that is, within the subjectivity of the individual. Through their spiritual faculties humans act, dominate, control the confines of their own existence with ever greater freedom and autonomy. On the other hand, paradoxically, this vision clashes with an acute sensitivity toward evil that is present in society and in humans, in their limits and sinfulness: we can mention the social upsets that marked the end of the medieval period, the Lutheran view of humans as *simul iustus et peccator* (at once just and sinner), the experience of many people during the Great Plague, the Thirty Years' War, and Jansenism.[81]

In both cases humans tend to prioritize their own subjectivity, their own thought, taking it as real, solid, and ultimate reality. While the Middle Ages generally considered human subjectivity as an accidental manifestation of the life of the soul, in the modern period the subjectivity of individuals is placed right at the center of human life. Man discovers himself no longer in the light of a distinct other (nature, cosmos, God, Christ) but within himself, within his own subjectivity that is autonomous and individual, which might be called selfhood as substance. The problem arising from concentrating on the subject is not only of an ethical kind, as if we were talking of a kind of exaggerated egotism. It is rather a question of a new understanding of humans in which human thought is considered real and supreme. The essence of man is shown up on the screen of consciousness with a clarity in which he becomes more and more lucid and free, ever more capable of dominating himself, his surroundings, and the whole wide world. The person is defined not so much in terms of ontology but of subjectivity: as someone capable of making a fully free, autonomous, and conscious decision. Perhaps we can say that while medieval anthropology was individualistic at an ontological level, modern anthropology is individualistic at a subjective or psychological level. The "person" begins to find expression as "personality."

The spirit of subjectivity gives a new impulse to the development of science and technology, concentrated more and more on understanding humans, on their immediate needs, on their will to dominate the universe. Gift and mystery are increasingly rationalized and instrumentalized; a perfect, complete clarity is sought after, entirely under human dominion. Rationalism consolidates.[82] The existence of God becomes a mere external guarantee of the order of the universal and of ethical action.[83] Humans neglect to praise God, they no longer refer everything to him. Anthropocentrism and naturalism abound. In the words of Gillespie, "Modernity ... was the consequence of

---

Racine, 2nd ed. (Paris: Gallimard, 1955), 16. Translated into English as *The Hidden God: A Study of Tragic Vision in the Pensées of Pascal and the Tragedies of Racine* (London: Routledge and Kegan Paul, 1964).

81. On the phenomenon of our sensitivity to sin, see J. Delumeau, *La peur en Occident, XIVè–XVIIIè siècles: Une cité assiégée* (Paris: Fayard, 1978), and *Sin and Fear: the Emergence of a Western Guilt Culture, 13th–18th Centuries* (New York: St. Martin's Press, 1991). On the Lutheran view, see O'Callaghan, *Fides Christi*, 35f. On people's experience during troubled times, see chapter 11, notes 32ff. and corresponding text.

82. See P. O'Callaghan, "L'incontro tra fede e ragione," 37–39.

83. See Taylor, *A Secular Age*, 221ff.

the attempt to resolve this conflict by asserting the ontic priority not of man or God but of nature."[84]

Several authors developed the notion of the centrality of the human subject. Among them probably the most influential is the seventeenth-century French philosopher René Descartes.[85] His expression of his doctrine of the *cogito*, the self-thinking "I," as ultimate and incontrovertible reality is considered by many the moment of the birth of modern philosophy.

Descartes and his dualistic heritage   Descartes, on the basis of human experience, distinguishes two things within humans, the *res cogitans* (the thinking substance) and the *res extensa* (corporeity, the material substance of humans), which correspond approximately to soul and body. He describes man "as an angel who drives a machine."[86] His is a dualistic understanding of humanity. Still, it should be noted that in spite of the apparent likenesses, the position of Descartes is quite different from that of Plato, for two reasons. First because he considers the body not as the product of a fall but rather as the instrument of the soul, its agent within the world, and holds that both body and soul are created by God. And second Descartes is different from Plato because he believes that human beings are *res cogitans* not because they are capable of thinking but rather because, in its subjectivity, thought itself is the immediate manifestation of the human spirit. For Descartes the *res cogitans* is "*intuitive* as to its mode; *innate* as to its origin; *independent of things*, as to its nature," in the words of Maritain.[87] Its purpose is not one of "animating" the body, as the scholastics taught, but that of thinking. *Cogito, ergo sum*: "I exist, I am, because I think." Within thought humans grasp their own existence, because being and thinking are equivalent to one another.

With Descartes, says Heidegger, "man becomes the measure and center of being. Man is at the foundation of the whole of being."[88] And, as Hannah Arendt writes: "The Cartesian solution to this perplexity [the discovery of the Archimedean point] was to move the Archimedean point into man himself, to choose as ultimate point of reference the pattern of the human mind itself, which assures itself of reality and certainty within a framework of mathematical formulas which are its own products."[89] With Descartes, says Karl Löwith laconically, "the Christian world was secularized."[90] This is the true "Copernican revolution" of anthropology. Neither the earth, nor God, nor Christ, is any longer the center, as they were for pagans, Greeks, Jews, and Christians, as the case may be; now humanity itself is at the center of all things.[91]

---

84. M. A. Gillespie, *The Theological Origins of Modernity*, 17. He continues: "While the new naturalistic beginning helped to ameliorate the conflict, it could not eliminate the antagonism at its heart without eliminating either God or man. However, one cannot abandon God without turning man into a beast, and one cannot abandon man without falling into theological fanaticism."

85. See especially the *Méditations* of Descartes.

86. Maritain, *Religion and Culture*, 24.

87. J. Maritain, *Three Reformers: Luther, Descartes, Rousseau* (London: Sheed and Ward, 1966), 57.

88. H. Heidegger, *Nietzsche* (Pfullingen: Neske, 1961), 2:61. Translated into English as *Nietzsche*, edited by D. F. Krell (San Francisco: HarperSanFrancisco, 1991).

89. H. Arendt, *The Human Condition*, 284.

90. K. Löwith, *Nietzsches Philosophie der ewigen Wiederkunft des Gleichen* (Berlin: Verlag die Runde, 1935), 99.

91. The position of Descartes has been critiqued frequently, starting during his lifetime, by P. Gassendi, T. Hobbes, A. Arnauld, and M. Mersenne: it is often said that his shift from thinking activity ("I think") to

As a consequence of this view, faith and theology, which are based on a revelation external to humans, are not excluded, but they become more and more superfluous. At the same time, paradoxically, the position of Descartes is anything but antireligious, because he considered God as the creator and guarantor of all that exists. In fact, many of the authors who follow his line of thinking (Leibniz, Berkeley, Malebranche, and others), tend to postulate the direct presence of "God" within human consciousness. Perhaps we might say of these authors, paraphrasing Paul (Gal 2:20), that it is no longer man who thinks, but God who thinks in him. On this basis, many modern authors, like Plato and Aristotle before them, attempt to offer an "ontological" demonstration of the existence of God, starting with human subjectivity.

As a result of this approach, we tend to lose a sense the existence of the world as a gift, to be contemplated and admired as a manifestation of God's love. Charles Taylor has noted that for this reason "modern humanism, in addition to being activist and interventionist, had to produce some substitute for agape," that is, for the gratuitous love that moves the world whose ultimate source is only God.[92] In an attempt to improve the world through ethics and technology, humans have in fact come to lose the meaning of the created world as a gift, from which arises the joyful duty to glorify and adore God in all things; we can verify in this period what Taylor has called "an eclipse of cult," a forgetfulness of the sacred obligation, superior to all others and at their root, of offering grateful praise to the one and only Lord of the universe.[93] Angelini observes: "One of the clearest markers of the modern period, in relation to different forms of Christian piety, is the massive loss of sensitivity in respect of liturgical celebration; liturgy has experienced a clear drop in the formative influence over Christian consciousness."[94]

Nihilism and the crisis of meaning   We can apply to this process the words of Heidegger already cited: "No other epoch has accumulated so great and so varied a store of knowledge concerning man as the present one.... But also, no epoch is less sure of its knowledge of what man is than the present one. In no other epoch has man appeared so mysterious as in ours."[95] Humans, in excluding an objective and external perspective on themselves—not inquiring into where they come from, where they are going, why they exist, who or what should be the point of reference for their lives—enter sooner or later into a deep crisis of meaning that easily ends up in nihilism, or at best in a postmodernist cul-de-sac of "weak thought" and the exclusion of the "metanarrative" (see the introduction). It is also true that when humans reject the perspective God himself gave them in faith, they tend toward self-sufficiency and,

---

the substance of the soul ("I am"), from the "idea" of perfection to the existence of a perfect Being, God, was overhasty, to say the least. The circularity of this "demonstration" of the existence of God and the attempt to found the objective truth of everything evident on a divine attribute has also been critiqued.

92. Taylor, *A Secular Age*, 27.

93. See O'Callaghan, "The Eclipse of Worship." On the loss of a sense of gratitude toward God in the modern period, see O'Callaghan, "La relación entre modernidad y evangelización."

94. G. Angelini, "Antropologia teologia: La svolta necessaria," *Teologia* 34 (2009): 322–49, 330.

95. See Introduction, note 2. The following words, frequently attributed to T. S. Eliot, are worth noting: "We know too much and are convinced of too little. Our literature is a substitute for religion, and so is our religion."

sooner or later, in many cases, toward practical atheism, what Taylor calls "exclusive humanism."[96] At the same time, human subjectivity becomes a univocal category shared equally by God and humans. Thus humans end up taking the creator's place, forgetting that their very existence (which is what makes thought and subjectivity possible) is truly a gift of the creator. In fact, humans over recent centuries have attempted to go beyond themselves, taking it that they are capable of "self-creation," of self-constructing their own identity and immortality down to the last detail, at a social level (as in the case of Marxism) or at an individual level (in line with Fichte, Nietzsche, and Sartre).

If humans are beings that, in knowing themselves, create or design their own identity, the result of this process cannot be but nihilism, because the product of the self-creation of humans, who have been created *ex nihilo*, will necessarily be ephemeral and transitory. This may be seen in the work *The Order of Things* (originally *Les mots et les choses*) of the anthropologist Michel Foucault, which speaks of the decisive presence within human life of death, on the basis of which all human projects, and the cosmos itself, are moving inexorably toward nothingness.[97] The same may be said of the studies of the scientist Jacques Monod, for example his work *Chance and Necessity*, in which he says that the universe is undergoing a long yet inevitable decline and cooling-off process that, having begun as anthropocentric, gradually has become anthropophobic and anticosmic.[98] We can see the classic process the Greeks described of humans who exalt themselves (*hybris*) but who eventually fall back into deep ruin (*nemesis*).

The Norwegian playwright Henrik Ibsen compared the modern effort of humans to understand themselves with the effort involved in peeling an onion in search of its core, its true essence. When one reaches the end of the process, the protagonist exclaims: "right to the very center, there are just layers and layers ... that are smaller and smaller.... Nature is facetious."[99] Hannah Arendt describes as follows the anti-mundane spirit the characterizes modernity:

The world loss of modern philosophy, whose introspection discovered consciousness as the inner sense with which one senses his senses and found it to be the only guarantee of reality, is different not only in degree from the age-old suspicion of the philosophers toward the world and toward the others with whom they shared the world; the philosopher no longer turns from the world of deceptive perishability to another world of eternal truth, but turns away from both and withdraws into himself.[100]

Returning to nature and the rediscovery of human singularity   At the same time it may be noted that humans, having excluded God because they find themselves incapable of dominating him with their own powers and having excluded themselves for

96. The ultimate purpose of Taylor's book *A Secular Age* is, he tells us, that of describing the *Entstehungsgeschichte* of "exclusive humanism" (26).

97. See M. Foucault, *The Order of Things: An Archaeology of the Human Sciences* (New York: Vintage, 1994).

98. See J. Monod, *Chance and Necessity: An Essay on the Natural Philosophy of Modern Biology* (New York: Alfred A. Knopf, 1972).

99. From the work of H. Ibsen, *Peter Gynt*, act 5; see the introduction to I. Yarza, ed., *Immagini dell'uomo: Percorsi antropologici nella filosofia moderna* (Rome: Armando, 1997), 16f.

100. H. Arendt, *The Human Condition*, 293.

more or less the same reason, over recent decades have directed their attention preferentially toward nature, often employing parareligious language. This may be seen in a good part of modern neopaganism, represented, for example, by so-called New Age religiosity, ideological ecologism, gender theories, and a univocal understanding of the rights of humans and animals.[101] In fact, an important part of contemporary scientific and philosophical anthropology places humans on the same level as animals, whether in the context of evolutionism or in behaviorist studies. Questions regarding history and tradition are avoided, as is the teleological argument (which deals with the end of humans), and obviously any possible reference to immortality, because all of this is ultimately unverifiable by science.

The twentieth-century scientist Arnold Gehlen, for example, considers the human being as an underdeveloped and deficient animal, from the zoological and biological standpoint, especially as regards its instincts.[102] Whereas most animals are born with well-developed instincts, the human pup is born with virtually none, defenseless and completely needful of the care of others. This is an obvious disadvantage from the point of view of autonomous and short-term survival as well as being a decisive factor in human socialization. However, Gehlen says, from other points of view this deficiency constitutes a net advantage for humans, for it allows them to be enriched by interacting with others in a gradual, complex, and extremely varied way. The initial instinctual underdevelopment of humans makes them extraordinarily adaptable and moldable. Humans are born nonspecialized, plastic, deeply "open" to many possible situations, opportunities, and circumstances. In brief terms, the place of nature in the formation and development of animals is occupied by that of culture in the formation of humans. Humans construct their own world through culture and interaction with others. In this way, according to Gehlen, whereas other animals filter everything they receive through their hard-wired instincts (excluding many elements), humans in principle are open to all and everything. In effect, humans can decide to accept or refuse, they can reinforce their natural tendencies, they can oppose their instincts, inclinations, and experience, they can project their own lives toward the future. In order to do so, in order to extend their power and dominion, humans seek out tools and instruments and establish agreed collaborations with others in a much more sophisticated, successful, and permanent way than animals do. Thus humans present themselves as finalized beings capable of directing their lives to an end that is common to all living beings: survival. All this, Gehlen adds, should not be attributed to a spiritual human soul but is rather a biological development that is much more advanced in humans than in animals.[103]

A similar line is to be found in the writings of the anthrobiologists Adolf Portmann and Francisco de Ayala. According to Portmann, humans have a "physiologically precocious birth"; by rights their birth should take place much later than it

---

101. See M. Introvigne, *Le nuovi religioni* (Milan: Sugarco, 1989); J. Vernette, *Le Nouvel Age: À l'aube de l'ère du Verseau* (Paris: Tequi, 1990); A. N. Terrin, *New Age: La religiosità del postmoderno* (Bologna: Dehoniane, 1993).

102. See A. Gehlen, *Man: His Nature and Place in the World* (New York: Columbia University Press, 1988). First published in 1940.

103. On this author, see J. L. Ruiz de la Peña, *Las nuevas antropologías: Un reto a la teología* (Santander: Sal Terrae, 1983), 107–28.

actually does if compared with the moment of birth of comparable mammals.[104] In spite of the tendency of these authors to explain everything on a biological basis, they realize that the religious question remains a fundamentally open one, especially (this is the position of de Ayala) in the context of the challenge posed by one's own death. Humans, in effect, experience an insuperable desire to survive, which goes beyond the confines of the empirical world.[105] Whereas animals ignore death, humans consider it as something decisive, as we can see in death rituals and the sense of life that is passing.[106] According to Portmann, humans, in the context of death, discover themselves as "self" (in self-consciousness), as "value" (in ethics), and as "finitude" (before the infinite, the divine).[107]

The value and limits of anthropocentrism   We have just seen that the anthropology deriving from Descartes's *cogito* has been, throughout the history of modernity, problematic from many points of view. Is this all that can be said? What has the Church's attitude been when faced with the growth of an anthropocentric view of the world that marks an important part of philosophical and scientific production over the past four centuries? The Church has had some reservations, of course, although the negative side of anthropocentrism did not leave a serious mark on the practical Christian lives of a great number of believers, who learned how to accept its fruits without forgetting to recognize their ultimate source (God, who creates and redeems). This movement, in spite of its limits, excesses, and one-sidedness, expressed something that was deeply valid and lasting for a Christian anthropology. John Paul II wrote in his encyclical *Fides et Ratio*:

Modern philosophy clearly has the great merit of focusing attention upon man.... Even in the philosophical thinking of those who helped drive faith and reason further apart there are found at times precious and seminal insights which, if pursued and developed with mind and heart rightly tuned, can lead to the discovery of truth's way. Such insights are found, for instance, in penetrating analyses of perception and experience, of the imaginary and the unconscious, of personhood and intersubjectivity, of freedom and values, of time and history. The theme of death as well can become for all thinkers an incisive appeal to seek within themselves the true meaning of their own life.[108]

Seven brief reflections may be made on this dynamic.

---

104. A. Portmann, *Biologische Fragmente zu einer Lehre vom Menschen* (Basel: Benno Schwabe, 1944), 45.

105. See *COH* 253–85.

106. See P. O'Callaghan and F. V. Tiso, "Death," in *Religions of the World: A Comprehensive Encyclopedia of Beliefs and Practices*, edited by J. G. Melton and M. Baumann, 2nd ed. (Santa Barbara, Calif.: ABC-CLIO, 2010), 2:866–74.

107. See A. Portmann, *Biologische Fragmente*, 45. The topic has been dealt with by many philosophers, such as K. Jaspers, M. Heidegger, L. Pareyson, and M. F. Sciacca.

108. John Paul II, *Fides et Ratio*, pars. 5 and 48. Benedict XVI, in "Faith, Reason, and the University: Memories and Reflections," a lecture at Regensburg on September 12, 2006, said the following: "This attempt, painted with broad strokes, at a critique of modern reason from within has nothing to do with putting the clock back to the time before the Enlightenment and rejecting the insights of the modern age. The positive aspects of modernity are to be acknowledged unreservedly: we are all grateful for the marvelous possibilities that it has opened up for mankind and for the progress in humanity that has been granted to us."

1. *The consolidation of a new individualistic religion.* On the one hand, the anthropocentric movement coincides historically with the consolidation of a somewhat anti-Christian and anticlerical attitude typical, for example, of the Enlightenment.[109] In some cases it was seen in an attempt to found a new religion, true and proper, in substitution of Christian faith. This may be seen, for example, in the work of Kant, *Religion within the Bounds of Reason.*[110] We are reminded of the enthronement of the goddess Reason in the cathedral of Notre Dame in Paris during the French Revolution. On the other hand, Christian spirituality and ethics, based on the commandment of love, cannot be lived out in the rarefied atmosphere of a closed human subjectivity, because Christians are—at least, they should be—radically other-centered, that is, directed through charity to the glory of God and the good of neighbor; the ultimate truth about humans is to be found in God, their creator. Human fulfillment takes place in the service of others and not in a closed individualism or eclectic spirituality.[111] If Feuerbach said that "the secret of theology is anthropology," the believer should say, on the contrary, that "the secret of anthropology is theology" or, better, "the secret of man is God."

2. *Overcoming the predominance of sin.* If Jesus the Christ came to the earth precisely as savior, humans—each and every human being—should consider themselves sinners, unredeemed, needful of reconciliation, and therefore incapable of finding within themselves the resources to overcome their own alienation, because salvation comes by divine grace. In this sense Augustine was right when he said that humanity is a *massa damnata.* One of the "dogmas" of the Enlightenment, however, is denial of the doctrine of original sin, and in that sense humans are considered to be in a position to save themselves.[112] Besides, deism (which separated ordinary, everyday life from the providential power of the creator), pantheism (which identifies the created world with God), and atheism (which denies God, or rather places humanity in his place) have undone all the seriousness of sin. On the other extreme, the Protestant Reformation and Jansenism considered humans above all else as sinners, thus neglecting to some degree questions regarding created nature and the dignity of each person. This position is in clear contrast with the optimism that marks the modern anthropocentric spirit. Yet the common result of both extremes has been that the consideration of the intrinsic dignity, goodness, and richness of human life, as well as its sociality, have become more and more disconnected from theological reflection, whether Protestant or Catholic, and, as a result, secularized.

3. *A proper evaluation of human life.* Unlike other periods of history, in the present historical moment humans are not considered, generally speaking, as as the fruit of God's work, worthy of being admired and represented artistically; at best, perhaps, they are considered either as organisms that produce things or as beings that stand

---

109. On the Enlightenment, see the classic work of F. Valjavec, *Geschichte der abendländischen Aufklärung* (Vienna: Herold, 1961).

110. See O'Callaghan, "Il compito della teologia," 38–46.

111. See H. de Lubac, *Catholicism: Christ and the Common Destiny of Man* (San Francisco: Ignatius, 1988); Benedict XVI, *Caritas in Veritate*, par. 53.

112. See Valjavec, *Geschichte der abendländischen Aufklärung*, 8ff. On original sin, see P. O'Callaghan, "Una lectura cristológica de la doctrina del pecado original," *Scripta Theologica* 46, no. 1 (2014): 161–80.

in need of assistance and compassion from society, specifically from the state. In this process the loss of the presence of Christian art (art carried out in a Christian spirit) has been of great importance. Besides, it has often been pointed out that a spirituality for simple, everyday life is lacking.[113] Little is said of the bond that should unite the grace of Christ with life in the world, with work, with civil professions, with family life. And, finally, reflection on the collective and social side of human nature has tended over recent centuries to become a monopoly of nonbelieving philosophers (especially in the area of sociology and political philosophy) who attempt to apply a purely secular or "lay" ethics to the situation of the world. This ethics initially seemed to open up to the existence of God (according to Kant, God is "a postulate of practical reason"), but it ended up by eliminating his public and private presence in order to defend autonomy and human freedom. In brief, it has seemed—Nietzsche had already said so—that Christians are against life: the glorification of God requires in one way or another the humiliation of man, and the exaltation of man points toward the disappearance, the "death" of God. In order for God to be God, humans have to be considered the negation, the sinners.

4. *A proper understanding of Christian subjectivism.* In all we have seen so far, it should be noted that Christian "subjectivism" has deep and ancient roots and is deeply linked with the spirituality and prayer of the Church. Augustine, for example, speaks of humans who look into their own hearts to know themselves and to know God. Looking toward themselves, they find God, and looking toward God, they rediscover themselves. "Deum et animam scire cupio," says Augustine. "Nihilne plus? Nihil omnino," he writes in an already cited text of his *Soliloquia*.[114] The soul turns to God, but God, in turn, within an ascending process, become present to the soul, which discovers God within its own interiority. Thus in the *Confessions* Augustine writes: "Intus eras et ego foris" (You were within me, yet I looked for you outside).[115] At the same time, the subjectivity forged in prayer and contemplation is not to be identified with simple solitude.

5. *The Christian rediscovery of human sociality.* In the modern period, as so many movements of robust Christian spirituality have demonstrated, the Spirit has kept placing his power and inspiration in the lives and hearts of the Church and of many believers; the life of prayer and piety has been maintained and consolidated; nature has corrected, to some degree at least, the errors of humans and regulated their lives; the Church has promoted an extraordinary variety of activities of a social kind, which are manifestations of the spirit of charity that they are animated by, especially in the area of education and health care; and the missions *ad gentes* have been ample and extraordinarily successful. All this reflects love and appreciation for humanity, a Christian anthropology that is strong, rich, and unitary, though implicit. Besides, at an institutional level the Church has taken important initiatives when faced with the "signs of the times" in relation to a progressive socialization, as we can see in the development of the social doctrine of the Church, especially from Leo XIII's encyclical

---

113. See C. Taylor, *Sources of the Self: The Making of the Modern Identity* (Cambridge, Mass.: Harvard University Press, 1989), 211–302.

114. Augustine, *Soliloquia* I, 7.

115. Augustine, *Confessiones* X, 27.

Rerum Novarum (1891) right up to the *Caritas in Veritate* of Benedict XVI (2009) and Francis's *Laudato Si'* (2015). Humanity, with all its complex problems, in the family and in society, has acquired an every greater importance in the Church's preaching.[116]

6. *Liturgical and ecclesiological renewal.* The twentieth century witnessed a powerful rediscovery of the intrinsically collective and social side of Christian life and of grace, especially in the liturgical movement and in ecclesiology; this may be seen in the writings of Casel, Guardini, Bouyer, Ratzinger, de Lubac, Congar, Philips, and many others, as well as in different documents of Vatican Council II, especially *Sacrosanctum Concilium* and *Lumen Gentium*. In fact, theological anthropology, which specifically concerns sanctifying and justifying grace, has traditionally been presented in a somewhat individualistic way in the sense that emphasis has been placed primarily on the relationship between grace and freedom, between God and the human individual. Throughout the past century, however, the Church has also managed to recuperate the collective and social side of humanity, taking into account the mediation of grace and the word of God, along with the implications of the life of grace for others, that is, in witnessing and the Christian apostolate.[117]

7. *The value of the world and of work.* At the same time, throughout the twentieth century there was a clear rediscovery of the intimate bond between authentic Christian spirituality and the lives of humans in the world and in society, and with it the depth (not only the amplitude) of the mission the Church is called to carry out. Christians rediscovered in the light of faith the most human of human realities: the family, service to society, social life. The theology of work is a definite novelty, and the sense of Christian secularity is better understood, as is the value of the created world (as may be seen with the so-called genitive theologies). To this rediscovery important contributions have been made by John Paul II.

Elements of the magisterium of John Paul II   The arduous rediscovery throughout the twentieth century of the value of humans and of the created world within the Christian economy of salvation was marked by two extremes: an exaggerated attention to the world and its intrinsic value, on the one hand, and an impatient aspiration to resolve all of society's problems in the name of Christian faith, on the other. Some authors would like to consider the human being as if God did not exist (the so-called theology of the death of God).[118] Facile confusion between the supernatural and the natural orders is frequent; there has been a loss of the sense of the sacred and the holy in the liturgy; compromises are made between the doctrine of the faith and concrete political action; and many forget that the Church, the pilgrim people of God, is not of the world, but exists for the world.

Given these challenges, it is fair to say that the key point of the teaching of John Paul II may be found in the defense of the dignity and freedom of humans, of each and every human being.[119] Still, it is important to note that this principle was taught

---

116. The book of C. S. Lewis, *The Abolition of Man*, 2nd ed. (London: Fount, 1999), is symptomatic.

117. See chapter 16, notes 171ff. and corresponding text.

118. On these theologies, see J. L. Illanes, *Cristianismo, historia, mundo* (Pamplona: Eunsa, 1973).

119. See G. Weigel, *Witness to Hope: The Biography of Pope John Paul II* (New York: HarperCollins, 1999), and the volume that completes this biography: G. Weigel, *The End and the Beginning: Pope John Paul II; The Victory of Freedom, the Last Years, the Legacy* (New York: Doubleday, 2010).

by the pope for deeply theological reasons. The Church defends humans, all human beings, with all their rights and duties, because it sees in them the action of God, the image of God, Christ himself, and their ultimate destiny, which is eternal life.[120] Since the collapse of communist Marxism (which attempted to eliminate the individual in the name of the progress of humanity) and the bankruptcy of uncontrolled capitalism (which was likewise disposed to dispense with the individual), the Church has become, over recent decades, a defender, perhaps among the most credible of defenders, of the dignity of humans. There is a paradox here. On the one hand, the purpose of the Church's existence is basically one of preaching the Gospel of the sovereignty of God, creator of all, and the salvation of a sinful world through the grace of Christ, our savior—that is, teaching humans their limits and sinfulness, as well as their obligation to submit themselves to God's law. On the other hand, the Church defends tirelessly the dignity of human beings, of each and every person, in obedience to God himself, because humans are made in his image and likeness and have become his children through faith in Jesus Christ; they are worth all the blood of Christ.[121] For this deeply theological reason, Paul VI said that the Church is "an expert in humanity" and John Paul II said that "man is the way of the Church."

A Christian Anthropology

In the coming chapters we shall consider theological anthropology from a clearly Christological standpoint, in three stages: methodological (we shall examine the teaching that Christ "fully reveals man to himself"); Christological, with the consideration of the human subject made in the image and likeness of Christ, which he, the perfect and filial image of the Father, brings to completion and perfection; and systematic, that is in the ultimate horizon of theological anthropology which is the doctrine of grace, that is, the life of Christ in the believer.

120. This is the basic motif of John Paul II's first, programmatic encyclical, *Redemptor Hominis*, March 4, 1979.

121. Thus writes Josemaría: "It is not right to offend human dignity and the dignity of the sons of God by not going personally to the aid of each one. The priest must do just that, with the humility of a man who knows he is only an instrument, the vehicle of Christ's love. For every soul is a wonderful treasure; every man is unique and irreplaceable. Every single person is worth all the blood of Christ." *Christ Is Passing By*, 80.

JESUS CHRIST, THE REDEEMER

A Living Perspective for a Christian Anthropology

If you say to me: "Show me your God," I will respond: "Show me your man."
THEOPHILUS OF ANTIOCH[1]

Man surpasses man infinitely: learn from your master your true condition, which
you ignore. Listen to God. BLAISE PASCAL

What does Christianity do? It reveals man to man. JOSEPH DE MAISTRE

By the loss of the unity which is possessed through the form of Jesus Christ,
the western world is brought to the brink of the void. DIETRICH BONHOEFFER

In the constitution of Vatican Council II, *Gaudium et Spes*, we read the following programmatic text: "In reality it is only in the mystery of the Word made flesh that the mystery of man truly becomes clear. For Adam, the first man, was a type of him who was to come, Christ the Lord. Christ the new Adam, in the very revelation of the mystery of the Father and of his love, fully reveals man to himself and brings to light his most high calling."[2] Karol Wojtyła, later Pope John Paul II, considers this text as "a key point of the Council's thought."[3] And Joseph Ratzinger, in an early commentary on the document, says that the constitution

1. Theophilus of Antioch, *Ad Autolycum I*, 2,7ff.; B. Pascal, *Pensées* (ed. Brunschvig), n. 438; J. De Maistre, *Du Pape* (orig. 1819) (Geneva: Droz, 1966), 240. Eng. tr.: J. M. De Maistre, *The Pope, considered in his Relations with the Church, Temporal Sovereignties, Separated Churches, and the Cause of Civilization* (New York: H. Fertig, 1975). I wish to thank Prof. Pedro Benítez for pointing out this text to me; D. Bonhoeffer, *Ethics* (New York: Macmillan, 1965), 118.

2. Vatican Council II, *Gaudium et Spes*, December 7, 1965 [hereafter "*GS*"], no. 22. In this chapter I have followed P. O'Callaghan, "Cristo revela el hombre al propio hombre," *Scripta Theologica* 41 (2009): 85–111; and "Il mistero dell'incarnazione e la giustificazione: Una riflessione sul rapporto antropologia-cristologia alla luce della *Gaudium et spes* 22," in *Il mistero dell'incarnazione e il mistero dell'uomo*, edited by M. Gagliardi (Vatican City: Vaticana, 2009), 87–97. The principal elements of this chapter have been published in O'Callaghan, "Europa: 'Cristo svela l'uomo all'uomo': La prospettiva del Vaticano II," *PATH* 11 (2012): 89–117.

3. K. Wojtyła, *Sources of Renewal: The Implementation of the Second Vatican Council* (San Francisco: Harper and Row, 1981), 75.

presents Christ as the eschatological Adam ... as the true image of God.... We are probably justified in saying that here for the first time in an official document of the Magisterium, a new type of completely Christocentric theology appears. On the basis of Christ this dares to present theology as anthropology and only becomes radically theological by including man in discourse about God by way of Christ, thus manifesting the deepest unity of theology.... [The text] points the way for theological reflection in our time.[4]

But what does this Conciliar teaching really involve?

The Meaning of a Conciliar Affirmation

The idea that Christ reveals to humanity what it means to be human has deep Patristic roots. The doctrine of the Trinity, Christology, and anthropology are closely bound up with one another in early Christian writings, as we shall see in chapter 7. The Christmas homilies of Pope Leo the Great on human dignity are well known; taking his cue from the work of redemption, he exclaims: "Agnosce, o christiane, dignitatem tuam!" (Recognize, O Christian, your dignity.... Think of the head of whom you are a member).[5] The expression found in *Gaudium et Spes*, "reveals man to man," is to be found in the writings of Joseph de Maistre from the early nineteenth century, though this author applies it to Christianity and not to Christ.[6] The idea has had a special echo during the twentieth century and, besides Vatican Council II, it was especially present in the teaching of John Paul II, from the time of his first encyclical, *Redemptor Hominis* (1979).[7]

John Paul II's Understanding of *Gaudium et Spes* (no. 22)

In *Redemptor Hominis* John Paul II starts from the fundamental affirmation of John the evangelist: "And the Word was made flesh and dwelt among us" (Jn 1:14).[8] Then he goes on to explain that the Church ceaselessly gazes upon, studies, and loves Christ, in action, at prayer, in contemplation. It does so, in the first place, to know God and his plan of salvation, to admire the great works of the creator. But besides, the Pope adds in his first encyclical, humans must enter ever more deeply into the mysteries of incarnation and redemption with a view to understanding man himself, and in this contemplative gaze discover his true dignity. In *Gaudium et Spes*, in the prepara-

4. J. Ratzinger, "The Dignity of the Human Person," in *Commentary on the Documents of Vatican II*, vol. 5: *Pastoral Constitution of the Church in the Modern World*, edited by H. Vorgrimler (London: Burns Oates, 1967), 159.

5. Leo the Great, *Sermo I in Nav. Domini*, 3.

6. Citation in note 1.

7. See the texts of de Lubac cited in P. O'Callaghan, "Cristo revela el hombre al propio hombre," 85. See also the text of Guardini cited in note 12, and the studies of P. Coda, "L'uomo nel mistero di Cristo e della Trinità: L'antropologia della 'Gaudium et spes,'" *Lateranum* 54 (1988): 164–94; T. Nascentes dos Santos, *Introdução ao discurso antropológico de João Paulo II: "GS" 22 e "GS" 24 no programa do actual Pontífice* (Rome: Athenaeum Romanum Sanctae Crucis, 1992); R. Tremblay, "L''Uomo' (Ef 4,13), misura dell'uomo di oggi e domani," in *Radicati e fondati nel Figlio: Contributi per una morale di tipo filiale* (Rome: Dehoniane, 1997), 13–43; Á. Cordovilla Pérez, "Il mistero dell'uomo nel mistero di Cristo," *Communio* (ed. italiana) 203–4 (2005): 154–66. On the Christology of *GS*, see T. Gertler, *Jesus Christus: Die Antwort der Kirche auf die Frage nach dem Menschsein; eine Untersuchung zu Funktion und Inhalt der Christologie im ersten Teil der Pastoralkonstitution "Gaudium et spes" des zweiten Vatikanischen Konzils* (Leipzig: St. Benno, 1986).

8. See John Paul II, *Redemptor Hominis*, pars. 1, 7, 8, 10. See also Wojtyła, *Sources of Renewal*, 69–83.

tion of which John Paul took part as a young council father, the text says, "Christus manifestat hominem" (Christ manifests/reveals man to man). But *Redemptor Hominis* is more specific and demanding. *Gaudium et Spes* seems to say, simply, that Christ manifests or shows man to man, he gives us new knowledge about humanity. But the encyclical says rather that Christ is the one who reveals who man is by redeeming him from sin, from death, from slavery. Christ is, in fact, the redeemer of man (many of John Paul's major documents contain the term *Redemptor* in the title), and thus not only does Christ explain to humans the truth about their nature and dignity, more or less well known beforehand, but actually restores the dignity lost through sin, constituting humans as children of God. In this process humans are revealed not only in their generic nature but as sinners redeemed, healed, and regenerated by Christ the redeemer. That is, humans are shown not as static beings, simply awaiting an as yet unknown revelation about their nature, as in the case of Plato's cave myth or with a Gnostic view of salvation, but rather as those who can lose their dignity (in part) and recuperate it again, obtaining a new, more elevated dignity.

The same position may be found further explained in John Paul's encyclical *Veritatis Splendor* (1987), where we read:

Only in the mystery of Christ's Redemption do we discover the "concrete" possibilities of man.... But what are the "concrete possibilities of man"? And of which man are we speaking? Of man dominated by lust or of man redeemed by Christ? This is what is at stake: the reality of Christ's redemption. Christ has redeemed us! This means that he has given us the possibility of realizing the entire truth of our being; he has set our freedom free from the domination of concupiscence.[9]

Within this movement of Christ's revelation and redemption we can discover important aspects of the life of humans that express their identity and dignity: freedom (through which they have lost their friendship with God but can receive this gift anew), historicity and temporality (because God's gift and free human action takes place within time), creation as a gift of existence, and humanity's destiny of immortality, aspects to which we shall return throughout this text. Christ shows humans, in other words, to be beings that are open to the divine gifts, open to being enriched, that is, dynamic beings. The fruit of this contemplation that the whole Church directs towards Christ, concludes John Paul II, is a deep sense of wonder, expressed not only in adoration of God but also as amazement at man and his dignity.[10]

In a strict sense, the Council and John Paul do not offer a simple theological understanding of humanity on the basis of God's plan and will for them but, in a strict sense, a Christian vision of humanity, or better, a Christological vision. Christ himself, in his incarnation and life, death, and resurrection, becomes *the living perspective for humanity*, being himself "resurrection and life" (Jn 11:25). In fact, "he knows what is in each man" (Jn 2:25). On the basis of the person and action of Christ, we can reach the fullest possible knowledge of what it means to be human, of our origin, nature, dignity, and destiny; from faith in his power, humans can fulfill their potentialities to the full; through Christ they can become what God always wanted them to be. That is what it means to say that Christ reveals man to man.

9. John Paul II, *Veritatis Splendor*, Encyclical Letter, August 6, 1993, par. 103.
10. See John Paul II, *Redemptor Hominis*, par. 10.

The Epistemological and Hermeneutical Question

The great majority of theologians admit in general terms that the one who reveals man to man is Jesus Christ. But in this affirmation there is a weighty challenge of an epistemological kind, which is the following: how do we know Christ? What is the true human and divine profile of Jesus of Nazareth? Could it not be that the image we have of Christ, which in turn should bring us to understand our own identity, is in real terms a simple projection of ourselves, of our interests, needs, and prejudices? And therefore, though we may start out wanting to know ourselves in Christ, we may end up simply knowing ourselves as we seem to be, and perhaps knowing ourselves not very well at that. Albert Schweitzer said on one occasion that each person does his own Christology, an interested Christology, covering Christ with his own cloak.

When we say that Christ reveals man to himself, it would seem at first that this is quite a straightforward affirmation: Christ, the perfect man, the true image of the Father (2 Cor 4:4, Col 1:15, Heb 1:3) enables us to know ourselves as we are or as we should be, made in God's image (Gn 1:26f.), even though we may have fallen on account of sin. He is presented before us as a perfect model of humanity. We might say that just as the humanity of Christ is a reflection of the divine nature, so also will man—who strives to conform his life as perfectly as possible to the model incarnated by Christ—be divinized, will become like God. This might be called an "assimilative" reading of the relationship between God and humans in Christ. But it is an insufficient one; things are more complex. To focus the question properly, we first need to take into account two epistemological discontinuities in humans' knowledge of God.[11]

The first discontinuity consists in the fact that humans are not, in the present moment, in every way like Jesus Christ, nor are they destined to be so in the future. This is so not only because Jesus is divine, whereas we are not, not only because Jesus is sinless, whereas we are not. It is also so because in Christ the fullness of God is corporally present (Col 2:9). It is true that Christ is "one of us," a man among humans. But it is also true that Christ is different from each person, from the sinner certainly but also from the faithful Christian in whom he lives and acts. According to the expression of Romano Guardini, Christ in relation to humanity is "the great contrast," because he is like humans in many things but not in all; he identifies with us in certain things but not in every one.[12] With the incarnation of the Word, between Christ and fallen humanity we may find what might be called a "differentiated solidarity," which may be understood in four stages.[13] I call it "differentiated" because, whereas

---

11. See O'Callaghan, "Cristo revela el hombre al propio hombre," 97ff.

12. Thus Guardini: "In our encounter with Jesus Christ is shown up the true essence of man; in his presence is revealed good and evil; in his presence humans encounter the consequences of their mentalities, 'their hearts are opened.' Christ is 'different' from the world; he is 'above' the world. Therefore he questions the world and obliges it to manifest itself. *Christ is the great contrast*, before whom the world shows up its true face. But at the same time he loves the world with a powerful, total, creative love, that is completely different from our own." R. Guardini, *Unterscheidung des Christlichen*, 3rd ed. (Mainz: Matthias-Grünewald, 1994), 1:32f.

13. See O'Callaghan, "Il mistero dell'incarnazione e la giustificazione," 93–97. On this issue during the preparation and reception of *GS*, no. 22, see the ample study of F. A. Castro Pérez, *Cristo y cada hombre: Hermenéutica y recepción de una enseñanza del Concilio Vaticano II* (Rome: Gregorian and Biblical Press, 2011).

the first stage involves a deep and permanent solidarity, in the last one there is no solidarity whatever. The four stages are as follows.

First, Christ is completely identified with humans with respect to human nature; in his everyday life, shared by all humans, the Father reveals what he wanted them always to be: a corporeal being, free, historical, social, capable of loving and living in communion with him: hungry and needful of nutrition, tired and needful of rest, rejected and needful of love. Christ shares with us our nature; in this sense, he is truly "one of us."[14]

Second, Christ lives in solidarity with humanity in a "mixed," temporal, or functional way, with respect to certain aspects of historical, fallen human nature, for example with respect to suffering, ignorance, and death. These characteristics of human life, while not identified with sin, are in some way linked with sin, and in being freely assumed by Christ they make our redemption possible. But at the end of time they will no longer be present in humans. We shall return presently to this latter point. For the moment it is enough say that there is not a simple specular or assimilative relationship between the man Jesus Christ and the common human condition; there is not a pure identity, a perfect solidarity. Christ makes himself like us but remains different from us.

Third, Christ also identifies himself with the human condition and contrasts himself with it in a "prophetic" key, through his actions and teaching. Certainly he consoles the downhearted, the weak, sinners: "Come to me, all who labor and are heavy laden, and I will give you rest. Take my yoke upon you, and learn from me; for I am gentle and lowly in heart, and you will find rest for your souls. For my yoke is easy, and my burden is light" (Mt 11:28–30). He is the "desideratus cunctis gentibus" (the one who is desired by all peoples; Hg 2:8, Vulgate). Besides, Jesus Christ is for humanity the norm to which all should conform their lives, the original vocation that humans should assimilate.

But, even more, during his earthly sojourn and in his preaching Jesus is considered a *skandalon* (scandal) for the Jews (1 Cor 1:23; see Mt 21:42). He puts the expectations of humans in crisis on repeated occasions; he provokes them and moves them toward conversion. Of him Simeon says to Mary, his mother: "Behold, this child is set for the fall and rising of many in Israel, and for a sign that is spoken against (and a sword will pierce through your own soul also), that thoughts out of many hearts may be revealed" (Lk 2:34f.). Doubtless the Beatitudes go to the heart of Jesus' teaching. In fact, they may be considered in a sense his spiritual autobiography.[15] But they do not correspond to the simple expectations of his listeners; rather they invert human expectations abruptly. They do not confirm human complacency; rather they challenge it. The evangelist Matthew observes: "And when Jesus finished these sayings, the

14. Pope Francis says that Christ "was far removed from philosophies which despised the body, matter and the things of the world. Such unhealthy dualisms, nonetheless, left a mark on certain Christian thinkers in the course of history and disfigured the Gospel. Jesus worked with his hands, in daily contact with the matter created by God, to which he gave form by his craftsmanship." *LS*, par. 98.

15. "The Beatitudes are the transposition of Cross and Resurrection into discipleship. But they apply to the disciple because they were first paradigmatically lived by Christ himself.... The Beatitudes present a sort of veiled interior biography of Jesus, a kind of portrait of his figure." J. Ratzinger/Benedict XVI, *Jesus of Nazareth: From the Baptism in the Jordan to the Transfiguration* (New York: Doubleday, 2007), 74.

crowds were astonished at his teaching, for he taught them as one who had authority, and not as their scribes" (Mt 7:28f.). Besides, the parables, full of apparent contradictions, surprise and disconcert his listeners. For this reason the disciples frequently say to him: "Explain to us the parable" (Mt 13:36). After having received the unexpected promise of the eucharist, John tells us that "after this many of his disciples drew back and no longer went about with him" (Jn 6:66), because they were no longer capable of assimilating the power and weight of his message. And Jesus himself recognizes this fact: "Yet you refuse to come to me that you may have life" (Jn 5:40). And elsewhere he says: "He who has ears to hear, let him hear" (Mt 11:15). In brief terms, the life and words of Jesus are anything but a comfortable confirmation of peoples' complacent expectations and reasonable aspirations: they are the "Gospel," the unexpected, prophetic, disconcerting novelty of the preaching of the kingdom.

Finally, Christ does not identify himself at all with humans as regards sin itself: "For we have not a high priest who is unable to sympathize with our weaknesses, but one who in every respect has been tempted as we are, yet without sin" (Heb 4:15). "For our sake [God] made him to be sin who knew no sin, so that in him we might become the righteousness of God" (2 Cor 5:21). In Christ the Father reveals his own holiness and the contrast between the historical human and fallen condition and God, the enormous divergence between humans in grace and in sin. Besides, it is obvious that if Jesus were a sinner he would be incapable of saving the world.

But there is a second epistemological discontinuity. Even if it were possible for humans to know the humanity of Christ perfectly and identify themselves with it successfully, they would still need to keep in mind that his humanity is not the perfect and complete reflection of God.[16] It is a faithful reflection, because the Lord teaches us that "he who has seen me has seen the Father" (Jn 14:9; see 12:45): the actions and words of Jesus truly reveal to us the will and person of the eternal Father. But it is not a perfect, total reflection. To affirm the contrary would be to fall into the Docetistic heresy, which envisages the absorption of the humanity of Christ by the divinity. The humanity of Jesus hides the Father at the same time that it reveals him. As Paul teaches, through revelation the believer does not know Christ any longer "from a human point of view" (2 Cor 5:16) because, all in all, the divine essence is completely unknowable if we begin with any created reality,[17] even the unsurpassable created condition of the humanity and life of Jesus Christ. In fact, if the Father did not reveal himself in Christ and through him (Mt 16:17), humans would not be in a position to know him. In brief terms, we can say that, in spite of the "transparency" of the humanity of Christ before the Father, the path to knowing God through the incarnate Word is a long one; it is a path of conversion, of faith, of purification, of God's light penetrating the lives of humans in time and eternity: it is a path of grace.

Before considering this path that disciples have to cover in order to come close to Christ, and in Christ to the Father, let us consider different historical manifestations of the relationship between anthropology and Christology.

16. This is the classic doctrine of the saving mediation of the humanity of Christ; see, for example, Thomas Aquinas, *Summa Theologiae*, translated and edited by T. Gilby (New York: McGraw-Hill, 1964–81) [hereafter "*S.Th.*"] III, q. 26, a. 2.

17. See Pérez de Laborda, "La preesistenza delle perfezioni in Dio," 279–98.

The Relationship between Anthropology and Christology

Many modern philosophers have come to consider "God" in his existence and attributes as a kind of projection of human aspirations. This was clearly the position of Ludwig Feuerbach, who held that the secret of theology is anthropology. It would seem, therefore, not that humans were made "in the image and likeness of God" but the other way around: humans made "God" in their own image and likeness. That is to say, every theocentrism may be understood as a kind of camouflaged anthropocentrism. Something of the kind happens with Christology insofar as it reflects in every period of history the needs and desires, the situations and aspirations, of humans. Even Christocentrism, which is so typical of Christian faith, can easily become, according to the logic of Feuerbach, a more or less masked form of anthropocentrism.[18] Humans think they are looking at Christ when in reality they are looking at a reflection of themselves with which they fall in love, like Narcissus in Greek mythology. Let us consider some authors who have systematically presented the relationship between Christ and humanity—first, those who explain Christology in terms of anthropology and then those who consider anthropology in the light of Christology.

Considering Christology from the Standpoint of Anthropology

Historically we can see that Christology has always developed side by side with anthropology. The following examples should suffice to show this.[19] In the context of the cultural ambience that marks the theology of the Greek Fathers, the principal aspiration of humans was that of being "divinized," that is, made immortal and wise through God's grace. Thus Christ is considered the perfect God-man, the one who communicates divine life to humans as the incarnate Word. That is to say, the doctrine of the incarnation goes side by side with a view of humanity in search of immortality and illumination.

Subsequently, in the period from Augustine to the Middle Ages up to Luther, Christ is considered principally as the savior of mankind—more specifically, as the one who reconciles sinful humanity with God; the purpose of the mission of Christ is one of overcoming guilt, temptation, and anxiety, because humans fear the possibility of being condemned forever on account of their sins. Christ is now looked upon as a benign and merciful savior who suffers to repair the sins of humanity; this gives us a "hamartocentric" view of Christ, one that is related essentially to sin. Again Christology is determined to some degree by the underlying anthropology, in this case the pervading conviction of human guilt.

---

18. On the relationship between Christology and anthropology, see W. Kasper, "Christologie und Anthropologie," *Theologische Quartalschrift* 162 (1982): 201–21; M. Bordoni, "Cristologia e Antropologia," in *Cristologia e Antropologia*, edited by C. Greco (Rome: AVE, 1994), 15–62; P. O'Callaghan, "Cristocentrismo y antropocentrismo en el horizonte de la teología: Una reflexión en torno a la epistemología teológica," in *Cristo y el Dios de los cristianos: Hacia una comprensión actual de la teología*, XVIII Simposio Internacional de Teología de la Universidad de Navarra, Pamplona 9–11 abril 1997, edited by J. Morales, J. J. Alviar, M. Lluch, P. Urbano, and J. Enériz (Pamplona: Servicio de Publicaciones de la Universidad de Navarra, 1998), 367–98.

19. For this explanation I have followed W. Pannenberg, "The Christological Foundation of Christian Anthropology," in *Humanism and Christianity*, edited by C. Geffré (New York: Concilium, 1973), 86–100.

From the time of the German Enlightenment (the *Aufklärung*) onward, openly anthropocentric understandings of Christ's identity abound. Interest shifts principally toward human morality, upright behavior that is needed to construct a healthy society. Christ therefore is presented as a model of virtue and goodness for the whole of humanity and for a just society. Romantic thought considers Christ as the model of a harmonic, strong, balanced, noble life; in the period in which personalism is important, Christ is considered as the perfect man in his personal relationship with others; fully open to his Father and to all humans, he is considered to be the source and model of communion.

In more recent times, with liberation theology, Christ is commonly considered as the one who, in solidarity with the weak and oppressed, dies at the hands of the public authorities on the cross, becoming in this way a model and inspiration for the liberation of the poor and persecuted. Also, here we can see how the anthropological horizon determines the profile of Christology. This, of course, is simply inevitable; the question, however, is this: is it enough? Does it faithfully represent the full divine-human identity of Christ? Or is it, rather, a projection of our ideas onto him?

As more specific examples we can consider two typical lines of modern Christology that emerge from the human situation, positions consolidated first of all in the ambit of liberal Protestantism. One is centered on personal religious experience, the other on the historicity of the Gospels and the life of Christ.

Christology and Religious Experience

First, let us consider the position of the nineteenth-century Lutheran Pietist F. D. E. Schleiermacher, and then the explanation of the Catholic theologian Karl Rahner. Schleiermacher's most influential work, called *The Christian Faith*, was published in 1820.[20] To understand humanity, our author does not start with the intellect, nor with the will, nor even with faith, but with the fundamental religious experience of all humans. This experience consists primarily of the awareness of their dependence on God, creator and savior of the world and of history. Schleiermacher says that Christ is our savior because he has communicated to us his own powerful awareness of the Father, on whom he depends as a Son. In that sense, certainly, Christ "reveals man to man" as one who depends on God radically. The problem with his explanation may be found in the purely psychological way in which this human awareness of God is obtained. For this awareness to come about, there is no need for Jesus to be the Son of God incarnate. The singularity of Christ is not to be found, therefore, in his divine-human identity but in the fact that he has communicated to many people with great efficacy his powerful awareness of depending on God as a Son. Besides, in this way only some aspects of the salvation humans need are taken into account. In spite of the fact that the Christological focus of Schleiermacher was criticized by Feuerbach as a kind of abusive "projection,"[21] it was proposed anew on several occasions throughout the twentieth century by authors such as Adolf von Harnack and Rudolf Bultmann. To some degree, with important reservations, a position of this kind was held by Karl Rahner and others.

20. See F. D. E. Schleiermacher, *The Christian Faith* (Edinburgh: T. and T. Clark, 1948). First published in 1820–22.

21. See L. Feuerbach, *The Essence of Christianity* (Buffalo, N.Y.: Prometheus Books, 1989).

Rahner develops his Christology on the basis of the human experience of transcendence.[22] Humans, he says, are essentially open to God in all their thoughts and actions; not only that, but the grace and calling of God are present in a germinal way within each person through the redemption carried out by Christ: this is what he calls the "supernatural existential."[23] Thus for Rahner, grace, more than the historical donation of the Holy Spirit, fruit of the Passover of Christ, is the historical working out of the transcendental openness of the human spirit to Being. His understanding has given rise to what has come to be known as the "anthropological turning" of twentieth-century theology.[24] According to Rahner, the transcendental openness of humans already contains the question about Christ. The common human situation, just as it is, offers the condition of possibility for the whole of Christology.[25] Thus the "hypostatic union," verified in Christ, may be considered as the supreme and definitive expression of human openness to the divinity. For this reason anthropology is always an incomplete Christology, whereas Christology is considered as an anthropology that transcends itself.

Among the advantages of Rahner's position is the strong connection he establishes between anthropology and Christology. Christ confirms humans in their native capacity to open their lives to the transcendent. Not only that: he makes such an openness possible. Among the limits we can observe is an excessively close assimilation between the identity of Christ (the supreme man) and that of humans (little christs). Rahner develops this position on the basis of a philosophically risky extension from a human subjectivity open to transcendence to the objectivity of the historical existence of the Son of God made man. As a result, Rahner's Christology remains somewhat flat because it cannot easily rise above being a mere anthropology.[26] In other words, it will be humans who reveal to us who Christ is (a Christology "from below"), not the other way around.

The Search for the Historical Jesus of Nazareth

In the nineteenth century began what came to be known as the *Leben-Jesu-Forschung*, the search for the true and historical Jesus. This search was undertaken

22. On the Christology of Rahner, see K. Rahner and W. Thüsing, *A New Christology* (New York: Seabury Press, 1980).

23. See, for example, K. Rahner, "Existential," in M. Buchberger and W. Kasper, eds., *Lexikon für Theologie und Kirche*, 3rd ed. (Freiburg: Herder, 1993–2001), 3:1301, and "Existenzial-übernatural," in *Sacramentum mundi: Theologisches Lexikon für die Praxis* (Freiburg: Herder, 1967), 1:591f. For an account of the limits of this explanation, see chapter 18, note 51 and corresponding text. For a critique, see P. Burke, *Reinterpreting Rahner: A Critical Study of His Major Themes* (New York: Fordham University Press, 2002); G. Mansini, "Experiential Expressivism and Two Twentieth-Century Catholic Theologians," *Nova et Vetera* (English ed.) 8, no. 1 (2010): 125–41. The article deals with Rahner and Lonergan.

24. See P. Eicher, *Die anthropologische Wende: Karl Rahners philosophischer Weg vom Wesen des Menschen zur personalen Existenz* (Freiburg: Universitätsverlag, 1970); C. Fabro, *La svolta antropologica di Karl Rahner* (Milan: Rusconi, 1974); K. P. Fischer, *Der Mensch als Geheimnis: Die Anthropologie Karl Rahners* (Freiburg: Herder, 1974).

25. "Man's true hominization therefore attains its apex in his divinization." International Theological Commission, *Theology, Christology, Anthropology*, 2.2 (Vatican City: Vaticana, 1982).

26. J. Ratzinger notes the insufficiency of Rahner's reflection as regards the historical dimension of human existence: J. Ratzinger, "Vom Verstehen des Glaubens: Anmerkungen zu Rahners *Grundkurs des Glaubens*," *Theologische Revue* 74 (1978): 177–86. See also Scola, Marengo, and Prades López, *La persona umana*, 35f.

on the basis of careful study of the Gospels employing the historical-critical method, with the precise intention of avoiding Christology's being determined by the projection of the human desires and aspirations of each period, that is, by religious experience such as that of Schleiermacher, rather letting it be determined by historical, documented, and certain data.

Among the protagonists of this movement, which began in the nineteenth century and covered much of the twentieth, may be mentioned D. F. Strauss, W. Wrede, A. Schweitzer, and E. Troeltsch. At present an important part of New Testament Christology moves in this direction.[27] The historian Troeltsch, for example, suggests that three criteria be applied to Biblical texts to ensure their historicity and trustworthiness: a rigorous historical critique (in order to identify the authentic text), correlation (to ensure the bonding and coherency between different aspects and stages of the text), and finally analogy (to confirm that the affirmations made are plausible and more or less in keeping with our experience).[28]

From many points of view, the criteria in question are reasonable. Still, the last one mentioned (analogy) could well become problematic if we end up judging the content of the Gospel on the basis of our human experiences, which are always limited, circumscribed to each period, and not as yet redeemed. Our experiences in fact may well filter and perhaps exclude elements that belong to divine revelation. The historical-critical method thus applied to the life of Jesus can easily fall victim to its own purported rigor. In fact, it is not infrequent for Biblical scholars to deny certain elements of the Gospel—for example, miracles, diabolic possession, and so on—that do not seem to fit into common human (modern) experience. In real terms, again, the result is a flat, impoverished Christology "from below"—assimilative, conformist, conservative, focused on passing and contingent human experiences, conditioned by history and sin and by the immediate needs of humans, not taking into account what we earlier called the "differentiated solidarity" of Christ with humanity.[29]

The historical understanding we have just presented begins with humans in their concreteness, historicity, deficiency, and sinfulness, according to the limits and poverty of the period they live in, of the culture and living situation of each. Christ is presented as the one who fills out—according to the judgment of humans themselves—what is lacking in each epoch. Christ is made to play the role of what Dietrich Bonhoeffer called the "God who fills in the gaps." In any case, there seems to be little interest in finding and knowing the authentic Jesus, because in real terms humans just keep inventing the Jesus they need; they work out an interested Christology, covering Christ, as Schweitzer said, with their own cloaks. The theologian Alfred Läpple ironically described the ambivalence of this process as moving "from the great God to the little Jesus; from the little Jesus to the big me!"[30]

27. The four-volume work of J. P. Meier, *A Marginal Jew: Rethinking the Historical Jesus* (New York: Doubleday, 1991), is well known. At the same time, the limits of the historical-critical method have been noted, especially by J. Ratzinger in his Christology in three volumes, *Jesus of Nazareth*.

28. See E. Troeltsch, *The Absoluteness of Christianity and the History of Religions* (London: S.C.M. Press, 1972). First published in 1902.

29. See notes 15ff. and corresponding text.

30. A. Läpple, *Jesus von Nazaret: Krit. Reflexionen* (Munich: Don-Bosco-Verlag, 1972), 16.

Christ: Source and Culmination of Humanity

Over and against the explanation just given, we can observe that if humans of every epoch have sought and found in Jesus of Nazareth the suitable model of their personal and collective aspirations, this does not constitute a priori a valid argument against what the faith teaches us about him. On the one hand, the positions mentioned earlier are not incompatible with one another (Christ as he divinizes, saves; as he saves, he liberates; as he liberates, he instructs; offering an example to be imitated, he opens the human heart to grace, etc.); besides, they are aspects of Jesus' identity that are all clearly to be found in the New Testament itself. On the other hand, everything human is contained in Christ, because he is the perfect man. As the evangelist John says, "He himself knows what was in man" (Jn 2:25), because when all is said and done, "all things were made through him, and without him was not anything made that was made" (Jn 1:3). In his incarnate divinity, Jesus Christ is more than the sum of universal reality, more than the sum of human aspirations, needs, and desires, because he is the Lord of history, "the Alpha and the Omega … who is and who was and who is to come, the Almighty" (Rv 1:8). Hence, in Christ is to be found all the good and positive aspirations present in humans—and perhaps many others besides of which we are as yet unaware.

At the same time, we need to ask: how is it possible to get out of this closed hermeneutic circle that seems to reduce Christology to anthropology? If we do not find this path, it will be humans who in every epoch will reveal Christ to himself with an inverted reading of the Gospel question "Who do men say that the Son of man is?" (Mt 16:13), and not the other way around, as Vatican II put it: "Christ reveals man to himself."

Understanding Anthropology on the Basis
of Christology

Several attempts have been made throughout the modern period to ensure that anthropology is Christologically mediated, not the other way around. Among the Protestant authors, the most important ones are the Calvinist Karl Barth and the Lutheran Wolfhart Pannenberg, among the Catholics, Hans Urs von Balthasar.

Karl Barth and human immortality   To understand the reality of human life and salvation on the basis of Christian faith, Barth holds that we must exclude any "previous anthropology" of a philosophical or cultural kind that could play the part of a pre-comprehension or previous fundamental structure for the faith, as if we possessed the faith in part before receiving it. Christ, sent by the Father, the true predestined one, is, for Barth, the only source of the dignity of humans, of human rights, of spirituality and ethics. "Christology must occupy all the space in theology," he says. "Christology is everything or it is nothing at all."[31] But why is this? Because, according to Barth, humans can speak of themselves in a meaningful way, as believers, only on the basis of eternity (and thus immortality), that is, from the perspective of God,

---

31. K. Barth, *Die kirchliche Dogmatik* II/1 (Zurich: Zöllikon, 1958), 114. Translated into English as *Church Dogmatics*, vol. 2.1 (Edinburgh: T. and T. Clark, 1957).

"who alone has immortality and dwells in unapproachable light" (1 Tm 6:16), the transcendent One, the totally Other. In that sense the immortal destiny of humans is revealed "perpendicularly" in Jesus Christ, only from him and in him. Thus Christ, and only he, reveals to us what we are. As Louis Bouyer wrote:

We had to wait for Karl Barth to come to the conclusion that the divine Word is not limited to responding to the questions which we asked ourselves before having heard it, but rather it begins to place these questions in a completely different way, and place other questions we simply had not thought about before. In fact the word of God begins above all by placing our very lives in question, we who pretend to speak of God with previous knowledge.[32]

The fact that Barth has concentrated the search for human identity on immortality is highly significant. As we saw in the previous chapter, the thrust for immortality, which is present and active in every action and reaction of humans, plays a central role in anthropology understood in a religious context.[33] Still, if humans without divine revelation know nothing previous of immortality, we may ask: how or why would they take an interest in it? The fundamental limit of Barth's position is that of excluding real dialogue between Christian faith, on the one hand, and the world, philosophy, and science, on the other. The verticality of his position tends sooner or later toward fideism.

The revelation of the love of God in von Balthasar   Like Barth, von Balthasar has been very critical of Christologies "from below," worked out on the basis of human experience.[34] He teaches that the appearing of God in Christ cannot follow the act of free human correspondence because the former elicits the correspondence of humans, not finding it present beforehand. Anthropology has to be thought out starting from Christ. Because Christ, in his being and life, is the *Gestalt*, that is, "the fundamental form" of humanity and of the whole of creation, what he calls "the concrete analogy of being."[35] According to von Balthasar, in Christ is definitively revealed the unconditioned love of the Father for humans, who are incapable, on the basis of their own situation or powers, to establish a relationship of communion with him. At the same time, following what he called the "aesthetic way," the path of beauty, humans are constituted in such a way as to recognize and allow themselves to get caught up in the divine donation, in the love of God revealed in Christ. Divine revelation is expressed, therefore, in the unity between the finite freedom of humans and the infinite freedom of God. Humans reach faith in God as they perceive that they are gratuitous-

32. L. Bouyer, *Le Père invisible: Approches du mystère de la divinité* (Paris: Cerf, 1976), 316. Translated into English as *The Invisible Father: Approaches to the Mystery of the Divinity* (Petersham, Mass.: St Bede's Publications, 1999).

33. See chapter 2, notes 13ff. and corresponding text (including bibliography); notes 39ff. below and corresponding text; chapter 4, note 42 and corresponding text; chapter 12, notes 105ff. and corresponding text; chapter 19, notes 167ff. and corresponding text.

34. See H. U. von Balthasar, *Karl Barth: Darstellung und Deutung seiner Theologie* (Olten: J. Hegner, 1951). Translated into English as *The Theology of Karl Barth: Exposition and Interpretation* (San Francisco: Ignatius, 1992). There is an important critique of Rahner in the work of H. U. von Balthasar, *The Moment of Christian Witness* (San Francisco: Ignatius, 1994). The work is better known by the original title, *Cordula*.

35. The notion of "form" (*Gestalt*) is the central category of Balthasar's entire work of theological aesthetics, *Glory of the Lord*, esp. volume 1, *Seeing the Form* (San Francisco: Ignatius, 1982).

ly loved in Christ; this principle is contained in the title of an important work of von Balthasar: love alone is worthy of belief.[36]

It should also be added that von Balthasar's Christology is characterized to the core by the Pauline principle of *kenosis*, or "emptying" (Phil 2:7), which expresses the internal dynamics of the redeeming work of the savior and of Christian ascetic practice, understood as renunciation of one's own life for love in view of the salvation of humanity (Lk 9:23f.). But von Balthasar's *kenosis* does not stop with the economy of human salvation: it is present besides within the divine essence, in the life of the Trinity, because the economy "was foreshadowed and made possible by the *eternal self-renunciation* of the Son in relation to the Father, in which the Son desires nothing but to be the adoring mirror-image of his source."[37] In real terms, this amounts to a kind of "assimilative" approach to the relationship between man and God, in which human life is (or should be) modeled on that of Christ, in the same way that the life of Christ is a faithful and perfect reflection of the Trinitarian life.

Von Balthasar's explanation insists opportunely, as does Barth's, on the objective priority of Christology over anthropology. However, at an epistemological level, that of the subjective appropriation of faith, it is not clear whether von Balthasar's Christology is truly anterior to his anthropology, because he speaks of unconditioned divine love on the basis of the human experience of love in general, especially that of the mother toward her small child. But the human experience of love, also that of the mother, is always limited, poor, ambivalent, and fallible.[38] And von Balthasar projects that love upward, toward God. At an epistemological level, again, it seems that the human being who attempts to obtain self-knowledge in Christ is little different than the one who attempts to do so by direct experience.

The eschatological approach to anthropology according to Pannenberg   In seeking out a Christological basis for anthropology, the Lutheran theologian Wolfhart Pannenberg distinguishes three paths, three possible epistemologies: the mythological, the philosophical, and the theological.[39] First, we can speak of a mythological epistemology. According to classic mythology, we know and interpret human and religious reality on the basis of what took place at the beginning, when the gods configured the world and gave it its laws. What is true with respect to the world and of humans, therefore, is situated in what took place at the beginning of history. And because the history of the first man is repeated in each and every individual, the myths that recount the beginnings are meant to be faithfully transmitted from one generation to

---

36. H. U. von Balthasar, *Love Alone [Is Credible]* (New York: Herder and Herder, 1969).

37. Von Balthasar continues: "Since the world is not God, the 'emptying' (Phil 2:7) that the Son accepted when he came into the world necessarily entailed for him a new relationship to God in the midst of creation. But this emptying was not something unfamiliar to him; it was foreshadowed and made possible by the *eternal self-renunciation of the Son* in relation to the Father, in which the Son desires nothing but to be the adoring mirror-image of his source.... The potentiality that he realized in the Incarnation even to the total renunciation of obedience unto death on the Cross had its foundation in the pure actuality of the eternal life of the Blessed Trinity.... So great is the inner richness of the eternal life of the Trinity that every aspect of Christ's Incarnation—the joyful union with the Father and the desolate abandonment by him—are but outward expressions of the inner possibilities of divine love." H. U. von Balthasar, *The Christian State of Life* (San Francisco: Ignatius, 1983), 188f.; emphasis added.

38. See P. O'Callaghan, "'Gli stati di vita del cristiano.'"

39. See Pannenberg, "The Christological Foundation of Christian Anthropology."

the next in order to maintain and reinforce the identity of the people to whom and through whom the myths are transmitted. This is done principally by courting the favor of the gods instead of their ire. On the basis of their own myths, then, each people will develop its own, potentially complete, anthropology, as we saw in chapter 2.

Second, we can speak of a philosophical epistemology. What is at issue here is not the truth about humanity present at the beginning and passed on by myths and popular traditions but rather the efforts of philosophers to identify what is continuous and permanent in human nature, what remains unvaried and intact under the ruins of history and the frailty of matter, what is human nature. According to Pannenberg, "The idea was that there is an identical human essence in all times, equal for all individuals."[40] The product of this knowledge is an immutable wisdom destined for the philosopher. Among the Greeks, this vision is present in Plato, Aristotle, and the Stoics, among others.

It may be observed that the two epistemologies just mentioned are not far from one another if seen from the anthropology they give rise to. In the first place, the knowledge obtained through myths is not unlike that deriving from philosophical thought because all human knowledge refers to what was seen at the beginning in the world of ideas (this is the case of Plato); in this case, both mythical and philosophical knowledge are rooted in the origin of humankind and should coincide with one another. In the second place, there is a profound affinity between the two systems (the mythological and the philosophical) because both provide elements of knowledge with respect to humans in terms of a substantially immutable nature; for this reason, this nature can be known not only at the beginning of history but also—unchanged—in the present moment and in any future moment. It may be observed that the immutability of humans is not so much a conclusion reached by anthropological inquiry but rather an implicit and decisive point of departure in this inquiry. In effect, if human nature were changeable in a meaningful or substantial way, any science, mythology, or philosophy would thereby become impossible. In other words, from an implicit pre-comprehension of human nature as something that is fixed and forever determined emerge two epistemologies, the mythological and the philosophical, differently focused but providing more or less the same conclusions contentwise.

Third, Pannenberg speaks of a theological epistemology, indeed, an eschatological one. He explains that, according to Christian faith, humans know themselves not only on the basis of what is transmitted from the beginning through myth and tradition, not only on the basis of what philosophers say about humans from their personal and present experience, but also on the basis of the promise of a new reality, the Gospel, the "good news." The Gospel, in effect, is to be found in Jesus Christ, the Word of God made man in the midst of our history, dead, buried, risen, and ascended into heaven, who promises to send us the Holy Spirit and who will return at the end of time to judge the living and the dead. He is "the new Adam," the new man, the new creation. "What is first and original is no longer supreme," Pannenberg states significantly.[41] And he concludes that "the Christian conception of man, taking into account the history that extends between the first and the second Adam, dissolves

40. Ibid., 90.
41. Ibid., 91.

the philosophical concept of substantial human nature, immutable over time, over history."[42]

Pannenberg recognizes that his eschatological approach to anthropology may be somewhat one-sided because it does not fully take into account the intelligibility of the beginning, the subject of protology, that is, the light present in the world from the moment of creation.[43] Therefore, to speak of the simple "dissolution" of human nature by history is not fully correct. Be that as it may, Pannenberg's position is substantially valid. In order to know humans, the entire human being as God projected it, it is not enough to scan the past and the present; we must also include the promise of a definitive future realization. The full truth about humans—or, better, the revelation of the full truth—is situated in the fulfillment of the future promise, in eschatology, in hope. In this sense the New Testament offers us not so much a new anthropology, complete and systematically described, but rather the presence and promise of a definitive life for sinners, who convert to and believe in Jesus Christ, beyond death, which he himself will bring to us. The fullness of human identity is not presently at our disposal. And even less so is our knowledge of that identity. We firmly hope it will be made present at the moment of eschatological resurrection. It is interesting to note that the fundamental elements of Christian anthropology consolidated during the Patristic period precisely in works concerning eschatology, especially those dealing with the resurrection of the dead (or the flesh).[44]

With the resurrection of Christ, therefore, not only do we come to know the unconditional love of God for humans but we also obtain the conviction that our future resurrection is already promised; in fact, it is already contained in that of the Lord, and with it, our definitive identity. God, in raising his Son from the dead forever, "reveals his mystery and his love for humans," paraphrasing the conciliar text cited earlier, "and brings to light [humans'] most high calling," that is, their eschatological vocation of living in perpetual communion with the Trinity. On the basis of the event of the resurrection of Jesus, a new Christian image of humanity begins to emerge in the minds and hearts of the apostles and disciples, a new and richer way of understanding, of dealing with, of considering, of loving, humanity. As they preached the

---

42. Ibid., 92.

43. Speaking of the Biblical texts that refer to Christ's action over the cosmos, Pannenberg writes: "the New Testament develops the idea of the Son of God in connection with the Jewish concept of preexistent divine wisdom and expresses it in terms of the concept of the Logos. In *Jesus—God and Man*, § 10.3 [Pannenberg's 1964 Christology] I linked these New Testament sayings to another group of New Testament Christological statements, those pertaining to the election or predestination of Jesus Christ to be the Head of a new humanity.... What is said here about the Son as Mediator of creation has primarily a 'final' sense. It is to the effect that creation will be consummated only in Jesus Christ.... Yet true though this is in the light of the New Testament statements, it is not the only aspect of the Son's mediation of creation. The final ordering of creatures to the manifestation of Jesus Christ presupposes that creatures already have the origin of their existence and nature in the Son. Otherwise the final summing up of all things in the Son (Eph 1:10) would be external to the things themselves, so that it would not be the definitive fulfillment of their own distinctive being. If, however, the creatures have their origin in the eternal Son or Logos, then as creatures aware of themselves they will be alienated from themselves so long as they do not perceive and receive the law of their own nature in this Logos." Pannenberg, *Systematic Theology*, 2:24f. On the theology of Pannenberg, see P. O'Callaghan, "Whose Future? Pannenberg's Eschatological Verification of Theological Truth," *Irish Theological Quarterly* 66 (2001): 19–49.

44. See O'Callaghan, "Risurrezione," 1223.

Gospel message, therefore, believers did not only announce the merciful love of God for humans but, even more so, they taught a new, amplified, enriched, anthropology.

Theological reflection on human nature, as we shall see in chapters 4 and 19, always begins with some kind of previous knowledge, however elementary, from concepts derived from our spontaneous experience, without which theological reflection could not even begin. Schleiermacher speaks of religious experience, Rahner of the transcendence of the spirit; Troeltsch considers the analogy between the life of Christ and that of humans; Barth starts with man's search for immortality, while von Balthasar concentrates on the love of a mother for her child, and Pannenberg on the epistemological priority of the future. All of them find, or should find, their basis in Jesus Christ, the Son of God made flesh, who invites us to believe and to follow him as disciples.

"Christ Fully Reveals Man to Himself" in the Context of Conversion and Eschatology

On the basis of what has emerged so far, we may ask the following question: what does it mean to say that "Christ reveals man to himself"? Three possible approaches may be made, which we call respectively, perpendicular, concordist, and integrating. First of all, for some authors, such as Karl Barth, Jesus Christ perpendicularly reveals all there is to be known about human nature; that is, there is nothing of particular importance that can be said about humanity above and beyond what we know through faith in God: all other sources and instances contribute little or nothing to Christian faith and salvation. This position, already described, runs the risk of ending up in fideism, of making theological discourse irrelevant to philosophy, science, and other forms of human knowledge. It would render an anthropologically responsible evangelization program meaningless and would facilitate secularization.[45] Interestingly, *Gaudium et Spes*, in no. 22, not only teaches that Christ reveals man to himself but also confirms the intrinsic value of the created order in a Christological light: "Since human nature as He [Christ] assumed it was not annulled, by that very fact it has been raised up to a divine dignity in our respect too. For by His incarnation the Son of God has united Himself in some fashion with every man."[46] In this sense we can say that the previous knowledge we have of human nature, from philosophy or science, should actually help us to know Jesus Christ and, in turn, to know humanity in the light of faith in him.

Second, we could take the expression "Christ reveals man to himself" in the sense that in him some new things about humanity are revealed to us. From him we receive new elements of knowledge that simply go beyond the elements we already have at

45. For a critique of Barth, see K. Stock, *Anthropologie der Verheißung: Karl Barths Lehre vom Menschen als dogmatisches Problem* (Munich: C. Kaiser, 1980).

46. Also: "He [Christ] Who is 'the image of the invisible God' (Col 1:15), is Himself the perfect man. To the sons of Adam He restores the divine likeness which had been disfigured from the first sin onward. Since human nature as He assumed it was not annulled, by that very fact it has been raised up to a divine dignity in our respect too. For by His incarnation the Son of God has united Himself in some fashion with every man. He worked with human hands, He thought with a human mind, acted by human choice and loved with a human heart. Born of the Virgin Mary, He has truly been made one of us, like us in all things except sin." *GS*, no. 22.

our disposal through science or philosophy. This position may be called concordist. To some degree it is valid, because Christ does provide us with new knowledge about humanity, especially as regards the beginning, the end, and the meaning of human life, all of which go beyond the knowledge available to us through science or philosophy. However, if things were focused systematically in this way, theology would end up paying the price for every new discovery made by science and human knowledge, for "every scientific advance would be a further blow to theology,"[47] that is, the scope of faith would have to diminish every time reason expands.[48]

Finally, taking an integrating approach, it is fair to say that "Christ reveals man to himself" in the sense that he, "revealing the mystery of the Father and his love," and bringing "to light his most high calling," as the Conciliar text affirms, offers humanity a unitary and definitive perspective from which to understand itself, a perspective that consists of the revelation of a single divine project that explains the why and the wherefore of the existence of humans, of their origin, of their being creatures and sinners, of their eschatological destiny of risen integrity and eternal glory. This does not exclude or compete with philosophy or science as autonomous disciplines. The very contrary is the case, in fact. Yet the theological light that derives from Christ does put the parts in their places. The path toward the truth about humans, as we have often said, passes through a search for unity, for human integrity. And Christ is the one who provides this unitary light, thus "revealing man to himself."

In real terms, the full truth about humankind exists only in the mind of God, in his mysterious design of creation and salvation; this design is known to humans through Jesus Christ to a degree that is not as yet complete and fully known to us. In real terms, God's eternal project about humanity can be fully known and accepted only in the context of the gift of faith, which requires a conversion of heart and a difficult commitment to overcoming sin. When we say that "Christ reveals man to himself," we do not say that Christ provides us with elements of a new "knowledge" that can be compared and verified scientifically and philosophically, that can be made easily available to the human intellect, that can be "added" onto other knowledges, as Gnostics might do.[49] What Jesus Christ reveals to humanity and to our understanding of the way of Christian life is expressed as a confrontation, reintegration, and re-dimensioning of the elements of knowledge that to an important degree may be obtained also by other means, putting together and integrating disunited elements that derive from science, philosophy, spontaneous reflection, and spiritual experience. Otherwise this knowledge in all its complexity and variety might well remain unintelligible and disconnected, as postmodern philosophers have well explained. In effect, Christ, the incarnate Logos, is the one who gives a unitary and harmonic intel-

---

47. In the words of Pannenberg, "The contingency of events in quantum physics and thermodynamics may be seen, of course, as an exception to the normal regulation of events in nature, as gaps in the scientific description of nature, which according to all our historical experience will be closed as research continues. To base what we say about God's work in natural events on these exceptions would be to fall victim to the fatal mistake of seeing God at work precisely in these gaps, so that every scientific advance would be a further blow to theology." *Systematic Theology*, 2:71.

48. See O'Callaghan, "L'incontro tra fede e ragione."

49. On Gnosticism, see H. Cornélis and A. Léonard, *La Gnose éternel* (Paris: D. Roge, 1960).

ligibility to everything that exists and that we know, in particular to human nature.[50]

Let us now consider three moments in Christian life in which the knowledge of Jesus Christ and the knowledge of humans come together: coming to faith and conversion, living in communion with the perfect man, and establishing a human identity in the context of resurrection and martyrdom.

Knowing Christ and Humanity through
Faith and Conversion

All humans, without exception, adopt a position and an understanding of life before Christ in the context of conversion from sin (Mk 1:15). Paul gives the reason for this: "All have sinned" (Rom 5:12), even though not all may be fully aware of it. Some, however, close up in their sin, refusing to recognize their guilt, and attempt repeatedly throughout history to "crucify the Son of God on their own account and hold him up to contempt" (Heb 6:6). In effect, Christ died on the cross for love of humans, sinful humans who killed him because they were not prepared to carry his "easy yoke" (Mt 11:29) and accept his saving word. For this reason, as I said earlier, Christ assumed death in a temporary and functional way in order to redeem humanity.[51]

Others, on the contrary, moved by the Spirit through the life, works, and words of Jesus, begin a long, personal path of conversion, a conversion of life, of mind, and of heart.[52] When Jesus asks, "Who do men say that the Son of man is?" (Mt 16:13), the disciples begin to respond: "Some say John the Baptist, others say Elijah, and others Jeremiah or one of the prophets" (Mt 16:14). "These various opinions are not simply mistaken; they are greater or lesser approximations to the mystery of Jesus, and they can certainly set us on the path toward Jesus' real identity," writes Benedict XVI. "Someone who holds this opinion can certainly love Jesus; he can even choose him as a guide for his own life."[53] Therefore Jesus asks again: "But who do you say that I am?" (Mt 16:15). And Peter, who at a personal level recognizes when faced with the divine power of Christ that he is "a sinner" (Lk 5:8), responds to Jesus: "You are the Christ, the Son of the living God" (Mt 16:16). This true knowledge of Christ, "in the spirit" (2 Cor 5:16), is the fruit of divine grace and of a long, drawn-out task of sowing and reaping undertaken by Christ in person: "Blessed are you, Simon Bar-Jonah! For flesh and blood has not revealed this to you, but my Father who is in heaven" (Mt 16:17).[54] The knowledge the believer has of the Lord, therefore, is not of a purely human or analytic

50. See O'Callaghan, "L'incontro tra fede e ragione."

51. See O'Callaghan, "Il mistero dell'incarnazione e la giustificazione," 95.

52. Thus the explanation of Guardini: "Understanding of Christ requires a complete conversion, not only of the will and the deed, but also of the mind. One must cease to judge the Lord from the worldly point of view and learn to accept his own measure of the genuine and the possible; to judge the world with his eyes. This revolution is difficult to accept and still more difficult to realize, and the more openly the world contradicts Christ's teaching, the more earnestly it defines those who accept it as fools, the more difficult that acceptance, realization. Nevertheless, to the degree that the intellect honestly attempts this right-about-face, the reality known as Jesus Christ will surrender itself. From this central reality the doors of all other reality will swing open, and it will be lifted into the hope of the new creation." R. Guardini, *The Lord* (London: Longmans, Green and Co., 1956), 535.

53. Ratzinger/Benedict XVI, *Jesus of Nazareth*, 292f.

54. On the question of evangelical patience in sowing, see P. O'Callaghan, *The Christological Assimilation of the Apocalypse: An Essay on Fundamental Eschatology* (Dublin: Four Courts, 2004), 76–79, 141–50, 249f.

kind, fruit perhaps of a long and difficult scientific and anthropological investigation; it derives principally from divine revelation, which produces in him conversion and faith. This is not any kind of knowledge, but the knowledge of the converted disciple, the knowledge of the one who has left all things to follow the Lord in faith (Mt 19:21). It is an objective knowledge because it reaches the full truth that is in Christ but with an objectivity that comes from the gift of faith.

The way of conversion lived by Christian disciples is a path that brings them to know and love Jesus more and more under the inspiration of God's grace. Fruit of this knowledge and love (or, better, of this "loving knowledge") is an ever more ample and rich knowledge of themselves in him. Christ, risen from the dead, becomes in person the living identity of Christians, to the extent that Paul can say of himself and of all believers, deeply convinced, "It is no longer I who live, but Christ who lives in me" (Gal 2:20). In him they discover, stage by stage, more and more as time goes by, their true identity.

Living in Communion with the Perfect Man

When the apostles were in the company of Jesus they felt unassailable, joyful, sure of themselves—perhaps at times too sure of themselves (Mk 9:33). When the Lord made it known that he was about to leave them, however, they seemed to lose this certainty, security, and strength. In fact, he had insisted with them that the secret of effective evangelization meant renouncing all purely human support (Mt 10): they had to purify themselves from all disorderly attachments and confide completely in him. And when he sent them to preach to the ends of the earth (Mt 28:20ff.), he made the following solemn promise: "I am with you always, to the close of the age" (Mt 28:20). So in what sense was Jesus with the disciples, and in what sense was he not?

When in the Gospel of John (13:34) Jesus announced that he was about to "return to the Father" (Jn 14:12), Peter was disconcerted, and the others with him. For this reason Jesus promised that he would send "another Paraclete" (Jn 14:16), the Holy Spirit, who would make his words, life, and works present in the minds and hearts of believers until his return in glory. For the two disciples on their way to Emmaus, the encounter with the risen Jesus was a source of new life, a spiritual resurrection (Lk 24). They had encountered the risen Jesus, and in him their definitive conversion, the meaning of their existence, their true identity, their lost dignity, their vocation. Unhurriedly they walked towards Emmaus, "looking sad" (Lk 24:17), but after their encounter with Jesus they returned to Jerusalem, the same people as before but now joyful and sure, filled with faith and hope, with new energy. In other words, the life, the words, and the actions of Jesus—perceived through his physical presence, through faith, through the action of the Holy Spirit, or, better, through all three at the same time—transformed the lives of the disciples, giving them a new understanding, a new sureness, a definitive mission. Jesus himself, it may be said, became their new and definitive "identity," and for this reason they became known as "Christians" (Acts 11:26).

This living communion with Jesus Christ does not mean, of course, that at a thematic or intellectual level the apostles knew more about anthropology than did the great philosophers of antiquity. They were not, simply put, "experts in Christianity." Rather, by living in Christ, with Christ, for Christ, that is, by living in communion with the perfect man, they had at their disposal—in an unelaborated way but implicitly, "on loan" as it were—the whole of Christian anthropology, all the richness of the mystery of salvation. In effect, it cannot be said that Peter knew more about man, at an intellectual and thematic level, than did the philosopher Socrates. But he knew that his life had in Christ an origin, a meaning, a direction, and a full, immortal future that the greatest philosophers of history could only suspect, dream of, and aspire to. Like Peter, any Christian who believes in Christ follows him and lives his life, becomes "an expert in humanity," to use an expression applied by Pope Paul VI to the Church. To the lame man in the temple, Peter said: "I have no silver and gold." As if to say: I have no human means, no esoteric knowledge, no sophisticated techniques, no medical qualifications, no extraordinary remedy. "But I give you what I have; in the name of Jesus Christ of Nazareth, walk!" (Acts 3:6). The richness and wisdom of Peter were real and efficacious, but they were not his "own"; they were not elements of knowledge under his dominion and control. Peter, a poor and ignorant fisherman, was certain that all he had and knew belonged to Christ, with whose eyes he saw, with whose strength he healed, with whose presence he consoled, with whose authority he taught. In effect, Peter, in the power of faith, was capable of communicating divine gifts to humans, as in the case of the lame man, with a miracle that clearly points to the final corporeal integrity promised by Jesus at the resurrection of the dead.

Christian Identity and Eschatological Resurrection

In the New Testament there is considerable insistence that the point of departure for Christian preaching is the resurrection of Christ. Christians, in fact, were defined as "witnesses to the Resurrection."[55] And it was said of them that "with great power the apostles gave their testimony to the resurrection of the Lord Jesus" (Acts 4:33). The resurrection of Jesus constituted the confirmation of the love of God for humanity and the promise of our future resurrection. Preaching the faith depended in a critical way on this bond between the risen life of Christ and of humans. To believe in the resurrection of Jesus was equivalent to accepting the future resurrection of humans. Belief in the resurrection spawned a new anthropology. Paul was deeply convinced of this (1 Cor 15:12–17):

Now if Christ is preached as raised from the dead, how can some of you say that there is no resurrection of the dead? But if there is no resurrection of the dead, then Christ has not been raised; if Christ has not been raised, then our preaching is in vain and your faith is in vain.... If Christ has not been raised, your faith is futile and you are still in your sins.[56]

It is interesting to note how Jesus spoke often of giving "peace" to the disciples, especially in the wake of his resurrection. "I give you my peace," he also said during the Last Supper. "Peace be with you" (Lk 24:36; Jn 20:19, 20:26), repeated the risen Lord, and Paul could conclude: "He is our peace" (Eph 2:14). Peace, in fact, is present when humans are aware of their own identity and accept and assimilate it without conflict. Peace, therefore, is a sign of consolidated identity. And this is the peace that the risen Jesus, reconciling us with the Father, has given us: "Peace I leave with you; my peace

55. See Acts 1:22, 2:24–32, 3:15, 4:2, 10:40f., 13:30.
56. See *COH* 89–93.

I give to you; not as the world gives do I give to you" (Jn 14:27). In this way also, by giving us his peace, "Christ reveals man to himself."

Martyrdom: A Manifestation of Christian identity

Christian faith in the resurrection and the anthropology this gives rise to are reflected clearly in the phenomenon of martyrdom, that exceptionally powerful witness to Christian faith that results from voluntarily renouncing the gift of life.[57] In the Old Testament, Daniel 12 and the books of the Maccabees (especially 2 Mc 7) reflect upon the unconditioned faith in God that is expressed in martyrdom.[58] The message is clear: God is faithful to us, and if humans are faithful to the divine will to the point of sacrificing the essential gift that God himself gave them (that is, life), they will receive it again, in fullness, in the future resurrection of the dead: "Give, and it will be given to you; good measure, pressed down, shaken together, running over, will be put into your lap. For the measure you give will be the measure you get back" (Lk 6:38). Besides, resurrection will constitute the moment of definitive realization for humans. This idea may be found in the words of Ignatius of Antioch as he goes toward his coveted martyrdom in Rome and writes to his fellow Christians: "Please, my brothers, do not deprive me of this life, do not wish me to die…. Allow me to contemplate the light, and then I shall be a man fully. Allow me to imitate the passion of my God."[59] In other words, for Ignatius, the definition, the true identity of humans, of believers, is eschatological, obtained through the power of God after death once they identify themselves with the cross of Jesus and thus share in his resurrection. As we saw earlier, anthropology is meaningless without the eschatological complement. If the latter is excluded, then the human being is broken and diminished, because the desired future fullness is filled with incertitude and anguish, and sooner or later with irrelevance.[60]

The Protological Aspect of Anthropology

We have already seen that the "eschatological" aspect of human identity, the basis of a renewed hope, is not easy to describe. When all is said and done, is it possible to develop a meaningful anthropology on the basis of a pure promise, of pure hope? Hope must refer to past memory and present experience in order to be fully human and relevant.[61] Augustine insisted in his *Confessions* on the principle *ex memoria spes* ("from memory, hope"), which means that it is not possible to reflect upon the future of humanity and the content of its hope if the latter has nothing to fall back on, an experience present in one's memory.[62]

We should note, however, that there is a strong bond between protology (the study of the beginnings of the created world) and future eschatological consummation. Three elements may be mentioned. First, as we saw, the future resurrection of humans is historically verified and faithfully witnessed by the Church in the resur-

---

57. See P. O'Callaghan, "La verità di Cristo nella storia: Testimonianza e dialogo," *PATH* 5 (2006): 95–109.

58. See *COH* 86f., 241f.

59. Ignatius of Antioch, *Ad Rom.* 6:2–3.

60. See *COH* 39–53.

61. See Ibid., 11f.

62. See Ibid., 4f.

rection of Jesus Christ.[63] Christians have seen the power of God with their own eyes. Second, the very power of the resurrection of Christ in the lives of Christians, which brings them to preach the "good news" even to the point of martyrdom, cannot but find in the fundamental constitution of humans a confirmation and profound resonance with the promise of resurrection, which rings true with the universal and irrepressible yearning toward immortality and human fullness. And third, scripture offers a clear vision not only of the eschatological end of humans but also of their origins, their creation, the subject of what is usually called protology. That is to say, scripture does not focus on anthropology exclusively from the eschatological standpoint; it also looks backward toward the beginnings of human existence when speaking of the creation of the world and of humans made "in the image and likeness of God" (Gn 1:27). And this vision, well developed in the Old Testament, is received in the New and brought to fullness in Christ, the perfect image of the Father. We shall consider this issue in the next chapter. After that we shall consider the topic of divine grace, which is none other than the very life of Christ in the believer.

63. See P. O'Callaghan, "Risurrezione," 1222f.

PART TWO   **THE HISTORICAL DEVELOPMENT OF THE DOCTRINE OF GRACE**

4 THE HUMAN BEING ACCORDING TO SCRIPTURE

Image of God and Son of God

Man is the first conversation nature has with God. J. G. GOETHE[1]

You formed man in your own image and entrusted the whole world to his care, so that in serving you alone, the Creator, he might have dominion over all creatures. EUCHARISTIC PRAYER IV

In the Biblical beginning ... the revealed truth concerning man as "the image and likeness" of God constitutes the immutable basis of all Christian anthropology. JOHN PAUL II[2]

Humans Made in the Image and Likeness of God in the Old Testament

Scripture does not have a developed and systematic anthropology. Yet both Testaments speak of the human being in a wide variety of ways.[3] This is especially so in the first book of the Bible, Genesis, which recounts the creation of the universe, the first stage of the Covenant that God established with his people and with humanity as a whole regarding its origin, its life, its Fall, and the promise of salvation. The fact that these texts are situated at the very beginning of scripture, though they are not the earliest ones of the Old Testament, is not without significance. Besides, the book of Genesis offers two principal accounts of the creation of humanity.

The first account chronologically, in Genesis 2:4b–3:24, usually called the "Yahvehist" account of creation, describes the origins of man, "drawn from the earth" (this is what the Hebrew word *adamāh*, applied to the first human, means), into whom God infuses the living spirit (*ruah*): "The Lord formed man from the dust of the ground, and breathed into his nostrils the breath of life; and man became a living

---

1. F. Heer, *The Intellectual History of Europe* (London: Weidenfeld and Nicolson, 1966), 335.
2. Pope John Paul II, *Mulieris Dignitatem*, Apostolic Letter, August 15, 1988, par. 6.
3. See Wolff, *Anthropology of the Old Testament*.

being" (Gn 2:7). In this account, humans are presented as unitary beings, similar to the animals. When they die, they will return to the earth they came out of. The same ideas are to be found frequently throughout the Old Testament, especially among the prophets and in the Psalms, somewhat less in the Wisdom literature. Besides, this description has much in common with the anthropologies typical of Eastern antiquity and, at a more general level, with that of some Greek philosophers. Genesis 2–3 may be said to provide the principal elements of the everyday anthropology of the Old Testament.[4]

The second account chronologically, in Genesis 1:1–2:4a, is a subsequent text, though scripture situates it before the "Yahvehist" account, perhaps due to its solemnity and objective importance. In it we find what is called the "Priestly" account of creation, so designated because the text has powerful liturgical resonances and expresses the need for humans to praise God for his great works.[5] In it humans are described not in terms of God piecing them together but in the light of their fundamental relationship with him and with the created world as a whole. It would be mistaken, therefore, to say that Genesis 1 represents a first stage in the process of creation (providing us with the original, perfect, human being), which later on would be completed with the addition of the bodily condition and the Fall (Gn 2–3). The latter was suggested by the philosopher Philo of Alexandria and received support from some Christian authors of Platonic inspiration.[6] Perhaps we may say that whereas Genesis 1 defines and considers humans from the point of view of God's overarching project and action, in a clearly liturgical context, Genesis 2–3 presents the self-same process from the point of view of the constitution of the human being. Both texts, in other words, recount the same fact of the creation of humans from two different perspectives. Whereas the Yahvehist text recounts the creation of humans as such, the Priestly text offers a description of God's act of creating.

The principal Biblical text that speaks of man made "in the image and likeness of God" is situated in Genesis 1, in the wider context of the creation of the world "in six days." God, according to this text, after having created the world, the firmament, plants, and animals, completed the process, before resting, by creating humans on "the sixth day." God said,

"Let us make man in our image, after our likeness; and let them have dominion over the fish of the sea, and over the birds of the air, and over the cattle, and over all the earth, and over every creeping thing that creeps upon the earth." So God created man in his own image, in the image of God he created him; male and female he created them. And God blessed them, and God said to them, "Be fruitful and multiply, and fill the earth and subdue it; and have dominion over the fish of the sea and over the birds of the air and over every living thing that moves upon the earth" (Gn 1:26–28).[7]

---

4. L. Perlitt, "Priesterschrift im Deuteronomium," *Zeitschrift für die alttestamentliche Wissenschaft* 100 suppl. (1988): 65–88, considers that Gn 2–3 has little influence on other books of the Old Testament.

5. On whether Gn 1:26ff. belongs to the so-called Priestly Source, see especially the works of Barr and Bruggemann in note 12.

6. See Philo of Alexandria, *De opificio mundi*, nos. 134–53.

7. In 2004 the International Theological Commission published an important document titled *Communion and Stewardship: Human Persons Created in the Image of God*. See also the recent studies of I. Egúzkiza Mutiloa, *El hombre creado a imagen de Dios en la teología del siglo XX: Las aportaciones de la teología positiva y su*

The first observation to be made on the text is that the expression "image of God" is seldom applied to humans in the Old Testament: just three times in the book of Genesis (1:26–28, 5:1–3, 9:6–7), once in the book of Sirach (17:3), and once in the book of Wisdom (2:23). Several other texts provide a paraphrase of Genesis 1:26–28, especially Psalm 8. Yet in comparison with the wide variety of texts that describe the nature and life of humans throughout the Old Testament,[8] the expression "image of God" is decidedly marginal and therefore, one might think, irrelevant. Perhaps for this reason the exegete Hermann Gunkel claimed that the expression "has no particular value in the Old Testament."[9] Still, it is undeniable that the expression "image of God" has had enormous weight throughout the history of Christian theology, in the New Testament and among the Church Fathers, both Eastern and Western, and also in scholastic and modern theology. It is fair to say that the idea of the "image of God" offers a point of departure and the fundamental structure for any anthropology inspired in Biblical and Christian faith. As John Paul II writes: "In the Biblical beginning ... the revealed truth concerning man as 'the image and likeness' of God constitutes the immutable basis of all Christian anthropology."[10]

Throughout this study I shall reflect frequently on the different implications of this programmatic text and of the corresponding New Testament ones on divine grace, which through Christ gives rise to the filial fullness of divine likeness in the believer. In the final section, which deals with Christian anthropology, we shall consider different ways in which the image of God is reflected in the lives of humans. Before doing so we shall examine Genesis 1:26–28 from a strictly exegetical viewpoint. The first thing to keep in mind is that there are two principal interpretations of the text: first, that the image of God expresses the close relationship between God and humans, and second, that the image of God refers to the mission of humans on earth, one of "dominating" or subduing the world created by God.[11] In considering the meaning of Genesis 1 we shall take into account a wide variety of twentieth-century Biblical studies.[12] It should become clear that the two interpretations are complementary.

recepción en el Concilio Vaticano II (Rome: Pontificia Università della Santa Croce, 2005); A. Aranda, Identità cristiana: I fondamenti, I: Teologia dell'imago Dei (Rome: Edusc, 2007). Interesting elements may be found in Pope Francis's encyclical Laudato Si'.

8. See H. W. Wolff, Anthropology of the Old Testament, and chapter 19.

9. H. Gunkel, Genesis, 4th ed. (Gottingen: Vandenhoeck & Ruprecht, 1964), 114. First published in 1901. Translated into English as Genesis (Macon, Ga.: Mercer University Press, 1997).

10. John Paul II, Mulieris Dignitatem, par. 6.

11. See the study of Stendebach in note 12, 392.

12. See, among other studies, J. Barr, "The Image of God in the Book of Genesis: A Study in Terminology," Bulletin of the J. Rylands Library 51 (1968): 11–26; Der Mensch als Bild Gottes, edited by L. Scheffczyk (Darmstadt: Wissenschaftliche Buchgesellschaft, 1969); J. M. Miller, "In the 'Image' and 'Likeness' of God," Journal of Biblical Literature 91 (1972): 298–304; D. Cairns, The Image of God in Man, 2nd ed. (London: Collins, 1973); J. F. A. Sawyer, "The Meaning of 'In the Image of God' in Genesis I–XI," Journal of Theological Studies 25 (1974): 418–26; A. G. Hamman, L'homme image de Dieu: Essai d'une anthropologie chrétienne dans l'Église des cinq premiers siècles (Paris: Desclée, 1987); G. J. Wenham, "Genesis 1–15," in Word Biblical Commentary, edited by B. M. Metzger, D. A. Hubbard, and G. W. Barker (Waco, Tex.: Word Books, 1987–2014) [hereafter "WBC"], 1:26–31; Jónsson, The Image of God; C. Westermann, Genesis (Edinburgh: T. and T. Clark, 1988), 4–13. In greater detail, see Westermann, Genesis 1–11; W. Vogels, "The Human Person in the Image of God (Gen 1,26)," Science et Esprit 46 (1994): 189–202; M. Welker, "Creation and the Image of God: Their Understanding in Christian Tradition

The Image and Likeness of God

In the coming paragraphs we shall consider the following eleven aspects of the image and likeness of God in humans: (1) the historical origin of the expression; (2) the distinction between "image" and "likeness" and the dynamic character of the human being; (3) the effect of sin on the image of God in humans; (4) the image of God and the filial character of human life; (5) the immortal destiny of humans made in the image and likeness of God and the sinfulness of homicide; (6) the fact that humans are made in the image of God as male and female; (7) the dominion that humans, made in the image of God, exercise over the created world; (8) the meaning and limits of human dominion over the earth; (9) human dominion over creation in other Old Testament texts; (10) the image of God as the root of human dignity; and (11) adoring God, the ultimate purpose of human life.

The following sections will consider the image of God in the light of Jesus Christ, perfect image of the Father.

The origin of the expression "image of God"   The description of man as the "image of God" is not unknown in the ancient East. In Babylonian and Egyptian literature, the idea is often applied to kings as representatives of God.[13] They alone are considered "images" of the divinity; the remainder of human beings are not. Besides, Egyptian kings frequently placed effigies in their own image in different parts of their territories to establish and proclaim their authority.[14] Exceptions may be found to this rule however. In a twentieth-century B.C. Egyptian text, King Merikare declares to his son: "Humans are images of the gods, issued from their members."[15] This would seem to mean that all humans are to be considered as images of God. Likewise, Platonic thought refers to an important likeness between the divine and the human; as a result humans are called to live ever more in conformity with the divine.[16]

Some authors consider the coincidence between Genesis 1 and other ancient texts merely verbal, of little or no interest from the theological point of view.[17] Besides,

---

and the Biblical Grounds," *Journal of Ecumenical Studies* 34 (1997): 436–48; F. J. Stendebach, "ṣelem," in G. J. Botterweck, H. Ringgren, and H.-J. Fabry, eds., *Theological Dictionary of the Old Testament* (Grand Rapids, Mich.: W. B. Eerdmans, 2003) [hereafter "*TDOT* "], 12:386–96.

13. The first modern author who established a connection between the image of God and royal power was probably J. Hehn, in *Zum Terminus 'Bild Gottes,'* in *Festschrift Eduard Sachau zum siebzigsten Geburtstag*, edited by G. Weil (Berlin: Reimer, 1915), 36–52. He was followed by S. Hermann, "Die Naturlehre des Schöpfungsberichtes: Erwägungen zur Vorgeschichte von Genesis 1," *Theologische Literaturzeitung* 86 (1961): 414–24; W. H. Schmidt, *Die Schöpfungsgeschichte der Priesterschrift: Zur Überlieferungsgeschichte von Genesis 1,1–2,4a und 2,4b–3,24* (Neukirchen-Vluyn: Neukirchen, 1964); H. Wildberger, "Das Abbild Gottes," *Theologische Zeitschrift* 21 (1965): 245–59, 481–501; G. von Rad, *Genesis: A Commentary* (London: SCM Press, 1985). On the concept of the image of God in ancient Egypt, see also E. Otto, "Der Mensch als Geschöpf und Bild Gottes in Ägypten," in *Probleme biblischer Theologie: Gerhard von Rad zum 70. Geburtstag*, edited by H. W. Wolff (Munich: Kaiser, 1971), 335–48; E. M. Curtis, *Man as the Image of God in Genesis in the Light of Ancient Near Eastern Parallels* (Ann Arbor, Mich.: UMI Dissertation Information Service, 1984); B. G. Ockinga, *Die Gottebenbildlichkeit im Alten Ägypten und im Alten Testament* (Wiesbaden: Harrassowitz, 1984).

14. See the works just cited of Curtis, Ockinga, and Otto.

15. Cited by Vogels, "The Human Person in the Image of God," from the *Instruction for King Mari-ka-Re*.

16. See, for example, Plato, *Thaetetus* 176a–b.

17. See, for example, Miller, "In the 'Image' and 'Likeness' of God," 209f; P. A. Bird, "'Male and Female

in his studies on the image of God in man, the influential Calvinist theologian Karl Barth has pointed out that the historical closeness between Christian and Jewish revelation and other religions has weighed heavily on the theological understanding of the issue throughout the twentieth century.[18] In effect, if revelation derives directly from God through the prophets and Christ, as Barth holds, coincidences between extra-Biblical texts and Biblical ones would be of scant relevance. This need not be so, however: revealed texts may well show up the meaning of extra-Biblical ones. The fact that the language used in Genesis 1:26ff. and other texts describing the royal dignity would seem to indicate that the texts in question are of some value at least in situating our understanding of the image of God in humans.

The distinction between "image" and "likeness" and the dynamic character of the human being   Whereas the Egyptian texts just mentioned state that man *is* the image of God, Genesis says rather that man is *made*, or created, in the image and likeness of God, that is, by an act of the divine creating will ("Let us make man in our image"). For this reason man cannot be considered as a spontaneous emanation of the divinity, as one who springs directly from the divine substance, as Platonists, Gnostics, and neo-Platonists thought. Thus, though made "in God's image," humans do not share in God's immutability and eternity because they are creatures, and thus open to change, to progress, and to growth (or to falling away, or even, perhaps, to disappearance). The human creature is essentially dependent on God's creating act.

Church Fathers such as Irenaeus of Lyons have seen in the distinction between "image" and "likeness" an indication of the contrast between seeing human nature as something that does not change (this is what the "image of God" means) and humans as open to change and growth, especially with respect to grace (this is what the "likeness of God" refers to).[19] With this distinction Irenaeus intended to take a clear position against a Gnostic view according to which humans are situated before God as fixed and unchangeable: the *psychicoi*, or spiritual ones, are destined to be saved because they are similar to God, whereas the *hylichoi*, those who belong to the material world, are destined for extinction. Important elements of Irenaeus's teaching are to be found among scholastic theologians, through Tertullian,[20] the Cappado-

He Created Them': Gen 1:27b in the Context of the Priestly Account of Creation," *Harvard Theological Review* 74 (1981): 129–59, 143. See also T. C. Vriezen, "La création de l'homme d'après l'image de Dieu," in *Lijst van de voornaamste geschriften van Prof. Dr. B. D. Eerdmans* (Leiden: E. J. Brill, 1943), 87–105; and F. Horst, "Face to Face: The Biblical Doctrine of the Image of God," *Interpretation* 4 (1950): 259–70, 259, who insist on the singularity and separated character of Biblical texts.

18. See notes 36ff. See P. O'Callaghan, "Is Christianity a Religion? The Role of Violence, Myth, and Witness in Religion," *Fellowship of Catholic Scholars Quarterly* 29, no. 4 (2006): 13–28. See also P. D. Miller, "God and the Gods: History of Religion as an Approach and Context for Bible and Theology," *Affirmation* 1, no. 5 (1973): 37–62, esp. 37ff.; O. Keel, B. Hartmann, *Monotheismus im Alten Israel und seiner Umwelt* (Einsidelen: Schweizerisches Katholisches Bibelwerk, 1980), 23ff.

19. See Irenaeus, *Adv. Haer.* V, 16, 2. On the position of Irenaeus, see A. Orbe, *Antropología de san Ireneo* (Madrid: BAC 1969), 118–48; Hamman, *L'homme image de Dieu*, 64–69.

20. The first author to link the image of God with human freedom was probably Tertullian: S. Otto, "Der Mensch als Bild Gottes bei Tertullian," *Münchener theologische Zeitschrift* 10 (1959): 276–82; A. G. Hamman, "L'homme, image de Dieu chez Tertullien," in *Autour de Tertullien: Hommage à René Braun*, edited by J. Granarolo and M. Biraud (Nice: Association des Publications de la Faculté des Lettres de Nice, 1991), 2:97–110, 105.

cians,[21] Augustine,[22] John Damascene,[23] and others. Thomas Aquinas explains that whereas the *image* refers to the intellectual and free constitution of man, that is, to his spiritual nature, the *likeness* belongs to the dynamics of moral virtue, that is, to what is spiritually changeable in him.[24] The *Catechism of the Catholic Church* puts it as follows:

Disfigured by sin and death, man remains "in the image of God," in the image of the Son, but is deprived "of the glory of God," of his "likeness." The promise made to Abraham inaugurates the economy of salvation, at the culmination of which the Son himself will assume that "image" and restore it in the Father's "likeness" by giving it again its glory, the Spirit who is "the giver of life."[25]

Still, from the strictly exegetical point of view, the two terms used, *ṣelem*, which means sculpture, material copy, and is usually translated as "image," and *demûth*, "likeness," correspondence with an original, are more or less equivalent, meant to strengthen one another, following the usual Semitic usage.[26] Perhaps it may be said that the term *demûth* in a sense attempts to attenuate the material emphasis present in *ṣelem*.[27] However, the interpretation of Irenaeus and the scholastics contains an important truth that may be summed up in two points: that (1) man is a being with an inalienable dignity, a permanent divine seal, received through the act of creation (the image), and, at the same time, (2) man is capable of development, growth, or de-

21. See for example, Basil, *Hom. I in orig. hom.*, 16–17.

22. According to Augustine, the terms "image" and "likeness" may not be distinguished: *Octoginta trium Quaest.*, q. 51; *De peccat. meritis et rem.* II, 7, 10. On this distinction in Augustine, see R. A. Markus, "'Image' and 'Similitudo' in Augustine," *Revue d'Études Augustiniens* 10 (1964): 125–43. See also notes 30ff below.

23. See John Damascene, *De fide orth.* 2, 12, cited by Aquinas as follows: "Secundum hoc Damascenus dicit quod id quod est secundum imaginem, intellectuale significat, et arbitrio liberum per se potestativum, quod autem secundum similitudinem, virtutis, secundum quod homini possibile est inesse, similitudinem." *S.Th.* I, q. 93, a. 9.

24. See Aquinas, *S.Th.* I, q. 93, a. 9.

25. *Catechism of the Catholic Church*, 2nd ed. (Washington, D.C.: United States Catholic Conference, 2000) [hereafter "*CCC*"], 705.

26. On this issue, see Wolff, *Anthropology of the Old Testament*, 183f. G. von Rad, *Das erste Buch Mose: Genesis*, 8th ed. (Gottingen: Vandenhoeck & Ruprecht, 1967, first published in 1950), 45, teaches that the term "image" is "better explained and clarified" by the addition of "likeness." According to Schmidt, *Die Schöpfungsgeschichte der Priesterschrift*, 133f., between the two terms *ṣelem* and *demûth* there is no difference of content, only of nuance. Wenham, in *Genesis 1–15*, 30, says the same thing. According to Miller, "In the 'Image' and 'Likeness' of God," 293f., they are equivalent terms, even though *demûth* (likeness) is introduced in order to limit, clarify, and modify *ṣelem* (image). Vogels, in *The Human Person in the Image of God*, 193, says the same thing, citing research undertaken after 1979 when the Tell Fakhariyah statue was discovered in Syria. It depicts the Aramaic prince Haddu-yis'i with inscriptions from the sixth century B.C. that present *demûth* and *ṣelem* as equivalents. On this topic, see also P.-E. Dion, "Image et Ressemblance en araméen ancien (Tell Fakhariyah)," *Science et Esprit* 34 (1982): 151–53; C. Dohmen, "Die Statue von Tell Fecherije und die Gottebenbildlichkeit des Menschen: Ein Beitrag zur Bildterminologie," *Biblische Notizen: Beiträge zur exegetischen Diskussion* 22 (1983): 91–106; D. M. Gropp and T. J. Lewis, "Notes on Some Problems in the Aramaic Text of the Hadd-Yith in Bilingual," *Bulletin of the American Schools of Oriental Research* 259 (1985): 45–61; P. Colella, "Immagine e somiglianza nell'iscrizione di Tell Fekheriyeh e nella Genesi," *Lateranum* 54 (1988): 34–57. Interestingly, in Genesis 1:27 and 9:6 only the term "image" is used, not "likeness," whereas in Gn 5:1, only "likeness" is to be found, and in Gn 5:3, both of them, but in reverse order. On the question of the synonymy of Biblical texts, see P. Niskanen, "The Poetics of Adam: The Creation of אדם in the Image of אלהים," *Journal of Biblical Literature* 128, no. 3 (2009): 417–36, esp. 421–24.

27. See M. Tábet, *Introducción al Antiguo Testamento*, vol 1: *Pentateuco y libros históricos*, 2nd ed. (Madrid: Palabra, 2008), 98.

cline according to the way he accepts the divine gifts (likeness). Paul's theology of the renewal of the image of God (Col 3:10; 1 Cor 15:49; Rom 8:29; 2 Cor 3:18) confirms this position. In his important study of Patristic anthropology, Adalbert Hamman says that the distinction between "image" and "likeness" underscores the unity between what humans are and what they should be, between what is given and what is obtained as the fruit of the action of the Holy Spirit and human effort.[28] Genesis 1:26ff. teaches, therefore, that humans are constituted as beings that are open to further divine gifts and, while being constituted with a God-given nature, may be considered as open, dynamic, and historical beings.[29]

The effect of sin on the image of God in humans   Drawing on the distinction between "image" and "likeness" just considered, some authors are of the opinion that the primordial (or "original") sin damaged humans to the extent of eliminating the image of God in them. This was the position of Augustine until the Pelagian controversy arose: sin destroyed the image of God in humans.[30] Later on, however, Augustine changed his position, saying that the image of God is rooted in the intellectual nature of the soul and cannot be lost.[31] At the same time, he taught that sin brings about a drastic reduction in the likeness of God in man.[32] He speaks frequently of a *regio dissimilitudinis* in the heart of humans, that is, an ample space within the fallen soul in which no trace of the action of God may be detected.[33] On this point Luther followed the early position of Augustine,[34] as did most Protestant authors for centuries,[35] until Karl Barth turned things around definitively.[36] Today, in fact, the common position among theologians is that the image of God remains substantially present in the human spirit with or without sin. That is to say, all humans, whether in God's grace or not, are made in God's image and likeness.

---

28. See Hamman, *L'homme image de Dieu*, 310.

29. See the article of G. D. Kaufmann, "The *Imago Dei* as Man's Historicity," *Journal of Religion* 36 (1956): 157–68. Kaufmann considers the formula "image of God" as an "analogia historicitatis" (a historical or dramatic analogue) in the sense that humans are determined by history and determine their own history.

30. Augustine, *De Gen. ad litt.* VI, 27:38.

31. Augustine, *Rectract.* II, 24, 2. See J. E. Sullivan, *The Image of God: The Doctrine of St. Augustine and Its Influence* (Dubuque, Iowa: Priory Press, 1963), 44.

32. See Markus, *"Image" and "Similitudo" in Augustine*, 142.

33. Augustine, *Conf.* VII, 10, 16.

34. Luther, *Enn. in Gen*, especially *WA* 42:45. On his doctrine, see A. Peters, "Bild Gottes IV," *Theologische Realenzyklopädie* 6 (1980): 512ff.; H.-M. Barth, "L'uomo secondo Martin Lutero: Alcune osservazioni sulla 'Disputatio de Homine' (1536)," *Studi Ecumenici* 1 (1983): 209–28; M. Lienhard, "Luther et sa conception de l'homme: Regards su le Commentaire de la Genèse (1535–1545)," *Positions Luthériennes* 40 (1992): 105–20; R. L. Wilken, "The Image of God in Classical Lutheran Theology," *Salvation in Christ: A Lutheran-Orthodox Dialogue*, edited by J. Meyendorff and R. Tobias (Minneapolis, Minn.: Augsburg, 1992), 121–32; C. D. von Dehsen, "The Imago Dei in Genesis 1:26–27," *Lutheran Quarterly* 11 (1997): 259–70.

35. See Pannenberg, *Systematic Theology*, 2:211. See also the Lutheran *Formula Concordiae: Solida Declaratio*, 1, 2f., in *Die Bekenntnisschriften der evangelisch-lutherischen Kirche*, 6th ed. (Gottingen: Vandenhoeck & Ruprecht, 1967), 848. See also the classic Lutheran work D. Hollaz, *Examen theologicum acroamaticum* (Stargard: Ernst u. Jenisch, 1707), q. 25 (§ 51).

36. In his earlier works, Karl Barth accepted the Protestant doctrine of the loss of the divine image through sin, but when he began to deal with the doctrine of creation, he abandoned this position. See *Die Kirchliche Dogmatik* I/1 (Zurich: Zöllikon, 1948), 238ff.; ibid., I/2, 307f.

The image of God and the filial character of human life   The text we are considering, Genesis 1:26–28, clearly expresses the relationship between God and man as the fruit of the former's creating action and, implicitly, the relationship established between man and other humans in that all are created "in the image and likeness of God." In this context Karl Barth places special emphasis on the social aspect of the "image of God." In effect, the latter is to be found in the relationship between God and humans, yet this relationship extends to all humans and is expressed in the phrase "male and female he created them" (Gn 1:27).[37]

Still, we may ask, What kind of relationship does the image of God establish between humans? Genesis 5, which coincides substantially with Genesis 1:26–28, makes an interesting adjunct, saying that the "image" of God in humans is basically filial in character and that they are capable of communicating this image to their descendants: "When God created man, he made him in the likeness of God. Male and female he created them, and he blessed them and named them man when they were created. When Adam had lived a hundred and thirty years, he became the father of a son in his own likeness, after his image, and named him Seth" (Gn 5:1–3). There is an obvious parallel between the two parts of the text: just as God made man in his image and likeness, and gave him the name "man" (*adamāh*), Adam, in turn, generated a son in his image and likeness, and named him Seth.[38] The name "Seth" means "the one who is called" or "placed," probably because he took the place of Abel, who, according to Genesis 4:8, had been killed by his brother Cain. But it is not only that Adam transmitted a likeness of his human nature to his son; besides, he handed on to his son the fact of his being in Adam's own image, and at heart being in the image and likeness of God.

From this reflection two observations may be made. First, the fact that being created in the image of God is communicated and handed on, in some way, by human generation, by the simple fact of being human. And second, that the expression "made in the image and likeness of God" has a clear filial connotation, even though the Old Testament does not explicitly teach that the human being, the believer, is a "son of God."[39]

As regards the first-person plural expression "Let us make man in *our* image, after *our* likeness" (Gn 1:26), it is quite common among Biblical scholars to say that the plural refers literally to the celestial court as agents of creation.[40] Still, Christian authors have frequently interpreted the expression, in the light of the New Testament,

37. Besides Barth (*Die Kirchliche Dogmatik* III/1, [Zurich: Zöllikon, 1945], 191ff., 205f.; ibid., III/2 [Zurich: Zöllikon, 1948], 323f.), on this issue see also Horst, *Face to Face*. Jónsson, in *The Image of God*, 203, observes the dependence of Barth on the philosophical personalism of Martin Buber, centered on the relationship "I-you-we." See also D. Bonhoeffer, who in *Schöpfung und Fall*, in *Dietrich Bonhoeffer Werke* (Munich: Chr. Kaiser Verlag, 1989), 3:58f., explains that the expression "Let us make man" presents humanity as a collectivity. In the English translation: D. Bonhoeffer, *Creation and Fall: A Theological Exposition of Genesis 1–3* (Minneapolis, Minn.: Fortress, 1997). The same position is held by Westermann, *Genesis*, 10f.

38. In the same way, Eve, when she had her son Cain, exclaimed: "I have acquired a man thanks to the Lord" (Gn 4:1).

39. See the beginning of chapter 13.

40. For a good summary, see D. J. A. Clines, "The Image of God in Man," *Tyndale Bulletin* 19 (1968): 53–103. See also Scheffczyk, ed., *Der Mensch als Bild Gottes*; Stendebach, "ṣelem," 394; G. F. Hasel, "The Meaning of 'Let us' in Gen 1:26," *Andrews University Seminary Studies* 13 (1975): 58–66.

in a Trinitarian way, seeing creation as an expression of the eternal dialogue between the Father, the Son, and the Holy Spirit.[41] This offers a further confirmation of the filial reading of the expression "image of God."

The immortal destiny of humans made in the image and likeness of God and the sinfulness of homicide   Genesis 9 offers an interesting paraphrase of Genesis 1:26ff. It reads: "And God blessed Noah and his sons, and said to them, 'Be fruitful and multiply, and fill the earth. The fear of you and the dread of you shall be upon every beast of the earth, and upon every bird of the air, upon everything that creeps on the ground and all the fish of the sea; into your hand they are delivered'" (Gn 9:1f.). Later on God addresses Noah and his sons as follows:

For your lifeblood I will surely require a reckoning; of every beast I will require it and of man; of every man's brother I will require the life of man. Whoever sheds the blood of man, by man shall his blood be shed; for *God made man in his own image*. And you, be fruitful and multiply, bring forth abundantly on the earth and multiply in it [and subdue it] (Gn 9:5–7).[42]

Man was sent by God to "dominate" over the fish and the birds (Gn 1:28) but not over other human beings. Because humans are made in the image of God, it is not permitted to harm them. To kill other humans is considered a grave offense to the creator. The fact that murder is illicit brings us to consider that humans are destined for immortality because they live not in the service of other corruptible creatures but exclusively in the service of God, who is eternal and immortal. This motive is taken up again openly in the book of Wisdom (2:23), which connects the image of God in man with the divine promise of immortality: "For God created man for incorruption, and made him in the image of his own eternity [in the Septuagint the Greek term used here is *epoiēsis*, which may be translated as "nature" or as "eternity"]." The book of Wisdom also indicates, by contrast, that the death of humans is not the will of God "because God did not make death, and he does not delight in the death of the living. For he created all things that they might exist" (Wis 1:13f.). In effect, "through the devil's envy death entered the world, and those who belong to his party experience it" (Wis 2:24).

Humans made in the image of God as male and female   Genesis 1:26–28 clearly links the "image of God" in humans to the distinction between the sexes and the propagation of the human species (Gn 1:27f.; see Gn 5:2):

So God created man in his own image, in the image of God he created him; *male and female he created them*. And God blessed them, and God said to them, "*Be fruitful and multiply*, and fill the earth and subdue it; and have dominion over the fish of the sea and over the birds of the air and over every living thing that moves upon the earth."

41. See, for example, Ps.-Barnabas, *Epistula* 5, 5 and 6, 12; Hillary of Poitiers, *De Trin.* IV, 17–20; and Cyril of Alexandria, *De dogmatum solutione*, 6, who teach that humans are made in the image of the Trinity. The same idea may be found in Augustine, *De Trin.* XII, 6, 6. On this issue, see G. T. Armstrong, *Die Genesis in der alten Kirche: Die drei Kirchenväter* (Tubingen: J. C. B. Mohr, 1962), 39; A. Struker, *Die Gottesebenbildlichkeit des Menschen in der christl. Literatur der ersten zwei Jahrhunderte; Ein Beitrag zur Geschichte u. Exegese von Gen 1:26* (Munster: Aschendorff, 1913), 81ff.

42. The Masoretic text that corresponds to Gn 9:6 does not contain the expression "and subdue it." On this question, see H.-J. Zobel, "rādâ," in *TDOT*, 13:330–36, esp. 336. Still, the teaching is to be found in Gn 9:1–4.

As mentioned already, Karl Barth insisted that the principal manifestation (what he calls the "definitive explanation") of the image of God in humans—of God who is a Trinitarian community of persons—is related precisely to their social character, which is discernible to a maximum degree in the communion of love between man and woman.[43]

The emphasis and priority given by Barth to this reading of Genesis has been accepted by some authors,[44] but not by the majority of exegetes.[45] On the one hand, it is clear that the sexual distinction is closely bound up with the divine blessing from which fruitfulness derives and which provides for the propagation of the human species. On the other hand, however, the blessing and the pressing invitation to propagate the species is also applied to the great sea monsters and birds, according to Genesis 1:21f.: "So God created the great sea monsters and every living creature that moves, with which the waters swarm.... And God saw that it was good. And God blessed them saying, 'Be fruitful and multiply and fill the waters in the seas, and let birds multiply on the earth.'" Yet it is clear that these animals are not made "in the image and likeness of God," nor are they meant to dominate and subdue the world. Hence it is not legitimate to establish a simple equivalence, as Barth does, between the image of God in man and "male and female he created them." Besides, it would be surprising if the author of the Priestly text, who always insists on the mystery of God's ineffability and transcendence (see Is 40:12–31), would attempt to establish a likeness, though it be analogous, between the triune God and human society.[46] Perhaps Wolfhart Pannenberg is right when he says that the text "allows us to conclude that

43. K. Barth, *Die Kirchliche Dogmatik* III/1, 219. As we saw earlier, Barth holds that being made in the image and likeness of God refers to the man-woman relationship and, in a wider sense, to the social character of humanity before the Trinitarian God: see *Die Kirchliche Dogmatik* III/2, 242–381.

44. The position of Barth is rejected by G. C. Berkouwer, *Man: The Image of God* (Grand Rapids, Mich.: W. B. Eerdmans, 1962), 73: "But this does not necessarily mean that the second clause gives a definition to the first; it does not necessarily imply that the image of God lies in the relationship between man and woman." The same position is to be found in P. Trible, *God and the Rhetoric of Sexuality* (Philadelphia: Fortress, 1978); M. C. Horowitz, "The Image of God in Man—Is Woman Included?," *Harvard Theological Review* 72, no. 3–4 (1979): 175–206; J. Goldingay, "The Bible and Sexuality," *Scottish Journal of Theology* 39 (1986): 175–88. According to Trible (*God and the Rhetoric*, 29n75), the interpretation of Barth may be considered at best an "interpretative indication" and point of departure. See also J. L. Thompson, "Creata ad Imaginem Dei, Licet Secundo Gradu: Woman as the Image of God According to John Calvin," *Harvard Theological Review* 81 (1988): 125–43.

45. Among exegetes unconvinced of this position, see P. Humbert, *Études sur le récit du paradis et de la chute dans la Genèse* (Neuchatel: Secrétariat Universitaire, 1940); L. Köhler, "Die Grundstelle der Imago-Dei-Lehre, Genesis 1, 26," *Theologische Zeitschrift* 4 (1948): 16–22. See also Wenham, *Genesis 1–15*, 31. Bird, in "*Male and Female He Created Them*," 155, is of the same opinion. In her influential study Bird concludes that the phrase "male and female he created them" "says nothing about the image which relates Adam to God nor about God as the referent of the image.... It relates only to the blessing of fertility.... The contemporary theologian-exegete is reminded that the Bible is often quite uninterested in, or unable to comprehend, the questions pressed upon the text from modern perspectives and experiences" (155). See also the critique of Barth's position by J. J. Stamm, "Die Imago-Lehre von Karl Barth und die alttestamentliche Wissenschaft," in *Antwort: Festschrift für Karl Barth* (Zurich: Evangelischer Verlag, 1956), 84–98. And Pannenberg concludes: "If we want to agree with Barth that the sexual relation corresponds to the trinitarian relation of the Father and the Son, then we must subordinate woman to man as Barth subordinates the Son to the Father." *Systematic Theology*, 2:206.

46. See Bird, "*Male and Female He Created Them*," 156. Some authors have suggested that the expression "male and female he created them," closely associated with the blessing and the divine invitation to propagate the species, belongs to the genealogical structure of the Priestly text (P). This would connect creation with the establishment of a cult by means of a genealogy made up exclusively of masculine names.

both man and woman are created equally in the divine image but not that the likeness consists of the relation between the sexes."[47]

Still, in the expression "male and female he created them," insofar as it is associated with the divine blessing and the pressing invitation to propagate the species, it is possible to find a further confirmation of the idea that humans are meant to subdue the created world. In effect, in order for them to exercise their dominion over the whole world, the propagation of the species is a necessary prelude. The propagation of the species is thus directed toward the task given by God to humans to dominate the whole world. As Wolff says: "The increase of mankind and dominion over the earth and the beasts are directly linked together."[48]

Human Dominion under God

To sum up so far what Genesis teaches us of the "image of God" in man, we may say that it probably has an extra-Biblical origin, gives expression to some degree to the relationship between God and man, and refers to the dynamic quality, openness, immortal destiny, dignity, and sociality of humans. But from the point of view of humans themselves, we may still ask what it actually means. What are the consequences for human life: what can humans, made in God's image, do that cannot be done by animals and other living beings? What does the "image of God" say of man's mission and destiny? What power does it confer?

Some authors would have it that to be made in the image of God means that humans possess a strong likeness, both bodily and spiritually, to God himself.[49] This interpretation, in a theologically sophisticated text such as the Priestly one, seems to involve a gross anthropomorphism.[50] In fact, some Church Fathers have suggested that being created in the image and likeness of God is undefinable for the simple reason that God himself, in whose image and likeness man is made, cannot be defined or described.[51] That is to say, God should be recognized, adored, obeyed, and loved, but he cannot be understood, defined, or dominated by humans: this would be idolatry. As a result, to investigate the nature of God with a view to understanding his created image would be completely out of place.[52]

47. Pannenberg, *Systematic Theology*, 2:206.

48. Wolff, *Anthropology of the Old Testament*, 162.

49. The first author to bring up the question in modern times was probably T. Nöldeke, in "Selem and demut," *Zeitschrift für die alttestamentliche Wissenschaft* 17 (1897): 183–87, followed by Gunkel, in *Genesis*. The author who made the position well known was Humbert, in *Études sur le récit du paradis*, 153–63, and then Köhler, in *Die Grundstelle*, 5f. For a summary of the different positions, see Miller, "In the 'Image' and 'Likeness' of God." See especially P. G. Duncker, "L'immagine di Dio nell'uomo (Gen 1,26–27): Una somiglianza fisica?" *Biblica* 40 (1959): 384–92.

50. See Wenham, *Genesis 1–15*, 30.

51. This was the position, for example, of Epiphanius, in *Panarion*, 70, 2, 7. Gregory of Nyssa, in *De opif. hom.* 16, holds that the image of God in humans, since it is perfect, is necessarily unknowable, because it is a reflection of the fullness of the archetype. On the idea of God involved here, see von Dehsen, *The Imago Dei*. This author explains that the notion of the "image of God" is connected in the mind of Israelites with idolatry. Hence it cannot be applied to humans. It just refers to God, not to a living artifact. See the section of this chapter headed "The Image of God, Root of Human Dignity," n. 69 and corresponding text.

52. As regards the image of God in humans, W. H. Schmidt, in *The Faith of the Old Testament: A History* (Oxford: Oxford University Press, 1986), 197, says: "Perhaps the concept of the 'image of God' cannot be strictly defined at all."

However, if we keep in mind the Egyptian origin of the term "image of God"—where it refers to the king, who represents God in the government of the world[53]—it is legitimate to say that man is made in the image of God not in the sense that he shares in the divine being, which is omnipotent and ineffable, but principally in the sense that he takes part in God's own action. After all, God alone is Lord of all that exists in the universe. In that sense, with Genesis 1:26–28 and Genesis 9:7, we can say that *God has destined humans to dominate and subdue the earth as his special representatives*. Humans are made in the image of the Yahweh, the Lord of the universe. Thus they partake in his Lordship. This position is commonly held by many Biblical scholars,[54] though not by all of them.[55] Besides, it is to be found among the Church Fathers and within several different theological traditions.[56]

In effect, God in his own inner essence cannot be known by humans, yet he has revealed himself to us as Lord, as sovereign.[57] He alone dominates and subdues and is therefore the source of all dominion and power. Thus, to be made "in the image and likeness of God" means that the human being, God's own ambassador or representative, partakes in this dominion "over the fish of the sea, and over the birds of the air"

53. See I. Engnell, *Studies in Divine Kingship in the Ancient Near East* (Oxford: Blackwell, 1967).

54. Jónsson, in *The Image of God*, 221, speaks of "ample agreement," of "an absolutely dominant position," with respect to this interpretation. Among the earlier studies, see especially D. T. Asselin, "The Notion of Dominion in Genesis 1–3," *Catholic Biblical Quarterly* 15 (1954): 277–94, and Schmidt, who in *Die Schöpfungsgeschichte der Priesterschrift*, 144, writes: "God is proclaimed wherever man is present.... Man is the witness to God." This is also the position of H. Gross, in "Die Gottesebenbildlichkeit des Menschen," in *Lex tua veritas: Festschrift für Herbert Junker* (Trier: Paulinus-Verlag, 1961), 89–100, and in "Gottebenbildlichkeit des Menschen im Kontext der Priesterschrift," *Theologische Quartalschrift* 161 (1981): 244–64, where he speaks especially of human dominion over animals. See also H. Ringgren, *Israelite Religion*, 2nd ed. (London: SPCK, 1969); N. C. Habel, *Literary Criticism of the Old Testament* (Philadelphia: Fortress, 1971), 24; H. D. Preuss, *dāmāh, demûth*, in *TDOT*, 3:250–60, 259; R. W. Klein, *Israel in Exile: A Theological Interpretation* (Philadelphia: Fortress, 1979); N. H. Snaith, "The Image of God," *Expository Times* 91 (1979): 20; J. C. L. Gibson, *Genesis* (Edinburgh: T. and T. Clark, 1981), 86; W. Janzen, *Still in the Image: Essays in Biblical Theology and Anthropology* (Winnipeg: Newton, 1982); Dohmen, "Die Statue von Tell Fecherije," 100; Dohmen, *Das Bilderverbot: Seine Entstehung und seine Entwicklung im Alten Testament* (Bonn: Hanstein, 1985), 282; E. Nielsen, "Über die Auffassung von der Natur im Alten Testament," in *Law, History and Tradition: Selected Essays by Eduard Nielsen* (Copenhagen: GEC Gads, 1983), 40–58, 54; E. Zenger, *Gottes Bogen in den Wolken: Untersuchungen zu Komposition und Theologie der priesterschriftlichen Urgeschichte* (Stuttgart: Verlag Katholisches Bibelwerk, 1983), 90; B. W. Anderson, "Creation and Ecology," in *Creation in the Old Testament* (Philadelphia: Fortress, 1984), 152–71; Vogels, *The Human Person in the Image of God*, 196–98; Goldingay, *The Bible and Sexuality*, 75; Wenham, *Genesis 1–15*, 30–32.

55. Authors such as Westermann, in *Genesis*, 11, do not accept this interpretation because it is based on an excessively close continuity between the divine and the human ambit. Still, we need to keep in mind that at a wider level the Biblical symbolism present throughout the Old Testament does not move in the direction suggested by Westermann: we can think of the animals sacrificed that represent Israel or of the high priest who represents the people before God and vice versa; see Wenham, *Genesis 1–15*, 31. J. M. Miller writes: "The priestly account presupposes essentially the same order of primordial events as do the Mesopotamian documents—i.e. the establishment of order in the universe, followed in turn by the creation of man, the resting of the gods, the establishment of kingship, a succession of pre-flood kings with fantastically long reigns, the great flood, and finally the re-establishment of kingship." "In the 'Image' and 'Likeness' of God," 303.

56. It would seem that the Socinians were the first in modern times to consider things in this way: see F. Socinus, *De statu primi hominis ante lapsum disputatio* (Racoviae: Typis Sebastiani Sternacii, 1610), 93. Likewise, Calvin was aware of this interpretation but was opposed to it: *Institutiones* 1, 15:4. From the standpoint of contemporary dogmatic theology, von Balthasar explains that humans are constituted in the image and likeness of God insofar as they act with finite freedom: *Theo-Drama*, 2:326–34.

57. On the question of Thomas's apophaticism, see the studies of M. Pérez de Laborda, "La preesistenza delle perfezioni in Dio," and "Il progresso nella conoscenza di Dio secondo san Tommaso."

(Gn 1:26). The capacity and invitation to subdue the earth do not as such constitute a definition of the image—the latter refers to the ineffable bond between creator and creature—but they are a direct consequence of being made in the image of God.[58] According to the Biblical text, therefore, every human being has received in God's name a participated royal power over creation. Man is made in the image of God, says Pannenberg, in the sense that "we may understand that our rule over creation is 'like' that of the Creator."[59]

The meaning and limits of human dominion over the earth Man is invited to exercise dominion over the earth and in doing so is accompanied by a special divine blessing (Gn 1:28). Divine blessing according to the Old Testament is always associated with life, fertility, fruitfulness, growth, prosperity, and success, with the fulfillment of the messianic prophecies.[60] Thus the task of humans, made in the image of God, will and always should be one of consolidating, developing, and confirming life on earth, not death and destruction.[61] Besides, the fact that man can relate to God directly as his own image, without having recourse to intermediate divinities, ushers into thought and culture the awareness and conviction of a demythologized world.[62] All that exists, without exception, has been created by God, and man, man alone, is constituted as divine ambassador before the world, capable of dominating other creatures. There is no "earth" that may be considered "divine"; there are no "divine" animals, or stars, or constellations. All creatures are subordinate to man and, through man, to God. In that sense we can say that the created universe is entirely "worldly," or "secular," that is, not divine. Within the material world, human creatures are supreme, for they are the only ones made in the image of God. "The heavens are the Lord's heavens, but the earth he has given to the sons of men" (Ps 115:16).

Genesis 1:28 uses two terms to describe the actions of humans made in the image of God with respect to the created world: "to subdue" (*kābaš*), a term that is applied to the world in general, and "to dominate" (*rādāh*), referred to living beings, also in Genesis 1:26.[63] The first term refers to an absolute form of dominion, obtained by force (Jos 18:1), by war (Nm 32:22, 29), even by crushing other peoples (2 Sm 8:1) and slaves (Neh 5:5). The other word, *rādāh*, "to dominate," is applied in the Old Testament also to royal dominion (Pss 72:8, 110:2; Is 14:6; Ezek 34:4),[64] as well as the process of treading the grape (Jl 3:13).

Nonetheless, it is clear that humans do not possess unlimited power over creation. God imposes a variety of restrictions to the power they are allowed to exercise. In the first place, humans do not dominate time and the seasons, for it will be a "greater light"

---

58. See Vogels, *The Human Person in the Image of God*, 197; E. Jacob, *Theology of the Old Testament*, 2nd ed. (London: Hodder and Stoughton, 1974); Wildberger, *Das Abbild Gottes*; Barr, *The Image of God in the Book of Genesis*. On this topic, see Jónsson, *The Image of God*, 224n40; Pannenberg, *Systematic Theology*, 2:204ff.

59. Pannenberg, *Systematic Theology*, 2:204.

60. See J. Scharbert, "brk (ברב)," in *TDOT*, 2:279–308; H. Ringgren, H. Cazelles, "hll (הלל)," in *TDOT*, 3:404–13; C. Westermann, *Blessing in the Bible and the Life of the Church* (Philadelphia: Fortress, 1978); Tábet, *Introducción al Antiguo Testamento*, 1:98f.

61. See Vogels, *The Human Person in the Image of God*, 197.

62. See Wolff, *Anthropology of the Old Testament*, 162.

63. Westermann teaches that the two terms are equivalent in *Genesis 1–11*, 147ff.

64. See Zobel, "rādâ."

that will govern the day and a "lesser light" the night, that is, the sun and the moon (Gn 1:14–18). Second, as we saw already, humans do not have power over the lives of others for the simple reason that one and all are made in the image and likeness of God. It is true that the Masoretic text of Genesis 9 does not speak of the "dominion" of humans over the earth.[65] Still, it does include the interesting, though implicit, teaching to the effect that human dominion over the earth is limited because human life is not in the hands of other humans: "Whoever sheds the blood of man, by man shall his blood be shed; for God made man in his own image" (Gn 9:6). As the fruit of the divine blessing, dominion exercised by humans must contribute to the preservation of creation under God's power, with full respect for human life. In short, human dominion is not exclusively of a royal or absolute kind because it is not exercised over other humans, also made in God's image. In the third place, humans have the power to subdue other creatures, and this may be observed in the fear and respect animals have, or should have, for them. God said to humans: "The fear of you and the dread of you shall be upon every beast of the earth, and upon every bird of the air, upon everything that creeps on the ground and all the fish of the sea; into your hand they are delivered" (Gn 9:2f.). According to the first-century Jewish work *The Life of Adam and Eve*, while Eve and Seth were on a journey, Seth was assaulted by a wild animal, and Eve cried out: "Cursed beast, are you not afraid to attack the image of God?" (v. 13). In the fourth place, God limits the power of humans over the earth, not allowing them eat of "the tree of life" (Gn 2:16). Fifth and last, we can observe that the content and ambit of human dominion are not fully known to us because, whereas the power of God is unlimited, that of humans is severely limited: "Of the Lord is the earth and everything it contains" (Ps 24:1).

Human dominion over creation in other Old Testament texts   The theme of human dominion over creation is to be found in two Wisdom texts of exceptional power and beauty. Both of them attempt to explain what it means for God to have created man in his image and likeness. They are Psalm 8 and Sirach 17.

In Psalm 8:3–9 we read:

When I look at your heavens, the work of your fingers, the moon and the stars which you have established; what is man that you are mindful of him, and the son of man that you should care for him? Yet you have made him little less than God, and crowned him with glory and honor. You have given him dominion over the works of your hands; you have put all things under his feet, all sheep and oxen, and also the beasts of the field, the birds of the air, and the fish of the sea, whatever passes along the paths of the sea. O Lord, our Lord, how majestic is your name in all the earth!

The likeness between Genesis 1:26–28 and Psalm 8 is obvious. Yet the latter text does not state that humans are made in the image and likeness of God. But it does say that we are made "somewhat less than God," "crowned with glory and honor." Besides, the text speaks openly of the dominion of man over the earth, especially over animals, and of the divine praise that should constitute the joyful ultimate fruit of exercising that dominion.[66]

---

65. See note 42.

66. Ps 8:7 says the same thing as Gn 1:26–28, according to Westermann, *Genesis*, 11. On Ps 8, see B. S. Childs, "Psalm 8 in the Context of the Christian Canon," *Interpretation* 23 (1969): 20–31.

In Sirach 17:1–12 we find a further ample gloss on Genesis 1:26–28. Although the first two verses of the text ("The Lord created …") evoke Genesis 2, the rest provide a rich description of the image of God in man (Gn 1). Again there is insistence on the dominion of humans over material creation: "The Lord created man out of earth, and turned him back to it again. He gave to men few days, a limited time, but granted them authority over the things upon the earth. He endowed them with strength like his own, and *made them in his own image*. He placed the fear of them in all living beings, and granted them dominion over beasts and birds" (Sr 17:1–4).

The rest of the passage (vv. 5–12) explains different aspects of the lives of humans, made in the image of God. We shall consider it later on.

The fact that man is destined to share in God's dominion over the earth is thus clearly present in the book of Genesis and in the rest of the Old Testament. God is the only Lord over creation. Yet humans have been created in his image and likeness, and this means that they have been sent and invited to share in God's work in the world. The second account of creation in the book of Genesis contains the same message though it uses different language: "The Lord God took the man and put him in the garden of Eden to till it and keep it" (Gn 2:15). The *Targumim*, or ancient Aramaic paraphrases of the Hebrew Bible, explains the latter text as follows: God placed man in the garden "so that he would give him worship according to the law."[67] In the words of the Lutheran exegete Gerhard von Rad, "Man is sent by God, and is destined to protect and extend his dominion over the earth."[68]

The image of God, root of human dignity   The term used, *ṣelem* ("image" in Aramaic), is translated in the Septuagint as *eikōn*, a term frequently used in the Old Testament to translate the term "idol," or sculpted image. We know that the prophets severely condemned the adoration of idols,[69] for their veneration contradicts the cult due exclusively to God.[70] The prophet Isaiah asks, "To whom then will you liken God, or what *likeness* compare with him?" (Is 40:18; see 46:5).[71] Yet humans have been made in the image of God. They are the highest beings in the material world. All creation is good, we are told frequently in Genesis 1, but with the creation of man the world acquired its definitive and supreme goodness: "And God saw everything that he had made, and behold, it was very good. And there was evening and there was morning, a sixth day" (Gn 1:31). In other words, there are no other "idols," no other divinities or images, between God and man.[72] The clear rejection of idolatry throughout the

---

67. See the *Targumim* on Gn 2:15.   68. Von Rad, *Genesis*, 70f.

69. See, for example, Nm 33:52; 1 Sm 6:5; 2 Kgs 11:18; 2 Chr 23:17; Hos 8:6; Jer 10:5, 9; Is 40:18, 42:17, 45:16 and 20, 46:5–7; Ezek 7:20, 16:17, 23:14. In these texts idols are always presented in an unfavorable light. See the comments of Stendebach, "ṣelem," 390f. On the theme of idolatry, see the interesting work of G. K. Beale, *We Become What We Worship: A Biblical Theology of Idolatry* (Downers Grove, Ill.: IVP Academic, 2008).

70. On the role of the first commandment in the Decalogue as the "integrating center" of the message of the Old Testament, see W. H. Schmidt, *Das erste Gebot: Seine Bedeutung für das Alte Testament* (Munich: Chr. Kaiser, 1969).

71. The term used in Is 40:18 is *demûth*, "likeness." The text of Isaiah is followed by these words, which are clearly opposed to idolatry: "The idol, a workman casts it, and a goldsmith overlays it with gold, and casts for it silver chains. He who is impoverished chooses for an offering wood that will not rot; he seeks out a skillful craftsman to set up an image that will not move" (Is 40:19f.).

72. On the equivalence between "image" and "idol" and their semantic and theological implications, see Barr, *The Image of God in the Book of Genesis*.

Old Testament thus becomes an affirmation not only of the absolute sovereignty of God over the earth and of our obligation to adore him unconditionally but also of the dignity of humans, supreme and ultimate creatures, God's confidants, destined to immortality, natural ambassadors for the whole of the created world. Idolatry not only offends the creator but also degrades human dignity. Thus, when humans badly treat other people, "made in the image of God" (Gn 9:6), not only do they offend them, but also their creator: "He who oppresses a poor man insults his Maker, but he who is kind to the needy honors him" (Prv 14:31).

In Jewish thought, says Abraham Heschel, the image of God in man is an expression above all of the inalienable dignity of the individual human being: "Man is man not for what he has in common with the earth, but for what he has in common with God."[73] "We must love man because he is made in the image of God," said Rabbi Akiba in the second century A.D.[74] Besides, according to Heschel, the obligation humans have to live a holy life is rooted in the fact that they are made in the image of God.[75]

In the same way that it is possible to distinguish between the divine plan of creating humans ("Let us make man in our own image") and of his being created in fact ("God created man in his image"), we may also distinguish the divine blessing of humans ("God blessed them") from the positive affirmation directed to them: "and he said to them" (Gn 1:28), an adjunct that is not present in the texts that refer to the blessing of birds and fish (Gn 1:22).[76] This removes any kind of automatism or mechanical element in the relationship between God and man and underscores the idea that humans have intelligence, free will, and dignity as personal interlocutors of God.

Adoring God: the ultimate purpose of human life and activity   The image of God in man, as we have seen, expresses in the first place the capacity of humans to establish a special and direct relationship with God. The second creation account confirms this: the dignity of human beings may be detected in the intimacy and immediacy between God and the creature, for example, when Yahweh is depicted as "walking in the garden in the cool of the day" (Gn 3:8).

Still, the fact that there is a special relationship between God and humans does not mean that the latter may be considered on a par with the creator, as if they were God's partners. It may not be said that the human being *is* the image of God; rather he is *made* in the image of God, depends on God entirely, and has a given existence. He is destined to dominate the earth and subdue it but only as God's representative

---

73. Heschel, *The Concept of Man in Jewish Thought*, 128. The same author says that the image of God exists in humans "to remind us that every thing found on earth was placed under the dominion of man, except human life, and to remind us that the body of man, and not only his soul, is endowed with divine dignity" (129). And he adds: "The divine likeness of man is an idea known in many religions. It is the contribution of Judaism to have taught the tremendous implication of that idea: the metaphysical dignity of man, the divine preciousness of human life" (131). On the image of God in humans according to recent Jewish thought, see D. S. Shapiro, "The Doctrine of the Image of God and Imitatio Dei," in *Contemporary Jewish Ethics*, edited by M. M. Kellner (New York: Sanhedrin Press, 1978), 127–51.

74. Rabbi Akiba, *Genesis Rabba*, 24, 8, cited by Heschel, *The Concept of Man in Jewish Thought*, 129.

75. Piety is the result of the imperative "Treat yourself as an image of God," says Heschel. "We can understand the meaning of the astonishing commandment: 'You shall be holy, for I the Lord your God am holy' (Lev 19,2). Holiness, an essential attribute of God, may become a quality of man. The human can become holy." Heschel, *The Concept of Man in Jewish Thought*, 132.

76. See Vogels, *The Human Person in the Image of God*, 196.

or ambassador. Thus in real terms the prime duty of humans is not that of dominating the earth but rather that of recognizing the absolute sovereignty of God, adoring and praising him.[77] Genesis 1 is, as we have already seen, a Priestly text, liturgical in structure, in which, above and beyond any descriptive elements, *God is meant to be praised*. In effect, once the account of the creation of the world is over, the people seem to exclaim: "And God saw everything that he had made, and behold, it was very good" (Gn 1:31). The second account of creation indicates openly what the Priestly text teaches, that is, that humans are meant to obey God and him alone (Gn 3). The same motive may be found in Psalm 8:2–10 and in other psalms.

In his study of the anthropology of the Old Testament, H.-W. Wolff explains that the destiny of man on the earth is fourfold: to live in the world, to love one's neighbor, to dominate creation, and to praise God.[78] The complex way in which the dominion of man over the material world is integrated with his duty to offer cult to God is expressed in the following text from the Roman Sunday liturgy: "For you laid the foundations of the world and have arranged for the changing of times and seasons; you have formed man in your own image and set humanity over the whole world in all its wonder, to rule in your name over all you have made, and for ever praise you in your mighty works, through Christ our Lord."[79] We shall consider this issue again in chapter 24, on human work.

The Image of God in the Light of Jesus Christ, Perfect Image of the Father

We shall now consider the doctrine of the image of God in humans in the context of the New Testament and the Church Fathers, that is, in the light of Jesus Christ, the perfect image of the Father.

The image of God and the constitution of man as body and soul   It is true that the number of Old Testament texts speaking of man made in the image of God is low.[80] This brings us to ask a simple question: why did the definition of humans "made in the image of God" become so important among the Church Fathers and in Christian theology as a whole?[81] To begin with, it should be said that among the former, two principal interpretations of the expression are given.

77. Thus T. N. D. Mettinger, "Abbild oder Urbild? 'Imago Dei' in traditionsgeschichtlicher Sicht," *Zeitschrift für die alttestamentliche Wissenschaft* 86 (1974): 404–24, 411. See also P.-E. Dion and D. Fraikin, "Ressemblance et Image de Dieu," in *Dictionnaire de la Bible, Supplément*, edited by H. Cazelles and A. Feuillet (Paris: Letouzey et Ané, 1985), 10:366–414, 378f.

78. See Wolff, *Anthropology of the Old Testament*, 223–29.

79. "Fifth Sunday Preface," *The Roman Missal*, edited by P. W. Carey, H. J. Nolan (Washington, D.C.: United States Conference of Bishops, 2011), 580.

80. The books of Sirach and Wisdom are not generally included in the Protestant canon. It is understandable, therefore, that some authors have attempted to diminish the value of the doctrine of the image and consider improper the centrality it takes on among the Church Fathers and medieval doctors. See K. L. Schmidt, "Homo Imago Dei im AT und NT," *Eranos-Jahrbuch* 15 (1947): 149–95.

81. See R. M. Wilson, "The Early History of the Exegesis of Gen. 1.26," *Studia Patristica* 1 (1957): 420–37; P. Schwanz, *Imago Dei als christologisch-anthropologisches Problem in der Geschichte der alten Kirche von Paulus bis Klemens von Alexandrien* (Halle: Niemeyer, 1970); S. Raponi, "Il tema dell'immagine-somiglianza nell'antropologia dei padri," in *Temi di antropologia teologica*, edited by E. Ancilli (Rome: Teresianum, 1981), 241–341, on the first commentaries of the Fathers. In a more general way, see also Hamman, *L'homme image de Dieu*.

Among Latin authors such as Irenaeus and Tertullian, the definition of man "made in the image of God" refers to the entire human being, body and soul.[82] These authors find in it an expression of the unity, integrity, and corporeity of humans. This is likewise the most common reading of the term among contemporary Biblical scholars.[83] The Fathers insisted on this aspect of the image of God to avoid a Manichean view of man that despises the body, God's own work of creation.[84] Likewise, Lactantius and others see the image of God in humans in terms of their erect posture, by means of which they are distinguished from animals and are capable of subduing them, showing in that way that they have been made to command the whole of creation.[85] The description given by the nineteenth-century philosopher Johann G. Herder is worth quoting:

The figure of man is distinguished from all others on earth on account of its erect posture. Besides, this erect position is what marks his activity organically, implying a perspective on the world and on things that is completely different from that of animals, which are inclined towards the ground. It is as if nature, once all the different possible forms of organic life on earth had been exhausted, wished to regale creatures with their most splendid ornament, their lord and second creator, a creature that, exalted above all the animals, would be like a god for them.[86]

However it is more common to find, among the Church Fathers, both East and West, a more spiritual reading of what it means for humans to have been created in the image of God. Following Philo of Alexandria and other authors inspired by Plato, many Fathers consider that the likeness of God in man is to be found in his *spiritual essence*, in the soul, and specifically in the intellect (*nous*).[87] This is so for two reasons. On the one hand, God is invisible and noncorporeal, and created spirit, made in God's image, should also be so. On the other hand, spirit and intellect distinguish humans from animals and other created beings, which, as we know, have not been

---

82. On Irenaeus, see E. Peterson, "L'immagine di Dio in sant'Ireneo," *La Scuola Cattolica* 69 (1941): 46–54; J. Fantino, *L'homme image de Dieu chez saint Irénée de Lyon* (Paris: Cerf, 1986). Irenaeus writes: "By the hands of the Father, that is the Son and the Spirit, man and not only a part of man was made in the image and likeness of God." *Adv. Haer.* V, 6, 1. On Tertullian, see O. Stéphan, "Der Mensch als Bild Gottes bei Tertullian," *Münchener theologische Zeitschrift* 2 (1959): 276–82.

83. See especially the works of Humbert and Köhler in note 49. See also Stamm, *Die Imago-Lehre von Karl Barth*. Stendebach, under ṣelem, 392, who holds that the image of God is present in the entire human being.

84. In the *Letter to Diognetus*, 10, 2, we read: "God loved humans, and for them created the world, giving them reason and intelligence; he modeled them according to his image, he sent them his Son, he promised them the kingdom of heaven, and will give it to those who love him."

85. See Lactantius, *De ira Dei*, 7, 4. Augustine also speaks of the erect posture (*De Gen. ad litt.* 6, 12), but does so principally to express the vocation of humans to look toward the heavens instead of subduing the earth. See also *De Gen. c. Manich.* I, 18, 29. The same idea is to be found in Aquinas, *S.Th.* I, q. 93, a. 6, ad 3, and among classic Protestant authors such as S. J. Baumgartner, C. G. Ammon, and J. G. Herder; see Pannenberg, *Systematic Theology*, 2:207n104.

86. J. G. Herder, *Ideen zur Philosophie der Geschichte der Menschheit* (Wiesbaden: Fourier, 1985), I, III, 6 (46). Translated into English as *Outlines of a Philosophy of the History of Man*, ed. T. Churchill (Farmington Hills, Mich.: Thomson Gale, 2005).

87. See Philo, *De opificio mundi* 69. On Philo's understanding of the image of God in man, see J. Giblet, "L'homme image de Dieu dans les commentaires littéraux de Philon d'Alexandrie," *Studia Hellenistica* 5 (1948): 93–118; J. D. Crossan, *Imago Dei: A Study in Philo and St. Paul* (Rome: Typis Pontificiae Universitatis Gregorianae, 1959); T. H. Tobin, *The Creation of Man: Philo and the History of Interpretation* (Washington, D.C.: Catholic Biblical Association, 1983).

created in the image and likeness of God. This position is openly taught by authors such as Clement of Alexandria,[88] Origen,[89] Didymus the Blind,[90] Athanasius,[91] Gregory of Nyssa,[92] Gregory of Nazianzen and Basil the Great,[93] and also Ambrose[94] and Augustine.[95] The latter asks, "Ubi imago Dei?" (Where is the image of God situated in man?), and he responds openly: "In mente, in intellectu" (In the mind, in the intellect).[96] That is to say, the image of God does not reside in the human body.[97]

More or less the same doctrine is to be found in medieval times,[98] for example,

88. See especially Clement of Alexandria, *Stromata* 5, 94, 5; *Protrepticus* 10, 98, 2–4. On Clement, see A. Mayer, *Das Gottesbild im Menschen nach Clemens von Alexandrien* (Rome: Herder, 1942).

89. See Origen, *De principiis* I, 1, 7, 24; *In Gen. I*, 13. Origen considers Christ as the Image of God according to his divinity, and not as God-man. Christ is the image of God, he says, in a contemplative sense, because he brings us to know the Father, manifesting him to the soul, and in an active sense because he brings to completion what was established by the divine intelligence. On the doctrine of Origen, see Crouzel, *Théologie de l'image de Dieu chez Origène* (Paris, Aubier-Montaigne, 1956).

90. Didymus the Blind, *In Gen. I*, 26–28, 55.

91. On the doctrine of Athanasius, see R. Bernard, *L'image de Dieu d'après saint Athanase* (Paris: Aubier-Montaigne, 1952); J. Roldanus, *Le Christ et l'homme dans la théologie d'Athanase d'Alexandrie: Étude de la conjonction de la conception de l'homme avec sa christologie* (Leiden: E. J. Brill, 1977).

92. See especially Gregory of Nyssa, *De hominis opificio*, 5. On his doctrine, see H. U. von Balthasar, "La philosophie de l'image," in *Présence et pensée: Essai sur la philosophie religieuse de Grégoire de Nysse* (Paris, Beauchesne, 1942), 81f.; J. T. Muckle, "The Doctrine of St. Gregory of Nyssa on Man as the Image of God," *Mediaeval Studies* 7 (1945): 55–84; R. Leys, *L'image de Dieu chez Saint Grégoire de Nysse: Esquisse d'une doctrine* (Brussels: L'Edition Universelle, 1951); J. Gaïth, *La conception de la liberté chez Grégoire de Nysse* (Paris: Vrin, 1953); T. Di Stefano, "La libertà radicale dell'immagine secondo san Gregorio di Nissa," *Divus Thomas* 75 (1972): 431–54; M. Girardi, "L'uomo immagine somigliante di Dio (Gen 1, 26–27) nell'esegesi dei Cappadoci," *Vetera Christianorum* 38 (2001): 293–314; G. Maspero, "Immagine (εἰκών)," *Gregorio di Nissa: Dizionario*, edited by L. F. Mateo-Seco and G. Maspero (Rome: Città Nuova, 2007), 320–24. As regards the relationship between image and divine image, says Gregory, "the whole of humanity, from the first humans to the last, is a single image of Being." *De hom. opif.*, 16. See G. Maspero and L. F. Mateo-Seco, eds., *The Brill Dictionary of Gregory of Nyssa* (Boston: Brill, 2009).

93. See Basil, *Hom. I in orig. hom.*, 7.

94. The *Hexameron* of Ambrose is decisive for Augustine. On the doctrine of the former, see G. A. McCool, "The Ambrosian Origin of St. Augustine's Theology of Image of God in Man," *Theological Studies* 20 (1959): 62–81.

95. See Augustine, *De Civ. Dei* XIII, 24, 2; *In Io. Ev. tr.* III, 4. On the doctrine of Augustine, see C. Boyer, "L'image de la Trinité, synthèse de la pensée augustinienne," *Gregorianum* 27 (1946): 173–99, 333–52; H. Somers, "Image de Dieu: Les sources de l'exégèse augustinienne," *Revue des Études Augustiniennes* 7 (1961): 105–26; P. Hadot, "L'image de la Trinité chez Victorinus et chez saint Augustin," in *Studia Patristica*, edited by F. L. Cross (Oxford: Oxford University Press, 1962), 6:409–42; Sullivan, *The Image of God*; Markus, *"Image" and "Similitudo" in Augustine*; J. I. Alcorta, "La imagen de Dios en el hombre, según san Agustín," *Augustinus* 12 (1967): 29–38; A. Turrado, "Nuestra imagen y semejanza divina: En torno a la evolución de esta doctrina en San Agustín," *La Ciudad de Dios* 181 (1968): 776–801; P. Agaësse, *L'anthropologie chrétienne selon saint Augustin: Image, liberté, péché et grâce* (Paris: Centre-Sèvres, 1986); M. C. Dolby Múgica, *El hombre es imagen de Dios: Visión antropológica de san Agustín* (Pamplona: Eunsa, 1993); M. T. Clark, "Image Doctrine," *Augustine through the Ages: An Encyclopedia*, edited by A. D. Fitzgerald and J. Cavadini (Grand Rapids, Mich.: W. B. Eerdmans, 1999), 440–42.

96. Augustine, *In Io. Ev. tr.* III, 4; see *De Gen. ad litt.* VII, 12; *Enn. in Ps. Sermo* 2, 16; *Enn. in Ps.* 42, 6. "Imago Dei intus est, non est in corpore ... sed est facta mens" (*Enn. in Ps.* 48, 11); "Fecit et hominem ad imaginem et similitudinem suam in mentem" (*Sermo I de Symbolo*, 2); "secundum solam mentem imago Dei dicitur" (*De Trin.* XV, 77, 11).

97. See Augustine, *De Trin.* XII, 7, 12.

98. See R. Cessario, *The Godly Image: Christ and Salvation in Catholic Thought from St. Anselm to Aquinas* (Petersham, Mass.: St. Bede's Publications, 1990); G. Dahan, *L'exégèse chrétienne de la Bible en Occident médiéval: XIIè–XIIIè siècle* (Paris: Cerf, 1999).

in Bernard of Clairvaux,[99] William of Saint-Thierry,[100] Bonaventure,[101] and Thomas Aquinas[102] right up to Calvin and classical Protestant theologians.[103] Besides, whereas during the twelfth through the thirteenth centuries there were important disputes on the way the human body shared in the image of God,[104] for different reasons interest among theologians and philosophers in the issue of the image of God waned as the medieval period progressed.[105]

99. See M. Standaert, "La doctrine de l'image chez Saint Bernard," *Ephemerides theologicae lovanienses* 23 (1947): 70–129; S. A. Iannello, "Dalla regio dissimilitudinis alla deificatio: L'uomo immagine e somiglianza di Dio in Bernardo di Chiaravalle," *Capys* 2 (2011): 75–96.

100. See L. Malevez, "La doctrine de l'image et de la connaissance mystique chez Guillaume de Saint-Thierry," *Recherches de science religieuse* 22 (1932): 178–205, 256–79.

101. The question of the image of God in Bonaventure has been extensively studied. See, for example, D. Scaramuzzi, "L'immagine di Dio nell'uomo nell'ordine naturale secondo san Bonaventura," *Sophia* 10 (1942): 259–74; B. Madariaga, "La 'imagen de Dios' en la metafísica del hombre según San Buenaventura," *Verdad y Vida* 7 (1949): 145–94; J.-P. Rézette, "Grâce et similitude de Dieu chez saint Bonaventure," *Ephemerides theologicae lovanienses* 32 (1956): 46–64; A. Schaefer, "The Position and Function of Man in the Created World According to Saint Bonaventure," *Franciscan Studies* 20 (1960): 261–316, 21 (1961): 233–382; A. Black, "The Doctrine of the Image and Similitude in Saint Bonaventure," *The Cord* 12 (1962): 269–75; A. Solignac, "L'homme image de Dieu dans la spiritualité de Saint Bonaventure," in *Contributi di spiritualità bonaventuriana*, edited by G. Zoppetti and D. M. Montagna (Padova: Studio teologico comune dei frati, 1974), 1:77–101; F. Chavero Blanco, *Imago Dei: Aproximación a la antropología teológica de san Buenaventura* (Murcia: Editorial Espigas, 1993).

102. See especially Aquinas, *S.Th.* I, q. 93. On his reflection, see A. Squire, "The Doctrine of the Image in the *De Veritate* of St. Thomas," *Dominican Studies* 4 (1951): 164–77; G. Lafont, "Le sens tu thème de l'image de Dieu dans l'anthropologie de saint Thomas d'Aquin," *Recherches de Science Religieuse* 47 (1959): 560–69; L. B. Geiger, "L'homme, image de Dieu: Àpropos de 'Summa Theologiae,' 1a,93,4," *Rivista di Filosofia Neo-scolastica* 66 (1974): 511–32; F. Conigliaro, "L'uomo *imago Dei* fine della creazione: Antropologia di Tommaso d'Aquino," *Ho Theológos* 5, no. 18 (1978): 5–100; J. J. Pelikan, "Imago Dei: An Explication of Summa Theologiae, Part 1, Question 93," in *Calgary Aquinas Studies*, edited by A. Parel (Toronto: Pontifical Institute of Medieval Studies, 1978), 27–48; D. J. Merriell, *To the Image of the Trinity: A Study in the Development of Aquinas's Teaching* (Toronto: Pontifical Institute of Medieval Studies, 1990); M. W. Dauphinais, "Loving the Lord Your God: The *Imago Dei* in Saint Thomas Aquinas," *The Thomist* 63 (1999): 241–67; G. M. Carbone, *L'uomo immagine e somiglianza di Dio: Uno studio sullo "Scritto sulle Sentenze" di san Tommaso d'Aquino* (Bologna: Edizioni Studio domenicano, 2003); L. Brenna, *L'immagine di Dio in san Tommaso d'Aquino: L'uomo alla luce di St I, 93* (Rome: Pontificia Università della Santa Croce, 2004); Egúzkiza Mutiloa, *El hombre creado a imagen de Dios*, 160–79; E. Reinhardt, *La dignidad del hombre en cuanto imagen de Dios: Tomás de Aquino ante sus fuentes* (Pamplona: Eunsa, 2005); M. W. Levering, "The Imago Dei in David Novak and Thomas Aquinas," *Thomist* 72 (2008): 259–311; A. Tubiello, "L'immagine di Dio nell'uomo: Appunti di umanesimo cristologico in Tommaso d'Aquino," *Capys* 2 (2011): 97–116.

103. According to Calvin, the image of God is situated in the soul: *Institutiones*, 1, 15:3. The same doctrine is to be found in later Lutherans such as D. Hollaz and J. F. Buddeus. On Luther, see notes 34f.

104. On this discussion, see R. Javelet, *Image et ressemblance au douzième siècle de saint Anselme à Alain de Lille* (Strasbourg: Letouzey et Ané, 1967), 1:196–207, 224–36.

105. In the later Middle Ages the centrality of the image of God in man was lost to some degree: see O. González de Cardedal, *El quehacer de la teología: Génesis, estructura, misión* (Salamanca: Sígueme, 2008), 575. This loss is frequently attributed to the falling away of Platonism, but the fact is that Platonism consolidated substantially throughout the Middle Ages. See S. Pinckaers, "Le thème de l'image de Dieu en l'homme et l'anthropologie," in *Humain a l'image de Dieu*, edited by P. Bühler (Geneva: Labor et Fides, 1989), 147–63, attributes the loss of the notion of the image of God to a growth in nominalist anthropology, with a new idea of freedom as indifference. On this issue, see also Rézette, *Grâce et similitude de Dieu*, esp. 50. The image of God is dealt with more in spirituality than in anthropology. On this issue, see R.-L. Oechslin, "Image et ressemblance, V: Des mystiques rhénans au Carmel réformé," in *Dictionnaire de Spiritualité*, edited by M. Viller et al. (Paris: G. Beauchesne, 1937–92), 7.2 (1971): 1451–63. However, the theme is present among the Renaissance authors: see C. E. Trinkaus, *In Our Image and Likeness: Humanity and Divinity in Italian Humanist Thought* (London: Constable, 1970); H. C. Baker, *The Image of Man: A Study of the Idea of Human Dignity in Classical Antiquity, the Middle Ages, and the Renaissance* (Gloucester, Mass.: Peter Smith, 1975).

The "image of God": Platonic or Christological? It seems that the strong emphasis placed by the Church Fathers on the expression "image of God" draws on the Platonism and neo-Platonism present in an important part of Patristic thought from the earliest centuries.[106] According to Platonic teaching, in effect, man, through contemplation and an ascetic life, is called to find his true self and overcome sin, in that way becoming "spiritual" and therefore more and more like God, who is pure Spirit, uncontaminated by matter. Understandably, Christian authors came to share this view in many ways. However, the real reason why the theme of the image of God came to occupy center-stage among the Church Fathers lies elsewhere.[107] Platonism was adopted by many of the Fathers as a philosophical and linguistic instrument in order to develop theological reflection in the light of faith.[108] The reason why the Fathers took a particular interest in the image of God in man has Christological roots: according to the New Testament, Jesus Christ, the Savior of the world, is, in person, the perfect image of the Father, as the letter to the Colossians teaches (1:15).[109] The Church Fathers therefore made use of this definition present in a small though relevant number of Old Testament passages, because they read them in the light of the New Testament. In the works of Scola and others "God speaks of himself through and in the humanity

106. On the Church Fathers' understanding of the image of God in humans, see Hamman, *L'homme image de Dieu*. Also Struker, *Die Gottesebenbildlichkeit des Menschen*; H. C. Graef, "L'image de Dieu et la structure de l'âme d'après les Pères grecs," *Vie Spirituelle, Supplément* 22 (1952): 331–39; P.-T. Camelot, "La théologie de l'image de Dieu," *Revue des sciences philosophiques et théologiques* 40 (1956): 443–72; G. A. Maloney, *Man, the Divine Icon: The Patristic Doctrine of Man Made According to the Image of God* (Pecos, Tex.: Dove Publications, 1973); R. Cantalamessa, "Cristo 'Immagine di Dio': Le tradizioni patristiche su Colossesi I,15," *Rivista di Storia e Letteratura Religiosa* 16 (1980): 181–212, 345–80; G. Visonà, "L'uomo a immagine di Dio: L'interpretazione di Genesi 1,26 nel pensiero cristiano dei primi tre secoli," *Studia Patavina* 27 (1980): 393–430; Raponi, "Il tema dell'immagine-somiglianza"; V. Grossi, *Lineamenti di antropologia patristica* (Rome: Borla, 1983); L. F. Ladaria, in *L'homme et son salut*, edited by B. Sesboüé, V. Grossi, L. F. Ladaria, and P. Lécrivain (Paris: Desclée, 1995), 100–108; F. G. McLeod, *The Image of God in the Antiochene Tradition* (Washington D.C.: The Catholic University of America Press, 1999); L. Dattrino, *Creati a immagine di Dio: La dignità dell'uomo nel pensiero dei Padri* (Vatican City: Lateran University Press, 2003); Egúzkiza Mutiloa, *El hombre creado a imagen de Dios*, 81–118, which presents the doctrine of Philo, Clement, Origen, Athanasius, and Gregory of Nyssa. Besides the authors mentioned in notes 87ff., see the monographic studies of W. J. Burghardt, *The Image of God in Man According to Cyril of Alexandria* (Woodstock, Md.: Woodstock College Press, 1957); W. R. Jenkinson, "The Image and the Likeness of God in Man in the Eighteen Lectures on the Credo of Cyril of Jerusalem (c. 315–87)," *Ephemerides Theologicae Lovanienses* 40 (1964): 48–71; P. Argárate, "El hombre creado a la imagen y semejanza de Dios en San Máximo el Confesor," *Communio* (ed. española) 30 (1977): 189–219.

107. "The Patristic doctrine of the likeness to God or to Christ is born then from a combination of Biblical and Hellenic ideas, in which the Christian element is naturally dominant." G. B. Ladner, "Der Bildbegriff bei den griechischen Vätern und der byzantinische Bilderstreit," in *Der Mensch als Bild Gottes*, edited by L. Scheffczyk (Darmstadt: Wissenschaftliche Buchgesellschaft, 1969), 144–92, 168. See also G. Söhngen, "Die biblische Lehre vom der Gottesebenbildlichkeit des Menschen," *Münchener Theologische Zeitschrift* 2 (1951): 52–76.

108. On the notion of the image of God in Plotinus, who was the principal representative of neo-Platonic thought, see P. Aubin, "L'"image" dans l'oeuvre de Plotin," *Recherches de science religieuse* 41 (1953): 348–79. On the different relationships between Christianity, Judaism, Gnosticism, and Platonism on the matter, see Jónsson, *The Image of God*, 55f.

109. See especially Irenaeus, *Adv. Haer.* V, 16, 2. See Scola, Marengo, and Prades López, *La persona umana*, 149ff.; Cantalamessa, *Cristo "Immagine di Dio"*; Hamman, *L'homme image de Dieu*; C. Spicq, *Dieu et l'homme selon le Nouveau Testament* (Paris: Cerf, 1961), 179–213; L. F. Ladaria, "La concepción del hombre como imagen de Dios y su reinterpretación en Cristo," *Miscelánea Comillas* 43 (1985): 383–99. On Christ as the true Image, see O. Procksch, *Theologie des Alten Testaments* (Gutersloh: Bertelsmann, 1950).

of his Son. Thus only in Him can man understand properly his having being created in the image and likeness of God, because he discovers himself to be image of the Image of God."[110] The "Image" explains the image; the "Image" accounts for the image. This, in real terms, is what is meant when we say, with *Gaudium et Spes*, no. 22, that "Christ reveals man to man."

The image of God in the New Testament It is principally Paul who presents Christ as the image of the Father, though the idea is not absent from John's teaching on the eternal generation of the Word and his incarnation (Jn 1:1-14). Paul speaks, for example, of those "who do not see the light of the gospel of the glory of Christ who is the likeness [*eikōn*] of God" (2 Cor 4:4). In the first chapter of the letter to the Colossians we read, "He [Christ] is the image [*eikōn*] of the invisible God, the first-born of all creation" (Col 1:15), a text that refers both to creation and to salvation.[111] In the letter to the Hebrews the same idea is to be found: "He [Christ] reflects the glory of God and bears the very stamp of his nature, upholding the universe by his word of power" (Heb 1:3).[112] In the Pauline doctrine is reinforced the idea of the believer living as an image of Christ.

It is interesting to note that in Genesis 1:26ff. man is said to be created "according" to the image of God, what exegetes call the *beth essentiae* (a "beth" of essence). The same expression may be found in Genesis 5:1 and 9:6. The text distinguishes, therefore, between the copy and the original. Obviously man is the copy. But Genesis 1:26f. does not specify who or what is the original. For this reason, the exegete Tryggve Mettinger suggested that the "man" spoken of in Gen 1:26f. is created according to a heavenly prototype, just as the tabernacle (or divine dwelling place) was made according to a heavenly model or form (*tabnît*: Ex 25:9, 40, 25:30, 27:8). Both humans and the prototype, Mettinger says, play the same "role of carrying out divine service in heavenly and earthly shrines in the praise of the Creator."[113] In the light of Wisdom literature, therefore, it may be plausible to say that the image in man of which scripture speaks refers to pre-existent Wisdom (Wis 7:26), or to the pre-existent Logos (Jn 1:1), or perhaps to the exalted Christ (2 Cor 4:4). Apart from the Christological opening this interpretation provides, the liturgical significance of the image of God in man is reinforced.

Man made in the image of God according to the Fathers The relationship between Christ as the perfect image of the Father and man made in the image of God is made explicit in the writings of Irenaeus,[114] Tertullian,[115] and Hillary of Poitiers. Irenaeus

---

110. See Scola, Marengo, and Prades López, *La persona umana*, 149f.; I. Biffi, *Il mistero dell'esistenza cristiana: "Conformi all'immagine del Figlio"* (Milan: Jaca Book, 2002).

111. On this central Pauline text, see T. Otero Lázaro, *Col 1,15–20 en el contexto de la carta* (Rome: Editrice Pontificia Università Gregoriana, 1999). See also Cantalamessa, *Cristo "Immagine di Dio."*

112. Philo uses this term to speak of the relationship between God and the Logos: see *BDAG* 99, s.v. ἀπαύγασμα.

113. Mettinger, *Abbild oder Urbild?*, 411.

114. See, for example, Irenaeus, *Adv. Haer.* V, 16, 2 and 36, 3; and A. Orbe, "El hombre ideal en la teología de s. Ireneo," *Gregorianum* 43 (1962): 449–91.

115. See Tertullian, *De Res.* 53:6–8, *Adv. Praxeam* 12:3–4. See Otto, *Der Mensch als Bild Gottes bei Tertullian*; Hamman, *L'homme, image de Dieu chez Tertullien*; J. Leal, *La antropología de Tertuliano: Estudio de los tratados polémicos de los años 207–212 d.C.* (Rome: Institutum Patristicum Augustinianum, 2001).

explains it as follows: "He has made man like God, and the image of God is the Son, according to the image in whose likeness man was made. And therefore he [the Son] appeared in the last times to show an image like himself."[116] Elsewhere he writes: "God made man in his image. And the image of God is the Son, in whose image man was made. That is why, in the last times, the Son was shown forth, to bring us to understand that the image was like himself."[117] And Tertullian, speaking of the creation of Adam from the earth, says: "Quodcumque enim limus exprimebatur, Christus cogitabatur" (All that was impressed on that earth was [God's] thought of Christ). And he comments: "The Father spoke to the Son, 'Let us make man in our image and likeness. And God made man,' who was to be modeled, 'in the image of God he was made,' that is of Christ. The Word in effect is God, the one who being in the form of God did not retain as a privilege being like God."[118]

Aurelius Prudentius offers the following brief formula: "Christus forma Patris, nos Christi forma et imago" (Christ is the form of the Father, and we are form and image of Christ).[119] And in Augustine the same idea is to be found: "We can understand that the likeness to God by which man was made is the selfsame Word of God, that is the only-begotten Son: on no account is man the very image and the exact likeness of the Father."[120] Finally, we may cite the following text of John Damascene: "Christ is the natural image of the Father; man is the image of God by imitation."[121]

Made in the image of which Christ?   What does the Christological understanding add to the different elements of the Old Testament theology of the image of God? To respond to this question, we should keep in mind that several Church Fathers, especially of the Alexandrian school, considered Christ as the image of God according to his *divinity*, whom they called the *Logos asarkos*, "the Word not incarnate."[122] As a result, the Christological reading of the image of God in man would refer principally to the spiritual side of man, that is, the human soul, and not to the body, a position described earlier on.[123] The *Logos asarkos* reading of the image of God in man, though valid to some degree, is not sufficient in that it does not take into account the

116. See Irenaeus, *Demostratio*, no. 22. Elsewhere he writes: "In times preceding it was said that man was created according to the image of God, but this was not manifested right away, because the Word, according to whom man was made, was as yet invisible, and for this reason the likeness had been easily lost. But when the Word became flesh, there was for both a solid basis: he revealed the truth of the image by becoming what his image was, and he reconstituted the likeness through the Word now visible, making man like the invisible Father." *Adv. Haer.* V, 16, 2.

117. Irenaeus, *Epideixis*, 33.

118. Tertullian, *De Res.*, 6:3–4. The following text is also worth citing: "The following passage distinguishes between the persons: 'And God made man, he made him in the image of God.' Why did he not say 'in his image' if there was one who made and none in whose image it was made? In fact there was one in whose image he acted, that is his Son, who in becoming the most perfect and truest man, ensured that the man that would then be formed from the earth, in the image and likeness of God, would be called his image." Tertullian, *Adv. Praxeam*, 12, 4.

119. Aurelius Prudentius, *Apotheosis* 309.

120. Augustine, *De Gen. ad litt.* 16:61.

121. John Damascene, *De imaginibus*, or. 3, 8. See J. J. Meany, *The Image of God in Man According to the Doctrine of Saint John Damascene* (Manila: San José Seminary, 1954).

122. See Origen, *De princ.* I, 2, 6, and Athanasius (Roldanus, *Le Christ et l'homme*, 40ff.) refer to it as the *logos asarkos*.

123. See notes 87ff.

realism of the incarnation and the power of the divine saving work that derives from the Word Incarnate. In fact, other Church Fathers, principally those who situate the image of God within the integrated body-soul constitution of humans, consider the image of God to be present in the *Logos ensarkos*, "the incarnate Word."[124]

As regards the specifically Christian understanding of the image of God in man, the following three questions may be asked. First, above and beyond what is stated in the Old Testament on the image of God in man, what does the notion of Christ as image add to human beings, made in God's image, in their direct relationship with God? Second, what does the Christian's belonging to Christ add to the task God assigned to humans to "dominate and subdue" the earth? And third, if being made "in the image of God" refers to the human activity of dominating the earth, why did the Church Fathers connect it principally to intellectual and contemplative activity, that is, to the human spirit, rather than to our bodily condition and activity in the world? We may respond in the following three stages.

Children of God in Christ   As we shall see in coming chapters,[125] the relationship between God and humans, made in his image, acquires a supernatural power and intimacy with the saving grace of Christ operating in them. In effect, through faith in Christ, the human being truly becomes a son of God (Gal 4:5f.; Rom 5:15f., 8:17–29; Eph 1:3f.; Jn 1:12; 1 Jn 3:1f.), a disciple, brother, and friend of Jesus Christ ("No longer do I call you servants, for the servant does not know what his master is doing; but I have called you friends, for all that I have heard from my Father I have made known to you" (Jn 15:15) and the temple of the Holy Spirit. Definitive fullness of the image of God in humans consists, therefore, in their divine filiation. Divine filiation provides the ultimate likeness of humans to God, the fullness of the image.

The Christian's share in the universal Lordship of Christ   Paul presents Christ as the Lord, who dominates the entire universe, especially from the moment of his resurrection, which is the fruit of his obedient fidelity to the Father in dying on the cross. Everything is his, John tells us (Jn 1:11), and at the end of time, all things will be subjected to him in a visible, tangible, and permanent way, and in him to the Father. As the fruit of his obedience and humility, that of his own unconditioned submission to the Father on the cross, "God has highly exalted him and given him the name which is above every name, that in the name of Jesus every knee should bend, in heaven and on earth and under the earth, and every tongue confess that Jesus Christ is Lord, to the glory of God the Father" (Phil 2:9–11). And in the first letter to the Corinthians we read (1 Cor 15:25–28):

For he must reign until he has put all his enemies under his feet. The last enemy to be destroyed is death [this will take place by means of the resurrection]. "For God has put all things in subjection under his feet" [Ps 8:6]. But when it says, "All things are put in subjection under him," it is plain that he is excepted who put all things under him. When all things are subjected to him, then the Son himself will also be subjected to him who put all things under him, that God may be everything to every one.

---

124. Irenaeus applies Col 1:15 to the incarnate Word, *Logos sarkos: Adv. Haer.* IV, 6, 6.
125. See also chapter 2, notes 25ff. and corresponding text, and chapter 13.

The same idea may be found in the letter to the Hebrews, which, like 1 Corinthians 15, just cited, provides a gloss of Psalm 8: "Now in putting everything in subjection to him, he left nothing outside his control. As it is, we do not yet see everything in subjection to him. But we see Jesus, who for a little while was made lower than the angels, crowned with glory and honor because of the suffering of death, so that by the grace of God he might taste death for everyone" (Heb 2:8–9). The same doctrine is presented in Jesus' solemn declaration during the Last Supper: "Now is the judgment of this world, now shall the ruler of this world be cast out; and I, when I am lifted up from the earth, will draw all men to myself" (Jn 12:31f.).

To the question "What does Christ our savior as image add to humans being made in the image of God?," three observations may be made. *First*, Christ, as our savior, frees us from sin, which, according to the book of Genesis (Gn 2–3), separated humans from their primordial task of dominating the earth while totally recognizing divine sovereignty, placing them, instead, within an abusive dominion that not only broke the bonds of love and trust uniting them to God but also introduced the seed of death and discord into the cosmos, into society, into human relationships, and into the very heart of the human being. Salvation brought by Christ reconciles and reestablishes within believers the original power to subject and dominate other creatures, by subjecting themselves to God. *Second*, in virtue of man's incorporation into Christ and of the gift of grace received through baptism, the image of God in man is manifested and reinforced and comes to fullness in such a way that humans can contribute, as children of God in Christ, to the restoration of the kingdom of Christ on earth through their work and by means of all human activities, for the glory of God. *Third* and finally, in the light of the incarnation and the resurrection, the role of the human body takes on particular value and importance, as we shall see now.

Man made in the image and likeness of God in body and soul   The text of Sirach 17, already cited, explains with surprising power and beauty that the reason God made man in his image and likeness, giving him intellect and wisdom, was to make it possible for him to dominate and subdue the earth. Thus it may be said that Christian contemplation and intellectual activity are anything but incompatible with the dominion over the earth that humans are invited to exercise in all their activities, including those of a bodily and manual kind. Even more: on account of their spiritual faculties and activities, humans manage to dominate the earth in a way that surpasses the action of any other created being. The text reads as follows (Sir 17:1–11):

The Lord … endowed [humans] with strength like his own, and made them in his own image. He placed the fear of them in all living beings, and granted them dominion over beasts and birds. *They received the use of the five powers from the Lord, a share of intelligence was given to them as a sixth, and as a seventh, reason—interpreter of his powers.* He made for them tongue and eyes; he gave them ears and a mind for thinking. He filled them with knowledge and understanding, and showed them good and evil. He set his eye upon their hearts to show them the majesty of his works *and privileged them to proclaim his marvels forever.* And they will praise his holy name, to proclaim the grandeur of his works. He bestowed knowledge upon them, and allotted to them the law of life.[126]

---

126. It is likely that the expressions of Sirach placed in italics, "They received the use …" and "privileged them …" are glosses of Stoic origin.

In this text we can observe, among other things, that the bodily character of humans and their physical action in relation to the created world are inseparable from their intelligence and will.[127] Not only is it clear that dominion over the created world exercised by man, made in God's image, is expressed corporally but also that intellectual activity necessarily requires a material complement, which Thomas Aquinas referred to in his epistemology when speaking of the *conversio ad phantasmata* (the turning towards mental images). It is interesting to note that according to Aquinas the soul united to the body is closer to the image of God than the separated soul on its own.[128] Gottlieb Söhngen sums this up in the following words: "Since the likeness of the new man with God is a likeness to Christ, this embraces the entire man, also the body."[129] We shall consider this affirmation principally in chapter 19.

Aspects of the Doctrine of Divine Grace in the Old Testament and the Synoptics

Besides teaching that man is made in the image of God, the Old Testament speaks of different ways in which God prepares the way for the New Testament doctrine of grace. Besides, it formulates some technical terms more directly.

Aspects of God's Gratuitous Action toward Humans

Five elements characterize God's way of acting toward humans according to the Old Testament: the blessing, the giving of life, the Covenant, salvation, and liberation.[130]

First, the Old Testament speaks of God's action toward humans in terms of the blessing (see, for example, Gn 12:1–3). To the king the Psalmist says: "You are the fairest of the sons of men; grace is poured upon your lips; therefore God has blessed you forever" (Ps 45:2). The notion of blessing includes that of election, guiding, leading, solicitude, and friendship with God for those who have been chosen. Man is invited to respond by blessing and thanking God for all his benefits; this may be found very often in the Psalms.

Second, the Old Testament teaches frequently that God is alive and is the source of all life. Being "alive" is what distinguishes God from all other "divinities," who jealously and in vain attract life and try to dominate it.[131] Ultimately only God can give

---

127. In a special way, Justin and many apologist Fathers taught that the whole human being is made "in the image and likeness of God," and this became an expression of his corporeity: Justin, *De Resurrectione*, 7. On his doctrine, see J. J. Ayán Calvo, *Antropología de san Justino: Exégesis del mártir a Gen. I–III* (Santiago de Compostela: Publicaciones del Monte de Piedad y Caja de Ahorros de Córdoba, 1988).

128. See Aquinas, *De Potentia*, q. 5, a. 10, ad 5.

129. Söhngen, *Die biblische Lehre*, 63.

130. See H. Conzelmann, W. Zimmerli, "χάρις, χαρίζομαι, χαριτόω, ἀχάριστος," in G. Kittel, G. Friedrich, and G. W. Bromiley, eds., *Theological Dictionary of the New Testament* (Grand Rapids, Mich.: W. B. Eerdmans, 1964) [hereafter "*TDNT*"], 9:372–415; H. Gross and F. Mussner, "Die Gnade nach dem Zeugnis der Hl. Schrift," in *Mysterium salutis: Grundriss heilsgeschichtlicher Dogmatik 4.2; Das Heilsgeschehen in der Gemeinde,* edited by J. Feiner and M. Löhrer (Einsiedeln: Benziger, 1965), 599–629.

131. On the "living God" in scripture, see the classic work of F. Mussner, *Zoë: Die Anschauung vom 'Leben' im vierten Evangelium unter Berücksichtigung der Johannesbriefe: Ein Beitrag zur biblischen Theologie* (Munich: K. Zink, 1952); see also F. Asensio, *Trayectoria teológica de la vida en el AT y su proyección en el Nuevo* (Madrid: CSIC, 1968).

life, and he does so magnanimously. Besides, only God can take it away. He is, after all, the God of the living (1 Sm 17:26–36; Ps 18:47), the source (Ps 36:10; Jer 2:13) from which life springs forth incessantly and abundantly (Dn 14:25). God is the one who infuses the *ruah*, or spirit, into humans, giving them the breath of life (Gn 2:7; Ps 104:29; Job 34:14f., 33:4; Wis 15:8, 11; Qo 3:20, 12:7).[132]

Third, God is the God of the Covenant. God has freely chosen a people and has wished to establish a Covenant with humans. He has committed himself to being faithful to it, demanding of humans that they be faithful in a corresponding way. This is a transversal doctrine in the Old Testament, with a wide variety of different expressions throughout the whole of scripture.[133]

Fourth, God's saving action is present throughout the whole of the Old Testament: his care, protection, and healing of the people are all directed ultimately toward the coming of Christ's kingdom. The history of salvation defines the correct profile of the doctrine of grace in the Old Testament. "Grace," writes Heinrich Gross, "is just a different expression of the salvation God gives to man."[134] At the same time, this author says:

The Old Testament concept of "grace" is complex like that of salvation. The basis of the notion of grace is the election which on no account can come from humans, but is rooted in their being made in the image of God. Throughout the course of revelation, important saving events are preceded therefore by acts of election. Those chosen must act in conformity with the election and reform their lives and behavior suitably. An essential element of this lifestyle is that of being on the way to God. The radical and complete response of humans to the call with which God has chosen them must be manifested in their personal union with God through faith.... Thus man becomes "just" in God's sight; this new ordering of life leads him to detachment from sin towards conversion to God for justification.... In the Old Testament view of things, this dynamic process as a whole of human salvation may be called grace.[135]

Fifth and last, the Old Testament speaks frequently of liberating divine interventions in the life of his people. These interventions give expression to God's omnipotence and love. At times they are public events, such as the liberation of Israel from Egypt. At times God's actions are more personal, for example, when humans discover that they cannot free themselves from sin in their own strength (Job 4:17, 14:4, 15:15; Ps 51:9–15) and they stand in need of God's merciful help. The conversion of humans is perceived as grace (Ps 31:1f.). This process of liberation is normally called redemption.[136] And the one who redeems is always and only God: "Truly no man can ransom himself, or give to God the price of his life, for the ransom of his life is costly, and can never suffice, that he should continue to live on forever and never see the pit" (Ps 49:7–9).

---

132. Qo = the book of Qoelet.

133. See the recent Hahn, *Kinship by Covenant*, esp. 37–213. For a *status quaestionis* of the doctrine of the Covenant, see ibid., 2–22.

134. Gross and Mussner, "Die Gnade nach dem Zeugnis der Hl. Schrift," 607.

135. Ibid., 607f.

136. See J. J. Stamm, *Erlösen und Vergeben im Alten Testament: Eine begriffsgeschichtliche Untersuchung* (Bern: Francke, 1940).

Grace language in the Old Testament   The Old Testament has no term, strictly speaking, for grace.[137] However, the verb *hānan* and the noun *hēn* are frequently used; both express the pity and mercy God has for humanity. *Hēn* is translated in Septuagint Greek as *charis*, which refers to God's benevolent love for humans, which guides the rapport between the creator and the creature. It is often associated with the term "mercy" in such a way that the expression "grace and mercy" is a frequent Biblical binomial that conveys the special way in which God communicates with humans. Besides, the Old Testament often applies the term *hesed* to God. It means "fidelity," the divine attitude that is at the heart of the Covenant. In the Septuagint it is translated as *elos*, that is, literally, "mercy."[138] *Hesed* is often associated with the term *emet*, which means "fidelity" in the strict sense of the word.[139] Finally, the Aramaic term *sedeq* ("divine justice") is not used in the Old Testament in a purely horizontal and juridical way, even though it does serve as a basis for rights and duties; it is always used as an expression of divine grace, that is, within a gratuitous and benevolent divine plan to bring humans to salvation.[140]

Still, it is in the New Testament that the reality of grace comes to the fore in a clear way in that the revelation of God's eternal design and the effective communication of grace reach their fullness in Christ.

God's grace in the New Testament   New Testament teaching on "divine grace" may be summed up in two ways: first, in the notion of "grace" in a strict sense; second, in different terms that express the gratuitous and benevolent relationship between God and humans, a relationship that begins with creation and is restored by the redemption obtained by Christ.[141] The New Testament theology of grace may be found principally in the Pauline and Johannine books, which provide a reflection on the human experience of the mystery of Christ. We shall consider them in the coming two chapters. In the Synoptic Gospels, however, the term "grace" is infrequently used, although the teaching of Jesus present in them is in perfect harmony with the image of a God who is benevolent, paternal, loving, merciful, and forgiving toward humans. Besides, the Synoptics present believers with a life project—incorporation into Christ and sharing in a kingdom of charity and justice in filial liberty—which is nothing

137. See G. Philips, *La grâce des justes de l'Ancien Testament* (Bruges: Beyaert, 1948); L. F. Ladaria, *Antropologia teologica* (Casale Monferrato: Piemme, 1982), 207–9.

138. On these terms, see N. Glueck, *Das Wort "hesed" im alttestamentlichen Sprachgebrauche als menschliche und göttliche gemeinschaftgemässe Verhaltungsweise* (Giessen: Töpelmann, 1927); K. D. Sakenfeld, *The Meaning of "Hesed" in the Hebrew Bible* (Missoula, Mont.: Scholars Press, 1978); H. Spiekermann, "God's Steadfast Love," *Biblica* 81 (2000): 305–27.

139. See F. Asensio, *Misericordia et veritas: El Hesed y 'Emet divinos, su influjo religioso-social en la historia de Israel* (Rome: Universitas Gregoriana, 1949).

140. See F. V. Reiterer, *Gerechtigkeit als Heil: "Sedac" bei Deuterojesaia* (Graz: Akademische Druck und Verlagsanstalt, 1976).

141. On the doctrine of grace in the New Testament, see J. Moffatt, *Grace in the New Testament* (New York: Richard R. Smith, 1931); H. S. Alivisatos and W. T. Whitley, eds., *The Doctrine of Grace* (London: Student Christian Movement Press, 1932); W. Manson, "Grace in the New Testament," in ibid., 33–66; C. R. Smith, *The Bible Doctrine of Grace and Related Doctrines* (London: Epworth Press, 1956); Conzelmann and Zimmerli, "χάρις, χαρίζομαι, χαριτόω, ἀχάριστος"; Gross and Mussner, "Die Gnade nach dem Zeugnis der Hl. Schrift"; E. Schillebeeckx, *Christ: The Christian Experience in the Modern World*, 2nd ed. (London: SCM Press, 1982), 72–653, esp. 77–104.

other than the life of grace in humans. Perhaps we may say that the Synoptics do not speak of grace because Jesus Christ is "grace in person."

According to Luis Ladaria:

With the term *grace* is meant in general the saving event of Jesus understood in different ways: the power of the Gospel, the manifestation of God's goodness, the remission of sin, the perennial intercession of Jesus before the Father. In the writings of Paul there is particular emphasis on the gratuitous character of salvation which the love of God has given us. In that sense Christ and his work *are* "grace" par excellence, the maximum gift or present that God can give humans.... Grace has an objective and cosmic dimension; to be 'in grace' means to live in the ambit of God. From a more subjective point of view ... grace may also be considered as divine favor which brings humans to live the life of Christ. In any case it is clear that in the New Testament grace is not primarily something that humans possess, but rather the benevolent attitude of God, accomplished and shown forth in Christ, who is the source of salvation for humanity. The life of those who believe in Christ is sustained by the overflowing love of God for all humanity.[142]

In the New Testament the notion of grace is enriched with an ample variety of concepts such as kingdom of God, union with Christ, life in Christ, eternal life, divine filiation, regeneration, new creation, predestination, justification, the living presence of the Holy Spirit, charism, life of faith, hope and charity, the gifts of the Holy Spirit, and so on. Much of this material is well developed in the Synoptic Gospels but is especially to be found in the writings of Paul and John, to which we shall now turn.[143]

---

142. Ladaria, *Antropologia teologica*, 212.

143. On the doctrine of grace in the Synoptics, see W. Manson, *The Doctrine of Grace in the Synoptic Gospels* (London: Methuen, 1919); M. Cambe, "La ΧΑΡΙΣ chez s. Luc," *Revue biblique* 70 (1963): 193–207.

5   GRACE AND JUSTIFICATION OF THE SINNER IN PAUL

It is no longer I who live, but Christ who lives in me.   GALATIANS 2:20

All have sinned and fall short of the glory of God, they are justified by his grace as a gift.
ROMANS 3:23

My grace is sufficient for you, for my power is made perfect in weakness.
2 CORINTHIANS 12:9

Let us now consider the doctrine of grace in the *corpus paulinum*.[1] In the face of
human sinfulness and the presumptuous attitude humans often have in performing
"good works," the apostle to the Gentiles insists above all on humans' absolute need
for the grace of Christ, God's pure gift, in order to be saved. Grace places us in a new

---

1. On Paul's doctrine of grace, among other works, see C. Baumgartner, *La grâce du Christ* (Tournai: Desclée, 1963), 22–32; G. Colzani, *Antropologia teologica: L'uomo paradosso e mistero* (Bologna: Dehoniane, 1997),
89–110; A. Ganoczy, *Aus seiner Fuelle haben wir alle empfangen: Grundriss der Gnadenlehre* (Dusseldorf: Patmos,
1989); Ladaria, *Antropologia teologica*, 210–12; P. O'Callaghan, *Fides Christi: The Justification Debate* (Portland,
Ore.: Four Courts, 1997), 169–85; H. Rondet, *Gratia Christi: Essai d'histoire du dogme et de théologie dogmatique*
(Paris: Beauchesne, 1948), 47–74, translated into English as *The Grace of Christ: A Brief History of the Theology
of Grace* (Westminster, Md.: Newman Press, 1967); J. L. Ruiz de la Peña, *El don de Dios: Antropología teológica
especial* (Salamanca: Sal Terrae, 1991), 248–60; J. A. Sayés, *La gracia de Cristo* (Madrid: BAC, 1993), 17–20.
More specifically on the anthropology of Paul, see P. Rousselot, "La grâce d'après saint Jean et d'après saint
Paul," *Recherches de Science Religieuse* 18 (1928): 87–104; L. Cerfaux, *Le chrétien dans la théologie paulinienne*
(Paris: Cerf, 1962), translated into English as *The Christian in the Theology of St. Paul* (New York: Herder and
Herder, 1967); G. Bof, *Un'antropologia cristiana nelle lettere di San Paolo* (Brescia: Queriniana, 1976); S. Lyon-
net, "Libertà cristiana e legge dello Spirito secondo s. Paolo," in *La vita secondo lo Spirito, condizione del cristiano*, edited by I. de la Potterie and S. Lyonnet (Rome: AVE, 1967), 201–34; Lyonnet, "Perfezione del cristiano
«animato dallo Spirito» e azione nel mondo secondo s. Paolo," in *La vita secondo lo Spirito*, 285–312; Lyonnet, "La vocazione cristiana alla perfezione secondo s. Paolo," in *La vita secondo lo Spirito*, 259–84; Lyonnet,
"L'antropologia di san Paolo," in *L'antropologia biblica*, edited by G. De Gennaro (Naples: Dehoniane, 1981),
753–64, 774–82; S. Zedda, "'Vivere in Cristo' secondo s. Paolo," *Rivista Biblica* 6 (1959): 83–92; J. D. G. Dunn,
The Theology of Paul the Apostle (Grand Rapids, Mich.: W. B. Eerdmans, 1998); J. M. G. Barclay, *Paul and the
Gift* (Grand Rapids: W. B. Eerdmans, 2015). An early version of this chapter was published as "La grazia e la
giustificazione nel pensiero di san Paolo," in *Paolo di Tarso: Tra Kerygma, cultus e vita*, edited by M. Sodi and
P. O'Callaghan (Vatican City: Vaticana, 2009), 103–16.

state by means of a "new creation" in which we become children of God through the power of the Holy Spirit and are freed from sin and slavery, introduced into a new life, and moved to witness our faith before humanity. The process, which begins with the predestination of humanity in Christ, unfolds and is revealed in his saving work and leads to the cosmic recapitulation of the whole universe, both material and spiritual. This is what Paul calls the divine "mystery." Let us look at the different stages and aspects of Paul's theology of grace.

Contextualizing Paul's Teaching: Justifying Grace and "Good Works"

Paul's doctrine on grace is meant to be interpreted above all in the context of his effort to avoid and overcome the deeply rooted human tendency, which is the fruit of sin, to self-justification by good works. According to Pauline writings, humans are not only creatures but also sinners, and for that reason their works are to some degree distorted and disordered at their very root. Hence only divine mercy, freely given, can save humanity and give ultimate value to human actions. In that sense, divine grace is opposed to "good works" only when the latter are considered and lived as a means necessary for salvation, with which humans attempt to present themselves before God autonomously and obtain recognition from him.

Paul uses the term "grace" (*charis*) about a hundred times. He does so always in the singular, to designate in general terms divine favor, specifically the saving event that took place in Jesus Christ and that brings about the forgiveness of sin and the interior renewal of believers. Christian life has its deepest roots in God's self-giving to humans and, only secondarily, in ethical behavior, though the latter is a necessary manifestation of living one's life under God's grace. Humans are sinners and need to be forgiven their sins and redeemed by Christ: "Since all have sinned and fall short of the glory of God, they are justified by his grace as a gift, through the redemption which is in Christ Jesus" (Rom 3:23f.).

The Way and the Content of Divine Grace: Jesus Christ

Justice has God as its source, Paul tells us. Yet the only way we have of obtaining it is through faith in his Son Jesus Christ.[2] This teaching is to be found in many texts, especially the following three from the letter to the Romans. First: "Therefore, since we are justified by faith, we have peace with God through our Lord Jesus Christ. Through him we have obtained access [by faith] to this grace in which we stand, and we rejoice in our hope of sharing the glory of God" (Rom 5:1f.). Second: "But now the righteousness [justice] of God has been manifested apart from law, although the law and the prophets bear witness to it, the righteousness of God through faith in Jesus Christ for all who believe" (Rom 3:21f.). Third: Paul also explains that in the Old Testament Abraham was justified not by his works but by faith in God (see Gn 15:6), on the basis of a promise not already verified; the Christian believer, in the same way, is justified by faith in Jesus Christ (Rom 4:24ff.).

---

2. See Dunn, *The Theology of Paul the Apostle*, 390–412.

Still, what really makes redemption (or salvation) through grace possible is the fact that we have been created through Christ, in Christ and for Christ, a theme frequently recurring in Pauline writings (see 1 Cor 8:6; Col 1:15–20; Heb 1:2–3, 10).[3] Christ came to save a world already created by him and directed to him from the very beginning. Grace, therefore, is not something violent, invasive, artificial, alienating, or marginal; rather it exists and acts in perfect continuity with the divine gift of creation. At the same time, it is a novelty, a divine gift, unexpected and undeserved.

It should also be added that Christ may not be considered as a mere means for making God's grace available to us because, according to Paul, the gift of God to humans is Jesus Christ himself. To live in grace means to "be (or to live) in Christ Jesus." In a central passage of the letter to the Galatians, Paul declares: "For I through the law died to the law, that I might live to God. I have been crucified with Christ; *it is no longer I who live, but Christ who lives in me*; and the life I now live in the flesh I live by faith in the Son of God, who loved me and gave himself for me" (Gal 2:19–21). There is no need to say, of course, that Christ lives not only in Paul but in all believers.

This incorporation into Christ, according to Paul, takes place through baptism with the sending of the Holy Spirit. We have been "baptized into Christ Jesus" (Rom 6:3). To explain this process, Paul uses the term "clothing": "For as many of you as were baptized into Christ have clothed yourselves with Christ" (Gal 3:27; see 2 Cor 5:2; Eph 4:24).

The New State of the Christian

According to Paul, believers in Christ live in a new state. But this does not simply mean that they have a new lifestyle following the example of the Master (Phil 2:5), imitating Jesus' virtues and attitudes through their own energies. The state of the new believer is more radical, for "it is no longer I who live, but Christ who lives in me" (Gal 2:20). For this reason, Paul contrasts the power of grace and human weakness that marks all kinds of ethical endeavor: "My grace is sufficient for you, for my power is made perfect in weakness.... For when I am weak, then I am strong" (2 Cor 12:9f.). Christ is present and active in the Christian believer, who, as a result, lives in him, with him, through him.[4] Paul employs a wide variety of expressions, closely bound up with one another, to explain this new life that derives from Christ's and becomes ever more present in the life of the believer. Seven may be mentioned.

First, a new creation. The life that comes from the gift of God in Christ is called by Paul "a new creation" (Gal 6:15).[5] The "new man" is meant to "put on the new nature, created after the likeness of God in true righteousness and holiness" (Eph 4:24). "If any one is in Christ, he is a new creation; the old has passed away, behold, the new

3. See P. O'Callaghan, *La metafisica cristiana: Teologia della creazione* (Rome: Pontificia Università della Santa Croce, 1998), 103–9.

4. On the life of Christ in humans, see P. O'Callaghan, "The Inseparability of Holiness and Apostolate: The Christian 'Alter Christus, ipse Christus' in the Writings of Blessed Josemaría Escrivá," *Annales Theologici* 16 (2002): 135–64, esp. 139–46.

5. See B. Rey, *Créés dans le Christ Jésus: La création nouvelle selon saint Paul* (Paris: Cerf, 1966); P. Stuhlmacher, "Erwägungen zum ontologischen Charakter der 'kainê ktisis' bei Paulus," *Evangelische Theologie* 27 (1967): 1–35; J. Reumann, *Creation and New Creation: The Past, Present, and Future of God's Creative Activity* (Minneapolis, Minn.: Augsburg, 1973).

has come" (2 Cor 5:17). God's work in humans is one of being "created in Christ Jesus for good works" (Eph 2:10). The human being, created in the image and likeness of God (Gn 1:26), is "recreated" in Christ according to his image (Rom 8:29).

On the one hand, this way of speaking evokes the original creation of all things in Christ and for Christ, which we have already mentioned. In that sense, "a new creation" is more than a mere metaphor. It is a true work of God, the only creator. On the other hand, the radical quality of this new creation may be seen in the fact that it has its starting point in sin, in "the old things" (2 Cor 2:17), and tends toward the newness of holiness.[6]

Second, divine filiation in the Spirit of Christ. The life of Christ in the believer produces in them a new reality, that of becoming a child of God, that is, divine filiation. In effect, Christ is the Son of God, and brotherhood with him makes us children of the Father. Paul explains that this is not a natural or original filiation but the fruit of a new creation, a kind of second and successive stage in human existence. For this reason, on several occasions he speaks of Christians as "children of God by adoption" (Gal 4:5; Rom 8:15f.; Eph 1:3f.).[7] At the same time, it is clear that the filiation received by grace gives rise to a life in the believer not unlike that of Christ. For this reason the Christian, son or daughter of God, becomes a "coheir" with Christ (Rom 8:17). Christ is the cause of this filial life (Rom 8:29) which he has merited for us on the cross (Gal 4:5).

The dynamics of divine filiation are made present in the life of the believer, Paul tells us, through the agency of the Holy Spirit in a process that the Christian to some degree tangibly experiences (Rom 8:14–16). By means of the Spirit we can call God our "Father" (Rom 8:15; Gal 4:6). The action of the Holy Spirit, new life in Christ, and divine filiation relate to one another as follows: the risen Christ, who entered the fullness of his filiation, is the one who sent the Spirit to transform us (Ti 3:6); the Holy Spirit, in turn, carries out the specific task of making Christians similar to Christ, of molding Christ in them, so that "Christ be formed in [them]" (Gal 4:19), making them children of God. Hence it is said that in the Spirit we can cry out "Abbà, Father" (Rom 8:14–16), "for through him [Christ] we both have access in one Spirit to the Father" (Eph 2:18). In chapter 13 we shall consider the topic of divine filiation in greater depth.

In the third place Paul teaches that the believer is made *an image of Christ*. Believers, having left behind the "old man," the image of Adam the sinner, have now "put on the new nature, which is being renewed in knowledge after the image of its creator" (Col 3:10). This is applied specifically to Christ, who is the "image of the invisible God" (Col 1:15). "Just as we have borne the image of the man of dust [Adam], we shall bear the image of the man of heaven [Christ]" (1 Cor 15:49). And in the let-

---

6. On the question of the believer sharing in the life of Christ, see Dunn, *The Theology of the Apostle Paul*, 389–410.

7. See S. Zedda, *L'adozione a Figli di Dio e lo Spirito Santo: Storia dell'interpretazione e teologia mistica di Gal 4,6* (Rome: Pontificio Istituto Biblico, 1962); B. Byrne, *Sons of God, Seed of Abraham: A Study of the Idea of the Sonship of God of All Christians in Paul against the Jewish Background* (Rome: Pontificio Istituto Biblico, 1979); J. M. Scott, *Adoption as Sons of God: An Exegetical Investigation into the Background of* υἱοθεσία *in the Pauline Corpus* (Tubingen: J. C. B. Mohr [Paul Siebeck], 1992).

ter to the Romans we read: "For those whom he foreknew he also predestined to be conformed to the image of his Son, in order that he might be the first-born among many brethren" (Rom 8:29). Finally, the second letter to the Corinthians speaks of the role of the Holy Spirit in bringing the image of God in humans to fullness: "And we all, with unveiled face, beholding the glory of the Lord, are being changed into his likeness from one degree of glory to another; for this comes from the Lord who is the Spirit" (2 Cor 3:18).

The divine filiation of the Christian is the manifestation of the life of Christ in him. Hence, being made in the image of God in Christ is simply equivalent to divine filiation, a notion already contained in the Old Testament, as we saw earlier, though it is fully developed only in the New Testament. The words of Angelo Scola are clear: "Both the notion of the image and that of filiation are used in revelation in a profoundly unitary way, both in respect of man and of Christ."[8]

Fourth, the presence of the Holy Spirit. On several occasions Paul speaks of the presence of the Spirit in humans as a specific and qualifying aspect of the new life of Christian believers: "Hope does not disappoint us, because God's love has been poured into our hearts through the Holy Spirit which has been given to us" (Rom 5:5). In effect, the Spirit is "sent" (Gal 4:6), is "supplied" (Gal 3:5), is "poured out on" (Ti 3:5) the believer. Besides, the Spirit is sent to live within the Christian: "the Spirit of God dwells in you" (Rom 8:9). If God is said to dwell in the midst of his people in the Old Testament, as in a temple, the temple of the Spirit now becomes the believing Christian.[9] "Do you not know that you are God's temple and that God's Spirit dwells in you. If any one destroys God's temple, God will destroy him. For God's temple is holy, and that temple you are" (1 Cor 3:16f.). "Do you not know that your body is a temple of the Holy Spirit within you, which you have from God? You are not your own; you were bought with a price. So glorify God in your body" (1 Cor 6:19f.). The presence of the Spirit, in other words, consecrates man to God and constitutes a pressing invitation to live a holy life. At the same time, Paul tells us, the presence of the Spirit is only a beginning, "the guarantee" or "first fruits" (2 Cor 1:22; 5:5; Eph 1:14; Rom 8:23). Christ is the "cornerstone in whom the whole structure is joined together and grows into a holy temple in the Lord, in whom you are built into it for a dwelling of God in the Spirit" (Eph 2:21f.). "Cornerstone" is a Petrine expression drawn from the Psalms (1 Pt 2:6f.).

Fifth, new life in Christ involves a liberation from evil. Paul speaks often of salvation by Christ as a work of liberation and redemption,[10] also in a cosmic sense: "For the creation waits with eager longing for the revealing of the sons of God; for the creation was subjected to futility, not of its own will but by the will of him who sub-

---

8. Scola, Marengo, and Prades López, *La persona umana*, 151.

9. See Y. M.-J. Congar, *Le mystère du Temple; ou, L'économie de la présence de Dieu a sa créature de la Genèse a l'Apocalypse* (Paris: Cerf, 1958).

10. See G. Bornkamm, "Die christliche Freiheit," in *Das Ende des Gesetzes: Paulusstudien*, 2nd ed., vol. 1 (Munich: Chr. Kaiser, 1952); J.-M. Cambier, "La liberté chrétienne selon s. Paul," in *Studia evangelica*, edited by K. Aland (Berlin: Akademie-Verlag, 1954), 2:315–43; Lyonnet, "Libertà cristiana e legge dello Spirito"; F. Mussner, *Theologie der Freiheit nach Paulus* (Freiburg: Herder, 1976); Dunn, *The Theology of Paul the Apostle*, 79–162, 334–441.

jected it in hope; because the creation itself will be set free from its bondage to decay and obtain the glorious liberty of the children of God" (Rom 8:19–21). The working of the Spirit has the same scope: "Now the Lord is the Spirit, and where the Spirit of the Lord is, there is freedom" (2 Cor 3:17). Also, in the letter to the Galatians Paul speaks of the "freedom which we have in Christ Jesus" (2:4). Alluding to those who attempt to submit believers to the slavery of the "works of the law," Paul reminds Christians that "for freedom Christ has set us free; stand fast therefore, and do not submit again to a yoke of slavery" (Gal 5:1). At the same time he insists that the new liberty should not provide the believer with an excuse for sinning: "For you were all called to freedom, brothers; only do not use your freedom as an opportunity for the flesh, but through love be servants of one another" (Gal 5:13).

Paul, in spite of the Stoic background of the language he uses, is not interested so much in the philosophical question of free will, that is, the human capacity to choose between different options. He speaks rather of the liberation of humans, of those who live under the slavery of evil and sin, of the law, of death, of concupiscence, and of fatalism, a liberation forged by divine grace. For Paul, in effect, center-stage is occupied by *liberation from sin*, because humans, according to Romans 7, are dominated by it as by a malevolent and personified power, though they have been regenerated by the grace of Christ, according to the teaching of the great Pauline letters (Gal 5 and Rom 8). Through this liberation the believer can still triumph over the "flesh," over the "old man," even though this will involve a battle that will last till the moment of death (Col 3:5–9; Rom 6:12–23, 8:5–13; Eph 4:17f.).[11] We can understand, however, that this is not just a battle against the weakness of the flesh, against the limits of created nature, but a true spiritual battle against the powers of evil, against a twisted idea of God.[12] "For we are not contending against flesh and blood, but against the principalities, against the powers, against the world rulers of this present darkness, against the spiritual hosts of wickedness in the heavenly places" (Eph 6:12).[13]

Paul likewise speaks also of *liberation from the law*, especially in the letter to the Galatians (3:1–5:12).[14] This is a more complex question. The apostle does not indeed encourage Christians to neglect the fulfillment of the will of God that the law expresses. The written Judaic law (or *Talmud*) is a divine guide for upright behavior. Still, the faithful fulfillment of the law is simply incapable of bringing about the justification of man. The law is not a source of sin, even though it can conceivably become an instrument of sin, because it shows up the sinful action of fallen humans and because humans tend to boast presumptuously of the good works carried out in conformity with it. According to Paul, in fact, the law is a pedagogue (Gal 3:24) in that it prepares for the coming of Christ. With exceptional insistence he teaches that new Christian converts from paganism are not obliged to take on the obligations laid down by the Judaic law, the rites, alimentary rules, circumcision, and so on. Still, the Christian is indeed obliged to live a holy life, following in everything the will of God (Gal 5:1–6; Col 2:16–23). The Holy Spirit is the one who interiorizes this divine will in all Christians, making not just an exterior observance, but the life of their lives: "But the fruit

---

11. See Dunn, *The Theology of Paul the Apostle*, 111–14.
12. See ibid., 114–19.   13. See ibid., 104–11.
14. See ibid., 128–61.

of the Spirit is love, joy, peace, patience, kindness, goodness, faithfulness, gentleness, self-control; against such there is no law" (Gal 5:22f.). And earlier (5:18): "If you are led by the Spirit you are not under the law."

Humans are also *liberated from death*. As in the Old Testament (Gen 3:17–19; Wis 1:13f., 2:23), Paul links death directly with sin: "Therefore ... sin came into the world through one man and death through sin, and so death spread to all men because all sinned" (Rom 5:12). And also: "The wages of sin is death, but the free gift of God is eternal life in Christ Jesus our Lord." And just as death entered the world on account of sin, it will be overcome at the final resurrection (1 Cor 15:35–58).[15]

Paul also speaks of *liberation from concupiscence and weakness*. God gives humans the help they need, especially when they experience weakness. When Paul complains about a "thorn in the flesh," the Lord responds to him: "My grace is sufficient for you, for my power is made perfect in weakness." And Paul concludes: "For when I am weak, then I am strong" (2 Cor 12:9f.). Convinced as he is of the promise of divine help, he exclaims: "I will all the more gladly boast of my weakness, that the power of Christ may rest upon me" (ibid.). The spirit lifts us up, whereas the flesh draws us down, he observes (Rom 8:4; Gal 5:16, 24f.). "But the free gift is not like the trespass. For if many died through one man's trespass, much more have the grace of God and the free gift in the grace of that one man Jesus Christ abounded for many" (Rom 5:15).

Lastly, man is *liberated from fatalism*, from the obscure power of evil, and from the sophisms of philosophers: "When we were children, we were slaves to the elemental spirits of the universe.... Formerly when you did not know God, you were in bondage to beings that by nature are no gods; but now that you have come to God, or rather to be known by God, how can you turn back again to the weak and beggarly elemental spirits, whose slaves you want to be once more?" (Gal 4:3, 8–9). Also: "See to it that no one makes a prey of you by philosophy and empty deceit, according to human tradition, according to the elemental spirits of the universe, and not according to Christ" (Col 2:8).

After considering liberation from different forms of evil, we can consider Paul's sixth expression of the life in Christ in believers, that is, *Christian justification*. According to Paul, the first effect or fruit of the new life in Christ, of incorporation into him, is the forgiveness of sin, that is, justification. The doctrine is well developed throughout his letters, especially in Romans and Galatians. As we saw already, the slavery from which man is liberated does not derive from matter, from the cosmos; neither is it equivalent to the simple limitations or weakness of the created condition. When he speaks of humanity and of the cosmos, Paul is not dualistic. The starting point for justification is, rather, sin itself, and therefore the work of regeneration (or "new creation") has salvation as its primary effect, that is, the forgiveness of sin, what he calls "justification." The universality of the offer of justifying grace is the other side of the coin of the universality of sin, because, as Rom 5:12 tells us, "all have sinned."

Paul speaks often of "reconciliation" between God and man (Col 1:20; Rom 5:11, 11:15; 2 Cor 5:18f.). However, though obvious, it should be kept in mind that reconciliation with God is not symmetric in Paul's mind, for the simple reason only man has sinned. In that sense "reconciliation" is above all a work of divine mercy, of pure grace,

---

15. On this issue, see *COH* 260–73.

of gratuitous forgiveness. Reconciliation takes place, certainly, but has its source exclusively in God, the only one who has been offended. And the conviction that God cannot be placated by the abundance of human good works is absolutely central for Paul. In the process of reconciliation, humans do not take the initiative, nor do they contribute directly to being justified. For this reason Paul says that "in Christ God was reconciling the world to himself, not counting their trespasses against them, and entrusting to us the message of reconciliation" (2 Cor 5:19).

When Paul states that Christ in different ways "became sin," this does not mean of course that he committed personal sin of any kind. The expression is meant to indicate that Christ has taken on himself the sin of humans, reconciling us with God in the most profound way possible: "For our sake he [God] made him [Christ] to be sin who knew no sin, so that in him we might become the righteousness of God" (2 Cor 5:21). And elsewhere: "Christ redeemed us from the curse of the law, having become a curse for us—for it is written 'Cursed be every one who hangs on a tree'" (Gal 3:13, citing Dt 27:26). Christ was not a sinner, but in his innocence he willingly made himself a sacrifice and victim for sin, indeed for sinners, and the sacrifice was efficacious precisely on account of his complete sinlessness, in that he did not need to expiate any personal sin. Paul tells us: "Walk in love, as Christ loved us and gave himself up for us, a fragrant offering and sacrifice to God" (Eph 5:2). And in the letter to the Hebrews we read: "He has appeared once for all at the end of the age to put away sin by the sacrifice of himself" (Heb 9:26).

Writing to the Christians at Corinth (2 Cor 5:19), Paul says that reconciliation with God means that faults are no longer "imputed" to humans (in Greek the term is *me logizomenos*, which literally means "not counted"; see also Rom 5:13).[16] This expression is frequently interpreted in the Lutheran tradition as indicating a merely extrinsic or forensic kind of justification of the sinner.[17] In other words, God would simply declare the sinner forgiven on the basis of Christ's sacrificial gesture. Christ is said to take our place before the Father in order to be chastised for us. It is true that the Biblical term *dikaio*, "to justify," is often used to translate the Aramaic "declare just."[18] In the New Testament, however, the declaration of innocence expresses only a part of the meaning of "the justification of the sinner." For this very reason a Christian neologism was created in Latin, *iustificatio*, which comes from *iustum facere*, literally "to make just."[19] Sinners are declared just and forgiven but also made just because they receive divine power and strength (*dynamis Theou*: Rom 1:16), as Lutheran scholars generally recognize today.[20] Through the work of Christ something takes place that goes beyond the exterior purity produced by Jewish purification rites. Speaking of baptism in the New Testament, Paul insists with considerable realism: "You were washed, you were sanctified, you were justified in the name of the Lord Jesus Christ and in the Spirit of our God" (1 Cor 6:11).

---

16. See *BDAG* 597f., s.v. λογίζομαι.

17. See O'Callaghan, *Fides Christi*, 187–91, 217–27.

18. See *BDAG* 249, s.v. δικαιόω .

19. See O'Callaghan, *Fides Christi*, 149–51.

20. Typical is the work of E. Käsemann, "The 'Righteousness of God' in Paul," *New Testament Questions of Today* (Philadelphia: Fortress, 1969), 168–82.

The seventh and last expression that Paul uses to describe the life in Christ is the obligation of believers to seek holiness. The proof of justification and sanctification is to be found in Christians' holiness of life. It is true that humans are not justified on the basis of good works, as we saw above. But good works must be present in the lives of those justified, as the fruit and manifestation of justifying grace. It is interesting to see how often Paul calls Christians simply "the saints," that is, those who live holy and virtuous lives.[21] The life of Christ in them moves them to live virtuously and spread around them the *bonus odor Christi*, "the good fragrance of Christ" (2 Cor 2:15). Conversely, sin, which is incapable of producing good works, is a sign that new life is not present and active in the person (Rom 1:29; Gal 5:18).

Holiness of life is present in the life of Christians, Paul says, in different ways. In the first place, new creation expresses itself above all as *agape*, that is, as gratuitous love for other people, what we call charity. This is the basic norm of the new life of grace. Love interprets the law (Gal 5:13); in fact "love is the fulfilling of the law" (Rom 13:10; see Gal 5:14f.). Love interprets all charisms in the Church (1 Cor 13); only through love is it possible to obtain the true good of other people (Rom 15:2-3). At the same time, it is clear that a generous love, inspired by the Holy Spirit, cannot be used as a cover-up for a decadent lifestyle, one of libertinage, because liberty and the love that comes from the Spirit have their limits (1 Cor 9:19).

Another manifestation of the new life Paul speaks of is called *parrhesia*, that is, courage, enthusiasm, fervor, frankness (2 Cor 13:12; 1 Thes 2:2; Eph 6:18-20).[22] Besides, there are many other manifestations of the life of Christ in Christians: the overcoming of social inequalities (1 Cor 7:21-23), loyalty and obedience to civil authorities (Rom 13:1), sharing goods with others (2 Cor 8:13; 1 Tm 6:17f.), and so on.

The Trinitarian and Personal Understanding of Grace in Paul

We have seen that the fruit of grace is the justification of the sinner before God. This takes place through the sharing in the life of Christ through the power of the Holy Spirit. In other words, the life of grace according to Paul is clearly Trinitarian. Grace establishes in the believer a differentiated relationship with the three divine persons. This goes "to the very heart of Paul's understanding of the beginning of salvation. These three aspects—justification by faith, participation in Christ and the gift of the Spirit—are not to be conceived as distinct and inconsistent 'models' or 'types.'"[23]

At the same time, it is interesting to note Paul's insistence on the personal char-

---

21. See for example Rom 1:7; 1 Cor 1:2, 6:1-2, 7, 14; 2 Cor 1:1, 8:4, 9:1-12, 13:12; Eph 1:1, 15, 18; 3:8, 18; 5:3; 6:18; Phil 1:1, 4:21-22; Col 1:1, 2, 4, 22, 26; 3:12; 1 Tm 5:10; Phil 5; Heb 3:1, 6:10, 13:24; 1 Pt 1:16.

22. See Smolders, "L'audace de l'apôtre selon saint Paul: La thème de la parrhesia," *Collectanea Mechliniensia* 43 (1958): 16-30; R. Fabris, *La virtù del coraggio: La "franchezza" nella Bibbia* (Casale Monferrato: Piemme, 1985); see D. Fredrickson, S. Winter, A. Mitchell, and W. Klassen in *Friendship, Flattery, and Frankness of Speech: Studies on Friendship in the New Testament World*, edited by J. T. Fitzgerald (Leiden: E. J. Brill, 1996); G. Scarpat, *Parrhesia greca, parrhesia cristiana* (Brescia: Paideia, 2001); BDAG 781f., s.v. παρρησία; *NIDNTTE* 657-59, s.v. παρρησία. 22, *New International Dictionary of New Testament Theology and Exegesis*, edited by M. Silva, 2 ed., 5 vols. (Grand Rapids, Mich., 2014) (hereafter NIDNTTE).

23. See D. Fee, *God's Empowering Presence: The Holy Spirit in the Letters of Paul* (Peabody, Mass.: Hendrickson, 1994), 827-45.

acter of divine grace.[24] In effect, justifying grace is the fruit of the call God directs to each person (Rom 8:29). And just as the call is personal, so also is the response. That is why he exhorts the Corinthians "not to accept the grace of God in vain" (2 Cor 6:1). Of himself he says that "by the grace of God I am what I am, and his grace toward me was not in vain" (1 Cor 15:10; see 2 Tm 1:6). In fact, "grace was given to each of us according to the measure of Christ's gift" (Eph 4:7); "each has his own special gift from God, one of one kind and one of another" (1 Cor 7:7). We may say, therefore, that the grace of God not only places the believer in a direct relationship with God but also, in the opposite direction, places God in a singular and unrepeated bond with each believer, with each and every person.

After we have seen the rich dynamics of the life of grace and justification in the writings of Paul, another question presents itself: to what purpose did God wish to give the paternal gift of himself to humans who believe in his Son made man? And two more questions: for what reason is someone "in the grace of God" or "in Christ"? And why are we destined to live as children of God, to receive the kingdom of God in inheritance? This brings us to consider two issues that are essential to Paul's doctrine of grace: the apostolic meaning of the life of believers and the divine plan to "bring together all things in Christ."

Living in Christ to Bring His Life to Humanity

Paul speaks of "grace" (*charis*) as a simple, unique reality that expresses and contains the gift of God in Christ Jesus to humanity. However, he also speaks of the presence in the life of the Church of charisms (*charismata*), that is, of special divine gifts that facilitate the communication of the Gospel to humanity, making its universal mission possible (1 Cor 12–13). In other words, Christian grace, though meant in the first place to justify each person, moves Christian believers to communicate their faith to other people, to evangelize. As Paul says, *caritas Christi urget nos*, "the love of Christ moves [or controls] us" (2 Cor 5:14).

Paul himself is an apostle. Paul applies the apostolic principle in the first place to himself, saying, for example: "To the weak I became weak, that I might win the weak. I have become all things to all men, that I might by all means save some" (1 Cor 9:22). By grace Paul felt obliged to evangelize, and he said: "If I preach the gospel, that gives me no ground for boasting. For necessity is laid upon me. Woe to me if I do not preach the gospel!" (1 Cor 9:16; see Rom 1:5, 12:13, 15:15f.). It is interesting to note that the grace of conversion Paul received on his way to Damascus was one not simply of personal conversion but rather of conversion for a new and universal mission.[25] Jesus said about Paul to Ananias: "Go, for he is a chosen instrument of mine to carry my name before the Gentiles and kings and the sons of Israel" (Acts 9:15f.). And to the Galatians Paul wrote that "he who set me apart before I was born, and had called me through his grace, was pleased to reveal his Son to me, in order that I might preach him among the Gentiles" (Gal 1:15f.). As a result, the grace of God in Paul became extraordinarily fruitful (2 Cor 12:5–10).

The polarity Paul teaches between faith and works clarifies two issues. The first

24. See L. Lorda, *La gracia de Dios* (Madrid: Rialp, 2004), 31f.

refers to the personal life of each believer: in effect, believers should not consider their own good works in a spirit of complacency but rather expect salvation from God alone in whom they believe and from whom they expect justification. We have already considered this matter. The second, however, refers to the antagonism between faith and works at an ecclesial, institutional, and social level.[26] In effect, to belong to Christ goes beyond a social belonging expressed in terms of a precise and scrupulous observance of a series of rules or actions of an institutional kind, the "works of the law," destined to reinforce barriers that separate believers from nonbelievers, rather than breaking them down. In other words, a merely passive belonging to the Church, to the saved community, is not sufficient to ensure individual justification or personal salvation. Faith is always necessary, for it opens humans to God's gifts not only for oneself but also for others.

Thus there are two possible, complementary readings of the Pauline opposition between faith and works: a more individual reading that considers the works of the person before God and the absolute need for faith, for trust, for humility, for salvation, and a more ecclesial or social reading that considers principally our common belonging to the Church, our adhesion to its doctrine and especially to the expansive and contagious (missionary, apostolic) character of Christian faith.

Christians are also apostles. In the person of Paul there is a strong bond between living in Christ and being an apostle, two inseparable aspects of his vocation. Still, we could ask if this same dynamic is to be found in the lives of other Christian believers. The response to the question is substantially positive in that all Christians are called both to holiness and to apostolate.[27] Three observations may be made.

First, the power and dedication of Paul's personal vocation to be the apostle to the Gentiles seems to cast a shadow over the apostolate of other Christians, even that of the other apostles (2 Cor 11:22-29): "I thank God that I speak in tongues more than you all" (1 Cor 14:18). "I worked harder than any of them [the apostles], though it was not I, but the grace of God which is with me" (1 Cor 15:10).

Second, it is still clear that the extraordinary apostolic drive of Paul constitutes anything but a negation of the evangelizing zeal of other Christians and of the other apostles. As may be seen in many of his letters, Paul counted on a wide variety of collaborators. We hear of the missionary efforts of believers such as Priscilla and Aquila, who on their own initiative instructed the preacher Apollo (Acts 18:26). Paul

25. See O'Callaghan, *Fides Christi*, 168-82.

26. See ibid. and especially these works of E. P. Sanders: *Paul and Palestinian Judaism: A Comparison of Patterns of Religion* (London: SCM Press, 1981), and *Paul, the Law and the Jewish People* (Philadelphia: Fortress, 1983). See also these works of J. D. G. Dunn: *Jesus, Paul and the Law: Studies in Mark and Galatians* (London: SPCK, 1990), especially the essays titled "The New Perspective on Paul," 183-206, and "Works of the Law and the Curse of the Law," 215-36, and *The Theology of Paul the Apostle*, 334-89. Recently, see the nuanced study of J. M. G. Barclay, *Paul and the Gift*.

27. On this issue, see W. A. Meeks, *The First Urban Christians: The Social World of the Apostle Paul* (New Haven, Conn.: Yale University Press, 1983), 51-73; R. L. Plummer, "A Theological Basis for the Church's Mission in Paul," *Westminster Theological Journal* 64 (2002): 253-71. See also J. P. Dickson, *Mission-Commitment in Ancient Judaism and in the Pauline Communities: The Shape, Extent, and Background of Early Christian Mission* (Tubingen: Mohr Siebeck, 2003), 86-132; E. J. Schnabel, *Paul the Missionary: Realities, Strategies and Methods* (Downers Grove, Ill.: IVP Academic Apollos, 2008), 248-55.

also counted on the collaboration of Barnabas on different apostolic trips (ibid.) and of Epaphras, the evangelizer of the Colossians (4:12). He warmly greets a wide variety of collaborators by name, especially at the end of his letters.[28]

Third, from the theological point of view, Paul insists on the bond between grace (the life of Christ in Christians) and "charisms," because both have the same Spirit at their source; besides, both are guided by love and directed toward love: "Now there are varieties of gifts, but the same Spirit; and there are varieties of service, but the same Lord; and there are varieties of working, but it is the same God who inspires them all in every one" (1 Cor 12:4-6). To speak, therefore, of private charisms, received for personal benefit, would be a contradiction in terms; all charisms are for the good of the Church and, through it, for humanity. Paul explains this extensively in his first letter to the Corinthians (12:7-11).

Predestination and "Recapitulation" of All Things in Christ

We have just seen that God's grace given to humans, the new life in Christ, has an intrinsically missionary purpose. To this must be added that the ultimate purpose of the communication of grace lies in the eternal plan of God in Christ for the world, that is, the "recapitulation" of all creation in Christ. This plan or design, hidden in God (the *mysterion* Paul speaks of in Colossians and Ephesians[29]) will be revealed in fullness at the end of time, but it has been revealed already in Christ, who is the center of salvation history. Therefore, Paul concludes, "When all things are subjected to him, then the Son himself will also be subjected to him who put all things under him, that God may be everything to every one" (1 Cor 15:28). Three considerations may be made.

First, as regards divine predestination. The point of departure for the divine plan, according to Paul, is predestination.[30] The salvation of the world is always rooted in predestination, present in God's original design. Paul speaks of Christians predestined "to know his will" (Acts 22:14), "predestined to be conformed to the image of his Son" (Rom 8:29), "predestined ... in love to be his sons through Jesus Christ, according to the purpose of his will" (Eph 1:5). It should be noted, however, that the principal object of predestination is Jesus Christ in person, who was, as Peter tells us, "predestined before the foundation of the world but was made manifest at the end of the times for your sake" (1 Pt 1:20). The fullest expression of this doctrine may be found in the first chapter of the letter to the Ephesians:

Blessed be the God and Father of our Lord Jesus Christ, who has blessed us in Christ with every spiritual blessing in the heavenly places, even as he chose us in him before the foundation of the world, that we should be holy and blameless before him. He predestined [from the Greek *proorizō*, literally, "decide previously"] us in love to be his sons through Jesus Christ, according to the purpose of his will, to the praise of his glorious grace which

---

28. See Tábet, "San Paolo ed i suoi collaboratori," in *Il deposito della fede: Timoteo e Tito*, edited by G. De Virgilio (Bologna: EDB, 1998), 53–79; E. E. Ellis, "Paul and His Coworkers," in G. F. Hawthorne, R. P. Martin, and D. G. Reid, eds., *Dictionary of Paul and His Letters* (Downers Grove, Ill.: InterVarsity Press, 1993) [hereafter "*DPL*"], 183–89.

29. See Deden, "Le 'mystère' paulinien," *Ephemerides theologicae lovanienses* 13 (1936): 405–42.

30. See chapter 12, notes 18ff. and corresponding text.

he freely bestowed on us in the Beloved. In him we have redemption through his blood, the forgiveness of our trespasses, according to the riches of his grace which he lavished upon us. For he has made known to us in all wisdom and insight the mystery of his will, according to his purpose which he set forth in Christ as a plan for the fullness of time, to unite [or "bring together," *anakefalaiōsasthai*] all things in him, things in heaven and things on earth (Eph 1:3-10).[31]

Four important elements of this text may be noted. *First*, Christians are said to be "predestined" or "chosen" in Christ. Their predestination, therefore, is an extension, as it were, of that of Christ; they may be considered as being "predestined in the One who is predestined." *Second*, the purpose of this predestination is that of bringing believers to be "holy and blameless," "in charity," living as "adopted sons" in holiness. *Third*, this all takes place through the work of Jesus Christ, that is, through grace received in God's Son, and, *fourth*, it takes place in order that God be "blessed" and "glorified." Throughout the writings of Paul we can observe how often the gradual development of the divine plan brings us to praise God, to thank him for his gifts,[32] "to the praise of his glorious grace."[33]

The second thing to be considered is this: does Paul's theology involve a *deterministic predestination?* When we speak of predestination and the divine plan of bringing all things under the effective dominion of God in Christ, we might ask: does this not justify to some degree a kind of determinism based on a divine plan in which everything has already been decided and preordained? We have already seen that the liberty Paul speaks of is identified not with "free will," in other words, with the autonomous capacity of each person to determine his own life and destiny, but rather with liberation from the slavery of sin. Besides, the reflection of Paul should be understood in the light of the destiny of the Jewish people, to whom was directed the divine promise (Rom 9-11). In his letter to the Romans Paul speaks of God as one who "has endured with much patience the vessels of wrath made for destruction" (Rom 9:22). And he says that God acts in this way "in order to make known the riches of his glory for the vessels of mercy, which he has prepared beforehand for glory" (Rom 9:23). But the question is still an open one: In Paul's doctrine of predestination, of election, of vocation, is there not a possibility of a kind of cosmic and human determinism? The following three observations may be made.

First, when Paul speaks of those who are lost or condemned, he is thinking of the chosen people losing God's promise in order that the Gentiles might be saved. In that sense, condemnation would not entail the necessary loss of certain individuals, known from all eternity, as if this was the price to be paid to obtain the salvation of the rest. Speaking of the destiny of the Jewish people, Paul says, in fact, that "the gifts and call of God are irrevocable" (Rom 11:29). Second, predestination does not involve an automatic salvation process for certain individuals. At every stage in the believer's life, a free response is required: "for those whom he foreknew he also predestined to be conformed to the image of his Son.... And those whom he predestined he also

---

31. On the exegesis of this text, see A. T. Lincoln, *Ephesians*, in WBC 42:8-44.

32. See Col 1:12; 1 Cor 1:4; 2 Cor 4:15, 9:11; Heb 13:15.

33. See Rom 1:5; 2:7, 10, 29; 5:2, 11; 6:4; 8:17, 18, 21; 11:36; 14:11; 15:7; 16:27; 1 Cor 1:29, 3:21, 10:31; 2 Cor 1:20; 3:18; 4:15, 17; 8:19; Gal 1:5; Eph 1:6, 12, 14, 18; 3:21; Phil 1:11, 4:20; 2 Thes 2:14.

called; and those whom he called he also justified; and those whom he justified he also glorified" (Rom 8:29f.). We shall return to this fundamental text in chapter 12. And third, grace given is not arbitrary in its effects but is meant to overcome sin and bring humans to salvation. Humans are involved deeply, fully, often painfully, in this process. Besides, in the letter to the Ephesians predestination is referred to Christ and, in him, to the Christian community, the Church. Paul never says of himself that he is predestined in person, though he frequently says that God has loved him personally, has saved and called and sent him. But he does not say that God has "predestined" him. The object of predestination is always Christ and, in him, the "we" of the Church.

Third and last, bringing all things together in Christ. In the letter to the Ephesians, just cited, Paul speaks of the *anakefalaiōsis* of all things in Christ (1:10).[34] The term is translated literally as a "summing up," a "leading back." Using the same word, Paul says in Romans 13:9 that every commandment is "summed up" in charity, because "love is the fulfilling of the law" (Rom 13:10). However, in the context of Ephesians 5:23 and Colossians 1:18, which speak of Christ as the head of the Church, *anakefalaiōsis* has often been translated as "recapitulation," which indicates the process of establishing Christ as the head of the whole of creation.[35] In effect, the "leading back" of the whole of reality to Christ involves all created things, not only humans, and not only the Church. Paul speaks in a graphic way of creation waiting "with eager longing for the revealing of the sons of God; for the creation was subjected to futility, not of its own will but by the will of him who subjected it in hope; because the creation itself will be set free from its bondage to decay and obtain the glorious liberty of the children of God" (Rom 8:19–21). The supreme moment of this recapitulation will be the bodily resurrection of the dead, promised for the end of time (1 Cor 15). Then all will be subject to God, who will be "everything to every one" (1 Cor 15:28).

34. See P. Tosaus Abadia, *Cristo y el Universo: Estudio lingüístico y temático de Ef 1, 10b en Efesios y en la obra de Ireneo de Lyon* (Salamanca: Publicaciones de la Universidad Pontificia Salamanca, 1995); *BDAG* 65, s.v. ἀνακεφαλαιόω.

35. See John Chrysostom, *In Eph*. I, 1, 10:9.

For God so loved the world that he gave his only Son, that whoever believes in him should not perish but have eternal life.   JOHN 3:16

If you knew the gift of God!   JOHN 4:10

We are called children of God, and so we are.   1 JOHN 2:1

The Terminology and Context of John's Theology of Grace

The letters of John speak of divine grace in a variety of ways. On the one hand, the evangelist seldom uses the term "grace"; he does so only on three occasions, in fact.[1] The first is in John 1:14: "And the Word became flesh and dwelt among us, full of grace and truth." It is interesting to note how "grace" and "truth" are closely associated in this passage.[2] The second is as follows: "From his fullness we have all received, grace upon grace" (Jn 1:16): what the Word possesses in fullness, grace, he communicates generously to humanity. And on the third occasion, in 2 John 1:3, he greets the Christian people with a typically Pauline formula: "Grace, mercy, and peace will be with us, from God the Father and from Jesus Christ the Father's Son, in truth and love."

On the other hand, on a few occasions John uses the expression "kingdom of God," typical of the Synoptics and probably equivalent to "eternal life," which, as we shall see, is very much present in the Johannine corpus. The following words that Jesus directs to Nicodemus are of particular interest: "Truly, truly, I say to you, unless one is born of water and the Spirit, he cannot enter the kingdom of God" (Jn 3:5). Besides, John speaks of Christ as savior: "savior of the world" (Jn 4:42), and later: "I did not come to judge the world but to save the world" (Jn 12:47). In these expressions the presence of grace—salvation as God's free gift—is clear.

---

1. See I. de la Potterie, "χάρις paulinienne et χάρις johannique," in *Jesus und Paulus: Festschrift für Werner Georg Kümmel zum 70. Geburtstag*, edited by E. E. Ellis and E. Grässer, 2nd ed. (Gottingen: Vandenhoeck & Ruprecht, 1978), 256–82.

2. See S. A. Panimolle, *Il dono della legge e la grazia della verità (Gv 1,17)* (Rome: AVE, 1973).

What is important to point out in John's writings is that the saving, gracious action of Christ toward humans is expressed especially with the term "life" or, more specifically, "eternal life," an expression found sixty-six times in the Johannine corpus.[3] The specific term "life," which is profoundly rooted in the Old Testament, is never defined by John but is simply used and presented in a wide variety of different situations.

At a fundamental level, there is real convergence between Paul's theology of grace and John's: God is the only one who saves. Still, their respective approaches are quite different. The theology of Paul, in simplistic terms, insists especially on the "healing," dynamic, and communicative side of grace offered to the sinner: grace is presented in terms of liberation, of divine power that changes the lives of humans, allowing them to fight against evil; it finds direct expression in human action and ethical questions. John's vision, on the other, concentrates more on "elevating grace," which divinizes humans and makes them contemplatives and children of God. It may be said that both apostles—from their own lived experience—attempt to express in their writings the impact that the life of Christ in the Spirit had on their own lives. If this impact oriented Paul more firmly in the line of missionary activity, it brought John to pay attention to the contemplation of the mystery of God.

The Dynamics of "Eternal Life" in John

The teaching of John on eternal life may be presented in eleven points: (1) eternal life comes from God, (2) through Christ, (3) through the sacraments of baptism and the eucharist in the power of the Holy Spirit, and (4) through faith. (5) The faith by which eternal life is accepted (6) is directed toward revelation of the light and life that comes from God as love. Hence, this life is (7) eternal and (8) present in the interior of humans. As a result, it may be concluded that (9) the believer becomes a son or daughter of God, being "born of God" and "remaining" in him, and (10) is moved to live a life centered on love. All this is made possible because (11) the world was made through the Word/Son, who became flesh to save humanity.[4]

Eternal Life Comes from God

New life has its origin in God, the source of all life. The communication of life is a gift and a divine initiative, not a human work. This conviction is fully consonant with

3. See D. B. Lyons, *The Concept of Eternal Life in the Gospel According to Saint John* (Washington, D.C.: The Catholic University of America Press, 1938); Mussner, *Zoé*; A. Feuillet, "La participation actuelle à la vie divine d'après le quatrième évangile," *Études johanniques* (Paris: Desclée de Brouwer, 1962), 175–89; *BDAG* 430f., s.v. ζωή; *NIDNTTE* 2:365–72, s.v. ζωή, esp. 371f.; *COH* 82, 152f.

4. On the doctrine of grace in John, see, for example, Baumgartner, *La grâce du Christ*, 32–38; Colzani, *Antropologia teologica*, 111–27; G. Manca, *La grazia: Dialogo di comunione* (Cinisello Balsamo: San Paolo, 1997), 40–55; Ruiz de la Peña, *El don de Dios*, 260–64; I. Sanna, *Chiamati per nome: Antropologia teologica* (Cinisello Balsamo: San Paolo, 1994), 234–37; Sayés, *La gracia de Cristo*, 20–22. Specifically on John's doctrine on grace, see Rousselot, *La grâce d'après saint Jean et d'après saint Paul*; B. Prete, "Dati e caratteristiche dell'antropologia giovannea," in *L'antropologia biblica*, edited by G. De Gennaro (Naples: Dehoniane, 1981), 817–70; I. de la Potterie, *La vérité dans saint Jean* (Rome: Biblical Institute Press, 1977); and especially V.-M. Capdevila y Montaner, *Liberación y divinización del hombre*, vol. 1: *La teología de la gracia en el Evangelio y en las cartas de San Juan* (Salamanca: Secretariado Trinitario, 1984). On the Johannine topic of "life," see also J. Frey, *Die johanneische Eschatologie* (Tubingen: J. C. B. Mohr [Paul Siebeck]), 1997–2000).

the Old Testament, which often speaks of God alone as the one who gives life. And so it is in John: "For God so loved the world that he gave his only Son, that whoever believes in him should not perish but have eternal life" (Jn 3:16).

"The Father has life in himself," John tells us (Jn 5:26). Hence, "no one can come to me unless the Father who sent me draws him; and I will raise him up at the last day" (Jn 6:44). And elsewhere: "No one can come to me unless it is granted him by the Father" (Jn 6:65). The same idea of gratuitous love may be found in other Johannine texts that use terms such as "draw" and "choose," in which the protagonist is Christ himself: "Now is the judgment of this world, now shall the rule of this world be cast out; and I, when I am lifted up from the earth, will draw all men to myself" (Jn 12:31f.). Thus Jesus can say: "You did not choose me, but I chose you and appointed you that you should go and bear fruit and that your fruit should endure" (Jn 15:16). The idea of "fruit that endures" refers, doubtless, to a life that becomes permanent in humans, that is, eternal life, because only God is capable of giving something that is eternal.

From God through Christ

Christ not only communicates life to believers—he is the only way to the Father—but he himself is the very life that is given.... This, of course, provides an indication of his own pre-existence and divinity as the "Word of life" (1 Jn 1:1). That Jesus Christ is life in person is a recurrent theme in the fourth Gospel: "In him was life, and the life was the light of men" (Jn 1:4). Of himself Jesus said the following: "I am the resurrection and the life" (Jn 11:25); "I am the way, and the truth, and the life; no one comes to the Father, but by me" (Jn 14:6); "For as the Father has life in himself, so he has granted the Son also to have life in himself" (Jn 5:26). Christ is the mediator, but his person may not be clearly distinguished from what he mediates: "God gave us eternal life, and this life is in his Son. He who has the Son has life; he who has not the Son of God has not life" (1 Jn 5:11f.).

As a result of his fullness of divine life, Christ is capable of communicating life to humans. "I came that they have life, and have it abundantly" (Jn 10:10; see Jn 3:16). In the priestly prayer of John 17, Jesus speaks as follows to his Father: "Father, the hour has come; glorify your Son that the Son may glorify you, since you have given him power over all flesh, to give eternal life to all whom you have given him." Then he concludes: "And this is eternal life, that they know you the only true God, and Jesus Christ whom you have sent" (Jn 17:1–3). The ultimate fruit of eternal life, therefore, is the knowledge of God and of the One he sent, Jesus Christ.

Life Coming through Baptism and the Eucharist in the
Power of the Holy Spirit

John explains to his fellow Christians the characteristics of the life he has received personally from the Lord Jesus. And he says that this life will be communicated to them also, though indirectly, through the sacraments. The evangelist says the following: "To all who received him, who believed in his name, he gave power to become children of God; who were born, not of blood nor of the will of the flesh nor of the will of man, but of God" (Jn 1:12f.). And this life is communicated by baptism and in the Spirit, as is explained principally in John 3, Jesus' discourse to Nicodemus; he speaks of the new birth, without which it is impossible "to see the kingdom of God" (Jn 3:3). This is the principal text: "Truly, truly, I say to you, unless one is born of water and the Spirit, he cannot enter the kingdom of God. That which is born of the flesh is flesh, and that which is born of the Spirit is spirit" (Jn 3:5f.). John the Baptist confirms this doctrine when he declares to his disciples: "He on whom you see the Spirit descend and remain, this is he who baptizes with the Holy Spirit" (Jn 1:33). And again to the Samaritan woman Jesus says: "Every one who drinks of this water will thirst again, but whoever drinks of the water that I shall give him will never thirst; the water that I shall give him will become in him a spring of water welling up to eternal life" (Jn 4:13f.).

Eternal life is made present in the lives of believers, besides, according to John 6:51–58, in their participation in the eucharist:

I am the living bread which came down from heaven; if any one eats of this bread, he will live for ever.... Unless you eat the flesh of the Son of man and drink his blood, you have no life in you; he who eats my flesh and drinks my blood has eternal life, and I will raise him up at the last day.... As the living Father sent me, and I live because of the Father, so he who eats me will live because of me.... He who eats this bread will live for ever.

The source of grace, therefore, is to be found in the incarnate Word, Jesus Christ, who invites us to eat his flesh and drink his blood. This life of Christ present in believers is what the Church Fathers later called "divinization." It may be said, in fact, that in the elevation of man to grace, the eucharist acts in some way as a prolonging of the incarnation. Still, we should add that this new reality of eternal life present in believers, with which they are divinized, is not automatic or anonymous in that it requires on their part a real reception by faith.

Reception of Eternal Life through Faith in Christ

Humans' acceptance of eternal life from Christ through the sacraments in the Holy Spirit is what John calls "faith."[5] He frequently insists on two issues. First, that faith is always faith in Christ, although it is directed at one and the same time to the Father. And second, John teaches that the one who believes in Christ in this very moment has eternal life: "Truly, truly I say to you he who hears my word and believes him who sent me has eternal life; he does not come into judgment, but has passed from death to life" (Jn 5:24).[6] "For this is the will of my Father, that every one who sees the Son and believes in him should have eternal life; and I will raise him up at the last day" (Jn 6:40).[7] However, we still need to ascertain what the object of this faith is, what is the content of the revelation believed in.

---

5. See J. Trütsch and J. N. Pfammatter, "Der Glaube," in *Mysterium salutis: Grundriss heilsgeschichtlicher Dogmatik*, vol. 1: *Die Grundlagen heilsgeschichtlicher Dogmatik*, edited by J. Feiner and M. Löhrer (Einsiedeln: Benziger, 1965), 791–903, esp. 805–16.

6. See Jn 3:15, 16, 18; 5:24; 6:40, 47; 10:28–30.

7. Summing up the doctrine of John, we can say that (1) to believe in Christ is equivalent to believing in God; belief in Christ is not a "first stage" of faith, because with the same faith with which we believe in the Son we also believe in the Father who sent him; (2) to have life (eternal) is equivalent to seeing life (that is, God); (3) to listen to the word of Jesus is equivalent to believing in the One who was sent by the Father; (4) eternal life consists of the passage from death to life and in knowing the Father who has sent his Son, Christ; (5) faith is a gift that makes eternal life possible in this life, as well as the vision of God in the next through the humanity of Christ.

Faith In the Revelation of Light and Life

Christ, according to John (14:6), is the way (through whom we believe), the truth, and the life (in whom we believe). The object of faith, what has been revealed to humanity, involves seeing God (truth, light) and having God (life). The Christian, in other words, is illuminated by God with truth and receives life from him. And not only that, for he receives life eternal, and with it immortality.

On the one hand, faith involves assent to the revealed truth: "We speak of what we know, and bear witness to what we have seen," Jesus says to Nicodemus (Jn 3:11). Frequently the Gospel invites the believer to accept the words of Jesus (Jn 12:47f.; 17:18).[8] On the other hand, and inseparably, faith consists of a union with Christ: "You refuse to come to me that you may have life," Jesus says to the Jews (Jn 5:40). "He who believes in me shall never thirst" (Jn 6:35). Jesus frequently uses expressions such as "come to me," "believe in me" (Jn 7:37f.). He invites the Jews to "continue in my word" (Jn 8:31). Likewise, the "beloved disciple" expresses his faith in Jesus by resting on his breast during the Last Supper (Jn 13:25).

These two aspects of faith in revelation, assent and union, truth and life, are at the same time inseparable: "That which was from the beginning, which we have heard, which we have seen with our eyes, which we have looked upon and touched with our hands, concerning the word of life" (1 Jn 1:1). For John, life and light always go together: Christ himself is "the bread of life" (Jn 6:35–48), "life" (Jn 11:25; 14:6), "the light of life" (Jn 8:12). Humans seek out these two things: light and life, knowledge and permanence, joy and movement; Christ gives both of them, inseparably, forever, intimately linked with one another. Man cannot see God (Jn 1:18), and so God in Christ gives him divine life so that he may do so. Let us examine this statement more closely.

In the Old Testament, believers listened to God mainly through the prophets. This was the case with Moses, for example, on Mount Sinai. But they did not see him. "No one has ever seen God," John tells us (Jn 1:18). Speaking to the Jews of his Father, Jesus said: "His voice you have never heard, his form you have never seen" (Jn 5:37; see 8:38, 15:24). On their own, humans are simply incapable of seeing God, of knowing him directly. For this reason, "the only Son, who is in the bosom of the Father, he has made him known" (Jn 1:18). More specifically, Jesus said: "He who has seen me has seen the Father" (Jn 14:9; see 8:19). And elsewhere: "And the Word became flesh and dwelt among us, full of grace and truth; we have beheld his glory, glory as of the only Son from the Father" (Jn 1:14).[9] God gives himself to humans, communicating new life through a new birth, because they are incapable of knowing him and loving him by their own means. With this gift the believer is given the power to "see," to contemplate, God. In other words, if humans did not "have" life, they would not be able to "see" or know life, that is, God. For this reason, according to the fourth Gospel, the infusion of life and the knowledge of truth go side by side in the sense that the former

---

8. See I. de la Potterie, "Οἶδα et γινώσκω: Les deux modes de la connaissance dans le quatrième Évangile," *Biblica* 40 (1959): 709–27; and *La vérité dans saint Jean.*

9. On this text, see Panimolle, *Il dono della legge e la grazia,* 297–319.

makes the latter possible.[10] In brief terms, John's Gospel leaves no space for Gnosticism, which we shall consider at the beginning of the next chapter.

One special moment in which God makes himself visible in Christ, according to John, is in the miracles Jesus performs, miracles or, as John calls them, "signs." In them we can "see" the power of God, and the works of God, which bring about faith (Jn 2:23, 6:2). At the same time, through miracles life is renewed, it is given again. A new relationship arises between light and truth, on the one hand, and life, on the other. For example, the miracle of the Cana marriage feast concludes with the following words: "This the first of his signs, Jesus did at Cana in Galilee, and manifested his glory; and his disciples believed in him" (Jn 2:11). The sick man at the sheep pool of Bethesda is healed by Jesus in that he is given new life, which is a work of the Father (Jn 5). The same may be said of the multiplication of the bread and fish (Jn 6:1–14). At the same time, Christ in his miracles gives light, for example, when he cures the man born blind (Jn 9:1–41). Then there is the special sign of the resurrection of Lazarus in which Jesus, as he invokes the power of the Father, gives life anew to the dead, while Lazarus comes into the light out of the darkness of the tomb (Jn 11).

Summing up the above, we may say that the Father is the source of all truth, light, and life; all of this is given to the Word and made available to humans through the incarnation so that they can believe in a way that is more suitable to and manageable by human nature. For this reason, man is also capable of rejecting divine life and light and truth by not believing, by not accepting what God has made visible. And this lack of faith is considered to be a source of guilt. In fact, for John the essential, true sin is incredulousness (Jn 3:18). In spite of the abundance of signs, many did not, in fact, believe in the word of Jesus, "they no longer went about with him" (Jn 6:66); "his own people received him not" (Jn 1:11). The same is true today. And this is due not to the obscurity of what we are supposed to believe in, to the objective difficulty in believing, but to the fact that humans do not want to perceive and believe in the eternal source of this light that is life. The one who believes, says John, cannot sin; faith is incompatible with the transgression: "No one born of God commits sin; for God's nature abides in him, and he cannot sin because he is born of God" (1 Jn 3:9). On the contrary, sin, the refusal to believe, causes humans to succumb to the paroxysm of killing the incarnate Son on the cross, inspired as they were by Satan, who "was a murderer from the beginning" (Jn 8:44). In effect, sinners attempt to destroy the incarnation, to block the divine source of life, all of which will bring about the divinely willed glorification of the resurrection of Christ.

The Revelation of God as Love

According to the fourth evangelist, as we have seen, in Christ is revealed light, truth, and life. But what is the source of it all? Where does the light arise? What does truth consist of? (This was the question Pilate asked Jesus: see Jn 18:38). What is life? According to John, our faith is directed to God himself as love, who gives himself (1 Jn 4:8.16). Again we recall the famous passage: "For God so loved the world that he gave his only Son, that whoever believes in him should not perish but have eternal life" (Jn 3:16).

10. On this issue in an eschatological context, see *COH* 156–70.

The message is developed in the first letter of John, which explains that the love of God, revealed in the incarnation of the Word, is, at the same time, the entire object of Christian faith, as well as its deepest motive. In effect, the Christian believes in God as love, because only a God who is love is worthy of being believed unconditionally, if we may paraphrase the title of a well-known work of von Balthasar.[11] The following text explains this principle beautifully (1 Jn 4:7–10, 16–18):

Beloved, let us love one another; for love is of God, and he who loves is born of God and knows God. He who does not love does not know God; for God is love. In this the love of God was made manifest among us, that God sent his only Son into the world, so that we might live through him. In this is love, not that we loved God but that he loved us and sent his Son to be the expiation for our sins…. So we know and believe the love God has for us. God is love, and he who abides in love abides in God, and God abides in him. In this is love perfected with us, that we may have confidence for the day of judgment, because as he is so are we in this world. There is no fear in love, but perfect love casts out fear. For fear has to do with punishment, and he who fears is not perfected in love.

To this should be added that the love of God revealed in Christ is Trinitarian in character. For this reason, the knowledge of God that comes from eternal life refers to the relationship between the Father and the Son. "This is eternal life: that they know you the only true God, and Jesus Christ whom you have sent" (Jn 17:3). And this, of course, involves the action of the Spirit (Jn 16:13–15):

When the Spirit of truth comes, he will guide you into all the truth; for he will not speak on his own authority, but whatever he hears he will speak, and he will declare to you the things that are to come. He will glorify me, for he will take what is mine and declare it to you. All that the Father has is mine; therefore I said that he will take what is mine and declare it to you.

The Life Given by Christ to the Believer Is "Eternal"

Because the life received by the believer comes from the faithful love of God made flesh in Jesus Christ (Jn 3:16), this love is unconditioned and faithful, that is, divine. As a result, it is eternal. It is eternal life, in real terms, because it is divine life. God, when he gives himself, does so according to his nature, that is, eternally, because "God is love" (1 Jn 4:16). In the Old Testament God is presented as the source of life in general, and the doctrine of John's Gospel is developed in continuity with it. However, the Old Testament does not speak of "eternal life," for this doctrine appears only in the New Testament. In effect, among the prophets and in the Psalms a certain doubt seems to hover over God's fidelity, over the reliability of his self-giving. From the moment of the incarnation of the Word, when the Son became flesh forever, there is no objective reason to doubt the fidelity of God's love for humans. Christian faith, understood as faith in Christ, the incarnate Word, becomes unconditional, because the self-giving of God in Jesus Christ is revealed as unconditioned and perpetual.

11. See von Balthasar, *Love Alone*.

Eternal Life Is Present in the Christian Believer

Because the love of God for humanity has been seen as unconditional, there is no reason that God would present himself in the life of Christians with a promise directed only to the future, of a purely eschatological kind. As we saw earlier, John teaches openly that the one who believes already has eternal life in this world.[12] For this reason the evangelist distinguishes clearly between eternal life (which is made present in the now of faith) and the resurrection of the dead (which will take place on the last day: Jn 6:39, 54), although Christ is the basis of both, for he is "the resurrection and the life" (Jn 11:25). Thus "eternal life" becomes a reality that is fully present in the believer, though in an interior and hidden way. This explains the most authentic mystical experiences of believers, those of love of God and neighbor. Already in this life believers to some degree see the Word and the Father in faith and enjoy the divine life that lives in them.

Some authors, such Rudolf Bultmann and Charles Dodd, have taken John's "presentism" in a unilateral way, to mean that the future eschatological complement of Christian grace is of little or no theological importance.[13] For these authors the expression "to have eternal life" indicates the openness of faith to the transcendence and grace of God here and now. Still, we may ask: should we not give ontological weight to the affirmations that speak of new life, or is it enough to speak of the simply existential value they have in John's teaching? What does the grace-driven passage from death to life consist of?[14] More specifically, is eternal life in John something that is imputed, in a forensic and existential way (as classic Lutheranism would have it), or does it involve a true and proper transformation of the human being?

The Essence and Fruit of Eternal Life

"See what love the Father has given us, that we should be called children of God; and so we are" (1 Jn 2:1). According to John, the new life of the Christian is not in name only (being "called" children of God) but is fully real ("and so we are"). The gift of eternal life involves not a new or renewed knowledge of an already existent situation, as a Gnostic might think, but rather a new, living union with Christ. In John's writings this position is expressed in three ways that are connected with one another: being born of God, being children of God, and sharing in the divine nature and living in God.

First, John 3:6 and 8 speak of believers being "born of the Spirit." Jesus explains this to Nicodemus: "Unless one is born anew [or "from above"], he cannot enter the kingdom of God" (Jn 3:3). And the surprise of Nicodemus (Jn 3:4) does not produce a further explanation or disclaimer on Jesus' part. In fact, he says the same thing again with greater insistence: "Truly, truly, I say to you, unless one is born of water and the Spirit, he cannot enter the kingdom of God" (Jn 3:5).

---

12. See Jn 3:15, 16, 18; 5:24; 6:40, 47; 10:28–30.

13. See, for example R. Bultmann, *History and Eschatology: The Presence of Eternity* (New York: Harper, 1962); C. H. Dodd, *The Parables of the Kingdom*, 6th ed. (London: Nisbet, 1960). On Bultmann and Dodd, see O'Callaghan, *The Christological Assimilation of the Apocalypse*, 30–48.

14. See Rv 3:1–2; Jn 3:24; 1 Jn 3:14–16.

Second, the result of receiving the gift of eternal life is that of becoming a child of God (1 Jn 3; see Jn 1:12f., 3:1–2).[15] It is clear that divine filiation is not simply a new aspect of the natural life of humans, which in some way is amplified and improved, but truly the fruit of a new generation, of being born again: "See what love the Father has given us, that we should be called children of God; and so we are.... Beloved, we are God's children now; it does not appear what we shall be, but we know that when he appears we shall be like him, for we shall see him as he is" (1 Jn 3:1f.).

Third, God "abides" or "remains" in the believer, Jesus teaches insistently,[16] especially in John's Gospel and first letter.[17] His teaching may be summed up in the following text: "Whoever confesses that Jesus is the Son of God, God abides (Greek, *meno*) in him, and he in God" (1 Jn 4:15). When Jesus promises the sending of the Spirit ("the Spirit of truth"), he says: "You know him, for he dwells with you, and will be in you" (Jn 14:17).

The Moral Life of Christians

It would seem at first glance that the living presence of God in man is the result of the good works of Christians, as the following texts would seem to indicate: "No man has ever seen God; if we love one another, God abides in us and his love is perfected in us.... God is love, and he who abides in love abides in God, and God abides in him" (1 Jn 4:12, 16); "If a man loves me," Jesus says, "he will keep my word, and my Father will love him, and we will come to him and make our home with him" (Jn 14:23); "He who says he abides in him ought to walk in the same way in which he walked" (1 Jn 2:6; see 2:10; 3:17, 24); "He who eats my flesh and drinks my blood abides in me, and I in him" (Jn 6:56).

These texts could make us think that God lives in man as the result of the latter's good works. But this is not the case. It is true that John insists on the symmetric character of the relationship between the action and the presence of God, on the one hand, and the rectitude of the human response, on the other. Still, upright human action is clearly the result of the presence of God in the believer, fruit of the divine initiative, of grace. "And from his fullness have we all received, grace upon grace" (Jn 1:16). God takes the reins of the lives of humans in such a way that they "can" no longer sin (1 Jn 3:9). The original source of divine presence in believers is God himself: "I in them and you in me, that they may become perfectly one" (Jn 17:23). The Christian is meant to bear abundant fruit—Jesus says, "He who abides in me and I in him, he it is that bears much fruit" (Jn 15:5)—but then he adds a critical phrase: "For apart from me you can do nothing" (ibid.). The same idea may be found in John 5:21: "For as the Father raises the dead and gives them life, so also the Son gives life to whom he will." This is what we have seen earlier: God and God alone gives life to humans. Christ acts through those who believe in him: "Truly, truly, I say to you, he who believes in

15. See M. Vellanickal, *The Divine Sonship of Christians in the Johannine Writings* (Rome: Biblical Institute Press, 1977).

16. See J. Heise, *Bleiben: "Menein" in den Johanneischen Schriften* (Tubingen: Mohr, 1967); B. Y. Tremel, "'Restare' negli scritti di san Giovanni: Fedeltà nella fede o nell'amore?" *Communio* (ed. italiana) 46 (1976): 43–56.

17. We shall consider the theme of "inhabitation" in chapter 14, notes 28ff. and corresponding text.

me will also do the works that I do; and greater works than these will he do, because I go to the Father.... Whatever you ask in my name, I will do it, that the Father may be glorified in the Son" (Jn 14:12f.).

The fruit of the presence of Christ in the Christian is to be seen precisely in two inseparable elements; in the observation of the commandments and in the love of one's neighbor: "If you love me, you will keep my commandments" (Jn 14:15). "By this we may be sure that we know him, if we keep his commandments" (1 Jn 2:3). And this commandment consists of love of neighbor (Jn 13:34; 1 Jn 2:7f.). This is the central theme of the first letter of John. "If anyone says, 'I love God,' and hates his brother, he is a liar; and he who does not love his brother whom he has seen, cannot love God whom he has not seen" (1 Jn 4:20). God loves humans, and they must communicate this love to their brothers and sisters (Jn 15:12, 17). "We know that we have passed out of death into life, because we love the brethren. He who does not love abides in death. Any one who hates his brother is a murderer, and you know that no murderer has eternal life abiding in him. By this we know love, that he laid down his life for us; and we ought to lay down our lives for our brethren" (1 Jn 3:14–16). "Every one who believes that Jesus is the Christ is a child of God, and every one who loves the parent loves the child" (1 Jn 5:1).

The World Was Created through the Word

To conclude this reflection on the notion of eternal life, the Johannine equivalent of grace, we may observe that there seems to be in John's writings a kind of repeated "dualism" between eternal life and the world, between light and darkness, between life and death, between faith and lying, and so on.[18] However, it would be mistaken to think that this rests ultimately on a real cosmic dualism for the simple reason that, according to scripture, the one who gives eternal life is the one who has created all these realities, the only one who created them, as John's Gospel tells us in the prologue, which is meant to offer us the interpretative key to the whole Gospel: "All things were made through him, and without him was not anything made that was made" (Jn 1:3f.).[19] Because the Word—light, life, truth—was God (Jn 1:1), light and darkness cannot be put on the same plane; neither can life and death, truth and lying. In effect, the Gospel of John does not provide a dualistic message but rather one that is deeply integrated and simple.

18. The position was first suggested by R. Bultmann. On this issue, see Y. Simoens, "Le dualisme johannique: Une question," *Nouvelle Revue Théologique* 137 (2015): 177–200.

19. On this text, see O'Callaghan, *La metafísica cristiana*, 94–103.

7 DIVINIZING GRACE IN THE EASTERN PATRISTIC TRADITION

Do not try to become like Zeus. PINDAR[1]

God became man so that man could become God. IRENAEUS OF LYONS[2]

The one who justifies, divinizes, because in justifying he makes us children of God. AUGUSTINE[3]

In the early centuries of Christian theology, the doctrine of grace developed in two principal, fundamentally convergent, directions. First, as a maturation of the teaching of Paul and John in the light of the pastoral and intellectual challenges of the Church's mission in different situations,[4] particularly in the context of the Gnostic heresy. And second, as a kind of "developed Christology": divine grace is described and understood on the basis of the insertion and manifestation of the life of Christ in believers, as the direct fruit of the incarnation of the Word, which makes the believer become a son or daughter of God. The term used to describe this process, particularly popular among Eastern Church Fathers, is *theosis*, or *theopoiēsis*, translated normally as "divinization." In the words of Lars Thunberg, "Divinization is simply the other side of incarnation."[5]

1. Pindar, *Ismicas* 5, 14.
2. Irenaeus, *Adv. Haer.* III, 18, 7; 19, 1; IV, 33, 4; V, praef.
3. Augustine, *Enn. in Ps.* 49, 2: "Qui autem justificat, ipse deificat, quia justificando, filios Dei facit."
4. On the history of the doctrine of grace, see J. van der Meersch, "Grâce," *Dictionnaire de théologie catholique* 6 (1915): 1554–1687; M. Flick and Z. Alszeghy, *Il vangelo della grazia. Un trattato dogmatico* (Florence: Libreria Editrice Fiorentina, 1964), §§ 59–63, with bibliography; Rondet, *Gratia Christi*; J. Martin-Palma, "Gnadenlehre: Von der Reformation bis zur Gegenwart," in *Handbuch der Dogmengeschichte*, edited by G. Tavard, A. Caquot, and J. Michl (Freiburg: Herder, 1980), III/5b, 6–199.
5. L. Thunberg, *Microcosmos and Mediator: The Theological Anthropology of Maximus the Confessor*, 2nd ed. (Chicago: Open Court, 1995), 432; see J. Alfaro, "Incarnazione e divinizzazione dell'uomo nella patristica greca e latina," in *Cristologia e antropologia* (Assisi: Cittadella, 1973), 81–104.

The Christian Response to the Gnostic Doctrine of Self-Redemption

The first great doctrinal and pastoral challenge the Church had to face in its first centuries was that of Gnosticism, which consolidated principally in the Egyptian city of Alexandria.[6] Our knowledge of Gnosticism is principally indirect, coming as it does from authors such as Irenaeus of Lyons, Origen, Hippolytus of Rome, and others. Yet it was a very influential movement, of considerable intellectual and religious weight. The key idea Gnostic authors developed in the context of the Christian doctrine of salvation was that the human spirit, a kind of spark of the divine substance, was capable of redeeming itself through the knowledge (gnosis, from which the term "Gnosticism" derives) of the divine mysteries.

Some Gnostic Authors

Basilides, a second-century author, used the term "grace" to indicate a spiritual reality only some privileged and spiritual persons (the pneumatikoi) had access to.[7] "Grace" was a kind of divine supplement moving the will to allow them to reach salvation; thus it has a pedagogical or supportive value as a remedy for human weakness. In this context, the Gnostic author Valentine developed a theory based on a strong cosmic and human dualism, insisting on the predestination of some individuals and the condemnation of others.[8] Marcion was one of the most influential figures among the Gnostics during the second century. He postulated a net opposition between the Old and New Testaments. Whereas the Old Testament speaks of a just God who creates a material world, the New Testament proposes a new understanding of God, revealed in Jesus Christ as merciful and saving, a vision destined, according to Marcion, to found a more spiritual, otherworldly life and destiny for humans. Marcion takes it that the "natural" man (who is carnal, not spiritual, immersed in and suffocated by matter), typified in the Old Testament, cannot perceive grace, cannot live a spiritual life. The "spiritual" man, however, represented in the New Testament, is already united with God and obtains salvation through ascetic practice and penance. The material world is corrupt and must be overcome; salvation, therefore, requires a flight from the world and everything in it.

6. For a brief introduction to Gnosticism, see Cornélis and Léonard, La Gnose éternel. See also K. Rudolph, Gnosis: The Nature and History of Gnosticism (San Francisco: Harper and Row, 1983); A. H. B. Logan, Gnostic Truth and Christian Heresy: A Study in the History of Gnosticism (Edinburgh: T. and T. Clark, 1996); G. Lettieri, "Lo gnosticismo: La sua essenza e le sue origini," Lateranum 64 (1998): 629–48. Among classic studies, see W. Bousset, Hauptprobleme der Gnosis (Gottingen: Vandenhoeck & Ruprecht, 1907).

7. See the classic study of A. B. C. C. Hilgenfeld, Die jüdische Apokalyptik in ihrer geschichtlichen Entwicklung: Ein Beitrag zur Vorgeschichte des Christentums nebst einem Anhänge über das gnostische System des Basilides (Amsterdam: Rodopi, 1966; originally published in 1857), and the more recent one of W. A. Löhr, Basilides und seine Schule: Eine Studie zur Theologie- und Kirchengeschichte des zweiten Jahrhunderts (Tubingen: J. C. B. Mohr, 1996).

8. See F.-M.-M. Sagnard, La gnose valentinienne et le témoignage de saint Irénée (Paris: Vrin, 1947); C. Markschies, Valentinus Gnosticus? Untersuchungen zur valentinianischen Gnosis mit einem Kommentar zu den Fragmenten Valentins (Tubingen: Mohr, 1992); P. Lampe, From Paul to Valentinus: Christians at Rome in the First Two Centuries (Minneapolis, Minn.: Fortress, 2003). For a brief summary of his position, see N. Russell, The Doctrine of Deification in the Greek Patristic Tradition (Oxford: Oxford University Press, 2004), 92–96.

Perhaps it might be said that for the Gnostics the distinction between "grace" and "nature" is situated between different individuals, whereas, according to Christian teachers, the dividing line is to be found in the heart of each and every human being.[9] In fact, among Gnostics an extreme and primitive form of predestinationism developed. Against it, Christian authors such as Irenaeus and Tertullian reacted energetically. Other authors, such as Clement of Alexandria and Origen, attempted to dialogue with Gnostics, in that way developing a genuine "Christian gnosis." The result of this process of theological clarification is the doctrine of "divinization."[10]

The Christian Adversaries of Gnosticism: Irenaeus, Tertullian, Clement

Irenaeus of Lyons, who lived during the second century A.D., reacted firmly against Gnostic teaching, in particular against its elitist and antimundane implications. He did so especially in his work *Adversus Haereses*. He insisted on the historical side of salvation: the saving action of God is deeply inserted into the created world, he says, into the flesh, into human history, giving rise to a process of salvation of humanity that develops throughout time. "If the flesh is not saved," he says, "then the Lord has not redeemed us with his blood."[11]

On the basis of the doctrine of the incarnation of the Word, Irenaeus attributes a very positive role to the material world as God has created it. He openly opposes Marcion by insisting on the deep, unbroken continuity between the Old and New Testaments, and therefore between creation and salvation, that is, on the essentially Jewish roots of Christianity. The Son of God made man is the one who carries ahead this process of "recapitulating" (a favorite expression of Irenaeus) the past, the present, and the future of creation so that humans may become children of God by adoption. In other words, humans are not saved at the beginning of their existence—they are not originally divine, as the Gnostics thought—but are saved by the free offering of God's grace in time. For this reason, as we saw earlier,[12] Irenaeus distinguishes between the image of God in man, which is not lost by sin in that it belongs to human

---

9. The classical distinction between "grace" and "nature" is posterior (see chapter 18).

10. On the doctrine of divinization among the Church Fathers, see esp. L. Baur, "Untersuchungen über die Vergöttlichungslehre in der Theologie der griechischen Väter," *Theologische Quartalschrift* 98 (1916): 467–91; 99 (1917): 225–52; 100 (1919): 426–44; 101 (1920): 28–64; M. Lot-Borodine, *La déification de l'homme: Selon la doctrine des Pères grecs* (Paris: Cerf, 2011; originally published in 1932–33); J. Gross, *La divinisation du chrétien d'après les pères grecs: Contribution historique à la doctrine de la grâce* (Paris: Lecoffre, 1938), translated into English as *The Divinisation of the Christian According to the Greek Fathers* (Anaheim, Calif.: A and C Press, 2002); G. Bardy, I. H. Dalmais, and E. Des Places, "Divinisation, I–III," *Dictionnaire de Spiritualité* 3 (1957): 1370–98; Y.-J. Congar, "La déification dans la tradition spirituelle de l'Orient," in *Chrétiens en dialogue: Contributions catholiques a l'Œcuménisme* (Paris: Cerf, 1964), 257–72; C. Schönborn, "Über die richtige Fassung des dogmatischen Begriffs der Vergöttlichung des Menschen," *Freiburger Zeitschrift für Philosophie und Theologie* 34 (1987): 3–47; J.-C. Larchet, *La divinisation de l'homme selon saint Maxime le Confesseur* (Paris: Cerf, 1996), introduction, 20–59; P. Urbano, *Theosis: La doctrina de la divinización en las tradiciones cristianas; Fundamentos para una teología ecuménica de la gracia* (Pamplona: Eunsa, 2001), 27–56, 107–30; Russell, *Deification*; M. J. Christensen and J. A. Wittung, eds., *Partakers of the Divine Nature: The History and Development of Deification in the Christian Traditions* (Grand Rapids, Mich.: Baker Academic, 2008); A. G. Cooper, *Naturally Human, Supernaturally God: Deification in Pre-Conciliar Catholicism* (Minneapolis, Minn.: Fortress, 2014).

11. Irenaeus, *Adv. Haer.* V, 2, 2.

12. See chapter 4, notes 19ff. and corresponding text.

nature, and the likeness of man to God, which can be lost, just as it can be gradually intensified. Even though Irenaeus's distinction does not derive from an exact exegesis of Genesis 1:26f., it certainly corresponds to the real situation of humans, created, fallen, and then saved. In this way, Irenaeus takes a position against Gnosticism and avoids any form of cosmic and anthropological dualism.

Irenaeus's understanding of divinization[13] begins with his interpretation of Psalm 82:6f.: "I say, 'You are gods, sons of the Most High, all of you; nevertheless, you shall die like men, and fall like any prince.'" The Bishop of Lyons frequently relates this text to the Pauline doctrine of adoptive filiation.[14] The expression "You shall die like men" is directed, he says, "to those who have not received the gift of adoption."[15] And this entire process takes place through Christ. The one who is Son of God by nature has become man to make us children of God by adoption.[16] Filial adoption makes humans "gods" because it brings them to partake in the divine fountain of life.[17] This process is the work of the Spirit, the "first fruits of our inheritance" (Heb 1:14), who cries out in the hearts of believers, "Abbà, Father!"[18] and gives them the seed of immortality.[19] All this directly involves the eucharist.[20]

The teaching of Irenaeus may be summed up in the following graphic expression: through the incarnation "God became man so that man could become God."[21] The incarnation of the divine Word brings about the divinization of believers.[22] Tertullian, insisting upon the realism of both creation and salvation, distinguishes openly between "nature" and "grace," which he considers to be two distinct orders.[23] And with a view to emphasizing the realism and value of the natural order, he explains that human freedom is not subject to the suffocating pressure of contrasting cosmic forces, as pagan fatalism suggested. For this reason, Tertullian speaks of the *anima naturaliter christiana* (the naturally Christian soul).[24] At the same time he recognizes in humans a *vitium originis* (an original vice), present at the beginning of their existence,[25] and in that sense "natural," although of course it will be overcome by baptism.[26]

Another important author from this period is Clement of Alexandria.[27] In his writings we find the same principle as in Irenaeus: the divine became human so that the human might become divine. Like Tertullian, Clement distinguishes in humans between natural and "other-worldly" life, even though the classic distinction between

13. On the doctrine of divinization in Irenaeus, see M. Aubineau, "Incorruptibilité et divinisation selon saint Irénée," *Recherches de science religieuse* 44 (1956): 25–52; Y. De Andía, *Homo vivens: Incorruptibilité et divinisation de l'homme selon Irénée de Lyon* (Paris: Études augustiniennes, 1986); J. Arroniz, "La inmortalidad como deificación en S. Ireneus," *Scriptorium Victoriense* 8 (1961): 262–87; Urbano, *Theosis*, 40f.; Russell, *Deification*, 105–10.

14. Irenaeus, *Adv. Haer.* III, 6, 1.
15. Ibid. III, 19, 1.
16. See ibid.
17. See Irenaeus, *Adv. Haer.* III, 18, 7.
18. See Ibid. V, 8, 1.
19. See Ibid. V, 5, 1.
20. See Ibid. IV, 18, 5.
21. Ibid. V, 8, 1.
22. See Tertullian, *De anima*, 21; *De Bapt.*, 5.
23. See Russell, *Deification*, 326f.; Leal, *La antropología de Tertuliano*.
24. See Tertullian, *Apol.* 17, 6.
25. See Tertullian, *De anima*, 41.
26. See Tertullian, *De praescrip. haer.* 13, 4.

27. On Clement, see G. W. Butterworth, "The Deification of Man in Clement of Alexandria," *Journal of Theological Studies* 17 (1915): 157–69; H.-I. Marrou, *Clement d'Alexandrie: Le Pédagogue*, vol. 1: Sources Chrétiennes 70 (Paris: Cerf, 1960), introduction, 38–42; D. A. Keating, *The Appropriation of Divine Life in Cyril of Alexandria* (Oxford: Oxford University Press, 2004); Urbano, *Theosis*, 41–43; Russell, *Deification*, 121–40.

the "natural" and the "supernatural" order is not yet consolidated. Fundamentally, divinization takes place through the power of Christ, yet it is also the result of the intellectual, moral, and ascetic effort of humans. It is at once a theological and a philosophical process.[28] Although the doctrine of Clement is Platonic from a conceptual and linguistic standpoint, it is entirely determined by the priority of the grace of God, who makes us children by adoption, as Clement says frequently.[29] In fact, on the basis of 2 Peter 1:4 ("We become partakers of the divine nature"), he describes grace as a sharing in the divine nature. Thus he lists the effects of baptism as follows: "Receiving baptism, we are illumined; being illumined, we become children of God; becoming children, we become perfect; becoming perfect, we become immortal. 'I said,' says scripture, 'You are gods, you are all sons of the most High,'" again citing Psalm 82:6f.[30]

Clement compares this doctrine with that of Plato, who in the *Theaetetus* speaks of the likeness of the soul to God.[31] His thought develops in a Platonic and dualist context that considers the human soul as a quasi-divine reality, as against the body, which is destined to extinction and corruption, not being divine.[32] In this context, Clement develops his theory of "true gnosis," gnosis of a Christian kind, which he presents as an attempt to overcome heretical Gnosticism.[33] The Christian Gnostic is a son of God, a temple of God, "already holy and divine, carrying God and carried by God."[34] For Irenaeus and Tertullian the duality between nature and grace involves the entire person, in body and soul (this derives from the doctrine of the resurrection of the flesh), whereas for Clement divinization refers principally to the soul.[35] Of this neo-Platonic position we can find relevant traces among other Christian theologians, most notably in Origen.[36]

28. See Russell, *Deification*, 139.

29. See Clement of Alexandria, *Stromata* 4, 26.

30. Clement of Alexandria, *Paedagogus*, 1, 26, 1.

31. Clement of Alexandria, *Paideia* 1, 2; 7, 1. See Plato, *Theaetetus* 176b.

32. According to Butterworth, "The Deification of Man in Clement of Alexandria," and L. Lattey, "The Deification of Man in Clement of Alexandria: Some Further Notes," *Journal of Theological Studies* 17 (1916): 257–62, this is a truly Christian doctrine with a Hellenic form and language. This is also the position of Gross, *La divinisation du chrétien d'après les pères grecs*, 161. On the other side, see E. Baert, in "Le thème de la vision de Dieu chez S. Justin, Clément d'Alexandrie et S. Grégoire de Nysse," *Freiburger Zeitschrift für Philosophie und Theologie* 12 (1965): 439–97, 473, and S. R. C. Lilla, in *Clement of Alexandria: A Study in Christian Platonism and Gnosticism*, 2nd ed. (Eugene, Ore.: Wipf and Stock, 2005), 186f., who consider Clement's doctrine of divinization to be basically Platonic and Gnostic. However, W. Völker, in *Der wahre Gnostiker nach Clemens Alexandrinus* (Berlin: Akademie Verlag, 1952), 606ff.; E. F. Osborn, in *The Beginning of Christian Philosophy* (Cambridge: Cambridge University Press, 1981), 113ff.; J. J. Sanguineti, in *La antropología educativa de Clemente Alejandrino: El giro del paganismo al cristianismo* (Pamplona: Eunsa, 2003); and Russell, in *Deification*, 123, consider it fundamentally Christian.

33. See Völker, *Der wahre Gnostiker nach Clemens Alexandrinus*.

34. Clement of Alexandria, *Stromata*, 7, 82, 2.

35. See ibid., 2, 106, 6.

36. On the doctrine of divinization in Origen, see Crouzel, *Théologie de l'image de Dieu chez Origène*, 160–79; J. Rius-Camps, *El dinamismo trinitario en la divinización de los seres racionales según Orígenes* (Rome: Pontificium Institutum Orientalium Studiorum, 1970); Russell, *Deification*, 140–54.

Divinization in the Context of Neo-Platonism and the Council of Nicaea

In the early centuries of Christianity, the Church Fathers dedicated their best energies to clarifying the doctrines of Christ and the Trinity. In the background was the debate over the more anthropological question of "divinization" (*theosis*), culminating in Christological declarations at the councils of Nicaea, Constantinople, Ephesus, and Chalcedon during the fourth and fifth centuries.

The Position of Arius and the Reaction of Athanasius

According to the third-century Alexandrian presbyter Arius, the divine Word, or *Logos*, is situated between the transcendence of the supreme divinity and the corruptible material world, between the incompatible and opposed extremes of spirit and matter.[37] The Word establishes a kind of bridge between them, he says, while at the same time giving expression to their discordance. In Platonic thought, in general terms, the material world cannot be reached directly by the divinity, it cannot be "divinized," because it is inherently corruptible. And in turn, the divine, spiritual world, which is immortal in character, can never make common cause with matter. What is divine (or immortal) always has been so and always will be so (the Logos, the gods, heroes, human souls). In the same way, what is worldly and corruptible depends, and will always depend, on matter. The dualism at the heart of Platonism leaves its mark on every aspect of life, of epistemology, of metaphysics, of ethics, and of spirituality. As a result, according to Arius, the Word made flesh spoken of in the New Testament can only be inferior to the Father, the supreme divinity. The Word is the first among creatures, the one through whom all others were made. Still, the Word is subject to the Father, as a kind of time-bound emanation of his being. To use a phrase often attributed to Arius, "there was a time when the Word was not."[38]

In opposition to Arius, Athanasius adopts a common expression of the Fathers in saying that "Christ was made man for us, so that we would become God."[39] He insists on this point while commenting on some central New Testament texts we have considered earlier (Jn 1:12–14, Gal 4:6): "He became human so that we might become divine."[40] To the doctrine of Arius Athanasius responds resolutely, saying that the divinization of human creatures is the very thing that requires the Word to be fully divine ("consubstantial to the Father," as Nicaea puts it).[41] With a kind of circular argument Athanasius explains that if the Word was not God in the full sense of the

37. On the position of Arius, see P. O'Callaghan, "L'incontro tra fede e ragione," 44–48.

38. This is so according to the historian Sozomen, *Historia Ecclesiastica* 1, 15, and Athanasius, in *Orat. I contra arianos*, 5, who in turn quotes Arius's work *Tales*.

39. Athanasius, *Adv. Arianos* 4, 2, 59; *Ep. de Syn.* 51.

40. Athanasius, *De Inc.*, 54.

41. See C. R. Strange, "Athanasius on Divinization," *Studia Patristica* 16, no. 2 (1975): 342–46; Roldanus, *Le Christ et l'homme*; S. A. Long, "Partakers of the Divine Nature: The Use of II Peter 1:4 by Athanasius," *Studia Patristica* 17 (1982): 1018–23; J. R. Meyer, "The Soteriology of Saint Athanasius of Alexandria: The Conformation of the Christian to Christ," *Excerpta e dissertationibus in sacra theologia* 22 (1992): 185–286; K. Anatolios, *Athanasius: The Coherence of His Thought* (New York: Routledge, 1998), 133–63; A. Pettersen, *Athanasius* (London: Geoffrey Chapman, 1995), 105–7; Russell, *Deification*, 166–88.

word, the doctrine of divinization, or salvation, would be impossible and Christian teaching would retreat necessarily into the realm of the symbolic.[42] If the Word is not God, he cannot divinize, he cannot save. At best he could help or instruct those who are already saved (as Gnostics might say). And the other way around: the fact that the Church has insisted on the full divinity of the Word means that it takes the doctrine of divinization not in a merely metaphorical sense but in a very real and ontological one. The whole person, body and soul, is divinized—not only the mind (*nous*), as Origen had suggested. The Word, wrote Athanasius, "being God, has assumed flesh, and being in the flesh, has divinized the flesh."[43] "Because now the flesh is risen, its mortality has been crushed and it has been divinized."[44]

Besides, for Athanasius as for the other Church Fathers, "filial adoption and divinization are one and the same thing."[45] "We are children and gods on account of the Word we carry within us," he says.[46] And, at the same time, "we are sons not as the Son is; we are gods, but not as he is."[47] The thought of Athanasius shifts from a notion of divinization understood as a simple putting aside of mortality and corruption to "the exaltation of nature through a sharing in the life of God. Divinization certainly is liberation from death and from corruption, but it is also adoption as children, it is the bond of love between the Father and the Son, and it is the entering in the kingdom of heaven in the likeness of Christ."[48]

The most complete explanation Athanasius gives of the full divinity of the Word is found in his discourse against the Arians. Man has been divinized, but not the Word, as Origen thought, because the latter was already eternally divine. In fact, "If the Word was a simple creature, the reparation of humanity would not have been possible," Athanasius says.[49] And elsewhere: "If the Son was a creature, man would have remained purely mortal and would never have been united with God; because a creature could not unite other creatures with the Creator if it stood in need of that union itself; neither could a part of creation save the rest if it needed to be saved."[50] The idea of Athanasius is clear and radical: the full (or consubstantial) divinity of the Word is the precise condition of the true divinization of humans. "Just as the Lord became man by assuming a body," Athanasius concludes, "we humans are divinized by the Word, assumed through his flesh, and in that way we receive eternal life in inheritance."[51]

Other Patristic Teachings

During the controversy with the Macedonians, Basil, Didymus the Blind, and other Fathers applied Athanasius's logic to the divinity of the Holy Spirit: if we be-

---

42. For a critique of Athanasius's argument, see M. Wiles, "Does Christology Rest on a Mistake?," in *Christ, Faith and History: Cambridge Studies in Christology*, edited by S. W. Sykes and J. P. Clayton (Cambridge: University Press, 1972), 3–12.

43. Athanasius, *Contra Arianos*, 3, 38.

44. Ibid., 3, 48.

45. Russell, *Deification*, 170. "Adoption, renewal, salvation, sanctification, grace, transcendence, illumination, and vivification are all presented as equivalents to deification" (177).

46. Athanasius, *Orat. II contra Arianos* 25. On this issue, see Russell, *Deification*, 170f. Athanasius situates the role and full divinity of the Holy Spirit in the equivalence between filiation and divinization. *Ep. Serap.*, 1, 25.

47. Athanasius, *Contra Arianos*, 3, 20. 48. Russell, *Deification*, 178.

49. Athanasius, *Orat. II contra Arianos*, 67. 50. Ibid., 69.

51. Ibid., 3, 34.

come adopted children of God through the work of the Holy Spirit, as scripture teaches, if the Spirit has divinized us, then he must be consubstantial with God. Basil says that by the work of the Holy Spirit the Christian "lives in God, has become like God, becomes God."[52]

Gregory of Nazianzen prayed that he would "become god to the same degree in which He [the Word] became man."[53] Cyril of Alexandria said that as we become children of God, "we are called gods by grace."[54] Finally, according to Maximus the Confessor, "Just as he [the Word-Son] descended and became man for us, without changing and without sin, dissolving with supernatural power the laws of nature, in the same way, as a result, we will rise up, and will be gods, through him, by the mystery of grace, without changing our nature in any way."[55] Maximus speaks of the seven mysteries that derive from the incarnation of the Word: theology, or knowledge of God; filial adoption by grace; equality with the angels; sharing in eternal life; the restoration of human nature; overcoming the law of sin; and the destruction of the tyranny of the devil.[56] He explains divine filiation as follows: "A son is one of whom it is said 'all that is mine is yours' [Lk 15:31, from the parable of the prodigal son]. Through divinization by grace I become, insofar as this is possible, what God is and is believed to be by nature and cause."[57] "Whoever is divinized through grace becomes all that God is, except in respect of the identification of essence."[58] Christians are "'gods' and 'sons' and 'body' and 'members' and 'part' of God, in name and in reality, on the basis of the divine plan and end."[59] Through birth from the Spirit, Maximus concludes, "man becomes a son of God and god through divinization by grace."[60]

The Theological Meaning of the Doctrine of Divinization

What does the divinization of humans by the Word really consist of? What does it produce in us? In what sense are we *divinized*, becoming "gods," becoming children of God? Athanasius offers the following explanation: "The Word became man so that we could become gods. He became visible in body in order to open to us the knowledge of the invisible Father; he accepted maltreatment from humans so that we would share in his immortality."[61] Pseudo-Dionysius the Areopagite offers the following description of what divinization entails:

52. Basil, *De Sp. Sancto* 39. On Basil, see Russell, *Deification*, 206–13.

53. Gregory of Nazianzen, *Or.* 29, 19. On Gregory, see D. F. Winslow, *The Dynamics of Salvation: A Study in Gregory of Nazianzus* (Cambridge, Mass.: Philadelphia Patristic Foundation, 1979); Russell, *Deification*, 213–25.

54. Cyril of Alexandria, *De Trin. dial.*, 4, 520c. See L. Janssens, "Notre filiation divine d'après saint Cyrille d'Alexandrie," *Ephemerides theologicae lovanienses* 40 (1938): 233–78.

55. Maximus the Confessor, *Ambig. ad Thom.* 211f. On Maximus, see P. M. Blowers, *Exegesis and Spiritual Pedagogy in Maximus the Confessor: An Investigation of the Quaestiones ad Thalassium* (Notre Dame, Ind.: University of Notre Dame Press, 1991); Larchet, *La divinisation de l'homme selon saint Maxime le Confesseur*; P. G. Renczes, *Agir de Dieu et liberté de l'homme: Recherches sur l'anthropologie théologique de saint Maxime le Confesseur* (Paris: Cerf, 2003); Russell, *Deification*, 262–95; A. G. Cooper, *The Body in St. Maximus the Confessor: Holy Flesh, Wholly Deified* (Oxford: University Press, 2005); M. Mira, *Apostolado y filiación divina: La relación interpersonal en Máximo el Confesor* (Valencia: Edicep, 2011).

56. See Maximus the Confessor, *Or. Dom.*, 1.

57. Maximus the Confessor, *Mystagogia*, 24.

58. Maximus the Confessor, *Ambig. ad Ioh.* 41.

59. Ibid., 7.

60. Ibid., 42.

61. Athanasius, *De Inc. Verbi*, 54.

Theosis is the assimilation and union with God insofar as this is possible. The common end of all hierarchy is a lasting love of God and of divine things, carried out in a holy way in God and in unity, and, in the first place, a total and irreversible surpassing of all that is opposed to it, the knowledge [*gnosis*] of what is, insofar as it is, the vision and knowledge of the holy truth, participation in the God of uniform perfection and of being One, insofar as this is possible, the intuition that fully satisfies any person who comes close to it, and at the same time nourishes that person intellectually.[62]

What divinization produces in humans consists, therefore, of the following three passages: from man to God; from ignorant to illuminated; from mortal to immortal. When humans are divinized they are illuminated by divine wisdom and receive the gift of immortality, becoming as God himself is, and so become children of God by adoption. As we already saw, John says more or less the same thing when he teaches that God, in Christ, gives us light (truth) and life.[63]

The Modern Critique of the Doctrine of Divinization

Some nineteenth- and twentieth-century Protestant authors, such as Ritschl and von Harnack, interpret the Patristic doctrine of divinization as a typical expression of the Hellenization of Christian doctrine, in particular, as an appearance of Platonic doctrine within Christian faith.[64] They propose that the doctrine be eliminated entirely, returning to the pure, simple Biblical doctrine of salvation by grace while avoiding the contamination of all Hellenic categories.

Substantially, the evaluation of the doctrine of divinization made by von Harnack is not valid, because he does not take into account the fact that Christian doctrine (especially as it has been explained by Irenaeus, Tertullian, Athanasius, the Cappadocians, and Maximus the Confessor) understands divinization entirely as a divine gift to the creature, to the nondivine. It is an expression of the priority of divine grace in salvation.[65] This kind of explanation is absent from classical Greek thought. Divinization in the Christian sense consists not in the actualization or in the revelation or in the purification of what was already divine and immortal (this is the Gnostic or Platonic position) but rather in the passage from darkness to light, from mortality to

---

62. Pseudo-Dionysius the Areopagite, *Hier. Eccl.* I, 4. The idea is extended in different writings of Thomas Aquinas. See L.-T. Somme, *Thomas d'Aquin, la divinisation dans le Christ: Traductions et commentaires* (Geneva: Ad Solem, 1998); A. Ara, "Deificazione dell'uomo e *visio Dei per essentiam:* Contributi alla definizione della dottrina in Tommaso d'Aquino," *Vivens homo* 18 (2007): 387–415.

63. See chapter 6.

64. See A. von Harnack, *Lehrbuch der Dogmengeschichte*, 3rd ed. (Freiburg: J. C. B. Mohr, 1894). For an analysis of von Harnack's thought, see J. Rivière, *Le dogme de la rédemption: Étude théologique* (Paris: V. Lecoffre / J. Gabalda, 1914), 411–35. See A. von Harnack, *History of Dogma* (New York: Dover Books, 1961). On the Greek understanding of divinization, see Urbano, *Theosis*, 32–37.

65. In recent Finnish dialogue between Lutherans, Catholics, and Orthodox, a new understanding of grace and divinization may be found, especially in the writings of T. Mannermaa. See C. E. Braaten and R. W. Jenson, eds., *Union with Christ: The New Finnish Interpretation of Luther* (Grand Rapids, Mich.: William B. Eerdmans, 1998); W. T. Cavanaugh, "A Joint Declaration? Justification as *Theosis* in Aquinas and Luther," *Heythrop Journal* 41 (2000): 265–80; S. Carletto, "Lutero, la divinizzazione e l'ontologia: Temi e figure della 'finnische Lutherforschung,'" *Annali di Studi Religiosi* 3, no. 3 (2002): 157–97. See also T. Mannermaa, "'In ipsa fide Christus adest': Der Schnittpunkt zwischen lutherischer und orthodoxer Theologie," in *Der im Glauben gegenwärtige Christus: Rechtfertigung und Vergottung: Zum ökumenischen Dialog* (Hanover: Lutherisches Verlagshaus, 1989), 11–93.

immortality, from slavery to sonship, through the power of God, the only one capable of recreating what he has already created. For this reason, as we already saw, the New Testament speaks of a "new creation," of a "new birth" of humans through the grace of God.

The Christian Specificity of the Doctrine of Divinization

Clement of Alexandria provides an interesting comparison between 2 Peter 1:4f. and a well-known text of Plato's.[66] In the second letter of Peter we read: "[Christ] has granted to us his precious and very great promises, that through these you may escape from the corruption that is in the world because of passion, and become partakers of the divine nature. For this very reason make every effort to supplement your faith with virtue and virtue with knowledge." And Plato writes: "The flight [from below to above] is a becoming like God according to one's own possibilities; becoming like God means becoming just and holy and at the same time wise."[67] Elsewhere Plato writes that God "elevates us up above the earth on account of our likeness to heaven, because we are not an earthly but a heavenly plant."[68] The result of the process of divinization (becoming like the divinity, overcoming concupiscence, obtaining justice and holiness) is comparable in both cases. Clement of Alexandria was right in this. However, the means to obtain divinization are clearly different in one and the other case. According to Peter, it is a divine gift ("granted to us his precious and very great promises"), whereas, according to Plato, man himself is the cause of his "sanctification," "purification," or "elevation." Through his own energies man adjusts himself more and more perfectly to what he is already, that is, divine. He does so through an ascetic way of life that brings about his divinization.[69] Man saves himself and, though illumined by God, he does not truly stand in need of divine grace.

It is interesting to note that the Latin rendering of "divinization" (*deificatio*, from *divinum facere*, "to render divine") is a strictly Christian neologism used, for example, by Augustine and Ruffinus.[70] There is no trace whatever of this term in classical Latin.[71] According to the Greek understanding, only that which is originally divine can exist and can live on as "divine." The Christian vision, however, is that God, when he gives himself to humanity, gives immortality to what was mortal, gives light to the one who was blind, gives sonship to the one who was enslaved.[72] Because man is not immortal but mortal, and God alone, who is the source of all life, gives him everlasting life.

---

66. Clement of Alexandria, *Paideia* I, 2; 7, 1. See notes 27ff. above and the corresponding text. On 2 Pt 1:4, see S. Hafemann, "'Divine Nature' in 2 Pet 1,5 within Its Eschatological Context," *Biblica* 94, no. 1 (2013): 80–99.

67. Plato, *Theaetetus* 176a–b (emphasis added), which speaks besides of man as *homoiosis Theou*, "of a substance that is similar to that of God." The same doctrine is to be found in Plato's *Republic* 501a–c, and *Laws* 716.

68. Plato, *Timaeus* 90.

69. On this issue, see O. Faller, "Griechische Vergöttung und Christliche Vergöttung," *Gregorianum* 6 (1925): 405–35; É. Des Places, *Syngeneia: La parenté de l'homme avec Dieu; D'Homère à la patristique* (Paris: C. Klincksieck, 1964).

70. See Various Authors, *Thesaurus Linguae Latinae* (Leipzig: G. Teubner, 1979), 5.1:403.

71. See P. G. W. Glare, ed., *Oxford Latin Dictionary* (Oxford: University Press, 1984), 505f.

72. Likewise, the word *iustificatio* (from *iustum facere*, "to make just") expresses the fact that before becoming just by God's grace, humans were not in a justified state but were sinners. See O'Callaghan, *Fides Christi*, 150f.

As we saw earlier, the divinization of the Christian believer means, among other things, that the latter is illuminated by God's grace (this point is developed especially by Augustine),[73] thus overcoming spiritual blindness.[74] Many Church Fathers, following the evangelist John, explain the sacrament of baptism and the action of the Holy Spirit as an illumination, as a *paideia* (or education) by God.[75] Von Harnack, however, asks if it would not be enough to limit the concept of divinization to this aspect, the noetic side of the Fathers' teaching, in that way identifying divinization with simple revelation. He insists that to speak of divinization in a literal sense would be too crass and physical[76] and would tend toward pantheism and a magical understanding of Christianity.[77] Von Harnack's interpretation, however, may lead sooner or later to a denial of the gratuitousness of salvation and a return, albeit implicit, to the Platonic doctrine of illumination or the Gnostic vision of salvation.

Trinity, Christology, and Divinization

As we saw earlier, divinization is a necessary corollary of the doctrine of Christ, the consubstantial Word of God made man. It is the direct result of the incarnation of the Word. If Christ was not God's own Word, man would not be divinized. This is the precise meaning of the Patristic adage "God became man so that man might become God." Besides, we might add, if the Word did not become flesh (a living and mortal man), humanity would not be saved. In this may be found the complementary conviction of the Fathers expressed in the following formula: *nihil sanatum nisi assumptum*, "what has not been assumed will not be healed or saved."[78] In these affirmations it becomes obvious that theological anthropology and the doctrine of grace are closely bound up with Christology. And Christology, of course, refers to the doctrine of the Trinity. If the Word (and then the Spirit) were not fully divine—with the power therefore to divinize man—it would be possible to speak not of a Trinity of consubstantial persons, but at best of a single divinity assisted by two subordinate hypostases, the Word and the Spirit (Arianism) or by historical manifestations of God (modalism). In the history of dogma these three doctrines—theological anthropology, understood in terms of gratuitous, ontological divinization; the Christology of the incarnate Word; and the Trinity of divine persons—involve, require, and explain one another directly.[79]

73. On the doctrine of divinization in Augustine, see V. Capánaga, "La deificación en la soteriología agustiniana," in *Augustinus magister* (Paris: Études augustiniennes, 1954), 2:745–54; P. Wilson-Kastner, "Grace as Participation in the Divine Life in the Theology of Augustine of Hippo," *Augustinian Studies* 7 (1976): 135–52; G. Bonner, "Augustine's Conception of Deification," *Journal of Theological Studies* 37 (1986): 369–86; J. Oroz Reta, "De l'illumination à la déification de l'âme selon Saint Augustin," in *Studia Patristica*, edited by E. A. Livingston (Leuven: Peeters, 1993), 27:364–82; A. Casiday, "St. Augustine on Deification: His Homily on Psalm 81," *Sobornost* 23, no. 2 (2001): 23–44; Urbano, *Theosis*, 112–30; Russell, *Deification*, 329–32; D. V. Meconi, *The One Christ: St. Augustine's Theology of Deification* (Washington, D.C.: The Catholic University of America Press, 2013).

74. See Athanasius, *De Inc. Verbi* 54.

75. See, for example, Cyril of Jerusalem, *Mystagogicae catecheses*.

76. See Von Harnack, *Lehrbuch der Dogmengeschichte*, 3:157–64. The same author (ibid., 2:47) speaks of a *physische Erlösungslehre*, a "physical doctrine of salvation."

77. See Von Harnack, *Lehrbuch der Dogmengeschichte*, 2:437f.

78. This motive may be found, for example, in Cyril of Alexandria, *Libr. 7–8 fragm. in Joan.* (on Jn 12:27), and in Gregory of Nazianzen, *Carmen de Inc. adv. Apoll.*, v. 36 and *Ep.* 101 (*Ad Cledonium I*).

79. See D. Fairbairn, *Grace and Christology in the Early Church* (New York: Oxford University Press, 2003).

The "Humanity" of Divinization

From the way the Church Fathers speak of divinization it is clear that they consider it as something very real that involves the created world at an ontological level. Modern authors such as von Harnack, on the contrary, see in it a kind of magic "physicalism" applied to the religious order, a kind of Greek metamorphosis. Besides, we can observe that in spite of being divinized through baptism all humans remain—as we can easily observe—both mortal and ignorant.[80] How can this contrast be understood? Two possible explanations may be offered. The first is that "divinization" is to be considered as a rhetorical or "enthusiastic" expression of the native, spiritual divinity present in each person (this is Gnosticism). The second is that it is something very real and ontological, yet hidden, that can be received and known only through faith. In effect, according to Christian doctrine, divinization produces a new life that is hidden, received through faith, which provides not only a token influence on the life of humans but vivifies it from within. As Paul says in his letter to the Galatians, "It is no longer I who live, but Christ who lives in me" (Gal 2:20). And elsewhere, "For you have died, and your life is hidden with Christ in God" (Col 3:3).

Hence, divinization, because is takes place through a free act of faith, supposes no violence upon humans nor any improper or magical intrusion into their lives. Rather, it requires a fully human and free openness to the new divine life, to which humans are destined from the moment of being created. If this was a magical process, as von Harnack suggested, humans would receive divine life in an anonymous way, never truly becoming aware of its presence. But in the case of divinization, the human being whole and entire is involved, including his history, soul, body, and faculties. Besides, the fact that this takes place in humans by the agency of the Word of God made man—the same Word through whom all things were made (Jn 1:3)—confirms the existence, in humans, of a strong continuity between being created and being divinized or saved.

Some Limits to the Concept of Divinization

As we have already seen, nowadays some authors have become somewhat ambivalent about the category of divinization.[81] Though Orthodox theology deserves a different judgment,[82] and though Augustine's explanation opened up a variety of alternative theological issues linked with divinization, Catholic theologians speak of it rarely nowadays, because it is conceived as Platonic, abstract, spiritualistic, and magical, closed to human history, novelty, and conversion. In order to provide a more ample contextualization for this theological category, it needs to be explained along with others. Four possible limits may be seen throughout the historical development of the notion of divinization.

---

80. See P. O'Callaghan, *La muerte y la esperanza* (Madrid: Palabra, 2004), 18–21.

81. The question of divinization is considered in a document of the International Theological Commission titled *Theology, Christology, Anthropology* (1981).

82. See, for example, P. Nellas, *Deification in Christ: Orthodox Perspectives on the Nature of the Human Person*, translated by N. Russell (Crestwood, N.Y.: St. Vladimir's Seminary Press, 1987); C. Yannaras, *Elements of Faith: An Introduction to Orthodox Theology* (Edinburgh: T. and T. Clark, 1991).

First, divinization could be seen to express human "anonymity" within the process of salvation, as von Harnack suggested. It would seem that from the incarnation onward, the world and humanity have already in some ways been divinized. Humanity is often defined by the Fathers as a *massa damnata* or a *massa redempta*. Against this argument it should be kept in mind, however, that theology has always considered both faith and sacrament to be necessary in order for the gift of divinization to be applied to the individual.[83]

Second, it would seem that the ethical or moral action of humans is not taken into account as something relevant in the divinized state. Contemplation, perhaps of a passive kind, would seem to be more central. Augustine, in fact, realized this with respect to the neo-Platonic view of "divinization."[84] The concrete works of humans appear irrelevant when compared to the personal response to divinizing grace, the contemplative life that arises out of the divine in humans. This is due to the fact that the doctrine of divinization developed principally in the context of Alexandrine theology, while the understanding of grace linked with moral action is more typical of Antiochene theology. To this criticism it should be observed that the divinization of Christians—as the expression of the life of Christ in them—is the source of a new life; this notion is often made present in Augustine's doctrine of *deificatio*, or divinization.[85] The ethical argument, therefore, is not excluded, though neither is it always sufficiently developed.

In Latin theology, in effect, especially that of Hillary of Poitiers and Augustine, the doctrine of *deificatio* occupies center-stage. The classic Patristic adage appears again in this affirmation of Augustine: "Taking the nature of the children of men, Christ has extended to them, by adoption, his own nature."[86] Still, Augustine's contribution to this doctrine goes beyond the Eastern understanding seen earlier. In fact, it involves quite an independent development, inspired directly by scripture.[87] Augustine explains his view not so much in terms of an ontological renewal of man, which is central for the Eastern Fathers, but rather in terms of the divine illumination of the human mind,[88] which gives a new orientation to the superior powers of humans by means of "a sharing in the vital properties of the divinity,"[89] through an

83. This is the position of Augustine and Thomas Aquinas. The former writes: "Omnis autem homo Adam; sicut in his qui crediderunt, omnis homo Christus, quia membra sunt Christi." *Enn. in Ps.* 70, 2, 1 (emphasis added). That is to say, all humans are born sinners but are justified one by one by means of their faith in Christ. And Thomas says the same thing: "Peccatum originale in Adam, quod est peccatum naturae, derivatum est a peccato actuali ipsius, quod est peccatum personale, quia in eo persona corrupit naturam; qua corruptione mediante, peccatum primi hominis derivatur ad posteros, secundum quod *natura corrupta corrumpit personam.* Sed *gratia non derivatur a Christo in nos mediante natura humana, sed per solam personalem actionem ipsius Christi." S.Th.* III, q. 8, a. 5, ad 1.

84. "'Becoming divine' through contemplation, *in otio deificari*, is a Platonic doctrine." Augustine, *Ep.* 10, 2. On this text, see G. Folliet, "*Deificari in otio*: Augustin, *Epistula* 10, 2," *Recherches Augustiniennes* 2 (1962): 225–36.

85. See Urbano, *Theosis*, 112ff.

86. Augustine, *Ep.* 140, 4, 10.

87. According to Bonner, *Augustine's Conception of Deification*, 370, there is close continuity between the Eastern doctrine of divinization and that of Augustine. This position is not accepted by a majority of scholars.

88. See A. Sage, "La dialectique de l'illumination," *Recherches Augustiniennes* 2 (1962): 111–23; Oroz Reta, *De l'illumination à la déification de l'âme.*

89. Urbano, *Theosis*, 128.

admirabile commercium, a "marvelous exchange" between God and man established by Christ. Augustine says: "ideo nos deos fecit, quia interiores oculos nostros illuminavit" (hence he has made us gods because he has illuminated our inner sight).[90] In other words, the process of divinization is clearly bound up with spiritual progress and with the ethical life of the Christian.

A third limit to the notion of divinization consists of the fact that the divinization of man seems to leave little space for human nature and for the concrete presence of Jesus Christ in the life of the Christian, to the point of making them all but irrelevant. A "pure" divinization would therefore seem to be a Christological corollary of monophysitism. That is to say, just as the humanity of Christ, for the monophysites, is absorbed into the divinity with the incarnation of the Word, in the same way man would be made divine and absorbed into God with divinization. Authors such as Pseudo-Dionysius and Maximus the Confessor, speaking of divinization, have attempted to clarify the specific role of the humanity of Christ in the development of the life of grace.[91] Specifically, they have attempted to overcome the tendency to artificially place one beside the other, that is, the imitation of the life of Christ (Christian ethics) beside the divinization of humans (the life of grace coming through a new creation), without integrating them sufficiently.

Pseudo-Dionysius, for example, places divinization in the human intellect, following the neo-Platonism of Proclus, and attempts to integrate ascetic practice with the new divine life of man. Maximus speaks of divinization principally in the ambit of the human will, speaking of the existence of three grades of spiritual life in the divinized man, which are consolidated, respectively, in purification, illumination, and union.[92] Divinization is expressed here in terms of spirituality, especially of mysticism. This was the case among ecclesiastical writers, such as Origen, Evagrius Ponticus, and Basil the Great and, later on, among others, Bernard of Clairvaux, Meister Eckhart, Nicolas Cabasilas, and Gregory Palamas.[93] Some authors approached the heretical extreme of presenting union with God, directly present in human nature, in a pantheistic fashion. Others, such as the Messalians (also called semi-Pelagians) during the controversy with Augustine, suggested that God is made present in the lives of humans by means of prayer and ascetic techniques, without the need for sacraments through which the life of Christ is communicated efficaciously. The fact is that the different explanations of the doctrine of divinization have never fully managed to express the doctrine of grace, with the consequent loss of the human, historical, social, and material richness of the term.

The fourth possible limit is that, whereas the notion of divinization expresses adequately the *terminus ad quem* of salvation, that is, union with God, assimilation to his life, it says little of the *terminus a quo*, the point of departure for this process, that is, fallen human nature. In that sense, it does not clarify properly the full range of human identity. The two points of departure for divinization are, as we have seen, ig-

90. Augustine, *Enn. in Ps.* 94, 6.

91. See Rondet, *Gratia Christi*, 94–96.

92. See Maximus the Confessor, *Capita ducenta ad theologiam Deique Filii in carne: Capita de caritate.*

93. On the views of Eckhart, see B. J. Farrelly, "La Trinidad divina y la deificación del hombre por el nacimiento del Hijo en el alma, según los escritos del Maestro Eckhart," *Sapientia* 60 (2000): 13–23.

norance and mortality, and at heart, sin. Still, above and beyond these elements, the doctrine of divinization says little about the situation of man in the world, about his way of acting, about Christian ethics.

Augustine, conversely, does consider the notion of *deificatio* in depth, describing not only the *terminus ad quem* but also, and at length, the *terminus a quo*. He does so frequently in his works, for example, when he illustrates the six fundamental freedoms Christ has won for us, bringing us from ignorance and error to the truth by means of the illumination of faith; from sin to divinization through justification; from disorderly to orderly passion through helping grace; from law to liberty through love; from death to immortality through resurrection; and from time to eternal life through the entrance of the divine into history.[94]

Summing up, we can say that whereas the doctrine of divinization develops in the East on the basis of the life and action of God in nature with a wide variety of expressions that connect with mystical theology, spiritual life, and contemplation, in Latin theology it is expressed more in the sphere of anthropology, that is, as a description of humans in themselves, with all that this implies for practical Christian life and ethics. As we have just seen, Augustine is of particular importance in this respect. We shall consider his teaching on grace in the next chapter.

---

94. See A. Trapè, *S. Agostino: Introduzione alla dottrina della grazia*, vol. 2: *Grazia e libertà*, 2nd ed. (Rome: Città Nuova, 1990), 81–88.

Omnes, quando oramus, mendici Dei sumus. AUGUSTINE[1]

Nos quoque per eius gratiam facti sumus quod non eramus, id est filii Dei. AUGUSTINE[2]

The nature of grace can be made plain only by describing its absence.
FLANNERY O'CONNOR[3]

To situate the teaching on grace of Augustine, bishop of Hippo, *Doctor gratiae*, first of all we need to consider the teaching of Pelagius, his principal adversary in the area of Christian spirituality and anthropology. Then we shall consider Augustine's own theology and finally the influence it had on Church teaching, on the question of semi-Pelagianism, and on that of predestination.[4]

The Christian Moralism of Pelagius

Pelagius and the Pelagians

Pelagius, a Breton monk who lived between the fourth and fifth centuries, of Stoic formation,[5] a commentator on Paul, went to Rome in 380 A.D. and dedicated his best energies to spiritual guidance and Church reform. Like many others, he was aware of a certain moral and spiritual decadence among Christians in Rome.[6] His works are known principally through Augustine, although the original text of his ample com-

---

1. Augustine, *Sermo* 83, 2: "All of us, when we pray, are simply God's beggars."
2. Augustine, *Ep. 140 ad Honoratum*, 4, 10: "By his grace we have been made what we are not, that is, children of God."
3. Flannery O'Connor, *Mystery and Manners: Occasional Prose*, edited by R. Fitzgerald and S. Fitzgerald, 8th ed. (New York: Farrar, Straus, and Giroux, 1979), 204.
4. I wish to thank Professor Vito Reale for his observations and suggestions on this chapter.
5. On the Stoicism of Pelagius, see H. Chadwick, *The Sentences of Sextus* (Cambridge: Cambridge University Press, 1959), 118–22; J. B. Valero, "El estoicismo de Pelagio," *Estudios Eclesiásticos* 57 (1982): 39–63.
6. See Rondet, *Gratia Christi*, 116.

mentary on the apostle to the Gentiles, titled *Expositiones XIII epistularum Pauli*, is now available.[7] From 411 onward he encountered firm opposition from the bishop of Hippo.[8] In 410 he left Rome with his disciple Celestius and went to the Holy Land. He was absolved from the accusation of heresy by local synods in 415, but in 416 synods at Carthage and Milevus condemned him along with Celestius. Pope Innocent I condemned Pelagianism in 417 at the request of Augustine.[9] Pelagius defended himself before the same Pope in his work *De libero arbitrio*, and later on before his successor, Pope Zozimus, whose verdict was not as severe as Innocent's. Pelagianism was condemned again in the Sixteenth Council of Carthage in 418, with the approval of Zozimus.[10] Pelagius died some years later.

Among the authors who in a broad sense may be considered "Pelagians," besides Celestius (who was condemned along with Nestorius at the Ecumenical Council of Ephesus in 431), we can mention Julian of Eclanus,[11] who was later on excommunicated, and some monks called "semi-Pelagians" from Hadrumentum in North Africa, who accused Augustine of neglecting the prayer and ascetic life of monks, and especially fraternal correction as a means of sanctification (Augustine responded to this accusation in his work *De corruptione et gratia*).

Pelagian Teaching

Scholars agree that Augustine's reading of Pelagius, though polemical, is fair. Nonetheless, the personal theological position of Pelagius is not completely clear. In fact, several modern authors have attempted to rehabilitate him as a Christian author.[12] In real terms we are not so much interested here in Pelagius's personal teach-

7. See the reconstruction of Pelagius's commentaries on Paul undertaken by A. Souter, *Expositiones XIII epistularum Pauli* (Cambridge: Cambridge University Press, 1922–31). On this text, see J. B. Valero, *Las bases antropológicas de Pelagio en su tratado de las Expositiones* (Madrid: Universidad Pontificia Comillas, 1980); S. Matteoli, *Alle origini della teologia di Pelagio: Tematiche e fonti della Expositiones XIII epistularum Pauli* (Pisa: F. Serra, 2011). On different writings of Pelagius in English translation, see B. R. Rees, *Pelagius: Life and Letters* (Rochester, N.Y.: Boydell Press, 1998).

8. At the beginning principally in *Sermo* 293 e 6; *Ad Marcellianum*, *De peccatorum meritis*; *De Spiritu et littera*; *Ep.* 140; besides, the theme is dealt with in major works such as *De natura et gratia*, *De perfectione iustitiae hominis*, and *De gratia Christi et peccato originali*.

9. Augustine, *Ep.* 181–83.

10. H. Denzinger, P. Hünermann, and A. E. Nash, eds., *Enchiridion symbolorum, definitionum et declarationum de rebus fidei et morum*, 43rd ed. (San Francisco: Ignatius, 2012) [hereafter "*DH*"], 222–30; Zozimus, *Ep. tract.*, *DH* 231.

11. See A. Bruckner, *Julian von Eclanum: Sein Leben und seine Lehre; Ein Beitrag zur Geschichte des Pelagianismus* (Leipzig: Hinrichs, 1897); F. Refoulé, "Julien d'Éclane, théologien et philosophe," *Recherches de sciences religieuses* 52 (1964): 42–84, 233–47.

12. Among them A. Souter, *Expositiones XIII epistularum Pauli*; G. De Plinval, "Recherches sur l'oeuvre littéraire de Pélage," *Revue de philologie* 60 (1934): 10–42; Pelagius, *The Letters of Pelagius and His Followers*, edited by B. R. Rees (Woodbridge: Boydell Press, 1991). On his theology, see J. Ferguson, *Pelagius: A Historical and Theological Study* (Cambridge: Cambridge University Press, 1956); T. Bohlin, *Die Theologie des Pelagius und ihre Genesis* (Uppsala: Wiesbaden, 1957); S. Prete, *Pelagio e il pelagianesimo* (Brescia: Morcelliana, 1961). Several authors evaluated these works critically during the 1960s: A. Corticelli, "Osservazioni su 'Pelagio e il pelagianesimo' di Serafino Prete," *Augustinianum* 2 (1962): 131–40; A. Trapè, "Verso una riabilitazione del pelagianesimo?," *Augustinianum* 3 (1963): 482–516; P. R. L. Brown, "Pelagius and His Supporters," *Journal of Theological Studies* 19 (1968): 93–114. See also G. Greshake, who in *Gnade als konkrete Freiheit: Eine Untersuchung zur Gnadenlehre des Pelagius* (Mainz: Grünewald, 1972), attempts to rehabilitate Pelagius. The latter work is criticized by G. De Plinval in "L'heure est-elle venue de redécouvrir Pelage?," *Revue des études anciennes* 19 (1973): 158–62;

ing as in the spiritual and theological current of thought called "Pelagianism," which developed out of what Pelagius and his followers taught.

Pelagianism attempts above all to explain the free moral action of humans in relation to the grace of God. It insists specifically on the need for conscious ethical effort on the part of humans. Creation is good because God made it such (Pelagius strongly insists on this point). Thus, our transgressions against the law are fully blameworthy. In his work *De natura* Pelagius speaks of the *impeccantia* of humans, that is, their native capacity not to sin.[13] He teaches that the *posse*, the ability to act freely, is a gift God gives with creation, whereas the *velle* (desire for the good) and the *esse* (concrete action) belong to humans themselves. For this reason, humans are capable of true merit before God. Humans sin freely and responsibly, with their actions not predetermined by forgetfulness of the law,[14] by the contagion of vice,[15] by the bad example of Adam.[16] The latter point is critical in Pelagius's thought: what we call "original sin" is the mere result of the bad example given by our first parents. When we say that humans are saved by the "grace" of God, what we mean is that they are saved through creation, by which they know the divine will, by the gift of the Law and the prophets,[17] and through the good example of others, especially that of Jesus Christ.[18] Pelagius does speak of the grace of the sacraments, with which God frees us from our previous sins and concupiscence. Yet "grace" for Pelagius is principally a *gratia externa*, an external divine help. As a result, humans can live good lives simply because they want to do so. And he concludes: "Since perfection is possible for humans, it is obligatory."[19] In the words of Celestius, Pelagius's disciple, "It is the easiest

---

A. Zumkeller, "Neue Interpretation oder Verzeichnung der Gnadenlehre des Pelagius und seines Gegners Augustinus?," *Augustinian Studies* 5 (1974): 209–26; P. Fransen, "Was Pelagius werkelijk pelagiaans?," *Bijdragen* 37 (1976): 86–93. On Pelagius, see also R. F. Evans, *Pelagius: Enquiries and Reappraisals* (London: Seabury Press, 1968); B. R. Rees, *Pelagius: A Reluctant Heretic* (Woodbridge: Boydell Press, 1988); N. Cipriani, "La morale pelagiana e la retorica," *Augustinianum* 31 (1991): 309–27; E. TeSelle, "Pelagius, Pelagianism," in *Augustine through the Ages: An Encyclopedia*, edited by J. C. Cavadini and A. D. Fitzgerald (Grand Rapids, Mich.: W. B. Eerdmans, 1999), 663–80; B. Quilliet, *L'acharnement théologique: Histoire de la grâce en Occident, IIIe–XXIe siècle* (Paris: Fayard, 2007), 83–100.

13. See Pelagius, *De natura*.

14. Pelagius, *Exp.* 32:8, 57:3, 367:15. The doctrine of the *oblivio legis*, the forgetting of the law, may be found in the earliest writings of Augustine, for example, *De lib. arb.* 3, 20.

15. See Pelagius, *Exp.* 58, 25; 59, 6. Again there is considerable coincidence with the *carnalis consuetudo* (carnal custom of young Augustine: *De lib. arb.* 3, 15. According to Pelagius, the *carnalis consuetudo* becomes a kind of second nature (*Exp.* 90, 19) or even an obsession (*Exp.* 352) in humans, even if this process develops slowly, given the fundamental good present in human nature. See Greshake, *Gnade als konkrete Freiheit*, 105.

16. Pelagius speaks of the bad example of Adam and others (*Exp.* 45). Every sin, being a free act, is in real terms mortal according to Pelagius (for Augustine, on the contrary, there is such a thing as "everyday" or "venial sins"), and so it is impossible to be just and unjust at one and the same time. *Exp.* 374, 15; 337f.

17. The law and the prophets give us reasonable precepts, says Pelagius (*Exp.* 134, 17; 197, 9). Pagans and those who lived before the time of Christ could respond to this "grace" by being "naturally just" (*Exp.* 23, 10). As a result, their works became "blessed" (*Exp.* 37, 13). Abraham, for example, was the archetype of the pagan in whom the law was written and who, in a sense, believed in the future Christ (*Exp.* 36, 1; 37, 21), who is "the purpose of the law" (*Exp.* 248, 14). For this reason, Pelagius insistently took exception to the error of the Manichaeans for having separated the two testaments.

18. Pelagius speaks of the educational value of the life and works of others (*paideia*), principally and definitively of those of Christ (*Exp.* 46–48; *Dem.* 8). See M. Michalski, "La doctrine christologique de Pélage," *Collectanea Theologica* 17 (1936): 143–64; A. Sage, "De la grâce du Christ modèle et principe de la grâce," *Revue des études anciennes* 7 (1961): 17–34.

19. E. Portalié, *A Guide to the Thought of Saint Augustine* (Chicago: H. Regnery, 1960), 188.

thing in the world to change one's own will with an act of the will."[20] Whoever does not do so, therefore, becomes fully guilty of sin.

The Reaction of Augustine

The principal theological defect Augustine saw in the moralizing doctrine of the Pelagians is that, before God, sin and human action *do not refer directly to the saving work of Christ*. Christ seems to be simply an exterior stimulus for the holy life of Christians, facilitating virtuous life by his heroic example.[21] Although Pelagius does not deny the divinity of Christ, he seems to make it superfluous in the work of redemption. It is of interest to note that his disciple Celestius was condemned, along with Nestorius, at the Council of Ephesus in 431. Nestorius, as is known, taught that the union between the divinity and the humanity of Jesus Christ was of a merely moral kind. In effect, just as the doctrine of divinization came to be associated with a monophysite Christology, so also was Pelagianism linked naturally with Nestorianism. In any case, it would seem that Pelagius did not recognize the absolute dependence of humans on God in all their actions. Pelagius's view of humanity, in comparison with Augustine's, is individualistic—nowadays we might say emancipated.[22] In the words of Peter Brown:

The Pelagian man was essentially a separate individual: the man of Augustine is always about to be engulfed in vast, mysterious solidarities. For Pelagius, men had simply decided to imitate Adam, the first sinner: for Augustine, they received their basic weakness in the most intimate and irreversible manner possible; they were born into it by the mere fact of physical descent from this, the common father of the human race.[23]

According to Augustine, in fact, "the healed man has had to achieve all that Pelagius had thought he possessed from the start."[24]

Augustine, Doctor of Grace

Augustine's Principal Works on Grace

Augustine's intellectual and spiritual formation[25] derives from neo-Platonism (from which he drew the doctrine of participation and the concept of God as the

---

20. Celestius, *De perf. iust.*, 6, 12.

21. According to Ladaria, in the teaching of Pelagius there is no intrinsic reference to Christ. Ladaria, *Antropologia teologica*, 217. The life of Christ would be a simple exterior stimulus, a supplement that helps us to act in a proper way. This is where Augustine begins his critique of Pelagius, in *De gratia christiana* I, 27:18. Pelagius speaks often of the *gratia externa* and presents the action of the human will excluding any kind of interior aid (Rondet, *Gratia Christi*, 121). Christ simply facilitates a virtuous lif.e: Ganoczy, *Aus seiner Fülle haben wir alle empfangen*, 119. The tendency of Pelagius to speak of a gradual assimilation of the believer to God as a work of *ratio* and of the *liberum arbitrium* is also hazardous.

22. "Pelagius wanted every Christian to be a monk," writes P. R. L. Brown, in *Augustine of Hippo: A Biography*, 2nd ed. (London: Faber and Faber, 2000), 348. See Pelagius, *Ad Demet.*, 10.

23. Brown, *Augustine of Hippo*, 367f.

24. Ibid., 376. See *De nat. et gratia*, 58:68.

25. Textbook studies of Augustine include J. Auer, *Das Evangelium der Gnade: Die neue Heilsordnung durch die Gnade in seiner Kirche*, 3rd ed. (Regensburg: F. Pustet, 1980), 29–32; Baumgartner, *La grâce du Christ*, 57–82; Colzani, *Antropologia teologica*, 167–85; Ganoczy, *Aus seiner Fülle haben wir alle empfangen*, 125–67; Ladaria,

source of all good), from the Old Testament (which teaches God's transcendence), from the New Testament and especially Paul (who insisted on the absolute gratuitousness of salvation and the common sinful state all humans are born in);[26] it draws on his polemics with the Manichees (from whom he learnt the need to affirm the goodness of created reality) and from his own moral and spiritual conversion (which made him conscious of the difficulties Christians suffer in being faithful, and of the constant need they have of God's grace). His basic spiritual conviction may be summed up in the following formula: "omnes, quando oramus, mendici Dei sumus" (all of us, when we pray, are simply God's beggars).[27] For Augustine, the Pelagian exaltation of the moral energies of man before God's grace is simply unthinkable. It is a moralizing and unacceptable betrayal of the blood of Christ.

Augustine's anti-Pelagian writings include, on the one hand, polemical works that need to be contextualized in order to be properly understood.[28] Augustine was a pioneer on many fronts in theology and Christian life, and some aspects of his teaching needed time in order to be understood and assimilated. On the other hand, he wrote basic theological treatises in which the polemical side was less present, among them *De Trinitate*, *De Civitate Dei*, and *Tractatus in Iohannem*. His doctrine on grace, especially in the context of Pelagianism, is to be found, for example, in *De peccatorum meritis et remissione et de baptismo parvulorum*, *Ad Simplicianum*, *De Spiritu et Littera*, *De natura et gratia*, *De gratia Christi et de peccato originali*, and *De gratia et libero arbitrio*.

From the standpoint of theological method, Augustine is not usually considered a deductive thinker who begins with a clear idea and draws out the consequences it contains. He may be described rather as a "circular" thinker: he begins with human experience (for example, with the phenomenology of sin), then considers the word of God in Christ, and subsequently returns to his phenomenological reflection with a new light, thus explaining the greatness of God and the misery of humans, as well as the mercy of God and the greatness of redeemed humanity. His theological method may be summed up in the classic formula or prayer *noverim te, noverim me* ("I will

Antropologia teologica, 216–22; G. L. Müller, *Katholische Dogmatik: Für Studium und Praxis Theologie* (Freiburg: Herder, 1995), 781–88; Rondet, *Gratia Christi*, 99–179; V.-M. Capdevila y Montaner, *Liberación y divinización del hombre*, vol. 2: *Estudio sistemático: Teología de la gracia* (Salamanca: Secretariado Trinitario, 1994), 75–96; Sanna, *Chiamati per nome*, 244–53; Sayés, *La gracia de Cristo*, 30–42; Lorda, *La gracia de Dios*, 177–93. Among more specific works on the doctrine of grace in Augustine, see especially A. Trapè, *S. Agostino: Introduzione alla dottrina della grazia*, vol. 1: *Natura della grazia*, and vol. 2: *Grazia e libertà* (Rome: Città Nuova, 1987–90); and also J. Chéné, *La théologie de saint Augustin: Grâce et prédestination* (Lyons: Mappus, 1962); A. Sage, "Preparatur voluntas a Deo," *Revue des études augustiniennes* 10 (1964): 1–20; Agaësse, *L'anthropologie chrétienne selon saint Augustin*; V. Grossi and B. Sesboüé, "Grâce et justification: Du témoignage de l'Écriture à la fin du moyen Âge," in *L'homme et son salut*, edited by B. Sesboüé, V. Grossi, L. F. Ladaria, and P. Lécrivain, 286–315; L. Arias, "San Agustín, Doctor de la gracia," *Salmanticensis* 2 (1955): 3–41; J. P. Burns, "Grace," in Cavadini and Fitzgerald, *Augustine through the Ages*, 391–98; Quilliet, *L'acharnement théologique*, 101–24. On the life of Augustine, see Brown, *Augustine of Hippo*. On the ethical implications of his thought, see J. Wetzel, *Augustine and the Limits of Virtue* (Cambridge: Cambridge University Press, 1992); on the spiritual side, see J. Burnaby, *Amor Dei: A Study of the Religion of St. Augustine*, 2nd ed. (London: Hodder and Stoughton, 1947).

26. See M. G. Mara, "Agostino e la polemica antimanichea: Il ruolo di Paolo e del suo epistolario," *Augustinianum* 32 (1992): 1–25; P. Fredriksen, "Paul," in Cavadini and Fitzgerald, *Augustine through the Ages*, 621–25.

27. Augustine, *Sermo* 83, 2.

28. For a summary of the principal works of Augustine with respect to Pelagianism, see Grossi and Sesboüé, *Grâce et justification*, 289–303; G. Bonner, "Against the Pelagians," in Cavadini and Fitzgerald, *Augustine through the Ages*, 41–47.

know you, I will know myself"). Man knows God, and, knowing God in the depths of his heart, as the *Confessions* teach, he knows himself and God, as we saw in the first chapter.

The Teaching of Augustine on Grace

In his doctrine of grace and salvation Augustine insists on three fundamental issues: first, the primacy of grace—which is both gratuitous and efficacious—in the lives of humans: *gratia semper invicta est*, he says, "nothing can defeat grace"; second, the decisive power of God's grace over human freedom, acting within the human spirit with a *suavitas amoris*, "the gentleness of love"; and third, the absolute need for grace, not only as an *adiutorium quo* (more or less equivalent to "actual grace"), but also as an *adiutorium sine quo non*, "the help without which it is not possible to act" (equivalent approximately to "elevating grace," which Adam had before sinning).[29] Augustine's teaching on grace, to be understood in the wider context of sin and human life, may be summed up in the following eight points.

The law   According to Augustine, the law (God's will and commandments) is good because it comes from God; it promotes the good and prohibits evil. However, merely acting in accordance with the law does not justify humans. Besides, to some extent the law presents itself as a temptation, because it makes evil known, which otherwise might not be known. At the same time, it helps us to know our weaknesses and limits. Hence the law has a pedagogical function that leads us to Christ's saving work. As can be seen, this is a clearly Pauline position.[30]

The sinfulness of humanity   Augustine teaches that man knows the principle of evil and sin through Christ: he says that *omnis homo Adam* (that is, every human is born a sinner), and *omnis homo Christus* (every human is, or can be, justified).[31] Specifically, the sinful situation of humans is known through the redemption Christ won for us. Knowing Christ, who redeems us, we come to know our sinful condition. Agostino Trapè writes:

Augustine deduces the theology of original sin from that of redemption, and not the other way around, as is often thought. Original sin constitutes a separation from God, because Christ has reconciled us with God; all of us share in it, because Christ has reconciled all; it is not only the imitation of the bad example of Adam, because redemption is not only the imitation of the good example of Christ. Two solidarities, therefore, of an opposite kind, but necessarily connected, with Adam and with Christ.[32]

---

29. See Baumgartner, *La grâce du Christ*, 65–67; C. Boyer, "*Adiutorium sine quo non*: Sa nature et son importance dans la doctrine de saint Augustin," *Doctor Communis* 13 (1960): 5–18; Trapè, *S. Agostino*, 2:330–32. Trapè explains this as follows: "Grace which gives the power—*auxilium sine quo non*—and grace which also gives the will: *auxilium quo*" (128).

30. See chapter 5, note 14 and corresponding text.

31. Augustine, *Enn. in Ps.* 70, 2, 1. The full text is "Omnis autem homo Adam; sicut in his qui crediderunt, omnis homo Christus, quia membra sunt Christi." On this text, see chapter 7, note 84.

32. A. Trapè, "S. Agostino," in *Patrologia*, vol. 3: *Dal Concilio di Nicea (325) al Concilio di Calcedonia (451): I Padri latini* (Casale Monferrato: Institutum Patristicum Augustinianum / Marietti, 1978), 409; see Trapè, *S. Agostino*, 1:140. Karl Adam gave this key to understanding Augustine in his work *Die geistige Entwicklung des heiligen Augustinus* (Augsburg: Haas und Grabherr, 1931), 38, translated into English as *Saint Augustine: The*

That is to say, Augustine understands and describes the reality of sin not only on the basis of the inner phenomenology of sin itself, which he understands deeply, but principally on the basis of the redemptive work of Christ in overcoming sin. In a strict sense, Christ the redeemer "reveals man to man" as a sinner.

Augustine believes that humans are born in a state of radical sinfulness, and for this reason the works of fallen humanity are sinful and defective.[33] Not all the works of *Christians* are sinful, however. Sinfulness before baptism is radical, for Augustine, because the intention of the sinner is deviant: the acts of humans are systematically stained by *cupiditas*, by vanity and human pride. Any human act from which full rectitude is lacking is sinful, he says; and from the beginning of human existence original sin has radically turned the will of humans away from God as the ultimate end. Human guilt lies, therefore, not so much in the sinfulness of concrete actions but rather in the fact that the person is in a *state of sin*, belonging to a humanity that may be described as a *massa damnata*. Augustine explains this doctrine with the use of a surprising expression that has cropped up frequently throughout history: "nemo habet de suo nisi mendacium et peccatum" (nobody has anything of their own that is not lying and sin).[34] Obviously it is an expression that needs further explanation.

The justification of the sinner   How can humanity's deeply rooted sinful state be overcome? According to Augustine, simply by the infusion of divine grace, which is *the love of God poured out on humans*, a reality humans experience as "being loved" by God. He frequently cites a passage of Paul from Romans 5:5: "Hope does not disappoint us, because God's love has been poured into our hearts through the Holy Spirit which has been given to us."[35] For Augustine, God's love is very tangible, concrete, and human. Commenting on Romans 5:5 he says that "Deus facit nos dilectores suos": God not only loves us, not only shows us his generous love, but "makes us his lovers," that is, makes us capable of loving him.[36]

This new life comes to humans by means of faith (which is a gift of God rather than a human response)[37] and of baptism (which incorporates us into Christ and the

Odyssey of His Soul (New York: Macmillan, 1967). As an example of how the doctrine of original sin reflects the parallel between Adam and Christ, see Augustine, *De pecc. orig.* 2. See also G. Philips, *L'union personnelle avec le Dieu vivant: Essai sur l'origine et le sens de la grâce créée*, 2nd ed. (Leuven: Leuven University Press, 1989), 45f.; G. Madec, *La patria e la via: Cristo nella vita e nel pensiero di sant'Agostino* (Rome: Borla, 1993); P. O'Callaghan, "Una lectura cristológica de la doctrina del pecado original."

33. See G. R. Evans, "Evil," in Cavadini and Fitzgerald, *Augustine through the Ages*, 340–44. On original sin in Augustine, see A. Sage, "Le péché originel dans la pensée de saint Augustin, de 412 a 430," *Revue des études augustiniennes* 13 (1967): 75–112; V. Grossi, "Il peccato originale nella catechesi di S. Agostino prima della polemica pelagiana," *Augustinianum* 10 (1970): 325–59, 458–92; P. Rigby, "Original Sin," in Cavadini and Fitzgerald, *Augustine through the Ages*, 607–14.

34. Augustine, *In Io. Ev. tract.* 5, 1.

35. See A.-M. La Bonnardière, "Le verset paulinien Rom., v. 5 dans l'œuvre de saint Augustin," in *Augustinus Magister* (Paris: Études Augustiniennes, 1954), 2:657–65. Rom 5:5 is cited more than a hundred times by Augustine.

36. Augustine, *De spir. et lett.* 32, 56.

37. Before his episcopal consecration, which took place in 397, Augustine taught that the preaching of the Gospel was a gift of God producing the faith (*De praed. sanct.* 3, 7ff.) and that faith was *our* response: "Nostrum est credere aut velle, illius [Dei] autem dare credentibus et volentibus facultatem bene operandi per Spiritum." *Explicatio quorumdam propositionum Epist. ad Romanos*, 61. This position was not far from the Pelagian vision of the *gratia externa*, that is, the grace of creation. Later on, however, Augustine modified

Church and makes us children of God and temples of the Spirit). "God wants to make you god not by nature, like the One whom he generated, but by grace and adoption."[38] For Augustine, the pastoral practice of the baptism of infants—which in his view is the liturgically typical form of this sacrament, not the baptism of adults—is indicative of the absolute necessity of grace and a clear sign of the original sinfulness of each and every human being.[39]

Thus baptism incorporates humans into Christ and, ipso facto, into the Church, the body of Christ. Augustine speaks of Christ together with the Church as the *Christus totus*, the entire Christ, head and members.[40] As the fruit of baptism, besides, the Holy Spirit lives in the souls of the just.[41] The Spirit is at the same time both giver and gift. Augustine frequently identifies charity in humans with the Holy Spirit; at the same time, he affirms, man is truly transformed by grace in his very nature, thus acting in a Godlike way: "Deus facit nos dilectores suos," a text just cited, and "amare Deum, Dei donum est" (to love God is itself a gift of God).[42] By means of the Spirit, Christ lives in the Christian; according to Augustine, through the Spirit Christ lives, loves, prays, and suffers in the one who believes.[43] As a result, the Father also lives in the person justified, and so "the entire Trinity lives in us."[44] This means not that the soul *contains* God but rather the other way around, that the soul lives in God: "Habitas in Deo ut contineraris" (You live in God so as to be contained by him).[45]

The divinization of believers   The fruit of justifying grace is the divinization of the human being.[46] "'You are as gods' (Ps 142:2): therefore we share in his life. Nobody should doubt it. Scripture has said it."[47] The basis for being divinized, according to Augustine, lies in the fact that one is created "in the image and likeness of God," a topic he reflected on extensively.[48] Being made in the image and likeness of God means for him that the whole person is made in the image of the Trinity. And this takes place through an *admirabile commercium* ("admirable exchange") with Christ. "We are made children of God, we are made gods."[49] Furthermore: "We partake of God in his holiness and justice, which makes us like God in an ontological way. We share in the Divinity through a divine way of seeing things, knowing them as they are in themselves, with a truly divine way of loving, taking joy in him in ourselves, living our eternal life from him, in him, with him."[50] In an expression already cited, he says: "He has made us gods, because he has illuminated our interior eyes."[51] As a result, Augustine explains,

---

his position profoundly: the preaching of the Gospel and working miracles do not contain any proper power capable of producing the faith in the one who listens if the interior operation of God in the soul is absent. *Ep.* 217, 2, 5; *Contra duas epistulas Pelagi* 1, 3, 7; *Ep.* 194, 4, 18.

38. Augustine, *Sermo* 166a.

39. See W. Harmless, "Baptism," in Cavadini and Fitzgerald, *Augustine through the Ages*, 84–91.

40. Augustine, *In epist. Io.* 1, 2; *In Io. Ev. tr.* 28, 1; *Enarr. in Ps.* 90, 2, 1.

41. See Augustine, *Ep.* 187. See V. Carbone, *La inabitazione dello Spirito santo nelle anime dei giusti secondo la dottrina di s. Agostino* (Vatican City: Tipografia poliglotta vaticana, 1961).

42. Augustine, *Sermo* 297, 1.

43. Augustine, *In Io. Ev. tr.* 140, 6.

44. Augustine, *De Trinitate* XV, 18, 32.

45. Ibid.

46. See chapter 7, esp. note 73.

47. Augustine, *Enn. in Ps.* 146.

48. See chapter 4 and Urbano, *Theosis*, 114–17.

49. Augustine, *Enn. in Ps.* 49, 2.

50. Augustine, *Sermo* 297, 8, cited in Urbano, *Theosis*, 122f.

51. Augustine, *Enn. in Ps.* 94, 6.

"You cannot do anything good if you are not illumined by the light of God, warmed up by the Spirit."[52] Through grace humans come ever closer to God.

Still, in the writings of Augustine this dynamic is to be understood principally on an existential plane[53] rather than an ontological one.[54] He works not with the Greek notion of human nature but rather with the moral and spiritual aspects of divine life in man. "Man shares in the properties of the divine nature: justice, wisdom, beatitude," he says.[55] Divinization is one and the same thing with the process of salvation and justification.

The role of "actual grace"   On account of God's grace, the human will is no longer disoriented and abandoned but is moved and directed by *caritas*, the love of God infused into it. As a result, the baptized enjoy a new *libertas*, the capacity to live a new life. At the same time, Christian believers enter into a state in which they cannot live without the punctual help of grace, what Augustine calls the *adiutorium quo*, for this supplementary impulse to the human will weakened by sin is not enough, though Pelagius thought it was. They need the repeated impulse of God's help in order to overcome the power of sin and do good works (this is what theologians would later call "actual grace"). Besides the *adiutorium quo*, however, humans also stand in need of the *adiutorium sine quo non*, that is, the grace without which the virtuous action has no value before God. In other words, God gives humans not only the grace to act well (*posse agere salutariter*) but the good action in itself (*agere salutariter*). God gives not only grace to act according to the law but also the good act in itself, as an efficacious grace (*gratia efficax*).[56] Hence grace is both *excitans* and *adiuvans*: not only does it incline the will toward the good but it also infallibly obtains and ensures the assent of the will.[57] Should this help from or act of God be absent, human life could, in principle, correspond materially to the divine will, but humans would not be capable of truly carrying out actions that are pleasing to God. In that sense, Augustine appropriately cites the words of Paul to the Philippians: "For God is at work in you, both to will and to work for his good pleasure" (2:13).[58]

This explains the insistence of Augustine not only on the prayer of praise and thanksgiving (also recommended by Pelagius) but also, and especially, on the prayer of petition. From the *Confessions* we can cite his famous prayer: "Da quod iubes et iube quod vis" (Give what you command, and then command what you want).[59] And elsewhere he advises Christians: "Fac quod potes, pete quod non potes" (Do what you can, ask what you cannot).[60]

52. Ibid., 91, 6. Augustine uses the expression *fervefactus a Spirito*.
53. Augustine cites Virgil's words "Trahit sua quemque voluptas" (Everyone is drawn by his pleasure) in *Tract in Ioh.* 26, 4.
54. This is the position of Oroz Reta in *De l'illumination à la déification de l'âme*.
55. See Augustine, *De diversis quaest.*, 46, 2.
56. Augustine, *De grat. et lib. arb.* 16, 32.
57. See J. P. Burns, *The Development of Augustine's Doctrine of Operative Grace* (Paris: Études Augustiniennes, 1980).
58. On this text, see, for example, Augustine, *De spir. et litt.*, 7, 11; 10, 11ff. On the relationship between grace and freedom in Augustine, see the recent work of L. Karfíková, *Grace and the Will According to Augustine* (Leiden: E. J. Brill, 2012).
59. Augustine, *Conf.* X, 29, 40.
60. Augustine, *De natura et gratia*, 43, 50.

Grace and freedom   According to Pelagius, salvation begins with human freedom; for Augustine it begins with grace. What Augustine attributes to grace and God's gift in Christ, Pelagius refers to the natural powers in man, given to humans at creation. The cause of salvation, for Augustine, is simply grace: salvation is *causa gratiae* (on account of grace).

Augustine speaks of the *gratia invicta* (invincible grace) that draws humans irresistibly toward God.[61] By it "they are guided in an inexorable and insuperable way [*indeclinabilter et insuperabiliter*] with the result that, in spite of their own weakness, they do not fall, they are not defeated by any hostile power."[62] Commenting on the Pauline phrase *virtus in infirmitate perficitur* ("power is made perfect in weakness"; 2 Cor 12:9), he says that the weak with the help of grace often triumph, whereas the "strong" without it may easily be lost.[63]

Augustine gives the impression, however, that God's grace accomplishes everything in humans. So what place is occupied by free will and human nature? What is the purpose of the powers and natural faculties of humans before the divine power of grace? Augustine's response is that the grace of God, *caritas*, does not violate human freedom because it is made present in humans always as a *delectatio victrix*, that is, as a pleasure that overcomes all resistance.[64] Grace respects human freedom deeply, presenting the human will its own proper object, which is the good. In a sense it can be said that God, through grace, "seduces" human beings, because grace is love. Hence, the divine power of grace is not incompatible with the apparent refinement of divine action in the lives of humans, because grace acts on the human heart and mind with a *suavitas amoris* that, in a certain sense, hides the powerful, persevering, faithful divine endeavor to overcome the resistance of the sinner.[65] In the *Confessions*, Augustine is personally aware of the great realism of the way God comes close to the human heart, even when it is immersed in sin: "Sero te amavi, pulchritudo tam antiqua et tam nova.... Mecum eras et tecum non eram" (Late have I loved you, beauty both ancient and new.... You were with me and I was not with you).[66]

Since the explanation he gives is mainly of an existential kind, Augustine does not distinguish clearly between the natural and the supernatural spheres. God loves humans by giving them the will to do good, and this divine presence becomes connatural to their recreated will. Grace gives a true joy to humans with respect to spiritual goods such as justice and the love of God.[67]

---

61. Augustine, *De corr. et grat.* 12, 38.62. Ibid.

63. Ibid.

64. See M. Djuth, "Freedom," in Cavadini and Fitzgerald, *Augustine through the Ages*, 495–98. See also I. Sciuto, "Il libero arbitrio nel pensiero medievale: Da Agostino al XII secolo," in *La libertà del bene*, edited by C. Vigna (Milan: Vita e pensiero, 1998), 123–45; M. Corbin, *La grâce de la liberté: Augustin et Anselme* (Paris: Cerf, 2012).

65. Augustine uses the expression *suavitas charitatis*, for example, in *Enn. in Ps.* 13.

66. Augustine, *Conf.* VII, 10, 27. "In the last analysis Augustine is less concerned with choosing, with doing, than with being, the elusive self, who one is and is meant to be, a person who spontaneously surrenders himself or herself unconditionally as enfleshed spirit to the One who alone offers fulfillment." S. J. Duffy, "Anthropology," in Cavadini and Fitzgerald, *Augustine through the Ages*, 24–31, 30.

67. See Augustine, *Sermo* 159, 3:3; *De gratia Christi* 21:22; *Enn. in Ps.* 118, 22:7.

Merit and perseverance   In some of his earlier works (written before his episcopal consecration, which took place in 397), Augustine speaks of a kind of human merit present before the reception of grace.[68] Starting in the year 398, the year in which he wrote his letter *Ad Simplicianum*, however, he abandons this approach and, in opposition to the Pelagians (and semi-Pelagians), denies the existence of any previous distinction between the members of nonredeemed humanity, the *massa damnata*, because one and all are sinners. First justification, in other words, is always pure grace.

Augustine's insistence on this doctrine is such that he may seem to be placing the universal saving will of God in doubt, suggesting the possibility of a predestination to condemnation for some people. Still, Augustine teaches at the same time that the works of the just, moved by grace, are really meritorious in that they fully involve humans in all their faculties. He reminds us that when all is said and done, "all the merits of the just are as many gifts of God."[69] And elsewhere: "God when he rewards our acts of charity in final judgment, crowns his own gifts."[70] He insists also on the fact that nobody is in a position to merit perseverance to the end in Christian life; this is possible only from God through assiduous prayer.[71] The position of Augustine is coherent: if final perseverance were the object of merit, the Christian would already be confirmed in grace and incapable of sinning.

Predestination and the primacy of God's action in salvation   Pelagius often used certain texts of scripture to defend his position on the intrinsic value of human works before God prior to receiving grace. He cited, for example, the following text of the prophet Zechariah: "Return to me, says the Lord of hosts, and I will return to you" (Zec 1:3). Augustine makes reference to other texts of scripture to confute this position, for example, Psalm 79:9: "Help us, O God of our salvation, for the glory of your name, deliver us, and forgive our sins, for your name's sake!"; Psalm 85:8: "The Lord will speak peace to his people, to his saints, to those who turn to him in their hearts"; and John 6:65: "No one can come to me unless it is granted him by the Father."

The priority of grace, according to Augustine, is reflected particularly in the question of predestination.[72] He inquires into the criterion God applies in conceding an invincible grace to some while denying it to others. The criterion cannot be human merit, he says, but only the *propositum Dei*, the immutable plan of God; along with divine foreknowledge the latter constitutes the basis for the doctrine of predestination. He offers the following definition of predestination: "praescientia et praeparatio beneficiorum Dei quibus certissime liberantur quicumque liberantur" (the fore-

---

68. Augustine, *De diversis quaest.* 68, 4; *Expos. quarundam propos. ex epist. ad Rom.* 60–64.

69. Augustine, *De dono persev.* 2, 4.   70. Augustine, *Ep.* 194, 5, 19.

71. Augustine, *De dono persev.* 6, 10.

72. See, for example, his work *De predestinatione sanctorum*. On the topic of predestination in Augustine, see V. Boublik, *La predestinazione: S. Paolo e S. Agostino* (Rome: Libreria Editrice Lateranense, 1961). This work has been critiqued by A. Trapè in "A proposito della predestinazione: S. Agostino e i suoi critici moderni," *Divinitas* 7 (1963): 243–84. See also G. Nygren, *Das Prädestinationsproblem in der Theologie Augustins: Eine systematisch-theologische Studie* (Gottingen: Vandenhoeck & Ruprecht, 1956); R. Bernard, "La prédestination du Christ total selon saint Augustin," *Recherches Augustiniennes* 3 (1965): 1–58; J. M. Rist, "Augustine on Free Will and Predestination," *Journal of Theological Studies* 20 (1969): 20–27; M. Lamberigts, "Predestination," in Cavadini and Fitzgerald, *Augustine through the Ages*, 677–79.

knowledge and preparation of divine benefits with which those who should be freed are in effect freed).[73]

In order to distinguish between those who have been predestined and those who have not, Augustine refers not to one's visible belonging to the Church (on the question of the relative and ambiguous visibility of the kingdom of God on earth, see especially his *De Civitate Dei*) but to final perseverance, which humans must ask God for assiduously. For this reason, some people outside the visible confines of the Church may be predestined, he says, whereas others who are within the Church visibly may not be. In any case, Augustine adds that the number of elect is fixed[74] and that it is small in comparison with those who will be lost.[75] This is predestination *ante praevisa merita*, previous to any human merit. Nonetheless, he does not admit the positive predestination of sinners to punishment, to eternal death.

Doubtless, as history has shown, difficulties abound in Augustine's doctrine of predestination, difficulties that are understandable given the polemical nature of many of his writings, as well as the topic in question. In the *first* place, Augustine does not seem to connect the *propositum Dei* with the salvation Christ has won for humanity on the cross, whereas predestination, in fact, has a Christological basis that is very much present in Paul.[76] *Second*, it would seem that Augustine calls the universal saving will of God (1 Tm 2:3ff.) into question.[77] The fact is that some of Augustine's expressions, for example, *massa damnata* and *vasa choleris* (vessel of anger) both of which are applied to humanity as a whole, do not seem to be compatible with God's universal saving will because grace is offered to some but not to others. In fact, Augustine says that grace would not truly be gratuitous if it were offered indistinctly to one and all.[78] Again we can see the tension between grace (given freely, magnanimously, without "previous rules," as it were) and nature (which has its own rules) brings about the severance between Christian spirituality (which attempts to study the workings of grace systematically) and philosophy (which reflects on the nature of humans and the cosmos).

We should keep in mind that Augustine, though he seems to speak of God as existing within time, teaches in fact that in God there is no time, because all is present to him.[79] Besides, he understands that the ultimate criterion for predestination is to

---

73. Augustine, *De dono persev.* 14:35.

74. Augustine, *De corr. et grat.* 13:39 and 42; *Ep.* 186:25; *Enchir.* 29; *De Civ. Dei* XXII, 1:2.

75. Augustine, *De corr. et grat.* 10:28; *Ep.* 190, 3:12.

76. See chapter 12, notes 18ff. and corresponding text.

77. This is the position of O. Rottmanner in *Der Augustinismus: Eine dogmengeschichtliche Studie* (Munich: Lentner, 1892). His position was contested by de Portalié, d'Alès, Gilson, and others. On the controversy, see F.-J. Thonnard, "La prédestination augustinienne et l'interprétation di O. Rottmanner," *Revue des Études Anciennes* 9 (1963): 250–87, and A. Sage, "La volonté salvifique universelle de Dieu dans la pensée de saint Augustin," *Recherches Augustiniennes* 3 (1965): 107–31. Augustine's principal text may be found in *De corr. et grat.*, 14. Still, elsewhere he writes: "If Christ died only for those who understand things, then we are wasting our time in the Church," *Ep.* 169, 1, 4.

78. See Augustine, *De dono persev.* 16.

79. See Rondet, *Gratia Christi*, 142. Speaking of time and eternity in God, Augustine says: "Apud Deum nihil deest, nec praeteritum igitur nec futurum, sed omne praesens est apud Deum" (*Conf.* XI, 16). He speaks also of the "hodiernus tuus aeternitatis" (your eternal today) (*Enn. in Ps.* 2, 6). It is also true that he speaks of God as if he was placing himself within time (see Rondet, *Gratia Christi*, 142). Agaësse sums up Augustine's position with respect to time and eternity in God with the following words: "Eternity involves time and is

be found in the ineffable mercy and justice of God. For this reason, he bases his reflection on the criterion of the universal saving will of God, at least in writings of a pastoral kind. He never says that Christ did not suffer for all. He writes: "Since we do not know who belongs to the number of the predestined and who does not, we should allow ourselves be guided by the benevolence of love, and desire that all would become blessed."[80] According to Brown, "Predestination, an abstract stumbling-block to the sheltered communities of Hadrumetum and Marseilles, as it would be to so many future Christians, had only one meaning for Augustine: it was a doctrine of survival, a fierce insistence that God alone could provide men with an irreducible inner core."[81]

The Church's Acceptance of Augustine's Teachings

In the Sixteenth Council of Carthage (418), convoked to discuss the position of Celestius, a disciple of Pelagius, three questions were dealt with, in response to which Augustine's position was decisively adopted.[82]

Original sin and infant baptism. Canon 2 indicates the absolute necessity for infants to receive the sacrament of baptism "for the remission of sins"; it would be mistaken, therefore, to teach that humans had not inherited something of the sin of Adam.[83]

The need for grace to fulfill the commandments. Canon 3 teaches that the grace of baptism not only justifies the sinner but also helps him not to sin again.[84] Citing John 15:5 ("Apart from me you can do nothing"), the idea that grace is exclusively meant to strengthen the human will in carrying out the will of God is rejected.[85]

The universality of sin. Against the optimistic teachings of Pelagius on the absence of sin in the baptized, the Council cites 1 John 1:8 ("If we say we have no sin, we deceive ourselves, and the truth is not in us") and refers to the experience of "good" Christians who frequently confess their sins[86] and recite every day without hypocrisy the Our Father, "and forgive us *our* trespasses" (emphasis added).[87] For this reason, holy Christians in the Church pray in all sincerity not only for others but also for themselves.[88]

---

contemporaneous with each and every instant, and with the development of time. Grace is at once transcendent to human action, because it is eternal and contemporaneous with every human action. It is neither before nor afterwards, but present and active with the passing of time. It is not therefore something irrevocable or closed on itself, as if God had fixed his design once and always, as if he chained himself to an irrevocable past." Agaësse, *L'anthropologie chrétienne selon saint Augustin*, 113.

80. Augustine, *De corr. et grat.* 15f.   81. Brown, *Augustine of Hippo*, 410.
82. *DH* 222–30.   83. Ibid. 223.
84. Ibid. 225.   85. Council of Carthage XVI, c. 5, *DH* 227.
86. Ibid., c. 6, *DH* 228.   87. Ibid., c. 8, *DH* 230.
88. Ibid., c. 7, *DH* 229: "Whoever says that when the saints say the Lord's prayer, 'Forgive us our debts,' that they say this not for themselves, because that petition is not now necessary for them, but for others who are sinners among their people, and that on this account each one of the saints does not say 'Forgive me my debts,' but 'Forgive us our debts,' so that the just man is understood to seek this for others rather than for himself, let him be anathema."

The "Semi-Pelagian" Controversy

The so-called semi-Pelagian position developed principally in a monastic context.[89] Some authors feared that a quietistic or passive reading of the works of Augustine could conceivably empty the value of Christian asceticism and the need for an uphill effort to follow the Lord closely. This position, though openly teaching the need of grace for justification, holds to the idea that the *initium fidei*, "the beginning of faith," depends on the human will, not on grace. This position would later on be called "semi-Pelagianism."

The Response of Augustine

In the year 418 Augustine wrote on the question in his *Letter 194* to the priest Sixtus in Rome (who later on became Pope Sixtus III). And in the years 426–27, he also wrote to the monks of Hadrumetum (in present-day Tunisia) his *Letters 214–15*, as well as his work *De gratia et libero arbitrio* (426). In these writings he spoke of the value of grace and freedom but concluded—at least this was the impression of the monks—that superiors should not correct their charges but simply pray for them. To clarify his position, he wrote his work *De correptione et gratia* in 427. When the priest Vitalus taught that the *initium fidei* depended on humans, Augustine rejected his position in his *Epistula 217 ad Vitalem*. Likewise he opposed the theology present in the monasteries of Victor at Marseilles and Lérins in his works *De praedestinatione sanctorum* and *De dono perseverantiae* (428–29), written shortly before his death. In fact, some important works of Vincent of Lérins (from his *Commonotorium* of 434) are clearly anti-Augustinian. Besides, John Cassian, the abbot of Marseilles, taught that some ordinary acts of our will precede the giving of God's grace. One thing is the exceptional conversions of people like Paul and Augustine, he says, quite another that of common persons. God, "as soon as he perceives in us a beginning of good will, right away he illumines, consolidates and moves it towards salvation; God gives growth to what he planted, or to what he has seen springing out of our effort."[90] Augustine also rejected this position.

Semi-Pelagianism after Augustine

The term "semi-Pelagianism" did not come to be used until the sixteenth century (in fact, perhaps the first time was during the controversy *de auxiliis* around the year 1600).[91] In the fifth and sixth centuries, however, the authors who defended this position were principally monks from Marseille and were therefore called "Masillians" or

---

89. See V. Grossi, "La crisi antropologica nel monastero di Adrumeto," *Augustinianum* 19 (1979): 103–33; D. Marafioti, "Il problema dell'initium fidei' in Sant'Agostino fino al 397," *Augustinianum* 21 (1981): 541–66; R. H. Weaver, *Divine Grace and Human Agency: A Study of the Semi-Pelagian Controversy* (Macon, Ga.: Mercer University Press, 1996); C. Leyser, "Semi-Pelagianism," in Cavadini and Fitzgerald, *Augustine through the Ages*, 761–66; Quilliet, *L'acharnement théologique*, 125–54. As regards Thomas Aquinas's interpretation of the question, see R. Hütter, "St. Thomas on Grace and Free Will in the *Initium fidei*: The Surpassing Augustinian Synthesis," *Nova et Vetera* (English ed.) 5 (2007): 521–54.

90. John Cassian, *Collationes* 13, 8.

91. See M. Jacquin, "A quelle date apparaît le terme semipélagien?," *Revue des Sciences Philosophiques et Théologiques* 1 (1907): 506–8.

Gauls. In fact, this doctrine was not equivalent to Pelagianism because the authors in question applied categories used previous to those of Pelagius present in many of the Eastern Fathers before Augustine. In the sense that "semi-Pelagianism" did not derive historically from Pelagianism, the expression is not exact.

The principal difficulty with the semi-Pelagian position lies in the synergism it postulates between the grace of God and human action (the *initium fidei*, or "the beginning of faith," and the *pius credulitatis affectus*, "the pious affect of believing").[92] Semi-Pelagian authors speak, for example, of the "good thief" who turns to Christ in the same way that the sick person turns to the doctor: this first movement, they would say, is not the fruit of grace. The spontaneous movement of human freedom toward the good, therefore, would precede grace, or at least would work side by side with it. To this it should be objected that if the *initium fidei* derives from humans themselves, why cannot the grace of justification, the *augmentum fidei*, or "increase in faith," develop within them through their own effort?

In any case, the error of semi-Pelagianism was condemned a hundred years after the death of Augustine, in the Second Council of Orange (529) presided over by Cesar of Arles. The path for this condemnation was prepared in the writings of Prosper of Aquitania,[93] for example, *De vocatione omnium hominum*, the *Carmen de ingratis*, and probably the *Indiculus Coelestinus*.[94] The Council of Orange taught what may be called a "moderate Augustinianism." Almost all the canons and chapters come directly from the writings of Augustine. Six questions are dealt with, among others, on grace and sin. Examples of the Council's conclusions follow.

First, the sin of our forefathers caused damage to the whole of the person, in body and soul, and this brought about above all the weakening of the will; besides, the order of creation has been disturbed.[95]

Second, human beings stand in need of grace to overcome the weakness of the will.[96] Only the action of the Holy Spirit moves us to authentic penance and purification.[97]

Third, grace precedes all human effort *before* justification. From grace proceeds prayer, the *initium salutis*, all efforts toward faith, all upright action, all preparation for grace, all merit;[98] thus a "semi-Pelagian" position is unacceptable.

Fourth, grace is present *within* justification itself: grace heals, frees from sin, directs us toward what is good, gives us the justice of Christ.

Fifth, grace also acts *after* justification, making it possible for believers to act in a way that is pleasing to God, to persevere, to observe vows, and to exercise great Christian virtues on account of the life of Christ in us, for the love of God.

---

92. On the *initium fidei*, see J. Chéné, "Que signifiaient 'initium fidei' et 'affectus credulitatis' pour les semipélagiens," *Recherches de Science Religieuse* 42 (1948): 566–88; M. Djuth, "Initium fidei," in Cavadini and Fitzgerald, *Augustine through the Ages*, 447–51.

93. See M. Cappuyns, "Le premier représentant de l'augustinisme médiéval, Prosper d'Aquitaine," *Recherches de théologie ancienne et médiévales* 1 (1929): 309–37; G. De Plinval, "Prosper d'Aquitaine interprète de saint Augustin," *Revue des Études Augustiniennes* 1 (1958): 339–55; A. Elberti, *Prospero d'Aquitania: Teologo e discepolo* (Rome: Dehoniane, 1999).

94. It is possible that this work, which dates from circa 442, mistakenly attributed to Pope Celestius and Augustinian in style and content, was written by Pope Leo the Great.

95. *DH* 372.

97. Ibid. 374.

96. Ibid. 389.

98. Ibid. 375.

Sixth, we have an absolute need for grace to avoid evil and do good. There is no predestination to condemnation. Besides, people are not predestined to evil, and the baptized have every possible opportunity of being saved; thus the Council taught the existence of a "sufficient grace" for all the baptized.

The following text of the Second Council of Orange, taken directly from Augustine's *De dono perseverantiae*,[99] synthesizes the content of the Council with respect to the need for grace:

If anyone says that mercy is divinely conferred upon us when, without God's grace, we believe, will, desire, strive, labor, pray, keep watch, endeavor, request, seek, knock, but does not confess that it is through the infusion and inspiration of the Holy Spirit that we believe, will or are able to do all these things as is required; or if anyone subordinates the help of grace to humility or human obedience, and does not admit that it is the very gift of grace that makes us obedient and humble, he contradicts the apostle who says: "What have you that you did not receive?" (1 Cor 4:7); and also: "By the grace of God I am what I am" (1 Cor 15:10).[100]

From the liturgical point of view, there are many ancient prayers that were inspired by the writings and preaching of Augustine, for example, the well-known *Actiones nostras* of the *Gregorian Sacramentary*: "Actiones nostras, quaesumus Domine, aspirando praeveni et adiuvando prosequere, ut cuncta nostra oratio et operatio a te semper incipiat et per te coepta finiatur" (Inspire our actions, O Lord, and accompany them with your help, so that all our prayers and works may have you as their beginning and their end).[101]

The Council of Orange was confirmed in 531 by Pope Boniface II. As a provincial council, to all appearances it was forgotten around the eighth century and taken up again only during the preparatory stages of the Council of Trent in the sixteenth century. In the meantime, greater emphasis came to be placed on the ethical side of Christian life and grace. The Augustinian position was handed on quite faithfully during the Middle Ages, without forgetting the concerns of the semi-Pelagians and the generally recognized need to avoid all passivity and quietism in Christian life. Particular emphasis is placed on the healing power of grace rather than on its irresistibility, more on the interior call than on its efficacious power.

Predestination and the Universal Saving Will of God

The teaching of Augustine on grace does not resolve two issues satisfactorily. First, the strictly anthropological one, because in emphasizing the place and presence of sin, the question of the created nature of the human subject and his free response to grace is neglected. And *second*, the question of predestination, on which, from the death of Augustine onward, there was an ample controversy that lasted for several centuries, indeed right up to modern times. In a period in which "the word of Augustine takes prevalence over the spirit of Augustine," as Henri Rondet puts it, a theology

---

99. Augustine, *De dono persev.* 23, 64.

100. Second Council of Orange, c. 6, *DH* 376.

101. *Gregorian Sacramentary*, in J.-P. Migne, ed., *Patrologiae cursus completus, series latina* (Paris: 1844–64) [hereafter "*PL*"], 78, 61c.

of "double-predestination" began to consolidate.[102] It can be summed up in the following formula of the seventh-century author Isidore of Seville: "Gemina est praedestinatio, sive electorum ad regnum, sive reproborum ad mortem" (There is a double predestination, that of the elect for the kingdom, that of the wicked for death).[103]

The controversy over predestination reached a culmination in the ninth century with the radical position of Gottschalk of Orbais, which was clarified at the Council of Quiercy in the north of France.[104] Gottschalk insists openly on double predestination because, following his reading of Augustine, all creatures need grace in order to live lives pleasing to God. His reasoning is as follows: "Since God is immutable, before the constitution of the world he predestined his elect to eternal life for ever through his free grace."[105] As a corollary of this position, says Gottschalk, it cannot be said that Christ died for all humans; he died only for the predestined. Gottschalk was condemned at a synod in Mainz (848) and later on in Quiercy (853) under Archbishop Hincmar of Reims, in the time of King Charles the Bald.[106] Hincmar was aware of the ethical, social, and political implications of Gottschalk's position and thus insisted on the realism of human freedom before grace; he did so with the help of the philosopher Scotus Eriugena, who spoke of the importance of the human will by returning to Eastern theologians previous to Augustine, such as Origen and Gregory of Nyssa. In any case, the universal saving will of God in Christ is taught. The Council of Quiercy made the following memorable statement:

Just as there has never been and there never will be anybody whose nature has not been assumed by Jesus Christ, our Lord, so also there is no man, there never has been and there never will be, for whom he has not suffered; still, not all are redeemed by the mystery of his suffering.... The chalice of salvation, which was prepared for our weakness by the divine power, has in itself the power to help all; but if it is not drunk, it does not save.[107]

The controversy has continued since then throughout the Middle Ages, during the Protestant Reformation (with Luther and especially with Calvin), then with Jansen and on the occasion of the *de auxiliis* controversy. As Rondet wrote, "In the perpetual oscillation between semi-Pelagianism and predestinationism, the theology of grace and predestination gradually centered the debate on the conciliation between grace and freedom, without ever eliminating the mystery."[108]

102. Rondet, *Gratia Christi*, 174.

103. Isidore of Seville, *II Sent.*, 6. See M. Jacquin, "La question de la prédestination aux Ve et VIe siècles," *Revue des Sciences Philosophiques et Théologiques* 1 (1906): 506–8.

104. See G. Morin, "Gottschalk retrouvé," *Revue Bénédictine* 42 (1931): 302–12; B. Lavaud, "Précurseur de Calvin ou témoin de l'Augustinisme: Le cas de Gotescalc," *Revue Thomiste* 37 (1932): 72–101; E. Aegerter, "Gottschalk et le problème de la prédestination au IXe siècle," *Revue d'Histoire des Religions* 111 (1937): 187–223; C. Lambot, ed., *Gottschalk d'Orbais: Œuvres théologiques et grammaticales* (Leuven: Spicilegium Sacrum Lovaniense, 1945); K. Vielhaber, *Gottschalk der Sachse* (Bonn: Röhrscheid, 1956); J. Jolivet, *Gottschalk d'Orbais et la Trinité: La méthode de la théologie a l'époque carolingienne* (Paris: Vrin, 1958). On this period see also Quilliet, *L'acharnement théologique*, 155–80.

105. Gottschalk of Orbais, *Fragmenta omnia*, art. 4 (*PL* 121, 368a). See also Hincmar of Reims, *De Praedestinatione* V (*PL* 125, 89), a document discovered in Bern in 1930.

106. See W. Grundlach, "Zwei Schriften des Erzbischofs Hinkmar von Reims," *Zeitschrift für Kirchengeschichte* 10 (1889): 92–145, 258–310; J. H. Schrörs, *Hinkmar, Erzbischof von Reims: Sein Leben und seine Schriften* (Hildesheim: G. Olms, 1967; originally published in 1884).

107. Council of Quiercy, cap. 4: *DH* 624.

108. Rondet, *Gratia Christi*, 168.

Nova lex est gratia ‛Spiritus Sancti. THOMAS AQUINAS[1]

Gratia Dei ponit aliquid in anima. THOMAS AQUINAS[2]

The Limits of Augustine's Theology, and the Search for an "Ontology" of Grace

Three aspects of Augustine's understanding of the workings of Christian grace may be noted: the priority of divine action (what would later be designated as "uncreated grace"), the human experience of grace (Augustine speaks of the *suavitas amoris*), and human ethical action that derives from grace. According to Augustine, anterior divine action—grace—produces a *delectatio,* a pleasing spiritual inclination in the soul, and divinizes believers *suaviter et fortiter* (gently and firmly), moving them through love to carry out good works. Not only that: it is *grace itself* that carries out the divine actions in humans.

The spiritual vigor and anthropological coherency of Augustine's explanation are obvious. The principal limit, however, lies in the tendency to neglect the proper dynamic of human nature itself, especially as regards human free will, which always retains its capacity to oppose grace. In continuity with Paul, Augustine speaks of Christian freedom in terms of liberation (from the slavery of sin, of death, etc.), but not as free will, that is, as the capacity for choosing, and the responsibility of humans to correspond to God's gifts. If in the context of Augustine's struggle against Pelagianism, a certain one-sidedness is understandable, this does not take away from the conviction that free human nature needs to be more fully integrated into the process of liberation that God carries out. For this reason, besides, Augustine does not systematically consider the question of what might be called the ontology of grace, that is, the created effect of grace in those who respond to the divine gift.[3] The theology

---

1. Aquinas, *S.Th.* I-II, q. 196, a. 1, co.: "The new law is the grace of the Holy Spirit."
2. Aquinas, *S.Th.* I-II, q. 110, a. 1, co.: "Grace places something in the soul."
3. On the question of "created grace" in Augustine, see G. Philips, "Saint Augustin a-t-il connu une 'grâce

of Augustine is concentrated principally on the supernatural order and its existential effects; it deals little with the natural order. Authors coming after him, radicalizing and simplifying his position, confusing besides the ontological with the existential aspects of his analysis, hold that the only relevant thing about the human being before receiving grace is sin and frequently quote in support of their position a well-known text of Augustine's: "nemo habet de suo nisi mendacium et peccatum" (nobody has anything of their own, if not lying and sin).[4] The use of Augustine's texts out of context has given rise over the centuries to not a few mistaken interpretations.

Medieval theologians and philosophers such as Thomas Aquinas fully accept the fundamental thrust of Augustine's teaching. However, they are more successful in expressing the realism of the life of grace with the help of new philosophical categories, especially those of Aristotle. Greater weight is given to Biblical and Patristic texts that speak of "new creation," of regeneration, of divine filiation, of divinization.[5] Grace is now considered not only on the basis of its origin in God ("uncreated grace") but also in terms of its objective and tangible effects on believers ("created grace"). Medieval authors speak of *gratia gratum faciens* (grace that makes the believer pleasing to God), of the *virtutes*, of the *habitus* of grace, and so on. For this reason, they begin to speak of different "kinds" or types of grace.[6] Distinctions arise, in understanding the life of grace, not so much on the basis of its origin, which is God alone, but rather in the function of the different aspects of human nature—being, actions, faculties, and so on—in which grace elevates, acts, and is present in life.

Early Medieval Interpretations

Two principal tendencies may be found among medieval authors. One is closer to an Eastern (perhaps semi-Pelagian) view of grace and takes into account the realism of human action and of the positive value of correspondence to God's gifts. The other is more in line with the development of the thought of Paul and Augustine, centered on God's action and initiative, while somewhat underestimating human nature and the realism of humans' free response to grace.[7]

Grace as a Stable Principle of Virtuous Action

According to the first tendency mentioned, it is generally held that divine grace in humans is not merely a punctual divine action that keeps the stimulus of sin at bay but rather a stable principle of virtuous action that acts in direct continuity with human nature that, like grace, derives from God's creating action. Starting with Augustine's doctrine of original sin, Anselm of Canterbury (eleventh century) teaches that the effect of grace is one of producing in the believer a *rectitudo*, or rectitude, in

créée'?" *Ephemerides theologicae lovanienses* 47 (1971): 97–116; P. J. Riga, "Created Grace in St. Augustine," *Augustinian Studies* 3 (1972): 113–30.

4. Augustine, *In Io. Ev. tr.* 5, 1.

5. J. B. Metz, in *Christliche Anthropozentrik: Über die Denkform des Thomas von Aquin* (Munich: Kösel, 1962), considers the medieval period to be anthropocentric because it is solidly based on the human.

6. See chapter 14, notes 84ff. and corresponding text.

7. I am grateful to Professor Robert Wielockx for the help he afforded me in preparing this chapter.

the potencies of the will and in virtuous action. Grace is experienced to some degree by humans and confers on them, besides, the *auxilium Dei moventis* (similar to what later on would be called "actual grace"), a stable capacity to resist temptation. In brief terms, God not only forgives sin but draws human life toward perfection.[8]

Peter Abelard, shortly after Anselm, presents an orderly lineup of Christian virtues.[9] What he calls the *gratia inhabitans* (grace living within) places the virtue of faith in the soul and constructs on that basis *caritas* and the other *virtutes*. This elevation gives humans a divine energy and power they experience as their own, in such a way that they stand in no need of punctual divine help in order to carry out upright moral actions. According to Abelard, God wanted humans to have true responsibility for the actions and autonomy in their lives.[10] Some aspects of his doctrine were condemned, however, at the Council of Sens in 1140 as a result of objections raised by Bernard of Clairvaux. For example, the following thesis was rejected: "quod liberum arbitrium per se sufficit ad aliquod bonum" (that free will is sufficient to carry out some particular good action).[11]

The difficulty experienced by these authors in expressing the truth of the encounter between divine grace and the free actions of humans is understandable. As yet they do not quite manage to differentiate between divine *concursus*, with which God moves things to act according to their nature (in continuity with God's creating action), on the one hand, and with actual grace, on the other.[12] Though the position of Abelard was in all probability semi-Pelagian or perhaps even Pelagian, he, together with Anselm, provided a strong impulse toward revitalizing the doctrine of grace in the context of a renewed anthropology.

Divine Grace as Charity

The principal representative of the second line of thought was Peter Lombard. A literalist follower of Augustine, he was the author of a highly influential medieval theological textbook called the *Sentences*. Lombard followed the anti-Pelagian writings of Augustine and held that the infused virtue of charity may be identified simply with the action of the Holy Spirit: "The Holy Spirit himself is the love or charity with which we love God and our neighbor."[13] That is to say, the lived charity of Christians is to be identified with the Holy Spirit, who acts in them.

This dynamic or punctual vision of grace was shared by some medieval authors

---

8. See Anselm, *De concordia praescientiae et praedestinationis et gratiae Dei cum libero arbitrio*, 4. It is true that Anselm greatly values the use of reason in the ambit of theological reflection. Still, it is also true that he reflects theologically on the basis of faith. On this topic, see A. Stolz, "Zur Theologie Anselms im Proslogion," *Catholica* 2 (1933): 1–24; B. Lohse, "Zur theologischen Methode Anselms von Canterbury in seiner Schrift 'Cur Deus Homo,'" in *Vernunft des Glaubens: Wissenschaftliche Theologie und kirchliche Lehre; Festschrift ze 60. Geburtstag von Wolfhart Pannenberg*, edited by J. Rohls and G. Wenz (Gottingen: Vandenhoeck & Ruprecht, 1988), 322–35; B. Goebel, *Rectitudo, Wahrheit und Freiheit bei Anselm von Canterbury: Eine philosophische Untersuchung seines Denkansatzes* (Munster: Aschendorff, 2001); Corbin, *La grâce de la liberté*.

9. See J. Jolivet, *La théologie d'Abélard* (Paris: Cerf, 1997).

10. See Peter Abelard, *Comm. in Rom. II*, 5, 1–5.   11. *DH* 725.

12. See Rondet, *Gratia Christi*, 185.

13. Peter Lombard, *I Sent.*, d. 17, aa. 1 and 6. On Lombard's doctrine of grace, see J. Schupp, *Die Gnadenlehre des Petrus Lombardus* (Freiburg: Herder, 1932). See also M. L. Colish, *Peter Lombard* (Leiden: E. J. Brill, 1994).

of a mystical bent, such as Pascasius Radbertus, Hugh and Richard of St. Victor, William of St. Thierry, and especially Richard Fishacre.[14] Later it was adopted by Luther. However, it was not accepted by major thirteenth-century medieval theologians[15] such as Bonaventure,[16] Albert the Great,[17] and Thomas Aquinas, as we shall soon see.

It should be kept in mind besides that Lombard was not entirely faithful to Augustine's position, because the latter did not simply identify infused charity with the action of the Holy Spirit. We have already cited Augustine's words, "Deus facit nos dilectores suos": through the action of the Holy Spirit (see Rom 5:5), "God makes us his lovers," that is, God transforms humans and makes them capable of loving him—not only of being loved by him but of really loving him—and of loving others with a divine love. In this discussion a position began to consolidate among medieval authors, especially among the many commentators on Lombard's *Sentences*, that emphasizes the distinction between *gratia increata* (the action of the Spirit of God on the soul) and *gratia creata* (the effect of this action produced continuously by God within the soul). The first one to use this distinction expressly was Alexander of Hales.[18]

The Doctrine of Grace in Thomas Aquinas

Whereas Augustine in his *Enchiridion* structures theology according to the scheme *fides, spes, caritas* (as does Aquinas in his late work the *Compendium theologiae*), in the time of Abelard and his disciples the study of theology begins to adhere to the following scheme: *fides, caritas, sacramentum*, that is, in the first place, faith (in God, man, and the created world), then charity (moral action and grace, which makes this possible), and finally sacrament (the means of salvation, Christ, the Church, the

14. See Philips, *L'union personnelle*; Colzani, *Antropologia teologica*, 190–202. More specifically, see Malevez, "La doctrine de l'image et de la connaissance mystique"; N. Den Bok, *Communicating the Most High: A Systematic Study of Person and Trinity in the Theology of Richard of St. Victor († 1173)* (Turnhout: Brepols, 1996). Fishacre understood the union between the Holy Spirit and the soul in parallel to the union between the two natures in Christ: just as in Christ the divine and the human natures are united in one person in a necessary and permanent way, so also the Spirit and the human will are united in a real union, though it is free and breakable. This is clearly a problematic reading. See F. Pelster, "Das Leben und die Schriften des Oxforder Dominikanerlehrers Richard Fishacre († 1248)," *Zeitschrift für katholische Theologie* 54 (1930): 518–53; A. M. Landgraf, "Caritas und Heiliger Geist," in *Dogmengeschichte der Frühscholastik*, I: *Gnadenlehre* 1 (Regensburg: F. Pustet, 1962), 220–37; Philips, *L'union personelle*, 71–73.

15. On this issue, see O'Callaghan, *Fides Christi*, 221–23; Philips, *L'union personelle*, 101–73.

16. Bonaventure understands grace as an active presence of the divine persons in the soul: in the just the Spirit is present, and through him, the entire Trinity, which confers "deiformity" to the soul and capacitates humans to enjoy God through knowledge and love. Grace, as a habit, renews the person, it is *gratia gratum faciens* or, better, a *deiformitas disponens animam* (a conformity to God that prepares the soul) (*Breviloquium* I, 5). The reception of grace takes place *patiendo divina*, "suffering," as it were, the divine action. See Rézette, *Grâce et similitude de Dieu*; L. Mathieu, *La Trinité créatrice d'après S. Bonaventure* (Paris: Les éditions Franciscaines, 1992); Colzani, *Antropologia teologica*, 203–5.

17. See A. Chacón, "Aspetti della dottrina sulla grazia giustificante in sant'Alberto Magno," *Annales Theologici* 2 (1988): 141–65.

18. According to Alexander, the presence of the Spirit is fruitful and efficacious and acts as a *forma transformans*, which makes of the soul a *forma transformata*. We can see, therefore, that the *gratia increata* and *gratia creata* are closely related to one another. See especially his *Summa Fratris Alexandri III*, III, inq. 1, tract. 1, q. 22, a. 2, sol. On his understanding of grace, see J. Auer, "Textkritische Studien zur Gnadenlehre des Alexander von Hales," *Scholastik* 15 (1940): 63–75.

sacraments).[19] This scheme is followed by Thomas Aquinas (thirteenth century) in his major work, the *Summa Theologiae.*

Aquinas's treatise on grace is not to be found in the *prima pars* of the *Summa Theologiae* (on God and the created world),[20] even though in this part he addresses two important questions that concern theological anthropology: predestination[21] and the divine "missions" of God toward humanity, and thus the doctrine of the Trinity's inhabitation of the souls of the just.[22] Nor is grace dealt with in the *tertia pars*, which considers Christology, salvation, the sacraments, and eschatology, although Thomas explains that all grace is *gratia Christi*, a sharing in the fullness of grace present in and deriving from our savior.[23] The study of grace, in fact, is situated at the end of his treatise on the foundations of moral life, that is, the *prima secundae*.[24] Alongside the law, Thomas defines grace as "an extrinsic principle of human actions." For him, as for Augustine, the purpose of grace is primarily that of perfecting the moral action of humans in such a way that it not only has its origin in God but is, besides, entirely and perfectly directed to God. By means of grace, human action, Aquinas tells us, "attingit ad ipsum Deum" (touches or hits off God himself).[25]

The principal aspects of Thomas's doctrine on grace are the following four, which will be elaborated in the systematic part of this work. In the first place, Aquinas introduces the question of grace in a strict sense when he speaks of "the new law," that is, the law of the Gospel, which justifies the sinner.[26] Even though it is expressed as a written law, he adds, the new law in real terms is none other than Christian grace. In this sense, the new law is to be identified not with the written law but rather with the "gratia Spiritus Sancti quae datur per fidem Christi" (the grace of the Holy Spirit which is given by faith in Jesus Christ).[27]

Second, for Aquinas, human moral action is determined by the *finis ultimus*, or ultimate end of human life. It is interesting to note that the question of the final end is dealt with at the very beginning of the *prima secundae*, as it entirely determines the structure of Thomas's ethics. The ultimate end of humans consists in their happiness and fulfillment in God, which is principally achieved by the beatific vision.[28] Thomas is aware that human nature on its own is simply incapable of reaching this end. Still, when he affirms that grace is an "extrinsic principle" of moral action, he is

---

19. See J. De Ghellinck, *Le mouvement théologique du XIIe siècle: Études, recherches et documents* (Paris: V. Lecoffre / J. Gabalda, 1914), 100.

20. See H. Bouillard, *Conversion et grâce chez S. Thomas d'Aquin: Étude historique* (Paris: Aubier-Montaigne, 1944); A. Galli, *La teologia della grazia secondo san Tommaso e nella storia* (Bologna: ESD, 1987); H. Lais, *Die Gnadenlehre des hl. Thomas von Aquin in der Summa contra Gentiles und der Kommentar des Franziskus Sylvestris von Ferrara* (Munich: K. Zink, 1951); W. A. Van Roo, *Grace and Original Justice According to St. Thomas* (Rome: Analecta Gregoriana, 1955).

21. See Aquinas, *S.Th.* I, q. 23. On the doctrine of predestination in Thomas, see J. M. Arroyo, *El tratado de la providencia divina en la obra de Santo Tomás de Aquino* (Rome: Edusc, 2009).

22. See Aquinas, *S.Th.* I, qq. 38 and 43. See chapter 14, notes 18ff. and corresponding text.

23. See Aquinas, *S.Th.* III, qq. 7–8. It is fair to say that the entire structure of the *Summa Theologiae* is Christocentric, including, of course, the part on divine grace. See M. Corbin, *Le chemin de la théologie chez Thomas d'Aquin* (Paris: G. Beauchesne, 1974); T. S. Hibbs, "*Imitatio Christi* and the Foundation of Aquinas's Ethics," *Communio* (English ed.) 18 (1991): 556–73.

24. See Aquinas, *S.Th.* I-II, qq. 106–14.

25. Aquinas, *S.Th.* I, q. 43, a. 3.

26. See Aquinas, *S.Th.* I-II, qq. 106–8.

27. Aquinas, *S.Th.* I-II, q. 106, a. 1.

28. See Aquinas, *S.Th.* I-II, qq. 2–5.

not denying its influence on human nature (as in Pelagius's *gratia externa*), and much less its relevance with respect to human nature. Thomas intends rather to say that grace is exclusively *a gift of God* that comes to us from without, not a spontaneous or natural development of human potentialities, though of course it does not contradict the latter. In this way he disassociates himself from both Pelagianism and semi-Pelagianism. In fact, he teaches that humans reach their ultimate end *only* through grace, because without it the action of the human being may be in material conformity with the divine will, but it does not fully reach God in person.

Third, it is also true that grace involves the totality of human nature and faculties, elevating them. Thomas frequently states that humans are *capax gratiae*, capable of receiving grace,[29] or, elsewhere, *capax Dei*, capable of God.[30] This does not mean that humans carry within themselves a positive capacity for grace (this is the case, of course, with different natural human activities such as seeing, knowing, and willing). In humans there is a real receptivity for grace, which Thomas calls a *potentia obedientiae* (an obeying potency).[31] For this reason, grace, when it is accepted by humans, does not change their basic nature, it does not produce a metamorphosis of human nature. At the same time, he continues, "gratia ponit aliquid in anima" (grace produces something in the soul),[32] what Aquinas calls a "nitor animae" (beauty or splendor of the soul),[33] given by God, or rather a "qualitas animae"[34] (a stable habit present in the soul), which he often calls "gratia gratum faciens" (grace that makes humans pleasing to God).

In brief terms, the first questions of the *prima secundae* on the ultimate end of man encounter their definitive explanations and fulfillment only at the end of the work, when the doctrine of grace is presented. Only through grace is the human being directed definitively and entirely to God, the only ultimate end. All Thomas's moral theology is based on the notion of the ultimate end, and the latter achieves its fulfillment only through grace.

Fourth and finally, the dynamics of sin is the point of departure for Augustine's doctrine of grace. But this is not the case for Thomas, in whose thought sin does not occupy such a central place, although it is dealt with thoroughly in the *prima secundae*.[35] The first man was created integral, Thomas teaches, but fell from this state.[36]

29. See Thomas Aquinas, *III Sent.*, d. 21, q. 1, a. 1, arg. 4; *S.Th.* III, q. 9, a. 2, co.; ibid., ad 3; also *S.Th.* I, q. 12, a. 4, ad 3; q. 93, a. 4, co.; *S.Th.* I-II, q. 106, a. 1, ad 1; q. 110, a. 4, ad 3. This doctrine has Augustinian roots: *De Trinitate* XIV, 8.

30. See Aquinas, *De Veritate*, q. 22, a. 2, ad 5; *De virtutibus in communi*, q. 4, a. 1, ad 5; *In Matth.*, c. 10, l. 2; *S.Th.* II-II, q. 18, a. 1, s.c.; *S.Th.* III, q. 4, a. 1, ad 2; q. 6, a. 2, co. In the latter article, Thomas connects the notion of *capax Dei* with that of the image of God in humans.

31. See for example *De Veritate*, q. 29, a. 3, ad 3.

32. See Aquinas, *S.Th.* I-II, q. 110, a. 1, co.

33. "Gratia est nitor animae," *De Veritate*, q. 27, a. 1, s.c. 1; *S.Th.* I-II, q. 110, a. 2, s.c.

34. See ibid.

35. See Aquinas, *S.Th.* I-II, qq. 71–89.

36. On original sin in Thomas, see P. De Letter, "Hereditary Guilt," *Irish Theological Quarterly* 20 (1953): 350–65; O. Magrath, "St. Thomas' Theory of Original Sin," *Thomist* (1953): 161–89; P. De Letter, "The Transmission of Original Sin," *Irish Theological Quarterly* 24 (1957): 339–45; J.-M. Dubois, "Transmission et rémission du péché originel: Genèse de la réflexion théologique de saint Thomas d'Aquin," *Revue des études anciennes* 19 (1983): 283–311; M.-M. Labourdette, "Aux origines du péché de l'homme d'après saint Thomas d'Aquin," *Revue thomiste* 85 (1985): 357–98.

In any case, for him the fundamental elements of the doctrine of grace may be considered quite independently of the question of sin. The reason for this lies in the fact that, whereas Augustine deals with of grace and sin in a predominantly existential way, Aquinas deals with it in a more ontological or metaphysical way.

Summing up the doctrine of Aquinas, we may say that (1) he gives greater attention than previous authors to the free will of humans and to their "nature," understood in a metaphysical rather than a physical way; (2) he deals with the complicated question of predestination elsewhere; (3) he teaches that the theological understanding of sin and evil is not constitutive of the treatise of grace; (4) he attempts to take into account the entire Pauline corpus and the whole of scripture through a sober exegesis; (5) his explanation is noticeably modest in that he says very little about his own spiritual and mystical experiences; and (6) he shifts from a certain voluntarism present in Augustine to a predominantly intellectual position. Voluntarism, as we shall now see, constitutes the central feature of the position of several authors that come after Thomas.

Blessed Duns Scotus and the Doctrine of Grace

Duns Scotus, a Franciscan theologian contemporaneous with Thomas Aquinas, developed a Christocentric understanding of grace closely bound up with creation, nature, and good works.[37] All in all, Scotus's anthropology may be best described as "personalist." His thought revolves around the following paradox: the more attention we pay to God, the less we emphasize humans and their dignity. Scotus considers God above all as love in that he created humans because he wanted there to be spiritual beings capable of loving. For this reason, he says that the incarnation of the Word would have taken place even if there had been no original sin, a position not held by Aquinas. Thus his language is centered on love and the will and less on faith and the intellect. In this way the dignity of human persons is emphasized. But for this reason also his theology is at times considered to be "voluntaristic."[38]

37. On his relationship with Aquinas and Ockham, see T. M. Osborne, *Human Action in Thomas Aquinas, John Duns Scotus, and William of Ockham* (Washington, D.C.: The Catholic University of America Press, 2014). On Scotus's own doctrine of grace, see P. Minges, *Die Gnadenlehre des Johannes Duns Scotus auf ihren angeblichen Pelagianismus und Semipelagianismus geprüft* (Munster: Aschendorff, 1906); Minges, "Der Wert der Guten Werke nach Duns Scotus," *Theologische Quartalschrift* 89 (1907): 79–93; P. Vignaux, *Justification et prédestination au XIVe siècle: Duns Scot, Pierre d'Auriole, Guillaume d'Occam, Grégoire de Rimini* (Paris: E. Leroux, 1934); W. Pannenberg, *Die Prädestinationslehre des Duns Skotus im Zusammenhang der scholastischen Lehrentwicklung* (Gottingen: Vandenhoeck & Ruprecht, 1954); W. Dettloff, *Die Lehre von der Acceptatio Divina bei Johannes Duns Scotus: Mit besonderer Berücksichtigung der Rechtfertigungslehre* (Werl: Dietrich Cölde, 1954); Dettloff, *Die Entwicklung der Akzeptations- und Verdienstlehre von Duns Scotus bis Luther: Mit besonderer Berücksichtigung der Franziskanertheologen* (Munster: Aschendorff, 1963); Dettloff, "Die antipelagianische Grundstruktur des scotischen Rechtfertigungslehre," *Franziskanische Studien* 48 (1966): 266–70; B. De Armellada, *La gracia, misterio de libertad: El "sobrenatural" en el beato Escoto y en la escuela franciscana* (Rome: Istituto Storico dei Cappuccini, 1997). On the Christocentric character of Scotus's theology, see I. Guzmán Manzano, "El primado absoluto de Cristo en Escoto: Nuevas perspectivas; Cristo el principio hermenéutico de la teología cristiana y fundamento de toda creación posible," *Naturaleza y Gracia* 55 (2008): 9–77.

38. The personal quality of the love of God for humans is reflected in the definition of "person" given by Scotus: "substantia incommunicabilis naturae rationalis" (an incommunicable substance of rational nature). *Lect.* I, d. 2, pars 32, qq. 1–4. See A. D. Conti, "I presupposti metafisici del concetto di persona in Scoto," in

Potentia Dei Absoluta and *Potentia Dei Ordinata*

Speaking of divine action, it is common for medieval authors to distinguish between *potentia Dei absoluta* and *potentia Dei ordinata*. The former refers to the unconfined range of possibilities and ways of doing things that God is capable of with no limits of any kind. The latter, the *potentia Dei ordinata*, however, refers to divine action that encounters what has already been established at creation: in this case, God acts in the world in a way that corresponds to created nature, in consonance with the revelation that has taken place in Jesus Christ. God "binds himself," as it were, to the nature of things as he has created them, not going beyond their limits, respecting their proper laws. In global terms, he is not, of course, "obliged" to do so, for God always acts with a pure, faithful, free will. Applying this logic to Scotus's understanding of grace, we may say that, on the basis of the *potentia Dei absoluta*, God would not be obliged to concede to humans the *habitus* of charity in order to lead them to eternal life. Neither would divine action be linked necessarily to the sacraments.[39] On the basis of the *potentia Dei ordinata*, however, Scotus teaches that God has established, in his wisdom, that nobody can become acceptable to him and justified without the *habitus* of charity[40] and without receiving the sacraments. God thus remains freely faithful to the obligations he took on in creating, revealing, and redeeming.

In the context of a deeply orderly and intellectualist theology such as that of Thomas Aquinas, the distinction between the *potentia Dei absoluta* and the *potentia Dei ordinata* would be more or less hypothetical. Everything has an intrinsically rational consistency, and it would be unthinkable for God not to adapt his self-imposed way of acting to the reality he has created, acting always in keeping with the *potentia Dei ordinata*. Thus Thomas's philosophy and theology, though distinct, move along side by side; they cannot contradict one another. Scotus, however, with his view of God as love, sees in this an excessively rationalistic view of reality in which God's magnanimity and generosity seem to be continually compromised and hampered, and in which the absolute gratuity of the supernatural order is not sufficiently underscored. With a view that is more centered on the pure and absolute gratuitousness of divine grace, the distinction between *potentia Dei absoluta* and *potentia Dei ordinata* becomes more relevant.

Divine Acceptance and the *Habitus Gratiae*

The nature of God for Scotus may be described as "gratia gratis dans" (grace that is given freely).[41] "God wants the happiness of humans," he says, "and only for this reason does he want the *habitus* of love, with the help of which he can bring them to

---

Etica e persona: Duns Scoto e suggestioni nel moderno, edited by S. Casamenti (Bologna: Edizioni Francescane, 1994), 87–99.

39. Duns Scotus, *Rep. Par.* I, q. 1. On this issue, see W. J. Courtenay, *Capacity and Volition: A History of the Distinction of Absolute and Ordained Power* (Bergamo: P. Lubrina, 1990); on the theological and political implications of the distinction, see F. Oakley, "The Absolute and Ordained Power of God," *Journal of the History of Ideas* 59, no. 3 (1998): 437–61; Oakley, "The Absolute and Ordained Power of God and King," *Journal of the History of Ideas* 59, no. 4 (1998): 669–90.

40. See Duns Scotus, *Rep. Par.* I, q. 1.

41. Duns Scotus, *II Sent.*, d. 27, cap. 7.

beatitude."[42] In other words, the prime element of the divine plan is to be found in the fact that God loves the human being and wants to make him happy; humans know, therefore, that they have been accepted by God. The means used in order to obtain this end—in this case the *habitus* of grace—are considered secondary, as subordinate and not really necessary. Thus we can say that things are necessarily good because God loves them and wills them, while the contrary affirmation—that the intrinsic good of things is a reflection of the love of God for them—does not have the same weight.[43]

God, in effect, by going beyond what he habitually does through grace and the sacraments, could conceivably offer grace in ways different from those he normally employs. The presence of the *habitus gratiae* may be considered as convenient and appropriate, but not necessary. In real terms we can say here that the end does not justify the means. As the medieval phrase has it, qui ordinate vult, prius vult finem quam media, "whoever wants in an orderly way, seeks the end before the means."[44] Scotus is aware of the role of religious experience in the lives of Christians, of the attraction to God, whom they can enjoy, of the facility they have in carrying out good actions, of the moral rectitude of their lives. Still, this does not mean that we can theologically deduce the presence in believers of the supernatural *habitus* of grace. That is to say, there are no infallible signs of the presence of grace. The counterpart of grace's being gratuitous is that we know very little of its presence and dynamism in our lives. The reason God justifies the sinner (the *ratio iustificationis*) and allows merit (the *ratio meriti*) are one and the same: they are pure divine will, the free *acceptatio* of human action on God's part.

In brief terms, according to Scotus the relationship between God and humans belongs to the category of Covenant (that is, it relates to the plan God has established in the order of salvation), and not so much to that of ontology (that is, with respect to the world that God has created). Hence the presence of a created *habitus* of grace as a means to obtain justification (through the sacraments, etc.) ultimately becomes contingent.[45]

---

42. Duns Scotus, *Lect. I Oxf.*, fol. 53 ra.

43. See Minges, *Der Wert der Guten Werke*, 78.

44. On this phrase, see H. Lennerz, "De historia applicationis principii 'omnis ordinate volens prius vult finem quam ea quae sunt ad finem' ad probandum gratuitatem praedestinationis ad gloriam," *Gregorianum* 10 (1929): 238–66.

45. The following is the position of Scotus according to McGrath: "For Scotus, the volition of the end necessarily precedes the volition of the means to that end, so that the precise means by which justification occurs is of secondary importance to the fact that God has ordained that it will occur. The increasing emphasis upon the priority of the extrinsic denomination of the divine acceptation over the possession of a habit of grace inevitably led to a marked reduction in interest in the question of how such a habit came about in the soul. Furthermore, Scotus' concept of covenantal causality eliminated the ontological difficulty felt by the theologians of the early Franciscan school over the possibility of the transition from nature to grace: for Scotus, God had ordained that this transition could be effected through a congruously meritorious disposition towards justification, so that there was no difficulty in abolishing the hiatus between the states of nature and grace." A. E. McGrath, *Iustitia Dei: A History of the Christian Doctrine of Justification* (Cambridge: Cambridge University Press, 1986), 1:163f.

The Orthodox Teaching of Gregory Palamas

We have seen that the key element of medieval theological anthropology lies in the relationship between uncreated and created grace, which usually are dealt with separately. The Orthodox tradition takes another approach. The best-known representative is Gregory Palamas, a fourteenth-century bishop of Thessaloniki, who pays more attention to uncreated grace than to created grace.[46]

Eastern theology attempts to be fundamentally theocentric and "apophatic." That is to say, it intends to avoid too many distinctions in the order of grace and prefers to insist on the "negative" side of our knowledge of God and his action, what we do not know, not what we do know. In his principal work, *Theophanes*, Palamas, who was a follower of Pseudo-Dionysius the Areopagite, employs a Platonic-style philosophy generally accepted by the Orthodox Church.[47] He reflects particularly on the doctrine of divinization, placing less emphasis on ethics and on the contingent presence of humans in the world, at least at an explicit level. His doctrine on grace is well developed and closely connected with Christian spiritual life, especially of a monastic kind. Besides, Palamas pays special attention to the nature of divine action.

Distancing himself from the Western tradition, which frequently deals with theological issues in terms of causality, Palamas considers grace through the prism of divine emanation. He affirms that God, in his essence or nature (*ousia*), is completely inaccessible and unknown. What humans receive with grace may be described in terms of "divine energies," uncreated forces that are distinct from the divine essence. Thus, says Gregory, "illumination of the soul by divine, divinizing grace, is not identified with the divine essence, but rather with divine energy."[48] Believers share not in the divine essence but in God's external irradiation, in the divine energies. This is to be understood in terms not of an operative presence of the cause in the effects but of an illuminating power that emerges eternally from the essence of the Trinity.[49]

Some Eastern authors who were contemporaries of Palamas (Barlaam, Alyndine) taught that the distinction between divine essence and energies or irradiation could compromise, to some degree, the simplicity of God, because the energies might be understood as intermediary beings that are neither created nor uncreated. Pope Gregory the Great, several centuries beforehand, had made the same observation

46. On Palamas, see M. Jugie, "Palamas," in A. Vacant et al., eds., *Dictionnaire de théologie catholique* (Paris: Letouzey et Ané, 1902–72) [hereafter "*DTC*"], 11:1735–76; E. Candal, "Innovaciones palamíticas en la doctrina de la gracia," *Miscellanea Giovanni Mercati* (Vatican City: Biblioteca Apostolica Vaticana, 1946), 3:65–103; C. Kern, "Les éléments de la théologie de G. Palamas," *Irénikon* 20 (1947): 6–33, 164–93; J. Meyendorff, *A Study of Gregory Palamas* (London: Faith Press, 1964); V. Lossky, *The Mystical Theology of the Eastern Church* (Cambridge: James Clarke, 1973); R. Flogaus, *Theosis bei Palamas und Luther: Ein Beitrag zum ökumenischen Gespräch* (Gottingen: Vandenhoeck & Ruprecht, 1997); Y. Spiteris, *Palamas: La grazia e l'esperienza; Gregorio Palamas nella discussione teologica* (Rome: Lipa Edizioni, 1998); A. N. Williams, *The Ground of Union: Deification in Aquinas and Palamas* (Oxford: Clarendon Press, 1999); B. D. Marshall, "*Ex Occidente Lux?* Aquinas and Eastern Orthodox Theology," *Modern Theology* 20, no. 2 (2004): 23–50. According to Lossky, in *The Mystical Theology*, Eastern theology on the whole does not accept the category of "created grace."

47. See Philips, *L'union personelle*, 248ff.

48. Gregory Palamas, *Capita physica, theologica, moralia et practica*, 68f.

49. Lossky, *The Mystical Theology of the Eastern Church*.

with respect to a similar doctrine taught by Theodoret of Cyrus.[50] Palamas responded to this accusation by saying that if the distinction between the divine essence and energies is not made, an identification is being established between the knowable and the unknowable, and divine transcendence is compromised.[51]

Some modern scholars, such as Gérard Philips, hold that Palamas, though avoiding the term "created grace," does not in real terms deny the divinizing effect of grace on humans.[52] Others suggest that Palamas's doctrine presents a false dilemma because there are simply no intermediaries within the dynamics of grace, either created (as the scholastics might say) or uncreated (according to the Eastern theologians), but simply God, who gives himself.[53] Others, finally, hold that while scholastic theology is based on Aristotelian categories and tends toward the "cosification" of grace, Eastern theology, developed in the context of Platonism, is expressed characteristically in terms of emanation, which would seem to suggest a certain continuity between God and the creature on the paradoxical basis of intending to respect and "protect" divine transcendence.[54]

Other Developments during the Middle Ages

The theology of grace developed in the late Middle Ages in three other important moments, closely connected with one another: nominalism, Renaissance humanism, and mysticism. All three help us situate and understand the posterior doctrine of the Protestant Reformation and the Council of Trent, as well as further developments during the modern period.

Nominalism

The term "nominalism" arose in the eleventh century during a series of controversies relating to the gnoseological theory that denied all ontological weight to the names (*nomina*) of things. In effect, according to nominalist thought, genres and species are simple mental constructions established on the basis of human convention. There is little or no relation between things as they are in themselves and the names we give them. Nominalism renounces metaphysics and excludes the application of reason to reflection on God.

Radicalizing the subtle and complex position of Duns Scotus, William of Ockham, an early fourteenth-century philosopher, took it that the divine will is not connected to world-bound rules of any kind.[55] What God does belongs necessarily to the category of the *potentia Dei absoluta*.[56] With Ockham, in other words, God's freedom

---

50. See Gregory the Great, *Moralium in Iob*, 18, 54:90. On the origins of the notion of divine energies, see J.-C. Larchet, *La théologie des énergies divines: des origines à saint Jean Damascène* (Paris: Cerf, 2010).

51. See Gregory Palamas, *Theopanes*, in J.-P. Migne, ed., *Patrologiae cursus completus, series graeca* (Paris: 1857–86) [hereafter "*PG*"], 150, 929.

52. See Philips, *L'union personelle*, 255f.

53. See Sayés, *La gracia de Cristo*, 353.

54. See, for example, Flick and Alszeghy, *Il vangelo della grazia*, 604.

55. On the thought of Ockham, see Vignaux, *Justification et prédestination*; A. Ghisalberti, *Guglielmo di Ockham* (Milan: Vita e pensiero, 1972).

56. See H. A. Oberman, "Some Notes on the Theology of Nominalism with Attention to Its Relation to

becomes purely arbitrary: thus God gives grace simply because he wishes to do so, in such a way that humans cannot fathom what it involves, how it is given, or what it is for. Like the *nomina*, which are external signs of things assigned by convention, the divine judgment by which humans are justified does not act on the human heart, does not transform human life. God, rather, declares humans just, accepted by him, but does not make them just. Justification, therefore, determines the destiny of humans from without, in such a way that there is no ontological regeneration or mutation. That is to say, the Holy Spirit acts on humans directly without created charity. The doctrine of Ockham speaks rather of the natural love of God and of the human capacity to do his will; this marks a return to an optimistic and humanistic Pelagianism.

Like Scotus, Gabriel Biel, who lived in the second half of the fifteenth century, teaches the doctrine of created grace.[57] However, he contemplates the possibility of God's leading the soul to beatitude without it, that is, exclusively on the basis of his acceptance of human works, without any reference either to the organism of grace or to the inward moral value of actions that in principle would be "meritorious."[58] At the same time, Biel teaches that man is capable of observing the divine law and of loving God above all things with his own strength. That is to say, the moral action of humans is extraneous to the justifying action of God, and vice versa.

Gregory of Rimini, a fourteenth-century Augustinian, was openly opposed to the optimistic doctrine of William of Ockham.[59] He taught, following the writings of Augustine, that human nature is deeply corrupted and that no human being can carry out a good action, even in the profane sphere, without the help of divine grace.[60] He understands original sin in the strong sense of the term (Augustine's *massa damnata*) and teaches the uselessness of pagan virtues, as well as dual predestination. The interesting thing is that Gregory, like Ockham, Biel, and other nominalists, teaches that the process of justification depends entirely on divine acceptance. A similar position may be found in a contemporary of Gregory's called Thomas Bradwardin. The latter, also inspired by Augustine, saw the danger of Pelagianism everywhere.[61] He tends, however, toward theological determinism and teaches a radical version of the

---

the Renaissance," *Harvard Theological Review* 53 (1960): 47–76; A. D. Muralt, "La toute-puissance divine, le possible et la non-contradiction," *Revue philosophique de Louvain* 84 (1986): 345–61; L. A. Kennedy, "The Fifteenth Century and Divine Absolute Power," *Vivarium* 27, no. 2 (1989): 125–52.

57. The works of Biel on justification are to be found in *Quaestiones de justificatione*, edited by C. Feckes (Munster: Aschendorff, 1929). On his doctrine, see principally C. Feckes, *Die Rechtfertigungslehre des Gabriel Biel und ihre Stellung innerhalb der nominalistischen Schule* (Munster: Aschendorff, 1925); H. A. Oberman, *The Harvest of Medieval Theology: Gabriel Biel and Late Medieval Nominalism* (Cambridge, Mass.: Harvard University Press, 1963); H. J. McSorley, "Was Gabriel Biel a Semipelagian?," *Wahrheit und Verkündigung (Festschrift M. Schmaus)*, edited by L. Scheffczyk (Munich: F. Schöningh, 1967), 2:1109–20; R. Schwarz, "Probleme in der spätmittelalterlichen Rechtfertigungslehre als Anstoss zur Reformation," *Münchener theologische Zeitschrift* 50 (1999): 25–42.

58. See G. Biel, *Collect* I., d. 17, q. 1, a. 2, concl. 1, 3.

59. See Vignaux, *Justification et prédestination*; L. Grane, "Gregor von Rimini und Luthers Leipziger Disputation," *Scottish Journal of Theology* 21 (1968): 29–49; B. McGinn, "Das auxilium speciale Dei in der Gnadenlehre Gregors von Rimini," in *Werk und Wirkung bis zur Reformation*, edited by H. A. Oberman (Leiden: De Gruyter, 1981), 195–240; M. Santos-Noya, *Die Sünden- und Gnadenlehre des Gregor von Rimini* (Frankfurt: P. Lang, 1990).

60. Gregory of Rimini, *II Sent.*, d. 26, q. 1, a. 1.

61. Thomas Bradwardin, *De causa Dei contra Pelagium et de virtute causarum ad suos Mertonenses*.

doctrine of predestination. It is interesting to note that an extrinsic view of justification is compatible both with an optimistic anthropology (such as Ockham's) and with a pessimistic one (such as Gregory's).

These "extrinsic" explanations of divine grace, based on the doctrine of divine *acceptatio*, did not, at least ostensibly, deny other central and arguably more tangible theological questions: Christian ethics, the role of the Church and the sacraments, priesthood, the papacy, and so on. With John Wycliff, a thirteenth-century English religious reformer, things began to change on this front also. Wycliff considered himself not a theologian but a practical reformer. He wanted to go beyond a rationalistic, Aristotelian theological reflection and attempted to base his position exclusively on the pure word of God in scripture (interpreting it on the basis of the text itself).[62] Not only did he accept the doctrine of double predestination but he also insisted that it is made manifest in a public and tangible way. Augustine took it that in the Church all Christians, both good and bad, those predestined to glory and those not, are mixed together until the time of judgment. Wycliff, however, anticipates the visible distinction between saints and sinners to the present moment.[63] For him the Church is identified with the community of those who are predestined to salvation, a community that at present is visible to some degree. Wycliff accepts the existence of a hierarchy and of the sacraments but holds that the predestined are the only ones who are capable of administrating the sacraments validly. An unworthy pope, bishop, or priest does not belong to the Church, does not validly administer the sacraments. This position, a kind of ecclesiological Pelagianism, had been rejected a millennium earlier by Augustine during the Donatist controversy. Though Wycliff's teaching attempted to bring about a much-needed reform in Church life, it contained significant anarchic potentialities. The latter would be detected frequently in later years, especially during the time of the Protestant Reformation. Wycliff's position was taken up and developed in particular by the early fifteenth-century Bohemian reformer Jan Hus, who was condemned to death for his errors.[64]

Renaissance Humanism

The Renaissance period (the fourteenth through sixteenth centuries) was a period of deep renewal in the humanities, art, literature, and religious life.[65] The context was certainly Christian, although classical cultural models were very much present. Economic, social, scientific, and cultural life consolidated within a new anthropological framework marked by the notion of human autonomy. Rational and scientific critique, also in relation to Biblical exegesis, became more and more important. It may be said that the all-pervading religious spirit of the epoch was interiorized, universalized, and to some degree separated from its Christian roots, causing thinkers to pay more attention to the content of ethics than to the dynamics of grace and sin. The

62. See M. Hurley, *Scriptura Sola: Wycliff and His Critics* (New York: Fordham University Press, 1960).

63. See J. Wycliff, *De Ecclesia*, ed. J. Loserth (London: Trubner, for the Wyclif Society, 1886).

64. See P. De Vooght, *L'hérésie de Jean Huss*, 2nd ed. (Leuven: Publications universitaires de Louvain; Bureaux de la RHE, 1975).

65. See W. K. Ferguson, *The Renaissance in Historical Thought: Five Centuries of Interpretation* (Cambridge, Mass.: Houghton Mifflin, 1948); A. Prandi, ed., *Interpretazioni del Rinascimento* (Bologna: Il Mulino, 1971).

free human person took on a ever more absolute identity. What Charles Taylor calls the "buffered identity" of humans is consolidated: individual personhood is lived in a more and more conscious way.[66]

One of the principal protagonists of this period was Erasmus of Rotterdam, who lived at the beginning of the sixteenth century.[67] Erasmus attempted to develop a more ample and universal religious Christian lifestyle by applying human reason to understanding the word of God. As well as being somewhat distant from the Catholic hierarchy, he was clearly opposed to the teaching of his contemporary, Martin Luther.[68] As a result he fell into a kind of halfway position between the exaltation of human dignity and service to God, between reason and revelation. A kind of "eclipse of worship" among Christians began to take shape, facilitating an ongoing process of secularization that has extended to our day.[69]

Late Medieval Mysticism

The third approach typical of the late Middle Ages may be seen in a growth in mysticism, starting with the twelfth-century doctrines of Hugh and Richard of St. Victor, William of St. Thierry, and others.[70] Mysticism is distinct from nominalism in two ways. On the one hand, it is spiritual and practical rather than philosophical and theological. On the other hand, whereas nominalism distinguishes the divine from the human, in that way opening the way to laicism and secularization, mysticism tends toward their fusion. Where mysticism unites the divine and human ambits to the point of confusing them, nominalism separates them, making them almost irreconcilable.[71] Besides, the growth of mysticism marks a decisive return to the classical category of divinization.

The mystical doctrine characteristic of the Middle Ages is often called the *devotio moderna*.[72] The novelty with respect to the Patristic age is to be found in the fact that the experience of union with the divine is in principle at the disposal, as it were, of any Christian. The universal call to Christian life begins, in fact, to become a common doctrine.

One of the best-known figures of this movement is the Flemish fourteenth-century spiritual author Meister Eckhart.[73] He describes the experience of grace us-

66. See Taylor, *A Secular Age*; on this work, see O'Callaghan, "The Eclipse of Worship."

67. On Erasmus, see L. Bouyer, *Erasmus and the Humanist Experiment* (London: G. Chapman, 1959); Quilliet, *L'acharnement théologique*, 237–58.

68. In their disputation over free will, which Erasmus affirmed and Luther denied, see L. F. Mateo-Seco, *M. Lutero: Sobre la libertad esclava* (Madrid: Emesa, 1978); G. Chantraine, "Erasmo e Lutero: Libero e servo arbitrio," in *Martin Lutero*, edited by K.-V. Selge (Milan: Vita e Pensiero, 1984), 37–47.

69. See O'Callaghan, "The Eclipse of Worship," 118–20.

70. See Malevez, *La doctrine de l'image et de la connaissance mystique*.

71. See Ganoczy, *Aus seiner Fülle haben wir alle empfangen*, 183. On this period, see B. McGinn, *The Presence of God: A History of Western Christian Mysticism* (New York: Crossroad, 1991–98).

72. By way of introduction, see R. R. Post, *The Modern Devotion: Confrontation with Reformation and Humanism* (Leiden: E. J. Brill, 1968); H. A. Oberman and J. H. Van Engen, eds., *Devotio Moderna: Basic Writings* (New York: Paulist Press, 1988).

73. See H. Rahner, "Die Gottesgeburt," *Zeitschrift für katholische Theologie* 59 (1935): 333–418; Rondet, *Gratia Christi*, 236–39; Ganoczy, *Aus seiner Fülle haben wir alle empfangen*, 181f.; Farrelly, *La Trinidad divina y la deificación del hombre*. On the philosophical implications of the doctrine of Eckhart, see M.-A. Vannier, "'Creatio'

ing the terminology of Thomas Aquinas but with very graphic expressions, full of paradox, often ambiguous. He frequently insists on the nullity of humans before grace.[74] The spirit, which is the maximum expression of human life, directly experiences the reciprocal exchange between the divine persons of the Trinity. In fact, Eckhart says that the soul can experience the birth of God within its very own being (and not only the birth of divine life in humans).[75] He takes it that the Father generates the Son eternally at the same time in himself and in the human soul.[76] Human and divine nature become mystically one and the same thing. The one justified not only is a son of God by adoption but becomes a Son by nature.[77]

On account of its ambiguities the doctrine of Eckhart was proscribed by the Church a short time after his death in Pope John XXII's 1329 bull *In agro Domini*.[78] Though this document does not constitute, in a strict sense, a formal condemnation by the Pope, in it the doctrine of Eckhart is taken as a material precedent for a kind of quietist pantheism. In effect, his writings, which describe Christian experience in a very direct and existential way, give the impression of an ontological fusion between God and the soul, a doctrine that of course is incompatible with the affirmation of the transcendence of God, the dependency of creation, the realism of grace and sin.[79] However, in spite of this ambiguity, Eckhart's teaching, in describing the action of the divine persons in the soul, offered a valid and lasting contribution to theology and spirituality.

With respect to the teaching of Eckhart, the spiritual theology of Jan van Ruysbroek is more precise.[80] He speaks of the *unio essentialis* between God and the soul, which is the result of the love of God for humans and the human experience of God. The Trinity abandons its quietude in order to communicate himself with the world, in order to attract humans again to himself, in that way going back to the beginnings (the classical scheme of *exitus-reditus*). For those who experience God, grace is a kind of pulsation, like the majestic flux and reflux of the ocean.

Other authors who belong to this movement include John Tauler and John Gerson.[81] Tauler takes up the idea of Eckhart according to which God reveals to humans their nullity through grace, as well as by exposing them to temptation in order to make them more receptive to the creator. Gerson, who was a follower of Bonaventure, is probably the author of the famous work of medieval spirituality, the *Imitation of Christ*. These different movements lead us now to a central moment in the history of the doctrine of grace, centered on Martin Luther and the Council of Trent.

---

et 'formatio' chez Eckhart," *Revue thomiste* 94, no. 1 (1994): 100–109; C. Cavicchioli, "Metafisica e mistica in Meister Eckhart," *Sapienza* 50 (1997): 407–44.

74. Meister Eckhart, *Sermons*, edited by M. de Gandillac (Paris: Aubier-Montaigne, 1942), 135f., 174.

75. Ibid., 106–12.   76. Ibid., 149.

77. Ibid., 87.   78. *DH* 950–80.

79. See Meister Eckhart, *Sermons*, 100f.

80. See P. Henry, "La mystique trinitaire du Bienheureux Jean Ruusbroec," *Recherches de science religieuse* 40 (1951): 335–68, 41 (1953) 51–75; P. Verdeyen, *Introduzione a Ruysbroeck* (Florence: Nardini, 1991).

81. See A. V. Müller, *Luther und Tauler auf ihren theologischen Zusammenhang neu untersucht* (Bern: Wyss, 1918); S. E. Ozment, *Homo spiritualis: A Comparative Study of the Anthropology of Johannes Tauler, Jean Gerson and Martin Luther (1509–16) in the Context of Their Theological Thought* (Leiden: E. J. Brill, 1969).

10 GRACE AND JUSTIFICATION IN LUTHER AND THE COUNCIL OF TRENT

Iustitia est fides Christi. MARTIN LUTHER[1]

Justification is a transition from the state in which man is born a son of the first Adam, to the state of grace and adoption as sons of God. COUNCIL OF TRENT[2]

The different ways of understanding grace during the medieval period prepare the way decisively for the radical change in Western Christianity that took place with the Protestant Reformation and the Council of Trent, the fruit of which was the Catholic Counter-Reformation. Let us consider first the doctrine of grace in the most important theologian of the Reformation, Martin Luther, and then in the Council of Trent.

Antecedents to Luther's Doctrine

Many currents of thought and spirituality prepared the way for Luther's teaching on grace and anthropology.[3] In the first place, *nominalism*. This philosophical vision, briefly explained in the last chapter, was very much present during the time of Luther's formation at Erfurt, especially through the teaching of Gabriel Biel.[4] As we saw, nominalism emphasizes especially (1) the extrinsic character of justification, fruit of divine "acceptance," with an ample application of the distinction between the *potentia Dei absoluta* (God who acts in an unbounded way) and *potentia Dei ordinata* (God who acts in accordance with his work of creation and redemption), and (2) a marked optimism with respect to the value of good works before God (in real terms, it amounted

1. M. Luther, *Die Vorlesung über den Römerbrief* (WA 56:255).
2. Council of Trent, DH 1524.
3. On the doctrine of Luther, see O'Callaghan, *Fides Christi*, 19–40, with an ample bibliography. For a summary of the issue, see B. Sesboüé, *Sauvés par la grâce: Les débats sur la justification du XVIe siècle à nos jours* (Paris: Facultés jésuites de Paris, 2009).
4. See Schwarz, "Probleme in der spätmittelalterlichen Rechtfertigungslehre."

to a kind of semi-Pelagianism). Luther, who at a young age, as a "scrupulous monk," strove diligently to carry out as many good works as possible in order to assure his own salvation, later reacted against this approach.

Then there was *mysticism*. Medieval mystical movements deeply influenced the thought and attitude of Luther, especially through Tauler and Gerson.[5] This may be seen in his writings (1) as a pessimistic anthropology in which humans are considered as being corrupted by and submerged in the power of sin and (2) in his teaching on the direct relationship between the soul and God in Christ, which in turn undoes the role of created mediations in the communication of God's gifts (the Church, sacraments, the law, etc.; a topic we shall return to at the end of chapter 16).

And finally, Luther was influenced by the *political situation*. The dissemination of his teachings was due in no small part to the volatile political situation of the period, especially in the context of the tense relationship between Rome and the mid-European states.

Luther's Approach

Luther's theological reflection considers the nature and action of God as they are perceived by the sinner. The starting point, the subject of theology, is the sinful human being. "Sola experientia fit theologum," he said; only experience makes the theologian.[6] The subject of theology, he says, "is God who justifies and saves" (that is, God in his saving action) and "humans who are guilty and lost."[7] Luther wishes to avoid what he calls a *theologia gloriae*, inspired by Aristotle, that is, a theology of rational transparency, of unassailable conclusions, of glory and clarity. He prefers to speak, rather, of the *theologia crucis*, that is, a theology that develops on the basis of a God who died on the cross for the sins of humanity, a theology that must include the complex dialectic of human sin and divine mercy.[8] This way of doing theology is based on humans' experience of saving grace and must take into account that humans before God are truly *sinners* (the justified, after all, are "simul iustus et peccator," Luther says, at the same time both just and sinner).[9]

---

5. See A. W. Hunzinger, "Luther und die deutsche Mystik," *Neue kirchliche Zeitschrift* 19 (1908): 972–80; Ozment, *Homo spiritualis*; K.-H. zur Mühlen, *Nos extra nos: Luthers Theologie zwischen Mystik und Scholastik* (Tubingen: J. C. B. Mohr, 1972). See chapter 9, notes 70ff. and corresponding text.

6. M. Luther, *WA Tischreden* 1:16.

7. M. Luther, *Enarratio in Ps. 51*.

8. See M. Lienhard, "Christologie et humilité dans la 'Theologia Crucis' du Commentaire de l'Epître aux Romains de Luther," *Revue d'histoire et de philosophie religieuses* 42 (1962): 304–15; W. von Löwenich, *Luther's Theology of the Cross* (Minneapolis, Minn.: Augusta, 1976); T. Beer, "La 'Theologia Crucis' de Lutero," *Scripta Theologica* 16 (1984): 747–80; A. E. McGrath, *What Was God Doing on the Cross?* (Grand Rapids, Mich.: Zondervan, 1992); H. Blaumeiser, *Martin Luthers Kreuzestheologie: Schlüssel zu seiner Deutung von Mensch und Wirklichkeit* (Paderborn: Bonifatius, 1995). On expressions of the *theologia crucis* posterior to Luther, see A. Toniolo, *La theologia crucis nel contesto della modernità: Il rapporto tra croce e modernità nel pensiero di E. Jüngel, H. U. von Balthasar e G.W.F. Hegel* (Milan: Glossa, 1995).

9. On this expression, see R. Hermann, *Luthers These "Gerecht und Sünder zugleich"* (Gutersloh: G. Mohn, 1960; originally published in 1930); R. Kösters, "Luthers These 'Gerecht und Sünder zugleich,'" *Catholica* 33 (1964): 48–77; J. Wicks, "Living and Praying as 'Simul Iustus et Peccator,'" *Gregorianum* 70 (1989): 521–48; G. Iammarrone, *Il dialogo sulla giustificazione: La formula "simul iustus et peccator" in Lutero, nel Concilio di Trento e nel confronto ecumenico attuale* (Padua: Messaggero, 2002).

Luther's Doctrine of Grace

Three principal stages may be detected in Luther's understanding of divine grace and justification, which refer respectively to God's action, to the human reception of justice, and to sanctification and good works.

God's Justification of Humans in Christ Jesus

The spirituality of good works lived by Luther before his conversion (which took place during what he calls his "Tower experience") may be summed up in the following medieval axiom: *Facienti quod est in se, Deus non denegat gratiam* ("God does not deny his grace to those who do all they possibly can").[10] According to this formula, it would seem that good works carried out by humans in some way attract the grace of God a posteriori, that God responds to human efforts. The change occasioned by Luther after his conversion involves what he saw as a radical reinterpretation of the notion of *iustitia Dei*, "the justice of God." In his early writings Luther considered divine justice as an attribute of divine nature (*iustitia Dei* in the subjective genitive) through which God judges the moral rectitude of human actions, rewarding or chastising humans: in other words, God is considered to be just because he recognizes human works as intrinsically "good" or "evil" and gives humans the corresponding recompense. This is a typically semi-Pelagian view. Later on, Luther came to understand *iustitia Dei* (in the objective genitive) as a divine action by which God justifies the sinner. This became his definitive position. In 1545 he wrote:

I greatly longed to understand Paul's Epistle to the Romans and nothing stood in the way but that one expression, "the justice of God" [Rom 1:17], because I took it to mean that justice whereby God is just and deals justly in punishing the unjust. My situation was that, although an impeccable monk, I stood before God as a sinner troubled in conscience, and I had no confidence that my merit would please him. Therefore I did not love a just and angry God, but rather hated and murmured against him. Yet I clung to the dear Paul and had a great yearning to know what he meant. . . . Night and day I pondered until I saw the connection between the justice of God and the statement that "the just shall live by faith" [Rom 1:17]. Then I grasped that *the justice of God is that righteousness by which though grace and sheer mercy God justifies us through faith*. Thereupon I felt myself to be reborn and to have gone through open doors into paradise. The whole of scripture took on a new meaning, and whereas beforehand the "justice of God" had filled me with hate, now it became for me inexpressibly sweet in greater love. The passage of Paul became a gate to heaven.[11]

In brief, according to Luther, divine justice cannot be considered as an attribute of divine nature with which God evaluates the moral stature of human actions, rewarding them a posteriori in a way that corresponds to their nature. Rather gratuitous divine action is what actively justifies the sinner. God makes the sinner just; he does the very thing the sinner is unable to do. The nature of God is that of acting, of giving, Luther would say, not that of being, of receiving.

---

10. See J. Rivière, "Quelques antécédents patristiques de la formule: 'Facienti quod est in se,'" *Revue des sciences religieuses* 7 (1927): 93–97; H. A. Oberman, "'Facientibus quod est in se est Deus non denegat gratiam': Robert Holcot O.P. and the Beginnings of Luther's Theology," *Harvard Theological Review* 55 (1962): 317–41.

11. M. Luther, *Praef. ad opera latina* (WA 54:185f.); emphasis added.

According to Luther, this divine justifying action is made present, tangibly and humanly, for us in Jesus Christ, especially on the cross. He defines Christ in a fully soteriological way, as "Deus pro me" (God for me).[12] Thus the life of the Christian consists essentially in a wonderful exchange (*admirabile commercium*) between Christ and the sinner: God sees his own Son in the justified believer: "Christus apparuit vultui Dei pro nobis" (Christ appears before God in our favor).[13]

The Human Reception of Justification

When Luther says that "faith alone" justifies humans, he really intends to say that only God justifies, because faith is the result, not the cause (even partially), of the justifying action of God in humans. Faith, in other words, is not a human work, not a pre-existing structure present in humans with which they accept God's gift. Rather it is the work of God in them and acts "in nobis et sine nobis" (in us and without us).[14] And because this takes place in Christ and through him, Christian justice, according to Luther, is necessarily a "fides Christi" (faith in Christ),[15] that is, a Christologically qualified faith. Christ becomes ours in taking our place before the Father.

Sanctification and Good Works

Sanctification and good works, in real terms, for Luther, are the fruit of the work of Christ in the believer. Christ becomes the new "person" of the new man. "Qui credit in Christum, evacuatur a se ipso," says Luther, "Whoever believes in Christ empties himself of himself,"[16] because Christ takes the believer's place before the Father. In fact, humans in themselves are sinners, and their works are wicked; but when Christ lives and acts within them, they carry out the works of Christ. This is why humans should be considered as *simul iustus et peccator*, "at the same time just and a sinner." The good works of Christians are the necessary fruit of the justifying power that acts in them, and they should be abundant.[17] Still, nobody should boast of their own works, Luther adds, but only in the Lord.

Interpretations of Luther's Teaching

The historical interpretation of the vast and complex theological corpus of Luther has been anything but univocal.[18] When he was still alive, his paradoxical, volcanic, uplifting, intuitive, and controversial way of speaking and writing occasioned an ample variety of theological reactions and interpretations that were more or less influential. There never was a single, unambiguous "Lutheran" theology. Three ways of understanding the father of the Reformation emerged.

First we may consider the doctrine of the *Schwärmer* (enthusiasts), such as Johannes Agricola, who died some twenty years after Luther. This popular Christian

---

12. M. Luther, *In ep. S. Pauli ad Galatas Comm.* (WA 40.1:298).
13. M. Lutero, *Die Scholien über den Römerbrief* (WA 57:215).
14. M. Luther, *De captivitate Babylonica* (WA 6:530).
15. M. Luther, *Die Vorlesung über den Römerbrief* (WA 56:255, 298, 482).
16. M. Luther, *In ep. S. Pauli ad Galatas Comm.* (WA 2:564).
17. See ibid., (WA 40.1:51).   18. See O'Callaghan, *Fides Christi*, 41–69.

movement saw in the doctrine of Luther a message of liberation, joy, and peace for afflicted and oppressed Christians. The *Schwärmer* considered themselves as "antinomian" (adversaries of the law) and held that good works were of no value whatever. Nor was the official teaching of the Church of any worth. It should be noted that Luther, though aware that many of his teachings were open to interpretations of this kind, was clearly opposed to the *Schwärmer*, insisting on the need for good works as a manifestation of faith in Jesus Christ. The absence of abundant good works, he said, is a sign of a lack of faith.[19] The justification of the sinner produces good works necessarily. As regards the Church and need for the sacraments, Luther took a firm position against the *Schwärmer* with respect to the sufficiency of the *verbum internum* (the word of God in the heart of man). He insisted that justification is the work of God in us (though it takes place *extra nos*), which requires a *verbum externum*, that is, the word of God publicly preached by the Church and personally received by humans.[20] As a result, therefore, for Luther, the Church, which he calls *creatura Verbi* (creature of the Word), with the sacraments and the ministry of preaching, is necessary in order for humans to be justified. Luther's theology was by no means antiecclesial.[21]

Second, several followers of Luther taught a systematically extrinsic view of justification, in particular his close collaborator Philip Melanchthon. This position was taken up in the common Lutheran confession, the so-called *Confessio Augustana*, in 1530. The central element of the process of justification, Melanchthon and the *Confessio* teach, is the declaration of justification, that is, extrinsic or "forensic" (legal) justification, the result of divine "acceptance." This idea has remained central in classical Lutheran thought (it is found, for example, in the 1577 Lutheran *Formula Concordiae*), and it attempts to express both the sinfulness of humans (who cannot *become* holy but can only be declared such) and the nominalist doctrine of justification as an *acceptatio divina*. Still, we should keep in mind that this teaching is Luther's only in part, for he based his understanding on the perpetual and profound exchange between Christ and the sinner (the *admirabile commercium*) that takes place through the word and the sacrament.

Third and finally, we have the position of a contemporary of Luther's by the name of Andreas Osiander, who was opposed to the doctrine of extrinsic justification and taught, on the basis of many texts of Luther, that Christ truly lives in the believer.[22] This is an aspect of Luther's thought neglected by Melanchthon. It is a kind of mystical Lutheranism (later it occasioned the development of what came to be known as "Pietism") and is not easy to explain theologically. In fact, it was sharply criticized by other Lutherans, and Calvin described it as a "crassa mixtura Christi cum fidelibus" (a coarse mixing up of Christ with the faithful).[23]

---

19. See M. Luther, *In ep. S. Pauli ad Galatas Comm.* (WA 40.1:266).

20. See M. Luther, *Resolutiones Lutherianae super propositionibus suis Lipsiae disputis* (WA 2:430).

21. See B. Gherardini, *Creatura verbi: La chiesa nella teologia di Martin Lutero* (Rome: Vivere, 1994); on Lutheran ecclesiology, see the 1993 document of the Lutheran-Catholic dialogue, Lutheran-Roman Catholic Joint Commission, *Church and Justification*, and the extensive commentary: P. O'Callaghan, "The Mediation of Justification and the Justification of Mediation: Report of the Lutheran/Catholic Dialogue: 'Church and Justification: Understanding the Church in the Light of the Doctrine of Justification' (1993)," *Annales Theologici* 10 (1996): 147–211.

22. See A. Osiander, *Von dem einigen Mittler,* E iib.

23. J. Calvin, *Institutiones christianae* III, 11, 10.

The different interpretations of the father of the Protestant Reformation spread so widely during his lifetime and after his death that in the year 1577 Lutherans felt the need to prepare a common profession of faith, the *Formula Concordiae*, which rejected both the antinomian position of the *Schwärmer* and the synergistic one of Osiander and others, affirming the extrinsic or forensic understanding of justification as the hallmark of authentic Lutheranism from that moment onward.

Other Aspects of the Protestant Understanding of Grace

Protestant authors without exception place particular emphasis on grace and its total gratuity. John Calvin taught that salvation is a free gift of God, yet he held more consistently than Luther to the reality of the sanctification of humans through God's grace.[24] At the same time, Calvinism on the whole gave less weight to the role of the Church, and especially that of the sacraments, in the communication of grace. On the other hand, the doctrine of the Zurich reformer Ulrich Zwingli places considerable weight on the value of good works.

Justification at the Council of Trent

Trent's Sixth Session

The ecumenical Council of Trent (1545–63) was convoked to confute the doctrinal errors that arose in the first part of the sixteenth century, especially among Lutherans, and to promote an overdue reform in the Church at a wider level. After several introductory sessions and a brief explanation (in the fifth session) of original sin, which is the point of departure for justification, the sixth session was inaugurated in 1547 (just a year after the death of Luther) and promulgated the decree on justification.[25] It may be considered as a small but complete and carefully crafted treatise on

24. See H. P. Santmire, "Justification in Calvin's 1540 Romans Commentary," *Church History* 33 (1963): 294–313; G. Bavaud, "La doctrine de la justification d'après Calvin et le Concile de Trent," *Verbum Caro* 22 (1968): 83–92; A. E. McGrath, "John Calvin and Late Medieval Thought: A Study in Late Medieval Influences upon Calvin's Theological Thought," *Archiv für Reformationsgeschichte* 77 (1986): 58–78; M. E. Brinkman, "Justification as Paradigm of Salvation in the Calvinistic Tradition," in *For Us and for Our Salvation: Seven Perspectives on Christian Soteriology*, edited by R. Lanooy (Leiden: Interuniversity Institute for Missiology and Ecumenical Research, 1994), 81–106; W. M. Thompson, "Viewing Justification through Calvin's Eyes," *Theological Studies* 57 (1996): 447–66. On the Calvinist approach to justification, see T. F. Torrance, "Justification: Its Radical Nature and Place in Reformed Doctrine and Life," *Scottish Journal of Theology* 13 (1960): 225–46.

25. On Trent's doctrine of justification, see F. Cavallera, "La session VI du concile de Trente," *Bulletin de littérature ecclésiastique* 44 (1943): 229–38; 45 (1944): 220–31; 46 (1945): 54–56; 47 (1946): 103–12; Cavallera, "Le Décret du concile de Trente sur la justification," *Bulletin de littérature ecclésiastique* 49 (1948): 21–31; 51 (1950): 65–76, 146–68; Cavallera, "La Session VI du concile de Trente: Foi et justification," *Bulletin de littérature ecclésiastique* 53 (1952): 99–108; A. Walz, "La giustificazione tridentina: Nota sul dibattito e sul decreto conciliare," *Angelicum* 28 (1951): 97–138; W. Joest, "Die tridentinische Rechtfertigungslehre," *Kerygma und Dogma* 9 (1963): 41–69; H. Jedin, "Le Concile de Trente fut-il un obstacle a la réunion des chrétiens?," *Union et désunion des chrétiens* (Paris: Desclée, 1963), 79–94; H. A. Oberman, "Das tridentinische Rechtfertigungsdekret im Lichte spätmittelalterlicher Theologie," *Zeitschrift für Theologie und Kirche* 61 (1964): 251–82; G. Philips, "La justification luthérienne et la Concile de Trente," *Ephemerides theologicae lovanienses* 47 (1971): 340–58; H. Jedin, *Geschichte des Konzils von Trient*, 2nd ed. (Freiburg: Herder, 1951), vol. 2; C. F. Allison, "The Pastoral and Political Implications of Trent on Justification," *One in Christ* 24 (1988): 112–27; F. Buzzi, *Il Concilio di Trento, 1545–1563:*

grace, very respectful of the Protestant position, followed by a series of canons that exclude certain doctrines considered incompatible with Catholic faith. With respect to Lutheran teaching, the fifth session had already insisted on the critical distinction to be observed between sin and concupiscence.[26]

At the sixth session three principal theological schools were present.[27] First was the Scotist school, which taught that faith and repentance constitute a preparation for justification (the need for grace to believe and repent is not denied, of course, but emphasis is placed on the *experience of grace* and on the realism of human response to it). Second was the Thomistic school, which retained the belief that faith and repentance are *effects of grace* in the strict and ontological sense of the word. And finally, the Augustinian school was represented principally by the Augustinian friar Jerome Seripando. In real terms, however, the doctrine of Augustine was the common patrimony of all the Council fathers present at Trent, as of Luther himself. It is fair to say that the Council fathers at Trent took Luther's theology seriously, reflecting in this Pope Paul II's efforts to find common ground with the Protestants, especially through the good offices of Cardinal Gaspar Contarini.[28]

The decree *De justificatione*, centered on the justification of adults (the baptism of infants was not a contentious issue for Lutherans and Catholics, though it was rejected by Anabaptists), is made up of five sections in sixteen chapters,[29] besides thirty-three canons.[30] It is usually called "first justification," justification for the first time, in order to distinguish it from second or later justification. The first three chapters of *De justificatione* situate the doctrine on justification and describe its beginning and preparation. The next six chapters (4–9) constitute the central part of the decree and deal with different issues regarding "first justification" (discussed in the following section). The next four chapters (10–13) consider the development and preservation of the life of grace: they teach that grace can increase, that its reception does not excuse anybody from fulfilling God's law (that is to say, the notion of *sola fides* cannot be interpreted in an antinomian way), and that believers cannot be certain of their own predestination and effective justification in that they will always need God's grace in order to persevere to the end. Two chapters (14–15) consider the question of the loss and recuperation of justifying grace; they teach that the state of the one justified can be lost but that sinners "rursus iustificari possunt" (can be justified anew)[31] through the sacrament of reconciliation. The last chapter (16) concludes the decree, insisting on the obligation incumbent on Christians to carry out good works, as well as dealing

---

Breve introduzione ad alcuni temi teologici principali (Milan: Glossa, 1995), 71–119; O'Callaghan, *Fides Christi*, 70–94, with bibliography; G. Colzani, "La nozione di 'giustificazione': Il senso del suo impiego nei dibattiti tridentini, la verifica di un modello di comprensione," in *La giustificazione (Associazione Teologica Italiana)*, edited by G. Ancona (Padua: Messaggero, 1997), 65–111; E. Benavent Vidal, "Actualidad de la doctrina de la justificación," *Anales Valentinos* 45 (1997): 1–17.

26. See *DH* 1515.

27. See A. Stakemeier, "Die theologischen Schulen auf dem Trienter Konzil während der Rechtfertigungsverhandlung," *Theologisches Quartalschrift* 117 (1936): 188–207, 322–50, 446–504.

28. See F. Hünermann, "Die Rechtfertigungslehre des Kard. Kaspar Contarini," *Theologische Quartalschrift* 102 (1921): 1–22.

29. *DH* 1520–50.   30. Ibid., 1551–83.

31. Ibid., 1542.

with the question of merit. According to Trent, the *ratio meriti*, the reason believers can merit God's grace, is directly Christological insofar as Christians can merit grace only in virtue of their belonging to the body of Christ.

First Justification

Trent describes justification as a process that moves from the state of sin to that of grace: "a passage from the state in which man is born a son of the first Adam, to the state of grace and adoption as sons of God."[32] In order to prepare themselves for justification, humans stand in absolute need of the grace of God, even though the call of grace makes itself deeply felt in the depths of their being (as described in the session's fifth chapter). In the sixth chapter the four stages of justification are presented: the reception of faith, repentance of sin through a solid trust in the mercy of God, the movement of grace bringing one to love God and hate sin, and the determination to receive baptism and live a Christian life.[33] At each stage of this process God takes the initiative, although humans are completely involved. All shades of Pelagianism and semi-Pelagianism are excluded.

The central part of this section is chapter 7, which describes the five "causes" of justification.[34] They are as follows. First is the final cause, which is "the glory of God and of Christ, and life everlasting." Second is the efficient cause, that is, "the merciful God who gratuitously washes and sanctifies, sealing and anointing with the Holy Spirit." Then, third, "the meritorious cause is the beloved only-begotten Son of God, our Lord Jesus Christ who . . . merited for us justification by his most holy passion on the wood of the Cross and made satisfaction for us to God the Father." There was no great divergence between Lutherans and Catholics with respect to these three causes of justification. However, as regards the other two, as we shall now see, there were more substantial differences.

In effect, the fourth cause of justification, the instrumental cause, is, according to Trent, the sacrament of baptism, "which is the sacrament of faith, without which no one has ever been justified." This declaration on the need for baptism reflects the ecclesial side of justification: Christians are baptized in and through the Church, which administers the sacraments. This refers, of course, to what the Council calls baptism *re aut voto*, that is, received either externally or by desire.[35] Lutherans, however, prefer to speak of *faith* as the instrument of justification. It should be noted that the decree adds that baptism is "the sacrament of faith" and that without it (that is, faith, for the original text says *sine qua* and *fides* is feminine) nobody can be saved. Although some affirmations of Luther suggest that faith is separable from the sacrament, and therefore from the Church, Trent teaches that in order to be saved faith must be directly linked with the sacraments, and therefore to the Church. The Council teaches also that faith is accompanied by the other theological virtues, hope and charity, in that faith should act through charity,[36] another issue that was called into question by Luther on account of a somewhat individualistic view of grace and of the need to disassociate faith from good works.

---

32. Ibid., 1524.   33. Ibid., 1526.
34. Ibid., 1529.   35. Ibid., 1524.
36. Ibid., 1530f.

The seventh chapter of the session speaks of the fifth cause, the formal cause of justification, "the single formal cause," as the text specifies. It is "the justice of God, not that by which he himself is just, but that by which he makes us just." The text insists, then, on the real and intrinsic character of the gift of justifying grace, distancing itself from the "extrinsic" view typical of classical Lutheranism. It speaks of "the justice which we have as a gift from him and by which we are spiritually renewed. Thus, not only are we considered just, but we are truly called just and we are just, each one receiving within himself his own justice, according to the measure which the Holy Spirit apportions to each one individually as he wills, and according to each one's personal disposition and cooperation."[37] Thus the decree teaches the possibility of and need to correspond to God's grace and accept it, but especially teaches that justification is not a mere declaration of justice, because in it the believer is really *made* just.

Tridentine doctrine on the formal nature of received justice ("the justice of God, not that by which he himself is just, but that by which he makes us just") is taken directly from Augustine[38] and shows how humans become just in virtue of the grace of God and not of their own works. The Augustinian Seripando, who was present at the Council, took it that humans, even when sanctified by grace, still remain immersed in sin.[39] For this reason he taught that, besides regeneration by grace, they need an extrinsic supplement of justice from God in order to be truly just; this came to be known as the "doctrine of double justice" and was unsuccessfully defended by Seripando at a disputation between Lutherans and Catholics that took place some years before Trent at Regensburg (in 1541).[40] For this reason, Trent insisted on the formula "a single formal cause" of justification: all God does for humans is to declare them just, forgive their sins, and truly regenerate their hearts, thus making them just.[41] The position of Seripando is therefore excluded. For this reason Trent rejects the position of those who maintain "that men are justified either by the imputation of Christ's justice alone, or by the remission of sins alone, excluding grace and charity which is poured into their hearts by the Holy Spirit and inheres in them, or also that the grace which justifies us is only the favor of God."[42]

Justifying grace, therefore, is a *gratia elevans*, a grace that elevates human nature, and not only *gratia sanans*, a grace that heals us from sin and its consequences. As Trent's decree on original sin says, "in renatis nihil odit Deus" (God has nothing to

37. Ibid., 1529.

38. See Augustine, *De Trinitate* XIV, 12, 15.

39. On Seripando, see D. Olivier, "Les deux sermons sur la double et la triple justice," *Öcumenica* 3 (1968): 39–69; V. Grossi, "La giustificazione secondo Girolamo Seripando nel contesto dei dibattiti tridentini," *Analecta Augustiniana* 41 (1978): 6–24; A. Marranzini, *Dibattito Lutero-Seripando su "Giustizia e libertà del cristiano,"* Pontificia Facoltà teologica dell'Italia meridionale (Brescia: Morcelliana, 1981); G. C. Cassaro, *Girolamo Seripando: La grazia e il metodo teologico* (Messina: Coop. S. Tommaso, 2010).

40. See O'Callaghan, *Fides Christi*, 53f.

41. See P. P. Pas, "La doctrine de la double justice au Concile de Trente," *Ephemerides theologicae lovanienses* 30 (1954): 5–53; Olivier, "Les deux sermons sur la double et la triple justice"; C. E. Maxcey, "Double Justice, Diego Laynez, and the Council of Trent," *Church History* 49 (1979): 269–78; J. F. McCue, "Double Justification at the Council of Trent: Piety and Theology in 16th Century Roman Catholicism," in *Piety, Politics, and Ethics,* edited by C. Lindberg (Kirksville: Sixteenth Century Journal, 1984), 39–56.

42. In c. 11, *DH* 1561.

hate in those reborn through baptism).[43] Although in the justified there remains a certain inclination to sin, called concupiscence, they are not sinners but just, children of God. If taken in an ontological, dogmatic sense, the Lutheran description of the believer as "simul iustus et peccator" (at one and the same time just and sinner) is not acceptable. In an existential and mystical sense, however, it expresses the experience of many saints.[44]

The eighth chapter of the decree on justification insists again on the absolute gratuitousness of justification: neither grace nor faith merits justification.[45] The ninth chapter then deals with the delicate theme of the certitude of being justified.[46] The popular Lutheran position gave rise to the idea that faith (a "fiducial faith") was needed for one to be sure of being justified, a faith without doubt or hesitation. Luther wished to obtain an absolute certainty of being in God's grace. The Council of Trent, however, taught that nobody is capable of having an absolute subjective certainty in this life of having been pardoned by God. Still, at an objective level believers should not doubt God's mercy, Christ's merits, nor the efficacy of the sacraments celebrated by the Church.[47] This faith, however, is not sufficient to produce certainty of being *personally* pardoned: "Whoever considers himself, his personal weakness and his lack of disposition, may fear and tremble about his own grace, since no one can know with a certitude of faith which cannot be subject to error, that he has obtained God's grace."[48] Thus a distinction is made between the certitude of faith and the certitude of personal salvation, that is, between the certitude of the Church and that of the individual.

Luther, Trent, and Modernity

Both the Protestant Reformation, initiated principally by Luther and Calvin, and the Catholic Counter-Reformation set in motion by Trent, set the scene decisively for the life of the Church and society at large in the following centuries. The key issue, which, regrettably, found expression in widespread misunderstanding, bloodshed, and secularization, was to be found in the living relationship between God's saving action, what we call grace, and human acceptance (or rejection) of that gift, that is, freedom. We shall consider some aspects of this in the coming chapter and later on (in chapter 20).

43. *DH* 1515.

44. See Wicks, *Living and Praying as "Simul Iustus et Peccator."* See the end of chapter 16 below.

45. *DH* 1532.

46. Ibid. 1533.

47. See H. Huthmacher, "La certitude de la grâce au Concile de Trente," *Nouvelle Revue Théologique* 65 (1933): 213–26; A. Stakemeier, *Das Konzil von Trient über die Heilsgewissheit* (Heidelberg: F. H. Kerle, 1947); V. Heynck, "Zur Kontroverse über die Gnadengewißheit auf dem Konzil von Trient," *Franziskanische Studien* 37 (1955): 1–17, 161; J. Alfaro, "Certitude de l'espérance et 'certitude de la grâce,'" *Nouvelle Revue Théologique* 94 (1972): 3–42.

48. *DH* 1534.

11 THE MODERN PERIOD

Grace, Freedom, and Anthropology

God is at work in you, both to will and to work for his good pleasure. PHILIPPIANS 2:13

God forgives sin by grace and at the same time frees human beings from sin's enslaving power and imparts the gift of new life in Christ. LUTHERAN-CATHOLIC JOINT DECLARATION ON JUSTIFICATION, NO. 24

The principal theological issue of the period that immediately followed Luther and Trent involved the relationship between grace and freedom. This is an expression of the tension, already present throughout the Middle Ages, between a transcendent, omnipotent God, on the one hand, and created human beings, who, though fallen, search for their rightful, God-given autonomy, on the other. Three episodes are of particular interest during the period: the *de auxiliis* controversy; the Augustinianism of Michael Baius, a theologian who worked in the years after Trent; and the theology of the seventeenth-century bishop Cornelius O. Jansen. Although in many ways Protestant thought developed quite independently of the theology and life of the Catholic Church during this period, the same basic questions were being asked between Calvinists and Arminians on the Protestant side, and between Jansenists and Jesuits among Catholics. Before describing the episodes just mentioned, something should be said about the classical distinction between "efficacious" and "sufficient" grace. Then, at the end of the chapter, we shall undertake a brief review of different aspects of the doctrine of grace that emerged over the centuries closer to us, the ninteenth and twentieth, up until the 1999 Lutheran-Catholic Declaration on Justification.

"Efficacious" and "Sufficient" Grace

Throughout the history of the Christian doctrine of grace and salvation, a theological challenge has frequently arisen in the following terms: is it possible to establish compatibility between the gracious action of God, who with sovereign and sublime power justifies, sanctifies, and leads humans to eschatological salvation, on the one hand, and the free, intelligent action and initiative of humans, on the other? That is to say: is it possible to reconcile grace and human freedom? Following Paul and Augustine, of course, the work of salvation should be considered primarily as a work of liberation, an overcoming of the slavery of sin through God's power, which leads humans to a state of freedom, the freedom of the children of God (Rom 8:21). Still, at creation humans receive the gift of free will, which in principle allows them to accept divine gifts responsibly, or to refuse them. Should they be unable to accept or reject grace, if "free will" is just a "mere word," as Luther said, humans would have no fundamental responsibility over their own lives, and it would be meaningless to speak of sin, or reward, or merit, or moral responsibility.

In fact, many scriptural texts attest to the real possibility of humans' freely resisting God's grace. In the book of Isaiah, God asks: "What more was there to do for my vineyard, that I have not done in it? When I looked for it to yield grapes, why did it yield wild grapes?" (Is 5:4). In Acts, we read the following words of Stephen: "You stiff-necked people, uncircumcised in heart and ears, you always resist the Holy Spirit" (Acts 7:51). And that of Jesus himself: "O Jerusalem, Jerusalem, killing the prophets and stoning those who are sent to you! How often would I have gathered your children together as a hen gathers her brood under her wings, and you would not!" (Mt 23:37). In the Gospel of John, Jesus gives voice to a certain bitterness in the face of the closed hearts of those who listened to him: "If I had not come and spoken to them, they would not have sin; but now they have no excuse for their sin.... If I had not done among them the works which no one else did, they would not have sin; but now they have seen and hated both me and my Father" (Jn 15:22–24). In fact, all the drama of the life, death, and resurrection of Jesus is occasioned by humans' resistance to God's grace: "He came to his own home, and his own people received him not" (Jn 1:11).

On the basis of texts like these, we can speak of a "sufficient" grace," that grace which gives humans the necessary help to respond to God's invitation and accept his gifts. This is a grace, however, that does not actually oblige the will but rather guides and inspires it; besides, it leaves open the possibility of acceptance or refusal, in such a way that the subject is responsible for meritorious action or for committing sin. The notion of "sufficient grace" gives weight and space to free human response to God's gifts.

At the same time, some texts from scripture speak clearly of the grace of God that cannot be resisted, what is often called "efficacious grace," or, by Calvinists, "irresistible grace."[1] For example, in the book of Ezekiel we read: "I will put my spirit within you, and cause you to walk in my statutes and be careful to observe my ordinances" (Ezek 36:27). Several texts of John's Gospel seem to suggest that God's power over humans is effective and infallible: "All that the Father gives me will come to me" (Jn 6:37; see Jn 6:39, 44, 65). And Paul says: "By the grace of God I am what I am, and his

---

1. The Synod of Dort (or Dordrecht), convoked in 1618–19 by the Dutch Reformed Church, defined five doctrinal elements as hallmarks of Calvinism: total depravity, unconditional election, limited atonement, irresistible grace, and perseverance of the saints.

THE MODERN PERIOD 201

grace toward me was not in vain. On the contrary, I worked harder than any of them, though it was not I, but the grace of God which is with me" (1 Cor 15:10). "God is at work in you, both to will and to work for his good pleasure" (Phil 2:13). In these texts there emerges another aspect of divine grace, that of its efficaciousness and infallibility. Theology calls "efficacious grace" the grace with which God obtains infallibly the purpose he proposes. Augustine spoke of a "gratia invicta," an invincible grace,[2] and spiritual authors speak of a habitual reluctance among humans that God himself is capable of overcoming. In this case, however, it would seem that human freedom loses out and becomes irrelevant.

In any case, two aspects of grace may be distinguished: there is a "sufficient" grace (which leaves real space for human response) and an "efficacious" or "operative" grace (which brings about necessarily in humans what God wants).[3] Priority is given to "efficacious grace" in Lutheran and Calvinist theology, as we saw, and also in the theologies of Baius and Jansen (see below). But the issue was of particular importance during a prolonged theological dispute that took place toward the end of the sixteenth century, the *de auxiliis* controversy.

The *De Auxiliis* Controversy

The Historical Stages of the Dispute

The *de auxiliis* controversy began in real terms during the time of the Counter-Reformation as the result of a public dispute that took place in Valladolid (Spain) in the year 1582 on the nature of Christ's freedom and merit.[4] The disputation proper started when some theologians, principally Jesuits, rejected the Thomistic doctrine of the *praedeterminatio physica*, or "physical predetermination," which—it was contended—grace exercises over the human will, and thus over human freedom in general. In the following year, staff at the University of Leuven in Belgium condemned a variety of propositions of the Jesuit authors, who insisted, understandably, on the real freedom of humans before grace.[5] In 1588 the Jesuit Luis de Molina published an influen-

2. Augustine, *De corr. et grat.* 12, 38. The eighteenth-century Baptist theologian John Gill puts it as follows: God's "act of drawing is an act of power, yet not of force; God in drawing the unwilling, makes willing in the day of His power: He enlightens the understanding, bends the will, gives a heart of flesh, sweetly allures by the power of His grace, and engages the soul to come to Christ, and give up itself to Him; he draws with the bands of love. Drawing, though it supposes power and influence, yet not always coaction and force: music draws the ear, love the heart, and pleasure the mind." J. Gill, *Exposition of the New Testament* (London: King's Arms, 1746), on Jn 6:44.

3. On the question of sufficient and efficacious grace, see Van der Meersch, *Grâce*, 1655–62; Flick and Alszeghy, *Il vangelo della grazia*, §§ 55–57.

4. On the *de auxiliis* controversy, see the classic works of G. Schneemann, *Controversiarum de divinae gratiae liberique arbitrii concordia* (Freiburg i.B.: Herder, 1881), and Van der Meersch, *Grâce*, 1644–77. See also Flick and Alszeghy, *Il vangelo della grazia*, §§ 59–63, with bibliography; Rondet, *Gratia Christi*; Martin-Palma, *Gnadenlehre*; L. Serenthà, "Predestinazione," in *Dizionario Teologico Interdisciplinare* (Turin: Marietti, 1977), 2:775–90, esp. 785; M. D. Torre, *Do Not Resist the Spirit's Call: Francisco Marín-Sola on Sufficient Grace* (Washington, D.C.: The Catholic University of America Press, 2013). On the beginnings of the controversy, see J. Stöhr, "En torno al primer período de la controversia 'de auxiliis,'" *Revista Española de Teología* 32 (1972): 323–54.

5. For example, L. Lessius, who taught at Leuven at the beginning of the seventeenth century. He was a disciple of F. Suárez and wrote *De gratia efficaci* (Antwerp, 1610).

tial work that became an entire program, entitled *Liberi arbitrii cum gratiae donis, divina praescientia, providentia, praedestinatione et reprobatione concordia* (The agreement of free will with the gifts of grace, divine foreknowledge, providence, predestination and condemnation). It was a commentary on Aquinas's doctrine of grace in which Molina took a position against Protestantism (especially the doctrine of predestination taught by Dutch Calvinists) and some Dominican university teachers from Salamanca, Spain, who were accused of having fallen into the Lutheran heresy. Among the Dominicans the best known author was Domingo Báñez, whose commentary on Thomas was published in 1584.

After a variety of disputes in 1594, the issue was sent to Rome. A commission of cardinals was set up by Pope Clement VIII in 1597 that nearly condemned Molina with an accusation of Pelagianism. In 1607, however, after 120 sessions in which the question was debated, Pope Paul V put an end to the dispute, excluding the accusation of heresy with respect to both sides, saying that Báñez and the Dominicans could not be accused of Calvinism or Lutheranism and that Molina was not to be considered Pelagian.[6] A critical issue was being dealt with in that both sides believed in the value of human freedom and the power of God and also in the reality and accessibility of theological truth. At the same time, the Pope, not wanting to condemn either side, confirmed the principle of the freedom of Christians in open theological questions.

The Positions of Báñez and Molina

The "Thomistic" position (represented by Báñez) emphasizes the primacy of God and his action over the human will[7] and takes up the idea of grace as a *praedeterminatio physica* in the life of the human being.[8] It should be noted that the latter expression is not to be found in the extant writings of Aquinas; in fact, it is not clear that the so-called Thomistic position is truly attributable to Aquinas. In any case, Báñez's teaching may be summed up in five points: (1) grace comes from God already sufficient or efficacious and (2) determines the orientation of the will toward a particular choice or way of acting. Thus it may be said that (3) divine concourse predetermines the free action of humans and that (4) their predestination is to be considered as *ante praevisa merita* in the sense that God predestines people before their foreseen merits and independently of their will. Finally, (5) God knows all things, also things future, and of them he has a simple, single knowledge; he also knows the future actions of humans because in God they are already infallibly decreed. In brief terms, within the process of the infusion of grace, the will of God is efficacious, determinant, and infallible even in the face of human freedom.

The position of Molina, however, insists on the realism of human freedom in the context of divine grace.[9] In this sense it is a clearly "modern" position. His teach-

---

6. *DH* 1997.

7. See W. R. O'Connor, "Molina and Báñez as Interpreters," *New Scholasticism* 21 (1947): 243–59.

8. See Y.-J. Congar, "*Praedeterminare* et *praedeterminatio* chez saint Thomas," *Revue des sciences philosophiques et théologiques* 23 (1934): 363–71.

9. See F. Stegmüller, *Geschichte des Molinismus* (Munster: Aschendorff, 1935); J. Peinado, *Evolución de las fórmulas molinistas sobre la gracia eficaz durante las controversias de auxiliis* (Granada: Universidad de Granada, 1968).

ing may also be described in five points that correspond to those of Báñez just mentioned: (1) God always and only gives humans sufficient grace, which becomes efficacious on account of the free reception of humans, because (2) the human will is not determined by a single factor, given that choice is always possible. "Human will is truly free only when, with all the different conditions, it could act in a different way," writes Molina.[10] As a result, (3) divine concourse acts in parallel with the free action of the human being, and (4) predestination must be considered as *post praevisa merita*, that is, decreed after the merits foreseen by God and in dependence on them. Furthermore, (5) in order to predestine *post praevisa merita*, God "foresees"—through what Molina calls the *scientia media* in God, a knowledge is situated somewhere in the middle between his knowledge of the possible and his knowledge of what really happens—the future reaction of humans within the particular circumstances of their lives, and gives them the graces sufficient to infallibly produce the effect he desires.[11] In fact, the theological novelty of the Molinist position lies in the doctrine of the *scientia media* in God, with which humans are truly free before God's offer of grace.

The Real Issues

Two fundamental questions arise within the *de auxiliis* controversy. The first concerns the relationship between divine grace and human freedom. The second, at a deeper level, refers to the nature of God himself, whether preeminence should be given to the divine will or to divine knowledge and wisdom.

The "Thomistic" position was the more classic one, in line with the theology of Trent's decree on justification, and reflecting the doctrine of both Luther and Augustine. Emphasis is placed especially on the all-powerful will of God, which cannot be conditioned or frustrated by creatures in any way. In effect, if anything external to God were in a position to condition his action, this would occupy God's own place, and divine transcendence would be compromised. In a strict sense, human freedom refers only to choices, but being free includes the possibility not of going against the will of God but rather of not being bound by any earthly good. As Luther held, man is free before creatures but not before God. The following texts of Aquinas may be given in support of this position: "The need and contingency of things is distinguished not from the divine will, which is a universal cause, but in respect of created causes, which the divine will has ordered in a way that is proportioned to their effects, that is, in a way that the cause of necessary effects is immutable, and that of contingent effects mutable."[12] Hence, "it is not contrary to freedom that God is the cause of the free act of the [human] will."[13] "Since no finite earthly good can oblige the will, we can say that the rational will is free."[14]

At the same time, the "Thomistic" position does not seem to give sufficient consideration to created human freedom, with the consequent personal responsibility of

10. L. de Molina, *Concordia*, q. 14, a. 13, disp. II.

11. See M. de la Taille, "Sur diverses classifications de la science moyenne," *Revue des sciences religieuses* 3 (1923): 7–23, 535.

12. Aquinas, *De malo* q. 16, a. 7, ad 15.   13. Ibid., q. 3, a. 2, ad 4.

14. Aquinas, *S.Th.* I, q. 82, a. 2, ad 2.

humans for their actions, guided by God in his infinite wisdom.[15] In effect, if human actions were predetermined—by nature or grace—the guilt for sin and evil would be attributable to God. This would go clearly against the fundamental intuition of Augustine, shared by Paul, Bernard, Bonaventure, and John Henry Newman, according to which *God moves the human will not physically, but rather by awakening love and willingness present in it*. This may be called "moral predetermination."[16] This movement that God insinuates in the soul—love—is stronger and greater than the concupiscence that leads to sin and overcomes sin while respecting human nature fully. In fact if we accept that the human will has been created by God with the precise and principal purpose of allowing man to respond to divine gifts, both natural and (especially) supernatural, the tension between grace and freedom is ever more attenuated.

It should also be said that the doctrine of Molina is not without its problems, especially in relation to the distinction within God of different kinds of knowledge.[17] In effect, Molina speaks of a *scientia media* in God, distinct both from the knowledge with which he knows all things and from the knowledge of possible future events. This distinction seems to indicate that there is within the divinity a kind of temporal scale that includes a before and an after, and this would be incompatible with the simplicity and eternity of the divine nature.[18] With Scola we can "observe that the prevalence of knowledge over will is the true discriminating factor between the two positions. Now it is not difficult to recognize that an explanation of this kind is problematic, because in God there is no real distinction between intellect and will."[19]

According to the eighteenth-century moral theologian Alphonsus Maria Liguori, it would be better to avoid terms such as *scientia media*, *praedeterminatio physica*, *reprobatio positiva*, and others of that kind, often used during the debate on grace and freedom. In the context of Christian prayer, Alphonsus, on the basis of his own spiritual and pastoral experience, is convinced that God confers efficacious grace for difficult actions and sufficient grace for ordinary actions. In any case, prayer, the petition to God that Augustine speaks of, is the great means of responding to divine grace.[20]

The Language of Grace

To conclude this presentation of the *de auxiliis* controversy, we can ask the following question: if the Church does not wish to reject either of the positions, even though they are clearly different from, even opposed to, one another, how can they

15. See the account of the critique made by B. Lonergan of Báñez's interpretation of Thomas: J. R. Brotherton, "The Integrity of Nature in the Grace-Freedom Dynamic: Lonergan's Critique of Bañezian Thomism," *Theological Studies* 75, no. 3 (2014): 537–63.

16. See Flick and Alszeghy, *Il vangelo della grazia*, § 61.

17. See R. Gaskin, "Molina on Divine Foreknowledge and the Principle of Bivalence," *Journal of the History of Philosophy* 32, no. 4 (1994): 551–71.

18. The Molinist doctrine of *scientia media* was criticized by N. Del Prado, *De gratia et libero arbitrio* (Fribourg: Ex typis consociationis sancti Pauli, 1907), and R. Garrigou-Lagrange, *God, His Existence and His Nature* (Albany, N.Y.: Preserving Christian Publications, 1993; originally published in 1914).

19. Scola, Marengo, and Prades López, *La persona umana*, 274.

20. See the work of Alphonsus, *Il gran mezzo della preghiera*, II. On this work, see J. Herrmann, *Tractatus de divina gratia secundum s. Alphonsi M. de Ligorio doctrinam et mentem* (Rome: P. Cuggiani, 1904), 399–496; J. F. Hidalgo, *Doctrina alfonsiana acerca de la acción de la gracia actual eficaz y suficiente: Estudio histórico-expositivo* (Turin: Marietti, 1954); Flick and Alszeghy, *Il vangelo della grazia*, § 58.

ultimately be understood and eventually reconciled? Perhaps it is fair to say that each position emphasizes a specific aspect of Christian life. The first, "Thomistic," position attempts to describe the ontology of grace, starting with God's action, without paying that much attention to the phenomenology of the human reaction in terms of psychological experience. The second position, that of Molina, expresses the dynamics of grace more in terms of the way humans experience it. We shall consider this ambivalence later on. The same movement is described from different angles, that of the divine giver and that of the human receiver, that of the divine creator and that of the creature.[21]

Baius's Interpretation of Augustine

The problem of the relationship between grace and freedom was considered by other influential authors in this period, especially Baius and Jansen, who were involved in different ways in the *de auxiliis* controversy. Michael Baius, a sixteenth-century university teacher in Leuven, took part in the final sessions of the Council of Trent.[22] In an attempt to establish a dialogue with Protestants, he developed a positive theology based on scripture and especially on texts of Augustine, whose writings he tended to cite somewhat out of context. It may also be noted that he neglected philosophical arguments.

Baius takes little interest in the theology of Thomas Aquinas, and thus in the question of the *gratia elevans* (that is, habitual, elevating or sanctifying grace), insisting especially on the *gratia sanans* (grace that heals the sinner). He pays attention especially to fallen humanity that stands in need of grace in order to overcome sin and live a virtuous life. In other words, he considered grace no longer as a habit, a state, but simply as a punctual action of the Spirit on the soul that keeps sin at bay.

According to Baius, "before" original sin, humans counted on the grace of *integritas*, or perfection, as something that is original or natural: "natural" in the sense that in the absence of this gift, humans would necessarily have become evil, losing all inclination toward the good. That is to say, humans have a moral need for grace, and therefore could not have been created without these gifts. For this motive, Henri de Lubac said that Baius had the tendency of "naturalizing the supernatural."[23] The loss of grace, he said, brings with it ipso facto the transmission of a corrupt nature. From this derives a strongly pessimistic view of humans without grace. In effect, according to Baius, when humans are not in a state of grace their will is corrupt and they no longer enjoy the

21. See also B. J. F. Lonergan, *Grace and Freedom: Operative Grace in the Thought of St. Thomas Aquinas* (Toronto: University of Toronto Press, 2000; originally published in 1942); J. Maritain, *Existence and the Existent: An Essay on Christian Existentialism* (Garden City, N.Y.: Doubleday, 1957), 99–112; C. Journet, *Entretiens sur la grâce* (Bruges: Desclée de Brouwer, 1961), 13–65, translated into English as *The Meaning of Grace* (New York: P. J. Kennedy, 1960).

22. See F.-X. Jansen, *Baïus et le baïanisme* (Leuven: Museum Lessianum, 1927); X.-M. Le Bachelet, "Baïus," *DTC* 2:38–111; Flick and Alszeghy, *Il vangelo della grazia*, § 13; G. Colombo, "M. Baio e il soprannaturale," *Scuola Cattolica* 93 (1965): 299–330; A. Vanneste, *Nature et grâce dans la théologie occidentale: Dialogue avec H. de Lubac* (Leuven: Leuven University Press, 1996), 185–228; Brambilla, *Antropologia teologica*, 88–95; Quilliet, *L'acharnement théologique*, 315–34.

23. H. de Lubac, *Surnaturel: Études historiques* (Paris: Aubier-Montaigne, 1946), 430. The work was never translated into English.

freedom of choice, becoming incapable of carrying out any good work. For this reason, he holds that the "virtues" of the pagan philosophers cannot be shared with believers because in real terms they are not imperfect virtues but rather camouflaged vices.

The result of Baius's way of explaining grace is that original sin is identified simply with concupiscence. Humans carry within themselves a deeply ingrained, primitive perversion, a desire and spontaneous orientation toward evil that is already sin. In particular—and this point was quite relevant in the context of the widespread missionary movement that sixteenth-century theology attempted to respond to—Baius held that all actions of the infidel are sinful. In his work *De libero arbitrio* he teaches that when they sin, pagans do so voluntarily (in the sense that they are moved to do so by an interior impulse that they are unable to resist) but not freely, because the action in question is produced inevitably.

The Sorbonne University in Paris took a position against the doctrine of Baius in 1560. Pope Pius V in the bull *Ex omnibus afflictionibus* (1567) condemned seventy-nine of his propositions. The condemnation was later on confirmed by Pope Gregory XIII (1579). Among them the following rejected positions are of particular interest:

25. "All works of infidels are sins, and the virtues of philosophers are vices."[24]

27. "Free will, without the help of God's grace, has only power for sin."[25]

38. "All love of a rational creature is either vicious cupidity, by which the world is loved, which is prohibited by John; or that praiseworthy charity by which when poured forth by the Holy Spirit in our heart, God is loved."[26]

39. "What is voluntarily done, even though it be done by necessity, is nevertheless freely done."[27]

41. "This measure of freedom, which is of necessity, is not found in the Scriptures under the name of freedom, but is merely the name for freedom from sin" (this means that humans do not have free will).[28]

55. "God would not have had the power from the beginning to create such a man as is born now."[29]

As it had already done at the Council of Trent with the decree on justification, the Church had to draw a line between two the extremes of literal Augustinianism on the one hand and open Pelagianism on the other. Later the doctrine of Baius was critiqued by Robert Bellarmine.[30]

Jansen and Jansenism

We already mentioned the title of Molina's book *Liberi arbitrii cum gratiae donis ... concordia*, which clearly taught the doctrine of human cooperation with grace and the realism of human freedom. This position provoked a decisive reaction on the part of

24. *DH* 1925f.   25. Ibid. 1927.
26. Ibid. 1938.   27. Ibid. 1939.
28. Ibid. 1941.   29. Ibid. 1955.
30. See G. Galeota, *Bellarmino contro Baio a Lovanio: Studio e testo di un inedito bellarminiano* (Rome: Herder, 1966); V. Grossi, *Baio e Bellarmino interpreti di s. Agostino nelle questioni del soprannaturale* (Rome: Studium Theologicum Augustinianum, 1968).

the bishop of Ypres in Belgium, Cornelius Jansen, who lived at the beginning of the seventeenth century. His work titled *Augustinus* was published posthumously in 1640.[31] In it he states that the doctrine of Molina is a true resurrection of the work of Pelagius.

Like Baius, Jansen took little interest in philosophy, and his reflection was centered above all on scripture and the Church Fathers, with quite a literal interpretation, often out of context, of the writings of Augustine.[32] In effect, Jansen was not a faithful disciple of his but rather a "misguided Augustinian" like Baius.[33] From 1649 onward, however, Jansenism developed considerably due to the works of several authors during the seventeenth and eighteenth centuries, such as Jean Duvergier de Hauranne, called "the curate of St. Cyran,"[34] Antoine Arnauld,[35] and Pasquier Quesnel.[36] It became very influential in countries with a strong Catholic spirituality, such as France and Belgium.

The Doctrine of Jansen

The teaching of Jansen is quite like that of Baius.[37] According to the former, humans were constituted from the beginning of their existence in a state of grace, in such a way that after original sin human nature became completely corrupt. Before the Fall, therefore, it was enough for Adam to have had "sufficient grace" to be able to avoid sin. Since the Fall, however, in order to avoid sin humans have always needed a special help, an "efficacious grace," which dominates the will in such a way that they cannot resist it. Thus Christian salvation and liberation has nothing whatever to do with human free will but refers to what humans achieve by exercising no resistance to grace. Jansen spoke in effect of a "voluntary necessity": the sinner gives in voluntarily to sin and can be freed only by means of efficacious grace, that is, through the irresistible attraction of the grace of God. Jansen uses the model of "the most powerful motive" and that of the "double delight" (what Augustine would call the *duplex delectatio victrix*), one of which is mundane and leads humans inevitably toward sin

31. The full title of Jansen's work is *Augustinus, seu doctrina sancti Augustini de humanae naturae sanitate, aegritudine, medicina adversus Pelagianos et Massilienses.*

32. On the continuity between Baius and Jansen, see the classic work of F. X. Linsenmann, *Michael Baius und die Grundlegung des Jansenismus: Eine dogmengeschichtliche Monographie* (Tubingen: Laupp, 1867). See also J. Orcibal, "De Baïus à Jansénius: Le *Comma Piarum*," *Revue des sciences religieuses* 32 (1962): 115–39.

33. See H. de Lubac, "Deux augustiniens fourvoyés: Baius et Jansenius," *Recherches de science religieuse* 21 (1931): 422–43, 513–40.

34. See J. Orcibal, *Jean Duvergier de Hauranne, abbé de Saint-Cyran, et son temps, 1581–1638* (Leuven: Bureaux de la Revue, 1947).

35. The most important work of Arnauld is called *De la fréquente communion* (1644). See A. R. Ndiaye, *La philosophie d'Antoine Arnauld* (Paris: J. Vrin, 1991). Also, Blaise Pascal was open to Jansenism: see M. Le Guern, *Pascal et Arnauld* (Paris: H. Champion, 2003); L. Kolakowski, *God Owes Us Nothing: A Brief Remark on Pascal's Religion and on the Spirit of Jansenism* (Chicago: University of Chicago Press, 1995).

36. See the work of Quesnel, *Abrégé de la morale de l'Évangile; or, Pensées chrétiennes sur les textes des 4 Évangélistes*, published in 1671. See J. A. G. Tans, ed., *La correspondance de Pasquier Quesnel: Inventaire et index analytique* (Leuven: Bureau de la RHE, 1989).

37. On Jansen, see J. Carreyre, "Jansénisme," *DTC* 8:478–529; L. Cognet, *Le Jansénisme* (Paris: PUF, 1961); A. Gazier, *Histoire générale du mouvement janséniste depuis ses origines jusquà nos jours*, 5th ed. (Paris: Librairie Ancienne H. Champion, 1923); J. Paquier, *Le Jansénisme: Étude doctrinale d'après les sources* (Paris: Bloud, 1909); T. J. Van Bavel and M. Schrama, eds., *Jansenius et le jansenisme dans les Pays-Bas: Mélanges Lucien Ceyssens* (Leuven: Leuven University Press, 1982); J. Orcibal, *Jansenius d'Ypres (1585–1638)* (Paris: Études augustiniennes, 1989).

and the other heavenly, orienting them to the good.[38] The only thing humans can do is to open themselves to this gift of God's grace, which overcomes, necessarily, the opposite inclination.

In brief terms, in the fallen state in which humans are presently situated, there is nothing but efficacious grace, which cannot be resisted. In this context Jansen proposes anew the classical doctrine of the *gemina praedestinatio*, according to which Christ died only for those who were predestined to glory, and infidels cannot carry out good actions. Paradoxically, however, in spite of Jansen's emphasis on the universal presence of sin and the power of salvation, humans end up being deprived of their sense of responsibility for sin.

The Influence and Condemnation of Jansenism

Jansenism was very influential among Catholics, especially in France, and contributed to the spread of a somewhat severe asceticism whose adherents were separated from the world, centered on sin and on human passivity before grace. It facilitated the development of what came to be known as "quietism," especially that of the seventeenth-century mystic Miguel de Molinos.[39] It is fair to say that this spiritual approach historically produced a tendency that was in many ways contrary to the intention of its authors. In effect, Jansenism facilitated the consolidation of the modern trust in the autonomy of human freedom that excludes divine grace and the resultant secularization of society. This is the position that is typical of the eighteenth-century authors Jean-Jacques Rousseau and François-Marie Arouet, called Voltaire.

Pope Innocent X condemned Jansen's work *Augustinus* in the constitution *Cum occasione* in 1653. The following propositions, for example, were rejected: "some of God's precepts are impossible to the just, who wish and strive to keep them, according to the present powers which they have";[40] "in the state of fallen nature one never resists interior grace";[41] "in order to merit or demerit in the state of fallen nature, freedom from necessity is not required in man, but freedom from external compulsion is sufficient";[42] and "it is semi-Pelagian to say that Christ died or shed his blood for all men without exception."[43]

Against the position of Quesnel, who guided Jansenism after the death of Arnauld, came the condemnation of Pope Clement XI in the constitution *Unigenitus Dei Filius* (1713), which rejects 101 propositions drawn from Jansenist works.[44] In the tenth proposition, for example, the following doctrine is rejected: "Grace is the working of the omnipotent hand of God, which nothing can hinder or retard."[45] In the thirty-ninth, the following position is rejected: "The will, which grace does not anticipate, has no light except for straying, no eagerness except to put itself in danger, no strength except to wound itself, and is capable of all evil and incapable of all good."[46]

---

38. Jansen, *Augustinus* 3, 6, 6.

39. See M. De Molinos, *Guía espiritual* (Rome, 1675), a work that was condemned by a Decree of the Holy Office in 1687: *DH* 2201–69, translated into English as M. De Molinos, *The Spiritual Guide Which Disentangles the Soul* (Glasgow: John Thomson, 1885).

40. *DH* 2001. 41. Ibid. 2002.

42. Ibid. 2003. 43. Ibid. 2005.

44. See L. Ceyssens, *Autour de l'Unigenitus: Recherches sur la genèse de la constitution* (Leuven: Leuven University Press, 1987).

45. *DH* 2410. 46. Ibid. 2439.

Despite the position taken by the Church, Jansenism spread farther and wider, especially in Italy in the area of Pavia and elsewhere, and was accepted by the so-called Synod of Pistoia in 1786.[47] Pope Pius VI condemned eighty-five propositions of this synod in the bull *Auctorem fidei* (1794). On the basis of the doctrine of Trent, this document rejects particularly the Jansenist doctrine of *duplex amor* (double love)[48] and teaches that humans did not lose the image of God with the Fall.[49]

Aspects of the Doctrine of Grace in the Nineteenth and Twentieth Centuries

The post-Tridentine controversies on grace were centered on truly critical questions for spiritual life and anthropology, especially regarding the relationship between grace and freedom. However, it is possible with hindsight to perceive gaps in theological and practical reflection. On the one hand, the controversies were at times very bitter, and this favored excessively rigid and critical ways of speaking about Christian life and spirituality. A certain absence of Biblical and Patristic doctrine meant that the wisdom, depth, and richness of the latter were missing, especially the warmth, power, and humanism that derives from the lives of the saints. On the other hand, several important aspects of Christian anthropology were neglected. Generally speaking, theological reflection on grace (and therefore on human freedom) was formulated in an individualistic way: the human being responds—or refuses to respond—to God's grace received within his own heart. The implications for moral theology were neglected, especially with respect to the social side of anthropology: in fact, there was hardly any reference to the ecclesial side of grace, to its sacramental and liturgical mediation, to Christian witnessing (and apostolate), to the Church's social teaching. Social and worldly aspects of human life were considered almost exclusively by philosophers, often in ways contrary to Christian faith. We shall deal with the latter issue in the last section of the text.

The Contributions of Petavius and Scheeben

During the seventeenth century the Patristic scholar Petavius (also called Denis Petau) left a clear mark on the renewal of the theology of grace.[50] By returning to the Greek Fathers, especially Cyril of Alexandria, he attempted to recuperate the primacy of "uncreated grace" over "created grace" in the relationship between God and humans.[51] Besides, he deals with the question of divine "appropriations," asking

---

47. See P. Stella, *Il giansenismo in Italia* (Rome: Edizioni di storia e letteratura, 2006); T. O'Connor, *Irish Jansenists, 1600–70: Religion and Politics in Flanders, France, Ireland and Rome* (Dublin: Four Courts, 2008).

48. Or *duplex dilectatio* (DH 2623).   49. DH 2624.

50. See D. Petau, *Opus de theologicis dogmatibus* (Barri: L. Guerin, 1864), esp. vol. 5 on Pelagius, Augustine, Trent, and justification. See also the brief work of D. Petau, *De adiutorio sine quo non, & adiutorio quo brevis dissertatio* (Paris: S. Cramoisy, 1651). On the theology of Petau, see M. Hofmann, *Theologie, Dogma und Dogmenentwicklung im theologischen Werk Denis Petaus: Mit einem biographischen und einem bibliographischen Anhang* (Bern: P. Lang, 1976).

51. According to Cyril, "Christ is formed [in you] through the Spirit, who regenerates in God through himself.... The Spirit is the true God and transforms into God, not by means of grace, but rather by offering, through himself, a sharing in the divine nature." Cyril of Alexandria, *De S. Trin. Dial.*, 7. On the doctrine of Cyril on divinization, see chapter 7, notes 27ff. and corresponding text.

whether in believers any trace of the life of the divine persons may be found. Petavius teaches that union with the Holy Spirit takes place "non interveniente ulla re vel qualitate creata" (without the intervention of anything or any created quality).[52] He explains that the three divine persons inhabit the justified. And he adds: "Sed solus Spiritus Sanctus quasi forma est sanctificans" (only the Holy Spirit sanctifies as if he was a form).[53] This brings us to an issue already dealt with by Peter Lombard regarding the close relationship between the Spirit and the formal cause of grace.

An important place in the history of the treatise of grace is occupied by the nineteenth-century German theologian Matthias-Joseph Scheeben.[54] He contributed in a substantial way to the modern understanding of Christian grace at a strictly dogmatic level, above all attempting to incorporate anew the Trinitarian and personalist side of grace and giving particular weight to the question of the formality of the life of grace. Important contributions were provided during the nineteenth century also by Joseph Adam Möhler,[55] John Henry Newman,[56] and others. During the twentieth century we can observe, besides the different efforts to reformulate the doctrine of grace,[57] a particular abundance of historical and Biblical studies on the matter.[58]

52. D. Petau, *Dogmata theologica*, 2nd ed. (Paris: L. Vivès, 1865), 3:460.

53. Ibid., 3:486.

54. The theology of grace in Scheeben is to be found principally in his work *The Mysteries of Christianity* (St. Louis, Mo.: Herder, 1946). On his theology, see K. Eschweiler, *Die zwei Wege der neueren Theologie: Georg Hermes, Matth. Jos. Scheeben; Eine kritische Untersuchung des Problems der theologischen Erkenntnis* (Augsburg: B. Filser, 1926); M. Donnelly, "The Indwelling of the Holy Spirit According to M. J. Scheeben," *Theological Studies* 7 (1946): 244–80; B. Fraigneau-Julien, "Grâce créée et grâce incréée dans la théologie de Scheeben," *Nouvelle Revue Théologique* 77 (1955): 339–58; N. P. Hoffmann, *Natur und Gnade: Die Theologie der Gottesschau als vollendeter Vergöttlichung des Geistgeschöpfes bei M. J. Scheeben* (Rome: Pontificia Università Gregoriana, 1967); G. Colombo, "Sull'antropologia teologica," *Teologia* 20 (1995): 223–60, 232; G. Tanzella-Nitti, *Mistero trinitario ed economia della grazia: Il personalismo soprannaturale di Matthias Joseph Scheeben* (Rome: Armando, 1997).

55. See especially J. A. Möhler, *Unity in the Church* (Washington, D.C.: The Catholic University of America Press, 1996). On his doctrine, see J. R. Geiselmann, *Die theologische Anthropologie Johann Adam Möhlers: Ihr geschichtlicher Wandel* (Freiburg: Herder, 1955).

56. See especially the work of J. H. Newman, *Lectures on the Doctrine of Justification* (London: Longmans, Green, 1838/74). On this work, see T. L. Sheridan, *Newman et la Justification* (Paris: Desclée, 1968); J. Morales, "La justificación en el pensamiento de John H. Newman," *Revista Agustiniana* 31 (1990): 867–88; and P. Njunge Cathogo, "The Relationship between Faith and Baptism in the 'Lectures on the Doctrine of Justification'" (PhD Diss., Pontificia Università della Santa Croce, 1999). See C. S. Dessain, "Cardinal Newman and the Doctrine of Uncreated Grace," *Clergy Review* 47 (1962): 207–25, 269–88. Newman's *Sermon Notes* (London: Longmans, Green, 1913), 31–45, 121f., 191f., 247, and 295f., are also important.

57. Specifically see K. Rahner, "Some Implications of the Scholastic Concept of Uncreated Grace," *Theological Investigations* (London: Darton, Longman and Todd, 1974), 1:319–46; *Gnade als Freiheit: Kleine theologische Beiträge* (Freiburg: Herder, 1968); and also *Foundations of Christian Faith*. On Rahner's way of explaining grace, see the presentation and critique of W. J. Hill, "Uncreated Grace—A Critique of Karl Rahner," *Thomist* 26 (1963): 333–56; G. Mansini, "Quasi-Formal Causality and 'Change in the Other': A Note on Karl Rahner's Christology," *Thomist* 52 (1989): 293–306; J. A. DiNoia, "Nature, Grace, and Experience: Karl Rahner's Theology of Human Transformation," *Philosophy and Theology* 7, no. 2 (1992): 115–26; M. Purcell, "Quasi-formal Causality; or, the Other-in-Me: Rahner and Lévinas," *Gregorianum* 78, no. 1 (1997): 79–93; Burke, *Reinterpreting Rahner*. Among Orthodox theologians, see the work of J. D. Zizioulas, *Being as Communion: Studies in Personhood and the Church* (Crestwood, N.Y.: St. Vladimir's Seminary Press, 1997). On his work, see D. H. Knight, ed., *The Theology of John Zizioulas: Personhood and the Church* (Aldershot: Ashgate, 2007). In the area of Lutheran theology, see, for example, Pannenberg, *Systematic Theology*, 3:97–236.

58. In the area of the history of dogma, see, *inter alia*, Rondet, *Gratia Christi*; Vignaux, *Justification et prédestination*; H. Schauf, *Die Einwohnung des Heiligen Geistes* (Freiburg: Herder, 1941); J. Auer, *Die Entwicklung der Gnadenlehre in der Hochscholastik: Mit besonderer Berücksichtigung des Kardinals Matteo d'Acquasparta*

Social, Liturgical, Spiritual, and Ecclesiological Renewal

Renewal in the personalist and social side of Christian anthropology is an important feature of recent theological reflection, especially in the area of ethics.[59] The Encyclical *Rerum Novarum* (1891) of Pope Leo XIII was followed by a long series of pontifical documents on the social doctrine of the Church that extended right up until Benedict XVI's encyclical *Caritas in Veritate* (2009). Of considerable importance was the renewal of liturgy, especially with the contributions of twentieth-century theologians such as Romano Guardini, Odo Casel, Louis Bouyer, Yves-Marie Congar, Joseph Ratzinger, and others. In effect, this theological effort reflects a will to make the dynamics of God's saving grace present, tangible, and public for the believing community. This period saw the consolidation of the doctrine of the sanctification of work and everyday life, understood in terms of living situations in which God's grace is made present, along with the holiness and apostolic witness of all Christians, especially the laity. Josemaría Escrivá and others contributed considerably to this tendency. Of particular importance was the renewal of ecclesiology that took place during the twentieth century, culminating in Vatican II's constitution *Lumen Gentium* (1965).[60] Of course, ecclesiology refers necessarily to the social aspect of theological anthropology. From the strictly anthropological standpoint, the contribution of Vatican II may to be found throughout the constitution *Gaudium et Spes* (1965), followed by the teaching of many popes, especially John Paul II. The principal issues will be considered in forthcoming chapters.

Recent Lutheran-Catholic Ecumenical Dialogue

Another important feature in the development in the theology of grace during the twentieth century concerned the theological *rapprochement* and ecumenical dialogue between Lutherans and Catholics.[61] With the 1999 *Joint Declaration on the Doctrine of Justification*, signed by the Lutheran World Federation and the Roman Catholic Church, a substantially common position has been established between both sides as regards the doctrine of justification.[62] This, of course, does not involve a cancellation

---

(Freiburg: Herder, 1942); O. H. Pesch, "Gottes Gnadenhandeln als Rechtfertigung des Menschen," in *Mysterium salutis: Grundriss heilsgeschichtlicher Dogmatik*, 4.2: *Das Heilsgeschehen in der Gemeinde*, edited by J. Feiner and M. Löhrer (Einsiedeln: Benziger, 1965), 831–920; Philips, *L'union personnelle*; McGrath, *Iustitia Dei*; Martin-Palma, *Gnadenlehre*.

59. An interesting contribution to the social aspect of grace has been made by some liberation theologians, for example, J. L. Segundo, *Teología abierta para el laico adulto*, vol. 2: *Gracia y condición humana* (Buenos Aires: C. Lohlé, 1969), and L. Boff, *A graça libertadora no mundo* (Lisbon: Vozes, 1976), translated into English respectively as J. L. Segundo, *A Theology for a New Humanity* (Dublin: Macmillan, 1980); L. Boff, *Liberating Grace* (Maryknoll, N.Y.: Orbis Books, 1987). On the work of Boff, see the critical observations of L. F. Ladaria, "Sobre el libro de L. Boff, *A graça libertadora no mundo*," *Estudios Eclesiásticos* 53 (1978): 135–36, especially as regards Boff's lack of Christocentrism.

60. See P. O'Callaghan, "The Holiness of the Church in 'Lumen Gentium,'" *Thomist* 52 (1988): 673–701.

61. See O'Callaghan, *Fides Christi*, 149–249.

62. For a summary of the ecumenical discussions that prepared the way for this document, see ibid., 95–145. The document is entitled *Joint Declaration on the Doctrine of Justification* and was prepared by the Lutheran World Federation and the Pontifical Council for Promoting Christian Unity (Grand Rapids, Mich.:

of the teaching of the Council of Trent. Trent wanted above all to clarify and define Catholic doctrine on justification; besides, its purpose was one of rejecting some aspects of Lutheranism that were popular in the sixteenth century. As we saw already, there is no such thing as a single, unitary Lutheran doctrine on justification. Trent, however, did insist on two central points which are reflected in the Joint Declaration: first, the inherent and ecclesial character of the divine work of justification in the believer, and second, the affirmation of the real cooperation of humans in the reception of grace and in the carrying out of good works. Both topics stand in need of further consideration in ecumenical dialogue. They will be studied throughout the systematic presentation of the doctrine of grace that we shall now undertake.

W. B. Eerdmans, 2000) [hereafter "*JDJ*"]. It is dated June 25, 1998, and was published on October 31, 1999, the "Day of the Reformation."

PART THREE THE CHRISTIAN THEOLOGY
OF GRACE

12   THE HISTORICAL WORKING OUT OF GOD'S PROJECT TO ESTABLISH AN INTIMATE AND PERPETUAL FILIAL COMMUNION OF HUMANS WITH THE TRINITY

> For those whom he foreknew he also predestined to be conformed to the image of his Son, in order that he might be the first-born among many brothers. And those whom he predestined he also called; and those whom he called he also justified; and those whom he justified he also glorified.   ROMANS 8:29–30

> We have invented the concept of "end," but in reality there is no end.
> FRIEDRICH NIETZSCHE[1]

> Mary, the One who impersonates truly the original, authentic idea of what man is, image of God.   POPE PAUL VI[2]

The Historical Working Out of God's Plan in Christ

As we read scripture we come to recognize, at the heart of the mystery of God's relationship with humans, a project of grace, a project of gratuitous and intimate love, which not only calls humans to existence but also invites them to share in the life of the Trinity, in a communion with the divine that is destined to last for ever. The content of this "project of grace" in favor of humans is mysteriously summed up in the person of Christ, the Word of God made man, and is communicated to them through the Holy Spirit, the Spirit of Christ, in the Church.

On the one hand, the gift of divine grace reveals the meaning of what precedes it: the created world as a whole, nature, and especially human beings created in the

---

1. F. Nietzsche, "The Four Great Errors," in *Twilight of Idols; or, How to Philosophize with a Hammer* (Oxford: Oxford University Press, 1998), no. 8.
2. Pope Paul VI, *Homily on the Solemnity of the Assumption*, August 15, 1966.

image of God, who are directed toward him and capable of responding freely to his call. Indeed, as Pope Francis writes, "The power and the light of the grace we have received" shows up "in our relationship to other creatures and to the world."[3] And this for a simple reason: God communicates his life to those whom he created for the very purpose of giving them his grace. Thus, humans perceive that not only is *grace* in the strict sense a gift of God but so also is being and life, nature, the whole of creation.[4] In real terms, the life of grace, which reaches fulfillment and completion with eternal life in communion with the Trinity, is what God had in mind when he created the world and a humanity capable of freely responding to his gifts. Simply put, grace explains the ultimate meaning of creation, of the natural and the supernatural.

On the other hand, however, the gift of communion with God is a true novelty in the lives of human beings, a supernatural reality, because it is not to be identified simply with the gift of creation. In real terms, God's invitation to communion with him cannot in any way be earned or obtained by humans through their own strengths, because it presupposes the free revelation and love of another person, that is, of a being who can reveal and give himself only in freedom, exclusively to a free, already existent, human being. The word of God is directed to humans, constituted as his privileged interlocutors, who are invited to enter his home, his family, his very life (Eph 2:19–20), in a communion of holiness and life that involves their whole beings, everything they are. Through this calling, God reveals himself definitively as a God of grace, of mercy, of love.

God's project of creation and grace has been developed and reaches perfection in a gradual way throughout history and in the hearts of humans, even though on God's side it is but a single project or plan, which Paul calls the *mystērion*, "the mystery which was kept secret for long ages but is now disclosed and through the prophetic writings is made known to all nations" (Rom 16:25f.; see 1 Cor 2:7, 1 Tm 3:16).[5] In his letter to the Romans Paul presents the narrative or stages of this single project that springs from the love and wisdom of God, especially in the following passage, which will be structural for this whole chapter: "For those whom he foreknew he also

---

3. *LS*, par. 221.

4. This is the thesis of G. Maspero and P. O'Callaghan in *Creatore perché Padre: Introduzione all'ontologia del dono* (Siena: Cantagalli, 2012).

5. Paul speaks of the *mystērion*, the divine "design," plan, or blueprint, full of wisdom, once hidden in God and now revealed in Christ. Doctrinally the notion of *mystērion* is rooted in Jewish apocalyptic literature (Dn 2:18f.), but it is applied in the New Testament to the work of salvation that Christ carried out by dying on the Cross (1 Cor 2:8). See B. L. Gladd, *Revealing the Mysterion: The Use of Mystery in Daniel and Second Temple Judaism with Its Bearing on First Corinthians* (Berlin: W. de Gruyter, 2009). It includes the call of the pagans to salvation (Rom 11:25) and is directed to the restoration of the universe in Christ as the only head (Eph 1:9f.). In Eph 3:8f., Paul writes, "Though I am the very least of all the saints, this grace was given, to preach to the Gentiles the unsearchable riches of Christ, and to make all men see what is the plan of the mystery hidden for ages in God who created all things." On the notion of "mystery" in Ephesians, see C. Reynier, *Évangile et mystère: Les enjeux théologiques de l'Épître aux Éphésiens* (Paris: Cerf, 1992). On this topic and the central position it occupies in Paul's theology, see Deden, "Le 'mystère' paulinien"; F. Hahn, "Der Begriff *Mysterion* im Neuen Testament," in *Die Weite des Mysteriums: Christliche Identität im Dialog; Festschrift für Horst Bürkle*, edited by H. Bürkle, K. Krämer, and A. Paus (Freiburg: Herder, 2000), 57–64; R. Penna, *Il mysterion paolino: Traiettoria e costituzione* (Brescia: Paideia, 2012); *BDAG* 661f., s.v. μυστήριον, 1, b; *NIDNTTE* 3:350–57, s.v. μυστήριον. The notion is at the heart of the theology of Louis Bouyer; see A. Catapano, *La sofiologia di Louis Bouyer: Prolegomeni per un'antropologia teologica* (Rome: Pontificia Università della Santa Croce, 2001).

predestined to be conformed to the image of his Son, in order that he might be the first-born among many brothers. And those whom he predestined he also called; and those whom he called he also justified; and those whom he justified he also glorified" (Rom 8:29–30).[6]

The project of grace that derives from the Trinity includes not only the creation of beings capable of freely listening and responding to the creator but also the predestination or election of humanity to partake in God's own life. Divine predestination, in turn, is presented to the individual human being in terms of a calling to communion with God, a calling that, once it has been freely accepted, produces in the first place the justification of humans (the effective donation of grace with which sin is forgiven) and, subsequently, their eschatological glorification (receipt of eternal life in the glory of Christ). Following this scheme proposed by Paul, therefore, the stages through which God's plan is expressed are five in number: divine knowledge, predestination, calling, justification, and glorification. The human being whom God has known and predestined is called to be justified and eventually glorified. All this takes place in Christ and in the power of the Holy Spirit. In this chapter we shall also consider the role of the human person in whom God's project has been implemented in the most perfect possible way, the one who is full of grace and therefore the prototype of humanity, the Virgin Mary, a role we shall consider at the end of the chapter.

Creation through the Word, the Basis of God's Saving Project

"For those whom he *foreknew* ..." (Rom 8:29). The term used by Paul here, *proegno*, translated normally as "foreknew," may be understood in two ways: "to know with anticipation" or "to choose."[7] Thus the common term "prognosticate." Romans 8:29 translates *proegno* in an ample sense as "foreknew." Romans 11:2 also uses "foreknew," but in the sense of "choosing": "God has not rejected his people whom he foreknew." When Paul teaches that God has "known" humanity, who will then be predestined, called, justified, and glorified, this of course does not involve a knowledge God obtains of creatures a posteriori, that is, a passive, received knowledge, typical of creatures, for the simple reason that God is the creator of all things, the origin of all beings, and especially of each and every human life: God is the one who implants intelligibility into creatures. In philosophical terms it may be said that the knowledge God has of creatures, especially of humans, precedes their existence at the deepest possible level. Not only that: divine knowledge *founds* that very existence. For the same reason, it is not a theoretical, abstract, or necessary knowledge of the world because it is at the root of the divine free act by which God created the world (with which he, as it were, "chose" the world to exist) and also every human being. This aspect of God's knowledge of the world is clarified by Paul in his letter to Galatians when he speaks of believers who have "come to know God, or rather *to be known by God*" (4:9). God's

---

6. On Romans 8:29–30, see K. Greyston, "The Doctrine of Election in Rom. 8:28–30," *Studia Evangelica* 2 (1964): 574–83.

7. Thus *BDAG* 866, s.v. προγινώσκω; *NIDNTTE* 4:139, s.v. προγινώσκω, NT.

knowledge is the basis of humans' relationship with God, which "does not have its basis in man's seeking (mysticism) or doing (legalism) or knowing (gnosticism), but it originates with God himself and is carried on always by divine grace."[8]

The doctrine contained in Romans 8:29 arises again in a rich and dense text from the letter to the Ephesians, which is in many ways similar to the Romans text in structure and doctrine. Here the Old Testament category of "choice" or "election" is used, alongside that of "predestination."[9] The text is likewise totally centered on Christ: "He [God] chose us in him [Christ] *before the foundation* [Greek *kataboles*, literally "founding"] *of the world*, that we should be holy and blameless before him. He *predestined* [*proorizo*] us in love [*en agape*] to be his sons through Jesus Christ, according to the purpose of his will, to the praise of his glorious grace [*charis*] which he freely bestowed on us in the Beloved" (Eph 1:4-6).

"Those whom he foreknew," and God "chose us before the foundation of the world": two expressions that come to say the same thing.[10] On other occasions in the New Testament, Christ prays in a special way to the Father, inviting his followers "to behold my glory which you have given me in your love for me *before the foundation of the world*" (Jn 17:24). "He [Christ] was destined *before the foundation of the world* but was made manifest at the end of the times" (1 Pt 1:20). It is clear, therefore, that the antecedent knowledge God had of creation in general, and of humans in particular, of which Romans 8:29 speaks, corresponds simply to the doctrine of the creation of all things in Christ. That is, the work of creation is the basis both of God's saving work carried out through Jesus Christ, God's Word made man, in the Holy Spirit, and of the knowledge he has of each and every creature.

The Creation of the World in Christ and for Christ, the Basis of a "New Creation"

Scripture teaches us not only that God is the maker of all existing things[11] but also that he created all things through the incarnate Word, Jesus Christ, as the evangelist John explains,[12] as does Paul, in saying that the world was made "in Christ, through him and for him."[13] On the basis of the Gospel of John, we can say that "the creating mediation of the Word is active, enduring and dynamic (and not merely passive, achieved once and for all, and static, as is the case with the *Logos* or Demiurge typical of Platonic and Stoic cosmogonies), because creation takes place not only *through* the Word, but also *in* the Word."[14] For Paul,

Christ is the mediator of creation as he is of salvation. His proper role goes beyond that of being a mere "exemplar" cause of creation, static and referred to the past, as in Pla-

8. R. N. Longenecker, *Galatians*, in *WBC* 41:180.

9. On the topic of predestination and election, see note 18. On the equivalence between the two, see Serenthà, "Predestinazione," 776.

10. See O. Hofius, "'Erwählt vor Grundlegung der Welt' (Eph 1,4)," *Zeitschrift für die neutestamentliche Wissenschaft* 62 (1971): 123–28.

11. See O'Callaghan, *La metafisica cristiana*, 33–49.

12. See ibid., 94–103, which referred especially to Jn 1:1–18.

13. See O'Callaghan, *La metafisica cristiana*, 103–9; the principal Pauline texts as regards creation are Rom 11:36; Eph 4:4–6; 1 Tm 6:13.15, and especially 1 Cor 8:5–6 and Col 1:15–20.

14. O'Callaghan, *La metafisica cristiana*, 99.

tonism. For Paul in fact creation takes place *in* Christ and, as if he wished to explain the radical character of the *in*, also *for* Christ's sake, directed *towards* him. Christ therefore is not a creature among creatures, harmoniously and hierarchically inserted among the rest. Neither is he a simple model, a prototype of abstract rationality that goes beyond time, unconnected from the things of the world. Creatures depend on him as much as they do on God.[15]

Speaking of the Christocentrism of the New Testament, Giacomo Biffi writes:

Each and every thing derives from him [Christ], the exemplary principle, their very nature; and every thing derives from him, efficient cause, their very existence. Each thing is a fragment of the immeasurable value that is contained in him; each thing receives only from him its proper meaning. All of us are the fruit of his act of love, which mysteriously humanizes the ineffable act of divine love which is at the source of existence of every creature.[16]

In the encyclical *Laudato Si'*, Pope Francis writes: "In the Christian understanding of the world, the destiny of all creation is bound up with the mystery of Christ, present from the beginning.... From the beginning of the world, but particularly through the incarnation, the mystery of Christ is at work in a hidden manner in the natural world as a whole, without thereby impinging on its autonomy."[17]

After these brief reflections, we can conclude that human beings live in peace with their created nature by living in conformity with the image of the Son of God made man. In Christ is to be found the fullness of perfect likeness to the Father; the Son of God, Jesus Christ, "was not 'yes' and 'no,' but in him it is always 'yes'" (2 Cor 1:19). From him we have received all God's gifts: "From his fullness have we all received, grace upon grace" (Jn 1:16).

The Predestination of Christ and of Humanity in Christ

The New Testament doctrine on predestination is similar to that of "election," always in the wider context of the Covenant God established with Israel and through Israel with the whole of humanity.[18] The universality of divine election may be found in

15. Ibid., 109.

16. G. Biffi, *Approccio al cristocentrismo: Note storiche per un tema eterno* (Milan: Jaca Book, 1994), 80; see also I. Biffi, "La solidarietà predestinata di tutti gli uomini in Cristo e la loro solidarietà in Adamo," *Teologia* 15 (1990): 277–82.

17. *LS*, par. 99.

18. For an overall view of the topic of predestination, see L. Serenthà, "Predestinazione." The following studies on predestination are classics: M.-J. Scheeben, *The Mysteries of Christianity*, 697–730, and Barth, *Kirchliche Dogmatik* II/1. On the doctrine of election, see H. H. Rowley, *The Biblical Doctrine of Election* (London: Lutterworth Press, 1950); T. C. Vriezen, *Die Erwählung Israels nach dem Alten Testament* (Zurich: Zwingli Verlag, 1953); K. Koch, "Zur Geschichte der Erwählungsvorstellung in Israel," *Zeitschrift für Allgemeine Wissenschaftstheorie* 67 (1955): 205–26; Brambilla, "Antropologia teologica," 160–72. For the Biblical understanding of predestination, besides the works already quoted, see Boublik, *La predestinazione*; Serenthà, "Predestinazione," 778f.; R. Fabris, "L'elezione-vocazione-predestinazione nei quattro vangeli," in *Elezione, vocazione, predestinazione* (Rome: Borla, 1997), 67–97; Fabris, "L'elezione-vocazione-predestinazione dell'umanità nel epistolario del Nuovo Testamento," in ibid., 127–56; I. Koncsik, "Prädestination—Menschliche Freiheit kraft göttlicher Freiheit?," *Wissenschaft und Weisheit* 68 (2005): 290–323; G. Tourn, *La predestinazione nella Bibbia e nella storia*, 2nd ed. (Turin: Claudiana, 2008); *NIDNTTE* 2:145–52, s.v. ἐκλέγομαι. For historical issues, see

the Songs of the Servant in Isaiah 42–55. The specificity of the New Testament, how-ever, lies in the fact that divine election or predestination is applied in the first place to Christ: God first predestined his own Son, Jesus Christ, to holiness and glory. And, on the basis of Jesus' foundational predestination, God has predestined humanity in-sofar as it belongs to his body, the Church, his children: "He predestined us in love to be his sons through Jesus Christ, according to the purpose of his will" (Eph 1:5). Still, throughout the history of theology, and especially in the centuries following Augustine, the Biblical doctrine of "predestination" has come to be interpreted in a somewhat individualistic way, between God and humans, as it were, and independent of Christ. Thus, in God's mind, independently of the incarnation of the Word, all the elect would already be predestined, one by one.

As we already saw, Augustine and the great majority of Christian authors did not come to the point of holding a doctrine of *gemina praedestinatio*, "double predesti-nation," according to which God has already predestined some to eternal glory and the rest to perpetual condemnation.[19] Still, from the time of Augustine onward the doctrine of predestination has tended to become more and more restricted to the re-lationship between God and the individual human being. In this development, the Church's struggle against Arianism played an important role. In effect, in order to avoid the subordinationism frequent in the years that followed the rejection of Ari-us's teaching at Nicaea, Jesus Christ was generally not designated as head, end, prin-ciple, or mediator of creation, as our intercessor before the Father, that is, as the pri-mordial object of divine predestination. In fact, such titles were common in theology and liturgy until the time of the Council. Nicaea insisted that Christ should be placed on the same plane as the Father, considered principally as the divine savior of the individual from sin, while the divine project of reconciling and "recapitulating" the entire created order falls into second place.[20] As regards the justified, predestination becomes a problematic category in the ambit of the controversy between Augustine and Pelagius, in an ascetic and spiritual context of a monastic kind that relegates the relationship between God and humans toward the interiority of the latter.

Stages of the Doctrine of Predestination in Scripture

According to the New Testament and especially Paul, the doctrine of predesti-nation is complex and may be understood in five stages: theological, Christological, ecclesiological, Marian, and cosmic.

The first stage is *theological* in character. In effect, predestination has the love of God as its one and only source. The initiative taken is purely divine, that is, totally gratuitous: "Those whom he [God] foreknew he also predestined" (Rom 8:29). The

---

A. Lemonnyer, H.-D. Simonin, R. Garrigou-Lagrange, and B. Lavaud, "Prédestination," *DTC* 12:2809–3022. On the philosophical implications of predestination, see A. Magris, *Destino, provvidenza, predestinazione: dal mondo antico al cristianesimo* (Brescia: Morcelliana, 2008). On the dogmatic and spiritual outworkings, see Colzani, *Antropologia teologica*, 285–309; F. Scanziani, "Destino—Destinazione—Vocazione," *La Scuola Cat-tolica* 132 (2004): 425–50; D. Albarello, "L'uomo, l'evocato: Una rilettura sistematica della 'predestinazione in Cristo,'" *Teologia* 32 (2011): 330–60; M. Levering, *Predestination: Biblical and Theological Paths* (Oxford; New York: Oxford University Press, 2011).

19. See chapter 8, notes 72ff. and 102ff., and corresponding text.
20. See *COH* 115–29.

term used by Paul here, *proōrizo*, simply means "to decide with anticipation," "to pre-determine."[21] The weight of the notion of "predestination" therefore derives from its subject, who is God. Only God predestines. In that sense, predestination is uncondi-tional and infallible; it does not depend in any way on human initiative. This leaves open the obvious problem of the meaning of human freedom in accepting God's gift of grace. We shall come back to this issue in chapter 16.

The second stage is the *Christological* aspect of predestination. The eternal plan of God, as we saw, is rooted in Christ, who is the true and only predestined one: "He [Christ] was predestined before the foundation of the world but was made manifest at the end of the times" (1 Pt 1:20). Clement of Rome wrote: "God chose the Lord Jesus Christ, and us in him."[22] Likewise, Thomas Aquinas explains that the first one to be predestined is Christ.[23] In effect, Christ is the one who, through his life, death, and resurrection, gives us the measure of the gratuitousness and unconditional character of the divine election. But, more specifically Paul teaches us that humans are predes-tined only indirectly, because all predestination takes place "in Christ" (Eph 1:4–5).[24] According to Serenthà, "The Pauline texts on mystery present the destiny of humans as conformity to the destiny of Christ, and therefore as an unheard-of reality ... in the sense that it is an access, in Christ, to a life that in a proper and exclusive way belongs to God and only by a free decision of his will can be given by God."[25]

We may say that the predestination of humans takes place, as it were, in two stag-es: in the relationship of Christ to the Father and in that between Christ and the rest of humanity. It would be mistaken to place the Father on the same plane as Christ, because this would mean that predestination is established simply between God and humans. Christ is not to be identified with the Father because he does not substi-tute for the Father or coincide with him but rather reveals his love. As he speaks of Christ in his letter to the Colossians, Paul writes: "For in him all the fullness of God was pleased to dwell [this is the predestination of Christ], and through him to recon-cile to himself all things [here, the predestination of humans in Christ], whether on earth or in heaven, making peace by the blood of his cross" (Col 1:19f.). In brief terms, God predestines Christ, but Christ, in turn, through the work of redemption, offers a share to humans in this predestination, in this unconditioned love of the Father. The Pauline doctrine of predestination (though not the language) is present also in the Gospel of John, for example, when we are told that Jesus is the way and the truth (Jn 14:6). In effect, Christ represents the fidelity of God toward humans (as the *truth*) and brings them to share in it (as the *way*) through the Holy Spirit, the Paraclete.[26]

---

21. See *BDAG* 873, s.v. προορίζω.   22. Clement of Rome, *Ep. ad Cor.*, 64.

23. See Aquinas, *S.Th.* III, q. 24.

24. In modern times, the author who has most insisted on the derived aspect of predestination has been Scheeben, even if he did not focus on the question from the standpoint of Christology. The latter is princi-pally the focus of K. Barth. On the latter's thought, see B. Gherardini, "Riflettendo sulla dottrina dell'elezione in Karl Barth," in *Barth contemporaneo*, edited by S. Rostagno (Turin: Claudiana, 1990), 105–17. According to Barth, the "Elected One" is not humanity as a whole or a particular individual but rather Jesus Christ, through whom election is extended from Israel to the Church: see *Kirchliche Dogmatik* II/1.

25. Serenthà, "Predestinazione," 778.

26. God's design, which Paul expresses using the term *mystērion* (see note 5), is expressed by John using the term "truth." The latter is identified with God's design over human history, expressed in De la Potterie, *La vérité dans saint Jean*.

The third stage of the dynamic of predestination is *ecclesiological*. For Paul, the plan of God in Christ refers directly not to human individuals but to the Church, that is, to the community of faith, his body. In the letter to the Ephesians, which is centered on the theology of the Church as the body of Christ (Eph 5), we read: "He chose *us* in him before the foundation of the world, that *we* should be holy and blameless before him. He predestined *us* in love to be his sons through Jesus Christ, according to the purpose of his will, to the praise of his glorious grace which be freely bestowed on *us* in the Beloved" (Eph 1:4–6). Clearly, the object of divine choice, in Christ, is the "we" of the Church.[27]

On several occasions Paul says that he was personally chosen by God as an apostle.[28] He writes, for example: "But when he who had set me apart before I was born, and had called me through his grace, was pleased to reveal his Son to me, in order that I might preach him among the Gentiles" (Gal 1:15f.). He states repeatedly that God offered him his grace.[29] For this reason he can say that "the life I now live in the flesh I live by faith in the Son of God, who loved me and gave himself for me" (Gal 2:20). Yet Paul never says he had been predestined by God.[30] We might say he is certain of his calling and mission but not of his salvation. He says, for example: "But with me it is a very small thing that I should be judged by you or by any human court. I do not even judge myself. I am not aware of anything against myself, but I am not thereby acquitted. It is the Lord who judges me" (1 Cor 4:3f.).

Predestination, therefore, is directed to Christ and his body, the Church. The latter does not simply include the elect as members, in a passive way. The Church actually partakes, through evangelization and in its apostolate and ministry, in the very process of the convocation of the elect. The unconditional character of God's love for Christ is extended to some degree toward the Church, and it cannot fail. Jesus promised the twelve, as he sent them out to evangelize all peoples: "I am with you always, to the close of the age" (Mt 28:20). Specifically to Simon Peter he said: "You are Peter, and on this rock I will build my Church, and the powers of death shall not

---

27. The same doctrine is found frequently in the Pauline corpus (as I have indicated by adding emphasis to the following): "Hope does not disappoint *us*, because God's love has been poured into *our* hearts through the Holy Spirit which has been given to *us*" (Rom 5:5; see Rom 5:11). God "did not spare his own Son but gave him up for *us* all, will he not also give *us* all things with him?" (Rom 8:32; see 8:35). "But thanks be to God, who gives *us* the victory through our Lord Jesus Christ" (1 Cor 15:57). "But it is God who establishes *us* with you in Christ, and has commissioned *us*; he has put his seal upon *us* and given *us* his Spirit in *our* hearts as a guarantee" (2 Cor 1:21f.; see 5:5). "The love of Christ controls *us*" (2 Cor 5:14; see 5:18). "Christ redeemed *us* from the curse of the law, having become a curse for *us*" (Gal 3:13). "For freedom Christ has set *us* free; stand fast therefore, and do not submit again to a yoke of slavery" (Gal 5:1). God "made *us* alive together with Christ" (Eph 2:5). "He has delivered *us* from the dominion of darkness and transferred *us* to the kingdom of his beloved Son, in whom *we* have redemption, the forgiveness of sins" (Col 1:13f.). See also 1 Thes 1:10, 2 Thes 2:10, 1 Tm 1:9, Ti 3:5.

28. See Rom 1:1; 1 Cor 1:1, 17; 2 Cor 1:1; Gal 1:1; Eph 1:1; Col 1:1; 1 Tm 1:1, 11; 2 Tm 1:1; Ti 1:1f.

29. See Rom 12:3, 15:15; 1 Cor 3:10; 2 Cor 12:9, 13:3; Gal 2:9, 20; Eph 3:17; Phil 4:13; 1 Tm 1:12.

30. In Acts, Ananias says to Paul after his conversion: "The God of our fathers appointed you to know his will, to see the Just One and to hear a voice from his mouth, for you will be *a witness for him to all men* of what you have seen and heard" (Acts 22:14f.). It is obvious that this refers to a divine election in function of the universal mission of Paul but not to his personal salvation. In fact, the term used, *procheirizō*, means "chosen," "appointed," "preferred for a particular task," but is not equivalent to "predestined." See *BDAG* 891, s.v. προχειρίζω.

prevail against it" (Mt 16:18). In the same way the letter to the Ephesians explains that the Church, the spouse of Christ, shares in the predestination of the elect: "as Christ loved the Church and gave himself up for her, that he might sanctify her, having cleansed her by the washing of water with the word, that he might present the Church to himself in splendor, without spot or wrinkle or any such thing, that she might be holy and without blemish" (Eph 5:25–27).

It is interesting to note that Augustine, in spite of the interpretations given later to his thought and writings, understands predestination in a predominantly Christological and ecclesiological way. He takes it that Christ's predestination as our head occupies the first place in God's plan: "That individual man was predestined to be our head, at the same time as a great multitude has been predestined to be his members."[31]

The fourth stage of predestination is *Marian*. It is common doctrine that the Virgin Mary was predestined by God on the basis of her mission as mother of the redeemer.[32] Bernard of Clairvaux said that Our Lady was "elected from all eternity, predestined and prepared by the Most High for himself, contemplated by the angels, designated beforehand by the patriarchs, promised by the prophets."[33] Pope Pius XII spoke openly of her predestination on the occasion of the proclamation of the dogma of the Assumption: "The sublime Mother of God, in mysterious union with Jesus Christ from all eternity, 'with the same decree' of predestination ... was lifted up in body and soul into the glory of heaven."[34] In Vatican II's *Lumen Gentium* we read: "The Father of mercies willed that the incarnation should be preceded by the acceptance of her who was predestined to be the mother of His Son." And later: [Mary was] "predestined from eternity by that decree of divine providence which determined the incarnation of the Word to be the Mother of God, the Blessed Virgin was on this earth the virgin Mother of the Redeemer, and above all others and in a singular way the generous associate and humble handmaid of the Lord."[35]

Fifth and finally, it may be said that the doctrine of predestination, closely associated with that of the "recapitulation" of all things in Christ (Rom 8:19–23), involves the whole of creation. This is the *cosmic* aspect of predestination, which was considered earlier when we examined Paul's teaching on grace.[36]

Open Questions on the Issue of Predestination

Recent reflection, in the wake of Karl Barth's theology of election, has recuperated the Christological, ecclesiological, Marian, and cosmic aspects of the mystery of

---

31. Augustine, *De praedestin. sanctorum*, 15, 31.

32. The doctrine of the predestination of Mary is related principally to that of the Immaculate Conception and the incarnation of the Word: see J. B. Carol, *The Absolute Primacy and Predestination of Jesus and His Virgin Mother* (Chicago: Franciscan Herald Press, 1981).

33. Bernard, *Hom.* 2, 4, on the excellence of Mary.

34. Pope Pius XII, *Munificentissimus Deus*, Encyclical Letter, November 1, 1950, in DH 3900–3904.

35. Vatican Council II, *Lumen Gentium*, November 21, 1964 [hereafter "LG"], nos. 56 and 61; emphasis added. On these texts, see G. Philips, *L'Église et son mystère au II. Concile du Vatican: Histoire, texte et commentaire de la constitution Lumen gentium* (Paris: Desclée, 1967). See also John Paul II, *Redemptoris Mater*, Encyclical Letter, March 25, 1987, pars. 8, 13.

36. See chapter 5, notes 34ff. and corresponding text.

divine predestination. Still, the fact remains that the divine decree by which humans are predestined does not resolve, on the whole, the problem of the freedom of individual human beings in receiving God's grace. Pannenberg explains it as follows:

Either from the beginning God assigned eternal salvation to only some of his creatures and passed over the rest, abandoning them from the outset to the final destiny of eternal damnation; *or* the universality of the divine will to save was preserved in principle, but in individual cases its efficacy was made to depend on the creaturely reaction and thus on the response of faith to the divine offer of grace, a response that has been calculated already in the divine foreknowledge and that is thus responsible for some being foreordained from the very first to eternal salvation, while others are left to eternal perdition.[37]

It is true that the divine origin of the decree of predestination explains its complete gratuity and unconditioned character. Still, it seems to indicate some kind of passivity or irrelevance on the part of human creatures. And it is not enough simply to say that grace is the "source" of freedom, "the power of divine communion that gives rise to freedom,"[38] as if the liberation that comes by grace need not take into account the previous constitution of humans as beings with a truly free will; on the basis of the latter they should be, in principle, able to accept or reject, with authentic responsibility, the gifts of God. Psalm 139:2–7 is worthwhile reading in this regard:

O Lord, you have searched me and known me! You know when I sit down and when I rise up; you discern my thoughts from afar. You search out my path and my lying down, you are acquainted with all my ways. Even before a word is on my tongue, you, o Lord, know it altogether. You are behind and before me, you lay your hand upon me. Such knowledge is too wonderful for me; it is high, I cannot attain it. Where shall I go from your Spirit? Or where shall I flee from your presence? ... For you formed my inward parts, you knitted me together in my mother's womb. I praise you, for you are fearful and wonderful. Wonderful are your works! You know me right well; my frame was not hidden from you, when I was being made in secret, intricately wrought in the depths of the earth. Your eyes beheld my unformed substance; in your book were written, every one of them, the days that were formed for me, when as yet there was none of them. How precious to me are your thoughts, O God! How vast is the sum of them!

This dilemma involving the relationship between grace and freedom, already mentioned in the context of the *de auxiliis* controversy and to which we shall return presently, brings us to consider the way in which predestination in Christ is concretized in the life of the believer, that is, through calling, or vocation.

The Christian Vocation and the Universal Call to Holiness

The word that God directs to the world is destined to produce a joyful and decided response on the part of creatures, all creatures (Bar 3:32–34):

But he who knows all things knows her [Wisdom], he found her by his understanding. He who prepared the earth for all time filled it with four-footed creatures. He who sends forth

---

37. Pannenberg, *Systematic Theology*, 3:444; see also what is said in ibid., 3:439–47.
38. Serenthà, "Predestinazione," 785. Greshake speaks in the same way in *Gnade als konkrete Freiheit*.

the light, and it goes, called it, and it obeyed him in fear; the stars shone in their watches, and were glad; he called them, and they said, 'Here we are!' They shone with gladness for him who made them.

Creatures not only come from God; they are meant to refer back to God as well.

The Biblical Doctrine of Vocation

Besides calling creatures in general, God calls humans in a special way: "Those whom he predestined he also called" (Rom 8:30). Within the development of God's project of grace, the notion of "vocation," or calling, adds to that of election/predestination two specific elements.[39] In the first place, the offer of grace is seen to require and bring about the free response of humans. God in fact through the grace of Christ made present by the Holy Spirit in the Church, calls humans, bringing about in them "suaviter et fortiter" (gently and firmly) a response that does not annul their intelligence, will, their temporal, bodily, and social condition, but rather stimulates, assumes, and elevates all five. As Albarello wrote, "Vocational choice is a creative entrusting of the human being to that special promise made by God, that calls on and stimulates the freedom of the creature."[40]

Second, God directs his call to humans one by one, in an exquisitely personal way, in and through the concrete circumstances of their lives, with the intention of establishing *with each one* a personal and perpetual relationship: "Thus says the Lord, he who created you, O Jacob, he who formed you, O Israel: 'Fear not, for I have redeemed you; I have called you by name, you are mine'" (Is 43:1). And the human response should, by right, correspond to the call, though it may take us some time to recognize it: "Here I am, for you called me," says the young boy Samuel on three occasions to the Lord's call (1 Sm 3:5, 6, 8).[41] As Thomas Aquinas acutely observed, "Since the soul has been made by God immediately, directly, the soul cannot be happy if it did not see God immediately"[42]—and we might add, if it did not respond to God directly, personally. The direct, immediate creation of the human soul by God and humans' being destined to perpetual communion with the Trinity sooner or later involves a personal calling on the part of the creator. "Cor ad cor loquitur," said J. H. Newman, "the heart speaks to the heart."[43] In fact, it may be said that the very notion of the human person is rooted in the vocation God directs to each one.[44]

Vocation is the fruit of divine initiative, not of human effort. "Biblical revela-

---

39. On the importance of the passage that bonds predestination and calling, see Scanziani, "Destino—Destinazione—Vocazione"; M. Bellet, *Vocazione e libertà* (Assisi: Cittadella, 2008; originally published in 1963); D. Albarello, "L'uomo, l'evocato"; C. Theobald, *Vocazione* (Bologna: Edizioni Dehoniane, 2011), 383–90.

40. Albarello, *L'uomo, l'evocato*, 389.

41. On individual vocation in the Old Testament, see the contributions of M. Conti and A. Sicari in A. Favale, ed., *Vocazione comune e vocazioni specifiche: Aspetti biblici, teologici e psico-pedagogico-pastorali*, 2nd ed. (Rome: LAS, 1993).

42. "Et quia anima immediate facta est a Deo, ideo beata esse non poterit nisi immediate videat Deum" (*Quodl.* X, q. 8, co.). "Homo est in potentia ad scientiam beatorum, quae in visione Dei consistit, et ad eam ordinatur sicut ad finem: est enim creatura rationalis capax illius beatae cognitionis, inquantum est ad imaginem Dei" (*S.Th.* III, q. 9, q. 2, co.).

43. This was Cardinal Newman's motto as cardinal.

44. On this affirmation, see O'Callaghan, "La persona umana tra filosofia e teologia."

tion speaks of a contrary movement to that by which humans attempt to transcend their lives: God wants to take the initiative in finding humanity," writes Hans Urs von Balthasar. He continues:

The fact that God never reveals himself in response to the cry of humans, to their desire to experience God, is very significant. God presents himself to Abraham with a completely unexpected promise, to Moses with a task that he had never foreseen, undesired and even stubbornly rejected ... to Isaiah who after contemplating God's glory exclaims: "Woe to me, for I am lost!" (Is 6:5), also on account of a painful and unpleasant mission. What is present in the Old Testament continues in the New, when God is encountered in Jesus Christ: humans are called to be sent with a mission and a power that comes from him, all over the world.... Even the mission of Jesus must pass this test; if he had given in to the temptation of an earthly Messianism, he would have reversed the situation and instead of allowing himself to be tested by God he would have tested God, the very sin of the people of Israel in the desert.[45]

The object of the call coincides with that of creation and predestination: to become children of God in Christ, "sons in the Son," through the power of the Holy Spirit. As we read in the letter to the Ephesians: "He [God] chose us in him [Christ] before the foundation of the world, that we should be holy and blameless before him. He predestined us in love to be his sons through Jesus Christ, according to the purpose of his will, to the praise of his glorious grace which be freely bestowed on us in the Beloved" (Eph 1:4–6).

Predestination and Vocation

The sixteenth-century Protestant reformer John Calvin distinguished between an exterior calling occasioned by the preaching of the Gospel and directed to all, and an interior calling that takes place in the power of the Holy Spirit, confers the capacity to believe, and is reserved to those who have been chosen by God.[46] For Calvin, who holds to the doctrine of double predestination, the distinction in question is a real one: humans are predestined by God either to glory (the chosen ones) or to condemnation. Besides, the distinction between the two kinds of calling may be considered valid in the sense that the mere proclamation of the Gospel cannot represent for those who receive it a clear proof of their having been chosen, for the latter requires besides the gift of the Spirit and personal acceptance. However, to some degree Calvin's doctrine is problematic because it would seem that God is not really attempting to bring about the salvation of all humans.[47] Besides, it looks as if he is establishing an a priori elitist distinction among those who hear the Word of God. In real terms, the intimate and personal character of election and calling need not be opposed either to the ecclesial mediations that God has wished to employ in order to establish communion between himself and humans, preaching among them, or to the adoring

---

45. H. U. von Balthasar, "Esperienza di Dio nella Bibbia dei Padri," *Communio* (ed. italiana) 5, no. 30 (1976): 4–15, 5f.

46. "Duplicem esse vocationis speciem. Est enim universalis vocatio qua per externam verbis praedicationem omnes pariter ad se invitat Deus.... Est altera specialis, qua ut plurimum solos fideles dignatur, dum interiori sui spiritus illuminatione efficit, ut verbum praedicatum eorum cordibus insideat." J. Calvin, *Inst. Christ.* III, 24:8.

47. This was the response of the Lutherans to Calvin in the *Formula della Concordia*, SD XI, neg. 3.

response that the whole Church owes to its Lord in both earthbound and heavenly liturgies. We have already seen that God predestines Christ in the first place, and in him the Church, the body of Christ, the mother that generates grace in humans. In effect, God's calling, the election of humans, is verified in the Church and through the Church. But it is clear that the calling, by its very nature, is personal. Humans are called one by one in the sense that the fruit of the call is one of personal communion with God. It is interesting to note that the Biblical terms for calling (*klēsis*) and Church (*ekklēsia*, "chosen community") have a common linguistic root.[48]

In these pages it is not possible, of course, to consider the question of Christian vocation in the widest sense of the word, in all its Biblical, spiritual, psychological, missionary, and ecclesial implications.[49] We may, however, reflect briefly on the following three aspects of Christian vocation.

The Christian Calling Involves the Entirety of Human Life and Personhood

God's call, directed to each and every person, is based on the original project of creation and predestination: "For those whom he foreknew he also predestined.... And those whom he predestined he also called" (Rom 8:29f.). Thus, to be called by God is not something accidental or artificially added on to human life. It is not something that is tacked on at a later moment to the personal and cultural characteristics of humans, covering up these latter. Certainly divine vocation does not depend on the virtues or talents previously possessed by humans. Quite the contrary: because God's calling is based on the divine project for humanity before the creation of the world, it includes and involves a priori every single aspect of the lives of humans, and therefore all their capacities, energies, talents, and projects.[50] No aspect of a person's life is excluded from their vocation. "Christian faith and calling affect our whole existence, not just a part of it," writes Josemaría Eserivá. "Our relations with God necessarily demand giving ourselves, giving ourselves completely. The man of faith sees life, in all its dimensions, from a new perspective: that which is given us by God."[51] For this

---

48. See *BDAG* 549, s.v. κλῆσις; 303f., s.v. ἐκκλησία.

49. On the question of vocation, see J. De Fraine, *Vocazione ed elezione nella Bibbia* (Bari: Paoline, 1967); G. Greganti, *La vocazione individuale nel Nuovo Testamento: L'uomo di fronte a Dio* (Rome: Pontificia Università Lateranense, 1969); A. Pigna, *La vocazione: Teologia e discernimento* (Rome: Teresianum, 1983); M. Conti, *La vocazione e le vocazioni nella Bibbia* (Brescia: La Scuola, 1985); J. Morales, "La vocación en el Antiguo Testamento," *Scripta Theologica* 19 (1987): 11–62; A. Bandera, *La vocación cristiana en la Iglesia* (Madrid: Rialp, 1988); Favale, *Vocazione comune e vocazioni specifiche*; F. Ocáriz, "Vocation to Opus Dei as a Vocation in the Church," in *Opus Dei in the Church: An Ecclesiological Study of the Life and Apostolate of Opus Dei*, edited by P. Rodríguez, F. Ocáriz, and J. L. Illanes (Dublin: Four Courts Press, 1994), 77–120; S. Légasse, M. Sauvage, and A. Godin, "Vocation," in *Dictionnaire de Spiritualité* 16 (1994): 1161–67; L. M. Rulla, ed., *Antropologia della vocazione cristiana*, 2nd ed., vol. 1: *Basi interdisciplinari*, vol. 2: *Conferme esistenziali*, vol. 3: *Aspetti interpersonali* (Casale Monferrato: Piemme, 1997); G. De Virgilio, ed., *Dizionario biblico della vocazione* (Rome: Rogate, 2007), esp. "Vocazione/Chiamata" by G. di Virgilio, in ibid., 987–1005; Bellet, *Vocazione e libertà*; Theobald, *Vocazione*; *NIDNTTE* 2:601–7, s.v. καλέω.

50. See J. L. Illanes, *Mundo e santidad* (Madrid: Rialp, 1984); A. Favale, "La vita come vocazione," in *Vocazione comune e vocazioni specifiche*, 31–71.

51. Josemaría Escrivá, "In Joseph's Workshop," homily in *Christ Is Passing By* (Dublin: Four Courts, 1975), no. 46. In one of his early writings, Josemaría described the Christian vocation in the following terms: "If you ask me how one recognizes a divine calling, how one comes to a realization of it, I will tell you that it is a new view of life. It is as if a light was lit within us: it is a mysterious impulse which urges one to devote one's

reason what truly gives us *unity of life* and a sense of being irreplaceable persons is the acceptance by each of us of our vocation, deeply assumed and lived to the full.[52] In real terms, those who are faithful to their vocation are faithful to themselves.[53] For this reason, the process of personal vocational discernment is closely linked with the concrete circumstances—personal, family, cultural, professional, temperamental, of character—in which each and every person lives and acts. Through these circumstances, which may seem banal and shifting, material and contingent, God's makes present to each person his concrete will, that is, his calling.[54] Doubtless, vocation is divine, and therefore it defines the lives of humans definitively, obliging them to fidelity, even though their knowledge of the exact profile and content of their vocation is not always fully clear.[55]

The Free Human Response to the Divine Call

Human response to vocation is, and should be, fully free. This is so not in the sense that response is indifferent or optional but in the sense that (1) when God calls he fully respects the free response of the person, in such a way that the latter is not constrained in a physical or moral way to respond positively but rather invited to lead a generous and trusting dedication to a life project whose shape and content are not yet fully known; and besides, (2) the response of humans involves the whole person of each, in all their concrete, social, corporeal, and historical concreteness. For this reason, human freedom with respect to vocation cannot be reduced to "a mere acceptance of a pre-constituted divine project, that is clearly and unmistakably knowable."[56] Vocation, in other words, is not a kind of ready-made "package" that drops down from heaven, designed and fashioned down to the last detail, as if it were "a copy of a theatrical score."[57] God wants and brings about in each person a completely personal and authentic response. That is because, as Gregory of Nyssa puts it, we are

---

noblest energies to an activity which, with practice, begins to take on the nature of an occupation. That vital force, which is something like an avalanche sweeping everything before it, is what others call a vocation.... Vocation leads us, without our realizing it, to take up a position in life and maintain it with eagerness and joy and a fullness of hope right up to the very moment of our death. It is a phenomenon which gives our work a sense of mission and which ennobles and gives value to our existence. Jesus, of his own accord, enters the soul—yours, mine.... That is the call." *Letter* 9-I-1932, no. 9, cited by A. Vázquez de Prada in *The Founder of Opus Dei*, vol. 1: *The Early Years* (Princeton, N.J.: Scepter, 2001), 227.

52. On "unity of life," see Ocáriz, "Vocation to Opus Dei," 83. See also John Paul II, *Christifideles Laici*, Apostolic Exhortation, December 30, 1988, pars. 17, 59f.

53. "The strongest obligation I am confronted with, the honest and substantial coherency of my being, coincide with the obligation I have before God who calls me." P. Rodríguez, *Vocación, trabajo, contemplación*, 2nd ed. (Pamplona: Eunsa, 1987), 19.

54. See C. Rocchetta, "Verso una rinnovata teologia della vocazione: Bilancio e prospettive," *Vivens Homo* 6 (1996): 79–99.

55. "Vocation, or divine calling, is not to be sought out in God's divine decrees, for this would be presumptuous, but in the signs of his will in our lives, this being much easier and practically sufficient." L. Sempé, "Vocation," *Dictionnaire de théologie catholique* 15, no. 2 (1950): 3170.

56. Ocáriz, "Vocation to Opus Dei," 83. On this issue, see also M. Bellet, *Vocation et liberté* (Paris: Desclée de Brouwer, 1963).

57. Scanziani, "Destino—Destinazione—Vocazione," 428. T. Citrini uses the binomial "copy or history of freedom" in "Teologia delle vocazioni: Il problema delle tipologie," in *Laicità e vocazioni dei laici nella Chiesa e nel mondo*, edited by A. Cargnel (Cinisello Balsamo Italy: Edizioni Paoline, 1987), 120–40.

"parents of ourselves."[58] We can say, therefore, that "every vocation is a creation."[59] As a result, the personal union with God that is the ultimate fruit of the human acceptance of divine vocation does not present itself as a kind of optional activity, a hobby, because it involves the human person in its entirety and is directed necessarily to eternal life, to the ultimate self-giving of God to humans, that is, to eschatological glorification.[60] Later we shall return to the question of human freedom in relation to the divine calling.

Humans' Calling and Apostolic Mission

Because vocation derives ultimately from the love of God for humans, its ultimate purpose is always that of bringing about the human response of love for God, that is, communion with the Trinity, or holiness. This is a totally unique, personal, and lasting love that Christians are invited to cultivate throughout their whole lives, in the context of complete fidelity.[61] At the same time, however, the call to love God above all things constitutes anything but a phenomenon of isolation. "For while God's call is addressed to the individual, it never concerns each person alone."[62] Rather it is a reality that involves relationship and communion with others because God, through the call to holiness, to the fullness of charity, inseparably calls humans to spread his love among other human beings. In other words, the call to holiness is inseparable from the call to apostolate, to ecclesial mission, to evangelization.[63] Every Christian vocation is missionary, apostolic, self-diffusing.[64]

Still, an enormous variety of different vocations is to be found in the Church. Yet each of them draws its specificity not from the level of holiness acquired, because one and all are called to holiness, but rather from the particular ecclesial mission each one is invited to carry out: a calling to a lay vocation, to marriage, to the ministerial priesthood, to a consecrated life.[65] Just as in the Church there is an ample range of charisms and gifts (1 Cor 12), there is likewise a great variety of missions, and thus of vocations.[66] Some of these may be considered special vocations, to be identified psychologically at particular moments of one's life and publicly discerned by the Church. This is so, for example, in the case of the ministerial priesthood. In other cases, however, people called by God may not be fully aware of the stages and ways in which God calls them. People in situations of this kind, as they look back over the lives they have

58. Gregory of Nyssa, *De vita Moysis*, 2:3.

59. C. Boureux, "La notion de vocation: Appel universel de Dieu, récit de l'homme," *Vie spirituelle* 78 (1998): 641–61, 651.

60. See U. Vanni, "La vocazione escatologica," in *Vocazione comune e vocazioni specifiche*, 423–37.

61. On the role of fidelity in Christian life, see J. Morales, *Fidelidad* (Madrid: Rialp, 2004).

62. *NIDNTTE* 2:606, s.v. καλέω.

63. On the inseparability of holiness and apostolate in Christian life, see A. Aranda, "Cristo presente en los cristianos," '*El bullir de la sangre de Cristo*': *Estudio sobre el cristocentrismo del beato Josemaría Escrivá* (Madrid: Rialp, 2000), 203–54; O'Callaghan, "The Inseparability of Holiness and Apostolate."

64. See J. Esquerda Bifet, "La vocazione missionaria," in *Vocazione comune e vocazioni specifiche*, 273–91. In the life and vocation of Paul, union with Christ is deeply bound up with his universal missionary vocation. See O'Callaghan, *Fides Christi*, 179–83.

65. See J. R. Villar, "Gli elementi definitori dell'identità del fedele laico," *Ius Ecclesiae* 23 (2011): 339–58.

66. Variety among vocations may also be expressed in terms of the different kinds of spirituality that people live.

lived, frequently discover, in the midst of many lived experiences, a project, a plan, a unitary narrative, that may be recognized as a response, or a series of responses, to the divine call they were receiving throughout a lifetime.[67]

Now, it is clear that God does not call all believers to carry out the same mission in the Church or to live according to the same spirituality. And so we may ask: Does God call all the baptized to holiness, to the fullness of Christian life, or only some? Is it licit to distinguish between the general mass of Christians, called to live honest and decent lives, and a group of chosen ones, people specially picked out by God to reach holiness in the fullest sense of the word?[68]

The Universal Call to Holiness

The doctrine of the universal call to holiness is a particular expression of God's universal saving will that is based, in turn, on the project of creation, on the decree of predestination in Christ such that humans would become children of God, living lives modeled on that of the Trinity.[69] The universality of God's saving will is also based on the universality of the divine image present in each person, which gives humans the capacity to enter into dialogue with God and to correspond to his offer of communion.

The Biblical basis for the universal call to holiness   The will of God to save all humans is expressed and carried out through the universal redemptive mediation of Christ, the fullness of the divine image and supreme expression of the divine saving will (Jn 12:47, 3:17). Christ gives expression to the universality of redemption in carrying out a work of reconciliation that reaches all creatures (Col 1:20). The New Testament assures us that God "desires all men to be saved and to come to the knowledge of the truth" (1 Tm 2:4). God sent his own Son in "expiation for our sins, and not for ours only but also for the sins of the whole world" (1 Jn 2:2). Christ *"died for all,* that those who live might live no longer for themselves but for him who for their sake died and was raised" (2 Cor 5:15). Faithful to the baptismal mandate of the Lord, "Go therefore and make disciples of all nations [*ethnē*], baptizing them in the name of the Father and of the Son and of the Holy Spirit" (Mt 28:19), the Church from the very outset was aware of the need to direct the word of God to all peoples, going beyond the boundaries established by the Israelitic Covenant, right to the very ends of the earth (Acts 1:8; see Acts 2:9–11, Eph 2:13–18). As a kind of summing up of the Beatitudes discourse, we can read Jesus' words to all the disciples: "You, therefore, must be perfect, as your heavenly Father is perfect" (Mt 5:48).[70] In real terms, to be "perfect" before the eternal Father means being like Christ, and in doing so becoming children

---

67. "Toute vocation singulière n'est que le récit de l'ensemble partiel des éléments qui ont contribué à la dessiner en fonction des destinataires de ce récit. Une vocation spécifique est la tentative d'ordonner, dans un récit signifiant, tout ce qui précède l'état de fait dans le quel se trouve le chrétien au moment où il tente d'expliquer qui il est sous le regard de Dieu." Boureux, *La notion de vocation*, 654.

68. This would seem to be the definitive position of von Balthasar, explained and evaluated in P. O'Callaghan, "'Gli stati di vita del cristiano.'" Von Balthasar does teach the universal call to holiness, yet the paradigm of Christian life is always that of the consecrated person.

69. See John Paul II, *Dominum et Vivificantem*, Encyclical Letter, May 18, 1986, par. 10; *General Audience*, May 3, 1986; Ocáriz, "Vocation to Opus Dei," 78ff.

70. The term "perfect" (*teleios*) is equivalent to the Hebrew *timîm*, frequently used in the Old Testament to

of God. Paul, in the first text of the New Testament, writes: "This is the will of God, your sanctification" (1 Thes 4:3).

According to the Old Testament, in fact, God does not take pleasure in the death of the malevolent but rather wants them to change their ways of acting and live, as the prophet tells us (Ezek 18:23). Scripture attests to the existence of a sufficient grace for conversion that is offered by God to each and every sinner. This may be clearly seen in the episode of the conversion of the repentant thief (Lk 23:39–43) as Christ was dying on the cross. Divine chastisement, trials, tribulations, and the need for patience before the fulfillment of the divine promise also prepare for this conversion (see Lk 22:28f.; 2 Pt 3:9). Heaven awaits the conversion of each and every sinner with the pained and patient devotion of the father of the prodigal son (Lk 15), and it rejoices with the exultation of the good shepherd who finds the lost sheep (Mt 18:12–14).

The theological and spiritual consolidation of the universal call to holiness   The doctrine of the universal call to holiness has always been taught by and lived in the Church, as may be seen, for example, during the sharp exchanges that took place in the ninth century (see chapter 8) on the question of predestination and in the controversies over the nature of grace and its efficacy that have been common over recent centuries.[71] With respect to the charismatic and elitist movements of his time, Augustine insisted especially that holiness was possible for all Christians. In doing so he took his cue principally from two texts of Paul: "What have you that you did not receive? If then you received it, why do you boast as if it were not a gift? ... As it is written, 'Let him who boasts, boast of the Lord'" (1 Cor 4:7 and 1:31).[72] The basis for the call of all humans to holiness is to be found, clearly, not within humans themselves, in that they belong, as Augustine says, to the *massa damnata*, but in the abundance of God's grace. For this reason, he says, there is no valid reason for putting off baptism. In real terms his homilies on the Christian's hope for holiness are homilies on equality: all, without exception, have the possibility of obtaining God's grace.

Several modern authors have insisted in a special way on the universal call to holiness, for example, Francis de Sales[73] and Thérèse of Lisieux.[74] In effect, the will of God to save all is not a mere "divine aspiration" but rather the efficacious will of a good, faithful, and omnipotent God and thus is really possible, on the basis of the death and resurrection of Christ and the sending of the Holy Spirit, a will that is prepared to stop only before sin, the willful closing of the human heart. Pope Bene-

---

speak of moral rectitude (Gn 6:9, 17:1; 2 Sm 22:24–27). In fact, the Septuagint translates this term into Greek as *teleios* (Dt 18:13). See D. A. Hagner, *Matthew 1–13*, in *WBC* 33A:135f.; *NIDNTTE* 4:470–80, s.v. τέλος, esp. 472.

71. In condemning Jansenism, the Church declared that nobody is predestined to remain *outside* the influence of Christ (*DH* 2305); besides, it declared that it would be erroneous to hold that outside the Church no grace whatsoever is to be found (*DH* 2429).

72. On the use Augustine makes of these texts, see P.-M. Hombert, *Gloria gratiae: Se glorifier en Dieu, principe et fin de la théologie augustinienne de la grâce* (Paris: Institut d'Études Augustiniennes, 1996), 19–24; Brown, *Augustine of Hippo*, 508–10.

73. See especially Francis de Sales, *Introduction to the Devout Life* and *Treatise on the Love of God*. On the teaching of Francis, see V. Balciunas, *La vocation universelle à la perfection chrétienne selon saint François de Sales* (Annecy: Académie Salésienne, 1952).

74. See Thérèse of Lisieux, *History of a Soul*. On her teaching, see A. M. Sicari, *La teologia di santa Teresa di Lisieux dottore della Chiesa* (Milan: Jaca Book, 1997).

dict XVI has noted that in a special way Josemaría Escrivá has reminded the whole Church of the universal call to holiness.[75] Writes Escrivá:

This is the great boldness of the Christian faith … to proclaim the value and dignity of human nature and to affirm that we have been created to achieve the dignity of children of God, through the grace that raises us up to a supernatural level. An incredible boldness it would be, were it not founded on the promise of salvation given us by God the Father, confirmed by the blood of Christ, and reaffirmed and made possible by the constant action of the Holy Spirit.[76]

In the words of Bisignano, "The vocation of the Church (which Paul VI termed 'the one who is called'), spouse of Christ, is the fundamental vocation of each and every one; a call to holiness, to communion in unity, to mission, lived out in a great variety of different ways, according to gifts, charisms and ministries, given by Christ for the growth of the Church."[77]

The Church's teaching on the universal call to holiness   This teaching that we are all called to holiness was solemnly proclaimed by Vatican Council II.[78] It may well be considered the principal interpretative key of the whole Council.[79] "The Church, whose mystery is being set forth by this Sacred Synod, is believed to be indefectibly holy," teaches the constitution *Lumen Gentium* in the fifth chapter. "Therefore in the Church, everyone whether belonging to the hierarchy, or being cared for by it, is called to holiness, according to the saying of the Apostle: 'For this is the will of God, your sanctification' (1 Thes 4:3)."[80] And the text continues:

75. See Pope Benedict XVI, *Verbum Domini*, Apostolic Exhortation, September 30, 2010, par. 48.

76. Escrivá, *Christ Is Passing By*, no. 133.

77. S. Bisignano, "Vocazione," in *Dizionario enciclopedico di spiritualità*, edited by E. Ancilli, 2nd ed. (Rome: Città Nuova, 1990), 3:2670–77, 2672.

78. See *LG*, chap. 5, nos. 39–42.

79. Pope Paul VI, *Sanctitas Clarior*, Apostolic Letter, March 19, 1969, in *Acta Apostolicae Sedis* 61 (1969): 150, said that the doctrine of the universal call to holiness was the most characteristic (*proprietas*) of the teaching of the Council, as well as being its ultimate purpose. On the relationship between the universal call to holiness and the holiness of the Church itself, see P. O'Callaghan, "The Holiness of the Church in 'Lumen Gentium,'" esp. 678–83. Karl Rahner called the Council teaching of the universal call to holiness "an amazing event": "For so far as the spontaneous attitude and outlook of the Church throughout almost two millennia is concerned with the truth embodied in this proposition [the universal call to holiness] has precisely *not* been self-evident. Of course *in point of fact* there always are Christians in all situations and walks of life who have been and are holy. But over and above this it has not been so immediately obvious that on God's side there is also a *positive vocation* and mission to marriage and to a worldly calling, to earthly tasks precisely as the manner positively ordained by God to the individual concerned, in which precisely he is to attain to the fullness of his Christian existence, the maturity of the baptismal grace bestowed upon him and in which he is to bring to their fullness the fruits of the Spirit." K. Rahner, "On the Evangelical Counsels," in *Theological Investigations* (London: Darton, Longman and Todd, 1977), 8:133–67, 136. See also the final report of the Special Synod of Bishops on the twentieth anniversary of the conclusion of Vatican Council II in the year 1985 (II, a, 4). Several of the presentations made during the International Congress *Attuazione del Concilio Ecumencio Vaticano II*, celebrated on the occasion of the jubilee year 2000, indicates the call to holiness as a central criterion for the interpretation of the Council documents. See R. Fisichella, ed. *Il Concilio Vaticano II: Recezione e attualità alla luce del Giubileo* (Cinisello Balsamo: San Paolo, 2000). M. Ouellet considers the universal call to holiness a "fundamental idea of the Council which draws on the Church's tradition, because in practice holiness was reserved only for those who made religious profession." M. Ouellet, *Actualité et avenir du Concile Oecuménique Vatican II*, interviewed by G. de la Tousche (Dijon: L'Échelle de Jacob, 2012), 45. "The universal call to holiness is one of the most important aspects of Vatican Council II," ibid., 188.

80. *LG*, no. 39.

The Lord Jesus, the divine Teacher and Model of all perfection, preached holiness of life to each and every one of His disciples of every condition. He Himself stands as the author and consummator of this lifestyle: "Be you therefore perfect, even as your heavenly Father is perfect" (Mt 5:48). Indeed He sent the Holy Spirit upon all men that He might move them inwardly to love God with their whole heart and their whole soul, with all their mind and all their strength (Mk 12:30) and that they might love each other as Christ loves them (Jn 13:34; 15:12).[81]

In John Paul II's 2001 apostolic letter *Novo Millennio Ineunte*, the same doctrine is taught:

It is necessary therefore to rediscover the full practical significance of chapter 5 of the Dogmatic Constitution on the Church *Lumen gentium*, dedicated to the "universal call to holiness." The Council Fathers laid such stress on this point, not just to embellish ecclesiology with a kind of spiritual veneer, but to make the call to holiness an intrinsic and essential aspect of their teaching on the Church. The rediscovery of the Church as "mystery," or as a people "gathered together by the unity of the Father, the Son and the Holy Spirit" [Cyprian], was bound to bring with it a rediscovery of the Church's "holiness," understood in the basic sense of belonging to him who is in essence the Holy One, the "thrice Holy" (Is 6:3). To profess the Church as holy means to point to her as the Bride of Christ, for whom he gave himself precisely in order to make her holy (see Eph 5:25–26). This as it were objective gift of holiness is offered to all the baptized.[82]

John Paul intends to situate the doctrine of the universal call to holiness as "the foundation of the pastoral planning in which the whole Church is involved at the start of the new millennium," making specific mention of the life of prayer, Sunday eucharist, the sacrament of reconciliation, the primacy of grace, listening to and proclaiming the word of God.[83] In fact, the theological, pastoral, and anthropological implications of the doctrine of the universal call to holiness are many and substantial. The following four may be mentioned. They correspond, respectively, to four dimensions of this call: the subjective, the objective, the ecumenical, and the cosmic.

Theological Implications of the Universal Call to Holiness

In the first place, God calls all the baptized to a holy life; each and every one receives a personal call to communion with the Trinity. In the universality of this call, as we saw earlier, may be found the Christian conviction of the dignity of each human being.[84] "God does not abandon any soul to a blind destiny. He has a plan for all and He calls each to a very personal and non-transferable vocation," writes Josemaría.[85] This aspect of the divine calling may be defined as the *subjective dimension* of the universal call to holiness.[86] From the fact that God in Christ calls all to holiness may be deduced the fundamental equality of all humans and thus the existence of a single

81. Ibid.

82. John Paul II, *Novo Millennio Ineunte*, Apostolic Letter, January 6, 2001, par. 30. The citation of Cyprian is taken from his work *De Orat. Dom*. 23 and is quoted in *LG*, no. 4.

83. John Paul II, *Novo Millennio Ineunte*, par. 31; see pars. 32–41.

84. See chapter 2, 54ff. and corresponding text, and chapter 25.

85. Josemaría Escrivá, *Conversations with Mgr Escrivá de Balaguer* (Dublin: Four Courts, 1968), no. 106.

86. See Ocáriz, "Vocation to Opus Dei," 90f. Ocáriz explains that this doctrine has been taught by many saints and masters of spirituality throughout history; see also J. Daujat, *La vita soprannaturale* (Milan: Ares, 1958), 561–73.

human race: "There is neither Jew nor Greek, there is neither slave nor free, there is neither male nor female; for you are all one in Christ Jesus" (Gal 3:28).[87]

Second, the call to holiness is appropriate and possible in every state in the Church (priesthood, consecrated life, laity) and in civil society (women and men, rich and poor, healthy and infirm, young and old, people who carry out all kinds of work and occupations). The distinction obtaining between different states in the Church refers primarily not to the place occupied by the call to holiness or to the possibility of receiving the divine calling and reaching holiness but to questions of an ecclesiological, apostolic, social, and historical kind. This is so because God does not call humans in the first place to a particular state but rather always and directly to holiness by means of the diverse states. Christian holiness is fundamentally the same for all (it consists of an ever more perfect communion with the Father though Christ in the Spirit), while the different states and life situations (ecclesial, civil, human, personal) and different spiritualities modulate in a wide variety of different ways the search for holiness and determine the specific mission each person is meant to carry out. This is what may be called the *objective dimension* of the universal call to holiness.[88]

As a result, the third implication of the universal call to holiness is that holiness is, or at least should be, the element that most unites Christians. Perhaps, indeed, it is the only thing that truly unites us. In other words, the reality of the universal call to Christian holiness does not only offer humans an interior liberation, fruit of justifying and sanctifying grace, but also gives us an exterior liberty in society and the Church, making it possible to enter "the glorious liberty of the children of God" (Rom 8:21) and to act with full freedom and responsibility in the world. The search for holiness should therefore constitute the "common denominator" of Christian believers. And this leaves wide open a vast "numerator" made up of a nearly infinite variety of different ways of focusing social, political, ecclesial, and spiritual life.[89] It is probably fair to say that problems and conflicts in the Church and in society arise, and may become more or less serious, when humans do not respond faithfully to this precise call to holiness and attempt to live their Christian faith seeking out alternative collective purposes and projects. This is what we may denominate the *ecumenical dimension* of the call to holiness.

Fourth, the doctrine of the universal call to holiness means that there is no objective obstacle present in the world, in life or in the human condition, that is capable of arresting a priori the power of the grace of God and of his calling. The apostle Paul proclaims this truth with intimate conviction: "For I am sure that neither death, nor life, nor angels, nor principalities, nor things present, nor things to come, nor powers, nor height, nor depth, nor anything else in all creation, will be able to separate us from the love of God in Christ Jesus our Lord" (Rom 8:38f.). That is to say, nothing

---

87. According to the praxis of the RigVeda, in the words of Raju, in "The Concept of Man in Indian Thought," 207, only one in ten thousand will reach perfect "renunciation," the Hindu equivalent of holiness.

88. See Ocáriz, "Vocation to Opus Dei," 90f.

89. Speaking to the faithful of Opus Dei, Josemaría describes as follows the variety of Christian lifestyles within the common search for holiness: "We are like fractions with the same denominator—and as many numerators as there are members, each in his or her own circumstances. A common denominator—with a distinctive spiritual doctrine, which spurs us to seek personal holiness," *Letter* 8-XII-1949, no. 29, cited by Vázquez de Prada in *The Founder of Opus Dei*, 3:219.

in the created order is in a position to annul divine grace because, as we already saw, all things have been created by the one who then calls all humans to holiness. To live the divine precepts is fully possible for humans (Dt 30:11–14), although, on account of their fallen condition, this may at times be superior to their strengths should God's grace be absent (1 Jn 5:3–4), which, of course, it is not. John Paul II, in the conclusive chapter of his 1993 encyclical *Veritatis Splendor*, insists on this very point.[90] This may be called the *cosmic dimension* of the universal call to holiness.

Still, it should be added that, along with divine grace, two other elements play a central role in making the way to holiness a real possibility for all the baptized: first, the sustenance and consolation of Christian charity, which God infuses into the hearts of the faithful,[91] and second, the catechetical, theological, and spiritual training that the Church at all levels is bound to impart to all the faithful.[92]

The Justification of the Sinner

"Those whom he called, he also justified" (Rom 8:30). God comes close to humans by calling them, seeking out their faithful response. However, in justifying the sinner God crowns his calling by an effective donation of divine grace, by which the believer is forgiven and sanctified and becomes really a child of God. When God justifies, not only does he come close to the human being, forgiving sin and offering his friendship, but carries out a deep—ontological—renewal of the concrete human being, of his life and action: the justified person becomes a "new creation," is regenerated as a child of God in Christ, enjoys the stable presence of the Holy Spirit, to use expressions central to Paul's theology. Or, in the terminology typical of John the evangelist, the believer is regenerated, acquiring a new, eternal life through which God himself lives and remains within the one who becomes really (and not only in name) a child of God. In the coming chapters different aspects of this transformation and new life will be considered in detail, as well as the concrete process of justification.[93] For the moment we shall consider two particular issues regarding the doctrine of justification: the presupposition of the state of sin that justifying grace eliminates and the faith required for the gift of justification to be received.

Sin as the Point of Departure for the Process of Justification

According to scripture, the point of departure for justification is the sinful human being.[94] This doctrine is developed principally by Paul in his letters to the Ro-

90. See John Paul II, *Veritatis Splendor*, pars. 102–5.

91. I attempt to explain this principle in P. O'Callaghan, "The Charism of the Founder of Opus Dei," *Annales Theologici* 14 (2000): 401–46.

92. The trust the Church places in the grace of God may not serve as an excuse for neglecting evangelization and catechesis, the theological and spiritual formation of Christians to which they have a right. See Pope Paul VI, *Evangelii Nuntiandi*, Apostolic Exhortation, December 8, 1975; J. Hervada, "Misión laical y formación," in *La Misión del laico en la Iglesia y en mundo*, edited by A. Sarmiento (Pamplona: Eunsa, 1987), 481–95.

93. On the topic of justification, see O'Callaghan, *Fides Christi*; for the Biblical part, see, ibid., 185–94; *NIDNTTE* 1:722–41, s.v. δικαιοσύνη.

94. See R. Penna, "Il tema della giustificazione in Paolo: Uno status quaestionis," in *La giustificazione (Associazione Teologica Italiana)*, edited by G. Ancona (Padua: Messaggero, 1997), 19–64.

mans and the Galatians.[95] "All have sinned and fall short of the glory of God, they are justified by his grace as a gift, through the redemption which is in Christ Jesus" (Rom 3:23f.). "As one man's trespass led to condemnation for all men, so one man's act of righteousness leads to forgiveness and life for all men" (Rom 5:18). "For you were washed, you were sanctified, you were justified in the name of the Lord Jesus Christ and in the Spirit of our God" (1 Cor 6:11). The Council of Trent, in the *Decree on Justification*, defines justification as "a transition from the state in which man is born a son of the first Adam, to the state of grace and adoption as sons of God, by means of the second Adam, Jesus Christ, our Savior."[96] And elsewhere Trent says: "Justification is not simply the forgiveness of sins, but also sanctification and the renewal of the inner man, through the free acceptance of grace and the gifts that accompany it, by which the unjust becomes just and the enemy a friend."[97] The Council adds: "Once the Gospel has been proclaimed, this transition cannot take place without the washing of regeneration or without the desire for the same."[98]

In effect, the call of God, which brings about justification, is not directed to human beings who find themselves in a neutral state before God but to people who carry within the centrifugal and destructive weight of sin, sin that is reaching out for reconciliation and salvation. In this we can see that the call of each one moves above and beyond the general plan of salvation and predestination of humans in Christ, because the human being to whom God directs his call is a sinner. The unconditional and faithful character of God's call—which seeks out a correspondingly faithful and grateful response from humans—is confirmed by the fact that God, in Christ, comes close to a *sinful humanity*. God intends to fully forgive the one who has offended him personally: "But God shows his love for us in that while we were yet sinners Christ died for us" (Rom 5:8).

The doctrine of faith as regards sin may be summed up in three points.[99] In the first place, the evil that is present in the world—death, suffering, corruption—finds its ultimate source neither in God (who is the absolute Good, love itself) nor in matter (which was created by God and in its simplicity and modesty carries within the seal of his goodness) but in the willing action of spiritual beings (both angels and humans) who rebelled against their creator and Lord by transgressing his commandments.[100] Second, the knowledge we have of sin as an offense to God is revealed to us not only (or principally) by our experience of evil and even by our conscience, which may accuse us of having transgressed the law of God. It is made known to us principally in the light of the death of Christ on the cross—a tragic icon of the God whose love was offered to, yet spurned by, humanity—and in the light of his resurrection from the dead[101] and by the action of the Spirit, who "will convince the world concerning sin

---

95. See chapter 5, notes 16ff. and corresponding text.

96. Council of Trent, *De iustificatione*, cap. 4, *DH* 1524, citing Rom 8:15.

97. Ibid., chap. 7, *DH* 1528.

98. Ibid., chap. 4, *DH* 1524.

99. On the question of sin in general and especially original sin, see O'Callaghan, *La metafisica cristiana*, 219–88.

100. On the relationship between evil in general and sin throughout the history of thought and theology, see O'Callaghan, *La metafisica cristiana*, 219–27.

101. See O'Callaghan, *La metafisica cristiana*, 227–34. On the way in which the saving work of Christ

and righteousness and judgment" (Jn 16:8).[102] Third, because human beings must always be considered as a synthesis of individuality and collective existence, sin should be understood not only as a purely individual phenomenon, deriving from each human in his relationship with God and confined therefore to private life, but as something that involves the human collectivity, all humans together. This is usually known as the doctrine of *original sin*.[103]

The Acceptance of Justifying Grace through Faith

According to the text of Paul we are glossing in these pages (Rom 8:29f.), calling (or vocation) is seen to precede justification. In effect, humans are justified when they respond freely to God's personal invitation, accepting his gift of grace through faith. The apostle to the Gentiles often insists on the idea that justification is the fruit of faith: "For we hold that a man is justified by faith apart from works of law.... Since God is one, and he will justify the circumcised on the ground of their faith and the uncircumcised through their faith" (Rom 3:28, 30). "Therefore, since we are justified by faith, we have peace with God through our Lord Jesus Christ" (Rom 5:1). "A man is not justified by works of the law but through faith in Jesus Christ.... So that the law was our custodian until Christ came, that we might be justified by faith. But now that faith has come, we are no longer under a pedagogue" (Gal 2:16, 3:24f.), that is, under the guidance of the law of Moses.

Still, two reservations arise in claiming that calling takes precedence over justification. First, if baptismal justification is received before a person enjoys the use of reason (the most typical case is that of an infant at baptism), how can we speak of a calling, a divine vocation received by humans in faith, which makes justification possible? And second, because a Christian vocation is normally recognized, consolidated, and accepted later on in life, that is, after justification through baptism, it would seem more correct to say that justification precedes calling.

In response to the first reservation, it may be observed that humans without the use of reason do not personally experience or recognize the divine call but still are truly justified (of course things are different in the case of an adult). The calling is there, however, and also the response, because the Church itself, though parents and

---

shows up humans as sinners, see chapter 3 and also P. O'Callaghan, "Una lectura cristológica de la doctrina del pecado original," *Scripta Theologica* 46, no. 1 (2014): 161–80.

102. See John Paul II, *Dominum et Vivificantem*.

103. On the history of the doctrine of original sin, see O'Callaghan, *La metafisica cristiana*, 235–44, and, for a systematic reflection, see 245–75. The doctrine of original sin may be summed up in the following formula of Paul VI, *Solemni Hac Liturgia*, Apostolic Letter, June 30, 1968: "We believe that in Adam all have sinned, which means that the original offense committed by him caused human nature, common to all men, to fall to a state in which it bears the consequences of that offense, and which is not the state in which it was at first in our first parents—established as they were in holiness and justice, and in which man knew neither evil nor death. It is human nature so fallen, stripped of the grace that clothed it, injured in its own natural powers and subjected to the dominion of death, that is transmitted to all men, and it is in this sense that every man is born in sin. We therefore hold, with the Council of Trent, that original sin is transmitted with human nature, 'not by imitation, but by propagation' and that it is thus 'proper to everyone'" (par. 16). The citation from the Council of Trent may be found in session V on original sin: c. 4, *DH* 1514. See the commentary of C. Pozo, *El credo del pueblo de Dios: Comentario teológico* (Madrid: BAC, 1968), 148–66, translated into English as *The Credo of the People of God: A Theological Commentary* (Chicago: Franciscan Herald Press 1980).

godparents, accepts and receives in the name of the baptized the call God directs to them.[104] So there is a calling, received in the name of the baptized through the faith of the Church, followed by justification. As regards the second reservation, it should be said that our knowledge of the complex dynamic of the Christian vocation arises and is consolidated often during a process that takes place over an extended period of time, because God gives himself to humans personally and within their temporal and historical coordinates, and thus repeatedly. As we saw earlier, the true profile of one's vocation is often recognized as such only after many years. Thus we can conclude that calling precedes justification.

Glorification and the Eschatological Purpose of All Grace

God's eternal plan, predestination, calling, and justification are always determined and understood in the light of the ultimate purpose God had when he created the world.[105] Without an ultimate reason, none of the previous stages of God's plan would have any meaning. Only the end explains the beginning. "We have invented the concept of 'end,' but in reality there is no end," declares Friedrich Nietzsche.[106] Without a purpose, without a consistent ultimate end, the whole process breaks down, all possibilities of development are emptied.

In the introduction I made reference to the central role eschatology plays in understanding Christian anthropology, specifically the human search for immortality (see chapter 2).[107] Besides, scripture speaks frequently of the idea that the life of grace is directed toward eschatological fulfillment: the life of grace, the gift of God's eternal love, constitutes a promise of reward, of glory, because although it contains within an eternal destiny, it will come to completion only in the future.[108] In that sense, from the believer's point of view, there is no substantial difference between the life of grace on earth and in eschatological glory.[109] Of course the life of grace, though very real, remains more or less hidden in this life, whereas in the next it will be revealed in all its realism and splendor, as the full, joyful and eternal fullness of divine life in humans. Glory, therefore, will constitute the definitive manifestation, the conclusive and perpetual blossoming of grace. According to Thomas Aquinas, the perfection of grace "in statu viae et patriae" (on the way and in the fatherland) is one and the same.[110] In creation and justification the power of God is fully and definitively committed, Aquinas adds, though in glorification it is not so to the same extent.[111] For this reason he says that grace is the "incohatio gloriae in nobis" (the beginning and guarantee of glory in us),[112] whereas the light of glory is "gratia consummata" (consummated grace).[113] To quote a phrase often attributed to Cardinal Newman but pro-

---

104. See *CCC* 1253.

105. On the epistemological priority of eschatology for Christian anthropology, see *COH* 25–31, 333f.

106. Cited in the first note to this chapter.

107. See also chapter 3.

108. On this issue, see Auer, *Das Evangelium der Gnade*, 140f.; Ruiz de la Peña, *El don de Dios*, 389–94; Sanna, *Chiamati per nome*, 376–80; Scola, Marengo, and Prades López, *La persona umana*, 342–45.

109. See the classic work of J. Kirschkamp, *Gnade und Glorie in ihrem innern Zusammenhang betrachtet: Eine dogmatische Studie* (Wurzburg: Bucher, 1878).

110. Aquinas, *De Veritate*, q. 27, a. 5, ad 6.　　　111. Aquinas, *S.Th.* I-II, q. 113, a. 9.

112. Aquinas, *S.Th.* II-II, q. 24, a. 3, ad 2.

113. Aquinas, *S.Th.* I, q. 95, q. 1, co.; *S.Th.* I-II, q. 111, a. 3, ad 2.

nounced by the Oratorian Federick W. Faber, a contemporary of the former, "Grace is not a different thing from glory. It is only *glory in exile*, while glory is but *grace at home*."[114] In fact, it has become quite common in theology over the past century to speak of the mystery of God's life in humans on earth in terms of "already but not yet," a expression first used by the Reformed exegete Oscar Cullmann.[115]

Continuity between Grace and Glory in the History of Theology

As Sanna writes, "Glorification is the last stage of the Father's work, and follows out the divine plan with which he predestined Christians to be conformed to the image who is the Son."[116] This is a common position in Christian theology.[117] According to Paul, God gives us his grace in order to obtain our eternal inheritance with Christ (Rom 8:17). For this reason the Christian is "no longer a slave but a son, and if a son then an heir" (Gal 4:7). Speaking of the vision of God, the apostle compares the present moment to eschatological fullness within a single process of salvation and incorporation into Christ: "For now we see in a mirror dimly, but then face to face. Now I know in part; then I shall understand fully, even as I have been fully understood" (1 Cor 13:12). John, besides speaking of our divine filiation (Jn 3, 1 Jn 3), explains that the life God gives to those who believe in Christ is eternal life, which is already present and active, though it is destined to last for ever in the place Christ prepares for his own (Jn 14:1–3). It is a life that brings us to share here on earth in God's own life, along with the future promise of resurrection. The present situation is, again, confronted with the eternal one: "Beloved, we are God's children now; it does not yet appear what we shall be, but we know that when he appears we shall be like him, for we shall see him as he is" (1 Jn 3:2).

Among the Eastern Church Fathers we have seen that the life of grace is expressed in terms of the process of the divinization of believers. Again the emphasis is on grace as a source of immortality, because to be "divinized" means first and foremost to become immortal, to live on forever. As Athanasius says, "The Word became man so that we could become gods. He became visible in body in order to open to us the knowledge of the invisible Father; he accepted the maltreatment of humanity so that we would share in his immortality."[118] In the theology of Augustine the doctrine of grace is clearly centered on the relationship between the dynamics of grace and sin and good works. Still, as is well known, the ultimate horizon of his anthropology is a living desire for peace and perpetual vision. Eternal life is "a holy and perpetual rest without any fatigue and weight; it consists not of an inactive laziness, but of an ineffable peace full of delightful activity."[119] In the background of Augustine's great work

---

114. F. W. Faber, *The Foot of the Cross or The Sorrows of Mary* (London: Richardson and Son, 1858), 24. The eighteenth-century American Calvinist Jonathan Edwards expressed the idea in the following formula: "Grace is but glory begun, glory is but grace perfected."

115. See O. Cullmann, *Salvation in History* (London: SCM Press, 1967); *Christ and Time: The Primitive Conception of Time and History* (Philadelphia: Westminster Press, 1964).

116. Sanna, *Chiamati per nome*, 377. 117. See *COH*.

118. Athanasius, *De Inc. Verbi* 54.

119. Augustine, *Ep. 55, ad Iannerion*, 9, 17: Eternal life involves "the praise of God, without effort of the members, without anxiety and concern; hence there is no succession of rest and work, and it cannot be said that activity begins as soon as rest ceases."

of political philosophy and theology, *De civitate Dei*, lies the promise of eternal life, that is, the city of God where justice will find a perpetual abode, in contrast with this world, the city of men, which is full of sin and corruption. Besides, we can remember his exclamation at the beginning of the *Confessions*: "You made us for you, Lord, and our heart is restless until it rests in you."[120] Still, when he insists on the need to pray for final perseverance, Augustine shows that there is a rupture between this life and eternity, which is always an unmerited gift of God. Likewise, according to Bonaventure, between grace and glory there is an essential connection. Grace, or the light of faith, is transformed into vision; the grace of hope into possession; the grace of charity into union with God.[121] Finally, the teaching of Thomas Aquinas, though centered on the question of created grace, is determined principally by the last end of humans, that is, eternal beatitude, which involves the never-ending vision of God.[122]

It is interesting to note that the eschatological aspect of the life of grace becomes less and less important for theologians in the modern period. This is so in Protestant thought, which is centered on the opposition between faith and works and in which justification, considered as a divine declaration of the innocence of the sinner, is clearly distinguished from the exclusively future realization of the eschatological promise. This may also be said, in the context of Jansenism, with respect to a kind of "instrumentalization" of grace in an ethical context: grace is seen only as a kind of punctual divine help to man to overcome temptation and avoid sin. Something of the kind has taken place in different moments of modern philosophy. In effect, for Hegel, human fullness is obtained in this world, not in the next.[123] For Kant, immortal life is unknown to us and is ethically irrelevant, or at best it should be considered a postulate of practical reason. Ethics, therefore, is focused on the present human situation, not on the eschatological end.[124] In practice, we can see in modern thought a shifting from an eschatological understanding of grace (which contains eternal life already in this life) toward an instrumental view of grace considered as a help or a stimulus for humans to behave well. This clearly constitutes an impoverishment. That is, grace is no longer directed toward eternal salvation but toward ethical behavior. Interesting, by contrast, is the following acute observation of Blaise Pascal: "It is true that the mortality or immortality of the soul must make an entire difference to morality. Even still, many philosophers have constructed their ethics independently of it. They discuss to pass an hour."[125]

Grace as Eschatological Promise in the Present Moment

We have just seen that the promise of eternal life is the motor of Christian life in the world, and it gives meaning to the life of grace.[126] But scripture, especially in the writings of Paul,[127] also speaks of grace as the premise of eschatological fulfillment in

---

120. Augustine, *Confessiones* I, 1, 1; see also IV, 10–13; IX, 10; *Ep.* 147, 8.
121. Bonaventure, *In II Sent.*, d. 27, a. 1, q. 3. 122. See *COH* x–xi, 330.
123. See ibid., 42–44. 124. On this issue, see *COH* 23f., 98f.
125. B. Pascal, *Pensées*, ed. Brunschvig, no. 219. 126. See *COH* 333–36.
127. See *NIDNTTE* 2:230–36, s.v. ἐπαγγαλία (promise, announcement).

the present moment (and as a seed that, though hidden, develops toward life everlasting, especially in the Synoptics).[128]

From the *Christological* point of view it may be said that the life of grace in believers reflects and reproduces to an important degree the reality, the drama, the life, and the narrative of Christ himself, the Word made flesh for our salvation. In effect, in him God's judgment of the world has already taken place along with its salvation, although it is a judgment that for humans will take place definitively only at the end of time, when God will be "everything to everyone" (1 Cor 15:28).[129] The certitude of justification, that is, of forgiving grace, is based on the resurrection of the one who has been crucified; besides, the permanence of glory depends on the risen Christ.[130] "Christ Jesus, who died, yes, who was raised from the dead, who is at the right hand of God, who indeed intercedes for us" (Rom 8:34).

The same may be said of the *Church*, which is

a living and enlivening setting, generated by the sacraments, by listening to the Word of God and by the gifts and charisms of the Spirit, in which we experience, at least in a germinal way, the fullness of new and eternal life.... The Christian believer experiences here on earth the first stages of risen life, a kind of anticipation of what one day will become definitive, when we will live in "the new heavens and the new earth" (Rev 21:1).[131]

In the sacraments, of course, divine grace is made present in the "now" of the Church (at the culmination of the eucharistic celebration, when the celebrant pronounces the words "This is my body"), which, however, contains a promise of future fulfillment (just after the consecration, the priest exclaims: "Come Lord Jesus"). In this sense the Church is essentially a pilgrim on earth. As Augustine says in a text cited by Vatican II's *Lumen Gentium*, the Church, "like a stranger in a foreign land, presses forward amid the persecutions of the world and the consolations of God."[132] After all, "here we have no lasting city, but we seek the city which is to come" (Heb 13:14).

Finally, the eschatological understanding of grace gives us the key to appreciate two fundamental and inseparable aspects of the life of grace: its realism and its hidden and enigmatic character. In effect, divine grace is marked essentially by a kind of "eschatological reserve." It is situated in the human space that opens toward the growth and interiorizing of faith, hope, and charity, and it is lived out within the chiaroscuro of human freedom. Believers do not see and touch and hear grace, they do not directly perceive divine life within themselves,[133] "for we walk by faith, not by sight" (2 Cor 5:7). Thus, concludes Paul, "Your life is hidden with Christ in God" (Col 3:3). Humans, in fact, believe in the life of grace and hope for its eschatological fulfillment, that is, they believe in the object of the promise. In this space opened up within history by the divine promise, humans are offered the opportunity, the risk, and the possibility of living in the world with a more or less generous spirit, which is required by the

---

128. See G. Gozzelino, *Nell'attesa della beata speranza: Saggio di escatologia cristiana* (Turin: Elle di Ci, 1993), 81–110.

129. On the dialectic between salvation and judgment, see *COH* 134–42.

130. See *COH* 184–86.

131. Scola, Marengo, and Prades López, *La persona umana*, 344.

132. Augustine, *De Civ. Dei* XVIII, 51, 2, in *LG*, no. 8.

133. See chapter 16, notes 106ff. and corresponding text, on the experience of grace.

day-to-day living out of Christian charity. Thus the realism and hidden character of grace opens a wide space for the exercise of human freedom and generosity.

Mary, "Full of Grace," Prototype of the Christian and of Humanity

Catholic theology has always insisted, and rightly so, on the singularity of the life and person of the Virgin Mary among all the faithful and within humanity itself.[134] Mary is the only person, as far as we know, to have been conceived without the stain of sin, the first one to have believed fully in Christ and his mission, becoming as a result the mother of the redeemer while conserving her virginity. She shared in the mission of Christ and that of the early Church in an incomparable way; she was assumed into heaven at the end of her earthly life, a privilege reserved to her;[135] she intercedes for all the faithful and partakes in the heavenly liturgy in a way that is hers alone, having been placed by God above all the angels and saints as their queen and that of the whole universe. At the moment of the Annunciation, her predestination was made manifest: the angel Gabriel gave her the title "full of grace" (Lk 1:28). As a result, having responded with complete fidelity to the divine calling, Mary will be called "blessed" (Lk 1:48) by all generations.

It might seem that this privileged and exceptional status reserved to Mary might distance her from the rest of humanity, placing her on an unreachable pedestal. In other words, Mary would certainly be the "full of grace," but for this very reason she would not be the supreme human prototype, a key point of reference for theological anthropology. More precisely, it might seem that by the fact of being exempted from any stain of original sin, Mary does not truly share in the lot of common humanity and cannot be considered a model for the Christian and for humanity as a whole.[136]

Mary in Recent Church Teaching

However, it should be noted that recent Mariology has amply developed the idea that Mary is not only the icon of God's grace but also the perfect model of the Christian and of humanity.[137] And the two aspects are not separable from one another:

---

134. It is interesting to observe the titles of the works of G. M. Roschini's *Mariologia*: vol. 2.1: *De Beata Maria Virgine considerata in sua singulari missione*; vol. 2.2: *De Beata Maria Virgine considerata in suis singularibus privilegiis*; vol. 2.3: *De singulari cultu Beatae Mariae Virginis* (Rome: A. Belardetti, 1942ff.). For a recent overview of Mariology, see A. Ducay, *La prediletta di Dio: Sintesi di mariologia* (Rome: Arcane, 2013).

135. The 1979 document of the Congregation for the Doctrine of the Faith, *Recentiores episcoporum Synodi*, has the following to say: "The Church in her teaching on what awaits humans after death, excludes any explanation that would take away from the Assumption of Mary what it has of unique, that is the fact that the bodily glorification of the Virgin is the anticipation of the glorification reserved for all the other elect," no. 6.

136. The principal elements of this section on Our Lady have been published in P. O'Callaghan, "María y el compromiso cristiano con la verdad," in *María, camino de retorno: Nueva evangelización y piedad mariana*, edited by A. Aranda (Pamplona: Eunsa, 2012), 277–92.

137. On the relationship between Mariology and anthropology, see M. X. Bertola, "Antropologia," in *Nuovo dizionario di mariologia*, edited by S. De Fiores and S. M. Meo (Cinisello Balsamo: Paoline, 1985), 87–100; Ildefonso de la Inmaculada, "María en la nueva creación," *Estudios marianos* 50 (1985): 167–208; Bertola, "Antropología y mariología," *Estudios marianos* 57 (1992): 277–308; L. Bouyer, *La trône de la sagesse: Essai sur la signification du culte marial*, 3rd ed. (Paris: Cerf, 1987); I. Siviglia, *Antropologia teologica in dialogo* (Bologna:

insofar as she is full of grace, she can also become a model of redeemed humanity, and therefore of humanity as a whole. This idea has been developed especially in the constitution *Lumen Gentium* of Vatican Council II, in Paul VI's apostolic exhortation *Marialis Cultus* (1974), and in John Paul II's encyclical *Redemptoris Mater* (1987). In *Lumen Gentium* we read, for example: "In the mystery of the Church, which is itself rightly called mother and virgin, the Blessed Virgin stands out in eminent and sin-gular fashion as exemplar both of virgin and mother.... In the most Blessed Virgin the Church has already reached that perfection whereby she exists without spot or wrinkle."[138] And Paul VI writes: "Faced with the incalculable expectancies of the human heart, in drama and torment, the Church invites us to look at the Mother, the One who impersonates truly the original, authentic idea of what man is, image of God."[139] Christianity, says John Paul II, "does not look to anything else except to form the Church in that ideal of holiness which is already formed and prefigured in Mary."[140] The principle according to which "Christ reveals man to man" is applicable to Mary in a derived way, John Paul says.[141] That is because Christian anthropology is essentially a Marian anthropology.

The role of Mariology, indeed of Mary herself, in the full understanding of hu-manity in the light of Christian faith, may be expressed in three moments.

Our Lady's Revelation of the "New Man" to Humanity

Mary, in her life and activity, in the mystery of her privileges, shows us how God envisaged humanity from the beginning. Several central elements of eschatological perfection were to be found already in her life, even on earth. According to the early Church Fathers, in her God revealed the new Eve, that is, he gave us the mother he wished us to have from the creation of the world: "Eve was an anthropological sketch of woman; Mary is the restoration and perfection of the project that failed."[142] Mary is "the face which is most like that of Christ," writes Dante.[143] "In you [Mary] there is mercy, in you piety, in you magnificence, in you is gathered up all that is good in crea-tures."[144] However, it should be noted that the primordial holiness of Mary does not make her less human than other human beings. In fact, because sin is not an inte-gral part of God's plan for humanity, it should be said that the transgression of God's

---

Dehoniane, 2007), 177–99; A. Amato, "Maria, paradigma dell'antropologia cristiana," *Maria la Theotokos: Conoscenza ed esperienza* (Vatican City: Vaticana, 2011), 369–90.

138. *LG*, nos. 63, 65.

139. Paul VI, *Homily on the Solemnity of the Assumption*, August 15, 1966.

140. John Paul II, *Discourse to the Roman Curia*, December 22, 1987.

141. "This eternal truth about the human being, man and woman—a truth which is immutably fixed in human experience—at the same time constitutes the mystery which only in 'the Incarnate Word takes on light ... (since) Christ fully reveals man to himself and makes his supreme calling clear,' as the Council teaches [*GS*, no. 22]. In this 'revealing of man to himself,' do we not need to find a special place for that 'woman' who was the Mother of Christ? Cannot the 'message' of Christ, contained in the Gospel, which has as its back-ground the whole of Scripture, both the Old and the New Testament, say much to the Church and to human-ity about the dignity of women and their vocation?" John Paul II, *Mulieris Dignitatem*, par. 2.

142. R. Laurentin, "Nuova Eva," in *Nuovo dizionario di mariologia*, edited by S. De Fiores and S. M. Meo (Cinisello Balsamo: Paoline, 1985), 1020.

143. Dante Alighieri, *Paradise* 32:86.

144. Ibid., 33:19–21.

law and perseverance in sin does not humanize people; quite the opposite: it destroys them, leading them to death.[145] Thus, precisely in virtue of her holiness, Mary is the most "human" of human beings, excepting of course her own Son, *perfectus Deus, perfectus homo*, who is the source of all holiness. Josemaría Escrivá writes: "'A great sign appeared in Heaven: a woman adorned with the sun, with the moon under her feet, and a crown of twelve stars about her head.' From this, you and I and everyone may be sure that nothing perfects our personality so much as correspondence with grace."[146] And Angelo Amato: "The dogma of the Immaculate Conception looked at from the anthropological point of view is a powerful sign of the great effectiveness of the grace of God that acts in creatures."[147]

Besides, Mary, on account of the faith with which she accepted God's calling,[148] thus becoming the mother of God, of the redeemer,[149] is a model and point of reference for humanity. Her charity and fortitude are made present in her virginity,[150] in her maternal solicitude for all humans,[151] and also in her fidelity at the foot of the cross as her Son dies.[152] The French philosopher Michel Henry, though aware of the contemporary difficulties to be found in the dogma of the virginity of Mary, comments that "this apparently absurd dogma expresses at heart the conviction that nobody is son or daughter of their father or even of their mother, but only of God."[153] The Assumption of Mary in body and soul into heaven shows the faithful that death and corruption do not belong to God's original plan, because humans are destined to immortality.[154] Death, in fact, entered the world on account of sin, and Mary (as far as we know) is the only one conceived without it, even though, like all humans, she came to the end of her earthly pilgrimage.[155] "The Mother of Jesus in the glory which she possesses in body and soul in heaven," *Lumen Gentium* says, "is the image and beginning of the Church as it is to be perfected in the world to come. Likewise she shines forth on earth, until the day of the Lord shall come, a sign of certain hope and comfort to the pilgrim people of God."[156]

It may also be said that Mary's special condition, a singularity of grace and moral perfection, reveals to humanity the need to be saved and inflames in humans a powerful nostalgia for the original purity once lost but now made available again: the present situation of humanity is not what God intended, whereas Mary is placed above and before us as an icon of human perfection, fruit of abundant divine grace generously accepted. This brings about in humans a real hope of attaining holiness. In effect, the Church contemplates Mary with admiration and hope: "Tota pulchra es tu Maria, et non est macula in te" (you are all beautiful, O Mary, and there is no origi-

145. On this issue, see P. O'Callaghan, "Il mistero dell'incarnazione e la giustificazione," 87–97, 94f.

146. Escrivá, *Furrow*, no. 443.

147. Amato, *Maria, paradigma dell'antropologia cristiana*, 375.

148. This is a central aspect of John Paul II's encyclical *Redemptoris Mater*, pars. 12–19.

149. See John Paul II, *Redemptoris Mater*, pars. 7ff.

150. See ibid., pars. 20, 32, 39.   151. See ibid., pars. 20–24, 42ff.

152. See ibid., pars. 18–19.

153. M. Henry, *C'est moi la vérité: Pour une philosophie du christianisme* (Paris: Seuil, 1996), 91, translated into English as *I am the Truth: Towards a Philosophy of Christianity* (Stanford, Calif.: Stanford University Press, 2003).

154. See *COH* 75f., 266f.   155. See Pius XII, *Munificentissimus Deus*.

156. *LG*, no. 68.

nal stain in you), we read in the liturgy of the feast of the Immaculate Conception;[157] Mary is *Sedes Sapientiae, spes nostra*, and *causa nostrae laetitiae*, "seat of wisdom," "our hope," and "cause of our joy." And the twelfth-century author Adam of St. Victor calls Mary "the mother of piety and the noble triclinium of the Trinity."[158]

Vatican Council II developed this theme, presenting Mary not only as a model of virtue who can make the path to holiness more amiable, coherent, and accessible from a moral standpoint, but also as an icon, image, and mother of the Church itself, and therefore as the most complete and definitive rendition and model of humanity springing directly from the mind and heart of God.[159]

Our Lady, Full of Grace: As Our Mother, the Most Solidary of All Humans

Earlier I mentioned that it would seem that Mary, who received an abundance of gifts from God, is placed above and beyond common mortals, superior to the human condition, a hierarchic and inaccessible figure, because she obtained by grace an exceptional facility and naturalness in living according to God's law in sublime faith, hope, and charity. However, it should be noted that divine grace does not, as its primary purpose, simply facilitate human or Christian life, thus making ethical life easier. Rather its objective is *to make the entire life of Christ present in the believer*. But of course the experience of the cross occupies in the life of Christ a decisive place. And precisely in Mary we can see how the abundance of grace brought her, as the first disciple of the Lord,[160] to what may be called "the dark night of the soul."[161] Josemaría Escrivá observes: "Don't forget: if God exalted his Mother, it is equally true that he did not spare her pain, exhaustion in her work or trials [*chiaroscuro*] of her faith."[162]

As in the case of her beloved Son, God did not allow Mary to live without suffering, upsets, misunderstandings of all kinds. It was on account of her mission as mother of the Church, which is a direct consequence of her vocation as mother of God with the fullness of grace, that she was and is closer to sinful human beings than anyone else. The one who is the mother of the redeemer and at the same time mother of the redeemed, through a kind of mystical solidarity, shares with suffering and persevering solicitude in the fortunes and disgrace of the whole of humanity. Mary suffered the limitations and wretchedness of the human condition not as a result of sin in her but because, in accepting God's calling for her to be the mother of God, she became also our mother and suffered out of love, with the present willingness and self-forgetfulness of a mother, what we suffer by inheritance. In other words, even though it may seem a paradox, the very fullness of grace in Mary, her charity, is what brought her extraordinarily close to humanity, living the greatest possible solidarity with all humans. And humans find in her only motives for hope, because she is not a sinner as we are but rather, though belonging to our race, being Eve, she showed with

---

157. Antiphon for the Solemnity of the Immaculate Conception.
158. In A. Amato, ed., *Testi mariani del secondo millennio* (Rome: Città Nuova, 1996), 3:436.
159. *LG*, nos. 63, 65, 68.
160. See John Paul II, *Redemptoris Mater*, par. 20.
161. See ibid., pars. 17–18. The Pope uses the classic terminology of John of the Cross and others.
162. Escrivá, *Christ Is Passing By*, no. 172.

her life the efficacy and attractiveness of the grace of God that overcomes sin, and becomes the new Eve, the new woman, the new model for humanity.

Our Lady: Living Her Mission in the Church as Woman, as Mother, and as Virgin

The Virgin Mary, full of grace, reveals to humanity the "new man" precisely as a woman, living in a feminine way her life as a mother and as a virgin. She carries out her unique mission in a specific way, a fully feminine way, "in a painful struggle of interiorizing, of patience, of waiting, of contemplation."[163] And *Lumen Gentium* teaches that "the Virgin has been a model of that motherly love with which all who join in the Church's apostolic mission for the regeneration of mankind should be animated."[164]

163. Bertola, "Antropologia," 96.
164. *LG*, no. 65.

13 CHILDREN OF GOD IN THE HOLY SPIRIT

The Life of Grace

Only through the Son could we learn what a Father truly is. JOSEPH RATZINGER[1]

And in the end ... everything else will turn out to be unimportant and inessential, except for this: father, child, love. JOHN PAUL II[2]

The central affirmation of Christianity as regards the human being is that humans are children of God. MICHEL HENRY[3]

The spiritual life is founded on a sense of divine filiation. JOSEMARÍA ESCRIVÁ[4]

Grace has God as its origin, as its only source. Grace is simply the life of God in humans. As we saw in the last chapter, grace is present at every stage of human life; it presides over a wide-ranging historical narrative composed of different stages that are, while distinct, inseparable from one another: creation, predestination in Christ, divine call, justification of the person and his gradual purification from sin, and, finally, eschatological communion with the Trinity in glory. We considered them in the previous chapter.

Of course Christian grace, which is the result of God's action, enters into a profound and meaningful symbiosis with the human being and all its faculties at an ontological and existential level. In other words, Christian teaching of grace does not only speak of the transcendence of its origin but also involves the deep, transformative insertion of God's life within created reality, in every single aspect of created

---

1. J. Ratzinger, *The God of Jesus Christ: Meditations on God in the Trinity* (Chicago: Franciscan Herald Press, 1979), 26.

2. John Paul II, *Reflections on Fatherhood*, in John Paul II, *Collected Plays and Writings on Theater* (Berkeley: University of California Press, 1987), 368.

3. Henry, *C'est moi la vérité*, 91.

4. Josemaría Escrivá, *Forge* (Dublin: Four Courts, 1988), no. 987.

reality, at every level, in every organ and faculty of human life. We may say that in humans divine grace, God's own life in humanity, takes on a narrative, a life of its own, a dynamic, a richness of color, of movement, of sound, of action. *In humans, grace becomes incarnate.* Of course grace cannot be simply identified with one more aspect of human nature that marks this life; nor may it be confused with the human essence in its natural constitution. And this is so because grace is the life of *God* in humans: it is the life of God (one and three) and therefore must be considered as essentially "uncreated" in character, as something that is divine in origin and divinizing in effect. At the same time it is the life of God in *humans*, and therefore gives rise to a reaction and response within the creature, a direct, tangible, and qualifying impact on the ontological structure of the human being. In this context, grace is often designated as "created grace," not because there is a created substance called grace but because creatures elevated by God's self-giving are truly modified, elevated, and enhanced, not just at an existential level but at an ontological one. In effect, as we have just seen, humans were created by God *for* grace; they were destined from the beginning of their existence for communion with the Trinity and structured in a corresponding way.[5]

In this chapter I develop the thesis that the essential and primary content of the giving and receiving of grace in humans is called divine filiation. The believer, identified with the only begotten Son of God through the power of the Holy Spirit, becomes at one and the same time a brother of Christ (God "predestined [us] to be conformed to the image of his Son, in order that he might be the first-born among many brothers" [Rom 8:29]) and, as a brother of Christ, ipso facto, a child of God in the fullest sense of the word, and, of course, a brother to all humans. In this filial transformation, the world, created in a filial way, is brought to fullness.[6] Of course this applies especially to human beings, made in the image and likeness of God in Christ.[7]

After this chapter we shall consider the following aspects of the regeneration and

---

5. The content of this chapter draws in the first place on scripture, on Biblical commentaries, on the Church Fathers, and on the writings of Thomas Aquinas and M.-J. Scheeben. See also F. Ocáriz, *Natura, grazia e gloria* (Rome: Edusc, 2003); Tanzella-Nitti, *Mistero trinitario ed economia della grazia*; P. O'Callaghan, "L'agire dello Spirito Santo, chiave dell'escatologia cristiana," *Annales Theologici* 12 (1998): 327–73; E. Burkhart and J. López Díaz, *Vida cotidiana y santidad en la enseñanza de San Josemaría: Estudio de teología espiritual*, 2nd ed. (Madrid: Rialp, 2011), 2:11–159.

6. Following the title of the work Maspero and O'Callaghan, *Creatore perché Padre*, and the work this is based on, O'Callaghan, *La metafisica cristiana*.

7. On the theological aspects of divine filiation, see S. I. Dockx, *Fils de Dieu par grâce* (Paris: Desclée de Brouwer, 1948); J. Jeremias, *Abba: Studien zur neutestamentlichen Theologie und Zeitgeschichte* (Göttingen: Vandenhoeck & Ruprecht, 1966), translated into English as *The Prayers of Jesus* (Philadelphia: Fortress, 1989); W. Marchel, *Abba, Père!: lLa prière du Christ et des chrétiens: étude exégétique sur les origines et la signification de l'invocation à la divinité comme père, avant et dans le Nouveau Testament*, 2nd ed. (Rome: Biblical Institute Press, 1971); F. Ocáriz, *Hijos de Dios en Cristo: Introducción a una teología de la participación sobrenatural* (Pamplona: Eunsa, 1972); M.-J. Le Guillou, *Le mystère du Père: foi des apôtres, gnoses actuelles* (Paris: Fayard, 1973); J. Galot, *Découvrir le Père: esquisse d'une théologie du Père* (Leuven: Sintal, 1985), translated into English as *Abba, Father, We Long to See Your Face: Theological Insights into the First Person of the Trinity* (New York: Alba House, 1972); F.-X. Durrwell, *Le Père: Dieu en son mystère*, 2nd ed. (Paris: Cerf, 1988); P. O'Callaghan, "'Perché tutto sia a lode della sua gloria': La paternità di Dio alla luce di Cristo," *Tertio millenio adveniente: Testo e commento teologico-pastorale*, edited by R. Fisichella (Cinisello Balsamo: San Paolo, 1996), 215–26; and O'Callaghan, "'That everything may be for his glory': the Paternity of God, Christ's own Perspective," in *Tertio millennio Adveniente. Preparing For the Year 2000*, edited by R. Fisichella, (New Hope, Ky.: Urbi et Orbi Communications, 1996), 207–18.

sanctification of believers who become children of God: the inhabitation of the Holy Spirit, the reality of created grace, infused virtues, the experience of grace that stimulates human freedom and makes human action meritorious. In this chapter we concentrate on the Biblical and historical development of the paternity of God revealed in Christ and the corresponding divine filiation of believers. We shall also consider the specific role of the Holy Spirit in the lives of the children of God.

God the Father in Religions and in the Old Testament

In order to understand the Christian doctrine of divine filiation we need to consider in the first place the fatherhood of God. It is interesting to note that the Old Testament speaks very little of God as a Father and of us as his children. In the New Testament, however, the fatherhood of God in Christ and the consequent filiation of believers are presented openly and repeatedly. Before considering the teaching of scripture, and to contextualize the issue, let us consider what has been said of God as a father in other religions and by philosophers.

God as a Father in Different Religions

The use of the image of a father to depict the divinity[8] "is one of the basic phenomena of religious history."[9] In fact, among the ancient Eastern people with whom Israel had considerable contact, God was frequently called "father." The same may be said of the classical religions of Greece and Rome. Their view was based principally on a mythical view of the world according to which humans (and gods) have been in some way "generated" by the divinity and descend naturally from God, who is therefore their father. The God of the Ugarit, El, was called "the father of humanity"; Baal, his son,

---

8. On the paternity of God in religions and in scripture, see the following works: R. Gyllenberg, "Gott der Vater im Alten Testament und in der Predigt Jesu," *Studia orientalia* 1 (1926): 3–140; A. Alt, *Der Gott der Väter: Ein Beitrag zur Vorgeschichte der israelitischen Religion* (Stuttgart: W. Kohlhammer, 1929); M. P. Nilsson, "Vater Zeus," *Archiv für Religionswissenschaft* 35 (1938): 156–71; G. Mensching, H.-J. Kraus, and J. Jeremias, "Vatername Gottes," in *Die Religion in Geschichte und Gegenwart*, edited by K. Galling, 3rd ed. (Tubingen: J. C. B. Mohr, 1964), 6:1232–38; Zedda, *L'adozione a figli di Dio*; G. Schrenk and G. Quell, πατήρ–πατριά–ἀπάτωρ–πατρικός, in *TDNT* 5:945–1022, esp. 948–59; P. Ternant, "Fathers and Father," in *Dictionary of Biblical Theology*, edited by X. Léon-Dufour, 2nd ed. (London: G. Chapman, 1978), 169–74; Jeremias, *Abba*; Marchel, *Abba, Père!*, 29–55; A. Schenker, "Gott als Vater–Söhne Gottes: Ein vernachlässigter Aspekt einer biblischen Metapher," *Freiburger Zeitschrift für Philosophie und Theologie* 25 (1978): 1–55; R. Hamerton-Kelly, *God the Father: Theology and Patriarchy in the Teaching of Jesus* (Philadelphia: Fortress, 1979), 21–28; Byrne, *Sons of God, Seed of Abraham*; R. Le Gall, "Appeler Dieu: 'Père,'" *Communio* (French edition) 6 (1989): 52–65; Scott, *Adoption as Sons of God*; K. Limburg, "La paternidad divina en el Antiguo Testamento: Algunas observaciones lingüístico-formales," in *Biblia, Exégesis y cultura*, edited by G. Aranda-Pérez, C. Basevi, and J. Chapa (Pamplona: Eunsa, 1994), 201–20; J. W. Miller, *Calling God "Father": Essays on the Bible, Fatherhood, and Culture* (New York: Paulist Press, 1999); A. Ohler, *The Bible Looks at Fathers* (Collegeville, Minn.: Liturgical Press, 1999); E. Cuvillier, "Filiation humaine et filiation divine: Jésus Fils dans l'Évangile de Matthieu," *Revue d'Éthique et de Théologie Morale* 225 (2003): 69–86; T. J. Burke, *Adopted into God's Family: Exploring a Pauline Metaphor* (Downers Grove, Ill.: Apollos InterVarsity Press, 2006); A.-M. Jerumanis, "La morale filiale del Nuovo Testamento," in *Figli nel Figlio: Una teologia morale fondamentale*, edited by R. Tremblay and S. Zamboni (Bologna: EDB, 2008), 45–60; *NITNTTE* 3, 677–84, s.v. πατήρ; 4, 522–46, s.v. υἱός; 3, 590–98, s.v. παῖς.

9. Schrenk and Quell, πατήρ, 951.

gave life to human couples, animals, and the earth; the Babylonian moon god Sin was defined "the father and parent of men and gods." Among the Egyptians, the Pharaoh was considered to be son (and image) of God in a literal and physical way.[10] The fact that God was considered a father was an indication of his absolute authority over humans. God's paternity also referred to his goodness, mercy, and care for them. As a result, the attitude of humans toward the divinity was meant to be twofold: on the one hand, one of recognition of their own ineptitude and dependence on the divinity and, on the other hand, one of a simple trust and love toward him, that is, piety.[11]

Among the Greeks, according to Homer, Zeus is considered to be the father of humanity and the universal god.[12] Zeus corresponds to the Hindu-European god-father Dyaus Pitar. The Latin equivalent is Jupiter, a name in whose root is to be found the term *pater*, "father." Titus Livius calls Jupiter *pater deum hominumque*, "the father of gods and men."[13] At a philosophical level, Platonists and Stoics likewise develop the notion of God as father. Plato considers the God who created the world as the "universal father" of the whole cosmos.[14] According to the Stoics, the paternal authority of God permeates the whole universe: for Epictetus and Cleantes he is the "creator, father, and supporter" of humans, and thus they are his children, close relatives of his.[15] "We all come directly from God and God is the father of gods and human beings."[16] In a like way, among the ancient mystery cults of regeneration and divinization it is said that the initiated ones were generated by the divinity; hence the divine is invoked as "father" in that it imparts to the faithful love, friendship, blessing, word, and knowledge.[17] Among the Gnostics, the supreme God is also described as a father or "first father."[18] We need to keep in mind, however, that the Gnostics believe that each human is a kind of a spark that emanates from the divinity and is enclosed in a human body: in that sense, divine "fatherhood" is generic in character and does not involve a personal relationship between God and man.[19]

Divine and Human Fatherhood in the Old Testament

The Old Testament uses the term "father" (Hebrew, *'āb*; Septuagint, *patēr*) frequently, almost always (1,200 times) applied to a human father, on very few occasions (fifteen) in a religious context, thirteen times as an adjective, and only twice when speaking to God in prayer.[20] In effect, human fatherhood, and the corresponding filiation, occupies a central place in the social life of Israel, which is structured princi-

---

10. See Marchel, *Abba, Père!*, 35–37.

11. See Mensching, Kraus, and Jeremias, "Vatername Gottes," 1233.

12. Homer, *Od.* 1:28. See Marchel, *Abba, Père!*, 39–41.

13. Titus Livius, *Bellum contra Sab.* I, 12, 4ff.

14. See Plato, *Timaeus* 28c, 41a; Schrenk and Quell, πατήρ, 954f.

15. See Epictetus, *Dissert.* I, 9, 7; Cleantes, *Hymn to Zeus*; Schrenk and Quell, πατήρ, 955.

16. Epictetus, *Dissert.* I, 3, 1.

17. See Schrenk and Quell, πατήρ, 953f.

18. See especially the *Gospel of Truth* from Nag Hammadi: K. Grobel, *The Gospel of Truth: A Valentinian Meditation on the Gospel* (London: Black, 1960).

19. See Schrenk and Quell, πατήρ, 958f.

20. See the references in note 8 above, especially those to Schrenk and Quell, πατήρ, 978–82; Ternant, "Fathers and Father," 170–72; Jeremias, *Abba*, 7–27; Marchel, *Abba, Père!*, 44–97; and Hamerton-Kelly, *God the Father*, 28–51. See also P. Ricoeur, "La paternité: Du fantasme au symbole," in *Le conflit des interprétations:*

pally as a patriarchy.[21] Fatherhood is considered a gift of the creator (Gn 1:27f.). A father carries the divine blessing (Gn 27) and is the head of the family that resides at his own home (Jos 24:15). His authority must always be respected (Ex 20:12, 21:15, 17; Prv 23:22). He has the responsibility to nourish, protect, and educate his children. He is also their priest (Ex 12:3ff.) and teacher.[22] The task of the father is one of ensuring that children are obedient to the Covenant and that they receive the necessary religious instruction. It is interesting to note that the early leaders in Israel were called simply "the fathers" (Pss 22:4, 106:7), which indicated, to say the least, the importance of this category.[23] In fact, the identity of Yahweh is validated by the term "the fathers" and is hence called "the God of our fathers."[24] In this case the title "father" is applied especially to Abraham, Isaac, and Jacob, bearers and mediators of the Covenant promises. Besides, human fatherhood and filiation were at the basis of all property rights. It may be noted that in the Old Testament, by contrast, "the concept of the mother or of motherhood is nowhere exalted to have religious significance or used in mythological presentations."[25]

Fatherhood in the Old Testament also assumes a spiritual meaning. The honorific title of "father," for example, is given to priest (Jgs 17:10, 18:19) and prophet (2 Kgs 6:21, 13:14).[26] In Rabbinic literature, the metaphor of father and son is applied clearly to the relationship between the teacher of the Torah and his student.[27]

God as Father in the Old Testament

In contrast with the extensive use of the term "father" for God in a variety of religions, some of which we saw earlier, the term is only rarely applied to God in the Old Testament. In effect, the God of Abraham, Isaac, and Jacob is above all Yahweh, the almighty Lord and king, who is benevolent and merciful toward those with whom he has established a Covenant. God is protector, patron, sovereign, Lord. Of course God's sovereignty is beneficent and may be said to have paternal traits that invite humans not only to submission but also to trust.[28] However, in the Old Testament taken as a whole, God is not presented as a father.[29] Still, it is possible to find interesting

---

Essais d'herméneutique (Paris: Éditions du Seuil, 1969), 458–86, translated into English as *The Conflict of Interpretations* (Evanston, Ind.: Northwestern University Press, 1974); F. Demelas, "Figli di Dio" nell'Antico Testamento e nella letteratura interestamentaria e apocrifa, in Demlas, *Figli per dono, figli per scelta: La verità sull'uomo nel rapporto nuovo tra i figli e il Padre* (Milan: Ancora, 2011), 53–102.

21. See N. A. Berdjaev, *Slavery and Freedom*, 108f. See C. L. Meyers, "Was Ancient Israel a Patriarchal Society?," *Journal of Biblical Literature* 133, no. 1 (2014): 8–27, which contests the classical patriarchy hypothesis.

22. See Ex 12:26f., 13:14ff.; Dt 6:7ff, 32:7; 46; Is 38:19.

23. See Schrenk and Quell, πατήρ, 976–78.

24. See Hamerton-Kelly, *God the Father*, 29, 34–38.

25. *NIDNTTE* 3:297–300, s.v. μήτηρ, 298.

26. See J. G. Williams, "The Prophetic Father," *Journal of Biblical Literature* 85 (1966): 344–48.

27. See H. L. Strack and P. Billerbeck, *Kommentar zum Neuen Testament aus Talmud und Midrasch*, 4th ed. (Munich: C. H. Beck, 1963–65), 3:340f.

28. See Ex 4:22; Nm 11:12; Dt 14:1; Is 1:2ff., 30:1, 9; Jer 3:14.

29. "The fact that divine filiation is attributed to the people of Israel and in some cases to individuals (the king, for example) is derived from the fact of the choice of grace, of the gratuitous election of Yahweh. If this act creates between God and his 'elect' a relationship of paternity, then this relationship is exclusively of a moral kind." R. Tremblay, "La primauté immédiate de Jésus le Christ sur l'être de l'homme appelé à agir moralement dans le monde," *Studia moralia* 22 (1985): 211–32.

texts that in an indirect way refer to God's fatherhood toward humans. These texts may be divided into four groups.

In the first place, there are texts that compare divine action with that of an earthly father in relation to his own children: "As a father has pity on his children, so the Lord pities those who fear him. For he knows our frame; he remembers that we are dust" (Ps 103:13f.). "For the Lord reproves him whom he loves, as a father the son in whom he delights" (Prv 3:12). "In the wilderness, where you have seen how the Lord your God bore you, as a man bears his son, in all the way that you went until you came to this place.... Know then in your heart that, as a man disciplines his son, the Lord your God disciplines you" (Dt 1:31, 8:5).

Secondly, most texts speaking of the fatherhood of God refer to Israel[30] or to the king of Israel[31] but neither to individuals nor to humanity as a whole. In effect, God is the father of Israel: "Is this the way you repay the Lord, you foolish and senseless people? Is not he your father, who created you, who made you and established you?" (Dt 32:6). "You are the sons of the Lord your God.... For you are a people holy to the Lord your God, and the Lord has chosen you to be a people for his own possession, out of all the peoples that are on the face of the earth" (Dt 14:1f.). "For you are our Father, though Abraham does not know us and Israel does not acknowledge us. You, O Lord, are our Father, 'our Redeemer from of old' is your name.... Yet, O Lord, you are our Father; we are the clay, and you are our potter; we are all the work of your hand" (Is 63:16, 64:8). And finally: "A son honors his father, and a servant his master. If then I am a father, where is my honor? And if I am a master, where is my fear?" (Mal 1:6).

With respect to God's fatherhood, the following passage of the prophet Hosea is particularly expressive and moving (Hos 11:1–4, 8):

When Israel was a child, I loved him, and out of Egypt I called my son. The more I called them, the more they went from me; they kept sacrificing to the Baals, and burning incense to idols. Yet it was I who taught Ephraim to walk, I took them up in my arms; but they did not know that I healed them. I led them with cords of compassion, with the bands of love, and I became to them as one who eases the yoke on their jaws, and I bent down to them and fed them.... How can I give you up, O Ephraim! How can I hand you over, O Israel! How can I make you like Admah! How can I treat you like Zeboiim! My heart recoils within me, my compassion grows warm and tender.

Yahweh desires ardently for Israel to respond as a son but discovers that his people is unfaithful as an adulterous wife toward her husband: "I thought how I would set you among my sons, and give you a pleasant land, a heritage most beautiful of all nations. And I thought you would call me, 'My Father,' and would not turn from following me. Surely, as a faithless wife leaves her husband, so have you been faithless to me, O house of Israel, says the Lord" (Jer 3:19f.).

On the basis of his fatherhood toward Israel, God is also considered father to the king. Making a comparison with Saul, God treats king David in a fatherly way: "I will be his father, and he shall be my son. When he commits iniquity, I will chasten him with the rod of men, with the stripes of the sons of men; but I will not take my steadfast love from him, as I took it from Saul, whom I put away from before you" (2 Sm

---

30. See Dt 32:6; Is 63:16 (twice), 64:7; Jer 31:9; Mal 1:6, 2:10.
31. See 2 Sm 7:14; 1 Chr 17:13, 22:10, 28:6; Ps 89:26 (see 2:7).

7:14f. = 1 Chr 17:13). Eastern kings were considered for the most part as adoptive sons of their own god—sons, however, who were often seen as capricious, despotic, and sensual. This was not meant to be the case of the king of Israel, who represents a God who goes beyond the carnal and materialistic order and sanctions the moral conduct of his children. However, the expression "you are my son" (Ps 2:7), taken from a psalm on royal consecration, is to be found in exactly the same form in a Babylonian formula of adoption.[32] Of course the texts that refer to royal filiation prepare the reader for the revelation of the unique filiation of Jesus Christ as the messianic promises recur, with greater frequency and precision.

Thirdly, the personal application of "father" to God is rare. The only clear text may be found in the book of Jeremiah: "Have you not just now called to me, 'My father, you are the friend of my youth?'" (Jer 3:4). However, it should be kept in mind that this invocation is situated within a prayer whose subject is Israel, the chosen people. Still, it is interesting to note that the different names given to people include direct references to fatherhood and to divine fatherhood: Eliab means "my God is father" (Nm 1:9), Abiram means "my father is exalted" (Nm 16:1), Abiezer means "my father helps" (Jos 17:2), Abijja means "my father is Yahweh" (1 Chr 7:8), and Abitub means "my father is goodness" (1 Chr 8:11).[33] Yet none of them openly designates man as a son of God.

Fourthly, in Wisdom and apocalyptic texts, we see a greater freedom in applying the title "father" to God: "Make his greatness known there, and exalt him in the presence of all the living; because he is our Lord and God, he is our Father for ever" (Tb 13:4; see Sir 51:10). In a messianic text in the book of Wisdom, we see how the just man, maltreated by his enemies, looks upon himself as a son of God (2:16–18):

We are considered by him as something base, and he avoids our ways as unclean; he calls the last end of the righteous happy, and boasts that God is his father. Let us see if his words are true, and let us test what will happen at the end of his life; for if the righteous man is God's son, he will help him, and will deliver him from the hand of his adversaries.

And the same book teaches this: "It is your providence, O Father, that steers its course, because you have given it [wisdom] a path in the sea, and a safe way through the waves" (Wis 14:3).

The Qumran manuscripts provide only one reference to God as father (1 QH 9:35f.). In Rabbinic Judaism of the first century after Christ, on some occasions God is called father, perhaps under the influence of the Gospel of Matthew, even though that title was not among the most important given to him.[34] Rabbi ben Zakkai, whose writings are contemporaneous with the earliest texts of the New Testament, spoke of God as "our heavenly Father."[35] Besides, God is referred to as "the father who is in

32. See Ternant, "Fathers and Father," 172. On Ps 2, see, for example, see E. Otto and E. Zenger, eds., "Mein Sohn bist du" (Ps 2,7): Studien zu den Königspsalmen (Stuttgart: Katholisches Bibelwerk, 2002); S. Janse, "You Are My Son": The Reception History of Psalm 2 in Early Judaism and the Early Church (Walpole, Mass.: Peeters, 2009).

33. See Schrenk and Quell, πατήρ, 969.

34. Thus Jeremias, Abba, 13. See Marchel, Abba, Père!, 85–97. S. V. McCasland, in "'Abba, Father,'" Journal of Biblical Literature 72, no. 2 (1953): 79–91, holds that the title "Father" for God was common in Palestinian Judaism.

35. See Yohanan ben Zakkai, Tos. B.Q. 7, 7.

heaven,"[36] an expression which may be found in the Lord's Prayer that Jesus taught. The expression shows that the specific fatherhood of God is transcendent.

God as Father in the Jewish Diaspora

Given their constant contact with the Greek and Eastern world, it is not surprising to find that the Jews of the Diaspora refer to God with less reserve as "Father," universal father, father of all. This is so especially of the first-century Jewish historian Flavius Josephus.[37] The same may be said of the Jewish philosopher Philo of Alexandria,[38] who uses this expression very frequently, observing that it is to be found in Homer ("Zeus"), Plato, and the Stoics, though not in scripture. Philo understands the work of creation as an act of generation by which the soul is infused into matter. At times the term "husband" is applied to God as well as "father," because God makes the conception and birth of all living things possible.[39] For the same reason, God is also called father and spouse of the soul.[40] Philo tells us that the wise man, Abraham in this case, is truly adopted as a son of God.[41] The fatherhood of God is also expressed in terms of mercy and providence and in the fact that God never inflicts evil on his children.[42]

The Meaning of Divine Fatherhood in the Old Testament

"It was not a process of reasoning by analogy that led Israel to God its Father," writes Ternant. "It was a lived experience, and perhaps a reaction against neighboring peoples."[43] With respect to other religious forms, the fact that God is hardly ever spoken of as father in the Old Testament indicates his complete transcendence over creation: God's relationship with the created world is not of a sexual kind. God does not relate to a pre-existing world in order to give life to humans or to the earth. Rather, God creates one and the other, out of nothing. God is father of humans insofar as he is their creator, not according to the extravagant theogonies typical of antiquity. The God that "calls on the grain" (Ezek 36:29) is completely unrelated to Baal, whose magic fecundates the world. According to the prophet Jeremiah, Baal is invoked by his followers to say to a tree, "'You are my father,' and to a stone, 'You gave me birth.' For they have turned their back to me [Yahweh], and not their face. But in the time of their trouble they say, 'Arise and save us!'" (Jer 2:27). In other words, the fundamental difference between Israel in its relationship with God and that of surrounding religions is to be found in the fact that the fatherhood of God is not of a biological or a mythological kind but is, rather, soteriological or, at a deeper level, creational:[44] "You are our Father; we are the clay, and you are our potter; we are all the work of

---

36. See Jeremias, *Abba*, 71–88; Marchel, *Abba, Père!*, 92–95.

37. Josephus Flavius, *Ant. Jud.*, 7, 380.

38. See Philo of Alexandria, *Op. Mund.*, 98; *Spec. Leg.* 1:96, 2:6. See Schrenk and Quell, πατήρ, 956f.; É. F. D. Bréhier, *Les idées philosophiques et religieuses de Philon d'Alexandrie*, 2nd ed. (Paris: J. Vrin, 1925), 74n3; P. Frick, *Divine Providence in Philo of Alexandria* (Tubingen: Mohr Siebeck, 1999).

39. See Philo, *Det. Pot. Ins.*, 147.   40. See Philo, *Som.* II, 273; *Mut. Nom.*, 205.

41. See Philo, *Sobr.*, 56.

42. See Philo, *Op. Mund.*, 135; *Decal.*, 90; *Spec. Leg.* I, 318; *Op. Mund.*, 75.

43. Ternant, "Fathers and Father," 171.

44. God's paternity "never refers to any other individual or to humanity in general. The basic difference between this usage and that of Israel's neighbors is that in the Old Testament God's fatherhood is not under-

your hand" (Is 64:8). Thus, to be a "son of God" is not a natural property of humans, because it is based on election and redemption, that is, on grace, as we shall soon see. God is paternally merciful and good, he forgives his children, he treats them with affection and kindness, and, at the same time, he requires of them respect, obedience, and radical submission, because first and foremost he is their creator and only Lord. In the words of Hammerton-Kelly:

Mosaic theology wanted to eradicate any hint of the mythological idea that God is the actual progenitor of his people, a notion that clung to the person of the high god El whom the patriarchs worshipped in the manner we have seen. Sexuality is to be emphatically excluded from the idea of God. In order to express this new and characteristically Mosaic theology, the Yahwists chose the image of adoption.[45]

Paul Ricoeur speaks likewise.[46]

Jesus Christ, the Only Begotten Son of God

Whereas in the Old Testament the term *'āb* or *patēr*, "father," is applied to God intermittently, as we have seen, the very opposite is the case in the New Testament. In fact, God is called "father" about 250 times throughout the New Testament, whereas it is used in a human and profane way less frequently (160 times). This marks a clear novelty with respect to what was taught under the law and the prophets. "Insofar as the personal invocation of God as '(my) Father' was evidently something new in Palestine ... Jesus' use of the term must have been surprising, and perhaps to some outrageous."[47]

Jesus' Teaching on Human Paternity

As regards human fatherhood (and motherhood), Jesus' teaching is in continuity with that of the Old Testament. He insists on the obligation of honoring father and mother (Mk 7:9ff., 10:19), in all sincerity, without falling into casuistry (Mc 7:10–13). The Gospels frequently refer to the tenderness and affection that there should be between parents and their children.[48] This became a central element of family life among believers and contributed not a little to the growth of Christianity and to the humanization of society at large.[49] Jesus himself lived in submission to Mary and Jo-

---

stood in a biological or mythological sense, but in a soteriological one. To be a child of God is not a natural state or quality; rather, it is grounded in the miracle of divine election and redemption." *NIDNTTE* 3:679.

45. Hamerton-Kelly, *God the Father*, 31f. "What is meant is not God's begetting, let alone God as an abstract cosmic principle, but his fatherhood as a disposition, attitude and action" (Schrenk and Quell, πατήρ, 978). "Through a dialectic process the term 'father' came to express the theological meaning of covenant and its relational character could be expressed through the symbolism of paternity as Israel perceived it. The formula of 2 Sam 7:14, 'I will be his father, and he shall be my son,' corresponds exactly to the classic formula: 'I will be your God, you will be my people' (Jer 7:23). But paternity does not found the covenant: on the contrary, the covenant gives meaning to paternity. Thus the primacy and initiative of God may be understood through a paternal vocabulary. The vicissitudes of the covenant find a suggestive interpretation through the expression of relationship with the people, the rebel and unfaithful son, before God." A. Milano, "Padre," in *Nuovo Dizionario di Teologia*, edited by G. Barbaglio and S. Dianich, 5th ed. (Milan: Paoline, 1988), 1067–96.

46. See P. Ricoeur, "La paternité."   47. *NIDNTTE* 3:682.

48. See Mt 17:14–21; Mk 5:40–43, 9:14–29; Lk 8:51–56, 9:37–43.

49. See the first chapters of R. Stark, *The Triumph of Christianity: How the Jesus Movement Became the*

seph (Lk 2:51). He was particularly respectful toward women and affectionate toward children, appreciative besides of their spiritual qualities (Mk 10:14).

Nonetheless, the obligation of the believer to follow Jesus is placed above the bond with father and mother (Mt 10:37; Lk 14:26). To "his parents" Jesus himself responded when they found him in the temple after losing him for several days: "How is it that you sought me? Did you not know that I must be in my Father's house?" (Lk 2:49). Just as sons and daughters are meant to leave home to get married (Gn 2:24; Mt 19:5), Jesus' disciples receive the call "to leave father and mother" (Mt 19:29), a precept he applies to them in a demanding (Lk 9:60) and radical (Lk 14:26) way. Thus obedience to parents is not an absolute. God alone claims absolute obedience. Also, Paul teaches Christians the obligation to honor their parents, as he does parents their obligation to look after and instruct their children (Eph 6:1ff.; Col 2:20f.). He also speaks of a spiritual paternity over believers as the fruit of his preaching (1 Cor 4:14ff.; Phil 10; 1 Tm 1:2–18; Ti 1:4f.; 1 Pt 5:13).[50] Finally, he teaches that new converts among the Gentiles truly belong to the people of God, the new Israel, in that they take their origin "from our fathers" (Rom 9:10; Heb 1:1f.).

Christ's Revelation of the Fatherhood of God

It is fair to say that the fatherhood of God is one of the most central doctrines of the New Testament.[51] Jesus very often uses the term "father" to speak of God: four times in Mark, fifteen in Luke, thirty-two in Matthew, and more than a hundred times in John. Christ reveals God as the one who always acts in a fatherly way. Three main consequences for the life of Christians may be drawn from his teaching and way of acting: trust, obedience, and hope.

1. According to the New Testament, the fatherly benevolence of God reaches each and every human being, Israelite or not (Mt 5:45; Lk 6:35). His mercy is abundant and universal (Mt 6:14f.; Lk 11:4), above all toward the afflicted and bewildered, for whom God has a powerful motherly and fatherly love (Lk 15:1–32). This experience of God invites us to trust. Because the fatherly solicitude of God is limitless (Mt 6:25–33; Lk 12:16–32), his children can live in peace and joy,[52] sure of the consolation of the Holy Spirit (Lk 11:13). The abundance of God's fatherly benevolence invites his children to live in the same way that their father lives, that is, to be "perfect as your heavenly Father is perfect" (Mt 5:48), in that way fulfilling God's will (Mt 7:21–27) in all

---

World's Largest Religion (New York: HarperOne, 2011). On this, see P. O'Callaghan, "I tempi dell'amore, della santità e della misericordia: Una riflessione sulle strutture di sostegno del matrimonio e della famiglia," in *Matrimonio e famiglia: La questione antropologica*, edited by H. Franceschi (Rome: Edusc, 2015), 49–64. This study is based on the work of the French author N. D. Fustel de Coulanges, *The Ancient City: A Study on the Religion, Laws and Institutions of Greece and Rome* (Boston: Lee and Shepard, 1874). See also the work of O. M. Bakke, *When Children Became People: The Birth of Childhood in Early Christianity* (Minneapolis, Minn.: Fortress, 2005).

50. See Schrenk and Quell, πατήρ, 1005f.; *NIDNTTE* 3:681.

51. See the works cited in note 8 above, especially Jeremias, *Abba*, 28–70; Marchel, *Abba, Père!*, 99ff.; Galot, *Découvrir le Père*, 132–57, on divine providence; and H. F. D. Sparks, "The Doctrine of the Divine Fatherhood in the Gospels," *Studies in the Gospels: Essays in Memory of R. H. Lightfoot*, edited by D. E. Nineham (Oxford: Blackwell, 1955), 241–62.

52. See Mt 6:8; Lk 10:41, 12:24–30.

sincerity (Mt 6:1–18) with the simplicity of little children (Mt 11:25; 18:2–5), imitating his goodness and mercy (Mt 5:7; Lk 6:36) with unrestrained confidence (Mt 6:25–34), forgiving others their faults (Mt 5:23), promoting a civilization of love.[53] "Sonship ... expresses the freedom of the baptized Christian, who needs to recognize no other tie but the will of God; it expresses the realization that God has committed himself to man; and it expresses the trust that grows out of his fatherhood."[54]

2. God's closeness to his children and their trust in him take away nothing of the other central aspect of the filial relationship between humans and God, *obedience*. And this is for two reasons: because obedience is easier where there is trust, and because the one who is Father is also creator and Lord. According to the New Testament, in effect, it is clear that the Father enjoys an unlimited authority over his children, in every aspect of their lives. Jesus himself lived this same obedience to his eternal Father (Mk 14:36; Jn 10:17f.), heroically but joyfully, to the extreme of death on the cross (Phil 2:8), and he invites the apostles to do the same thing (Mt 19:17; Mk 7:8; Jn 14:15.21): "If you keep my commandments, you will abide in my love, just as I have kept my Father's commandments and abide in his love" (Jn 15:10).

3. Because the eternal Father is Lord, he is presented in scripture also as judge and king,[55] who gives eternal life to those who believe. And here we can see how an essential complement to divine filiation emerges in the New Testament: *hope in the promise of eternal inheritance*. Whereas "the slave does not continue in the house for ever; the son continues for ever" (Jn 8:35). Whoever receives eternal life through faith will remain in "the Father's house" forever: "In my Father's house are many rooms; if it were not so, would I have told you that I go to prepare a place for you? And when I go and prepare a place for you, I will come again and will take you to myself, that where I am you may be also" (Jn 14:2f.). Paul teaches the same thing: "It is the Spirit himself bearing witness with our spirit that we are children of God, and if children, then heirs, heirs of God and fellow heirs with Christ, provided we suffer with him in order that we may also be glorified with him" (Rom 8:16f.). Divine filiation thus takes on a clear eschatological profile: the children of God hope for the eternal inheritance.

The Father of Jesus Christ

It should be noted, however, that the real reason for the New Testament's sea change on the question of God's fatherhood and the consequent divine filiation of believers is not to be found simply in the reinforcement of the fatherly traits of God revealed by Jesus, which had been somewhat neglected in the Old Testament. According to Jesus' teaching, it is not simply that God acts in an ever more paternal way toward himself and us; God behaves in a fatherly way because God is a Father, he always was and always will be a Father, and because he has a Son, consubstantial with himself, the Word made flesh, Jesus Christ in person: "Before the world was created, God is already the love of the Father and the Son. And if he can become our Father and the standard of measurement of all fatherhood, it is because he himself is a Father from all eternity."[56] Jesus never calls God "the father of Israel," as if his own filiation was

---

53. See Mt 5:44f.; Lk 6:35.
54. O. Michel, *Der Brief an die Römer*, 13th ed. (Göttingen: Vandenhoeck, 1965), 197.
55. Schrenk and Quell, πατήρ, 995–97.   56. Ratzinger, *The God of Jesus Christ*, 27.

subordinate to that of the people, but rather calls him "my Father."[57] In the presence of the disciples he does not call him "our Father," but "your Father,"[58] as if to make it clear that his own filiation is original and cannot be transferred to anybody else. He calls himself "the Son" (Mk 13:32), "the beloved Son," that is, the only one who is truly Son (Mk 12:6, 1:11, 9:7, etc.). We may also note that Jesus, in order to express his transcendent or divine identity, does not present himself as the "Son of God" (although the disciples did: Mt 16:16; Lk 4:41), a title applicable to a generic divinity (Mt 27:54),[59] but rather as the "Son of Man," a title with clear messianic connotations.[60]

The fact that Jesus called God "my Father" is not the final result of a gradual development in the Old Testament and Rabbinic doctrine of God as Father. It is based on a special and unexpected divine revelation of the singular filiation of Jesus, of the radical intimacy between him and his Father (Mt 11:25–27):

I thank you, Father, Lord of heaven and earth, that you have hidden these things from the wise and understanding and revealed them to children; yes, Father, for such was your gracious will. All things have been delivered to me by my Father; and no one knows the Son except the Father, and no one knows the Father except the Son and any one to whom the Son chooses to reveal him.

And in the prologue of John's Gospel we read the following text: "And the Word became flesh and dwelt among us, full of grace and truth; we have beheld his glory, glory as of the only Son from the Father.... No one has ever seen God; the only Son, who is in the bosom of the Father, he has made him known" (Jn 1:14, 18).

Three observations may be made with respect to the New Testament texts that speak of Jesus' singular divine filiation. First, there is a strong continuity between Jesus' filiation and his being sent by the Father to redeem the world and submit all things to God: "For I have not spoken on my own authority; the Father who sent me has himself given me commandment what to say and what to speak. And I know that his commandment is eternal life. What I say, therefore, I say as the Father has bidden me" (Jn 12:49f.).[61] We can see that the sovereignty of God, his omnipotence, the central divine attribute in the Old Testament, is not weakened in the New Testament with the revelation of his paternity.[62] Still, we may say that divine Lordship becomes paternal with the coming of Christ. In the second place, the way Jesus directs his mind and heart to the Father is very direct, intimate, and familiar. He uses the term "Abba," especially in dramatic and demanding moments of his ministry, for example, in Gethsemane: "Abba, Father, all things are possible to you; remove this cup from me; yet not what I will, but what you will" (Mk 14:36). "Abba" in Aramaic evokes a relationship of trust and intimacy with one's own father and is frequently used by very young children. In the Gospel of Mark (14:36), though written in Greek, the original expression is conserved, as it is in Romans 8:15 and Galatians 4:6.

---

57. See Mt 7:21, 11:27; Lk 2:49, 22:29.   58. See Mt 5:45, 6:1, 7:11; Lk 12:32.

59. See M. Peppard, *The Son of God in the Roman World: Divine Sonship in Its Social and Political Context* (Oxford: Oxford University Press, 2011).

60. On the Christological title "son of man," see O'Callaghan, *The Christological Assimilation*, 54–58; for some recent overviews of the vast literature on the topic, see M. Casey, *The Solution to the "Son of Man" Problem* (New York: T. and T. Clark, 2007); M. Müller, *The Expression "Son of Man" and the Development of Christology: A History of Interpretation* (Oakville, Conn.: Equinox, 2008).

61. See Schrenk and Quell, πατήρ, 998f.   62. Ibid., 1010f.

Thirdly, Christ's filiation finds its maximum expression in his prayer, which is often doxological in character, that is, expressing praise and thanksgiving.[63] On the occasion of the resurrection of Lazarus, we read: "And Jesus lifted up his eyes and said, 'Father, I thank you that you have heard me. I knew that you hear me always, but I have said this on account of the people standing by, that they may believe that you did send me'" (Jn 11:41f.). During the Last Supper, he says: "Now is my soul troubled. And what shall I say? 'Father, save me from this hour'" (Jn 12:27). The same attitude may be found in the Lord's priestly prayer (Jn 17), of which we read: "He lifted up his eyes to heaven and said, 'Father, the hour has come; glorify your Son that the Son may glorify you'" (Jn 17:1). The doxological aspect of Christ's prayer may also be found in the prayer of his followers.[64] For believers in Christ, says Paul, "there is one God, the Father, from whom are all things and for whom we exist, and one Lord, Jesus Christ, through whom are all things and through whom we exist" (1 Cor 8:6). In his letter to the Ephesians we hear that Christians have "one Lord, one faith, one baptism." And, as a result, there is only "one God and Father of us all, who is above all and through all and in all" (Eph 4:5f.).

The Theology of the Father and the Son

According to the New Testament, the relationship between the Father and the Son has four principal properties: singularity/exclusivity, priority, assimilation, and equality. Let us consider them one by one.[65] Regarding the first, the *singularity* or exclusivity of this relationship, the letter to the Hebrews compares the priesthood of Christ with that of the Old Testament figure Melchizedek for the simple reason that the latter was "without father or mother or genealogy, and has neither beginning of days nor end of life, but resembling the Son of God he continues a priest for ever" (Heb 7:3).[66] In the silence surrounding the paternity of Melchizedek (Gn 14:18ff.) we can detect a cryptic reference to the priest-king who is to come, without an earthly father. While Levitical priesthood was communicated from one generation to the next, always from father to son, Melchizedek becomes the type and prophetical prefiguration of the pre-existent Son born of God and with no earthly father: "The Son of God, not descended from the tribe of Levi, is the pre-existent and eternal High Priest."[67]

The meaning of the virginity of Mary, of which Luke speaks, moves in the same direction. "And behold, you will conceive in your womb and bear a son, and you shall call his name Jesus. He will be great, and will be called the Son of the Most High" (Lk 1:31f.). This son will have a dignity that is above that of the patriarchs of the Old Testament: "And the Lord God will give to him the throne of his father David and he will reign over the house of Jacob for ever; and of his kingdom there will be no end" (Lk 1:32f.). All this will take place, says Gabriel to Mary, because "the Holy Spirit will come upon you, and the power of the Most High will overshadow you; therefore the child to be born will be called holy, the Son of God" (Lk 1:35). The dogma of the virginity of Mary teaches us that at the deepest level humans are fundamentally children of God, a thesis that is applicable in the first place to Christ, of course, but also, in Christ, to the rest of humanity. In effect, Jesus was *supposed to be* a son of Joseph

---

63. Ibid., 1002f.
64. Ibid., 1007f.
65. See Galot, *Découvrir le Père*, 60–69.
66. *NIDNTTE* 3:267–69, s.v. Μελχισέδεκ.
67. *NIDNTTE* 3:681.

(Lk 3:23), but in real terms he was the Son of God. For this reason, according to Paul, Christ's divine filiation is clearly distinct from ours: Paul speaks of God's "own Son" (Rom 8:32) and attributes to him the work of creation (Col 1:13ff.).

As for the second property of the relationship between the Father and the Son, the New Testament insists on the fact that, at least in his incarnate condition, the Son is always subject to the Father, who enjoys *priority* over the Son. The Father always conserves his paternal prerogatives (Mt 11:26f., 24:36, 26:39). The resurrection of Jesus is attributed to the Father (Acts 2:24; 1 Thes 1:10; 2 Cor 4:14). The one who chooses and calls Christians (1 Thes 2:13f.) and the apostles (Gal 1:15f.), the one who justifies the sinner (Rom 3:26–30, 8:30), is the Father. Jesus is the mediator, the only mediator (1 Tm 2:5), but is sent by the Father (Gal 4:4; Rom 8:3). The Father sacrifices him (Rom 8:32), commends a task to him (Jn 17:4), and gives him special words to say (Jn 12:49). The Father is the source of all things (1 Cor 8:6). The Son will be subject to him at the end of time and forever (1 Cor 15:28). In fact, Jesus himself perceives that "the Father is greater than I" (Jn 14:28). As we shall see, these affirmations cannot be interpreted as if Christ was personally subordinated to the Father, as Arius suggests in his exegesis of some of the Biblical texts just cited.

The third property of the relationship between Father and Son as seen in the New Testament is the *assimilation* of Christ to the Father, principally in the way he unconditionally dedicates his life and energies to carrying out the will of God, as a manifestation of his unreserved—that is, filial—trust and gratitude. This property seems to nourish his very union with his Father: "My food is to do the will of him who sent me, and to accomplish his work" (Jn 4:34). It is expressed also in the fact that Jesus does not define his own identity as Son by distinguishing himself on purpose from the Father, but rather by assimilating himself to his Father always and in everything. Christ works on the Sabbath because the Father does (Jn 5:17). He does what he sees his Father doing (Jn 5:19). The Father has given all judgment to the Son (Jn 5:22); of himself Jesus says: "I can do nothing on my own authority; as I hear, I judge; and my judgment is just, because I seek not my own will but the will of him who sent me" (Jn 5:30). He also says: "For this reason the Father loves me, because I lay down my life, that I may take it again. No one takes it from me, but I lay it down of my own accord. I have power to lay it down, and I have power to take it again; this charge I have received from my Father" (Jn 10:17f.). In the words of Durrwell, "According to John, obedience is the seal that consecrates and manifests filiation."[68] The perfection of this assimilation emerges especially in the obedience of Jesus in Gethsemane and on the cross (Mk 14:36). On the basis of this assimilation, we can say not only that Christ reveals the Father but that he himself, in person, is the revelation of the Father. The fatherly traits of God are expressed perfectly in the whole life of Christ and in his every action. For this reason, Jesus says of himself that he *is* the truth (Jn 14:6) and proclaims: "He who sees me sees him who sent me" (Jn 12:45); "He who has seen me has seen the Father" (Jn 14:9).

The assimilation of Christ to the Father does not take place in a gradual way, through a progressive overcoming of subordinate imperfection, because of the fourth property of his relationship to the Father: in the depths of his being, Christ is *equal* to the Father. Paul speaks often of "the Father of our Lord Jesus Christ" (Rom 15:6;

---

68. Durrwell, *Le Père*, 206.

2 Cor 1:3, 11:31; Eph 1:3; see 1 Pt 1:3).[69] For this reason Jesus is to be placed on the same level as the Father: "The grace [*charis*] of the Lord Jesus Christ and the love [*agapē*] of God and the fellowship [*koinonia*] of the Holy Spirit be with you all" (2 Cor 13:14).[70] John goes even further.[71] He calls Jesus the only begotten Son, that is the only, beloved Son (Jn 1:14, 18; 3:16, 18; 1 Jn 4:9). He underscores the singular character of divine paternity with respect to Jesus' filiation (Jn 20:17), the perfect union between the will (Jn 5:30) and activities of Christ with the Father (Jn 5:17–20). He speaks of the miracles they perform together (Jn 5:36, 11:41–44), of their mutual, intimate knowledge and love (Jn 5:20, 23; 10:15; 14:31; 17:24ff.), of their reciprocal glorification (Jn 12:28, 13:31f., 17:1, 4f.). "I and the Father are one" (Jn 10:30), Jesus concludes.

Those who listen to Jesus understand his declarations as professions of equality with the Father in a strict sense (Jn 1:34 and 49, 5:17f., 10:33, 12:27, 19:7). And Jesus himself confirms the veracity of this proclamation in two ways: first, with the words "Before Abraham was, I am" (Jn 8:58) and those in which he describes his living in "the bosom of the Father" (Jn 1:18; 1 Jn 1:1; Jn 5:25, 10:36, 11:4); and second with his life, accepting death on the cross precisely on account of being proclaimed "equal with God" (Jn 5:18; see 11:49, 18:14, 19:7).

Jesus Christ, the Servant-Son

Summing up what we have just said, we can affirm that the obedience of Jesus to the Father is not the obedience of a slave; it is the obedience of the consubstantial Son: full, free, transparent, heroic, filial, lived out "in the glorious liberty of the children of God" (Rom 8:21). Yet the paradox is that his filial condition brings him to obey as a servant, as a slave. Besides fulfilling the will of the Father on the basis of the divine glory present in his spirit,[72] the identification of the Son of God with the human condition (Phil 2:7) brings him to also obey human beings: Mary and Joseph (Lk 2:51); Nicodemus, who comes to speak with him late one evening (Jn 3); the centurion who leads him to heal his own servant (Mt 8:5–9). To the disciples the fact that Jesus, the Son of God and messiah, presents himself as a servant, a slave, is deeply disconcerting.[73] He does not seek human glory, nor does he attempt to crush those who listen to him: "he will not break a bruised reed or quench a smoldering wick, till he brings justice to victory; and in his name will the Gentiles hope" (Mt 12:20f.). He describes his own way of acting in the following terms: "Whoever would be great among you must be your servant, and whoever would be first among you must be your slave; even as the Son of Man came not to be served but to serve, and to give his life as a ransom for many" (Mt 20:26–28; see also Mk 10:45).[74] Or, as we read in Luke's Gospel, "For which is the greater, one who sits at table, or one who serves? Is it not the one who sits at table? But I am among you as one who serves" (Lk 22:27). Paul

---

69. On the different ways of speaking of Paul, see Schrenk and Quell, πατήρ, 1006–10.

70. This liturgical and Trinitarian formulation appears frequently throughout the New Testament.

71. Schrenk and Quell, πατήρ, 999–1001.

72. J. Ratzinger/Benedict XVI, *Jesus of Nazareth*, vol. 1: *From the Baptism in the Jordan to the Transfiguration* (New York: Doubleday, 2007), 1–8.

73. On the connotations of the terms "slave" and "servant" in the New Testament, see *BDAG* 259f., s.v. δοῦλος; *NIDNTTE* 1:767–73, s.v. δοῦλος.

74. On the centrality of this text in Matthew's Gospel, see O'Callaghan, *The Christological Assimilation*, 227–30.

repeats the same idea: "Christ Jesus, who, though he was in the form of God, did not count equality with God a thing to be grasped, but emptied himself, taking the form of a servant, being born in the likeness of men. And being found in human form he humbled himself and became obedient unto death, even death on a cross" (Phil 2:6–8). Though it may seem deeply paradoxical, the fact that Jesus is God's Son brings him to give himself completely to serve and save humanity, doing the Father's will in all things: the Son willingly becomes a slave.

The Divine Filiation of Christian Believers

Whoever receives the grace of believing in Christ, whoever follows him, becomes his disciple, friend, and brother, and for this very reason becomes a son or daughter of God.

Becoming a Child of God through Faith in Christ

According to the New Testament, believers become children of God (Jn 1:12) by adoption (Rom 8:23, 9:4; Gal 4:5; Eph 1:5). This is a work of divine grace: "To be called a son of God is the highest honor and the richest gift of grace. The words 'shall be called' indicate that it all depends on God's verdict.... A man cannot make himself a son of God; he has to be given the name by which he becomes a son."[75] This is made possible, according to the Synoptics, on the basis of Jesus' identification with his disciples (Mt 18:5, 25:40), becoming their brother (Mt 28:10), master (Mt 10:24, 19:16, 23:8), and friend (Jn 15:12–15). It is the fruit of divine initiative accepted in faith, which brings the believer to become a disciple. As we have seen already, this doctrine is taught clearly by Paul and John.[76] God frees us from slavery and adopts us as his children through baptismal faith, which makes us one with Christ (Gal 3:26ff.) and members of his body (Eph 5). Christ is the only begotten Son, who shares with his brothers the paternal heritage (Rom 8:17, 29; Col 1:18). The interior agent of filial adoption is the Holy Spirit; the Spirit also witnesses the adoption of Christians, inspiring in their hearts the trusting prayer "Abba, Father" (Rom 8:14–17; see also 8:29; Gal 4:5–7):

For all who are led by the Spirit of God are sons of God. For you did not receive the spirit of slavery to fall back into fear, but you have received the spirit of sonship. When we cry, "Abba! Father!," it is the Spirit himself bearing witness with our spirit that we are children of God, and if children, then heirs, heirs of God and fellow heirs with Christ, provided we suffer with him in order that we may also be glorified with him.

Christians, as they pray the Our Father, express an awareness of being loved with the same love with which the eternal Son is loved: "See what love the Father has given us, that we should be called children of God; and so we are" (1 Jn 3:1). The New Testament explains how the Christian directs filial prayer to God in different ways: as blessing, doxology, belief, and petition.[77]

---

75. A. Schlatter, *Der Evangelist Matthäus*, 5th ed. (Stuttgart: Calwer, 1959), 140.

76. See chapter 5, note 7, and chapter 6, note 15, and corresponding text.

77. In the New Testament there are prayers of blessing: Rom 1:7, 1 Cor 1:3, 2 Cor 1:2; of doxology: Rom 15:6, 2 Cor 1:3, Eph 1:3; of believing: 1 Cor 8:6, Eph 4:6; of petition: Eph 5:20, Col 1:12.

Is God the Father of All Humans?

Now we can pass on to an important question: is God the father of all human beings? Are all humans children of God? As we saw, Plato, the Stoics, and adherents to many Eastern religions were convinced that he was: God is considered the father of all people and creatures.[78] In the Old Testament, however, the paternity of God over humans was focused in a very restrictive way, first because it is applied only to Israel, the people of the Covenant, and their kings, and not to individuals one by one, and secondly because the filiation of Israel before God, in the light of Jesus' teaching, may be considered something generic because it depends both on the fulfillment of the will of God (Mt 21) and on the affirmation of his mercy (Lk 15).

As regards New Testament teaching, what can be said? Three observations may be made. First, as we have already seen, Jesus' divine filiation is not a simple add-on to his person and existence; it is, rather, his deepest and most authentic identity. He is the eternal Son, and he is so by nature, eternally. In that sense, the fatherhood of God is fully and substantially expressed in the relationship with his Son. As a result, all filiation of any kind present in the created order and saving economy, if it exists, cannot but depend on his: all filiation shares necessarily in that of the Son. Second, humans can truly become children of God (1 Jn 3:1), but only as the result of being adopted by God in Christ (Rom 8:15; Gal 4:5) in the Spirit.[79] Schnackenburg, in his commentary on John's Gospel, says that "one becomes a child of God not by natural birth, but by a supernatural event, carried out by God alone."[80] Paul's letter to the Ephesians teaches, in fact, that before baptism believers were "by nature children of wrath" (Eph 2:3). Thus we cannot say that they were "born" children of God, because in real terms they were born sinners "like the rest of mankind," that is, like the pagans.[81] Paul believed that to be children "by adoption" expresses not only the complete gratuity of this gift and its realism but also the original sinfulness of humans, their state when they were not (yet) children of God. The divine filiation of believers, therefore, is opposed to their previous state, that of slavery, the state in which, according to Paul, humans were born. John says more or less the same thing: humans are born not as children of God but in slavery

---

78. See notes 5ff. above and Schrenk and Quell, πατήρ, 990f.

79. Paul uses the term "adoption" to speak of the doctrine of final resurrection (Rom 8:23) and of the divine predestination of believers through Christ (Eph 1:5). On the Pauline meaning of adoption, see J. M. Scott, "Adoption, Sonship," in *DPL* 15–18. The term is rooted in Old Testament usage, for example, 2 Sm 7:14. See also *BDAG* 1024, s.v. υιοθεσια.

80. R. Schnackenburg, *The Gospel of John* (New York: Crossroad, 1982), 1:420. On the contrary, F.-X. Durrwell considers the use of the term "adoption" inappropriate when applied to divine filiation and says that the meaning of divine filiation in Paul is always natural; he thinks that it would be better "to avoid the word 'adoption' in the translations of Pauline texts" (Durrwell, *Le Père*, 82).

81. According to G. Harder, φύσις, in *The New International Dictionary of New Testament Theology*, edited by C. Brown (Exeter: Paternoster Press, 1980), 2:656–62, 660, "by nature" (*phusei*) in Eph 2:3 means "by birth." The same position is held by F. F. Bruce in *The Epistles to the Colossians, to Philemon, and to the Ephesians* (Grand Rapids, Mich.: W. B. Eerdmans, 1984), 248. This author observes that Paul uses the same terminology to say that Peter and he were "born" Jews. *BDAG* 1069, s.v. φύσις, 1, interprets it as meaning "as descendants of Adam." H. Schlier, in *Der Brief an die Epheser: Ein Kommentar* (Dusseldorf: Patmos, 1957), 99, on the contrary, says that "by nature" means "insofar as it relates to us, to our proper being." On Ephesians 2:3, see J. Mehlmann, *Natura filii irae: Historia interpretationis Eph 2,3, ejusque cum doctrina de peccato originali nexus* (Rome: Pontificia Institutum Studiorum Orientalium, 1957).

(Jn 8:33–44). Jesus "clearly did not teach the idea that God is the Father of all human beings. Rather, he linked divine fatherhood to a person's relationship to God."[82]

Third, this brings us to ask if for Jesus all humans had some kind of filial relationship with God.[83] According to Matthew, God's paternal goodness reaches all persons and created beings, "for he makes his sun rise on the evil and on the good, and sends rain on the just and on the unjust" (Mt 5:45). God, in fact, treats all humans, saints and sinners, in a truly paternal way. But he does the same with the birds of the air, who would not normally be considered children of God: "Look at the birds of the air: they neither sow nor reap nor gather into barns, and yet your heavenly Father feeds them. Are you not of more value than they?" (Mt 6:26). As Pope Francis writes, "In talking with his disciples, Jesus would invite them to recognize the paternal relationship God has with all his creatures."[84]

Thus, on the basis of Biblical texts, it is not possible to say that all humans are children of God in the full sense of the word, although they are objects of God's common paternal action. It is clear that the filial condition belongs, in a strict sense, only to those who believe in the teaching of Jesus about his Father and follow him as disciples (Mt 23:8f.; Lk 6:35f.), becoming his friends and brothers.

Perhaps we can say that all humans may be considered children of God in differentiated ways.[85] Filiation in other words is an analogous term. In the first place, of course, divine filiation is fully applicable only to Christ, the only begotten Son of God, the Father's only Son by nature, with whom God "is well pleased" (Mk 1:11). Second, filiation is applicable to the saints in heaven, the baptized welcomed by God into glory, who have obtained the eternal inheritance of his children (Rom 8:16; see Lk 22:28–30; 1 Pt 4:13), not only as a promise but as a perpetual reality. Third, all baptized Christians in the state of grace are adoptive children of God in the fullest sense of the word even though they are still pilgrims on earth. Fourth, the baptized who are in the state of grave sin may be considered children of God in an ample sense because, having lost divine grace, they have forfeited the eternal inheritance, yet have not lost their baptismal character. The Biblical point of reference is the young (or "prodigal") son, who left his father's home and squandered his fortune, according to the Gospel of Luke (15:11–31). According to this parable, God looks out and waits for his son to come back, with all the mercy and patience of a father, with the intention, if possible, of restoring his son's filial dignity, which has not been fully lost: "for this *my son* was dead, and is alive again; he was lost, and is found" (Lk 15:24). Sinners do not enjoy the condition and privileges of being children of God,[86] but in the merciful heart of the Father they are still seen as his beloved children. Fourth, we can speak of those who never received baptism and justifying grace. It may be said that they are children of God in an ample sense, partly because they are created "in the image and likeness of God" (this expression has filial connotations, as we saw in chapter 4) and partly because everything God does is paternal because God *is* Father: hence the whole of creation, especially humans,

---

82. *NIDNTTE* 3:682.

83. I have followed the analysis of Schrenk and Quell, πατήρ, 990f.

84. *LS*, par. 96.

85. Aquinas, in *S.Th.* I, q. 33, a. 3, and q. 41, a. 3, applies the notion of analogy to filiation, especially between that of the eternal Son and believers who become children of God by adoption.

86. See M. Schmaus, *Katholische Dogmatik* III/2: *Die göttliche Gnade* (Munich: Max Hueber, 1956), 239.

cannot but be related to him in a generically filial way or, for that matter, in an antifilial way. In this sense Josemaría Escrivá teaches that "all humans are children of God."[87] Fifth and finally, perhaps we may mention condemned Christians, who, though constituted as children of God, have lost the heavenly inheritance forever, and their baptismal filiation, instead of being a source of joy and consolation, is rather a source of perpetual suffering, shame, and frustration.[88]

Whatever the case, there are some texts in the New Testament that present the paternity of God without any explicit Christological anchor, as if a kind of generic paternity and filiation was to be found within the order of creation besides that which derives from the grace of Christ.[89] In the letter to the Hebrews, God, as creator of the human soul, is called "the father of spirits" (Heb 12:9). According to James, God is creator of the stars, "the father of lights" (Jas 1:17). And in the letter to the Ephesians we hear of "the Father, from whom every family [or paternity] in heaven and on earth is named" (Eph 3:14f.).[90] Let us consider the latter text in greater detail.

What Is the Relationship between Divine and Human Paternity?

Paul writes, "For this reason I bow my knees before the Father [pater], from whom every family [patria] in heaven and on earth is named" (Eph 3:14f.). In this text, Paul teaches that every family or relationship of descendants (patria), whether heavenly or earthly, derives in some way from the pater who is the origin of all things. To understand this text fully, we must ask the following question: should the term patria be interpreted following the literal meaning of the term within the Greek lexicon (especially as found in the Septuagint and the New Testament) or in the light of the term pater, with which it is compared by association?

Let us consider the first possibility. In the Septuagint, patria is not a univocal term. It may be translated "offspring" or "home" or a group of families, peoples, or tribes. It may also be used to express a "superior family," which, according to the Rabbinic tradition, is constituted by the angels.[91] In the Pauline writings the term patria is to be found only in the text we are considering, Eph 3:15. Still, in the New Testament patria is found on a few more occasions and is translated as "family" or "homeland" (Heb 11:4). First, that of David ("Joseph ... was of the house and lineage of David," Lk 2:4). Second, that of "the families ... blessed in Abraham" ("and in your posterity shall all the families of the earth be blessed," Acts 3:25). Third, in Hebrews 11:4: "For people who speak thus make it clear that they are seeking a homeland." In this context Ephesians 3:15 teaches simply that every family, every group of people, every spiritual

---

87. Escrivá, *Christ Is Passing By*, no. 64. On this issue, see Burkhart and López, *Vida cotidiana y santidad*, 2:69–71.

88. See *COH* 189–221.

89. See *NIDNTTE* 3:682f., s.v. πατριά.

90. On this text, see the commentaries of Schrenk and Quell, πατήρ, 1017f.; Schlier, *Der Brief an die Epheser*, 159–61; M. Barth, *Ephesians* (Garden City, N.Y.: Doubleday, 1984), 1:379–84; Bruce, *The Epistles*, 324f.; *NIDNTTE* 3:514–22, s.v. ὄνομα; A. T. Lincoln, *Ephesians*, in *WBC* 42:201–4.

91. See Schlier, *Der Brief an die Epheser*, 159f. As regards the angels, see *B. Sanh* 98b, and Strack and Billerbeck, *Kommentar zum Neuen Testament aus Talmud und Midrasch*, 1:744, 3:594. See also *BDAG*, 788, s.v. πατριά, 3; T. Muraoka, *A Greek-English Lexicon of the Septuagint* (Walpole, Mass.: Peeters, 2009), 540.

union, including those among angels, finds its origin in God, who is Father.[92] Even if the letter to the Ephesians on the whole is centered on the Church, in this text God's paternity reaches the whole of reality, all family relationships, including both Israel and other peoples, the *ethnē*, that is, both Jews and Gentiles (Eph 3:1). According to G. Schrenk, the text should be interpreted as follows: "From the Father of Jesus Christ we look towards all *patria* which finds its strength and unity in this Father.... There is a connection between the Father and every *patria*."[93] And not much more may be said.

Let us now consider the second interpretation. The play of words, technically called "paronomasia," between *patēr* and *patria* is undeniable. One refers openly to the other. We argue that *patria* should be understood in the light of *patēr*, not the other way round. *Patēr* would be the original, as it were, and *patria* the copy. According to Ephesians 3:15, then, the Father of Jesus Christ should be considered as the archetypal Father, the father of all, and source of all paternity (the Greek original has *ex ou*, translated as "from whom"). In fact, the Latin text of both the *Vulgata* and the *neo-Vulgata* translate *patria* as *paternitas*, "paternity," offering in that way a more elevated, restrictive, and demanding interpretation of *patria*. Thus Ephesians 3:15 would mean that from the Father "all paternity in heaven and on the earth takes its name." The paternity of God thus extends to the whole of creation. This interpretation is common among the Church Fathers: Clement of Alexandria,[94] Athanasius,[95] Theodoret of Cyrus,[96] and Jerome.[97] The same interpretation is accepted by Biblical exegetes[98] and among contemporary theologians.[99]

92. The text reads: *ex ou pasa patria*, literally, "from whom every single descendant." The adjective *pasa* without a previous article is not normally translated as "all" but rather as "each one." As a result, it is not precise to translate *patria* in an abstract way; rather it should be concrete, as "family," or "offspring." The correct word in Greek for "paternity" should be *patrotēs*. See Schrenk and Quell, πατήρ, 1017.

93. Schrenk and Quell, πατήρ, 1018f.

94. "All offspring find their source in God the Creator." Clement of Alexandria, *Strom.* 6:7; see *Comm. in Io.*, 1:3.

95. "God as Father of the Son is the only true father, and all created paternity is a shadow of the true one." Athanasius, *Orat. contra Arian.* 1:23, 24.

96. "God is fully and truly Father, because he was not Father first, and then became Son, but he was always Father and Father by nature. Other fathers, whether corporeal or spiritual, have received this name from on high.... He has his paternity not because he has received it from another, but because he himself confers paternity to others." Theodoretus of Cyrus, *Comm. in Eph. 3*, 14f.

97. "God allows the term 'paternity' to be given to creatures. Thus by analogy with his own paternity we can understand paternity among creatures.... In the same way as the one good makes all other things good, as the one immortal God has given immortality to others, as the one that is truth imparts the name of truth, so also the one Father, being the only creator of all things and the cause of the existence of everything that exists, makes it possible also for other creatures to receive the name of Father." Jerome, *Comm. in Eph. 2, 3, 14*. "Our term 'paternity' now can be used in the light of the knowledge that God is the Father of our Lord Jesus Christ. Since the only generated Son is not so by adoption, but by nature. Also by adoption it is permitted to other creatures to share in paternity and thus they can receive the name 'father.'" Jerome, *Comm. in Eph. 2, 3*.

98. This is the position of Luther, according Schrenk and Quell, πατήρ, 1018n20. See also J. A. Robinson, *St. Paul's Epistle to the Ephesians* (London: Macmillan, 1903), 84: "So far from regarding the Divine fatherhood as a mode of speech in reference to the Godhead, derived by analogy from our conception of human fatherhood, the Apostle maintains that the very idea of fatherhood exists primarily in the Divine nature, and only by derivation in every other form of fatherhood, whether earthly or heavenly." E. Percy, *Die Probleme der Kolosser- und Epheserbriefe* (Lund, Sweden: Gleerup, 1946), 277n30: "But then the thought in this passage is obviously that God as the Father of believers is Himself the prototype of every fatherly relationship and therewith of every reflection of that in which God stands to His children"; see also Bruce, *The Epistles*, 324f. The point is "not that God is the name-giver ... but that every πατριά is so named after the πατήρ." Schrenk and Quell, πατήρ, 1017.

99. See for example K. Barth, *Dogmatics in Outline* (New York: Philosophical Library, 1949), 43.

Against this interpretation, some commentators say that *patria* is not an abstract name but always a concrete one and thus cannot be translated as *paternitas*.[100] Others, however, hold that it is legitimate to translate it as "paternity," which is quite close to "descendant."[101] Heinrich Schlier asks why all paternity refers ultimately to the "Father" in Ephesians 3:15 and responds: "For the same motive for which in Eph 3:9 the Father is spoken of as creator, that is, to counter the Gnostic error."[102] According to Ephesians 3:8f., in effect, Paul says that he has received the grace "to preach to the gentiles the unsearchable riches of Christ and to make all men see what is the plan of the mystery hidden for ages in God who created all things." And just as every creature receives existence directly from God and not from an inferior divinity (such as the Demiurge, as the Gnostics thought), all paternity finds its direct source in the eternal Father. There are no alternative fatherhoods, therefore, to that of the eternal Father. Hence, concludes Schlier, God "is *patēr* not only as redeemer, but also as creator."[103] The same idea is to be found, he says, in Ephesians 4:6, which speaks of "one God and Father of us all, who is above all and through all and in all."

The question regarding the proper interpretation of Ephesians 3:15 may be expressed in another way: When we say that God is Father, is this just a simple projection of our language, fruit of our experience of human paternity, onto God? Or do we affirm that this is what God is in himself? In other words, do we call God "Father" on the basis of our previous experience of paternity and filiation, or do we speak of all paternity and family bonds on the basis of the fact that God is Father? In brief terms, do we *call* God Father,[104] or *is* he truly Father? That is to say, is being a Father a simple anthropomorphic metaphor for God, a way of speaking of what is unknown to us, or is it a reality, which offers a fundamental light by which we may explain all the rest?

On the basis of the analysis just made, we may conclude by saying that being a Father is more than a simple metaphor for God, because if it were not so, the filiation of Christ would be purely nominal, not unlike the divine paternity the Old Testament applied to Israel or to the king, and the doctrine of the Trinity would easily fall into modalism. The reading just offered is confirmed in the discourse of Jesus on hypocrisy when he says: "And call no man your father on earth, for *you have one Father*, who is in heaven" (Mt 23:9). It is true that the prime purpose of the text is one of helping believers to avoid a vain search for honorific titles, especially that of "master,"[105] so

100. Lincoln, *Ephesians*, 203; Barth, *Ephesians*, 1:382: "This beautiful expression can at best be considered a homiletic corollary to 3,15."

101. See W. F. Arndt and F. W. Gringrich, *A Greek-English Lexicon of the New Testament and Other Early Christian Literature*, 4th ed. (Chicago: University of Chicago Press, 1957), 642. According to J. H. Moulton and G. Milligan, in *The Vocabulary of the Greek Testament Illustrated from the Papyri and Other Non-literary Sources* (Grand Rapids, Mich.: W. B. Eerdmans, 1985), 498, *patria* means "a group of persons structured by descent from a common father or ancestor."

102. Schlier, *Der Brief an die Epheser*, 160.

103. Ibid.

104. Some feminist scholars consider paternity a metaphorical way of referring to God. If this is the case, logically, there would be no difficulty in saying that God is also Mother. To say that God is Father and not Mother, therefore, would amount to a kind of idolatry. On this, see especially S. McFague, *Metaphorical Theology: Models of God in Religious Language* (Philadelphia: Fortress, 1982), 4–7; E. A. Johnson, *She Who Is: The Mystery of God in Feminist Theological Discourse* (New York: Crossroad, 1997), 33ff.; M. Daly, *Beyond God the Father: Toward a Philosophy of Women's Liberation* (Boston, Mass.: Beacon, 1985). Daly writes: "If God is male, then the male is God" (*Beyond God the Father*, 19).

105. In this text, "father" is probably equivalent to "master": see D. A. Hagner, *Matthew 14–28*, in *WBC*

as not to take anything away from God's glory (Mt 5:16). Still, the theological reason runs deeper: "one alone is your Father,"[106] because in reality all paternity derives from his. As the philosopher Michel Henry says, "No man is the son of another man, or of a woman, but only of God."[107] In other words, the *analogatum princeps* of fatherhood is divine, not human, paternity, even though, from the epistemological point of view, we need some experience of human fatherhood in order to be able to recognize and appreciate divine fatherhood. Ratzinger wrote: "The biblical Father is not a heavenly double of human fatherhood. He contributes a new aspect and is a divine critic of human fatherhood. God establishes his own standard of measurement."[108] And as Benedict XVI put it: "Critics of religion have said that speaking of the 'Father,' of God, is a projection of our ancestors in heaven. But the opposite is true: in the Gospel Christ shows us who is the father and as he is a true father we can understand true fatherhood and even learn true fatherhood."[109]

Theological Issues Concerning Divine Filiation

On the basis of the previous analysis, we can formulate some theological reflections on the divine filiation of those who are incorporated into Christ through baptism and faith. First we shall consider the question of the father-son paradigm with which the believer looks upon the created world and himself. Then we shall consider the realism of the state of the adopted son or daughter of God, based on the idea that the believer partakes in the relationship that exists, in the Spirit, between the Father and the Son. Finally we shall consider some spiritual and practical consequences that derive from the filial condition of the Christian. In the coming chapters we shall return frequently to considering the different aspects of the filial condition of the believer, for example, when speaking of Christian liberty, of the theological virtues, of work, and so on.

The Basic Paradigm of Human Existence:
Father-Son or Master-Slave?

We have seen that according to the New Testament, the relationship between the Father and the Son—in which the believer shares truly by grace—has four particular characteristics: singularity/exclusivity, priority, assimilation, and equality.[110] To some degree these marks are replicated in the lives of children of God by adoption.

It is worth reflecting on the paradox expressed in the simultaneous and apparently contradictory affirmation of the priority of the Father over the Son and of the equality of the Son with respect to the Father. This doctrine, which is deeply present

---

33B:661; see the study of S. Byrskog, *Jesus the Only Teacher: Didactic Authority and Transmission in Ancient Israel, Ancient Judaism and the Matthean Community* (Stockholm: Almqvist & Wiksell, 1994), 299f.

106. "The fact that in nature there is only one God and one Son of God does not mean that others be called gods and sons by adoption. In the same way the fact that there is one Father and one Master does not bar the existence of others who are improperly called masters and fathers." Jerome, *Comm. in Mt.*, 4, 23:10.

107. Henry, *C'est moi la vérité*, 91.

108. Ratzinger, *The God of Jesus Christ*, 26.

109. Benedict XVI, *The Spirit and the "Abba" of Believers*, General Audience, May 23, 2012.

110. See notes 65ff.

in the whole of the New Testament, was made explicit at the Council of Nicaea, which taught the full and eternal consubstantiality (and thus equality) of the Word with the Father, against the Arian doctrine.[111] In effect, Arius, reasoning in the context of neo-Platonic, hierarchical categories, taught that the generation of the Son from the Father necessarily required the former's subordination to the latter, because every form of derivation or generation involves inferiority. Thus filiation requires the submission and obedience typical of slaves. In other words, whoever obeys is inevitably considered subordinate and inferior. Nicaea teaches, however, that the Son, though deriving from the Father because he is generated by him, is equal to the Father.[112] For a theological understanding of the world, created through Christ and for Christ, this supposes a radical and surprising novelty from the philosophical standpoint as well.

In his major work *The Phenomenology of Spirit*, Hegel describes the consolidation of human self-knowledge in the context of the relationship with other people. In fact, he explains that this relationship conditions and defines human self-knowledge.[113] Those who know themselves, however, experience the inclination of wishing to subordinate others to themselves, striving to oblige these others to do their own will. Though recognizing the individuality of others, humans experience the desire to eliminate and annul it in order to be able to victoriously proclaim their own individuality. The collective and the individual are in conflict. Of course Hegel does not attempt to obtain the total elimination of the other for the simple reason that the affirmation of one's own individuality always requires the affirmation of the other. However, two figures emerge, according to Hegel, two structural figures that are dialectically opposed to one another, in society and in every aspect of human life: the master and the slave, the one who dominates and the one who is dominated. "There thus arises the master-slave relationship. The master is the one who succeeds in obtaining recognition from the other, in the sense that he imposes himself on the other's value. The slave is the one who sees his own true self in the other."[114] All relations in society, Hegel says, are expressions of this basic relationship between master and slave, among them, that which obtains between father and son. In the words of Paul Ricoeur, paraphrasing Hegel, "Paternity and filiation may be recognized only in the light of the relationship slave-master."[115] Thus the fundamental structure of the world and of society, their deepest and most authentic key, is the relationship master-slave. It is present, Hegel says, also among the Stoics, for whom "the master recognizes individuality and liberty only in the self and not in the slave, while the slave recognizes it only in the master but not in himself."[116]

In continuity with Hegel, the psychoanalysis of Sigmund Freud considered the relationship between father and son in light of the fundamental relationship master-

111. *DH* 150.

112. See O'Callaghan, "L'incontro tra fede e ragione," 44–49. See chapter 7, notes 37ff. and corresponding text.

113. See F. Copleston, *History of Philosophy*, vol. 7, part 1: *From Fichte to Hegel* (New York: Doubleday, 1965), 180–88; Berdjaev, *Slavery and Freedom*, 59–72.

114. Copleston, *History of Philosophy*, 7.1:180. See Ricoeur, *La paternité*, 463–70.

115. Ricoeur, "La paternité," 464. "There is father because there is family and not the other way around; and there is family because there is morality and not the other way around." Ricoeur, "La paternité," 468.

116. Copleston, *History of Philosophy*, 7.1:185.

slave, of dominion and submission. In order to become oneself, says Freud, the son must separate himself from his own father and reject the source, thus affirming his own individuality and autonomy.[117] As is well known, Freud's problematic vision of paternity and filiation has been very influential.

However, in the light of the mystery of Christ, savior of the world, Son of God and equal to the Father, the master-slave paradigm is inverted. The fruit of Christ's saving work is the establishment of a new paradigm, that of father-son, or, better, the reestablishment of an old paradigm that was present when God created the world and loved humans into existence. The effective predominance of the master-slave paradigm within certain aspects of life is the result of the Fall, of sin, which Christ came to redeem. This means that the father-son relationship (in which filial subordination, obedience, and receptivity are compatible with equality, liberty, self-determination, peace, trust, and love) cannot be included within the master-slave paradigm (where subordination, obedience and receptivity find expression in terms of inferiority, slavery, passivity, alienation, violence, mistrust, humiliation, and hate). The practical predominance throughout the twentieth century of Hegel's master-slave dialectic is in real terms one of the most eloquent results of the sin of humans, and therefore of humanity's need for salvation.

John Paul II observes that the master-slave paradigm seems to be more present nowadays in peoples' minds than is Christian wisdom, which is rooted in the filial fear of God.[118] Modern philosophies of arrogance and submission, of dominion and oppression, he says, stem from this paradigm. The only power capable of overcoming this philosophy is to be found in the Gospel, where the master-slave paradigm is radically inverted by the father-son paradigm. The Pope concludes that "original sin attempts to abolish paternity, destroying its rays which permeate the created world, placing the truth that is Love in doubt and leaving humanity alone and lost with the sensation of a master-slave relationship."[119] The saving incarnation of the Word-Son, however, restores the original order and establishes anew in the world the father-son paradigm. The latter becomes the interpretative key for the Christian way of understanding the world. "And in the end," John Paul writes, "everything else will turn out to be unimportant and inessential, except for this: father, child, love."[120]

Christian Divine Filiation Is a Sharing in the Original Filiation of the Divine Word

Peter speaks openly of a "sharing" (in Greek the term used is *koinonia*, normally translated as "communion") of the believer in the divine nature (2 Pt 1:4).[121] In effect, the Christian believer shares in divine life by participating in a person, that of Christ the Lord, or, more precisely, in a subsistent relationship, that which exists between

---

117. On the issue, see A. Milano, "Padre," 1069–78.

118. See John Paul II, interviewed by V. Messori, *Crossing the Threshold of Hope* (London: J. Cape, 1994), 227–29.

119. Ibid., 228.

120. John Paul II, "Reflections on Fatherhood," 368.

121. On the importance of this text, see Jerumanis, *La morale filiale del Nuovo Testamento*, 51; Tremblay, *La primauté immédiate de Jésus le Christ*, 216.

the Father and the Son. This doctrine may be found, as we have already seen, in the expression Paul frequently uses, that the believer *lives in* Jesus Christ.[122] This involves an intimate union, a personal identification of the believer with Christ. Humans become ipso facto children of God to the extent to which they are identified with Christ, because he is the Son of God in the fullest sense of the word. This gives rise to a moral and spiritual program of identification with Christ,[123] which brings us to share his sentiments (Phil 2:5) and his very life (Gal 2:20), death (Rom 6:8; Col 2:20), and resurrection (Col 3:1),[124] becoming "sons in the Son."[125] As we shall see presently, this identification takes place through the power of the Holy Spirit.

In God there is but one filiation, that of the only begotten Word (Jn 1:18). God does nothing other than love his own Son. If the divine filiation of humans is true (though adoptive), as John and Paul teach (1 Jn 3:1, Gal 4:6, Rom 8:15, etc.), it cannot have any basis or reason other than the filiation of the Word, the one who, to use an expression of Thomas Aquinas, "is said to be only Begotten by nature, but also first-Born, in that from his natural filiation descends the filiation of many, through likeness and participation."[126]

The believer's filial condition is explained, therefore, as a true transcendental participation in the supernatural order.[127] The filiation of the Word, "Son by nature,"[128] is the cause, Thomas says. He is subsistent by participation who possesses every perfection and fullness;[129] he is God's instrument in communicating divine goods to humanity,[130] the model to whom the participant is conformed.[131] The divine filiation of the believer is therefore that of Jesus: it is a *similitudo participata filiationis*

---

122. See chapter 5 on the anthropology of Paul; see also O'Callaghan, "The Inseparability of Holiness and Apostolate," 139–46.

123. See R. Tremblay and S. Zamboni, eds., *Figli nel Figlio: Una teologia morale fondamentale* (Bologna: EDB, 2008).

124. On the Pauline usage of *syn*, "with" Christ, see Dunn, *The Theology of the Apostle Paul*, 401–4.

125. The expression *filii in Filio* may be found in É. Mersch, "Filii in Filio," *Nouvelle Revue Théologique* 65 (1938): 551–82, 681–702, 809–30. See also Philippe de la Trinité, "Filiation Adoptive," *Ephemerides Carmeliticae* 16 (1965): 71–117; Ocáriz, *Hijos de Dios en Cristo*, and a further developed version of the latter, "La santísima Trinidad y el misterio de nuestra deificación," *Scripta Theologica* 6 (1974): 363–90. For a philosophical justification of this expression, see M. Henry, *C'est moi la vérité*, 142–67.

126. Thomas Aquinas, *In Io. Ev.* 1, 14, l. 8. Commenting on John's text "And from his fullness have we all received, grace upon grace" (Jn 1:16), Thomas points out three elements: "The preposition *from* indicates that the grace of Christ is the original cause of grace received by humans; it then indicates the consubstantiality of his grace with ours; lastly, it indicates partiality, that is, finite participation in the fullness of his grace." *In Io. Ev.* 1, 16, l. 10.

127. See F. Ocáriz, *Hijos de Dios en Cristo*; Ocáriz, *La santísima Trinidad y el misterio de nuestra deificación*; M. Sánchez Sorondo, *La gracia como participación de la naturaleza divina según Santo Tomás de Aquino* (Rome: Pontificia Università Lateranense, 1979); C. Bermúdez Merizalde, *Aspectos de la doctrina de la gracia en los comentarios de Santo Tomás a las epístolas paulinas: Vida de gracia e identificación con Cristo* (Rome: Pontificia Università della Santa Croce, 1990); L.-T. Somme, *Fils adoptifs de Dieu par Jésus Christ: La filiation divine par adoption dans la théologie de saint Thomas d'Aquin* (Paris: Vrin, 1997).

128. Aquinas, *S.Th.* III, q. 45, a. 4, co.

129. See Aquinas, *S.Th.* III, q. 7, a. 1.

130. See ibid., ad 3.

131. "Sed quae necessitas ut Verbum Dei pateretur pro nobis? Magna: et potest colligi duplex necessitas. Una est ad remedium contra peccata, alia est ad exemplum quantum ad agenda." *In Symb. Apost. Exp.*, a. 4 (ed. Marietti, 913).

naturalis,[132] "a participated likeness of the natural filiation" of Christ. We shall return to this topic in the coming chapter.

The Christian believer is not only liberated from the slavery of sin, of death, and so on, but is also elevated above the creaturely condition, completely under God's sovereign power. Humans, though they become "sons in the Son," are still creatures, radically subordinate to the creator, as they strive to assimilate their lives to the Father's will. Nonetheless, in a sense the son or daughter of God acquires a kind of parity with God and is placed in a position where he can look at God face to face in a kind of equality by grace that permits a familiarity and unlimited trust that children have with their own parents. As Maximus the Confessor says: "Whoever is divinized by grace becomes all that God is, except with respect to the identity of essence."[133]

The Christian Lives the Life of a Child of God

Consideration of divine filiation for a Christian cannot be looked upon as a simple devotion like any other, for the simple reason that the filial condition is not just another aspect of the Christian way of life. Divine filiation is the fundamental ontological condition of being Christian, of the "new creation," and it is what gives meaning to every other aspect of God's project of grace. The Christian is a child of God just as much as God is Father. And God is Father because he has a Son made man, Jesus Christ. Divine filiation ontologically determines what the Christian is in God's sight and before the world: a son by adoption. All the different elements that go to making up the life of grace—supernatural elevation, sanctifying grace, theological virtues, and gifts of the Holy Spirit—flow from it and are expressions of it. As a result, divine filiation should determine critically the practical living out of Christian life.

In effect, the "filial equality" Christians have with God by grace is reflected in a series of basic and inseparable elements of Christian spirituality and ethics: in the imitation of the life and behavior of Christ; in prayer and the living of daily life in trust and simplicity, that is, by faith; in the responsible and sincere effort to do the will of God for love, freely, in everything, as something of one's own, that is, in Christian obedience; in the effort to bring God's sovereignty to prevail in the world; in living charity as service to those most in need; in the joyful hope of receiving the eternal inheritance due to those who live in the Father's house, which consists of the eternal communion with the Trinity.

Adoptive divine filiation is, in real terms, the fundamental condition of the new creature in Christ called to communion with the Trinity. The life of the children of God is defined by the theological virtues (especially faith, hope, and charity) and consists of the human virtues, lived in the midst of human activities and all created realities, which, with filial love, become holy and pleasing to God. The son or daughter of God looks at, contemplates, and admires the world with all the enthusiasm that arises from his love for the eternal Father, the world's creator. He feels completely at home in a world

---

132. Aquinas, *S.Th.* III, q. 3, a. 5, ad 2; q. 23, a. 3, co.; q. 24, a. 3, co. "Illud quod fit ignitum, per ignem oportet fieri, quia nihil consequitur participationem alicuius, nisi per id quod est per naturam suam tale: ideo, adoptionem filiorum oportet fieri per Filium naturalem." Aquinas, *In Eph.*, 1, 5, l. 1.

133. Maximus the Confessor, *Ambig. ad Ioh.* 41.

created by God, living in a secular way that insertion into the world, with filial joy, "passionately loving the world."[134] Josemaría Escrivá explains this as follows:

Divine filiation is a joyful truth, a consoling mystery. It fills all our spiritual life, it shows us how to speak to God, to know and to love our Father in heaven. And it makes our interior struggle overflow with hope and gives us the trusting simplicity of little children. More than that: precisely because we are children of God, we can contemplate in love and wonder everything as coming from the hands of our Father, God the Creator. And so we become contemplatives in the middle of the world, loving the world.... God the Father, in the fullness of time, sent to the world his only begotten Son, to reestablish peace; so that by his redeeming men from sin, 'we might become sons of God' (Gal 4:5), freed from the yoke of sin, capable of sharing in the divine intimacy of the Trinity. And so it has become possible for this new man, this new grafting of the children of God (Rom 6:4–5), to free all creation from disorder, restoring all things in Christ (Eph 1:5–10), who has reconciled them to God (Col 1:20).[135]

Being Children of God through Grace: The Action of the Holy Spirit as Gift

According to scripture, humans become children of God through the power of the Holy Spirit.[136] In real terms, of course, the Holy Spirit is the true inner protagonist of the life of grace. "The Spirit helps us in our weakness," we read in Paul's letter to the Romans, "for we do not know how to pray as we ought, but the Spirit himself intercedes for us with sighs too deep for words" (Rom 8:26). We have already cited the principal Pauline texts on divine filiation, Romans 8:14–17 and Galatians 4:6f., which remind us of the fundamental role played by the Spirit. In Romans we read: "For all who are led by the Spirit of God are sons of God. For you did not receive the spirit of slavery to fall back into fear, but you have received the spirit of sonship. When we cry, 'Abba! Father!' It is the Spirit himself bearing witness with our spirit that we are children of God, and if children, then heirs, heirs of God and fellow heirs with Christ" (Rom 8:14–17). And in Galatians: "Because you are sons, God has sent the Spirit of his Son into our hearts, crying, 'Abba! Father!' So through God you are no longer a slave but a son, and if a son then an heir" (Gal 4:6f.). Josemaría Escrivá writes: "The action of the Paraclete within us confirms what Christ had announced—that we are children of God."[137]

The work of the Spirit among the faithful may be distinguished into two inseparable stages. First, the Spirit produces an identification of the believer with Christ, molding his life into that of Christ, converting the believer into an *alter Christus, ipse Christus,* "another Christ, Christ himself."[138] And second, as a result, the Spirit is the

---

134. The expression is that of Josemaría, taken from the title of a homily published in *Conversations with Msgr Escrivá de Balaguer,* nos. 113–23.

135. Escrivá, *Christ Is Passing By,* no. 65. On the doctrine of divine filiation in Josemaría, see Burkhart and López, *Vida cotidiana y santidad en la enseñanza de San Josemaría,* 2:11–159.

136. On this issue we have followed the outline of O'Callaghan, "L'agire dello Spirito Santo." See also the audience of Benedict XVI titled *The Spirit and the 'Abba' of Believers,* dated May 23, 2012.

137. Escrivá, *Christ Is Passing By,* no. 118.

138. See Aranda, "Cristo presente en los cristianos"; O'Callaghan, "The Inseparability of Holiness and Apostolate."

one who cries out "Abba, Father" in the heart of believers, bringing them to know and take delight in the Father and the Son in the mystery of their reciprocal love, both gratuitous and infinite, in the ineffable bond that may be expressed in the following complementary declarations: "Jesus lifted up his eyes and said, 'Father, I thank you that you have heard me. I knew that you hear me always, but I have said this on account of the people standing by, that they may believe that you sent me'" (Jn 11:41f.), and "A voice came from heaven, saying, 'This is my beloved Son, with whom I am well pleased'" (Mt 3:17).

The Spirit Molds Christ in the Believer

The New Testament teaches that the action of the Holy Spirit adds no new or diverse thematic content to the work and teaching of Christ. The Spirit has no teaching of his own. Rather the Spirit is the one who applies, communicates, and makes present, from the beginning of the Church's life, in the hearts of believers, the content of revelation and grace that derive completely from the words and works of Jesus, the only Word of the Father, the "Christ." It is true that humans are moved by the life and example of Christ and gradually become his disciples, but God is the one who reveals that Jesus is the Christ, that is, the One who has been anointed by the Spirit: "Blessed are you, Simon Bar-Jona! For flesh and blood has not revealed this to you [that Jesus is the Christ, the Son of the living God], but my Father who is in heaven" (Mt 16:16f.).

All this is, in fact, the work of the Spirit: "But the Paraclete, the Holy Spirit, whom the Father will send in my name, he will teach you all things, and bring to your remembrance all that I have said to you" (Jn 14:26; see Jn 15:26f.).[139] The Spirit, therefore, does not teach the faithful new or diverse things with respect to what Jesus revealed or explained. The Spirit is the "paraclete," the consoler, but the *other* Paraclete—Jesus is the first Paraclete (1 Jn 2:1)—"to be with you forever" (Jn 14:16). "He will glorify me," Jesus says, "for he will *take what is mine* and declare it to you" (Jn 16:14). In the life of the Church the Spirit carries out what the Son did for his disciples while on earth, making the eternal love of the Father immediate and tangible. According to Gregory of Nyssa, the Spirit of God "accompanies the Word and reveals its efficacy."[140] In the elegant expression of Gregory of Nazianzen, "Christ is born, the Spirit moves; he is baptized, the Spirit gives witness; he is tempted, the Spirit leads him; he carries out works of power, the Spirit accompanies him; he ascends into heaven, the Spirit is his inheritance."[141] And Thomas Aquinas writes: "All that is done by the Holy Spirit is done also by Christ."[142] With respect to the work of Christ, therefore, the action of the Spirit may not be considered in any way discontinuous, separated, violent, elitist, contrary, or parallel.[143] It is one and the same work.

139. See M. Tábet, "Lo Spirito Santo, testimone di Gesù," *Annales Theologici* 12 (1998): 3–34, esp. 5–16. "The witness of the Spirit is presented in the fourth gospel as a certification directed not so much to the historical present of Jesus, but to the Church throughout the ages" (31).

140. Gregory of Nyssa, *Or. catech.*, 2, cited by John Damascene, *De fide orth.* I, 7.

141. Gregory Nazianzen, *Oratio theologica*, 5, 29.

142. Thomas Aquinas, *In Eph.*, c. 2, l. 5: "Sic autem habemus accessum ad Patrem per Christum, quoniam Christus operatur per Spiritum Sanctum: *si quis autem Spiritum Christi non habet, hic non est eius.* Et ideo quidquid fit per Spiritum Sanctum, etiam fit per Christum." And elsewhere: "Salus generi humani quae perficitur per Filium incarnatum et per donum Spiritui Sancti." *S.Th.* I, q. 32, a. 1, co.

143. See the title of the book of B. Gilliéron, *Le Saint-Esprit, actualité du Christ* (Geneva: Labor et Fides,

The Spirit Brings the Christian to Share in the Relationship between the Father and the Son

It has often been observed that the action of the Holy Spirit, though absolutely central at every stage of Christian life, particularly in the life of grace, is normally expressed and experienced in a hidden, humble, silent, we might say "kenotic," way, a way that is difficult to describe, to objectify.[144] When the Christian is "divinized" by the Spirit, when he shares in the filiation of the eternal Son of the Father, entering into God's inner life, when he is made capable of praying with the total confidence of children, the same Spirit who divinizes reminds him in his creaturely and sinful heart that filial union with God takes place always as a gift, a gift that derives from and reflects the infinite and transparent dialogue and self-giving that constitutes the inner Trinitarian bond between the Father and the Son.[145]

It may be said, therefore, that the Holy Spirit acts within humans in a hidden and secret way, insofar as he makes the sharing in the life of the Trinity operative and present in them, which is what divine filiation is. The Father always gives everything to the Son, and the Son, in receiving all, glorifies the Father in all. This reciprocal paterno-filial donation, lived eternally and unreservedly, is identified with the very action of the Spirit and expresses at one and the same time the fullness of his divin-

---

1978). And this from Karl Barth: "The Holy Spirit ... is God himself, insofar as he is capable, in an ineffably real way, without losing out on being God, to be present to the creature, and in virtue of that presence, to give life to the creature." *Kirchliche Dogmatik* I/1, 515f. In the words of M.-J. Le Guillou, "The Spirit interiorizes the knowledge of the mysteries of Christ within Christians," in "Le développement de la doctrine sur l'Esprit Saint dans les écrits du Nouveau Testament," in *Credo in Spiritum Sanctum: Atti del Congresso Teologico Internazionale di Pneumatologia*, edited by J. Saraiva Martins (Vatican City: Vaticana, 1982), 1:729–39, 734. The Spirit is "the mediation that determines all the rest," according to the Lutheran J. Baur, in "La pneumatologia luterana del XX secolo," in *Credo in Spiritum Sanctum*, 1:681–85, 682. And H. Mühlen explains that the mediations of Christ and the Spirit are not two alternative or parallel mediations, in "Das Christusereignis als Tat des Heiligen Geistes," in *Mysterium Salutis* III.2:513–45, 514f. He says that "the Holy Spirit, as the divine 'person' that is 'closest' to us, cannot be considered a 'mediator' in the analogical sense as Christ is the mediator of the Father; rather, he is the mediation which mediates himself, which mediates everything to everything else, but which of itself has no need for mediation.... With the Holy Spirit we do not have a relationship of one to another, face-to-face, because he is the 'immediateness' (not mediated and mediating himself) of our encounter with Christ.... We are in relationship with Christ only through his Spirit, in such a way that the experience of the Spirit (that is the experience of the mediation that mediates itself) is materially—though not formally—experience of Christ" (514ff.). "In the giving of grace, we should distinguish between a mediation of our relationship with Christ—and with Christ to the Father—: Christ 'intermediates' *himself* to us as the origin, within time, of the Holy Spirit, through this very Spirit ... and in this way he places himself before his Church as a spouse. But the Spirit of Jesus also 'intermediates' *himself* in the concrete and historical working out of the 'tradition,' the office and the sacrament. In that way he 'intermediates' on the one hand Christ to us, being numerically identical in Christ and in us; on the other hand he 'intermediates' us with Christ, being immediateness itself in the personal relationship through which the Church is facing Christ as a spouse" (542f.).

144. See O'Callaghan, "L'agire dello Spirito Santo," 338–43.

145. Thus the conclusion of the work of Mühlen: "The anonymity, the unnamed-ness of the Holy Spirit is a personal peculiarity of his: we can only speak of the Spirit speaking of the Father and the Son, from whom we can eventually arrive at the following provisional conclusion: the experience of the Spirit is, originally, the experience of the dual divine 'we' [of the Father and the Son] and the experience of the historical insertion in the plural 'we' of the disciples. Insofar as the dual divine 'we' has been revealed through the Cross as total self-donation, as self-surpassing, the experience of the Spirit is always, at the same time, the experience of the donation and the surpassing that takes place in us, and this is so in a double direction: through Christ toward the Father and toward the rest of humanity." Mühlen, "Das Christusereignis," 542f.; emphasis added.

ity, consubstantial with the Father and the Son. The Spirit identifies us with Christ, making us his brothers, friends, and disciples, and Christ, in turn, reveals God to us as our Father. In the brief formulation of Basil the Great we read: "Just as the Father is contemplated in the Son, so also the Son is contemplated in the Spirit."[146] In the words of Matthias J. Scheeben:

The Holy Spirit comes to our soul and becomes present formally in it in his own Person, as the outpouring and pledge of the fatherly love with which the Father loves us, his adoptive children. He comes to us as the flower of the sweetness and loveliness of God; in a word, as the *osculum* or kiss of the Father and Son which we receive in the innermost recess of our soul.[147]

And Ratzinger writes:

The Spirit is found at the beginning as the guide and leader of humanity, although he can scarcely be perceived. He leads us to the Son, and through the Son he leads us to the Father.... The Spirit is recognized by his faithfulness to the Word that has been spoken.... This forgetfulness of self, which is characteristic of him, and the fact that he does not give witness concerning himself, this is what gives Jesus authority with the world.... If he reveals himself to be the Spirit of the Trinity, the Spirit of the one God in three persons, this is precisely because he does not appear as a separate and separable self, but disappears into the Father and the Son.[148]

The Spirit Communicates to the Believer the Sense of Divine Filiation

The Spirit, therefore, may be considered as the one who expresses and unfolds fully and continuously in the life of the children of God both the fullness of the giving of the Father to the Son and the fullness of the obedient and filial glorification of the Father by the Son. The Spirit is, in the words of John Paul II, "the direct witness of the reciprocal love" of the Father and the Son.[149] The Spirit is the gift that convinces believers, in the depths of their hearts, that their divine filiation is a pure gift of God. Josemaría Escrivá expresses this as follows: "I felt the action of the Lord which gave rise in my heart and on my lips, with the power of imperious necessity, the tender invocation: *Abba, Pater!*"[150] In the power of the Spirit which establishes and vivifies the paterno-filial bond between Christians and the Father, humans become aware (1) of the *Father* of whom they are beloved children and from whom they have freely received all things;[151] (2) of the *Son* with whom and (above all) through whom they have

---

146. Basil, *De Spiritu Sancto*, 26, 64.

147. Scheeben, *The Mysteries of Christianity*, 160.

148. Ratzinger, *The God of Jesus Christ*, 101, 104.

149. John Paul II, *Dominum et Vivificantem*, par. 34. And, in the words of William of Saint Thierry: "Man is caught up, in a sense, in this embrace, in this kiss of the Father and the Son which is the Holy Spirit; he sees himself united to God with the same charity that goes to make up the unity of the Father and the Son" (*Speculum fidei*). On the role of the Holy Spirit in Christians' perceiving that they are children of God, see Burkhart and López, *Vida cotidiana y santidad en la enseñanza de San Josemaría*, 2:33–37.

150. Escrivá, *Letter*, January 9, 1959, 60, cited in Burkhart and López, *Vida cotidiana y santidad en la enseñanza de San Josemaría*, 2:36.

151. Thomas Aquinas teaches that the Spirit is present in the believer *ex affectu filialis amoris*. *In Rom.* (ed. Marietti), no. 645; see Aquinas, *In Gal.*, nos. 210ff.).

become children of the Father and of whom they have become brothers; (3) of the *Church*, the body of Christ, from which and in which they live their supernatural filiation and fraternity,[152] and (4) of the *Spirit* in the very act of giving himself to humans.

152. "The prayer of the Spirit of Christ in us and ours in him is not solely an individual act but an act of the entire Church. In praying our heart is opened, not only do we enter into communion with God but actually with all the children of God, because we are one body. When we address the Father in our inner room in silence and in recollection we are never alone. Those who speak to God are not alone. We are within the great prayer of the Church, we are part of a great symphony that the Christian community in all the parts of the earth and in all epochs, raises to God." Benedict XVI, "The Spirit and the 'Abba' of Believers."

14 DIVINE LIFE IN HUMANS

God's "Inhabitation" of Man's Soul and "Created Grace"

If a man loves me, he will keep my word, and my Father will love him, and we will come to him and make our home with him.   JOHN 14:23

Deus facit nos dilectores suos.   AUGUSTINE[1]

Per se primo, non fit gratia, sed gratum.   FRANCIS SUÁREZ[2]

We have considered the life of grace from the perspective of its one and only origin, God: the project or plan of divine love that finds its first expression in the work of creation is expressed in terms of predestination and calling, and culminates in justification and glorification. In the previous chapter we considered the fundamental condition of human beings in grace, that is, adopted divine filiation, with its Christological and pneumatological (and therefore Trinitarian) structure.

Still, scripture speaks of grace as present and active in humans using a wide variety of expressions, mainly Biblical in origin, that refer openly to anthropological and ontological factors, for example, regeneration, new creation, new life, eternal life, liberation. These expressions tell us that the human being, though divinized, does not *become* God but always remains a creature. A human is a creature, however, that has been regenerated, renovated, vivified, elevated, liberated, created anew. For this reason we need to consider the effect of grace on the human creature, that is, the way in which God's self-giving transforms humans and brings them to the fullness of their nature.

It should be noted, however, that the dynamics of the gift of grace cannot be limited to metaphysical categories that describe the inanimate world. The life of grace

---

1. Augustine, *De spir. et lett.* 32:56: "God makes us his lovers."
2. F. Suárez, *De gratia*, 8, 3, 13: "It is not grace that is given in the first place, but rather that one is made pleasing," that is, that humans are made pleasing to God.

must be understood and described in a "personalistic" way, a way in which humans, by God's grace, live in communion with the Father, the Son, and the Holy Spirit.[3] In order to give priority to this personalistic side of grace within humans, we shall consider in the coming chapters three different ways in which they live and act within the divine presence of grace.[4]

First, we shall consider the *objective-metaphysical* side of grace: humans in grace are transformed, ontologically elevated, renewed to the depths of their being. This aspect of grace is often to referred to as "created grace" and will be considered under that name in this chapter. We shall also consider the life of grace insofar as it goes beyond the objective and metaphysical to the *psychological-moral* aspects of grace, in the sense that humans are renewed by grace in their faculties and personal actions. When he gives himself to humans, God, in effect, infuses into them truly divine powers, often called "infused virtues," powers with which humans, freely, though in complete submission to God, act in a Christ-like and Spirit-like way (we shall consider this in chapter 15). In the third place, in continuity with the other two aspects of grace, we can speak of a *personal-existential* side to the life of grace, in that humans can really *experience* God's life within their lives, which influences their free will and makes their actions meritorious before God (see chapter 16). Finally, because God is the one and only source of grace, we shall briefly conclude the systematic part of this treatise on Christian anthropology by considering the question of the *need for grace* in different ambits of human life (see chapter 17).

The Trinity and Grace: The Exemplarity of the Eternal Processions and Temporal Missions

Through revelation we can recognize that God acts and communicates in two ways: *ad intra* in the "eternal processions" and *ad extra* in creation and the donation of grace to spiritual creatures.[5] Thomas Aquinas called the latter "divine missions."[6] The first is substantial and necessary and belongs to divine nature as such, to the *immanent Trinity*, whereas the second is participated in by creatures and is free, belonging to the *economy of grace*, to God's action *ad extra*. Obviously the two orders are distinct from one another, just as we distinguish between the necessity of God and the contingency of the creature, between divine life and created life. Still, because

3. On the importance of the personalistic aspect of divine grace, see G. Gloege, "Der theologische Personalismus als dogmatisches Problem: Versuch einer Fragestellung," *Kerygma und Dogma* 1 (1955): 23–51; H. Volk, "Gnade und Person," in *Theologie in Geschichte und Gegenwart*, edited by J. Auer and H. Volk (Munich: Zink, 1957), 219–36.

4. I adopt this tripartite distinction from J. Auer, *Die menschliche Willensfreiheit im Lehrsystem des Thomas von Aquin und Johannes Duns Scotus* (Munich: M. Hueber, 1938); see also Auer, *Die Entwicklung der Gnadenlehre in der Hochscholastik*; Flick and Alszeghy, *Il Vangelo della grazia*; Rahner, "Some Implications of the Scholastic Concept of Uncreated Grace"; G. Colzani, "Dalla grazia creata alla libertà donata: Per una diversa comprensione della tesi dell'"habitus,"" *Scuola Cattolica* 112 (1984): 399–434.

5. See A. Staglianò, *Il mistero del Dio vivente: Per una teologia dell'Assoluto trinitario* (Bologna: Dehoniane, 1996), 519–78; L. F. Mateo-Seco, *Dios Uno y Trino* (Pamplona: Eunsa, 1998), 522–83; P. Coda, *Dalla Trinità: L'avvento di Dio tra storia e profezia* (Rome: Città Nuova, 2011), 535–83; L. F. Mateo-Seco and G. Maspero, *Il mistero di Dio uno e trino: Manuale di teologia trinitaria* (Rome: Edusc, 2014), 243–51.

6. See Aquinas, *S.Th.* I, q. 43.

the gift of grace involves a sharing in Trinitarian life itself and, more specifically, in the paterno-filial relationship between God and the Son, we may say that grace is communicated *ad extra* in a way that is analogous to the way divine life is possessed and communicated by God *ad intra*. In that sense, the human being in grace is placed *in the likeness of the Trinity*: he is identified with the Son in the power of the Spirit, thus becoming capable of relating to God in a filial way. The Trinitarian processions are said to be prolonged outside God, *ad extra*, toward the created world through the missions of the Son and the Spirit. This involves and transforms the created being that is called and elevated to communion with God, bringing it back to its source.[7] As Aquinas says, "Id quod substantialiter est in Deo, accidentaliter fit in anima participante divinam bonitatem" (That which takes place substantially in God, takes place accidentally in the soul sharing in divine goodness).[8] This partaking or sharing involves a kind of prolonging of the divine processions.

The first procession, the generation of the Son by the Father, is prolonged *ad extra* with respect to *filial generation*. The second, that of the Spirit, is prolonged *ad extra* according to *love*, self-donation. As Augustine teaches, the Spirit "exit non quomodo natus, sed quomodo datus" (proceeds not as one who is born but as one who is given).[9] We can say, therefore, that the fruit of the divine missions consists of divine filiation offered as a gift. Thus the *result* of elevation by grace consists of a prolonging of the procession of the Son, and therefore in divine filiation, whereas the *mode* of elevation refers to the second procession, that of the Spirit: becoming children of God is given to believers, because it does not belong to them by nature, but is given by the one who is the hypostatic "gift." It is therefore correct to say that the Christian, through grace, is a "son," generated by God, but not a "spirit." And we can understand why the Spirit reminds us that we are children of God: "It is the Spirit himself bearing witness with our spirit that we are children of God" (Rom 8:16), children by God's gift, and thus children by adoption (Rom 8:23; Gal 4:5). Believers become, as it were, God's equals, by grace of course. As a result, Thomas tells us, "Assumptio quae fit per gratiam adoptionis, terminatur ad quandam participationem divinae naturae" (The assumption that takes place by the grace of adoption obtains a kind of participation in the divine nature).[10] And elsewhere: "Filiatio adoptionis est participata similitudo filiationis naturalis" (Adoptive filiation is a participated likeness in natural filiation), that is, in the filiation of Christ.[11] And finally, the spiritual creature "fit particeps divini Verbi et procedentis Amoris" (shares in the divine Word and in love that proceeds).[12]

Each and every divine operation proceeding from the Trinity belongs necessarily to all three divine persons, to whom must be predicated a common efficient causality *ad extra* in the production of grace: the Trinitarian project of our sanctification, like

7. Thomas says: "Anima per gratia conformatur Deo. Unde ad hoc quod aliqua Persona divina mittatur ad aliquem per gratiam, oportet quod fiat assimilatio illius ad divinam Personam quae mittitur per aliquod gratiae donum." *S.Th.* I, q. 43, a. 5, ad 2.

8. Aquinas, *S.Th.* I-II, q. 110, a. 2, ad 2.   9. Augustine, *De Trinitate* V, 14, 15.

10. Aquinas, *S.Th.* III, q. 3, a. 4, ad 3.

11. Aquinas, *S.Th.* III, q. 23, a. 4. And Thomas speaks in *S.Th.* III, q. 3, a. 5, ad 2, of the *similitudo participata filiationis naturalis*.

12. Aquinas, *S.Th.* I, q. 38, a. 1, co.

that of our creation, refers to the Trinity in unity. As Augustine says, "Inseparabilia sunt opera Trinitatis" (The works of the Trinity are inseparable).[13] God always acts through the Son and in the Holy Spirit. Still, in comparison with the work of creation, God's giving of grace has a peculiarity all its own: whereas the *origin* of grace involves a common Trinitarian action, the *effect* of grace places the creature in a *differentiated relationship* with the three persons.[14] In other words, if from the point of view of the unity of divine action *ad extra* we can say that the entire Trinity makes us children of God, from the point of view of the result of this divine action, the believer is made to share in divine life, becoming *a child of the Father in the Son through the Holy Spirit*.[15] With the gift of grace, God places the human creature, who now lives out an existence beyond itself, in a relationship that is not dissimilar to the one that obtains between the divine persons: the offering of grace is not a simple operation *ad extra* like creation;[16] it is a special operation *ad extra* with the purpose of placing believers *ad intra*, that is, "placing" them within the Trinity. If in the created world we may find the *vestigia Trinitatis*, traces of Trinitarian life, in grace is to be found a faithful reflection in humans of God's own life, God one and three.

Grace and Inhabitation of the Human Soul by the Trinity

Scripture speaks frequently of the "inhabitation" of the soul in grace by the divine persons, in a variety of ways.[17] It uses the term most clearly with respect to the Holy Spirit, who is called "the guarantee (or seal, in Greek, *arrabōn*) of our inheritance" (Eph 1:14). The life of grace, the dignity and proper works of the children of God, find in this inhabitation their founding presence: "For all who are led by the Spirit of

13. Augustine, *Sermo* 213, 6. See the following monographic number of *PATH* 11 (2012): *"Pisteuomen eis hena Theon": Ripensare l'Unità di Dio alla luce della rivelazione trinitaria.*

14. Josemaría Escrivá writes: "Our heart now needs to distinguish and adore each one of the divine Persons. The soul is, as it were, making a discovery in the supernatural life, like a little child opening his eyes to the world about him. The soul spends time lovingly with the Father and the Son and the Holy Spirit, and readily submits to the work of the life-giving Paraclete, who gives himself to us with no merit on our part, bestowing his gifts and the supernatural virtues!" *Friends of God: Homilies by Josemaría Escrivá* (1974), no. 306. And, in the words of Bernadot: "The Father comes to the soul as the source of life and peace: he is the Creator, who, after generating the creature, places it in its proper place; he is the Father who surrounds his son with goodness and unspeakable tenderness…. The Word, as the fountain of light: thought of the Father, his living Word, his Image, unites himself with my intelligence to introduce me into the supernatural knowledge of the divinity…. The Holy Spirit, source of love: Love of the Father and the Son, their mutual kiss, eternal Movement and ineffable Ecstasy of their love, consummation of their life, unites himself with my will to introduce me into the supernatural love of the Father and the Son." M. V. Bernadot, *De la eucaristía a la Trinidad* (Barcelona: Luis Gili, 1946), 53.

15. See Ocáriz, "La santísima Trinidad y el misterio de nuestra deificación."

16. M.-J. Scheeben noticeably insists on the distinction between the donation of grace and that of creation, that is, between the generation of the children of God and the work of creating the world: "Our natural relationship to God as our Creator and Lord is accounted for simply by the infinity of the divine nature and our dependence on it…. God can give existence to finite beings because He is being itself…. But the case is otherwise with the grace of divine filiation, with the gratuitous communication of the divine nature to creatures. God's power to communicate His nature externally and to beget children of grace is conceived by us not on the ground of his creative power, but as correlative to the infinite generative power by which He communicates His nature substantially and begets a Son equal to Himself." Scheeben, *The Mysteries of Christianity*, 141f. Rather than a "new creation," the giving of grace should be considered as a real divine generation, Scheeben says.

17. See chapter 6, notes 16ff. and corresponding text.

God are sons of God" (Rom 8:14; see 5:5).[18] John teaches that God the Father makes his home in those who believe in his Son: "Whoever confesses that Jesus is the Son of God, God abides in him, and he in God" (1 Jn 4:15). And we find the same thing in John 14:23: "If a man loves me, he will keep my word, and my Father will love him, and we will come to him and *make our home* with him." The same may be said of the Spirit: "If you love me, you will keep my commandments. And I will pray the Father, and he will give you another Counselor, *to be with you for ever*, the Spirit of truth, whom the world cannot receive, because it neither sees him nor knows him; you know him, *for he dwells with you*, and will be in you" (Jn 14:15–17).[19] As a result, Paul considers the baptized as God's temples, and even as divine "lodgings."[20] "Do you not know that you are God's temple and that God's Spirit dwells in you?" he writes (1 Cor 3:16). And later: "Do you not know that your body is a temple of the Holy Spirit within you, which you have from God? You are not your own" (1 Cor 6:19). From this Paul draws important consequences: "You were bought with a price. So glorify God in your body" (1 Cor 6:20). "For we are *the temple of the living God*" (2 Cor 6:16). "In him [Christ] you also are built into it for a *dwelling place of God* in the Spirit (Eph 2:22).

Pope Pius XII once observed that divine indwelling will always be

a hidden mystery, which during this earthly exile can only be dimly seen through a veil, and which no human words can express. The Divine Persons are said to indwell inasmuch as they are present to beings endowed with intelligence in a way that lies beyond human comprehension, and in a unique and very intimate manner which transcends all created nature, these creatures enter into a relationship with Them through knowledge and love.[21]

To develop our reflection on the doctrine of indwelling, two questions may be considered: what kind of presence does God's indwelling in the soul involve? And what relationship is there between indwelling and grace?

May God Be Considered as the "Quasi-formal Cause" of Grace?

During the twentieth century it was frequently held that God is the "quasi-formal" cause of grace in the believer. This idea was developed first in the works of Maurice de la Taille and Karl Rahner.[22] Both authors offer the following explanation of the life of grace: besides the efficient divine causality in the donation of grace, priority should be accorded to God's self-communication to humans by means of grace, through which God becomes a quasi-constitutive principle of the created being while not losing his absolute ontological priority.[23] Grace is given, therefore, not for the purpose

18. On the question of God's inhabitation of the soul, see Flick and Alszeghy, *Il vangelo della grazia*, § 96.

19. See Heise, *Bleiben; NIDNTTE* 3:272–77, s.v. μονή.

20. See *NIDNTTE* 2:511–21, s.v. ἱερός.

21. Pope Pius XII, *Mystici Corporis*, Encyclical Letter, June 29, 1943, in *DH* 3815. See also Pope Leo XIII, *Divinum Illud Munus*, Encyclical Letter, May 9, 1897. Other Church documents may be found in Flick and, Alszeghy, *Il vangelo della grazia*, § 99.

22. This position has presented first of all by M. de la Taille in "Actuation créée par un acte incréé, lumière de gloire, grâce sanctifiante, union hypostatique," *Recherches de science religieuse* 18 (1928): 253–68, and then by K. Rahner in "Some Implications of the Scholastic Concept of Uncreated Grace."

23. See K. Rahner, *Foundations of Christian Faith: An Introduction to the Idea of Christianity* (London: Darton, Longman and Todd, 1978), 126ff.

of making God a known and loved "object" of the believer but rather so that the latter would live off the "unobjectifiable" experience of the transcendent, in continuous openness to it. According to this theory, humans would come to know and love God one and three by sharing directly in divine life; it might be said that God knows and loves himself in and through them. Without going so far as to say that God becomes the formal cause of grace (in which case humans would become absorbed by God in their very being), some authors describe this explanation of the divine presence using the terminology "quasi-formal cause."

The point of reference that explains this union is, according to Rahner, the beatific vision. In the eschatological vision, God in person unites himself directly to the blessed by making them capable of acting in a "deiform" way, knowing God on the basis of his own essence. Thomas Aquinas says, in fact, that in the vision of God "essentia divina est quod videtur et quo videtur" (the divine essence is that which is seen and that by which it is seen).[24] In glory, humans see God because he unites himself to them by means of the *lumen gloriae*. On the basis of the close continuity between grace and glory, Rahner argues that the life of grace on earth is subject to the same workings as the beatific vision: the Trinity unites itself directly to the human spirit in knowledge and love. He concludes, therefore, that the indwelling of the Trinity, already on earth, consists in the Trinitarian action on the spirit of the believer as a quasi-formal cause.

The explanation of Rahner is significant because it emphasizes the intimate and personal aspect of the relationship between God and humans in grace. However, this union seems to be presented in an excessively immediate way that removes from the creature its ontological autonomy and freedom before God. As regards Rahner's interpretation of Thomas Aquinas, three things should be noted. Above all, Thomas does not teach that humans will in any way be absorbed by God in vision. When he says that "the very divine essence becomes the intelligible form of the intellect,"[25] he means that this is not so on the level of nature but on an intentional or representative level.[26] Secondly, between grace and glory there is continuity but not identity. The same parameters may not be applied to one and the other, as Popes Leo XIII and Pius XII explained when comparing and contrasting indwelling and the beatific vision.[27] And finally, Thomas explained his view of divine indwelling while insisting on the importance of "created grace" and excluding, ever more clearly as the years went by, the possibility that God would enter into a relationship with the soul that is comparable with the way the soul relates to the body, that is, at a formal or quasi-formal level. Let us now consider how the position of Thomas evolved.

24. Aquinas, *Summa contra Gentiles* [hereafter "SCG"] III, 51. In the *Compendium theologiae*, 105, Thomas writes: "Ipse Deus fiat forma intellectus ipsum cognoscentis."

25. Aquinas, *S.Th.* I, q. 12, a. 5, co.

26. This is the position of Cajetan, *In S.Th.* I, q. 12, a. 2. See *COH* 168f. On this point, C. Fabro, in *La svolta antropologica di Karl Rahner*, criticizes Rahner's interpretation of Aquinas.

27. See Flick and Alszeghy, *Il vangelo della grazia*, § 100.

What Is the Relationship between Divine Indwelling and Grace?
The Response of Aquinas

The common presence by immensity of God in all things (by his presence, power, and essence) as the cause of all creation does not provide a sufficient explanation for the indwelling of the Trinity in the soul.[28] As we have seen in scripture, God dwells in humans in a deeply intimate, singular, and personal way. This indwelling involves God's being present not as the cause in its effects but as the cause of supernatural life, that is, divine, Trinitarian life, on which the personal relationship with God is based.

What places us in direct contact with God is our supernatural activity, especially that which stems from the theological virtues, more or less as happens with the beatific vision. In the earthly state of humans, this takes place in an incomplete and hidden way, while in heaven it will take place face to face and fully, according to a difference that is one of grade but not of essence. The divine missions and the exercise of the theological virtues therefore offer the context in which we can consider this new formality of the indwelling of God in the soul in grace.

On the question of God's indwelling the soul, the thought of Aquinas shifted gradually but in a significant way during his lifetime.[29] In his early work, the *Commentary on the Sentences of Peter Lombard*, Thomas speaks of the indwelling of the Trinity in accordance with the following principle: "Per prius recipimus Spiritum Sanctum quam dona eius" (First we receive the Spirit, and then his gifts).[30] As a result, he concludes, God is present in the soul of the just "prout res est in sua similitudine" (as something is present in what is similar to it).[31] And elsewhere, in the same work, he writes: "Efficitur in nobis similitudo ad propria personarum" (On us is impressed a likeness to what is proper to the [divine] persons).[32] In other words, Thomas understands the presence of God in the just as a kind of assimilation to the persons of the Trinity produced in the soul by the action of God. God, in the Trinity of persons, would as it were be the "exemplar cause" of the life of grace. On this point Thomas is not far from the position of Peter Lombard that we already considered, in which charity is identified with the action of the Holy Spirit.[33]

In the *Summa contra Gentiles* the same position is to be found. Thomas says: "Id quod in nobis a Deo est, aliquo modo Deum imitatur" (Whatever is present in us is

---

28. On being the cause of all creation, see Aquinas, *S.Th.* I, q. 8, a. 3.

29. In the thought of Thomas, there was a considerable evolution in the explanation he gave of the nature of Trinitarian inhabitation. See Philips, *L'union personnelle*, 141–57; J. L. González Alio, "La inhabitación de la Santísima Trinidad," *Excerpta e dissertationibus in sacra theologia* 6 (1982): 1–106; J. Prades López, *"Deus specialiter est in sanctis per gratiam"*: *El misterio de la inhabitación de la Trinidad en los escritos de santo Tomás* (Rome: Pontificia Università Gregoriana, 1993). See also Flick and Alszeghy, *Il vangelo della grazia*, §§ 95–101, with a bibliography; L. F. Mateo-Seco, "Divino huésped del alma," *Scripta Theologica* 31 (1999): 453–69.

30. Aquinas, *I Sent.*, d. 14, q. 2, a. 1, qc 2, co.

31. "Unde sicut Spiritus Sanctus invisibiliter procedit in mentem per donum amoris, ita Filius per donum sapientiae; in quo est manifestatio ipsius Patris, qui est ultimum ad quod recurrimus. Et quia secundum receptionem horum duorum efficitur in nobis similitudo ad propria personarum; ideo secundum novum modum essendi, prout res est in sua similitudine, dicuntur personae divinae in nobis esse, secundum quod novo modo eis assimilamur; et secundum hoc utraque processio dicitur missio." Aquinas, *I Sent.*, d. 15, q. 4, a. 1, co.

32. Aquinas, *I Sent.*, d. 15, q. 4, a. 1, co.

33. See chapter 9, notes 13ff. and corresponding text.

from God, and in a certain sense it imitates God himself).[34] However, in this work is to be found an important shift from what might be called an "assimilative" understanding of indwelling (which we have just considered) to a "relational" understanding. Thomas describes the indwelling presence as follows: "Omne autem amatum in amante est" (Whatever is loved is present in the one who loves).[35] In his commentary on 2 Corinthians 6:16 ("We are God's living temple") this new approach is confirmed in the following dense text: "God is present in the saints through their own operation, with which they reach God and in a sense comprehend him; this operation is to love and to know: in fact it is said that the lover and the knower contain within themselves the realities they love and know."[36] Just as God is present in Christ corporally, says Thomas in his commentary on the letter to the Colossians (2:9), "he is also present in the soul of the just through the operation with which they reach God through love and knowledge."[37]

In comparison with what he wrote in his first texts, now Thomas is openly affirming the distinction between the divine and human subjects, the one loved (God) and his lovers (believers). If God is said to be present in humans, then, this is not only in the sense that human action is elevated and assimilated in some way to that of God but also in the sense that God is present in humans as a person directly known and loved, as a present "other." When it is said that humans know and love somebody else, it means that they are in a position to direct themselves to that person because, without being that person, they carry him within, in mind and heart, as a known and loved person.

The final doctrine of Thomas is to be found in the *Summa Theologiae*. Speaking precisely of the divine missions, he explains divine indwelling in the following terms:

God is to be found commonly in things by essence, by power and by presence, as the cause in the effects that share in his goodness and perfection. Beyond this common presence there is a special one reserved for rational creatures, in which it is said that God is present like the known thing in the one who knows, and the loved thing in the one who loves [*sicut*

---

34. "Ea quae a Deo in nobis sunt, reducuntur in Deum sicut in causam efficientem et exemplarem. In causam quidem efficientem, inquantum virtute operativa divina aliquid in nobis efficitur. In causam quidem exemplarem, secundum quod id quod in nobis a Deo est, aliquo modo Deum imitatur. Cum ergo eadem virtus sit Patris et Filii et Spiritus Sancti, sicut et eadem essentia; oportet quod omne id quod Deus in nobis efficit, sit, sicut a causa efficiente, simul a Patre et Filio et Spiritu Sancto. Verbum tamen sapientiae, quo Deum cognoscimus, nobis a Deo immissum, est proprie repraesentativum Filii. Et similiter amor quo Deum diligimus, est proprium repraesentativum Spiritus Sancti. Et sic caritas quae in nobis est, licet sit effectus Patris et Filii et Spiritus Sancti, tamen quadam speciali ratione dicitur esse in nobis per Spiritum Sanctum. Quia vero effectus divini non solum divina operatione esse incipiunt, sed etiam per eam tenentur in esse ... nihil autem operari potest ubi non est, oportet enim operans et operatum in actu esse simul, sicut movens et motum: necesse est ut, ubicumque est aliquis effectus Dei, ibi sit ipse Deus effector. Unde, cum caritas, qua Deum diligimus, sit in nobis per Spiritum Sanctum, oportet quod ipse etiam Spiritus Sanctus in nobis sit, quandiu caritas in nobis est." Aquinas, *SCG* IV, 21, 2.

35. "Omne autem amatum in amante est. Necesse est igitur quod per Spiritum Sanctum non solum Deus sit in nobis, sed etiam nos in Deo." Aquinas, *SCG* IV, 21, 3.

36. "In sanctis [Deus] est per ipsorum sanctorum operationem, qua attingunt ad Deum, et quodammodo comprehendunt ipsum, quae est diligere et cognoscere: nam diligens et cognoscens dicitur in se habere cognita et dilecta." Aquinas, *II ad Cor.* VI, l. 3.

37. "Item est in mentibus sanctis per operationem, quae per amorem et cognitionem attingunt Deum. Et ideo Deus est in eis secundum gratiam, sed non corporaliter, sed secundum effectum gratiae; nec est plenitudo, sed secundum aliquos effectus terminatos." Aquinas, *II ad Col.*, l. 2.

cognitum in cognoscente et amatum in amante]. And because the creature with reason, who knows and loves, reaches God with its operation [*sua operatione attingit ad ipsum Deum*], it is said, precisely on account of this special way of being, that God is not simply in the rational creature, but also that he dwells in it as in his temple [*sicut in templo suo*].[38]

Elsewhere in the *Summa*, Thomas confirms this doctrine, saying that "Deum esse ... sicut obiectum cognitum et amatum" (God is present in the soul in grace as a known and loved object).[39]

It is clear for Thomas that the believer is divinized by grace, that is, made to be like God. In the *Summa Theologiae* he says so openly: "Gratia enim causatur in homine ex praesentia divinitatis, sicut lumen in aëre ex praesentia solis" (Grace is brought about in humans by the presence of God, just as light in the air through the presence of the sun).[40] The supernatural virtues reflect to a degree God's way of acting, with which the Son and the Spirit proceed from the Father. Concretely, the believer becomes a child of God by sharing in the relationship between the Father and the Son. He becomes capable of acting in a divine, filial way. Still, the human being in grace is not absorbed into God either in being or in action.[41] This is a central affirmation of Christian faith that Aquinas never loses sight of.

The result of Aquinas's mature position, which insists on the distinction between God and divinized humans, is an affirmation of the need for the elevation of human beings through the infusion of grace, which is what makes them capable of knowing and loving God in his Trinitarian life. If this sanctifying elevation of the human being and faculties did not take place, it might be said that God loves humans and in a general way divinizes them, but it would not be possible to truly say that God has created humans capable of knowing and loving him. In that sense the divine commandment to love God with all one's heart and soul and mind and strength (Mt 22:37) would be meaningful only at the level of nature—in that all creatures naturally tend toward their creator[42]—but not at the level of grace, not at a personal level, because there would be no true otherness between persons who love one another. If at a hypothetical level the human being had the same nature as God, no elevation would be required in order to establish communion with him, as happens between two human persons, who can easily develop a friendship on the basis of belonging to the same human species. Still, the very fact that humans are creatures means that they stand

---

38. "Est enim unus communis modus quo Deus est in omnibus rebus per essentiam, potentiam et praesentiam, sicut causa in effectibus participantibus bonitatem ipsius. Super istum modum autem communem, est unus specialis, qui convenit creaturae rationali, in qua Deus dicitur esse sicut cognitum in cognoscente et amatum in amante. Et quia, cognoscendo et amando, creatura rationalis sua operatione attingit ad ipsum Deum, secundum istum specialem modum Deus non solum dicitur esse in creatura rationali, sed etiam habitare in ea sicut in templo suo." Aquinas, *S.Th.* I, q. 43, a. 3, co. In an earlier text we read: "Deus dicitur esse in re aliqua dupliciter. Uno modo, per modum causae agentis, et sic est in omnibus rebus creatis ab ipso. Alio modo, sicut obiectum operationis est in operante, quod proprium est in operationibus animae, secundum quod cognitum est in cognoscente, et desideratum in desiderante. Hoc igitur secundo modo, Deus specialiter est in rationali creatura, quae cognoscit et diligit illum actu vel habitu. Et quia hoc habet rationalis creatura per gratiam ... dicitur esse hoc modo in sanctis per gratiam." *S.Th.* I, q. 8, a. 3, co.

39. Aquinas, *S.Th.* I, q. 8, a. 3, ad 4.

40. Aquinas, *S.Th.* III, q. 7, a. 13, co.

41. For a further explanation, see Flick and Alszeghy, *Il vangelo della grazia*, §§ 100f.; J. L. Lorda, *Antropología teológica* (Pamplona: Eunsa, 2009), 442–45.

in need of the infusion of divine grace so that they can reach God directly, so that the human being "sua operatione attingat ad ipsum Deum" (by his action can reach God directly). This brings us to a consideration of the nature of that grace that elevates or sanctifies the human being and its faculties, what is often called "created grace."[43]

What Is the Relationship between Divine Indwelling and "Created" Grace?

We have seen that God's indwelling in the soul requires the created human being to be elevated to divine life through the infusion of grace. In technical terms we might say that "uncreated grace" requires "created grace."[44] Still, with respect to the relationship between indwelling and created grace, three observations may be made.

First, the "capacity" received by humans to know God as he is can never become a kind of autonomous capacity humans possess. Divine filiation is always adoptive, it is always and only a gift. Thomas Aquinas says so, as follows: "Ubicumque est aliquis effectus Dei, ibi sit ipse Deus effector" (Wherever is to be found a divine effect, God himself who acts is present there).[45] Therefore, to understand the notion of indwelling fully we need to keep in mind not only the idea of the presence of the divine persons in the soul, a presence that can bring about the contemplation of God, but also the idea that the human being is possessed by God and made capable of loving him. The mystery of indwelling, in effect, is rooted in the fact that the basis of our "possessing" God lies in the previous fact that God possesses creatures. The life of grace is life in the Trinity. Perhaps for this reason, it is not completely exact to speak of God indwelling humans; it would be better to say that humans indwell God. This is the position of Augustine, who wrote: "Habitas in Deo ut contineris" (Live in God so as to be contained in him).[46] And Bonaventure spoke in the same way, saying that "habere Deum est haberi a Deo" (to have God is to be possessed by God).[47] And Aquinas also says something of the kind: "Necesse est non solum Deus sit in nobis, sed etiam nos in Deo" (It is not just that God is present in us, but also that we are in him).[48]

Second, in the text of the *Summa Theologiae* on divine indwelling that we analyzed earlier, Aquinas speaks of the Trinity, made present in humans not only as the origin and source of grace, not only as the exemplary cause of the life of grace but specifically as the object of knowledge and love of the human being regenerated by grace, "sicut obiectum cogitum et amatum." He is of the opinion that humans are not only known and loved by God (called, justified, etc.) but also made capable of knowing and loving God one and three, and therefore able to direct their lives to him as children at prayer, at work, and in all kinds of activities. In order to carry out this sublime function it

---

42. See chapter 17, notes 34ff. and corresponding text.

43. On the importance of this category, see Colzani, "Dalla grazia creata alla libertà donata"; Auer, *Das Evangelium der Gnade*, 149–52.

44. See Colzani, "Dalla grazia creata"; A. Chacón, "El tratado sobre la gracia en la 'Summa contra gentiles,'" *Scripta Theologica* 16 (1984): 113–46; J.-M. Garrigues, "La doctrine de la grâce habituelle dans ses sources scripturaires et patristiques," *Revue Thomiste* 103, no. 2 (2003): 179–202. The latter study considers the presence of the notion of "created grace" in the New Testament and also in Irenaeus, Maximus the Confessor, and others.

45. Aquinas, *SCG* IV, 21, 2.   46. Augustine, *De Trinitate* XV, 18:32.

47. Bonaventure, *Breviloquium*, 5, c. 1.   48. Aquinas, *SCG* IV, 21.

is necessary that the faculties of humans—especially intellect and will—be elevated and amplified in an suitable way through grace. The Church teaches that when grace turns into glory and humans can see God face to face, they will receive the gift of the *lumen gloriae*, which makes the vision of God both possible and beatific.[49] Likewise, during their earthly pilgrimage humans need sanctifying grace and the theological virtues (faith, hope, and charity) in order to know, love, and dialogue with God as *filii in Filio*, "children in the Son." God dwells in the soul, therefore, not only as the source of grace but as the *only adequate object* of the new human capacity to know (through faith) and love (through charity). As a result, Thomas can conclude: "By the gift of grace, the creature gifted with reason is elevated not only to use the created gift freely, but also to enjoy the divine Person itself."[50] In Thomas's explanation, however, it is not clear how a created reality can elevate human faculties to the point of producing an immediate knowledge of God.

Third, as we have already seen, Peter Lombard, taking his cue from the anti-Pelagian writings of Augustine, teaches that the infused virtue of charity may be identified simply with the very action of the Holy Spirit: "The Holy Spirit itself is the love or the charity with which we love God and neighbor."[51] According to this position, however, it would seem that in a sense the action of the believer has been absorbed by that of God and that humans are no longer capable of acting on their own account, with their whole being, freely, before God. Interestingly, in fact, Lombard's teaching does not truly correspond to Augustine's. The latter teaches that with the infusion of the Holy Spirit "caritas Dei dicta diffundi in cordibus nostris non qua nos ipse diligit sed qua nos facit dilectores suos" (we say that the love of God is infused into our hearts not just in the sense that God loves us, but in that he makes us his lovers).[52] In other words, humans are not only loved by God but as the result of this love become capable of loving God. A similar phrase of Augustine's is to be found in the sixth session of the Council of Trent on justification,[53] which is cited with a view to avoiding an extrinsic or forensic understanding of grace suggested by some Lutherans. In effect, after teaching that the only efficient cause of grace is God himself, Trent says that the only formal cause of justification is "iustitia Dei, non qua ipse iustus est, sed qua nos iustos facit" (the justice of God, not that by which he is just, but that by which he makes us just).[54]

Why "Created Grace"?

Aquinas openly inquires into the created consistency of grace when he asks "utrum gratia ponit aliquid in anima" (whether grace places something in the soul).[55]

---

49. "The soul needs the 'light of glory' to be elevated, see God, and enjoy him." Council of Vienne (1312), in *DH* 875. See also *COH* 168f.

50. "Per donum gratiae gratum facientis perficitur creatura rationalis, ad hoc quod libere non solum ipso dono creato utatur, sed ut ipsa divina persona fruatur." *S.Th.* I, q. 43, a. 3, ad 1. He also says: "Illud solum habere dicimur, quo libere possumus uti vel frui. Habere autem potestatem fruendi divina persona, est solum secundum gratiam gratum facientem." *S.Th.* I, q. 43, co.

51. Peter Lombard, *I Sent.* d. 17, aa. 1 and 6.

52. Augustine, *De spiritu et littera* 32, 56. On the question of created grace in Augustine, see chapter 9, note 3.

53. See *DH* 1529.

54. The text is in Augustine, *De Trinitate* XIV, 12:15.

55. See Aquinas, *S.Th.* I-II, q. 110, a. 1. See also *II Sent.* d. 26, a. 1; *De Veritate*, q. 27, a. 1.

As he gives a substantially positive response to the question, he puts forward a fundamental intuition of his, saying that (1) humans (with or without sin) do not have the capacity to know and love God face to face, person to person, and this is so because God completely transcends every created nature; but, at the same time, (2) human nature is in a position to be elevated to divine life, or divinized, because it is "capax gratiae" (capable of receiving grace). And this elevation takes place by way of efficient causality, not because God becomes the formal or quasi-formal cause of grace. In fact, although the soul may be said to be the life of the body at the level of formal causality, says Thomas, grace is the life of the soul at that of efficient causality.[56] For this very reason, besides the original and foundational understanding of divine life as uncreated grace, we must speak of a created grace.

Grace, Thomas says, derives from the love of God.[57] Still, when we say that God loves humans, it should be added that he does not love them in a merely human way. In effect, the human will is normally moved to love by an existing good that is already present in things and persons. As a result, human love does not bring about the good that is present in the thing or person loved, but rather encounters it pre-existing and is moved to love on account of it. Hence we have to say that the goodness present in creatures has been implanted in them by the very act of creation. God, in fact, when he loves a creature, does not find in it an already established good that he encounters and admires and loves; rather, God freely gives goodness to creatures as he creates or recreates them. And the same may be said of the life of grace: when God loves humans and wishes to elevate them to communion with him, he gives them a new life that elevates their nature, in that way intensifying the being and goodness of humans.[58] In that sense, humans become pleasing to God and are made capable of responding to his life, of reaching him, touching him, and enjoying his presence. And although love between humans does not really create a new good, because it presupposes that it already exists in the loved person, the love of God toward creatures consists always and only in the giving of a new good to them. Thus the grace of God consists not in a mere complacency or admiration on God's part before creatures but

---

56. "Deus est vita animae per modum causae efficientis, sed anima est vita corporis per modum causae formalis. Inter formam autem et materiam non cadit aliquod medium, quia forma per seipsam informat materiam vel subiectum. Sed agens informat subiectum non per suam substantiam, sed per formam quam in materia causat." Aquinas, *S.Th.* I-II, q. 110, a. 1, ad 2. On the distinction between efficient and formal causality in the offering of grace, see also *De Ver.*, q. 27, a. 1, ad 1 and ad 10; *S.Th.* I-II, q. 111, a. 2, ad 1.

57. "Quia enim bonum creaturae provenit ex voluntate divina, ideo ex dilectione Dei qua vult creaturae bonum, profluit aliquod bonum in creatura. Voluntas autem hominis movetur ex bono praeexistente in rebus, et inde est quod dilectio hominis non causat totaliter rei bonitatem, sed praesupponit ipsam vel in parte vel in toto. Patet igitur quod quamlibet Dei dilectionem sequitur aliquod bonum in creatura causatum quandoque, non tamen dilectioni aeternae coaeternum. Et secundum huiusmodi boni differentiam, differens consideratur dilectio Dei ad creaturam." *S.Th.* I-II, q. 110, a. 1, co. "Una quidem communis, secundum quam diligit omnia quae sunt, ut dicitur Sap 9; secundum quam esse naturale rebus creatis largitur.... Alia autem est dilectio specialis, secundum quam trahit creaturam rationalem supra conditionem naturae, ad participationem divini boni. Et secundum hanc dilectionem dicitur aliquem diligere simpliciter, quia secundum hanc dilectionem vult Deus simpliciter creaturae bonum aeternum, quod est ipse. Sic igitur per hoc quod dicitur homo gratiam Dei habere, significatur quiddam supernaturale in homine a Deo proveniens." *S.Th.* I-II, q. 110, a. 1, co.

58. On the intensification of the act of being in those elevated by grace, see F. Ocáriz, "Partecipazione dell'essere e soprannaturale," in *Essere e libertà: Studi in onore di Cornelio Fabro* (Rimini: Maggioli, 1984), 41–53.

in a true act of giving being in which God "ponit aliquid in anima," as Aquinas says, "he places something in the soul."[59]

Elsewhere, Aquinas speaks in a realistic way of created grace in humans with respect to the Pauline doctrine of "new creation." He says:

Creation is a movement from nothing to being. There is a double being, the being of nature and the being of grace [*esse gratiae*]. The first creation took place when creatures were produced by God from nothing.... It is proper, therefore, that there would be a new creation with which the being of grace is produced, which in real terms is a "creation out of nothing," because those who are not in grace, it is as if they are nothing.[60]

Hence Aquinas frequently calls the grace by which God justifies or sanctifies the soul "gratia gratum faciens" (grace which makes one pleasing [to God]), because it makes humans truly endearing to God and capable of knowing and loving him. This provides an echo of what Augustine spoke of when he said that "God made us his lovers" and also "quia amasti me, fecisti me amabilem" (because you made me, you made me lovable).[61]

What Is the Ontological Constitution of Created Grace?

After explaining that "gratia ponit aliquid in anima," Aquinas specifies that sanctifying grace is present in the soul as an "accident," specifically as a quality of the soul,[62] a habitual gift infused by God: "Id enim quod substantialiter est in Deo, accidentaliter fit in anima participante divinam bonitatem" (That which is present as a substance in God, is given in the soul in an accidental way when it shares in the divine goodness).[63] In using Aristotelian language here, Aquinas intends to present the doctrine of grace in parallel with that of nature. With grace, humans are moved gently and promptly (*suaviter et prompte*), in accordance with nature, to obtain the eternal good.[64] When he says that grace is like an "accident" in the soul, he is not saying that it is something secondary or of little importance. In fact, he is perfectly aware that humans can reach their last end only by means of grace. He says, besides, that one single grace is worth more than the whole of the natural order. What Aquinas wants to avoid is an extrinsic view of the life of grace, the separation of grace and nature, in two directions, (1) that which understands grace only in the order of efficient causality (i.e., God infuses grace), passing over the formal causality (as created grace, which inclines the very human being toward God),[65] and (2) that which considers grace as a complete living substance contiguous to the soul (in effect, if grace were not an acci-

59. See note 57.

60. "Creatio enim est motus ex nihilo ad esse. Est autem duplex esse, scilicet esse naturae et esse gratiae. Prima creatio facta fuit quando creaturae ex nihilo productae sunt a Deo in esse naturae, et tunc creatura erat nova, sed tamen per peccatum inveterata est.... Oportet ergo esse novam creationem, per quam producerentur in esse gratiae, quae quidem creatio est ex nihilo, quia qui gratia carent, nihil sunt." *II ad Cor.*, 5, 17, l. 4. "Esse naturale per creationem Deus causat in nobis nulla causa agente mediante, sed tamen mediante aliqua causa formali; forma enim naturalis principium est esse naturalis. Et similiter esse spirituale gratuitum Deus facit in nobis nullo agente mediante, sed tamen mediante aliqua forma creata, quae est gratia." *De Veritate*, q. 27, a. 1, ad 3. See *De veritate*, q. 27, a. 2 ad 7, and *De virtutibus*, q. 1, a. 10, which speak of *quoddam spirituale esse*.

61. Augustine, *Enn. in Ps.* 191:5.

62. Aquinas, *S.Th.* I-II, q. 110, a. 2. On this issue, see Auer, *Das Evangelium der Gnade*, 166–69.

63. Aquinas, *S.Th.* I-II, q. 110, a. 2, ad 2.

64. "Infundit aliquas formas seu qualitates supernaturales, secundum quas suaviter et prompte ab ipso moveantur ad bonum aeternum consequendum." Ibid.

65. See *S.Th.* I-II, q. 110, a. 2, ad 1.

dent, it would necessarily be a separate substance, a divine substance, for that matter, God himself who gives his own life).[66] Thus the life of grace in the soul can only be an accident implanted in the soul by God that makes the perpetual relationship between God and humans possible. As the sixteenth-century theologian Francis Suárez said, "Per se primo, non fit gratia, sed gratum" (It is not grace that is given in the first place, but one is made pleasing), that is, humans are made pleasing to God.[67]

Besides, according to Thomas, grace is not a virtue; it may not be identified with faith, hope, or charity.[68] And the reason is simple: the faculties or powers presuppose always a pre-existing nature, an essence out of which they arise. And thus, although the infused virtues elevate the faculties, grace is what elevates nature as a whole: "The light of grace, which is a sharing in the divine nature," Aquinas says, "is a reality that goes beyond the infused virtues that derive from that light, and are ordered toward it."[69] For this reason we need to distinguish between the infused virtues, which perfect the different human faculties, and sanctifying grace, which perfects and elevates the soul in itself.

Thus Aquinas concludes that the life of grace is situated not in the powers or faculties of the soul but rather in its essence, because through grace the whole human being, with all its faculties, is regenerated as a child of God. Nothing of what is human, material and spiritual, temporal and immortal, ontological and phenomenological, is excluded from the life of grace. Hence, "just as humans intellectually share in divine knowledge through the power of faith, and in the will in divine love through the power of charity, so also humans according to their nature share in the divine nature, by likeness, with a kind of regeneration or recreation."[70] The *Roman Catechism* (or *Catechism of the Council of Trent*, published in 1566) sums up the principal elements of Thomas's description of grace, saying that it is "a divine quality that inheres in the soul, a kind of splendor and light, which takes away all the stains of the soul and makes it more beautiful and luminous."[71]

Grace in the Context of the Lutheran-Catholic Dialogue

The question of the consistency of created grace has been of considerable importance since the time of Luther, as well as in the Lutheran-Catholic dialogue that has taken place over recent decades. We have seen that classic Lutheran theology[72] spoke of justification in predominantly forensic terms, that is, as a juridical and extrinsic

---

66. "Omnis substantia vel est ipsa natura rei cuius est substantia, vel est pars naturae, secundum quem modum materia vel forma substantia dicitur. Et quia gratia est supra naturam humanam, non potest esse quod sit substantia aut forma substantialis, sed est forma accidentalis ipsius animae." Aquinas, *S.Th.* I-II, q. 110, a. 2, ad 2.

67. F. Suárez, *De gratia*, 8, 3:13.   68. See Aquinas, *S.Th.* I-II, q. 110, a. 2.

69. "Sicut igitur lumen naturale rationis est aliquid praeter virtutes acquisitas, quae dicuntur in ordine ad ipsum lumen naturale; ita etiam ipsum lumen gratiae, quod est participatio divinae naturae, est aliquid praeter virtutes infusas, quae a lumine illo derivantur, et ad illud lumen ordinantur." *S.Th.* I-II, q. 110, a. 2, co.

70. *S.Th.* I-II, q. 110, a. 4, co.

71. *Roman Catechism* II, 2, 50.

72. On this specific topic, see P. O'Callaghan, "L'uomo giustificato, nuova creatura in Cristo: Una riflessione intorno all'attuale dibattito ecumenico," in *Giustificati in Cristo: Elementi per una riflessione ecumenica; Atti del II Simposio Internazionale, Facoltà di Teologia del Pontificio Ateneo della Santa Croce*, edited by J. M. Galván (Vatican City: Vaticana, 1997), 129–64; O'Callaghan, *Fides Christi*, 31–40, 218–28. See chapter 10.

process, because according to Luther, divine justice is "extra nos, pro nobis, in Christo" (outside of us, for us, in Christ).[73] And in classical Lutheranism the idea prevailed that God simply pardons our transgressions by not imputing our sin to us. Catholic doctrine, however, insists on a real coming together of divine pardon and the regenerating infusion of grace. Grace is considered to transform the soul, making it holy, forgiving sin, and setting in motion the process of sanctification. Understood in this way, however, Catholic teaching was often rejected by Protestants because it seemed that the Christian believer, from the moment of being justified, became the "proprietor" of a divine treasure, of a personalized relationship with God, to some degree dependent on one's personal efforts or under one's own dominion. With this new reality, it was suggested, the justified believer would experience no need to perpetually recognize God's gifts, especially those of divine pardon and the personal and direct action of the Spirit of Christ on the soul. The "state of grace" would thus be a kind of human "work" and would give rise to a sense of practical autonomy in the ethical sphere,[74] a motive therefore of pride and misplaced trust in one's own works.[75]

It should be noted that the Protestant reformers by no means neglected the classic teaching on personal sanctification that results from justification, though they were considered distinct from one another. As we saw earlier, this fact is confirmed especially in the firm rejection on the part of Luther of the antinomianism of the *Schwärmer*, his more enthusiastic followers. Besides, it should be kept in mind that the scholastic doctrine of "created grace," which might seem to be problematic for the Protestants, expressed, in continuity with Augustine, a firmly anti-Pelagian position and a decisive assertion of the transcendence and unconditioned character of divine action.[76] In fact, the confusion present in the writings of some Protestant authors between the *favor Dei* and the *favor hominis*, both equally extrinsic, could actually prejudice divine transcendence and promote a Pelagian view of Christian life.[77] In recent times, in fact, several Protestant authors have come to recognize the Biblical notion of the real infusion of God's love as an active gift of the Spirit in the hearts of the faithful (Rom 5:5), a power (*dynamis*),[78] a gift to some extent "adhering" (*adhaerens*) to the human spirit and justifying it.[79]

73. See M. Luther, *Sermo die S. Matthiae*, in *WA* 1:139. See also the ample documentation from the agreement between Lutherans and Catholics undertaken in the United States (1984) in H. G. Anderson, T. A. Murphy, and J. A. Burgess, eds., *Justification by Faith: Lutherans and Catholics in Dialogue*, VII (Minneapolis, Minn.: Augsburg, 1985), esp. nos. 98–101.

74. Melanchthon frequently reprimanded Catholics for this way of understanding. However, his reprimand may well reflect a nominalistic conception of freedom (and grace) as a *positive* "contributor" to salvation. Anderson, Murphy, and Burgess, *Justification by Faith*, no. 10.

75. After pride and excessive self-confidence, according to Luther, follows "a terrorized conscience." On the way Reformed theologians attempted to console the consciences of terrorized Christians in their perception that they were not doing enough to win salvation, see Anderson, Murphy, and Burgess, *Justification by Faith*, nos. 22, 24, 39, 62.

76. On this issue, see C. Morerod, "La philosophie dans le dialogue catholique-luthérien," *Freiburger Zeitschrift für Philosophie und Theologie* 44 (1997): 219–40; Morerod, *Oecuménisme et philosophie: Questions philosophiques pour renouveler le dialogue* (Paris: Parole et silence, 2004); O'Callaghan, *Fides Christi*, 222–26.

77. See J. Calvin, *Institutiones christianae* III, 11, 2.

78. See *NIDNTTE* 1:775–82, s.v. δύναμις. See the study of E. Käsemann in the next note.

79. Modern New Testament exegesis has brought about a significant turnabout in Protestant thought in this area, according to the 1985 document of the workgroup of Evangelical and Catholic theologians, in *Lehrverurteilungen—kirchentrennend? Materialien zu den Lehrverurteilungen und zur Theologie der Rechtferti-*

On the other side, as we saw at the start of chapter 13, recent Catholic theology has developed a renewed awareness of the personal and interpersonal side of grace, fruit of "uncreated grace," which comes from God, who gives his very life to humans. In that way it is possible to avoid a certain tendency to "reify" grace (what Germans call *Verdinglichung*), as if it were to be understood only in terms of created grace.[80]

In any case the 1999 *Lutheran-Catholic Joint Declaration on Justification* had the following to say:

We confess together that God forgives sin by grace and at the same time frees human beings from sin's enslaving power, and imparts the gift of new life in Christ. When persons come by faith to share in Christ, God no longer imputes to them their sin and through the Holy Spirit effects in them an active love. These two aspects of God's gracious action are not to be separated, for persons are by faith united with Christ, who in his person is our righteousness (1 Cor 1:30): both the forgiveness of sin and the saving presence of God himself.[81]

In this text, the "created" aspect of grace—the presence of grace in humans—is expressed in three ways: "God ... imparts the gift of new life in Christ"; "God ... effects in them an active love"; and "persons are by faith united with Christ." There is a question of emphasis here between the Lutheran and Catholic views of grace, but the doctrine is fundamentally the same.

In simplistic terms, Lutheran theology has traditionally held that grace is simply God's direct and personal action on the soul, which forgives sin, "creates" faith, and directly transforms ethical action, in such a way that "good works" are substantially the fruit of grace, that is, divine "works," in those who have been justified. In other words, grace is real in the created realm but is understood in somewhat "actualistic" terms. Alberto Bellini observes:

When the Reformation teaches that sanctification follows on necessarily from justification, it is not speaking of the sanctification of humans in their essence, an ontological sanctification, as Catholic theologians would say, but a moral sanctification.... In fact,

---

gung, edited by K. Lehmann and W. Pannenberg (Freiburg: Herder, 1989), 35–75. "Because the love of God which remains 'outside us' is truly infused into our hearts (Rom 5:5), not being other than the gift of the Holy Spirit ...; as such it unites us with Christ, it fills us with trust and joy, it makes us capable of a new life, a life which we do not owe to ourselves, because it is a question of fraternity with Jesus and the gift of the Spirit" (Rom 5:48). In this development an important role was played by the Lutheran exegete E. Käsemann in "Gottesgerechtigkeit bei Paulus," *Zeitschrift für Theologie und Kirche* 58 (1961): 367–78, translated into English as: "The 'Righteousness of God' in Paul," *New Testament Questions of Today* (Philadelphia: Fortress, 1969), 168–82. More recently, however, the Lutheran theologian E. Jüngel, in *Das Evangelium von der Rechtfertigung des Gottlosen als Zentrum des christlichen Glaubens: Eine theologische Studie in ökumenischer Absicht* (Tubingen: J. C. B. Mohr [Paul Siebeck], 1998), has taken exception to this reading, insisting that an "extrinsic" reading of justification is more faithful to the Lutheran tradition. Jüngel's work has been translated into English as *Justification, the Heart of the Christian Faith: A Theological Study with an Ecumenical Purpose* (London: Bloomsbury, 2014). On this issue, see O'Callaghan, *Fides Christi*, 187–91. More recent opinions are those of D. A. Campbell, *The Deliverance of God: An Apocalyptic Rereading of Justification in Paul* (Grand Rapids, Mich.: W. B. Eerdmans, 2009); J. D. G. Dunn, "Paul and Justification by Faith," in *The Road from Damascus: The Impact of Paul's Conversion on His Life, Thought, and Ministry*, edited by R. N. Longenecker (Grand Rapids, Mich.: W. B. Eerdmans, 2009), 85–101; N. T. Wright, *Justification: God's Plan and Paul's Vision* (Downers Grove, Ill.: InterVarsity Press, 2009); and J. M. G. Barclay, *Paul and the Gift*.

80. On the way "created" or "sanctifying" grace came to be "reified" or depersonalized during the late Middle Ages as a result of an improper understanding of the doctrine of merit and mediation, see C. Möller, "La grâce et la justification," *Lumen Vitae* 19 (1964): 532–44, esp. 539f.

81. *JDJ* 22.

sanctification is a new life, which the Christian, justified in the goodness of the judgment and mercy of God, begins to carry out under the action of the Holy Spirit present in the soul.[82]

This understanding of the life of grace is expressed in Protestant theology in the conviction that any grace experience that humans may have can only be an "experience of the Spirit," in an extrinsic or ambiguous relationship with created reality.

Catholic doctrine, however, insists more on "created," or "sanctifying grace," understood as a stable and transforming reality, interpersonal and relational, placed by the continuous action of God on the human spirit.[83] It draws on a rich and demanding view of the doctrine of creation. This is so because human beings, "made in the image and likeness of God" (Gn 1:26), created therefore "in Christ, through Him and for Him" (Col 1:15-20), are in a position to accept this new reality—a new creation—without bringing about a metamorphosis of their nature and, at the same time, without becoming mere passive spectators in a theater in which God is the only actor. In the Catholic view of things, divine grace, the action of Christ's Spirit, cannot but find in the believer "registers" that are fully human and with which it is possible to establish an ontological and experienced relationship with God that may be less ambiguous and elusive than the one that Lutheran theology proposes. In the coming chapters, on the theological virtues and on the experience and free reception of grace, we shall consider the question of this relationship again.

Different Kinds of Grace

Theologians frequently speak of different aspects or divisions of divine grace in humans. We have already come across different kinds: sanctifying grace, actual grace, habitual grace, and so on. The Calvinist theologian Karl Barth, however, considered this tendency inappropriate because Christ himself is grace, according to Paul, and thus grace is single, simple and unique in the sense that divine action is unique and simple.[84] From the point of view of "uncreated grace," therefore, it makes no sense to speak of different kinds or classifications of grace because all grace comes from the Father, through the Son, in the Holy Spirit, and has as its only scope that of bringing humans to share in the life of the Trinity as children of God. Still, from the point of view of the subject who receives grace, it is inevitable that we end up speaking of different classifications or divisions of grace, for grace is much like a single pure-white light that is refracted into a rainbow of colors by a prism. These divisions cor-

---

82. A. Bellini, "La giustificazione per la sola fede," *Communio* (ed. italiana) 7 (1978): 30–73, 69.

83. On different explanations of grace in the theology of justification, see Möller, "La grâce et la justification."

84. See K. Barth, *Die Kirchliche Dogmatik* IV/1 (Zurich: Zöllikon, 1953), 88–92. Voltaire explains the same idea in his very own way: "Were Paulus Emilius, Scipio, Cato, Cicero, Caesar, Titus, Trajan, and Marcus Aurelius to revisit that Rome which they formerly raised to some consideration, you must own that they would be a little staggered at your determinations concerning grace. What would they say to your debates on St. Thomas's grace of health, on Cajetan's medicinal grace, on external and internal grace, on gratuitous, sanctifying, actual, habitual, co-operating grace, on effectual grace which is sometimes ineffectual, on sufficient grace often insufficient, on versatile and congruous grace, sincerely, would they understand it more than yourselves or I?" Voltaire, "Grace," *The Philosophical Dictionary* (London: Wynn and Scholey, 1802), 181–85, 181f.

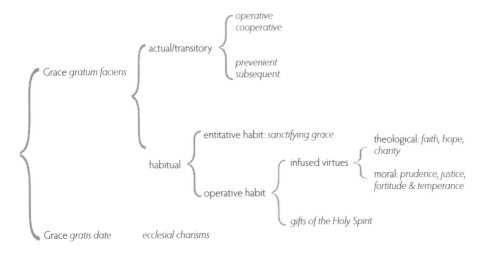

Figure 14-1

respond, in an approximate way, to different aspects of the lives of humans and of their ontological structure, elevated by grace. God, in fact, is simple, but humans are not. Therefore, grace does not melt or "metamorphose" human nature. Humans are individual and social, composed of essence and potencies, free and at the same time determined, temporal yet immortal. Because grace regenerates the entire being of the human person, not only one faculty or part, it must involve the regeneration of all the faculties and facets of human life. The fact of speaking of divisions or classifications of grace is a simple corollary of the classical adage according to which grace does not destroy nature but perfects it.

On the basis of the Pauline texts of 1 Corinthians 12:7–13:13, the *Summa Theologiae* of Thomas Aquinas,[85] and other works,[86] the following six classifications of grace may be made by way of illustration. Church documents have often made use of these terms. Many of these different aspects of the life of grace have been considered in previous chapters, especially the historical ones (chapters 7–11); see figure 14-1.

Grace Gratum Faciens and Gratis Data

This first distinction corresponds to the fact that the justified are at one and same time individuals and members of society and the Church. God first gives to the individual grace that is *gratum faciens*, the grace "per quam ipse homo Deo coniungitur" (by which humans themselves are united with God),[87] grace that makes humans "pleasing to God." The term *gratum faciens* applied to grace was used for the first time by the thirteenth-century theologian Alexander of Hales. It provides the widest de-

---

85. See Aquinas, *S.Th.* I-II, q. 111, aa. 1–5.
86. See Van der Meersch, *Grâce;* Flick and Alszeghy, *Il vangelo della grazia;* Auer, *Das Evangelium der Gnade,* 36–40, 213–15.
87. Aquinas, *S.Th.* I-II, q. 111, a. 1, co.

scription of what divine grace achieves in relation to the individual because it includes many other aspects of supernatural life.

At the same time, the believer can receive from God graces called *gratis data*. The term is derived from the end of the Gospel text of Matthew 10:8, translated in the Vulgate as "gratis accepistis, gratis date" (you received without paying, give without pay). The beginning of this Gospel passage, at the very heart of Matthew's discourse on the mission of the twelve apostles, speaks of the special gifts given by Jesus to his disciples to facilitate their mission ("Heal the sick, raise the dead, cleanse lepers, cast out demons"). They are gifts or special charisms whose purpose is to facilitate the mission of the Church.[88] According to Thomas Aquinas, grace *gratis data* is that grace "per quam unus homo cooperatur alteri ad hoc quod ad Deum reducatur" (by means of which humans bring others closer to God).[89] Such gifts are received by those justified in benefit of others, not of themselves. Hence they are distinguishable from grace that is *gratum faciens*, that sanctifies the individual.[90] At the same time charisms have the same divine source as all other graces and share the same purpose.

In any case, the meaning of this distinction is as follows: the fact that some people in the Church have received certain gifts and special charisms does not make them automatically holier at a personal level than those who have not received them. Rather, these gifts facilitate and even oblige Christians to spread the good news to all humanity, to evangelize. As they carry out their apostolic task, of course, Christian believers may well grow in holiness, but indirectly as it were, because the charismatic gifts they have received are meant not for their personal sanctification but for the Church and the efficacy of her mission. All are called to holiness, but not all are meant to carry out the mission of the Church in the same way. Thus not all have received from God the same charismatic gifts. Paul insinuates this distinction when he insists on the difference between different gifts, especially on the superiority of the gift of charity above all others: tongues, prophecies, healing, and so on (1 Cor 13).

By way of example, the graces received through priestly ordination are destined entirely to the edification of God's faithful and not to the spiritual good of the one being ordained. At the same time, the growth or otherwise in holiness of the priest will depend for the most part on the fidelity and generosity with which he administers these gifts. We shall consider the issue further in chapters 16 and 22.

It is interesting to note that for Aquinas *gratum faciens* grace, which makes humans pleasing to God, should be considered superior to grace *gratis data*, that is, to ecclesial charisms.[91] This is so because, whereas the former orders humans directly to their last end, God, the latter does so only indirectly in that they serve others and help

---

88. See A. George and P. Grelot, "Charisms," in *Dictionary of Biblical Theology*, edited by X. Léon-Dufour, 2nd ed. (London: G. Chapman, 1978), 68–71.

89. Aquinas, *S.Th.* I-II, q. 111, a. 1, co.

90. According to Thomas, in Christ grace *gratum faciens* is not clearly distinguished from grace *gratis data*: "Sicut gratia gratum faciens ordinatur ad actus meritorios tam interiores quam exteriores, ita gratia gratis data ordinatur ad quosdam actus exteriores fidei manifestativos, sicut est operatio miraculorum, et alia huiusmodi. In utraque autem gratia Christus plenitudinem habuit: inquantum enim divinitati unita erat eius anima, plenam perficiendos. Sed alii sancti, qui moventur a Deo sicut instrumenta non unita, sed separata, particulariter efficaciam recipiunt ad hos vel illos actus perficiendos. Et ideo in aliis sanctis huiusmodi gratiae dividuntur: non autem in Christo." *S.Th.* III, q. 7, a. 7, ad 1.

91. Aquinas, *S.Th.* I-II, q. 111, a. 1, ad 3.

to bring them closer to God. In other words, for Thomas the purpose of charismatic gifts in the Church is none other than one of facilitating and promoting personal holiness, union with God.[92] The call to holiness is universal and essential to the divine economy; the different charismatic gifts are always directed to that end.

Actual Grace and Habitual Grace

Within the category of *gratum faciens* grace it is possible to distinguish between a transitory grace, an impulse of grace, usually called "actual grace," and a grace that is present in believers as a stable habit infused by God, called "habitual grace." This division corresponds to the fact that in human beings it is possible to distinguish between concrete, transitory movement of the will and intellect, on the one hand, and their essence, on the other.

Thomas Aquinas does not use the term "actual grace" literally (in fact, the expression belongs to post-Tridentine theology); he speaks rather of the "divinum auxilium quo nos movet ad bene volendum et agendum" (the divine help that moves us to want to do good),[93] or, to use a more compact formula, the "auxilium Dei moventis" (the help of God who moves).[94] When we consider the question of the need for grace in different ambits of human life, we shall consider the question of actual grace again.

"Habitual grace," is described by Thomas as the "habituale donum nobis divinitus inditum" (the habitual gift infused in us by God),[95] that is, the grace received as a stable habit, equivalent to the "state of grace," which may be lost only through grave sin.[96] That this grace is habitual does not mean that it is the product of human effort, of repeated virtuous actions, or that it cannot be lost, but rather that God has infused it stably into the human soul. And, as regards grace, we should remember Thomas's principle already cited: "Ubicumque est aliquis effectus Dei, ibi sit ipse Deus effector" (Wherever there is any divine effect, there God who acts is present).[97] On the basis of "habitual grace" we can speak of the notion of the "state of grace."

Sanctifying Grace, Infused Virtues, and Gifts of the Holy Spirit

Habitual grace may be distinguished, in turn, into an ontological habit called "sanctifying grace" (an expression used for the first time at the Council of Trent)[98] and an operative habit, which consists of the infused virtues and the gifts of the Holy Spirit. Sanctifying grace is an ontological habit with which God justifies and sanctifies the soul in its being.[99] With the operative habit of the infused virtues, however, the powers of the soul are elevated. In humans, the distinction between these two aspects of grace corresponds, as is obvious, to the distinction between essence and potencies.

---

92. "Gratia autem gratum faciens ordinat hominem immediate ad coniunctionem ultimi finis; gratiae autem gratis datae ordinant hominem ad quaedam praeparatoria finis ultimi." Ibid., a. 5, co.

93. Aquinas, *S.Th.* I-II, q. 111, a. 2, co.

94. Or rather "auxilium Dei moventis animam ad bonum." Ibid., q. 112, a. 2, co.

95. Ibid., q. 111, a. 2, co.

96. See Garrigues, "La doctrine de la grâce habituelle"; G. Del Pozo Abejón, "Renovar la tradición de la gracia habitual," *Revista Española de Teología* 69 (2009): 151–203.

97. Aquinas, *SCG* IV, 21, 2.

98. See Trent's decree on justification (*DH* 1528), also in the encyclical of Pius XI, *Casti Connubii* (1930), in *DH* 3714.

99. See Aquinas, *S.Th.* I-II, q. 110, a. 2, co.: "aliquod habituale donum a Deo animae infunditur."

In the proper sense of the word, "grace" is sanctifying grace: it is a quality present in humans—not a transitory gift—that divinizes them, makes them holy, children of God; it is the stable principle of supernatural life, the habit that derives from divine action, which becomes rooted in the essence of the soul and allows the one who receives it to become a child of God, that is, to exercise Christian virtues and fulfill the commandments of God's law. In that sense, the Christian is not just "called" a child of God but is so really (1 Jn 3:1). This does not mean, of course, that humans are confirmed in grace in this life; as Thomas says: "Homo non habet cor suum firmatum in Deo" (The heart of man is not fixed on God forever).[100] Only in heaven, when humans see God face to face, will they be able to love him forever, without being ever able to sin. Sanctifying grace, in fact, can only be lost through grave sin, although it can be obtained again through the contrition of the sinner and divine pardon, in virtue of the infinite merits of Christ.

The infused virtues are good operative habits introduced by God into the soul along with sanctifying grace; they are frequently distinguished as theological (faith, hope, and charity) or moral (especially the cardinal virtues of prudence, justice, fortitude, and temperance; Wis 8:7). The infused virtues are distinguished from the acquired or human virtues because, whereas the latter are consolidated through effort and repetition, in the former "Deus in nobis sine nobis operatur" (God acts in us, but without us).[101] Finally, we can speak of the gifts of the Holy Spirit, which are "quidam habitus perficientes hominem ad hoc quod prompte sequatur instinctum Spiritus Sancti" (certain habits that perfect humans in such a way that they can promptly follow the inspiration of the Holy Spirit).[102] These gifts are traditionally considered to be seven in number. We shall consider the infused theological virtues and the gifts of the Holy Spirit in the coming chapter.

Operative and Cooperative Grace

With respect to the free action of humans before God's offer of grace, we can distinguish between "operative grace" and "cooperative grace."[103] Augustine was the first to introduce this idea.[104] Aquinas has it that habitual and actual grace, "insofar as they heal and justify the soul, or make it pleasing to God, are called 'operative grace'; insofar as they act as a principle of meritorious action that proceeds also from human free will, they are called 'cooperative.'"[105] From the point of view of God, who gives grace, operative and cooperative grace are one and the same thing. They are distinguished only on the basis of the different effects they have on the lives of those justified.[106]

---

100. Aquinas, *S.Th.* I-II, q. 109, a. 8, co.

101. Ibid., q. 55, a. 4.

102. See ibid., q. 68, a. 4, co.

103. See F. Zigon, "Gratia operans et gratia cooperans juxta S. Thomam," *Ephemerides theologicae lovanienses* 5 (1928): 614–29; Lonergan, *Grace and Freedom.*

104. See Augustine, *De gratia et lib. arb.* I, 17, 33.

105. "Inquantum animam sanat vel iustificat, sive gratam Deo facit, dicitur *gratia operans,* e inquantum vero est principium operis meritorii, quod etiam ex libero arbitrio procedit, dicitur *cooperans.*" *S.Th.* I-II, q. 111, a. 2, co. The same doctrine is to be found in Trent: *DH* 1548–50.

106. "Gratia operans et cooperans est eadem gratia, sed distinguitur secundum diversos effectus." *S.Th.* I-II, q. 111, a. 2, co., ad 4.

Efficacious and Sufficient Grace

During the post-Tridentine controversies on grace it became common to distinguish between an "efficacious grace" (the effect of which does not depend on human consent) and a "sufficient grace" (which may be rendered inefficacious on account of free human resistance), instead of "operative" and "cooperative" grace.[107] Thomas Aquinas, without openly espousing the notion of "efficacious" grace, does mention a grace that infallibly obtains its effect.[108] On the one hand, the fact that the Church opposed semi-Pelagianism was evidence that there was such a thing as "efficacious grace." The condemnation of Jansenism, on the other hand, was an indication that we could also speak of a "sufficient grace" that could be resisted. This is clearly a delicate and mysterious issue because it attempts to explain at once the primacy of God in the order of salvation as well as human responsibility with respect to one's eternal destiny. It may be said that whereas impenitence, that is, persevering in resistance to grace, depends exclusively on humans, conversion proceeds from God not only with respect to the grace offered but also in the sense that consent itself is the fruit of grace. According to the principle we have already seen—that distinctions in the ambit of grace are determined by the different effects it has on the creature, not on the part of God, who is the origin of all grace—it is likely that Aquinas would not agree with the followers of Báñez, who claimed that grace is given by God already efficacious or sufficient.

Prevenient and Subsequent Grace

According to the times of grace in humans (that is, taking into account the fundamental fact that grace is made present temporally and historically during the lives and narratives of humans), we may distinguish, within the category of actual grace, between "prevenient" and "subsequent" grace.[109] We have already considered the notion of predestination, which is essential to the theology of grace. The notion of God's prevenient action is clearly present in scripture: "My God goes before me with his love" (Ps 59:11). In describing God's gift of grace, Augustine lists four stages: "Ut esses, ut sentires, ut audires, ut consentires, prevenit te misericordia eius" (The mercy of God precedes you so that you can be, feel, hear, and consent).[110] And Thomas mentions five effects of grace that follow on chronologically from one another: "sanatio animae, bonum velle, bonum efficaciter operare, in bono perseverare, ad gloriam pervenire" (healing the soul, wishing the good, doing the good efficaciously, persever-

---

107. See Hidalgo, *Doctrina alfonsiana acerca de la acción de la gracia*; Flick and Alszeghy, *Il vangelo della grazia*, §§ 54–58; Auer, *Das Evangelium der Gnade*, 39f., 240–49.

108. See Aquinas, *S.Th.* I-II, q. 112, a. 3: "Donum gratiae excedit omnem praeparationem virtutis humanae." As regards God, who acts, grace is efficacious "ad id ad quod ordinatur a Deo, non quidem coactionis, sed infallibilitatis, quia intentio Dei deficere non potest (Augustine, *De praedest. Sanct.*) quod per beneficia Dei certissime liberantur quicumque liberantur. Unde si ex intentione Dei moventis est quod homo cuius cor movet, gratiam consequatur, infallibiliter ipsam consequitur" (*S.Th.* I-II, q. 112, a. 3). Aquinas reminds us that "defectus gratiae prima causa est ex nobis, sed collationis gratiae prima causa est a Deo" (*S.Th.* I-II, q. 112, a. 3, ad 2).

109. On the question of grace and time, see M. Flick, *L'attimo della giustificazione secondo S. Tommaso* (Rome: Università Gregoriana, 1947).

110. Augustine, *Sermo* 176, 5. See also *Contra Julianum op. imperf.* I, 95 and 131.

ing in the good, obtaining glory).[111] Of the five elements of the human narrative of grace, we can say that the first is "prevenient" with respect to the second, the second with respect to the third. Or we can say that the second is "subsequent" with respect to the first, the third with respect to the second, and so on. Again, as we saw earlier, grace is still one and simple insofar as it derives from God; the time distinction is due to the fact that grace assumes the temporal cadence of human life; it does not destroy nature, but perfects it.[112]

Other Terminological Issues Related to Grace

Another four distinctions may be mentioned, several of which have already appeared. First, we may speak of the distinction between "uncreated grace" and "created grace." The former corresponds to God's own action insofar as he gives himself benevolently to humans; the latter refers to the transformative effect on the creature who receives grace. Second, we have distinguished between "healing grace" (*gratia sanans*, an Augustinian expression) and "elevating grace" (*gratia elevans*, first used by the thirteenth-century theologian Philip the Chancellor). Both of them may be considered inseparable effects of grace *gratum faciens*. "Healing grace" cures the mortal wounds produced by original and personal sins; "elevating grace" refers to the lifting up of human nature in order to be able to live a life in intimate communion with God. Third, it is possible to distinguish between an "internal grace" and an "external grace." Rooted in the spirituality of the Old Testament, the distinction reflects the fact that God gives his grace to the very heart of the human person (thus grace is "internal") but does so also through created mediations such as the prophets, the Church, the sacraments, preaching of the word, and Christian apostolate (the same grace is also called "external"). Finally, we can distinguish between *gratia Dei* and *gratia Christi*. All grace conceded to humans after the Fall is called *gratia Christi*, "the grace of Christ," and not only *gratia Dei*, because it is offered to humans in virtue of the merits of Christ. Still, according to Thomas and most Christian authors, grace before the Fall should also be designated as *gratia Christi*.[113]

---

111. Aquinas, *S.Th.* I-II, q. 111, a. 3, co. The doctrine is present in Augustine, *De natura et gratia*, 31.

112. "Gratia non diversificatur per hoc quod est praeveniens et subsequens, secundum essentiam, sed solum secundum effectum." *S.Th.* I-II, q. 111, a. 3, ad 2.

113. See Aquinas, *S.Th.* I-II, q. 2, a. 7, co.

15 GRACE AND CHRISTIAN LIFE

The Infused Virtues and Gifts of the Holy Spirit

Christus est vita nostra, quoniam totum principium vitae nostrae et operationis est Christus.
THOMAS AQUINAS[1]

Faith in the intelligence, hope in the memory, charity in the will.   JOHN OF THE CROSS[2]

Speramus Deum nobis, non vero propter nos.   THOMAS DE VIO CAJETAN[3]

Hope does not disappoint us, because God's love has been poured into our hearts through the Holy Spirit which has been given to us.   ROMANS 5:5

We have just considered what might be called the "objective-metaphysical" side of grace: humans, through the gift of God, are transformed, ontologically elevated, renewed to the depths of their being and faculties by divine grace. On the basis of this elevation we shall now consider the "psychological-moral" side of the life of grace, that is, the renewal that God brings about within the faculties and actions of the human person. In effect, with grace God infuses truly divine powers into the soul, usually called "infused virtues," powers with which Christians act as God's children in a truly Christ-like and pneumatological way. These virtues may be theological and moral (principally faith, hope, and charity) and are integrated with the gifts of the Holy Spirit, which may be understood as a kind of prolongation of the infused virtues. Because the content proper to each of these virtues is studied in fundamental, moral, and spiritual theology, we shall consider them in this chapter in a limited perspective as elements proper to the life of grace.[4] Classic theology speaks of them as

1. Aquinas, *In Ep. ad Philipp.*, I, l. 3: "Christ is our life, because the only source of our life and action is Christ."
2. John of the Cross, *The Ascent of Mount Carmel* II, 6, 1.
3. Cajetan, *In II-II S.Th.*, q. 17, a. 5, n. 8: "We believe in God for our own benefit, but not on the basis of what we can achieve."
4. Among the moral theology textbooks that give particular importance to the infused virtues, see L.

"operative habits," calling them supernatural virtues and gifts, or what we might call the supernatural organism.

As we saw earlier, the divine project of making us children of God in Christ through the Holy Spirit reaches the essence—the inner being—of the spiritual creature, before reaching its potencies and faculties. The human being is divinized, elevated, and transformed in its nature: this is why we speak of "created grace." According to Aquinas, sanctifying grace is an infused habit that perfects human nature prior to perfecting its faculties, because "grace in itself is in the essence of the soul before being in its potencies."[5] At the same time, our sharing in divine nature involves not just an empowering of our human faculties but also a true transformation of the human being. Humans' own acts in grace reach God directly, as it were:[6] they are therefore truly the fruits of grace, gifts that are not due to human nature, and therefore accidental. "Accidental," of course, is understood in the technical sense of the word in that these gifts do not derive from the natural, created condition of humans. In other words, the elevation to the life of children of God brings with it a kind of sharing in God's own life by means of a form that is accidental in the creature.

The presence of infused virtues is the result of divine indwelling. According to Aquinas, "It is said that God dwells in the saints spiritually as in a family home, in that their minds are made capable of God through knowledge and love. And also if they do not know and love in act [in actu], by grace they have the habit of faith and charity."[7]

The Theological and Acquired Virtues

On the basis of many scriptural texts, the Church speaks of the theological virtues and their relationship with acquired (or human) virtues.

The Church's Teaching on the Theological Virtues

The Council of Trent teaches that "humans through Jesus Christ ... receive in justification, together with the remission of sin, all these gifts infused at the same time: faith, hope and charity."[8] All three are present also in the baptized infant even before

---

Melina, J. J. Pérez-Soba Díez del Corral, and J. Noriega Bastos, *Camminare nella luce dell'amore: I fondamenti della morale cristiana* (Siena: Cantagalli, 2008); E. Colom and A. Rodríguez Luño, *Scelti in Cristo per essere santi*, (Rome: Edusc, 2003–14). See particularly J. Noriega Bastos, "Il dinamismo teologico dell'agire umano nel rinnovamento della teologia morale," *Annales Theologici* 24 (2010): 425–36.

5. See Aquinas, *S.Th.* I-II, q. 110, a. 4. "Gratia, secundum se considerata, perficit essentiam animae, inquantum participat quandam similitudinem divini esse. Et sicut ab essentia animae fluunt eius potentiae, ita a gratia fluunt quaedam perfectiones ad potentias animae, quae dicuntur virtutes et dona, quibus potentiae perficiuntur in ordine ad suos actos." *S.Th.* III, q. 62, a. 2, co. "Gratia est prima specie qualitatis, quamvis non proprie possit dici habitus, quia non immediate ordinatur ad actum, sed ad quoddam esse spirituale quod in anima facit." *De Veritate*, q. 27, a. 2, ad 7.

6. "Cognoscendo et amando, creatura rationalis sua operatione attingit ad ipsum Deum." Aquinas, *S.Th.* I, q. 43, a. 3, co.

7. "Sed spiritualiter dicitur Deus inhabitare tamquam in familiari domo in sanctis, quorum mens capax est Dei per cognitionem et amorem, etiam si ipsi in actu non cognoscant et diligant, dummodo habeant per gratiam habitum fidei et charitatis." Aquinas, *In I Cor. 3*, l. 3 (on 1 Cor 3:17: "If anyone destroys God's temple, God will destroy him. For God's temple is holy, and that temple you are").

8. Council of Trent, *Sess. VI de iustificatione*, cap. 7, *DH* 1530.

he enjoys the use of reason.[9] Scripture speaks openly of them in three important texts of Paul (1 Thes 1:2–3; Rom 5:1–5; 1 Cor 13:8–13; see also 1 Thes 5:8; Gal 5:5f.; Col 1:4f.; Heb 10:22–24; 1 Pt 1:21f.):

We give thanks to God always for you all, constantly mentioning you in our prayers, remembering before our God and Father your work of faith, and labor of love, and steadfastness of hope in our Lord Jesus Christ [1 Thes 1:2–3].

Therefore, since we are justified by faith, we have peace with God through our Lord Jesus Christ. Through him we have obtained access to this grace in which we stand, and we rejoice in our hope of sharing the glory of God. More than that, we rejoice in our sufferings, knowing that suffering produces endurance, and endurance produces character, and character produces hope, and hope does not disappoint us, because God's love has been poured into our hearts through the Holy Spirit which has been given to us (Rom 5:1–5).

Love never ends; as for prophecies, they will pass away; as for tongues, they will cease; as for knowledge, it will pass away. For our knowledge is imperfect and our prophecy is imperfect; but when the perfect comes, the imperfect will pass away.... For now we see in a mirror dimly, but then face to face. Now I know in part; then I shall understand fully, even as I have been fully understood. So *faith, hope, love abide, these three; but the greatest of these is love* (2 Cor 13:8–13).

These three theological virtues bring the divinized creature to believe and to hope in God one and three, and to love him in a way that goes beyond natural human capacities, as a true sharing of divine life. Thanks to the theological virtues, believers can know what only God knows, what goes beyond the powers of human reason; they can hope for what derives from divine benevolence alone, and what humans do not dare to request or aspire to; they can love what God loves and as God loves, in a disinterested way, loving in him and through him all created things. As virtues they contain a true life and dynamism of their own, an exercise of divine knowledge, desire, and will that is directed by God's own power toward God and the things of God.

The theological virtues relate to one another, and in real terms their proper acts cannot be exercised in a neatly independent way.[10] In scripture they appear in all their harmonic relationships: faith produces hope and moves us to charity; hope, based on faith, increases charity, and in turn it is reinforced by charity in desiring a union that is not yet realized; faith, in order to be true, must find confirmation in God's self-giving love and expression in works of charity. "Thus wonderfully interwoven," we read in *Lumen Fidei*, "faith, hope and charity are the driving force of the Christian life as it advances towards full communion with God."[11] In the words of the exegete Bornkamm, "The triad of faith, hope and love is the quintessence of the God-given life in Christ."[12]

The object of the theological virtues is always God, who is infinite and eternal. Hence it is not possible to believe, to hope, or to love too much, simply because faith, hope, and love are directed toward an infinite divinity. We can always believe more, with more trust, abandon, and depth, because the mystery of God is ineffable and infinitely rich in its intelligibility; besides, God is completely worthy of trust because

9. See Council of Vienne, *DH* 904.

10. See especially H. U. von Balthasar, "Die Einheit der theologischen Tugenden," *Communio* (Deutsche Ausg.) 13 (1984): 306–14.

11. Francis and Benedict XVI, *Lumen Fidei*, par. 7.

12. G. Bornkamm, *Paul* (New York: Harper and Row, 1971), 219.

he is truth itself. One can always hope more because the one who has wished to share his life with humans forever is an infinitely desirable God, capable of satiating all the longings of the human heart. And it is always possible to love God more, because God is infinitely lovable, being love itself. But the fact that humans can believe in God, hope in him, and love him requires the presence of grace. The power at the root of these virtues is God in person, and humans share in the divine life as they receive them and live according to them, steeped in adoration and praise.

The Relationship between the Theological Virtues and Classic Virtue Ethics

It is interesting to note that in classic reflection on the ethical life, that of the Stoics, for example, the exercise of faith, hope, and charity was not included, on the whole, within the ambit of virtuous action.[13] In effect, the Stoic attempts to live freely, adapting himself to the rules and dictates of nature.[14] Humans certainly tend to believe, to hope, and to love, and this is not indifferent for everyday social life, for proper ethical behavior. But in classic "virtue ethics," faith, hope, and charity are not virtues in the strict sense of the word because their exercise does not necessarily bring humans to their ultimate end of personal realization. Other human virtues are more highly considered by the Stoics, the "cardinal" virtues, especially fortitude, justice, courage, wisdom, temperance, prudence, and the like. It is interesting to note that the latter virtues promote a virtuous life, the ethical perfection of the individual, what nowadays we would call his autonomy. Faith, hope, and charity, however, always involve other persons and refer necessarily to dependency and solidarity, to the lack of autonomy.[15] Whereas the strength of the Stoic philosopher (note that the word "virtue" comes from the Latin *vis*, "strength") belongs to himself and finds expression in a well-defined individuality,[16] the strength of Christians has as its source the Spirit of Christ, who dwells in them (Gal 2:20; Phil 1:21). In fact, the strength of the Christian is to be found paradoxically alongside his weakness and, as a result, in the fact that one belongs (and must belong) to a community (whether civil or ecclesiastical). "For the sake of Christ, then, I am content with weaknesses, insults, hardships, persecutions, and calamities; for when I am weak, then I am strong" (2 Cor 12:10).[17] Strong,

13. On classical ethics, especially those of the Stoics, and on the transition between the latter and Christian ethics, see M. Spanneut, *Le stoïcisme des Pères de l'Église: De Clément de Rome à Clément d'Alexandrie* (Paris: Seuil, 1957); M. Forschner, *Die stoische Ethik: Über den Zusammenhang von Natur-, Sprach- und Moralphilosophie im altstoischen System* (Stuttgart: Klett-Cotta, 1981).

14. This is what the Stoics called l'*oikeiosis*. On the topic among the early Stoics, see T. Engberg-Pedersen, *The Stoic Theory of Oikeiosis: Moral Development and Social Interaction in Early Stoic Philosophy* (Aarhus: Aarhus University Press, 1990).

15. Professor A. Malo made this observation.

16. "What saves us?," Epictetus asked. "What do we need in order to be freed from the chains, from the abyss?" And he responds: "We need the will. There is nothing stronger in man." *Diss.* II, 17. And Marcus Aurelius said: "The wise man never pulls back after having made up his mind." *De benef.* IV, 34. And elsewhere: "He must be like a rock against which all the waves crash" (49).

17. On the Pauline notion of "weakness," see Rom 5:6, 7:5, 8:26; 1 Cor 1:25, 4:10; 2 Cor 10:1. For example, 1 Cor 1:27f.: "God chose what is foolish in the world to shame the wise, God chose what is weak in the world to shame the strong, God chose what is low and despised in the world, even things that are not, to bring to nothing things that are." Also 2 Cor 11:30: "If I must boast, I will boast of the things that show my weakness." Then Paul writes that God said to him: "'My grace is sufficient for you, for my power is made perfect in weak-

that is, with the power that comes from God. Stoic virtues are essentially individual, but Christian virtues are always social, rooted in charity.

It is also true that Christian theology has made its own the classic teaching on individual virtues found in Aristotle and the Stoics.[18] But it has opened them, one by one, to the light of charity and of its intrinsic complement, humility. Charity has become for Christian ethics the "forma virtutum" (the form of all virtues).[19] Before God and neighbor the infused virtue of charity molds and configures all the other virtues from within and places them in a close relationship with one another. For the same reason, the virtue of humility becomes central for the ethical and spiritual life of Christians, because all human energies, whether of grace or of nature, derive from God, who should be revered, adored, and obeyed. In that sense, Christian humility is not the same thing as the simple modesty the Stoics spoke of. Rather, as Aquinas says, "Principium et radix humilitatis est reverentia quam quis habet ad Deum" (The principle and root of humility is reverence towards God).[20] In antiquity, on the contrary, humility was considered by many as a simple sign of weakness, of a lack of strength or *vis*, that is, of virtue.[21] Nietzsche sees it simply as a strategy the weak employ in order not to be crushed by the strong.[22]

Infused and Acquired Virtues

Acquired virtues, commonly called human virtues, differ from infused virtues that derive from sanctifying grace in three ways.[23] First, they are different in terms of the way the person comes to acquire them: from God directly in the case of the infused virtues, or from free, conscious, upright, deliberate, and repeated actions with respect to the acquired virtues.[24] Second, human and infused virtues usually have different objects: the human virtues, in fact, direct the free will toward goods that are

---

ness.' I will all the more gladly boast of my weaknesses, that the power of Christ may rest upon me. For the sake of Christ, then, I am content with weaknesses, insults, hardships, persecutions, and calamities; for when I am weak, then I am strong" (2 Cor 12:9f.). Later he writes: "For he [Christ] was crucified in weakness, but lives by the power of God. For we are weak in him, but in dealing with you we shall live with him by the power of God" (2 Cor 13:4). See BDAG 142, s.v. ἀσθένεια, 2a; NIDNTTE 1:420–24, s.v. ἀσθένεια, NT 3; A. D. Black, *Paul, Apostle of Weakness*, 2nd ed. (New York: Peter Lang, 2012).

18. That Stoicism all but disappeared as a predominant philosophy some few centuries after the appearance of Christianity is probably due to the fact that the latter assumed and improved upon its best features: see E. Elorduy, "Misión de la Estoa en la filosofía perenne," *Revista de filosofía* 6 (1947): 5–55. On the presence of Stoicism in the writings of Paul, see T. Engberg-Pedersen, *Paul and the Stoics* (Edinburgh: T. and T. Clark, 2000).

19. See Aquinas, *S.Th.* II-II, q. 62, a. 4; q. 23, a. 8. The expression originally comes from Peter Lombard, *Glossa maior*.

20. Aquinas, *S.Th.* II-II, q. 161, a. 6, co.

21. "I am not convinced either when I hear people making a great distinction between personal and social virtues. No virtue worthy of its name can foster selfishness. Every virtue necessarily works to the good both of our own soul and to the good of those around us. We are all of us men and all likewise children of God, and we cannot think that life consists in building up a brilliant curriculum vitae or an outstanding career. Ties of solidarity should bind us all and, besides, in the order of grace we are united by the supernatural bond of the Communion of Saints." Escrivá, *Friends of God*, no. 76.

22. F. W. Nietzsche, "Maxims and Arrows," in Nietzsche, *Twilight of the Idols* (Oxford: Oxford University Press, 1998), no. 31.

23. On this question, see E. Colom and A. Rodríguez Luño, *Scelti in Cristo per essere santi*, 1:13–18.

24. See Aquinas, *S.Th.* II-II, q. 45, a. 2.

not simply the knowledge and love of God, whereas the infused virtues, at least the theological ones, are directed in the first place toward God.

Third, the acquired and infused virtues differ principally in that, although the former provide a certain acquired facility to carry out a given action, the latter confer on the subject the capacity to carry out actions in a way that is pleasing to God and reaches God, as supernatural acts. In effect, acquired virtues consolidate with time by means of a willing and repeated reinforcement of natural inclinations toward a present good. Classic ethics, whether Platonic, Aristotelian, or Stoic, has given pride of place to this kind of action. But only with the infused virtues can humans direct their lives fully toward God as the true ultimate end, and merit, with God's grace, the response of his love. The infused virtues do not necessarily make it easier to fulfill the corresponding actions. Rather they ensure that these actions, whether easy or difficult, become fully and personally pleasing to God. Still, it is also true that, beyond the capacity to carry out actions that are supernaturally pleasing to God, the infused virtues (1) communicate to humans a kind of inclination toward the actions in question; (2) confer on them an unforeseeable capacity to carry out good actions, even to the point of heroism and martyrdom, which in real terms are the fruits of faith, hope, and charity (this may occur in people without exceptional natural gifts); and (3) make the ultimate end alive and present in the minds and hearts of humans.

Still, the human or acquired virtues are very important in living an upright Christian life led by the infused virtues. The acquired virtues should be fully integrated into the infused. For example, fortitude without charity could conceivably become violent, disrespectful of other people. And charity without fortitude might easily fall into sentimentalism, the tomb of true love. The following example may be useful in understanding the complementarity between infused and acquired virtues: in order to exercise the profession of a judge, the person in question needs not only technical and experiential knowledge to be able to deliberate correctly, but also the title of judge for a particular circumscription, with a competence established by the public authority. Without the former, deliberations made may well be unjust or mistaken; without the latter, they will be null in any case. In a similar way, in the absence of acquired virtues we can carry out virtuous acts only with difficulty and the supernatural organism infused by God may well remain stagnant, atrophic. Yet without infused virtues our actions will not be fully pleasing to God in that they will not obtain their ultimate end to the full: they will be sterile, like the action of a needle without thread.[25] "Apart from me you can do nothing," Jesus said (Jn 15:5). "Sine tuo numine, nihil est in homine, nihil est innoxium," we read in the hymn *Veni Sancte Spiritus*: "Without your strength, Lord, there is just nothing in humans; there is nothing that is not harmful."

In effect, human virtues, once they have been informed from within by a supernatural end, find their ultimate meaning and most sublime motive, and, though fully human, they become truly Christian. And these virtues, being divinized in the Christian, show up the ultimate significance of human action and become truly, authentically human. On the contrary, the life of grace and the presence of the infused virtues

---

25. This image is drawn from the writings of Josemaría Escrivá, *The Way*, no. 967.

becomes precarious and easily open to hypocrisy and infidelity if the firm basis of consolidated human virtue is missing. But the human virtues, if they are not elevated by divine grace, may contribute to the improvement of the human person, they do not bring that person personally close to God. Josemaría Escrivá explains it in these terms:

In this world of ours there are many people who neglect God. It may be that they have not had an opportunity to listen to his words, or that they have forgotten them. Yet their human dispositions are honest, loyal, compassionate, and sincere. I would go so far as to say that anyone possessing such qualities is ready to be generous with God, because human virtues constitute the foundation for the supernatural virtues.... It is true that in themselves such personal qualities are not enough, for no one is saved without the grace of Christ. But if a man fosters and cultivates the seeds of virtue within him, God will smooth out his path, and such a person will be able to become holy because he has known how to live as a man of good will.... You may perhaps have noticed other cases which are in a certain sense just the opposite; so many people who call themselves Christians because they have been baptized and have received other sacraments, but then prove to be disloyal and deceitful, insincere and proud, and ... they fail to achieve anything. They are like shooting stars, lighting up the sky for an instant and then falling away to nothing.[26]

We shall now consider the theological virtues, one by one. They constitute the warp and woof of Christian life and are key elements of Christian apostolate. First of all we consider faith, the foundation of Christian life.

The Infused Virtue of Christian Faith

Situating Christian Faith between
Religion and Philosophy

According to scripture, both Old and New Testament, what best describes the essence of the relationship between God and humans is faith (in Greek, *pistis*).[27] It expresses at once both the sovereignty of God and the dependence of the creature. In order to situate faith properly in the widest religious, philosophical, and anthropological context possible, the following four preliminary observations may be made.

First, though Christian faith connects spontaneously with human trust, it is not identified with it; it is not a simple natural blossoming of confidence between people.[28] Whereas trust is present in the healthy human subject (humans naturally tend

26. Escrivá, *Friends of God*, nos. 74f. Elsewhere he writes: "But along with these timid and frivolous types, we also find here on earth many upright individuals pursuing noble ideals, even though their motives are often not supernatural, but merely philanthropic. These people face up to all kinds of hardship. They generously spend themselves serving others, helping them overcome suffering and difficulties. I am always moved to respect and even to admiration by the tenacity of those who work wholeheartedly for noble ideals. Nevertheless, I consider I have a duty to remind you that everything we undertake in this life, if we see it exclusively as our own work, bears from the outset the stamp of perishability" (no. 208).

27. See R. Bultmann, in *TDNT* 6:176–82, s.v. πίστις; *BDAG* 818–20, s.v. πίστις; *NIDNTTE* 3:759–72, s.v. πιστεύω.

28. On the relationship between faith and human trust, see G. Lingua, "Le forme dell'affidarsi," in *La fede: Evento e promessa*, edited by P. Coda and C. Hennecke (Rome: Città Nuova, 2000), 73–86. Some theologians have attempted to reformulate the theology of the act of faith on the basis of an attitude of "original trust," a theme that has been developed by psychologists, for example, O. F. Bollnow, in *Wesen und Wandel*

to trust, to confide), faith is brought about and determined by its proper object, that is, by God, who reveals. In fact, simple human trust needs to be formed and disciplined because it can be twisted by duplicity and deception. That is, trust does not create its object but rather presupposes it and is supported by it. In other words, from the fact that humans are structured as trusting beings[29] we can deduce neither the exact profile of the divinity in which they believe nor the dynamics of faith, which does not find in the human being its proper origin.[30] The life of faith is a very human reality, doubtless, but faith is a central aspect of the *life of God* in humans. Yet it is clear that the human register with which revelation and faith best "dialogue" is trust, that tendency, written deeply into the human subject, to confide in, to accept the word of another person.

Second, on the margin of a Judeo-Christian context, what distinguishes religious life, in a general sense, is that truth is understood as something that already exists, whole and complete, in such a way that there is no such thing as a "new revelation."[31] In effect, classic thought focuses the actuation of a truth that is already existent and potentially known, to be discovered gradually and more perfectly with the passage of time. This idea is to be found in the "non-Biblical" expression present in the book of Qoelet, "Nihil novum sub sole" (There is nothing new under the sun) (Qo 1:9).[32] In this context, "faith," as a way to know truth by trusting other persons, would be a simple correlate of the obscurity of the known truth, a sign of the mental limitations of humans and of their dependence on others. It is the conception of faith typical of Gnostic thought, which opposes *gnosis* and *pistis*, knowledge and faith:[33] the first is the mark of spiritual persons, the second of the rest of humanity. Among the Stoics, the term "faith" (*pistis*) has human value but no particular religious value.[34] On the contrary, Christian faith is marked specifically by the novelty of the word of God pronounced within human history and directed to particular persons: the Gospel.[35] Gospel novelty does not contradict what already exists and is known to us by reason or knowledge; still, by faith reality is elevated and enriched with novelties that human reason cannot reach on its own, while it establishes a personal—or, better, an

---

der Tugenden (Frankfurt am M.: Ullstein, 1960). Among them, see B. Welte, *Was ist Glauben? Gedanken zur Religionsphilosophie* (Freiburg: Herder, 1982); H. Küng, *Does God Exist? An Answer for Today* (London: Collins, 1980); Pannenberg, *Anthropology in a Theological Perspective*; P. A. Sequeri, *Il Dio affidabile* (Brescia: Queriniana, 1996). Küng's attempt to deduce faith from trust was criticized by Pannenberg.

29. See A. Peyrefitte, *La société de confiance: Essai sur les origines et la nature du développement* (Paris: Odile Jacob, 1995).

30. See Lingua, "Le forme dell'affidarsi," 83.

31. See for example, chapter 2, notes 25ff., and chapter 3, notes 39ff. on Pannenberg.

32. See R. E. Murphy, *Ecclesiastes*, in *WBC* 23A:8.

33. See Cornélis and Léonard, *La Gnose éternel.*

34. According to R. Bultmann, in *TDNT* 6:182: "Primarily, then, πίστις is an attitude of man to himself, not to others." "Man is born for fidelity [πρὸς πίστιν γέγονεν], and the one who overthrows it overthrows the human distinctiveness." Epictetus, *Diss.* 2.4.1. If we abandon fidelity, we destroy friendship and even the State (2.4.2–3). Even the deity is faithful, so if we wish to please the gods we too must be faithful (2.14.12f.). Epictetus quotations found in *NIDNTTE* 3:761.

35. See von Balthasar, *Theo-Drama*, 2:394–416. The same may be said for Judaism and mystery religions. "Along with Judaism and Christianity, the mystery religions stand out in that they expect faith in their divinities and in the revelations and teaching delivered by them (e.g., the cult of Isis and Osiris). In this way salvation (which in the mystery religions was equated with divinization) was promised to the believer." *NIDNTTE* 3:761.

interpersonal—relationship between God and each person. It may be said that if the existence of religious "faith" is seen as a sign of weakness in paganism or Gnosticism, in Christianity it is a source of richness and strength, because it corresponds to the correct relationship between God, who reveals, and humans, who believe.

A third observation is this: in classic antiquity, religious "faith," such as it was, referred to mythical traditions received by humanity. However, as Socrates and Plato showed, these traditions are often in open contrast with the results of philosophical reflection.[36] They are not always trustworthy and need purification and reform. In fact, according to these authors, authentic religious and philosophical life requires reason, intellect, and philosophy, not only myth received by "faith." Pure faith, in this view, would be an expression of an imperfect religion, the religion of one who did not as yet enjoy full knowledge. For the Greeks, "faith," therefore, is clearly surpassed by reason: just as the *logos* took the place of *mythos*, so also reason should ultimately take the place of faith. The relationship between faith and reason in the Christian sense, however, is not conflictive but positive, as we shall see presently.

The fourth observation is that the religious faith that marked antiquity is not in a position to guide humans to their ultimate end because the divinities in whom one might trust are not worthy of unconditioned faith. Thus such faith should not be regarded as a virtue. This may be the case either because the divine is inaccessible (the case of the Platonic Good, or the Unmoved Mover of Aristotle), because it is limited (as with Plato's Demiurge) or perhaps egoistic or envious, or because, simply, it does not exist (the principle of idolatrous religions). In effect, in the classic period the relation between humans and the divine was lived out not so much in the key of faith or trust but rather through mutual collaboration or, at best, through contemplation, in the efforts made by an elite to assimilate divine wisdom. But Christian faith is different from all that insofar as it is determined and profiled by the action of Yahweh throughout history.

The Profile of Christian Faith Is Determined by God, Who Acts and Reveals Himself

In scripture "faith" is what best describes the relationship between God, who acts and reveals himself, on the one hand, and humans, who recognize God's action and accept revelation, on the other.[37] The expression "he'emīn" (to believe) in scripture re-

---

36. See P. O'Callaghan, "Evangelizzazione e luoghi della fede: Una riflessione in base all'enciclica *Fides et ratio*," in *Comunicazione e luoghi della fede*, edited by N. González Gaitano (Vatican City: Vaticana, 2001), 109–46, esp. 123–28.

37. On faith in scripture, see J. Alfaro, "Fides in terminologia biblica," *Gregorianum* 42 (1961): 463–505; E. D. O'Connor, *Faith in the Synoptic Gospels: A Problem in the Correlation of Scripture and Theology* (Notre Dame, Ind.: University of Notre Dame, 1961); P. Benoit, "La théologie des Évangiles synoptiques: La foi," *Exégèse et théologie* (Paris: Cerf, 1961), 143–59, translated into English as *Jesus and the Gospel* (London: Dartman, Longman and Todd, 1974); J. Dupont, "Faith," in *Dictionary of Biblical Theology*, edited by X. Léon-Dufour, 2nd ed. (London: G. Chapman, 1978), 158–63; Trütsch and Pfammatter, *Der Glaube*; H. Wildberger, "'Glauben' im AT," *Zeitschrift für Theologie und Kirche* 65 (1968): 129–50; R. Schnackenburg, "Glauben im Verständnis der Bibel," *Christliche Existenz nach dem Neuen Testament* (Munich: Kösel, 1967), 61–85; F. Sedlmeier, "La fede nel Primo Testamento," in *La fede: Evento e promessa*, edited by P. Coda and C. Hennecke (Rome: Città Nuova, 2000), 129–43; Tanzella-Nitti, *Lezioni di teologia fondamentale*, 121–74. See especially Francis and Benedict XVI, *Lumen Fidei*.

fers almost always to Yahweh and is related to the term "emunah" (fidelity), a term applicable to God as faithful, solid, worthy of trust. Thus "to believe means to abandon oneself trustingly to God who is faithful, to the promises and the Covenant, to find in his faithfulness a sure refuge, to recognize his interventions in history, to listen to and receive his Word as worthy of trust, to practice justice in observing the Law."[38] As Giuseppe Angelini says, "Christian faith is nothing other than the faith necessary in any case for humans to live, but it is the form which such a faith takes on when faced with the historical revelation of God; thus it is a Christological revelation, which fully shows up the truth of the destiny of humans."[39] At the same time, Rossé observes, faith "is not a part of the DNA of humans, it is not written into them as a kind of predisposition or talent which, in certain circumstances, rises up and flourishes.... Humans ... do not carry within themselves, on account of their religious understanding of God, the possibility of putting together cross and God."[40] Thus the God who is revealed "does not correspond to the questions and representations humans have of God."[41] Indeed, the profile and dynamic of faith is defined by the God who is revealed, not by the humans who believe. God does not respond to humans; rather humans are invited to respond to God.[42]

Yet we may ask: what is faith? On the part of humans, it finds expression as abandonment to God, trusting in him, recognizing his presence, listening to his word, practicing justice, and so on. But on God's part, what is faith? What does God actually give? According to the encyclical *Lumen Fidei* of Francis and Benedict, faith is primarily a light that comes from God: "Faith is a light, for once the flame of faith dies out, all other lights begin to dim. The light of faith is unique, since it is capable of illuminating every aspect of human existence.... It is a powerful light which brightens the journey of a successful and fruitful life."[43] Because it comes from God, the encyclical goes on to explain, the light of faith finds expression in two ways: as totality and as truth.

First, because God is the creator of humans and their savior, their only God, faith takes on necessarily a note of totality in their lives: "Faith enriches life in all its dimensions." And later: "For Abraham, faith in God sheds light on the depths of his being, it enables him to acknowledge the wellspring of goodness at the origin of all things and to realize that his life is not the product of nonbeing or chance, but the fruit of a personal call and a personal love." Furthermore, "Faith knows that God has drawn close to us, that Christ has been given to us as a great gift which inwardly transforms us, dwells within us and thus bestows on us the light that illumines the

38. Ardusso, "Fede," 612.

39. G. Angelini, *Teologia morale fondamentale: Tradizione, Scrittura e teoria* (Milan: Glossa, 1999), 590.

40. G. Rossé, "La fede secondo san Paolo," in *La fede: Evento e promessa*, 145–52, 145f.

41. Ardusso, "Fede," 613f.

42. According to Louis Bouyer, who refers to Barth, "The divine Word does not limit itself to respond to the demands that we place before it before listening to it, but it begins by putting them in a very different way, and to put others to which we had not even thought. Not only that: the word of God brings us above all to place our very selves in question, we who pretend to speak of God with a causal knowledge." Bouyer, *Le Père invisible: Approches du mystère de la divinité* (Paris: Cerf, 1976), 316. On this issue, see O'Callaghan, "Il compito della teologia."

43. Francis and Benedict XVI, *Lumen Fidei*, pars. 4, 7.

origin and the end of life."[44] Faith expresses, in the words of Giuseppe Ardusso, "the many different aspects of the 'reaction of humans' before the multifaceted 'action of God.' ... The relationship between humans and God, designated if you wish by the synthetic term 'to believe,' involves humans entirely in their interior life and external behavior, in such a way that the essential sin is one of apostasy, of superstition and idolatry," that is, of not believing, or of believing in a partial way.[45] John confirms that the most fundamental sin is that of incredulity (Jn 3:18).

And second, through Jesus Christ, who definitively reveals the person and plan of the Father, faith reaches its culmination and maximum perfection because it makes the *whole truth* present.[46] Giuseppe Colombo writes as follows: "Christian faith considers it has excellent motives to connect the question of truth with Jesus Christ. It has taken these motives fundamentally from the 'history of Jesus of Nazareth,' transmitted by the first disciples who believed in him.... There is no such thing in fact as Christian faith without the previous historical knowledge of Jesus of Nazareth."[47] The faith of humans in Christ is supreme not only because what he reveals is true but also because in person he is "the truth" (Jn 14:6). And Giovanni Moioli observes:

Faith is a complex attitude of humans who say to Jesus Christ: "You are my truth," that is, "You measure the truth of my way of being human." The truth of humanity, in fact, is to be found not in humans but in the humanity of Jesus Christ.... The grace of the faith operates not only bringing us to accept truth, but, even before truth, bringing us to accept the reference to Jesus Christ. Of that reference the believing subject says: "This reference is my truth, I must assume the form of this truth."[48]

This is what the New Testament calls the "obedience of faith" (Rom 1:5, 16:26; see 2 Cor 10:5f.).[49]

The Narrative of Faith in the Old Testament

Faith belongs not only to the individual who opens his heart to God but to the entire people of God as it lives out its pilgrim journey.[50] Faith is manifested and consolidated, therefore, within history, within the narrative of the pilgrimage of God's people. God revealed himself first to Abraham, often called "our father in the faith" (Gn 12:1–4; Rom 4:12; Gal 3:6f.; Heb 11:8f.), and to the other patriarchs. Then he revealed himself to Moses and accompanied him as he brought Israel out of Egypt into the promised land (Ex 3:1–15). Moses responded to this divine gesture with a faith in which "he endured as seeing him who is invisible" (Heb 11:27). From that time on-

---

44. Ibid., pars. 4, 6, 11, 20.

45. Ardusso, "Fede," 611f.

46. "Today more than ever, we need to be reminded of this bond between faith and truth.... Faith without truth does not save, it does not provide a sure footing. It remains a beautiful story, the projection of our deep yearning for happiness, something capable of satisfying us to the extent that we are willing to deceive ourselves. Either that, or it is reduced to a lofty sentiment which brings consolation and cheer, yet remains prey to the vagaries of our spirit and the changing seasons, incapable of sustaining a steady journey through life." Francis and Benedict XVI, *Lumen Fidei*, pars. 25, 24.

47. G. Colombo, *Professione "teologo"* (Milan: Glossa, 1996), 25–27.

48. G. Moioli and C. Stercal, *L'esperienza spirituale: Lezioni introduttive* (Milan: Glossa, 1992), 20.

49. See *NIDNTTE* 4:549–51, s.v. ὑπακούω, esp. 550. See also D. B. Garlington, *Faith, Obedience, and Perseverance* (Tubingen: J. C. B. Mohr [Paul Siebeck], 1994), 13–31.

50. See Francis and Benedict XVI, *Lumen Fidei*, pars. 8–14.

ward, Israel "believed in the Lord and in Moses his servant" (Ex 14:31). The principal fruit of divine revelation received in faith was the Covenant with Israel, which stays alive in the faith of the people and determines every aspect of the life of the chosen people. Faith may be found in the fidelity of the Jews to the divine precepts and in hearing the word of God (Ex 19:3–9, Dt 9:23). In real terms, the history of the people of God is the history of its faith (Heb 11:30ff.) and, at times, of its lack of faith. In order to keep this faith alive, the Israelites celebrated annually the memory of the great gestures of God in their favor (Ex 12:26, 13:8; Ps 136) as they enjoyed the support and encouragement of the prophets, especially Isaiah, Jeremiah, and Ezekiel. All the prophets promised that one day God would renew and transform the hardened hearts of humans (Is 6:9f., Ezek 36:26), giving them a lasting and definitive faith (Rom 10:9f.). These promises, often repeated, are directed ever more to the messiah who is to come.

Faith in God as a Christologically Qualified Faith

As the letter to the Hebrews says, Jesus is "the pioneer [or author] and perfecter of our faith" (12:2). Christians, who are disciples of the Lord, define themselves as "those who have believed," "those who believe" (Acts 2:44, 1 Thes 1:7), that is, believers. Content-wise their faith is substantially identical to that of the Old Testament, but it is now directed to the word and person of Christ,[51] the Word of God made flesh.[52] To believe in God is equivalent to becoming a disciple of Christ (Lk 8:20). Christ's disciples are prepared to follow and believe in him even to the point of sacrificing their own lives, for him and with him, showing in no better way their absolute trust in the one who can raise them up from the dead (Rom 4:24f.). Subsequently, through acceptance of the witness of the disciples and divine illumination, faith germinates among the people, as faith in God, the God of Jesus Christ (Acts 15:7; 1 Cor 15:2). This, in turn, becomes the faith of the Church.[53] According to Paul, salvation, which comes from justifying grace, is always received in faith, which must be considered a divine gift that humans have no way of obtaining as the fruit of their own works (Rom 3:28; Gal 2:16). Faith is not a human "work" but rather the result of the freely received gift of revelation and justification.

Whereas the Jews who believed—as did Abraham, their "father in the faith"— had *life* because they received it as descendants of the great patriarch, John tells us that "whoever believes in the Son has *eternal life*." There is a movement here from the "life" that Abraham hands on to the "eternal life" that Christ gives to those who

---

51. The Jewish philosopher Martin Buber, in his work *Two Types of Faith* (New York: Harper Torchbooks, 1961), attempted to establish opposition between an Old Testament faith and a New Testament faith. The former would be the *fides qua*, trust in God; the second would be the *fides quae*, the doctrinal content of the faith. The position has been questioned frequently, for example, by H. U. von Balthasar in "Fides Christi," in *Sponsa Verbi* (Einsiedeln: Johannes-Verlag, 1960) and by D. Flusser in "Bubers 'Zwei Glaubensweisen,'" in *Zwei Glaubensweisen*, edited by M. Buber, 2nd ed. (Zurich: Manesse Verlag, 1994), 186–247. See C. Caltagirone, "Teologia della fede e elementi di antropologia fondamentale," in *Teologia fondamentale*, edited by G. Lorizio, A. Sabetta, and P. Sguazzardo (Rome: Città Nuova, 2004), 2:341–96, esp. 357n57.

52. See Francis and Benedict XVI, *Lumen Fidei*, pars. 15–18.

53. "Faith is not a private matter, a completely individualistic notion or a personal opinion: it comes from hearing, and it is meant to find expression in words and to be proclaimed" (ibid., par. 22; see pars. 37–49).

believe. This doctrine is taught repeatedly by John (e.g., Jn 3:36). Belief in God is expressed now as faith in Christ (Jn 12:44, 14:1). Faith becomes a living and present reality in the believer, and on account of it the Christian is raised up even in this life (Jn 11:25f.), becomes a child of God (Jn 1:12), "does not come into judgment [literally "condemnation"], but has passed from death to life" (Jn 5:24).

Besides, faith produces in humans a new knowledge. In fact, for John "to believe" means "to know."[54] For this reason we say that Jesus in whom we believe is, in person, "the truth" (Jn 12:36). At the end of time, faith will reach the perfection of full light, and in that moment "we know that when he appears we shall be like him, for we shall see him as he is" (1 Jn 3:2). Paul says the same thing: "For now we see in a mirror dimly [in faith], but then face to face. Now I know in part; then I shall understand fully [in glory], even as I have been fully understood" (1 Cor 13:12). In the words of Rossé, "in effect, faith 'is to be found in the "yes" of God to his promises' (2 Cor 1:20). It has a particular name: faith 'in Christ Jesus': faith is the acceptance of the Gospel which has as its content the saving work of God carried out by and manifested in Jesus Christ crucified and risen in favor of a humanity that is far from God."[55] As a result, we may say with John, "this is the victory that overcomes the world, our faith" (1 Jn 5:4). And for Paul, through faith the actions of Christians are filled with divine power (1 Cor 3:4; 1 Thes 1:5).

According to the New Testament, then, what best defines the Christian disciple is faith in Jesus Christ: "Faith comes from [ek] what is heard, and what is heard comes by [dia] the preaching of Christ" (Rom 10:17). To be "in Christ Jesus" (Rom 8:1) means to have faith. The fact that "Christ lives in me" has as a result that "I live in the faith of the Son of God" (Gal 2:20). In the words of Kertelge, "In virtue of faith in Jesus, believers are 'in Christ' and, as such, 'in possession' of the Spirit, that is to say, made by the Spirit suitable for life and moved to fulfill 'the law of the Spirit.'"[56] John often explains that the Christian is bound to believe in Christ (Jn 2:11, 3:16–18, 14:1) because the latter has been sent by the Father (Jn 11:42; 17:3, 8, 21), and in the messiah (11:27); as a result, the believer *must recognize both the divine filiation of Christ and his humanity* (1 Jn 4:1–4, 5:5). The encyclical *Lumen Fidei* employs an expression, "the light-filled life of Jesus," used by the exegete Helmut Schlier. In effect, the entire luminous life of Jesus confronts the entire life of humans and engenders faith: "together with hearing and seeing, Saint John can speak of faith as touch."[57]

Scripture, however, does not teach that Christ himself believed, that he was bound to the Father by faith.[58] According to the letter to the Hebrews, in fact, Christ is the "the

---

54. See Alfaro, "Fides in terminologia biblica," 500–502; Tanzella-Nitti, *Teologia fondamentale*, 135f. "Faith and knowledge are not two processes distinct from each other, but instructive coordinates that speak of the reception of the testimony from different standpoints (Jn 6:69, 17:8; 1 Jn 4:6). Faith alone receives the testimony and possesses knowledge; conversely, those who know the truth are pointed to faith. The hearer should understand that both are involved in salvation: acceptance of the testimony as well as the personal response and reformation that conform to the testimony." *NIDNTTE* 3:770.

55. Rossé, "La fede secondo san Paolo," 146.

56. K. Kertelge, *"Rechtfertigung" bei Paulus: Studien zur Struktur und zur Bedeutungsgehalt des paulinischen Rechtfertigungsbegriffes* (Munster in Westfalia: Aschendorff, 1967), 213.

57. Francis and Benedict XVI, *Lumen Fidei*, pars. 30f.

58. The New Testament uses the phrase "to believe in Christ" forty-two times and "faith in Christ" nine times.

pioneer [Greek, *archegon*] and perfecter [*teleioten*] of our faith" (12:2).[59] He is the one who perfectly reveals the saving love of the Father; from him comes the light. He is thus the one who makes faith possible, precisely because he is the one who sees the Father. For this reason Jesus can say that "he who has seen me has seen the Father" (Jn 14:9). According to several texts of scripture,[60] many theologians[61] and Church documents,[62] we may say that Christ enjoyed a direct vision of the Father during his earthly sojourn.

To say that in Christ is to be found the fullness of faith is correct in the sense that in him is to be found the fullness of light, which in the *eschaton* will take the place of faith definitively: Christ sees now what we believe. In this sense, paradoxically, the one who "has" faith to a maximum degree no longer has faith, but rather vision, the fullness of light. The reason Thomas Aquinas holds that Jesus enjoyed the fullness of light on earth was that he had to eventually hand it on to us.[63] Faith, according to scripture, refers to what is not seen (Heb 11:1). Now if Christ did not enjoy the vision of God on earth, he would have been like all his followers, and, as Matthew writes, "If a blind man leads a blind man, both will fall into a pit" (15:14). The Pauline expression *pistis Christou* (Gal 2:16, 3:22), therefore, should be understood according to the objective genitive, "faith *due* to Christ," and not the subjective genitive, "the faith *of* Christ."[64]

59. On Heb 12:2, see A. P. Wikgren, "Patterns of Perfection in the Epistle to the Hebrews," *New Testament Studies* 6, no. 2 (1960): 159–67; N. C. Croy, "A Note on Hebrews 12:2," *Journal of Biblical Literature* 114, no. 1 (1995): 117–19; BDAG, 997, s.v. τελειωτής. The term "fulfillment/perfection" means "one not to be transcended by subsequent improvements."

60. For example, Mt 11:27; Mk 14:26; Jn 1:18, 8:55. See also Jn 3:11–32, 5:19, 7:29, 8:38, 17:5.

61. For a presentation of different positions, see L. Iammarrone, "La visione beatifica di Cristo viatore nel pensiero di san Tommaso," *Doctor Communis* 36 (1983): 287–330; J. Galot, "Le Christ terrestre et la vision," *Gregorianum* 67 (1986): 429–50; J. A. Riestra, "Cristo e la fede nella cristologia recente," *Aquinas* 30 (1987): 271–87; J.-P. Torrell, "La vision de Dieu 'per essentiam' selon saint Thomas d'Aquin," in *Recherches Thomasiennes: Études revues et augmentées* (Paris: Vrin, 2000), 177–97; R. Wielockx, "Incarnation et vision béatifique: Aperçus théologiques," *Revue des sciences philosophiques et théologiques* 86, no. 4 (2002): 601–39; T. J. White, "The Voluntary Action of the Earthly Christ and the Necessity of the Beatific Vision," *Thomist* 69 (2005): 497–534; T. G. Weinandy, "The Beatific Vision of the Incarnate Son: Furthering the Discussion," *Thomist* 70 (2006): 605–15; M. Hauke, "La visione beatifica di Cristo durante la Passione: La dottrina di San Tommaso d'Aquino e la teologia contemporanea," *Annales Theologici* 21 (2007): 381–98; N. J. Healy, "The Filial Mode of Christ's Knowledge," *Nova et Vetera* (English ed.) 11, no. 2 (2013): 341–55.

62. See the decree of the Holy Office in 1918, *DH* 3645–47; Pope Pius XII, *Mystici Corporis* (*DH* 3812); Pope Pius XII, *Haurietis Aquas*, Encyclical Letter, May 15, 1956 (*DH* 3924). In a discourse for priests in Kinshasa (Zaire) on May 15, 1980, Pope John Paul II said: "Jesus was able to fulfill his mission thanks to his total union with the Father, because he was one with him: in his condition as a pilgrim on the ways of the world ('viator') he was already in possession of the end ('comprehensor') toward which he had to bring all others." See also *CCC* 473f. "Jesus' teaching is not the product of human learning, of whatever kind. It originates from immediate contact with the Father, from 'face-to-face' dialogue—from the vision of the one who rests close to the Father's heart." Ratzinger/Benedict XVI, *Jesus of Nazareth* 1:7. In *Lumen Fidei* we read: "To enable us to know, accept and follow him, the Son of God took on our flesh. In this way he also saw the Father humanly, within the setting of a journey unfolding in time" (par. 18).

63. See Aquinas, *S.Th.* III, q. 7, a. 11; q. 8, a. 1; q. 9, a. 2.

64. The latter interpretation is not to be found among the Church Fathers but has become popular in the past century or so. For the history, see R. B. Hays, *The Faith of Jesus Christ: An Investigation of the Narrative Substructure of Galatians 3:1–4:11* (Chico, Calif.: Scholars Press, 1983), 142–47. Paul "explicitly, unambiguously, and repeatedly speaks of *pistis* as something exercised by believers (e.g., Rom 1:8, 10:17; 1 Cor 15:14; Gal 5:5; 1 Thes 3:2) and uses *pisteuō* with human beings as subject (e.g., Rom 1:16, 4:5; 1 Cor 1:21; Gal 3:22). Moreover, in the critical statement of Gal 2:16, Christ functions as the object of the verb between two instances of the phrase *pistis Christou*." *NIDNTTE* 3:769.

In an ample sense we can translate *pistou Christou* also as "the fidelity of Christ," his filial trust, which corresponds to the complete trustworthiness of the Father. It is true that the basic attitude of Christ before the Father is one of total filial trust.[65] And, as we already saw, Christ is the source and model of the filial bond that unites the Christian with God. In the words of Sequeri, "Faith that saves is above all the appropriation of that special way of identifying God that qualifies Jesus of Nazareth."[66] But the union of Christ with the Father is not the *analogatum princeps* of Christian faith as such,[67] because that union involves several elements that go beyond simple trust and self-abandonment, such as confession of faith (which includes intellectual knowledge) and obedience.[68]

A "Definition" of Faith: Hebrews 11:1

Chapter 11 of the letter to the Hebrews, which deals entirely with the nature, narrative, and dynamics of faith, offers the following definition of this virtue: "Now faith is the *assurance* of things hoped for, the *conviction* of things not seen." "Of things hoped for" obviously refers to God, whom believers desire to possess eternally. "Things not seen" also refers to God. It should be noted, however, that the translation just offered, from the Revised Standard Version, is not quite precise. "Assurance" translates the Greek *hypostasis*. Yet the Vulgate and neo-Vulgate translate it as "substantia" (substance), which refers to an objective reality experienced by humans and rooted in God. It would be more correct to translate *hypostasis* as "foundation" or "basis." And "conviction" translates the Greek *elenchos*, which really should be translated as "proof," that is, the basis of conviction. That is to say, both *hypostatis* and *elenchos* should be translated objectively, not subjectively.[69] Of course "assurance" does arise

---

65. This may be seen especially in the attitude of Jesus toward the Father. In his rapport with the Father von Balthasar finds some central elements of Jewish faith, elevated to divine perfection: "The total fidelity to the Father in different circumstances of life, primacy is always given to the will of the Father, abandonment of oneself to the initiative of the Father, without the pretext of knowing beforehand the historical way of concrete realization." Ardusso, "Fede," 615.

66. Sequeri, *Il Dio affidabile*, 244.

67. Von Balthasar focuses the question differently in *Fides Christi*. He holds that the *fides Iesu* becomes the "paradigm of paradigms": "What Jesus makes us share in may be called the prototypical faith insofar as Jesus carries out within himself the Old Testament attitude of total faith in God." H. U. von Balthasar, *Glory of the Lord*, vol. 7: *Theology: The New Covenant* (Edinburgh: T. and T. Clark, 1989), 146. More or less the same position is taken up by G. Ebeling in *Word and Faith* (Philadelphia: Fortress, 1963); R. Guardini, *The Humanity of Christ: Contributions to a Psychology of Jesus* (New York: Pantheon Books, 1964); J. Guillet, *La foi de Jésus Christ* (Paris: Desclée, 1980); A. Bastoni, "La *fides Christi* in Hans Urs von Balthasar," *La fede: Evento e promessa*, 197–218; G. Canobbio, ed., *La fede di Gesù: Atti del convegno tenuto a Trento il 27–28 maggio 1998* (Bologna: Dehoniane, 2000).

68. See Alfaro, "Fides in terminologia biblica," 500–504.

69. Benedict XVI, in the encyclical *Spe Salvi* (par. 7), explains the difficulties experienced by Lutherans in this area: "To Luther, who was not particularly fond of the *Letter to the Hebrews*, the concept of 'substance,' in the context of his view of faith, meant nothing. For this reason he understood the term *hypostasis/substance* not in the objective sense (of a reality present within us), but in the subjective sense, as an expression of an interior attitude, and so, naturally, he also had to understand the term *argumentum* as a disposition of the subject. In the twentieth century this interpretation became prevalent—at least in Germany—in Catholic exegesis too, so that the ecumenical translation into German of the New Testament, approved by the Bishops, reads as follows: 'Glaube aber ist: Feststehen in dem, was man erhofft, Überzeugtsein von dem, was man nicht sieht' (Faith is: standing firm in what one hopes, being convinced of what one does not see). This in itself is not incorrect, but it is not the meaning of the text, because the Greek term used (*elenchos*) has not the subjec-

in the believer because there is a "foundation," and "conviction" because there is a "proof." But faith may not be identified with the anthropological categories of assurance and conviction because they are the fruit of faith, and faith is the source of both.

Benedict XVI, in the encyclical *Spe Salvi*, insists upon the objective (though eschatological) realism of Christian faith, as well as its deep continuity with hope:

> Faith is not merely a personal reaching out toward things to come that are still totally absent: it gives us something. It gives us even now something of the reality we are waiting for, and this present reality constitutes for us a "proof" of the things that are still unseen. Faith draws the future into the present so that it is no longer simply a "not yet." The fact that this future exists changes the present; the present is touched by the future reality, and thus the things of the future spill over into those of the present and those of the present into those of the future.[70]

Benedict goes on to explain faith as an infused virtue, following the teaching of Thomas Aquinas:

> Faith is a *habitus*, that is, a stable disposition of the spirit, through which eternal life takes root in us and reason is led to consent to what it does not see. The concept of "substance" is therefore modified in the sense that through faith, in a tentative way, or as we might say "in embryo"—and thus according to the "substance"—there are already present in us the things that are hoped for: the whole, true life.[71]

In brief, what is presented to the minds of believers is not a "truth" as such (or a "value" or conviction) that comes to be known and appreciated but rather the reality of God's own life infused into their lives, though in a germinal way, a life which humans are invited to receive and which bring them to consent to divine revelation.[72] Faith in that sense is not a mere supplement to the weakness of reason; it is a new light, an infused light, God's precious gift.

Faith as an Infused Light

From the Christian standpoint, therefore, faith may be described as an infused theological virtue that unites humans directly to their ultimate end, God, revealed in Christ as the one who is totally true and worthy of trust.[73] With faith only do humans come to know God as an infinitely intelligible, objectively known reality. Our knowledge of God in faith is the fruit of God's own personal revelation through Christ in

---

tive sense of 'conviction' but the objective sense of 'proof.' Rightly, therefore, recent Protestant exegesis has arrived at a different interpretation: 'Yet there can be no question but that this classical Protestant understanding is untenable' (H. Köster, *TDNT* 8:586)." This is confirmed by *BDAG* 1041, s.v. ὑπόστασις, 3; ibid., 315, s.v. ἔλεγχος, "the act of presenting evidence for the truth of something." See also W. L. Lane, *Hebrews 9–13*, in *WBC* 47B:328f.

70. *Spe Salvi*, par. 7; emphasis added.

71. Ibid., quoting Aquinas, *S.Th.* II-II, q. 4, a. 1.

72. "Only now, in the midst of everything that man may think or experience, in the midst of all that is known as 'world,' rises a point that does not belong to the world; a place into which one may step; a room one may enter; a power on which one may lean; a love to which one may give oneself. This is reality, different from the reality of the world, more real than the world. Faith is the act of seizing this reality, of building one's life on it, of becoming part of it." Guardini, *The Lord*, 199.

73. On the structure of Christian faith, see J. Mouroux, *I Believe: The Personal Structure of Faith* (London: G. Chapman, 1959); P. Coda and C. Hennecke, eds., *La fede: Evento e promessa*; Caltagirone, *Teologia della fede*; Tanzella-Nitti, *Teologia fondamentale*, 140–48.

the power of the Spirit. The light of faith opens to the human intelligence "all the treasures of wisdom and knowledge" (Col 2:3). We may say that in a real sense humans through faith share in the knowledge that God has of himself. Thomas Aquinas says: "Per potentiam intellectivam homo participat cognitionem divinam per virtutem fidei" (Through the power of their intellect humans share in divine knowledge by the virtue of faith).[74] Still, faith does not require of humans a delirious or irrational jump in the dark, into emptiness, because it is the result in them of the acceptance of the gift of divine revelation, which is a strong light, a virtue, a loving infused divine power. As the philosopher Michel Henry says, "To believe is not a surrogate of a vision that is still absent."[75] When spiritual authors speak of the "darkness of faith" or of the "dark night of the soul," this obscurity refers in the first place to the greatness and depth of the mystery of God, which cannot be comprehended or dominated by a limited human intellect and which has been weakened by sin that makes humans reluctant to trust other people. Faith, which is accepted revelation, is above all a sharing in divine life, a light, a luminosity that is not as yet definitive. Objectively, therefore, in the life of the believer light enjoys dominion over darkness, although subjectively believers may be more aware of the darkness than the light because they have not yet obtained the fullness of beatific vision.[76] John of the Cross described faith in the following terms: "With no other light or guide, than the one that burned in my heart. This guided me more surely than the light of noon, to where he was awaiting me."[77]

Characteristics of the Virtue of Faith

Four observations may be made on the dynamic of the virtue of faith. First, Christian faith is a filial virtue in the sense that those who believe become, in the Spirit, disciples, friends, and brothers of Christ and, by that very fact, children of God: "In accepting the gift of faith, believers become a new creation; they receive a new being; as God's children, they are now 'sons in the Son.'"[78] On a human plane, children confide completely in their parents, "knowing" that if they cannot understand and do "everything," their parents can. In real terms, only a Father is worthy of the unconditioned faith and unlimited trust that is asked of Christians, because he has revealed himself with all-powerful transparency through his Son Jesus Christ in the Spirit. Jesus himself said: "*No longer do I call you servants*, for the servant does not know what his master is doing; but I have called you friends, for *all that I have heard from my Father I have made known to you*" (Jn 15:15). Elsewhere in the New Testament, being a slave is presented as the opposite of being a son. In fact, filial faith takes away all fear, calculation, and reserve in one's relationship with others: "Do not fear," Jesus said to Jairus, the ruler of the synagogue, "only believe" (Mk 5:36).[79] Besides, through faith

74. Aquinas, *S.Th.* I-II, q. 110, a. 4, co.; see Francis and Benedict XVI, *Lumen Fidei*, par. 36.

75. Henry, *C'est moi la vérité*, 108.

76. On beatific vision and faith, see *COH* 124, 133f.

77. John of the Cross, in his poem "En una noche oscura": "En la noche dichosa / En secreto, que nadie me veía / Ni yo miraba cosa / Sin otra luz y guía, / sino la que en el corazón ardía. / Aquesta me guiaba / Más cierto que la luz de mediodía, / A donde me esperaba, / Quien yo bien me sabía." English translation from *The Collected Works of Saint John of the Cross*, edited by K. Kavanaugh and O. Rodríguez (Washington, D.C.: ISC Publications, 1991), 51.

78. Francis and Benedict XVI, *Lumen Fidei*, par. 19.

79. See Tanzella-Nitti, *Teologia fondamentale*, 145.

humans "abandon all things to God freely," that is, with the freedom that marks the lives of the children of God (Rom 8:21).[80]

Second, through faith human reason, opened to the whole truth (Jn 16:13)—to God, the very source of truth—can reach its ultimate fullness.[81] Perhaps it may be said that reason, understood in a merely rationalistic and individualistic way, is "saved" and elevated and perfected by faith. In this way the presence of faith in the life of Christians shows that human life is directed to the knowledge of truth, the whole truth.[82]

Third, theological faith helps us understand the dynamics and profile of the faith or trust due to other creatures.[83] The one who believes in God is in a position to see and contemplate the whole of reality—especially other human beings—as something created by God. Therefore he recognizes them in general terms as worthy of esteem and trust. It is obvious that humans could not live out their lives and reach fulfillment if they were not recipients of trust on the part of others. Besides, the believer considers things, people, and events always in the light of faith, not only because they are all created by God but also because they are directed to him and finalized in him (this is called providence). The virtue of faith, in other words, moves humans to consider all that happens to them from the perspective of God, the God who is faithful to creation, to nature, to the Covenant, to promises made, to institutions established to communicate his gifts, and especially to humans made in his image and likeness. With Paul Christians can exclaim: "Omnia in bonum": "We know that in everything God works for good with those who love him" (Rom 8:28). At the same time, faith, as a theological virtue, regulates and limits the kind of trust that should be placed in creatures. The latter, in effect, are not worthy of the total and unconditioned faith that is meant for God alone, who is the fullness of truth, revealed in Christ Jesus, "Light of the world" (Jn 8:12, 9:5). The Christian, therefore, is trustful toward the world and toward other people in general terms, but is not, or at least should not be, either utopian or naïve. In the words of *Lumen Fidei*:

The light of faith is capable of enhancing the richness of human relations, their ability to endure, to be trustworthy, to enrich our life together. Faith does not draw us away from the world or prove irrelevant to the concrete concerns of the men and women of our time.... Faith makes us appreciate the architecture of human relationships because it grasps their ultimate foundation and definitive destiny in God.[84]

Fourth, just as all creatures are, generally speaking, worthy of faith because God, in whom we believe, created them, they are also, in a certain sense, the way or source

---

80. Vatican Council II, *Dei Verbum*, no. 5.

81. This is a fundamental aspect of John Paul II's encyclical *Fides et Ratio* and of the entire magisterium of Benedict XVI. See also P. Coda and G. Sgubbi, eds., *Il risveglio della ragione: Proposte per un pensiero credente* (Rome: Città Nuova, 2000), and especially G. Maspero and M. Pérez de Laborda, eds., *Fede e ragione: L'incontro e il cammino; In occasione del decimo anniversario dell'enciclica Fides et ratio* (Siena: Cantagalli, 2011), which contains my study "L'incontro tra fede e ragione," 35–59.

82. In Francis and Benedict XVI's *Lumen Fidei*, par. 34, we read that faith "illumines the material world, trusts its inherent order and knows that it calls us to an ever widening path of harmony and understanding. The gaze of science thus benefits from faith: faith encourages the scientist to remain constantly open to reality in all its inexhaustible richness. Faith awakens the critical sense by preventing research from being satisfied with its own formulae and helps it to realize that nature is always greater."

83. See Lingua, "Le forme dell'affidarsi."

84. Francis and Benedict, *Lumen Fidei*, par. 51.

of faith. In effect, our faith in God is mediated in a privileged way by certain created elements that God himself has wished to associate with his revelation and saving action. Above all, revelation that gives rise to faith is mediated by Christ in his humanity, the direct and immediate fruit of the incarnation, and therefore the direct object of faith that receives divine revelation. Besides, faith includes other elements linked with the communication of revelation: the word of God announced by the prophets and the Church, body of Christ, which in the word and sacraments makes the life and grace of Jesus Christ present to humanity and becomes therefore the place of faith, the human space "in which" faith is received and exercised along with other believers. Finally, faith refers to humans themselves, made in the image of God, and especially to justified humans because, being children of God, *alter Christus*, *ipse Christus*, they become, or at least should become, transparent mediators of the good things God wishes to communicate to all humans. Through all these elements, therefore, the light of faith is communicated, handed on from one generation to the next, and must be guarded as a divine treasure.[85] In *Lumen Fidei* we read:

The light of Christ shines, as in a mirror, upon the face of Christians; as it spreads, it comes down to us, so that we too can share in that vision and reflect that light to others.... It is impossible to believe on our own. Faith is not simply an individual decision which takes place in the depths of the believer's heart ... between an autonomous subject and God. By its very nature, faith is open to the "We" of the Church; it always takes place within her communion.... Those who receive faith discover that their horizons expand as new and enriching relationships come to life.[86]

The Infused Virtue of Christian Hope

Hope in Ancient Philosophy

Among Greek philosophers there was no developed reflection on hope.[87] "The notion of hope does not appear to have been a fundamental religious attitude in Greek and Roman cultures."[88] Aristotle considers it a mere passion, brought about by the *bonum futurum arduum possibile*, that is, by the absent good, difficult to obtain, yet considered reachable. Greek mythology does give some weight to hope (*elpis*), for example, in the myth of Pandora's box: hope in effect is the last thing to be lost. But in real terms hope is considered as a simple fact, a characteristic of human life, and certainly not a virtue to be cultivated unconditionally. The reason for this is simple: the future, toward which hope necessarily points, is, according to the classic and universal myth of eternal return, a simple replica of the past.[89] Nothing substantially new will happen that is not already present: "Nihil novum sub sole" (There is nothing

---

85. Tanzella-Nitti, *Teologia fondamentale*, 145–47.

86. Francis and Benedict, *Lumen Fidei*, pars. 37, 39.

87. On hope in Greek literature and Biblical exegesis, see R. Bultmann and K. H. Rengstorf, *TDNT* 2:517–35, s.v. ἐλπίς, esp. 507–16; F. Van Menxel, *Elpis, Espoir, Espérance: Études sémantiques et théologiques du vocabulaire de l'espérance dans l'Hellénisme et le Judaïsme avant le Nouveau Testament* (Frankfurt: P. Lang, 1983); *BDAG*, 319, s.v. ἐλπίς; *NIDNTTE* 2:183–89, s.v. ἐλπίς.

88. *NIDNTTE* 2:183.

89. See this work of M. Eliade: *Cosmos and History: The Myth of the Eternal Return* (New York: Harper and Row, 1959).

new under the sun) (Qo 1:9). Thus there is no space for a hope directed toward the future. In antiquity there is no equivalent of what Christians call the Gospel, or "good news," the kingdom of heaven as a radical novelty introduced by God into the history of the world with the coming of Christ, a novelty that the created world anticipates, in a sense, but does not as yet contain. For the Greeks, in fact, to hope firmly in the advent of a definitively new or better reality in the future would be a utopia, a sign of naïveté. Realistically speaking, the future will be more or less like the past; it does not promise anything especially new. Hence in Greek thought there is no cosmic or theological basis for considering hope a virtue. According to Bultmann, Greeks hold that hope easily deceives humans because only a god can be sure of its expectations; specifically, he claims that the Stoics had little interest in the phenomenon of hope.[90] Understandably, Paul concludes that pagans are those who live "without hope" (Eph 2:12).

Christian Revelation Gives Rise to Hope

The New Testament speaks frequently about hope, which, like faith, is brought about by divine revelation. However, "it is a remarkable fact that the word group plays no significant role in the Gospels. Indeed, the noun *elpis* is totally absent in those books."[91] Perhaps this is so because Christ himself, in person, is "our hope" (1 Tm 1:1).[92] To say, "I hope" means simply that "Christ lives in me"; his words, his actions, his saving work, his union with the Father reach out to humans, and fill them with hope. Of course if the Gospels do not speak openly of hope, Paul and John do, in that they speak of the working out of the life of Christ in the lives of believers.

According to Paul, hope is a consistent, coherent reality. First, "Hope is never egocentric, but always focused on Christ and on God. Its heart is not the blessing of the individual but the universal kingly rule of God, who will be 'all in all' (1 Cor 15:28)."[93] Its content principally includes eschatological realities: the resurrection of the body (Rom 8:18–23; 1 Thes 4:13ff.), the heritage of the saints (Eph 1:18), eternal life (Ti 1:2), glory (Rom 5:2; 2 Cor 3:7–12; Eph 1:18; Col 1:27; Ti 2:13), the vision of God (1 Jn 3:2f.)— in a word, salvation (1 Thes 5:8), one's own and others' (2 Cor 1:6f.; 1 Thes 2:19). Second, hope rests not on good works but on the gracious action of God in Jesus Christ. Hope, in effect, is founded on God (1 Tm 5:5, 6:17; 1 Pt 1:21, 3:5), on his love (2 Thes 2:16), on his call (1 Pt 1:13–15), on his power (Rom 4:17–21), on his truthfulness (Ti 1:2; Heb 6:18), and on his fidelity to the promises (Heb 10:23) that are expressed through scripture (Rom 15:4), through the Gospel (Col 1:23), and principally in the person of Christ (1 Tm 1:1; 1 Pt 1:3, 21). Third, "Hope is a gift of the Father's grace, offered as a message of salvation (Col 1:23).... Through the power of the Holy Spirit, who is given to us as first fruits (Rom 8:23), we receive a superabundance of hope (Rom 15:23), for his indwelling in believers is the guarantee of their resurrection (Rom 8:11)."[94]

In effect, the old Covenant was centered on a promise to which God would give

---

90. See R. Bultmann and K. H. Rengstorf, *TDNT* 2:507.
91. *NIDNTTE* 2:185.
92. Thus *Christ our Hope*, the title of the first volume of the trilogy of which this work is a second volume.
93. *NIDNTTE* 2:187.
94. Ibid.

future fulfillment, a promise destined to bring about the salvation of humanity. In the Christian economy this hope is actualized because, with the coming of the messiah and the sending of the Holy Spirit, the work of salvation is already being carried out, alongside the ultimate promise of the eternal fullness of divine love, the eternal inheritance of the children of God, eternal life, final resurrection, and glory. Believers in Christ hope to receive from God what only God can give: communion with the Trinity and the perfect and perpetual beatitude that follows from it. For the saints, "God chose to make known how great among the Gentiles are the riches of the glory of this mystery, which is Christ in you, the hope of glory" (Col 1:27). Through Christ "we have obtained access to this grace in which we stand, and we rejoice in our hope of sharing the glory of God" (Rom 5:2).

God as the Object and Source of Hope

We have said that only God is in a position to give definitive fulfillment to the profound desire for infinite happiness present in each person, a desire that seeks out eternal fulfillment and perpetual contentment. This is so because God is infinitely good (and therefore desirable), all-powerful (capable of giving what he has promised), merciful (disposed to forgive all faults), and faithful to his word (and therefore prepared to give the everlasting life he has promised). The fact that humans have this desire for infinite and perpetual happiness is itself an indication that they are in a position to accept God's gift. In this sense, Thomas Aquinas says, humans are *capax Dei*. Therefore, we can conclude that hope is a virtue only because it is theological. No creature is in a position to fulfill the desire for infinite and perfect happiness present in the human heart; no one other than God, therefore, may be considered a suitable object of true and unconditioned hope on the part of humans. Aquinas explains this as follows: "Hope must be considered a virtue in the sense that humans, with the help of divine aid, desire to obtain eternal life. Still, if one seeks human help in obtaining the perfect good, whether for oneself or for another, while excluding divine help, then this attitude may become vicious."[95]

As in the case of faith, God is not simply the object of human hope. He is the object because previously he has been the motor or source of hope. Humans hope in God because he gives them the power, the virtue, to do so. God reveals himself as love in the depths of their being, through Christ in the Holy Spirit. Indeed the Spirit may be considered "the cause and power of hope."[96] According to scripture, precisely the Spirit is the source of hope (Gal 5:5), the one who illuminates hope (Eph 1:17f.) and fortifies it (Rom 15:13), bringing humans to pray (Rom 8:25–27) and act through hope in union with the body of Christ (Eph 4:4). God promises eternal life to those who believe in his Son and makes present in their hearts, through the Spirit, the certain hope that this promise will be fulfilled as an intimate, joyful, and stable conviction. With serenity and insistence the Spirit whispers in the hearts of Christians: "This is possible," "That is worthwhile." Thus hope is full of certainty (2 Cor 3:12; Heb 3:6), of consolation (2 Thes 2:16; Heb 6:18), of joy (Rom 12:12; 1 Thes 2:19; Heb 3:6), and

---

95. Aquinas, *Q. disp. de spe*, a. 1, co.
96. See *COH* 33–36.

of enthusiasm (Rom 5:2; 1 Thes 2:19; Heb 3:6); hope does not allow humans to be discouraged by suffering or tribulation in the present moment, because all that is of little weight compared with the promise of glory (Rom 8:18), especially when difficulties are lived and accepted with "constancy" (Rom 8:25, 12:12, 15:4; 1 Thes 1:3), a constancy that manifests (Rom 5:4) and confirms (2 Cor 1:7) hope. Hope is indeed a gift infused by God, a gift that brings about in humans (and requires of them) an openness, a goodness, a simplicity, a generosity, a capacity to recognize and accept what is freely given. These attitudes and human virtues facilitate the reception of the virtue of theological hope, and they are reinforced, in turn, by hope.

Some Characteristics of Christian Hope

Six observations may be made regarding this theological virtue. First, hope is a filial virtue, a manifestation of the spirit of divine filiation in the Christian, because it refers in the first place to the eternal inheritance of the children of God (Rom 8:17), that is, the promise of perpetual participation, face to face, in the life that unites the Father and the Son in their perpetual dialogue of love in the Spirit. In effect, by hope the Christian is convinced that "the slave does not continue in the house for ever; the son continues for ever" (Jn 8:35). The hope of the children of God anticipates in this life the perpetual joy of heaven, according to the promise of the Lord: "In my Father's house are many rooms; if it were not so, would I have told you that 'I go to prepare a place for you'? And when I go and prepare a place for you, I will come again and will take you to myself, that where I am you may be also" (Jn 14:2f.). As Josemaría Escrivá says, "The certainty I derive from feeling—from knowing—that I am a son of God fills me with real hope which, being a supernatural virtue, adapts to our nature when it is infused in us, and so is also a very human virtue."[97]

Second, the theological virtue of hope gives fulfillment and meaning to the longing for immortality present in the human heart. Because the search for immortality is fundamental to Christian anthropology as a whole, we can say that the way we understand and live hope plays a basic role not only in the lives of humans but also in the way we understand anthropology in general.[98] The philosopher Gabriel Marcel said, in fact, that "hope is perhaps the very material out of which the soul is made."[99] At the same time, the presence of hope in the life of the Christian shows up the fact and intensifies the conviction that humans are destined to immortality.

Third, following Augustine and John of the Cross it may be said that the human faculty with which hope best pairs off is memory. According to the former, hope is configured by what is present in one's memory, and therefore, *ex memoria spes*: hope is molded, facilitated, profiled on the basis of memory, of the lived narrative of each person's life, of human identity consolidated over the years.[100] Likewise, John of the

---

97. Escrivá, *Friends of God*, no. 208. On his teaching on hope, see P. O'Callaghan, "La virtù della speranza e l'ascetica cristiana in alcuni scritti del Beato Josemaría Escrivá, Fondatore dell'Opus Dei," *Romana* 12 (1996): 262–79; Burkhart and López, *Vida cotidiana y santidad*, 2:364–83.

98. On the centrality of the dynamics of hope in human life, see especially the works of Gabriel Marcel; on his thought, see O'Callaghan, "La metafísica de la esperanza y del deseo en Gabriel Marcel."

99. Marcel, *Etre et avoir*, 117.

100. On the notion of memory in Augustine, see *De Trinitate* IX–XV and especially *Confessiones* X–XI.

Cross speaks of the need to purify one's memory in order to be able to hope in a fully Christian way; thus the mind and affections toward creatures are freed so as to be able to hope in God alone.[101]

Thomas Aquinas, however, argues that hope in humans refers principally to the will.[102] Still, he explains that the passion of hope, provoked by the *bonum futurum arduum*, depends on what he calls the *existimatio possibilitatis*, that is, the conviction that the absent and arduous good can really be obtained.[103] This judgment depends not only on human reason but also on the experience each one of us has had during our lifetime, on what we have lived and experienced, and therefore on our own memory and narrative identity. In that sense, as it develops throughout time, hope pairs off principally with memory. "What hope is for future things, memory is for past things," he says.[104] It is interesting to note that Aquinas holds that those who experience hope most powerfully are infants and drunkards,[105] because they may be unaware of the obstacles present in obtaining the arduous good they desire; they do not have the experience that makes a negative spontaneous human reaction both reasonable and balanced in the face of the absent arduous good.[106] On the contrary, when

---

On his thought, see the classic work of P. Laín Entralgo, *La espera y la esperanza: Historia y teoría del esperar humano* (Madrid: Alianza, 1984; originally published in 1956), 56–70. See the recent P. E. Hochschild, *Memory in Augustine's Theological Anthropology* (Oxford: Oxford University Press, 2012). Augustine speaks of remembering "within myself, in the great hall of my memory for there are to my hand heaven, earth and sea, and all I have been able to perceive in them, except what I have forgotten. I meet myself there, too, and recall myself, what, when and where I have done something, and my reaction when I did it. Everything is there which I have personally experienced, or believed and remember. Out of the same store, I continually weave into the past new and newer images of things which I have experienced, or, on the basis of experience, have believed. *And from these too I fashion future actions, events, and hopes,* and reflect on all these things again as if they were there." *Conf.* X, 8, 14.

101. See John of the Cross, *Ascent to Mount Carmel*, especially books II and III. On this work, see Laín Entralgo, *La espera y la esperanza*, 115–31. "Since our aim is the union of the soul with God in hope, according to the memory, and since that which is hoped for is that which is not possessed, and since, the less we possess of other things, the greater scope and the greater capacity have we for hoping, and consequently the greater hope, therefore, the more things we possess, the less scope and capacity is there for hoping, and consequently the less hope have we. Hence, the more the soul dispossesses the memory of forms and things which may be recalled by it, which are not God, the more will it set its memory upon God, and the emptier will its memory become, so that it may hope for Him Who shall fill it. What must be done, then, that the soul may live in the perfect and pure hope of God is that, whensoever these distinct images, forms, and ideas come to it, it must not rest in them, but must turn immediately to God, voiding the memory of them entirely, with loving affection." *Ascent to Mount Carmel* III, 15:1. John also says that "the three faculties of the soul—understanding, memory, and will—are brought into this spiritual night, which is the means to Divine union, it is necessary first of all to explain in this chapter how the three theological virtues—faith, hope, and charity—which have respect to the three faculties aforesaid as their proper supernatural objects, and by means whereof the soul is united with God according to its faculties, produce the same emptiness and darkness, each one in its own faculty." *Ascent to Mount Carmel* II, 6, 1. D. Doyle, in "From Triadic to Dyadic Soul: A Genetic Study of John of the Cross on the Anthropological Basis of Hope," *Studies in Spirituality* 21 (2011): 219–41, explains that in the early writings of John of the Cross there is a close bond between faith, hope, and charity, on the one hand, and intellect, memory, and will on the other. In his later writings, however, Doyle observes that hope is presented as rooted in the soul itself, in which the desire of the entire person to share in the wisdom and love of God is to be found.

102. Aquinas, *S.Th.* II-II, q. 18, a. 1.

103. *Ibid.* I-II, q. 40, a. 5, co.

104. Aquinas, *Q. disp. de spe*, q. 1, co.

105. Aquinas, *S.Th.* I-II, q. 40, a. 6, co.

106. On the dynamics of the human passions with respect to reason, see *S.Th.* I, q. 76, a. 5. Thomas concludes that the passions are "rationales per participationem" (rational by participation). *S.Th.* I-II, q. 56, a. 4, ad 1.

people have unpleasant memories of harsh experiences in the past, their spontaneous (passional) reactions when faced with new experiences or promises will tend to be negative. Their passional reactions will then be those of despair, not hope, what we perhaps normally call "pessimism." But if they have had more positive experiences, it will normal for them to react with hope, perhaps we could say with "optimism." So it is with the dynamics of the passion of hope.

Still, we should keep in mind that the infused theological virtue of hope develops in the context of the passion of hope. Two observations may be made. First, that the virtue of hope constitutes a central aspect of the inner life of Christians in which the subject experiences or "suffers" the powerful presence of God, a kind of divine "passion." Second, the place of memory is occupied in the theological virtue of hope by Christian memory, that is, by the living and contemporary narrative of the history of salvation: the words of the prophets, the life of the people of God, the psalms and other Old Testament prayers, wisdom literature, and above all the rich and open-ended narrative of the life of Jesus Christ: his incarnation, teaching, life, death, resurrection, and sending of the Spirit. This living reality is made present in the hearts of believers along with the virtue of hope through the action of the Holy Spirit, which moves them to live a fully Christian life, in persevering consideration and contemplation of the word of God contained in scripture and, if necessary, in heroic correspondence to divine grace.[107] In brief, Christians hope on the basis of their Christic and pneumatological identity communicated by baptism, consolidated through Christian life, and deepened in the contemplation of the word of God.

But how does the virtue of hope actually purify the memories of the baptized? In two stages. First, the presence of the life of Christ in the mind and heart of the Christian through grace and the virtues (the "Christ who lives in me" of which Paul speaks in Gal 2:20) purifies the memory and therefore the identity of humans, shaped at least to some degree by the effects of original and personal sin, as well as by the limited and historical condition of humans. In that way hope is made ever more alive and present. Second, Christians can to a certain degree be directly involved in the purification of their own memories under the sway of virtue, and therefore in the consolidation of their deep narrative identity as Christians, in such a way that every event and action is memorized or remembered in the proper way.[108] Let us consider the latter point more closely.

On the one hand, a human can consider a negative experience (such as an illness or the death of a loved one) as a source of upset, frustration, and rebellion, and thus remember it in a negative way (or with a negative "tag"). For the future this memory

107. John of the Cross often speaks of the need for active purification: "All the things that [man] hears, sees, smells, tastes, or touches, he must be careful not to store up or collect in his memory, but he must allow himself to forget them immediately, and this he must accomplish, if need be, with the same efficacy as that with which others contrive to remember them, so that there remains in his memory no knowledge or image of them whatsoever. It must be with him as if they existed not in the world, and his memory must be left free and disencumbered of them, and be tied to no consideration, whether from above or from below, as if he had no faculty of memory; he must freely allow everything to fall into oblivion as though all things were a hindrance to him; and in fact everything that is natural, if one attempt to make use of it in supernatural matters, is a hindrance rather than a help." *Ascent to Mount Carmel* III, 2, 14.

108. On the dynamics of human memory, see A. Malo, *Essere persona: Un'antropologia dell'identità* (Rome: A. Armando, 2013), 131–38.

becomes a wellhead of bitterness, of anger, of despair. The memory in question may be forgotten at a conscious level, yet it incisively influences the person's reflection, judgment, and behavior. It will reduce and condition the dynamic of hope in that person, occasioning negative and pessimistic reactions. It is also true, however, that a negative experience may be lived, assimilated, and remembered with a positive "tag" when a human, before losing conscious awareness of the event lived, focuses on it willingly in the proper way with the help of God's grace. For example, a person may experience an illness as an occasion of sharing with others, as an opportunity to learn compassion and humility, to become more patient; believers besides may identify their lives more fully with the suffering of Christ and may joyfully discover that the apparent disgrace offers them the opportunity to co-redeem the world, that resurrection follows the cross.

On the other hand, positive experiences, such as professional success, a happy family life, and stable and good relationships with others may be experienced with an egoistical sense of self-complacency or with joyful gratitude. The same event may be memorized, therefore, with a vicious, egoist tag in which other people are despised or with a virtuous tag of grateful recognition toward God and others, with realism, detachment, and humility. In this way humans, with the help of divine grace, can shape their own memories, their own narrative identities, in a fully human and Christian manner, and do so in such a way that the infused virtue of hope is absorbed deeply, becoming life of their lives, their true identity, their "dominant passion,"[109] lived with all the naturalness of the children of God.[110]

The fourth observation that may be made regarding the theological virtue of hope is that, though Christians hope in God and in God alone (as the only source of all good things), hope is also directed toward other creatures, especially other human beings. And this is so for a truly theological reason: they are made in the image and likeness of God and are destined to glory. Besides, the last end of humans is inseparable from that of humanity as a whole; Christian hope includes both final judgment and the resurrection of the dead, that is, the certainty that God will establish a new world in which his sovereignty and truth will be eternally present and recognized. In this state, humans will enjoy "a new earth in which righteousness dwells" (2 Pt 3:13).[111] Christians therefore look upon life in the world, on history as a whole, with hope. Josemaría writes: "Far from separating me from the things of this earth, hope draws me closer to these realities in a new way, a Christian way, which seeks to discover in everything the relation between our fallen nature and God, our Creator and Redeemer."[112]

At the same time, faith teaches us that humans are sinners and creatures and are not meant to become objects of an unconditional hope that may be attributed to God alone. Hence theological hope, far from drawing humans away from the world, from

---

109. This expression was often used by Josemaría to designate the different aspects of the apostolic lives of Christians.

110. On the resurrection of the dead as the resurrection of the life once lived, of the memory and narrative identity of the person, see *COH* 109–12.

111. See *COH* 118–20.

112. Escrivá, *Friends of God*, no. 208.

great projects and ambitions, vivifies all noble human hopes from within, giving us motives for optimism, avoiding idolatries and false expectations, purifying ambitions, directing all human projects and ventures to the glory of the creator. Christian hope thus offers a guarantee of objectivity in the performance of one's work and life in society: the Christian manages to avoid the disappointments and letdowns that accompany poor, passing, false, and disproportionate hopes; hoping in God alone as their ultimate end, Christian believers manage to direct their daily tasks towards the future, with work and effort. Thus hope as a theological virtue plays a decisive role in the sanctification of all human activities, especially work.[113]

Fifth, hope thus takes on a practical, everyday quality. It becomes

a patient, disciplined, confident waiting for and expectation of the Lord as our Savior. It demonstrates its living character by the steadfastness with which it waits, by the patient bearing of the tension between the now (as we walk by faith and not by sight, 2 Cor 5:7) and our future manner of life (Rom 8:25; 1 Thes 1:3). This waiting is something active, for it involves overcoming. Therefore those who hope are comforted and confident (2 Cor 5:8; 1 Thes 4:18; 2 Thes 2:16).... Genuine hope involves the abandonment of all calculations of the future, the humble recognition of the limits set to our knowledge, the submission of our wishes to the demands of the battle for life to which we have been appointed. The goal of our hope calls us to "watch and pray," to be as diligent and committed as the athlete who competes for an earthly crown and makes the necessary sacrifices (1 Cor 9:25). Hope becomes the motive for personal purity (1 Jn 3:3), spurring us on to strive for that holiness without which no one can see God (Heb 12:14). Filled with the longing to return home to his Lord, Paul seeks his glory in pleasing Christ (2 Cor 5:8–9). Hope requires us to hold fast our confession without wavering (Heb 10:23), and to be ready to give an answer to anyone who asks about that hope (1 Pt 3:15). Finally, New Testament hope is a joyful waiting (Rom 12:12) that gives courage and strength. It protects the inner self as a helmet protects the head (1 Thes 5:8). As a ship is safe when at anchor, our life is secured by the hope that binds us to Christ, our great High Priest who has entered the sanctuary (Heb 6:18–19).[114]

Sixth, in classical thought hope is considered a personal, individual passion. Following the Aristotelian explanation, the *bonum futurum arduum* (the absent arduous good) is made *possibile* simply through the investing of one's own energies of intelligence, psychic and physical effort, according to the ancient aphorism *nil difficile volenti*. In this case it is clear that the sum of good things that human hope can obtain will never exceed the sum of good things that are already present at the disposal of humanity. To get maximum benefit out of hope would become, therefore, a technical question, one of self-knowledge, with little space for love, risk, or self-giving. The difference introduced by Christian hope, however, is a radical one: the *bonum futurum arduum* becomes *possibile* not only through the effort of humans, or with the help of other people, but especially through the unexpected gift that comes from God, grace in all its different aspects. And because divine gifts come also through other persons, Christian hope becomes a truly social, communitarian, and relational virtue.

Thus humans hope not only in God but also in others; in the same way as they believe in God and trust others, they love God and love others. In effect, hope rests

---

113. See O'Callaghan, "La virtù della speranza e l'ascetica cristiana"; see also chapter 24.
114. *NIDNTTE* 2:188.

on faith (Rom 4:18; 5:1f., 15:13; Gal 5:5; Heb 6:11f.; 1 Pt 1:21), although it is directed toward invisible goods (Rom 8:24; Heb 11:1) and is nurtured by charity (Rom 5:5; 1 Cor 13:7).[115] Charles Péguy represents hope as a little girl being led by her two big sisters that are faith and charity.[116] In *Lumen Fidei* we read: "In union with faith and charity, hope propels us towards a sure future, set against a different horizon with regard to the illusory enticements of the idols of this world yet granting new momentum and strength to our daily lives."[117]

This brings us now to consider the theological virtue of charity.

The Infused Virtue of Christian Charity

Love in Classical Thought

Among ancient philosophers and writers love is considered as a lived reality, in principle as something good or useful to society, as an integral and inevitable aspect of human life.[118] Humans undeniably love one another and often hate one another. Perhaps it is more correct to say that they act and orient their lives according to the love present in their hearts, which is what in real terms drives and configures their lives. Their actions indicate where their will is pointing: they love as they are. Thus, according to the expression of Augustine, "pondus meum, amor meus" (my weight is my love).[119] And Aquinas says: "All agents act on the basis of a love."[120]

According to the Stoics, however, love between humans is not considered a virtue in the strict sense of the word because it easily becomes an occasion—indeed a source—of suffering, of bitterness and disturbance in their lives. Instead of contributing to the fulfillment of humans, love is often considered a brake and a limit on their development. Specifically the notion of *agapē*—free, self-giving love—is substantially absent from pre-Biblical Greek.[121] According to Seneca, "Compassion is a weakness, an illness; it is strange for the wise."[122] For the Stoics, it would be better on the whole to avoid loving because it is a source of suffering, affliction, and disgust. Humans are meant to reach their ultimate end, on the contrary, by detaching themselves progressively from everything they are surrounded by: material goods, social relationships, things they do, projects they undertake, other persons—and all that to obtain what they call *apatheia*, or indifference. The Stoic Cicero explains that the wise person is meant to live without *pathē*, or suffering, not under the sway of

---

115. Benedict XVI, in *Spe Salvi*, pars. 2–3, speaks of the continuity—almost an identity—between faith and hope. On this issue, see also F. Kerstiens, *Die Hoffnungsstruktur des Glaubens* (Mainz: Matthias-Grünewald, 1969).

116. See C.-P. Péguy, "On the Mystery of Hope, from 'The Portal of the Mystery of the Second Virtue,'" *Communio* (English ed.) 21 (1994): 504–25.

117. Francis and Benedict XVI, *Lumen Fidei*, par. 57.

118. Cicero writes: "We are moved by nature itself to love those whom we have generated, and from this derives among humans a reciprocal sense of interest for one another, on account of which it is necessary that a man, for the simple fact of being a man, is not extraneous to another one." *De finibus* IV, 19:62; 20:65.

119. Augustine, *Conf.* XIII, 9, 10.

120. Aquinas, *S.Th.* I-II, q. 28, a. 6, co. On this question, see Berdjaev, *Slavery and Freedom*, 55–57.

121. See Quell, in *TDNT* 1:21–36, s.v. ἀγάπη; *BDAG* 6, s.v. ἀγάπη; *NIDNTTE* 1:102–15, s.v. ἀγαπάω. "The noun *agapē* is only a late construction and occurs very rarely outside the Bible." *NIDNTTE* 1:102.

122. See Seneca, *De clementia* II, 3:4, 4.

the passions.[123] Seneca says that "our philosophers [the Stoics] repress affections and passions, while the peripatetics [followers of Aristotle] simply moderate them."[124] He adds that the dominion of the passions is what makes humans most like the gods.[125] According to Marcus Aurelius, humans must allow themselves to be guided by reason, not by desire, anger, compassion, or repentance. "The first precept," he says, "is not to allow yourself to be impressed by anything."[126]

Here we encounter the paradox of humans who seek fulfillment by not loving, by not giving or committing themselves. In effect, the Stoics held that humans should not dedicate their lives to demanding causes; they should not give, receive, or accept: they should not love. Just like faith and hope, love in classical thought is not considered a virtue because the creatures humans tend to love are not capable of returning them that love—perfect, infinite, gratuitous, committed—that they deeply long for. Only God, the Father of our Lord Jesus Christ, can do this. The God who is love is the one who makes charity possible as a virtue.

Charity as a Theological Virtue

Against the background of Stoicism, the theological virtue of charity stands out as a complete novelty. Charity is none other than the sharing by humans, through grace, of the flux of inter-Trinitarian love with which God loves himself, the mutual love between the Father and the Son, which is the Holy Spirit. Thomas Aquinas describes this as follows: "God does not act with mercy except out of charity, because he loves us as something of himself [amat nos tamquam aliquid sui]."[127] Having been created for love and called to love,[128] humans perceive in the act of charity the most faithful and expressive likeness to God.[129] It expresses in a sense the fullness of the Trinitarian image in humans. Christ, the perfection of the divine image, is the first to reveal charity: "While we were yet sinners, Christ died for us" (Rom 5:8); loving us first (1 Jn 4:10), he shows us through his saving mission the limitless love of God for creatures.[130] Three aspects of the virtue of charity may be noted.

Above all, the first commandment of the new Covenant (and of the old) is this: "You shall love the Lord your God with all your heart, and with all your soul, and with all your mind, and with all your strength" (Mk 12:30; see Lv 19:18). In effect, God may be considered the object of charity, being the only one who can fully satisfy the infinite capacity for love present in the human heart. This love is meant to define the entire existence of the Christian, and to endure forever: "So faith, hope, love abide, these three; but the greatest of these is love" (1 Cor 13:13).

Second, at a deeper level, it should be said that God is the fount or source of charity. The same love with which God gives himself to humans, through the Son in the Holy Spirit, is the origin of the charity with which humans love both God and neighbor. As Augustine said, "amamus Deum cum Deo" (we love God with God himself).[131]

123. See Cicero, *Tusc. Disp.* 4, 18:41f.   124. Seneca, *Ep.* 116.
125. Ibid., 73:13.   126. Marcus Aurelius, *Med.* IV, 49.
127. Aquinas, *S.Th.* II-II, q. 30, a. 2, ad 1.
128. See John Paul II, *Familiaris Consortio*, Apostolic Exhortation, November 22, 1981, par. 11.
129. See Aquinas, *De Caritate*, a. 1, ad 8.   130. See Jn 3:16; 1 Jn 3:16–4:9.
131. Augustine, *Sermo* 34, 2, 3; 169, 14.

In this sense we might say that God loves himself through humans. Aquinas puts it as follows: "The Father through the Holy Spirit loves not only the Son, but also himself and us."[132]

And third, charity should not be considered a mere movement of divine love before which humans behave as passive spectators, as if the love of God were something to be merely contemplated and admired. Through charity believers share to the very depths of their being in the power of the love of God, because they are divinized: with grace, nature and all the faculties of humans are elevated, and charity is received as an infused power or virtue with which they are made capable of loving God at a personal level, and loving others as God loves them. The virtue of charity, in fact, transforms humans, making them lovers of God. Augustine said it in a text already mentioned: "Deus facit nos dilectores suos" (God has made us his lovers).

Some Characteristics of the Virtue of Charity

The following six observations may be made on the dynamics of Christian charity. First, like faith and hope, the theological virtue of charity may also be considered a filial virtue because it consists precisely in a sharing, through the power of the Spirit, in the mutual, total, and eternal love that exists between the Father and the Son. In the *Catechism of the Catholic Church* we read: "The practice of the moral life animated by charity gives to the Christian the spiritual freedom of the children of God. He no longer stands before God as a slave, in servile fear, or as a mercenary looking for wages, but as a son responding to the love of him who 'first loved us' (1 Jn 4:19)."[133] The same *Catechism* cites the following text of Basil the Great: "If we turn away from evil out of fear of punishment, we are in the position of slaves. If we pursue the enticement of wages, ... we resemble mercenaries. Finally if we obey for the sake of the good itself and out of love for him who commands ... we are in the position of children."[134] Because the love by which Christians love God is a sharing in the life of the Trinity, this love is to be considered primordially filial rather than spousal.[135]

---

132. Aquinas, *S.Th.* I, q. 37, a. 2, ad 3.

133. *CCC* 1828.

134. Basil, *Regulae fusius tract.*, prol. 4, in *CCC* 1828.

135. In God is to be found both paternity and filiation—the Father generates the Son eternally—independently of the work of creation and salvation, as is taught by the Council of Nicaea (325). Thus God acts always *ad instar generationis*, whether *ad intra* or *ad extra*, and the fruit of sharing in divine life, which comes from the grace of baptism, has as a result *the real divine filiation of the believer* (see chapter 13). That God is Father and Christians, his sons and daughters, is not a symbolic way of speaking: God is Father because he has always had a Son; thus God is the origin of all paternity (see chapter 13, notes 90ff. and corresponding text). In that sense God defines what paternity is about. It is not necessary to affirm, however, that within the divine inner life there is a spousal relationship between the Persons, because the Son has no other origin than that of the Father. The spousal relationship, such as it is, belongs exclusively to the economy, that of creation and salvation, and may be used as a category or symbol to express certain aspects of the way in which God relates to humans and how humans can respond to his love. According to scripture, in fact, the spousal relationship between God and humanity is applied principally to the relationship between Christ and the Church, as Eph 5, Rv 21, and *LG*, no. 6, indicate, or between God and Jerusalem in the Old Testament (Hos 1–3). Human love—which counts on spousal love as its maximum and paradigmatic expression—may be used to speak of divine love because humans love God and others with the one heart. The spousal character can indicate the totality or unconditioned quality of the love between God and humans, as well as the supernaturally fruitful character of a life fully dedicated to God. To say, however, that each believer is a "spouse" of God (or of Christ)

We can observe here a singular convergence between Christian charity and the liberty of the children of God (Rom 8:21). This makes sense because the proper act of the free person is that of loving. It is possible to love freely only because we want to. Still, freedom is not a simple correlate of charity—in fact, the sinner is also free and responsible for his actions—but is expressed and fulfilled to the maximum degree in charity on account of the latter's constitutive orientation toward the good. In the words of Thomas Aquinas we can say, "Quanto aliquis plus habet de caritate, plus habet de libertate" (the more one has of charity, the more one has of liberty).[136]

Second, the virtue of charity brings the faculty of the human will to completion and perfection because the will, although open to the infinite good, is incapable of attaining that good with its own power. The presence of charity in the life of the Christian reveals the fact that the definitive vocation of humans is that of loving. "The fulfillment of all our works is love," writes Augustine. "This is our end; for this we run, towards this goal we advance; when we reach it, we shall find repose."[137] And elsewhere, "Pedes tui, caritas tua est" (Your feet are your love).[138]

Third, the subject of the virtue of charity is the other person, of course, but the virtue finds expression in two different and complementary ways, *according to the person loved*, God or humans as the case may be. In the first place, charity is expressed as love for God: "Charity loves God on account of God, and therefore the proper object of love is God."[139] Still, to "love God" does not mean that humans are capable of actually giving something to God. And this is for the simple reason that all they possess they have received from God in the first place. To "love God" means, rather, that humans can and must recognize that they have received all they have at their disposal from the creator of the universe. This might seem to be a poor love, but in real terms such recognition is the maximum expression of human dignity, the recognition of having been made in the image and likeness of God. Love for God is expressed in adoration, in joyful praise, in thanksgiving, in Christian cult (charity "is the principle of religion," Aquinas says),[140] in obedience to the will of God, in dedication to his service, in zeal for the things of God (Jn 2:17): "If you keep my commandments, you will abide in my love, just as I have kept my Father's commandments and abide in his love" (Jn 15:10). "That humans would dedicate themselves entirely to God, bonded with him through a spiritual union, is what truly belongs to charity," says Thomas Aquinas.[141]

Besides, the same charity infused by God into humans finds expression in gratuitous love for one's neighbor. But this is not a new or different virtue; rather it is the same virtue infused into humans by God, with which they direct their minds and hearts to God. God loves humans while making them at the same time capable of lov-

---

may give the impression of situating God and humans on the same plane in the origin of a new life. In other words, a real and non-symbolic reading of the spousal character of the love between God and humans could well condition divine sovereignty. In fact, the Old Testament does not accept the practice of pagan religions based on the marriage between gods and humans (see chapter 13), because this would compromise divine transcendence.

136. Aquinas, *In III Sent.* d. 29, q. 1, a. 8.   137. Augustine, *In Ep. Io. tr.* 10, 4.
138. Augustine, *Enn. in Ps. 33*, 2, 10.
139. Aquinas, *S.Th.* II-II, q. 23, a. 4, ad 2; q. 24, a. 1, ad 3.
140. Ibid., q. 89, a. 1, ad 1.
141. Ibid., q. 82, a. 2, ad 1.

ing; in that way he shows his limitless and free love for humanity through the lives of those elevated by grace. Thomas Aquinas says that "the charity with which we formally love our neighbor, is a kind of sharing in divine charity, which is God himself."[142] Humans are convinced they are loved by God, and, full of gratitude, amazement, and joy, they feel moved to love their neighbors, communicating to them the gifts received from God for them (Mt 10:8): "Gratis accepistis, gratis date" (You received without paying, give without pay).

The mutual bond between the two inseparable aspects of charity—love for God and for neighbor—is of course fundamental in Jesus' message,[143] and it is also an unequivocal sign of Christian perfection (Mt 5:43–48). "If any one says, 'I love God,' and hates his brother, he is a liar; for he who does not love his brother whom he has seen, cannot love God whom he has not seen. And this commandment we have from him, that he who loves God should love his brother also" (1 Jn 4:20f.). Like all human love, the exercise of charity toward another person is a finite, limited act because it is the act of a creature. It becomes Christian "charity," properly speaking, in that it is lived as it were "in a divine way," that is, as an unconditioned and faithful commitment to one's neighbor, just as God wants him or her to be, in spite of the refusals, offenses, sins, lack of recognition, or other limits on the part of the human loved. In that sense Christians strive to love—or rather they are moved to love—in the same way as they are loved by God, who "makes his sun rise on the evil and on the good, and sends rain on the just and on the unjust" (Mt 5:45). Recognizing the magnanimity of the love of God for humans, they feel moved to love their neighbor generously, magnanimously, perseveringly, unconditionally.[144] "The cause of the love of God is God; the measure of love is in not having any measure," said Bernard.[145]

For this reason the Gospel places special emphasis on the need to forgive those who have occasioned offense. In effect, the act of forgiving is perhaps the most sublime manifestation of Christian charity, that is, of the action of God, who loves humans through those who believe in him. If it is true that Christians through charity love their neighbor "in a divine way," this does not mean that such a love is strange or mysterious, unrecognizable to one who has not received such a gift.[146] In fact, in the early centuries of Christianity it was common to speak of the impact of the lived charity of Christians on pagans. The latter knew they were sincerely loved by believers; what they were unable to comprehend, however, was the hidden source of such a faithful, generous, and self-sacrificing love. We shall return to a consideration of the dynamics of lived Christian charity in chapter 22 when we consider the social nature of humans.

Fourth, charity is closely bound up with both faith and hope, as we have already seen.[147] In real terms, charity is expressed as faith, and faith as charity; the same mutual relationship may be also applied to hope and charity.

142. Ibid., q. 23, a. 2, ad 1.
143. See Mt 22:37–39; Mk 12:30f.; Lk 10:27.
144. "Magnanimity means greatness of spirit, a largeness of heart wherein many can find refuge. Magnanimity gives us the energy to break out of ourselves and be prepared to undertake generous tasks which will be of benefit to all." Escrivá, *Friends of God*, no. 80.
145. Bernard of Clairvaux, *De diligendo Deo*, I.
146. See Benedict XVI, *Deus Caritas Est*, Encyclical Letter, December 25, 2005, pars. 19–42.
147. Aquinas, *S.Th*. II-II, q. 17, aa. 7–8.

In effect, faith is bound up with charity in two ways. First, faith is an expression of charity. Paul says so: "For in Christ Jesus neither circumcision nor uncircumcision is of any avail, but faith working through love" (Gal 5:6). Without good works, faith is dead (Jas 2:26). But second, charity is also an expression of faith. The fact that we do not perceive the fruits of our acts of charity toward others with recognition and thanksgiving, always and immediately, is a sign that true charity is lived as an act of faith, of trust.[148] In effect, humans, when they give themselves to others, do not usually perceive the results right away. In that sense, in living charity they do not seek, as a subjective end, their own benefit; they simply wish to allow Christ to live in them and work through them: they wish to be an *alter Christus*, doing the will of the Father. Thus they seek not their own, directly perceived, benefit and gratification, but simply and solely that of the other. In effect, God moves believers so that their charity is truly *agapē*: gratuitous, generous, joyful and often discrete (Mt 6:3; Mk 12:42f.). Thus Christian charity consists primarily not so much in the imitation of the charitable behavior of others but in docility to the inspiration of the Holy Spirit, who has been poured out into our hearts (Rom 5:5). This docility helps us to think only of doing things for the glory of God (Mt 5:16);[149] it brings us to discover the true material and spiritual needs of our neighbors, one by one, and to help them refer their lives to God. Gregory Nazianzen observes that "the works of charity are the only ones that allow for no delay."[150]

Besides, while practicing this virtue humans are invited to follow Christ, always obedient to the Father with filial love, prepared to sacrifice himself on the cross. In this is expressed and revealed the greatest possible love for God and for neighbor (Jn 15:13): "The clearest proof of the reliability of Christ's love is to be found in his dying for our sake."[151] On the basis of the believer's union with the cross of Christ, human suffering is redeemed in that it becomes an occasion to manifest an unconditional love. At the same time, the close bond between suffering and love that the Stoics spoke about is inverted.[152] Suffering, when necessary, becomes the price willingly paid to show love for God and neighbor.

But it is also true that within lived charity we can find a clear expression of Christian hope, because humans, when they love, cannot but desire to be happy. With charity humans give themselves, that is, they exercise faith in not seeing the fruit of their donation. But at the same time they hope, dreaming of the prize, because they wish to be loved in return for their dedication. Thus the objective end of charity is to be found in humans' realization of ultimate beatitude. It is true that this reward, the prize of love, is never complete in this life but rather refers to the eschatological

---

148. "Put love where there is no love and you will find love." John of the Cross, *Letter to Mary of the Incarnation*, July 6, 1591.

149. See P. O'Callaghan, "Gloria de Dios."

150. Gregory Nazianzen, *Sermo 14 de pauperum amore*, 38.

151. Francis and Benedict XVI, *Lumen Fidei*, par. 16.

152. Suffering is often the price to pay for love. Josemaría Escrivá puts it as follows: "I am very fond of repeating these artless but very expressive verses: 'My life consists in loving / And, if with loving I'm familiar, / 'Tis because I've sorrowed much; / For there's no finer lover / Than one who's suffered much" (*Mi vida es toda de amor / y, si en amor estoy ducho, / es por fuerza del dolor, / que no hay amante mejor / que aquél que ha sufrido mucho*). *Friends of God*, no. 68.

promise: "Do not let your left hand know what your right hand is doing, so that your alms may be in secret; and your Father who sees in secret will reward you" (Mt 6:3f.). God himself in his infinite love is the promised prize; in real terms it is a prize already possessed but still under the shadow and provisionality of faith and hope.

Fifth, the role of charity is singular in Christian life because it is the perfection and form of all other virtues,[153] that "which unites them perfectly" (Col 3:14, "sundesmos tēs teleiotētos," literally, "the bond of perfection"). Charity directs human action toward God as the ultimate end because it unites the human will to the will of God. From this is derived the specificity of charity's role in Christian life: it brings all the virtues together as the fullness of the law, directing them symphonically, as it were.[154] Hence in real terms, without charity no virtue is Christian in the full sense of the word (1 Cor 13:2f.). Without charity, faith and hope remain dead or unformed (Jas 2:17), even though they do not disappear.[155] For humans in the state of grave sin it is true that the capacity to believe in God and to hope for his pardon stays intact. However, these are acts that on their own do not justify the sinner but, as we shall see, need the complement of the proper act of charity, moved by God's grace. Besides being a living expression of faith and hope, it should also be said that charity is actually what moves humans to believe (only love is worthy of faith: the content of the faith that is recited in the Nicene Creed is a summary of the history of God's love for humans, culminating in Christ)[156] and to hope (the "arduous good" that humans hope for is God, who gives himself, the one who is most lovable). Charity also becomes an essential part of the cardinal virtues: prudence, justice, fortitude, and temperance. Augustine explains this as follows: "To live well is nothing other than to love God with all one's heart, with all one's soul and with all one's efforts; from this it comes about that love is kept whole and uncorrupted (through temperance). No misfortune can disturb it (and this is fortitude). It obeys only God (and this is justice), and is careful in discerning things, so as not to be surprised by deceit or trickery (and this is prudence)."[157]

And sixth, charity is the source of all Christian virtues and attitudes. In contrast with "the works of the flesh," Paul speaks of the fruits of the Spirit in the life of the Christian: "The fruit of the Spirit is love, joy, peace, patience, kindness, goodness, faithfulness, gentleness, self-control; against such there is no law" (Gal 5:22f.). And Thomas Aquinas suggests the following twelve effects of charity: spiritual life, the observation of the commandments, protection against the adversary, beatitude, forgiveness, illumination, joy, peace, friendship, freedom, divine filiation, the expulsion of fear.[158]

---

153. See Aquinas, *S.Th.* II-II, q. 62, a. 4; q. 23, a. 8.
154. See Mt 22:36–40; Rom 13:10; Gal 6:2.
155. See Council of Trent, *DH* 1578.
156. See Francis and Benedict XVI, *Lumen Fidei*, pars. 26–28.
157. Augustine, *De moribus eccl. cath.* I, 25, 46, cited in *CCC* 1809.
158. See Aquinas, *S.Th.* III, q. 89, a. 6.

The Infused Moral Virtues

With baptism the virtues of faith, hope, and charity are infused into the believer. "In the justification of man," says the Council of Trent, "along with the remission of sin the justified receive through Jesus Christ to whom they belong, all these infused gifts: faith, hope and charity."[159] However, it is common doctrine that the moral virtues—in particular the four cardinal virtues, prudence, justice, fortitude, and temperance—are also infused along with sanctifying grace and the theological virtues.[160] These virtues have the same material object as the corresponding human ones, but, as supernatural virtues informed by charity, they give humans the capacity to carry out actions that surpass human energies alone and orient them to God as their last end. The infused virtues not only add the capacity to carry out supernatural acts[161] but confer a certain facility to live the virtues before God with a heroism that may be shown in diverse ways—in martyrdom, in celibacy, in virtuous actions carried out in a hidden way or in difficult circumstances—and also in unforeseen situations and among the simple, the very young, people with little Christian formation, and so on.[162] The unifying center of the infused virtues, as we saw earlier, is the virtue of charity, and their model is the life of Jesus Christ. As disciples of Christ the saints are (or at least should be) models of virtue, for they have known how to make the life of Christ present in their own lives, responding with refinement and integrity, with heroic perseverance, to the inspirations of the Holy Spirit.

The infused moral virtues direct human action to the proper use of created goods, according to their condition as children of God. Their purpose is not a merely human one—for example, that of self-mastery—as in the case of the Stoic description of virtue, but rather the full development of free will before God, who gives himself. Only by means of an ever-increasing self-possession, thanks to an equitable and sober use of created goods, can human freedom open itself easily to a total love, the gift of self, the service of others for the love of God.

Scholastic theologians have seen in the four cardinal infused virtues an important aspect of healing grace applied to the wounds inflicted on human nature by original sin (the *vulnera peccati*). Prudence perfects the intellect as it heals ignorance; justice perfects the will, healing it from malice; fortitude perfects the irascible appetite, providing healing for weakness (*infirmitas*); and finally, temperance perfects the concupiscible appetite, healing it from disorderly desires (*concupiscentia*).

---

159. Council of Trent, *DH* 1530.

160. See Aquinas, *S.Th.* I-II, q. 63, a. 3. On the infused moral virtues, see R. Garrigou-Lagrange, "Les vertus morales dans la vie intérieur," *Vie spirituelle* 41 (1934): 225–36; E. Niveut, "Les vertus morales surnaturelles," *Revue Apologétique* 59 (1934): 395–406; A. Lanfranco, *La necessità delle virtù morali infuse secondo S. Tommaso* (Casale Monferrato: Unione Tipografica Botto, Alessio & C., 1942). See also W. C. Mattison, "Can Christians Possess the Acquired Cardinal Virtues?," *Theological Studies* 72 (2011): 558–85.

161. See Aquinas, *S.Th.* I-II, q. 63, a. 4.

162. See ibid., q. 68, a. 1, ad 1; II-II, q. 159, a. 2, ad 1; III, q. 7, a. 2, ad 2.

The Virtues and Passions of Christ in the Christian

Christ is the most authentic and complete model of moral life for Christians.[163] But he is more than that. His life constitutes and contains the power and energy behind and within the moral lives of Christians, members of his body. That is, Jesus' life not only presents us with a constant example of lived virtue but also provides us with an abundance of grace to put it into practice. Indeed, the believer can say with Paul that "Christ lives in me" (Gal 2:20). His prudence, or correct judgment in carrying out his mission, taking into account all the circumstances, is a reflection of Christ's perfect charity, which seeks out the best way to speak of the Father to the hearts of humans and save them.[164] His justice is revealed in a special way in Jesus' redemption of humanity, giving back to the Father what is his due, what humans had taken away from their creator by sinning, then as a just judge of the living and the dead at the end of time,[165] and finally in the restoration of true divine justice to humanity and the world.[166] Fortitude, as a tension toward the arduous good, is shown in Jesus particularly in his zeal for the things of the Father, in his witness to the truth, in his firmness when correcting, in his resistance to temptation, in his exercise of patience, and especially in his death on the cross.[167] Temperance, finally, informs the entirety of the balanced and serene relationship between Jesus and created goods, as a living example that teaches us to aspire to greater goods.[168]

The moral life of Jesus also teaches how the passions, which he wished to fully take on along with human nature,[169] must be oriented toward the good according to God's design. The passions may become damaging only because of the disorder introduced by sin. Yet when they are made subject to reason through the will that is oriented toward the good, they are of considerable help in living upright lives because they manifest what God wants humans to do. A passion born under the light of faith and properly oriented by the will in the exercise of the moral virtues can come to express the intensity of the Christian's love for God. Jesus himself said that he had come "to cast fire upon the earth; and would that it were already kindled" (Lk 12:49). Christ, in taking on our passions, has healed them, making it possible for believers to dominate them and reorder them to God's service, making it possible, besides, to love both God and the world passionately.[170]

In real terms, the infused moral virtues are directly connected with the theological virtues. The *Catechism of the Catholic Church* relates them to faith, hope, and charity: "The theological virtues are the foundation of Christian moral activity; they animate it and give it its special character. They inform and give life to all the moral virtues."[171]

---

163. See John Paul II, *Veritatis Splendor*, pars. 6–27.

164. See Mk 7:37 and Acts 10:38; see also Lk 19:1–10.

165. See *COH* 138–42.   166. See Mt 3:15–27:4; Lk 23:47; Jn 16:11; 1 Jn 3:7.

167. See Mt 4:10; Jn 2:17 and 18:37; 1 Pt 2:21–23.   168. See Mt 6:33f.; Lk 21:34.

169. See Mt 23:13–33 and 26:38; Lk 22:15; Jn 2:15 and 11:36.

170. This is the title of a homily by Josemaría Escrivá: "Passionately Loving the World" (October 8, 1967), in *Conversations with Mgr Escrivá* (Dublin: Four Courts 1968), nos. 113–23.

171. *CCC* 1813; see *CCC* 1841, 2095.

The Gifts of the Holy Spirit

As we already observed, scripture presents the Holy Spirit as the source of the life of grace in the sanctified creature.[172] This role is also made present in the Church's liturgy and in theological tradition, which speaks of the Spirit as "fons vivus, ignis, caritas" (living fountain, fire, and love).[173] Spiritual theology and the Church Fathers underscore a special relationship between docility to the Holy Spirit and the consolidation of the life of grace. However, this docility may not be considered a mere pre-existing human disposition with which people more easily welcome God's grace, because docility is made possible by grace itself, specifically by the seven gifts of the Holy Spirit.[174] "The moral life of Christians is sustained by the gifts of the Holy Spirit. These are permanent dispositions which make man docile in following the promptings of the Holy Spirit."[175]

The Gifts of the Holy Spirit

The notion of the gifts of the Holy Spirit is suggested in scripture. The just man in the Old Testament says to God: "teach me to do your will, for you are my God! Let your good spirit lead me on a level path" (Ps 143:10). Likewise, according to the New Testament the Spirit guides believers in their journey to the heavenly fatherland: "For all who are led by the Spirit of God are sons of God ... and if children, then heirs, heirs of God and fellow heirs with Christ" (Rom 8:14, 17). Yet the scriptural basis for the gifts is to be found in a well-known passage from the prophet Isaiah (Is 11:1-3):[176]

---

172. See chapters 5–6 and 13, notes 136ff. and corresponding text.

173. From the hymn "Veni Creator Spiritus."

174. On the theology of the gifts of the Holy Spirit, see the classic work of the seventeenth-century author John of St. Thomas, *The Gifts of the Holy Spirit*, edited by W. Farrell (London: Sheed and Ward, 1950). See also J. Biard, *Les dons du Saint-Esprit: Dons, charismes, fruits, béatitudes d'après saint Thomas d'Aquin et les Épîtres de saint Paul* (Avignon: Aubanel, 1930); R. Bernard, "Le vertu infuse et le don du Saint-Esprit," *Vie spirituelle* 42 (1935): 65–90; J. De Blic, "Pour l'histoire de la théologie des dons avant Saint Thomas," *Revue d'Ascétique et de Mystique* 22 (1946): 117–79; H. Vignon, *De virtutibus et donis vitae supernaturalis* (Rome: Pontificia Universitas Gregoriana, 1953); M. Llamera, "Unidad de la teología de los dones según santo Tomás," *Revista Española de Teología* 15 (1955): 3–66, 217–79; G. Bardy, F. Vandenbroucke, S. Rayez, and M.-M. Labourdette, "Dons du Saint-Esprit," in *Dictionnaire de Spiritualité* 3 (1957): 1579–1641; G. Kostko, *Doni dello Spirito Santo e vita morale: San Tommaso nella Somma teologica* (Rome: Angelicum, 1997); O. Lottin, "Les dons du Saint-Esprit du XIIe siècle à l'époque de St. Thomas d'Aquin," in Lottin, *Psychologie et morale aux XIIe et XIIIe siècles* (Leuven: Abbaye du Mont César, 1949), 3:329–456; Lottin, "Les dons du Saint-Esprit de St. Thomas d'Aquin à Pierre Auriol," *Psychologie et morale aux XIIe et XIIIe siècles*, 4:667–736; M.-M. Philipon, *Les dons du Saint-Esprit* (Paris: Desclée de Brouwer, 1964); M. Schmaus, *Katholische Dogmatik*, vol. III/2: *Christi Fortleben und Fortwirken in der Welt bis zu seiner Wiederkunft: Die göttliche Gnade* (Munich: M. Hueber, 1951), § 195; S. M. Ramírez and V. Rodríguez Rodríguez, *Los dones del Espíritu Santo* (Madrid: 1978); Auer, *Das Evangelium der Gnade*, 132–37; P. J. Wadell, *Friends of God: Virtues and Gifts in Aquinas* (New York: P. Lang, 1991); M. Turner, *The Holy Spirit and Spiritual Gifts: Then and Now* (Carlisle: Paternoster, 1996); R. Gerardi, *Alla sequela di Gesù: Etica delle beatitudini, doni dello Spirito, virtù* (Bologna: Dehoniane, 1998); J. Sesé, "Los dones del Espíritu Santo y el camino hacia la santidad," *Scripta Theologica* 30 (1998): 531–57; Lorda, *Antropología teológica*, 510–15.

175. *CCC* 1830.

176. In this text, "the Spirit of Yahweh gives the king the skills needed to reign. They are listed in three pairs." J. D. W. Watts, *Isaiah 1–33*, in *WBC* 24:209. The pairs are "wisdom and understanding," "counsel and might [or heroism]," and "knowledge and fear of the Lord."

There shall come forth a shoot from the stump of Jesse, and a branch shall grow out of his roots. And the Spirit of the Lord shall rest upon him, the spirit of wisdom and understanding, the spirit of counsel and might, the spirit of knowledge and the fear of the Lord. And his delight shall be in the fear of the Lord. He shall not judge by what his eyes see, or decide by what his ears hear.

The text of the Vulgate translation, around which an important part of the theology of the gifts developed, also mentions the gift of piety instead of speaking for the second time of the gift of fear. The neo-Vulgate, however, omits it. In any case, Isaiah 11 has traditionally received a messianic interpretation, applicable in the first place to Christ. In the *Catechism of the Catholic Church* we read: "The seven gifts of the Holy Spirit are wisdom, understanding, counsel, fortitude, knowledge, piety, and fear of the Lord. They belong in their fullness to Christ, Son of David. They complete and perfect the virtues of those who receive them. They make the faithful docile in readily obeying divine inspirations."[177]

Besides, the gifts are presented as signs of the missionary anointing carried out by the Spirit; the capacity to anoint is possessed fully by Christ (that is, "the Anointed One") and shared in by Christians with the gifts of the Spirit.[178] The Fathers speak of the existence of the gifts of the Spirit, though the understanding of the gifts was not theologically developed until medieval theologians linked them with the seven-fold messianic gifts that find expression in the Church's liturgy.

The Theology of the Gifts

Thomas Aquinas offers the following definition of the gifts of the Holy Spirit: "They are supernatural habits infused by God into the powers of the soul so that the person can promptly and easily receive the lights and movements of the Holy Spirit."[179] And Pope Leo XIII, in his encyclical on the Holy Spirit, writes: "The just man, that is to say he who lives the life of divine grace, and acts by the fitting virtues as by means of faculties, has need of those seven gifts which are properly attributed to the Holy Spirit. By means of them the soul is furnished and strengthened so as to obey more easily and promptly His voice and impulse."[180] In effect, the gifts are experienced as the fruit of a special presence of the Spirit within the soul in grace. They provide humans with a kind of intuitive affinity (sensitivity, docility, promptness) for divine things, as well as the action of the same Spirit as the motor of the acts that the gifts inspire. The Spirit moves humans to act "ultra modum humanum" (beyond the human way of doing things).[181] Through the gifts humans in the state of grace easily overcome their natural resistance to pain and sacrifice; they judge situations and happenings with a supernatural logic that provides a more direct union with the will of God than could be obtained by the exercise of the virtue of prudence, often to the point of heroism and martyrdom.[182] Jesus gives an example of this when he tells

177. CCC 1831.
178. See John Paul II, *Dominum et Vivificantem*, pars. 15 and 16.
179. Aquinas, *S.Th.* I-II, q. 68, a. 4, co. On Aquinas's theology of the gifts, see *S.Th.* I-II, q. 68.
180. Leo XIII, *Divinum Illud Munus*, par. 9.
181. See Aquinas, *S.Th.* I-II, q. 68, a. 2.
182. See John Paul II, *Veritatis Splendor*, pars. 90–94.

his disciples, "You will be dragged before governors and kings for my sake, to bear testimony before them and the Gentiles. When they deliver you up, do not be anxious how you are to speak or what you are to say; for what you are to say will be given to you in that hour; for it is not you who speak, *but the Spirit of your Father speaking through you*" (Mt 10:18–20).

What do the gifts add to the virtues? We may respond in technical terms by saying that in the case of the virtues, the causal rapport between divine and created action is one of "concursus," that is, between first causality and second causality, whereas in the case of the gifts the relationship is more one of principal and instrumental causality. In the exercise of the gifts, God, besides moving creatures according to their nature, guides them: the initiative is taken by the Holy Spirit, and humans correspond to it by consent.[183] The virtues do not spare humans the effort of thinking things through rationally, the need to overcome doubt or ponder judgment, the suffered choice of recognizing the good and putting it into practice, that is, the effort required to exercise the virtue of prudence. The gifts, however, carry within them a kind of innate prudence that brings the believer to perceive the good clearly and practice it rapidly with docility and ease, in spite of the obstacles. It may be said that the gifts give believers a kind of operative, filial "connatural-ness" for the things of their Father, God (Rom 8:14). In the human life journey, perhaps the virtues may be compared with the oars of a boat and the gifts to the wind in the sails. Thomas refers specifically to the relationship between the gifts and the *sequela Christi*, discipleship of Christ, especially as regards the cross: "The virtues are ordered simply to carrying out the good, whereas the gifts are ordained to conform humans to Christ, especially with respect to what he suffered, because in his Passion in the first place the gifts shine out."[184]

The Content of the Seven Gifts of the Holy Spirit

The gifts of the Holy Spirit are traditionally seven.[185] They are usually listed as: wisdom, understanding, counsel, fortitude, knowledge, piety, and fear of the Lord. In an approximate way, according to some authors, the first four are said to perfect the intellect, the other three to strengthen the will. Their content, according to the commentary of Thomas Aquinas in different parts of the *Summa Theologiae* and elsewhere, is as follows:

• With the gift of *wisdom* believers obtain a loving knowledge of God as the cause of all things and human actions are more easily directed toward him, who is the ultimate end of human life. Scripture establishes an opposition between earthly and divine wisdom (Jas 3:13–18; 1 Cor 2:6–16). With this gift God gives believers "the ability

---

183. "Dona sunt quidam habitus perficientes hominem ad hoc quod prompte sequatur instinctum Spiritus Sancti, sicut virtutes morales perficiunt vires appetitivas ad obediendum rationi." Aquinas, *S.Th.* I-II, q. 68, a. 4, co.

184. "Ista dona traduntur in Scriptura secundum quod fuerunt in Christo, ut patet Isaiae XI; dixerunt quod virtutes ordinantur simpliciter ad bene operandum; sed dona ordinantur ad hoc ut per ea conformemur Christo, praecipue quantum ad ea quae passus est, quia in passione eius praecipue huiusmodi dona resplenduerunt." *S.Th.* I-II, q. 68, a. 1, co.

185. See the catechesis of Pope Francis on the gifts of the Holy Spirit in his audiences from April 9 to June 11, 2014.

to distinguish between spirits" (1 Cor 12:10), the capacity to perceive what is eternal, to make a just evaluation of what happens around them in the light of faith.

• The gift of *understanding* favors a deeper intelligence of the mysteries of faith and helps us to recognize what is properly ordered to them. Through the gift of intellect the believer comes to know God not only in "in a mirror dimly" (1 Cor 13:12), but with a foretaste and anticipation of heaven; Thomas considers this gift as the highest one for theologians, although Bonaventure considered that this place is occupied by wisdom.

• The gift of *counsel* allows us to recognize in a special way divine providence, the role created things play in God's plans and how to orient them to his glory and our salvation. Science continues and completes the gifts of intellect and wisdom. It facilitates the integration of all forms of knowledge in relation to divine revelation, what Bonaventure called the "reductio omnium artium ad theologiam,"[186] for "the Lord is a God of knowledge, and by him actions are weighed" (1 Sm 2:3).

• The gift of *knowledge* provides humans with a special docility to understand what the will of God is in each and every moment, along with whatever is necessary for our salvation and that of others; it is the gift of risk and action, which guides the practical decisions of believers: "I have counsel and sound wisdom, I have insight, I have strength. By me kings reign, and rulers decree what is just; by me princes rule, and nobles govern the earth" (Prv 8:14–16).

• The gift of *fortitude* gives humans strength in circumstances in which doing the will of God in obtaining the arduous good requires true heroism, in the struggle against temptations, against fear, persevering in good works until the end of one's life, also with the possibility of martyrdom. The Psalmist often repeats that God himself is his strength (Pss 18:1, 22:20, 28:7, 59:10, 118:14).

• By the gift of *piety* the Holy Spirit leads Christians to an awareness of their divine condition as children of God, bringing them to live every moment in a filial way.

• Finally, the gift of the *fear of God* leads believers to firmly abhor sin. It is the fruit of filial reverence for God, which rejects everything that separates us from our eternal Father, all-powerful and eternal, before whom creatures are but a breath (Job 4:9, 7:7; Pss 39:6, 7, 12; 90:9; 94:11; 144:4). The believer in the Old Testament is defined as the one who "fears the Lord" (Sir 3:7, 6:17, 15:1, 21:7, 32:18, 34:16), although in the New Testament John tells us, "One who fears is not yet perfect in charity" (1 Jn 4:18). The fear of the Lord is considered the beginning of all wisdom, that is, of all true knowledge of God (Prv 1:7, 9, 10; 15:33). It is assumed but not eliminated by filial love and piety (1 Jn 4:17f.).

186. See chapter 1, note 78.

Justification, Merit, Experience, and Mediations

> Where there is necessity, there is no liberty; where there is no liberty, there is no merit; where there is no merit there is no judgment.   BERNARD OF CLAIRVAUX[1]

> God when he rewards our acts crowns his own gifts.   AUGUSTINE[2]

> Grace changes us and the change is painful.   FLANNERY O'CONNOR[3]

> Grace, a divine compulsion, both gentle and affectionate.   JOSEMARÍA ESCRIVÁ[4]

In the preceding chapters we considered God's love for us in terms of "uncreated grace" and God as one who gives himself to humans, adopting them as his children in the Holy Spirit. Then we looked into the dynamics of the supernatural organism, fruit of God's action, which remains stably present and active in believers; this is often referred to as "created grace." But another important issue still needs to be considered, an articulated and complex one that refers to the relationship between divine grace and free human response, what we have called the personal-existential aspect of the life of grace. Catholic doctrine speaks openly of a human "cooperation" with grace.[5] Historically, however, the use of the term "cooperation" has been called into question, especially in Lutheran theology, because it would seem to compromise the

---

1. Bernard of Clairvaux, *De gratia et lib. arb. II*, 5: "Ubi necessitas est, libertas non est; ubi libertas non est, nec meritum ac per hoc nec iudicium."

2. Augustine, *Epist.* 194, 5:9.

3. F. O'Connor, *The Habit of Being: Letters* (New York: Farrar, Straus and Giroux, 2007), 307;

4. Escrivá, *Letter 2.2.1945*, no. 22, cited in A. Vázquez de Prada, *The Founder of Opus Dei*, vol. 2: *God and Daring* (New York: Scepter, 2003), 424n76. "Una coacción divina, suave y cariñosa."

5. Several Church documents speak of the "cooperation" of humans with divine grace. See *DH* 248, 1525, 1529, 1535, 1554, 1559, 2354, 3009, 3756. In documents from Vatican Council II, the term "cooperation" is used principally to explain the dynamics of structural relationships within the Church but not with God. Still, cooperation with divine grace is mentioned in *LG*, no. 61, referring to Mary, and in *Apostolicam Actuositatem*, par. 11), referring to Christian spouses.

absolute transcendence and freedom of God's action by the created (and sinful) actions of humans. Although important agreements have been established in the area of grace in recent times, some tensions remain between Lutherans and Catholics on this point, which we shall consider first. Then we shall examine a series of issues in which the relationship between grace and freedom emerges: the process of justification, what Thomas Aquinas calls the effect of "operative grace" in humans, then, the doctrine of merit, which he calls the effect of "cooperative grace,"[6] which also involves the question of the value of "good works." Then we shall consider the question of the experience of grace and its role in the fully free and human acceptance of God's gifts, principally with respect to the interior response of humans. Finally, we shall reflect on created mediations of grace and their role in the process of reception of God's gifts in the external ambit of human life. Perhaps we can sum up the content of this chapter with the following affirmation: *humans respond to divine grace with their whole being, with their whole life, body, and spirit.* That is to say, the freedom of believers before grace is human freedom, incarnate freedom, created freedom.

Grace and Freedom in Lutheran-Catholic Dialogue

The question of the relationship between grace and freedom was of considerable importance in the time of the Protestant Reformation and in the ensuing period. Classical Lutheranism rejected in general terms the notion of the free human will with respect to grace because, when faced with the omnipotence of God who gives himself, man is but a poor and sinful creature, incapable of opposing divine power. The exercise of free human will—"cooperation"—would be restricted to the created or profane order, to the relationship between human beings.[7] That is to say, humans may be free before creatures but are not so before God.

Catholic theology, however, considered Lutheran insistence on the sinful perversion of humans as excessive, seeing in it a negative and superficial judgment on humanity and on the work of creation as a whole, or perhaps as an expression of a kind of divine arbitrariness, which shows itself as the passivity of humans before God. Lutherans, on their side, held that Catholics insisted too much on the goodness of the created world and in particular on the value of "good works," entrusting to the latter the successful outcome of their own salvation rather than placing their trust unreservedly in their creator and savior, making divine grace a kind of add-on to human nature and the free human being a "cooperator" of God in the fullest sense of the word.[8]

Christianity, though it preaches the good news of redemption and of the forgiveness of sin, reveals at the same time the total dependence of humans on God as creatures and sinners. It is true that humans can act freely before other creatures, in the sense that they can choose one thing or another, freely give life to a project along with

6. See Aquinas, *S.Th.* I-II, q. 113, prol.

7. On this issue, see O'Callaghan, *Fides Christi*; Mateo-Seco, *M. Lutero*, 167–212. Lutherans, in fact, speak of "two kingdoms," the divine and the human.

8. Luther, in his work *De Servo Arbitrio*, states: "Thus the human will is placed between two as a beast. If God rides, it wills and goes where God wants.... If Satan rides it, then it wills and goes where Satan wants. The will cannot choose or search for one or the other rider." *WA* 18:635. See also the Lutheran *Formula Concordiae, Solida Declaratio* II, 59, which compares the human being before grace to a stone.

other people, take and use God's good creatures; in that sense humans "co-operate" with one another. Still, the action of humans before God (*coram Deo*), creator and redeemer, is objectively different from that before creatures, because they have received all they have from God, including the very faculty of acting freely. And because God's action is incommensurable with that of humans, the term "cooperation" in the context of grace seems to be misplaced. Even the expression "grace *and* freedom" may be misconstrued, because the action of God and the free action of creatures are simply incommensurable with one another. Perhaps we may say that before divine love, which gives itself, humans are free in the sense that they can recognize God's grace as a good and accept it—or perhaps they can refuse it. By definition, those who receive do not contribute anything to themselves: they can receive the divine gift, or they can refuse it; they can open their hearts, or they can close them. This is what Luther intended to say when he stated that in the ambit of grace, the nonfreedom of humans is the *cardo rerum*, a critical element of his doctrine.[9]

An important question clearly remains open. At an ontological and existential level, we need to insist on the distinction between divine action and that of the creature because they are, respectively, the action of the creator and the creature. Still we may ask: do believers, while trusting ultimately in God as their savior, have to renounce all trust in and complacency toward creatures, toward themselves and their sentiments, toward other people, toward the rest of creation? Or, even more specifically: can the concrete choices that humans carry out between different created things, through which they exercise in a limited though authentic way their freedom and dominion and build up the human city, be separated from human action before the creator and his grace? Might not an excessive distinction between receiving grace, on the one hand (understood as an essentially unfree action), and human action before creatures, on the other (an essentially free action), involve the danger of an excessive separation between Christian life and human life? Might it not pave the way toward secularization?

To deal with this theme adequately, let us consider two basic aspects of the life of grace in which freedom is involved: justification and merit.

The Process of Justification

The moment in which grace is infused into the believer, for sanctification and forgiveness of sin, is normally called "justification."[10] The process of justification is

---

9. Luther, *De Servo Arbitrio* (WA 18:786).

10. On the topic of justification, see O'Callaghan, *Fides Christi*. We have already considered the 1999 agreement between Lutherans and Catholics (*JDJ*). Recent bibliography on the issue, understandably, is quite ample. Among other works, see P. Holc, *Un ampio consenso sulla dottrina della giustificazione: Studio sul dialogo teologico cattolico–luterano* (Rome: Pontificia Università Gregoriana, 1999); A. Birmelé, "Uniti nella giustificazione," *Il Regno—Documenti* 45 (2000): 127–36; Cavanaugh, "A Joint Declaration?; J. Ratzinger, "Wie weit trägt der Konsens über die Rechtfertigungslehre?," *Communio* (Deutsche Ausg.) 29 (2000): 424–37; A. Maffeis, "Giustificazione," in *Teologia*, edited by G. Barbaglio, G. Bof, and S. Dianich (Cinisello Balsamo: San Paolo, 2002), 721–37; M. Root, "Aquinas, Merit and Reformation Theology after the Joint Declaration on the Doctrine of Justification," *Modern Theology* 20, no. 1 (2004): 5–22; C. J. Malloy, *Engrafted into Christ: A Critique of the Joint Declaration* (New York: Peter Lang, 2005); J. Piper, *The Future of Justification: A Response to N. T. Wright* (Wheaton, Ill.: Crossway Books, 2007); Dunn, "Paul and Justification by Faith"; Wright, *Justification* (which was written as a response to Piper). See chapter 12, notes 93ff. and corresponding text.

described by the Council of Trent as "a transition from the state in which man is born a son of the first Adam, to the state of grace and adoption as sons of God, by means of the second Adam, Jesus Christ, our Savior."[11]

Two Aspects of Justification: The Forgiveness of Sin and the Sanctification of Humans

The process of justification consists of two inseparable stages: the forgiveness of sin and the sanctification of the person. Classical Lutheranism often limited justification to the first moment, forgiveness, understood as a simple non-imputation of the offense by God, whereas the real sanctification of the sinner through the infusion of divine life was excluded or would follow at a later moment. The fear of Lutherans was a legitimate one: admitting an intelligent and free cooperation on the part of humans could conceivably compromise the full gratuitousness of justification, and therefore the transcendence of God over creatures. However, the difficulty with the Lutheran position is twofold. First, in the conviction that humans always remain in sin (which is simply not imputed) and enter into a relationship with God through a pure "fiducial faith." It should be noted, however, that an important part of more recent Lutheran theology, on the basis of important texts of Luther, has recuperated the double aspect of justification,[12] as well as a greater involvement of free human action in the acceptance of God's gifts. Second, it is clear that a simple non-imputation of sin does not reflect Biblical teaching to the full. Commenting on the expression "Love covers a multitude of sins" (1 Pt 4:8; see Tb 12:9; Ps 84:3; Prv 10:12; Jas 5:20), Thomas Aquinas observes: "It is said that love covers sins before God who sees all things: this can only mean that he actually destroys them."[13]

Four Stages in the Process of Justification

Aquinas spends most of his treatise on justification examining the different stages of the process of humans being justified.[14] He insists on the fact that justification requires not only the grace-filled action of God but also, inseparably, the movement of free will on the part of humans, because grace, though prior, acts with full respect to human nature.[15] The process consists, in the first place, of a movement of faith toward God (a *conversio ad Deum*), and this begins and continues exclusively on the basis of divine grace.[16] As a result, grace itself brings about in humans a reaction against sin (a *destestatio*), inclining them to move away from their sinful behavior for the simple reason that it offends God.[17] These two stages involve not only the primacy

---

11. *DH* 1524.

12. See chapter 14, notes 72ff. and the corresponding text.

13. Aquinas, IV *Sent*. d. 22, q. 1, a. 1, ad 2. "The meaning of 'cover' in its context in 1 Peter is neither to conceal sin illegitimately (as in Ps 31:5, LXX), nor precisely to atone for it, but rather to obliterate it or make it disappear." J. R. Michaels, *1 Peter*, in *WBC* 49:247.

14. See Aquinas, *S.Th.* I-II, q. 113, aa. 3–8.

15. "Deus autem movet omnia secundum modum uniuscuiusque.... Homo autem secundum propriam naturam habet quod sit liberi arbitrii.... Ita [Deus] infundit donum gratiae iustificantis, quod etiam simul cum hoc movet liberum arbitrium ad donum gratiae acceptandum, in his qui sunt huius motionis capaces." Ibid., a. 3, co.

16. See Aquinas, *S.Th.* I-II, q. 113, a. 4.

17. "Oportet quod mens humana, dum iustificatur, per motum liberi arbitrii recedat a peccato, et accedat

of grace in the process of justification but also the fact that the first movement of the will takes place toward God, while the second, the consequence, is against sin. The reason for this is simple: humans detest sin "quia est contra Deum" (because it is against God).[18] Contrition for sin, in other words, has a supernatural origin and motive; it cannot be considered as a simple reaction to a sense of guilt, as disappointment due to failure, to sorrow, or to remorse stemming from the sinful act and its tangible deleterious effects. Grace is what moves the will toward God and against sin. On its own, however, the will is incapable of achieving this. At the same time, humans can, freely and responsibly, resist the inclination that God places in their souls and shut themselves off to the grace of justification.

Thus, for Thomas Aquinas, the stages of the process of justification[19] are four: the donation of grace; the "motus liberi arbitrii in Deum" (the movement of free will toward God); the "motus liberi arbitrii in peccatum" (the movement of free will against sin); and the effective forgiveness of sin by the infusion of grace.[20]

Other Issues Concerning Justification

Aquinas mentions three further issues when studying the topic of justification. In the first place, he says that it is an instantaneous process because it is a work of God, who gives grace.[21] This does not mean that the process of justification may not well be the fruit of an extended preparation lasting for long period of time, which always takes place under the impulse of actual grace.[22]

Second, in comparing the works of creation and justification, Thomas considers the latter as God's greatest work on earth,[23] "secundum quantitatem absolutum" (according to absolute quantity), because it is a process in which the *terminus ad quem*, the point of arrival, is none other than the divinization of the human being.[24] In fact, "the effect of grace in one person is greater than the good of nature of the whole universe."[25] He adds, however, that from the point of view of the *terminus a quo*, the point of departure, creation is a greater divine work than justification because its starting

---

ad iustitiam." This takes place "secundum detestationem et desiderium.... Oportet igitur quod in iustificatione impii sit motus liberi arbitrii duplex, unus quo per desiderium tendat in Dei iustitiam; et alius quo detestetur peccatum." Ibid., a. 5, co.

18. "Propter hoc enim ille qui iustificatur, detestatur peccatum, quia est contra Deum, unde motus liberi arbitrii in Deum, praecedit naturaliter motum liberi arbitrii in peccatum, cum sit causa et ratio eius." Aquinas, *S.Th.* I-II, q. 113, a. 8, co.

19. See Aquinas, *S.Th.* I-II, q. 113, aa. 6–8.

20. The teaching of Trent on justification is similar to that of Thomas in many respects. From the VI session on justification we read that the faithful "are disposed to that justice when, aroused and assisted by divine grace, receiving faith by hearing, they are freely moved toward God, believing that to be true which has been divinely revealed and promised, and this especially, that the sinner is justified by God through his grace, 'through the redemption which is in Christ Jesus.'" *DH* 1526.

21. See Aquinas, *S.Th.* I-II, q. 113, a. 6. See also Flick, *L'attimo della giustificazione*.

22. In effect, as Thomas notes, the action of the human will requires time and deliberation. Such deliberation, however, "non est de substantia iustificationis, sed via in iustificationem." Aquinas, *S.Th.* I-II, q. 113, a. 6, ad 1.

23. See Aquinas, *S.Th.* I-II, q. 113, a. 9.

24. Ambrose writes: "Non minor est novas rebus dare quam mutare naturas." *De mysteriis*, 53.

25. "Sed bonum gratiae unius maius est quam bonum naturae totius universi." Aquinas, *S.Th.* I-II, q. 113, a. 9, ad 2.

point is ontological nothingness. Besides, he affirms that both creation and justification are greater divine works than glorification because justifying grace makes humans already *dignus gloriae*, fully worthy of eternal glory. Glorification is the natural blossoming of justification.

Third and finally, Thomas teaches that justification is not in a strict sense a miraculous work. This is so because it is not "supra naturam" (above nature), as miracles are, because "anima humana naturaliter est gratiae capax" (the human soul is naturally capable of grace).[26] Miraculous works, on the contrary, go beyond nature, surpassing its normal rules and laws. Besides, with respect to the visibility of the miracle and the admiration it may produce, the process of justification is normally something quite simple and discrete, prepared for over a long period and usually lived without extraordinary exterior manifestations. As an exception to this rule Thomas mentions the conversion of Paul.[27] In effect, the miracle may well occasion a powerful experience; still, the work of justification is greater than any miracle because in it humans are divinized, whereas in the miracle nature is simply modified, and perhaps only temporarily. Besides, Aquinas adds that the purpose of miracles is one of preparing the way to conversion or of manifesting the work of justification. Thus Jesus explains in the Gospel that the visible miracle reveals an invisible justification (Mt 9:6).

Grace, Merit, and Good Works

The doctrine of merit—that humans can merit grace from God—has been taught by Church Fathers such as Tertullian and Augustine, was common during the Middle Ages, and has long been considered to be Catholic teaching par excellence.[28] Though Catholic theologians taught that salvation was the fruit of grace, they also spoke of merit, as if humans could add something to their own supernatural gifts through their own strengths. And this, understandably, did not seem correct to Protestants. In fact, the Protestant Reformation is often presented first and foremost as a battle against the doctrine of merit.[29] Yet it should be noted that the doctrine of merit is not a secondary one for Catholics. According to Flick and Alszeghy, "The Catholic doctrine of merit ... is not a mere marginal add-on to the gospel of grace, because it constitutes one of its most central aspects. Without it, it would be impossible to understand this gospel."[30]

---

26. See Aquinas, *S.Th.* I-II, q. 113, a. 10.

27. Thomas, following Augustine, says: "Quando homo convertatur ad Deum, primo quidem conversione imperfecta, et postmodum ad perfectam deveniat, quia caritas inchoata meretur augeri, ut aucta mereatur perfici." On other occasions, however, "Tam vehementer Deus animam movet ut statim quandam perfectionem iustitiae assequatur," as in the case of Paul. See ibid., a. 10, co.

28. On the doctrine of merit in an ecumenical context, see P.-Y. Émery, *Le Christ, notre récompense: Grâce de Dieu et responsabilité de l'homme* (Neuchatel: Delachaux, 1962); Y.-J. Congar and V. Vajta, "Mérite," in *Vocabulaire œcuménique*, edited by Y.-J. Congar (Paris: Cerf, 1970), 231–79; J. D. Quinn, "The Scriptures on Merit," in Anderson, Murphy, and Burgess, *Justification by Faith*, 82–93; W. D. Lynn, *Christ's Redemptive Merit: The Nature of its Causality* (Rome: Libreria Editrice Gregoriana, 1962); J. P. Wawrykow, *God's Grace and Human Action: Merit in the Theology of Thomas Aquinas* (Notre Dame, Ind.: University of Notre Dame Press, 1995).

29. According to the *Realenzyklopädie für protestantische Theologie und Kirche*, 3rd ed. (Leipzig: Hinrichs, 1908), 20:506, "The Reformation was principally a battle against the doctrine of merit."

30. Flick and Alszeghy, *Il vangelo della grazia*, § 139.

Merit and Eschatological Reward

Protestants for the most part accepted the Biblical doctrine of a future "reward," which was centered on eternal life, understood in a strictly eschatological sense, as the fruit of the divine promise, which will be obtained only in the future.[31] The *Apologia* of the *Confessio Augustana*, written by Melanchthon in 1530, presents Lutheran doctrine in the following terms: "We recognize that eternal life is a recompense because it is due not to our merits but on account of the [divine] promise."[32] So the question should be asked: are merit and eschatological reward not the same thing? In principle, merit refers to humans' possibility of being enriched in this life by meritorious actions, whereas the eschatological reward will be given in the next life to those who were faithful to the will of God. Thus two important differences arise between merit and reward. First, on the side of humans: whereas "merit" refers to the present moment, to the action of Christians on earth, the reward is exclusively eschatological. Second, on God's side: whereas the possibility of merit, according to classical theology, is based on the supernatural organism present *in humans* as the fruit of God's action in them, the eschatological prize will be given to humans from without, simply on the basis of the promise made to them by God. At the end of this section, we shall return to these questions, which express two fundamental though connected aspects of the mystery of salvation: the extrinsic side, referring to God's action, and the intrinsic side, referring to the human being in grace.

The Idea That Humans Can "Merit" Anything from God

At first glance it would seem simply unthinkable that humans could "merit" something from God, above all in the order of grace. In effect, merit, the *ius ad praemium*, the "right to being rewarded," is verified between equals, for example, when one person merits payment for an agreed task. But between God and humans this equality is not present, at a most radical level. Everything humans have is received, without merit; in the commutative order, humans have no rights to grace.[33] In the *Catechism of the Catholic Church* we read: "With regard to God, there is no strict right to any merit on the part of man. Between God and us there is an immeasurable inequality, for we have received everything from him, our Creator."[34]

Still, the Gospel, in continuity with the Old Testament,[35] speaks of the reward of

---

31. "Many oppositions may well be eliminated simply by considering and analyzing the equivocal term 'merit' in relation to the true meaning of the Biblical word 'reward.'" Lehmann and Pannenberg, *Lehrverurteilungen—kirchentrennend?*, nos. 4, 7–9. See G. Bornkamm, *Der Lohngedanke im Neuen Testament* (Lunenburg: Heliand, 1947); J. A. Burgess, "Rewards, but in a Very Different Sense," in Anderson, Murphy, and Burgess, *Justification by Faith*, 94–110.

32. P. Melancthon, *Apologia Confessionis Augustanae*, in *Die Bekenntnisschriften der Evangelisch-Lutherischen Kirche*, edited by H. Lietzmann, H. Bornkamm, H. Volz, and E. Wolf, 6th ed. (Gottingen: Vandenhoeck und Ruprecht), 141–404.

33. "Inter Deum et hominem est maxima inaequalitas: In infinitum enim distant, et totum quod est hominis bonum, est a Deo." Aquinas, *S.Th.* I-II, q. 114, a. 1, co.

34. CCC 2007.

35. *Pace* E. P. Sanders (*Paul and Palestinian Judaism: A Comparison of Patterns of Religion* [London: SCM Press, 1981]), "it would be naïve ... to think that in mainstream Judaism, and particularly in the popular imagination, good deeds were not regarded as meritorious." *NIDNTTE* 1:729f., s.v. δικαιοσύνη. "Even in modern

eternal life as the result of faith in this life (e.g., Jn 3:36) and also of the "hundred times more" that the faithful will receive in this life (Mk 10:30; Lk 18:30). It speaks besides of rewards for good works (1 Cor 9:24; Phil 3:14), of recompense (Mt 5:12, 10:41f.; Lk 6:35; 1 Cor 3:8), of the crown of glory (1 Cor 9:25; 2 Tm 4:8; 1 Pt 5:4; Rv 2:10), of the treasure to accumulate in heaven (Mt 6:20), of the inheritance we can expect (Gal 3:18; 1 Pt 1:4; Mk 10:17).[36] It is true, however, that these promises are spoken of with reserve. In the parable of the vineyard (Mt 20:1-16), for example, the workers are meant to obtain a wage that is proportionate to the work they perform. But the text clearly shows that the wages eventually given will depend primarily on the generosity of the owner of the vineyard. On the one hand, payment is agreed between the contracting parties; on the other hand, when the workers insist on proportionality between the work done and the wages received, the owner responds: "Friend, I am doing you no wrong; did you not agree with me for a denarius? Take what belongs to you, and go; I choose to give to this last as I give to you. Am I not allowed to do what I choose with what belongs to me? Or do you begrudge my generosity?" (vv. 13–15).[37] The parable clearly teaches that the logic of the kingdom of God is diverse from human logic. The conclusion is that an exact map of the dynamics of merit between God and humans is impossible to provide.

At a theological level the doctrine of merit is present and developed by Church Fathers, especially Tertullian,[38] who introduced the term *meritum* into Latin theology, and Augustine. Still, it was during the Middle Ages that the doctrine developed and consolidated.[39] In this period authors considered what makes it possible to speak of merit in the context of grace, the so-called *ratio meriti*. According to Thomas Aquinas, there are five reasons for an act to be meritorious.[40]

---

times a Jewish scholar can acknowledge that he grew up worrying that his good deeds would not outweigh his sins: 'On the unerring scales of God's justice, would my righteousness offset my sinfulness and tip the scales to eternal life, or would the heavy weight of this or that sin, alone or in combination, bring the scales down on the side of eternal punishment?'" E. Rivkin, *A Hidden Revolution: The Pharisees' Search for the Kingdom Within* (Nashville, Tenn.: Abingdon Press, 1978), 22. Although there was no well-defined and consistent doctrine on the subject among the rabbis, the evidence suggests that, in the minds of many, merits were indeed weighed against demerits and that those who had accumulated a preponderance of the former were deemed righteous. This notion is reflected in Lk 18:9 and the parable that follows; see further A. Marmorstein, *The Doctrine of Merits in old Rabbinical Literature* (London: Oxford University Press, 1920). Against the position of Sanders, see D. A. Carson, P. T. O'Brien, and M. A. Seifrid, eds., *Justification and Variegated Nomism* (Grand Rapids, Mich.: Baker Academic, 2001).

36. On the topic of reward in the Synoptics and Paul, see M.-F. Berrouard, "Le mérite dans les évangiles synoptiques," *Istina* 3 (1956): 191–209; F. V. Filson, *St. Paul's Conception of Recompense* (Leipzig: J.C. Hinrichs, 1931); G. Didier, *Désintéressement du chrétien: La rétribution dans la morale de saint Paul* (Paris: Aubier-Montaigne, 1955). And on reward in scripture on the whole, see Flick and Alszeghy, *Il vangelo della grazia*, § 134; *NIDNTTE* 3:321-27, s.v. μισθός.

37. See also Mt 6:4, 18, 20; 19:29, 25:21–23; Mk 10:21; 2 Tm 4:7–8; 1 Cor 3:8.

38. See Flick and Alszeghy, *Il vangelo della grazia*, § 135, and G. Hallonsten, *Meritum bei Tertullian: Überprüfung einer Forschungstradition* (Malmö: Gleerup, 1985).

39. See Flick and Alszeghy, *Il vangelo della grazia*, § 136; J. Czerny, *Das übernatürliche Verdienst für Andere: Eine Untersuchung über die Entwicklung dieser Lehre von der Frühscholastik an bis zur Theologie der Gegenwart* (Fribourg: Universitätsverlag, 1957); K. Froehlich, "Justification Language in the Middle Ages," in Anderson, Murphy, and Burgess, *Justification by Faith*, 143–61.

40. See Flick and Alszeghy, *Il vangelo della grazia*, § 139. On Thomas, see Wawrykow, *God's Grace and Human Action*.

First, from the Biblical reflection just made we can say that the only way possible to speak of merit is "secundum praesuppositionem divinae ordinationis" (according to the presupposition of divine ordering).[41] This is the first and most basic condition for supernatural merit: its measure and inner dynamics are established entirely by God himself. "Human merit before God in Christian life derives from the fact that *God has freely disposed to associate humans with the work of grace.*"[42] God, the creator of the universe, has no debts with anybody. Aquinas suggests that God has debts only with himself, in the sense that he committed himself with humans when he established a Covenant with them: "Inquantum debitum est ut sua ordinatio impleatur" (he has the debt of fulfilling his own ordering), of being faithful to his own decisions.[43] We can speak of merit, therefore, only because God is faithful to the word he has given. According the *potentia Dei ordinata*, God will give humans what he promised them.

Second, merit, of course, refers not only to God but also to humans. There must therefore be conditions on the part of humans that make it possible. Merit obviously requires the *freedom* of the subject. Without the free exercise of his faculties, it is not possible to speak of human action and therefore of merit. The result or fruit of merit, or reward, comes from God alone but responds directly, according to scripture, to the works humans accomplish with a free will. In order to be able to act freely before God, as we have seen, humans receive the infused virtue of charity.[44]

A third condition for merit is that of *historicity*. Merit is possible if humans are still pilgrims on earth, awaiting their eternal reward. When a believer has reached eternal life, he may no longer be described as *homo viator*, a pilgrim, and by definition can no longer merit, because there is nothing more, at a substantial level, to receive from God.

Still we must ask the following question: how can these three conditions be reconciled with one another? The first resides, as it were, entirely in God (his promises of rewarding human actions). The other two (freedom and historicity) are clearly human conditions. God's promise remains within his divinity; freedom and historicity belong to the creaturely condition. How are they reconciled? In the late Middle Ages, William of Ockham developed a doctrine of merit of an extrinsic kind, which might be described in terms of a "causality of Covenant," according to which merit depends purely and simply on the divine ordering and does not refer to human conditions. That is to say, merit is not *ex natura rei*; it is not referred to the actions or situation of the one who merits.[45] This is a typically nominalistic way of focusing the problem. It is not infrequently found among Protestant authors and specifically among Lutherans, who have traditionally considered justification an extrinsic action, fruit of God's *acceptatio* of humans.

41. Aquinas, *S.Th.* I-II, q. 114, a. 1, co.

42. *CCC* 2008; emphasis added.

43. Aquinas, *S.Th.* I-II, q. 114, a. 1, ad 3. See Wawrykow, *God's Grace and Human Action.*

44. "Vita aeterna in Dei fruitione consistit. Motus autem humanae mentis ad fruitionem divini boni, est proprius actus caritatis, per quem omnes actus aliarum virtutum ordinantur in hunc finem, secundum quod aliae virtutes imperantur a caritate." Ibid., a. 4, co.

45. On this topic, see McGrath, *Iustitia Dei,* 1:116; Dettloff, *Die Entwicklung der Akzeptations- und Verdienstlehre von Duns Scotus bis Luther.* See chapter 9, notes 37ff. and corresponding text.

In its explanation of the *ratio meriti*, the Council of Trent takes up a well-known axiom of the Middle Ages: "Christus solus meruit" (the only one who truly merits is Christ). And here we find the solution to the dilemma.[46] The Council teaches that our merit is based always and only on our participation in the merit of Christ, the only one who truly merits, insofar as we are members of his body, the Church. Thus the text of Trent: "Jesus Christ himself as the 'head into the members,' and 'as the vine into the branches' continually infuses his power in the justified, a power which always precedes their good works, and which accompanies and follows them, and without with they would on no account be pleasing and meritorious before God."[47] And Cardinal Cajetan, glossing Galatians 2:20, says: "I merit, but not I, for Christ merits in me; I fast, but not I, because Christ fasts in me."[48] This is what Eastern theology commonly calls *synergeia*, the mutual exchange between the will of God and that of humans.

As a result—and this is the fourth condition of a meritorious action—we may say that merit is made possible only because humans are in the state of grace,[49] redeemed by Christ, participating in his body with the charity that comes from the Spirit. Those who are divinized, made children of God, become capable of meriting the gifts that derive from the paternal goodness of God. In the person of Christ, the head, who infuses grace into his members, is combined the "divine" condition (preordination, the eternal plan of God to reward good actions) and the "human" conditions (freedom moved by charity, the pilgrim state).

To better express the a priori need for grace in order to merit, it is common to cite the Augustinian phrase taken up by the Church: "prima gratia non cadit sub meritum" (first grace does not fall under merit).[50] Without grace, in effect our actions may well form habits—perhaps good habits if developed on the basis of good actions—which prepare the way for grace but do not have supernatural value before God. At the same time, the fulfillment of good actions carried out in the grace of God requires actual grace, with which God inspires us and moves us to act according to his will.

The fifth and final condition, to which the previous conditions must be added, obviously, is that meritorious actions must also be upright; they must be in conformity with the will of God. In effect, according to the Gospel, the eschatological prize depends on the rectitude of the actions performed: they must be good and upright, in agreement with God's will.

Here we can observe that the first condition connects with the last, just mentioned. The divine promise (divine preordination) of making the good action of the justified meritorious is connected with the will of God for humanity in general (obedience to natural and positive law) and with the will of the concrete human individual (fidelity to the personal vocation of each one). In other words, the divine promise of rewarding good human actions is not disconnected from created reality, which is

---

46. See McGrath, *Iustitia Dei*, 1:110.

47. Council of Trent, *DH* 1546. See ibid., c. 2, *DH* 1552.

48. T. Cajetan, *De fide et operibus* (1532).

49. Sharing in the divine nature, being adopted as children of God and therefore heirs of the heavenly inheritance, and receiving besides the Holy Spirit is, according to Aquinas, "sufficiens causa vitae aeternae." *S.Th.* I-II, q. 114, a. 3, ad 3.

50. See *DH* 388, 1532, 1913.5; see also Aquinas, *S.Th.* I-II, q. 114, a. 5.

the first stage of the project of grace: that is, the project of creation with which God has presented humans as free and historical and in the project of grace with which God, in Christ, has given humans the ability to participate and the filial capacity to merit his gifts.[51]

On the basis of the Gospel declaration "We are unworthy servants; we have only done what was our duty" (Lk 17:10), Origen and some scholastics took it that meritorious acts can only be of an exceptional and heroic kind, because the acts that we are merely obliged to perform do not merit anything for us.[52] Suárez considers this a mistaken position, because every good act undertaken by humans on earth, even the most simple and ordinary ones, when undertaken freely and for love in God's grace, is meritorious.[53]

The Intention to Merit

Theologians ask if each and every good work carried out in grace, in order to be meritorious, must be consciously ordered to God as our ultimate end. Some scripture texts seem to indicate that Jesus promises recompense to those who carry out good actions in his name or for his cause.[54] Still, in Jesus' presentation of final eschatological judgment, the just are presented as having accomplished good works without any special awareness of having served or cared for Jesus directly (Mt 25:40). We may conclude, therefore, that they should have at least a virtual intention to receive the fruit of merit as a true and proper gift of God.[55] A liturgical prayer reads as follows: "O God, strength of those who hope in you, graciously hear our pleas, and since without you mortal frailty can do nothing, grant us always the help of your grace, that in following your commands we may please you by our resolve and our deeds."[56] In practice, God's children will naturally and frequently offer their works and lives to God, even without an actual intention, including in this filial offering actions that might be considered indifferent. For one who lives in charity, Thomas says, every free act is meritorious[57] as long as it is in conformity with God's will. In any case, it is common theological opinion that Christians should offer their works to God as much as they can, with conscious acts of charity, rectifying their intention frequently.

The Object of Merit

We may now ask what humans in grace can actually merit, that is, what is the object of their meritorious action. Medieval theology, including that of Thomas Aquinas, distinguishes two kinds of merit, merit *de condigno* and merit *de congruo*.[58] The first kind, *de condigno*, corresponds to what believers can merit in the strict sense of the word: what God has committed himself to giving them for their good actions. The

---

51. On the unity of the divine project of grace, see the beginning of chapter 12.
52. See Origen, *Comm. in Rom.* 3, 3.
53. F. Suárez, *De gratia*, 12, 5, citing Dionysius the Carthusian.
54. See Mk 9:41; Lk 9:48; and also Col 3:17.
55. Thus Aquinas, *II Sent.*, d. 40, q. 1, a. 5, ad 6.
56. Collect prayer from the eleventh Sunday in ordinary time.
57. Aquinas, *De malo*, q. 2, a. 5, ad 7.
58. See J. Rivière, "Sur l'origine des formules 'de condigno' et 'de congruo,'" *Bulletin de littérature ecclésiastique* 28 (1927): 75–88; McGrath, *Iustitia Dei*, 1:110ff.

second, *de congruo*, corresponds to what seems appropriate, apposite, reasonable. In the first case, God's fidelity to his promise is at stake, in the second his liberality and magnanimity. The Council of Trent speaks of merit, and, although it does not use this terminology, the distinction is present. In fact, when the Council speaks of merit, it understands it principally in the first sense, as merit *de condigno*.[59] There are three areas to be considered, according to Aquinas.[60]

First, humans can merit *de condigno* three things: eternal life, which, as we already saw, is in continuity with grace itself[61] (in that sense, glory adds nothing substantially new to the life of those in grace); the increase of sanctifying grace, and with it an increase in the infused virtues and in the gifts of the Holy Spirit;[62] and finally, the grade of glory: in effect, humans who merit can determine more or less the grade of glory they will enjoy in heaven.[63] The same doctrine is taught by Trent.[64] The fact that all good actions carried out in the grace of God produce in Christians an increase in holiness is of singular relevance for everyday Christian life.

Second, humans can merit *de congruo* many other things, whatever it is licit to ask God for and desire from him. Through their good works, or with prayer, it is possible to obtain, for example, an increase in grace for others, the conversion of sinners, and divine favor toward the holy souls in purgatory, besides other temporal benefits for oneself and for others.[65] As regards the latter, Thomas Aquinas adds that God gives temporal goods to the just, "quantum eis expedit ad perveniendum ad vitam aeternam" (insofar as it is appropriate for them to obtain eternal life).[66] Only Christ, however, as head of the mystical body and author of salvation, is in a position to merit *de condigno* in favor of others.[67]

---

59. See Council of Trent, *DH* 1585.

60. See Aquinas, *S.Th.* I-II, q. 114, a. 3.

61. See chapter 12, notes 105ff. and corresponding text. "Valor meriti attenditur secundum virtutem Spiritus Sancti moventis nos in vitam aeternam … secundum dignitatem gratiae, per quam homo, consors factus divinae naturae, adoptatur in filium Dei, cui debetur hereditas ex ipso iure adoptionis." Ibid., a. 3, co.

62. See Aquinas, *S.Th.* I-II, q. 114, a. 8.

63. Human individuals rejoice to different degrees in heaven, and therefore in the beatific vision: see Aquinas, *S.Th.* I, q. 12, a. 6. The Council of Florence (1439) teaches that vision corresponds to the merit of each one: "by the diversity of merits, one [possesses it] more perfectly than the other." *DH* 1305.

64. Council of Trent, *De justificatione*, c. 32, *DH* 1582, rejects the following statement: "that the good works of the man justified are in such a way the gifts of God that they are not also the good merits of him who is justified, or that the one justified by the good works, which are done by him through the grace of God and the merit of Jesus Christ (whose living member he is), does not truly merit an increase in grace, eternal life and the attainment of that eternal life … and also an increase in glory." See Flick and Alszeghy, *Il vangelo della grazia*, § 140.

65. See J. Czerny, *Das übernatürliche Verdienst für Andere*.

66. Aquinas, *S.Th.* I-II, q. 114, a. 10, co.

67. Each one is moved by God "per donum gratiae ut ipse ad vitam aeternam perveniat." Thus *de congruo* merit does not go beyond the ambit of the justified individual. "Sed anima Christi mota est a Deo per gratiam non solum ut ipse perveniret ad gloriam vitae aeternae, sed etiam ut alios in eam adduceret, inquantum est caput ecclesiae et auctor salutis humanae (Heb 2,10)." Ibid., a. 6. "Christo data est gratia non solum sicut singulari personae, sed inquantum est caput Ecclesiae, ut scilicet ab ipso redundaret ad membra. Et ideo opera Christi hoc modo se habent tam ad se quam ad sua membra, sicut se habent opera alterius hominis in gratia constituti ad ipsum." *S.Th.* III, q. 48, a. 1, co. On the merit of Christ, see C. de Bouëssé, "La causalité efficiente instrumentale et la causalité méritoire de la Sainte Humanité du Christ," *Revue Théologique* 44 (1938): 256–98; Lynn, *Christ's Redemptive Merit*; B. Catâo, *Salut et rédemption chez S. Thomas d'Aquin: L'acte sauveur du Christ* (Paris: Aubier-Montaigne, 1965); P. O'Callaghan, "La mediación de Cristo en su Pasión (Estudio del tema

From these two points we can draw a conclusion: the just can be sure through faith that their good works obtain for them an increase in grace, a deepening in friendship with God, but cannot be certain they will help other people in the precise way they desire. The reason for this lies in the fundamental condition for intercession before God: the acceptance of the divine will on the part of humans,[68] besides the disposition of forgiving one's neighbor.[69]

Third and finally, humans cannot merit a series of things they might desire, for example, repentance of their own grave sin,[70] because, as we shall see presently, whoever is not in grace can simply not merit. Nor can humans merit the grace of final perseverance (*perseverantia viae*),[71] among other reasons because, if it were possible for them to do so in the present moment, they would be certain of their salvation and confirmed in grace and therefore, ipso facto, incapable of sinning.[72] We may note that all the merits acquired by a person living in the grace of God are lost with mortal sin, but they can be revived when the sinner turns back to God and is justified anew.[73] In Latin this is usually called *reviviscentia*.

The Increase and Loss of Grace

Our creaturely condition, marked by the limits of a finite liberty, requires that the life of grace be subject to the historical dimension of humans' correspondence to the divine will: humans can accept the gift of divine grace, they can oppose it, and they can lose it through sin.[74] The universal saving will of God does not mean that there are no grades or differences in the gift conceded: there are different vocations, different charisms, different responsibilities within the one people of God.[75] Thus there are different grades and profiles of holiness. Both factors—human correspondence to grace and divine liberality—determine the fact that grace may be present in individuals with different grades and intensities, even though the critical factor in holiness, according to Thomas Aquinas, is the second, the gift of God.[76] This variety re-

---

en la Suma Teológica de Santo Tomás)," *Scripta Theologica* 18 (1986): 771–98, esp. 784–92, on the relationship between the merit and action of Christ.

68. See Aquinas, *S.Th.* I-II, q. 114, a. 6, ad 3; *CCC* 2611, 2677.

69. See *CCC* 2631.

70. See Aquinas, *S.Th.* I-II, q. 114, a. 7.

71. See ibid., a. 9. See chapter 17, notes 49ff. and corresponding text.

72. Nor is it possible to merit final perseverance *de congruo*, says Thomas. "Frustra peteretur a Deo in petitionibus orationis dominicae." Still, it is true that "etiam ea quae non meremur, orando impetramus." *S.Th.* I-II, q. 114, a. 9, ad 1.

73. See Aquinas, *S.Th.* III, q. 89, a. 5.

74. The question of the believer's growth or loss of the life of Christ is a classic one. It is to be found in Jerome (*Adv. Iov.* II, 1) and in writings from later during the Middle Ages and Church documents, specifically in Trent: see *DH* 891, 1535, 1573f., 1582. Against Calvin, the Church teaches that Christian justice can be lost with each grave sin (against Luther) and forever (against Wycliff). See Flick and Alszeghy, *Il vangelo della grazia*, § 144; Auer, *Das Evangelium der Gnade*, 179–82.

75. See Mt 10:41f. and 25:14–30; Lk 12:48; 1 Cor 12:11.

76. "Ex parte subiecti, gratia potest suscipere magis vel minus, prout scilicet unus perfectius illustratur a lumine gratiae quam alius. Cuius diversitatis ratio quidem est aliqua ex parte praeparantis se ad gratiam, qui enim se magis ad gratiam praeparat, pleniorem gratiam accipit. Sed ex hac parte non potest accipi prima ratio huius diversitatis, quia praeparatio ad gratiam non est hominis nisi inquantum liberum arbitrium eius praeparatur a Deo. Unde prima causa huius diversitatis accipienda est ex parte ipsius Dei." Aquinas, *S.Th.* I-II, q. 112, a. 4, co.

fers, of course, not to the fundamental aspects of God's plan for humanity—creation and predestination—but rather to the intensity with which this project is confided by God to each one and carried out by that person. In the case of actual grace, we can see a diversification of God's gift during the personal history of each person; in the case of sanctifying grace, there is a gradualness of an accidental form that inheres in the soul, in the same way that a person might be more or less wise or more or less virtuous.[77]

The Council of Trent teaches that "each one receives justice within, according to his own measure which 'the Holy Spirit distributes to everyone as he wills' (1 Cor 12:11), and according to each one's own disposition and cooperation."[78] This justice grows with good works carried out before God and with a humble and penitent prayer.[79] Justification does not depend, therefore, on a kind of fundamental option, which in a sense would reduce the concrete value of each single act in determining once and for all our personal orientation toward God. The Church teaches that, besides the stable commitment of faith, divine justice should be conserved and grow with the practice of the commandments and, in the first place, with the exercise of charity.[80] There is no such thing as a state of sinless perfection that the just cannot either intensify or lose,[81] as the Begards and Beguins taught in the thirteenth and fourteenth centuries and Miguel de Molinos in the eighteenth century.

The possibility of losing friendship with God through sin, forfeiting the filial inheritance and merits gratuitously acquired, rejecting God's justice and returning to the slavery of sin, is well documented in scripture. In the book of the prophet Ezekiel[82] we read: "But when a righteous man turns away from his righteousness and commits iniquity and does the same abominable things that the wicked man does, shall he live? None of the righteous deeds which he has done shall be remembered; for the treachery of which he is guilty and the sin he has committed, he shall die" (18:24). Scripture teaches that there is a sin that leads to death and a sin that does not (mortal and venial sin, respectively): the former changes the fundamental condition of the Christian, from being just and pleasing to God to deserving condemnation, whereas the latter weakens the orientation of the will toward the good and, albeit indirectly, places the life of grace in danger by inclining the person toward mortal sin.[83] Paul speaks openly of the possibility of "falling from grace" (Gal 5:4).

The Council of Trent has also taught the existence of venial sin, with which believers remain just before God.[84] According to Aquinas, venial sin does not diminish charity,[85] but when it is not rectified continually through daily penance, it disposes

---

77. On the question of the degrees of glory in Protestant theology, E. Disley, "Degrees of Glory: Protestant Doctrine and the Concept of Rewards Hereafter," *Journal of Theological Studies* 42 (1991): 77–105.

78. Council of Trent, *DH* 1529.

79. See ibid., 1574 and 1535.

80. See *DH* 1536; see also on this point *DH* 2001, 2406, and 2619 and John Paul II, *Veritatis Splendor*, pars. 65–70.

81. See *DH* 891–92 and 2257.

82. See Flick and Alszeghy, *Il vangelo della grazia*, §§ 141–45; Auer, *Das Evangelium der Gnade*, 177–79.

83. Among other texts, see Jn 15:6; Gal 5:19–21; Eph 5:3–5; Col 3:5–11; 1 Cor 6:9ff., 9:26f., 10:11f.; see Pope John Paul II, *Reconciliatio et Paenitentia*, Apostolic Exhortation, December 2, 1984, par. 17.

84. See *DH* 1537.

85. See Aquinas, *De malo*, q. 7, a. 2; *S.Th.* I-II, qq. 88–89; *S.Th.* II-II, q. 24, a. 10.

believers to mortal sin. Trent does not accept the doctrine of those, such as Calvin,[86] who hold that charity cannot be lost, and rejects the position of those who "say that a man once justified can sin no more, nor lose grace, and that therefore he who falls and sins was never truly justified."[87] Besides, Trent teaches that "those who by sin have fallen away from the received grace of justification, will again be able to be justified (*rursus iustificari*) when, roused by God through the sacrament of penance, they by the merit of Christ shall have attended to the recovery of the grace lost."[88]

Reward and Merit: Final Observations

In the context of denial of this doctrine of merit mentioned earlier on, the following observations may be made. First, Protestant theologians for the most part have expressed serious reservations on the question of the theological value of "good works." They suspect that the root of this emphasis is to be found in a conviction on the part of believers that they are able to approach God with their own strength, thus falling into a vain and sterile spirit of self-complacency.[89] For this reason Rudolf Hermann suggested that Luther was opposed to the doctrine of good works not because they were superfluous in Christian life[90] but on account of the temptation, difficult to overcome, of wanting to be "presentable" before God with one's own deeds.[91] In effect, when Christians carry out good works they should remember, as Augustine said, that "all the merits of the just are so many gifts of God" and that "God when he rewards our acts of charity in final judgment, he crowns his own gifts."[92] In other words, the value of good works carried out by the just depends in the first place not on the effort or fatigue or commitment they require but on the humble and thankful charity with which they are carried out.[93]

Second, as we saw earlier, whereas Catholic theology speaks of merit, Protestant theology prefers the Biblical term "reward." When classical Lutheranism speaks of

---

86. See note 96. 87. *DH* 1573.

88. *DH* 1542.

89. Thomas says that "homo bene operando sibi proficit, vel alteri homini, non autem Deo." And he adds: "Deus ex bonis nostris non quaerit utilitatem, sed gloriam, idest manifestationem suae bonitatis, quod etiam ex suis operibus quaerit. Ex hoc autem quod eum colimus, nihil ei accrescit, sed nobis. Et ideo meremur aliquid a Deo, non quasi ex nostris operibus aliquid ei accrescat, sed inquantum propter eius gloriam operamur." *S.Th.* I-II, q. 114, a. 1, ad 2.

90. See O'Callaghan, *Fides Christi*, 34–36.

91. "[Luther] ... attempted to struggle not against works as such ... but against the *presentability* of works before God." R. Hermann, "Willensfreiheit und gute Werke im Sinne der Reformation," in *Gesammelte Studien zur Theologie Luthers und der Reformation* (Gottingen: Vandenhoeck & Ruprecht, 1960), 44–76, 64.

92. Augustine, *De dono persev.* 2:4; *Epist.* 194, 5:19.

93. Thomas suggests the possibility that other virtues may be considered as the source or principle of merit. However, he explains that charity, having God as its ultimate end, "pro obiecto, movet alias virtutes ad operandum." *S.Th.* I-II, q. 114, a. 4, ad 1. When asking whether it would be more correct to focus merit in terms of human effort and dedication, observing at the same time that charity diminishes effort rather than increasing it, he replies that things we do become difficult for two reasons: In the first place, on account of the inherent difficulty of great works, and in this case charity "facit aggredi opera maxima." In the second place, when a person does not have a ready will, "ex defectu ipsius operantis." And he concludes: "Et talis labor diminuit meritum, et a caritate tollitur." *S.Th.* I-II, q. 114, a. 4, ad 2. Aquinas suggests that faith, patience, and fortitude are meritorious, as we see in the lives of martyrs. Still, the point is that "fidei actus non est meritorius nisi fides per dilectionem operetur (Gal 5); actus patientiae et fortitudinis non est meritorius nisi aliquis ex caritate haec operetur (1 Cor 13)." *S.Th.* I-II, q. 114, a. 4, ad 3.

"reward" it is understood that the prize of eternal life that humans, justified in this life in an extrinsic or forensic way, will receive is situated in *an eschatological future*. Doubtless, glory adds something new to the state of grace, for humans in heaven are no longer pilgrims and sinners; they will contemplate the glory God forever, receiving the *lumen gloriae*. Still, according to Catholic doctrine it is clear that the life of grace begins and consolidates here on earth, in profound harmony with the present lives of humans, and it blooms definitively into eternal glory. Were we to accept a purely "consequent" view of eschatology (on the basis of which the "last things" will be fulfilled only at the end of time) and exclude all "realized eschatology,"[94] we would have to avoid applying the doctrine of merit to the present moment of our lives. But in a theological system that combines consequent and realized eschatology, the doctrine of merit, as something that directly involves both the present and the future situations of believers, cannot be excluded. This point was made in different texts of both Calvin and Luther.[95]

In any case, the 1999 Lutheran-Catholic *Joint Declaration on the Doctrine of Justification*, though it does not use the language of "merit," speaks of the "fruits" of good works carried out in grace.[96] It reads as follows:

We confess together that good works—a Christian life lived in faith, hope and love—follow justification and are its fruits. When the justified live in Christ and act in the grace they receive, they bring forth, in biblical terms, good fruit. Since Christians struggle against sin their entire lives, this consequence of justification is also for them an obligation they must fulfill. Thus both Jesus and the apostolic Scriptures admonish Christians to bring forth the works of love.[97]

Grace, Freedom, and the Ascetic Life of Christians

In Christian spirituality it is frequently held that in order to persevere in the state of grace and grow in Christian life, it is paramount that a person engage in *ascetic struggle* (also called "spiritual combat"), that is, the effort to overcome sinful inclinations in the fallen nature of humans and acquire virtue. In the *Catechism of the Catholic Church* we read: "The way of perfection passes by way of the Cross. There is no holiness without renunciation and spiritual battle (2 Tm 4). Spiritual progress entails the ascesis and mortification that gradually lead to living in the peace and joy of the Beatitudes."[98] Scripture expresses this praxis with the categories of vigilance and tension between the logic of the world and that of God. Besides, the lives of the

---

94. See *COH* 50–53.

95. According to Calvin, "Since God is rich and liberal in doing good, he rewards the graces he confers on us as if they were virtues of our own, because when he gives them to us, he has made them ours." *Institutiones* 2. And in some earlier texts of Luther the same position may be found, for example, in one dated about 1514: "Opera mea, id est, Christi, quae per participationem etiam mea sunt, dicam quod non sint mea, sed Regi." Luther, *In Ps. 44*, in *WA* 3:257.

96. See Root, "Aquinas, Merit and Reformation Theology."

97. *JDJ* 37.

98. *CCC* 2015. On the importance of Christian ascetic struggle, see *CCC* 405, 407–9, 921, 979, 1426, 1496, 1523, 2516, 2725–51, 2849. See this document of the World Council of Churches: F. Fleinert-Jensen, *Entre l'effort et la grâce: Essai sur la justification de l'homme* (Geneva: World Council of Churches, 2005).

saints have frequently shown this to have been so throughout history. The trials that God sends, and even temptations, are experienced frequently in this life and show up the concrete way Christians live the virtues of charity, hope, and humility.[99] Likewise Vatican Council II teaches the need to struggle in order to continuously orient toward God the heart and the world, a world marked by sin and of struggle between good and evil.[100]

Still, several important questions need to asked in the wider context of the doctrine of merit: if "good works" and ascetic struggle are not objectively the causes of grace but rather its fruits, why should we insist on the ascetic life of Christians, lived conscientiously with effort and perseverance—we might even say with stubbornness? What is the meaning of Christian struggle, the effort to follow Christ, to recognize and overcome one's defects? And with what spirit should Christians live out their conscious, constant effort, which, according to spiritual authors, constitutes the essential element of Christian life? It is clear that Christians live out the effort to overcome their habitual reluctance before the duties of conscience; to overcome their fallen will, historical and contextualized; and to follow divine inspiration, as something of their own. But if there is such a thing as "grace," the gift of God that strengthens the will, illuminates the intellect, elevates and heals all the faculties, why insist that Christians should positively struggle to live an upright life? And not only that: why should they be encouraged to assume apostolic commitments toward others? It would seem that the more attention is paid to God and his gifts, the less needs to be paid to our own situations, actions, and merits. The greater our confidence in God, the less we can place in ourselves and our own energies. In brief: the more grace is present, the less is our need for struggle and effort. It would seem that the best thing would be simply to abandon oneself completely in God's hands and not make any particular effort, as the seventeenth-century Quietists thought.

To resolve this apparent dilemma we should keep in mind, as has been frequently said, that grace received is none other than the life of Christ in the believer. Hence grace not only elevates the human faculties, divinizing them, but reproduces within humans the principal tenets and stages of the historical life of Jesus Christ on earth: birth, family life, work, fatigue, joys, friendships, sorrows, glory. The logic of the incarnation does not allow us to consider the dynamics of grace exclusively as a kind of *theologia gloriae*, the theology of glory, without the complement of the *theologia crucis*, the theology of the cross. Divinizing grace, in effect, is not only a source of light, power, consolation, and sweetness, all of which facilitate our actions. The life of grace is the life in believers of the mystical body of Christ, who during his earthly pilgrimage takes on something of the joys, sorrows, and glories of all humans who have lived on the earth, who were redeemed by him. Paraphrasing the text of Galatians 2:20, often cited, the Christian can say, "It is no longer I, member of the body of Christ, who struggle. It is no longer I, but Christ who struggles in me."

The conclusion is as follows: even if it is true that the grace of God facilitates the lives of believers, in the sense that it makes the supernatural final end and the personal presence of the eternal Father more living and present within us, we still have

99. See Sir 2:4–5:10–11; Jas 1:12.
100. See *GS*, no. 37.

to say that grace is what moves humans to struggle, to make an effort: to act, to work, to overcome difficulties, to accept, to believe and trust, to be humble, that is, to conform themselves to Christ, sharing his very sentiments (Phil 2:5). Grace, as it divinizes, awakens, purifies, and stimulates all human energies penetrates every layer and recess of the human structure. Grace does not dispense humans from everyday effort. Quite the contrary: grace precedes, accompanies, and completes their actions in such a way that they are directed entirely to God. It may be said that the Christian believer pays the full price for the gradual purification this process requires. Prosper of Aquitania, a contemporary of Augustine's, said that "the elect receive grace not in order to remain indolent, but to make them work well."[101] The grace of God inclines, inspires, invites humans to an effort that must permeate every nook and cranny of their souls, one that penetrates every single faculty. Objectively, therefore, ascetic struggle, even when it involves human action solicited with intelligence by humans, is the fruit of God's grace in them.[102]

No differently than nonbelievers, Christians are spared neither effort nor dedication nor suffering. Grace certainly facilitates life, because, while it gives meaning and purpose to human existence, it also gives humans the strength and perseverance that accompany actions carried out for love. However, it is also true that grace brings believers to share more in the redeeming work of Christ, in such a way that the Christian, made *alter Christus, ipse Christus* by grace, becomes also a co-redeemer with him: "And if [we are] children, then heirs, heirs of God and fellow heirs with Christ, provided we suffer with him in order that we may also be glorified with him" (Rom 8:17). As Josemaría Escrivá said, the calling of God, and grace with it, often "complicates our life."[103] "Allow yourself," he wrote, "to be formed by the rough or gentle strokes of grace."[104] As Flannery O'Connor writes, "grace changes us, and change is painful."[105]

By way of conclusion we may ask: does Christian struggle produce a growth in holiness, or does holiness move us toward ascetic struggle? We can say that ascetic struggle produces a growth in holiness in the sense that it opens the human heart to divine gifts, as long as we keep in mind that the grace of God in the first place brings about the opening of the heart. In real terms ascetic struggle is the fruit of the intelligent though sometimes pained acceptance of grace by humans, and this

101. Prosper of Aquitania, *De vocatione omnium gentium*, 2:35. On this question, see Weaver, *Divine Grace and Human Agency.*

102. Thomas asks why it is more difficult to persevere in grace under Christ than under Adam. He responds showing that the grace of God won by Christ must be inserted deeply but gradually into the souls of humans, born sinners and carriers of the *fomes peccati*. In fact, "facilius homo per gratiae donum perseverare poterat in statu innocentiae, in quo nulla erat rebellio carnis ad spiritum, quam nunc possumus, quando reparatio gratiae Christi, etsi sit inchoata quantum ad mentem, *nondum tamen est consummata quantum ad carnem*. Quod erit in patria, ubi homo non solum perseverare poterit, sed etiam peccare non poterit," *S.Th.* I-II, q. 109, a. 10, ad 3.

103. See Escrivá, *Forge*, no. 902: "I didn't think God would get hold of me the way he did, either. But, let me tell you once again, God doesn't ask our permission to complicate our lives. He just gets in: and that's that!" And also, in *Friends of God*, no. 21: "Jesus comes up to the boats tied up alongside and goes into one of them, which is Simon's. How naturally the Master comes aboard our own boat! 'Just to complicate our lives,' you hear some people complain. You and I know better, we know that Our Lord has crossed our paths to complicate our existence with gentleness and love."

104. Escrivá, *Forge*, no. 874.

105. O'Connor, *The Habit of Being*, 307.

takes place with full respect to one's humanity and concrete situation. Thus sincere ascetic struggle to serve God—in obedience to his commandments—is not the cause of holiness but must be considered as a clear sign or manifestation of holiness being consolidated. The ascetic life of Christians, therefore, even though it is experienced as one's own effort, in reality consists of the impulse to allow oneself to be conformed progressively, in the power of the Holy Spirit, to the doctrine, life, death, and resurrection of Jesus Christ.

The Experience and Certitude of Grace

In order to be able to speak of a freedom and grace it is necessary to consider the question of spiritual experience. The free response with which humans accept divine grace, in effect, is not a simple option made by humans in a voluntaristic, unconscious, or athematic way, without any presupposition, a pure choice made out of nothing, or perhaps out of darkness, irrationality, or emptiness. God's grace illumines the intelligence and inclines the will; it stimulates the imagination and stirs up the memory; it brings us face to face with our lives and identity; it makes the lives of other people present in a corporeal and sensory way through sacramental signs. In effect, grace acts within the person but also through exterior mediations: the Word of God, the example of others, sacramental actions, and so on. And people realize that something is happening, that God is speaking to them, inspiring them. They long for truth, they find meaning, they experience love. Hence we can say that humans' response to grace is brought about in a way that is fully in keeping with the nature and concrete situation of the persons involved, especially with their intellect and affectivity. Augustine speaks of the *suavitas amoris*, the way in which God, through grace and without violating human nature, "seduces" humans and makes them react positively to his gifts. Thomas, in his treatise on the theological virtues, explains that the supernatural action of God in humans becomes within them a kind of "passion."[106] In brief terms, in order to be able to accept God's grace in a fully intelligent, willing, and human way, humans must be able to encounter and experience a reality that is divine (grace) yet in a truly human way,[107] that is, to experience grace as grace.

The Experience of Grace: A Historical Perspective

In the modern period the topic of religious experience has been somewhat neglected by Catholic theologians. On the one hand, from the time of the Protestant Reformation onward they wished to avoid the tendency, present in lived spirituality, toward a kind of pietistic subjectivism, which besides, in many cases, was antiecclesiastical. To this may be added that a certain rationalism played a real part in mod-

---

106. Elsewhere, Thomas speaks of human knowledge by "connatural-ness," referred to in the first place as philosophical knowledge but applicable to the order of religious experience. See M. D'Avenia, *La conoscenza per connaturalità in S. Tommaso d'Aquino* (Bologna: Edizioni Studio domenicano, 1992). See chapter 15 on the theological virtues.

107. On the experience of the divine in Jesus Christ, see P. O'Callaghan, "Il cristiano come *ipse Christus* e l' 'umanità' della grazia divina," in *Cristo nel cammino storico dell'uomo: Atti del Convegno Internazionale di Teologia, Roma, 6–8 settembre 2000*, edited by J. M. Galván (Vatican City: Vaticana, 2002), 229–54.

ern Catholic theology. Taking their cue from Descartes and others, some rationalistic authors propounded that "clear and distinct ideas" made the experience of God more or less superfluous. Besides, the so-called masters of suspicion, such as Nietzsche, Feuerbach, Marx, and Freud, considered all kinds of religious experience in a negative light. Finally, during the twentieth century the Catholic Church reacted energetically against "modernism," which seemed to identify God himself with the experience of God in a vision of human nature that seemed to be confused with the divinity.[108]

In spite of this, a growing tendency within Catholic thought gave ever greater weight to religious experience while avoiding the pitfalls of subjectivism, rationalism, and immanentism.[109] Some Protestant authors made an important contribution to this process, especially the early eighteenth-century Lutheran pietist Friedrich Schleiermacher.[110] In the philosophical area, phenomenology and hermeneutics have clarified many issues. In the ambit of twentieth-century Catholic theology, perhaps the most important contribution has come from Jean Mouroux.[111] Besides, Karl Rahner[112] and Hans Urs von Balthasar[113] have made useful contributions. The latter states that the category of experience "is indispensable when faith is understood as the encounter of the whole person with God."[114]

The Value and Ambivalence of Religious Experience

The concern that emerged during the modernist controversy in the early twentieth century was real and relevant: experience of the divine is an experience lived by humans, but it is, or at least it should be, an experience of God. Grace is experi-

108. On the phenomenon of modernism, see the following studies of G. Colombo: "Esperienza e rivelazione nel pensiero di G. Tyrrell," *La Scuola Cattolica* 6 (1978): 544–68; "La nozione di 'esperienza' nel magistero antimodernista," *Teologia* 4 (1979): 297–313; "La nozione di 'esperienza' e la teologia cattolica d'inizio secolo," *Teologia* 6 (1981): 183–88. See especially Pope Pius X, *Pascendi Dominici Gregis*, Encyclical Letter, September 8, 1907.

109. For a history of the different stages of the debate on the experience of grace, see J. Ratzinger, "Faith and Experience"; A. Bertuletti, "Il concetto di 'esperienza,'" in *L'evidenza e la fede*, edited by G. Colombo (Milan: Glossa, 1988), 112–81. See also the essays of W. A. Beinert, "Die Erfahrbarkeit der Glaubenswirklichkeit," in *Mysterium der Gnade*, edited by H. Rossmann and J. Ratzinger (Regensburg: Pustet, 1975), 134–45; L. Scheffczyk, "Die Erfahrbarkeit der göttlichen Gnade," in *Mysterium der Gnade*, edited by Rossmann and Ratzinger, 146–59; Von Balthasar, "Esperienza di Dio nella Bibbia dei Padri"; A. Nichols, "Experience," in *The Shape of Catholic Theology* (Edinburgh: T. and T. Clark, 1991), 235–47.

110. On the question of experience in philosophy and specifically in Schleiermacher, see A. Bertuletti, "Il concetto di 'esperienza' e la teologia," *Teologia* 6 (1981): 85–121. Schleiermacher has the following to say: "The doctrines of Christian faith are expressions of pious-emotive Christian conditions present in language." *Der christliche Glaube*, 2nd ed., 1831, § 15.

111. See his principal work, J. Mouroux, *L'expérience chrétienne: Introduction à une théologie* (Paris: Aubier-Montaigne, 1952), translated into English as *The Christian Experience: An Introduction to a Theology* (London: Sheed and Ward, 1955). On his thought, see J. Alonso García, *Fe y experiencia cristiana: La teología de Jean Mouroux* (Pamplona: Eunsa, 2002).

112. See K. Rahner, "Ateismo e 'cristianesimo implicito,'" in *L'ateismo contemporaneo* (Turin: SEI, 1970), 4:91–108; Rahner, "Reflections on the Experience of Grace," *Theological Investigations* (London: Darton, Longman and Todd, 1982), 3:86–90. On Rahner's understanding, see Bertuletti, *Il concetto di "esperienza,"* 155–63, and the critical comments of Scola, Marengo, and Prades López in *La persona umana*, 319–22.

113. See especially Balthasar, *Glory of the Lord*, vol. 1. On his thought, see Bertuletti, *Il concetto di "esperienza,"* 163–65.

114. Von Balthasar, *Glory of the Lord*, 1:219.

enced by humans but comes from God and is meant to direct the human heart to its creator. Yet God cannot be identified with humanity: *Deus semper maius!* "Left on its own, experience is satisfied with too little," observes Rémi Brague in a cryptic way.[115] Humans are satisfied with too little because religious experience is not a mere human experience but, rather, the experience of God, of the eternal. In other words, religious experience is not—it should not be—an end in itself. It does not begin and end within the human sphere but points towards God—the true God, the totally Other, personally experienced—and not toward an idea of God that humans have invented. John Paul II writes: "What we experience is not absolute: it is neither uncreated nor self-generating. God alone is the Absolute."[116] Even though lived by humans, true religious experience is the result of divine initiative. Besides, experience is always particular, concrete, but at the same time it seems to refer to the universal, to the whole, to the eternal, to the unconditional. Hence it is necessary to undertake a careful discernment in order to distinguish between common human experience, which may contain an (apparently) transcendent component, and the authentic experience of God's action in the soul.[117]

Three different understandings of religious experience may be suggested, going from the more particular to the more general. In the first place, there are extraordinary mystical experiences that are well documented by students of spirituality.[118] Doubtless, mystical experiences do exist, yet they do not constitute the only valid form of experiencing divine grace. If the general experience of grace were identified with mystical experience, experience could easily become an elitist phenomenon, destined only to certain exceptional individuals. The common, everyday, experience of grace by believers who strive to be faithful to their baptismal vows seems to be excluded, and this would not be acceptable.[119]

Second, some authors have attempted to amplify the category of religious experience to include other religions, seeing in them the presence of God, who acts in the depths of the human soul.[120] These studies show to some degree something Christians are convinced of, that humans are made in the image of God and that they experience a natural tension toward the divine that finds expression in religious vision and praxis. Still, it cannot be said that this in a true sense is an experience of God's grace, which, from the moment of the incarnation, has always been an experience of the life of Christ in humans.

---

115. R. Brague, "Was heisst christliche Erfahrung?," *Communio* (Deutsche Ausg.) 5 (1976): 481–82, 482.

116. John Paul II, *Fides et Ratio*, par. 80.

117. On the metaphysical question behind that of experience, see F. Alquié, *L'expérience*, 4th ed. (Paris: PUF, 1970). John Paul II writes in *Fides et Ratio*, par. 48: "Deprived of what Revelation offers, reason has taken side-tracks which expose it to the danger of losing sight of its final goal. Deprived of reason, faith has stressed feeling and experience, and so run the risk of no longer being a universal proposition."

118. The writings of F. Suárez were particularly important in this respect. See A. Stolz, *Teologia della mistica* (Brescia: Morcelliana, 1940), translated into English as *Doctrine of Spiritual Perfection* (Eugene, Ore.: Wipf and Stock, 2013). See also the bibliography listed in P. O'Callaghan, "The Mysticism of Paul of Tarsus," in *In Dialogue with God: Mystics in World Religions*, edited by K. Acharya, U. Vaidya, L. Namjoshi, and M. Iturbe (Mumbai: Somaiya, 2009), 161–82.

119. See M.-L. Gondal, "Le mystique est-elle un lieu théologique?," *Nouvelle Revue Théologique* 108 (1986): 666–84.

120. See the different positions presented in Acharya et al., eds., *In Dialogue with God: Mystics in World Religions*.

Third, it has become quite common, especially with the studies of Karl Rahner, to consider the experience of grace as a thematic expression of the generic or athematic experience of depth present in humans as such.[121] In real terms, should this be the case, the experience of grace would coincide more or less with general human experience, and it would not be possible to say that this is the result of divine action through Christ in the Spirit. If these three forms of "religious" experience are to be excluded, how can we discern what is truly the Christian experience of grace?

The Theological Study of Religious Experience

The first thing to consider is the language used to refer to the religious experience of humans. Linguistic expressions of experience may be situated between two kinds of affirmation. On the one hand there are affirmations of a descriptive or phenomenological kind, which attempt to express and communicate the experience as it presents itself to the subject. On the other hand, there are affirmations of an ontological kind, which attempt to discover the essence of the objective reality that lies behind experience, that *of which* humans have had experience. Logically, the two affirmations require one another, yet may not be identified. It is obvious that the study of religious experience cannot stay at the first, empirical, level. It is necessary to go further and attempt to discover the reality that has produced or provoked the experience in question, that is, what is really going on behind or within the experience. To understand this two-stage dynamic, we can take the example of the medical doctor attempting to cure a patient. The first stage in this attempt is the anamnesis, the investigation of the problem, gathering all the information and data possible, all the symptoms. Then, at a second stage, the doctor elaborates the diagnosis, suggesting with greater or lesser precision the illness that is at the root of the upset. The experience of pain, greater or lesser, may derive from a real and objective illness that is more or less grave, or perhaps it may refer to no illness at all. This is why it is important to distinguish between the two moments of religious experience: it may refer to simple, common human experience, or it may truly be the experience of God acting within the soul. The same thing may be applied to the spiritual direction of souls; like the doctor, the director must help the person to see, appreciate, and live his personal experiences in an objective and more or less typical framework. One thing is what the person feels, another what is really happening.

Something of the kind may be said of the experience of grace. The experience in question should be documented, studied, correlated, integrated, described.[122] Then, at a second stage, systematic or dogmatic theology attempts to express in a sober, universal, and communicable language the objective dynamic of God's action in humans present in the experience. The experience of the grace of God in the human soul is rich, varied, fascinating, unforeseeable, subjective, perhaps poetic, whereas dogmatic affirmations that attempt to describe what is really happening are, and should be, on the contrary, simple, sober, and objective.

Two important difficulties emerge, however, (1) with respect to the anteriority of religious experience over dogmatic reflection and (2) with regard to the ambivalence

---

121. See note 112 and also Schillebeeckx, *Christ: The Christian Experience in the Modern World.*
122. See the studies in the final volumes of *Dictionnaire de Spiritualité.*

of religious experience itself. First of all, let us consider the question of the role religious experience plays in relation to dogmatic reflection. Anyone making objective dogmatic conclusions deriving from scientific or systematic theological reflection should be in a position to wisely interpret, measure, and filter the empirical data that are found in spiritual experience. However, such conclusions are always, or almost always, based on the concrete experience of the work of God in the sphere of human life: dogma is the fruit of experience, of lived Christianity. But how can dogma interpret experience? Does this involve a vicious circle? Which comes first: dogma that interprets experience or experience that comes to be expressed in terms of dogma? In the dynamics of divine grace this idea is particularly relevant. All language that attempts to objectively describe the reality of grace is based on the lives and experience of those who have in fact accepted the grace of God and is inspired in them. This may be seen frequently in the psalms and prophetic works. It is particularly present, of course, in the life, death, and resurrection of Jesus Christ, our savior, in whom "the whole fullness of deity dwells bodily" (Col 2:9). The same may be said of Mary, the one who is "full of grace" (Lk 1:28); in Paul, convinced that the grace of God in him "was not in vain" (1 Cor 15:10); and in all the other saints.

By way of example, we may say that from the repeated human experience of the care God has for his people in the Old Testament it is possible to deduce, with the help of reason and in the light of faith, a series of objective theological truths: that God is good toward humans, that God is faithful to his promises, that God is all-powerful.[123] From the encounters early Christians had with the risen Christ it became possible for them to deduce not only the veracity of the resurrection of Jesus, which took place within history, but also the fact that the God who brought his Son back from the dead is a God who saves and loves humans in an unconditional way. This, in turn, provided them with a critical conviction from which to affirm the full divinity of Jesus Christ. Human experience, in other words, is indispensable in order to explain a dogmatic discourse in a coherent way, at least in a Christian context. Experience gives rise to dogma.

The second difficulty refers to religious experience itself. In effect, human experience of any kind is—or can be—deeply ambivalent, because it is present within the ambit of individual human subjectivity and affectivity. Experience always belongs to someone, someone who is situated socially, culturally, humanly, psychologically, and so on. From the epistemological point of view, to this ambivalence is added the fact that strong religious experiences occur in a small number of people and not frequently during their lifetimes. The best-known case is that of Paul: on the experience of his encounter with the risen Lord on the road to Damascus, a very intense and personal experience, is based an important part of Christian theology, especially as regards vocation, grace, and mission.[124] The same may be said of the experience of Augustine, present in his *Confessions* and other works. From the point of view of Christian faith itself, it should be kept in mind besides that religious experience is affected at its deepest root by the emotional ambivalence present in humans, which derives from

---

123. On this movement, see P. O'Callaghan, "Il realismo e la teologia della creazione," *Per la filosofia* 12 (1995): 98–110.

124. See O'Callaghan, "The Mysticism of Paul of Tarsus."

the disorder introduced by sin. From such an experience, therefore, it would seem to be difficult to deduce a doctrine that is rigorously applicable to all situations.

Let us look at a further experience in the area of grace and justification, particularly in the context of Lutheran-Catholic dialogue. Classical Lutheranism would say, "God in Christ covers over our sins" or "humans are convinced of their incurable condition as sinners" or "the believer is *simul iustus et peccator*," at the same time just and sinner. These affirmations, properly understood, are perfectly acceptable in the context of Catholic spirituality:[125] they are experiences existentially perceived in the first person, capable of describing the genuine dynamics of God's action in human life. Still, at a dogmatic level, that is, at the level of objective revealed reality, they are easily misunderstood expressions. In effect, if God forgives our sins, it is not enough for him to cover them up: he must necessarily eliminate them. As Thomas Aquinas writes in a text already cited, "It is said that love covers sins before God who sees all things: this means that he actually destroys them."[126] If God is revealed as merciful, humans may consider themselves truly justified and loved, and not only convinced that God is merciful. At an existential level, the Christian, illuminated by the Spirit, may be convinced at one and the same time of being both "saint and sinner." This is not an uncommon experience among believers.[127] Still, if the grace of God is present in the Christian, he is a saint, not a sinner. As Trent teaches, "in renatis nihil odit Deus" (God hates nothing in those who have been regenerated).[128] Still, it is true that in the baptized is to be found concupiscence, or *fomes peccati*, the tendency toward sin, which "originates in sin and inclines towards sin."[129] And yet concupiscence is not sin but rather an inclination that convinces humans of the need to request divine help, to struggle and not be sure of their own perseverance. We can see, therefore, how affirmations that derive from the phenomenology of religious experience do not coincide perfectly with those deriving from a dogmatic discourse.

We could likewise quote the medieval expression "Facienti quod est in se, Deus non denegat gratiam" (For the one who does all they can, God does not deny grace),[130] which is not unlike the more popular phrase "God helps those who help themselves." Lutherans consider the expression semi-Pelagian because it seems to indicate that the beginning of the Christian pilgrimage, the *initium fidei*, depends on humans and not on God. Thus, while at a dogmatic level the statement may be considered problematic, it would seem to be acceptable at an existential and concrete level because it expresses the common Christian experience of wishing to act well and to be rewarded by God, in spite of the presence of sin. Still, this experience needs to be completed with the sober, dogmatic conviction that the beginning of Christian action, in this case the desire to do everything that is humanly possible, is always the fruit of the prevenient grace of God, which acts in us before we have any experience of it or take any initiative in our spiritual life.

125. Teresa of Avila (seventh *Soliloquia*) spoke in the same way.
126. Aquinas, *IV Sent*. d. 22, q. 1, a. 1, ad 2.
127. See Wicks, "Living and Praying as 'Simul Iustus et Peccator.'"
128. *DH* 1515.
129. Ibid.
130. On this expression, see O'Callaghan, *Fides Christi*, 23f.

How can we understand and explain these apparently opposed expressions of the life of grace and the dynamic of justification (*simul iustus et peccator; facienti quod est in se*, etc.)? Perhaps we may say that at the level of human experience they are correct or, better, that they are valid expressions of the concrete spiritual phenomenology of Christian life. However, in a moral, dogmatic, or ontological sense they need to be understood and explained with precision. In other words, there is a spiritual, kerygmatic, concrete, and practical sense in which they are acceptable (because they describe the experience the Christian subject commonly has of grace in the ambit of a personal struggle), yet in a precise metaphysical, literal, abstract, and ontological sense they may be false.

In other words, different expressions of Christian grace, before being described in ontological, dogmatic terms, stand in need of an experienced and intuitive phenomenology.[131] At the same time, these same experiences need to be submitted to a rigorous, abstract, and sober theological reflection in order to ensure the truth of the faith, applicable in principle to all believers.

The Incarnation of the Son: A Living Criterion for the Discernment of Religious Experience

According to scripture, the experience of God is marked in a supreme and definitive way by the fact that the invisible God (Jn 1:18), who lives in an inaccessible light (1 Tm 6:16), has become visible among creatures in Jesus Christ (Col 1:15). God has come close to humans in an extraordinarily tangible way that takes the human senses fully into account (1 Jn 1:1–3):

That which was from the beginning, which we have *heard*, which we have *seen* with our eyes, which we have *looked upon* and *touched* with our hands, concerning the word of life— the life was made manifest, and we saw it, and testify to it, and proclaim to you the eternal life which was with the Father and was made manifest to us—that which we have *seen* and *heard* we proclaim also to you, so that you may have fellowship with us.

Thus, according to Scola, "this seeing, hearing and touching must ... enter into the normal relationship of grace with [the believer], in such a way that the logic of the Incarnation is insuperable."[132] In the incarnation of the Son/Word of God, of his life, death, and resurrection, we can find the key to understanding and discerning Christian experience, the experience of grace, which is none other than the life of God in the believer (Gal 2:20; Phil 3:10–12).[133] For Paul, the Christian's experience of weakness also becomes a place where divine action is shown forth as a reflection

---

131. See Flick and Alszeghy, *Il vangelo della grazia*, § 146; Philips, *L'union personnelle*, 106, 182.

132. Scola, Marengo, and Prades López, *La persona umana*, 321.

133. On this way of understanding things, see Scola, Marengo, and Prades López, *La persona umana*, 319–22. This position was formulated by Schillebeeckx in *Christ: The Christian Experience in the Modern World*. Jesus experienced in a living way his own filial condition, and in this way understood his own identity and destiny. The apostles, in turn, experienced Christ as their Lord and master, living, dead, and risen, and through this experience came to understand their lives, identities, and missions. The notion of Schillebeeckx is fundamentally valid, although his Christology is reductive from certain points of view. See the critique by L. Scheffczyk, "Christology in the Context of Experience: On the Interpretation of Christ by E. Schillebeeckx," *Thomist* 48, no. 3 (1984): 383–408, and also the comments of Bertuletti in *Il concetto di "esperienza,"* 145–54.

of that "weakness" with which Christ has redeemed us (2 Cor 6:4–10, 12:9f., 13:3–9). "The same sentiments of Christ Jesus" (Phil 2:5) are to some degree reproduced in the Christian.[134] Authentic experience of grace in the believer, therefore, reflects faithfully, though poorly, the experience of Christ himself, which is none other than his filial experience of the eternal Father.[135]

Let us now consider four issues that refer to the experience of divine grace: the certitude of the state of grace, the meaning of the cross in Christian experience, the role of incertitude in Christian life, and the role of the Church with respect to the experience of grace.

The Certitude of the State of Grace

As we saw earlier, humans can in different ways have deep experiences of a "transcendental" kind. However, it is not clear whether these are, strictly speaking, experiences of grace, experiences of God, derived from the Spirit of Christ. Perhaps they are simply natural human experiences in which even sin or some pathological alteration might play a part. Such experiences are not necessarily a sign of the presence of the state of sin in a person's soul. The Council of Trent teaches that "whoever considers himself, his personal weakness and his lack of disposition, may fear and tremble about his own grace, since no one can know with a certitude of faith which cannot be subject to error, that he has obtained God's grace."[136] The question has been considered frequently throughout the history of theology when dealing with the "certitude" humans on earth can have of being in the state of grace.

Speaking of grace, Thomas Aquinas teaches that there are three ways of knowing our situation before God with certitude.[137] The first involves knowledge acquired by revelation. Someone may be sure of being in God's grace through a special revelation of a prophetic or mystical kind. This is an uncommon experience, however, which God may give to some people for the sake of others and is directed especially to those who carry out special missions in the Church.[138]

Second, it is possible to know things as they are in themselves, directly, when we perceive them not only in their effects but also in their origin (*principium*). The *principium* of grace of course is God alone, whom we do not know directly in this life but only eschatologically, in beatific vision. Therefore, Christians cannot achieve certainty of being in the state of grace because it belongs only to the saved in heaven.[139] Aquinas quotes in this respect the words of Paul: "With me it is a very small thing

---

134. See G. Barbaglio, *Emozioni e sentimenti di Gesù* (Bologna: EDB, 2009), 7–154.

135. See chapters 3, and 13, notes 47ff. and corresponding text.

136. *DH* 1534.

137. See Aquinas, *S.Th.* I-II, q. 112, a. 5.

138. "Et hoc modo potest aliquis scire se habere gratiam. Revelat enim Deus hoc aliquando aliquibus ex speciali privilegio, ut securitatis gaudium etiam in hac vita in eis incipiat, et confidentius et fortius magnifica opera prosequantur, et mala praesentis vitae sustineant." Ibid.

139. "Homo cognoscit aliquid per seipsum, et hoc certitudinaliter. Et sic nullus potest scire se habere gratiam. Certitudo enim non potest haberi de aliquo, nisi possit diiudicari per proprium principium.... Nullus autem posset scire se habere scientiam alicuius conclusionis, si principium ignoraret. Principium autem gratiae, et obiectum eius, est ipse Deus, qui propter sui excellentiam est nobis ignotus. Et ideo eius praesentia in nobis vel absentia per certitudinem cognosci non potest. Et ideo homo non potest per certitudinem diiudicare utrum ipse habeat gratiam." Ibid.

that I should be judged by you or by any human court. I do not even judge myself. I am not aware of anything against myself, but I am not thereby acquitted. It is the Lord who judges me" (1 Cor 4:3f.).

Third, Thomas says that it is possible to know things through signs or effects, that is, indirectly, through so-called objective and indirect experiences.[140] Those justified may perceive in their lives, he says, that they enjoy the things of God (*delectari in Deo*), that they despise mundane things (*contemnere res mundanas*), that they are not aware of mortal sin; that they experience a certain sweetness toward the things of God.[141] In his work *De Veritate* he adds the presence in human life of the works of charity and of the detestation of evil.[142] In his commentary on the Apostles' Creed, he says: "Hoc est enim signum quod diligamus Deum, si verba illius libenter audimus" (This is a sign that we love God: that we listen willingly to his words).[143] Other spiritual authors speak of the experience of spiritual consolation, of Christian courage, of interior fortitude, of inner peace and joy in the heart, of the love of God that places created things on a second plane, of the attraction of the things of the spirit. With these experiences, humans can presuppose the presence of the state of grace without ever enjoying a complete certitude that Christ lives in them. Besides, all these "signs" are connected with a wide variety of everyday life experiences.[144] Therefore, we can conclude that the ambivalence inherent in religious experience will remain with us always until the moment that we see God face to face.

Grace and the Cross

In order to understand the richness and complexity of the experience of divine grace in human life, we need to complete our reflection with a central Christian notion of special importance, the deepest expression of the incarnation of the Word, that is, the presence of the cross, of the suffering of the Son of God, in believers. It is not only a question of the suffering that results from personal guilt, as this is not necessarily linked with grace. The fact is that grace reproduces in the disciple the most authentic traits and experiences of the life of the sinless master, of "Christ who lives in me." The presence of the cross can be a clear sign of the presence of the grace of Christ in the lives of humans. It is present also in the darkness of the Christian pilgrimage, in trials and temptations, in the sentiment of having been abandoned by God, and so on. Von Balthasar observes: "The Bible's reflective experience

---

140. See the reflection of Mouroux in *L'expérience chrétienne*, 354–65.

141. "Cognoscitur aliquid coniecturaliter per aliqua signa. Et hoc modo aliquis cognoscere potest se habere gratiam, inquantum scilicet percipit se delectari in Deo, et contemnere res mundanas; et inquantum homo non est conscius sibi alicuius peccati mortalis.... 'Vincenti dabo manna absconditum' (Apoc 2,17) quod nemo novit nisi qui accipit, quia scilicet ille qui accipit, per quandam experientiam dulcedinis novit, quam non experitur ille qui non accipit. Ista tamen cognitio imperfecta est." Aquinas, *S.Th.* I-II, q. 112, a. 5. See also *S.Th.* II-II, q. 97, a. 2, ad 2.

142. "Aliquis habens caritatem potest ex aliquibus probabilibus signis coniicere se caritatem habere; utpote cum se ad spiritualia opera paratum videt, et mala efficaciter detestari, et per alia huiusmodi quae caritas in homine facit." Aquinas, *De Veritate*, q. 10, a. 10, co. See also *IV Sent.*, d. 9, q. 1, a. 3, arg. 2. On this issue, see G. Philips, *L'union personelle*, 112.

143. Aquinas, *In Symb. Apost.*, 2.

144. Nichols, in "Experience," 237ff., speaks of the bond between religious experience and common, secular experiences. See also A. Forest, *Consentement et création* (Paris: Aubier-Montaigne, 1943).

is marked in a special way: it is the fruit of renunciation, which has been proven by temptation…. Only the renunciation of all partial experience and all subjective counter-assurance of possessing what has been experienced, the whole of being, the divine mystery is given to us as an initiative. God needs disinterested receivers in order to pour into them his essential disinterest."[145]

Of course the incertitude regarding grace does not come from God, who shows himself to be entirely trustworthy toward humans,[146] as we learn in an objective way from the life, death, and resurrection of Jesus Christ: "God so loved the world that he gave his only Son" (Jn 3:16). The incertitude derives rather from the fact that humans live as pilgrims on a path of faith, not having yet reached the fullness of light in the heavenly fatherland (1 Cor 13:12), and as sinners who carry within something of the original germ of distrust toward the creator.[147] For this reason, the faith of Christians is certain, because its object is the saving action of God in history. The (objective) certainty of the faith, the faith of the Church, is at the basis of all certitude with respect to personal salvation but does not coincide with it. Faith, in fact, perfects the intellect, and with faith it is possible to arrive at a real certitude. Yet the imperfection and fickleness of the will and the appetites is still present, and on account of it the believer cannot enjoy the certitude of being in the grace of God and cannot count on the virtue of charity.[148]

The Meaning of Incertitude: Space for Freedom, Defeating Idolatry

Humans' incertitude of grace acting within them plays a double role in Christian life. On the one hand, it becomes a space in which the free human will is moved and can react with more or less generosity to God's gifts. If humans were to count on an immoveable and absolute certainty of the presence and action of God in their lives—whether related to the state of grace or to the dynamic of actual grace—the pilgrim human will would never be fully moved or provoked. The entire life of the Christian would be predetermined and programmed. Freedom in the context of grace would be a "mere word," as Luther suggested. There would be no space for risk, for generosity, for creativity, for the adventure of love.[149] In the Song of Songs we read (3:1f., 5:6):

On my bed at night I sought him whom my heart loves—I sought him but I did not find him. I will rise then and go about the city; in the streets and crossings I will seek him whom my heart loves. I sought him but I did not find him…. I opened to my lover—but my lover

---

145. Von Balthasar, "Esperienza di Dio nella Bibbia dei Padri," 7, 14. He bases this position on Blondel: see M. Ossa, "Possession de l'être et abnégation dans la philosophie de Maurice Blondel," *Revue d'Ascétique et de Mystique* 38 (1962): 483–509.

146. See Sequeri, *Il Dio affidabile*.

147. On this topic, see John Paul II, *Dominum et Vivificantem*, pars. 27ff.

148. "Quod de ratione scientiae est quod homo certitudinem habeat de his quorum habet scientiam, et similiter de ratione fidei est quod homo sit certus de his quorum habet fidem. Et hoc ideo, quia certitudo pertinet ad perfectionem intellectus, in quo praedicta dona existunt. Et ideo quicumque habet scientiam vel fidem, certus est se habere. Non est autem similis ratio de gratia et caritate et aliis huiusmodi, quae perficiunt vim appetitivam." Aquinas, *S.Th.* I-II, q. 112, a. 5, ad 2.

149. On the value and relevance of risk-taking in human life, see P. Wust, *Ungewissheit und Wagnis*, 4th ed. (Munich: Kösel, 1946).

had departed, gone. I sought him but I did not find him; I called to him but he did not answer me.

This is the adventure of Christian life, the adventure of love. To the question of the dynamics of human freedom before grace and the other gifts of God we shall return later.

On the other hand, our subjective incertitude of grace reminds us every moment that religious experience is not an end in itself but refers to another (God) who is distinct from our self. It expresses the radical otherness of God with respect to the creature and defeats all possible idols created by the human imagination. Certainly religious experience is human, it is personal though shared with others, but if it is authentic, it has its source not in humans but in God, the totally Other.

Lutheranism and the Ecclesial Aspect of the Experience of Grace

The question of the human experience of grace was central in the thought of Luther, also for reasons of a more personal kind.[150] Above all Luther was determined not to place any trust in good works; neither did he wish to direct his impassioned and tempestuous search for salvation toward a possible experience of divine favor toward his person. Both Luther himself and the Council of Trent wanted to "avoid all certainty and presumption with respect to one's personal condition, any complacent certainty of being in the grace of God, self-delusion with respect to one's own defects, tranquillized sentiments as a criterion for a salvation already obtained, moral laxity as a result."[151] To the question "How can humans live before God in full awareness of their sin and weakness?," Christians should respond by directing their gaze directly to the word of divine forgiveness in Christ. When Luther rejected the value of good works, he did not think such works did not have the power to manifest the state of grace. He saw, rather, in the Catholic emphasis on good works an attempt to find a created substitute for the fiducial faith in God as the only source of salvation: humans seeking out the certainty of salvation in themselves and their actions and not in God.

Still, the difficulty of the Lutheran position is not that of Christians directing their attention to God, to his forgiving Word, Jesus Christ. Both Catholics and Lutherans, in fact, agree in saying that believers should place their faith exclusively

---

150. See K. Lehmann and W. Pannenberg, "The Justification of the Sinner," in Lehmann and W. Pannenberg, *The Condemnations of the Reformation Era: Do They Still Divide?* (Minneapolis, Minn.: Fortress, 1990), 29–69, nos. 24, 33, 158f., and Lehmann and Pannenberg, *Lehrverurteilungen—kirchentrennend?*, esp. 34f. and 53–56. At times the words "assurance" and "certitude" are considered equivalent, when in real terms they are not. The first expresses in principle a "certitude" obtained thanks to a promise of help from another; the second, a pure subjective certitude. See also Pesch, *Gottes Gnadenhandeln als Rechtfertigung des Menschen*, 871–77. J. Maritain writes that he is convinced of the subjectivism of Luther, in "Luther ou l'événement du moi," in Maritain, *Trois réformateurs: Luther, Descartes, Rousseau*, 2nd ed. (Paris: Plon, 1925), 5–72, translated into English as J. Maritain, *Three Reformers: Luther, Descartes, Rousseau* (London: Sheed and Ward, 1966). According Lehmann and Pannenberg in *Lehrverurteilungen—kirchentrennend?*, 54, however, Luther had no intention of being subjectivist. Subjectivism is more present in Pietistic Lutheranism and especially in the writings of Schleiermacher: see O'Callaghan, *Fides Christi*, 58f., 66f.

151. Lehmann and Pannenberg, *Lehrverurteilungen—kirchentrennend?*, 56.

in him.[152] The controversial point refers to the possibility that created mediations linked with the justifying word of God (preaching, the sacraments, the Church, religious experience, good works, etc.), might become the real object, though partial and subordinate, of the trust of Christians who wish to obtain peace and be sure of salvation. According to Catholic theology, trust in God is associated with the consolation of good works,[153] with visible elements of the Church,[154] and with external manifestations of Christian piety. God, in fact, uses created "mediations" to express his paternal and reassuring presence. Perhaps we may say that the difference between the Lutheran position and the Catholic one with respect to justification lies not so much in the fact that the latter takes place "by faith alone" but rather in relation to the question of the Church and the mediation of salvation.[155] This is so because the grace God gives to humans touches not only their inner lives, their spirits, but also the corporeal, social, external side of human existence. Hence an important role in Christian experience is played by tradition, also by liturgical tradition: the Church itself should be considered a "place of experience."[156] In fact, grace is directed to the entire person, and the whole human being is meant to respond to it. Let us now consider the question of created mediations.

Grace and Visible Mediations

The Ecclesial Dimension of the Experience of Grace

The Council of Trent teaches that the instrumental cause of justification is the sacrament of baptism, while for Lutherans it would be rather an unconditioned or fiducial faith. According to the Council, therefore, the tangible point of reference for the certitude of justification is a visible action of the Church, exterior to humans and perceived by the latter as something objective and tangible. For Lutherans, however,

152. The U.S. ecumenical document *Justification by Faith*, edited by Anderson, Murphy, and Burgess, teaches as follows: "Our entire hope of justification and salvation rests on Christ Jesus and on the gospel whereby the good news of God's merciful action in Christ is made known; we do not place our ultimate trust in anything other than God's promise and saving work in Christ. This excludes ultimate reliance on our faith, virtues, or merits, even though we acknowledge God working in these by grace alone," no. 4, repeated in a conclusive way in no. 157.

153. Luther, at least during a certain period of life, expressed his trust in God looking toward the objective value of the sacraments, especially that of penance: see Lehmann and Pannenberg, *Lehrverurteilungen—kirchentrennend?*, 54. He rejected the doctrine of "contritionism" developed by Gabriel Biel, who considered perfect contrition the true and proper condition in which to receive sacramental absolution, attempting in this way to "give greater importance to the power of the keys and to absolution" (55). The Council of Trent, however, demands of penitents only an imperfect contrition, called "attrition" (*DH* 1678). On the delicate issues that relate justification, baptism, and penance, see the long *excursus* in Lehmann and Pannenberg, *Lehrverurteilungen—kirchentrennend?*, 56–66, which speaks of the disappearance of the practice of the sacrament in Reformed Christendom (59–60). On the question of contrition and attrition within the debates on justification, see G. Bavaud, "La justification par la foi: Quelle est la racine de la divergence entre catholiques et protestants?," *Nova et Vetera* 68 (1993): 250–62.

154. "The reformers on their side thought that the rejection of their point of view meant that Catholics had a positive interest in keeping believers in a state of incertitude." Lehmann and Pannenberg, *Lehrverurteilungen—kirchentrennend?*, 54f.

155. This is the position of O. H. Pesch in *Frei sein aus Gnade: Theologische Anthropologie* (Leipzig: St. Benno, 1986), 243–46. See also O'Callaghan, "The Mediation of Justification and the Justification of Mediation."

156. See Ratzinger, "Faith and Experience," 353–55.

the fundamental element is the personal faith of each person in God, interiorly experienced. Still, Trent specifies expressly that baptism is "the sacrament of the faith," adding "without which (that is, 'without the faith') no one has ever obtained justification."[157] In other words, the Council does not separate the ecclesiological and sacramental side of grace from that of personal faith in God. The point of reference for the efficacy of the act of justification is always faith: Paul says so: "We hold that a man is justified by faith" (Rom 3:28). However, such faith must necessarily have an ecclesial complement, among other reasons because it is the faith of the Church. The Lutheran position, centered rather on "fiducial faith," can easily tend toward individualism, as Lutheran authors openly recognize,[158] and is centered principally on personal piety, as the Lutheran Pietist tradition and the theology of Schleiermacher show. Clement Maria Hofbauer observed that the Protestant Reformation "arose because the Germans had and still have a need to be pious."[159] The German *Catechism for Adults* takes up the question of the ecclesial aspect of the experience of grace when it teaches that "'certitude' is possible only in the community of the Church, in mutual encouragement and comfort of the grace and hope that comes from it, as well as being carried along by the one 'we' of faith and hope."[160]

We have already seen that at an individual level, grace may be perceived in the lives of believers in their joy in the things of God, in despising worldliness, in not being aware of mortal sin, in a sense of satisfaction with all that is directly related to God, in carrying out good works, and so on. However, because the human being is not only an individual but also a member of a collectivity, other indications may well be added, such as convinced and active belonging to the ecclesial community, which brings with it a spirit of sincerely listening to the Word of God, faithful fulfillment of the Church's law and liturgical life, reception of the sacraments, sharing, and fraternal charity.

Why Divine Grace Should Be Mediated

From revelation we learn that God has wished to communicate his grace through created mediations, primarily through the humanity of his incarnate Son; then through the Church, the body of Christ, which is an extension in time, space, and history of his humanity, the place in which the power of God is made present through Word and sacraments; and finally through the angels and saints, who contribute to purifying, illumining, and perfecting the just.[161]

Still, we may ask: why did God wish to communicate his grace through created mediations in the first place?[162] In a hierarchic-Platonic context, mediations of one kind or another, both spiritual and material, would be considered necessary in the

---

157. *DH* 1529, which says *sine qua*.

158. See, for example, W. Pannenberg, *Anthropology in a Theological Perspective*, 13f.; W. Pannenberg, *Systematic Theology*, 3:458f.

159. Cited in the German Catholic Catechism: M. Jordan, ed., *The Church's Confession of Faith: Catholic Catechism for Adults* (San Francisco: Ignatius, 1987), 200.

160. Ibid., 208.

161. See Aquinas, *S.Th.* I-II, q. 112, a. 1.

162. See P. O'Callaghan, "La mediazione cristiana," in *Inaugurazione dell'Anno Accademico 1998–99 della Pontificia Università della Santa Croce* (Rome: 1998), 83–105.

relationship between the divine and the creature. Their existence reveals the operative limit of divine nature when faced with intractable matter. But in the Christian vision of the world, God stands in no need of any mediator. He has created all things, each and every single creature, material and spiritual, directly, with his own "hands." At a personal (or interpersonal) level God can communicate directly, and will do so definitively in heaven, when the faithful will see God "face to face" (1 Cor 13:12). The power of God knows no limit with respect to creation.[163] But if this is the case, why did God want some creatures to enjoy the capacity of mediating his presence and saving power?

The reason is simple and at the same time profound: in this way, free human will (which may be considered the last stage of the mediation between God and humans) is moved and elevated in the most human way possible, that is, in a way that respects the intrinsic corporeity, historicity, and sociality of humans, as well as the concrete existential situation in which each one lives. In this way God comes close to humans not only as love but also with love, with a love that takes on the concrete human situation in the deepest possible way. Thus, humans are not forced or conditioned beyond their concrete possibilities. God, besides, does not manifest himself directly to humans in this life; rather, through the most simple, humble, and material human means, he avoids imposing himself forcefully on the free will of humans, though he invites one and all, *suaviter et fortiter*, to open their hearts to grace. Mediations are not necessary for God but are perfectly appropriate to human nature.

Let us return to this question: why does an all-powerful God, a God who has created the universe directly, make use of mediations to establish communion with humans? The purpose of mediation between the creator and the creature refers to the non-reciprocal relationship between the transcendent creator, who creates humans and intends to invite them to share his inner life forever, on the one hand, and the spiritual creature, metaphysically contingent and sinful besides, on the other. At an objective and ontological level, this mediation makes the close union between humans and God possible. At a subjective or existential level, however, it is meant to make humans aware not only of the filiation God offers them as a gift but also of their own inherent and perpetual otherness and distinction with respect to the creator, as well as their incapacity to enter into communion with God through their own energies. In other words, Christian mediation expresses both the gratuity of all that exists outside God (the created world and grace) and the inherent otherness of humans before their creator and savior.

Thanks to the experience and perspicacity of the saints, we can better understand the place and dynamic of mediations in Christian life. By faith, hope, and charity, the saints are aware of their close union with God, of their filial familiarity with him. They are children of God, disciples, friends, and brothers of Christ, carriers of the Spirit. They live in close communion with the Trinity. At the same time, as an interior exigency of holiness itself, they are aware of being sinners before God, as well as of the fact that they are and always will be creatures, and that their union with God is exclusively due to the divine gift. For this very reason the saints have an ex-

---

163. See O'Callaghan, "L'incontro tra fede e ragione," 44–49.

traordinary recognition of and sensitivity not only to God, but also to the mediations through which union with God has come to them in the most human way possible. This recognition on no account means that the saints are unaware of the possible defects present in created mediations, imperfections that are more or less inevitable, because they do not substantially obstruct the offer of divine grace.

The saints, in fact, are deeply grateful to the Church, the body of Christ,[164] and to the institutions through which they have received divine grace: the sacraments and the Word of God (and therefore, Christian priesthood), the angels, the saints, and, in a special way, the Virgin Mary. They also show gratitude to all those who have accompanied and assisted them on their way toward eternal life. They are not impatient and overly demanding with created mediations, but understanding and benevolent, just as God has been with them. This awareness was very much present in the life of Josemaría Escrivá, who lived this spirit with great naturalness in the midst of everyday life.[165] We may contrast the ways in which the Curé d'Ars and Jean-Jacques Rousseau considered created mediations. Speaking of the priesthood, John Vianney wrote: "If we realized what is the priesthood, we would die, not of fright, but of love, because it is he who gives us the Christ."[166] Yet his compatriot Rousseau complained of "the endless witnesses, infinite witnesses between God and I! There is no end to those who keep telling me what others have told them. Humans, so many humans, between God and myself!"[167]

A human being cannot obtain eternal union with God by returning to a primitive ideal knowledge of the divinity, lost—as Platonists would say—by the fall of spirit into matter, that is, by eliminating mediations.[168] Nor is it possible to obtain such a union by forgetting the unpleasantness of life lived on earth, as a kind of antimundane spiritualism might suggest. The perpetual presence and evocation of created mediations also in the eschaton will serve as a constant reminder to the just not only of God's refinement in wishing to attract humans to himself with an exquisite respect for their created condition, but also of their humanity, of their freedom and personal history,[169] and of the fact that eternal beatitude is an unmerited pure gift.[170]

164. Augustine contrasts the Church with the "city," making it clear that whereas the city is the associative result of human life, the Church is the body of Christ: "The city has no other source of happiness than humans, because the city is but a multitude of humans that live in concord" *Ep. ad Macedon.*, 3.

165. See Escrivá, *Christ Is Passing By*, no. 18; *Furrow*, no. 712; *Forge*, no. 592; the chapter of *Furrow* on "Naturalness," nos. 554–66; and Escrivá's reflections on the hidden and ordinary character of Christian life in the homily "Christ Triumphs through Humility," in *Christ Is Passing By*, nos. 12–21.

166. "Oh! que le prêtre est quelque chose de grand! S'il se comprenait, il mourrait.... Dieu lui obéit: il dit deux mots et Notre Seigneur descend du ciel à sa voix et se renferme dans une petite hostie.... Si l'on comprenait le prêtre sur la terre, on mourrait, non de frayeur, mais d'amour." Quoted in A. Monnin, *Esprit du Curé d'Ars: Saint J.-B. M. Vianney dans ses catéchismes, ses homélies et sa conversation* (Paris: Tequi, 1934; originally published in 1864), 113. See the section headed "Grandeur du prêtre" in *Jean-Marie Vianney curé d'Ars: Sa pensée, son coeur*, edited by B. Nodet (Paris: Mappus, 1956), 99–103.

167. J.-J. Rousseau, *La Profession de foi de Vicard Savoyard*, in *Œuvres* (Paris: Hachette, 1856), 4:89.

168. See the document of the Congregation for the Doctrine of the Faith on the role of mediations in Christian meditation, *Orationis Formas* (1989).

169. Irenaeus, in his reflection on the mediation of Christ, speaks of the familiarity that the incarnation of the Word established between God and humans: *Adv. Haer.* III, 18:7. Maximus the Confessor uses the same terminology: Christ "is mediator on account of his familiarity with both poles." *Epist.* 12. See also his *Quaestiones ad Thass.*, 60.

170. On the question of "mediation" in beatific vision, which is "face to face" with God, see *COH* 184–86.

Christian Apostolate

The Church, in preaching the Word of God, administering the sacraments, and witnessing to the salvation God has communicated in Christ, does not make the grace of God present in a mechanical or passive way.[171] Moved by the Spirit of Christ, the Church overflows with divine gifts and is therefore essentially missionary and active in communicating them. The Church, as Vatican Council II says, thus becomes "sign and instrument both of a very closely knit union with God and of the unity of the whole human race."[172] The grace of God is communicated to believers in order to be communicated in turn to the whole of humanity. For this very reason, Jesus constituted the College of the Apostles and sent his disciples to evangelize everywhere. "You received without paying, give without pay" (Mt 10:8), the Lord said to the twelve. Then, after the resurrection, at the end of Matthew's Gospel we read: "And Jesus came and said to them, 'All authority in heaven and on earth has been given to me. *Go therefore and make disciples of all nations*, baptizing them in the name of the Father and of the Son and of the Holy Spirit, *teaching them to observe all that I have commanded you*; and behold, I am with you always, to the close of the age'" (Mt 28:18–20). Humans therefore commit their free will not only in receiving God's grace personally but also in becoming, with all their being, efficacious instruments in the communication of this grace to others. We have already seen how the life of Christ present in Paul was the very thing that moved him—we might even say the thing that "forced" him—to spread his faith among others, insofar as this depended on him: "The love of Christ compels us" (2 Cor 5:14). According to Augustine, "The human condition would be abject if God could not communicate his word to humans *through other humans*."[173] The same idea is present in Basil the Great's theology of the Spirit: "In the same way as bodies become resplendent and transparent when they enter into contact with the ray of light, and thus communicate a powerful beam from within themselves, so also those who carry the Spirit and are illumined by the Spirit, become themselves spiritual, and project grace toward others."[174]

The same dynamic may be found in the lives of all Christians, as may be seen in the writings, the life, and the apostolic works of Josemaría Escrivá, in which he describes the baptized Christian as *alter Christus, ipse Christus*.[175] Christians, in effect, are not simple objects or depositories of a series of revealed doctrines or exemplary Christian virtues that refer indirectly to Christ. That is, they are not mere extrinsic instruments for the communication of grace. According to Josemaría, Christ himself

171. On the topic of witness, see P. O'Callaghan, "El testimonio de Cristo y de los cristianos: Una reflexión sobre el método teológico," *Scripta Theologica* 38 (2005): 501–68; and O'Callaghan, "L'articolazione tra parola e evento nella *Dei Verbum*, chiave della testimonianza cristiana," in *Parola e testimonianza nella comunicazione della fede: Rilettura di un binomio critico alla luce del Concilio Vaticano II*, edited by Á. Granados and P. O'Callaghan (Rome: Edusc, 2013), 299–322. In the latter volume, see also the texts of Angelini and Prades.

172. *LG*, no. 1.

173. Augustine, *De doct. christ.*, prol., 6.

174. "Et quemadmodum corpora nitida perlucidaque, contacta radio, fiunt et ipsa supra modum splendida, et alium fulgorem ex sese profundunt, ita animae, quae Spiritum ferunt, illustranturque a Spiritu, fiunt et ipsae spirituales, et in alios gratiam emittunt." Basil, *De Spiritu Sancto*, 9:23.

175. See O'Callaghan, "The Inseparability of Holiness and Apostolate"; O'Callaghan, "*Lumen Christi*: Il paradigma del cristiano nel mondo," *PATH* 9 (2010): 171–83.

acts directly in the world in and through Christian believers, and that in spite of their limits, defects, and lack of virtue: "The same grace which gives rise to Christian virtues, though still far from perfection, acts and works through the Christian on other people, preparing them for faith and conversion."[176]

However, it is not enough to say that Christians are simply "capable" of cooperating in the communication of the saving power of God to other creatures: as believers they are also obliged to do so, obliged by God's grace, just as Paul was, as when he said, "Caritas Christi urget nos" (the love of Christ moves [or controls] us) (2 Cor 5:14) and "Woe to me if I do not preach the gospel!" (1 Cor 9:16). Christian apostles (that is, all believers) are aware that God calls all the baptized without exception, for the call to holiness is universal. Thus they are aware of the central role they play in giving life to that calling.[177]

At the same time, the attention of those who receive the benefit of Christian apostolate is and must be directed to God and not to those who have made present to them the love of God.[178] That is what the Lord wanted when speaking to his disciples: "Let your light so shine before men, that they may see your good works and give glory to your Father who is in heaven" (Mt 5:16). As we have seen, religious experience, if it is genuine, is always an experience of God, an experience of his grace.

176. O'Callaghan, "The Inseparability of Holiness and Apostolate," 152. The same idea may be found in the writings of the founder of Opus Dei when he speaks of Christians offering the world the *bonus odor Christi* (2 Cor 2:15), the "good fragrance of Christ," of their carrying out an apostolate as a *compelle intrare* (Lk 14:23). He also speaks of his life motto: "To hide and to disappear is for me, so that only Jesus may shine forth." See O'Callaghan, "The Inseparability of Holiness and Apostolate," 160–63.

177. On Christian apostolate, see F. Ocáriz, "Evangelizzazione, attrazione e proselitismo," *PATH* 13 (2014): 429–38.

178. On this issue, with particular reference to John the Baptist and Escrivá, see O'Callaghan, "*Lumen Christi*: Il paradigma del cristiano nel mondo."

The braying of the donkey does not reach the heavens.   ITALIAN PROVERB

Seek out merit, look for the cause, try to find justice: and discover that you will find nothing but grace.   AUGUSTINE[1]

After having spoken of the life of divine grace in humans and their free response, this part of the book shall be concluded by presenting an overview of an issue that, though obvious, is central to this treatise: that of the need for grace to obtain salvation and live in communion with the Trinity. Without God's gift of grace, humans are simply not justified or saved. God's grace holds absolute primacy in Christian life, it stands above all the rest.

Two Perspectives of the Need for Divine Grace

Two complementary perspectives lie behind the affirmation that we stand in need of grace. One is of a more ontological or metaphysical kind, which refers to God as creator and humans as creatures who require "elevating grace" (*gratia elevans*), the grace by which God lifts up humans to the condition of filial adoption, makes them pleasing to him, and establishes with them a personal relationship. The second perspective is more closely linked with the history of salvation and refers to God as savior and humans as sinners. Here it is common to speak of "healing grace" (*gratia sanans*), which forgives sin and heals the wounds sin inflicts. With the donation of divine grace, in effect, humans are elevated in their being, faculties, and potencies; at the same time saved from the state of disgrace incurred on account of sin; and healed from its consequences. And this is possible only because God takes the free initiative to do so.

We already have spoken of the Church's insistence on the need for grace to carry out every act ordered to supernatural union with God. We saw this especially in the

---

1. Augustine, *Sermo* 185: "Quaere meritum, quaere causam, quaere iustitiam; et vide utrum invenias nisi gratiam."

context of the teaching of Pelagius, Baius, and Jansen, as well as in the doctrine of Paul.[2] The Church teaches the need for divine grace not simply in the sense that grace confers a certain facility to carry out good works, illumining the intellect and moving the will, but even more so in the sense that it provides the capacity to do so. Grace is not a mere supplement to top up our weakened energies: no effort, sacrifice, or prayer can bring us salvation if God does not freely offer his grace. The spiritual actions of humans reach the throne of God—*attingit ad ipsum Deum*, Aquinas says in a text already cited[3]—only if they first stem from the divine initiative. In fact, as Paul says, the Spirit "intercedes for us with sighs too deep for words" (Rom 8:26). According to John, Jesus clearly said to the disciples: "Without me you can do nothing" (Jn 15:5). Scripture also points out that every beginning of conversion is the work of God: God begins in us all good works (Phil 1:6), he is the one who adds new faithful to the Christian community (Acts 2:48), he moves the hearts of those who listen to the preaching of the apostles (Acts 16:14), he illumines, inspires, converts.

Augustine tells us that his consideration of the Pauline text "What have you that you did not receive? If then you received it, why do you boast as if it were not a gift?" (1 Cor 4:7) convinced him that "he was mistaken in thinking that faith, by which we believe in God, was not also a gift of God, but that it proceeded from what we possess."[4] And in the sixth-century *Gelasian Sacramentary* we read that "tibi sine te placere non possumus" (we cannot be pleasing to you [God] if you do not concede it to us).[5] We have already cited the following text, again belonging to the Augustinian tradition, present among the teachings of the Second Council of Orange. It is unacceptable to say

that mercy is divinely conferred upon us when, without God's grace, we believe, will, desire, strive, labor, pray, keep watch, endeavor, request, seek, knock, [while not confessing] … that it is through the infusion and inspiration of the Holy Spirit that we believe, will or are able to do all these things as is required; or if anyone subordinates the help of grace to humility or human obedience, and does not admit that it is the very gift of grace that makes us obedient and humble, contradicting the Apostle who says: "What have you that you did not receive?" (1 Cor 4:7); and also: "By the grace of God I am what I am" (1 Cor 15:10).[6]

The gift of grace, therefore, is not the result of human effort or initiative, of acquired virtue, and not even of humility and obedience. All this, in fact, is the result of divine self-giving.

The Different Ambits of Human Life in Which We Need Grace

Before speaking of the nature of grace in the *Summa Theologiae*, Thomas Aquinas considers in a detailed way the issue of the need for grace in different stages and

---

2. See chapter 5, the beginning of chapter 8, and chapter 11, notes 22ff. and corresponding text.
3. Aquinas, *S.Th.* I, q. 43, a. 3.
4. Augustine, *De praedest. sanctorum*, III, 7.
5. See *Gelasian Sacramentary* (PL 74, 1194c) and the *Gregorian Sacramentary* (PL 78, 186c).
6. Council of Orange II, DH 376. This text provides a summary of Augustine, *De praedest. sanctorum*.

ambits of human life, which correspond to different aspects of human action.[7] The following seven aspects may be considered.

Knowing the Truth

In the first place, Aquinas asks if grace is needed "to know what is true."[8] On the one hand, it is obvious that in order to know the mysteries of faith, the Trinity, the incarnation, and so on, humans stand in need of divine revelation. On the other hand, however, humans do not need divine grace to know truth in a generic sense because they possess by means of their creation a natural capacity to know things (including the existence and attributes of God), and this capacity has not been removed or destroyed by sin, even though our energy and capacity to know may have been affected. Of course, though they may have no need for special divine grace to know what is true, humans certainly need the divine *concursus*, with which they carry out all actions that belong to created nature. But it is clear that this *concursus* is not identified in any way with grace because it belongs to the natural metaphysical constitution of humans.[9]

The knowledge of God as the basis and prime cause of everything that exists is in fact the proper object of human reason, and humans have access to it, in principle, without the help of grace. With this natural knowledge humans can understand the principal moral and religious truths. This doctrine, based on scripture (Wis 13; Rom 1–2) and amply developed by medieval authors, has been taken up by the Church in Vatican Councils I and II and frequently commented upon in twentieth-century and more recent Church documents.[10] In the encyclical *Casti Connubii* of Pius XI, for example, it is said that the moral truths that refer to marriage and sexuality are accessible to the human intellect.[11] In the encyclical *Humani Generis* Pope Pius XII taught that the knowledge of God and of his law can be acquired "absque divinae revelationis divinaeque gratiae auxilio" (without the help of revelation and of divine grace).[12] And in the encyclical of John Paul II *Fides et Ratio*, the same position is repeated insistently.[13]

Still, revelation, and with it divine grace, become *morally* necessary for humans in their present situation marked by original and personal sin, so that God—as the foundation and first cause of the created world—may be known "ab omnibus expedite, firma certitudine et nullo admixto errore" (by all easily, with firm certitude and without error), to use the expression of Vatican Council I.[14] Counter-Reformation

---

7. Aquinas, *S.Th.* I-II, q. 109, aa. 1–10.

8. See ibid., a. 1. For a historical overview, see Flick and Alszeghy, *Il vangelo della grazia*, § 28; Auer, *Das Evangelium der Gnade*, 216–22.

9. "Semper indigemus divino auxilio ad cogitandum quodcumque, inquantum ipse movet intellectum ad agendum." Aquinas, *S.Th.* I-II, q. 109, a. 1, ad 3. On the question of divine *concursus*, see O'Callaghan, *La metafisica cristiana*, 164f.

10. See Vatican Council I, *Dei Filius*, DH 3005, 3031–33; Vatican Council II, *Dei Verbum*, nos. 3, 6.

11. See Pope Pius XI, *Casti Connubii*, Encyclical Letter, December 31, 1930, in *Acta Apostolicae Sedis* 22 (1930): 579f.

12. See Pope Pius XII, *Humani Generis*, Encyclical Letter, August 12, 1950, in *DH* 3890.

13. See John Paul II, *Fides et Ratio*, pars. 19–22.

14. Vatican Council I, *Dei Filius*, DH 3005.

theology, assuming in part the position of Luther, Calvin, and others, considered that "in many things man errs if not illumined and directed by God."[15] The same principle may be applied to the knowledge of natural law and what constitutes upright moral behavior.[16] We need to keep in mind in this area that the ultimate questions of human reason regarding truth, the good, the cause of all things, and the meaning of love have a strong existential and religious impact on people's lives. In practice, reason cannot deal with them without being conditioned in one way or another by the will. Also, in this sense we can take it that grace becomes morally necessary and acts invisibly to direct the will in a proper way toward truth and goodness.[17] When everything is taken into account, the help of grace is morally necessary for those who do not know revelation in order to fulfill the will of God, follow the dictates of conscience, and eventually be saved.[18]

Doing Good and Avoiding Evil

In a series of articles Aquinas asks if grace is necessary "to do good and avoid evil."[19] His response, understandably, is measured but substantially positive: divine grace is needed to do good and avoid committing sin. As regards the first part, "doing good," he distinguishes between the conditions in which humans have lived historically: the "prelapsary" condition, that which obtained before original sin, and the "postlapsary" condition, after the Fall. Before the Fall, humans could do good, with a way of acting proportionate to their nature. They could carry out good actions, actions that reflected the will of God. Still, when creating humans, God elevated them to the order of grace. Without this *gratia elevans*, humans were not in a position to carry out perfect actions because such actions, though upright in themselves, did not have the supernatural power to reach God in his Trinitarian intimacy.[20] And this supernatural power is called by Thomas "the principal necessity of grace."[21] Thus the Council of Orange, which takes up the doctrine of Augustine, says: "Whenever we carry out anything good, God works in us and with us [*Deus in nobis atque nobiscum*] so that we can act."[22] The liturgy expresses this conviction whenever the Christian community directs its prayer to the Father, through Christ, in the Holy Spirit.

In the fallen state, however, humans are capable of carrying out some good actions, Thomas says, "sicut aedificare domos, plantare vineas, et alias huiusmodi" (like

---

15. R. Bellarmine, *De gratia et lib. arb.*, l. 5, c. 3. Bellarmine lists eleven ways in which human ignorance may be expressed as a result of the original Fall: *De amiss. gratiae et statu peccati*, l. 6, c. 9.

16. See the document of the International Theological Commission, *In Search of a Universal Ethic: A New Look at the Natural Law* (2009), and P. O'Callaghan, "Algunas reflexiones sobre identidad cristiana, laicidad y ley natural," in *Identidad cristiana: Coloquios universitarios*, edited by A. Aranda (Pamplona: Eunsa, 2006), 200–214. See also chapter 2 of *LS*.

17. See *GS*, no. 22.

18. See *LG*, no. 16. See also chapter 12, notes 37ff. and corresponding text.

19. See Aquinas, *S.Th.* I-II, q. 109, aa. 2, 4, 8, 9.

20. On the question of *gratia elevans* and its importance in the Christian vision of the origins of humanity, see O'Callaghan, *La metafísica cristiana*, 264–66.

21. "Homo post peccatum ad plura indiget gratia quam ante peccatum, sed non magis, *quia* homo ante peccatum indigebat gratia ad vitam aeternam consequendam, quae est principalis necessitas gratiae," *S.Th.* I, q. 95, a. 4, ad 1.

22. Council of Orange II, *DH* 379.

building houses, planting vines, and things of the kind).[23] For fallen humans, doing good is a source of fatigue, and they need not only *gratia elevans*, which directs good actions to God in person, but also *gratia sanans*, healing grace that purifies the heart and facilitates upright action. Thus Aquinas adds: "Magis est natura humana corrupta per peccatum quantum ad appetitum boni, quam quantum ad cognitionem veri" (Human nature is more corrupt as regards the appetite to the good than with respect to the knowledge of what is true).[24] In practical terms, this means that it is more difficult to do good than to know truth.

In order to avoid sin, humans stand in need of divine grace.[25] Since the Fall, says Thomas, as distinct from before, some sin is more or less inevitable.[26] "Humans cannot avoid sin for a long period of time without sanctifying grace, because they are drawn toward temporal goods as if they were the last end; therefore it becomes impossible for them to be attracted by the moral good."[27] It should be said, however, that even after the Fall it is possible to avoid mortal sin, though not every venial sin.[28] Besides, if humans, though regenerated through baptism, are in the state of mortal sin, they will be capable of avoiding further grave sins one by one, but only with enormous effort will they be able to avoid further mortal sin for an extended period of time.[29] To live one's life avoiding all venial sin should be considered a special privilege, one that God, as far as we know, has granted only to the Virgin Mary.[30] In any case, without divine help it is impossible to remain immune from light faults.[31]

The habitual state of humans is such that they need to ask God pardon frequently for their faults. This doctrine is present throughout the whole of scripture: "Woe is me! For I am lost; for I am a man of unclean lips, and I dwell in the midst of a people of unclean lips; for my eyes have seen the King, the Lord of hosts!" (Is 6:5). "Who can say, 'I have made my heart clean; I am pure from my sin'?" (Prv 20:9; see 24:16). "Surely there is not a righteous man on earth who does good and never sins" (Qo 7:20). "Let not many of you become teachers, my brethren, for you know that we who teach shall be judged with greater strictness. For we all make many mistakes, and if any one makes no mistakes in what he says he is a perfect man, able to bridle the whole body also" (Jas 3:1f.). "If we say we have no sin, we deceive ourselves, and the truth is not in us" (1 Jn 1:8). The same principle may be found in the liturgy: all Christians are invited to frequently ask God to forgive their faults and sins.

---

23. Aquinas, *S.Th.* I-II, q. 109, a. 2, co.   24. Ibid., *S.Th.* I-II, q. 109, a. 2, ad 3.

25. For a historical overview, see Flick and Alszeghy, *Il vangelo della grazia*, § 32.

26. "Secundum statum quidem naturae integrae, etiam sine gratia habituali, poterat homo non peccare nec mortaliter nec venialiter." *S.Th.* I-II, q. 109, a. 8, co.

27. Aquinas, *De Ver.*, q. 24, a. 12, co.

28. It is impossible to avoid every single venial sin, Thomas says, "propter corruptionem inferioris appetitus sensualitatis, cuius motus singulos quidem ratio reprimere potest (et ex hoc habent rationem peccati et voluntarii), non autem omnes, quia dum uni resistere nititur, fortassis alius insurgit; et etiam quia ratio non semper potest esse pervigil ad huiusmodi motus vitandos." Aquinas, *S.Th.* I-II, q. 109, a. 8, co.

29. "Antequam hominis ratio, in qua est peccatum mortale, reparetur per gratiam iustificantem, potest singula peccata mortalia vitare, et secundum aliquod tempus, quia non est necesse quod continuo peccet in actu. Sed quod diu maneat absque peccato mortali, esse non potest." Aquinas, *S.Th.* I-II, q. 109, a. 8, co.

30. See Aquinas, *S.Th.* III, q. 27, a. 3; Pope Pius IX, *Ineffabilis Deus* (1854), on the Immaculate Conception of Mary, in *DH* 2803.

31. See Council of Trent, De justificatione, c. 23, *DH* 1573.

In real terms, Thomas insists on the need, in order to carry out any good action, to request the "auxilium Dei moventis" (the help of God which moves the soul toward the good),[32] equivalent to what later would be called "actual grace," in order to overcome the weakness and ignorance that derive from sin.[33]

Loving God above All Things

Then Aquinas asks if grace is necessary "to love God above all things."[34] He replies in substance, and perhaps surprisingly, that it is not. The reason is that all created nature, not only human nature, is objectively inclined toward God in the very depths of its being. For this reason, as we saw earlier, humans are *capax Dei*.[35] Aquinas concludes, therefore, that "to love God above all things is natural for humans." With their own energies, they can know and love God above all other creatures,[36] because God is objectively more knowable and more lovable than any other being.[37] Because fallen humans easily tend to love created things, which are immediately accessible, in a disorderly way, as if God did not exist, they need God's healing grace to overcome this disorder and love God above all other things. In any case, it is clear that the love of God "above all things" may not be identified with the supernatural love with which humans partake in the intimate life of the Trinity. For the latter, of course, humans need the infused virtue of charity, which adds to the natural love of God that all creatures have the capacity to love God in a personal, filial, and supernatural way, with joy and promptness.[38]

Meriting Eternal Life

Thomas asks if humans need God's grace "to merit eternal life." Merit is the blossoming, the direct fruit, of grace within the good works of believers. He responds that merit is "finis excedens proportionem naturae humanae" (an end that goes beyond human nature) and is thus the effect of grace.[39] He does not deny that there is such a thing as human merit that people can obtain.[40] However, in order to merit an increase in grace, that is, to merit before God, humans must be in the state of grace. Without grace it would be impossible to merit grace or eternal life from God. As the medieval authors put it, "prima gratia non cadit sub meritum" (first grace cannot be merited).[41] In the previous chapter we considered the reality of "merit" in the lives of

---

32. Aquinas, *S.Th.* I-II, q. 109, a. 9.

33. "Remanet etiam quaedam ignorantiae obscuritas in intellectu, secundum quam ... quid oremus sicut oportet, nescimus [Rom 8]. Propter varios enim rerum eventus, et quia etiam nosipsos non perfecte cognoscimus, non possumus ad plenum scire quid nobis expediat." Ibid., a. 9, co.

34. "Utrum homo possit diligere Deum super omnia ex solis naturalibus sine gratia." Aquinas, *S.Th.* I-II, q. 109, a. 3.

35. See chapter 9, notes 29ff.

36. Aquinas, *S.Th.* I-II, q. 109, a. 3, co.

37. By nature the human being "diligit Deum super omnia, prout est principium et finis naturalis boni." Aquinas, *S.Th.* I-II, q. 109, a. 3, co.

38. See Aquinas, *S.Th.* I-II, q. 109, a. 3, co. and ad 1.

39. See ibid., a. 5, co.

40. "Opera perducentia ad aliquod bonum homini connaturale, sicut laborare in agro, bibere, manducare, et habere amicum." Ibid.

41. See *DH* 388, 1532, 1913; Aquinas, *S.Th.* I-II, q. 114, a. 5.

humans and in the context of grace, which precedes and accompanies all human action.[42]

Preparing for Grace

Thomas teaches that humans need God's grace "to prepare themselves for grace." This is not the *gratia habitualis*, or the state of grace, because the latter is the point of arrival of the process of justification. It refers rather to the "auxilium Dei moventis" (actual grace),[43] which prepares humans to receive habitual grace. Aquinas employs the image of light, which is necessary for humans to begin to see because it awakens the soul. In this way he excludes the position of the semi-Pelagians, who taught that the *initium fidei*, the beginning of faith, was the fruit of human action.[44]

Repenting of Sin

Grace is also necessary for people to repent of sin, that is "for conversion."[45] Speaking of the repentance of the sinner, Aquinas distinguishes between the act of sin and the sinful state that follows from it, that is, between the *actus* and the *reatus*. Humans could, in principle, repent of a particular sinful act (or behavior) without the help of grace, by reasoning things out, for example, as they realize that they are ruining their lives and will not obtain happiness. But "Non est idem resurgere a peccato quod cessare ab actu peccati" (One thing is to rise up from sin, another is to desist from committing sin).[46] In effect, to understand that sin is a true personal offense to God and to return to the offended God with all one's heart, it is entirely necessary that God take the pardoning initiative through grace. Only God can bring about conversion and forgive sin,[47] in that way making it possible to make reparation for human transgression.[48] Humans are not capable of submitting themselves anew to God through conversion if God does not come close to them and illumine them. Still, God's offer of forgiveness is guaranteed in general terms for the whole of humanity by the saving death of Christ on the cross and is made abundantly accessible to the faithful in the sacrament of penance.

The Grace of Perseverance

Finally, in clear continuity with Augustinian tradition, Thomas teaches that the grace of God is necessary "to persevere to the end" in the life of grace.[49] For this reason we are exhorted to implore the grace of perseverance, for example, in the Our Father

---

42. See Flick and Alszeghy, *Il vangelo della grazia*, § 139.

43. See Aquinas, *S.Th.* I-II, q. 109, a. 6.

44. See Flick and Alszeghy, *Il vangelo della grazia*, §§ 36–41.

45. See Aquinas, *S.Th.* I-II, q. 109, a. 7.

46. Ibid., co.

47. "Cum enim decor gratiae proveniat ex illustratione divini luminis, non potest talis decor in anima reparari, nisi Deo denuo illustrante, unde requiritur habituale donum, quod est gratiae lumen." Ibid.

48. As regards reparation of sins, "similiter ordo naturae reparari non potest, ut voluntas hominis Deo subiiciatur, nisi Deo voluntatem hominis ad se trahente." Aquinas, *S.Th.* I-II, q. 109, co.

49. See Aquinas, *S.Th.* I-II, q. 109, a. 10. On the question of final perseverance, see J. Gummersbach, *Unsündlichkeit und Befestigung in der Gnade nach der Lehre der Scholastik* (Frankfurt: Verlag der Carolus-Druckerei, 1933); A. Michel, "Persévérance," *Dictionnaire de théologie catholique* 12, no. 1 (1933): 1256–1304; A. Minon, "De incertitudine perseverantiae finalis," *Revue Ecclésiastique de Liège* 35 (1948): 188–92; J. Sagüés,

(Mt 6:9–13). The same message is to be found in Luke 21:36: "But watch at all times, praying that you may have strength to escape all these things that will take place, and to stand before the Son of man." And also in Colossians 4:2: "Continue steadfastly in prayer, being watchful in it with thanksgiving." "Pray at all times in the Spirit, with all prayer and supplication," writes Paul to the Ephesians, and "to that end keep alert with all perseverance, making supplication for all the saints" (Eph 6:18). And the Church in its liturgy prays to God constantly for the perseverance of all believers until the end of their lives: "O God all-powerful and merciful, you have given to the human race help to be saved and the gift of eternal life, look benevolently on your servants and comfort the souls of those whom you have created, so that at the moment of their death they can deserve to present themselves without stain of sin, before you, their Creator."[50] Augustine considers *ex professo* the gratuitous origin of the gift of perseverance in his last work written against the semi-Pelagians, *De dono perseverantiae*. He cites Cyprian's commentary on the *Our Father*[51] and Ambrose's work *De fuga saecula*, which says that we should ask for the grace of perseverance "since our heart and our thoughts are not in our power (2 Cor 3:5)."[52] According to Augustine, to resist evil to the very end is a gift of God but also to die in the state of grace.[53] "Hoc est donum Dei suppliciter emereri potesti" (the gift of perseverance may be merited by a prayer of petition).[54] The Councils of Carthage and Orange take up this doctrine.[55]

Some Protestant authors understood that Catholic theologians held that, after having received the gift of justification, Christians could conserve and develop the new life on their own with meritorious works yet without the constant influence of the grace of Christ.[56] The Council of Trent, however, teaches that the justified person "cannot persevere in received justice without a special help from God."[57] It speaks, in fact, of perseverance in grace as "a very great gift" (*magnum donum*) of which nobody can be certain.[58]

Thomas speaks of three kinds of perseverance: firmness in virtues even in the face of difficulty; the habit of perseverance to the very end; and, finally, "perseverantiae continuatio" (continued perseverance) with respect to a particular good to be conserved until the end of time. Humans have a need for grace with respect to all three. Still, as regards the last one, they need from God the "divinum auxilium ipsum dirigente et protegente contra tentationum impulsus" (the divine help which orients and protects them from the impulse of temptation).[59] The latter must be requested

---

"¿Se puede evitar todo pecado venial?," *Estudios Eclesiásticos* 31 (1957): 205–18; Flick and Alszeghy, *Il vangelo della grazia*, §§ 148–54.

50. Collect for the Mass *ad postulandum gratiam bene moriendi*.

51. Cyprian, *Comm. in Pater noster*, 2, 4. See chapter 8, notes 68ff. and corresponding text.

52. Ambrose, *De fuga saeculi* I, 1. He also cites Lk 18:1 and 1 Thes 5:17.

53. See Augustine, *De dono persev.*, 17.

54. Ibid., 6, 10.

55. *DH* 228–30, 241. "The assistance of God ought to be implored always, even by those who have been reborn and healed, that they may arrive at a good end, or may be able to continue in good work" (DH 380). The text is inspired by the writings of Prosper of Aquitaine.

56. On this topic, see W. Joest, "Die Rechtfertigungslehre des Konzils von Trient," *Kerygma und Dogma* 20 (1963): 41–69.

57. Council of Trent, session VI, c. 22, *DH* 1572. See especially chap. 13 of the same document, *DH* 1541.

58. See Council of Trent, session VI, c. 16, *DH* 1566.

59. Aquinas, *S.Th.* I-II, q. 109, q. 10, co.

humbly from God. Perseverance, even though it cannot be merited, may be obtained through prayer[60] or, as Robert Bellarmine suggests, by continuous prayer.[61]

The meaning of this doctrine is quite clear: should humans merit perseverance in grace once they have received it, they could consider themselves in a sense confirmed in grace and therefore certainly predestined, no longer really pilgrims passing through a time of trial. Besides, as was said earlier, if humans have a need for actual grace not only to avoid sin but also to request divine help, they can not persevere in Christian life without divine grace.

60. See, ad 1.
61. According to Robert Bellarmine, Christians should request perseverance daily. *De iustif.*, l. 3, c. 13.

PART FOUR   CHRISTIAN ANTHROPOLOGY

That which is above us is none of our business.   SOCRATES[1]

The supernatural is the real.   EVELYN WAUGH[2]

All things can be happy about themselves, except humans, and this shows that their existence is not limited to this world like that of other beings.   GIACOMO LEOPARDI[3]

Man carries within himself a tendency that transcends all possible vital values and is directed toward the divine; on account of this it may be said that man is a seeker of God. MAX SCHELER[4]

Theological Anthropology and Christian Anthropology

In this fourth and last section of the book we shall consider what it means to be human *in the light of Christian faith* or, more concretely, in the light of saving grace, that is, the life of Christ present in the believer. The previous section dealt with grace in a strict sense and was based simply on Christian revelation. This one will consider a series of issues that are also the object of philosophical and scientific reflection. In chapter 1 they were called "mixed questions." We shall attempt here to offer a Christian response to the great issues humans formulate concerning their lives and existence in the light of faith and experience, that is, in the light of the plan God has for humanity and has revealed to us in faith. In effect, different aspects of created reality, especially of human nature, can be known fully and integrally only when they are illuminated by the free action of God on the world. As Benedict XVI said, "Faith is not a parallel world of feelings that we can still afford to hold on to, rather it is the key that encompasses everything, gives it meaning, interprets it and also provides its in-

---

1. This is the response he gave to those who asked what heaven was, according to Minucius Felix, Lactantius, and others.
2. E. Waugh, *Brideshead Revisted* (London: Penguin, 2000), 83.
3. G. Leopardi, *Zibaldone* I, 119.
4. M. Scheler, *Die Stellung des Menschen im Kosmos* (Munich: Nymphenburger, 1947), 91f.

ner ethical orientation: making clear that it is to be understood and lived as tending towards God and proceeding from God."[5]

Divine grace, as we know, regenerates the human being, purifies and prepares it for filial and perpetual communion with God. But the doctrine on grace does not contain the entirety of anthropology because it presupposes an already existing human structure. As we saw, human nature remains substantially unchanged when humans "lose" the state of grace through sin. Nonetheless, it is true that *grace illumines the whole of humanity*, which was created by God with the precise purpose of being elevated to the state of grace and of living in perpetual communion with him. As Maximus the Confessor, speaking of the life of grace, wrote: "On account of divinization all things exist and have stability and are created."[6] In effect, created reality, when it is illumined by God, is revealed in fullness as the fruit of his love; sin is seen to be an offense to him; humans come to perceive that they are made in the image of God, which is the point of departure for filial elevation; human freedom is understood in the context of gift and reception (or rejection); history and temporality as the human space that allows for God's action and human response within time; human sociality as a form of mediation employed by God to communicate his gifts; human work as an ambit in which God's grace may be made present in the world, thus definitively establishing divine sovereignty over the whole of creation; and, finally, the concept of the human person, which may be understood fully only on the basis of the unconditioned, Trinitarian love with which God created humans and called them to holiness and glory. As we said, all these aspects of being human are fully open and accessible to philosophical and scientific reflection. Yet the light of faith illumines the more paradoxical and hidden aspects of human life to the core. For this reason von Balthasar concludes that "no other, mythical or religio-philosophical anthropology can attain a satisfactory idea of man, an idea that integrates all the elements, but the Christian one."[7]

With a view to situating the topics this section of the book will deal with, the following pages will look into issues of a systematic and epistemological kind. It will deal, on the one hand, with the relationship between the life of grace in a strict sense (what is normally called the "supernatural order") and ordinary human life, on the other (the "natural order"). In a Christian context the distinction is obligatory not only for historical reasons but because Christian holiness and the life of grace cannot, in a strict sense, be explained in terms of the pure, natural coordinates of human life understood on the basis of philosophy, science, and common human experience. Not all humans are Christians, not even hidden ones. To say that they are should be considered condescending, even insulting, to them.[8] The life of grace is a true novelty for humans, a "new creation." Still, grace and nature not only exist side by side; they exist for one another: on the basis of God's single eternal design, they are simply inseparable. But they may not be identified *tout court*, except, of course, in the mind

---

5. Benedict XVI, discourse to seminarians in Freiburg, Germany, September 24, 2011.

6. Maximus the Confessor, *Epist.* 24.

7. Von Balthasar, *Theo-Drama*, 2:343.

8. See G. D'Costa, "Vatican II and the Status of Other Religions on Salvific Structures," in *Faith, Word and Culture*, edited by L. Bergin (Dublin: Columba Press, 2004), 9–24.

and heart of God. Proof of this distinction may be seen in the fact that those who are not in grace are still human persons, even though they have not reached the perfection they are destined for.

Our reflection on the natural and the supernatural will introduce the other human polarities this section will cover, which consider different fundamental aspects of the human being "made in the image and likeness of God" in Christ, in the context of the gift of grace received in faith:

· *as a union of body and soul* in different moments of philosophical, theological, and scientific reflection (chapter 19);

· *as a free being* (chapter 20) in the context of the polarity between freedom and determination;

· *as a temporal and historical being* (chapter 21) in which the polarity between time and eternity is to be found;

· *as a social being* (chapter 22) based on the polarity between the social and individual sides of human life;

· *as a sexual being* (chapter 23) created by God masculine and feminine; and

· *as a worker*, a child of God who lives and acts in the world (chapter 24), in which the polarity heaven-earth is present.

In an epilogue and conclusion to the text, we shall consider the genesis and nature of the concept of *the human person* (chapter 25), which may be considered the mature fruit of Christian reflection on humanity and the most beautiful and enduring contribution Christianity has made to anthropology.

What Is the Significance of the Natural and the Supernatural?

The Gospel of John teaches us that through faith in Christ humans become carriers of a life that is different from mortal, earthly life, a new life, regenerated, "eternal life." Likewise, Paul speaks of a "new life" or a "new creation" of the Christian that is the fruit of grace received in faith. But what does this "eternal life" consist of, this mysterious and invisible "life of grace," this "new life," this "new creation"? And how does it relate to life as we know it—natural, common, everyday life—at an ontological, epistemological, and existential level? Is the "new life" of the Christian simply a new lifestyle, a renewed ethics based on radical discipleship of Christ and obedience to his commandments? Certainly a renewed ethics constitutes an important, indeed integral, part of the new life of the Christian. But in real terms the renewed ethical commitment Christians assume at baptism takes place at a second stage: Christian ethical commitment springs forth from the new life present in each one.[9] John speaks of the need to "be born again" (Jn 3:3). And Paul speaks of Christ as the one "who lives in me" (Gal 2:20). Christian life is, indeed, my life, but it is the life of Christ in me, another life, a new life. "To live in Christ, to exist in Christ, means that the life of the Christian is a life that emanates from his or her union with Christ; he is the source

9. See chapter 5, notes 21ff., and chapter 6, notes 17ff. and corresponding text.

of this life, its exemplar and author, on the basis of his active presence in the Christian."[10]

At an elementary and objective level, we may say that the "new life" distinguishes the believer in Christ from the nonbeliever, the baptized from the nonbaptized. But in what way? On the one hand, Christians cannot always say that their lifestyle is notably superior to that of non-Christians from the ethical point of view. It very often is, but may not necessarily be so. Besides, through divine grace, which regenerates humans and reconciles them with God, they become aware of the sinfulness present in their lives. In effect, Christians share with the rest of humanity the same desires and difficulties, the same need to struggle, the same perception of the limits of human life, of suffering and illness, and, at heart, of mortality itself. Yet Christians are convinced that salvation is not due, in the first place, to good works, but to grace, God's gift, the new life. Nor do they forget, on the basis of the lives of the saints, that grace is capable of truly renewing humans, of producing consolidated virtue, of making saints. In that sense, the "superiority" of Christianity is due to God's grace, not necessarily to human response.

If it is possible to speak of an objective difference between the believer and the nonbeliever, it involves the relationship between two orders that surpass the ethical order insofar as they are situated at the very source of human action: *the order of human nature*, humanity as it is created by God, the common condition of all humans, and *the order of divine grace*, the supernatural order, vivified by faith in Christ. These orders might be said, hypothetically, to relate to one another in three possible ways: extrinsic, partial, and intrinsic.

An Extrinsic Rapport

It might said that the life of grace (the new life, the supernatural order) is a kind of superstructure artificially grafted onto human nature. The use of the terms "gratuitous" and "grace" when referring to the new life of Christians is meant to indicate that the latter is a gift to them, a gift that derives from the love of God, in continuity and integrated with other gifts. However, the term "gratuitous" may also refer to something unnecessary and superfluous, something arbitrary, extrinsic, and artificial with respect to nature itself, as when we say, "That was a gratuitous remark!" If meant in this sense the term "grace" would be a mere linguistic accessory that speaks in general, but noncommittal, terms of God's self-giving to humans. With this understanding, grace would simply be juxtaposed with human nature, with everyday life, with common human nature, and thus would become more or less irrelevant. Consisting of a kind of mysterious, magical, or elusive elevation of human nature, it would exercise no true influence on the real lives of humans who live and work along with others in the midst of the natural world. Understandably, this extrinsic understanding of the supernatural order, though present to some degree in other periods, is substantially absent nowadays.

---

10. Baumgartner, *La grâce du Christ*, 24.

A Partial Relationship

The life of grace and the entire supernatural order could be thought of in terms of *gratia sanans* alone, which considers grace as a source of healing, a light for the intellect and impulse for the will that God gives humans in order to overcome sin and sinful inclinations. This aspect of grace, of course, is of considerable importance (it is dealt with especially by Augustine and later on by Jansen). However, if the supernatural is limited to this alone, the two orders will sooner or later come into conflict with one another: the weaker human nature is (that is, the fallen human being with his own energies), the more need it has for grace or supernatural assistance; the stronger humans are, the less need they have for divine help. Thus, although strong humans would have little need for God, the weak ones would be very dependent on him. This interpretation, according to which grace is situated first in continuity with and then in opposition to fallen human nature, tends to produce a secularized view of the world. According to this scheme of things, when humans are eventually reconciled with God at the end of time and sin is defeated forever, the distinction between the two orders will actually have to disappear entirely.

An Intrinsic Relationship

The integration between the natural and supernatural orders may also be focused in terms of the simple and basically valid spiritual intuition of the writer Georges Bernanos with which he concludes his *Diary of a Country Priest:* "All is grace," he says. In effect, everything that God does in the world (creation, redemption, calling, sanctification, elevation, glorification) is done freely, gratuitously, out of love, that is, by grace. God has only one project, only one all-embracing design, as we saw in chapter 12. God's action, of whatever kind, may not be demanded of him. Now, if *all* God does is the result of his free love, why should he give a differentiated statute to the order of grace, distinct from that of created nature, on the very basis of that gratuitousness? Why speak of two orders? Would it not be simpler to speak of a single one in which "all is grace"? This is the point that will be considered in this chapter: why should we maintain a kind of duality within God's unique design and plan for humanity?

Using the Terms "Natural" and "Supernatural"

It is true that contemporary theology uses the terms "natural" and "supernatural" infrequently. Still, documents of Vatican Council II,[11] as well as the *Catechism of the Catholic Church,*[12] refers often to the "supernatural order." The theologian Henri de Lubac, who, more than anybody else, dealt with the question during the twentieth century, said on one occasion that "the supernatural order is essential to Christianity, as is for example the idea of revelation or that of Incarnation or that of sacrament."[13] Likewise, Walter Kasper, speaking of the modern challenge of secularization, states:

11. See Vatican Council II, *Apostolicam Actuositatem*, nos. 6–8, 24, 30; *Christus Dominus*, October 28, 1965, nos. 17, 20, 28, 35; *Inter Mirifica*, December 4, 1963, no. 6; *LG*, nos. 12, 61; *Optatam Totius*, October 28, 1965, nos. 11, 21; *Presbyterorum Ordinis*, December 7, 1965, no. 16; *Sacrosanctum Concilium*, December 4, 1963, no. 122.

12. The term is used about thirty times in *CCC*.

13. De Lubac, *Surnaturel*, 325.

"The crisis of the supernatural is the root of the present crisis in the Church in the Western world."[14] Doubtless the terms "natural" and "supernatural" may be misunderstood. Still, it would seem necessary to identify an appropriate way for speaking of the Biblical message regarding the specificity and novelty of being Christian with respect to the created, natural world. With Olivier Boulnois we may say that "throughout the vicissitudes of the supernatural, it is possible to read and detect all the difficulties of Christian anthropology."[15]

The Relationship between the Natural and the Supernatural: Historical Pointers

As we saw, the distinction between the natural and supernatural orders is already present among the Church Fathers and early ecclesiastical writers as an expression of Pauline and Johannine teaching on "new life," "new creation," salvation as the fruit of grace rather than works, "eternal life," and so on. Irenaeus, Clement of Alexandria, and Tertullian, for example, make the distinction. Origen writes: "Nothing God has made can go against nature ... but there are things that are beyond nature: they are the things that God can do by elevating man beyond human nature."[16] The term *hyperfuēs* ("superessential" or "supernatural") is used by the Fathers to refer, in the first place, to God himself in his action in the world,[17] especially with respect to divine actions that exceed the ordinary workings of nature: the virginal conception of Jesus Christ, his incarnation, the eucharist, miracles.[18] The Latin term *supernaturalis* is used for the first time, probably, by Rusticus in the sixth century.[19] The distinction is developed and applied by Pseudo-Dionysius the Areopagite during the same period in his work *De mystica theologica*, and, later on, during the eighth century, by John Damascene.[20] The one who first used the counterpoised terminology "natural"-"supernatural" was probably the ninth-century philosopher and theologian Scotus Eriugena, in his work *De divisione naturae*. In the theology of Augustine and in that of some of his followers there is a strong insistence on the predomination of the order of grace over that of fallen nature. That is, before God (*coram Deo*) humans are understood in terms of *grace*, and in that sense are destined to salvation, or as *sinners* worthy of condemnation. However, at a theological level it would seem that the consistency and value of the natural order are neglected.

The Middle Ages saw the introduction of Aristotelian categories into anthropology. Human nature as such began to be considered as a reality in itself, open to a philosophical and scientific reflection quite independent of the life of grace. Under the influence of Aristotle, the question of the individuality and dignity of each and

---

14. W. Kasper, "Natur-Gnade-Kultur: Zur Bedeutung der modernen Säkularisierung," *Theologische Quartalschrift* 170 (1990): 81–97, 91.

15. O. Boulnois, "Surnaturel," in *Dictionnaire critique de théologie*, edited by J.-Y. Lacoste (Paris: PUF, 1998), 1112–16, 1112; English translation: *Encyclopedia of Christian Theology* (London: Fitzroy Dearboy, 2005).

16. Origin, *Adv. Cels.* V, 23.

17. Ibid.

18. See Maximus the Confessor, *Exp. orat. dom.* (PG 90, 893b).

19. In a translation of Rusticus undertaken by Isidore of Pelusius, *Epist.* 44.

20. John Damascene, *De fide orth.* 81, 4, 8.

every person as a component of nature became more central, without making explicit reference to supernatural life and the reasons of faith. The first medieval author to have reflected on the relationship between the natural and the supernatural order was Philip the Chancellor.[21] Shortly after him, in a systematic way, came Thomas Aquinas.[22] Most posterior efforts at clarifying the question have been based on the latter's writings.[23]

Thomas Aquinas on the Relationship between the Natural and the Supernatural

According to Aquinas, "nature" in each human being refers to the common metaphysical nucleus of humans as beings created with intelligence and will, made in body and soul in the image and likeness of God. It is this created spiritual nucleus that gives humans their native capacity to enter into a relationship with God, and therefore to be open to the life of grace and to the possibility of divinization. The "supernatural" order, however, refers to the concrete, historical realization of this native openness to the divine through the infusion of grace by Christ, which sanctifies those who receive it freely, elevating them beyond their created and natural condition, placing them in the state of adoptive divine filiation. With this new life humans are capable of living in intimacy with God, their last end, which will reach plenitude in beatific and perpetual vision in communion with the Trinity.

Thomas's position may be summed up in three points. First, the supernatural order is situated above and beyond the natural limits and possibilities humans have (and will have) at their disposal: "Gratia excedit conditionem naturae creatae" (Grace exceeds the condition of created nature).[24] On several occasions, in fact, Thomas teaches that the good contained in a single grace is superior to the natural good of the whole universe.[25] Second, this new order is not opposed to that of nature because it involves its fulfillment and perfection: "Supernaturale non tollit sed perficit naturam" (The supernatural does not take away nature but rather perfects it).[26]

---

21. See Thomas Aquinas, Albert the Great, and Philip the Chancellor, *The Cardinal Virtues*, edited by R. E. Houser (Toronto: Pontifical Institute of Mediaeval Studies, 2004); W. H. Principe, ed., *Philip the Chancellor's Theology of the Hypostatic Union* (Toronto: Pontifical Institute of Mediaeval Studies, 1975).

22. Thomas uses this terminology principally in his treatise on the theological virtues: *S.Th.* I-II, qq. 62ff.

23. On the history of the question of the supernatural and the place it occupies in Aquinas, see de Lubac, *Surnaturel*; J. Alfaro, *Lo natural y lo sobrenatural: Estudio histórico desde santo Tomás hasta Cayetano, 1274–1534* (Madrid: Consejo Superior de Investigaciones Científicas, 1952); H. de Lubac, *Augustinisme et théologie moderne* (Paris: Aubier-Montaigne, 1965), translated into English as *Augustinianism and Modern Theology* (New York: Herder, 1969); J.-H. Nicolas, *Les profondeurs de la grâce* (Paris: G. Beauchesne, 1969); C. Ruini, *La trascendenza della grazia nella teologia di san Tommaso d'Aquino* (Rome: Pontificia Università Gregoriana, 1971); G. Colombo, *Del soprannaturale* (Milan: Glossa, 1996); Various Authors, "Surnaturel: Une controverse au coeur du thomisme au XXᵉ siècle," *Revue thomiste* 109 (2001); Boulnois, "Surnaturel"; S. A. Long, *Natura Pura: On the Recovery of Nature in the Doctrine of Grace* (New York: Fordham University Press, 2010); L. Feingold, *The Natural Desire to See God According to St. Thomas Aquinas and His Interpreters*, 2nd ed. (Ave Maria, Fla.: Sapientia Press of Ave Maria University, 2010). For a more recent summary of the debate, see C. M. Cullen, "The Natural Desire for God and Pure Nature: A Debate Renewed," *American Catholic Philosophical Quarterly* 86, no. 4 (2012): 705–30.

24. Aquinas, *S.Th.* I-II, q. 112, a. 1, co.; q. 114, a. 2, co.; a. 5, co.

25. See ibid., q. 113, a. 9, ad 2.

26. See Aquinas, *III Sent.*, d. 24, q. 1, a. 3, co.; *IV Sent.*, d. 2, q. 4, a. 4, *s.c.* 1; *S.Th.* II-II, q. 188, a. 8, co.

And third, Aquinas often says that humans are "capax gratiae" (capable of receiving grace).[27] That is to say, in humans is to be found a *potentia obedientialis* for grace.[28] This expression may be explained as follows.

The natural activities of humans, such as seeing, understanding, and walking, take place predictably during their lives. In order to carry them out they possess by nature a corresponding *potentia activa* that is activated and perfected through the operation in question over the simple passage of time. Yet humans do not possess an *active capacity* for grace, in the sense that they do not have the germinal structures that might allow for a gradual and spontaneous development of divine life in their souls. It is also true, however, that human openness to grace is not a purely passive capacity that would remain extrinsic to them, and that because they are truly *capax gratiae*, and grace received really transforms them—regenerates, recreates, and elevates their faculties—without substantially altering their nature. That is, grace does not produce in humans a *metamorphosis*, or change in nature. The meaning of the *potentia obedientialis*, therefore, is as follows: humans possess a native openness to grace without having the proper power capable of actively fulfilling this openness.

Still, two important questions are left open. First, in distinguishing between the natural and the supernatural, how can we avoid understanding the human being in terms of a "two-plane" structure, as two separate worlds artificially connected with one another? We already saw that Thomas situated his treatise on grace at the end of his study of fundamental moral theology (*S.Th.* I-II). The work was determined entirely by his understanding of Christian grace in its eschatological and teleological aspects. In effect, Aquinas considers moral action and the life of grace (ibid., qq. 109–14) on the basis of the single last end of humans (ibid., qq. 1–5). Following Aristotle, he teaches that human nature is structured in a teleological way in that it tends toward its proper end. Still, he says that there is in fact *only one last end for humans*,[29] and it is supernatural in character in that it is directed toward perfect contemplation in the definitive possession of God, the result of which is human beatitude in their entire being, spiritual and corporeal.[30] In real terms, there are not two distinct last ends, one for the natural order and another for the supernatural order. Of course human beings, one by one, can miss out on their supernatural last end by falling into grave sin and remaining in it, but in real terms there is no viable alternative to the supernatural end. If they fall and remain in sin, they will be lost; if they remain in grace, they will share in God's life forever. "Aut vitis, aut ignis," said Augustine, "either the vine," in union with Christ, "or the fire," that is, definitive separation from him.[31]

The oneness of the last end is based on the fact that there is only one God, and therefore only one divine plan: as we already saw, creation, predestination, vocation, justification, and glorification are inseparable within divine action. Whatever humans do, whatever happens to them, in the natural and the supernatural sphere, is

---

27. "Est enim creatura rationalis capax illius beatae cognitionis inquantum est ad imaginem Dei." *S.Th.* III, q. 9, a. 2, co. "Anima rationalis secundum naturam suam capax est eius [i.e., visionis beatae] prout scilicet est ad imaginem Dei facta." *S.Th.* III, q. 9, a. 2, ad 3. See also *S.Th.* I, q. 12, a. 4, ad 3; q. 93, a. 4, co.

28. See, for example, *De Veritate*, q. 29, a. 3, ad 3.

29. Aquinas, *S.Th.* I-II, q. 1, a. 7.

30. See ibid., qq. 5–6.

31. Augustine, *In Io. Ev. tr.*, 15, 6.

carried out in dependence on God and tends toward and is included within their last supernatural end. Only in communion with God will humans find their perfect and definitive self-realization. Just as the object of the human intellect is the *universale rerum*, Thomas says, the object of the human will is the *universale bonum*, all good things, which is to be found in God, Trinity of persons, and only in him.[32] Other created beings are participated goods for humans, whose longing for fullness can be satisfied by God only through the beatific vision. In brief, the union of the natural and supernatural orders is situated primarily in God, not in humans, because God is simple, whereas humans are not.

The second question is the following: Is the desire or longing for God (of which Augustine speaks unforgettably at the beginning of his *Confessions*) entirely the fruit of grace in humans, or is it rooted in human nature itself? Do humans, *capax Dei*, desire communion with God because, through grace, he insinuates this longing into their hearts as something totally new and unexpected? Or is it something that is written into human nature, hard-wired as it were, in the original and unchangeable constitution of humans made in the image of God, spiritual beings?

According to Thomas, the desire or appetite for God is rooted in the very intellectual and volitive constitution of humans, in their spiritual nature: "Omnis intellectus naturaliter desiderat divinae substantiae visionem" (Every intellect naturally desires to see the divine substance).[33] At the same time, he insists, this desire does not imply on the part of humans a positive exigency of being fulfilled. They stand in absolute need of God-given grace in order to be justified, just as they need the creative act of God in order to exist. And the grace of God is certainly not present at the created beginning of their existence, not even in a germinal way: it needs to grow and consolidate throughout life as the fruit of the supernatural action of God. In any case, later on we shall attempt to clarify what the "natural desire to see God" really means.

The Position of Duns Scotus

Like Thomas, Duns Scotus understands humans as intellectual beings capable of receiving beatific vision and therefore open to supernatural life.[34] The concrete realization of this capacity depends, of course, on God's free gift, which requires, according to Scotus, a contingent and unforeseeable act of God. The problem that might arise from this position lies in the possibility that the complete gratuitousness of divine grace enters into dialectic opposition to the supreme human inclination toward the realization of their desire for God. If the desire to see God is structural or natural in humans, how can divine grace be gratuitous? The alternatives are the following: either the natural appetite for God is frustrated, or the supernatural realization of humans must take place necessarily. The latter is the position (optimistic, as we can see) taken by Scotus.

---

32. "Obiectum autem voluntatis, quae est appetitus humanus, est universale bonum; sicut obiectum intellectus est universale verum. Ex quo patet quod nihil potest quietare voluntatem hominis, nisi bonum universale. Quod non invenitur in aliquo creato, sed solum in Deo, quia omnis creatura habet bonitatem participatam." Aquinas, *S.Th.* I-II, q. 2, a. 8, co.

33. Aquinas, *SCG* III, 57, 4.

34. See the classic work of Minges, *Die Gnadenlehre des Johannes Duns Scotus*, and the more recent ones

"Pure Nature," Cajetan, and His School

In the sixteenth century Thomas di Vio Caetano, or Cajetan, took a position against Scotist "necessity" with respect to grace. In his commentaries on the works of Thomas Aquinas he insists that supernatural life (and therefore beatific vision) remains outside and beyond the natural and spontaneous appetite of humans.[35] Cajetan teaches that there is no appetite or natural desire in humans directed toward the beatific vision; should there be, as Scotus had suggested, it would have to be fulfilled always, and, as a result, the supernatural order would no longer be gratuitous. The desire to see God, Cajetan teaches, is exclusively the fruit of grace. The *potentia obedientialis* in humans, he says, is a kind of purely passive receptivity. In other words, in believers we may find two life planes connected with one another accidentally, the natural and the supernatural. Authors begin to speak of "pure human nature," a nature that is complete in itself, needless of grace, open to an exclusively philosophical inquiry.

In taking this position, Cajetan closely follows the Aristotelian doctrine expressed in the following phrase of his predecessor, the fifteenth-century theologian Dionysius the Carthusian: "Naturale desiderium ultra naturalem capacitatem se extendere nequit" (The natural desire does not go beyond the capacity of nature).[36] Only in this way, says Cajetan, can we maintain the complete gratuitousness of the supernatural order. Should humans naturally desire to see God with their own energies, they would have to count on the real capacity to give fulfillment to that desire, and grace would no longer be freely given.

The position of Cajetan is shared by his contemporary, the theologian Sylvester of Ferrara, called the Ferrariensis. The latter writes:

If God was the natural end [of man], that is, the end toward which nature inclines, although the end is obtainable only in a supernatural way, this would mean that nature inclines the subject to a condition that would be impossible for it to produce for itself. But an appetite present in every being which cannot be satisfied in any way by nature would be useless to nature as a whole.... It is absurd to desire something by a natural appetite (the only form of natural inclination) without man in any way being able to reach this end with his own natural capacities, because nature of itself has inclinations only within the limits of nature.[37]

---

of De Armellada, *La gracia, misterio de libertad*, and O. Boulnois, *Duns Scoto: Il rigore della carità* (Milan: Jaca Book, 1999). See also Feingold, *The Natural Desire to See God*, 47–65.

35. See B. Hallensleben, *Communicatio: Anthropologie und Gnadenlehre bei Thomas de Vio Cajetan* (Munster: Aschendorff, 1985); R. Cessario, "Cardinal Cajetan and His Critics," *Nova et Vetera* (English ed.) 3, no. 1 (2005): 109–18; Feingold, *The Natural Desire to See God*, 101–82.

36. Dionysius the Carthusian, *De lumine christianae theoriae* I, a. 56. Cajetan has the same teaching: "Non videtur verum, quod intellectus creatus naturaliter desideret videre Deum: quoniam natura non largitur inclinationem ad aliquid, ad quod tota vis naturae perducere nequit; cuius signum est, quod organa natura dedit cuilibet potentiae quam intus in anima posuit." *In primam*, q. 12, a. 1. On this issue and these citations, see M. Beer, *Dionysius' des Kartäusers Lehre vom Desiderium naturale des Menschen nach der Gottesschau* (Munich: Max Hueber Verlag, 1963); De Lubac, *Augustinisme et théologie moderne*, 201–3; Feingold, *The Natural Desire to See God*, 67–79.

37. Franciscus Silvestri Ferrarense, *Opera* (Venice, 1535), 1:39–41.

Positions of the kind are held by Luis de Molina,[38] Francis Suárez,[39] and Robert Bellarmine.

Luther, Baius, and Jansen

The position of Luther, who was also a contemporary of Cajetan, is similar, though focused in an Augustinian way, that is, centered on the opposition between grace and sin in humans. The gratuitousness of salvation, of new life, imposes a clear distinction between the sinful human being (fallen nature) and the justified person. In other words, human "nature" has no particular theological value, no native openness to the divine. This position tends towards fideism and, sooner or later, secularization. Baius, in teaching that the gifts and grace of God are an integral part of human nature, enters into the same logic but with different results: if all is grace, then nothing is grace. In the same way, Jansen holds that in humans the demand for supernatural life is intrinsic to them.[40]

New Approaches to the Notion of the Supernatural in the Twentieth Century

Explanations centered on two accidentally connected planes brought theologians to speak of a "pure nature" that can be understood entirely on its own terms, with no structural reference to the supernatural, to the life of grace. According to this doctrine, the *potentia obedientialis* would be a purely passive receptivity to God's grace. The supernatural would belong, therefore, to another world, an unknown world, perhaps an irrelevant and unreal world, entirely unlinked to the one we know and live in. This position clearly tends toward secularization.

Throughout the twentieth century an understandable reaction may be detected against the (not always understood) distinction between two clearly separated orders and especially the idea of "pure nature." This reaction arose within an important theological movement called modernism.[41] Given the challenge of rampant secularization, modernist thinkers rightly insisted anew on the natural inclination of humans toward God that is written into their nature, on the religious character of the whole of human life and society. In some cases, however, it seemed as if there could be a quasi-physical exigency for grace: humans would be constituted from the beginning of their existence as an organism that is positively directed toward an ever more actualized relationship with God. Among the authors who contributed decisively to this awareness during the first half of the twentieth century may be included the philosophers Maurice Blondel and Pierre Teilhard de Chardin.[42]

---

38. The same position is taken up in a nuanced way by L. de Molina in *Concordia*, 16f. See chapter 11, notes 4ff. and corresponding text.

39. See de Lubac, *Augustinisme et théologie moderne*, 185–200. F. Suárez says: "Appetitus autem naturalis sequitur ex potentia naturali" (The natural appetite follows the natural power). *De gratia*, prolegom. 4, 1.

40. See chapter 11, notes 22ff. and corresponding text.

41. Among other works, see S. Casas, ed., *El modernismo a la vuelta de un siglo* (Pamplona: Eunsa, 2008). See chapter 16, note 108.

42. Blondel, of course, was an adamant opponent of modernism. John Paul II commended him for "being one of the first to discern what was at stake in the modernist crisis and the errors that were involved in it." (*Letter*, February 19, 1993; available on www.vatican.va); see also G. Tanzella-Nitti, "La proposta

However, perhaps the author who has done most to re-situate our understanding of the supernatural during the past century was Henri de Lubac, especially in his book *Surnaturel*, published first in 1946. On the basis of a wide-ranging study of the Church Fathers, de Lubac openly opposes the position of Cajetan, which, as we saw, proposes a clear distinction between the natural and the supernatural.[43] He likewise rejects the notion of "pure nature," for the divine plan is one and unique. Humans naturally experience a desire to see God, he says, and it is unthinkable that they would have been created outside this condition.[44] The gratuitousness of salvation and elevation links to the more fundamental gift of creation. Interestingly, de Lubac's book occasioned an ample controversy. Pope Pius XII's encyclical *Humanae Generis* (1950) states that some authors "destroy the gratuity of the supernatural order, since God, they say, cannot create intellectual beings without ordering and calling them to the beatific vision."[45] It is quite possible that the Pope's words refer to the position of de Lubac. After some years, in 1965, de Lubac published another essay, somewhat more nuanced, called *The Mystery of the Supernatural*.[46] He insists again that the Church Fathers are opposed to the notion of "pure nature," that the *potentia obedientialis* includes a positive tendency toward the beatific vision, and that there are not two last ends but only one, that of beatific vision.

De Lubac is not mistaken, of course, when he states that historically there was never such a thing as "pure nature." Humans, in effect, were always in a state (1) of grace, that is, of supernatural elevation, (2) of sin, or (3) of redemption through grace. Historically, in other words, "pure nature" never existed. Still, from the point of view of theological reflection, the notion of "pure nature" may be considered a useful hypothetical category (von Balthasar calls it a *Hilfsbegriff*, an auxiliary concept),[47] in that it describes those aspects of the historical and empirical human condition created by God and shared by all, aspects that may be known philosophically but that do not change substantially whether humans are in the state of grace or of sin.[48] Besides, from the point of view of God's power, there is no need to say that God could not but elevate spiritual beings, made of intellect and will, to grace, to the supernatural order. We may conclude, therefore, that the affirmation of the universal destiny of humanity to beatific vision is correct de facto, historically, but not of absolute necessity, as de Lubac seems to suggest.

apologetica di Maurice Blondel (1861–1949): Una rilettura del metodo dell'immanenza nel 150° della nascita," *Annales Theologici* 25 (2011): 45–74.

43. See C. Cardona, "Rilievi critici a due fondamentazioni metafisiche per una costruzione teologica," *Divus Thomas* (Piacenza) 75 (1972): 149–76; J. Milbank, *The Suspended Middle: Henri de Lubac and the Debate Concerning the Supernatural* (London: SCM, 2005); S.-T. Bonino and M. W. Levering, eds., *Surnaturel: A Controversy at the Heart of Twentieth-century Thomistic Thought* (Naples, Fla.: Sapientia Press of Ave Maria University, 2009); Feingold, *The Natural Desire to See God*, 317–95.

44. De Lubac seems to identify the desire to see God with Christian vocation: "This desire is nothing other than the call." De Lubac, *Surnaturel*, 487.

45. *DH* 3891.

46. See H. de Lubac, *Le mystère du surnaturel* (Paris: Aubier-Montaigne, 1965), translated into English as *The Mystery of the Supernatural* (New York: Herder and Herder, 1967). This work should be taken alongside the historical study published the same year, titled *Augustinisme et théologie moderne*.

47. Von Balthasar, *Karl Barth*, 278–335.

48. See Cardona, "Rilievi critici a due fondamentazioni metafisiche," esp. 150–62.

According to the theologian Karl Rahner, the life of a human before God, in its different aspects, both natural and supernatural, is reduced decisively to a single gratuity.[49] In his early writings Rahner held to the need for "pure nature" to save the gratuitousness of the supernatural.[50] But later on he taught that, from the moment of universal redemption brought about by Christ, human nature itself has been ordered in each and every person directly to grace through what he calls an "supernatural existential," even though many people may be unaware of its presence during their lives.[51] They are to be considered "anonymous Christians." As we already saw, this position has important ecclesiological and pastoral consequences. The Church's preaching, for example, would principally involve awakening the human spirit and making thematic what is already profoundly present and active in it. Faith that first existed in an "athematic" or implicit way now becomes, through the action of the Church, "categorical" (thematic) and explicit. Rahner writes: "There is present in the transcendental experience an unthematic and anonymous, as it were, knowledge of God. Hence the original knowledge of God is not the kind of knowledge in which one grasps an object which happens to be present itself directly or indirectly from outside. It has rather the character of a transcendental experience. Insofar as this subjective, non-objective luminosity of the subject in its transcendence is always orientated towards the holy mystery, the knowledge of God is always present unthematically and without name, and not just when we begin to speak of it."[52] And elsewhere: "Because the universal and supernatural will of God is working for human salvation, the unlimited transcendence of man, itself directed of necessity towards God, is raised up consciously by grace, although possible without explicit thematic reflection, in such a way that the possibility of faith in revelation is thereby made available to the being who possesses unlimited transcendence of knowledge and freedom."[53] In brief terms, the "natural-supernatural" polarity is verified, according to Rahner, on the level of knowledge (first athematic, then thematic) but not on that of ontology (nature, elevated nature).

Also, the theologian Juan Alfaro deals with this question when speaking of human nature as a reality that is open to the infinite, of the intellectual creature open to the whole of truth, who knows God, however, only through analogous concepts.[54] In

49. See chapter 3, notes 22ff., and chapter 14, notes 22ff. and corresponding text.

50. See K. Rahner, "Concerning the Relationship between Nature and Grace," in Rahner, *Theological Investigations* (London: Darton, Longman and Todd, 1974, 1:297–318, originally published in 1939)

51. Some authors have found difficulty with Rahner's doctrine of the supernatural existential because, "to the extent that this 'existential' is conceived as a kind of 'medium' or 'linking reality,' one may object that this is a useless supposition, whereby the problem of the relationship between nature and the supernatural is not resolved, but only set aside." H. de Lubac, *The Mystery of the Supernatural* (New York: Herder and Herder, 1967), 132n2. E. Schillebeeckx, in "L'instinct de la foi selon S. Thomas d'Aquin," *Revue des sciences philosophiques et théologiques* 48 (1964): 377–408, 397, has the same observation to make. See also the critique of J. Colombo, "Rahner and His Critics: Lindbeck and Metz," *Thomist* 56 (1992): 71–96; J. B. Metz, *Faith in History and Society: Toward a Practical Fundamental Theology* (New York: Seabury Press, 1980), 161–63. P. Rulands, in "Das übernatürliche Existential," *Zeitschrift für katholische Theologie* 123 (2001): 239–68, attempts to justify Rahner's position regarding the supernatural existential, saying that it refers more to his baptismal theology than to that of grace.

52. K. Rahner, *Foundations of Christian Faith: An Introduction to the Idea of Christianity* (London: Darton, Longman and Todd, 1978), 21.

53. K. Rahner, "Anonymous and Explicit Faith," in *Theological Investigations* (London: Darton, Longman and Todd, 1979), 16:52–59, 55.

54. Alfaro, *Lo natural y lo sobrenatural*; Alfaro, *Cristologia e antropologia* (Assisi: Cittadella, 1973); Alfaro, *De la cuestión del hombre a la cuestión de Dios* (Salamanca: Sígueme, 1988).

the present moment, humans do not have a perfect knowledge of God, which will be revealed only in the beatific vision. In the same way, the definitive good for the will comes only through grace. So there is no inner, ontological exigency in humans for grace. Alfaro teaches that without supernatural elevation a kind of natural happiness would be possible for humans; this happiness, however, would not be clearly opposed to human nature but would rather leave humans subject to the law of mobility and therefore of dissatisfaction. With grace and the beatific vision, we may say, the intellect and the will are, as it were, definitively immobilized in God.

Two issues need to be clarified with respect to Thomas Aquinas's teaching on the positions just described (those principally of Cajetan and de Lubac), which refer, respectively, to the correspondence between capacity and desire to see God and the nature of this desire.

The Correspondence between Desire and Capacity

If humans desire to see God, according to Cajetan's interpretation of Thomas Aquinas, they need to count on the active capacity that will allow them to follow through on that desire. This is the clear affirmation of Dionysius the Carthusian, already stated: "The natural desire does not go beyond the capacity of nature"; what we desire we must be capable of doing. Robert Spaemann observes that sixteenth-century Thomists interpreted Aquinas in line with the following Aristotelian principle: "If nature had given the stars the tendency to move by themselves, it would have also given them the organs necessary for that movement."[55] Applying this principle to the natural-supernatural distinction, we might say that if God had given humans a desire for him, he would also have given them the positive capacity to realize the corresponding union. But Spaemann notes the limits of this cosmological reading of the life of grace:

Thomas's specifically anthropological reflections disappear on account of the fact that man transcends himself. An effort is made to understand man by analogy with celestial bodies. The conception of nature that is present here moves in the direction that brings about the Cartesian-Spinozean definition of substance as that which may be conceived without the concept of any other thing. This fictitious anthropological hypothesis of a pure nature begins its triumphal march, with all the consequences this occasions.... Man defines himself no longer on the basis of a transcending tendency.[56]

In brief, the rule that works for stars and stones may not be applied *tout court* to humans, to the person. What happens to pure matter may be applied only analogously to the human spirit, even though the latter exists with the specific purpose of informing the material body directly.[57]

Natural human inclination may be understood in two ways, Thomas says. On the one hand, there are objects such as stones that move naturally and always downward: their inclination and capacity coincide. On the other hand, "it is said that something is natural to someone in that it inclines naturally, even if it does not have the power to obtain what it desires; for example, it is said that a woman conceives a child naturally

---

55. Aristotle, *De caelo* II.8.290a30–33.
56. Spaemann, "Sulla nozione di natura umana," 34.
57. See chapter 19, notes 84ff. and corresponding text.

which of course, is not possible without receiving the seed from her husband."[58] In other words, according to Thomas, humans may desire to have things they are incapable of obtaining. This is the case with regard to the beatific vision. The existence of this desire, therefore, does not contradict a priori the doctrine of salvation by grace, as Dionysius and Cajetan thought. Thomas openly considers the problem with respect to the *beatitudo*, that is, perfect human happiness, and asks if humans are capable of obtaining what they desire through their own natural means. He responds by saying that God has given humans free will with which they can convert: hence humans can desire happiness, but it will always be God who makes them happy.[59] In this explanation Thomas cites and accepts another Aristotelian principle, of a more personalist kind, according to which "that which we can do thanks to our friends in a sense we can do it by ourselves."[60] In brief, in the things that have to do with humans themselves, with the human spirit, with the communion between them and God and one another, we find situations in which they desire the good without being able to obtain it directly. The non-coincidence between desire and capacity is necessary in order to respect the free relationships between persons, in order to maintain human sociality in the face of an isolating individualism. Thus we can conclude that the Aristotelian principle stated by Dionysius the Carthusian and accepted by Cajetan— "the natural desire does not go beyond the capacity of nature"—may not be applied simply to humans in their relationship with God and with others and cannot be used to justify a doctrine of "pure nature."

The Consistency of the "Desire" to See God

According to the position generally attributed to Cajetan and his school, humans do not possess a natural desire to see God. At the other extreme, that of de Lubac and other twentieth-century authors, this desire is present and consistent among all humans.[61] What can be said of this contrast? On the one hand, we may say that the saints, whose lives are deeply penetrated by divine grace, desire to see God, and desire it more and more during their earthly sojourn:[62] "My eyes are ever toward the Lord" (Ps 25:15); "I am weary with my crying; my throat is parched. My eyes grow dim with waiting for my God" (Ps 69:3). At the end of the hymn of charity, Paul says: "For now we see in a mirror dimly, but then face to face. Now I know in part; then I shall understand fully, even as I have been fully understood" (1 Cor 13:12). And elsewhere he exclaims: "I am hard pressed between the two. My desire is to depart and be with Christ, for that is far better" (Phil 1:23). As we saw earlier, the dynamic of the theological virtues produces such a desire, a kind of "passion" for God, in humans.[63]

---

58. "Alio modo dicitur aliquid alicui naturale, quia habet naturalem inclinationem in illud, quamvis in se non habeat sufficiens illius principium ex quo necessario consequatur; sicut mulieri dicitur naturale concipere filium, quod tamen non potest nisi semine maris suscepto." Thomas Aquinas, *De Veritate*, q. 24, a. 10, ad 1.

59. Aquinas, *S.Th.* I-II, q. 5, a. 5, ad 1.

60. Aristotle, *Ethica Nicomachea* III.3.1112b27–28, cited by Aquinas in *S.Th.* I-II, q. 5, a. 5, ad 1.

61. John Milbank, in his work *The Suspended Middle*, takes a position in favor of de Lubac and against three authors: Feingold, *The Natural Desire to See God*; S. A. Long, *Natura Pura*; and B. Mulcahy, *Aquinas's Notion of Pure Nature and the Christian Integralism of Henri de Lubac: Not Everything Is Grace* (New York: P. Lang, 2011).

62. See *COH* 156f.

63. On the notion of desire in scripture, see *NIDNTTE* 2:241–44, s.v. ἐπιθυμέω. See chapter 15.

On the other hand, however, humans as sinners seek out the darkness in order to hide their sin, fleeing from the face of God (Gn 3:8; Jn 1:5, 3:19) and from the divine light. Thus Psalm 14:1 says: "The fool says in his heart, 'There is no God.'" But in real terms the sinner is fleeing, because he realizes that light is seeking him out and in a sense finding him, trying to unsettle his conscience and provoke his conversion. The impulse toward God is present in every person, though perhaps only vaguely.

In fact, Christ is the light of the world (Jn 8:12, 9:5), and his presence, words, and works produce ipso facto a separation between saints and sinners: "Behold, this child is set for the fall and rising of many in Israel, and for *a sign that is spoken against*," Simeon says, "that thoughts out of many hearts may be revealed" (Lk 2:34f.).[64] Before Jesus humans can recognize themselves as those who search for God or those who flee from the divine presence. We can say that openness to God, the capacity to see him, the desire to open ourselves to the whole truth, is present in every person, at least at an athematic level, perhaps weakly and feebly. The fact is that all are made "in the image and likeness of God." The spiritual nature of the human soul, open to the *universale rerum* and the *universale bonum*, shows this. This knowledge of God and desire for him can become more and more thematic, intense, and efficacious with the infusion of grace and the development of Christian life. But if there were no initial natural openness in the human spirit to God, eventual openness to the divine in receiving grace would be the result of pure faith (fideism); it would be a simple, irrational jump in the dark.[65] The act of faith would have no moral connotation (it could make no appeal to conscience), and Christian evangelization would constitute simply an act of arbitrary violence to humanity. In fact, the existence of this natural openness of the human spirit to God is what makes humans truly responsible for their actions and prevents secularism.

According to Thomas Aquinas, the notion of the "desire to see God" should be understood in an analogous way. We already saw that he speaks of at least two ways of understanding the natural human inclination toward God.[66] On the basis of his thought,[67] later authors have worked out a distinction between an "innate desire" and an "elicit desire" to see God.[68] The "innate desire" is occasioned in humans by objects proportionate to their nature and may be found in real terms in all created beings;[69] a stone, for example, possesses the inclination or the natural appetite to fall. This desire in humans cannot be referred, therefore, to God and to his intimate Trinitarian life because it would involve a necessary union with God,[70] and humans would have no need for sanctifying grace and infused charity in order to live in union with God. The "elicit desire," however, derives from the knowledge either of the works of God or of the limits of the created human condition. In effect, in recognizing their limits

---

64. See *COH* 182f.

65. See ibid., 43f.

66. See notes 56ff.

67. See the texts listed by Feingold in *The Natural Desire to See God*, 34–43. They are the following: *SCG* III, 25 and 50; *Comp. Theol.* I, 104.

68. See especially the works of Silvester in Feingold, *The Natural Desire to See God*, 183–96, and those of F. Suárez in ibid., 221–59.

69. See Feingold, *The Natural Desire to See God*, 404–6.

70. As regards the difficulties in explaining the doctrine of beatific vision adequately, see *COH* 161–70.

humans can desire to transcend them and in that way direct their lives to the one who has created them. That is, the elicit desire is occasioned by the indirect knowledge we have of God through creatures.[71] It is with this logic that Thomas demonstrates the existence of a "natural desire to see God" in angels and humans.[72] Thus the explanation of Jacques Maritain:

There is in the human intelligence a natural desire to see in his essence the same God it knows from the things he has created.... But this desire to know the *first Cause in its essence* is a desire that does not know what it asks, like the sons of Zebedee, when they asked to sit at the right hand and the left of the Son of Man [Mt 20:20–23].... Because to know the first Cause in its essence or without the mediation of anything else is to know the first Cause differently than as a first Cause.[73]

The "Pressure" of the Supernatural on the Natural: The Epistemological Relevance of a Distinction

Summing up what we have seen in this chapter, we can say that the natural and the supernatural coincide in the indivisible simplicity of the divine essence, plan, and action. They meet also in the concrete person, in everyday Christian existence and experience. "The supernatural is the real," said Evelyn Waugh.[74] *Le surnaturel, c'est du réel précis*, said the cinematographer Robert Bresson, "the supernatural is precisely what reality is."[75] But whereas God is simple, the human being is not. In the structure of humans a distinction obtains between what has been created by God, on the one

---

71. Vatican Council I, *Dei Filius*, 2, 1, DH 3026.

72. See Aquinas, SCG III, 50 and 51; *S.Th.* I-II, q. 3, a. 8: "Si igitur intellectus humanus, cognoscens essentiam alicuius effectus creati, non cognoscat de Deo nisi an est; nondum perfectio eius attingit simpliciter ad causam primam, sed remanet ei adhuc naturale desiderium inquirendi causam. Unde nondum est perfecte beatus. Ad perfectam igitur beatitudinem requiritur quod intellectus pertingat ad ipsam essentiam primae causae. Et sic perfectionem suam habebit per unionem ad Deum sicut ad obiectum, in quo solo beatitudo hominis consistit, ut supra dictum est." Milbank, in *The Suspended Middle*, 24, does not accept the distinction between innate desire and elicit desire of the supernatural. This is also the case with Bouillard in *Conversion et grâce chez S. Thomas d'Aquin*, and "L'idée de surnaturel de le mystère chrétien," *L'homme devant Dieu: Mélanges offerts au père Henri de Lubac* (Paris: Aubier, 1963), 3:153–66. Still, it may be observed that Milbank is probably reading Thomas in a somewhat neo-Platonic way, following the epistemology of Pseudo-Dionysius and Augustine, drawing therefore on the doctrine of divine illumination, which "skips over" created reality, as it were, that is, over the phenomenon in itself. According to this author, the object of the intellect would be not reality as it is known but a partaking in reality as it is known to the divine being: that is, the intellect knows not the object but rather a ray of divine light. This epistemology, of course, eliminates ipso facto the distinction between innate and elicited desire for God. This position is further explained in J. Milbank and C. Pickstock, *Truth in Aquinas* (New York: Routledge, 2001). See the comments of Long, *Natura Pura*; Mulcahy, *Aquinas's Notion of Pure Nature*, 191–94. C. M. Cullen, in *The Natural Desire for God*, 703, holds that for de Lubac and Milbank, "as in the Platonic tradition, we are divine-like beings called home. For classical Thomists, we are rational animals, at home in this natural world, and our ever seeing God face to face will involve an utter transformation of our cognitional apparatus." On the critical and specific role played by the creature in the communication of the truth of faith, see the first part of O'Callaghan, "El testimonio de Cristo y de los cristianos."

73. J. Maritain, "Approches de Dieu," in *Oeuvres* (Fribourg: Éditions Universitaires, 1985), 10:9–99, 87.

74. See note 2.

75. Robert Bresson directed, among others, a film on Bernanos's book *Diary of a Country Priest* in 1951. The phrase is cited by G. Chantraine in "Le Surnaturel: Discernement de la pensée catholique selon Henri de Lubac," *Revue thomiste* 109 (2001): 31–50, 50.

hand, and the elevated supernatural world of grace that brings them to share in the divine life, on the other. Of course the natural order is directed (in God's mind and in its own created dynamics) toward gratuitous elevation to the supernatural order, in communion with God. But the former does not contain the potentialities that make the realization of the latter possible. It would not be correct to say that the supernatural order is marked merely by gratuitousness and that the order of nature (fruit of God's creating act) is consigned to necessity. The work of creation is just as much the fruit of God's free will,[76] of Trinitarian love, as is grace, and it is destined to glory in virtue of its original purpose.[77]

The fact that in the lives of humans there is a distinction or polarity between the natural and the supernatural is of great importance, especially at an epistemological level, in understanding the mystery of humanity and the world in the light of faith. Nature is not grace, but it contains to some degree the logic of grace; the grammar of nature points toward the supernatural life. Between the two orders a distinction is to be found, but not a separation, much less an independent existence or opposition, because in real terms between them is to be found a living polarity,[78] a polarity that is expressed in a derived way in other polarities that mark Christian life: Church and state; Christianity and the world; growth of the kingdom of God and human progress; and so on.[79] In an approximate sense we can say that supernatural life "pressurizes" natural life, informing it, illuminating it, purifying it, filling it with joy, love, and liberty—with a "pressure" of grace that in a sense "seduces" humans, what Augustine called the *suavitas amoris*. While avoiding an identification of grace with nature (and the integralist understanding of human life, ethics, and political science that derives from it), divine grace may be seen as pressurizing human nature and "bringing out the best" in it, as it were, whereas human nature channels and applies grace to the concrete situations humans live in. Grace and nature combine in a kind of Hegelian synthesis—without the *Aufhebung*.

In the coming chapters we shall consider several aspects of the natural constitution of humans (body-soul, freedom, historicity, sociality, activity, personhood) in the light of the gift of divine grace according to the logic of the distinction and union between the natural and supernatural orders as described above. Three examples of this dynamic of the double-order polarity may be cited to explain this, thus concluding the chapter.

First, whereas human free will takes no part in the work of creation, it is present

---

76. The expression applied by Vatican Council I to God's work of creation is *liberrimo consilio*. DH 3025.

77. "To live in grace means to live and obtain fulfillment from the God who created us. There is no need to add the relationship of grace to that of creation, because one is the perfection of the other. In his nature, in the depths of his fundamental inclinations, man created by grace tends towards God as his fulfillment, and all other possible goods are included in that total good, and all inclinations are summed up in that fundamental inclination. Not only before God, but towards God. God is not only present in man as the one who gives being, but as the one who gives himself, as the fulfillment of being. To lose this grace or leave it inoperative and inert is to destroy oneself. Man without grace is in fact that 'useless passion' [Sartre], this creature who strives to be God without ever finding anything but himself." M.-J. Nicolas, *Évolution et christianisme: De Teilhard de Chardin à saint Thomas d'Aquin* (Paris: Fayard, 1973), 144f. See chapter 12, notes 105ff. and corresponding text.

78. See chapter 1, notes 35ff. and corresponding text.

79. An important manifestation of this polarity is to be found in the Christian understanding of secularity; see M. Rhonheimer, *Christentum und säkularer Staat: Geschichte-Gegenwart-Zukunft* (Freiburg: Herder, 2012).

in natural human action and in the acceptance of divine grace; this free action shares in the consequent process of divinization. As Augustine says, "Qui ergo fecit te sine te non te iustificat sine te" (He who created you without you does not justify you without you).[80] Besides, the life of grace, the fruit of supernatural elevation, can be lost through the free act of grave sin, but in this process humans do not lose their own nature or existence destined for immortality.

Second, supernatural life relates to the natural order also by the fact that humans develop historically, not only in appearance (as would be the case of a tree that grows from a seed) but in a very real way. This is so because the definitive identity of the human being is not entirely given with nature but consolidates, stage by stage, throughout time and history. In real terms it is achieved only eschatologically, at the end of time. In effect, through the exercise of free will, which accepts the gifts of God, humans live out their lives within time and history, intensifying and enriching their own existence right up to the moment of final consummation. The fact that there is such a thing as the supernatural order illumines this process and makes it possible, at least in part. An integralist view of humanity, ethics, and the world, however, in which the natural and the supernatural are inextricably bound together and identified, would not be in a position to accept the dynamic nature-history.[81]

And third, besides, the reality of supernatural life, given to us by a tri-personal God, finds a strong confirmation of the binomial natural-supernatural in the fact that humans are essentially social not only in the order of nature but also in that of grace. Grace comes to humans as a gift from the other, that is, "from beyond" and, in a derived way, through other people. Humans do not give themselves grace; the same logic of gratuitousness necessarily demands alterity, and, as a result, mediation, the foundational mediation of Christ and the participated mediation of the Church acting through the sacraments and the word. If this communication of goods were not possible, we could not speak of a nature capable of growing, of intensifying, of becoming ever more assimilated to the divine. For Thomas Aquinas the fundamental idea is the following: the being that tends toward the perfect good, even though it requires the help of another in order to obtain it, is more noble than the being capable of obtaining an imperfect good counting only on its own resources.[82] For this reason we can say that in the fundamental openness and receptiveness of humans to the other it is possible to speak of a "natural" desire to see God in which the subject does not possess the capacity of bringing that desire to fruition, as Dionysius, Cajetan, and others thought.[83] In brief, the historical antinomies relating to the problem of the supernatural and the natural may be resolved more easily by taking into account the profoundly social nature of humans.

---

80. Augustine, *Sermo* 169, 3.

81. For a critique of the lack of historical perspective in Karl Rahner's *Hearers of the Word*, see J. Ratzinger, "Salvation and History," in *Principles of Catholic Theology: Building Stones for a Fundamental Theology* (San Francisco: Ignatius, 1987), 153–71.

82. See, for example, *S.Th.* I-II, q. 5, a. 5, ad 2, even though Thomas takes it from Aristotle, *De Caelo* II.12.292a22. "Illud quod est perfectum secundum ordinem suae naturae, indiget adiuvari ab eo quod est altioris naturae, sicut homo, quantumcumque perfectus, indiget adiuvari a Deo. Et hoc modo virtutes indigent adiuvari per dona, quae perficiunt potentias animae secundum quod sunt motae a Spiritu Sancto." *S.Th.* III, q. 7, a. 5, ad 1.

83. See notes 30f.

19 THE HUMAN BEING

Union of Body and Soul

Without a superior idea there can neither be a man nor a nation. Yet there is only one superior idea on earth: the idea of the immortality of the human soul. All the other superior ideas that humans live off derive from this one. F. DOSTOEVSKY[1]

It is only shallow people who do not judge by appearances. The true mystery of the world is the visible, not the invisible. OSCAR WILDE[2]

The unity of soul and body is so profound that one has to consider the soul to be the "form" of the body. CATECHISM OF THE CATHOLIC CHURCH[3]

So far we have spoken of the human being as a unity, that is, simply, as a person. However, when it comes to describing human nature, all scientific, philosophical, and theological anthropologies speak in a variety of different ways of the different "components" that go to make up the human being, for the most part using terms such as "soul" (or "spirit") and "body." More recently it has become common to speak of the "mind" or the "brain." Humans, we are told, are composed of two fundamental elements or aspects, more or less linked with one another, the body and the soul.

In this chapter we shall consider how, throughout history, theological reflection has influenced the efforts of philosophers and scientists in explaining the relationship between the body and the soul (or spirit). First we shall look into the development of the notion of body and soul in antiquity. Then we shall consider the way that scripture describes the human being and the different aspects of its life. Third we shall reflect on how Christian theology has approached the relationship between soul and body, first among the Church Fathers up to the Middle Ages and then in different

1. F. Dostoevsky, *A Writer's Diary* (Evanston, Ill.: Northwestern University Press, 1993).
2. O. Wilde, *The Picture of Dorian Gray*, chap. 2.
3. *CCC* 365.

Church teachings on the matter. Fourth we shall consider the effort made during the modern period to clarify the relationship between body and soul with the consolidation of two opposed positions: a materialistic monism with which all body-soul duality is denied and a spiritualist dualism with which it is strongly affirmed. Fifth we shall concentrate on different moments of the contemporary debate that deal with the origins of humans (evolution and "hominization") and the relationship between mind and brain. And finally we shall consider how recent Christian theology has explained the process of understanding the union between body and soul in the wider context of the challenges of science.

Before considering the different ways in which the duality between body and soul has been understood by philosophers, we may observe that it is also the fruit of spontaneous human experience. This is so in two directions. In the first place, we experience ourselves as beings belonging to two worlds, two levels of reality that seem to be impenetrable to one another: on the one hand, we see ourselves as *subjects* who in their interiority contemplate, think, decide, recollect; on the other hand, we grasp our existence as *objects* that exist outside and beyond their own subjectivity, to all appearances independent of it. In this way we perceive ourselves spontaneously as "soul" and "body," made up of "thoughts and things." At the same time, humans realize that these "two worlds" are intimately related, completely bound up with one another, they connect deeply, and they are inseparable. In humans is to be found a world of thought: the active part is fast, inertia-free, spiritual, the part that lifts us up, that transcends us, that goes beyond. But there is also the passive, heavy, bodily part: slow, reluctant, full of inertia, material, the part that seems to drag us down. The contrast between the two in human activity may bring us to think of two discordant elements that constitute human existence in a dialectical way. At the same time, it may be observed that although the "spiritual" identity of humans (subjectivity) remains, as it were, enclosed in itself, objective bodily life opens us to the outside, to the other, to relationships, to the world, serving as an organ of communication and therefore as an expression of human sociality. On the basis of this common experience, the question of the structure of humans as body and soul arises necessarily.

In the second place, as we saw in chapter 2, humans know themselves as subjects that seek in all circumstances to survive, to transcend, to become permanent and immortal. All religions confirm the validity of this pervasive human inclination, particularly Christianity, which promises to humans in God's name that they are destined to eternal life and final resurrection. At the same time, we are all convinced of our mortality: that, at the end of life on earth, the human being disappears and dissolves. And there are no exceptions to the rule: death belongs to the law of nature, for all die. From this contrast—the quest for immortality and the evidence of mortality—spontaneously emerges the conviction of a kind of duality in the human being, that which exists between the spirit, or the soul (which would be immortal), and the body (which is mortal).

Let us consider how this has been explained throughout history.

The Soul and the Body in Antiquity

The doctrine of the soul in its relationship to the body has had a long history.[4] Among primitive peoples the term "soul" is spoken of for the most part in *cosmological* and *religious* terms, that is, in an attempt to understand the *unity* of the universe (this gives rise to the notion of cosmic soul), or in describing the relationship between humans and the divinity.[5] Yet the earliest philosophical understandings of the human soul arose in an ethical and religious context rather than a cosmic or scientific one.[6] The Presocratics looked on the soul not primarily in physical and cosmological terms but in anthropological, intuitive, and mystical ones. The notion of the soul as "breath" or "fire" is common among many peoples, and for this reason death is represented as an "escape" (or at least as an absence) from the body of that breath or fire. The Greek philosophers of the sixth through the fifth century B.C. naturalist school, such as Diogenes, Anaximander, and Anaximenes, identified the soul with "air" or "breath." For Heraclitus it was composed of fire. Both Democritus and Epicurus, as well as the Stoics, considered it to be composed of refined, mobile atoms. At an individual level it was thought to be mortal and corruptible, yet to belong to the living organism of the cosmos, vivified by the *Anima mundi*, the "world soul." With the Orphics the fundamental attributes of the soul—that of "breath" and that of "consciousness"—came together in a vision that later on found expression in the doctrine of the "transmigration of souls," what we now call "reincarnation."

At a strictly philosophical level, the human soul has been understood in two principal ways. First, Plato developed an anthropology of the human composite of body and soul, in a clearly "dualistic" and spiritualist key, in which the true identity of the human being is taken to be the soul. Second, taking a more rational, empirical, and metaphysical approach, Aristotle developed an understanding of the human being involving the "substantial unity" of body and soul. These two tendencies have recurred frequently throughout the history of anthropology.

Plato's Understanding of the Soul

Plato received the notion of the purification and salvation of the soul from the Orphic sects through Pythagorism. He considers souls to be of celestial origin, par-

---

4. For this section and for the whole chapter I closely follow P. O'Callaghan, "Soul," (2002), found at www.inters.org/soul. See also E. Arbman, "Untersuchungen zur primitiven Seelenvorstellung mit besonderer Rücksicht auf Indien," *Le Monde Oriental* 20 (1926): 85–222 and 21 (1927): 1–185; W. Stettner, *Die Seelenwanderung bei Griechen und Römern* (Stuttgart: Kohlhammer, 1934); L. Lévy-Bruhl, *L'âme primitive* (Paris: F. Alcan, 1927), translated into English as *The "Soul" of the Primitive* (London: Allen and Unwin, 1965); Q. Huonder, *Gott und Seele im Lichte der griechischen Philosophie* (Munich: Max Hueber, 1954); H.-D. Saffrey, "Origine en Grèce de la croyance en l'immortalité de l'âme," *Lumière et vie* 4, no. 24 (1955): 11ff.; E. Rohde, *Psyche: Seelencult und Unsterblichkeitsglaube der Griechen* (Darmstadt: Wissenschaftliche Buchgesellschaft, 1961; originally published in 1891); T. Tracy, "The Soul as Boatman of the Body: Presocratics to Descartes," *Diotima* (1979): 195–99; J. N. Bremmer, *The Early Greek Concept of the Soul* (Princeton, N.J.: Princeton University Press, 1983); D. Frede and B. Reis, eds., *Body and Soul in Ancient Philosophy: Gesellschaft für antike Philosophie* (Berlin: W. de Gruyter, 2009).

5. See Rohde, *Psyche*; Lévy-Bruhl, *L'âme primitive*.

6. See K. Joël, *Der Ursprung der Naturphilosophie aus dem Geiste der Mystik* (Jena: Diederichs, 1906); R. R. Marett, *The Threshold of Religion*, 3rd ed. (London: Methuen, 1929).

ticles broken off of the infinite spirit (Greek, *pneuma*) that enter material bodies in order to breathe.[7] Given their heavenly origin, souls, if they behave in an upright way and attain complete purification, will eventually be reintegrated into their primitive spiritual source. If they live unworthy lives, however, they will be reincarnated as often as necessary in the bodies of plants or animals until they have undergone full purification.[8] Though certain cosmological elements linger in this description, Plato's understanding of the soul is principally of an ethical and religious kind. This is confirmed by his idea that soul and body are fundamentally antagonistic and that the former "enters" the latter as the result of a primitive fall or sin.[9]

Plato attributes three properties to the human soul. First, the soul is the "principle of life." Although every body moved from without is inanimate, every body that moves from within, by itself and for itself, is animate, that is, living. Every aspect of reality is regulated, as it were, by its own soul. The sun, the stars, and the earth all have their own.[10] Second, the human soul is "immaterial." What is proper to the soul is thought, and by it the soul relates to the intelligible world. Significantly, Plato rejects the theory of Pythagoras, according to whom the soul is the simple result of the harmony (Greek, *krasis*) among the elements.[11] Moreover, Plato says that the human soul is composed of three parts: the rational soul, situated in the brain and destined to direct superior human activities; the passional soul, situated in the thorax and source of the noble passions; and the concupiscible soul, situated in the abdomen, source of the gross appetites.[12] Third, the passional and concupiscible parts of the soul are mortal, whereas the rational soul is of itself immortal and eternal: "Of all the things man possesses, his soul is the closest to the gods, and its properties are most divine and true."[13]

In the *Phaedo* Plato offers a series of reasons to account for the soul's immortality. He begins with an analogy with the cyclical rule of natural things: just as death follows on from life, so also life must follow on from death. Next he offers the example of humans' knowing in the present moment by means of reminiscence or recognition of what they once saw in a previous existence; of course this would be impossible were the soul not immortal. He continues by saying that the soul, on account of its simplicity and affinity to the celestial ideas, is immutable and pure and thus imperishable, whereas the body and everything composed corrupts and dissolves.[14] And finally he says that the soul "precedes" the body, with which it is united in an accidental and not entirely natural way, as a pilot does a ship or a rider to a horse.[15] In that sense the body is not fully human: man *is* his soul; perhaps we may say that man is a soul using a body.[16] In this Plato follows the Orphic doctrine according to which

---

7. See J. Burnet, "The Socratic Doctrine of the Soul," *Proceedings of the British Academy* 7 (1915): 235–59; Rohde, *Psyche*; J. M. Rist, *Man, Soul and Body: Essays in Ancient Thought from Plato to Dionysius* (Aldershot: Variorum, 1996); B. Silva Santos, "La inmortalidad del alma en el 'Fedón' de Platón: Cohesión y legitimidad de la prueba final (102A–177B)," *Angelicum* 77 (2000): 275–97; Frede and Reis, *Body and Soul in Ancient Philosophy*.

8. See *COH* 76–78.

9. See Plato, *Phaedrus* 248ff.; *Republic* VII, 514ff.

10. See Plato, *Laws* 898d.

11. See Plato, *Phaedo* 93b.

12. See Plato, *Republic* 441c.

13. See Plato, *Laws* 726a.

14. See Plato, *Phaedo* 70–80; *Republic* 608–11.

15. See Plato, *Phaedo* 246a, 247c. See Tracy, "The Soul as Boatman of the Body."

16. See Plato, *Alcibiades Major* I, 130a–131a.

the body may be considered as the "tomb" of the soul.[17] As a result, death constitutes a liberation for humans.[18]

Plato's ideas have been taken up frequently throughout the history of thought, especially by the neo-Platonic thinkers Plotinus and Porphyry, as well as by the Stoics. Seneca writes: "Nam corpus hoc animi pondus ac poena est" (The body is a weight and chastisement for this soul).[19] The Platonic understanding of the soul has been enormously influential over the centuries for several reasons. On the one hand, it expresses a way of thinking consonant with the basic thrust of many other philosophies and religions, particularly Eastern ones,[20] and it has the merit of rationally enhancing pre-critical and intuitive descriptions of the soul, giving them a metaphysical basis. On the other hand, from the ethical and religious standpoint it offers a coherent and enduringly attractive account of the origin and nature of the soul.[21] However, its drawbacks are not easily overcome, mainly because the strictly anthropological and metaphysical underpinnings of Platonism are constantly put under strain by its inherent dualism and the scarce attention it pays to the human body, to matter, and to the findings of science. Platonism defends the immortality and dignity of the human individual, certainly, but the presence of humans (of human souls) in the world and their relationship to the cosmos and to other humans remain clearly problematic. This is where Aristotle's contribution comes in.

Aristotle's Understanding of the Soul

The definitive position of Aristotle is found in his work *De anima*, deeply influenced by his scientific findings and cognizant of the psychosomatic unity of the human being.[22] Here Aristotle speaks unhesitatingly of a direct union between body and soul, such that the soul is said to be the "substantial form" of the body, even though he does not use this expression literally. This has given rise to the "hylomorphic theory" (from the Greek *hylē*, "matter," and *morphe*, "form"), on account of which it is said that the soul is the form of the body.

Aristotle begins by affirming that "the soul is that by which in the first place we live, feel, move and understand" and adds that "it cannot be either without the body, or be a body, because it is not a body, but something of the body."[23] It is the first prin-

---

17. Plato employs a play on words between *sōma* (body) and *sēma* (tomb) in *Cratylus* 400bc. See also *Gorgias* 493a. The same position may be found in Plotinus: "For the soul the body is a prison and a tomb." *Ennead.* IV, 8, 3.

18. See Plato, *Phaedo* 64e; *Gorgias* 524b.

19. Seneca, *Epist.* 120, 14.

20. See M. Eliade, "Soul," in *The Encyclopedia of Religion*, edited by M. Eliade and C. J. Adams (New York: MacMillan, 1986), 13:426–65.

21. See M. Elkaisy-Friemuth and J. M. Dillon, eds., *The Afterlife of the Platonic Soul: Reflections of Platonic Psychology in the Monotheistic Religions* (Leiden: Brill, 2009).

22. See Aristotle, *De anima*. On his thought, see J. Philoponus, *Commentaire sur le* De anima *d'Aristote* (Paris: Publications universitaires de Louvain, 1966); F. Inciarte, "Der Begriff der Seele in der Philosophie des Aristoteles," in *Seele: Ihre Wirklichkeit ihr Verhältnis zum Leib und zur menschlichen Person*, edited by K. Kremer (Leiden: E. J. Brill, 1984), 46–65; Blumenthal, *Aristotle and Neoplatonism in Late Antiquity*; M. Amarose, "Aristotle's Immortal Intellect," *Proceedings of the American Catholic Philosophical Association* 75 (2002): 97–106; Polansky, *Aristotle's De Anima*.

23. Aristotle, *De anima*, II.2.414a.

ciple of corporeal living beings, though distinct from matter; it is the source of the body's life. The soul "is the first act and the final act (Greek, *entelechia*) of the natural body which is in potency to life."[24] Thus the soul can be considered either as an "entitative principle," which constitutes a living organism out of a potentially living body, or as an "operative principle," or source and root of all the vital acts of the organism. According to Aristotle, there are three kinds of "soul" that inform matter: the *vegetative* soul, principle of nutritive, growth, and reproductive actions; the *sensitive soul*, origin of knowledge, appetite and sensitive movement; and the *rational soul*, principle of rational knowledge and attraction. For him it would be incorrect to say that the soul lives; rather, one should say that the entire human being lives in virtue of the soul.[25]

As regards the spirituality and immortality of the human soul, Aristotle holds that in the human being there are intellectual operations that only an intellectual substance separated from the body can accomplish (the *nous poietikos*). The separate substance is therefore incorruptible and immortal, of divine origin, what he calls the "agent intellect." However, the natural "forms" are not a separated substance, and they corrupt when the union of matter and form decomposes. What happens, then, to humans when they die? On the basis of the writings of Aristotle, it is not clear whether the "agent intellect" is particular and unique in *each* human being, a question we considered earlier.[26] If it is not unique, in effect, human immortality would be attributed not to the individual but only to the human collectivity. Humanity would be immortal, but the individual would not.

In any case, from a careful examination of the thought of Plato and Aristotle it is clear that the understanding of the soul is conditioned, stage by stage, by the understanding of the body—its origin, nature, and destiny—and vice versa. A key point may be found, certainly, in the understanding of the mortality of the human being and its destiny after death. For Plato, whose religious ethics move humans predominantly toward immortality in the afterlife, death is a liberation, the releasing of a soul from the dead weight of matter. For Aristotle, whose metaphysics, closely connected with the empirical order, binds humans intrinsically to the sensitive and material world, death seems to imply the destruction of nature and the loss of human individuality, at least in part. It is precisely in the context of death and the promise of immortality through resurrection that Judeo-Christian revelation has provided probably its most enduring contribution to anthropology and to our understanding of the relationship between body and soul.

The Human Being in Scripture

When scripture speaks of humans, it uses three terms closely bound up with one another: *basar*, that is, "flesh" (translated in the LXX as *sarx*); *nefesh*, approximately equivalent to "soul" (usually translated in the LXX as *psuchē*); and *ruah*, or "spirit"

---

24. Ibid., 1.412a.

25. See Aristotle, *Metaphysics*, VII.11.1037a.

26. See chapter 2, note 41, with the corresponding texts on the debate on the question of the agent and possible intellects in Aristotle.

(in Greek, *pneuma*).[27] Besides, scripture frequently uses two other terms to speak of the human being: *lēb* (heart) and *refa'im* (shades of the dead). The first three terms refer to the entire human being, in a unitary sense, even with different nuances: *basar* emphasizes weakness, corruptibility, and dependency, *nefesh* individual vitality, while *ruah* speaks of the divine source of the living being. Thus the human being "is" *basar* and *nefesh* and receives *ruah*. The other two terms have more concrete meanings.

Basar

The term *basar* (living flesh, body)[28] designates *the whole human being*,[29] as weak, mortal, and visible. Out of the 273 times the term is found in the Old Testament, it is applied 104 times to animals; in effect, in their mortal bodily condition humans share the vital condition and destiny of animals. From the use of this term in the Old Testament, three aspects of human life are clarified: its weakness and mortality, its relationship with others, and the contrast between human life and that of the divinity.

First of all, in effect, the term *basar* evokes weakness and mortality. According to Genesis 6:12, the "flesh" is connected with sin and corruption among humans. In Isaiah 40:6, "flesh" is the ephemeral part of the human being: "All flesh [that is, all humanity] is grass, and all its beauty is like the flower of the field." Psalm 78:39 reminds us that humans "are but flesh, a wind that passes and comes not again." In the second place, *basar* is often used to indicate a blood relationship between people. Humans are said to be "of one flesh," that is, of one race or family. In the Old Testament the Aramaic expression *kol basar* ("all flesh") means "all living beings" or "all humans."[30] It refers not to human individuality but rather to the common features of humans, human collectivity—the capacity to enter into contact with others, to share the life of the world, of animals, of other humans—that is, the social, corporeal, and mundane condition of human beings. In the third place, the term *basar* has an important though negative theological connotation. It expresses not simply the contrast between spirit and matter but rather the distinction between creator and creature. When it is said that the human being, the entire human being, is *basar*, this refers to its radical contingency before God, its weakness and inconsistency, its creaturely condition. In fact, the term is never applied directly to Yahweh, because he is the sovereign of the whole universe;[31] in him there is nothing weak, corruptible, or mortal.

The term "flesh" (*sarx*) is found anew in the New Testament with a similar meaning but also with a surprising shift.[32] According to Paul, "flesh" is presented as that which is *opposed to God* from the ethical point of view (Rom 7:5f.; 1 Cor 1:26–29). Thus,

---

27. For an introduction to Biblical anthropology, see H. W. Wolff, *Anthropology of the Old Testament*, 6th ed. (Philadelphia: Fortress, 1974); G. Ravasi, *Breve storia dell'anima*, 2nd ed. (Milan: A. Mondadori, 2004), 71–111; H. Schwarz, *The Human Being: A Theological Anthropology* (Grand Rapids, Mich.: W. B. Eerdmans, 2013), 5–13.

28. See D. Lys, *La chair dans l'Ancien Testament "Bâsâr"* (Paris: Editions Universitaires, 1967).

29. See Ps 56:5–12; Job 34:15; Jer 17:5.

30. On this topic, see G. Kretschmar, "Auferstehung des Fleisches: Zur Frühgeschichte einer theologischen Lehrformel," in *Leben angesichts des Todes: Beiträge zum theologischen Problem des Todes; Helmut Thielicke zum 60. Geburtstag*, edited by M.-L. Henry et al. (Tubingen: J. C. B. Mohr [Paul Siebeck], 1968), 101–37, esp. 108–11.

31. See Jer 32:27; Job 12:10; Pss 136:25, 65:3, 145:21.

32. See V. Pasquetto, "Il lessico antropologico del Vangelo e delle lettere di Giovanni (I)," *Teresianum* 47 (1996): 103–47; *BDAG*, 913–16, s.v. σάρξ; *NIDNTTE* 4:251–62, s.v. σάρξ.

he says, the life of the Christian should not be lived "according to the flesh" (Rom 7:5), that is, sinfully. The same notion may be found in the Rule of the Community from Qumran, one of whose members says: "I belong to wicked mankind, to the company of ungodly flesh" (1QS 11:9). In fact, to live according to the flesh brings humans to death (1 Cor 15:10). Thus the term "*sarx* can function almost as shorthand for the present evil world and for human existence apart from God, both of which have a drive that is opposed to God.... Fleshly life is life lived in pursuit of one's own ends, in independence of God or of the law of God, in contrast to living in accordance with the direction of the Spirit."[33]

At the same time, sinners are saved by means of the solidarity of Christ with human flesh (Rom 1:3). In turn, John speaks openly of the union of the God with the flesh: "And the Word was made flesh and dwelt among us" (Jn 1:14), he says, in the prologue of his Gospel. To carry out the work of redemption, God does not step back from the weakness and corruptibility of the flesh but divinizes it from within through the incarnation.

Nefesh

The term *nefesh*,[34] the Biblical word closest to what we call "soul," appears 750 times in the Old Testament, generally referring to a being "that breathes,"[35] with an etymology close to terms like "throat," "mouth," and "breath." Likewise, it is associated with "blood": breath and blood, of course, are both clear signs of life. "For the life [*nefesh*] of a living body [*basar*] is in its blood" (Lv 17:11; Dt 12:23). In fact, throughout the Old Testament *nefesh* designates life in general, or the living human being, and is applied to the human individual about seventy times.

The human being becomes a living *nefesh* upon receiving "the breath of life": "Then the Lord God formed man of dust from the ground, and breathed into his nostrils the breath of life [*nismat*]; and man became a living being [*nefesh*]" (Gn 2:7). In 1 Kings 17:17ff. the *nefesh* is said to leave the child and to return only when the prophet Elijah uses mouth-to-mouth resuscitation. As soon as the breath ends, life comes to a close. When Rachel's *nefesh* departs, she dies (Gn 35:18). In the *Targumin*, Genesis 2:7 is interpreted as follows: "And man became a talking being." *Nefesh*, therefore, is associated with a variety of manifestations of human life, especially of an interior kind, such as the passions, affections, and desires, to a degree that it may be considered equivalent to human interiority, the seat of love and affection, of thought and knowledge,[36] of joy (Ps 86:4), of fear (Ps 6:4), of piety (Pss 104:1, 35; 143:8), of trust (Ps 57:2), and of memory (Dt 4:9). It refers also to a human's "personality," to his psychology or the idiosyncrasy of humans as a people. Exodus 23:9 speaks thus, for example, of Israel, just after the Jews have left Egypt: "You know the heart [*nefesh*] of a stranger, for you were strangers in the land of Egypt."

At the same time, it is clear that *nefesh* is not equivalent simply to the spiritual

---

33. *NIDNTTE* 4:258, 262.

34. See D. Lys, *Néphésh: Histoire de l'âme dans la révélation d'Israël au sein des religions proche-orientales* (Paris: Presses Universitaires de France, 1959).

35. See Ex 23:12, 31:17; 2 Sm 16:14.

36. See Ex 23:9; Job 16:4; Prv 12:10.

part of humans, the soul understood in the Platonic sense. Isaiah 29:8 explains that when humans are hungry, their *nefesh* is empty. Hence we can understand that *basar* and *nefesh* are used indistinctly to speak of the entire human being. Substantially they are synonymous, even though they express different aspects of the same human life.[37] According to Johannes Pedersen, the Israelites are quite capable of distinguishing between body and soul; still they do not consider them as two independent forms of existence: the flesh is weak, but the soul is stronger; the soul is greater than the body, but the body is the most perfect manifestation of the soul.[38] Yet the unity of body and soul is essential to Judaism.

Ruah

At the same time, the Old Testament teaches that man is *ruah*, the spirit that comes from God.[39] Etymologically the term designates a wind or breeze.[40] The *ruah* is what makes it possible for humans to breathe, and thus it links naturally with *nefesh*, human vitality. Normally the term is applied to the spirit of Yahweh, who is both gift and creative power.[41] In humans it is possible to say that there is a living openness to God. By means of the *ruah* God gives life to humans and communicates with him. The strength of the *ruah* admits different levels. The prophets, for example, are considered "men of the spirit" (Nm 27:19; Hos 9:7), and when the prophets are missing or are prevented from prophesying (Jer 20:9; Am 2:12) it is said that the Spirit is quenched (1 Thes 5:19).

In the New Testament, the terms "soul" (*psuchē*) and "spirit" (*pneuma*) are used according to a variety of different meanings.[42] *Psuchē* keeps its connotation of psychical life with respect to the soul or the individual, also according to the words of Jesus (Mk 14:34).[43] In the Gospel of Matthew Jesus speaks openly of the possibility of "killing the soul" (Mt 10:28; see Jas 5:20).[44] As his passion and death come close, Jesus says that his soul (*psuchē*) "is very sorrowful, even to death" (Mk 14:34). The human spirit (*pneuma*) is also present, referring to individual interiority,[45] though a series of texts, mostly from the Pauline corpus, link the human spirit to the divine Spirit.[46] It is clear, however, that *pneuma* is not the same thing as *psuchē*, just as the *ruah* is not identified with *nefesh* (1 Thes 5:23; Heb 4:12). On the cross, in the moment of death, John openly proclaims that Jesus "gave up his spirit (*pneuma*)" (Jn 19:30).

Summing up, we may say that scripture proposes a kind of tripartite anthropol-

37. See Job 14:22; Pss 16:9–10, 63:2, 84:3, 4.

38. See J. Pedersen, *Israel: Its Life and Culture* (Atlanta, Ga.: Scholars Press, 1991; originally published in 1946), 1:171.

39. See D. Lys, *Rûach, le souffle dans l'Ancien Testament: Enquête anthropologique à travers l'histoire théologique d'Israël* (Paris: Presses Universitaires de France, 1962).

40. See Gn 3:8; Ex 10:3; Is 7:2.

41. See Job 33:4, 34:14f.; Pss 33:6, 51:12f., 104:29f.; Is 31:3; Ezek 11:19, 36:26f.

42. See *BDAG*, 1098–1100, s.v. ψυχή; 832–36, s.v. πνεῦμα; *NIDNTTE* 4:725–34, s.v. ψυχή; 3, 802–23, s.v. πνεῦμα.

43. See Lk 2:35; Acts 2:43, 15:24; Rom 2:9; 2 Pt 2:8.

44. On this text, see A. Fernández, "'No temáis a los que matan el cuerpo, pero no pueden matar el alma': Interpretación patrística de Mt 10,28," *Burgense* 28 (1987): 85–108.

45. See Mt 5:3; Acts 17:16; 1 Cor 2:11; 2 Cor 2:13; Heb 12:23.

46. See Rom 1:9, 8:10, 8:16; 1 Cor 6:17; 2 Cor 12:18; Gal 6:18; and also Lk 1:80; Acts 18:25.

ogy:[47] humans are living flesh (*basar*), with a vitality (*nefesh*) that is the fruit of the divine breath (*ruah*). The same idea may be found in the New Testament: "May the God of peace himself sanctify you wholly; and may *your spirit and soul and body* be kept sound and blameless at the coming of our Lord Jesus Christ" (1 Thes 5:23).[48] However, it is clear that neither the Old Testament nor the New attempts to provide a philosophically precise anthropology; rather they both give a concrete, living, existential description of human life in its unity, of the person living in a triple nexus of relationships: (1) with the world, the cosmos, and other living beings (*basar* is common to all living beings, though they are animated by their own breath, *nefesh*); (2) with other humans (beings of the same flesh); and (3) with God, who created humans and constituted them as such with the infusion of the *ruah*. In other words, each human being is flesh, that is, mundane, material, secular, and limited; is soul, with an immanent living dynamism that makes him or her superior to other types of living beings; and is spirit, insofar as he receives all from God to whom he is always open.

The ultimate dignity of humans, then, is determined by the latter's response to the word of God; this response is measured in scripture not so much in terms of contemplation (as in Greek thought) as from listening to the word that God communicates, and therefore from *faith*.

Lēb

The psychical and somatic aspects of the human being are combined, according to the Old Testament, with the frequently used term *lēb* (in Greek, *cardis*), that is, "heart."[49] According to Wolff, "The most important word in the vocabulary of Old Testament anthropology is generally translated 'heart.' ... It is the commonest of all anthropological terms."[50] Sensitive, affective, voluntary, and inaccessible actions are rooted in the heart. The heart is the organ of identity both of the individual and of the people. In it is situated the memory of the great works of God that should be handed on to future generations. Besides, sin is not situated only in the flesh nor holiness in the soul, for both sin and holiness are situated in the heart; from it arise the decisions that involve the entire life of the human being, for good and for evil. In the words of Eichrodt, "heart" is "a comprehensive term for the personality as a whole, its inner life, its character. It is the conscious and deliberate spiritual activity of the self-contained human ego.... That which comes out of the heart is quite distinctively the property of the whole inner man, and therefore makes him, as a consciously acting ego, responsible for it."[51]

Lēb is somewhat analogous to the New Testament term *nous*,[52] which is normally

---

47. Still, "it is precarious to try to construct a tripartite doctrine of human nature on the juxtaposition of the three nouns." F. F. Bruce, *1 & 2 Thessalonians*, in *WBC* 45:130. Here "Paul's intention was not to offer an anthropological definition. Rather he sought to emphasize his desire that God would preserve his readers as complete human beings." C. A. Wanamaker, *The Epistles to the Thessalonians: A Commentary on the Greek Text* (Grand Rapids, Mich.: W. B. Eerdmans, 1990), 207.

48. G. H. Van Kooten, *Paul's Anthropology in Context: The Image of God, Assimilation to God, and Tripartite Man in Ancient Judaism, Ancient Philosophy and Early Christianity* (Tubingen: Mohr Siebeck, 2008).

49. See *BDAG*, 508f., s.v. καρδίς; *NIDNTTE* 2:622–26, s.v. καρδία.

50. Wolff, *Anthropology*, 40.

51. W. Eichrodt, *Theology of the Old Testament* (London: SCM Press, 1967), 2:143f.

52. See Schwarz, *The Human Being*, 16.

translated as "mind," and frequently used by Paul.[53] *Nous* refers not to a detached rationality, however, but to a state of mind, or an attitude of human beings, whether drawn down by sin (Rom 7:22; 1 Cor 14:14; 2 Tm 3:8) or inspired with understanding through the Spirit (1 Cor 14:19), that leads toward conversion (*metanoia*, that is, "beyond the mind"), bringing believers to have "the mind of the Lord" (1 Cor 2:16).

Refa'im: The Dead

Given the insistence throughout scripture on the unitary character of humans, body and soul, it makes sense to ask what may be said of humans in the context of death. Doubtless, in the Old Testament all cult of the dead is strongly discouraged with the intention of avoiding all possible idolatry.[54] Besides, at least in the early books of scripture, human immortality is spoken of principally in the context of fame, family, and abundance of goods and children, that is, as a collective, world-bound immortality, the immortality of the people, and not so much that of the individual in a spiritual context.[55] At the same time, the Old Testament teaches that a part or aspect of the human being survives in *she'ol*, or the underworld, what is collectively called the *refa'im*, "the dead," or "the shades."[56] The root of the word is *râfa*, that is, what is considered weak and languid. The *refa'im*, therefore, are in a way replicas of humans, poor but real shades of their earthly existence, personal nuclei, unconscious, undifferentiated, lethargic, sleepy.[57] The term *refa'im* is used principally in the plural, as a collective term, hardly ever in the singular. The quality of life of the *refa'im* is low: the *refa'im* cannot praise God,[58] and they do not know what is happening on earth (Job 14:21ff.), although some texts speak of a kind of awareness they enjoy (1 Sm 28:8-19). Still, it is true that, just as *she'ol* does not coincide with the physical place of burial, so also the *refa'im* may not be identified with the corpses of the dead. We may say, therefore, that according to the older parts of scripture, something spiritual of humans survives after death, apart from the memory of the people.[59]

---

53. See *BDAG* 680, s.v. νοῦς; *NIDNTTE* 3:425-35, s.v. νοῦς.

54. See, for example, Lv 19:31, 20:6; Is 8:19. The Old Testament detected in the cult of the dead the danger of idolatry, in opposition to God's power over the future. On this question, see L. Wächter, *Der Tod im Alten Testament* (Stuttgart: Calwer, 1967), 187f.; J. Ratzinger, *Eschatology: Death and Eternal Life* (Washington D.C.: The Catholic University of America Press, 1988), 84f. See also the classic work of A. Lods, *La croyance à la vie future et le culte des morts dans l'antiquité israélite* (Paris: Fischbacher, 1906). See also *COH* 78f.

55. See *COH* 79f.

56. P. Karge, *Rephaim: Die vorgeschichtliche Kultur Palästinas und Phöniziens; Archäologische und religionsgeschichtliche Studien* (Paderborn: Schöningh, 1917); D. J. Ryan, *Rpum and Rephaim: A Study in the Relationship between the Rpum of Ugarit and Rephaim of the Old Testament* (Dublin: National University of Ireland, 1954); A. Caquot, "Rephaïm," in *Dictionnaire de la Bible, Supplément,* edited by H. Cazelles and A. Feuillet (Paris: Letouzey et Ané, 1985), 10:344-57.

57. See Job 26:5; Na 3:18.

58. See Is 38:18; Pss 88:11ff., 30:10; Sir 17:22.

59. See C. Pozo, *La teología del más allá,* 3rd ed. (Madrid: BAC, 1992), 200-210, translated into English as *Theology of the Beyond* (Staten Island, N.Y.: St. Pauls, 2009).

The Human Composite of Body and Soul in the Church Fathers and the Middle Ages

The different aporias of Old Testament anthropology are clarified to some degree in the New Testament, as we saw earlier on, and this takes place, of course, in light of the teachings, life, death, and resurrection of Jesus Christ. Besides, the "definition" of the human being offered by the book of Genesis and elsewhere ("made in the image and likeness of God") may be appreciated in all its power in and through the saving work of Christ, who is the perfect image of the Father (Col 1:15). On the one hand, by faith in Christ, Son and image of God, humans become children of God. On the other, the doctrine of the incarnation of the Word reveals, in the clearest way possible, that the human body is worthy of God and is destined—on the basis of the promise of final resurrection that has already "taken place" in Christ—to eternal life.[60] On the basis of the life, teaching, and person of Christ an extended reflection begins on the nature of humans in which two tendencies or sensibilities are found alternately: the first, that humans are souls with annexed and subordinate bodies (the Platonic line) and the second, that humans are unitary compositions of body and soul (the Aristotelian line). It is probably fair to say that the latter position has ended up taking center-stage in philosophical thought, even though Platonism, at least terminologically, has been predominant for a long period of time and every so often has made strong comebacks.

The Patristic Period

On the face of things, Christians, at least during the first centuries, took a greater interest in ethics and religion than they did in the findings of science and its implications. This may be seen in a generalized acceptance of Platonic anthropological categories that express a net distinction, indeed opposition, between soul and body. Platonism was considered to be more pliable to Christian revelation and reflection than was Aristotle's thought because it focused on upright human behavior and asceticism, on the eternal reward for the individual who is faithful to God, though it has a somewhat pessimistic attitude toward a world in urgent need of being saved. The Aristotelian understanding, however, saw the world in terms of an unbreakable unity between body and soul, which better explained the sociality and secularity of human life, that is, humans' living, bodily insertion in the world, but had greater difficulties in dealing with immortality and heavenly destiny.

It would be mistaken, however, to consider early Christianity in a dualistic light, and this for distinctly theological reasons. Body-soul "dualism"—whether of a Platonic or a Gnostic variety—speaks of a double divine origin for the universe, unthinkable in a Judeo-Christian monotheistic context. Body-soul dualism tends to identify matter with nothingness (Plotinus) or with evil (Manes, Priscillian), which is clearly contrary to faith in a free creation of all things *ex nihilo*, material and spiritual, in divine freedom and love. The doctrine of the resurrection of Christ, and its

---

60. See O'Callaghan, "Resurrection," IV, 3 (2002), at www.inters.org/resurrection.

promised extension to believers at the end of time, completely obviates any essential antagonism between body and soul. It is understandable, therefore, that Christian writers from the beginning unanimously taught the fundamental unity of the human being.[61] Two principal expressions of this doctrine may be found, that of the school of Antioch, which insisted on the formation of humans from the dust of the earth and emphasized primarily the unity of the human being, and that of the Alexandrian school, which considered the spiritual soul as the defining element of the human composite.[62] The same basic arguments recurred throughout the Middle Ages, right up to the Council of Vienne, held in 1312, and afterward.[63]

According to Justin Martyr, man is an *anthropos sarkikos*, who lives naturally in the flesh.[64] He asks: "Is man to be identified with the soul on its own? No, it is the soul of man. Is the body man? No, it is man's body. Neither of them is of itself man, who is a rational animal. Man is the result of the composition of both."[65] Athenagoras, another second-century author, speaks in the following terms: "Every human nature is made up of an immortal soul and a body adapted to it in the moment of creation; it was not the soul alone, not in separation from the body, to which God destined creation and life ... but rather to humans, composed of body and soul.... A single living being is formed out of body and soul, a being that suffers as much as the soul and the body suffer."[66] In opposition to the Gnostics, who denied final resurrection and considered that matter had been created by the evil principle, Irenaeus of Lyons emphasized the original goodness of the flesh and developed this doctrine in strictly Christological terms.[67] Tertullian followed Irenaeus's Christological approach, extending it to the sacramental realm in an audacious Christian "materialism" clearly opposed to the Gnosticism of Valentinus. "Caro cardo salutis," he declares, "The flesh is the hinge of our salvation."[68] As a result, though in man both body and soul are present, neither component can be said to be prior to the other.

Other Fathers of a more Platonic bent, such as Clement of Alexandria, Origen, and Gregory of Nyssa in the East and Lactantius and Augustine in the West, attributed a clear priority to the soul over the body in explaining the dignity of the human being made in the image of God, in the face of the undeniable corruptibility of matter.[69] They did not deny the unity of the human composite but considered human

---

61. See A. Orbe, "La definición del hombre en la teología del siglo II," *Gregorianum* 48 (1967): 522–76; A. Fernández, *La escatología en el siglo II* (Burgos: Aldecoa, 1979).

62. See G. Greshake, "'Seele' in der Geschicte der christlichen Eschatologie," in *Seele: Problembegriff christlicher Eschatologie,* edited by R. Friedli and W. Breuning (Freiburg: Herder, 1986), 107–58, esp. 108–27; Grossi, *Lineamenti di antropologia patristica,* 11–84.

63. For the following sections, from the historical standpoint see J. L. Ruiz de la Peña, *Imagen de Dios: Antropología teológica fundamental* (Santander: Sal Terrae, 1988). On the Council of Vienne, see notes 104f.

64. See Pseudo-Justin, *De resurrectione,* 7.

65. Ibid., 8.

66. Ibid., 15.

67. See Irenaeus of Lyons, *Epideixis,* 71; *Adv. Haer.* V, 28. See F. F. Bovon, "The Soul's Comeback: Immortality and Resurrection in Early Christianity," *Harvard Theological Review* 103, no. 4 (2010): 387–406.

68. Tertullian, *De carnis resurrectione,* 8.

69. On Origen and Augustine, see F. Refoulé, "Immortalité de l'âme et résurrection de la chair," *Revue d'histoire et de philosophie religieuses* 163 (1963): 11–52. On Clement, see M. G. Bianco, "Clemente alessandrino: Il farmaco dell'immortalità (*Protr.* X, 106, 2)," in *Morte e immortalità nella catechesi dei Padri del III–V secolo,*

nature on the basis of the specificity of the human soul. Still, the position of Origen moved away from common Christian theological tradition with a vision of the pre-existent soul that is very close to classical Platonism.[70] He had no doubt but that God had created matter but had done so in order to punish wayward souls.

Openly opposed to Manichaean dualism with respect to matter, Augustine drew deeply on the doctrine of Plato: "The better part of man is his soul," he says, "the body is not all man, but the inferior part of man."[71] Nonetheless, Augustine did reject the Platonic notion of the pre-existence (or native divinity) of the human soul, as well as its temporal precedence over the body. As regards the origin of the soul, he accepted neither Plotinus's emanationism nor Origen's doctrine of the simultaneous creation of all souls at the beginning of time. The theology of original sin and its transmission inclined him earlier towards the theory of "traducianism," popularized by Tertullian, according to which the souls of children are drawn from those of their parents and are not created as such by God.[72] Yet he remained undecided between this and the theory of "individual creationism," first taught by Lactantius, which with time became the doctrine most commonly accepted by Christians.[73] Augustine, in fact, thought that body and soul are mutually necessary elements of the human composite. The human being is not the body alone or the soul alone; when both are united at the same moment, humans come into being. "It would be false," says Augustine, "to say that man consists of the mind [Latin, *mens*; Greek, *nous*], and then go on to say that what is in the flesh is not human."[74] It is clear, however, that Augustine envisaged the union between body and soul in terms of hierarchical and dynamic interaction. He states that man is a rational soul that *uses* a mortal and earthly body. Analogously, the body as such does not feel, but rather the soul feels through the body.[75]

Church Teaching on the Body and the Soul

During the Patristic period, the principal purpose of the official interventions of the Church in the area of anthropology was one of overcoming the errors of Manicheans and Gnostics, establishing the common divine origin of both body and soul,

---

edited by S. Felici (Rome: Las, 1985), 63–73. On Lactantius, see P. Caspar, "La création de l'âme humaine et l'animation immédiate de l'embryon chez Lactance," *Anthropotes* 2 (1991): 189–98. On Gregory of Nyssa, see E. Peroli, "Platonismo e cristianesimo: Gregorio di Nissa e il problema dell'anima," *Medioevo* 22 (1996): 1–38.

70. From Plato (*Phaedrus* 248c–d) Origen took the ideas of human pre-existence and that souls are bound to bodies as a result of their fall (*De princ.* 2, 9, 6f.; 1, 7, 4f.). On this question, see P. Kübel, *Schuld und Schicksal bei Origenes, Gnostikern und Platonikern* (Stuttgart: Calwer, 1973), 88ff., 95ff. Irenaeus took a clearly opposed position to Plato on this point, challenging the idea that a previous life can be demonstrated on the basis of previous memory (*Adv. Haer. II*, 33, 2 and 5).

71. Augustine, *De civitate Dei*, XIII, 24. On Augustine, see F. Rego, *La relación del alma con el cuerpo: Una reconsideración del dualismo agustiniano* (Buenos Aires: Gladius, 2001).

72. See Augustine, *Ep.* 190, to Optatus. The same position is to be found later on in Luther. See G. Ebeling, *Lutherstudien* (Tubingen: J. C. B. Mohr, 1982), 2.2:46–59. On this question, see H. Karpp, *Probleme altchristlicher Anthropologie: Biblische Anthropologie und philosophische Psychologie bei den Kirchenvätern des dritten Jahrhunderts* (Gutersloh: Bertelsmann, 1950); R. J. O'Connell, *The Origin of the Soul in St. Augustine's Later Works* (New York: Fordham University Press, 1987); and the critique of J. M. Rist, *Augustine: Ancient Thought Baptized* (Cambridge: Cambridge University Press, 1996), 317–20.

73. See Lactantius, *De opificio Dei*, 19, 73.

74. Augustine, *Sermo* 154, 10, 15.

75. See Augustine, *De Genesi ad litteram*, III, 7.

and explaining human nature in the framework of the divine plan of creation and incarnation. With that aim the following points were clarified. First, the soul is not a part of God, nor is it an emanation of the divinity,[76] but rather it is created by God directly and without intermediaries,[77] that is, *ex nihilo*, with no pre-existing matter.[78] Second, souls do not pre-exist "ab aeterno" (from all eternity), as Origen said, nor are they enclosed in bodies as a punishment for sin.[79] Third, the Church professed solemnly the original goodness of matter, of the body and the world, as true creatures of God, condemning the errors of Gnostics and their teachings on the perversity of marriage and procreation; this was confirmed on several occasions at the Synod of Braga in 561, at Lateran Council IV in 1215, and at the Council of Florence in 1442.[80]

Fourth, Church teaching insisted above all on the close union between body and soul. It did so in three ways. First, by saying that the unity between body and soul is based on the single creative act of God, the only "creator of all things, visible and invisible."[81] Second, by teaching the central role is played by the doctrine of the final resurrection of the whole of the human being "in the same flesh," which will take place at the end of time;[82] resurrection makes it clear that the ultimate and perpetual destiny of humans is the union of body and soul. And finally, by declaring that the union between body and soul is based on the analogy of the "hypostatic union," that is between the divine person of the Word and human nature assumed in Jesus Christ: "Just as a man is intelligent soul and flesh, so also Christ is God and man."[83] We shall return to this point in the next section.

The Debate on the Human Composite during the Middle Ages

Christian anthropology during the Patristic period is Christological in approach, though linguistically and conceptually still Platonic. Things change somewhat during the Middle Ages. In rather simplistic terms it may be said that Christology and Platonism are replaced, respectively, by eschatology and Aristotelianism. The questions being asked here relate to the anthropological implications of the eschatological salvation won by Christ: how can a part of the human composite survive death? And how is the body saved? What categories can we use to understand human nature?

In the early Middle Ages, under the influence of Augustine, the approach of Bonaventure and Hugh of St. Victor is still decidedly Platonic. According to the latter, God created the soul and not the body in his image and likeness; that is why it is im-

---

76. See the classic work of W. Götzmann, *Die Unsterblichkeitsbeweise in der Väterzeit und Scholastik bis zum Ende des 13. Jahrhunderts: Eine philosophie- und dogmengeschichtliche Studie* (Karlsruhe: F. Gutsch, 1927).

77. See *DH* 190 and 360; this teaching was taken up again in the twentieth century by Pius XII in *Humani Generis, DH* 3896.

78. See *DH* 190, 360, 685.

79. See *DH* 403, 456.

80. See *DH* 457–63, 802; 1333 and 6, respectively.

81. See Nicene-Constantinopolitan Creed, *DH* 150.

82. See *DH* 72, 76, 325, 540, 574, 684, 801. On the term "the same flesh" referring to final resurrection, see P. O'Callaghan, "La fórmula 'Resurrección de la carne' y su significado para la moral cristiana," *Scripta Theologica* 21 (1989): 777–803. On the wider anthropological implications of final resurrection, see *COH* 106–12.

83. See *Quicumque* Creed, *DH* 76.

mortal.[84] Yet on account of its union with the soul, the body partakes in the latter's immortality as a "beneficium creationis" (benefit of creation). Body and soul are complete substances, accidentally united to one another, and the separated soul, therefore, may be considered as a person in its own right. And just as the body did not give the soul its personal being in being united with it, neither will it take it away when it corrupts at death. As a result, final resurrection is of little theological import. Bernard considers the soul as a pilgrim lodging within the human being. "Nobilem hospitem habes, o caro," he says, "nobilem valde, et tota salus tua pendet de eius salute. Da honorem hospiti tanto. Tu quidem habitas in regione tua: anima vero peregrina et exul apud te est hospitata" (You have a noble lodger, O flesh, truly noble, and all your salvation depends on its state of health. Honor your lodger, then. You live in your region, and the pilgrim, exiled soul is your lodger).[85]

The decisive twist comes, however, with the introduction of Aristotle's thought through the agency of his Arabic and Jewish commentators Averroes, Avicenna, and Maimonides, whose influence made itself felt during the thirteenth century. Gilbert de la Porrée and William of Auvergne consider the human being in a more harmonic way, following the Aristotelian perspective of the soul as the form of the body: the soul is to the body what form is to matter, that is, the "informing" function of the soul is essential both to its own nature and to the body that it constitutes as human. According to this position, the separated soul without the body, even though it may be considered as a "subject," may not be taken as a "person" in the strict sense of the word because in it the full perfection that belongs to human nature deriving from the union of body and soul is not expressed: it survives after death in a state that is not fully natural, awaiting to be joined with its own body at final resurrection. The apparently insuperable tension between the Aristotelian doctrine of substantial union between body and soul and the Platonic vision of the immortality of the soul and its metaphysical independence from the body is given a decisive clarification, if not a definitive solution, in the writings of Thomas Aquinas.[86]

---

84. See Hugh's work *De arra anime: L'inizio del dono*, translated and edited by M. Fioroni (Milan: Glossa, 2000). See P. Rorem, *Hugh of Saint Victor* (Oxford: Oxford University Press, 2009).

85. Bernard, *De adventu Domini, Sermo 6, 3*.

86. Regarding that tension, see J. Mundhenk, *Die Seele im System des Thomas von Aquin: Ein Beitrag zur Klärung und Beurteilung der Grundbegriffe der thomistischen Psychologie* (Hamburg: F. Meiner, 1980; originally published in 1934); E. Bertola, "Il problema dell'immortalità dell'anima nelle opere di Tommaso d'Aquino," *Rivista di filosofia neo-scolastica* 65 (1973): 248–302; A. C. Pegis, "The Separated Soul and Its Nature in St. Thomas," *St. Thomas Aquinas 1274–1974: Commemorative Studies*, edited by A. A. Maurer (Toronto: Pontifical Institute of Medieval Studies, 1974), 1:131–58; Pegis, *St. Thomas and the Problem of the Soul in the Thirteenth Century* (Toronto: Pontifical Institute of Medieval Studies, 1976); J. Moreau, "L'homme et son âme, selon saint Thomas d'Aquin," *Revue philosophique de Louvain* 74 (1976): 5–29; A. Lobato Casado, ed., *L'anima nell'antropologia di S. Tommaso d'Aquino: Con allocuzione di S.S. Giovanni Paolo II; Atti del congresso della Società internazionale S. Tommaso d'Aquino (1986)* (Milan: Massimo, 1987); R. Pietrosanti, *L'anima umana nei testi di S. Tommaso: Partecipazione, spiritualità, immortalità* (Bologna: ESD, 1996); B. C. Bazán, "The Human Soul: Form and Substance? Thomas Aquinas' Critique of Eclectic Aristotelianism," *Archives d'Histoire Doctrinale et Littéraire du Moyen-Age* 64 (1997): 95–126; S. L. Brock, "Tommaso d'Aquino e lo statuto fisico dell'anima spirituale," *L'Anima: Annuario di Filosofia 2004*, edited by V. Possenti (Milan: Mondadori, 2004), 67–87, 323–26; S. Simonetti, *L'anima in san Tommaso d'Aquino* (Rome: A. Armando, 2007); A. Lobato Casado, "El ser humano y su alma: Introducción al tratado del alma en Santo Tomás de Aquino," *Angelicum* 87 (2010): 657–81.

The Contribution of Thomas Aquinas

It should be noted that Aquinas attempted to overcome the tension between the Platonic and Aristotelian tendencies for theological and Christian reasons.[87] The human soul is the form of a body because of the kind of substance it is, he says (the term "substance" must be understood as something that exists per se). It is neither a pure spirit nor a separated substance but rather an intellectual substance that informs, "shapes," or configures the body. The novelty introduced by Aquinas over the teaching of Aristotle was as follows: whereas the latter considered nondivine substances as composed, generally speaking, of "matter" and "form," the former considered each substance as a composition of essence and the individual "act of being" (Latin, *esse*, existence). In every creature there is a composition between potency and act: both Aristotle and Aquinas accepted that. Yet according to Aquinas the act need not correspond in every case to a particular substantial form, nor potency to matter, as Aristotle held. The soul is a substance in that it is composed of essence (that of a spiritual form) and act of being deriving directly from the divine creating action.[88] Although this position is not completely guaranteed by Aristotelian metaphysics, as we already saw, it gives man full metaphysical individuality or incommunicability,[89] a teaching Aquinas insisted upon against commentators on Aristotle such as Averroes, who in a sense had attempted to "Platonize" Aristotle.[90] Besides, because it includes no materiality in its own structure, the soul is simple and incorruptible: "The body is not united to the soul accidentally, because the very being of the soul is also the being of the body, thus being common to both."[91] In technical terms, it may be said that the soul communicates being to the body at the level of formal, not efficient, causality.

The question Aquinas faced, however, was the following: can an incorruptible spiritual substance be the form of a corruptible body, constituting with it a substantial unity of being?[92] His reply was in the affirmative, for the soul's very purpose is to communicate the being by which it subsists to the body.[93] Still, four observations may be made. First, the rational soul is the form of the body not through its potencies and capacities, as Avicenna held, but by its very essence. Though subsistent, it is proper for the soul to "inform" the body; the soul, in turn, stands in need of the body for its own perfection:[94] "Humanae animae competit uniri corpori" (The human soul is meant to be united to the body).[95]

Second, the rational soul is the one and only form of the human body, being at the same time vegetative, animal, and rational. By a single act of being the human soul is the form of the body and of all its functions. Thus there are no intermediaries of any

---

87. See especially *S.Th.* I, q. 75. For other issues related to the human soul, see ibid., qq. 75–90.
88. See Aquinas, *SCG* II, 87.
89. See ibid., 75; *De Unitate Intellectus contra Averroistas*, no. 2.
90. Thus C. Fabro, *L'anima: Introduzione al problema dell'uomo* (Rome: Studium, 1955), 269.
91. Aquinas, *Q. de anima*, a. 1, ad 1.   92. See Aquinas, *II C. Gent.*, 56.
93. See ibid., 68–72.   94. See Aquinas, *S.Th.* I, q. 51, a. 1.
95. Aquinas, *S.Th.* I, q. 51, a. 1. On the text, G. Trapp, "*Humanae animae competit uniri corpori* (STh I q51, a1, c): Überlegungen zu einer Philosophie des menschlichen Ausdrucks," *Scholastik* 27 (1952): 382–99. Brock writes specifically: "The soul is the form of the body properly speaking in function of knowledge and truth." "Tommaso d'Aquino e lo statuto fisico dell'anima spirituale," 69.

kind between the body and the soul. The fact that a particular human being does not exercise all his faculties only means that these faculties are in potentiality relative to the person's acts; the situation is different with God, of course, for whom the power of acting and act itself are identical with the simple divine substance.

Third, the soul as such is not temporarily prior to the body, though metaphysically it is in that it is a form that is independent of the body as regards its being: "The body receives being from the soul; thus the human soul communicates to the body the being in which it subsists; therefore when the body is removed the soul remains."[96] This is what makes it possible to speak of the "incorruptibility" of the soul (Aquinas prefers to apply the term "immortality" to the human being who participates in divine life through the gift of grace). Aquinas demonstrates the incorruptibility of the soul not on Platonic but on distinctly Aristotelian premises. The soul can, potentially, know all things material and can transcend itself; therefore, it must be immaterial and hence incorruptible.[97] Aquinas also gives weight to the universality of humans' desire for immortality.[98]

Fourth, the separated soul may be considered human but is not to be identified simply with the human being. Nor may it be considered a "person" in the sense that to be a person corresponds to what is most perfect in nature.[99] After death the soul retains a natural tension (*commensuratio*) with "its" own body,[100] a tension that will be overcome at final resurrection in such a way that the soul united to the body will be more like God than when separated from the body because it possesses its nature more perfectly.[101] Still, Thomas adds, "The soul separated from the body will have another way of understanding, not by abstraction or phantasms, but in a way that is like separate, non-corporeal substances," such as angels.[102]

Summing up, we can say that Aquinas insisted on the formulation *anima forma corporis* for three kinds of reason: (1) theological, to avoid the body-soul duality's becoming a dualism of a double origin of humans; (2) anthropological, to avoid the Averroist position, which could compromise the dignity of each individual human being on the basis of the doctrine of a common separated intellect present in all humans; and (3) scientific, on the basis of a healthy trust in empirical observation and scientific discourse, both of which indicate a close, essential union between body and soul, between matter and spirit.

Difficulties with Thomas's Position

Two points still remained unclear in Aquinas's explanation: the *unicity* of the human soul and the statute of the *separated soul*. First, just after the death of Aquinas

---

96. Aquinas, *Q. de anima*, a. 14, ad 10.

97. See Aquinas, *S.Th.* I, q. 75, a. 6. See D. R. Foster, "Aquinas on the Immateriality of the Intellect," *Thomist* 55, no. 3 (1991): 415–38; for a fuller explanation, see *COH* 24f.

98. See Aquinas, *S.Th.* I, q. 75, a. 6, co.

99. Ibid., q. 29, a. 3, co.

100. See Aquinas, *SCG* II, 80 (ed. Marietti, n. 1621).

101. See Aquinas, *De Pot.*, q. 5, a. 10, ad 5.

102. "Intelligere cum phantasmate est propria operatio animae secundum quod corpori est unita. Separata autem a corpore habebit alium modum intelligendi, similem aliis substantiis a corpore separatis, ut infra melius patebit." *S.Th.* I, q. 75, a. 6, ad 3.

in 1274, the bishop of Paris, Stephen Tempier, and later the archbishop of Canterbury, Robert Kilwardby, as well as his successor John Peckham, rejected as false the Thomistic thesis of the unicity of the soul, all of them maintaining the existence of three different souls, or three different "forms" (*morphe*), in each human being.[103] The "plurimorphic hypothesis," which in real terms comes closer to Plato than to Aristotle, was followed by most of the scholars of that epoch, among them the leader of the Franciscan "spiritual" faction, Pier di Giovanni Olivi.[104] The plurimorphic theories, however, in spite of appearing to resolve certain difficulties, had one weak point: they were unable to explain and guarantee the unity of the human being, for an accidental union between different forms can give rise only to several distinct substances: "Forma dat esse" (Form gives being), as the scholastics said.[105]

As a result, authors such as Richard Knapwell and John of Paris began to re-propose Aquinas's theory of the soul as the only form of the body, insisting that body and soul are not truly distinct realities.[106] Finally, Aquinas's position was taken up at the Council of Vienne in 1312, which states that "substantia animae rationalis seu intellectivae, vere, per se et essentialiter humani corporis forma" (the substance of the rational soul truly, of itself and essentially, is the form of the human body).[107] Interestingly, the doctrinal point of departure for this statement is at heart Christological: the same conciliar decree taught, against Olivi, that the unity/oneness of the saving humanity of Jesus Christ is what points to the substantial unity of human beings in general.[108] The Word was united to the whole human being, body and soul, and not to the body through the soul. However, the text of Vienne does not state that the soul is the only form of the body, but the context seems to indicate that this is the case.[109]

---

103. On Tempier, see É. Tempier, *La condamnation parisienne de 1277*, edited by D. Piché and C. Lafleur (Paris: J. Vrin, 1999).

104. On the thought of Olivi, see B. Jansen, "Die Seelenlehre Olivis und ihre Verurteilung auf dem Vienner Konzil," *Franziskanische Studien* 21 (1934): 297–314; R. Schneider, *Die Einheit des Menschen: Die anthropologische Formel 'anima forma corporis' im sogenannten Korrektorienstreit und bei Petrus Johannis Olivi; Ein Beitrag zur Vorgeschichte des Konzils von Vienne* (Munster: Aschendorff, 1973); C. Bérubé, *De l'homme à Dieu selon Duns Scot, Henri de Gand et Olivi* (Rome: Istituto storico dei Cappuccini, Collegio S. Lorenzo, 1983); Various Authors, "Pier di Giovanni Olivi," *Archivium Franciscanum Historicum* 91, nos. 3–4 (1998).

105. Aquinas, *De Veritate*, q. 28, a. 8, ad 8; *Q. de anima*, a. 10, ad 2.

106. See the work of R. Knapwell, *De unitate formae*, in *Medieval and Renaissance Texts and Studies*, edited by F. E. Kelley (Binghamton, N.Y.: Center for Medieval and Early Renaissance Studies, 1982).

107. *DH* 902.

108. See *DH* 900.

109. The moral consequences of this approach may be found in John Paul II's *Veritatis Splendor*, which cites the Council of Vienne: "A freedom which claims to be absolute ends up treating the human body as a raw datum, devoid of any meaning and moral values until freedom has shaped it in accordance with its design. Consequently, human nature and the body appear as *presuppositions or preambles*, materially *necessary* for freedom to make its choice, yet extrinsic to the person, the subject and the human act. Their functions would not be able to constitute reference points for moral decisions, because the finalities of these inclinations would be merely 'physical' goods, called by some 'pre-moral.' To refer to them, in order to find in them rational indications with regard to the order of morality, would be to expose oneself to the accusation of physicalism or biologism. In this way of thinking, the tension between freedom and a nature conceived of in a reductive way is resolved by a division within man himself. This moral theory does not correspond to the truth about man and his freedom. It contradicts the Church's teachings on the unity of the human person, whose rational soul is *per se et essentialiter* the form of his body. The spiritual and immortal soul is the principle of unity of the human being, whereby it exists as a whole—*corpore et anima unus*—as a person. These definitions not only point out that the body, which has been promised the resurrection, will also share in glory. They also remind

Second, it is easy to understand that Aquinas's position concerning the situation of the soul, once separated from the body, remained unclear. Thomas himself was keenly aware that after death the separated soul does not fulfill its essential purpose, that of "in-forming" the body.[110] Averroists at Padua kept insisting that there is only one immortal intellect, common to all humans. Conversely, followers of Alexander of Aphrodisias, such as Peter Pomponazzi, claimed that man has no immortal intellect. Intellectual operations depend, indeed, on the body, Pomponazzi said, but this does not mean that there is an independent intellectual substance. On account of its capacity to know universal ideas, he said, the human soul may be considered not an individual entity but rather one that is common to all humans.[111] In different directions both schools (Averroists and followers of Pomponazzi) came to deny personal immortality. However, the Lateran Council V (1513) with the approval of Pope Leo X, rejected the proposition that "the human soul is mortal or that it is one for all humans."[112] At the beginning of the modern period, we can see that the fundamental intuitions of Thomas Aquinas were vindicated.

Fideism, Dualism, and Protestantism

The teaching of the Protestant Reformers Luther, Calvin, Zwingli, and others differed little from that which was taught commonly during the Middle Ages as regards the union between body and soul, at least materially.[113] Nobody questioned the common doctrine of the composition and unity of body and soul, though the latter was understood, at least implicitly, in a Platonic and spiritualist sense, more centered on individual salvation after death (the immortality of the soul) than on eschatological consummation at the end of time (resurrection).[114]

Yet under the influence of nominalism and Augustinianism, a subtle change began to take place. It was no longer generally accepted that the existence and nature of the soul could be arrived at by rational deduction, whether in Aristotelian or Platonic terms. This position was not without precedent. In the fourteenth century Peter Au-

---

us that reason and free will are linked with all the bodily and sense faculties. The person, including the body, is completely entrusted to himself, and it is in the unity of body and soul that the person is the subject of his own moral acts" (par. 48).

110. On the fact that the soul separates from the body only temporarily and that this separation (death) is the result of sin, see COH 262–67.

111. See the work of P. Pomponazzi, *Tractatus de immortalitate animae*, edited by B. Mojsisch (Hamburg: F. Meiner, 1990; originally published in 1516). On his thought, see E. Gilson, "Autour de Pomponazzi: Problématique de l'immortalité de l'âme en Italie en début du XVIe siècle," *Archives d'Histoire Doctrinale et Littéraire du Moyen-Age* 28 (1961): 163–279; A. H. Douglas, *The Philosophy and Psychology of Pietro Pomponazzi* (Hildesheim: G. Olms, 1962); G. Cenacchi, "Secolo XVI: Problema dell'immortalità e interpretazioni del 'De Anima' di Aristotele; Rilievi critici sulle teorie alessandriaste, tomiste e della Scuola di Pietro Pomponazzi," in *L'anima nell'antropologia di S. Tommaso d'Aquino*, edited by A. Lobato Casado (Milan: Massimo, 1987), 521–33; W. I. M. Van Dooren, "Pomponazzi als Leitbild oder: Wie verhält man sich zu einem Philosophen der Vergangenheit," *Philosophica* (1988): 57–67; J. L. Treloar, "Pomponazzi's Critique of Aquinas' Arguments for the Immortality of the Soul," *Thomist* 54, no. 3 (1990): 453–70.

112. The Council rejects the position of those who say that the soul "mortalis sit, aut unica in cunctis hominibus." *DH* 1440.

113. On the relationship between Luther and Lateran Council V, see C. Stange, *Luther und das fünfte Laterankonzil* (Gutersloh: Bertelsmann, 1928).

114. On the anthropology of Luther, see Barth, "L'uomo secondo Martin Lutero."

reolus and William of Ockham had taught that there was no reason to attribute the immaterial acts of knowing and willing to an immaterial form or soul, the existence of which can be known only by faith. Likewise, Pomponazzi said that it is not possible to demonstrate the immortality of the human soul by reason. Cardinal Cajetan was also convinced that the immortality of the soul is as unknown to humans as the mystery of the Trinity or the incarnation of the Word,[115] and opposed Lateran V's suggestion that philosophers should teach students how to justify this doctrine rationally.[116] (It is interesting to note that Cajetan explained the supernatural order in an extrinsic way, as we saw in chapter 18.)

Perhaps on account of a certain pessimism present in the later Middle Ages, the doctrine of the survival of the soul after death and its final reintegration at resurrection came ever more strictly under the sway of the theological virtues of faith and hope and no longer under reason.[117] Ockham, for example, though accepting by faith the existence of an immaterial and incorruptible form in man, was not prepared to say that this form informs matter directly. He endorsed the opinion according to which there are in the human being several substantial forms, at least a form of corporeity and one of the intellectual soul, or perhaps three distinct forms.[118] It would seem, therefore, that the loosening of the bond between soul and body and the gradual reappearance of Platonic dualism were accompanied by an ever-growing difficulty of reflecting on the ontological reality of the soul in purely rational terms. Immortality was no longer considered a "natural" quality of the human soul, but rather was seen as a gift of divine grace. In other words, dualism and fideism seemed to move side by side.

Understandably, in these circumstances philosophers began to turn their attention to the human soul in terms of tangible human subjectivity, leaving aside its ontological aspects.

Human Subjectivity and Modern Philosophy

It may be said that the existence, subsistence, and immortality of the human soul have become, after the existence of God, the principal, unquestioned, "article of faith" of modern philosophers.[119] Yet they explain and reflect upon the soul's existence and properties not in metaphysical but in subjectivistic terms. The soul is looked upon

115. See M. F. Manzanedo, "La inmortalidad del alma humana según Cayetano," *Angelicum* 76 (1999): 309–40.

116. The Council spoke of the rational aspect of our knowledge of the soul and its immortality in *DH* 1440. See S. Offelli, "Il pensiero del concilio Lateranense V sulla dimostrabilità razionale dell'immortalità dell'anima," *Studia Patavina* 1 (1954): 7–40; C. F. J. Martin, "On a Mistake Commonly Made in Accounts of Sixteenth-Century Discussions of the Immortality of the Soul," *American Catholic Philosophical Quarterly* 69 (1995): 29–37.

117. On this question, see *COH* 316f.

118. See M. M. Adams, "Ockham on the Soul: Elusive Proof, Dialectical Persuasions," *Proceedings of the American Catholic Philosophical Association* 75 (2002): 43–77.

119. Pieper showed this to be the case in his work *Death and Immortality*. The modern period is frequently considered a period of unconfined anthropological optimism. By way of example, Voltaire said that "of all animals man is the most perfect, the happiest and the one who lives longest." *Remarques sur les pensées de Pascal*, in *Oeuv. Comp.*, edited by L. Moland (Paris: Garnier, 1877–85), 22:28.

not as a reality that founds immaterial actions but mainly as an element that localizes human thought, consciousness, and subjectivity. Whereas during the Middle Ages being was identified as an "ens creatum" (a created being), Heidegger explains, modernity considers being "only insofar as it is placed by humans who represent and produce."[120] This takes place in an intellectual climate in which a kind of metaphysical skepticism prevails, induced by nominalism and reinforced by the fideism that derives from Protestant thought.[121]

In any case, the doctrine of the soul in its relationship to the body is focused in two different ways, according to the canons of dualism or monism. Let us consider them one by one.

Radical Dualism and the Supremacy of the Soul

The humanism of the Renaissance did not put the soul at the center of things; the true center, rather, was human subjectivity, as may be seen, for example, in the writings of Marcellus Ficinus.[122] Intent on countering the inroads of skeptical empiricism, the seventeenth-century philosopher Descartes attempted to establish a kind of "clear and distinct idea," an incontrovertible point of certitude going beyond all doubt, in observing that human thinking and existence always go together. "I can be sure of nothing else but that I think," he would say; and, as a result, "Cogito, ergo sum" (I think, therefore I am).[123] We are able to doubt everything, he says, except the fact that we think. Thus we are sure we exist. As a result, Descartes considers the soul itself as a thinking subjectivity, the self-thinking self. In this process, he observes, thought is distinct from both the body and sensation; the soul, in fact, operates on the basis of "innate" ideas and relates to the body only accidentally. Body and soul are thus separate substances, the *res extensa* and the *res cogitans*, respectively, and there is no true substantial union between them. "I *have* a body to which I am closely united," he says. "Nonetheless, since on the one hand I have a clear and distinct idea of myself, according to which I am only a thing that thinks and not something extensive, it is certain that I, that is, my soul, by which I am what I am, is completely and truly distinct from my body."[124] Though Descartes insists that the union between body and soul is very close, his vision is undoubtedly dualistic. The human being consists of two complete though mutually linked substances: he is an animal controlled by a spiritual soul. The soul exercises its influence on the vital spirits of the pineal gland, where it is located, and in return it receives images and sensations from the corporeal organs.

120. M. Heidegger, *Off the Beaten Track*, edited by J. Young and K. Haynes (Cambridge: Cambridge University Press, 2002), 58–83, 83.

121. See K. Stock, "Seele VI: Theologisch," in *Theologische Realenzyklopädie*, edited by G. Krause and G. Müller (Berlin: De Gruyter, 1999), 30:759–73; M. A. Gillespie, *The Theological Origins of Modernity*.

122. On the thought of Ficino, see A. B. Collins, *The Secular Is Sacred: Platonism and Thomism in Marsilio Ficino's Platonic Theology* (The Hague: Nijhoff, 1974); B. Mojsisch, "Zum Disput über die Unsterblichkeit der Seele in Mittelalter und Renaissance," *Freiburger Zeitschrift für Philosophie und Theologie* 29 (1982): 341–59.

123. R. Descartes, *Principia philosophiae* I, 10. On his position, see Tracy, "The Soul as Boatman of the Body"; E. M. Curley, "The Immortality of the Soul in Descartes and Spinoza," *Proceedings of the American Catholic Philosophical Association* 75 (2002): 27–41; J. Skirry, "A Hylomorphic Interpretation of Descartes's Theory of Mind-Body Problem," *Proceedings of the American Catholic Philosophical Association* 75 (2002): 267–83. See chapter 2, notes 85ff. and corresponding text.

124. Descartes, *Meditationes* VI.

Nicholas Malebranche takes up the basic thrust of Descartes's arguments, affirming, however, that the soul does not exercise any real influence over the body or vice versa. Rather, the desires of the soul provide God with the "occasion" for producing the required reaction in the body.[125] Baruch Spinoza radicalizes Descartes's doctrine in a pantheistic fashion by affirming that body and the soul are two modes of one substance, coinciding, respectively, with extension and thought. In other words, there is a strict psycho-physical parallelism between "body" and "soul." Both terms designate the same reality: the soul is the "idea of the body," whereas the body is the object of the mental idea that constitutes it. Instead of "soul," Spinoza speaks preferentially of "mind" (Latin, *mens*).[126] The understanding of the relationship between body and soul is expressed by G. W. Leibniz with the aid of his theory of monads, simple, indivisible, incorruptible, closed, incommunicable substances out of which everything is composed. Leibniz thinks that body and soul relate to one another in a purely exterior fashion, working side by side synchronically in that the creator establishes a primordial harmony between them.[127] Similar ways of speaking of the soul are to be found in the works of authors such as Goethe, Hölderlin, and Moses Mendelssohn.

Understandably, the problematic side of the equivalence Descartes and others established between soul and consciousness would come to the fore with the passing of time. Immanuel Kant censured Descartes, Mendelssohn, and Leibniz for uncritically affirming continuity between the psychological and metaphysical spheres. It is not legitimate, he said, to deduce the existence of a soul that is substantial, simple, incorruptible, personal, spiritual, and immortal from the subjective experience of thinking.[128] The soul may be said to exist, Kant says, but only as an idea or "postulate of practical reason." That is to say, were there no such thing as the human soul, it would be impossible to develop a consistent religious and ethical system. He considers the doctrine of final resurrection, however, as merely symbolic or even superfluous, of no interest theologically. He explains it as follows:

Now, the perfect accordance of the will with the moral law is *holiness*, a perfection of which no rational being in the sensible world is capable of at any moment of his existence. Since, nevertheless, it is required as practically necessary, it can only be found in a *progress in infinitum* towards that perfect accordance, and on the principles of pure practical reason it is necessary to assume such a practical progress as the real object of our will.... Now, this endless progress is only possible on the supposition of an *endless* duration of the *existence* and personality of the same rational being (which us called the immortality of the soul).[129]

125. See M. Merleau-Ponty, *L'union de l'âme et du corps chez Malebranche, Biran et Bergson* (Paris: J. Vrin, 1978).

126. See Curley, "The Immortality of the Soul in Descartes and Spinoza."

127. On the thought of Leibniz, see M. D. Wilson, "Leibniz: Self-Consciousness and Immortality in the Paris Notes and After," *Archiv für Geschichte der Philosophie* 58 (1976): 335–52.

128. See I. Kant, *Critique of Pure Reason*, translated by F. M. Müller, 2nd ed. (New York: Macmillan, 1922), II, II, 1, 640f.

129. I. Kant, *Critique of Practical Reason* (London: Longmans, Green, and Co., 1898), 218f. See the critique of Kant's position by Gevaert, "L'affermazione filosofica dell'immortalità," esp. 119.

The Soul and the Self as a Product of Matter

The eigtheenth-century Scottish philosopher David Hume developed a skeptical approach to the question of the soul, in open opposition to Descartes. He argued that human selfhood is but a "bundle of perceptions," a kind of theater in which different apprehensions present themselves and make us aware of knowing things. In other words, consciousness derives from the presence of objects perceived, not from a pre-existent spiritual soul. Hume does not deny the soul (or better, the *mind*) as such as a spiritual substance, but he affirms simply that we have no way of demonstrating its existence. The philosopher Paul H. d'Holbach explains this further, saying that we have no reason "to believe we have been privileged by nature: we are subject to the same vicissitudes to which all its other products are subjected. Our so-called prerogatives are founded on a simple error."[130] In a like fashion William James, passing from Hume's agnosticism to an explicit materialism, concluded that the soul does not exist at all but is merely a collection of psychic phenomena.[131] Bertrand Russell would graphically describe the spirit as "matter in the gaseous state."

A distinct phenomenon facilitating the decline of Descartes's understanding of the soul developed in the area of experimental psychology toward the end of the nineteenth century and the beginning of the twentieth. The psychologies of Freud, Jung, and Adler took no interest in "the soul" as such. All three, however, in spite of significant variants, developed psychologies "of the deep" and came to appreciate that the mind does not operate only at a conscious level, as Descartes and others as much as said by identifying the soul with conscious thought. The mind has a life of its own, much of which is "unconscious" or "subconscious." Though the notion of "depth" had not been lost in classical thought—we may think of Augustine's *cor* (or to the corresponding Biblical term, *leb*) and of Bonaventure's *apex*—Freud's symbolic equivalent of the "soul" remains entirely self-referential, unrelated to God or religion, in such a way that psychoanalysis and psychotherapy took the place of spiritual life (mysticism) and redemption. Against Descartes, depth psychologies also "rediscovered" that the human mind is deeply influenced and determined by somatic influences of all kinds, a notion to which Aquinas, with his doctrine of the soul as the only substantial form of the human body, gave full expression. In the first half of the twentieth century, Nicholas Berdjaev severely critiques Descartes and his followers: "The old dualism which comes from Descartes, is absolutely false and out of date. Such a dualism does not exist. The life of the soul permeates the whole life of the body, just as the bodily life has its effects upon the life of the soul. There is a vital unity of soul and body in man."[132]

Some twentieth-century authors of the phenomenological school, such as Edmund Husserl, attempted to go beyond mere descriptive psychology and claimed to develop a renewed *ontology* of the human spirit. However, experimental psychology, due to the fact that it insisted on the psychosomatic unity of the human being, tend-

---

130. P. H. D'Holbach, *Système de la nature; ou, Des lois du monde physique et du monde moral* (New York: G. Olms, 1994; originally published in 1821), 1:107.

131. On the thought of William James, see H. Ey, *La conscience*, 2nd ed. (Paris: PUF, 1968).

132. N. A. Berdjaev, *Slavery and Freedom*, 31.

ed for the most part to deny its spirituality, immortality, and free will.[133] Something of the kind is to be found in Marxist thought. In linking realism with materialism, Marxists considered the "soul" as a mere epiphenomenon or product of matter and denied its existence as a spiritual substance. Friedrich Engels once asked: "What is original, spirit or nature? According as one responds to this question, philosophers divide in two great schools. Those who affirm the originality of spirit over nature admit in one way or another the creation of the world.... Those for whom nature is original belong to the different schools of materialism."[134] For materialists the "soul" as such does not exist. It is a conventional term used to express the unstable and alienating epiphenomenon of individual human life. Psychical and conscious life are considered the highest product of matter (of the physical world). They are the product of that particularly complex form of matter called the "human brain."

Soul and Body in the Context of Modern Science

Modern science has given special attention, directly and indirectly, to the human soul in two directions: in dealing with the evolutionist hypothesis and in relation to the mind-body problem developed by philosophers and neurologists during the twentieth century.

Evolutionism and Hominization

In 1859 Charles Darwin published his famous work *The Origin of the Species by Means of Natural Selection*, in which, among other things, he put forward his theory that humans are simply a more evolved form of primate.[135] Though many of his findings have since been thoroughly revised and even reversed, the original thesis he put forward, that humans are direct descendants of the higher primates, was destined to become extremely popular. Besides, on the basis of evolutionary and genetic continuity with lower animals, and therefore with the biological, chemical, and physical world, it began to be argued that man could have evolved ultimately from even lower forms of life, and this would render superfluous the hypothesis of a spiritual soul, created by God and infused into humans. Though many scientists and philosophers accepted Darwin's position and followed through on it, theologians, many Christian philosophers and scientists expressed reservations. On the basis of what seemed to be the contrary teaching of scripture, they perceived that evolutionism questioned the unity and transcendental character of man. Given, however, that humans probably share 99.5 percent of the evolutionary history of higher primates and 95 percent of their genetic patrimony,[136] it is understandable that scientists and philosophers

133. See A.-T. Tymieniecka, ed., *Soul and Body in Husserlian Phenomenology: Man and Nature* (Boston: D. Reidel, 1983).

134. F. Engels and K. Marx, *Ludwig Feuerbach and the End [or Outcome] of Classical German Philosophy* (London: Union Books, 2009; originally published in 1886).

135. For an introduction to the topic of evolution, see L. Galleni, "Evolution" (2002) at www.inters.org/evolution; F. Facchini, "Uomo, identità biologica e culturale," in *Enciclopedia filosofica* (Milan: Bompiani, 2006), 12:11928–33. Specifically on Darwin, see G. Monastra, "Darwin, Charles Robert," in *DISF* 2:1669–90.

136. See J. Marks, *What It Means to be 98% Chimpanzee: Apes, People, and Their Genes* (Berkeley: University

would continue attempting to come up with other possible explanations of the evolutionist phenomenon. Several Christian thinkers and others during the nineteenth and early twentieth centuries formulated what was known as the "transformist" hypothesis, which explained that the human body proceeds, ultimately, from nonhuman parents, yet the soul is created directly by God.[137] Becoming a human being (what is generally called "hominization") may be considered, therefore, as a process that is staged over an extended historical period.[138]

On the face of things, the transformist hypothesis simplifies things a lot in that the body is seen as the reserve of science, whereas the soul is put aside for the study of theologians and philosophers. This clear distinction is made, however, at the price of resurrecting the old dualistic understanding of body and soul, whether in a Platonic or a Cartesian key.

Though some Christian theologians reacted at first against these positions, theological reflection continued. In the 1950 encyclical *Humani Generis* Pope Pius XII made it clear that the evolutionist hypothesis—specifically with respect to the origin of the human body from already existing living matter—is not a priori contrary to Catholic faith.[139] This teaching was confirmed and made more precise by John Paul II,[140] who referred to evolution as a "theory," no longer as a "hypothesis," and by Benedict XVI, who insisted on the compatibility between the doctrine of creation and evolutionary theories, properly understood.[141]

However, it should be noted that the evolutionist theory of staged hominization, even in mitigated form, is still problematic from a philosophical standpoint, for it can easily be seen to mark a return to the plurimorphist explanations common throughout the Middle Ages, or even to outright dualism. Should the human body already possess a complete "form" of its own (vegetative, sensitive) before the creation and infusion of the soul, the latter can hardly be considered as the *unica forma corporis*, and the difficulties typical of the dualistic interactionist theories of Descartes and others will crop up anew. Although we do not know how a link was established between the higher primates and *homo sapiens*, the adjective "human" should qualify "the body" only insofar as it is united to the soul; and this in order to avoid a dualistic extrinsic view.

According to Church teaching, in effect, the "human body" begins to exist only

---

of California Press, 2003); T. S. Mikkelsen et al., "Initial Sequence of the Chimpanzee Genome and Comparison with the Human Genome," *Nature* 437 (2005): 69–87.

137. Among the Christian thinkers, see, for example, A. Gardeil, "L'évolutionnisme et les principes de S. Thomas," *Revue thomiste* 1 (1893): 27–45, 316–27, 725–37; M. D. Leroy, *L'évolution restreinte aux espèces organiques* (Paris; Lyons: 1891); J. A. Zahm, *Evolution and Dogma* (Chicago: D. H. McBride, 1896).

138. See, for example, K. Rahner, *Hominisation: The Evolutionary Origin of Man as a Theological Problem* (Freiburg: Herder Palm, 1969).

139. See Pius XII, *Humani Generis*, DH 3897.

140. The principal interventions of John Paul II on the topic of evolution are the following: address to the participants in the International Symposium Christian Faith and Evolution Theory, April 26, 1985; *Humans Are Spiritual and Corporeal Beings*, General Audience, April 16, 1986; message to the participants in the Plenary of the Pontifical Academy of the Sciences, October 22, 1996, and *The Holy Spirit's Role in the Incarnation*, General Audience, May 27, 1998, no. 5.

141. See the address of His Holiness Benedict XVI to members of the Pontifical Academy of Sciences, October 31, 2008.

when the human soul is created. It should be added, of course, that science may well be in a position to establish that the evolutionary history and genetic pattern of humans coincide more or less with those of higher primates. Yet such a morphological or genetic continuity is not enough to postulate a direct causal link between nonhuman progenitors and *homo sapiens* unless we endorse a reductionistic view of all truly human behavior. Strictly speaking, such a "missing link" is not within the field of scientific research but rather leans toward philosophical (and not only theological) inquiry. Besides, it should be noted that differences between humans and primates are notably consistent, as recent research has shown.[142]

The Mind-Body Relationship

The growth of experimental psychology during the twentieth century spawned a wide variety of schools and scientific approaches to the question of the soul and human specificity. Of particular importance were the "methodological behaviorism" of B. F. Skinner and the "logical behaviorism" of Gilbert Ryle.[143] In simple terms, "behaviorists" consider humans as highly complex machines whose laws and workings can be deduced by scientific observation of their external behavior. Platonic or Cartesian dualisms are strictly excluded.

142. According to P.-P. Grassé, in *L'évolution du vivant: Matériaux pour une nouvelle théorie transformiste*, *Sciences d'aujourd'hui* (Paris: Albin Michel, 1978), translated into English as *Evolution of Living Organisms: Evidence for a New Theory of Transformation* (New York: Academic Press, 1977), when one attempts to establish parallel features between humans and primates, the real danger arises of making an unjustified projection. On the important differences between humans and primates, see V. Marcozzi, *Però l'uomo è diverso* (Milan: Rusconi, 1981). "The grammatical categories: name, subject, verb, are not known to chimpanzees. The great monkeys show no capacity to put information in order, to distinguish between truth and falsehood, to learn and/or construct rapports between phenomena and relationships, forms of behavior typical of humans." M. Goustard, "L'éthologie cognitive et affective des singes supérieurs (gibbons, chimpanzés, gorilles, orang-outans) à l'épreuve e la différence anthropologique," *Revue des questions scientifiques* 1 (1991): 34–80, 75. T. Dobzhansky, in *The Biology of Ultimate Concern* (London: Rapp and Whiting, 1969), 76, writes: "Not only do inferior animals not know what death is; neither do the superior ones." J. Van Lawick-Goodall, *In the Shadow of Man* (London: Fontana, 1973), 271, states: "It is only through a real understanding of the ways in which chimpanzees and men show similarities in behavior that we can reflect with meaning on the ways in which men and chimpanzees *differ*. And only then can we really begin to appreciate, in a biological and spiritual manner, the full extent of man's uniqueness." "Culture is an exclusive property of the human species," observes T. Dobzhansky in "L'evoluzione e l'ominizzazione," in *Le origini dell'uomo: L'evoluzione oggi*, 7th ed., edited by V. Marcozzi (Milan: Massimo, 1972). The same thing about culture is said by T. W. Deacon, *The Symbolic Species: The Co-evolution of Language and the Brain*, 2nd ed. (New York: W. W. Norton, 1998). Facchini describes the following features of humans that make them superior to other animals: "(a) establishing a conscious rapport with one's surroundings, controlling it, organizing it, inventing new responses to external stimuli; (b) the systematic fabrication of ever more perfect tools according to a project which foresees certain gestures and reveals abstractive and innovative capacities; (c) the capacity to give life to strong and lasting family bonds in the relationships between parents and children; (d) the capacity to go beyond the purely biological side of life through freely carried out actions and altruistic and extra-biological forms of behavior, distinct from properties, laws and projects of a biological kind, and which can become meaningful as regards gratuitousness, art, religion and ethics; (e) symbolic communication carried out through language and other symbolic forms; (f) the accumulation and transmission of behavioral forms not by genetic or strictly parental means; (g) the possibility of choosing between different alternatives, also in similar circumstances ... that is, self-determination or freedom; (h) the tendency towards a complex social life rich in symbolism." Facchini, "Uomo, identità biologica e culturale," 12:11931.

143. See B. F. Skinner and J. G. Holland, *The Analysis of Behavior: A Program for Self-instruction* (New York: McGraw-Hill, 1961); Skinner, *Beyond Freedom and Dignity*; G. Ryle, *The Concept of Mind* (London: Hutchinson, 1949).

Criticisms of behaviorism, however, were not long in coming.[144] In fact, the perennial dilemma of the relationship between body and soul comes to the fore again in terms of the relationship between mind (which takes the place of "soul" or "spirit") and body. Against empiricists, materialists, and behaviorists, the existence of the mind is unequivocally affirmed. Yet it still may be asked: what is the relationship between the self, subjectivity, and the mind, on the one hand, and the biological, chemical, and physical organism usually termed the brain, on the other? A wide variety of explanations drawing on neurobiology, the cognitive sciences, information theory, computer science, linguistics, and sociology has been suggested.[145] We may mention the theory of identity (Feigl) with the associated question of artificial intelligence, that of emergentism (Bunge), and that of interactive dualism (Popper, Eccles).

Helmuth Feigl, taking issue with the behaviorist position in his 1958 work *The "Mental" and the "Physical,"* insists on the real existence of the human mind.[146] The human being is more than an automated mechanism driven by stimulus and response. Human behavior, at least in part, is directed by a self-conscious self. Hence the "self" cannot be identified with behavior as such but with the interior principle of behavior. The mind, however, according to Feigl, is identified purely and simply with the brain. He takes this approach because of what he calls "the principle of economy," according to which there is no need to multiply unnecessarily the causes of any phenomenon (this is a classical application of the principle of "Ockham's razor"). If, therefore, all human processes, events, and mental states (mental teleology, behavioral intentionalism, cognition, willing choice) can be explained adequately on the basis of the workings of the brain, there is no need to postulate the existence of a spiritual principle of life. Feigl takes it that this is the case: if cerebral processes could be mapped in sufficient detail on a screen as it were, human action and development could be suitably predicted. Leaving aside for the moment the fact that many philosophers and neurologists refuse to identify the mind (or soul) with the brain, what Crick called the "binding problem" still remains and can be stated as follows: what keeps such structures in place, first of all, and, even more important, where did their form or structure originate?[147]

The "emergentist materialism" of Mario Bunge rendered Feigl's reductionist view obsolete.[148] Matter is all that exists, according to Bunge, but within reality matter ex-

144. The critique has been undertaken by authors such as H. Feigl, "The 'Mental' and the '"Physical,'" in *Concepts, Theories, and the Mind-Body Problem*, edited by H. Feigl, M. Scriven, and G. Maxwell (Minneapolis: University of Minnesota Press, 1958), 370–497; M. Bunge, *The Mind-Body Problem: A Psychobiological Approach* (Oxford: Oxford University Press, 1980); R. Rorty, *Philosophy and the Mirror of Nature*, 2nd ed. (Princeton, N.J.: Princeton University Press, 1980).

145. For an overall view, see J. Seifert, *Das Leib-Seele-Problem und die gegenwärtige philosophische Diskussion: Eine systematisch-kritische Analyse*, 2nd ed. (Darmstadt: Wissenschaftliche Buchgesellschaft, 1989); D. Pinkas, *La matérialité de l'esprit: La conscience, le langage et la machine dans les théories contemporaines de l'esprit* (Paris: La Découverte, 1995); J.-M. Maldamé, "Sciences cognitives, neurosciences et âme humaine," *Revue thomiste* 98 (1998): 282–322; J. R. Searle, "Deux biologistes et un physicien en quête de l'âme: Crick, Penrose et Edelman passés au scalpel de la critique philosophique," *La Recherche* 287 (1998): 62–77; J. J. Sanguineti, A. Acerbi, and J. Á. Lombo, eds., *Moral Behavior and Free Will: A Neurobiological and Philosophical Approach* (Morolo: If Press, 2011); J. J. Sanguineti, *Neuroscienza e filosofia dell'uomo* (Rome: Edusc, 2014).

146. See note 144.

147. See F. Crick, *The Astonishing Hypothesis: The Scientific Search for the Soul* (London: Touchstone, 1995).

148. On this question, see G. Del Re, "The Question of the Soul," *La Nuova Critica* 30 (1997): 75–98.

presses itself in qualitatively distinct levels of being. Each level supposes the anterior one yet surpasses it ontologically. Common experience does not allow us to understand everything in purely physical terms. Bunge accepts that the mind *is* the brain but adds that the human brain differs qualitatively and not only quantitatively from any other known material object. The human being must thus be distinguished both from the biosphere and from his nearest genetic relative, the chimpanzee. The principal property of Bunge's emergentist materialism is what he calls "plasticity," that is, the aptitude of the brain to program and organize itself. The theory of emergentism attempts to find a better theory to fit the facts than does the reductionist identity theory. Similar attempts may be found in recent works of a variety of different authors.[149] However, insofar as they generally begin with a monistic view of reality from which higher levels of life are seen to spontaneously emerge, it is difficult to shake off the impression that such levels are merely quantitative improvements of the lower ones. In real terms, little space is left for human intentionality, freedom, or transcendence.[150]

Mind-body dualism continues to be popular among philosophers and scientists. Authors such as Karl Popper and John Eccles are probably still the best-known representatives.[151] Popper approaches the problem of the mind-body relationship from the perspective of his theory of the "three worlds." Apart from the world of physical entities (World 1) and of mental phenomena such as subjective experiences, consciousness, etc. (World 2), there is also a world comprising the products of the mind: history, scientific theories, social institutions, works of art, and so on (World 3). The existence of World 1 cannot be doubted. Yet Popper holds that real existence must be attributed to the other two as well in that their empirical effects can be experienced and checked because they really act on the inferior worlds. It is evident that the products of the mind (World 3) are what most decisively influence and transform physical reality (World 1). As a result, it must be said that there exist real beings that are incorporeal. But World 3 exercises its influence on World 1 only through the workings of the mind, World 2, which, according to Popper, is a real entity that surpasses the purely physical and corporeal, even though it stands in need of them in order to act. In other words, the mind is *distinct from* the brain, even though it interacts closely with it. Thus it is the self that possesses the brain, not the other way around. Popper, in fact, quite openly adopts the explanation popularized by Plato: the self (the soul) is like a tiller to a boat or like a pianist to a piano. The position of Popper has been accepted by other renowned philosophers and neurophysicists such as John Eccles, André Green, Roger Penrose, and Robert W. Sperry.[152] Though confirming the need

149. For example, J.-P. Changeux, *Neuronal Man: The Biology of Mind* (Princeton, N.J.: Princeton University Press, 1997); D. C. Dennett, *Consciousness Explained* (Boston: Little, Brown, 1995); G. M. Edelman, *Neural Darwinism: The Theory of Neuronal Group Selection* (New York: Basic Books, 1987); E. Boncinelli, *Il cervello, la mente e l'anima* (Milan: Mondadori, 1999).

150. See Maldamé, "Sciences cognitives."

151. See especially K. R. Popper and J. C. Eccles, *The Self and its Brain: An Argument for Interactionism* (Berlin-Heidelberg: Springer, 1977); J. C. Eccles, *Evolution of the Brain: Creation of the Self* (London: Routledge, 1989); K. R. Popper, *Knowledge and the Body-Mind Problem: In Defence of Interaction* (London: Routledge, 1994).

152. See A. Green, *La causalité psychique: Entre nature et culture* (Paris: Odile Jacob, 1995); R. Penrose, *Shadows of the Mind: A Search for the Missing Science of Consciousness* (Oxford: Oxford University Press, 1994);

to retain the presence of a nonmaterial principle of action in the human being, this position tends, however, to return to the problematic "plurimorphic" positions of Plato and Descartes.

Recent Theological Proposals on the Human Soul

After the preceding survey it would seem that only two viable alternatives remain as regards the existence and substantiality of the human soul: dualism and monism. Either the human soul exists as a separate (or at least separable) substance that controls the body from without (Plato, Descartes, Popper), in principle a "spiritual" substance produced by the divinity and capable of meaningful survival after death, or, alternatively, it designates a configuring form totally bound up with the unitary psychosomatic structure of humans, which simply dissolves at death. Understandably, the Christian doctrine of creation and eschatological fulfillment cannot accept either as a unique solution. Many attempts were made by theologians throughout the twentieth century to express anew what is intended traditionally by the human soul, especially in the context of the challenges presented by the sciences. We shall briefly examine Karl Rahner's understanding of "hominization" and the Lutheran Wolfhart Pannenberg's explanation of human identity in the context of eschatological salvation. Both suggest what might be termed "actualistic" understandings of the human soul.[153]

The Origin of Humans according to Karl Rahner

Rahner suggests that the origin of life may be attributed entirely to God in the realm of primary causality (creation) yet entirely to generation as regards secondary causality (that is, evolution).[154] God can thus be considered as the real and transcendental basis of the evolutionary process of the world. That is to say, God works at the very heart of creation in and through secondary causes, without ever replacing or interrupting them. Divine causality, in other words, acts from within a finite causality, elevating and empowering it to go beyond its own potentialities. God's action, therefore, is what brings about the creature's self-transcendence; this is what scientists might call "emergentism." Applying this principle to humans, Rahner says that both God and pre-hominids are fully the cause of the entire human being. God's power brings out the full potential of the pre-hominid state, constituting humans as persons, thus going beyond the biological chain of reproduction. As a result, the uniqueness, irreplaceability, and spirituality of the human person is rooted in the creating and empowering action of God. "Emergentism" leads both to "personhood" and "grace." For this reason, Rahner concludes, the evolution of humanity from primates is not problematic.

Rahner's hominization theory, on the face of things, offers a reasonably coherent

R. W. Sperry, "Mind-Brain Interaction: Mentalism, Yes; Dualism, No," *Neuroscience* 5 (1980): 195–206; Sperry, *Science and Moral Priority* (New York: Columbia University Press, 1983).

153. On this period, see G. Greshake and G. Lohfink, *Naherwartung, Auferstehung, Unsterblichkeit* (Freiburg: Herder, 1975).

154. See Rahner, *Hominisation*. On the position of Rahner, see the presentation of G. Canobbio, *Destinati alla beatitudine: Breve trattato sui Novissimi* (Milan: Vita e pensiero, 2012), 40–42.

solution to the dilemma posed by evolution. But it does so at a cost.[155] First, there is no good reason that the divine action that brings finite beings to transcend themselves should be reserved to individuals that are genetically identifiable as humans. Put another way, the difference between human and nonhuman beings can only be quantitative, not qualitative; "spirit" would constitute simply a more evolved state of matter.[156] Second, if divine efficient causality is what brings about the self-transcendence of finite beings, the actions attributed to the beings in question may remain unrelated to their respective natures. Thomas Aquinas teaches that in the order of creation, and specifically in that of the spirituality of the human soul, "nulla actio convenit alicui rei, nisi per aliquod principium formaliter ei inhaerens" (no action can be performed by a subject without any principle that is inherent in that same subject).[157] And elsewhere: "Non dicimus quod calor calefacit, sed calidum" (We do not say that heat makes something hot, but that a certain hot body makes something else hot).[158] That is, immaterial actions of whatever kind (knowing, loving, acting freely) can be meaningfully attributed to humans only if they derive from a proper immaterial substance, that is, the human soul. Otherwise they can be attributed only to some distinct immaterial reality—an external, common "agent intellect," perhaps, or to God himself. It would be more correct to say that the direct action of God on man at the level of primary causality involves the creation of the human soul, the unique form that makes it possible for humans to will, to know, to be open to God, and so on.

The Place of the Soul in Contemporary Protestant Theology

A number of twentieth-century Reformed authors, such as H. Thielicke, P. Althaus, O. Cullmann, K. Barth, and W. Pannenberg, commonly deny the "natural" immortality of the human soul and, as a result, its substantiality as a metaphysical co-principle of the human being.[159] Some Catholic theologians have tended to move in the same direction.[160] The theology of the first Reformers, however, had not traditionally denied the immortality and substantiality of the human soul. Quite the contrary, in fact, although they emphasized that such a belief was a tenet of faith and, as such, was unattainable by reason alone.[161] This change of perspective has been mainly due to the preference contemporary authors have given to pure Biblical exegesis (scripture speaks openly of final resurrection and not so much of the immortality of the soul) and to an attempt at "de-Hellenizing" historical Christianity, thus calling the existence of the soul into question.

---

155. Rahner's position has been criticized by Ladaria in *Antropologia teologica*, 138; J. Maritain, *Approches sans entraves* (Paris: Fayard, 1973), 1:105–62, translated into English as *Untrammeled Approaches* (Notre Dame, Ind.: University of Notre Dame Press, 1987); C. Schönborn, "L'homme créé par Dieu: Le fondement de la dignité de l'homme," *Gregorianum* 65 (1984): 337–63; L. Scheffczyk, *Einführung in die Schöpfungslehre*, 3rd ed. (Darmstadt: Wissenschaftliche Buchgesellschaft, 1987), 87f.

156. This might involve a confusion between "instrumental" and "secondary" causality. Schönborn's critique of Rahner in "L'homme créé par Dieu" moves in this direction.

157. Aquinas, *S.Th.* I, q. 79, a. 4.   158. Ibid., q. 75, a. 2, co.

159. See *COH* 313–18.

160. For example, G. Greshake, N. Lohfink, and J. L. Ruiz de la Peña.

161. See B. Gherardini, "Immortalità e risurrezione in Karl Barth," *Euntes Docete* 12 (1959): 182–211.

However, it seems that the main difficulty Reformed theologians encounter with the doctrine of the immortality and substantiality of the human soul lies elsewhere. In modern philosophy the soul had come to be understood in terms of subjectivity and of a human aspiration to the absolute (for Lessing the soul is "an infinite striving," for Fichte the combination of knowledge and deed, for Nietzsche, "the will to power"). In such a context, an immortal soul is perceived as a source of autonomous human action and thus a threat to the traditional Lutheran doctrine of justification by faith alone, by grace alone, as if the human being could offer to God something that had not first been received from him.[162] According to Karl Barth, if God alone is immortal (see 1 Tm 6:16), the human soul cannot be such.

Leaving aside the variety of questions involved in the denial of the immortality of the soul from a theological standpoint, some Reformed theologians in recent times have attempted to recuperate the notion of the soul.[163] Others, such as the Lutheran theologian Wolfhart Pannenberg, have put forward what might be termed an "actualistic" or dynamic understanding of what has traditionally been called the human soul.

Pannenberg's View of the Origins of Humanity

Pannenberg takes it that modern science has demonstrated that the "soul" is not an object as such but rather an aspect of the dynamism of life and of human behavior.[164] Hence it would make no sense to speak of the immortality "of" the soul. Besides, he notes that Christian hope is founded on the notion of novelty, not on that of stability and continuity. Pannenberg admits, however, that Christian theology has historically accepted the notion of the subsistence and survival of the soul as a vital principle, for reasons not necessarily bound up with an uncritical assimilation of Platonism. The doctrine, in fact, is closely related to salvation and resurrection and was put forward in order to ensure that *human identity* between the earthly and the risen state is maintained. The so-called immortality of the soul is what made it possible for resurrection to take place; the "soul" as the *forma corporis* was seen to retain the scheme, project, genetic code, or *eidos* (that is, the image) of the individual human being. Pannenberg considers, however, that a subsistent immortal soul capable of surviving death and ensuring final resurrection should in principle be in a position to undergo new human experiences. But this would actually disqualify its very reason of being, for new experiences (those involved, for example, in purgatorial purification and the intercession of the saints) would provide the soul with a distinct identity, as if the human person was present in plenitude. As an alternative, Pannenberg suggests that human identity during the intermediate period between death and resurrection (what is usually called "intermediate eschatology") would be better guaranteed if such identity were retained or "codified" in God himself, because it is only "in Him" that our lives and histories can be made immortal.[165]

---

162. See A. Ahlbrecht, *Tod und Unsterblichkeit in der evangelischen Theologie der Gegenwart* (Paderborn: Bonifatius, 1955), 112–20.

163. See, for example, C. Hermann, *Unsterblichkeit der Seele durch Auferstehung: Studien zu den anthropologischen Implikationen der Eschatologie* (Gottingen: Vandenhoeck & Ruprecht, 1997).

164. See Pannenberg, *Systematic Theology*, 2:175–275 and 3:527–646.

165. See *COH* 109ff.

Still, Pannenberg's position regarding the immortality and substantiality of the human soul does not give sufficient consistency to created reality as such. In a Christian context he is correct in considering God as the only one capable of granting immortality or permanence to the human being in its concrete lived identity. However, not unlike Rahner, he is mistaken in seeking out human identity (and thus immortality) exclusively in the concrete history of the person, not rather in the human subject of that history. Humans, before having a personal history and developing a concrete identity of their own, were already human, with a spiritual dignity written into their very being. In fact, the doctrine of the immortality of the soul is meant not only to guarantee the identity of the singular history of each human being but also to ensure the metaphysical identity of that person's being human. Pannenberg's opposition between (eschatological) novelty and (Platonic) stability is problematic for the same reason. In the absence of a metaphysically stable subject, no novelty would be possible or meaningful because any novelty would presuppose a discontinuity with respect to what was previously present. "Novelty" must be the novelty of something. The subject of such a "novelty" in Pannenberg—certainly for as long as the intermediate period between death and resurrection lasts—could be only God himself, the objective Spirit, of which the individual human being (the "subjective spirit") would be a simple derivation or manifestation.

Concluding Reflections

Three observations may be made to conclude this chapter on the union between body and soul that constitutes the human being. The first refers to the knowability of the existence and immortal character of the human soul, the second to the precise nature of the union between the two, and the third to the contribution Christian theology has made to the philosophical and scientific challenges of understanding human nature.[166]

The Knowability of Human Immortality

We have seen throughout this chapter that the theme of the human soul (or, if you wish, the human spirit) is historically transversal. It has been present in many different ways in all ages and areas of thought: theology, philosophy, art, science. All this would seem to indicate that the human soul really exists. From the point of view of Christian faith, it is essential in order to affirm the singular and irreplaceable dignity of each human being, made in the image and likeness of God, as well as its eschatological destiny. In the words of Giacomo Canobbio, "The soul is, at heart, the condition of possibility so that eternal life can be given to the concrete person."[167] In a 1979 document of the Congregation for the Doctrine of the Faith the following explanation of the soul is given.

---

166. See the following works in Italian: J. P. Lieggi, ed., *Per una scienza dell'anima: La teologia sfidata; Corso di aggiornamento dell'Associazione Teologica Italiana* (Milan: Glossa, 2009); Canobbio, *Destinati alla beatitudine*, 31–48.

167. G. Canobbio, *Il destino dell'anima: Elementi per una teologia* (Brescia: Morcelliana, 2009), 120.

The Church affirms that a spiritual element survives and subsists after death, an element endowed with consciousness and will, so that the "human self" subsists. To designate this element, the Church uses the word "soul," the accepted term in the usage of Scripture and Tradition. Although not unaware that this term has various meanings in the Bible, the Church thinks that there is no valid reason for rejecting it; moreover, she considers that the use of some word as a vehicle is absolutely indispensable in order to support the faith of Christians.[168]

Still, this does not mean that the affirmation of the existence and subsistence of the human soul can be taken as a simple postulate of faith. This is so, as we saw, because it is a proper and transversal argument emerging from the history of philosophy and religion (the explanations of a Platonic, Thomistic, and subjectivistic kind are well known).[169] Besides, it is due to the fact that "the soul" forms a presupposition for any explanation of human life that intends to go beyond the limits of empirical materiality, reflecting on human immortality and offering a solid basis for moral commitment.[170] In effect, should the thrust toward immortality be based on a pure promise of faith, or if it were a superstructure invented by humans themselves, all anthropology would remain flat and insipid, open to the grossest forms of materialism, because it would have to consider as alienating the human drive toward immortality and permanence experienced by each person.[171] In fact, Vatican Council II teaches that the human being "rightly follows the intuition of his heart when he abhors and repudiates the utter ruin and total disappearance of his own person. He rebels against death because he bears in himself an eternal seed which cannot be reduced to sheer matter."[172]

According to Maldamé, the soul

is a power of unification because it guarantees the unity of different forms of behavior. It is a power of reflection, which makes it possible for humans to direct their gaze toward themselves, to make all their actions and thoughts the object of observation. The soul is a power of transcendence: humans are always dissatisfied with what they have and what they are. The soul is a power of freedom: it founds the underived capacity for decision and responsibility.[173]

---

168. Congregation for the Doctrine of the Faith, *Letter on Certain Questions Concerning Eschatology*, May 17, 1979, no. 3.

169. See the study of Gevaert, "L'affermazione filosofica dell'immortalità."

170. Blaise Pascal said: "It is true that the mortality or immortality of the soul must make an enormous difference for morality. Strangely, however, philosophers for the most part have constructed their ethical systems independently of it." *Pensées*, no. 219.

171. "But Christians are asked to 'give an account for their hope' (1 Pet 3:15). Indeed ... Christian eschatology makes sense not only because the divine promise of eternal life to believers exists, but also because such a promise is seen to be anthropologically and rationally meaningful to humans. And if we say that the soul's spirituality (and immortality) is rationally knowable, that can be only because the soul is naturally spiritual, and therefore incorruptible. If it cannot be shown that immortality is structurally rooted in the human constitution, then faith may well become fideistic, and hope utopian." *COH* 22. On our knowledge of human immortality, see *COH* 19–25.

172. *GS*, no. 18. See also *CCC* 362–67.

173. Maldamé, "Sciences cognitives," 321.

The Unity between Body and Soul

Better than other explanations, the hylomorphism of Thomas Aquinas (as seen earlier in this chapter) seems to be in a position to overcome the difficulties of both monistic and dualistic accounts of the rapport between body and soul.[174] Thomas was openly opposed to the theory of the Arabic commentator on Aristotle, Averroes, according to whom there is only one "possible" intellect common to all humans, separate from their bodies and coinciding with the motor intelligence of the world, the only one that is eternal and immortal. Thomas was likewise opposed to the position of Avicenna, who taught the oneness of the "agent intellect." And he did so for a simple reason, deeply rooted in Christian faith: if the agent intellect were one for all humans, we could guarantee the unity of the human race but not the dignity of each and every human individual and thus their personal freedom and inalienable rights. In fact, each "man" would be a simple exemplar of the species, a passive instrument in which the action and thought of the collectivity (or divinity) are reflected. "Hic homo intelligit" (This man thinks):[175] in this simple phrase Thomas sums up his thought on the individuality of the human soul, from which there arises the dignity and relevance of the free action of each person, which we shall consider in the next chapter. In the explanations of both Rahner and Pannenberg, the "soul" would become, rather, a kind of divine dynamism that is activated in each person. And if it were, the senses and imagination of the individual would play a merely accidental and decorative role in human knowledge.[176]

The Contribution of Theology to the Philosophical Challenge of Understanding Human Nature

On the basis of the study of science, as well as that on religious and philosophical grounds, we have come to speak of the need to have a unifying principle of the individual, a spiritual, "informing" center of their lives, the soul, *anima forma corporis*. If science has insisted mainly on the psychosomatic unity of the human person, and thus on the inseparability of body and soul, of matter and spirit, philosophy for the most part has favored distinguishing the body from the soul to a greater or lesser degree, with a certain tendency toward dualism. In any case, Christian revelation has given substantial reasons to explain the nature of the union and the distinction. Four may be mentioned.

First, on the basis of the oneness and simplicity of God's creative act it makes sense to say that the human soul is the only form of the human body. Second, on the basis of the doctrine of the hypostatic union of Christ (the divine nature and the human nature in a single divine person) we come to know that the divine Word is united with humanity whole and entire, not with the body through the soul. And because Christ "reveals man to himself," we can deduce that the spiritual soul is the only

---

174. See L. Borghi, "L'antropologia tomista e il body-mind problem: Alla ricerca di un contributo mancante," *Acta Philosophica* 1 (1992): 279–92.

175. Aquinas, *S.Th.* I, q. 76, a. 1. On this text, see J.-B. Brenet, "Thomas d'Aquin pense-t-il? Retours sur *hic homo intelligit*," *Revue des sciences philosophiques et théologiques* 93 (2009): 229–50.

176. See Aquinas, *SCG* II, 76; *S.Th.* I, q. 79, aa. 4–5.

form of the human being in its entirety. Third, in the light of the doctrine of universal resurrection at the end of time we can accept the possibility of a merely temporary survival of the separated soul while it awaits the final and definitive union that God wanted for humans from the beginning. And fourth, apart from situating the dignity of the human person in the fact that the soul was created directly by God in a non-mediated way, Christianity attributes metaphysical priority to this specifically spiritual co-principle of the human being.[177] "To affirm the soul," writes Canobbio, "means saving and guarding the dignity of the human person, which cannot be reduced to a complex combination of biological phenomena that are destined to come to an end, in the human sense, at death, in order to continue in an undifferentiated form of matter."[178]

177. On the theme of creation and of the infusion of the soul in the *nasciturus*, see Caspar, "La création de l'âme humaine et l'animation immédiate de l'embryon chez Lactance"; Caspar, "La problématique de l'animation de l'embryon: Survol historique et enjeux dogmatiques," *Nouvelle Revue Théologique* 113 (1991): 3–24, 239–55, 400–413; L.-M. Antoniotti, "La vérité de la personne humaine: Animation différée ou animation immédiate," *Revue thomiste* 103 (2003): 547–76; D. A. Jones, *The Soul of the Embryo: An Enquiry into the Status of the Human Embryo in the Christian Tradition*, 2nd ed. (London: Continuum, 2005).

178. Canobbio, *Destinati alla beatitudine*, 48.

Sed quid eligimus, nisi prius eligamur?   AUGUSTINE[1]

The image of God in man means intellect, free will and power over oneself.
JOHN DAMASCENE[2]

The Christian religion is the religion of freedom—although it may come about that this
freedom is perverted into unfreedom under the influence of superstition.   G. W. F. HEGEL[3]

The Christian doctrine of grace constitutes the true doctrine of freedom.
NICOLAS BERDJAEV[4]

Modernization is a passage from fatalism to choice, from a world of rigid necessity to one
of frenzied possibilities.   PETER BERGER[5]

The Image of God and Human Freedom

God made humans in his image and likeness (Gn 1:27). The first consequence of
God's act is the imperative invitation humans receive to exercise dominion over the
earth as he blesses them. Under God's sovereign power, though as his children, they
receive the capacity and responsibility of administering the entire material universe.[6]
That is to say, humans live before God as responsible beings in that they respond to
what they have received. According to scripture, the task and mission humans receive to exercise dominion over the earth is not of a merely external or transitory
kind because they are also given the capability in the depths of their being and in
all their faculties to be able to carry out the task effectively. It is not a simple com-

---

1. Augustine, *Sermo* 34: "But what can we choose if we have not been chosen?"
2. John Damascene, *De fide orth.* II, 12.
3. G. W. F. Hegel, *Elements of the Philosophy of Right*, edited by A. W. Wood and H. B. Nisbet (Cambridge: Cambridge University Press, 1991), no. 270 (303).
4. N. A. Berdjaev, *Freedom and the Spirit*, 2nd ed. (London: G. Bles, 1935), I, no. 199.
5. P. L. Berger, *A Far Glory: the Quest for Faith in an Age of Credulity* (New York: Doubleday, 1992), 75.
6. See chapter 4, notes 49ff. and corresponding text.

mission; they are structured in order to exercise dominion. In fact, the meaning of humans' existence and activity is precisely that of being able to direct themselves to God in profound adoration as they exercise dominion over the earth. It is traditional to associate the image of God in humans with their spiritual constitution. That is correct: humans were created with the spiritual faculties of intellect and will, and this is what makes them capable of exercising dominion over animals and the material world (Sir 17:1–10). The dominion of humans have over the earth is carried out in the free and conscious exercise of the spiritual faculties God has given them. At the same time, the exercise of human spiritual faculties is fully present in the material world to which humans belong in and through the body, of which the soul is the "form." Thus humans exercise their dominion over the created world, and likewise their freedom, in and through their entire being, spiritual and material, body and soul, as individuals and as members of the collectivity, directed to God and at the same time to the world. Living as a free human being, therefore, is not a "part" or an "aspect" of life but belongs to the entire human being.

The Centrality of Freedom to the Christian View of the World

Throughout the history of Christian theology, freedom has been considered essential to humans, a sign of the image of God in them.[7] Tertullian said, for example:

As long as man possesses now, as something of his own, the good things God has placed at his disposition, and insofar as they become his property and of his nature, he has been given by constitution the freedom and the power to decide, like a needle in the balance, for the good given him by God, in such a way that the good from now on is generated by man through his own will.[8]

The same doctrine may be found in the writings of Gregory of Nyssa, Augustine, and Bernard of Clairvaux.[9] Thomas Aquinas, in the prologue to his treatise on Christian moral theology (which is inseparable from his anthropology, the *S.Th.* I-II and II-II), cites an important text of John Damascene that says: "Per imaginem significatur intellectuale et arbitrio liberum et per se potestativum" (The image of God in man means intellect, free will and power over oneself).[10] Descartes teaches the same

---

7. See the philosophical study of F. Botturi, "Libertà," in *Enciclopedia filosofica*, 7:6393–6450, which has been used amply throughout this chapter.

8. Tertullian, *Adv. Marc.* II, 6, 4–5.

9. "Beings that are subject to change never remain the same, but pass continuously from one state to another through a change which works always, for good and for bad.... Now, to be subject to change is to be born continuously.... But here birth does not take place by an extraneous intervention, as in the case of bodily beings.... It is the result of a free choice and we are thus, in a sense, our own parents, creating ourselves as we wish, and with our choice giving ourselves the form we want." Gregory of Nyssa, *De vita Moysis* II, 2–3; see also his *Hom.* 6. And Augustine: "The age of the body does not depend on our will. In this sense nobody, from the corporeal point of view, grows when they want to grow, nor are they born when they want to be born. But wherever birth depends on the will, also growth depends on the will" (*In Ep. Io. ad Parthos* III, 1). "Voluntas, quia est in nostra potestate, libera est nobis" (The will, since it is in our power, is free for us). *De lib. arbit.* III, 3, 8. And Bernard: "Ubi consensus, ibi voluntas ... et ubi voluntas ibi libertas. Et hoc est liberum arbitrium" (Where there is consent, there is will, and where there is will, there is freedom. And this is free will). *De gratia et libero arbitrio* 1, 2.

10. John Damascene, *De fide orth.* II, 12. See Aquinas, *S.Th.* I-II, prol.

thing: "Freedom formally considered is the reason of the image and likeness of God in man."[11] Also, the constitution *Gaudium et Spes* of Vatican Council II says that freedom is to be considered "an exceptional sign of the divine image" within humans.[12] We can mention Hans Urs von Balthasar among recent theologians who see the image of God principally in human freedom—what he calls "finite freedom."[13]

Distinguishing between Freedom and Free Will

Situating the Dynamics of Human Freedom between Restrictions and Aspirations

We speak of human freedom normally as a fact, a physical and/or moral reality. When we say that someone is free, this refers, in the first place, to their interior and exterior state, which allows them to overcome physical or moral restrictions to their actions. Humans spontaneously desire and seek after this freedom in the sense that they strive to overcome all kinds of hindrances and limitations: they desire to be educated; to open horizons; to go beyond the restrictions, closures, and claustrophobias they experience; to enjoy the widest possible space of movement; and so on. It is clear that this aspect of freedom—understood as an absence of interior and exterior restriction—is completely necessary for people to live in a healthy and dignified way. Humans, in effect, need space for free movement, they need to experiment mentally, to play, to choose, to move. This is an indication of the openness of the human spirit toward the other, toward the infinite. Besides, on the basis of this freedom humans are given the opportunity of choosing between different options, of determining their life projects with autonomy and responsibility, of exercising what is normally called "free will."

At the same time, common experience tells us that in reaching out toward this unconfined freedom of movement we cannot, in fact, grasp or reach the infinite for the simple reason that humans are finite and limited beings: as creatures, as particular persons, as corporeal and cultural beings. In this sense, the desire for an infinite and unconfined freedom, without limits of any kind, is and always will be illusory and impossible for humans. "We know well that man does not begin with freedom but with the limit and with the threshold that cannot be passed," said Michel Foucault. "There is not a single culture in the world in which it is allowed to do absolutely everything."[14] Ancient philosophers understood this well, as is reflected in their description of the dialectic typical of human life between *hybris* (pride and presumption, especially with respect to the gods) and *nemesis* (the inevitable retribution, ending in collapse or ruin): humans attempt to act beyond their powers, to flourish beyond their true possibilities, and later collapse irremediably into nothingness and irrelevance. In brief, in one sense humans are free, yet in another they are not. In real terms, humans are both free and determined at the same time. That is what it means to say that humans have a finite freedom.

11. Botturi, "Libertà," 6411.   12. *GS*, no. 17.
13. See von Balthasar, *Theo-Drama*, 2:316–34.
14. M. Foucault, *Folie et déraison: Histoire de la folie à l'âge classique* (Paris: Plon, 1961), translated into English as *Madness and Civilization: A History of Insanity in the Age of Reason* (London: Routledge, 2009).

The Meaning of Human Freedom

In this chapter we shall ask two sets of questions. First, where does this space of freedom that marks the life of every person come from? Are humans constituted as free by the circumstances in which they are born? Or are they free on the basis of their own natural constitution, because they are made that way? Or rather is freedom a space humans open for themselves, employing their own energies and means, or do they do this with the help of other people? Once we have established the provenance of freedom in this sense, we can ask a second set of questions: What is the meaning of human freedom? What do humans want to be free for? What do they obtain by their free actions? Are such actions truly relevant? Do they produce something that goes beyond their concreteness and finitude? Do they reach out in any way to the infinite and the eternal? These two sets of questions may be summed up in the distinction made by the philosopher Isaiah Berlin between *freedom from* and *freedom for*.[15] The first is equivalent to freedom from restriction, from limit, as described earlier, that is, the fact of being capable of acting more or less freely. The second responds rather to the purpose of the free act, that is, the meaning or sense of free human action, what it can really achieve.

To understand the meaning and reach of human freedom in the light of faith, we shall reflect on three things. First we shall briefly present what philosophers and theologians have said throughout history about freedom. Second we shall consider the dynamics of human free action from a phenomenological point of view in the wider context of the Christian vision of God, of humanity, and of the world. Third, in the last section of the chapter we shall draw some practical consequences from this reflection.

Historical Pointers to the Meaning of Human Freedom

Freedom and Society in Greek Thought

The Greek term for "freedom" is *eleutheria*; the adjective *eleutheros* designates, literally, someone who "belongs to the people."[16] The notion of human freedom originally arose, therefore, in the context of a group of individuals who make up a single community. Freedom does not refer simply to the individual but to the autonomy of the state and of the collectivity.[17] The one who is "free" enjoys full political rights and

---

15. See I. Berlin, *Liberty*, 2nd ed. (Oxford: Oxford University Press, 2005).

16. On the notion of freedom in Greek thought, see A.-J. Festugière, *Liberté et civilisation chez les Grecs* (Paris: Revue des jeunes, 1947), translated into English as *Freedom and Civilization among the Greeks* (Allison Park, Pa.: Pickwick, 1987); M. Pohlenz, *Griechische Freiheit: Wesen und Werden eines Lebensideals* (Heidelberg: Quelle & Meyer, 1955), translated into English as *Freedom in Greek Life and Thought: History of an Ideal* (Dordrecht: D. Reidel, 1966); T. C. Anderson, "Aristotle and Aquinas on the Freedom of the Mathematician," *Thomist* (1972): 231–55; M. Zanatta, "Aspetti della libertà nel pensiero greco," in *Antonio Rosmini e l'idea della libertà*, edited by A. Autiero and A. Genovese (Bologna: EDB, 2001), 45–81; S. Natoli, *Libertà e destino nella tragedia greca* (Brescia: Morcelliana, 2002); A. Squilloni, *Libertà esteriore libertà interiore: Due aspetti del pensiero greco* (Florence: Olschki, 2004). On the etymological question, see Pohlenz, *Griechische Freiheit*, 185f.; *BDAG* 316f., s.v. ἐλεύθερος; *NIDNTTE* 2:172–78, s.v. ἐλευθερία; Zanatta, "Aspetti della libertà nel pensiero greco," 46–48.

17. Thus T. Hobbes, *De cive*, 10, 8.

is therefore not subjected to any despot. The slave, however, is not free because he is subjected unconditionally to someone else.[18] According to H.-G. Gadamer, in the classical Greek world freedom was identified with the "freedom of action and choice of one who is master of self, as distinct from the slave, who cannot follow his own will but the caprice of the master. Freedom in this sense was the mark of political status, precisely the condition of the free man."[19] Freedom, therefore, was a social or political condition of humans, not a native or natural one. For the Greeks it is not correct to say that humans are born free; but rather, at best, to say that they become free.

In the Greek view, even though some humans may be considered "free" within a particular societal grouping, all humans are bound recognize their limits, their lack of freedom, in the face of the necessity (*ananke*), destiny (*moira*), and fate (*tyche*) imposed by the cosmos. To be free, therefore, involves obeying nature, following its commands.[20] According to Stoic thought, humans are "impotent before the presupposition of a pervasive universal necessary *Logos*.... The fundamental figure of Stoic freedom is the act of wisdom that adheres to necessity.... It is the rational acceptance of fate and support for its necessity.... The true freedom of the sage consists of willingly following what would otherwise drag him to his destiny."[21] As Seneca says, "Ducunt volentem fata, nolentem trahunt" (Destiny leads whoever is willing, and drags whoever is not).[22] For the Greeks, in brief, humans—or at least some of them—may be free before the state and before others, but they are always slaves before the cosmos. In this dynamic we can perceive (1) the tension already mentioned between the human aspiration to freedom and the limits humans must accept and (2) the doctrine contained in Genesis 1:26f. on the dominion God invited humans to exercise over the world.

Human Freedom and the Divine

According to Plato, "Freedom coincides with the rational dominion one has over self, over one's impulses, passions, states of pleasure and pain, the exercise of the primacy of soul over body, which makes it possible for humans to know the good."[23] Freedom lies in self-sufficiency, *autarkeia*, says Seneca. According to Socrates, "Not having need of anything is divine, having need of very little is very close to the divine: now the divine is perfection itself and whatever is closer to the divine is closer to perfection."[24] To be free, or unencumbered, then, in a sense, is to be divine. This notion is developed in Judaism and neo-Platonism, through Philo and Plotinus, respectively.

---

18. On the question of slavery, see Manning, "Stoicism and Slavery in the Roman Empire"; P. Garnsey, *Ideas of Slavery from Aristotle to Augustine* (Cambridge: Cambridge University Press, 1996).

19. H.-G. Gadamer, "Kausalität in der Geschichte," *Kleine Schriften* I: *Philosophie, Hermeneutik* (Tubingen: J. C. B. Mohr, 1967), 192–200, 198.

20. "As regards the useful, what is prescribed by the law is an obstacle for nature, that is, what is prescribed by nature is free." Antiphon, *Die Fragmente der Vorsokratiker*, ed. H. Diels, 2:346–52, B 44, translated into English as *The Elder Sophists*, edited by R. K. Sprague (Columbia: University of South Carolina Press, 1972).

21. Botturi, "Libertà," 6398.

22. Seneca, *Epist.* 107, 10. See S. Bobzien, *Determinism and Freedom in Stoic Philosophy* (Oxford: Clarendon Press, 1998).

23. Plato, *Prot.* 356. See also R. Muller, *La doctrine platonicienne de la liberté* (Paris: Vrin, 1997); Botturi, "Libertà," 6395.

24. Thus Socrates, according to Xenophon, *Memorabilia* I, 6, 10.

As Botturi writes: "Differently from the Stoics, for Philo [the Jewish philosopher from Alexandria] freedom is a gift (or grace) of God and not a structural characteristic of man."[25] According to Philo, humans discover themselves, in faith, as open to an omnipotent God to whom they respond in word and prayer. "The virtuous man," Philo says, "has a great freedom of word, and not only does he have the courage to speak and shout, but also that of raising his voice in reprimand [toward God] from the depths of his sincere faith and pure sentiments."[26] With the help of Old Testament revelation, Philo explains that the relationship between God and humans is not of a competitive kind: humans encounter ample spaces of freedom within their living rapport with the omnipotent God. The awareness of being guided by God, by his providence, has relevant social consequences: whoever believes flees from slavery just as he flees from idolatry.

In the context of neo-Platonic thought, the third-century philosopher Plotinus has offered an important contribution to our understanding of freedom, not so much that of humans but rather the foundational freedom of God, who is the One.[27] In continuity with the Stoic vision of freedom as conformity with nature, Botturi says,

the power and novelty of Plotinus's explanation consist of shifting the discourse on freedom toward God (that is, the one), in speaking of divine freedom for the first time by identifying full freedom with the one itself.... In oneness, not in a limited and extrinsic sense, but in an intrinsic and ontological one, is to be found the root of freedom. Wherever there is identity of being [hypostasis], essence [ousia], and activity [energeia], there is to be found freedom in fullness.[28]

The typical expression of freedom, "being lord of oneself," is thus seen as improper and out of place, in Plotinus's view, in that it attempts to indicate a duality of being an object for oneself.[29] God is free, however, precisely because he is One. And the same may be said, on another level, of humans. As a result, the freedom of humans is simply to be found in the contemplation of God, who is free: "the soul is free when it aspires to the good through the intelligence, and in this aspiration it will not find any obstacle."[30] Humans are free when they share by way of contemplation in the freedom, that is, in the unity, of God himself: "The soul, united and guided by the intelligence, separates itself from the material multitude and from the passions, that is, from the kingdom of otherness, and exercises itself in knowledge and contemplation, bringing about that simplification [haplotēs] that frees it. How can a simple nature, not divided between act and potency, be free?"[31] In real terms, Plotinus thought that the human being will be free, as Plato had already said, when the soul is definitively liberated from the body.

---

25. Botturi, "Libertà," 6399.

26. Philo of Alexandria, *Quis rerum divinarum heres sit*, 19; this is what Philo calls *parrēsia*, a term that is used frequently in the New Testament.

27. See especially Plotinus, *Enn.* VI, 8. On his thought, see the introduction by G. Leroux, *Traité sur la liberté et la volonté de l'Un: Ennéade VI, 8 (39)* (Paris: J. Vrin, 1990); A. Ousager, *Plotinus on Selfhood, Freedom and Politics* (Aarhus: Aarhus University Press, 2004).

28. Botturi, "Libertà," 6399. See Plotinus, *Enn.* VI, 7, 47–54.

29. See Plotinus, *Enn.* VI, 12, 30ff. "The one however will be exactly that which it has wanted to be, and to affirm that it wishes and acts in conformity to its nature is the same thing as saying that its essence is as it wishes and as it acts." *Enn.* VI, 13, 9f.

30. Ibid., VI, 7, 1f.

31. Botturi, "Libertà," 6400. See Plotinus, *Enn.* VI, 4, 25f.

Christian Reflection on Human Freedom

In the New Testament, the noun *eleutheria* (freedom) is never used in the secular sense of political freedom (in contrast with the numerous instances of such a meaning in Flavius Josephus). This feature—strange to moderns—no doubt reflects the fact that the recovery of Israel's political independence no longer played a significant part in the thinking of the New Testament writers. Jesus unambiguously swept aside all misunderstanding here. He and his kingdom do not live by this external freedom. Otherwise it would not have been so readily abandoned (Jn 18:36). Even in those places where Jesus stressed his earthly authority (Mt 28:18), he drew no conclusions about claims for political freedom. Time and again he disappointed all the late Jewish expectations of a political messiah. His teaching had a quite different aim. The kind of freedom he preached was that which comes through returning to the Father (Mt 4:17; Lk 24:47; Jn 8:34–36). The New Testament also dissociates itself from the idea of freedom as the power to do whatever we want with our lives. The believer's hope is rather "that the creation itself will be liberated [*eleutherōthēsetai*] from its bondage to decay and brought into the glorious freedom [*tēn eleutherian tēs doxēs*] of the children of God" (Rom 8:21). True *eleutheria* is to be found "where the Spirit of the Lord is" (2 Cor 3:17), for it consists of "the freedom we have in Christ Jesus" (Gal 2:4), the freedom for which "Christ has set us free [*eleutherōsen*]" (5:1). Even the verb *eleutheroō* is used in the New Testament exclusively for the salvation from sin that has been provided by Jesus Christ (Jn 8:32, 36; Rom 6:18, 22; 8:2, 21; Gal 5:1). The adjective *eleutheros*, however, often has the secular meaning of being socially free in contrast to being a slave (1 Cor 7:21–22, 12:13; Gal 3:28; Eph 6:8; Col 3:11; Rv 6:15), and it may be used with reference to being released from a law (Rom 7:3). In Gal 4:22–31 Paul employs the term initially in its social sense, but that leads to the specifically New Testament idea of being free in Christ. The characteristic of those who have been spiritually freed is not that they contrast with slaves but that even in their freedom they are slaves of Christ and to one another (1 Cor 9:19; Gal 5:13; 1 Pt 2:16; Rom 1:1; Phil 1:1). The *apeleutheros kyriou*, "the Lord's freedman," is at the same time the *doulos Christou*, "Christ's slave" (1 Cor 7:22).[32] As Paul Claudel put it, "The Christian is the only one who is free in a world of slaves."[33]

In this context, from the very beginning Christians understood their identity in terms of an open acceptance of the solidity and relevance of human liberation and freedom. They do not subject themselves blindly to the civil authority as if it enjoyed divine status. They develop a relationship with the God of Jesus Christ, who is intensely personal, living, superior to all things—in a word, liberating.[34] They live in charity with one and all, thus indicating their conviction that society is not predetermined but can be changed and improved.[35] They avoid all fatalism, magic, and

---

32. The whole paragraph is taken from *NIDNTTE* 2:175f.

33. P. Claudel, *Inter mortuos liber*, in *Journal*, edited by J. Petit, F. Varillon (Gallimard: Paris, 1969), 2:859.

34. P. Veyne, *Quand notre monde est devenu chrétien: 312–394* (Paris: A. Michel, 2010), translated into English as *When Our World Became Christian 312–394* (Cambridge: Polity, 2013); G. Bardy, *La conversion au christianisme durant les premiers siècles* (Paris: Aubier-Montaigne, 1947), 146–57.

35. See R. Lane Fox, *Pagans and Christians* (New York: A. A. Knopf, 1987); Veyne, *Quand notre monde est devenu chrétien*. See also Benedict XVI, *Deus Caritas Est*, pars. 19–25.

astrology.[36] Tatian writes that Christians are "no longer led by necessity [*heimarmene*] and they have abandoned the stars that are said to make the laws."[37] And Clement of Alexandria explains why this is the case:

A foreign star has risen, a new star that breaks the old power of the constellations [Jesus Christ]. It shines out with a new light that is not physical. It opens new and salutary paths. This star is the Lord, who came to the earth to guide humankind, to bring those who believe in Christ from the kingdom of *heimarmene* to that of providence.... Just as the birth of the Savior has made the power of the horoscope and necessity depart in flight, the baptism of the Savior has freed us from the fire of his suffering, because we all follow him.[38]

Following the thought of Paul, Augustine deals with the question of freedom in a clearly Christian context, that is, on the basis of divine grace, with which humans are freed from sin and its consequences.[39] The Christian, therefore, is one who has been liberated by God's grace, thus becoming his son or daughter. Augustine inquires into the source of evil, of sin.[40] Evil, he says, does not come either from matter, as the Manichaeans held, or from God, who is all good: therefore, it can only come from free human will. In Botturi's words, "Evil does not derive from an inferior being, which would be in a position to dominate it. Neither does it derive from a superior being, God, who cannot be evil.... Only the *voluntas* itself and its *liberum arbitrium* can introduce disorder."[41] In other words, God has constituted humans in such a way that they are truly responsible before him for the evil they commit. According to Augustine, the weight and importance of free will may be deduced not so much from the immediate phenomenology of human action, from the conviction of its true value, as from the theological challenge of evil and the salvation of humans. As a result, he says, in order to escape from the slavery of sin, humans are completely needful of divine grace, a topic that of course is central to Augustine. But it is also true that the reception of the divine gift by humans is a free act, in the sense that they are capable of rejecting divine pardon or opening themselves to grace. Likewise, Maximus the Confessor associates human freedom with divine grace in the work of divinization. He sees freedom to be at the heart of a process of assimilation, as the realization of the image of God inscribed in human nature from the very moment of creation.[42]

The principal object of the reflection of medieval authors is rather the dynamics of *free will*, the particular way in which the human will acts, of its relationship with reason and with the appetites and passions, that is, with the free human act.[43]

---

36. See Bardy, *La conversion au christianisme*, 134–45; G. Picasso, G. Piana, and G. Motta, eds., *A pane e acqua: Peccati e penitenze nel Medioevo; Il "Penitenziale" di Burcardo di Worms* (Novara: Europìa, 1986), 82f., which details the strenuous penances imposed by Bucardus of Worms in the early eleventh century for sins of superstition and magic.

37. Tatian, *Ad Graec.* 9, 2.

38. Clement of Alexandria, *Exc. ex Theodoto*, 76.

39. On Paul, see chapter 5, notes 10ff.; chapter 8, notes 61ff. and corresponding text.

40. M. Huftier, *Libre arbitre, liberté et péché chez saint Augustin* (Leuven: Nauwelaerts, 1966); T. D. J. Chappell, *Aristotle and Augustine on Freedom: Two Theories of Freedom, Voluntary Action and Akrasia* (New York: St. Martin's Press, 1995); Sciuto, "Il libero arbitrio nel pensiero medievale."

41. Botturi, "Libertà," 6401. Augustine writes: "Nulla res alia mentem cupiditas comitem faciat, quam propria voluntas et liberum arbitrium." *De lib. arb.*, 1, 11, 21.

42. See Maximus the Confessor, *Ambig. in Io.* 7, 42.

43. On the topic of freedom throughout the Middle Ages, see O. Lottin, "Libre arbitre et liberté depuis s.

Freedom is no longer considered primordially in the ambit of theology as a divinely worked liberation but rather in that of anthropology and ethics. Anselm founds human freedom on the will; human action is determined by its end or purpose, indicated by reason and freely chosen by the will.[44] In the thought of Thomas Aquinas, this concatenation is based on the fact that the free act arises within the entire human being because it is the fruit of the *encounter* between reason, which seeks truth, and the will, which is directed toward the good.[45] In other words, Aquinas held that the free act derives from and belongs to the human being in its entirety, spirit and body.

After Aquinas, with the development of voluntarist (or nominalist) thought during the later Middle Ages, we can observe a clear impoverishment in the discourse on human freedom.[46] Emphasis is placed almost exclusively on free will itself, as pure choice, disconnecting it from intellect and ultimate purpose. In effect nominalists held that the role of reason is more or less excluded from human action, and

Anselme jusqu'à la fin du XIII siècle," in Lottin, *Psychologie et morale aux XIIe et XIIIe siècles* (Leuven: Abbaye du Mont César, 1942), vol. 1; E. Stadter, *Psychologie und Metaphysik der menschlichen Freiheit: Die ideengeschichtliche Entwicklung zwischen Bonaventura und Duns Scotus* (Munich: Schöningh, 1971); G. Makdisi, D. Sourdel, and J. Sourdel-Thomine, eds., *La notion de liberté au Moyen Age: Islam, Byzance, Occident. = The Concept of Freedom in the Middle Ages: Islam, Byzantium, and the West* (Paris: Les Belles Lettres, 1985); F.-X. Putallaz, *Insolente liberté: Controverses et condamnations au XIIIè siècle* (Fribourg: Éditions universitaires de Fribourg Cerf, 1995); Sciuto, "Il libero arbitrio nel pensiero medievale"; A. M. Ghisalberti, "L'evoluzione del tema della libertà nella filosofia medievale," in *Antonio Rosmini e l'idea della libertà*, edited by A. Autiero and A. Genovese (Bologna: EDB, 2001), 83–108.

44. Anselm, *De lib. arb.* III. Specifically on Anselm, see Goebel, *Rectitudo, Wahrheit und Freiheit bei Anselm von Canterbury*.

45. Thomas Aquinas says: "Totius libertatis radix est in ratione constituta." *De ver.*, q. 24, a. 3, co. "Radix libertatis est voluntas sicut subiectum, sed sicut causa, est ratio. Ex hoc enim voluntas libere potest ad diversa ferri, quia ratio potest habere diversas conceptiones boni." *S.Th.* I-II, q. 17, a. 1, ad 2. "Thomas attributes to reason the *specificatio* of the act of the will and to the will its *exercitium:* from the judgment of reason the choice receives its specifying object and with it its moving end, while the fulfillment of the act is in the will, whose movement takes place in the power of the structural attraction which the good exercises over the will." Botturi, "Libertà," 6406. The will is equipped with the power of self-determination, which impedes it from being moved necessarily by any object. It can always decide not to direct itself to a possible object of choice and not want it. See *S.Th.* I-II, q. 10, aa. 2–4; *De malo*, 6 and ad 7. On Aquinas, see G. Montanari, *Determinazione e libertà in san Tommaso d'Aquino* (Rome: Libreria editrice della Pontificia università Lateranense, 1962); P. Pagani, "Tommaso: La libertà della differenza," in *La libertà del bene*, edited by C. Vigna (Milan: Vita e pensiero, 1998); F. Bergamino, *La razionalità e la libertà della scelta in Tommaso d'Aquino* (Rome: Edusc, 2002).

46. Among Franciscan authors the topic of freedom is central. On Bonaventure, see V. C. Bigi, "Il concetto e il valore della libertà in S. Bonaventura," *Incontri Bonaventurani* 8 (1973): 45–64; V. Ristori, *La libertà in san Bonaventura: Non potestà di scelta ma possesso di sé in Dio* (Rome: Ed. Laurentianum, 1974); C. Fabro, "La libertà in san Bonaventura," in *San Bonaventura maestro di vita francescana e di sapienza cristiana*, edited by A. Pompei (Rome: Pontificia facoltà teologica San Bonaventura, 1976), 3:507–35. On Pier di Giovanni Olivi, see F. Simoncioli, *Il problema della libertà umana in Pietro di Giovanni Olivi e Pietro de Trabibus* (Milan: Vita e pensiero, 1946); G. Bonafede, "L'Olivi e la difesa del libero arbitrio," *Italia francescana* 25 (1950): 93–101. On Duns Scotus, see B. M. Bonansea, "Duns Scotus' Voluntarism," in *Studies in Philosophy and the History of Philosophy* (1965): 83–121; H. Borak, "Libertà e prudenza nel pensiero di Duns Scoto," *Laurentianum* 10 (1969): 105–41; Stadter, *Psychologie und Metaphysik der menschlichen Freiheit*; L. D. Roberts, "John Duns Scotus and the Concept of Human Freedom," in *Deus et homo ad mentem I[oannis] Duns Scoti* (Rome: Societas Internationalis Scotistica, 1972), 317–25; D. C. Lagston, "Scotus' Conception of Human Freedom," in *L'homme et son univers au Moyen Âge*, edited by C. Wenin (Louvain-la-Neuve: Éditions de l'Institut supérieur de philosophie, 1986), 2:815–21; S. Gaine, *Will There Be Free Will in Heaven? Freedom, Impeccability, and Beatitude* (London: T. and T. Clark, 2003). On Ockham, see Ghisalberti, *Guglielmo di Ockham*; D. W. Klark, "Ockham on Human and Divine Freedom," *Franciscan Studies* 38 (1978): 122–60.

the will is no longer directed toward the good as its proper end. As a result, the free act is considered to be a simple act of self-determination, a pure choice, marked by indifference, arbitrariness. and contingency. "Libertas est quaedam indifferentia et contingentia," says William of Ockham, "Freedom is a kind of indifference or contingency."[47] And elsewhere he declares that freedom is "the capacity with which I can do something in an indifferent and contingent way, in such a way that I am in a position to cause that effect, or not cause it."[48] Still, nominalist reflection on human freedom does not lose its theological roots entirely because this freedom is considered to be a reflection of divine freedom, which is also arbitrary and contingent.

From the sixteenth century onward, in an openly religious context, the theme of human freedom plays out on center-stage. Martin Luther's open denial of free will is particularly important and situates the debate. He based his denial on the Christian need to affirm the grace of an all-powerful God over the human will and to contrast that with the excessively nominalist tendency to consider freedom in terms of indifference and pure choice. In theological terms, he saw things as follows: if God freely predestines humans and gives them his grace, they are no longer free; or, to put it the other way around, if humans are truly free, God is no longer such.[49] At best, humans could behave freely and responsibly, according to Luther, in their relationship with the created world, with other humans. Yet before God humans are to be considered simply slaves, entirely dependent on their Lord for everything they are and do.[50] To speak of the relevance of freedom in the face of an all-powerful and eternal God would be a kind of idolatry. As we saw earlier, the same dilemma was posed during the controversy called *de auxiliis* regarding the question of the efficacy of divine grace. Luther's determinism is, in fact, theologically derived. According to the reading Hans Blumenberg gives to modernity, Christian theology has not allowed humans to be themselves on account of the weight of sin. In order to "legitimize modernity," as he says, it is necessary to eliminate not only the suffocating shadow of sin but also the presence of divine grace (and thus Christian religion) because it is contrary to human freedom and blocks human autonomy, growth, and flourishing. In effect, the modern period has witnessed the emergence of a purely human form of freedom, independent of God, that attempts to affirm itself in contraposition to Christian freedom.

At the same time, partly as a result of these unresolved theological controversies, modern thought has provided some interesting explanations of the dynamics of human freedom from a strictly philosophical and anthropological angle, some of which

47. William of Ockham, *I Sent.*, 6. "The free will is therefore the causal principle preceded by nothing whatever, radically contingent, on the ontological plane (the adage *omne quod movetur ab alio movetur* does not apply) and on the psychological (being indifferent to any motivation)." Botturi, "Libertà," 6408. "In this context, teleology loses all relevance. Ockham does not hold that the will tends naturally to the infinite good, since there are no apodictic reasons to prove the existence of such a good, and given that the finality of the universe is not philosophically demonstrable" (ibid.). Voluntaristic thought involves "the radical capacity for self-determination which allows it to want and not to want whatever thing, including the supreme good.... It is autonomous in respect to the good itself" (ibid., 6409).

48. William of Ockham, *Quodl.* I, 16.

49. On this topic, see O'Callaghan, *Fides Christi*, 19–40.

50. This is the central thesis of Luther's 1525 work *De servo arbitrio*. On this work, see J. Brantschen, "De Servo oder de Libero Arbitrio: Luther und Thomas im Gespräch," *Freiburger Zeitschrift für Philosophie und Theologie* (1966): 239–58; Mateo-Seco, *M. Lutero.*

are more determinist (see the next two headings), others of which insist on the reality and centrality of human freedom (see the following three).[51]

Modern and Contemporary Determinisms

Humans, according to the seventeenth-century philosopher Baruch Spinoza, are a perfect image of God insofar as they reproduce in themselves two divine attributes: thought (the soul) and extension (the body): "The mind of man is a part of the infinite intellect of God (and the body is a part of God's infinite extension). Hence, when we say that the mind knows this thing or that we simply say that God, not as infinite, but as he manifests himself in the nature of the mind, insofar as he constitutes the essence of the mind, has this or that idea."[52] Within this pantheistic understanding, the human individual can hardly be considered free. "Those who believe they are free are mistaken," Spinoza says, "and their opinion is due to the fact that they are aware of their actions, but not of the causes that determine their actions; that is, their idea of freedom is that they do not know the cause of their actions."[53] In other words, humans think they are free but in real terms they are simply ignorant. Elsewhere Spinoza says: "In the human mind there is no absolute or free will, but the mind is made to will this or that by a cause that is also determined by a further cause, and this in turn by another, and so on to infinity."[54] In spite of this explanation, Spinoza considers God to be supremely free. In that sense humans, insofar as they belong to the divine substance, may also be considered to be free.[55]

Thomas Hobbes considers freedom from an anthropological angle and concludes that the processes of human life are mechanical in character. Thus there is no space for freedom.[56] He holds that "the cause of the will is not the will itself, but something that is not in its own power."[57] G. W. F. Hegel, in line with Spinoza, affirms that what we call "human freedom" is simply the result of our ignorance of the necessity of things. Even within the process of the coming to consciousness of the Absolute Spirit—that is, the dynamics of divine life—there is no freedom. Hegel identifies freedom with the rational essence of reality and history. Thus freedom does not, strictly speaking, involve individuals, but rather the Absolute Spirit in its turning around itself through a dialectic of alienation in nature and in history: "The truth of the particular determination of free will is the universal determination of the will: that is, freedom."[58] Darwin speaks of "the necessary character of the evolutionary process,

51. On the question of freedom in the modern period, see, *inter alia*, J. Laporte, *La conscience de la liberté* (Paris: Flammarion, 1947).

52. Baruch Spinoza, *Ethica*, prop. 11, coroll. On Spinoza, see J. Préposiet, *Spinoza et la liberté des hommes* (Paris: Gallimard, 1967).

53. Spinoza, *Ethica* II, prop. 35, scol.   54. Ibid., prop. 48.

55. Ibid. I, prop. 32, 17.

56. Hobbes speaks of the rigid causal connection of matter in movement: T. Hobbes, *The Elements of Law Natural and Politic*, I: *Human nature* (Oxford: Oxford University Press, 1994), chap. 12; *Leviathan*, edited by A. D. Lindsay (London: J. M. Dent, 1914), vol. 1, chap. 6. On the thought of that period, see the classic work of J. Rickaby, *Free Will and Four English Philosophers: Hobbes, Locke, Hume and Mill* (London: Burns and Oates, 1906).

57. T. Hobbes, "Liberty and Necessity," in *The English Works* (London: John Bohn, 1860), 4:239–78, 274.

58. G. W. F. Hegel, *Encyclopedia of the Philosophical Sciences in Basic Outline* (Cambridge: Cambridge University Press, 2010), § 480. On Hegel, see H. Röttges, *Der Begriff der Freiheit in der Philosophie Hegels* (Frankfurt: Universität, 1963); C. Fabro, "La libertà in Hegel e san Tommaso," *Sacra Doctrina* 66 (1972): 165–86;

with respect to which freedom is only a name of what results from causal combinations."[59]

Throughout the twentieth century it has been frequently held by both philosophers and scientists that humans are fundamentally determined beings. In spite of personal aspirations toward freedom that many experience, tangible evidence presents humans as clearly circumscribed beings, drawn along by inflexible, impersonal and unconscious laws. Faced with the crushing power of destiny, humans are small and insignificant, continually dominated by their impulses and instincts, both physical and psychic.

Determinism has received serious support from the human sciences over the past century or so, especially in the area of neurobiology.[60] It is also worthwhile mentioning the behaviorism of B. F. Skinner as enunciated in his 1971 work *Beyond Freedom and Dignity*. This American author states:

Autonomous man is a device used to explain what we cannot explain in any other way. He has been constructed from our ignorance, and as our understanding increases, the very stuff of which he is composed vanishes.... To man *qua* man we readily say good riddance. Only by dispossessing him can we turn to the real causes of human behavior. Only then can we turn from the inferred to the observed, from the miraculous to the natural, from the inaccessible to the manipulable.[61]

In his novel *Walden Two* the same author writes: "I deny openly that there is such a thing as human freedom. I have to deny it, because to the contrary my program would be completely absurd. You can't have a science about a subject matter which hops capriciously about. Perhaps we can never *prove* that man isn't free; it's an assumption. But the growing outcome of the science of behavior makes it more and more plausible."[62]

Over recent decades many neuroscientists have been of the opinion that human free will is but apparent. Experiments seem to show that the "conscious" (and therefore "free") decision to react to a particular stimulus is preceded by a previous cerebral activation. The scientist Benjamin Libet registered cerebral activity several hundred milliseconds before subjects expressed their "conscious" intention to do this or that.[63] The conclusion would seem to be that the awareness of having made a decision is simply a biochemical appendix to the event itself, in which there is no real influence on the actions of the person. According to Patrick Haggard, "We have the

---

L. Cortella, "Hegel: Libertà e storia," in *La libertà del bene*, edited by C. Vigna (Milan: Vita e pensiero, 1998), 289–317.

59. Botturi, "Libertà," 6423.

60. See chapter 19, notes 130ff.

61. Skinner, *Beyond Freedom and Dignity* (Harmondsworth: Penguin Books, 1973), 196.

62. Skinner, *Walden Two* (Indianapolis, Ind.: Hackett, 1976; originally published in 1948), 241f.

63. See especially the work of B. Libet, A. Freeman, and K. Sutherland, eds., *The Volitional Brain: Towards a Neuroscience of Free Will*, 2nd ed. (Exeter: Imprint Academic, 2004); B. Libet, *Mind Time: The Temporal Factor in Consciousness* (Cambridge, Mass.: Harvard University Press, 2005). The same conclusion has been drawn by John D. Haynes; see C. S. Soon, M. Brass, H. J. Heinze, and J. D. Haynes, "Unconscious Determinants of Free Decisions in the Human Brain," *Nature Neuroscience* 11, no. 1 (2008): 543–45. See also A. Suárez and P. Adams, eds., *Is Science Compatible with Free Will? Exploring Free Will and Consciousness in the Light of Quantum Physics and Neuroscience* (New York: Springer, 2012).

sensation of choosing, but in reality this is not the case."[64] The scientist Itzhak Fried describes the process in brief terms: "At a certain stage, things which are predetermined become present in consciousness."[65]

The Meaning of Determinism

As we have seen, in Greek antiquity it was taken for granted that human life was determined by nature, by the cosmos, by destiny: by the sun or the stars, and always, directly or indirectly, by the gods. In more recent times, language and symbols have changed because things have been focused in a more scientific and anthropological way. Yet the conclusion is the same: humans are moved and controlled in all their relevant actions by unconscious, hidden impulses, by different kinds of psycho-physical conditionings. In other words, freedom as the power of self-determination should be considered a mere illusion. What we call "human freedom" is worth nothing, it has no purpose, and it is irrelevant.

Perhaps for those who refuse to consider their own lives openly, or accept responsibility for their actions, the very possibility of acting freely becomes problematic, anguish-filled, to be avoided at all costs. In other words, the history of thought seems to indicate that, alongside the aspiration to freedom (typical of the modern period), there is to be found among humans the hidden desire *not* to be free, a preference to lose their freedom, to flee from the obligation of deciding and taking responsibility, to avoid the challenge, the queasy feeling and empty space of indeterminism, in order to identify themselves in a detached and guiltless way with everything they consider to be permanent and solid. Determinist thinkers could perhaps accept the existence of a human aspiration to freedom while considering it a pure illusion, a form of alienation, fruit of an overheated imagination. "Nothing is more unbearable for humans and society than freedom," observes one of Dostoevsky's characters.[66] According to the Hindu writer Sri Aurobindo, "The whole world aspires to freedom; still, each creature loves its chains."[67] And Paul Claudel exclaims: "My God, I am free. Free me from freedom!"[68] According to this way of thinking, truth is identified with permanence and acceptance; indetermination belongs to the ambit of risk and free choice and is considered as something hostile.

The Affirmation of the Realism of Human Freedom

In spite of what has just been said, it is fair to say that human freedom—understood in terms of external and public liberation and in a derived way as the interior dynamism of free will—has become the principal motif of the modern period, especially in the context of the philosophy of the Enlightenment: humans live meaningful

---

64. Cited by K. Smith in "Taking Aim at Free Will," *Nature* 477 (2011): 23–25, 24; see P. Haggard, Y. Rossetti, and M. Kawato, eds., *Sensorimotor Foundations of Higher Cognition* (Oxford: Oxford University Press, 2008).

65. I. Fried, R. Mukamel, and G. Kreiman, "Internally Generated Preactivation of Single Neurons in Human Medial Frontal Cortex Predicts Volition," *Neuron* 69 (2011): 548–62.

66. F. Dostoevsky, *The Brothers Karamazov* II, 5, 5.

67. A. Ghose, *Thoughts and Aphorisms* (Pondicherry: Sri Aurobindo Ashram, 1958).

68. P. Claudel, "L'esprit et l'eau," in Claudel, *Cinq grandes odes: Suivies d'un Processionnal pour saluer le siècle nouveau*, 3rd ed. (Paris: Éditions de la Nouvelle revue française, 1913).

lives only if they are free, that is, only if they manage to really overcome the interior and exterior constrictions that hamper and restrict their development. As a result, the principal purpose of society and the laws of the state should be that of guaranteeing maximum freedom, within the bounds of the possible, to all citizens.[69] "Freedom is the new religion, the religion of our time," said the poet Heinrich Heine.[70]

For many modern thinkers the affirmation of human freedom is simply taken for granted. Descartes says, for example: "It is so manifest that there is freedom in our will, and that we have complete power to either assent or not assent to many things, that this must be numbered among the first and most common notions innate in us."[71] On this point he is not far from the voluntarism of the nominalists, who—by inverting the order between intellect and will—consider free will as the most excellent and perfect of human faculties. The human being is defined in this sense as someone who is free from all bonds, and also from the need to project life toward the future. A similar vision, though clearly nihilistic in style, may be found in the writings of Jean-Paul Sartre.[72]

It is also evident to Kant that humans are free and morally responsible; indeed, humans are free because they are responsible.[73] When faced with the moral law, humans intuit their moral duty, as well as the possibility of transgressing it; in this way they become aware of being free and responsible. Likewise, Henri Bergson writes: "Freedom is a fact and, among the facts that are present to us, there is none clearer."[74]

---

69. This is the position defended especially by J. Rawls in his theory of distributive justice: *Political Liberalism* (New York: Columbia University Press, 1993).

70. See H. Heine, *English Fragments*, translated by S. Norris (Edinburgh: R. Grant and Son, 1880).

71. R. Descartes, *Principles of Philosophy* (Dordrecht: Kluwer, 1983), I, 39 (18). The text continues as follows: "And this was very obvious a little earlier, when we were striving to doubt everything and had gone so far as to imagine that some very powerful author of our origin was attempting to deceive us in every way; for we nevertheless experienced in ourselves the freedom to be able to abstain from believing those things which were not absolutely certain and confirmed. For no things can ever be better known of themselves and better proved than those which did not seem doubtful at that time" (ibid.). According to Descartes, in the words of Cornelio Fabro, freedom would be "the autonomy of man before truth insofar as he is responsible for truth. This autonomy is what constitutes the essence of the *cogito* and shows that truth is a human thing, because I have to actuate it in order for it to exist: from this position Descartes holds that judgment consists in the conformity of the will and free commitment (*engagement*) of my being." Fabro, *Introduzione all'ateismo moderno*, 977. On the doctrine of Descartes, see É. Gilson, *La liberté chez Descartes et la théologie* (Paris: F. Alcan, 1913); H. Bouchilloux, *La question de la liberté chez Descartes: Libre arbitre, liberté et indifférence* (Paris: Honoré Champion, 2003).

72. See Botturi, "Libertà," 6435f.; M. A. Schaldenbrand, *Phenomenologies of Freedom: An Essay on the Philosophies of Jean-Paul Sartre and Gabriel Marcel* (Washington, D.C.: The Catholic University of America Press, 1960). According to J.-P. Sartre, "Man is the being through whom nothingness comes to the world." *Being and Nothingness*, translated by H. E. Barnes (New York: Washington Square Press, 1984), 24. "Thus freedom as the requisite condition for the annihilation of nothingness is not a property which belongs among others to the essence of the human being. We have already noticed furthermore that with man the relation of existence to essence is not comparable to what it is for the things of the world" (ibid., 25). According to Sartre, there is no natural presupposition of free action, neither freedom, nor essence, nor values, nor God. All in all, "man is a useless passion" (ibid., 615).

73. See Kant, *Critique of Practical Reason*, 1–9. See M. Stockhammer, *Kants Zurechnungsidee und Freiheitsantinomie* (Cologne: Kölner Universitäts-Verlag, 1961); A. Capizzi, *La difesa del libero arbitrio da Erasmo a Kant* (Florence: La Nuova Italia, 1963); H. E. Allison, *Kant's Theory of Freedom* (Cambridge: Cambridge University Press, 1990); F. Chiereghin, *Il problema della libertà in Kant* (Trent: Verifiche, 1991).

74. H. Bergson, *Essai sur les données immédiates de la conscience* (Geneva: A. Skira, 1945), 170, translated

Also Romano Guardini speaks of the immediate awareness we have of our own freedom: "Freedom means belonging to oneself. I experience myself as free when I realize I belong to myself: when I realize that in acting I depend on myself, that the action does not pass through me, in that way seeking out something else, but it arises in me, and therefore it is mine in a special sense, and in it I am myself."[75]

Perceiving Freedom in the Context of Faith in God

The contrast with the two positions we have seen—closed determinism and an all-too-obvious freedom—seems difficult to overcome. The former compromises the individual self-determination of the subject in the name of the omnipresence of nature or of a divine principle, whereas the latter seems to maintain human individuality and its free autonomy at the cost of this divine presence. Still, it has often been observed that it is precisely the Christian vision of God, of creation, and of humans that has made it really possible for us to speak of human freedom in due depth. It is undeniable that human freedom is theologically contextualized. The question needs to be considered carefully. Speaking of human freedom, Hegel writes:

When individuals and nations have once got in their heads the abstract concept of full-blown liberty, there is nothing like it in its uncontrollable strength, just because it is the very essence of mind, and that as its very actuality. Whole continents, Africa and the East, have never had this Idea, and are without it still. The Greeks and Romans, Plato and Aristotle, even the Stoics, did not have it. On the contrary, they saw that it is only by birth (as, for example, an Athenian or Spartan citizen), or by strength of character, education, or philosophy (the sage is free even as a slave and in chains) that the human being is actually free. *It was through Christianity that this Idea came into the world.* According to Christianity, the individual as such has an infinite value as the object and aim of divine love, destined as a mind to live in an absolute relationship with God himself, and have God's mind dwelling in him: i.e., man is implicitly destined to supreme freedom.[76]

Perhaps the one who has best explained the theological basis of freedom is not Hegel but his great adversary, Søren Kierkegaard. According to the Lutheran philosopher, human freedom is neither absolute (that is, divine, in the sense that Spinoza understood it) nor obvious (in the sense of Descartes and Bergson) but is rooted in the individual's decision of faith before God. He criticizes the autonomous ethics of Kant as illusory, "like the blows Sancho Panza applied to his back."[77] According to Kierkegaard, the basis of freedom can be only God, and not any god, but the all-

---

into English as *Time and Free Will: An Essay on the Immediate Data of Consciousness* (Whitefish, Mont.: Kessinger, 1945). On Bergson, see A. Pessina, *Il tempo della coscienza: Bergson e il problema della libertà* (Milan: Vita e pensiero, 1988).

75. R. Guardini, "La libertà vivente," in Guardini, *Persona e libertà: Saggi di fondazione della teoria pedagogica* (Brescia: La scuola, 1990), 93–116, 101. Also, according to A. Millán-Puelles in *La libre afirmación de nuestro ser: Una fundamentación de la ética realista* (Madrid: Rialp, 1994), 207, human freedom is obvious, and its existence need not be demonstrated.

76. Hegel, *Encyclopedia*, § 482.

77. Kierkegaard, *Diary* X/2, A 396. On Kierkegaard, see R. Jolivet, "La liberà e l'onnipotenza secondo Kierkegaard," in *Studi kierkegaardiani*, edited by C. Fabro (Brescia: Morcelliana, 1957), 170–74; G. Malantschuk, "La dialectique de la liberté selon S. Kierkegaard," *Revue des sciences philosophiques et théologiques* 42 (1958): 711–25; I. Adinolfi Bettiolo, "Kierkegaard: Libertà e ragione," in *La libertà del bene*, edited by C. Vigna (Milan: Vita e pensiero, 1998), 319–50.

powerful, free God we come to know through Christian faith, because "only an all-powerful being can take on himself fully as he gives himself, and this relationship is what constitutes the independence of the one who receives."[78] Further, "Existence is … freedom and free activity, transcendence and history, which cannot be objectified in any form of knowledge, *but rather believed*."[79] Luther had already said something of the kind: "Man has free will only in the sense that God himself was the one who gave it to him."[80]

This somewhat fideistic approach to the question offers a complete inversion of the position of Blumenberg, considered in chapter 2, according to whom both God and grace impede the proper working out of human freedom. According to Kierkegaard, God and his giving of grace is the very thing that *founds* freedom, that makes free action, reception (or rejection) of the gift, ultimately possible and relevant. Without divine grace, as the English poet Thomas Grey said, humans may well be "wasting their sweetness on the desert air."[81] Ambrose of Milan had already said: "Ubi fides, ibi libertas" (Where there is faith, there is freedom). And the Orthodox writer Nicholas Berdjaev writes: "The Christian doctrine of grace constitutes the true doctrine of freedom."[82] The philosopher Alasdair MacIntyre observes: "Acknowledgement of dependence is the key to independence."[83] It is interesting to note the way in which the philosopher Johann Herder contrasts animals with humans: "While the animal is faithful to its species, man has chosen as his divinity not necessity, but free will."[84]

The Perception of Freedom in a Personalistic Context

Speaking of Spinoza and of determinism, it was said earlier that "humans think they are free but in reality they are not." Descartes, on the contrary, says that humans declare themselves to be free because they perceive it directly on the clear and distinct screen of the *res cogitans*, that is, "Man thinks he is free, and therefore he is." According to Kierkegaard, humans are free, truly free, but they acquire this conviction through Christian faith: "Man thinks he is free because he *believes* he is free." Still, we need to consider the question carefully: if the latter position is acceptable, moral life

---

78. S. Kierkegaard, *Diary* VII, A 171.

79. Botturi, who in "Libertà," 6427, explains Kierkegaard's position as follows: "Only in the choice for God, like that of Abraham, freedom coincides with faith, and despair is completely extirpated, because in relation to oneself, wanting to be oneself, the I is based transparently on the power that placed it." And later: "Only faith respects the true nature of the rapport between finite freedom and infinite freedom, in which only the latter is in a position to give independence, because only 'omnipotence can take itself up as it gives itself,' and constitute 'the independence of the one who receives.' Only God, that is, is 'good': only an all-powerful God can produce 'the most fragile thing of all' things, a nature independent of omnipotence. 'Creation from nothing expresses … that omnipotence can make us free'" (6428).

80. "Homo est liberi arbitrii, ita sane, si Deus illi suum concederet." Luther, *De servo arbitrio*, 49 (WA 18:637).

81. "Full many a flower is born to blush unseen, and waste its sweetness on the desert air." T. Grey, *Elegy Written in a Country Churchyard*.

82. Berdjaev, *Freedom and the Spirit*, I, 216n199.

83. A. MacIntyre, *Dependent Rational Animals: Why Human Beings Need Virtues*, 2nd ed. (La Salle, Ill.: Open Court, 1999), 85.

84. J. G. Herder, *Ideen zur Philosophie der Geschichte der Menschheit* (Wiesbaden: Fourier, 1985), translated into English as *Reflections on the Philosophy of the History of Mankind* (Chicago: University of Chicago Press, 2001), I, III, 6.

458 CHRISTIAN ANTHROPOLOGY

and the defense of freedom become exclusively a product of Christian faith. Whoever believes accepts the eternal responsibility of his actions before the creator; whoever does not is spared the trouble. We should note, however, that other authors consider humans can rationally discover the weight and realism of freedom, the relevance of the free act, not only in the subjective perception of their spirit, not only through their faith in God, but also in their relationship with other people. They are usually called the personalists.

According to the twentieth-century philosopher Emmanuel Lévinas, freedom is situated not in human initiative but in the original relationship of responsibility of humans for one another.[85] Something of a kind was taught in the previous century by Jules Lequier[86] and then by Karl Jaspers. The latter has the following to say:

We are aware of our freedom when we recognize imperatives addressed to us. It is up to us whether we carry them out or evade them. We cannot seriously deny that we make a decision by which we decide concerning ourselves, and that we are responsible.... Man's freedom opens up to him, along with the uncertainty of his being, an opportunity to become what he can authentically be.... The freer man knows himself to be in this lucid certainty, the more aware he becomes of the transcendence through which he is.... The more authentically free a man is, the greater his certainty of God. When I am authentically free, I am certain that I am not free through myself.... Man's freedom opens up to him, along with the uncertainty of his being, an opportunity to become that which he can authentically be.[87]

That is to say, humans discover they are free in the context of social relationships, with other people and more concretely with God, that is, in the context of love and faith.

Another author who explains freedom in this way is Gabriel Marcel.[88] He says

---

85. See E. Lévinas, *Autrement quêtre ou au-delà de l'essence* (Dordrecht: Kluwer, 1978), translated into English as *Otherwise than Being or Beyond Essence* (Pittsburgh, Pa.: Duquesne University Press, 2009). "The relation with the Other, discourse, not only calls into question my freedom, the appeal coming from the other to call me to responsibility; it is not only the speech by which I divest myself of the possession that encircles me by setting forth an objective and common world, but it is also sermon, exhortation, the prophetic word." E. Lévinas, *Totality and Infinity: An Essay on Exteriority* (Pittsburgh, Pa.: Duquesne University Press, 2000), 213. "Responsible freedom, understood as a revision of the idea of freedom as independence, if this means autonomy of the *causa sui*" (239). As a result, says Botturi, "freedom is ... the independent exercise of the constitutive dependence of the relationship established on the basis of others, in which we may verify a coincidence between passivity and activity. The logic of freedom is that of gratuity, in opposition to that which is opposed by necessity and independence, and refers ultimately to an 'an-anarchic' origin for the good." Botturi, "Libertà," 6439; see Lévinas, *Totality and Infinity*, 199.

86. Lequier says: "The human person! A being that can do something without God! Who can, if it pleases him, prefer himself to God, who can want what God does not want, and not want what God wants, that is a new God who can offend the other. A prodigy that makes one tremble: man deliberates and God awaits." J. Lequier, *Oeuvres complètes*, edited by J. Grenier (Neuchatel: Éditions de la Baconnière, 1952), 225. "I am a person responsible for myself, I am my own work, responsible to God who made me creator of myself" (ibid.). On Lequier, see J. Grenier, *La philosophie de Jules Lequier* (Paris: Les Belles Lettres, 1936), and on freedom, see P. Pagani, *Libertà e non-contraddizione in Jules Lequier* (Milan: F. Angeli, 2000); A. del Noce, introduzione a J. Lequier, *Opere*, 3–124, esp. 78–83.

87. K. Jaspers, *The Way to Wisdom: Introduction to Philosophy* (New Haven, Conn.: Yale University Press, 1954), 64, 66f.

88. See especially Marcel's conference "Liberté et grâce," in Marcel, *Le mystère de l'être*, 2:109–25, and my study: P. O'Callaghan, "El enigma de la libertad humana en Gabriel Marcel," *Anuario Filosófico* 23 (1990):

that "man is a being to whom has been given the singular faculty of affirming or denying himself, according to whether he affirms being and opens himself to it, or denies being and closes himself up to it: because it is in this dilemma where the essence of freedom is to be found."[89] Freedom, according to Marcel, is situated in a response to an "appeal" that being addresses to man; it essentially consists not of an act of free will but rather of an act of "acceptance," of "reception," of "consent" to being offered as a gift.[90] Freedom, therefore, is not so much an attribute with which humans are born, to be exercised in an individualistic or creative context (Marcel is highly critical of the weight attributed to freedom by the agents of the French Revolution). Freedom cannot be easily observed at an empirical, measurable level. The free act is rather that act by which I open myself, I receive and accept a gift or a grace from another person (or I offer such a gift), an act that, even though I may not be completely aware of it when it is being performed, contributes to making me free and by means of which I acquire an ever greater state of deeply experienced intersubjective fullness with others. Only within this process—which Marcel would consider a "mystery," not a "problem"—can I begin to observe and be aware of the fact of "being free."[91] Openness to and reception of the gift of another refers not only to what other people give me but also to what God gives us. Thus Marcel prefers not to say that humans are self-determined but rather that they are "*sur-déterminées*" (determined by what comes from above).[92] Breaking definitively with Blumenberg's opposition between grace and freedom, Marcel's understanding of freedom "presupposes the intimate relationship that unites freedom and grace. In the last analysis, according to the response we give to this question—the most difficult of them all—we can take a position with respect to the existence of God."[93]

The Degree to Which Humans Are Determined

The denial of free will by some scientists and philosophers, described earlier, is reasonable from many points of view because humans are doubtless limited beings, determined in many ways. This is also true with respect to their relationship with God, the only true sovereign. Luther explains the nonfreedom of humans in the context of the undeniable sovereignty of God over all creatures. But it is also true that humans say they are free because they are speaking of the Cartesian experience of freedom, understood in terms of a decision made by the individual with clear and transparent awareness. However, in real terms, Cartesian awareness is not enough to show we are free, because if science has shown us one thing, it is that the dynamic of the free act is more hidden, more mysterious, more personal, more profound, more

---

139–52; R. Celada Ballanti, *Libertà e mistero dell'essere: Saggio su Gabriel Marcel* (Genoa: Tilgher, 1991). For an introduction to Marcel, see my study "Gabriel Marcel," in *Philosophica: Enciclopedia filosófica online* (2009), at *http://www.philosophica.info/archivo/2009/voces/marcel/Marcel.html*.

89. Marcel, *Etre et avoir*, 175.

90. G. Marcel, *Du refus à l'invocation*, 6th ed. (Paris: Gallimard, 1940), 73, translated into English as *Creative Fidelity* (New York: Fordham University Press, 2002).

91. O'Callaghan, "El enigma de la libertad humana," 151. See chapter 1, notes 43ff. and corresponding text.

92. Troisfontaines, *De l'Existence a l'Etre*, 1:319.

93. Marcel, *Le mystère de l'etre*, 2:110.

subtle, than Descartes would allow because it touches off the very depths of human personhood, in the subconscious, where my life is involved with that of others—and with that of God. The neurobiologist Michael Gazzaniga holds that neuroscientists who consider the question of human freedom should think of a complex net full of different interactions rather than of a series of processes working in parallel. The specific moment in which we become clear-mindedly aware of a decision, therefore, does not have all the importance attributed to it by authors such as Libet and Haggard. In other words, the moment of conscious awareness is not to be identified as the moment of freedom, as Descartes thought it was.[94] That is because in the end, as Gazzaniga suggests, "the brain is determined, but the person is free."[95]

Without "grace"—or, more amply, without the offering and reception of gift, without the social or relational character of humans, without corporeity, and therefore without the different unresolved human polarities—our reflection on freedom simply cannot take off. A solitary free action, if such a thing was possible, might be free, but it would be entirely irrelevant. The free act is not localized, therefore, in one part, in one aspect, in a hidden corner, of the soul, in the brain, in the pineal gland, or whatever, because it necessarily involves the entire human being, spiritual and corporal, individual and collective, mundane and open to the transcendent. Henri Bergson insists on this idea especially: "We are free when our acts emanate *from our whole personality*, when they express it."[96] And Karl Jaspers writes: "We realize we are free when we recognize what others expect from us."[97] A further confirmation of this may be found in the writings of Jürgen Habermas when he explains that humans are never free "on their own": "Nobody can enjoy freedom on their own, or at the cost of others. For this reason, freedom cannot be understood in a merely negative way, as a simple absence of constriction. Understood in an intersubjective way, freedom is different from the free will of an isolated individual. Nobody is truly free until all are free."[98] Likewise, Marcel avoids speaking of "freedom" on its own, always speaking of "freedom and fraternity," "freedom and grace," "freedom and existence," "freedom and gift," "freedom and hope," and so on.[99] Thus he concludes that what is most important in the life of a human is "freedom from myself," that is, liberation, which comes to him or her as a gift.[100]

94. See M. S. Gazzaniga, *Who's in Charge? Free Will and the Science of the Brain* (New York: Ecco Press, 2011).

95. M. S. Gazzaniga, "My Brain Made Me Do It," *Defining Right and Wrong in Brain Science: Essential Readings in Neuroethics*, edited by W. Glannon (New York: Dana Press, 2007), 183–94, 191.

96. Bergson, *Essai sur les données immédiates de la conscience*, 136: "Bref, nous sommes libres quand nos actes émanent de notre personnalité entière, quand ils l'expriment, quand ils ont avec elle cette indéfinissable ressemblance qu'on trouve parfois entre l'oeuvre e l'artiste."

97. Jaspers, *The Way to Wisdom*, 64, cited approvingly by Marcel in *Le mystère de l'etre*, 2, 114.

98. J. Habermas, "Dialog zu Gott und der Welt," with E. Mendieta, *Jahrbuch für politische Theologie* 3 (1999): 190–211, 209.

99. See O'Callaghan, "El enigma de la libertad humana," 139n1.

100. G. Marcel, *La dignité humaine et ses assises existentielles* (Paris: Aubier-Montaigne, 1964), 191f.

A Phenomenology of Free Human Action

The historical study just presented helps us understand that being free is not a simple issue. It is not obvious that we are free. Though freedom is central to human life and involves the whole of human personhood, paradoxically, we do not "dominate" our freedom. We observe it unfolding in front of us. The question we intend to consider in the coming pages, with the aid of a straightforward phenomenological reflection, is not so much whether humans experience themselves as free (which they may to a greater or lesser extent) but rather if they are so truly: that is, if the voluntary acts human beings carry out are really *influential and relevant*, if a free human act in its finitude is capable of giving life to a lasting reality, or perhaps even to a reality that becomes infinite and permanent.

The Ways in Which We Are Free

To begin this reflection we can consider two possible ways in which people normally say they are "free."[101] In the first place, humans frequently say they are free when they are doing what they spontaneously want to do, when they do not experience any significant discrepancy between what they desire and what they do. They manage to control their own lives, with effort perhaps, and simply take it for granted that they are acting freely.[102] However, it should be kept in mind that this common experience is not incompatible with a determinist view of the human being, who may well be moved by his passions and hidden impulses, as an important part of modern psychology from Freud onward has confirmed. And then, even though humans experience themselves as free, they may not in fact be so because, perhaps, they are deceived by a taste of freedom without having the substance. This is the valid critique directed by Spinoza against a simplistic or obvious understanding of freedom; in the words of Botturi, "A certain psychological evidence of freedom, of feeling oneself free, is undeniable in human experience, but against it rises up Spinoza's objection on the disparity between psychological evidence and ontological effectiveness: we can be determined and feel that we are free."[103] To demonstrate the ambivalence of this way of understanding human freedom, it is interesting to note how the Stoics struggled systematically against their spontaneous, passional inclinations with a view to not being slaves to their passions; following this path, they taught, humans become truly free, that is, indifferent to their passions and to external stimulation.[104]

This argument brings us to the second way in which humans commonly claim to be free, that is, when they manage to distance themselves from a series of options among which they can choose. The free act is situated in the indifference the subject

---

101. The following pages are adapted from O'Callaghan, "El enigma de la libertad humana."

102. F.-P. Maine de Biran understands human freedom in terms of the *effort* humans have to exercise: "Freedom, or the idea of freedom … is nothing other than the sentiment of our activity and our power of acting and of producing the constitutive effort of the self." *Essai sur les fondements de la psychologie*, in Maine de Biran, *Oeuvres complètes* (Geneva: Slatkine Reprints, 1982), 8–9:250.

103. Botturi, "Libertà," 6445. This position has been criticized by Jules Lequier, according to whom our freedom is demonstrated neither by choice (Lequier, *Oeuvres*, 210) nor by the effort to overcome obstacles to our will.

104. See notes 35ff.

experiences in the face of a variety of possible choices, none of which impose themselves. Here humans experience themselves as free, as non-determined, before a variety of different stimuli. This is normally what we refer to when speaking of "free will." With Descartes and Marcel we can observe that this elementary expression of human experience, though valid, corresponds to the lowest possible grade of freedom.[105] It is true that humans are free when they choose with complete indifference among a range of options (if this was ever possible). However, with this exercise of freedom nothing truly relevant is obtained as the fruit of their action. At best they may have a poor sensation of acting freely, but they achieve literally nothing by it. Or perhaps we could say that such a free act places on one side of the balance a supplementary weight, introducing the arbitrary into human action. In this case, when humans choose, they would exercise a merely illusory dominion over things. It might seem that they are obtaining something as the fruit of their free action, but in real terms nothing human is really produced, nothing new, or relevant, or enriched, or permanent. If human freedom, therefore, involves complete indifference in the choice between different options, in real terms we are affirming the meaninglessness of free action, a total lack of commitment (*engagement*).

In the coming pages the following thesis shall be presented: the free human act normally involves a choice between two or more options. In its materiality and immediacy it is a mere choice. Yet beyond or above the choice between different options is situated a choice between two different planes, two ways of perceiving the good, two ways in which humans can mold and reinforce their identity: either in terms of the acceptance of reality as gift or in terms of the rejection of reality as a gift. The possibility of a relevant exercise of human freedom or otherwise refers, therefore, sooner or later, to the ultimate source of all gifts—that is, God.

Three Possible Choice Frames

We can consider three examples of this dynamic, three examples of choosing between different created objects. First, humans choose between two things in which the subject perceives an identical level of goodness, for example, between two equal apples. Certainly this involves a free choice, but with this action nothing real is achieved; there is no progress or novelty. One may have the sensation of acting freely, a true choice may be made, but it is a simply irrelevant or arbitrary action. In fact, in acting in this way one perceives that the proper object of the human will cannot be mere choice, the pure variety of options, but rather the good: in fact, we ask, "What *should* I choose?" The multiplicity of options in real terms gives humans an illusory dominion. In many ways it contributes to suffocating and disorienting the human will rather than stimulating it. We may think of Buridan's donkey, which died because it was unable to choose between two identical piles of hay.

Second, alternatively humans may choose between things they perceive to possess an objective difference of goodness, for example, between something that is worth $10 and something worth $1,000. Again this is a true and proper choice, because the human is not forced to choose the superior quantity. However, if the greater quantity

---

105. See Marcel, in *Le mystère de l'être*, 2:111, where he quotes Descartes.

is chosen, again an irrelevant choice is made from an anthropological standpoint, a choice that could just as easily be made by an animal that spontaneously gives priority to a superior form of alimentation while refusing an inferior one or by a computer that calculates the value of a property and "chooses" it. So-called consequentialist ethics move in this direction: ethics deal with measuring the good that can be obtained through a particular line of action and choosing the most advantageous one. From the human point of view, with a choice of this kind, no contribution is made to reality; we act in a humanly irrelevant way, doing more or less what we are programed to do. In the words of Marcel, this is an act "that anybody can carry out, and it does not contribute anything to the creation, as it were, that I make of myself."[106]

Third and finally, we may present the scenario of choosing between two clearly different things, one of which is perceived spontaneously as inferior and the other as superior, for example, between bread and cake. The choice of the "inferior" object, the bread instead of the cake in this case, cannot be explained on the basis of the indifference of the will or on the basis of the spontaneous acceptance of a greater good, but only on the basis of an ulterior motive, rationally known, a motive that goes beyond immediate gratification.[107] In this case one might choose bread instead of cake in order to avoid tooth decay or diabetes. It is possible, of course, that through this way of acting one might attempt to live life in an attitude of indifference in the face of good or evil, joy or suffering, love or hate: this is typical of the ascetic practices of Stoicism and Buddhism. Something of the kind may be said of one who sleeps less in order to have more time for other activities or the person who decides not to love in order not to suffer eventually the consequences of a failed love, and so on. In other words, humans act freely; often against their spontaneous inclinations, they renounce a particular good in order to attain indifference and therefore freedom before the created world, before others, perhaps before God. But to what purpose? What meaning does such an act have?

A Choice between Two Planes

Now, if it is licit to speak of a relevant free act, it is clear that in performing it the human being—in concretely choosing between two or more particular options—chooses in real terms something that goes beyond the particular options, between two different planes, levels, or projects intrinsically bound up with the concrete choices. If the objects to be chosen were situated on a single plane (as in the first two examples mentioned earlier), the apparently "free" choice would remain in the ambit of the banal, the arbitrary, the irrelevant, as we saw already. Such a "free act" simply produces nothing. What gives weight to the free act, what makes it relevant, in fact, is the purpose that is sought (and that may not be obtained): the end, purpose, plan, scope, or incentive that goes beyond the concrete action, even though it is inseparable from the latter. And when humans act motivated by such an end, in real terms they are attempting to identify themselves with (or construct) a project or image that constitutes, or should constitute, their own identity, to some degree already

---

106. Marcel, *Le mystère de l'être*, 2:21.
107. See *LS*, par. 162.

defined, to some degree still needing to be defined fully. This is normally called the "ultimate end." In effect, when humans act freely they identity themselves with something that does not coincide completely with a particular choice, something that can be achieved only intentionally. Besides their concrete choice, humans are attempting to make common cause with a project or vision that is not as yet achieved (a vocation, life project, the will of God, etc.). When they act in this way they realize, often a posteriori, that they acted freely, that they built a part of their lives, with a freedom that changed their destiny for good (or for bad), that is to say, a freedom that has become relevant.

Choosing between Planes: Platonism and Christianity

Now we can ask a further question: what do these "planes" that humans choose between actually consist of, what kind of consistency do they have? They involve not only human subjectivity but surrounding reality: society, the world, and the entire cosmos to which humans belong and are related, because the free act derives from the entire human being and is linked with reality as a whole. We can mention two possible approaches to reality (there are others, of course), two possible planes, which correspond approximately to the Platonic and the Christian worldviews.

As a first example let us consider the cosmology, the ethics, and the anthropology typical of Platonism, in the most ample and generic understanding of the word, without getting involved in finer details.[108] At the heart of this ethical and cosmic vision there is a clear double-plane or dualistic structure, between spirit, which is immortal, and matter, which is corruptible, between the intelligible world and the sensitive world. Platonic ethics are understood in such a way that humans in performing each action make common cause with the search for or consolidation of immortality (the good, the eternal, the one, the spirit, whatever is permanent) or with the consolidation of mortality (evil, corruption, matter, multiplicity, the provisional). In each action people are called to identify themselves with eternal, spiritual values and at the same time distance themselves from matter, corruption, temporality, the senses, impermanence, and so on. They do so by overcoming the immediate attraction of the latter, that is, the immediately perceived goods, which are corruptible, ephemeral, material, sense-bound. The human life project, the identity one wishes to achieve according to the Platonic scheme, is, or should be, one of obtaining the immortality that corresponds to a perfectly spiritual state. Particular choices should reinforce all that moves in this direction and avoid all that moves in the opposite. From this example we can observe that what critically determines the dynamics of moral choice, what gives meaning to human freedom and relevance to the free act, is the fundamental structure of reality, of the cosmos and of humanity, in their relationship with God.

If this principle is applied to the Christian economy and to the vision of the world it contains, things change a lot and become more complex and subtle. On the one hand, certainly, the fundamental consistency of the choice between two planes in each particular action remains unvaried: humans must obtain whatever is eternal and immortal and leave behind whatever does not last, whatever is corruptible

---

108. See chapter 2, notes 33ff., and chapter 19, notes 7ff. and corresponding text.

and ephemeral. That is to say, the Christian, like the Platonist, seeks eternal life and strives to distance the self from anything that could bind to a corruptible temporality, following the exhortation of the Lord in Matthew's Gospel: "Store up treasures in heaven" (6:20).[109] The reception of this Platonic intuition by Christian authors from the beginning is significant. In Augustine it is very clear.[110] According to Aquinas, likewise, the ultimate end of human action cannot but be eternal beatitude, and this determines—or should determine—every other choice.[111] On the other hand, however, in spite of the structural likeness between Platonic and Christian ethics, the profound diversity of the fundamental configuration of created reality and of humans themselves between the two makes the dynamics of human action very different for a Platonist and a Christian.

For a Platonist the distinction between the two planes is obvious: one must distance oneself systematically from the call of matter, of the empirical, of the senses, and make common cause with the spirit, with the intellect, with ideas, with the good spiritually perceived, with the true intuitively grasped, with all that derives from the world of ideas. According to Christian doctrine, however, God is the author of all created beings, and also, therefore, of material ones that are apparently corruptible, of all that derives from the passions, the senses, and so on. All this is destined besides to live on forever through the resurrection of the dead.[112] For this reason the particular choice that commences with a material, sensitive, immediate, or temporary stimulus does not necessarily involve a distancing from immortality, a detachment from "spiritual" and permanent values, from the true good. In real terms, the passions—when they are properly ordered—constitute the voice, the call, of God.[113] And for the same reason, to identify oneself with a "spiritual" reality—an idea, for example—does not necessarily bring us closer to truth and immortality because the "idea" may be mistaken, false, the result of human pride. Berdjaev observes that "many universal common abstract ideas are evil in an exalted form."[114] Thus the Christian does not choose in a Platonic way because the two planes are no longer simply those of spirit and matter; they refer to the way in which created reality as a whole is perceived. Let us consider this proposal more carefully.

The Exercise of Human Freedom before Creation Perceived as a Gift

The Christian sees the world and everything that is in it as God's creation. God has created all things from nothing, without any presupposition. In other words, he has created it as a pure gift.[115] Nothing within the created world could have obliged him to do so in any way. If there *had* been something existent "before" or "outside" the work of creation (perhaps prime matter or divine spirits), it would have conditioned to some

---

109. See *COH* 110f., 272f.

110. See ibid., 158.

111. See Aquinas, *S.Th.* I-II, q. 1.

112. See *COH* 109–12.

113. "Passiones animae … inquantum sunt ordinatae a ratione, pertinent ad virtutem." Aquinas, *S.Th.* I-II, q. 24, a. 2, ad 3.

114. Berdjaev, *Slavery and Freedom*, 249.

115. See Maspero and O'Callaghan, *Creatore perché Padre*.

degree God's intervention, which would therefore not have been fully free. The follow-ing three affirmations, therefore, are rigorously equivalent: God creates freely; God cre-ates as a pure gift; God creates out of nothing (*ex nihilo*). And, on the basis of faith in creation, Christians are meant to act and react before the world in a way determined by creation's fundamental gift structure. When humans make a particular choice between different options, they can act with two fundamental perceptions or intrinsic inten-tions: either the choice is made with a view to reinforcing the will to autonomous power over reality, excluding the native dominion God has over all things, that is, rejecting created reality as a gift (this is a sinful action), or the choice reflects and recognizes reality as a divine gift and in that way intensifies more and more the human's adoring dependence on the One who is the author of the world before him or her (this is a virtu-ous act). In this way, the free human act is, ipso facto, an act of rejecting the gift, an act of closure, or an act of divine praise, a "eucharistic" act.[116] As the book of Wisdom sug-gests, "It is a mark of insight to know whose gift she [Wisdom] was" (8:21).

In the first case, the free act expresses and consolidates the dominion of humans over created beings, as if God did not exist; in the second, the free will reinforces the subjection of humans to their creator. In one case, created beings are treated as objects to be manipulated and possessed arbitrarily; in the other case, they are per-ceived and treated as a gift that is received, admired, used, enjoyed, and shared, whose existence as a gift is joyfully recognized. In one case the dependence of things on humans is strengthened, independently of God (with man placing himself as a god over creation); in the other case human dependence on God is reinforced in the use of creatures that, in turn, should be submitted to him through humans (in that way contributing to the establishment of the concrete dominion of God over the world). In effect, as we have already seen, humans express the fact that they have been created in the image and likeness of God not only by their dominion over creatures, but, even more so, by their adoring submission to God.[117] In brief, according to the Christian vision of the world, the choice between different planes that is intrinsic to each and every practical choice takes place not so much between the spiritual and the material as between the personal and filial submission to God, who gives himself, and the au-tonomous dominion of humans over the created world: that is, between the grateful acceptance of God's gift and its self-sufficing rejection.

From the Christian standpoint, no human act, no free act, should express con-tempt for created goods, even the simplest material ones, because they are made by God as a manifestation of his glory and as a gift for humanity. Contempt for and ma-nipulation of any creature (for example, its gratuitous destruction or the perversion of its intrinsic purpose) as a creature (that is, as the product of God's love offered to humans as a gift) constitutes ipso facto an offense to the creator because it involves the rejection of the gift in the very act of its being given.[118] But not only is the creator affronted; the creature itself is despised insofar as it is used by humans in any way that affirms, intensifies, and shapes their autonomy before God, that is, when their

---

116. On the "eucharistic" side of Christian reflection with respect to modernity, see P. O'Callaghan, "La relación entre modernidad y evangelización," *Scripta Theologica* 45 (2013): 41–64.

117. See chapter 4, notes 76ff. and corresponding text.

118. This is a central element of Pope Francis's encyclical *LS*, especially chap. 2.

inner truth (that of being creatures, and thus of being God's gift) is not recognized and respected.[119] In the encyclical *Lumen Fidei* we read: "The Decalogue appears as the path of gratitude, the response of love, made possible because in faith we are receptive to the experience of God's transforming love for us."[120]

To sum up: the interior choice (between two planes) of the external free act (which generally consists of a choice between different particular options, also small ones and often apparently irrelevant ones) is to be found either in using the created good as a received good recognized as such before the creator or in considering it as a "disposable" reality, like unformed matter, which serves only to extend the power of humans, their dominion, their independence and autonomy before the creator. For this reason I have said that the reality and relevance of the free act are determined not on the basis of how the act itself is experienced (consciously wanting to do this or that or experiencing indifference before a variety of options[121]) but from the structure of reality that humans have before them and in which they are inserted.

Why Pantheisms Render Human Freedom Irrelevant

Considering things hypothetically, if there was no such thing as creation *ex nihilo*, that is, if the universe was not entirely God's free gift of existence, the only thing that would exist would be the whole of reality, the metaphysically unitary amalgam of all that exists: the divine, the human, the cosmos, matter, or whatever we may call it. In this case it would not be possible to exercise human freedom in a relevant way. This is basically the position of Spinoza, of Hegel, and of atheistic scientism, because pantheisms, total or partial as they may be, tend necessarily to suffocate human freedom and impose determinism. In effect, for the pantheist what exists is the whole, which has never changed and will never change. At best, humans living in a pantheistic world will become interested spectators of reality but never truly actors.

In the Platonic vision of things, something of the kind may be said, because there is a metaphysical gradation and continuity between all things, from the supreme Good down to prime matter, and thus the human will is never truly confronted with the dilemma of a real choice. With Christianity, however, the human will is confronted to the core with willing action on account of the net distinction between a sovereign creator and a created world entirely subordinate to yet distinct from him. In every action, in effect, humans, though they may not realize it fully, recognize God as God, as supreme Lord, as the creator who gives them a universe that should not be manipulated or maltreated, as the Lord to whom humans submit themselves in a free and filial way. On the contrary, humans may equally well act as "gods" over creatures to manipulate them with an arbitrary dominion, thus making them slaves of their immediate needs or caprice. In brief, free action is relevant, it is efficacious, and its effects are potentially eternal because there is a net distinction between the creator and the creature, that is, because God creates *ex nihilo*, because God creates freely. In brief: the freedom of God as God is the very thing that makes humans free as humans.

---

119. On the way in which eschatological recompense reflects our relationship to the cosmos, see *COH* 201–5.

120. Francis and Benedict XVI, *Lumen Fidei*, par. 46.

121. See nos. 4, above, 1, and 2.

These considerations on the dynamics of the interior action of humans go well beyond the logic of a purely intentionalistic ethics because there are human actions that *objectively* involve contempt for the creator in the destruction of his gift of creation, with the concomitant will of being "gods" over the created world. This is the case, for example, with homicide, with different forms of genetic manipulation, with the destruction of the environment. And the fact that such actions may be carried out with apparent "good intentions" makes no substantial difference. Each action itself contains and expresses its own intention, the recognition or rejection of God's sovereignty.

Divine and Human Freedom

The possibility of a purely free action without presuppositions of any kind may be attributed to God alone as creator, even though humans may strive to be "divine" in this way (we may think of Sartre's explanation of freedom). The upright exercise of created, finite freedom on the part of humans consists, properly speaking, of the use of creatures (including themselves) with full respect to their nature, as icons of the love of God, in other words, in the grateful acceptance of gift.[122]

On the one hand, the free act is carried out by humans in a positive, active way, often choosing between different options, employing in the process all their faculties of intelligence, will, imagination, and experience. On the other hand, however, such an action is lived in objective terms as a passion, that is, as a reception and acceptance of God's gifts (or as a rejection of such gifts), even though at a visible and phenomenological level it shows up as an active agency. The relevance of free action, therefore, is not so much in action, in production, in results, in making things happen, in spite of the appearances. It may rather be found in the objective passiveness of an intelligent and humble acceptance of gift. In Jane Austen's novel *Mansfield Park* the young protagonist, Fanny Price, seems to be, with respect to the other characters in the book, a limited, passive person, submissive, oversensitive, not very creative, and unsure of herself. Paradoxically, however, in everything that she does and does not do, she is the one who determines the destiny of all the other persons of the story, many of whom have much more "personality" than she has. In such a case we could say: free action is not primarily in doing, but in accepting. And if acceptance always requires a "yes" to the one who gives, it is often expressed as a "no" to an immediate appeal. As the neuroscientist Vilayanur Ramachandran put it: "Our conscious minds may not have free will, but they have, rather, a 'free won't'!"

---

122. The nineteenth-century philosopher Martin Deutinger explains this as follows: "In man, nature and freedom confront each other as opposites. This opposition can only be resolved by the revelation of a higher, divine Will, in such a way that man, in attaching himself to this Will, touches both the ground of being and the ground of freedom. On the other hand, if man negates the divine Will, he also negates the ground of freedom, and hence the ground of being too, setting himself in contradiction to both. If free choice is to be genuinely free, therefore, it must acknowledge a being—namely, freedom—superior to both existence and relation. If there were a necessary being superior to freedom, it would dissolve all relative freedom and all choice. We must assume an absolute Will if we wish to comprehend the law found in the relative will. This Will, this higher personality, is absolute because it is not bound up with existence but is one with being.... Being is freedom, and freedom is being." M. Deutinger, "Die Denklehre," *Grundlinien der positiven Philosophie* (Regensburg: G. J. Manz, 1844), 3:393f., cited by von Balthasar in *Theo-Drama*, 2:334f.

Final Reflections on Free Human Action

Three observations may be made.

The Entire Human Being Is Free

We have seen throughout this chapter that human freedom—or, more precisely, free human action—is intrinsically referred to every single aspect of human life: to intelligence and will; to the rest of humanity and its individual members; to the body and the cosmos, which are part of our being; to time, without which we cannot act humanly; and, above all, to God, source of our being and of all gifts. We have already cited Henri Bergson, who says: "We are free when our acts emanate from our whole personality, when they express it."[123] Freedom, therefore, is not a localized or circumscribed part of the human being, it is not a human "faculty"; rather it is an expression of the entire human being, in all its relationships.

To an Important Degree the Free Human Act Is Irreversible

The free act is a human act; therefore, it is a finite act, limited time-wise. Within the contingency and banality of life, humans choose from a variety of possible options. However, this contingency and banality are only apparent. What makes a human act important or relevant is not its limited quality but the fact that in its finitude it obtains (or can obtain) something that is greater than itself, in that it is instrumental in enriching the person (or, alternatively, something that can destroy it definitively). This is so because the free act does not, in a strict sense, construct the human, society, and the world (as Marx and Sartre thought) but rather opens its life to the gift of another and especially to the gift of God. From this conviction the adventure of freedom takes its origin. Without the gift offered, the free act would be null: human beings would be walking around in circles, producing nothing. Those who act freely in real terms commit themselves before others, and therefore, though they act freely, in a sense they lose their freedom, they reduce or narrow down their lives by committing themselves to a particular ambit within their field of choice.[124] Yet this free act is what makes humans grow, and at the same time solidifies and directs their lives, for good or for evil. The free act, therefore, is to an important degree irreversible. What is done cannot be undone (although sin, of course, can be undone by divine pardon). If with the same will people were capable of deciding and then of undoing the decisions they had made, their free acts would have no consistency, no power, no relevance; they would be pure appearance.

Free Will Is Involved in Human Liberation

Paul insists often that humans, in becoming children of God in Christ, are no longer slaves because they have received the gift of liberation, the liberty of the chil-

---

123. Bergson, *Essai sur les données immédiates de la conscience*, 136.

124. Speaking of the different currents of history, John Paul II wrote a letter to his biographer G. Weigel dated January 12, 1995, in which the Pope said that in the currents of history "it is the 'turning point' that is most important, as when a train enters a switch where an inch decides its future direction." Weigel, *The End and the Beginning*, 424.

dren of God. And this liberation by grace consists not only in the tangible help that God gives humans in order to overcome the different slaveries that result from sin (what was earlier on called "healing grace") but also in the presence by faith of a new reality, of an infinite space, divine and eternal, never dreamed of: that of eternal life, which comes from perpetually partaking in the divine life that makes them children of God ("elevating grace"). Christians on earth live immersed in this divine reality, what we might call this divine space, which is much greater and wider than themselves, "the freedom of the glory of the children of God" (Rom 8:21), even though they may not always experience it as such. This new life has been placed at the disposal of humans to enjoy it, to communicate it, to bring it to fruition (Mt 25:14–30), always and only as divine grace. The weight of the choice made by Christians in accepting the infinite divine gift of grace is extraordinary, even though it takes place by means of finite actions that to all appearances may seem banal and of no apparent transcendence, because in each human action the treasure of the life of grace and divine filiation is placed at center-stage: to increase it (by merit) or to lose it (by sin). "The good of grace in one person," says Thomas Aquinas, "is greater than the natural goodness of the whole universe."[125]

Within the Christian economy we can better perceive how to reconcile the two fundamental understandings of human freedom mentioned at the beginning of this chapter: the fact of being free (or liberated) and free will, that is, the true capacity for choice that each human individual possesses. Christian liberation, in effect, is above all a gift, a liberating gift that can, in principle, become definitive (with eternal life) and in a certain sense infinite. Of course it is a gift that must be accepted repeatedly by humans through free choices that build up virtue with intelligence, creativity, and generosity, often also with fatigue and in darkness. The point of departure for the free act, therefore, is grace in the most ample sense of the word: the gift of creation, talents received, opportunities offered by others, and, last but not least, supernatural life, the theological virtues. Only in the context of divine grace can we understand, express, and respect the mystery of human freedom in all its amplitude. Nicholas Berdjaev, as we already saw, wrote that "the Christian doctrine of grace constitutes the true doctrine of freedom." But grace that liberates must be accepted by the creature capable of doing so; paraphrasing the prologue of John's Gospel, we may say that grace is not "made flesh" if it is not freely accepted; in this case it has no value or relevance in the created sphere.

If we consider things from the angle of Stoic ethics, we can say that "liberation," that space of freedom or indifference that humans open for themselves, in which they move and with which they manage to reduce as much as possible life's suffering and distress, has to be won with effort, stage by stage, as the direct fruit of their own free choices often repeated.[126] That is to say, the Stoic must gradually conquer liberty on his own. Something of the kind may be said with regard to Eastern asceticism (Hinduism and Buddhism). In the Christian economy, however, liberation obtained

---

125. "Sed bonum gratiae unius maius est quam bonum naturae totius universi." Aquinas, *S.Th.* I-II, q. 113, a. 9, ad 2.

126. It is generally accepted that the philosophical ethics of Pelagius, which does not recognize the need for grace, was Stoic in character: see chapter 8. See also Valero, "El estoicismo de Pelagio."

by humans is extensive and ample because it is the freedom of the children of God; however, it is not primarily the fruit of repeated human free action, the result of the exercise of their own free will, which is always created and limited, but the fruit of grace. Humans are given the possibility of accepting with all their being the quasi-infinite gift of eternal life, freely offered and liberating. In other words, it is only in the context of gift and divine grace that we can understand and measure the meaning and value of human freedom, where freedom is freed, where freedom is loved, where freedom is defended passionately. As Aquinas said, the more that humans have charity, the more they have liberty.[127]

In the concrete situation of humans, these two understandings of human freedom (liberation and free will) refer to one another directly. On the one hand, humans aspire to liberation in every ambit of their lives—spiritual, material, social, and political, all of which offer a wider space to move—as something that is in part procured by their own effort, and in part received from without. In obtaining and establishing an ever-greater space of movement, humans then manage to exercise their free will more and more amply. This is so because they can enjoy a wider and richer range of options and dispositions among which they can choose. In brief, liberation is what makes the exercise of free will possible. On the other hand, however, free will is often exercised with a view to opening up ever-wider spaces, that is, obtaining greater liberation for oneself or for others. Yet most of the time experience shows us that the liberation we desire, whether promised or possessed, is not consistent or long lasting, among other reasons because free will on its own is not capable of obtaining or erecting anything that can last forever. We can understand, therefore, that throughout the history of humanity "liberty" has been considered above all as a great and noble aspiration, deeply felt, but one that often becomes an illusion, unobtainable, something that slips through our fingers as soon as we attempt to grasp it or control it.

In the Christian economy, however, things do not work in this way. Historically, human freedom in both senses, inseparably, has been defended passionately by Christians because free will is the greatest gift God has given humans in the order of creation and liberation is the greatest gift he has promised to those who believe in the order of grace. God in effect liberates humans, offering them the gift of grace that liberates, but previously God gave them the capacity to accept (or reject) this gift with intelligence and awareness (free will). In other words, with the gift of grace, human free will, is made capable of cooperating in the fullest sense in the process of human liberation.

---

127. "Quanto aliquis plus habet de caritate, plus habet de libertate." *III Sent.*, d. 29, q. 1, a. 8, *s.c.* 1. On this question, see L. Clavell, "La libertà conquistata da Cristo sulla Croce: Approccio teologico ad alcuni insegnamenti del Beato Josemaría Escrivá sulla libertà," *Romana* 17 (2001): 240–69.

21   THE TEMPORALITY AND HISTORICITY
OF THE HUMAN BEING

Man is a synthesis of the temporal and the eternal.   SØREN KIERKEGAARD[1]

Christianity is not a historical magnitude; rather history is a Christian magnitude.
HENRI DE LUBAC[2]

The world is full of the old Christian virtues gone mad.   G. K. CHESTERTON[3]

History is built up by memory; the loss of memory is the disappearance of history.
NICOLAS BERDJAEV[4]

Man alone has a history, that is, he does not live only by his biological heritage
but also by tradition.   KARL JASPERS[5]

We have spoken frequently in previous chapters of human nature, that is, of those
aspects of the human being that are, as it were, stable, fixed, inalterable, what might
be called the physical, biological, psychological, and spiritual DNA of humans: their
corporeal, intellectual, volitive, social, religious nature, all of which respond to the
question "What is the human being?" Common nature is the foundational aspect of
human life that makes all sociality and communication possible. In effect, humans
are in a position, for better or for worse, to communicate with one another because
they share the same nature. And nature is stable in humans: "La nature est toujours
la même," said Jean D'Alembert, "Nature is always the same."[6]

---

1. S. Kierkegaard, *The Concept of Anxiety: A Simple Psychologically Orienting Deliberation on the Dogmatic Issue of Hereditary Sin* (Princeton, N.J.: Princeton University Press, 1980), 85.
2. H. de Lubac, *Paradoxes, suivi de nouveaux paradoxes,* 2nd ed. (Paris: Éditions du Seuil, 1959), 108.
3. Chesterton, *Orthodoxy,* 15.
4. Berdjaev, *Slavery and Freedom,* 197.
5. Jaspers, *The Way of Wisdom,* 66.
6. J. D'Alembert, *Discours préliminaire de l'Encyclopédie,* ed. M. Malherbe (Paris: Vrin, 2000), 118.

However, if we wish to be faithful to Christian patrimony, philosophy, and science itself, we need to take into account the other aspect of human life, in contrast, though not in contradiction, with human nature: *human historicity* (including temporality), which involves central aspects of life, such as progress, evolution, tradition, memory, development, mobility, and dynamism.[7] The human being, in effect, is a being that changes, that shifts, that moves forward and backward, that makes progress and can diminish; humans live consciously from the memory of the past yet project themselves toward the future, as they live rooted in the present moment. Though human nature is maintained, it consolidates, is affirmed, is made manifest, comes back again and again, becomes permanent and basically invariable,[8] whereas history seems to relativize human existence.[9] In fact, it would seem that history is opposed to nature, to fixity, to the natural law, to the stable essence of things. The Greek philosophers were aware of the dilemma between nature and history, some of them (such as Parmenides) saying that all is fixed because all change is apparent, others (such as Heraclitus) that everything that exists is in flux and is changing because every being is ephemeral. As a compatriot and contemporary of D'Alembert, Denis Diderot, said, "La nature est encore à l'ouvrage" (Nature is still at work).[10] In real terms, as we shall see, we need to say that human nature is historical in the sense that not all is determined from the outset of human life and in the present moment; human nature is open and teleological, that is, directed toward an end. This is explained by the philosopher Luigi Pareyson as follows: "On account of his indefinite advancement man develops, but is not reduced to his history, because man has history, but is not history.... Thus, to speak of the historicity of man is only possible in the sense of a programmed plasticity, in which reason is not an instrument but a norm."[11]

Within the Christian economy there is no need to consider things in terms of a radical alternative between nature and history. God created the world with established laws, with perennial inclinations. If they are not recognized and respected, nature ends up destroying itself.[12] At the same time, within the vastness of the divine project, development, evolution, progress, change, tradition, intensification, and perfection are all possible. This does not take place following a law of necessity because it is also possible for the world to go into reverse, to decline, to deteriorate, to slip backward, to decay, to decompose. That is to say, there is such a thing as history. For this reason we

7. On the philosophy and theology of history, see W. H. Walsh, *An Introduction to the Philosophy of History*, 3rd ed. (New York: Harper and Row, 1967); J. Cruz, *Filosofía de la historia* (Pamplona: Eunsa, 1995); P. Rossi, "Storia e storiografia," in *Enciclopedia filosofica*, 11:11130–48.

8. See the suggestive and provocative study of S. Pinker, which defends the fundamental stability of human nature, though in a determinist way: *The Blank Slate: The Modern Denial of Human Nature* (New York: Viking Press, 2002).

9. Pico della Mirandola, speaking of the creation of Adam, placed the following words in God's mouth: "I did not give you, Adam, either a particular place, or a special appearance, or any prerogative for yourself, in order to ensure that that place, that appearance, those prerogatives which you desired, would become your possession as your own, according to your desire and your will." *Discorso sulla dignità dell'uomo*, edited by F. Bausi (Parma: Fondazione Pietro Bembo U. Guanda, 2003), 11, translated into English as *On the Dignity of Man*, edited by C. G. Wallis, P. J. W. Miller (Indianapolis, Ind.: Hackett, 1998).

10. D. Diderot, "De l'interprétation de la nature," in *Œuvres complètes* (Paris: A. Belin, 1818), 58, 1, 455.

11. L. Pareyson, *Esistenza e persona*, 4th ed. (Genoa: Il melangolo, 1992), 198f.

12. See Francis, *LS*, chap. 2.

can say that Christian anthropology is a dramatic anthropology.[13] Within the Christian vision, history finds its ultimate meaning at the culmination of this process, what is called the Parousia, the coming of Christ the savior as judge in glory at the end of time: then history will reach its conclusion with the resurrection of the living and the dead and with their definitive judgment.[14] Hope in the return of Christ confirms and manifests the original divine design in a definitive way. Only at final judgment will the extraordinarily complex dynamism of history be known, along with its fruitful interacting with created nature. As Bonaventure said, history is like a poem; we shall be in a position to appreciate its beauty in a single breath only when it is complete.

In this sense, according to Christian faith, "nature" (which is the fruit of God's creative action) and "history" (the result of God's action as well as the free acceptance or rejection of humans) find their point of convergence in the creative and saving work of God. We shall now consider "human historicity" in the context of what we have termed the "historical event." Then we shall look into the different ways in which human historicity has been interpreted by philosophers and theologians.

The Historical Event, Human Historicity, and Hermeneutics

The term "historical" may be understood and applied to human life in two basic ways: as event and as interpretation.

The Historical Event

In order for a human act or event to be considered properly speaking "historical," three conditions must be met. The first condition is that it should be a free act performed by one or more individuals. We considered this extensively in the previous chapter. If there was no such thing as a truly free human act, there would be no such thing as history. At best, we could speak of a simple natural development but not of a historical event. The growth of a tree, for example, represents a real process of a living being, a process of enrichment, progress, and development, but the stages of its growth cannot be considered as historical events in the strict sense of the word because the tree already contains in a germinal way all the possibilities of its own future development and needs only the appropriate conditions (climate, nutrition, and the passage of time) to achieve them. Likewise, an earthquake or volcano may be a very damaging event, very influential in terms of the lives of many people, something that may be remembered many years later (it may even "change the course of history"). It is an event, certainly, but it is not a historical event in the strict sense of the word. The term "nature," in effect, comes from the Latin *nascor*, "to be born," and refers to the origin of things, not so much to their present way of acting. But the historical event is born of the freedom of the individual human at a particular point of time. Using the terminology of Martin Heidegger, we may say that humans are distinct from other things in that the latter—inanimate things, animals, and plants—are simply given,

---

13. See Angelini, "Antropologia teologia: La svolta necessaria."
14. See *COH* 39–148.

while humans really *exist*, because only they are capable of establishing a conscious rapport with all the possibilities of their existence.[15] With this understanding, "freedom expressed in temporal action is the fundamental factor that guides and governs history."[16] For this reason, "the historical past is not the efficient cause of history, but rather its immanent condition."[17]

Within the free act, as we have seen already, human reason is present—the mind, thought, imagination, a project, a dream. In that sense, the history of the world is always the history of thought, of thoughts that lie at the heart of actions, that is to say, history is spiritual. According to Robin Collingwood, whereas nature is simply a phenomenon observed by humans, historical events refer not to mere phenomena but to the thought that lies behind or within them.[18] For him, in the words of William Walsh, "the central concept of history is the concept of action, that is of thought that is expressed as external behavior."[19] This may be called the "idealist" reading of history, shared to an important degree by the twentieth-century Italian philosophers Giovanni Gentile and Benedetto Croce,[20] what Wilhelm Dilthey (and German thinkers, generally speaking) express in the distinction between *Naturwissenschaften*, "nature sciences," and *Geisteswissenschaften*, "sciences of the spirit."

The second condition for an event to be historical is that it must exercise a more or less tangible and permanent *effect* on society, on other people, on the world—an effect that is knowable and to some degree measured and documented. A free act that does not go beyond the individual who carries it out (a sublime thought, for example) is not, strictly speaking, a historical event. In this sense, it should be said that the historical event is what really changes the course of history. The past cannot be changed because it is given, but the future can be modified.[21] Thus history is lived out fundamentally as a handing on, a transmission of the present, a tradition.[22]

15. M. Heidegger, *Being and Time*, translated by Joan Stambaugh (Albany: State University of New York Press, 1996), §§ 9 and 72.

16. Cruz, *Filosofía de la historia*, 79.

17. A. Millán-Puelles, *Ontología de la existencia histórica* (Madrid: CSIC, 1951), 60.

18. "To the scientist, nature is always and merely a 'phenomenon,' not in the sense of being defective in reality, but in the sense of being a spectacle presented to his intelligent observation; whereas the events of history are never mere phenomena, never mere spectacles for contemplation, but things which the historian looks, not at, but through, to discern the thought within them.... For history, the object to be discovered is not the mere event, but the thought expressed in it.... After the historian has ascertained the facts, there is no further process of inquiring into the causes. When he knows what happened, he already knows why it happened." R. G. Collingwood, *The Idea of History* (Oxford: Clarendon Press, 1946), 214.

19. Walsh, *An Introduction to the Philosophy of History*, 52.

20. This vision of history is described by Giovanni Gentile: "History in real terms is the history of the concrete thinking act, with which the historian creates at once his historiography and his respective history; for this reason Mommsen wrote the history of Rome, but at the same time he projects onto the screen of reality, on which he investigates his own thought, a determined historical reality, a specific Rome, a Roman republic which is not that of Livius, nor that of anyone else who might have wished to know it." *Sistema di logica come teoria del conoscere*, 2nd ed. (Bari: Laterza, 1922), 2:251. The same idea may be found in B. Croce: "History is like the knowledge of the eternal present," in *Theory and History of Historiography*, edited by D. Ainslie (London: George G. Harrap, 1921), 47.

21. Thomas Aquinas writes: "The power and strength of things existent extends to that which is and that which will be, but not to that which once was; thus there is no need to attribute further possibilities to things past." *SCG* II, 84, no. 1686.

22. On this topic, see J. Ortega y Gasset, *Historia como sistema*, edited by J. Novella Suárez (Madrid: Biblioteca Nueva, 2001).

The third condition that marks a historical event is that it contributes to form and give shape to what we call history, that immeasurably vast symphony of events and effects, that unitary human reality, accumulated over time, that is the ultimate result of the intersection and intermingling of nature and events, of things and persons. Like nature, history in this sense seems to refer back to some kind of subject that acquires with the passage of time an ever richer and more definitive profile. This aspect of history as a single developing subject has been understood and explained, especially by Hegel.

Summing up, we may say that the historical event is the fruit of a human act that influences others and the world and, at the same time, reaches a permanent meaning, value, and content that contribute to the whole of reality. All three elements must be present simultaneously: freedom, efficacy for the collectivity, and unity (which entails permanence). The first (freedom) refers to the source of the historical event, the second (efficacy) to its realism and influence, and the third (unity) to its permanent reception. In anthropological terms, the first speaks of the individual, the second of the collectivity, the third of immortality. If one or another of the three was missing, it would be difficult to speak of historical events, and thus of the historicity of humanity.

Historical Interpretation

We have just said that the "historical event" is the concrete, free, external expression of individual thought. Still, we should add that the term "historical" is often understood in a different sense, referring not so much to the events themselves but to the interpretation of events. That events are open to interpretation indicates that they are relative and conditioned.[23] In effect, a reality (a form of thought or government, a law, a scientific theory, or a form of artistic expression) is often called "historical" in the sense that it has consolidated in a contingent way, is marked by a particularity given to it by a concrete moment, and it fuses later on with other realities that rise up out of contingency. In other words, what is "historical" would seem to belong not to what is permanent, to the truth, but simply to the things that pass; it has a relative and conditioned value, referred to the moment in which it took place. Thus historicity is a mark, for example, of culture, of the structures of sin, of popular customs, of languages, and so on. In its extreme version, this aspect of human historicity may be called "historicism."[24]

On account of the phenomenon of historical relativity, when we study a written document or a reality lived in another period or country, it is necessary for us to understand the cultural, social, and intellectual context of the period or country

---

23. On this issue, see M. Marassi, "Storia, filosofia della," in *Enciclopedia filosofica*, 11:11111–30.

24. According to "historicism," there is no such thing as "nature," because all is in flux. For this reason, in fact, history does not even exist. This position is defended in different ways by Dilthey, Troeltsch, Spengler, Mannheim, Ortega y Gasset, and Sartre. The following is the position of Ortega y Gasset: "Man has no nature. Man is not his body, but rather a drama.... Life is a gerundive and not a participle, a 'faciendum' and not a 'factum.' Life is doing, action." *Historia como sistema*, 32f. "History is the proper way of being of reality, whose substance, precisely, is variability; that is, the very opposite of all substance. Man is insubstantial. That is all we can say!" J. Ortega y Gasset, "Pasado y porvenir para el hombre actual," in *Obras completas* (Madrid: Alianza, 1983), 9:646f., translated into English as *History as a System, and Other Essays toward a Philosophy of History* (New York: Norton, 1961).

in question in order to be able to interpret it correctly. This process is usually called "hermeneutics." In effect, hermeneutics—the term means "interpretation"—is necessary precisely because thought is historical. According to Hans-Georg Gadamer, all knowledge *is* interpretation because the past—the flux of history—becomes more and more a substantial presupposition, one that is often unconscious, of our knowledge of the things that we encounter.[25]

Event and Interpretation

Now, how do the two meanings of the term "historical" relate? We can say that there are events that spring from free actions, but insofar as they are rooted in rational decisions they stand in need of interpretation. But who does the interpreting? And which of the two has priority: the event (free, efficacious, permanent), or the effect, insofar as it is conditioned and contingent and therefore open to interpretation? We may say that, in a strict sense, the former has precedence over the latter. If there were no historical events, events that have truly changed history, it would not be possible to speak of historical effects that change the epistemological categories of different periods and human situations and, in turn, require the application of hermeneutics. If all was fixed, if all was nature, if nothing changed, there would be no historical events or historical effects. There would therefore be no need to interpret history, only a need to know reality and, perhaps, know it ever better. All changes, however, would be apparent. Language in this case would not be a living reality that reflects meanings that change but would become ever more perfect and definitive in expressing the fixed richness of reality; in its meaning it would remain necessarily univocal with the passage of time. If things were what they were, truth would be more or less clear and a historically conditioned interpretation would become circumstantial and needless. All this would be verified should there be no historical events.[26] But because there *are* historical events, there will always be a need for hermeneutics. From this we may conclude that hermeneutics becomes necessary precisely because there have been and there are historical events that have changed the situations of individuals and societies, that have modified meaningfully our ways of thinking and understanding reality, that is, our fundamental epistemological categories.[27]

Before considering the need or otherwise for hermeneutics, what we need to show in the first place is that (1) historical events do take place that really influence the development and progress of humans and the world and (2) their influence is consistent and permanent. Once this has been established, it will be possible to reflect upon the

---

25. On the importance of hermeneutics Gadamer opines as follows: "The appearance of a historical consciousness is in all likelihood the most important revolution that has taken place after the coming of the modern age. Its spiritual contribution probably surpasses what we recognize as the contribution of the natural sciences, a contribution which has visibly transformed the life of our planet. Historical consciousness, which marks contemporary man, is a privilege (perhaps also a dead weight) which has not been imposed on any preceding generation." H.-G. Gadamer, *Le problème de la conscience historique* (Leuven: Publications universitaires de Louvain Béatrice-Nauwelaerts, 1963), 7.

26. K. Rahner tended to neglect precisely the historical side of the human being in the first sense, though not in the second, especially in his early work *Hearers of the Word*. On this topic, see Ratzinger, "Vom Verstehen des Glaubens"; Ratzinger, "Salvation and History," esp. 162–71.

27. See O'Callaghan, "Il compito della teologia," 48f.

question of a hermeneutic of history and to establish its workings and laws. In this chapter it shall be shown that our awareness of the realism of history is made possible to an important degree by Christian faith in the history of salvation. As Henri de Lubac put it, "Christianity is not a historical magnitude; rather history is a Christian magnitude."[28]

Pointers for an Understanding of History

We shall now consider a series of interpretations of the meaning of history, understood not from the angle of hermeneutics but from that of the dynamics of the historical event. Different ways may be suggested to understand human action and its permanent efficacy on humans, on society, and on the world within a temporal time frame. Each of them reflects, in real terms, different anthropologies, for the most part quite opposed to one another. Three principal interpretations may be given: that which is typical of Greek thought, founded on the image of a circle; the Christian view of history, represented by an ascending line (or spiral) that begins at creation and ends with eschatological consummation in God, fruit of the confluence of divine and human action; and, finally, the modern view of history—known from the time of Voltaire onward as the "philosophy of history"—symbolized again by an ascending line that derives from humanity and points back to it. Paradoxically, as we shall see, the position that denies history (the first) and that which affirms it as an autonomous reality (the third) end up coinciding with one another. And we shall see why the second position, the Christian view of history, which considers both God and humans as the true protagonists of history, is the only one fully capable of sustaining a solid historical understanding of humanity and society, the only one capable of keeping alive the possibility of a truly historical event.

Greek Determinism and the Myth of Eternal Return

The view in question is typical not only of the classical Greek world but also of many other peoples, cultures, philosophies, and religions. We begin with the cosmos—the earth, the moon, the sun, and the stars—and we observe a surprising regularity that marks the whole of it. Humans experience themselves, they act and understand themselves, as present within great cosmic cycles, those of the stars, of the sun, of the moon: days, weeks, months, years, and epochs follow one another, endlessly. At the same time, humans consider themselves not as superior to the universe but rather as a minor, subordinate, insignificant part of it. They also live under the dominion of the great cosmic cycles. In ancient times, stars generally were considered as divinities, immutable and immortal, to which humanity is meant to subject itself. Humans are what they appear to be: tiny insignificant motes of dust lost in the vastness of the universe or grains of salt that dissolve in the immense ocean of the cosmos, never to be found again. Because the whole of the universe turns continually in great circles, repeating these movements endlessly, humans take it for granted that they also share in this vast process of growth, decadence, destruction, death, and resurrection

28. De Lubac, *Paradoxes*, 108.

(on this topic, Mircea Eliade's book *The Myth of the Eternal Return* is a classic).[29] Small changes, variations, and minor modulations there may be, of course, but on the whole what happens today in the lives of humans is substantially identical to what happened yesterday and what will happen an infinite number of times in the future.

According to the Hindu cosmology described in the *Upanishads*, the following process may be verified. The universe develops and moves within cycles of enormous duration. One year of Brahma, that is, the ultimate reality present in every existing thing (what is often called "being"), is equivalent to three trillion solar years. Once the Brahma, in turn, has been repeated a hundred times, the whole world will be destroyed and everything will begin again "from nothing." Humans live within this process, reincarnating all the times it is necessary for them to purify and compensate, through good works, for the accumulated sum of their actions (*karma*) and obtain perfection.[30] Still, there is no stable, eternal end, no definitive consummation, at least in the Christian sense of the term.

According to Plato, every cosmic or social event reflects the fundamental paradigm of the eternal world of the ideas; time moves on in a cyclical process on the basis of a perfect, numerical proportion.[31] It is also true, however, that in the *Republic* Plato speaks of the human aspiration toward a perfect political constitution.[32] Also for Aristotle, the rotary movements of the heavens mark the cyclical eternity of time. In Greek thought, what is, what never changes, is the *periodos*, the period of rotation of the heavens.[33]

In Eastern thought as a whole, says Ethelbert Stauffer, "history is none other than a phenomenon within the cosmos."[34] Primacy is occupied not by the person, the individual in his free actions, but rather by the universal, the ideal. Only that which does not change, what is immutable, is real. The individual in his existence and action is a passing factor and communicates nothing substantially new to the future. All there is, is the typical, what is repeated time and again. This idea is to be found in the book of Qoelet (1:9), which solemnly states: "Nihil novum sub sole" (There is nothing new under the sun). In real terms, "Greek and Roman thinkers never thought that history was a linear work of human freedom."[35]

In any case, the cyclical doctrine typical of the ancient Greek world may be expressed in two different ways, one historiographical, the other metaphysical.[36]

The historiographical expression of eternal return   Ancient historians recounted history for two principal reasons. Some, as in the case of Thucydides in his *Peloponnesian Wars*, did so in order to study the dynamics of the cycles of development within

---

29. See Eliade, *Cosmos and History.*

30. On the meaning of reincarnation in the context of Christian faith, see *COH* 76–78.

31. Plato, *Timaeus* 33a–38e.

32. Aristotle, *Physica* 223b19.

33. See H.-G. Gadamer, "Die Kontinuität der Geschichte und der Augenblick der Existenz," in Gadamer, *Kleine Schriften* I: *Philosophie, Hermeneutik* (Tubingen: J. C. B. Mohr, 1967), 149–60, 154f.

34. E. Stauffer, cited by M. Schmaus, *Katholische Dogmatik*, IV/2: *Von den letzten Dingen* (Munich: M. Hueber, 1953), § 293.

35. Cruz, *Filosofía de la historia*, 95.

36. For the following, see especially J. L. Illanes, "La historia entre el nihilismo y la afirmación del sentido," *Anuario filosófico* 27, no. 1 (1993): 95–111; Cruz, *Filosofía de la historia.*

society, to discover the common traits of human psychology that are always repeated, cyclically, from one age to the next. What has taken place is studied and recounted in order to ensure that in the future, when things of a similar kind recur, people will know what to do because the same things will repeat time and again in the life of the world. Paradoxically, history is studied *because there is no history*, because there are no meaningful epochal changes. Cicero designates historiography as the "lux veritatis" (the light of truth), and elsewhere he says: "Historia magistra vitae" (History is the teacher of life).[37] Others, for example, Herodotus in his *Histories*, recount events with a slightly different end in mind, that of ensuring that the great works and gestures of heroes are not forgotten, especially those of the battlefield. The ultimate purpose that Herodotus proposes coincides in real terms with that of Thucydides, because telling history is a matter, above all, of providing a criterion or an inspiration for future generations to behave as did their forebears, not so much a matter of knowing what "really" happened, as if the historical event was of value in itself. In brief, the historical event is "typical," not singular.

The metaphysical expression of eternal return   The cyclical vision of the Greeks is also expressed in a metaphysical mode. It is said not only that the same kind of event is repeated in a cyclical way as historiography but that the same material and spiritual world turns and returns eternally with slight, non-permanent modulations and variations. Prime matter and spirit are eternal and indestructible, and in their perpetual dialectical interaction a constant process is verified—a process of growth, maturity, decay, death, new birth, and so on.

The two expressions of the doctrine of eternal return are often confused and mixed with one another, but they are not identical. The first is acceptable from many points of view; it is certainly not contrary to a Christian view of history, precisely in that the latter does not intend to leave aside human and cosmic nature, which is determined and perennial, which finds expression in the laws of history. "La nature est toujours la même," said D'Alembert in an already cited expression. And in a phrase commonly attributed to Mark Twain: "History does not repeat itself, but it does rhyme." The second form of the doctrine of eternal return, however, the metaphysical one, is not reconcilable with Christian doctrine of creation and the history of salvation. Let us see why.

The metaphysical vision is present, for example, in the fifth-century B.C. philosopher Empedocles and especially among the Stoics.[38] According to the latter, the universe is subject to constant transformations, fluctuations, generations, and corruptions until a final conflagration is produced, with the destruction of all individuals, leaving only the principles and eternal forms. After this "annihilation," the process begins once again with a new universe. This means that there is no creative novelty in being; in fact, this implies a kind of pantheism, because the divinity is directly involved in the process. From the anthropological and ethical point of view, the result of the Stoic understanding of the world consists of the idealization of necessity,

---

37. Cicero, *De Oratore* II, 9.

38. See E. R. Bevan, *Stoics and Sceptics* (Oxford: Clarendon Press, 1913); M. L. Colish, *The Stoic Tradition from Antiquity to the Early Middle Ages* (Leiden: E. J. Brill, 1985).

with the elimination of the efficacy of individual free will. Humans must necessarily identify themselves with their proper destiny, excluding from their own hearts all the noble human aspirations toward infinity and personal realization, accepting—stoically, as it is said—the contingent situation as it is because, in spite of appearances, there is no real change, no true growth or decadence. In spite of the human desire to improve the world, there is no hope. This view provides is a kind of asceticism, a bitter, passive, resigned "spirituality," based on the faithful fulfillment of the impersonal and inflexible "will" of the cosmos. The second-century philosopher and Roman emperor Marcus Aurelius directs the following "prayer" to the cosmos: "All that is in harmony with you, O Cosmos, is in harmony with me. Whatever for you comes at the right moment, for me is neither too early nor too late. For you are all things, in you are all things, to you all things return."[39]

An anthropological critique of eternal return   The doctrine of eternal return is based on a noble, firm, serene philosophical vision that is capable of producing good for the individual and for society. However, it is totally lacking in optimism, hope, and joy because it includes no possibility of a better future life, no novelty of divine *kairos*, no salvation history, no divine promise. In effect, as Karl Löwith notes, in the cyclical visions of the world hope is absent because no new future is expected.[40] The future, in effect, relates to the past in a purely specular way and does nothing but replicate it. The ultimate result for human life is therefore tedium, emptiness, a sense of futility. All the same things come back again and again, all is determined and produced inexorably; no alienation is definitively overcome; no war is won forever.

Augustine, who has a particularly deep understanding of ancient thought, was well aware of the doctrine of eternal return and criticized it harshly for anthropological reasons in the light of Christian faith and hope: "I cannot imagine a more terrible vision than this one," he says.[41] And in his work *De Civitate Dei* he describes in a graphic, ironic way how Socrates will marry time and again the fearsome Xanthippe, how he will drink the poison any number of times, how he will discuss deep questions with the Sophists again and for ever, without rest, without success.[42] Augustine presents all this within his wide vision of humanity aspiring to definitive and eschatological fullness, perfect goodness and happiness, all emerging from the human heart under God's grace.[43] And he realizes that, in spite of certain points of contact he had with ancient thought, the divide between Christianity and Greek thought on this front is insuperable.

A scientific and theological critique of eternal return   Besides the difficulties of an anthropological and ethical kind present in the theory of eternal return, there are others of a scientific and theological nature. Copernicus, in the fifteenth century, showed that the world is not the center of the universe but simply a planet that spins around

---

39. Marcus Aurelius, *Soliloquia* 4, 23.

40. "The pagan doctrine is hopeless, for hope and faith are essentially related to the future, and a real future cannot exist if past and future times are equal phases within a cyclic recurrence without beginning and end." Löwith, *Meaning in History*, 163.

41. Augustine, *Epist.* 166, 9.   42. Augustine, *De Civ. Dei* XII, 20.

43. See *COH* 158f.

the sun. After him, Kepler showed besides that the orbits of the planets are not circular but in fact elliptical. Nowadays, physicists are convinced that the universe is not a simple fixed space but rather a process of expansion and even of growth.[44] From the theological point of view, Augustine explains that according to the Greeks, God, when he formed the finite world, employed a finite number of reasons. Sooner or later, therefore, the things he made should by rights come back again and again and thus repeat indefinitely.[45] A similar argument is used by Plotinus and Nietzsche.[46] The error of this explanation, says Augustine, lies in the fact that "it measures the divine mind with the human mind that is mutable and limited, while God is absolutely immutable and infinite and capable of numerating all the innumerable things without changing his thought."[47] The infinity of God leaves open the possibility of the verification of a potentially infinite number of different events.

The Christian View of History

The Christian economy, based on an all-powerful, eternal, and infinite God making himself present in the world and in all human affairs, culminating in the incarnation of the Word, Jesus Christ, breaks decisively with the cyclical vision of history typical of ancient thought. In fact, times do not repeat; the successive stages are not entirely typical and foreseeable; there are net and definitive changes, realities that come on the scene that were not present beforehand, although they may have been the objects of prophetic promise. According to scripture, in fact, time is not only *chronos*, time that passes, but also *plēroma*, future plenitude that has taken place in Christ and is directed toward eschatological fullness; more specifically, time is *kairos*, occasion, opportunity, a moment of grace, the unforeseeable intervention of God in history.[48] On the basis of the foundational event of creation, in effect, a series of unpredictable events begin to take place in which we can observe a powerful interplay between divine action and human reaction: the sin by which humans rejected the friendship God offered them, followed by the work of salvation through the word and power of God made present within human history itself, the predictions of the prophets. And above all, the culminating, determinative moment of this history is the incarnation of the eternal Word, Jesus Christ.

The scope of the incarnation of the Word   In simple yet profound terms we may say that before the event of the incarnation, God was not incarnate; afterward, he was, he is now, and he will be: so forever, for "His kingdom will be without end" (Lk 1:33),

---

44. See *COH* 45f.; G. F. R. Ellis, *The Far-Future Universe: Eschatology from a Cosmic Perspective* (Philadelphia: Templeton Foundation Press, 2002).

45. See Augustine, *De Civ. Dei* XII, 13; Cruz, *Filosofía de la historia*, 96f.

46. See Plotinus, *Enn.* V, 7, 2, and K. Löwith, *Nietzsche's Philosophy of the Eternal Recurrence of the Same* (Berkeley: University of California Press, 1997), 169–88.

47. Augustine, *De Civ. Dei* XII, 13.

48. On the question of time in scripture, see J. M. Casciaro, "El tiempo y la historia en San Pablo," in *Estudios sobre la cristología del Nuevo Testamento* (Pamplona: Eunsa, 1982), 335–57; BDAG, 1092, s.v. χρόνος; 829f., s.v. πλήρωμα; BDAG 497f., NIDNTTE 2:586–92, s.v. καιρός. See also J. Mouroux, *Le mystère du temps: Approche théologique* (Paris: Aubier-Montaigne, 1962). On Mouroux, see the careful study of P. A. Benítez Mestre, *La teología del tiempo según Jean Mouroux* (Rome: Edusc, 2009).

a phrase repeated literally in the symbol of faith, the creed.[49] In other words, God intervenes, he changes the course of history without changing himself—he changes history in a creative, loving, and efficacious way without destroying the past (except insofar as sin is present in it) but bringing creation to full reconciliation and plenitude. With the incarnation, Augustine says as he comments on the doctrine of eternal return, "circuitus illi iam explosi sunt" (those circles have been obliterated).[50] The incarnation of the Word (which includes, of course, the entire life, death, and resurrection of Jesus), is the most decisive and efficacious historical event that has ever taken place because (1) it changed the course of history in a radical, almost unrecognizable, way and also because (2) it sets the stage for what will bring human history to its fulfillment and completion with the Parousia. It is an event that fulfills the second and third conditions mentioned earlier for a particular human action to be counted as a "historical event": the saving incarnation is efficacious with respect to the collectivity and contributes and gives definitive consistency to history as a whole. "Propter te [Verbum Dei] factus est temporalis, ut tu fias aeternus," says Augustine, "For you the Word of God became temporal so that you might become eternal."[51] But what can be said of the first condition for something to be counted as a "historical event," the fundamental one, that of the exercise of human freedom? Does that take place when the Word becomes incarnate? Would it not be more correct to say that the incarnation of the Word is, above all, a divine act that takes place within our history but not, properly speaking, a human historical event?

The role of Mary   We should add here, in fact, that the incarnation of the Word, God's greatest and in a sense only gift to humankind—because in it all his gifts are included and their meaning revealed—becomes possible and concrete through human collaboration (or cooperation), that of Mary of Nazareth, and later on through the human obedience of Jesus (Jn 10:17; Heb 10:7–9) and that of humans. The forebears of humanity, Adam and Eve, had "made history" with their free, historical rejection of God's grace at the beginning of creation. This event, as a culpable refusal to accept divine friendship, had truly changed the course of history, drawing humans away from their true end.[52] Now Mary, the new Eve, accepts and embraces in the name of all the greatest grace possible, the very source of grace for humanity, Jesus Christ, because "from his fullness have we all received, grace upon grace" (Jn 1:16). Accepting God's call in the apparent passivity, silence, and everydayness of her prayer, she is the human being who, under the inspiration of the Holy Spirit, changes definitively the course of human history, making definitive communion with God possible.[53] Her finite, free, time-bound, apparently modest act makes the infinite work of redemption and divinization possible.

It is clear, therefore, that the incarnation of the Word is not a "typical" event, one

49. *DH* 150.

50. Augustine, *De Civ. Dei* XII, 20, 4.

51. Augustine, *In I Io.*, 2, 10.

52. On original sin as an "event," see O'Callaghan, *La metafísica cristiana*, 250–53. See also O'Callaghan, "Una lectura cristológica de la doctrina del pecado original."

53. "Congruum fuit beatae Virgini annuntiari quod esset Christum conceptura.... Quarto, ut ostenderetur esse quoddam spirituale matrimonium inter Filium Dei et humanam naturam. Et ideo per annuntiationem expetebatur consensus virginis loco totius humanae naturae." Aquinas, *S.Th.* III, q. 30, q. 1, co.

among many that could be repeated any number of times, but an event that is totally singular and unrepeatable.[54] This is referred to frequently in the letter to the Hebrews when the term "ephapax" (only one time) is repeatedly applied to the life and saving work of Christ, expressing its universal sufficiency and efficacy. In effect, "He has no need, like those high priests, to offer sacrifices daily, first for his own sins and then for those of the people; he did this *once for all* when he offered up himself" (Heb 7:27).[55] Irenaeus insists particularly on the once-off, or non-typical, character of the incarnation against the Gnostics.[56] We could say that Christ, God's *only* Son, in saving humanity from sin through the *only* supreme and definitive sacrifice on the cross, becomes the One who gives to each one the possibility of establishing with God, within time, a personal and unrepeatable relationship.

The incarnation of the Word as a manifestation of the historicity of human life   From what we have just seen, we can say that the incarnation is the very event that reveals and "makes historical" (free, efficacious, and definitive before God) all the particular actions of humans. It is not as if such actions were not historical before the coming of Christ. But in the light of the incarnation of the Word, which takes place "only once," we begin to read human history in a new way, in the light of faith, as a process that is irreversible and unique. This faith-vision decisively excludes a pure deterministic specularity between past and future based on the doctrine of eternal return. To this may be added that with the free human act that is projected toward the future in a non-predetermined way, neither past nor future is destroyed or dissolved. What has been obtained and established in the historical present is carried ahead and, in a certain sense, assumed forever by history.[57] For this reason history cannot be seen as a mere succession of more or less relevant events that pass on, each one of them falling into the scrapheap of irrelevance or forgetfulness. Rather, what constitutes the life and identity of humans is their history, their biography, narrative, or drama. Through it they consolidate freely and gradually their own identity, eternity, and destiny until the end of time. The end of history coincides, therefore, with the fulfillment or consummation of history: this takes place for each individual at death,[58] and for the whole created universe, at the Parousia, or definitive return of Christ.[59] In other words, for the Christian history is rooted and understood always as a kind of history of salvation, and history in a general sense, though not to be identified with salvation history, receives its ultimate meaning from this story of grace, of sin, and of salvation.

Sacred and profane history   Hegel said that "all history moves toward Christ and from Christ. The appearance of the Son of God is the axis of history."[60] However, the way in which Christ reveals the sense of history is based on faith. Therefore, observes Karl Jaspers, "the flaw in this view of history is that it can have meaning only for be-

---

54. On this point Christianity is clearly distinct from the Hinduism of the *Bhagavad-gita*, according to which the "incarnations" of the divinity (*avatara*) repeat cyclically. See C. Dawson, "The Christian View of History," in Dawson, *The Dynamics of World History* (London: Sheed and Ward, 1957), 233–50, 236.

55. See Heb 9:12, 26, 28; 10:2. On the term, see *BDAG*, 97, s.v. ἅπαξ; 417, s.v. ἐφάπαξ.

56. See Irenaeus, *Adv. Haer.* III, 16, 6.   57. See *COH* 109–12.

58. See O'Callaghan, "La muerte del cristiano."   59. See *COH* 39–73.

60. Cited by Jaspers in *Way to Wisdom*, 99.

lieving Christians." However, he adds: "Even Western Christians have not built their empirical view of history on their faith but have drawn an essential distinction between sacred and profane history."[61] In effect, sacred history should not be confused with profane history. Still, it is true that sacred history has always offered a warm and powerful light with which to understand the meaning of universal history as a whole, just as the "pressure" of the supernatural brings us to fully understand the natural in its inner dynamic and ultimate end. The incarnation of the Word, indeed the whole of salvation history, has awakened humans' appetite for history—and not just for the lessons history offers (these can easily be manipulated and turned into ideology) but also for real history in itself, because history is where persons act freely.

Augustine was among the first Christian thinkers to come up with a true and proper "theology of history."[62] In his work *De Civitate Dei* he explains that there are three human "histories" that interact with one another. In the first place, the history of the "city of God," that is, the progressive formation of redeemed humanity, which finds ultimate expression in eternal life. Then there is the history of sin, that of the destruction and damage wrought by humanity's refusal to accept God's gifts, a history that, like the first, could conceivably become permanent if humans close themselves off from God definitively. Third and finally, there is the history of the human city, that of society, which can be studied, documented, and analyzed with greater or lesser precision. The first two are of a mystical or transcendent kind and are difficult to describe and profile empirically, although they are extremely real and influential, because they "pressurize" empirical history; in fact, only God knows fully their meaning and development. Perhaps "providence" would be a better term to designate them.

Still, these three "histories" all meet and intermingle in a myriad of ways. But the city of God and the city of men are mixed with one another during the Church's earthly pilgrimage and are not easy to distinguish at an empirical level, like the grain and the weeds the Gospels speak of (Mt 13:24ff.).[63] The twentieth-century philosopher Raymond Aron observes: "Humans make history, but they do not know the history they make."[64] Discernment between different "histories" and the definitive manifestation of history will take place only at the end of time with final judgment. Only then will we be able to know with certitude where good and evil lie and have been situated. We might add that Augustine's attempt to explain history, even though it was pioneering and very influential, offers quite a negative and pessimistic view of humanity and the world.

---

61. Ibid.

62. See C. Dawson, "Augustine and the City of God (1930)," in *The Dynamics of World History* (London: Sheed and Ward, 1957), 294–325; W. Kamlah, *Christentum und Geschichtlichkeit: Untersuchungen zur Entstehung des Christentums und zu Augustinus "Bürgerschaft Gottes,"* 2nd ed. (Stuttgart: W. Kohlhammer, 1951); J. L. Illanes, "Historia VI: Teología de la historia," *Gran Enciclopedia Rialp* (1972): 27–33; G. Baget-Bozzo, "La teología de la historia en la 'Ciudad de Dios,'" *Augustinus* 35 (1990): 321–65.

63. Jesus speaks in the Gospel of the fact that the people are "with him" or "against him," those who gather with him and those who scatter (Mt 12:30). Elsewhere he says that "he that is not against us is for us" (Mk 9:40). Yet this belonging to Jesus or otherwise will not be perfectly clear until the end of time (Mt 25:31–46).

64. R. Aron, *Introduction à la philosophie de l'histoire: Essai sur les limites de l'objectivité,* 8th ed. (Paris: Gallimard, 1948), 168, translated into English as *Introduction to the Philosophy of History: An Essay on the Limits of Historical Objectivity* (Boston: Beacon Press, 1961), 168.

Among the different ways in which Christians have considered history, we can distinguish between two models, two ways of interpreting it: the apologistic and the apocalyptic. The former attempts to understand history by looking toward the past, the latter by moving toward our future hope.

The apologistic interpretation of history   According to the apologistic view, history is considered in the main as the development and fulfillment of the past. It is an understanding that became frequent with the establishment of the Christianity as a state religion. In effect, from the time of the Edict of Milan (313), under Constantine, Christianity gradually became the official religion of the Roman Empire, systematic persecution of Christians came to end, and evangelization was facilitated. This situation occasioned also a tendency toward a certain superficiality and decadence in Christian life: "Since the Church gained princes for its cause," writes Jerome at the end of the fourth century, "it grew in power and riches, but diminished in virtue."[65] History was understood in an optimistic way, according to which the past (coinciding more or less with the history of the Roman Empire) is considered to constitute a kind of positive preparation for the Gospel, a *praeparatio evangelica*, which is part of divine providence, that facilitates the preaching of the Gospel and the advent of the Christian religion. This position is explained in detail by Eusebius of Caesarea in his work *Ecclesiastical History*. The Roman Empire, he says, is fused irrevocably with the universal kingdom of Christ. The kingdom of Christ is established firmly on earth, and the emperor is his representative. Herman Dörries sums up Eusebius's understanding in the following formula: "One God, one *Logos*, one emperor."[66] This vision of history is characterized by the expression "Pax Romana, pax Christiana" (The peace of Rome is the origin and guarantee of Christian peace). For developing this theory Eusebius came to be known as "the first political theologian of the Christian Church."[67]

This position was maintained solidly for many centuries in regions where Christianity was the dominant religion of the Empire. An interesting description of this position, though somewhat exaggerated, overly optimistic, and ingenuous, may be found in the work of Otto von Freising, *Chronicon sive historia de duabus civitatibus*, from the early twelfth century. He says: "I have attempted to write the history of the two cities, that of God and that of man. Looking closely at the facts, however, I have come to realize that the two merge with one another when kings and peoples are all Christian. In fact there is only one city, the *civitas christiana*, the Church of kings and peoples, and therefore only one history."[68] Otto is speaking of a society in which all were Christians, in which it was common to speak of the "holy Roman empire," of the divine right of kings, who enjoyed a power similar to that of the pope, by whom they were crowned. We can say that to some degree the notion of the Church as pilgrim and missionary, sent by the Spirit to imitate and propagate the simple life of its

---

65. Jerome, *Vita Mal. Monach.* 1.

66. H. Dörries, *Konstantin der Grosse* (Stuttgart: Kohlhammer, 1958), 146f. translated into English as *Constantine the Great* (New York: Beacon Books, 1962).

67. H. Eger, "Kaiser und Kirche in der Geschichtstheologie Eusebs von Ceasarea," *Zeitschrift für die Neutestamentliche Wissenschaft* 38 (1939): 97–115.

68. Otto of Freising, "Chronicon sive historia de duabus civitatibus," in *Monumenta Germaniae Historica* (Hannover: Hahn, 1978), 20:83–301.

founder, had been lost. The citizen was, indeed had to be, automatically a Christian, even by force. Besides, Christian holiness was in practice considered something exceptional because it was destined for the few.

This position was maintained, with a variety of nuances, more or less during the Renaissance period, right up to beginnings of modernity. Among the last authors to defend it we find the great seventeenth-century preacher Jacques-Bénigne Bossuet, who teaches in his work *Discours sur l'histoire universelle* (1681) that the Church is nothing other than "a society of peoples of Christian confession." According to Bossuet, everything that happens is situated within God's plans, and history is simply the map opened by divine providence. This affirmation might be valid were it not for the fact that Bossuet and others were tempted to provide concrete and univocal interpretations of divine providence, rationalizing it, reducing it to a purely human level, and in that way instrumentalizing it. As an example, Bossuet held that the defeat of England by France guided by Joan of Arc in the fifteenth century was a clear sign that God did not want France and England to be united. In response to this it can be said that providence exists, but only God, as Augustine reminded us, knows the complexity of its interactions.[69] In a text already cited, Raymond Aron said that "humans make history, but they do not know the history they make."

The apologistic understanding of history, consolidated over many centuries, has lost its influence in the modern epoch, and this is due in part to the experiences and challenges of evangelizing the new world, in part to a more spiritualist and invisible view of the action of the Church and God that arose with Protestantism, in part due to the terribly destructive Thirty Years War, and in part due to the Enlightenment, within which humans began to consider their own dignity and rights on an exclusively anthropological, autonomous basis, and not so much on the basis of God's creative, saving, and providential action in Christ.[70]

The apocalyptic interpretation of history   The other typically Christian understanding of history looks not toward the past, as fertile ground in which God gradually prepares the advent of his kingdom, but rather toward the future, in which the eschatological promises that God revealed in Christ will at last reach fulfillment.[71] According to this interpretation, the past is considered as a world of darkness, of sin, of unintelligibility; the future however, is seen as the promised moment of light and liberation. This way of looking on history typically tends to consolidate during world history (differently from the apologist vision) in moments of special difficulty, of the persecution of believers, of the precariousness of their lives. Besides, the living promise of the Parousia was particularly alive in the early times of the Church. All this facilitated the growth of an apocalyptic understanding of history. Besides, the New Testament (Rv 20:4–7) speaks of the advent of the millennium (from which derives the term "millennialism" or "chilialism."[72] In effect, among the early Church

69. See O'Callaghan, *La metafisica cristiana*, 173–83.

70. See also Vatican Council II, *Dignitatis Humanae*, December 7, 1965.

71. On the central place occupied by the apocalyptic and the eschatological in the Christian theological view, see O'Callaghan, *The Christological Assimilation.*

72. On millennialism, see *COH* 241–49. The term "chilialism" comes from the Greek *chilos*, one thousand.

Fathers (Justin, Irenaeus, and, for a period of his life, Tertullian) the idea was commonly held that in a short space of time a new epoch would be inaugurated on earth, lasting for a thousand years, in which the devil would be chained and the world governed by Christ and the saints. At the end of this period the devil would be unleashed again, it was said, and after a period of intense trial and persecution for Christians, Christ would come again definitively with the Parousia. These understandings gradually became obsolete as the Christian Church became firmly established in society, even though they have reappeared not infrequently throughout history, especially in moments of trial and persecution and around the turn of the millennium.

Of particular interest is the doctrine of the Calabrian abbot Joachim da Fiore, who was especially influential after his death at the end of the twelfth century.[73] This author spoke of three epochs or ages in human history: that of the Old Testament, in which God the Father acted, an epoch marked by the law and by slavery and personified by married people; that of the New Testament, the epoch of God the Son, characterized by liberation from the law, in which the point of reference was the Christian priesthood, the ecclesiastical hierarchy, the visible Church; and the epoch of the Holy Spirit, an epoch of perfect and spontaneous freedom in which human mediations will no longer be needed in order to receive God's grace, in which an anti-hierarchical attitude toward the Church will consolidate, and in which the point of reference is consecrated life. Some of Joachim's followers (for example, the so-called spiritual Franciscans) even suggested a date for the beginning of the new and definitive world age, the year 1260 A.D.

Of course the doctrines of Joachim, if wrongly interpreted, contain significant theological difficulties as regards ethics (the attempt to go beyond positive and natural law), the role of states in the Church (the relationship between laity, priests, and religious), and above all with respect to the doctrine of the Trinity, because it would seem that the action of the three persons is successive or even disconnected.[74] Augustine had already said that "inseparabilia sunt opera Trinitatis" (the works of the Trinity are inseparable) from one another.[75] The Fourth Lateran Council, celebrated in 1215, convoked among other reasons to clarify the position of Joachim, insisted on the simple unity of the three persons: "Tres quidem personae, sed una essentia, substantia seu natura simplex omnino" (Three persons, but only one essence, substance, that is, nature, that is absolutely simple).[76] The same Council took a position in favor of Peter Lombard when he affirmed that God—Father, Son, and Holy Spirit—is

73. See M. Reeves, *Joachim of Fiore and the Prophetic Future* (London: SPCK, 1976); H. Mottu, *La manifestation de l'Esprit selon Joachim de Flore: Herméneutique et théologie de l'histoire d'après le "Traité sur les Quatre Evangiles"* (Neuchatel: Delachaux et Niestlé, 1977); D. C. West and S. L. Zimdars-Swartz, *Joachim di Fiori: A Study in Spiritual Perception and History* (Bloomington: Indiana University Press, 1983); J. Grzeszczak, *Dall'età dello Spirito Santo al New Age: Gioacchino da Fiore nella nuova religiosità* (Rome: Pontificio Ateneo della Santa Croce, 1997); O'Callaghan, "L'agire dello Spirito Santo," 349–54; A. Stagliano, *L'Abate calabrese: Fede cattolica nella Trinità e pensiero teologico della storia in Gioacchino da Fiore* (Vatican City: Vaticana, 2013).

74. Joachim was criticized by Bonaventure. See J. Ratzinger, *Die Geschichtstheologie des heiligen Bonaventura* (Munich: Schnell und Steiner, 1959). He was also criticized by Thomas Aquinas. See J.-I. Saranyana, *Joaquín de Fiore y Tomás de Aquino: Historia doctrinal de una polémica* (Pamplona: Eunsa, 1979). See also the critique of H. de Lubac in note 79.

75. Augustine, *Sermo* 213, 6.

76. *DH* 800.

"one single supreme reality,"[77] an affirmation that was considered "heretical and non-sensical" by Joachim.[78] Besides, the doctrine of Joachim seems to suggest that God's action in a sense does not really take nature into account and does not respect the laws inscribed into it or the sacramental economy established with the incarnation of the Word. In a great variety of forms, the position of Joachim has arisen again and again in philosophies throughout the second millennium, from Hegel to Marx, from Engels to Nietzsche.[79]

Still, taking into account the pessimism present in Augustine's influential position, the apocalyptic view of history has the advantage of emphasizing the positive value of history, of great human events, as a series of singular moments, moments of grace, occasions and opportunities (*kairoi*) created by God to make humans partake in the God's saving plan. This point was made by Joseph Ratzinger in his study of the history of salvation in Bonaventure.[80]

History and hope   In spite of the appearances, both positions—the apologistic and the apocalyptic—have shared a common view of Christian hope, which only with an extreme interpretation can become problematic. Hope, in fact, is an infused virtue that comes from God and has God as its proper object; hence its presence and efficacy cannot be measured, calibrated, or understood within worldly parameters, either as regards the past (God's great works, or *magnalia Dei*) or as regards his future intervention in history (the return of Christ in glory).[81] Christians look upon the world and on history in a contemplative but humble way, in a committed but modest way, with a gaze of faith and hope. Grace and the virtues act with the chiaroscuro of saving grace won by Christ on the cross and received by humans. Saving grace cannot be measured empirically, nor is it open to human analysis. At the same time, with both interpretations the path toward the secularization of Christian faith (and of the Christian view of history) has been facilitated. Let us now consider this experience.

The Enlightenment as a Secularization of the Christian Vision of History

The modern understanding of history, like the Christian one, may be expressed with the symbol of a line, an ascending line, which suggests the growth and progress of humanity, in which is affirmed both the realism and the efficacy of individual freedom over nature and society with respect to the construction of the future and the one-way and unrepeatable path of human history as it moves toward its culmination. The principal difference, however, between the Christian and the modern secularized view lies in the fact that the latter constitutes a closed and hermetic process because any intervention of God in his mysterious, gratuitous, and creative providence is excluded.[82] As Ernst Troeltsch says, "Modern thought is affirmed as an autonomous

---

77. DH 803f.   78. Ibid.

79. This process has been carefully considered in the ample study of H. de Lubac, *La postérité spirituelle de Joachim de Flore*, 2 vols. (Paris: Lethielleux Culture et vérité, 1979).

80. See note 74.

81. See *COH* 39–73.

82. On the modern philosophy of history, see C. Dawson, *The Dynamics of World History* (London: Sheed and Ward, 1957); Walsh, *An Introduction to the Philosophy of History*; Cruz, *Filosofía de la historia*.

and mundane formation before a theological formation."[83] Historically speaking, several factors have facilitated the process of the secularization of the notion of history, among them the development of science and technology and the secularization of the practice of Christian faith (see chapter 2).

The first is the development of science and its follow-up, technology and the Industrial Revolution. The development of science and technology reinforced humans' conviction of their capacity to dominate nature and the world, controlling them, transforming and improving them, even without God's help. Knowledge became less and less identified with wisdom, which moves toward contemplation, joyful recognition, and an ever-deeper understanding of reality (in fact, it refers ultimately to the world's mysterious maker) and more identified as an accumulation of technical data with which it becomes possible to control and dominate the world ever more effectively. Over recent centuries we have observed an unprecedented development of the sciences, the Encyclopedist movement, technology, and the Industrial Revolution, in which humans attempt to "enclose" all human knowledge in an accessible whole of ordered parts; in that way, it was thought, humanity would be capable of dominating all that can be known.

The second factor in the secularization of history is that the practice of Christian faith has been tending to diminish in modern times, while a secularized view of the world has been developing, at least in certain ambits. In a sense people attempt to hold onto the fruits of the rich humanism that Christian faith and life have made possible within thought and human civilization (the notion of the dignity and value of the person, freedom and human rights, a universal society, the equality of all, love, socialization, history, etc.). It seems as if modernity has disconnected from its living, ultimate source: people have held onto the gifts while letting go of the divine giver.[84] The action of a provident God who moves history as its Lord—an action that humans are invited to recognize and join with commitment, intelligence, freedom, effort, and above all gratitude and praise—has been replaced by humans themselves, who act in society, to design the world as they want it to be within a process that is more accessible and easier to control but closed in on itself. In fact, within this process religion has come to be considered by some as a way of escaping from worldly responsibility, that is, as the "opium of the people," to use the words of Karl Marx, by others as an obstacle to progress. The motors of history are no longer providence and divine grace but autonomous work, the work of humans in the world along with others. The dogma of original sin is for the most part left aside, and a somewhat ingenuous optimism prevails alongside a conviction that human progress is necessary and inevitable. Perhaps God is considered as the one who has set the process going, but the world no longer returns the compliment by directing its adoring, grateful gaze toward its one and only Lord.[85] Two protagonists of this period may be mentioned: Voltaire and Comte.

---

83. E. Troeltsch, *Aufsätze zur Geistesgeschichte und Religionssoziologie* (Tubingen: J. C. B. Mohr, 1925), 7.

84. See O'Callaghan, "La relación entre modernidad y evangelización."

85. See the ample analysis undertaken by Taylor, *A Secular Age*. On this work, see O'Callaghan, "The Eclipse of Worship."

Voltaire's "philosophy of history"   Voltaire (F.-M. Arouet), in his 1756 *Essai sur le moeurs et l'esprit des nations*, is among the first to speak openly of a true "philosophy of history," consciously avoiding any kind of theology of history based on the history of salvation. In this vision, all divine "interventions" are excluded: providence, grace, judgment, reward, punishment. Not only that: Voltaire excludes the doctrine of original sin and renders that of salvation irrelevant.[86] God exists, certainly, but as mere guarantor of the workings of the world, which he set in motion in past ages. This is a deist approach to the world, described with the image of the watchmaker God, of God as the great architect, as the *deus ex machina*. But God, once the world was in movement, left it in the hands of humans. They are the only ones in a position to control the earth; with fatigue and effort they give the world the form it has, its shape, its *telos*, its purpose. With Voltaire the scope and value of human freedom becomes almost absolute,[87] to the point that the existence of others as free beings is seen at times as a limit and threat to the rest instead of being the source of and opportunity for the exercise of one's free will as charity. Voltaire considers humans as beings that determine themselves and, as a result, govern the whole world, designing autonomously the course of their own history. The individualistic logic of Luther, present in his work *De servo arbitrio* (which teaches that as long as God is free, humans cannot but be slaves) is turned radically around: "If humans are free, then God is not," and "If humans act, then God does not."

Comte's scientific sociology   Auguste Comte, the nineteenth-century founding father of modern sociology, offers a new and influential interpretation of history of a scientific kind.[88] He speaks of three successive stages in the history of the world and of thought. The first is the stage of theology, centered on myth and meant for primitive peoples (where humans trust divinities in an uncritical way); the second is the stage of philosophy, centered on reason and on the contemplation of truth (in which humans come to know the mysteries of the universe through reason and remain immobile before them); and the third is the stage of science, positive knowledge of facts, which brings humans to action (here things are known with clarity, without the obscurity that characterizes the mysteries). The first stage is that of the child, the immature person; the second is that of the adolescent, going through different stages of crisis and growth; and the third is that of the adult, serene master of his own life and destiny. Besides, growth in knowledge is attributed not so much to the maturation of individuals, but to that of humanity itself and of the world as a whole (here there is a clear resonance with Hegel).

Certainly this is an optimistic period for human thought, the occasion of important intellectual, scientific, and cultural enrichment for humanity. Humans are taught to trust themselves and their own resources, their own capacities to resolve problems. It would seem that they no longer stand in need of salvation, of the Church, of God. The "dogma" of "necessary progress" begins to consolidate, according to which things

---

86. See Voltaire, "Whatever is right," *Philosophical Dictionary*, 351–59, 358.

87. Ibid., 284ff.

88. See A. Comte, *The Positive Philosophy*, edited by H. Martineau (New York: AMS Press, 1974). For a critique of the position of Comte, see Walsh, *An Introduction to the Philosophy of History*, 155–58.

improve inevitably in the world, at all levels, perhaps in spite of appearances. In a special way an interesting idea emerges that has never really been uttered throughout the history of Christianity: that human history will be fulfilled within history itself. In other words, Christian eschatology itself passes through a secularizing process because humans are considered to construct their own future and bring the world to achieve its ultimate purpose. The perfections and possibilities available to humans remain closed within this world as it is, placed fully at the disposal of humans.[89]

The limits of the modern vision of history   The modern vision of history is certainly attractive in the sense that humans see themselves as exclusive, responsible, and irreplaceable protagonists of the adventure of their own lives and the world's future. At the same time, there are important limitations. Four may be mentioned. The first is that the true protagonists of human history will necessarily be a small number of persons, few in comparison with the whole human population. As we have often seen, only eschatological salvation—the promise of immortality—is in a position to guarantee the full realization of humans taken one by one, to express the irreplaceable dignity of each person. Hegel thought, for example, that the great personages of history—Alexander the Great, Napoleon, and others—could allow themselves, if necessary, the luxury of disposing of the lives of a large number of persons for the good of humanity as a whole.[90] According to the Christian vision, on the contrary, any person—even the very weakest one, and perhaps especially that one—can correspond to God's gifts and contribute to changing the world and history, deeply influencing the lives of other people, reaching holiness and the eternal glory of heaven. This is clearly the case with the life of Mary. The "modern" understanding of history, from the anthropological standpoint, would be clearly reductionist, mundane, elitist, and conducive to racism.

The second limitation may be found in the careless optimism that marks the dogma of necessary progress, which, in spite of appearances, hides a secret despair, because at best only the human collectivity will be in a position to enjoy a better future (as Karl Marx held). The individual, however, even if he has contributed a great deal to the common good of humanity, is struck down and eliminated forever by death and is rendered incapable of enjoying the fruit of his work. We have already noted that according to Augustine, the true motor of life and of society is precisely the perspective and promise of a perfect, eternal, future fulfillment for the individual and for society.

The third limitation lies in the promise of an internal end of history that will take place within history itself. This becomes a pure illusion, a utopia, as many twentieth-century authors have conclusively shown.[91] In particular, this may be seen in the collapse of Marxist ideology. The failure of the modern promise of a perfect society has

---

89. See *COH*, 42–46.

90. Hegel writes: "It is even possible that such men may treat other great, even sacred interests, inconsiderately, conduct which is indeed obnoxious to moral reprehension. But so mighty a form must trample down many an innocent flower, crush to pieces many an object in its path." G. W. F. Hegel, *Lectures on the Philosophy of History* (London: G. Bell and Sons, 1914), 34.

91. On the topic of utopia, see Cruz, *Filosofía de la historia*, 181–94. On its dynamics, see K. Mannheim, *Ideology and Utopia: An Introduction to the Sociology of Knowledge* (New York: Harcourt, Brace, 1953); R. Dahrendorf, *Pfade aus Utopia: Arbeiten zur Theorie und Methode der Soziologie* (Munich: Piper, 1967); M. Buber, *Pfade in Utopia* (Heidelberg: L. Schneider, 1950).

constituted not simply a disappointment that might be overcome with the passage of time but a true tragedy, because a system that promised to give humans their lost dignity anew has, in real terms, taken it away.[92] The historical results of this failure and disappointment, as we have already seen, were often attempts to escape: fleeing toward the world (hedonism) and fleeing from the world (the neo-Gnostic and New Age movements, etc.).

Now we come to the fourth limitation. Throughout the nineteenth century several authors began to realize that thought forms closed to transcendence were moving toward bankruptcy and the old doctrines of eternal return were making a strong comeback. This was the case with Friedrich Engels, a close collaborator of Karl Marx. In his work *The Dialectics of Nature* he teaches that matter is subject to a process of eternal return; following a law of absolute necessity, matter will destroy its most sublime fruit, that is, the thinking intellect, even if the latter will resurface time and again as the years go by.[93]

In the reappearance of the doctrine of eternal return Friedrich Nietzsche played an important role.[94] Speaking of the Superman, he looks with contempt on simplicity, tenderness, and humility as signs of human weakness, values promoted by Christians who—he claims—hate life. At the same time, paradoxically, he comes to the conclusion that human life itself is completely futile. It is interesting to note that his thought, after so many centuries of "progress," of self-affirmation by humans, goes back to the doctrine of eternal return, typical of ancient fatalism. According to Nietzsche: "Everything goes, everything returns; eternally rolls the wheel of existence. Everything dies, everything blossoms forth again; eternally runs on the year of existence. Everything breaks up, everything is integrated anew; eternally the same house of existence builds itself. All things separate, all things again greet one another; eternally true to itself remains the ring of existence."[95] And then, in *The Gay Science*, he asks himself:

The heaviest burden: What if, some day or night, a demon were to steal after you into your loneliest loneliness and say to you: "This life, as you now live it and have lived it, you will have to live once more and innumerable times more; and there will be nothing new in it, but every pain and every joy and every thought and sigh ... must return to you—all in the same succession and sequence—even this spider and this moonlight between the trees and even this moment and I myself. The eternal hourglass of existence is turned over again and again—and you with it, speck of dust!" Would you not throw yourself down and gnash your teeth and curse the demon who spoke thus? Or have you once experienced a tremendous moment when you would have answered him: "You are a god, and never have I heard anything more divine!" If this thought were to gain possession of you, it would change you as you are, or perhaps crush you. The question in each and every thing, "do you want this once more and innumerable times more?" would lie upon your actions as the greatest weight. Or how well disposed would you have to become to yourself and to life to crave nothing more fervently than this ultimate eternal confirmation and seal?[96]

92. See Courtois and Kramer, *The Black Book of Communism*.

93. See Engels, *Dialectics of Nature*.

94. On Nietzsche's understanding of the eternal return, see Löwith, *Nietzsches Philosophie der ewigen Wiederkunft des Gleichen*; D'Iorio, *La linea e il circolo*.

95. Nietzsche, *Thus Spake Zarathustra*, 201.

96. F. Nietzsche, *The Gay Science*, translated by W. Kaufmann (New York: Random House, 1974), IV, no. 273 (341).

Something of the kind may be found in Albert Camus's work *The Myth of Sisyphus*.[97] According to "the philosopher of the absurd," humans continually attempt to reach the peak of their capabilities without ever managing to do so. The hero Sisyphus, drawn from Greek mythology, carries a large stone toward the top of a mountain and, when he is about to reach it, the stone slips from his grasp and he experiences the frustration and bitterness of seeing it roll back down into the valley. He returns to pick it up anew, and drags it up again toward the top. But the same thing happens. And so on again and again, endlessly. Life, which we thought was fully under our control, is seen to be a permanent useless absurdity, repeated time and again.

Summing up, once it is forgotten that God is the only one who is capable of bringing humans to their transcendent end, the result is a return to the doctrine of the eternal return and, sooner or later, to nihilism. In effect, modern extreme rationalism empties evermore the concrete historical moment, attempting to put reason in its place as an absolute (that is, separated from the act, with which humans enter into relationships with others and with reality) and as a totality (that is, as the exclusive horizon and measure of knowledge). Likewise, postmodern thought attempts to abolish history, eliminating the optimistic titanism of the rationalist and the idealist.[98] According to Heidegger, man in the modern period has lost the path (*Holzwege*) and attempts to live off the emotion of the present, fleeting moment.[99]

Conclusion

Following from what we saw in the previous chapter on human freedom, the historical event at heart is the free human act that accepts and receives God's gifts, whether in the ambit of creation (using created goods truly as creatures) or in that of supernatural grace, that is, of personal communion with the Trinity. It may also be the act, likewise historical, with which humans can reject these gifts, giving rise to sin. This acceptance and reception (or refusal and rejection) involves all human faculties and produces in the life of the individual a permanent effect that contributes to the formation of history, which will be revealed in fullness at final judgment at the end of time, when Christ returns in glory. If such an original divine gift did not exist—creation, grace—this history (and the historical awareness that derives from it) would remain an illusion, weakened or even eliminated. As de Lubac put it, "History is a Christian magnitude."

97. See A. Camus, *The Myth of Sisyphus and Other Essays* (New York: Vintage, 1959).

98. On titanism, see von Balthasar, *Theo-Drama*, 2:420–26.

99. On this issue, see C. Vigna, *Il frammento e l'intero: Indagini sul senso dell'essere e sulla stabilità del sapere* (Milan: Vita e pensiero, 2000). Reference is being made to Heidegger's work *Off the Beaten Track*.

We are here on earth to do good to others. What the others are for, I just don't know.
ATTRIBUTED TO W. H. AUDEN

All should be my ministers in distributing the graces and gifts they have received from me.
CATHERINE OF SIENA[1]

That humans are social beings who relate closely to those of their own species is more than obvious. That human sociality has been considered throughout the history of anthropology as something deeply ambivalent, however, is undeniable. In this chapter we shall attempt to describe certain moments of this history of the reality and ambivalence of the social condition. Then we shall consider how the fact of human sociality and its dynamism may be interpreted in the light of faith in order to understand its origin, purpose, and inner meaning. Finally we shall attempt to clarify the notion of human sociality by reflecting on the equality of human beings.

Human Sociality, Its Dynamism, and Its Ambivalence

Throughout the history of philosophy, human sociality has sometimes been considered as something natural and appropriate, sometimes as an improper situation for humans, an alienated state that must be overcome.

Humans as Social Beings

Aristotle teaches openly that man is a *zōon politikon*, "a social animal." In an important passage of his *Politics*, he explains that whereas for humans sociality is necessary and unavoidable, the opposite—asociality—is a characteristic only of divinities or animals:

1. Catherine of Siena, *Dialogs* I, 7.

The proof that the state is a creation of nature and prior to the individual is that the individual, when isolated, is not self-sufficing; and therefore he is like a part in relation to the whole. But he who is unable to live in society, or who has no need because he is sufficient for himself, must be either a beast or a god: he is no part of the state. A social instinct is implanted in all men by nature."[2]

It is evident, says Aristotle, that humans are social beings in the sense that they stand in need of one another in order to reach fulfillment. This is a consequence of the practical truth of human life; from this Aristotle deduces that sociality is a fundamental aspect of human nature itself. Throughout history, the Aristotelian position has been taken up, and sometimes exaggerated—for example, by different forms of collectivism that attempt to understand humanity in exclusively social terms. According to Marx, for example, "The human essence is no abstraction inherent in each single individual. In reality the human essence is the ensemble of the social relations."[3] Feuerbach, in turn, teaches openly that the essence of humans may be found only in the community.[4]

The Human Being as an Individual

Several ancient authors, though they share the experience of Aristotle as regards the social side of humans, read it differently, seeing in human sociality a sign of weakness, of imperfection, of impropriety, of removal from the divine, because they take it that the divine, by nature, is solitary and self-sufficient. Likewise, the perfect human should be solitary and self-sufficient, individual and androgynous, as we shall see in the next chapter. All sociality, therefore, would be a source and sign of alienation for humans, something that should be overcome.

This is the line followed by Plato, according to whom the human being is identified with its own spiritual soul and must strive to overcome the claims deriving from living in a body, which is an instrument of communication and sociality. According to the individualist philosophy of Epicurus, in order to obtain peace and happiness, humans need only themselves, not the city or the state (*polis*); nor do they need institutions, nobles, or even God.[5] Man is a fully autonomous being. "Do not fool yourselves, O humans," says Epicurus in a text attributed to him by Epictetus and Lactantius, "do not allow your judgment be bypassed, do not fall into error. There is no such thing as a natural society of reasoning beings that relate to one another.... Let each one think of himself."[6] In a less radical way, neo-Platonic authors and some spiritualistic Christian authors considered with suspicion strong affirmations with respect to human sociality. Plotinus, for example, was convinced that "it is not possible to live happily in society, 'with a body.'"[7]

---

2. Aristotle, *Politics* I.2.1252b28–1253a29. This text is preceded by the following explanation: "The community that is the result of several villages is the state [*polis*], which reaches already, as it were, the limits of complete self-sufficiency: as a format which makes life possible, in real terms it exists in order to make possible a happy life. Thus every state exists by nature, if by nature there exist also the first communities. In fact it is their end and the nature is the end: for example that which each thing is when it developed fully, we call it its nature, whether it be of a man, of a horse, or of a thing."

3. K. Marx, *Thesis on Feuerbach* (Moscow: Progress, 1969), VI.

4. See Feuerbach, *The Essence of Christianity*.

5. See G. Reale, *Storia della filosofia antica*, 8th ed. (Milan: Vita e pensiero, 1988), 2:174f.

6. Ibid., 2:259.   7. Plotinus, *Enn.* I, 4, 16.

In modern philosophy we not infrequently encounter this monadic, individu-alistic vision—that, for example, of Leibniz, according to whom what is primary in humans is their individuality. The same tendency is to be found in Kant, Hobbes, Nietzsche, and other authors. According to this line of thought, the relationship of humans with God and with others would be accidental, contractual, established a posteriori. That is, the human being exists first as an autonomous individual, *a se*; only later on does he establish more or less intense relationships with other individu-als, according to needs or likes, and lives *ab alio*. Hence sociality would not be fun-damental in human nature but accessory, not essential but useful, not natural but conventional, not original but subsequent, not under the sway of nature but under that of freedom—and therefore, in real terms, optional. According to an important part of modern philosophy, the human being is primarily an *ens a se*. Thus the root of human dignity is located in the individuality of a separate subjectivity, requiring no recourse to a divinity, to a creator who would act as guarantor of that dignity. In the context of the autonomous individual, other individuals represent simply situations of advantage or disadvantage. The best situation we could hope for would be a kind of "complementarity pact" between monadic individuals that would allow each one give to the others what they are lacking. As a result, the others are seen as mere objects or instruments, according to what they possess or what they are capable of doing, not so much to what they are. We can understand, therefore, why Thomas Hobbes described the human being using a famous expression: "Homo homini lupus" (Man is a wolf for man).

Something of the kind may be found in the writings of some modern authors of the existentialist school, who warn against the dangers of depersonalization through socialization and gregariousness. They rightfully fear that humans, as they immerse themselves in the company of others, will be drawn along by them to the point of losing themselves, renouncing their own responsibilities, becoming "depersonalized." According to Martin Heidegger,

The public "surrounding world" is already at hand and taken care of in the surrounding world nearest to us. In utilizing public transportation, in the use of information services such as the newspaper, every other is like the next. This being-with-one-another dissolves one's own *Da-sein* completely in the kind of being of "the others" in such a way that the oth-ers, as distinguishable and explicit, disappear ever more. In this inconspicuousness and "unascertainability," the "they" unfolds its true dictatorship. We enjoy ourselves and have fun the way *they* enjoy themselves. We read, see, and judge literature and art the way *they* see and judge. But we also withdraw from the "great mass" the way *they* withdraw, we find "shocking" what *they* find shocking. The "they," which is nothing definite and which all are, though not as a sum, prescribes the kind of being and everydayness.[8]

According to Simone Weil, the greatest danger for humans is not to be found in the tendency of the collectivity to compress and inhibit the person but rather in the ten-dency of the person himself to be drowned by the collectivity, allowing himself to be compressed by it.[9] In other words, where Marx, following Hegel, sees the individual as the fundamental expression of alienation for humans, Heidegger and other ex-

---

8. Heidegger, *Being and Time*, 119.
9. See S. Weil, *Ecrits de Londres et dernières lettres*, 10th ed. (Paris: Gallimard, 1957).

istentialists, following Kierkegaard, see in human collectivity the origin of the true loss of humanity. Jean-Paul Sartre, for example, teaches that "Hell [the state that best represents a failed humanity] is other people."[10]

Moving beyond the Impasse

Christian faith needs to reflect on the following phenomena: on the one hand, the concrete and evident fact of human sociality and, on the other, the latter's ambivalence, whether this tends toward individualism or gregariousness, as the case may be. On the basis of God's original design and purpose, we shall attempt to understand (1) whether God constituted humans from the start as essentially social beings and (2) what are the meaning and purpose of this sociality. This chapter concentrates on the social condition of humans in general, whereas the next one looks into the sociality specific to the sexual condition of humans, that is, the distinction between man and woman.

A Christian Reflection on Human Sociality: Man as a Being *ab Alio*

The starting point to understanding human sociality must be the fact that according to Christian faith in creation, humans are constituted entirely as beings *ab alio* or, better, *ab Alio*, in that they have their exclusive origin in another, who is God. Humans had no preceding existence outside of God's thought and action. Humans have not given existence to themselves, not even partially; rather they have received it entirely from God. In this affirmation we can sum up Christian teaching on both the creation of humans in the image and likeness of God and on that of the call to interpersonal communion with him. The nature and lives of humans make sense only with respect to a project that began outside them, in God. The simplest, most precise, and theologically rigorous definition of the human being is this: "made in the image and likeness of God" (Gn 1:27). As a result, human beings are essentially beings in relation, in relation at all levels but fundamentally with respect to the creator who gives them existence. Besides, the Old Testament doctrine of Covenant is deeply rooted in that of the union God wishes to establish not only with humans individually, one by one, but specifically with his own people.

This fundamental aspect of human life—that we proceed in our entire existence *ab alio*, from another—finds full expression in the possibility of entering into a relationship with other human beings, also created by God and members of the same race. For this reason we can say that humans are social, relational, to the very core of their being. This fact may be expressed in three ways. First, because the eternal project that God has thought out for each person—ultimately, his vocation—develops and reaches fulfillment through and with other people because God has wanted to give to humans his many gifts—existence, grace, talents, happiness, eternal life—through others and along with others. Second, the human being develops as a person, as a human being, in communicating to others the gifts God has confided to

10. From J.-P. Sartre's drama, *Huis-clos*.

him or her through the exercise of the virtue of charity, the "form" of all virtues. And third, we may posit a certain likeness between the communion of the divine persons and that of all humanity.[11]

In effect, the first account of creation in the book of Genesis explains that humans live out the fact of being made in the image of the creator not only in their relationship with God and in "dominating" the material world but also in relation to others, specifically in the relationship between man and woman: "So God created man in his own image, in the image of God he created him; *male and female he created them*" (Gn 1:27). The second account of creation in Genesis explains the same thing in a different way. The human being created by God is presented as incomplete in the absence of another who is similar: "Then the Lord God said, 'It is not good that the man should be alone; I will make him a helper fit for him'" (Gn 2:18). We shall return to these texts presently. In any case it is clear, according to Church teaching, that humans are fundamentally social beings: "For by his innermost nature man is a social being, and unless he relates himself to others he can neither live nor develop his potential."[12]

The sociality intrinsic to humans, typical of Christian thought, finds its principal expression in the fact that each human being, in spite of possible appearances to the contrary, depends at a very profound level on other people: this may be seen at the beginning of their lives, in their education and growth, in their development and maturation, in the process of salvation that takes place in and through and with the Church, and at the end of time, when the redeemed are incorporated definitively into the communion of saints, the heavenly Jerusalem, with the resurrection of the dead and final judgment.[13] Human sociality is a condition that God has wanted for humans, and makes its presence felt in each and every aspect of their life and nature. Still, it is not enough to insist on the mere fact of human sociality, confirmed by Christian revelation. Besides, we must ask why there is such a thing as human sociality: why did God want humans to be linked with one another at such a deep level, in such a way that a chemically pure individualism would be simply impossible even if humans tried their level best to achieve it? What, therefore, is the purpose of sociality in God's plan?

In order to understand the issue, let us take one step backward and consider the question of human equality.[14]

Attempting to Understand Human Equality

Humans clearly relate to God in a condition of inferiority and submission: before their creator they recognize themselves as ontologically dependent and morally weak. Perhaps they may be tempted to *hybris*, the will to become more than they really are. Of course believers are children of God, and in that sense his equals, but they

11. See *GS*, no. 24.

12. Ibid., 12. See chapter 4, notes 43ff. and corresponding text.

13. On the intrinsically social aspect of eternal life, see *COH* 176–79.

14. See P. O'Callaghan, "The Anthropological Roots of Communion," in *The Ecclesiology of Communion Fifty Years after the Opening of Vatican II*, edited by B. Leahy (Dublin: Veritas, 2013), 3:287–301.

are adopted children, children by grace. On the contrary, humans relate to the material cosmos as superior beings, capable of knowing, guarding, and dominating the things that surround them; perhaps they may be tempted to manipulate nature, but the latter, inexorably, makes its voice and vengeance felt, as the present-day ecological problem shows.[15] Finally, humans relate to other human beings as their equals. Before others, humans perceive themselves in a situation of equality, as individuals who belong to the same race, with the same nature.

Although we intuit our fundamental equality with other humans, the differences between them are all too obvious, in such a way that "equality" between humans seems to be a mirage, a pure aspiration with no basis in reality, a way of speaking that results from cynicism, ingenuity, or envy.[16] Distinctions between humans stand out clearly: distinctions between man and woman, between sick and healthy, between old and young, between tall and small, between weak and strong, between intelligent and ignorant, between poor and rich, between those who suffer much and those who have suffered little, between those who have received a good education and those who have not, between those who have enjoyed good fortune and human success and those for whom life has been to all appearances a failure. It would seem, therefore, that there is anything but equality between humans. What role does the creating God play in that?

Historical Pointers on Human Equality

We may note that in classical antiquity persons were not generally considered equal. On the contrary, it was accepted, in theory and in practice, that the great majority were slaves (or something of the kind) by nature and should be considered as inferior to the rest.[17] According to Aristotle, "It is clear that some are free and others are slaves by nature."[18] The few who are free, however, have the right to live and act in different ways; they can govern their own lives, as well as those of their slaves, and run society and the state. Among the Greeks, equality was to be found, but only among the free, among citizens, who enjoyed equal rights before the law, the possibility of running society and speaking freely, what they called the *parrhesia*.[19] Equality, such as it was, was to be found in law, therefore, not in nature. According to Aristotle, for the organization of the city, there is equality "for the mass formed out of the free who do not go against the law."[20] In other words, the value or dignity of each person

---

15. See Pope Francis, *LS*.

16. "The idea of equality may at a given moment have a practically useful significance, it may be a fight for the liberation and dignity of man. But in itself the idea of equality is futile, in itself it does not mean the raising of every man but an envious glance at one's neighbor. And all the while personalism on the other hand is based upon the equality of all men in the sight of God." Berdjaev, *Slavery and Freedom*, 205. "A socially leveling process is necessary, not in order to equalize and depersonalize men and women, but precisely in order to differentiate and diversify them, to bring to light personal qualitative distinctions which are concealed and suppressed by a class structure of society" (215).

17. See the collection of texts made by Garnsey, *Ideas of Slavery from Aristotle to Augustine*. See also O. Pétré-Grenouilleau, *Les traites négrières: Essai d'histoire globale* (Paris: Gallimard, 2004); Pétré-Grenouilleau, ed., *Dictionnaire des esclavages* (Paris: Larousse, 2010).

18. Aristotle, *Politics* I.1255a1–2.

19. See especially the works of the jurist Clistinus (sixth century B.C.), of Teseus of Euripides in his work *The Supplications*, vv. 405ff., and of Thucydides, *The Peloponnesian Wars* II, 36.41. Finally, see the myth of Protagoras, explained by Plato in *Protag.* 320c.

20. Aristotle, *Politics* III.1286.37.

depended on his moral qualities;[21] human equality did not find its roots in human nature as such. In the Roman Empire, creator of law and social peace, only the father, the *paterfamilias*, had full rights. Women, children, slaves, and the inhabitants of the provinces were considered inferior and subjugated to him.[22] In this period, "culture was limited principally to a chosen minority ... the class of propertied citizens," over against a numerous proletariat made up of slaves, freed-persons, and country dwellers, whose condition "was little more than that of beggars."[23]

Still, some exceptions to this rule may be found. Herodotus declared that equality among humans, at least as regards the law (what was called *isonomia*), is "the most beautiful name."[24] The sophist Antiphone proclaimed: "By nature we are all created equal in every way, barbarians and Greeks."[25] Successively, the Stoics introduced the anthropological principle of universalism. According to Cicero, all share alike in the same *logos*, or reason, which controls the universe.[26] Likewise, Seneca said that all humans are equal on the basis of common human reason: "Nature imposes on me the obligation of being useful to all humanity, whether they are slaves or free, born free or freed. Wherever there is a human being, there is an opportunity to do good."[27] The second-century Roman jurist Florentinus said that "slavery is an institution of the *ius gentium*, with which someone, against the nature of things, takes over the other as their property."[28] Clearly these authors did not exclude the notion of natural human equality. Yet such an awareness was made explicit by the third-century jurist Ulipan, who said that "with respect to civil law, we take it that slaves have no position. But as regards natural law, this is not the case. According to natural law, all humans are equal."[29]

The Contribution of Christian Faith to the Awareness of Human Equality

It is fair to say that the message of the fundamental equality of all humans is to be found in a special way in Christian revelation and life.[30] According to the Old Testament, all have been made in the image and likeness of God. The book of Wisdom stresses the natural, essential equality of all humans, principally in the context of the transitoriness and frailty of human life, in the suffering of birth and death (Wis 7:1, 3-6). Still, humans are not said to have any likeness to or equality with God (2 Mc 9:12), in contrast to the Greek veneration of heroes based on the desire to be "like God." In fact, "the Old Testament echoes with majestic monotony the question 'Who is like God?'"[31]

21. See Aristotle, *Ethica Nic.* V.6–7.

22. See W. Kern, "Der Beitrag des Christentums zu einer menschlicheren Welt," in *Handbuch der Fundamentaltheologie*, edited by W. Kern, H. J. Pottmeyer, and M. Seckler (Freiburg: Herder, 1985), 278–314, esp. 288–96.

23. M. I. Rostovtzeff, *Geschichte der alten Welt*, vol. 2: *Rom* (Bremen: Carl Schünemann, 1942), 453, 458.

24. Herodotus, *Histories* III, 8.

25. From H. Diels, *Die Fragmente der Vorsokratiker: Griechisch und deutsch* (Berlin: Weidmann, 1903), B 44, B 2.

26. Cicero, *De repub.* I, 6, 18; I, 32, 49; III, 22, 33.

27. Seneca, *De vita beata* 24, 3.

28. Florentinus, *Digest.* 1, 5, 4.

29. Ulpian, *Digest.*, 15, 17, 32.

30. See *NIDNTTE* 2:548–51, s.v. ἴσος.

31. G. Stählin, in *TDNT* 3:352, s.v. ἰσότης.

In the New Testament, before God, who calls to filial and eternal union all humans, who live before a single savior of all, Jesus Christ (1 Tm 2:5), before one Spirit (1 Cor 12:13), in the context of an ecclesial mission destined for all humans, a natural and spontaneous conclusion emerges: all humans enjoy a fundamental equality before God, and therefore with one another, a real equality in the strongest, deepest, and most lasting sense of the word. God deals with each and every human with the love of a father; all are made in his image and likeness; all have been redeemed by the blood of Christ and called to holiness. Paul says so clearly on repeated occasions: "There is neither Jew nor Greek, there is neither slave nor free, there is neither male nor female; for you are all one in Christ Jesus" (Gal 3:28). And elsewhere: "For by one Spirit we were all baptized into one body—Jews or Greeks, slaves or free—and all were made to drink of one Spirit" (1 Cor 12:13). And finally: "Here there cannot be Greek and Jew, circumcised and uncircumcised, barbarian, Scythian, slave, free man, but Christ is all, and in all" (Col 3:11).

The same message may be found in the Old Testament, according to Philo of Alexandria: "We humans are all brothers, because God is our common Father."[32] Thus, he concludes, "Nobody is a slave by nature."[33] Abraham Heschel asks: "What is the Sabbath?" And he answers: "A reminder of every man's royalty; an abolition of the distinction between master and slave, rich and poor, success and failure.... The Sabbath is an embodiment of the belief that all men are equal and that equality of men means the nobility of men. The greatest sin of man is to forget that he is a prince."[34]

Speaking of the human person in the early Christian centuries, Meslin writes: "Humans are no longer defined, as Roman Law laid down, on the basis of an individual statute of an ethnical, sexual, social, or political kind; neither were they defined, as the Stoics said, on the basis of a natural equality; rather they were alike in the equality of being creatures, all of them children of the one God."[35] The third-century Christian writer Lactantius observed that "God, who generates and enlightens all humans, wished them to be equal.... Nobody is a slave for him, no one a master. If he is for all one and the same Father, then we are all his children with the same right. Nobody is poor for God, except the one who is lacking in justice."[36]

Christianity and Slavery

It has sometimes been suggested that slavery came into the world through sin: humans are enslaved on account of their transgressions. "Slavery is of two kinds, one of the body and the other of the soul," says Ambrose. "It is true that man dominates the body, but sin and passion dominate the soul, and of these only freedom of spirit liberates a man from his slavery."[37] Still, Christian faith teaches that humans have been liberated by God, becoming his children. God is Father, but he is also Lord. In a dense

---

32. Philo of Alexandria, *De decalogo*.   33. Philo of Alexandria, *De spec. legibus* 2, 69.

34. Heschel, *God in Search of Man*, 417.

35. M. Meslin, "La personne," in *Les grandes inventions du christianisme*, edited by R. Rémond (Paris: Bayard, 1999), 47–69, 51.

36. Lactantius, *De ira Dei*, 14; see Lactantius, *Institutiones divinae* V, 14ff. See also Ambrose, *In Luc.* 9, 29.

37. Ambrose, *Epist.* 7, 24. See R. Klein, *Die Sklaverei in der Sicht der Bischöfe Ambrosius und Augustinus* (Stuttgart: Steiner Verlag Wiesbaden, 1988).

and suggestive text, Athanasius says: "Being slaves by nature, we direct ourselves to God as Lord."[38] Humans, in fact, are born slaves of sin; when they are freed through baptism, they become children, living their freedom in willing service, submission, and obedience to God, who is Father and Lord. Becoming "slaves of Christ" freed believers from being slaves to humans; on account of baptism nobody could belong to another as their personal property.[39] Still, this submission to God is meant to find expression in terms of free service to one's brothers (Mt 20:28). Paul says that "the Lord's freedman" is at the same time "Christ's slave" (1 Cor 7:22). The paradox at the heart of Christian life, on account of which Christian believers are both slaves and free—or rather, freely live as servants—is to be found first and foremost in the life of Jesus Christ himself, who, being the Son, willingly became the servant of all, to the point of dying ignominiously on the cross.[40]

The legal institution of slavery remained in use for an extended period even in nations evangelized by Christians, although things began to change with the coming of Constantine as emperor.[41] Slavery remained, however, within the economic and juridical structures. Still, all Christians, masters or slaves, considered one another as "one in Christ," living their "slavery" as a free reciprocal service between equals. It is interesting to note that some Christian authors taught equality for Christians as regards the soul while maintaining their condition as slaves with respect to the body.[42] Masters, therefore, in their political and social action could dominate the bodies but not the souls of their slaves, which came under the free dominion of each person. This explanation, however, though realistic in some situations, does not hold up when Christian faith excludes all kinds of dualistic anthropology.

The Modern Recognition of the Christian Root of Equality

The critical role Christianity played in the genesis of the idea of equality between all humans, without exception, has been pointed out by modern philosophers.

---

38. Athanasius, *C. Arianos* II, 51.

39. See, for example, Gregory of Nyssa, *Hom. in Eccl.*, 4, on the friendship between slave and freeman. On Gregory and the Cappadocians, see R. Klein, *Die Haltung der kappadokischen Bischöfe Basilius von Caesarea, Gregor von Nazianz und Gregor von Nyssa zur Sklaverei* (Stuttgart: F. Steiner, 2000).

40. See chapter 13, notes 72ff. and corresponding text.

41. The historian of law H. J. Berman writes: "Under the influence of Christianity, and also under the influence of Stoic and neo-Platonic ideas adopted by Christian philosophy, changes were made: (1) in family law, giving the wife a position of greater equality before the law, requiring mutual consent of both spouses for the validity of a marriage, making divorce more difficult (which at that time was a step toward women's liberation), and abolishing the father's power of life or death over his children (*patria potestas*); (2) in the law of slavery, giving a slave the right to appeal to a magistrate if his master abused his powers and even in some cases the right to freedom if the master exercised cruelty, multiplying modes of manumission of slaves, and permitting slaves to acquire rights by kinship with freemen; and (3) in the relation between strict law and equity, strengthening the concept of equity and tempering the strictness of general prescriptions. Finally, (4) the great collections of law compiled by the Emperor Justinian and his successors in the sixth, seventh, and eighth centuries were inspired in part by the belief that Christianity required that the law be systematized as a necessary step in its humanization." H. J. Berman, *Law and Revolution: The Formation of the Western Legal Tradition* (Cambridge, Mass.: Harvard University Press, 1983), 167.

42. See Garnsey, *Ideas of Slavery from Aristotle to Augustine*, 40f., 119–23. According to Philo, *Quod omnis probus liber sit*, 17–19, slavery may be applied in one sense to bodies, in another to souls. The masters of bodies are humans, whereas souls have their vices and passions.

J.-J. Rousseau published an important work of political philosophy in 1755 titled *Discours sur l'origine et les fondements de l'inégalité parmi les hommes* (Discourse upon the Origins and Foundation of Inequality among Humans). In *The Social Contract* he made the following observation:

The patriotic spirit is an exclusive spirit which brings us to look upon those who are not fellow citizens as foreigners or even enemies. That was the spirit of Sparta and Rome. To the contrary, the spirit of Christianity brings us to consider all humans as our brothers, as children of God. Christian charity does not allow us to make an odious distinction between the compatriot and the foreigner.... It indistinctly embraces the whole of the human race. It is true that Christianity, because of its *holiness*, is opposed to the particular social spirit.

And elsewhere he writes: "The ideas of natural law and the common fraternity of all human beings spread quite late and have made slow progress in the world; only Christianity has universalized them to a sufficient degree."[43]

Hegel said the same thing: "In Christianity the individual, personal mind for the first time becomes of real, infinite, and absolute value; God wills that all men shall be saved. It was in the Christian religion that the doctrine was advanced that all men are equal before God, because Christ has set them free with the freedom of Christianity."[44] The nineteenth-century political philosopher Alexis de Tocqueville wrote that "Jesus Christ came to earth in order to make it understood that all members of the human species were naturally similar and equal."[45] And, more recently, Max Horkheimer, in an essay on religion, places equality and freedom on the same plane: "If we intend to conserve equality, then we must limit freedom, but if we wish to leave freedom, then there is no more space for equality."[46] Finally, the contemporary philosopher Jürgen Habermas explains as follows the dynamics of our knowledge of human equality:

For the normative self-understanding of modernity, Christianity does not represent only a precedent or catalyst. Egalitarian universality—from which derives the ideas of liberty and social cohesion, autonomous behavior and emancipation, individual moral conscience, human rights, and democracy—is a direct heritage of the Jewish ethic of justice and the Christian ethic of love. This heritage has been continually assimilated, criticized, and reinterpreted without substantial transformations. Even today we have no viable alternatives. With the challenges that rise up today out of the post-national constellation, we continue to be nourished by this source. All the rest is postmodern chatter.[47]

Our Knowledge of Human Equality: A Matter of Faith or of Reason?

What can we draw from our conviction of the fundamental equality of all humans? Is it just a doctrine of faith? Or is it fully accessible to reason? That is to say:

---

43. J.-J. Rousseau, *Political Writings*, edited by C. E. Vaughan (Oxford: Oxford University Press 1962), 2:166, 1:453.

44. G. W. F. Hegel, *Lectures on the History of Philosophy* (Bristol: Thoemmes Press, 1999), 1:48.

45. A. De Tocqueville, *Democracy in America* (Indianapolis, Ind.: Liberty Fund, 2012), 733.

46. M. Horkheimer, *Die Sehnsucht nach dem ganz Anderen* (Hamburg: Fursche-Verlag, 1970), 70.

47. J. Habermas, "Dialog zu Gott und der Welt," 191f. On the relationship between universalism and individualism, see Dumont, *Essais sur l'individualisme*; A. Laurent, *L'histoire de l'individualisme* (Paris: PUF, 1993).

Can it only be defended by Christian believers *as* believers, or may it be shared by nonbelievers? Or might we not say, perhaps, that humans are equal in spirit but not in body, as some Christian authors suggested during debates on slavery?

It is important to emphasize that at the beginning of the Reformation, the affirmation of the freedom and equality of all Christians—members of the hierarchy, consecrated men and women, lay faithful—was of particular importance to Protestants, who based their conviction on the doctrine of faith in Christ. In Reformed and Lutheran theology the question of human equality was frequently considered in an interior and spiritual way based on faith in Jesus Christ, who saved us from sin. In Germany the so-called *Reformatio Sigismundi* (in the fifteenth century)[48] invited Christians to eliminate all kinds of slavery: "Nobility and power and material goods do not help us to come close to God. All enjoy the same freedom before heaven."[49] The third article of the declaration of the emancipated peasantry in Germany in 1525 proclaimed: "Until now it has been customary to consider us all as people in need of mercy, since Christ has redeemed us and rescued us all with his precious blood, the pastor just as the highest dignitary, to the exclusion of no one. And it is in conformity with Scripture that we are free and wish to be free."[50] And Luther himself said:

This is clear for us ... that in the measure in which we call ourselves Christians there is no inequality or preference of persons, but one is like the other, man, woman, young, old ... prince or peasant, lord or servant.... But then, if we pay attention to the exterior reality and our way of acting ... inequalities come to the surface and differences arise among Christians, not insofar as they are Christians, not as regards the Christian essence, but as regards the latter's fruit.[51]

Secular forms of equality, "which are determined by earthly law and righteousness, are confronted in the New Testament by another kind of equality that is established by the love of Christians and by the divine gifts of grace."[52]

We can see how the affirmation of human equality has been justified mainly on the basis of the work of Christian redemption, that is, on the basis of faith in salvation, without referring to the original project of God's creation of humans, made of spirit and matter, body and soul, in the image and likeness of the creator, and therefore knowable by reason. The French Enlightenment authors insisted on the values of *liberté* and *égalité* as the fruits of human reasoning. Their approach to both, however, remained at an abstract and formal level, somewhat like their overall aspirations, which were easy to enunciate theoretically but difficult to put into practice at a social and juridical level. Even if *égalité* was the watchword of the French Revolution, in practice it "was exclusively an affair of an evolved bourgeois society, which hankered after equality with the nobles. The 'people,' however, the middle and lower classes,

48. See U. Altmann, *Reformatio Sigismundi* (Leipzig: Zentralantiquariat der Deutschen Demokratischen Republik, 1984). The document was associated with the Council of Basilea in the fifteenth century.

49. The text is cited by O. Dann in "Gleichheit," in *Geschichtliche Grundbegriffe: Historisches Lexikon zur politisch-sozialen Sprache in Deutschland*, edited by R. Koselleck and W. Conze (Stuttgart: Klett-Cotta, 1974), 2:997–1046, 1005.

50. Cited by T. Mayer-Maly in "Zur Rechtsgeschichte der Freiheitsidee in Antike und Mittelalter," *Österreichische Zeitschrift für öffentliches Recht* NF 6 (1955): 399–428, 418n123.

51. M. Luther, *Wochenpredigten über Mt 5–7* (1530), in WA 32:536f.

52. G. Stählin, *TDNT* 3:348.

were kept far from such aspirations."[53] The same attitude may be found in some modern authors who preceded the French Revolution, especially Hobbes[54] and Locke.[55] In this context, humans are considered, in an individualistic way, more and more as sovereign rational beings separated from a superior rationality (that of God), who artificially construct order within society.[56]

We have already seen that human equality may be considered philosophically and juridically. The Stoics, especially Seneca, told us that human nature is common to all. For this reason several authors have situated the genesis of the doctrine of human equality in Stoic philosophy, and also in later Roman jurisprudence, rather than in Christianity.[57] It is interesting to note, however, that Christian authors have taken a clearly rational and philosophical approach to the topic of equality.[58] Still, it is fair to say that the living presence of Christian faith has been critical in the passage from a restricted, theoretical awareness of equality to its practical universalization. Rousseau said as much in the text cited earlier. Roberto Gatti has the following to say:

Referring the notion of human equality to revealed faith and supernatural life does not involve an emptying of the political weight of the principle of equality but implies the imperative of distinguishing always, in different historical circumstances and taking into account the structural limits of human action in the world, the way in which the conviction of equality as a coming together of rights deriving from human dignity ... consolidated in concrete terms: either through individual charity or through the effort to conform human institutions according to justice (which is the *minimum of charity*).[59]

In practice, however, nonredeemed human reason experiences many difficulties in reaching this truth. Voltaire wrote: "Equality is at the same time both the most nat-

---

53. Dann, "Gleichheit," 1016f. See Kern, "Der Beitrag des Christentums," 296.

54. According to Hobbes, equality in the state of nature unreservedly renders legitimate the authority of the sovereign, "to the end he may use the strength and means of them all as he shall think expedient for their peace and common defense." *Leviathan* II, 17. As a result, natural equality generates, by consent, political inequality between an all-powerful sovereign, the "mortal God," and the subjects, who only in the conservation of life maintain a right untouchable by the sovereign (14). See R. Gatti and A. Spadaro, "Uguaglianza," in *Enciclopedia filosofica*, 12:11833–44, 11835. On this basis, and with the idea of monarchy, is born the theory of modern absolutism.

55. Locke deals with the question in his *Treatise on Governance* II. Because the individual is looked upon as a rational egotist, the state is present to ensure proper social relationships (IX, §§ 123–31). Thus it is necessary to maintain equality before the law.

56. On this question, see, for example, G. Sartori, *Democrazia: cosa è*, 5th ed. (Milan: Rizzoli, 1993).

57. See H. Cancik, "Gleichheit und Freiheit: Die antiken Grundlagen der Menschenrechte," in *Vor Gott sind alle gleich*, edited by G. Kehrer (Düsseldorf: Patmos, 1983), 997–1046. See also the classical contribution of R. H. Tawney, *Equality* (London: William Pickering, 1994; originally published in 1931).

58. This was done by Augustine in *De Civ. Dei* XI, 21; 23, 5; 24, and by Thomas Aquinas and Francis of Vitoria.

59. Gatti and Spadaro, "Uguaglianza," 11834. See also J. Maritain, *Les droits de l'homme et la loi naturelle* (New York: Éditions de la maison française, 1942), translated into English as *The Rights of Man and Natural Law* (New York: Gordian Press, 1971). Here we see verified what Benedict XVI applied to the role of the Church in political life: "The Church cannot and must not take upon herself the political battle to bring about the most just society possible. She cannot and must not replace the State. Yet at the same time she cannot and must not remain on the sidelines in the fight for justice. She has to play her part through rational argument and she has to reawaken the spiritual energy without which justice, which always demands sacrifice, cannot prevail and prosper. A just society must be the achievement of politics, not of the Church. Yet the promotion of justice through efforts to bring about openness of mind and will to the demands of the common good is something which concerns the Church deeply." *Deus Caritas Est*, par. 28.

ural and the most chimerical thing."[60] And the nineteenth-century novelist Honoré de Balzac said that "equality may perhaps be a right, but no human power is capable of turning it into a reality."[61] "No human power," Balzac says. Is that really the case? Perhaps we can say that in real terms the power of God made present in Jesus Christ our Lord is capable of converting the elitist "right" into a universally recognized and lived "fact"; for as Paul wrote in a text already cited, "in Christ Jesus you are all sons of God, through faith. For as many of you as were baptized into Christ have put on Christ. There is neither Jew nor Greek, there is neither slave nor free, there is neither male nor female; for you are all one in Christ Jesus" (Gal 3:26–28). Still, the universal conviction that there is equality between all human beings will be fully reached only at the end of time; in the meantime, the logic and power of the kingdom and grace of God will "pressurize" human life and thought to ensure that it becomes a deeply lived and properly understood conviction in every age.

Relationship with Others and the Meaning of Human Equality and Inequality

If according to Christian faith all humans are equal at a fundamental level, the following question emerges: why do inequalities exist in the first place—clear differences between people, visible, tangible, and lasting differences? The reply to this question, theologically speaking, should give us an important key to understanding the inner meaning of human sociality.

Thomas Aquinas openly attempts to clarify the meaning of inequality between created beings in asking "utrum inaequalitas rerum sit a Deo" (whether the inequality of things derives from God).[62] To begin his reflection Thomas cites a well-known text of Origen, according to whom inequality between created beings, and specifically that which exists between humans, refers directly to the dialectic between God and evil.[63]

According to Origen, God created all rational beings at the beginning of time, simultaneously, for all eternity. All were alike, fully spiritual, and lived in a state of contemplation of the Word. The differences between them arose, historically, from the intensity of their freely committed sin. The angels did not sin but retained the primordial dignity they still possess; humans sinned, to a greater or lesser degree, and were placed in human bodies on earth in a way that reflected their guilt; finally, some spirits sinned in a particularly grievous way and were placed in hell: the devil and the fallen angels. The present inequality between the three kinds of originally equal spirits corresponds, therefore, to the intensity and nature of their sin. At the end of time, says Origen, an *apokatastasis*, or universal reconciliation, will take place in which all spiritual beings without exception will return to their primitive state of equal dignity, contemplating anew the Word. In other words, equality among humans

---

60. Voltaire, *The Philosophical Dictionary* (London: Wynn and Scholey, 1802), 151.

61. H. De Balzac, *Histoire des treize* (Paris: Librairie Nouvelle, 1856), translated into English as *The Thirteen* (New York: Macmillan, 1898).

62. See Aquinas, *S.Th.* I, q. 47, a. 2.

63. See Origen, *De Principiis* I, 6:1–4; II, 3:1–5; III, 6:1–9.

is foundational, original, and spiritual; the divergences and inequalities are the result of sin and are made manifest in corporeal life.

The Origenist position certainly offers a complete and coherent explanation that takes into account human freedom and the fundamental equality among humans. In that sense it is fully Christian. However, it is not without its problems. It is based, in fact, on the doctrine of the pre-existence of souls and on the notion that human nature was not originally corporeal but spiritual, in that the body was created merely as an instrument of punishment and purification. In particular, the theme of inequality is focused in a problematic way. According to scripture, in fact, God created humans gratuitously, with different talents and gifts, as the parable of Matthew's Gospel teaches (Mt 25:14–30). Inequality and diversity, in other words, find their root in God's creative action, not in sin.

Responding to the question of the inequalities between created things (whether or not they have their origin in God), Aquinas responds: "Sicut divina sapientia est causa distinctionis rerum propter perfectionem universi, sic et inaequalitatis. Non enim esset perfectum universum, si tantum unus gradus bonitatis invenitur in rebus" (Divine wisdom is the cause of the distinction present in things on account of the perfection of the universe; the same may be said of inequality. The universe, in effect, would not be perfect if in it there was only one grade of goodness).[64] In other words, says Thomas, the divergences between created things are not defects, flaws to be overcome, but rather the sources or occasions of their perfection because they were created by God "propter perfectionem universi." But how can we explain this? Should it not be considered an injustice on God's part to create things, also humans, diversely? Might it not occur that these inequalities occasion or foment an unjust and sinful discrimination? Why has God foreseen inequality; indeed, why has he constituted humans as different from one another?

The following text of Catherine of Siena may offer us a useful line of response. She places the following words in God's mouth:

I distribute the virtues quite diversely, I did not give all of them to each person, but some to one, some to others.... I shall give principally charity to one; justice to another; humility to this one, a living faith to that one.... And so I have given many gifts and graces, both spiritual and temporal, with such diversity that I have not given everything to one single person, so that *you may be constrained to practice charity* towards one another.... I have willed that one should need another and that *all should be my ministers in distributing the graces and gifts* they have received from me.[65]

The saint's intuition is simple and profound: God not only creates humans as social beings, in the sense that human individuals simply *exist* that relate to others. God creates and/or allows differences between humans with a view to bringing them to exercise charity one with the other. Thus they can live their sociality as a free dedication in charity, as disinterested donation and reception. In effect, if God had created all humans equal from the very beginning—equal in everything, down to the last detail, without any needs, and all with the same talents and capacities—human

---

64. Aquinas, *S.Th.* I, q. 47, a. 2, co.
65. Catherine of Siena, *Dialogs* I, 7, in *CCC* 1937.

sociality would remain as a purely decorative fact, without meaning or relevance. We may say that God ensured that there would be inequalities to ensure that humans are urged—and in a sense coerced—to contribute, each one according to his possibilities, to the enrichment of the other. In this way, to some degree, they overcome inequalities without ever eliminating them, because human creatures are always beings in need, eternally open to enrichment. The ultimate source of human sociality is God, who creates humans. Its meaning and dynamism is given by the virtue of charity, but the opportunity to live charity is provided in the main by the inequalities that exist between persons. The need of the other person thus becomes a kind of divine calling, such that the one who has in abundance can pass on what God has given him to the one who is in need. A classic work of early medieval spirituality, the *Libellus de diversis ordinibus*, often attributed to Reimbaldus, teaches: "Love in others what you do not possess, because the other can love in you what he does not possess; in this way, what you do and what he does will be good for him and for you."[66]

In effect, God could have constituted humans from the beginning perfectly made, down to the last detail, with their eternal vocation and destiny fully realized. However, his plan of salvation has developed in an essentially historical way throughout the course of time. In other words, God has preferred to communicate gifts and graces to humans (1) who freely receive them (chapter 20), (2) within a temporal and historical process (chapter 21), and (3) through other people (this chapter). In the optic of faith, therefore, freedom, historicity, and sociality belong fully and permanently to humans made in the image and likeness of God and composed of body and soul. In the light of Christian faith, the ultimate meaning of human equality (in the context of really existing inequalities) is to be found in the fact that humans can receive and communicate and exchange the gifts of God with one another. Let us consider this issue more closely.

Giving and Receiving

God gives humans goods and talents not only for themselves but with a specific purpose: that of passing them on to others who stand in need of them. This way of acting shows no sign of weakness or limitation on the part of God, who stands in no need to use subordinate mediations in acting *ad extra*, as Platonic cosmogonies held. Indeed, the very opposite is the case: the fact of establishing human mediations to communicate his gifts shows the greatest possible perfection in God.[67] God gives humans his gifts, they accept them and make them their own as creatures, and they share them with others. There is therefore a deep equality among humans in the sense that all can communicate something to others and at the same time are in a position to receive from them. What opens up the possibility of giving and receiving among humans—the living core of their sociality—is precisely the existence of a wide variety of inequalities and differences among them. Without such inequalities and imperfections between people, there would be little practical opportunity of giving

---

66. Reimbaldus, *Libellus de diversis ordinibus et professionibus que sunt in aecclesia*, 15.

67. On mediation in the order of grace and salvation, see Thomas Aquinas *S.Th.* I-II, q. 5, a. 5, ad 2, and also chapter 16, notes 157ff. and corresponding text.

oneself to others to live charity. According to words of *Gaudium et Spes* frequently cited by John Paul II, "Man, who is the only creature on earth which God willed for itself, cannot fully find himself except through a sincere gift of himself."[68] Still, giving of oneself to others requires a real knowledge of them in their true situation and needs; the concrete profile of lived charity is determined by the person loved, not by the one loving.[69]

And yet a further observation should be made. Those who are capable of enriching others might well consider that they are superior to them and thus stand in need of the latter in a very superficial sense. But in real terms this is not the case, for two reasons.[70] In the first place, it is not the case because gifts and talents of whatever kind have their origin only in God (and should be received and used always in recognition of the creator for his glory). Thus self-giving to others is objectively an act of reception and acceptance, because what is given has in the first place been received, whether from other people or ultimately from God himself, the source of all good things, or, more precisely, always *from* God and often *through* other people. In this sense, humans do not really give; rather they hand on what they have received. On this account, "the one who does not give is ungrateful to the One who filled him with gifts," writes Augustine.[71] Or, to cite the subtitle of a book by Xavier Lacroix, *Donner la vie, c'est la recevoir*, "To give life is to receive it."[72] Still, it is true that those who give are enriched, not on the basis of their own "treasure" but because in giving themselves generously they open themselves to the generosity of God, accumulating treasures in heaven (Mt 6:20). On the text "For to him who has will more be given" (Mk 4:25), Augustine comments: "God will give more to those who use for others what they have received: God fills up what he has given from the beginning."[73] The Lord encourages his disciples in the following terms: "Give, and it will be given to you; good measure, pressed down, shaken together, running over, will be put into your lap. For the measure you give will be the measure you get back" (Lk 6:38).

In the second place, the fact of receiving something as a gift from someone else (in this case, recognizing one's own needfulness) in itself constitutes an act of donation to the one who gives, that is, a gift of profound humanity. In effect, those who recognize themselves in need before others enrich their lives not only with the goods received but with the donation they make of themselves in opening themselves up to one from whom they have received the gift. Hence, just as the giver should not take vain credit for giving, neither should the receiver feel humiliated or frustrated by the fact of receiving. In fact, Jesus places the following words on his disciples' tongues: "We are unworthy servants; we have only done what was our duty" (Lk 17:10). And Jesus himself reminds them, "You received without paying, give without pay" (Mt 10:8), a text that goes to the very heart of Matthew's mission discourse. Likewise Paul speaks of the "abundance" of Christians and exhorts them: "As a matter of equality

---

68. *GS*, no. 24.

69. See chapter 15, notes 139ff. and corresponding text.

70. On the fundamental dynamics of giving and receiving, see the reflections of MacIntyre, *Dependent Rational Animals*, on what he calls "recognized dependency."

71. Augustine, *Sermo* 260, 2.

72. See X. Lacroix, *Le corps retrouvé: donner la vie, c'est la recevoir* (Paris: Bayard, 2012).

73. Augustine, *De doct. christiana* I, 1, 1.

your abundance at the present time should supply their want, so that their abundance may supply your want, that there may be equality" (2 Cor 8:14).[74]

It may even happen, in fact, that receiving requires more effort, humility, trust, openness, and humanity toward others (in real terms, toward God) than does giving, because it demands the quintessential attitude of the creature, which is one of gratitude.[75] In any case, both giving and receiving are fully human acts in that they manifest human dignity and the fundamental equality between humans. Perhaps we can say, in the light of faith and of human experience, that human equality is expressed in the certitude that *all* are beneficiaries of the divine gifts: "Your Father who is in heaven … makes his sun rise on the evil and on the good, and sends rain on the just and on the unjust" (Mt 5:45). Pope Leo the Great exhorted the faithful to fast and give alms "in such a way that, also in the midst of unequal fortunes, the disposition of soul of all the faithful may be of equal caliber."[76] Gregory the Great describes as follows the condition of equality of all Christians: "In sancta Ecclesia unusquisque et portat alterum et portatur ab altero" (In the holy Church, each one carries the other and is carried by the other).[77] In this context Paul VI spoke of a "civilization of love," and John Paul II repeated often that "love is the native vocation of every human being."[78]

To sum up, God gives humans his gifts in abundance. Humans are called to accept them with humility and gratitude. As a proof of the latter, they are likewise called on to communicate them generously to others, to share them with the rest of humanity. A shared good, based on the original divine donation that is gratefully received and willingly handed on, produces a "new good," previously nonexistent, a good that is shared by many. It has its origin in God but belongs also to the giver and the receiver. In this way, humans enjoy the good received and show forth their awareness of its quality as a gift by thanking the creator and sharing it with other creatures. The good that originally comes from God and is shared by humans, reinforcing the unity between them, though without producing a uniform leveling out between one and all, may be called *communion*.

Egotism, individualism, and antisocial attitudes may be present both in the fact of not giving what one has received from God for others and in that of not opening oneself to what has been offered as a gift by another. In both cases, humans do not wish to consider themselves in debt to anybody, not even to God, and it is here that we discover the essence of sin: not recognizing ourselves as creatures and sinners before God, from whom alone all good things come.

Inequalities and Discrimination

What may be said of the inequalities that develop and consolidate in the context of sin, that is, human closure before the needs of others, the refusal to share with oth-

---

74. This "abundance" can hardly refer to "economic prosperity; rather it is their enrichments by grace as in 1 Cor 1:7." R. P. Martin, *2 Corinthians*, in *WBC* 40:267.

75. See P. J. Leithart, *Gratitude: An Intellectual History* (Waco, Tex.: Baylor University Press, 2014). See chapter 20, notes 115ff. and corresponding text.

76. Leo the Great, *Sermo 6 de Quadragesima*, 2.   77. Gregory the Great, *In Ezech. II*, hom. 1, 5.

78. John Paul II, *Familiaris Consortio*, par. 11.

ers goods that have been received? *Gaudium et Spes* reads: "The equal dignity of persons demands that a more humane and just condition of life be brought about. For excessive economic and social differences between the members of the one human family or population groups cause scandal, and militate against social justice, equity, the dignity of the human person, as well as social and international peace."[79] But what goods can really become a source of discrimination between humans? Is it possible that there are inequalities that, instead of becoming sources and opportunities of enrichment because they open spaces for donation and reception, as we just saw, actually damage and corrode human dignity and make humans permanently closed in on themselves? How can we distinguish between the inequalities that God creates and permits *propter perfectionem*, to take up an expression of Thomas Aquinas, and those that humans create and maintain *propter seipsos*, "for themselves," in order to reinforce their own security, to turn in on themselves and stay closed up within their own egotism and self-sufficiency, before God and before others?

Different Kinds of Inequality

Three kinds of inequality may be mentioned. In the first place are those that are simply not wanted by God, being connected directly to sin, to infidelity to one's vocation, and so on. The Christian *sic et simpliciter* cannot accept them. In the second place there are inequalities that God positively wants, if it is legitimate to read the will of God from the way in which God has constituted nature and humanity:[80] race, sex, the fact of being born in a certain place and time, one's specific vocation, genetic constitution, or level of holiness. These differences—which do not affect the fundamental equal dignity of humans open to divine and human gifts—should be accepted and loved by the persons who possess them and by others because in these elements (and others) is manifested the will of God for them. Pope Francis writes: "Valuing one's own body in its femininity or masculinity is necessary if I am going to be able to recognize myself in an encounter with someone who is different. In this way we can joyfully accept the specific gifts of another man or woman, the work of God the Creator, and find mutual enrichment."[81] In the *third* place, there are divergences between persons which are the result not only of God's gifts and decision, but also of human action, social life, history and culture, divergences that correspond more or less to God's will. These are distinctions that God wills to some degree, and certainly allows. Perhaps we may say he wants them *secundum quid*, that is on the basis of a higher purpose. This is the case with issues such as intelligence and education, professional and social opportunities, riches and success. On the basis of the logic we have seen in this chapter, we can say that God has wanted (or permitted) that some have these goods in greater abundance than others *in order to communicate them* to the latter: intelligence and education, to instruct; professional and social opportunities as well as material riches, in order to facilitate the lives of others. "If we make something our own," Francis says, "it is only to administer it for the good of all. If we do not, we burden our consciences with the weight of having denied the existence of others."[82]

---

79. *GS*, no. 29.

80. See the document of the International Theological Commission, *In Search of a Universal Ethic.*

81. *LS*, par. 155.   82. Ibid., 95.

A Christian Focus on Political Action?

Material prosperity has been considered an unmistakable sign of divine favor toward humans at different stages in history: at times throughout the Old Testament, in Calvinistic thought, or in some modern forms of "prosperity religion." Still, the message at the heart of the New Testament is to be found in the fact that, in general terms, those who have little in this life are to be considered especially blessed by the Lord (Mt 5:3). In any case, we can say that God has wanted to give humans certain goods but also that he has destined the created world for *all* humans. Thus the fact that some have more than others does not mean that they can egoistically hold onto them for their own exclusive benefit, against the reasonable claims of others (this is what the social doctrine of the Church calls the "social mortgage of private property"[83]), or, even worse, to consider themselves more favored by God. From the point of view of the practice of social justice, the following question may be asked: is it obligatory to *oblige* people to share their excessive spiritual and material goods (thus facilitating justice at the expense of the institutionalization of charity), or would it be better to leave to people the possibility of communicating their goods freely to others (thus avoiding the institutionalization of charity but not guaranteeing, at least in the short term, greater justice)? A more complete reflection would be required to answer these questions fully.

83. Pontifical Council for Justice and Peace, *Compendium of the Social Doctrine of the Church* (London: Burns and Oates, 2005), nos. 176–84. *LS*, par. 93 speaks of "social mortgage."

23   HUMANS CREATED IN THE IMAGE OF GOD
AS MAN AND WOMAN

There are deep differences, at the level of every cell, between the male and female brain.
LOUANN BRIZENDINE[1]

Naturam expelles furca, tamen usque recurret.   HORACE[2]

From the very beginning they appear as a "unity of the two."   JOHN PAUL II[3]

One of the most obvious distinctions between persons is the sexual one, between man and woman, between male and female. Sexual difference manifests itself not only physiologically, but also psychologically and with differentiating features in the areas of affectivity and cognition.[4] In this chapter, however, we cannot consider in

---

1. L. Brizendine, *The Female Brain* (New York: Morgan Road Books, 2006).

2. Horace, *Epist. I*, 10, 24: "Throw out the natural with a fork, and it will come back all the same." The same idea is to be found in P. N. Destouches: "chassez le naturel, il revient au galop" (hunt out the natural, it will return with a gallop), from the work *La Belle orgueilleuse*.

3. John Paul II, *Mulieris Dignitatem*, par. 6.

4. The bibliography on the matter, of course, is vast, and many issues are still controversial and unsettled. See, for example, the bibliographical study of J. A. Riestra, "Los movimientos feministas y su significación teológica," *Estudios marianos* 62 (1996): 3–42, and the reflection of C. Burke, "Il ruolo umanizzante della sessualità," *Studi Cattolici* 492 (2002): 100–108. As regards the scientific side of sexual differences, see S. E. Rhoads, *Taking Sex Differences Seriously* (San Francisco: Encounter Books, 2004); L. Sax, *Why Gender Matters: What Parents and Teachers Need to Know about the Emerging Science of Sex Differences* (New York: Doubleday, 2005). Recently, see M. Ingalhalikar et al., "Sex Differences in the Structural Connectome of the Human Brain," *Proceedings of the National Academy of Sciences* 2 (December 2013). See also L. Irigaray, *Speculum of the Other Woman* (Ithaca, N.Y.: Cornell University Press, 1985); Irigaray, *An Ethics of Sexual Difference* (London: Continuum, 2004). N. Chodorow, in *The Reproduction of Mothering: Psychoanalysis and the Sociology of Gender* (Berkeley: University of California Press, 1999), explains that women tend to develop in a way that is directed toward looking after others, sharing between people, and this not only on account of the education they receive but also for psychological reasons. L. Brizendine says: "The female brain has tremendously unique aptitudes—outstanding verbal agility, the ability to connect deeply in friendship, a nearly psychic capacity to read faces and tone of voice for emotions and states of mind, and the ability to defuse conflict. All of this is hardwired into the brains of women. These are the talents women are born with that many men, frankly, are not. Men are born with other talents, shaped by their own hormonal reality" (*The Female Brain*, 8).

depth the complex issues that refer to the psychological, sociological, and human differences between men and women and the corresponding myriad social implications, but rather we shall consider the theological statute of the difference, considering it on the basis of the creation of human persons, of their present action, of their divine vocation and their destiny to final resurrection. Following and applying what was presented in the previous chapter on human sociality, on human equality, giving and receiving, we will look at the origin and eventual purpose of the distinction between man and woman, considering this distinction on the basis of God's creating action and the eschatological destiny of all humans. The Church teaches the fundamental equality of man and woman, as well as their obvious differences. And the dynamics of their relationship is situated within this fundamental social polarity of equality and difference we considered in chapter 22. As von Balthasar writes: "The man/woman relationship can stand as a paradigm of that community dimension which characterizes man's entire nature."[5]

In recent decades the Church has spoken frequently on the question of the relationship between man and woman in the light of theology;[6] Pope John Paul II spoke specifically of the "feminine genius." The most recent document of the Holy See on the collaboration of man and woman in the Church (2004) has the following to say:

It is appropriate to recall that the feminine values mentioned here are above all human values: the human condition of man and woman created in the image of God is one and indivisible. It is only because women are more immediately attuned to these values that they are the reminder and the privileged sign of such values. But, in the final analysis, every human being, man or woman, is destined to be "for the other." In this perspective, that which is called "femininity" is more than simply an attribute of the female sex. The word designates indeed the fundamental human capacity to live for the other and because of the other.[7]

In the history of anthropology as a whole, consideration of the issues of the emancipation of woman and of the rapport between man and woman is quite recent (having begun in a serious way in the nineteenth century). Hence we shall examine first some moments of modern history related to the topic. This will be followed by Biblical, historical, and theological considerations.

---

5. Von Balthasar, *Theo-Drama*, 2:365.

6. Of particular importance in the magisterium of John Paul II is the apostolic letter *Mulieris Dignitatem* and also the *Letter to Women*, June 29, 1995, which refers to a message directed to the General Secretary of the fourth World Conference on the Woman in Beijing, Gertrude Mongella, dated May 26, 1995. Among Catholic theologians, see T. Beattie, *New Catholic Feminism: Theology and Theory* (London: Routledge, 2006), who, in contrast with Church teaching, attempts to justify the priestly ordination of women and other practices. For an approach that is closer to Church teaching, inspired by H. U. von Balthasar, see M. M. Schumacher, ed., *Women in Christ: Toward a New Feminism* (Grand Rapids, Mich.: W. B. Eerdmans, 2004). On the question of the ordination of women, see the exhaustive work of A. Piola, *Donna e sacerdozio: Indagine storico-teologica degli aspetti antropologici dell'ordinazione delle donne* (Cantalup: Effatà, 2006), which gathers up and presents the many studies undertaken over previous decades on this topic, culminating in John Paul II, *Ordinatio Sacerdotalis*, Apostolic Letter, May 22, 1994.

7. Congregation for the Doctrine of the Faith, *Letter to the Bishops of the Catholic Church on the Collaboration of Men and Women in the Church and the World*, May 31, 2004, no. 14.

The Contemporary Debate between
Sex and Gender

It may fairly be said that throughout the twentieth century three principal stages have been verified in the secular understanding of feminine identity, with positions that have challenged philosophical and theological reflection in a variety of different ways.[8] In the first place, we can speak of a "feminism of equality," which under the inspiration of the French Revolution has insisted upon equality between the genders in their social rapport. The best-known author here is Simone de Beauvoir, whose ideas on the subject may be seen in her 1949 work *The Second Sex*.[9] According to de Beauvoir, femininity is not given by nature but is just a social and civil construct: "Woman is not born, woman you become," she declared. To be a woman, in other words, is not something that is given with birth but rather a state that is reached and determined, consciously and freely, without "natural" presuppositions. Woman therefore needs to be emancipated, de Beauvoir argues; she must reject the identity proposed by the official culture, which is predominantly male chauvinist. Besides, the female is not to be considered "another" with respect to the male. According to de Beauvoir, while a man lives free from his body by means of his rationality, for a woman her body is still her destiny, especially on account of motherhood. Hence, she proposes, nature must be overcome by culture.[10] The basis for a systematic distinction between sex and gender—that is, between nature and culture—is clearly to be seen in the work of de Beauvoir.

The second stage of this process may be called a "feminism of difference." The best-known exponent of this position is Luce Irigaray, also French, who expressed her views in her 1974 work *Speculum*.[11] When Irigaray wrote this work, the social and political emancipation of women had been more or less achieved. The key issue shifted to the question of the postmodern focus on the individual with respect to the surrounding culture. Men and women are different, Irigaray says clearly. Yet specifically feminine identity has been neglected on account of the arbitrary domination of the male. She attempts to overcome a notion of neutral, common human nature that excludes all reference to the body. Irigaray holds that human thought is not in fact neutral but still predominantly male. The title of one of her books shows this concern: *To Speak Is Never Neutral*.[12] She proposes, therefore, that women should produce their own form of thinking from the standpoint of themselves and the whole world, on the basis of their own bodies. She suggests that they must create a feminist philosophy, a feminist theology, a feminist economy, and so on.[13]

---

8. See P. F. De Solenni, *A Hermeneutic of Aquinas's "Mens" through a Sexually Differentiated Epistemology: Towards an Understanding of Woman as Imago Dei* (Rome: Edusc, 2003), 23–65; G. Angelini, "Passaggio al postmoderno: Il *gender* in questione," in *Maschio e femmina li creò*, edited by G. Angelini (Milan: Glossa, 2008), 263–96, esp. 276–94.

9. S. de Beauvoir, *The Second Sex* (New York: Vintage, 1989). The following works may also be mentioned: B. Friedan, *The Feminine Mystique* (Harmondsworth: Penguin, 1963), and K. Millet, *Sexual Politics* (London: Virago, 1985; originally published in 1969).

10. The likeness to Sartre as regards the denial or at least malleability of human nature is undeniable.

11. See Irigaray, *Speculum*.

12. See L. Irigaray, *To Speak Is Never Neutral* (London: Continuum, 2002).

13. On feminist theology, see especially the work of Daly, *Beyond God the Father*.

In the "feminism of difference," Angelini observes that "the most elementary evidence is removed, the evidence that binds the word, and with it the complex process of the meaningfulness of the real, to the encounter between male and female."[14] That is to say, given the depth of the distinction between being man and being woman in human language, it will be no easy task to consolidate a feminist thought system clearly separated from general thought. Besides, Angelini adds, "the perspective which provides the perception of the meaning of all things is not defined in reference to one gender or another, but in the encounter between the two, and therefore from their symbolic interchange ... thanks to the practical encounter between man and woman."[15] In other words, from the point of view of Christian faith, it is not so much a matter of developing a feminist philosophy or theology starting with woman, or even one that starts with man (for this would denote an individualistic starting point), but rather a matter of developing one on the basis of the living union between them, a union made up of donation, reception, and acceptance.

Regarding the third stage, returning to some degree to the position of de Beauvoir, more recently specialists have begun to speak of the "theory of gender."[16] In simple terms, this theory denies that the polar scheme of the sexes—male and female—is paradigmatic, because the identity of each person is defined not by his or her sex but rather by the person's gender. "Sex" is determined biologically and is fixed, but "gender" is a highly plastic category. In contrast with a "feminism of difference," the different features of a "feminine sensibility" are not the expression of a feminine nature but rather the historical and cultural configuration of an image of womanhood imposed by human will, specifically by men. The most influential contemporary defender of this position is Judith Butler. The title of her 2004 book is *Undoing Gender.*[17] Butler above all intends to overcome the classic heterosexual paradigm, the fundamental and "immovable" polarity between man and woman, dominated by nature. On the one hand, each person, with his or her own "gender," is present in society. On the other hand, each one must emancipate him- or herself from their own gender, throwing off all dependence on the "truth" of nature or culture. Butler writes as follows: "Gender itself becomes an artifice free from every bond."[18] This, of course, is not an easy position to maintain, as Francis Bacon said several centuries ago: "Nature is often hidden, some times it is overwhelmed, but very seldom is extinguished."[19] And P. N. Destouches said: "Hunt out the natural, it will return with a gallop."[20]

Doubtless there is a certain tension between sex and gender, similar to the tension that exists on a broader level between nature and culture.[21] But is also true that

14. Angelini, "Passaggio al postmoderno," 286.

15. Ibid., 280f.

16. It is suggested that there are five (or more) genders: masculine heterosexual, feminine heterosexual, homosexual, lesbian, bisexual, transsexual, and undifferentiated.

17. See J. Butler, *Undoing Gender* (New York: Routledge, 2004).

18. J. Butler, *Gender Trouble: Feminism and the Subversion of Identity*, 2nd ed. (London: Routledge, 1999), 6.

19. F. Bacon, *Essays.*

20. P. N. Destouches: *chassez le naturel, il revient au galop*: "hunt out the natural, it will return with a gallop," from the work *La Belle orgueilleuse.*

21. See G. Solé Romeo, *Historia del feminismo: Siglos XIX y XX* (Pamplona: Eunsa, 1995). On this question, see J. Burggraf, "Gender," in *Lexicon: Ambiguous and Debatable Terms Regarding Family Life and Ethical*

the idea of "gender" as an independent and perfectly plastic aspect of human existence is somewhat exaggerated, with a surfeit of ideology[22] and a deficit of science.[23] A unitary anthropology, developed by Aristotle and Thomas Aquinas and based on the doctrine of the *anima forma corporis*, which affirms the close relationship between body and soul, destined to rise up together at the end of time, leaves little space for such a tension, while a dualistic, Platonic, Gnostic, or Cartesian anthropology might well embrace it more generously.[24]

The Theological Meaning of the Distinction between Man and Woman

At the level of God's creation it has been asked, at times implicitly, at times explicitly, if the distinction between man and woman corresponds simply to the will of God, if it is to some degree the result of sin, or if God wanted it *secundum quid*, that is, as a means to obtain an ulterior aim. In particular, we should consider whether the distinction between man and woman relates to some degree to the fact that humans were created "in the image and likeness" of God. As regards our eschatological destiny, we can inquire into the final statute of the distinction between man and woman, and especially whether this distinction will remain in their risen state. In reality, both approaches—starting with creation and starting with eschatology—should by rights coincide if we accept the idea that according to many authors (in particular Irenaeus, Origen, and Thomas Aquinas) the end of human life involves a return to the original perfection and serves as its definitive confirmation.

In the next section we shall consider what scripture has to say about the matter. In the following one we shall look at a series of explanations elaborated by philosophers and theologians on the origin of the distinction between man and woman as creatures and the consequent relationship that has arisen between them. After that we shall reflect on the way that woman has been spoken about throughout the course of history, especially as regards the important contribution Christianity made to giving expression to her dignity. Finally, the central part of the chapter deals with the "complementary" relationship between man and woman in the light of the faith, as a "unity of two," especially in recent theology and Church teaching.

Questions, edited by the Pontifical Council for the Family (Front Royal, Va.: Human Life International, 2006), 399–408; S. Zanardo and M. Forcina, "Differenza sessuale," *Enciclopedia filosofica*, 7:2851–61.

22. On the controversies around the world conferences on the woman in Cairo (1994) and Beijing (1995), see D. O'Leary, *The Gender Agenda: Redefining Equality* (Lafayette, La.: Vital Issues Press, 1997). On the legal implications of the category of "gender" in the Italian context, see L. Palazzani, *Sex/gender: Gli equivoci dell'uguaglianza* (Turin: G. Giappichelli, 2011). Pope Francis has frequently spoken of an "ideology of gender." In one audience (April 15, 2015) he asked if "gender theory is not, at the same time, an expression of frustration and resignation, which seeks to cancel out sexual difference because it no longer knows how to confront it," cited in *LS*, par. 155.

23. See Ó. Alzamora Revoredo, "An Ideology of Gender: Dangers and Scope," *Lexicon*, 465–82; De Solenni, *A Hermeneutic of Aquinas's Mens*, 67–84.

24. On the influence of the Cartesian approach to the theory of gender, see Taylor, *Sources of the Self*, 161f.; De Solenni, *A Hermeneutic of Aquinas's Mens*, 81–84.

Biblical Data: The Genesis Creation Narratives

The first chapters of the book of Genesis speak of the creation of man and woman in two separate accounts, in Genesis 1–2:4a and 2:4b–3:24.

The Creation of Man and Woman in the
Image and Likeness of God

In the first chapter of Genesis[25] we read (1:26–28):

Then God said, "Let us make man in our image, after our likeness; and let them have dominion over the fish of the sea, and over the birds of the air, and over the cattle, and over all the earth, and over every creeping thing that creeps upon the earth." So God created man in his own image, in the image of God he created him; *male and female he created them.* And God blessed them, and God said to them, "Be fruitful and multiply, and fill the earth and subdue it; and have dominion over the fish of the sea and over the birds of the air and over every living thing that moves upon the earth."

Humans, the only creatures to be made "in the image and likeness of God," are presented in a clearly differentiated way, as male and as female. At the end of the account, the author adds: "And God saw everything that he had made, and behold, it was very good" (Gn 1:31). This text expresses something of the divine approval of and complacency toward the entire work of creation in its greatness and harmony, presided over by man and woman. This divine complacency finds an ulterior confirmation in a later text of Genesis (5:1–3), in which the children of the first couple are presented as having been made "in the image" of both God and their parents.[26] Dominion over the earth, to which God insistently invites humans, is directly associated with fruitfulness and human reproduction, fruit of the divine blessing, which is given precisely through the union of man and woman. In brief, the fact that humans have been made in the image and likeness of God is expressed, according to Genesis, in a special way in the fundamental human sociality expressed in the binomial man-woman. That is to say, human sociality—especially the foundational relationship between man and woman—exists in order for humanity to carry out its vocation to dominate the earth while at the same time submitting itself to God and bringing all things to him.

The Formation of Woman from Man

In the second chapter of Genesis the distinction between man and woman is spoken of in a more extensive though enigmatic way than in the first chapter. The creation of humans is described in the following terms: "The Lord God formed man of dust from the ground, and breathed into his nostrils the breath of life; and man became a living being" (Gn 2:7). The human being is presented first of all in the mascu-

25. On the Biblical question, see, for example, Horowitz, *The Image of God in Man*; Bird, "'Male and Female He Created Them,'" and the whole of chapter 4.

26. In effect, Gn 5:1–3, which substantially repeats Gn 1:26–27, adds, however, an interesting novelty: that the "image" has a clear filial side to it: "When God created man, he made him in the likeness of God. Male and female he created them, and he blessed them and named them man when they were created. When Adam had lived a hundred and thirty years, he became the father of a son *in his own likeness, after his image*, and named him Seth." See chapter 4, notes 37ff. and corresponding text.

line form: his name, *Adamah*, means "the one who has been taken from the ground." Successively, God gives fulfillment to his project or dream for humanity by placing him in paradise, "in the garden of Eden to till it and keep it" (Gn 2:15), with only one express prohibition: "Of the tree of the knowledge of good and evil you shall not eat, for in the day that you eat of it you shall die" (Gn 2:17). In this way God expresses the obligation of humans to cultivate and take care of the earth while remaining always subject to God, the only Lord of heaven and earth.

At the same time, according to the text, God recognizes that man is not perfectly content and fulfilled with the simple company of water and plants. For this reason he says: "It is not good that the man should be alone; I will make him a helper fit for him" (Gn 2:18). It is as if he were saying that to live in relation to other living beings belongs to the very structure of man as created by God. As a result God creates the animals and birds, who are brought to man to receive their names from him. In this way—giving names to the creatures—man expresses his vocation to exercise domin-ion over creation. Still, the text observes that "for the man there was not found a helper fit for him" (Gn 2:20). The Congregation for the Doctrine of the Faith docu-ment on collaboration of men and women says: "The term 'help' here does not refer to an inferior, but to a vital helper."[27] With a view to finding a helper that will be similar to Adam, God makes the woman, drawn out of man himself, and presents her to him.[28] As Pope Francis has written, "Woman is not a replica of man; she comes directly from the creative act of God."[29] Adam's exclamation of recognition and accep-tance of the woman is joyful and spontaneous: "This at last is bone of my bones and flesh of my flesh [that is, she is like man, of the same nature, just as man is like God]; she shall be called Woman ['ishsha] because she was taken out of Man ['ish]" (Gn 2:23). With man finding at last a perfect companion, the author of the book of Genesis con-cludes the narration by saying: "Therefore a man leaves his father and his mother and cleaves to his wife, and they become one flesh" (Gn 2:24).[30] Man and woman, in fact, though presented as two distinct individuals, are at the same time equal and form "one flesh"; they have just one life, they have an origin and destiny in common, and they form a lasting communion, "a unity of two," as John Paul II often repeated. The human being is presented again, in language different from that in Genesis 1:27, as an intrinsically social being, with a sociality that has the distinction and union of man and woman as its point of departure.[31]

Besides, the text of Genesis points out the ultimate purpose of the distinction and union between man and woman. The exegete Phyllis Bird explains it as follows:

Gen 1:27 contributes the notion, rightly understood if wrongly isolated and absolutized in traditional interpretation, that sex, as differentiation and union, is intended for procre-

27. Congregation for the Doctrine of the Faith, *On the Collaboration of Men and Women*, no. 6. The term used in Gn 2:18 is *ezer neghed*. See W. E. Phipps, who in "Adam's Rib: Bone of Contention," *Theology Today* 33, no. 3 (1997): 263–73, writes that "the term 'ezer neghed' is best translated as a companion or partner similar to him" (271).

28. On the creation of woman from man, see J. B. Pritchard, ed., *Ancient Near Eastern Texts Relating to the Old Testament*, 3rd ed. (Princeton, N.J.: Princeton University Press, 1978).

29. Francis, General Audience, April 22, 2015.

30. On this text, see P. Gilbert, "Une seule chair," *Nouvelle Revue Théologique* 100 (1978): 66–89.

31. See ibid., 88.

ation—a divinely given capacity and power conceived both in terms of blessing and command. But the word that activates the endowment addresses the species, not the individual, and is limited in its application by the setting in which it is spoken, a limitation made explicit in the qualifying amplification, "and fill the earth."[32]

Likewise, the *Talmud of Rashi* (the full name of the rabbi who wrote it in the tenth century was Shlomo Yitzaki), in a passage on Genesis 2:24 speaks of the close bond between man and woman on the one hand and between them and human procreation on the other, commenting: "It is in their child that they become one flesh."[33]

The Fall of Man and Woman

In the third chapter of Genesis is to be found an account of the Fall of our first parents. Tempted by the serpent, the first couple do not obey the divine command, here voiced by the woman, called Eve: "We may eat of the fruit of the trees of the garden; but God said, 'You shall not eat of the fruit of the tree which is in the midst of the garden, neither shall you touch it, lest you die'" (Gn 3:2–3). The woman was fooled by the serpent, the text tells us; she gave the fruit to her husband, and both of them ate it and thus fell into sin, one being the accomplice of the other. The realization of their nudity and the will to hide are presented by the text as manifestations of their shame of being seen after the sin, seen by the other, by the accomplice in sin, and above all by God, their creator and Lord, who had entrusted them with the created world, God who "walked in the garden in the cool of the day" (Gn 3:8). God calls them in the garden, seeking them out (Gn 3:9). And man, no longer able to hide, tries to excuse himself, placing the blame on his companion: "The woman you gave to be with me, she gave me fruit of the tree, and I ate" (Gn 3:12). In other words, guilt is recognized but shifted or transferred. The woman, a gift of God to man, "bone of my bone, flesh of my flesh," is made to carry blame: besides, her identity seems to be changed because in the mind of the man she has become, through her sin, a temptation, a problem, and a wound, and therefore a threat to his life. In fact, man also seems to put the blame on God ("the woman *you* gave to be with me"), perhaps considering the gift insufficient or improper, and therefore to be rejected. Sin, as we have seen, lies in the non-recognition of gift. The woman, in turn, puts the blame on the serpent, on the material world inferior to humans: "The serpent beguiled me, and I ate" (Gn 3:13). The result is that all three, the man, the woman and the serpent, are responsible for the sin in different ways and are punished. For this original offense, our first parents—and on account of them the whole of humanity—forfeit their primitive familiarity and friendship with God.

To the serpent God says: "Because you have done this, cursed are you above all cattle, and above all wild animals; upon your belly you shall go, and dust you shall eat all the days of your life" (Gn 3:14–15). The man is chastised and punished with the fatigue of work, the very means by which he should have been able to exercise his dominion over the earth as a joyous original vocation, and with death (Gn 3:17–19):

32. Bird, "'Male and Female He Created Them,'" 157.
33. Cited by J. Eisenberg in *Et Dieu créa Ève* (Paris: A. Michel, 1979), 176.

Because you have listened to the voice of your wife, and have eaten of the tree of which I commanded you, "You shall not eat of it," cursed is the ground because of you; in toil you shall eat of it all the days of your life; thorns and thistles it shall bring forth to you; and you shall eat the plants of the field. In the sweat of your face you shall eat bread till you return to the ground, for out of it you were taken; you are dust, and to dust you shall return.

In a sense it may be said that with this punishment man's masculinity is mortified and diminished. And the woman is punished with birth pangs and with an involuntary submission to man: "I will greatly multiply your pain in childbearing; in pain you shall bring forth children, yet your desire shall be for your husband, and he shall rule over you" (Gn 3:16). In other words, that aspect of the original divine vocation to exercise dominion over the earth through the fruitfulness of motherhood is affected by suffering and ambivalence; it is presented as an evil. In woman maternity lived with joy and independence is mortified.

The Meaning of "He Shall Rule over You"

But does scripture mean to say that man would "rule" over woman as a punishment for sin? After they commit the first sin, the union between man and woman remains, certainly, and at an objective level it tends toward the original purpose of human life, which is that of sharing a common dominion over the earth through work and procreative fruitfulness. Following their sin, however, this dominion is no longer exercised in a harmonious way because, in the union between man and woman, the text says, the woman tends to be subjected to the man, seeking in him her strength and therefore recognizing her own weakness. Still, the man tends to abuse this weakness and dominate not only the material world but also the woman, treating her as an object, as a thing among things, as an inferior reality, not as a person, another "I," "bone of my bones, flesh of my flesh." The expression in Genesis—"Your desire shall be for your husband, and he shall rule over you"—does not describe a precept, it is not an explicit manifestation of the will of God, and it does not reflect an immutable aspect of natural human life. Rather it expresses a negative condition that persists, and will continue to persist, between man and woman, generation after generation, as the historical, contingent (and therefore redeemable) sign of their sin. Besides, from the moment of their fall onward, the text says, woman is no longer called *'ishsha* ("taken from your husband") but is rather called *hawwah*, that is, "the mother of all the living" (Gn 3:20). She goes from being a spouse and a woman, the book of Genesis tells us without further explanations, to become a mother. Sin seems to establish an alternative between being a woman and a mother.

In real terms, however, the great chastisement for the first sin is our first parents' loss of familiarity with God, their loss of closeness to him: "The Lord God sent him forth from the garden of Eden" (Gn 3:23). "When humanity considers God its enemy, the relationship between man and woman becomes distorted. When this relationship is damaged, their access to the face of God risks being compromised in turn."[34] Still, as the same text tells us (Gn 3:15), God does not completely abandon humans; in fact, he promises them a savior in their moment of maximum disgrace.

---

34. Congregation for the Doctrine of the Faith, *On the Collaboration of Men and Women*, no. 7.

Many things could be said about these texts. One point is worth mentioning. It is clear that the relationship between the man and the woman, originally marked by harmony and equality, is decisively affected by sin, by the original Fall. This fact, witnessed by scripture, has given rise to theological reflection that considers the texts that refer to the man-woman distinction in an primordially hamartiological sense, that is, in terms of sin, of the Fall, of death, neglecting somewhat the original vocation to communion, the original invitation to dominate the earth, the original human sociality present in the relationship between equals, man and woman, a situation that is diminished but not destroyed by sin. An example of this sin-centered reading of Genesis is to be found in the so-called Gospel of Philip, a second-century Gnostic Christian text, in which the following words may be read: "When Eve was still in Adam, death did not exist; it began to exist when she was separated from him."[35]

Different Explanations of the Distinction between Man and Woman

There are several possible ways to account for the distinction between man and woman in the history of philosophy and theology, one more surprising than the next. Before attempting to provide a theological account of the distinction, we shall mention three authors: Plato, Philo of Alexandria, and Gregory of Nyssa.

The Platonic Myth of the Spherical Man

In the discourse of Aristophanes in Plato's *Symposium* we find an interesting and influential explanation of the origin of the sexual distinction in humans.[36] Aristophanes recounts the myth according to which Zeus creates the first man, the *universale ante rem*, as a solitary and perfect being, and therefore androgynous, who is without sexually distinctive features. Because the human being in this situation enjoys too much strength and his existence becomes a threat to the divinity, Zeus decides to diminish his powers. He does so by dividing the human being into two parts: man and woman. The sexual distinction does not belong, therefore, to the original nature of humans, thought out by the divinity, but has as its origin a divine action inspired by the god's fear when faced with the excessive power of an androgynous, solitary, powerful human being. From the time of the division of man into masculine and feminine, love grows between them, and, as a result, sociality arises as a sign of weakness that plays second fiddle to the original, aspired-after androgynous autonomy. In this way, through socialization, Zeus achieves his purposes in that man is weakened and cannot struggle successfully against the gods but depends completely on them and has to fall back on their intercession and protection. "From that time onward," concludes Aristophanes, "reciprocal love was born among humans and it attempts to reconstitute the ancient nature, saving it and making of the two a unity."[37]

---

35. J. M. Robinson, *The Coptic Gnostic Library: A Complete Edition of the Nag Hammadi Codices* (Leiden: Brill, 2000), 2:141.

36. Plato, *Symposium* 191c–d. Benedict XVI, in *Deus Caritas Est*, par. 11, reflects on this myth to explain the social character of humans.

37. Plato, *Symposium* 191d.

In this passage of Plato we find a clear resonance with the Biblical text, with which it is more or less contemporaneous: "The two will be one flesh" (Gn 2:24). But there is an important difference between them. According to Plato, the distinction between man and woman, and, as a result, human sociality, is considered as a kind of anticipated punishment meted out by a weakened and threatened divinity. That is, apart from indicating the limits of the divinity (God's "anthropophobia," we might say), human sociality is to be considered fundamentally as a defect, a limit to human nature. The distinction between man and woman, and the consequent sociality, are considered as weaknesses and imperfections to be overcome, and when they are, man will reappear reconstituted in his original nature, that is, androgynous, autonomous, individualist.

The Two-Stage Explanation of Philo

The Jewish philosopher Philo of Alexandria, contemporaneous with Jesus Christ, has influenced Christian thought considerably in different areas, particularly as regards the distinction between man and woman. In his work *The Creation of the World* he explains, following a Midrashic interpretation of Genesis, that the two accounts of the creation correspond in general terms to two chronologically successive stages in the creation of humanity.[38] The first account (Gn 1) would refer to the spiritual, original man, constituted in an asexual state, androgynous, ideal, that is, made in the image of God. This is so because, according to scripture, in God there is no sexual distinction. Humanity according to Genesis 1 is the celestial, ideal, perfect man. In the second account (Gn 2–3), however, along with the Fall of humans comes the sexual differentiation, and the distinction between man and woman emerges. The passages that speak of shame and the need to wear clothes (Gn 3:7) are interpreted by Philo as the dressing of human souls with a physical body. The dominion of man over woman is also considered as an acquired right on account of her infidelity to him. As a result, we come to the conclusion that the creation of man and woman was not the direct and primary will of God (which referred only to humanity and the animals) and that "original sin" was of a sexual kind, connected therefore with the will of man to dominate woman. According to Hultgård, Philo used "the story of the fall ... to illustrate the superiority in each human being of the masculine principle, the mind [*nous*], over the feminine, the senses [*aisthesis*]. Adam, who represents the mind, is seduced by Eve, who represents the senses, and this occurs, says Philo, because pleasure [*edone*] is associated with the senses, and through them 'the sovereign mind' deceives."[39]

For obvious reasons, this vision is difficult to reconcile with Christian doctrine. Still, certain aspects of this explanation left their mark on Christian theology,[40] especially that of the Alexandrians, Clement, Origen, Maximus the Confessor, and others. A case in point is Gregory of Nyssa. Let us consider his position.

---

38. Philo of Alexandria, *De opif. mundi*, nos. 134–53.

39. A. Hultgård, "God and Image of Woman in Early Jewish Religion," in *The Image of God: Gender Models in Judaeo-Christian Tradition*, edited by K. E. Børresen (Minneapolis, Minn.: Fortress, 1995). See Philo, *De opif. mundi*, 153–65.

40. F. Asensio, "¿Tradición sobre un pecado sexual en el Paraíso?," *Gregorianum* 30–31 (1949): 30:490–520 on Ambrose, 31:35–62 on Augustine; ibid., 163–91, on Isidore, Alcuin of York, Bernard, Duns Scotus, and

The Creation of Man and Woman according to
Gregory of Nyssa

In his work *De hominis opificio* Gregory of Nyssa explains that "Adam" designates the complete and perfect man, made in the image of God, which prefigures the Christ, the true archetype of humanity, because God's plan for humanity is fully present in him alone.[41] This may be seen, Gregory says, in the Adam-Christ typology typical of the New Testament. He further explains that the sexual distinction appeared in the context of sin, the first sin. However, he is attentive to explain carefully the relationship between the sexual distinction and original sin. According to Gregory, the duality man-woman is not the result of two separate "stages" of creation, as Plato and Philo thought, but rather something that took place first of all in the creative mind of God, in his foreknowledge of the work of creation. God in effect created humans in a differentiated way, as man and woman, because, in wanting to create them free,[42] he foresaw the possibility of sin and rebellion. In order to ensure the unity of the human race and reduce the danger of the spread of sin and destruction, he established that the development and growth of humanity would take place through sexual reproduction. This, in real terms, was a kind of security measure designed to limit the damage that could be caused by sin. When humans sin, their transgressions easily occasion a contagion of evil, combat, vengeance, hostility, murder, and the rest. But when humans are united with one another by bonds of blood and kinship, it becomes more difficult for them to destroy one another; hence the propagation of the effects of sin may not be halted, but they are certainly slowed down. In other words, the social origin of humanity, the ultimate, theological root of human sociality, according to Gregory, is not to be found in the positive divine plan. Rather it is an emergency measure intended to avoid the excesses of the destructive solitude that comes from sin. The sinner, having lost familiarity with God and others, is obliged, in spite of all, to live with and get on with others, to depend on other persons.

The position of Gregory offers a subtle, coherent, and intelligent account of the origin of human sociality, in particular of the sexual condition of humans. On the whole, it has been quite influential in the history of Christian anthropology and spirituality. However, it presents several drawbacks. In the first place, according to Gregory, the social condition of humans and their sexual differentiation are not direct consequences of sin but rather its distinctive sign. Virginity, which refers to the original state of humans, at least in God's mind, would be more perfect in the sense of being more original, more in keeping with God's innermost intentions for humanity.[43] As a result, marriage is necessarily considered as a concession to weakness and a sign (though indirect) of human sinfulness. Gregory called marriage "a sad tragedy

---

Ruysbroeck; ibid., 362–90 on Justin, Epiphanius, Gregory of Nyssa, Maximus the Confessor, and John Damascene. See also G. Aranda-Pérez, "Corporeidad y sexualidad en los relatos de la creación," in *Teología del cuerpo y de la sexualidad*, edited by P. J. Viladrich and J. Escrivá Ivars (Madrid: Rialp, 1991), 19–50.

41. See Gregory of Nyssa, *De hominis opificio*, nos. 16–17.

42. See, for example, Clement of Alexandria, *Stromata* 3:17.

43. On the topic of virginity in Gregory, see L. F. Mateo-Seco, "Virginity," in *The Brill Dictionary of Gregory of Nyssa*, 777–83. See especially the work Gregory wrote on this subject, his first written work: *De virginitate*. He considers virginity as a mark of God himself.

... that was instituted as the compensation for having to die."[44] It should be said, of course, that Gregory and other Church Fathers have always excluded any *causal* relationship between original sin and the dynamics of human sexuality.

Second, it is clear that in the anthropological vision formulated by Gregory of Nyssa the *imago Dei* corresponds to the superior part of the human being, the *nous*, or intellect. Specifically, the image of God in humans has little or nothing to do with human sociality or with the bodily condition but rather relates to their spiritual individuality. As we have seen, this position does not correspond fully to what scripture teaches.

Third, as a consequence, Gregory presents Christ as the perfect man, the ideal image of God. This does not correspond fully to the reality of the incarnation of the Word, to Christ's perfect humanity, concrete, masculine, and fully involved in family and social life.[45] Gregory presents things as if Jesus did not have a clear sexual identity, incorrectly interpreting Paul's programmatic text: "There is neither Jew nor Greek, there is neither slave nor free, there is neither male nor female; for you are all one in Christ Jesus" (Gal 3:28). The text of the Congregation for the Doctrine of the Faith already cited explains that Galatians 3:28 refers not to an asexual Christ but to the fact that "in Christ the rivalry, enmity and violence which disfigured the relationship between men and women can be overcome and have been overcome."[46]

Summing up, we may say that according to the line followed by Gregory of Nyssa, the sexual distinction between humans, the basis of human sociality, is not related to the image and likeness of God in them but becomes something secondary, profane, perhaps problematic. Besides, this explanation normally presents the woman as the inferior element of the human couple. Let us now consider this issue.

The Understanding of Women in the History of Philosophy and Theology

Christianity has, from the beginning, offered a strong and decisive contribution to a proper understanding of woman and her equality to man. Still, it is undeniable that in the history of philosophical and theological thought her dignity and role in society have frequently been considered in an openly negative way.[47]

The Inferiority of Woman in Greek Thought

Plato, as we saw earlier, held that man is closer than woman to the original model of being human. Woman is considered as an inferior human being.[48] This explains to some degree the common discrimination toward women in ancient Greece, as well as

---

44. Gregory of Nyssa, *De Virginitate* 3.12.

45. On the Christology of Gregory, see L. F. Mateo-Seco, "Christology," in *The Brill Dictionary of Gregory of Nyssa*, 139–52.

46. Congregation for the Doctrine of the Faith, *On the Collaboration of Men and Women*, no. 12.

47. On this topic see especially A. Scola, "L'imago Dei e la sessualità umana: A proposito di una tesi originale della *Mulieris Dignitatem*," *Anthropotes* 1 (1992): 61–73, and Scola, Marengo, and Prades López, *La persona umana*, 172–79.

48. See, *inter alia*, J. O'Faolain and L. Martines, eds., *Not in God's Image: Women in History from the Greeks to the Victorians* (London: Temple Smith, 1973).

polygamy, the priority of having sons rather than daughters, infanticide, and so on. A similar position encounters a biological justification in the thought of Aristotle. To his mind, in the process of human reproduction the man plays the active role, while the woman is purely passive in the reception of new life. The male, therefore, gives life; the woman just receives and nourishes it. As a result, says Aristotle, "the male is superior by nature, the woman inferior, one commands, the other is commanded, because in the context of the equitable distribution of virtue, in one there is the courage of deliberation, in the other of subordination."[49]

The Woman in Jewish Thought

The Old Testament presents woman prevalently as a socially inferior individual, as can be seen, for example, in Moses's law of repudiation (Dt 24:1). Among the Jews, women did not have the possibility of creating and spreading literary texts, a task that could be undertaken only by priests, Levites, scribes, sages, officials, and merchants, professions from which women were excluded by law or were absent by convention or custom.[50] Still, throughout the Biblical text the unequal and problematic relationships between the sexes, when they are present, are seen to be the fruit of sin and not of the original created constitution of humans, made in the image of God, male and female. Nevertheless, many women played very important roles in the history of the chosen people.[51]

The Christian Contribution to the Dignity of Women

W. H. Frend observes that "the attitude of Jesus towards women was revolutionary.... For him the sexes were equal."[52] In Jesus' mind, in sinning the woman was not more guilty than the man, as the account of the woman caught in adultery shows (Jn 8:1–11). Christ gave particular attention to the poorest and most neglected women in society, the widows (Mk 12:40, 41–44; Lk 7:12–16). Indeed, the order of deacons was instituted to an important degree to ensure that they were cared for (Acts 6:1). There were many widows among the newly converted Christians (Acts 9:39–41). Quite probably the special place they occupied in the early Church was not unrelated to the veneration Christians had for Mary, the mother of God, who was also a widow. As James says: "Religion that is pure and undefiled before God and the Father is this: to visit orphans and widows in their affliction, and to keep oneself unstained from the world" (Jas 1:27; see Acts 5:3).

The same appreciation for women may be found in the writings of Paul: man and woman were both created in the image of God and possess an equal dignity before Christ (Gal 3:28), the perfect image. It is interesting to note that among those converted through the ministry of Paul, "the converts we hear most about are women ...

---

49. Aristotle, *Politics* 1260a.

50. See Hultgård, "God and Image of Woman in Early Jewish Religion."

51. On the issue, see the information gathered by I. Sassoon in *The Status of Women in Jewish Tradition* (Cambridge: Cambridge University Press, 2011).

52. W. H. C. Frend, *The Rise of Christianity* (London: Darton, Longman and Todd, 1986), 67. Pope Francis was struck by "the way Jesus considered women in a context less favorable than ours, because women in those times were relegated to second place" (General Audience, April 15, 2015).

many of them leading women."[53] In the early centuries, Chadwick tells us, "Christianity seems to have been especially successful among women. It was often through the wives that it penetrated the upper classes of society in the first instance."[54] And Stark says, "Women were especially drawn to Christianity because it offered them a life that was so greatly superior to the life they otherwise would have led."[55] By way of example, Chadwick writes that Christians "regarded unchastity in a husband as no less serious a breach of loyalty and trust than unfaithfulness in a wife."[56] With the advent of Christianity, all humans, both men and women, became *equally* believers by baptism. Infanticide (especially that of girls) and abortion were severely prohibited; monogamous and indissoluble marriage was established, which "clearly indicates the equal dignity of the spouses;"[57] the free consent of the spouses was defended, and the age of marriage (especially for the girl) was raised (for the Romans the minimum age was twelve years); the custom of arranged marriages was avoided, as was marriage between blood relatives.

In medieval times, according to the historian Jacques Le Goff, "the idea that woman is equal to man determined the Christian concept of woman and influenced the vision and attitude of the medieval Church."[58] The same author, speaking of the legal regulation of marriage, says: "I believe that respect for women is one of the great innovations of Christianity.... The dispositions of the Lateran council [1215] made it impossible for marriage to take place without the agreement between the spouses, the man and the woman."[59] "In Christianity," write Pelaja and Scaraffia, "what constitutes the essence of marriage is the agreement of the couple and not fecundity: in marriage for this reason sterility is not a reason for separation, which was always believed in ancient society to be a woman's illness."[60] In the times of early Christianity, pagan Roman women had to have at least three children "in order, when the father died, to be free from all kinds of supervision of goods."[61] Besides, in Christian society adultery was punished equally for man as for woman.[62] Also to be noted is the power and influence of feminine spirituality in the Church well before modern times.[63]

Throughout the course of history, woman has been seen, says Agnoli, as

53. Frend, *The Rise of Christianity*, 99.

54. H. Chadwick, *The Early Church* (Harmondsworth: Penguin, 1967), 58. According to M. R. Salzman, in *The Making of a Christian Aristocracy: Social and Religious Change in the Western Roman Empire* (Cambridge, Mass.: Harvard University Press, 2002), in the Roman senatorial class between the years 283 and 423 A.D., fifty percent of the men were Christians, as were eighty-five percent of the women.

55. R. Stark, *The Triumph of Christianity*, 122.

56. Chadwick, *The Early Church*, 59.

57. F. Agnoli, *Indagine sul cristianesimo: Come si costruisce una civiltà* (Casale Monferrato: Piemme, 2010), 47.

58. J. Le Goff, "Il cristianesimo ha liberato le donne," *Un lungo Medioevo* (Bari: Dedalo, 2006), 89–101, 89f. See also his article "Medioevo: Quando il cristianesimo liberò le donne," *Avvenire*, January 21, 2007.

59. Le Goff, "Il cristianesimo ha liberato le donne," 92.

60. M. Pelaja and L. Scaraffia, *Due in una carne: Chiesa e sessualità nella storia* (Rome: GLF editori, 2008), 15.

61. G. Duby and M. Perrot, eds., *A History of Women in the West* (Cambridge, Mass.: Belknap Press of Harvard University Press, 2002).

62. Pelaja and Scaraffia, *Due in una carne*, 17; Le Goff, "Il cristianesimo ha liberato le donne," 94.

63. See P. Ranft, *Women and Spiritual Equality in Christian Tradition* (New York: St. Martin's Press, 1998). See also the catechesis of Benedict XVI in his General Audiences from October 1, 2010, to April 6, 2011, on the spiritual life of women mystics mainly during the Middle Ages. The catechesis was focused as a commentary on the "feminine genius" of which John Paul II spoke in *Mulieris Dignitatem*, par. 31.

secondary and marginal, relegated to her rooms in the Greek world; under the perpetual supervision of man, father or husband, like an object, in the Roman world; a hostage of male power among the German peoples; open to repudiation and juridically inferior in the Jewish world; victim of infinite abuse and violence, including infanticide, in China and India; an inferior form of reincarnation in traditional Hinduism; subjected to polygamy, a humiliating affirmation of her inferiority, in the Muslim and animist world; victim in many different cultures of real physical mutilation; subjected to repudiation by the male, in all ancient cultures, the woman became with Christianity God's own creature, on the same level as man.[64]

Understanding of the Relationship between Man and Woman

If things are as we have just seen, if it is true that Christianity has promoted an elevated vision of woman and her equality with man at a practical level, how can we explain the following text of Paul to the Christians of Corinth: "For a man ought not to cover his head, since he is the image and glory of God; but woman is the glory of man. (For man was not made from woman, but woman from man. Neither was man created for woman, but woman for man.) That is why a woman ought to have a veil on her head, because of the angels" (1 Cor 11:7–10)? From the exegetical point of view it would seem that Paul is attempting to combine Genesis 1:27 and Genesis 2:7 in a Midrashic context.[65] Although it is clearly a complex text to interpret, it is difficult to avoid the impression that for Paul only man is in the fullest sense made in the image of God, while woman needs to strive, in Christ, to obtain a kind of spiritual masculinity or asexuality.[66]

The fourth-century ecclesiastical writer Ambrosiaster, commenting on Genesis 2:23 ("This at last is bone of my bones and flesh of my flesh") and 1 Cor 11:7 ("For a man ... is the image and glory of God; but woman is the glory of man"), teaches that Eve did not receive her soul from God but that, along with the body, she received it directly from Adam. By intrinsic constitution and divine will, and not only as the contingent and passing result of sin, woman was placed under the dominion of man.[67] Augustine rejects this interpretation, observing, fairly, that the image and likeness of God in "man" refers to their being "male and female," according to Genesis 1.[68] In fact, the view of human sexuality proposed by Augustine is substantially positive, moder-

---

64. Agnoli, *Indagine sul cristianesimo: Come si costruisce una civiltà*, 42f.

65. J. S. Jervell, *Imago Dei: Gen 1,26 f. im Spätjudentum, in der Gnosis und in den paulinischen Briefen* (Göttingen: Vandenhoeck & Ruprecht, 1960), 292–312. On 1 Corinthians 11:7–10, see W. O. Walker, "1 Corinthians 11:2–16 and Paul's Views Regarding Women," *Journal of Biblical Literature* 94 (1979): 94–110.

66. On this topic, see L. Fatum, "Image of God and Glory of Man: Women in the Pauline Congregations," in *The Image of God*, edited by K. E. Børresen (Minneapolis, Minn.: Fortress, 1995). K. Vogt, in "'Becoming Male': A Gnostic and Early Christian Metaphor," in the same volume, explains that for Gnostic thought it was typical to consider the destiny of woman to be like that of man; Gnostics speak of "woman transformed into man." See the eighth Code of the library of *Nag Hammadi*, the so-called *Zostrianos*, in Robinson, *The Coptic Gnostic Library*, 4:392, which says: "Flee from the slavery of femininity, and choose the salvation of masculinity."

67. See Ambrosiaster, *Comm. in 1 Cor 8*, 5–7: "Vir enim ad imagine Dei factum est, non mulier." See also his *Comm. in I Tim 2*, 9–10, and his *Liber quaestionum Veteris et Novi Testamenti*. On the thought of Ambrosiaster, see K. E. Børresen, "God's Image, Man's Image? Patristic Interpretation of Gen.1,27 and I Cor.11,7," in *The Image of God* (Philadelphia: Fortress, 1995), 187–209, esp. 191–95.

68. See Augustine, *De Gen. ad litt.* 10, 1.

ate, and humane.[69] Sexual life became problematic in his writings only on account of the presence of original sin.

Still, the position of Ambrosiaster was not an isolated one.[70] We have already examined that of Gregory of Nyssa. During the episcopal synod at Macon in France in 585, according to an account to be found no longer in the acts of the synod but only in the writings of Gregory of Tours, some bishops asserted that woman should not be considered human at all.[71] Others present at the synod, taking their cue from Genesis 1:27 and from the devotion Christians had for the mother of God, took an opposite position. In any case, whatever the result of the synod, the fact that Gregory had expressed the issue in these terms is not indifferent. Reservations on the status of women as made in the image of God in the fullest possible sense have not been lacking throughout the history of theology.[72] Let us consider briefly the teaching of Thomas Aquinas.

Thomas Aquinas's Understanding of Woman

Aquinas[73] draws from Aristotle[74] the idea that woman is an "animal imperfectum" (an imperfect animal),[75] or, as he said elsewhere, a "mas occasionatus" (a defective male).[76] "When a girl is born," he says, "this happens on account of the weakness of the creative power (masculine), or perhaps because of an indisposition of matter,

69. On this question, see the "ascetic" reading of Augustine undertaken by P. R. L. Brown, *The Body and Society: Men, Women and Sexual Renunciation in Early Christianity* (New York: Columbia University Press, 1988), and the revision undertaken by the same author: Brown, *Augustine of Hippo,* 500ff. The extreme reading of Augustine done by U. Ranke-Heinemann in *Eunuchs for the Kingdom of Heaven: Women, Sexuality and the Catholic Church* (New York: Doubleday Books, 1990), has been contrasted by D. G. Hunter in "Augustine's Pessimism? A New Look at Augustine's Teaching on Sex, Marriage and Celibacy," *Augustinian Studies* 25 (1994): 153–77. See also T. J. Van Bavel, "Augustine's View on Women," *Augustiniana* 39 (1989): 1–53.

70. For example, in the writings of Origen, Gregory of Nyssa, Ambrose, and Jerome. In fact, Augustine took a position clearly opposed to that of Jerome in his *Sermo 397,* edited by F. Dolbeau in "Nouveaux sermons de saint Augustin pour la conversion des païens et des donatistes (V)," *Revue des études augustiniennes* 39 (1993): 57–108.

71. See H. Leclercq, "Macon," in *Dictionnaire d'archéologie chrétienne et de liturgie,* vol. 10, coll. 747–55, esp. 754f.; K. J. von Hefele, *Histoire des conciles d'après les documents originaux* (Paris: A. le Clere et Cie., 1869–78), 3.1:208–14, translated into English as *A History of the Christian Councils, from the Original Documents,* 2nd ed. (Whitefish, Mont.: Kessinger, 2009). See the summary of the doctrine of Gregory of Tours in his *Historia Francorum,* 8, 20.

72. See the studies of Børresen mentioned frequently throughout this chapter.

73. On woman in the writings of Aquinas, see K. E. Børresen, *Subordination and Equivalence: The Nature and Role of Woman in Augustine and Thomas Aquinas* (Mainz: Matthias-Grünewald, 1981), 141–311; J. F. Hartel, *Femina ut imago Dei in the Integral Feminism of St. Thomas Aquinas* (Rome: Pontificia Università Gregoriana, 1993); De Solenni, *A Hermeneutic of Aquinas's "Mens,"* esp. 149–64.

74. See Aristotle, *De generatione animalium* IV.2.767a10–13.

75. See Aquinas, *S.Th.* I-II, q. 102, q. 3, ad 9. On this text, see M. Nolan, "The Aristotelian Background to Aquinas' Denial that 'Woman is a Defective Male,'" *Thomist* 64 (2000): 21–69, esp. 56–68. The conclusion Nolan's careful study takes from Aquinas (and Bonaventure) is the following: "We should deny that woman is defective ... though man has greater *vigor animi* and *robur corporis* than woman (IV Sent., 25, 2, 1 ad 1)" (69). The same line is taken by De Solenni in *A Hermeneutic of Aquinas's "Mens."* See also P. Camus, "Le mythe de la femme chez saint Thomas d'Aquin," *Revue thomiste* 76 (1976): 243–65, 394–409; T. Rossi, "Il corpo muliebre nell'articolo 1 della q. 92, I pars," *Antropologia Tomista (Atti del IX Congresso Tomistico Internazionale),* Pontifical Academy of St. Thomas (Vatican City: Vaticana, 1991), 105–10.

76. Aquinas, *In I Cor.* 11, lect 2.

or because of some external mutation, for example when humid winds blow from the south."[77] Therefore, he concludes, "Femina est aliquid deficiens et occasionatum" (The woman is faulty and defective).[78]

It should be kept in mind, however, that the position of Thomas is determined to an important degree by the most reputable biology of the time, that of Aristotle, developed some fifteen hundred years beforehand and substantially unchanged in the meantime. As we saw above, Aristotle considers the woman as the weak and passive stage of human reproduction. Therefore, Aquinas adds—and the addition is important—that the woman is inferior as regards the particular nature but not as regards universal human nature, because this depends directly on the will of God.[79] And when God instituted human nature, he positively created not only male but also female, whose existence corresponds simply to God's will. Thomas says besides that the image of God is present in man and in woman principally with respect to the human mind. And in the mind, he says, there is no sexual distinction.[80] Besides, Thomas explains, Eve was formed "from the rib of Adam" (Gn 2:21f.) in order to indicate her fundamental equality with him.[81]

In conclusion, says Aquinas, woman is naturally subject to man because man possesses a more vigorous nature and a reasoned capacity to decide.[82] Then he goes on to explain the Pauline text already cited, 1 Corinthians 11:7 ("Woman is the glory of man") as follows: "In a secondary sense the image of God is in man in a way in which it is not in woman, in that man is the beginning and end of woman, just as God is the beginning and end of creation."[83] Although the explanation of Aquinas is far from adequate, he strives to avoid an extreme reading of the Biblical texts of other authors who actually deny that the image of God is present in woman.[84] Paul himself goes on to explain to the Corinthians: "Nevertheless, in the Lord woman is not independent of man nor man of woman; for as woman was made from man, so man is now born of woman. And all things are from God" (vv. 11f.). And he concludes: "If any one is disposed to be contentious, we recognize no other practice [that of women covering their heads in Church], nor do the Churches of God" (v. 16).

Equality and Difference between Man and Woman

On the whole, Christian authors have attempted to teach that man and woman are equal because they are made in the image and likeness of God. But what kind of equality is involved? It is not sufficient simply to say that this equality is on the level of spirit, of the soul, all the while considering it as secondary or irrelevant on the level of

---

77. See Aquinas, *S.Th.* I, q. 92, a. 1, ad 1.

78. Ibid.

79. Ibid.

80. See *ibid.*, q. 93, a. 6, ad 2.

81. Ibid., q. 92, a. 3, co.: "Conveniens fuit mulierem formari de costa viri ... ad significandum quod inter virum et mulierem debet esse socialis coniunctio. Neque enim mulier debet dominari in virum, et ideo non est formata de capite. Neque debet a viro despici, tanquam serviliter subiecta, et ideo non est formata de pedibus."

82. See Aquinas, *S.Th.* I, q. 92, a. 1, ad 2.

83. Ibid., q. 93, a. 4, ad 1.

84. On the question in Calvin, see *Institutiones christianae* I, 15, 4. See Thompson, *Creata ad imaginem Dei.*

the body and sociality. As we saw earlier, the image of God in a human is not limited to the individual, immortal spirit, the *nous* or soul; it includes to the fullest possible extent the person's body, history, free action, and entire social life. For this reason, as Paul already suggested in a text just mentioned (1 Cor 11:11), the fundamental equality between man and woman does not require denying the differences between them or, more specifically, the *complementary* quality of their relationship, or as John Paul II calls it, their reciprocity.[85] As the nineteenth-century philosopher Pierre J. Proudhon said, "Man and woman can be equivalent before the Absolute; but they are not equal, nor can they be, either in the family or in the State."[86] In the preceding chapter we saw that the fundamental equality of humans means anything but uniformity, but it may be expressed in two elements: in their common reason and human nature, on the one hand (as was put forward by the Stoics), and in their capacity to give and receive, on the other (this was the fruit of Christian reflection); in fact, what provides the opportunity for people to exchange goods with one another is the difference that exists between them.

Man and Woman as a "Unity of the Two"

The image of God in man and woman may be understood in two very different ways. The first excludes woman from being made in the image of God. Only man would have been made truly in the image and likeness of God. The other reading of Genesis 1:27 identifies the image of God *tout court* with humans as social beings, and specifically with the foundational form of sociality, which is the spousal relationship between man and woman. The latter reading, promoted during the twentieth century by Karl Barth, is not without historical precedents.[87] According to some Jewish authors—for example, the third-century Rabbi Eleazer ben Pedat—the expression "male and female" is simply equivalent to the "human being." Hence, he concluded, "any man who has no wife is not a man in the true sense of the word, because it is said 'he made them male and female, and he called him Adam.'"[88] The latter, however, constitutes an unsatisfactory reading of scripture. In effect, to be made "in the image and likeness of God" cannot be considered as a simple equivalent of "male and female." The fact is that the epithets "male" and "female" are never applied to God in the Bible; they are applied only to animals and humans. The male/female distinction is not a divine absolute. "To be male and/or female," says Vogels, "is therefore something which humanity has in common with the other living creatures, the animals. Male and female is an aspect of creation, not of the creator."[89] As Erich Przywara says when speaking of the image of God in humans:

85. John Paul II, *Mulieris Dignitatem*, par. 7.

86. P.-J. Proudhon, *De la justice dans la Révolution et dans l'Eglise* (Paris: Marcel Rivière, 1930).

87. On this question, see Vogels, "The Human Person in the Image of God (Gen 1,26)," esp. 198–200.

88. Rabbi Eleazar ben Pedat, *Yebam.* 62b–63a, cited by Vogels in *The Human Person in the Image of God*, 199. The same author adds, however, that man is not truly so if he has no land, that is, property, of his own.

89. Vogels, *The Human Person in the Image of God*, 199.

There is not on the one hand a "closure" to the sexual aspect, in such a way that humans would not be such outside the sexual relationship between male and female. But neither is there, on the other hand, a "limitation" to the spiritual in the image of God against an intra-cosmic creaturely sexuality: thus man would not be man if not in the spiritually personal "interiority of the image of God."[90]

Avoiding, however, the two extreme readings of Genesis 1:27 just mentioned—one that excludes women from being in the image of God and the other that makes the image simply equivalent to the union between man and woman—it is possible to hold to a strong bond between male and female, precisely in the sense that the union between them is an important expression of the image of God in humans. This reading became common throughout the twentieth century and beforehand. Of particular importance are the writings of Matthias J. Scheeben and Hans Urs von Balthasar.[91] Among Protestant theologians, the author who has insisted most on this, as we saw, was Karl Barth;[92] among Catholics, interesting pointers are to be found in the spousal theology of Erich Przywara.[93] The position is presented in an authoritative way in John Paul II's 1988 apostolic letter *Mulieris Dignitatem*. Pope Francis has also spoken of this relationship.[94]

The Meaning of "Unity of the Two"

According to Genesis 1:27, John Paul II says, man and woman *were created together* in the image and likeness of God: "The woman is another 'I' in a common humanity. From the very beginning they appear as a 'unity of the two', and this signifies that the original solitude is overcome."[95] Besides, continues John Paul, the distinction between man and woman is linked directly with marriage and the transmission of life. Three aspects of human life converge and become inseparable from one another according to the book of Genesis: (1) man and woman are persons because they are created in the image and likeness of God; (2) the image of God is present in them in their unity composed of two persons; and therefore (3) this unity, reflecting the presence of God within the created order, is intrinsically ordered to fruitfulness and procreation, to new human life made in the image of God. In brief, the image of God is more perfect insofar as it exists in man and woman together, in their union and fruitfulness. It is not simply a matter of equal dignity between man and woman, placed beside one another and compared mathematically as individual "images of God," but also a matter of the presence of God's image *in their very unity*. In the liturgy of the rite of marriage, the Church prays: "You have given humanity the gift of existence and you have exalted them to an incomparable dignity; in the union between man

90. E. Przywara, *Mensch: Typologische Anthropologie* (Nuremberg: Glock and Lutz, 1958), 134, cited by von Balthasar, *Theo-Drama*, 2:369ff.

91. See Von Balthasar, *Theo-Drama*, 2:365–82.

92. Karl Barth teaches decisively that being made in the image and likeness of God refers principally to the relationship between man and woman and, at a more general level, to the community character of humans before the Trinitarian God. See *Die Kirchliche Dogmatik* III/2 (Zurich: Zöllikon, 1948), 242–381.

93. See E. Przywara, *Mensch: Typologische Anthropologie*.

94. See especially Francis, General Audiences for April 15 and 22, 2015.

95. See John Paul II, *Mulieris Dignitatem*, par. 6. On this document, see the reflections of D. Tettamanzi, *Grandi cose ha fatto in me l'Onnipotente* (Milan: Ancora, 1989); Scola, "L'imago Dei e la sessualità umana."

and woman you have placed an image of your love."[96] Man and woman are present in creation as

two diverse but inseparable realities, of which one is the fullness of the other, and both are ordered to a supreme definitive union.... Double, without the multiplication of one in two, simply two poles of a single reality, two diverse actuations of a single being, two *entia* in one *esse*, one existence in two lives, but certainly not two diverse fragments of a totality that might be recomposed as in a puzzle.[97]

In brief, the sexual distinction between humans and its social meaning are integral parts of their being made in the image of God. Thus human sexuality is elevated to a level that is superior to mere animal sexuality.

New Testament Teaching

We may still ask is it correct to take a single Old Testament text (Gn 1:27) and deduce so many consequences from it? This is a question John Paul II asks in his catechesis on human love, *Man and Woman He Created Them*.[98] The Pope shows that the doctrine of the "unity of the two" is present also in the New Testament. On the one hand, he observes that Jesus dealt with women in a particularly respectful and delicate way, bringing them to share in his ministry; this was completely exceptional for that period in history. On the other hand, speaking of the matter of the indissolubility of marriage to the scribes (Mt 19:3–12), Jesus refers to what took place at the beginning of human history with the creation of man and woman (Mt 19:4–6):

Have you not read that he who made them from the beginning *made them male and female* [we may note here that the one who in his own person is the perfect image of the Father cites Genesis 1:27 as an authoritative text] and said, "For this reason a man shall leave his father and mother and be joined to his wife, and the two shall become one"? So they are no longer two but one. What therefore God has joined together, let not man put asunder [that is, the image of God is present not only in the two taken separately but precisely in their divinely sealed union].

And when the Pharisees ask him about the injunction of Moses allowing the Israelites to repudiate their wives, Jesus explains that this possibility does not correspond to God's original will but is rather a exception occasioned by sin and infidelity: "For your hardness of heart Moses allowed you to divorce your wives, but from the beginning it was not so" (Mt 19:8). In other words, Jesus himself takes the beginning, the creation of man and woman, as an authoritative point of departure. Hence the tolerance of Moses becomes unacceptable to anyone who believes in the God who has created humans—man and woman—in his image and likeness. The work of Christ, in fact, is that of bringing all things back to the original situation, in which God was the sovereign of the whole world (Jn 12:32; 1 Cor 15:28), overcoming original sin and the ensuing hardness of heart, giving grace, renewing friendship with God, reconciling man with woman.

---

96. Second Preface to the Ritual Mass for Marriage.

97. A. Frank-Duquesne, *Création et procréation: Métaphysique, théologie et mystique du couple humain* (Paris: Éditions de Minuit, 1951), 42–46.

98. See John Paul II, *Man and Woman He Created Them: A Theology of the Body*, edited by M. Waldstein (Boston: Pauline Books and Media, 2006).

The value of the human sexual distinction is confirmed by the Christian doctrine of final resurrection. According to the common position of the Church Fathers, the sexual distinction will remain unvaried at final resurrection at the end of time and forever,[99] thus becoming a perpetual manifestation of God's original design for humanity and the universe.

Summing up, we may make four observations. First, human life as lived by man and woman is to a degree a reflection (or image) of divine love, a manifestation of the glory of God, because man and woman *together* are and act in the image and likeness of God. Second, the union between the two does not destroy the individuality of each one, because it is a unity (or, better, "communion") of two persons, not an eventual amalgamation of two individuals in one single reality (as was suggested in Aristophanes's discourse in Plato's *Symposium*). Through their very union each one can and should develop his or her masculine or feminine personality to the full. Third, we have seen that human equality and inequality find expression, among other things, in humans' capacity to give and receive. Still, it would be a mistake to say that the capacity to give corresponds primarily to the masculine principle and that of receiving to the feminine, as Aristotle suggested, because both man and woman give, and, beyond that, as we saw earlier, both receive and are enriched, by God and by other people. At the same time, what makes the interchange and enrichment possible—the fruit of love between man and woman—is at once their fundamental human equality as well as the wide variety of real differences that exist between them.

And fourth, the result, fruit, and proof of the authenticity of the union between man and woman, which reflects something of the communion that is present in God himself, the God who gives life, is new human life, the children who are at the same time made in the image of their parents and in the image of God, just as their parents in their union express their having been made in the image of God. As Clement of Alexandria writes, "Human beings [*anthropos*] are in the image of God insofar as they co-operate, through their human nature, in the birth of new human beings."[100]

These elements are coherent with one another and inseparable. Sin makes its presence felt in breaking up one or more of the elements of this living and dynamic structure of the image of God in man and woman.[101] However, marriage and family life, in keeping this unity intact, become an open path to holiness.[102] Pope Francis says: "The difference between man and woman is not meant to indicate opposition or subordination, but is for the sake of communion and generation, always in the image and likeness of God.... The removal of difference in fact creates a problem, not a so-

---

99. See Augustine, *De Civitate Dei* XXII, 17. See *DH* 407, against the position of Origen. See *COH* 103f. In the context of the ideology of gender, see the interesting reflection of S. Coakley, "The Eschatological Body: Gender, Transformation and God," in Coakley, *Powers and Submissions: Spirituality, Philosophy and Gender* (Oxford: Blackwell, 2002), 153–67.

100. Clement of Alexandria, *Paedag.* 2, 10, 83, 2.

101. In Gn 1:28 "we have a clear statement of the divine purpose of marriage: positively, it is for the procreation of children; negatively, it is a rejection of the ancient oriental fertility cults. God desires his people to be fruitful. His promise makes any participation in such cults or the use of other devices to secure fertility not only redundant, but a mark of unbelief." Wenham, *Genesis 1–15*, 33.

102. See especially John Paul II's *Familiaris Consortio* and *Gratissimam Sane*, Apostolic Letter, February 2, 1994. See besides, R. Díaz Dorronsoro, *La naturaleza vocacional del matrimonio a la luz de la teología del siglo XX* (Rome: Edusc, 2001).

lution.... God entrusted the earth to the alliance between man and woman: its failure deprives the earth of warmth and darkens the sky of hope."[103]

The Human Family as the Basis of Human Sociality

In response to what has just been said we can make the following observation: conjugal love is not the only way in which human sociality and love can be expressed between persons. There are many other ways in which it can be shown: civil life, life in society, friendship, fraternity, professional relationships, and so on. So why does scripture seem to give priority to the union between man and woman, to the spousal relationship, to family, as the ultimate paradigm of human love? The response is probably the following: the practical and ontological basis for all sociality is to be found in the family (just as birth is at the origin of all life), and thus it is founded, directly or indirectly, on the love between man and woman and modeled on this love, which is, in turn, the clearest possible reflection or image we know of the love of God for humanity. Humans come to the world as intrinsically social beings directly from the relationship between their own parents. All other forms of socialization are successive to, and in real terms dependent on, this relationship. In fact, the family precedes chronologically and logically other manifestations of human sociality; it offers the basic model of love, of living with others, of socialization. The family is the place where one learns to love, to establish relationships, to recognize and accept differences between people, to trust, to forgive, to "make a sincere gift of self." In the family people learn to love and to be loved, they learn that love is to be found precisely in living as children with their parents; they learn besides that the most direct path to loving God, the Father of all, is to live as his children.[104] "In the 'unity of the two,' man and woman are called from the beginning not only to exist 'side by side' or 'together,' but they are also called to exist mutually 'one for the other,'" writes John Paul II. And elsewhere he writes:

The text of Genesis 2:18–25 shows that marriage is the first and, in a sense, the fundamental dimension of this call. But it is not the only one. The whole of human history unfolds within the context of this call. In this history, on the basis of the principle of mutually being "for" the other, in interpersonal "communion," there develops in humanity itself, in accordance with God's will, the integration of what is "masculine" and what is "feminine."[105]

---

103. Francis, General Audience, April 15, 2015. See my study "I tempi dell'amore, della santità e della misericordia. Una riflessione sulle strutture di sostegno del matrimonio e della famiglia," *Matrimonio e famiglia. La questione antropologica*, edited by H. Franceschi (Rome: Edusc, 2015), 49–64.

104. "I wonder if the crisis of collective trust in God, which does us so much harm, and makes us pale with resignation, incredulity and cynicism, is not also connected to the crisis of the alliance between man and woman. In fact the biblical account, with the great symbolic fresco depicting the earthly paradise and original sin, tells us that the communion with God is reflected in the communion of the human couple and the loss of trust in the heavenly Father generates division and conflict between man and woman." Francis, General Audience, April 15, 2015.

105. John Paul II, *Mulieris Dignitatem*, par. 7.

24 HUMANS, MADE IN THE IMAGE OF GOD, AT WORK IN THE WORLD

My Father is working still, and I am working. JOHN 5:17

The essence of man is not to be found in what he is, but rather in what he is able to do. A. HESCHEL[1]

The Orthodox author Nicholas Berdjaev made the following observation:

Labor is the greatest reality of human life in this world, it is a primary reality.... In labor there is both a truth of redemption ("in the sweat of your face shall you gain your bread") and a truth of the creative and constructive power of men. Both elements are present in labor. Human labor humanizes nature; it bears witness to the great mission of man in nature. But sin and evil have perverted the mission of labor. A reverse process has taken place in the dehumanization of labor, an alienation of human nature has taken place in the workers.... Man has been seized with the desire to be not only the master of nature, but also the master of his brother man, and he has enslaved labor.[2]

Humans Created by God and Placed in the World to Work

The fact that the human person, male and female, has been created by God as a deeply unitary being, with a soul that acts as "the form of the body," has the following important consequence: that humans are fully material, "mundane" beings, profoundly inserted into and truly belonging to the created material world, with which they share not only limitations, restriction, and mortality but also openness, communication, and dynamism.[3] That is to say, humans exist as beings in relation not only

1. Heschel, "The Concept of Man in Jewish Thought," 115.
2. Berdjaev, *Slavery and Freedom*, 220f.
3. On the insertion of humans into the cosmos and their intrinsic belongingness to the created world, see von Balthasar, *Theo-Drama*, 2:346–55.

with respect to God and to other people but also with respect to the world, which is the natural habitat into which they are most authentically "inserted" and "situated": "The heavens are the Lord's heavens, but the earth he has given to the sons of men" (Ps 115:16). And just as it is impossible to establish a net separation between body and soul (for the soul is the form of the body, and the body is the full expression of the human spirit), is it impossible to completely distinguish between human beings and the cosmos/world in which they live and act. Between the two there is a living and fruitful polarity and symbiosis. On the one hand, in effect, humans, made in the image of the creator, as his representative (Gn 1:26f.), are meant to "give form" to the cosmos, to shape the world by having dominion *over* the earth, thus contributing to making it completely subject to God. On the other hand, however, humans are conditioned *by* the world and live out their lives and vocations precisely in the ambit of this worldly condition. And this is not just a temporary, passing phase: at the end of time the "resurrection of the dead" will be accompanied and contextualized by the advent of the "new heavens and the new earth,"[4] a renewed cosmos which will become our common home.

Each and every human being, made "in the image and likeness of God," lives out his existence as a person through a proper free, personal, and irreplaceable action. Still, humans' freedom is always a situated and limited freedom: situated within history and within a series of concrete circumstances, referred to a variety of specific people, in a living and creative confrontation with the world as it is, through which the voice of nature may be perceived, the voice of the creator from whom humans have received the task and summons to mold and dominate the earth.[5] This is the sense of the "mundane" (or "secular") character of human existence in the light of faith: humans have received from God the charge to "exercise dominion" over the earth and at the same time the blessing as well as the spiritual and physical capacities indispensable to carry out that charge.[6] It is up to them to contribute to the definitive establishment of the sovereignty of God over the whole of creation. For this reason the dominion humans exercise and should exercise over the earth—through their work and all human activities—is always a sharing in the sovereignty over the world that Christ won by dying on the cross and rising up to a new life. This is the destiny of humans on earth: to dominate the world under God, in filial contemplation, that is, without fear or anguish, yet with the effort and commitment that come from considering the world as something of their own because it was created by their Father, who is Father of all (1 Cor 3:22f.), striving to govern the world along with other humans, who are also children of God.

Therefore we conclude our reflection of the consequences of the theology of the image of God (chapters 19–24) with this brief study of the theology of human work. God, in fact, calls humans to rule the world as his ambassadors and children, as we saw in chapters 4 and 13; he gives them the possibility of acting with freedom and re-

---

4. See *COH* 115–29.

5. On the importance of "natural law," see International Theological Commission, *In Search of a Universal Ethic*. See also P. O'Callaghan, "Algunas reflexiones sobre identidad cristiana, laicidad y ley natural." Francis's encyclical *LS* also deals with this issue.

6. See chapter 4, notes 48ff. and corresponding text.

sponsibility (chapter 20, on the image of God and freedom), the space or time to project their lives into the future (chapter 21 on the image of God, time, and historicity), and the possibility of sharing divine gifts with other creatures, especially with other human beings (chapters 22–23 on the image of God and human sociality). The work of humans—indeed, human activity on earth of any kind—presupposes and includes all these fundamental aspects of human constitution and life. As scripture teaches, "The Lord God took the man and put him in the garden of Eden to till it and keep it" (Gn 2:15). It is interesting to note that the term for "work" normally used in Aramaic (*'avad*) can be translated also to mean "give cult to God," "serve the Lord," and "carry out the Levitical [priestly] service."[7] In effect, when humans carry out God's command to cultivate and rule the earth, they carry out the divine will and at the same time glorify the creator, thus becoming "perfect as your heavenly Father is perfect" (Mt 5:48).

Historical Pointers on the Meaning and Value of Human Work

Modern studies of the genesis and development of human work often refer to the critical role played by human activity in the lives of humans and their development.[8] Work, that demanding activity in which humans invest their best intellectual, psychical, and physical energies in the world about them, belongs to the very definition of being human. According to Emmanuel Mounier, "Man is essentially an *artifex*, a creator of forms, a doer of works ... the form of being human is to act."[9] The human being is always a *homo faber*.[10] In effect, from time immemorial humans have established through work an ever greater dominion over nature.[11]

7. See F. Brown, C. A. Briggs, and S. R. Driver, *A Hebrew and English Lexicon of the Old Testament: With an Appendix Containing the Biblical Aramaic* (Oxford: Oxford University Press, 1951), s.v. עָבַד.

8. The work of Arendt, *The Human Condition*, cited in the first section, has been very influential. The author distinguishes between "labor," "work," and "action." See also D. Sölle, *To Work and to Love: A Theology of Creation* (Philadelphia: Fortress, 1984); the anthology of A. Negri, ed., *Filosofia del lavoro: Storia antologica* (Milan: C. Marzorati, 1980); G. Morra and F. Totaro, "Lavoro," in *Enciclopedia filosofica*, 7:6251–62. In Church teaching, see *GS*, nos. 33–39, and John Paul II, *Laborem Exercens*, Encyclical Letter, September 14, 1981. On the former document, see P. Smulders, "L'activité humaine dans le monde," in *L'Église dans le monde de ce temps: Constitution pastorale "Gaudium et spes,"* edited by Y. M. J. Congar, P. Delhaye, and M. Peuchmaurd (Paris: Cerf, 1967); on the latter, Y. Ledure, "L'encyclique de Jean Paul II sur le travail humain," *Nouvelle Revue Théologique* 105 (1983): 218–27. See also the study of J. L. Illanes, *La santificación del trabajo: El trabajo en la historia de la espiritualidad*, 10th ed. (Madrid: Palabra, 2001), translated into English as *The Sanctification of Work: Aspects of the Teaching of the Founder of Opus Dei*, 3rd ed. (New York: Scepter, 2003), which I have used extensively in this chapter. On the theology of work, see also M.-D. Chenu, *Pour une théologie du travail* (Paris: Seuil, 1955), translated into English as *The Theology of Work: An Exploration* (Chicago: H. Regnery, 1966); J. De Finance, *Essai sur l'agir humain* (Rome: Presses de l'Université Grégorienne, 1962); K. V. Truhlar, *Il lavoro cristiano: Per una teologia del lavoro* (Rome: Herder, 1966); V. Tranquilli, *Il concetto di lavoro da Aristotele a Calvino* (Milan: R. Ricciardi, 1979); Rodríguez, *Vocación, trabajo, contemplación*; J. L. Illanes, "Lavoro," in *Dizionario enciclopedico di spiritualità*, edited by E. Ancilli, 2nd ed. (Rome: Città Nuova, 1990), 3:1404–9.

9. E. Mounier, *La petite peur du XXe siècle* (Neuchatel: Éditions de la Baconnière, 1959), 20, translated into English as *Be Not Afraid: A Denunciation of Despair* (New York: Sheed and Ward, 1962).

10. See A. Tilgher, *Homo faber: Storia del concetto di lavoro nella civiltà occidentale; Analisi filosofica di concetti affini*, 2nd ed. (Rome: G. Bardi, 1943), translated into English as *Homo faber: Work through the Ages* (Chicago: Regnery, 1965).

11. Isaac Asimov speaks of the beginnings of human work and of the way in which humans began to use fire: "Fire is a concentrated source of energy. With its use, the amount of energy at the disposal of a single

Work among the Greeks

The seventh-century B.C. author Hesiod had the following to say: "Through works men become rich in herds and wealthy, and when they work they are much preferred by the immortals. Work is no misfortune, but laziness is a disgrace."[12] However, in spite of the importance work and human activity have always had for human life, philosophers for many centuries have looked upon it as something negative and damaging to the integral development of humans. In classical antiquity, for example, a substantially negative attitude toward work prevailed, especially manual work, meant only for slaves. Plato excluded the mechanical arts from the government of the state.[13] Aristotle considered all kinds of physical work as vile in that they oppress the human intelligence.[14] The Stoics Cicero and Seneca exalted leisure (*otium*) as superior to work. At best, the ancients presented work as a kind of *imitatio naturae*, an "imitation of nature." The reasons for this attitude are several. On the one hand, the Platonic conception of human nature left its mark because in order to reach the end of perfect contemplation, humans were meant to separate themselves from the material world. In the Mesopotamian world it was said that humans were created by the gods with a view to rescuing the latter from the fatigue and dead weight of work. In that way the gods could center their lives on leisure and peaceful activities: humans existed so that the gods need not work. Obviously the fact that physical work was grueling and backbreaking left its mark on this attitude: work was worthy only of slaves. Interestingly, the value of work begins to be appreciated only once the institution of slavery has begun to wane. "Work in antiquity does not have the moral value that has been attributed to it after twenty centuries of Christianity," writes Claude Mossé. "Contempt for manual work appeared to many as the counterpart of slavery and, at the same time, as the cause of the stagnation of technology."[15]

Work in Christian Theology

The book of Genesis clearly refers to the fatigue present in physical work as a chastisement for sin (Gn 3:17). According to many Church Fathers, in fact, the purpose of work is principally one of personal purification.[16] This may be seen in Athanasius's *Life of St. Anthony*,[17] in the writings of John Cassian[18] and Augustine,[19] and in

---

human being is so much greater than is to be found in his own body that it can be considered virtually limitless. It is for this reason that the 'discovery of fire' is beyond doubt the greatest single human achievement. It alone freed him completely from bondage to the limited energy supply of his own body, eked out by that of the animals he domesticated.... Here is an unmistakable physical achievement in the manner of utilizing energy, which marks out man (and pre-man) from all other animals. No other species, however intelligent, makes even the most fumbling attempt to use fire, whereas no tribe of man is known today, however primitive, that does not use fire." I. Asimov, *Life and Energy* (Garden City, N.Y.: Doubleday, 1962), 12.

12. Hesiod, *Works and Days*, 308–11.   13. Plato, *Repub.* 369ff.

14. Aristotle, *Politics* 1328bff.

15. C. Mossé, *Le travail en Grèce et à Rome* (Paris: Presses Universitaires de France, 1966), 81, translated into English as *The Ancient World at Work* (New York: Norton, 1969).

16. See Illanes, *La santificación del trabajo*, 46ff.

17. See Athanasius, *Life of Anthony*, 3, according to Illanes in *La santificación del trabajo*, 39.

18. See John Cassian, *De institutis coenobiorum* 2, 14. See the texts cited by Illanes in *La santificación del trabajo*, 39f.

19. See J. L. Illanes, "Trabajo y vida cristiana en San Agustín," *Revista Agustiniana* 38 (1997): 339–77.

Benedict's *Rule*.[20] As such, work was considered on the whole an activity unworthy of humans, also perhaps because it was presented in scripture as a punishment for sin (Gn 3:17–19). Besides, the reflection of Thomas Aquinas on work did not go beyond the generally accepted position of Christian authors.[21] He never spoke of the hidden life of Jesus, his years of work and family life. He said that Jesus' "entrance of Christ into the world,"[22] in fact, began only at his baptism in the Jordan. Bonaventure took a similar position.[23] The famous late medieval work of spirituality *The Imitation of Christ* pronounces a severe judgment against the role of work in Christian life, considering it as one of the elements that cause special misery and unpleasantness for the devout Christian.[24] In fact, some authors from the Middle Ages stated categorically that Jesus, before beginning his public life, did not work at all.[25]

Something of the kind may be said of Luther and Calvin.[26] The Protestant reformers valued human work and related it to creation, that is, to the original design of God for humans and for the world. Still, they did not consider work as an action that is capable of sanctifying humans because of the damage done to them by sin. They thought that Christian life involves principally a "fiducial" faith and leaves little space for "good works." In spite of the existence of some exceptions in the modern period—for example, in the writings of Francis de Sales[27]—the topic of work is substantially neglected in works of Christian spiritual theology and ethics. Vatican Council II made an important contribution in placing work in its essential place in human and Christian life,[28] as did spiritual impulses in the Church at the time, especially the work of Josemaría Escrivá.[29]

Work in the Renaissance and the Industrial Revolution

It is interesting to note that in the late Middle Ages and during the Renaissance period some authors, such as Pico della Mirandola, Erasmus, and Thomas More (in the fifteenth and sixteenth centuries) made a special effort to promote a renewed awareness of the value of human work within society.[30] In the modern period, in fact, work came to be placed more and more at the center of human attention.[31] This re-

20. See Benedict, *Regula Monasteriorum* 48, 8.

21. See especially the work of Aquinas, *Contra impugnantes Dei cultum et religionem*, which defends the option of mendicant religious orders to abstain from manual work.

22. "His quae pertinent ad ingressum eius in mundum." Aquinas, *S.Th.* III, q. 27, *praef.*

23. See Bonaventure, *Quaestiones disputatae de perfectione evangelica*, q. 2, aa. 2–3.

24. See Thomas à Kempis, *Imitatio Christi* I, 22 and 25, III, 26. The same idea may be found in the popular work by the fifteenth-century abbot García Jiménez de Cisneros, *Ejercitatorio de la vida espiritual*.

25. See the work *Meditationes vitae Christi*, attributed to Bonaventure but probably written by James of Cordone. See Illanes, *La santificación del trabajo*, 55f.

26. See H.-J. Prien, *Luthers Wirtschaftsethik* (Gottingen: Vandenhoeck & Ruprecht, 1992); G. Wingren, *Luthers Lehre vom Beruf* (Munich: Kaiser, 1952); A. Biéler, *L'umanesimo sociale di Calvino* (Turin: Claudiana, 1964); Thompson, "Creata ad Imaginem Dei."

27. See Illanes, *La santificación del trabajo*, 62–64.

28. See ibid., 13ff. See the bibliography mentioned in note 8.

29. On the notion of work and its sanctification in Josemaría, see the homilies "In Joseph's Workshop" in *Christ Is Passing By*, nos. 39–56, and "Work of God," in *Friends of God*, nos. 55–72. See the studies of Rodríguez, *Vocación, trabajo, contemplación*, and Illanes, *La santificación del trabajo*, chap. 7; E. Burkhart and J. López Díaz, *Vida cotidiana y santidad en la enseñanza de San Josemaría*, 3:19–251.

30. See Illanes, *La santificación del trabajo*, 60.

31. On the growing centrality of human work in the period of the Enlightenment, see F. Valjavec, *Geschichte der abendländischen Aufklärung*, 198ff.

newed awareness coincides materially with the secularization of society and the moving away from religious practice. The Protestant Reformation played a certain part in this process.[32] The writings of John Locke were particularly influential, because they insisted on the right to property of body and work.[33] De Lubac sees in the growing importance given to work in recent centuries an attempt "to flee fatality, which, from time immemorial was considered invincible."[34] Voltaire encouraged one and all to carry out some worthy task in order to provide for their own sustenance and for the good of humanity, because in work three evils are overcome: boredom, vice, and need.[35]

One of the first authors to name work as the principal motor for the development of humans and of the world as a whole is Karl Marx. He pays little attention to *homo sapiens*, as had Augustine, Avicenna, and Aquinas, or to the *homo volens* of Scotus, Descartes, and Kant; he is interested rather in *homo faber*,[36] the man who works, who produces, who constructs, who expresses his own dignity in a supreme way through work, no longer interpreting the world but rather transforming it, to take up Marx's well-known expression.[37] According to Marx and his followers, human work should be considered the motor of all human progress, the power that draws human society toward the future, to its full realization.[38] Likewise Hannah Arendt speaks of work as creative and as what distinguishes humans from other living beings.[39]

Thus work, from being a mere instrument and means in antiquity—a poor and simple means, to be avoided if at all possible—becomes in the modern period central, almost an end in itself, an end with which the *homo faber* has come to identify his existence. With this identification in an ever more technological context, however, humans can easily become slaves anew because inevitably they become not just the subjects but also the objects of transformations and manipulation by others.[40] As in

---

32. See Taylor, *Sources of the Self*, 211–27.

33. See J. Locke, *Two Treatises of Civil Government* (London: J. M. Dent, 1924), II, 27f.

34. H. de Lubac, "Affrontements mystiques," in *Oeuvres complètes* (Paris: Cerf, 2006), 4:233–406, 246.

35. See Voltaire, *Candide; or, The Optimist* (London: 1823).

36. The animal "produces only under the dominion of immediate physical need, whilst man produces even when he is free from physical need and only truly produces in freedom therefrom. An animal produces only itself, whilst man reproduces the whole of nature. An animal's product belongs immediately to its physical body, whilst man freely confronts his product. An animal forms only in accordance with the standard and the need of the species to which it belongs, whilst man knows how to produce in accordance with the standard of every species, and knows how to apply everywhere the inherent standard to the object. Man therefore also forms objects in accordance with the laws of beauty.... It is just in his work upon the objective world, therefore, that man really proves himself to be a *species-being*." K. Marx, *Economic and Philosophic Manuscripts of 1844* (Moscow: Progress, 1959), 32.

37. See K. Marx and F. Engels, *Theses on Feuerbach* (London: Union Books, 2009).

38. See the work of the neo-Marxist Ernst Bloch, *The Principle of Hope* (Cambridge, Mass.: MIT Press, 1986). On this see P. O'Callaghan, "Hope and Freedom in Gabriel Marcel and Ernst Bloch," *Irish Theological Quarterly* 55 (1989): 215–39.

39. Arendt, *The Human Condition*, 86.

40. Nietzsche was aware of this dynamic. He wrote: "How frugal our educated and uneducated have become concerning 'joy'! More and more, *work* gets all good conscience on its side; the desire for joy already calls itself a 'need to recuperate' and is starting to be ashamed of itself. 'One owes it to one's health'—that is what one says when caught on an excursion in the countryside. Soon we may well reach the point where one can't give in to the desire for a *vita contemplativa* (that is, taking a walk with ideas and friends) without self-contempt and a bad conscience. Well, formerly it was the other way around: work was afflicted with a bad

antiquity, some are free, others are oppressed as slaves, either because of the work they do or because they have no work to do. In fact, since the time of the early Industrial Revolution onward the question arises not only of liberation *through* work but also of liberation *from* work.[41] The experience of recent centuries shows not so much the need to choose between work and effort, on the one hand, and contemplation/repose/leisure on the other; nor does it seem to indicate a way of combining them materially. Rather it shows the need to integrate them formally and establish between them an adequate hierarchy.

Human Work, Rest, and Common Priesthood

Let us consider now what scripture has to say about work and human activity.

Human Work in Scripture

We have already seen that God destined humans to rule over and care for the world (Gn 1:26–28), placing them in paradise to "cultivate and guard it" (Gn 2:15).[42] On the whole, scripture speaks positively about work and human activity. Sin has not substantially changed our destiny, for "paradise was not a life of leisured unemployment."[43] But sin has introduced a kind of disorder into all human activity on account of which we do not easily recognize the sovereignty of God in which we, his children, share. In effect, man is lord over creation as the image of God, but his dominion is vicarious, not proper. The earth in which the Israelites lived was always considered to be "the property of Jahweh."[44]

Work, Rest, and the Sabbath

The fact that humans were meant to work in fulfillment of a divine mandate is situated within the Old Testament in the context of the Sabbath rest.[45] The following classic texts are well known (Dt 5:12–14):

Observe the sabbath day, to keep it holy, as the Lord your God commanded you. Six days you shall labor, and do all your work; but the seventh day is a sabbath to the Lord your God; in it you shall not do any work, you, or your son, or your daughter, or your manservant, or your maidservant, or your ox, or your ass, or any of your cattle, or the sojourner

---

conscience. A person of good family *concealed* the fact that he worked if need compelled him to work. The slave worked under the pressure of the feeling that he was doing something contemptible: 'doing' was itself contemptible. 'Nobility and honor are attached solely to *otium* and *bellum*'—that was the ancient prejudice." F. Nietzsche, *The Gay Science*, edited by B. Williams (Cambridge: Cambridge University Press, 2001), no. 184 (389).

41. See S. Semplici, "Uomo," in *Enciclopedia filosofica*, 12:11913–28, 11925f.

42. On work in the Old Testament, see Wolff, *Anthropology of the Old Testament*, 128–33. This author considers a variety of different human activities, such as waking, working, sleeping, and resting. See also A. Richardson, *The Biblical Doctrine of Work* (London: SCM Press, 1963); M. Riber, *Il lavoro nella Bibbia* (Bari: Edizioni paoline, 1969).

43. G. J. Wenham, *Genesis 1–15*, in *WBC* 1:67.

44. See Jos 22:19, Hos 9:3, Ps 85:2, Jer 16:18, Ezek 36:5.

45. See N.-E. A. Andreasen, *The Old Testament Sabbath: A Tradition-Historical Investigation* (Missoula: University of Montana, 1972); D. A. Carson, ed., *From Sabbath to Lord's Day: A Biblical, Historical, and Theological Investigation* (Eugene, Ore.: Wipf and Stock, 1999).

who is within your gates, that your manservant and your maidservant may rest as well as you.

And in the book of Exodus essentially the same prescription is to be found (20:8–11):

Remember the sabbath day, to keep it holy. Six days you shall labor, and do all your work; but the seventh day is a sabbath to the Lord your God; in it you shall not do any work.... For in six days the Lord made heaven and earth, the sea, and all that is in them, and rested the seventh day; therefore the Lord blessed the sabbath day and made it holy.

And finally: "Six days you shall do your work, but on the seventh day you shall rest; that your ox and your ass may have rest, and the son of your bondmaid, and the alien, may be refreshed" (Ex 23:12).

The Jewish scholar Abraham Heschel comments on these texts as follows:

Lift up your eyes and see: who created these. Six days a week we are engaged in conquering the forces of nature, in the arts of civilization. The seventh day is dedicated to the remembrance of creation and the remembrance of redemption, to the liberation of Israel from Egypt, to the exodus from a great civilization into a wilderness where the word of God was given. By our acts of labor during the six days we participate in the works of history; by sanctifying the seventh day we are reminded of the acts that surpass, ennoble and redeem history.... The Sabbath, as experienced by man, cannot survive in exile, a lonely stranger among days of profanity. It needs the companionship of the other days. All days of the week must be spiritually consistent with the seventh day.... In the language of the Jew, living *sub specie aeternitatis* means living *sub specie Sabbatis*.[46]

Thus not only should human work reflect, extend, and perfect the divine work of creation and providence, all done for the glory of God, but to work for the glory of God means that humans must relive and reproduce in their lives that blending of activity and rest, of conquering and remembering, inaugurated by God when he created the world. Yet we must keep in mind that during our earthly pilgrimage the unredeemed side of human nature does not facilitate a serene integration of work and rest, which are often lived by fallen human beings as forms of self-affirmation and escapism, respectively.

The Old Testament insistence on the Sabbath rest shows, besides, that work has an intrinsically social side to it, because it is meant to express the need to look after the weaker members of society, servants, and children, who are looked upon as equals before the Lord, and even domestic animals. We are meant to praise God along with other creatures. The Biblical texts just cited show that work exists in relation to rest or, more precisely, in function of what rest is meant to express: divine praise and service to our neighbor. Rest serves as a permanent corrective to all human attempts to confuse the means (self-affirming human activity, constructing the world) with the end (salvation, giving glory to God), ensuring we never forget that God is the only Lord, that only grace can save us. The Psalmist expressed this conviction well: "Unless the Lord builds the house, those who build it labor in vain. Unless the Lord watches over the city, the watchman stays awake in vain. It is in vain that you rise up early and go late to rest, eating the bread of anxious toil; for he gives to his beloved sleep" (Ps 127:1f.). Work, in other words, may exclude neither God nor neighbor.

---

46. Heschel, *God in Search of Man*, 417f.

Human life is directed by God to the "promise of entering his rest" (Heb 4:1; see vv. 1–11); the term "rest" in this text of the letter to the Hebrews refers to the Sabbath rest,[47] and has clearly eschatological connotations.[48] In effect, eschatological consummation, God's own gift, eternal rest in God, is the direct fruit not of human work but rather of God's grace.[49] Still, the fact that humans are saved by God's grace does not exclude the idea that there will be authentic human activity in heaven.[50] In the words of Heschel:

The meaning of the Sabbath is to celebrate time rather than space. Six days a week we live under the tyranny of things of space; on the Sabbath we try to become attuned to *holiness in time*. It is a day on which we are called upon to share in what is eternal in time, to turn from the results of creation to the mystery of creation; from the world of creation to the creation of the world.[51]

Augustine spoke of the heavenly reward as "a holy and perpetual rest free of all fatigue and weight; yet it involves not an inactive indolence but an ineffable peace full of delightful activity.... It involves the praise of God, without effort of the members, without anxiety and concern; hence there is no succession of rest and work, and it cannot be said that activity begins as soon as rest ceases."[52] Pope Francis observes that "we tend to demean contemplative rest as something unproductive and unnecessary, but this is to do away with the very thing which is most important about work: its meaning." Rest "is another way of working, which forms part of our very essence. It protects human action from becoming empty activism; it also prevents that unfettered greed and sense of isolation which make us seek personal gain to the detriment of all else."[53]

Wisdom literature frequently pays attention to the issue of work and human activity, especially in a practical and moral context. Laziness is condemned out of hand (Prv 6:6–11, 12:24, 24:30–34), and work, even of the most humble kind, is positively evaluated (Prv 31:10–31; Sir 38:25–34). Those who carry out a manual task, says the book of Sirach, "keep stable the fabric of the world, and their prayer is in the practice of their trade" (38:34). In other words, work itself becomes prayer. At the same time, the author of this book says, "He who devotes himself to the study of the law of the Most High will seek out the wisdom of all the ancients, and will be concerned with prophecies" (39:1), which seems to indicate that contemplation and study are superior to physical work.

Human Work in the New Testament

The contribution of the New Testament to the Old Testament view of work moves in five directions. First, in continuity with the Old Testament, Christ reminds his disciples in no uncertain terms that without God's grace their work and activity are of no use: "Without me you can do nothing" (Jn 15:5). God seeks human collaboration, but only he can save the world. Thus the Christian understanding of work is based on the

---

47. See *BDAG*, 523f., s.v. κατάπαυσις.
48. W. L. Lane, *Hebrews 1–8*, in *WBC* 47A:98.
49. *COH* 156–61.
50. See ibid., 170–81.
51. A. J. Heschel, *The Sabbath: Its Meaning for Modern Man* (New York: Noonday Press, 1993), 19.
52. Augustine, *Ep. 55 ad Iannerion*, 9:17.
53. *LS*, par. 237.

doctrine of the incarnation of the Word and of Christ's Passover, because in it God gives his definitive "yes" to the world and to history (1 Cor 1:18–20). Besides, Christ saves humanity, overcoming, though gradually, the disorder introduced by sin, preparing the world so that God can eventually become "everything to everyone" (1 Cor 15:28). The entire work of salvation is a divine work, done by God in Christ.

In effect, second, it is clear that the central "place" of the Sabbath in the Old Testament is now occupied by Christ himself, "for the Son of Man is Lord of the Sabbath" (Mt 12:8). Paul writes to the Romans: "I appeal to you therefore, brethren, by the mercies of God, to present your bodies as a living sacrifice, holy and acceptable to God, which is your spiritual worship" (Rom 12:1). And D. A. Hagner comments: "The demands of the sabbath commandment, however they be construed, must give way to the presence and purpose of Jesus, and not vice versa."[54] Perhaps we may say that the fact and the form of human work derive ultimately from God as creator of the world and of humans, but they are actuated in and through the life and power of Christ present in each and every Christian. Paraphrasing Galatians 2:20, we might say not only that Christ "lives in me" but also that Christ "works in me." While working, the Christian believer "is thrice blessed. The one who works is himself blessed in his reception of divine grace to carry through his labors for the glory of God; those who receive the results of such tasks done in a new spirit and with a new quality are benefited also; and in all God is himself glorified."[55]

Third, the simple observation that Jesus himself worked is highly significant; in fact, for many years he carried out a manual task: he was "the carpenter's son" (Mt 13:55).[56] And he did so assiduously for many years, as we can see, among other things, in his capacity to work tirelessly during his public ministry. Of himself he said: "My Father is working still, and I am working" (Jn 5:17). Paul also worked diligently both as a tentmaker and as an apostle, perceiving in the midst of his striving the grace of God present in him: "By the grace of God I am what I am, and his grace toward me was not in vain. On the contrary, *I worked harder than any of them* [the other apostles], though it was not I, but the grace of God which is with me" (1 Cor 15:10). Besides, Paul, who earned his living in the exercise of a manual trade, roundly condemned the behavior of some Christians who were "living in idleness, mere busybodies, not doing any work" (2 Thes 3:11; see vv. 6–15). Whereas Jesus said that "the laborer deserves his wages" (Lk 10:7), Paul states: "If anyone will not work, let him not eat" (2 Thes 3:10).

Fourth, in chapter 8 of Romans Paul speaks repeatedly of the fact that creation is reconciled—that is, brought back to God—in and through the life and activity of the children of God. And this is not an automatic or mechanical process, for creation glorifies God through humans:

---

54. D. A. Hagner, *Matthew 1–13*, in *WBC* 33A:330.

55. H. D. McDonald, "Work," in *New Bible Dictionary*, edited by N. Hillyer and J. D. Douglas (Leicester: Inter-Varsity Press, 1986), 1248.

56. See C. C. McCown, "ὁ τέκτων," in *Studies in Early Christianity*, edited by S. J. Case (New York: Century, 1928), 173–89; E. Lombard, "Charpentier ou maçon?," *Revue de théologie et de philosophie* 36 (1948): 161–92; P. H. Furfey, "Christ as Tektón," *Catholic Biblical Quarterly* 17 (1966): 324–35; R. A. Batey, "Is Not This the Carpenter?," *New Testament Studies* 30 (1984): 249–58.

For the creation waits with eager longing for the revealing of the sons of God; for the creation was subjected to futility, not of its own will but by the will of him who subjected it in hope; because the creation itself will be set free from its bondage to decay and obtain the glorious liberty of the children of God. We know that the whole creation has been groaning in travail together until now; and not only the creation, but we ourselves, who have the first fruits of the Spirit, groan inwardly as we wait for adoption as sons, the redemption of our bodies" (Rom 8:19–23).

Fifth and finally, in the dialogue between Jesus and the sisters Martha and Mary (Lk 10:38–42) we find an interesting expression of the dilemma mentioned above between work and contemplation (Sir 38:34–39:1). In this text (Lk 10:39–42) it is said that Mary

sat at the Lord's feet and listened to his teaching. But Martha was distracted with much serving; and she went to him and said, "Lord, do you not care that my sister has left me to serve alone? Tell her then to help me." But the Lord answered her, "Martha, Martha, you are anxious and troubled about many things; one thing is needful. Mary has chosen the good portion, which shall not be taken away from her."

Jesus makes it clear that the materiality of manual work, such as it is, requires the inner complement of a deeper attitude, one of contemplation, thanksgiving, and praise, listening to the word of God, in order for such an activity to be fully pleasing to God (we considered this question when studying the doctrine of merit). "Attention to the word of God supplies an integrating center and makes possible a singleness of vision. This is the one necessary thing."[57]

The Common Priesthood of Believers

In the book of Exodus God speaks to Moses, saying: "You shall be to me a kingdom of priests and a holy nation. These are the words which you shall speak to the children of Israel" (Ex 19:6). In God's mind, this is the identity of the Jewish people: a kingdom of priests and a holy nation. In spite of the fact that the expression "a kingdom of priests" is unique in the Old Testament,[58] Heschel claims that "the great dream of Judaism is not to raise priests [Levites, etc.], but a people of priests; to consecrate all men, not only some men."[59] The twelfth-century Jewish philosopher Maimonides observed, in fact, that not only the Levites were consecrated to God, for "every human being born into this world whose spirit stirs him and whose intellect guides him dedicates himself to the Lord in order to minister to Him and worship Him and to come to know Him, and the one who acts in conformity with God's design … becomes sanctified with sublime holiness."[60]

The first letter of Peter repeats Exodus 19:6 almost to the letter. It declares to believers: "You are a chosen race, a royal priesthood, a holy nation, God's own people, that you may declare the wonderful deeds of him who called you out of darkness into his marvelous light" (1 Pt 2:9).[61] In his letter to the Romans Paul writes: "I appeal to

---

57. J. Nolland, *Luke 9:21–18:34*, in *WBC* 35B:605.

58. J. I. Durham, *Exodus*, in *WBC* 3:263. On this text, see also R. B. Y. Scott, "A Kingdom of Priests (Exodus XIX 6)," *Oudtestamentische Studien* 6 (1950): 213–91.

59. A. Heschel, *God in Search of Man*, 419.

60. Maimonides, *Mishneh Torah, Shemitah ve-Yobel*, 13, 12f., cited in ibid.

61. See J. M. Ramsey, *1 Peter*, in *WBC* 47:107–10.

you therefore, brethren, by the mercies of God, *to present your bodies as a living sacrifice*, holy and acceptable to God, which is your spiritual worship" (Rom 12:1). It is clear that "the sacrifice God looks for from humans is no longer that of beast or bird in the temple, but the daily commitment of life lived within the constraints and relationships of this bodily world."[62]

On the basis of these texts and others (e.g., Rev 1:6, 5:10, and 20:6), it is common doctrine that Christians are truly made priests by baptism, sharing validly in the priesthood of Christ, though not as ministers. The notion is widely commented on by the Church Fathers.[63] It is of particular importance to Protestant authors.[64] Vatican Council II's *Lumen Gentium* explains it as follows:

The baptized, by regeneration and the anointing of the Holy Spirit, are consecrated as a spiritual house and a holy priesthood, in order that through all those works which are those of the Christian man they may offer spiritual sacrifices and proclaim the power of Him who has called them out of darkness into His marvelous light (1 Pt 2:4–10). Therefore all the disciples of Christ, persevering in prayer and praising God (Acts 2:42, 47), should present themselves as a living sacrifice, holy and pleasing to God (Rom 12:1). Everywhere on earth they must bear witness to Christ and give an answer to those who seek an account of that hope of eternal life which is in them (1 Pt 3:15).[65]

---

62. J. D. G. Dunn, *Romans 9–16*, in *WBC* 38B:717.

63. Especially Origen, Ambrose, Augustine, Gregory the Great, and others. Origen has the following to say: "Do you not realize that to you also—that is to the whole Church and to all believers—has been given a priesthood? Listen to what Peter says to the faithful: 'You are a chosen race, a royal priesthood, a holy nation, God's own people.'" *In Lev. hom.*, 9, 1. "If I renounce everything I possess, if I carry the Cross or follow Christ, I have offered a holocaust on the altar of God.... If I mortify my body and abstain from all concupiscence, if the world is crucified for me and I for the world, then I have offered a holocaust on God's altar and I become a priest of my own sacrifice." Ibid., 9, 9. And Gregory the Great, *Altare Dei est cor nostrum, Moral.* 25, 7:15.

64. See for example T. F. Torrance, *Royal Priesthood*, 2nd ed. (Edinburgh: T. and T. Clark, 1993).

65. *LG*, no. 10. Besides, the decree *Presbyterorum Ordinis*, no. 2, reads: "The Lord Jesus, 'whom the Father has sent into the world' (Jn 10:36) has made his whole Mystical Body a sharer in the anointing of the Spirit with which he himself is anointed. In him all the faithful are made a holy and royal priesthood; they offer spiritual sacrifices to God through Jesus Christ, and they proclaim the perfections of him who has called them out of darkness into his marvelous light. Therefore, there is no member who does not have a part in the mission of the whole Body; but each one ought to hallow Jesus in his heart, and in the spirit of prophecy bear witness to Jesus." Bibliography on the matter has been abundant over the past fifty years. On the topic of the common or royal priesthood of the faithful in Vatican Council II, see Y.-J. Congar, *Sacerdoce et laïcat devant leurs taches d'évangélisation et de civilisation* (Paris: Cerf, 1962), translated into English as *A Gospel Priesthood* (New York: Herder and Herder, 1967); P. Drilling, "Common and Ministerial Priesthood: *Lumen Gentium*, Article Ten," *Irish Theological Quarterly* 53 (1987): 81–99; A. Elberti, *Il sacerdozio regale dei fedeli nei prodromi del Concilio ecumenico Vaticano II, 1903–1962* (Rome: Pontificia università Gregoriana, 1989); M. Michalski, *The Relationship between the Universal Priesthood of the Baptized and the Ministerial Priesthood of the Ordained in Vatican II and in Subsequent Theology: Understanding "essentia et non gradu tantum," Lumen gentium, no. 10* (Lewiston, N.Y.: Mellen University Press, 1996); A. Aranda, "El sacerdocio de Jesucristo en los ministros y en los fieles: Estudio teológico sobre la distinción 'essentia et non gradu tantum,'" in *La formación de los sacerdotes en las circunstancias actuales*, edited by L. F. Mateo-Seco et al. (Pamplona: Sepunsa, 1990), 207–46. From after the Council, see A. M. Carré, *Sacerdozio e laicato* (Turin: SEI, 1963); F. F. Ramos, ed., *Sacerdocio ministerial y laical* (Burgos: Aldecoa, 1970). On the doctrine of Paul VI, see A. Bonetti, ed., *Sacerdozio regale: Pagine del magistero di Paolo VI sui laici* (Vatican City: Vaticana, 2000). See also M. Adinolfi, *Il sacerdozio comune dei fedeli* (Rome: Antonianum, 1983); P. J. Rosato, "Priesthood of the Baptized and Priesthood of the Ordained," *Gregorianum* 68 (1987): 215–66; P. Rodríguez, "Sacerdocio ministerial y sacerdocio común en la estructura de la Iglesia," *Romana* 3 (1987): 162–76; J. M.-R. Tillard, "Sacerdoce," in *Dictionnaire de Spiritualité* (Paris: Beauchesne, 1990), 14:1–37; J. Castellano, "Sacerdozio dei fedeli," in *Dizionario enciclopedico di spiritualità*, edited by E. Ancilli, 2nd ed. (Rome: Città Nuova, 1990), 3:2199–2202; G. Hintzen, "Das gemeinsame Priestertum aller Gläubigen und das besondere Priestertum des Dienstes in der ökumenischen Diskussion," *Catholica* 45 (1991): 44–77;

The royal, priestly role of Christians entails not only obedience to Christ as "the rule of kings on earth" (Rv 1:5) but also participation in his rule over others: "and they shall reign on earth" (Rv 5:10). But even more, it involves ensuring that God is loved and praised in all human activity: the Christian's life should be a self-offering of gratitude. Besides, the fact that such a sacrificial self-offering can be made in a real way in the midst of suffering links suffering and praise together in Christian life (Phil 2:17). It is clear that "the living sacrifice, holy and pleasing to God" would involve sanctified human work carried out by believers who thus "reverence Christ as Lord." And Peter continues saying that believers should "always be prepared to make a defense to any one who calls you to account for the hope that is in you" (1 Pt 3:15), that is, to engage in Christian apostolate.

Work in Recent Church Documents

Both in Vatican Council II documents (*Gaudium et Spes*, no. 3) and in later papal teaching (especially John Paul II's 1981 encyclical on work, *Laborem Exercens*[66] and Francis's 2015 encyclical *Laudato Si'*)[67] the Church has encountered in scripture itself the deep meaning of the rediscovery of the anthropological meaning of work present throughout the modern period.[68] In effect, work should be considered not as an activity directed only to the purification of the individual's sinful tendencies and still less as an activity unworthy of humans, because the task of working and ruling the earth, according to the book of Genesis, is something previous to the original fall (Gn 1:27f., 2:15),[69] and humans are invited to rule over the earth by submitting themselves to God along with the rest of humanity as priests of creation. In *Gaudium et Spes* we read:

G. Chantraine, "Synodalité, expression du sacerdoce commun et du sacerdoce ministériel," *Nouvelle Revue Théologique* 113 (1991): 340–62; D. Coffey, "The Common and Ordained Priesthood," *Theological Studies* 58 (1997): 209–36; L. Campagnoli, *Il sacerdozio comune dei battezzati: Bilancio storico e prospettive future* (Rome: Apostolato della preghiera, 2007); P. J. Philibert, *Le sacerdoce des baptisés: Clé d'une Église vivante* (Paris: Cerf, 2007); J. Martín Gómez, *Sacerdocio común-sacerdocio ministerial: Presupuestos teológicos y consecuencias pastorales* (Toledo: Instituto Superior de Estudios Teológicos San Ildefonso, 2008); J.-M. Hennaux, "Le rapport intrinsèque du sacerdoce ministériel et du sacerdoce commun des fidèles: Pour une symbolique du sacerdoce," *Nouvelle Revue Théologique* 131 (2009): 211–24; E. Castellucci, "Sacerdozio," in *Dizionario di ecclesiologia*, edited by G. Calabrese, P. Goyret, and O. F. Piazza (Rome: Città Nuova, 2010), 1229–42; J. López Díaz, "Sacerdocio común," *Diccionario de San Josemaría Escrivá de Balaguer*, edited by J. L. Illanes (Burgos: Monte Carmelo, 2013), 1079–83.

66. See R. Buttiglione, *L'uomo e il lavoro: Riflessioni sull'enciclica "Laborem exercens,"* 2nd ed. (Bologna: CSEO, 1984).

67. See *LS*, pars. 124–29.

68. See Illanes, *La santificación del trabajo.*

69. In the words of Escrivá, "From the beginning of creation man has had to work. This is not something that I have invented. It is enough to turn to the opening pages of the Bible. There you can read that, before sin entered the world, and in its wake death, punishment and misery (Rom 5:12), God made Adam from the clay of the earth, and created for him and his descendants this beautiful world we live in, *ut operaretur et custodiret illum* (Gen 2:15), so that we might cultivate it and look after it.... We must be convinced therefore that work is a magnificent reality, and that it has been imposed on us as an inexorable law which, one way or another, binds everyone, even though some may try to seek exemption from it. Make no mistake about it. Man's duty to work is not a consequence of original sin, nor is it just a discovery of modern times. It is an indispensable means which God has entrusted to us here on this earth. It is meant to fill out our days and make us sharers in God's creative power. It enables us to earn our living and, at the same time, to reap 'the fruits of eternal life' (Jn 4:26) for 'man is born to work as the birds are born to fly' (Job 5:7).... To this you might reply

To believers, this point is settled: considered in itself, this human activity accords with God's will. For man, created to God's image, received a mandate to subject to himself the earth and all it contains, and to govern the world with justice and holiness; a mandate to relate himself and the totality of things to Him Who was to be acknowledged as the Lord and Creator of all. Thus, by the subjection of all things to man, the name of God would be wonderful in all the earth.[70]

Conclusion: A Christian View of Work

To conclude this chapter, we can consider four aspects of human work in the context of Christian faith. In the first place, as we have already seen, work is the fulfillment of a task God confided to humans when making them "in his image and likeness." Through work, humans take care of the created world, they exercise dominion over the earth and bring it to completion in a way that is filially subject to God. This may be seen in a special way in the life on earth of Christ himself, image of God and savior of the world.

In the second place, for a Christian work is lived as a sharing in the redeeming work of Christ. And this is for two reasons. Principally because Christ, in saving humans, gives back to them the divine friendship they lost through sin and renews in them the image of God, and with it the pressing invitation to "exercise dominion" over the earth. And it is also because Christ, in dying on the cross, in rising from the dead, and in sending the Holy Spirit, has established the sovereignty of God over the created world once and for all, in such a way that those who belong to his mystical body share—through prayer, penance, work, and apostolate—in the effective establishment of divine sovereignty as his "co-redeemers."[71] "Since Christ took it into his hands," Josemaría Escrivá writes, "work has become for us a redeemed and redemptive reality."[72]

The third aspect of human work in the Christian context is that, even though the task of ruling the earth was confided to humans before the Fall, the influence of sin makes its presence felt in the vital context in which they work, that is in the hearts of humans. Humans should live out their "rule of service" in accordance with their filial identity, in a spirit of freedom, joy, trust, and sharing, fully directed toward God

---

that many centuries have gone by and very few people think along these lines; that most people, when they work, do so for very different reasons: some for money, some to support their families, others to get on in society, to develop their capabilities, or perhaps to give free play to their disordered desires, or to contribute to social progress. In other words, most people regard their work as something that has to be done and cannot be avoided.... This is a stunted, selfish and earthbound outlook, which neither you nor I can accept. For we have to remember and remind people around us that we are children of God, who have received the same invitation from our Father as the two brothers in the parable: 'Son, go and work in my vineyard.' (Mt 21:28). I give you my word that if we make a daily effort to see our personal duties in this light, that is, as a divine summons, we will learn to carry them through to completion with the greatest human and supernatural perfection of which we are capable. Occasionally we may rebel, like the elder of the two sons, who replied to his father, 'I will not,' (Mt 21:29), but we will learn how to turn back repentant and will redouble our efforts to do our duty." *Friends of God*, no. 57.

70. *GS*, no. 34.

71. See P. Rodríguez, "*Omnia traham ad meipsum:* Il significato di Giovanni 12, 32 nell'esperienza spirituale di Mons. Escrivá de Balaguer," *Annales Theologici* 6 (1992): 5–34.

72. Escrivá, *Christ Is Passing By*, no. 47.

(a dominion that is expressed as patient, attentive, prudent, persevering, respectful, in solidarity, free, and joyful). The introduction of sin inclined them rather toward a "rule of destruction," with them vainly attempting to live as if the creator did not exist (with a dominion that is impatient, uncontrolled, careless, egoistic, idolatrous, and sad).[73] The latter may be easily seen in the common negligence accorded to natural law and the present ecological crisis.[74] As a result, to carry out work in an upright way poses for the Christian important moral challenges. Among the latter may be added the fact that with the introduction of sin, death, misery, and suffering entered into the world. In the present historical moment, human work is carried out by many under the sign of corruption, fatigue, and often dissatisfaction. Still, for believers, united in the cross of Christ, this fatigue acquires an eternal value, as John Paul II says in *Laborem Exercens.*[75]

Fourth and finally, human work carried out according to the will of God and for his glory offers the believer the opportunity of communicating the faith to other people (Christian apostolate), for work itself is apostolate. Christ indeed instructs his disciples: "Let your light so shine before men, that they may see your good works and give glory to your Father who is in heaven" (Mt 5:16).

73. In the Aramaic text of Gn 1:28, the term "dominate" derives from a double root: "to subject" (*kābaš*), which means "to take possession of a territory," and "to dominate" (*rādāh*), which expresses the notion of pasturing, guiding, governing. We can say, therefore, that humans, when they "dominate," when they work, should act as *shepherds* of the created world: see chapter 4, notes 63f. and corresponding text.

74. See notes 5–6.

75. John Paul II writes: "The Christian finds in human work a small part of the Cross of Christ and accepts it in the same spirit of redemption in which Christ accepted his Cross for us. In work, thanks to the light that penetrates us from the Resurrection of Christ, we always find a *glimmer* of new life, of the *new good*, as if it were an announcement of 'the new heavens and the new earth,' in which man and the world participate precisely through the toil that goes with work. Through toil—and never without it. On the one hand this confirms the indispensability of the Cross in the spirituality of human work; on the other hand the Cross which this toil constitutes reveals a new good springing from work itself, from work understood in depth and in all its aspects and never apart from work." *Laborem Exercens*, par. 27.

25   THE HUMAN PERSON

Christianity's Contribution to Anthropology

Christianity created language. From the very beginning it has been, and still is, a strengthening power of language.   F. SCHLEIERMACHER[1]

It is a mistake to attribute to the person as person the operation that characterizes nature. MAXIMUS THE CONFESSOR[2]

Person and nature are realities that are simply incommensurable with one another. ROBERT SPAEMANN[3]

A person is a person because of people. ZULU PROVERB

Coming to the last chapter of this text, we shall return to the question dealt with in the first chapter: who is the human being? In the light of Christian faith in divine grace through Christ, the reply must be: the human person, Christianity's foremost contribution to anthropology.

In the first place, as we already saw, humans exist and live as beings in relationship, social beings, *ens ab alio*, or, better, *ens* (or *entia*) *ab Alio*. In effect, humans have been created in the image and likeness of God, constituted in complete ontological dependence on the creator, yet are capable of entering into filial and perpetual communion with the Trinity and with other humans, who are children of God like them. Humans, in the depth of their being, exist and act totally in relationship, in solidarity, even when they do not recognize it, even though they try to avoid it; each is an *ens ab alio*, a being that has received existence and life *from* another, God, and *through*

---

1. F. D. E. Schleiermacher, "Die Aphorismen von 1805 und 1809," *Hermeneutik*, edited by H.-G. Gadamer and O. Kimmerle (Heidelberg: C. Winter, 1959), 31–50, 38, translated into English as *Hermeneutics: the Hand-written Manuscripts* (Atlanta, Ga.: Scholars Press, 1986).

2. Maximus the Confessor, *Opusc. theol. pol.* 10.

3. Spaemann, *Sulla nozione di natura umana*, 29.

others, humans like themselves. We come to know ourselves not only by asking, "what is the human being?" but also, and more fundamentally, "who is the human being?" For this reason an anthropology that intends to be complete must always approach these questions from the perspective of God's action manifested definitively in Jesus of Nazareth, his only-begotten Son made man, his only, ultimate, and supreme Word.

At the same time, the human being may not be considered as a pure, abstract relationship up in the air, living exclusively on the basis of his origin. Humans may not be considered as a kind of transient spark temporarily emanating from the divine substance and returning subsequently into nothing. On the basis of their origin in God, humans receive a quasi-infinite dignity; the seat of this dignity is in human beings themselves, who contain a special value: the dignity of a being who, though ontologically dependent on the creator, is not God but rather a spiritual, immortal, and corporeal being with the inherent capacity (intelligence and free will) to define its own destiny even independently of God, to the point of being able to rebel against him.[4] That is: a being in itself, corporeal and free, with its own narrative and a clear individual otherness with respect to other creatures.

The one who has been constituted as an *ens ab alio* is therefore, at the same time, an *ens a se*, a being that exists of itself. This distinct and separate existence, this inalienable individuality of humans before the creator on whom they depend completely, and on others, is what in philosophy and theology is called the "person."[5]

The Genesis of the Notion of "Person" in Greek Philosophy

It is fair to say that the notion of "person" is a an almost pure product of the philosophical reflection that started under the assimilation, practice, and preaching of Christian faith. Considering the classical anthropology of the Greeks, it is possible to

4. See *COH* 189–221.

5. This section has made use of central parts of O'Callaghan, "La persona umana tra filosofia e teologia." Of course bibliography on the topic of the person is ample. Among theological works, see S. Schlossmann, *Persona und Πρόσωπόν im Recht und im christlichen Dogma* (Kiel: Lisius & Tischer, 1906); C. Andresen, "Zur Entstehung und Geschichte des trinitarischen Personsbegriffs," *Zeitschrift für die neutestamentliche Wissenschaft* 52 (1961): 1–38; W. Pannenberg, "Person," in *Die Religion in Geschichte und Gegenwart*, edited by K. Galling, 3rd ed. (Tubingen: J. C. B. Mohr, 1961), 5:230–35; J. Ratzinger, "On the Understanding of 'Person' in Theology," in Ratzinger, *Dogma and Preaching* (Chicago: Franciscan Herald Press, 1985), 181–96; A. Milano, *Persona in teologia: Alle origini del significato di persona nel cristianesimo antico*, 2nd ed. (Rome: Edizioni dehoniane, 1996); M. Bordoni, "Il contributo della categoria teologica di persona," in *La teologia per l'unità dell'Europa*, edited by I. Sanna (Bologna: Dehoniane, 1991), 47–62; J. D. Zizioulas, "Personhood and Being," in Zizioulas, *Being as Communion: Studies in Personhood and the Church* (Crestwood, N.Y.: St. Vladimir's Seminary Press, 1997), 27–65. Among philosophical works, see F. A. Stentrup, "Zum Begriff der Hypostase," *Zeitschrift für katholische Theologie* 1 (1877): 57–84, 361–93; 2 (1878): 225–58; M. Nédoncelle, "Prosopon et Persona dans l'antiquité classique: Essai de bilan linguistique," *Revue des sciences religieuses* 22 (1948): 277–99; A. Pavan and A. Milano, eds., *Persona e personalismi* (Naples: Dehoniane, 1987); J. Seifert, *Essere e persona* (Milan: Vita e pensiero, 1989); J. F. Crosby, "The Incommunicability of Human Persons," *Thomist* 57 (1993): 403–42; E. Berti, "Individuo e persona: La concezione classica," *Studium* 91 (1995): 515–28; J. A. Lombo, *La persona en Tomás de Aquino: Un estudio histórico y sistemático* (Rome: Apollinare Studi, 2001); see also Various Authors, *Person: Historia y grandeza de un concepto*, "Espíritu" 59 (2010).

reconstruct quite a complete picture of the principal elements of human nature.[6] In effect, ancient anthropology managed to describe with precision and depth central aspects of being and acting humanly. It did not manage, however, to integrate the corporeal and spiritual sides of anthropology in a single integrated reality and was thus unable to give a sufficient account of the concrete human individual, that of *being someone*.

Etymological Origins of the Term "Person"

The term "person" derives probably from the Greek *prosōpon*, which appears in the lexicon of ancient philosophy in the context of tragic drama and is usually translated as "face."[7] The word *prosōpon* connects easily with the term *prosōpeion*, or "mask." In effect, the whole of Greek theater, especially of the tragic kind, was considered the place in which conflicts between the rational and universalist necessity of a unitary and harmonic world (the Greek ideal), on the one hand, and individual human freedom, on the other, were represented and resolved. "It was in the theater that man attempted to 'become a person,'" observes Marcello Bordoni.[8] On the stage of the world, in the presence of other people, humans attempted to affirm their own personal value, their own ideas, their own individuality; they attempted to overcome the rational and impersonal force of necessity without, however, generally managing to do so.

In both Aristotle and Plato the multiplicity of beings, the fact of the existence of a variety of individuals, is in real terms a sign of their imperfection. Multiplicity must be overcome in order to achieve the harmonic unity of all beings. Plato, in his work *Laws*, for example, teaches that the cosmos does not exist on account of humans but the other way around: humans exist on account of the cosmos.[9] For Platonists, the human ideal is that of being absorbed into the universal mind. To remain locked into one's own corporeal individuality would involve an unresolved imperfection. Even though the neo-Platonist Plotinus came much closer to recognizing the value of a distinct human individuality, in real terms he was unable bring this project to completion.[10] Also, Porphyry considered the individual as a unique whole of different properties.[11] That is to say, the individual exists on account of the whole, the multiplicity for the all. Analogously, according to Aristotle individuals cannot be defined, and philosophy is interested in them only insofar as they are members of a species or class.[12] Humans discover, with frustration and bitterness, that their own individuality is nothing other than a mask, a presumption, a problem, a defect to be overcome.

The Genesis of the Concept of "Person"

The use of the term "person," the notion of "personal" human dignity, situated above created authority, office, profession, lifestyle, and so on, is to be found in the

---

6. See, for example, Groethuysen, *Anthropologie philosophique*, 13–102.
7. On the use of the term *prosōpon* in a Biblical context, see BDAG 887f., s.v. πρόσωπον.
8. Bordoni, "Il contributo della categoria teologica di persona," 49.
9. Plato, *Laws* 903c–d.
10. See A. H. Armstrong, "Form, Individual and Person in Plotinus," *Dionysius* 1 (1977): 49–68.
11. See Porphyry, *Isag.* 7, 20–26.
12. See Aristotle, *Metaph.* 1036a5–6.

works of several ancient authors. In Mesopotamia (present-day Iraq), a thousand years before Christ, there is evidence that there was a direct legal rapport between transgression and responsibility, which seems to indicate the idea of an accountable individual and, at heart, the person.[13] The same may be found in the writings of the Stoic Cicero.[14] As Brunschvig says, "From Stoicism humans have learned to say 'I.'"[15] Human dignity, however, is based not on the inviolability of human life, or on the relationship of humans with a supreme God who liberates them from all created authority, but rather on the rationality common to all humans. This rationality confers dignity on humans and obliges them to act with responsibility. In a more Christian context this sense of human dignity as likewise developed by many modern philosophers.[16]

At the beginning of this text we saw that throughout the Old Testament and especially in the New, humans begin to perceive their value as individuals, their inalienable dignity and that of the other members of their race, within a process that moves from the revelation of the God of the Covenant to the incarnation of his Son, Jesus Christ. In fact, the basis for the doctrine of the human person is fully present in the New Testament. Of particular importance, as we have already seen, is the fact that humans have been created "in the image and likeness of God."[17] Likewise, the idea that each and every one is *called* contains an implicit doctrine of the person.[18] Still, this doctrine has developed and been made explicit only gradually during the early Christian centuries in the context of the doctrines of Christology and of the Trinity.

The Theological Basis for the Concept of Person

Knowing the Person and "Becoming" a Person

Reflecting on the saving work of Christ, we can come to appreciate the notion of person and, in virtue of this knowledge, the Christian reflection of three persons in God. From the fact that in God there are three persons arises the possibility of applying the term "person" also to the human individual. Still, the fact of man becoming a person does not depend on the work of salvation carried out by the eternal Son made man; that is, it is not a soteriological or eschatological doctrine but rather a protological one in that it belongs to the original creation of humans. Christian salvation does not make man a person but rather provides us with the conviction through faith that to be a person is his original, natural, common condition. To be a person therefore is not the result of a hope-filled promise, nor is it situated in self-realization or future becoming; it is located rather in the original situation, created and present, of humans, of any human being whatsoever. Being a person finds its roots not in the incarnation of the eternal Son of the Father but in creation, the work of the Father through the Son in the Holy Spirit. Humans become persons not when they receive

13. Meslin, "La personne," 48.
14. See Cicero, *De officiis* 1:30, 106.
15. Cited by Meslin in "La personne," 49.
16. See notes 53ff. and the corresponding text.
17. On the explanation of Theophilus of Antioch, Gregory of Nyssa, Gregory the Great, Leo the Great, Bonaventure, and Thomas Aquinas, see the summary given by W. Pannenberg in *Systematic Theology*, 2:176f. and n2.
18. See chapter 12, notes 39ff. and corresponding text.

the gift of saving grace and eternal glory from Christ, nor in their encounter with other persons, as if becoming a person were a kind of "event" within one's own history. Humans *are* persons insofar as they have been created by God as such in the image of his Son, even though we may come to realize this to the fullest possible extent only in the light of the history of salvation.

The notion of the human person consolidated and became explicit during the Patristic period in three principal stages: with the confession of the consubstantiality of the Word with the Father and of the Holy Spirit with both, with the application of the term "person" to the three hypostases in God, and finally with the application of the term "person" to the human individual.

The Christological Consolidation of the Notion of Personhood

The first moment of consolidation of the notion of person coincided with the confession of the full divinity of the divine Word with the eternal Father against the Arians at the Council of Nicaea (325). The Alexandrian presbyter Arius had taught that the divine Logos, the Son, who temporarily became "flesh" to save humanity from corruption, is not co-eternal with the Father but was rather "created," generated, or produced by him in time as a kind of "second God" who acts as the creator (or "Demiurge") of other creatures.[19] "There was a time when the Logos did not exist," said Arius.[20] Of course if there was a moment when the Logos or Son was not existent, there must have been a time, "before" the generation of the Word, when there were no persons in God (what is said of the Son may be extended to the Holy Spirit). That is, there was a time when "the Father" existed on his own, a phase in which God was strictly "uni-personal," living in a non-Trinitarian unity. For God, to be Trinity, and thus to be personal (in three persons), would take place "after" or on account of creation. It would therefore be something accidental in God himself—historical, contingent, non-permanent, accessory—something that sooner or later might be eliminated. In fact, from Arianism it is straightforward to pass on to modalism.

In reality, however, the God of Christians creates not individuals who later on acquire a "personal" existence but rather true and real persons from the beginning of their existence because God is, in the depths of his eternal being, *always personal*, tri-personal. God was never Father "alone"; he was always a Father because, from before time began, he forever generates a Son who is consubstantial with him, loved infinitely in the Holy Spirit. And just as God does not *become* a person with the passing of time, through the events and happenings that take place in the divine life, in a like way humans do not "become" persons in a certain moment or period of their earthly existence, of their personal history, but rather in the very moment of their creation as individuals. We can conclude, therefore, that an anthropology understood on the basis of a "uni-personal" view of God is not in a position to found a rigorous doctrine of the human person.

---

19. We have already considered the anthropological implications of the doctrine of Arius in chapter 7, notes 37ff. and corresponding text.

20. Cited by Aquinas, *S.Th.* III, q. 16, a. 9, co.

The Distinction between Person and Nature

We can see during the Patristic period, in the context of the clarification of the doctrine of the Trinity, a semantic and philosophical consolidation of the distinction between nature/substance (in Greek, *physis/ousia*)[21] and subject (in Greek, *hypostasis*),[22] apart from the identification of the latter with the notion of "person" (*prosōpon*). This was the second theological stage in defining the notion of person. Classical philosophical thought began with a monistic view of reality. As a result, the individual was considered as a mere exemplar of the human species, or perhaps as the product or emanation of the divine substance. Individuality as such, therefore, added nothing new or specific to human existence. The category of "created individual existence" was of no particular relevance. The Christian doctrine on Christ and the Trinity, however, turned this approach on its head. The Church Fathers, when faced with the spread of reductive or one-sided explanations of the Christian mystery (what is called "heresy"), were forced to find a new language and a new metaphysics to explain a revealed reality that could not be adequately expressed with the common categories of the period: the Trinity, three persons in one substance, in one nature, and Christ, one person, the eternal Son, who subsists in two natures, the divine and the human. The heretical position systematically reduces the revealed mystery to the metaphysical scheme in which nature corresponds directly with hypostasis. Let us look at three examples of this process.

In the first place, the neo-Platonic view of reality—that, for example, of Plotinus—considered the possibility of the presence of three different hypostases in God: the One, the Nous (or mind), and the World-Soul.[23] However, this was a connected, hierarchically subordinate triad constituted in three stages or levels that moved from the highest to the lowest, in metaphysical continuity with the created world and also with matter. In other words, each hypostasis was distinguished from the others in that it had its own nature: three diverse hypostases corresponded to three different natures, hierarchically distinct and ordered to one another. Besides, the triad existed in the function of the material cosmos: the Nous and the Soul were considered to be divine emanations that exist in order to give form to pre-existing matter, in order to create the world. In brief: three hypostases, three natures. But this is not Christian teaching.

Second, according to Sabellius, the "three persons" referred simply to three aspects, roles, modes, or moments of the one and only divine substance; this doctrine became known as "modalism." Again, therefore, we find that *one* nature corresponded to *one* hypostasis, even though this has been manifested in three different ways throughout salvation history.

Third, in the fifth century, Nestorius—it might be more precise to speak of "Nestorianism"—attempted to resolve the problem of the union of the divine with the human nature in Christ by reducing the personal union between the natures

---

21. On the term *ousia*, see *BDAG* 740, s.v. οὐσία.
22. On the term *hypostasis*, see *BDAG* 1040f., s.v. ὑπόστασις.
23. Plotinus, *Enn.* V, 1. See Armstrong, *Form, Individual and Person in Plotinus.*

(called "hypostatic," that is, in the person) to the level of a merely moral bond. Again the same philosophical stance emerged: each nature refers to *one* person or subject. In Christ, therefore, the two natures would be united with two subjects or persons, the divine personhood of the Word and the human personhood of Jesus of Nazareth. With two hypostases and two natures, the Plotinian and Sabellian logic was repeated. Out of this insufficient explanation arose the need for Christian thinkers to go beyond the fundamental metaphysical paradigm, that one substance/nature would correspond to one individual or *suppositum*, or vice versa.

In this process of semantic and philosophical clarification the Western theologian Tertullian played an important role. He was the first to employ the Latin expression that later became normative: *una substantia, tres personae*.[24] In the East, the Cappadocian Fathers of the fourth century (Gregory of Nyssa, Basil the Great, and Gregory of Nazianzen[25]), with their formulation "one substance, three hypostases," brought this long spiritual, theological, and semantic process to a conclusion: they gave priority in God to the "hypostases" (what is proper to each person) over "nature" or substance (that which is common to all three), because it identifies "hypostasis" with "person." The Western reception of this terminology (*persona/natura*) is to be found, for example, in the written correspondence between Basil and Pope Damasus and in the Christological declarations of the ecumenical councils of Ephesus and Chalcedon. No longer did "nature" constitute what is most fundamental in being; this place was now occupied by "person," what is most perfect among all existing beings. That is to say, individuality and personhood was not a simple accidental and problematic *function* placed alongside the substance; it was no longer a simple "epiphenomenon" of being.

The Application of the Trinitarian Notion of "Person" to Humans

As regards the third stage of the theological and philosophical consolidation of the notion of human person, Augustine was probably the first author to apply the originally Trinitarian term "person" to humans with a view to designating the concrete exemplar of the human species, defined on the basis of the spiritual substance made in the image and likeness of God. "Personae nomine non speciem significari,

---

24. Tertullian, *Adv. Praxeam* 11–12. Praxeas, who is referred to in this work, was a modalist.

25. On Gregory of Nyssa, see L. Turcescu, *Gregory of Nyssa and the Concept of Divine Persons* (Oxford: Oxford University Press, 2005); Turcescu, "Person," in *The Brill Dictionary of Gregory of Nyssa*, 591–96. Gregory explains that there are three sides to the notion of person. In the first place, the terms *hypostasis* and *prosōpon* are used indistinctly, and they designate the person as particular circumscription, particularity, a unique amalgam of properties (this is close to the position of Porphyry). Second, Gregory distinguishes "person" from nature (*physis*) in the same way as one distinguishes the individual from the species: while the person can be numbered, nature cannot. And third, Gregory explains the person on the basis of the *relation*: whereas Porphyry speaks of Socrates as the son of Sofroniscus, Gregory refers to the apostles Peter or Paul. Peter is the son of Jonah, born in Bethsaida, the brother of Andrew. Something of the kind may be said of the divine persons. Turcescu writes: "The Father proceeds from no other cause, i.e., he is ungenerated, and is the one who generates; the Son is generated from the Father as the Only-begotten, and through himself and with himself makes known the Holy Spirit who proceeds from the Father; moreover, all things (including the Holy Spirit) come into existence from the Father through the Son." And he concludes: "The Father is the cause, the Son is from the cause or directly from the first, and the Spirit is from the cause (i.e. from the Father) through that which is directly from the first (i.e. through the Son)." Turcescu, "Person," 593.

sed aliquid singulare atque individuum," Augustine says, "The name 'person' does not designate the species, but rather the singular and individual."[26] And later: "Singulus quisque homo, qui ... secundum solam mentem imago Dei dicitur, una persona est et imago Trinitatis in mente" (The individual human being is a person).[27]

The twentieth-century philosopher Xavier Zubiri offers the following observations on the genesis of the notion of the human person:

Greek metaphysics here encounters significant limitations, stemming from the idea of the possible actuation of a potency by an act, or of a possible Platonic participation of some realities with respect to others. But above all it has a fundamental and serious limitation: the complete absence of the concept and the very term "person." It took the titanic effort on the part of the Cappadocian Fathers to divest the term *hypostasis* from its characteristic of pure *hypokeimenon*, from its characteristic of *subjectum*, and of substance, to bring it close to the juridical sense the Romans had given the term "person," as distinct from the pure *res*, the thing. It is easy to speak during the course of philosophy of what a person is in respect of the *res naturalis*, for example in Descartes and above all in Kant. But it should not be forgotten that the introduction of the concept of person in its specificity was the work of Christian thought and of the revelation that thought refers to.[28]

Hegel had it that "it must be nearly one and a half millennia since the freedom of personality began to flourish under Christianity and become a universal principle for part—if only a small part—of the human race.... It was primarily in the Christian religion that the right of subjectivity arose, along with the infinity of being-for-itself."[29]

The Human "Person" in Theology

We have already seen that the value or dignity of the individual is central in the Old and New Testaments. Even leaving aside the generally benevolent attitude of Jesus toward humanity as a whole, all his works and words proclaim the dignity of individual human life. Paul expresses this in the first person with his well-known expression: "*I* have been crucified with Christ; it is no longer *I* who live, but Christ who lives in *me*; and the life *I* now live in the flesh *I* live by faith in the Son of God, who loved *me* and gave himself for *me*" (Gal 2:20). Several centuries would go by until this original intuition and light, at the very heart of Christian faith, would find a philosophically rigorous expression. Many definitions of the human person were offered before and during the Middle Ages in an attempt to describe with ever greater precision the personhood of humans.

The Medieval Definitions of "Person"

Of particular importance was the definition of the person offered by the Christian philosopher Boethius in the early sixth century: "naturae rationalis individua substantia" (an individual substance of rational nature).[30] Boethius's idea was taken

---

26. Augustine, *De Trinitate* VII, 6, 11.

27. Ibid., XV, 7, 11.

28. X. Zubiri, *Man and God* (Lanham, Md.: University Press of America, 2009), 235f.

29. G. W. F. Hegel, *Elements of the Philosophy of Right*, 92, 223.

30. Boethius, *De persona Christi et duabus naturis*, 3.

up by John Damascene, who says that the person is "that which, expressing itself by means of its operations and properties, manifests itself in such a way that it is distinguished from others of the same nature."[31] In the early Middle Ages, Richard of St. Victor expresses the concept in two ways: "Persona est existens per se solum iuxta singularem quemdam rationalis existentiae modum.... Persona est rationalis naturae individua [vel incommunicabilis] existentia" (The person exists of itself as a singular only according to a determined mode of rational existence; the person is a singular [or uncommunicable] existence of rational nature).[32] Alan of Lille offers the following definition: "Hypostasis proprietate distincta ad dignitatem pertinente" (The person is a hypostasis with distinct property qualified by proper dignity).[33] Thomas Aquinas defined the person as "subsistens in rationali natura" (that which subsists in a rational nature).[34] Bonaventure, following Alan of Lille, says: "Persona de sui ratione dicit suppositum distinctum proprietate ad dignitatem pertinente" (The person of itself means what subsists with distinct property and proper dignity).[35] Finally, Duns Scotus affirms that the person is "substantia incommunicabilis naturae rationalis" (an incommunicable substance of rational nature).[36]

What It Means to Be a Human Person

On these definitions of the person three observations may be made. In the first place, they are almost always to be found in treatises that do not concern anthropology as such or the doctrine of grace but rather Christology, especially Trinitarian theology. The concept of "person" is applied in the first place to God. For this reason Aquinas says that God is person "ex significatione sua" (in the original sense of the word),[37] whereas humans may be designated "persons" only in an analogical way.[38] That is to say, the *analogatum princeps* of the person is the divine; humans are persons only in a derived, though real, sense. In the words of Berdjaev, "It might be said that the awareness of God as person preceded the awareness of man as person."[39] And the phenomenologist Max Scheler says: "The idea of 'person' applied to God is not an anthropomorphism! In fact God is only perfect and pure person, while that *quid* we call by the name 'man' is only an imperfect and analogically understood 'person.'"[40]

Second, the structure of the definition is almost always the same: the person is presented as a subject, as an individual substance (*individua substantia, existens per se,*

---

31. John Damascene, *Dialectica* 43.

32. Richard of St. Victor, *De Trinitate* IV, 21–22, 23.

33. Alan of Lille, *Theolog. regulae*, 32. From the etymological point of view, Alan claims unconvincingly, the term "persona" means *res per se una*.

34. Aquinas, *S.Th.* I, q. 29, a. 3. On the notion of person in Thomas, see H. C. Schmidbaur, *Personarum Trinitas: Die trinitarische Gotteslehre des heiligen Thomas von Aquin* (Emming: St. Ottilien, 1995); Lombo, *La persona en Tomás de Aquino*. See also G. Emery, *The Trinitarian Theology of Saint Thomas Aquinas* (Oxford: Oxford University Press, 2007).

35. Bonaventure, *In I Sent.* I, 1 resp.

36. Duns Scotus, *Lectura* I, d. 2, pars 32, qq. 1–4. See H. Mühlen, *Sein und Person nach Johannes Duns Scotus: Beitrag zur Grundlegung einer Metaphysik der Person* (Werl: Dietrich-Coelde, 1954).

37. Aquinas, *S.Th.* I, q. 29, a. 3.

38. See ibid., ad 2; a. 4, ad 4.

39. Berdjaev, *Slavery and Freedom*, 33.

40. M. Scheler, *Die Stellung des Menschen im Kosmos*, 15.

subsistens, substantia incommunicabilis, etc.), yet a substance marked by a specific characteristic, that of rationality, and thus, of course, of spirituality and infinitude, which is precisely what distinguishes humans from animals.[41] Let us remember that for the Stoics the notion of rationality was central in order to describe human individuals and their dignity.

The third observation is that in a strict sense "person" is not a simple attribute, among others, of human nature.[42] It is more correct to say the following: an attribute belonging to the nature of the human individual (rationality, spirituality) is what identifies this human individual not only as an exemplar of the species, but as an irreplaceable and eternal being, a person. Thomas Aquinas affirms specifically that "persona est id quod perfectissimum est in tota natura" (the person is that which is most perfect in the whole of nature).[43] By knowing the specific nature of humans (rational, corporeal, etc.) we can affirm that *that* individual is a person. Being a person is not a simple "attribute" of human nature; as Robert Spaemann says, "Person and nature are realities that are simply incommensurable with one another."[44] At the same time, being a person is not rooted in human nature or its rationality, at least if we apply the Aristotelian notion of rationality (humans who share a rationality that is common to all).[45] Thomas Aquinas retains always an individualized and personalized notion of rationality, as when he says, "Hic homo intelligit" (This concrete man [person] thinks). Using different language, Kierkegaard explains the special character of the person as a single individual in the following terms: "The paradox of faith is this, that the single individual is superior to the universal, and determines its relationship with the Absolute through its relationship with the Absolute; it does not determine its relationship with the Absolute through its relationship with the universal."[46] That is to say, humans possess their dignity not as members of humanity, not because others recognize them as such, not on the basis of their rationality, not because of their nature, but because they are creatures of God, made one by one "in his image and likeness." Berdjaev suggests that "personhood is not formulated by the world of objects but by subjectivity, in which lies hidden the power of the image of God."[47]

The Metaphysical Incommunicability of the Person

The person is defined in Patristic and medieval descriptions as an *ens a se,* an individual distinct from others. Given this emphasis, it might seem that these descriptions neglect or exclude the foundational relationality of being a person, which refers directly back to the creator. Still, we need to understand the significance of this emphasis on "incommunicability." Against the interpretations of Aristotle offered by

41. Thomas speaks of the "infinity" of humans present in their rationality: "Naturae autem intellectuales maiorem habent affinitatem ad totum quam aliae naturae; unaquaeque intellectualis substantia est quodammodo omnia, in quanto totius entis comprehensiva est suo intellectu; quaelibet autem alia substantia particularem solam entis participationem habet." SCG III, 112.

42. Thomas writes: "Forma significata per hoc nomen persona, non est essentia vel natura, sed personalitas." *S.Th.* I, q. 39, a. 3, ad 4.

43. Aquinas, *S.Th.* I, q. 29, a. 3, co.

44. Spaemann, *Sulla nozione di natura umana,* 29.

45. See chapter 2, note 41.

46. Kierkegaard, *The Concept of Anxiety,* prolegom. II.

47. Berdjaev, *Slavery and Freedom,* 45.

Averroes and other commentators who spoke of a collective human nature,[48] Thomas Aquinas attempted to explain and defend the immortality and individuality of each human being, as well as the substantiality and realism of the person, as something that is ontologically "incommunicable" with respect to other persons. In this effort he insisted on the individuality and subsistence, after death, of the soul of each person,[49] and therefore on the irreplaceable and personal character of humans and their inalienable dignity. Yet he was speaking not of an incommunicability of a psychological, existential, or personalistic kind (this would be the case of humans closed in on themselves) but of a metaphysical kind. Humans are capable of establishing relationships with others precisely insofar as they *do not* lose their own individuality and metaphysical incommunicability; if it were lost, humans would no longer have value in themselves, they would have no proper dignity, and nobody could establish a meaningful relationship with them. Communion implies relationship, of course, but it also involves the fundamental condition of an ontologically incommunicable individuality that has been received from God. The fact that each is an *ens ab Alio* becomes the basis for the capacity of each to live as an *ens cum aliis*, a being capable of entering into multiple relationships with others. We have already seen that the notion of the individual and its inner dignity was firmly rooted among medieval thinkers well before the time of the Renaissance.

Still, this insistence on the individuality of human persons, on their ontological incommunicability, though correct as an expression of the dignity of each person, in practice tended to overshadow the fact that the human person is essentially a being in relationship with others. We have already considered the intrinsically social aspect of human existence, the sense of dependence we have on one another, the central role of mediation. All this should be applied to the notion of person.

The Loss and Rediscovery of the Human Person in the Modern Period

Leaving the ontological definition of the person typical of the Middle Ages, the modern understanding came to be focused more and more on human subjectivity; there was a shift toward a more psychological, conscious, subjective identity of the person. The "person" was no longer presented as an ontological entity but rather as a psychological one.

When we see someone, observed Descartes, what really happens is that we see hair, clothes, etc., and say "there's a man"; this affirmation is exclusively the result of their mental faculty of judging.[50] In other words, if man is a "person," he is so because he has been designated as such by others. According to John Locke, the person is an intelligent, thinking being with a capacity to reason and reflect, conscious of his own identity, permanence, and continuity in time and space. That is, person is equivalent to human consciousness.[51] Still, "from our not having any notion of the substance of

---

48. See chapter 2, note 41.   49. See Aquinas, *S.Th.* I, q. 75, a. 6.
50. Descartes, *Méditations* II, 7, 32.

51. According to Locke, there are two possible ways of understanding individuality: the first is the monadic way of Leibniz, whereby God is considered the monarch of spirits; the second involves not considering

spirit, we can no more conclude its non-existence than we can, for the same reason, deny the existence of the body."[52] According to David Hume, human consciousness is a simple aggregate of sensations and perceptions; thus it is meaningless to speak philosophically of the "person." Marx attempted to rescue the notion of being a person from the subjective sphere by saying that being human is situated in living united with other people, in a social relationship.[53] However, the affirmation of human individuality (or, better, individualism) should be considered as the most fundamental form of alienation and must be suppressed. Likewise, the notion of person was weakened in both Kant[54] and Hegel.[55] Against the position of the latter, Kierkegaard reacted vigorously.[56] Yet perhaps the most decisive negation of the dignity of the person during the nineteenth century may be found in the vitalism of Nietzsche.[57]

---

the soul as a substance. As a result, the "I" designates that thinking activity which "is concerned about itself" and, above all, which remembers itself, "whatever substance it is made of, whether spiritual or material." J. Locke, *An Essay Concerning Human Understanding*, edited by J. W. Yolton (London: J. M. Dent, 1993), II, 27, 15–19 (185–87).

52. Locke, *An Essay Concerning Human Understanding*, II, 23, 5 (150f.).

53. On Marx, see chapter 24, notes 36f.

54. For Kant, it is the subject that imposes on the object its forms, at a sensitive and intellectual level. Denying the possibility of any metaphysics, Kant holds that the object is constituted by the subject, at the level of knowledge though not of ontology. See especially his *Anthropology from a Pragmatic Point of View*, translated by R. B. Louden (Cambridge: Cambridge University Press, 2006). Hence, according to Kant, what we call "person" is in fact the experience of our own internal unity. The person is the consciousness that, by virtue of the internal senses, has its own identity within the different states of its own existence. See L. Prieto López, "La persona in Kant," *Espíritu* 59, no. 139 (2010): 117–42, esp. 142. See my critique of the Kantian approach in O'Callaghan, "Il compito della teologia."

55. According to Hegel, the individual human being adds nothing to humanity as such. In turn, humanity is the self-manifestation of Reason, of the Idea, of the Spirit. Thus body and matter can never become autonomous and individualized, because they are simply necessary manifestations of the life of the Spirit. The human individual, therefore, has no particular relevance. The Spirit is manifested not through the minute and irrelevant epiphanies that constitute the lives of individuals but in the great moments of history, of peoples and civilizations, in which the state is supreme. In a like way, Fichte and Schelling consider the person a simple moment in the self-consciousness of the Absolute.

56. Differently from Hegel, Kierkegaard gives primacy to the human individual (the "single individual") and not to the collectivity, to faith and not to reason, to ethics and not to logic. But his position also goes against the tide of modernity because the human "I" is not considered to be self-sufficient, because it exists essentially in relation to God. Human freedom is central (chapter 20, notes 16ff.), not because it is autonomous but because it is a sign of the limit and fallibility of humans before God.

57. Nietzsche, perhaps more than anyone else, has contributed philosophically to emptying the notion of person. Speaking of Schopenhauer, he says that "man is an animal who is not yet completely determined." Humans are not yet a definitive species but rather an "embryo of the man who is meant to come." Man is brought along by life, he says, through three metamorphoses, which he details in *Thus spake Zarathustra*. In the first stage, man is a *camel*: "many heavy things are there for the spirit, the strong load-bearing spirit in which reverence dwells: for the heavy and the heaviest longs for its strength. What is heavy? So asks the load-bearing spirit; then it kneels down like the camel and wants to be well laden.... All these heaviest things the load-bearing spirit takes upon itself; and like the camel, which, when laden, hastens into the wilderness, so hastens the spirit into its wilderness" (33f.). At this stage humans carry the chains they impose on themselves through morals and religion; they deny all exuberance and the beauty of life. In the second stage, man becomes like a *lion*: "man from being weak, mediocre, obedient, religious, moralistic, must be transformed into a man who is strong, autonomous, a law unto himself and absolute lord of his own acts, who is not meant to give an account of what he does either to God or to society, but only to himself" (34f.). At this stage, humans experience repugnance toward the little, mediocre man. The only norm for the strong man is not a "you must" but rather an "I want," which knows no limit, expressing itself without scruples. The strong man must be a "superman," marked by daring, with no qualms or sensitivity. This is described by Nietzsche in

The Consolidation and Ambivalence of Personalism

During the twentieth century the "phenomenological" school developed side by side with the "personalist" school, partly as a reaction against the anti-humanism of the nineteenth century just mentioned.[58] The first to use the term "personalism" was Charles Renouvier, who in 1903 attempted to place the theological elements implicit in the notion of person at the disposal of a secular philosophy, disconnecting them from their original link with Christian thought.[59] Edmund Husserl attempted to clarify the meaning of inter-human relationships, specifically the distinctions between the "I"-"it" and the "I"-"you."[60] Yet this provided only a phenomenological description of the human person, not an ontological one. Analogously, Max Scheler speaks of the person as that which is above all other things, organizations and communities, that is, concrete being, which is at the heart of human action. And the basis of all this, Scheler adds, is to be found in the relationships between humans. In this sense, the human being is to be considered as an *ens ab alio*. Still, because not all human relationships have the same strength and value, not all humans would enjoy to the same degree the quality of being "persons."[61] Likewise, the philosopher Martin Buber speaks of the discovery of the person within the community, of human relationship, citing Feuerbach approvingly: "The being of man is to be found only in the community, in the union of man with man, a unity that is based only on a reality of the difference between you and me."[62] Humans first discover the other, the "you," and on that basis discover themselves, the "I"; then, as the third stage in the process, they discover the "we," the community, what in real terms makes the entire process possible in the first place. When humans make this discovery, they become philosophically "illuminated" or "saved"; they go beyond the impersonal human condition (*der Mensch*) and become persons (*die Person*).[63]

The fact is that among some personalist authors the idea has consolidated that the person is to be considered as *distinct* from the individual, subjectivity from the

---

his work *Beyond Good and Evil* (Chicago: H. Regnery, 1966). Last of all, in the third stage, the human ideal of freedom not fully realized corresponds not to power, to violence, to injustice, or to arbitrariness but rather to innocence, sincerity, justice, love, the full realization of what life offers, without resentment, egotism, jealousy, like a *small child*. Like a child, the innocent man knows how to say "yes" to life and loves the reality of all its manifestations, the pleasant and the unpleasant ones. All supernatural and eschatological elements are excluded. Life is loved as it is. Also, death is a marvelous manifestation of the power of nature. The place of God, says Nietzsche, is taken by the god Dionysius, who represents the exuberance of life, embracing the innocent with joy.

58. On personalism, see for example J. M. Burgos Velasco, *Reconstruir la persona: ensayos personalistas* (Madrid: Palabra, 2009).

59. See C. Renouvier, *Le personnalisme: Suivi d'une Étude sur la perception externe et sur la force* (Paris: F. Alcan, 1926).

60. See E. Husserl, *Ideen zu einer reinen Phänomenologie und phänomenologischen Philosophie: Allgemeine Einführung in die reine Phänomenologie* (The Hague: Nijhoff, 1950–52), translated into English as *Ideas: General Introduction to Pure Phenomenology* (Hoboken, N.Y.: Taylor and Francis, 2014).

61. See M. Scheler, *Formalism in Ethics and Non-formal Ethics of Values: A new Attempt toward the Foundation of an Ethical Personalism* (Evanston, Ill.: Northwestern University Press, 1973; originally published in 1916).

62. Buber, *Das Problem des Menschen*, 82.

63. See ibid., 126ff.

thing,[64] the *pour-soi* from the *en-soi*, to use Sartre's terminology. Still, the real distinction between person and individual, typical of personalists, is not always accepted by other philosophers,[65] who insist on the presence in humans of an incarnate spirituality, concluding that wherever there is a biologically living human organism, there is a rational human being and therefore a person.[66] In that sense, though it may be legitimate to distinguish conceptually between person and individual, the concrete, living human individual is always a person, no more and no less. Paul Ricoeur explains that the contemporary return of some philosophers to the idea of person in the wake of the previous anti-humanist season is motivated also by the exhaustion of the terms used to describe what the human being is (individual, subject, I, personality, consciousness) and of their respective philosophies.[67] Still, Ricoeur takes it that personalism has not always managed to define and recuperate the person adequately. He concludes with a provocation: "Meurt le personnalisme, revient la personne" (Once personalism dies, the person returns, remains, and takes over).[68]

In real terms, the difficulty in defining the "person" derives from the fact that to be a person is not a simple attribute of human nature, however spiritual or elevated that may be. Every effort to define it brings us to compare it with other elements of human nature we already know. And in this process the "person" is easily domesticated, reduced, emptied, controlled. As Stefanini and Rivi observe, the undefinability of the person "corresponds to the ethical and theoretical instance of removing it from all kinds of dominion."[69] In real terms, the only "comparison" that does not empty the reality of the person as we attempt to define it is the fundamental one: the divine person, God himself, Trinity of persons, in whose image and likeness humans are made.[70]

---

64. Maritain writes, "as individuals were are subject to the stars." Maritain, *Trois réformateurs*, 17. Gabriel Marcel writes: "The individual is just a statistical element; besides, there is no place for statistics except on the plane of the 'on' [the 'one']." Marcel, *Du refus à l'invocation*, 151. According to Louis Lavelle, the individual is "a coming together of different influences that act within humans, one more thing among others, an element of nature which suffers and retains within itself the living movement which passes through it. The person is not to be found however unless there is interiority, subjectivity, secret and free communion of being with itself." Lavelle, *Les puissances du moi* (Paris: E. Flammarion, 1948), 164f.

65. For example, Cornelio Fabro and Pierre Descoqs, cited by L. Stefanini and F. Riva in "Persona," in *Enciclopedia filosofica*, 9:8526–35, 8532.

66. This position contrasts to some degree with the following explanation of Maritain: "As an individual, each one of us is a fragment of the species, a part of this universe, a singular point within the vast web of cosmic, ethnic, historical, law-bound powers and influences, subject to the determinism of the physical world. But each of us is also a person, and as a person is not subject to the stars, it subsists whole and entire with the same subsistence of the spiritual soul, and this is a principle in each one of creative unity, independence and freedom." J. Maritain, "La personne et le bien commun," in *Oeuvres complètes* (Fribourg: Editions universitaires, 1990), 9:167–237, 190.

67. See P. Ricoeur, "Meurt le personnalisme, revient la personne," in *Lectures 2: La contrée des philosophes* (Paris: Éditions du Seuil, 1992), 195–202, 198f.

68. Thus the name of the conference just cited.

69. Stefanini and Riva, *Persona*, 8533.

70. "When one speaks of the person, one refers both to the irreducible identity and interiority that constitutes the particular individual being, and to the fundamental relationship to other persons that is the basis for human community. In the Christian perspective, this personal identity that is at once an orientation to the other, is founded essentially on the Trinity of divine Persons. God is not a solitary being, but a communion of three Persons.... In effect, no person is as such alone in the universe, but is always constituted with others and is summoned to form a community with them.... It follows that personal beings are social beings

Person and Faith

A similar process to the one we have just seen in modern philosophy may be found also in the ambit of Protestant theology during the twentieth century. Among Protestants, anthropological thought is focused preferably on the basis of the category of Christian salvation and personalism.[71] When Luther said that "fides facit personam" (faith makes the person),[72] he said something that was very true, that is, that humans obtain their full potentiality only through faith, grace, and justification; besides, through faith we come to know and appreciate our unsurpassable dignity before God as "persons." Still, in the expression of Luther the risk of undervaluing the dignity and original quality of the person may be present in that the latter is deeply affected by sin. The Lutheran theologian Emil Brunner said, for example, that becoming a person takes place in the very act of responding to the Word of God. In this way he introduced a distinction between the capacity to communicate and the concrete act of communicating.[73] Other authors, such as the Lutheran Helmut Thielicke, were aware of this tendency and of the danger of reducing the concept of person to a pure interpersonal dynamic, though it be with God.[74]

In effect, it is in the context of faith in Christ that humans discover definitively that they are persons because they recognize themselves as loved with the solidity and constancy of a creative divine love; they see themselves as beings who live in an unmovable relationship with God that reaches the depths of their essence. Through faith, besides, they are made capable of obtaining the perfection to which God has destined them as human persons: holiness and eternal filial communion with the Trinity. Still, this does not mean that humans are constituted ontologically as persons through faith or throughout their history, for example, when they are forgiven their sins. To say so would constitute a profound betrayal of the Christian message, which teaches (1) that God wants all to be saved (1 Tm 2:3–6) through his Son Jesus Christ, who came to save what was lost (Mt 18:22), and (2) that each and every human being, without exception, is made in God's image and likeness. It is true that Christian revelation presents Christ above all as the savior of humanity, and in this context humans are first seen to be sinners, needful of redemption. But the modality and object of the saving work of Christ should be contextualized on the basis of the fact that Christ in the first place is the creator of the world and of man.[75] In the New

---

as well. The human being is truly human to the extent that he actualizes the essentially social element in his constitution as a person within familial, religious, civil, professional, and other groups that together form the surrounding society to which he belongs." International Theological Commission, *Communion and Stewardship*, nos. 41f.

71. On this issue, see the work of H. Mühlen, "Das Vorverständnis von Person und die evangelisch-katholische Differenz," *Catholica* 19 (1964): 108–42.

72. M. Luther, *WA* 39.1:293. On Luther's doctrine, see W. Joest, *Ontologie der Person bei Luther* (Gottingen: Vandenhoeck & Ruprecht, 1967). The words of Luther continue as follows: "persona facit opera." That is so say, "faith makes the person, and the person through the power of faith carries out good works."

73. See E. Brunner, *Dogmatique* (Geneva: Labor et Fides, 1965), 2:69; see also E. Brunner, *Wahrheit als Begegnung: Sechs Vorlesungen über das christliche Wahrheitsverständnis* (Berlin: Furche, 1938), translated into English as *The Divine-Human Encounter* (London: SCM Press, 2012).

74. See H. Thielicke, "Die Subjekthaftigkeit des Menschen," in Scheffczyk, ed., *Der Mensch als Bild Gottes*, 352–58.

75. See ibid.

Testament we learn that Christ could not be our savior if he were not in the first place our creator (Jn 1:3; Col 1:15). And just as the Word is the other-in-God, humans created through the Word are to be considered as persons distinct from their creator, as other-from-God.[76]

The 2004 document of the International Theological Commission, *Communion and Stewardship*, gathers up the principal elements of Christian personalist thought as follows: "Man is not an isolated individual but a person—an essentially relational being. Far from entailing a pure actualism that would deny its permanent ontological status, the fundamentally relational character of the *imago Dei* itself constitutes its ontological structure and the basis for its exercise of freedom and responsibility."[77]

Conclusion: The Central Role of the Human Person

The phenomenological and personalist explanations of humanity provide us with an interpersonal view of the human being while leaving aside at times the ontological and "untouchable" character of being a person, which is a reflection of the foundational, creative relationship of humans with the Trinity. The following questions still need a response: what can we say of the human individual who is meant to establish meaningful relationships with others but is not able to do so? Can we say that such a one is a person? The Christian response is clear: human beings are persons independently of whether or not they think, act meaningfully, or are accepted and recognized by others. Perhaps for this reason von Balthasar teaches that "it will not do simply to replace the so-called 'theo-ontological' categories of philosophy with 'personalogical' categories, that is, to dissolve Being and its relationships."[78] In any case, Romano Guardini reacted against this reductionism of the person. The person, he says, means "being there in itself and disposing of self. The person means that in my very being I cannot, when all is said and done, be possessed by any other instance, but that I belong to myself."[79] Thus, he concludes incisively, "the person does not arise from the encounter, but only acts within it."[80]

76. Pope Benedict XVI, in *Caritas in Veritate*, par. 3, writes: "As a spiritual being, the human creature is defined through interpersonal relations. The more authentically he lives these relations, the more his or her own personal identity matures. It is not by isolation that man establishes his worth, but by placing himself in relation with others and with God. Hence these relations take on fundamental importance. The same holds true for peoples as well. A metaphysical understanding of the relations between persons is therefore of great benefit for their development. In this regard, reason finds inspiration and direction in Christian revelation, according to which the human community does not absorb the individual, annihilating his autonomy, as happens in the various forms of totalitarianism, but rather values him all the more because the relation between individual and community is a relation between one totality and another. Just as a family does not submerge the identities of its individual members, just as the Church rejoices in each 'new creation' (Gal 6:15; 2 Cor 5:17) incorporated by Baptism into her living Body, so too the unity of the human family does not submerge the identities of individuals, peoples and cultures, but makes them more transparent to each other and links them more closely in their legitimate diversity."

77. International Theological Commission, *Communion and Stewardship*, no. 10.

78. Von Balthasar, *Theo-Drama*, 2:268.

79. R. Guardini, *Welt und Person: Versuche zur christlichen Lehre vom Menschen*, 2nd ed. (Wurzburg: Werkbund, 1940), 94, translated into English as *The World and the Person* (Chicago: Regnery, 1965).

80. Ibid., 107.

SELECTED BIBLIOGRAPHY

The following bibliography contains a selection of the principal textbooks and source materials in theological anthropology cited frequently throughout the text, wherever possible in English original or translation. A list of principal abbreviations has been included preceding the introduction.

Ancona, G. *Antropologia teologica: Temi fondamentali.* Brescia: Queriniana, 2014.

Anderson, H. G., T. A. Murphy, and J. A. Burgess, eds. *Justification by Faith: Lutherans and Catholics in Dialogue,* VII. Minneapolis, Minn.: Augsburg, 1985.

Arendt, H. *The Human Condition.* 2nd ed. Chicago: University of Chicago Press, 1959.

Auer, J. *Das Evangelium der Gnade: Die neue Heilsordnung durch die Gnade in seiner Kirche.* 3rd ed. Regensburg: F. Pustet, 1980.

Barth, K. *Church Dogmatics,* vol. 4: *The Doctrine of Reconciliation,* part 3. Translated by G. W. Bromiley. Edinburgh: T. and T. Clark, 2004.

Baumgartner, C. *La grâce du Christ.* Tournai: Desclée, 1963.

Berdjaev, N. A. *Slavery and Freedom.* London: G. Bles, 1943.

Botturi, F. "Libertà." In *Enciclopedia filosofica,* 7:6393–6450. Milan: Bompiani, 2006.

Colzani, G. *Antropologia teologica: L'uomo paradosso e mistero.* 2nd ed. Bologna: Dehoniane, 1997.

De la Potterie, I. *La vérité dans saint Jean.* Rome: Biblical Institute Press, 1977.

De Lubac, H. *Le mystère du surnaturel.* Paris: Aubier-Montaigne, 1965. Translated into English as *The Mystery of the Supernatural.* New York: Herder and Herder, 1967.

Dunn, J. D. G. *The Theology of Paul the Apostle.* Grand Rapids, Mich.: W. B. Eerdmans, 1998.

Guardini, R. *The End of the Modern World.* Wilmington, Del.: ISI Books, 1998.

Heschel, A. J. *God in Search of Man: A Philosophy of Judaism.* Cleveland, Ohio: World Publishing, 1963.

Illanes, J. L. *La santificación del trabajo: El trabajo en la historia de la espiritualidad.* 10th ed. Madrid: Palabra, 2001. Translated into English as *The Sanctification of Work: Aspects of the Teaching of the Founder of Opus Dei.* 3rd ed. New York: Scepter, 2003.

International Theological Commission. *Theology, Christology, Anthropology.* Vatican City: Vaticana, 1982.

John Paul II, Pope. *Redemptor Hominis.* Encyclical Letter. March 4, 1979.

Jónsson, G. A. *The Image of God: Genesis 1:26–28 in a Century of Old Testament Research.* Stockholm: Almqvist and Wiksell, 1988.

Journet, C. *Entretiens sur la grâce*. Bruges: Desclée de Brouwer, 1961. Translated into English as *The Meaning of Grace*. New York: P. J. Kennedy, 1960.

Ladaria, L. F. *Antropologia teologica*. Casale Monferrato: Piemme, 1982.

Lonergan, B. J. F. *Grace and Freedom: Operative Grace in the Thought of St. Thomas Aquinas*. Toronto: University of Toronto Press, 2000.

Lorda, J. L. *Antropología teológica*. Pamplona: Eunsa, 2009.

Marcel, G. *The Mystery of Being*. 2 vols. Lanham, Md.: University Press of America, 1983.

McGrath, A. E. *Iustitia Dei: A History of the Christian Doctrine of Justification*. 2 vols. Cambridge: Cambridge University Press, 1986.

Mouroux, J. *L'expérience chrétienne: Introduction à une théologie*. Paris: Aubier-Montaigne, 1952. Translated into English as *The Christian Experience: An Introduction to a Theology*. London: Sheed and Ward, 1955.

O'Callaghan, P. *Christ Our Hope: An Introduction to Eschatology*. Washington, D.C.: The Catholic University of America Press, 2011.

———. *Fides Christi: The Justification Debate*. Portland, Ore.: Four Courts, 1997.

———. *God Ahead of Us: The Story of Divine Grace*. Minneapolis, Minn.: Fortress, 2014.

Ocáriz, F. *Natura, grazia e gloria*. Rome: Edusc, 2003.

Pannenberg, W. *Anthropology in a Theological Perspective*. Edinburgh: T. and T. Clark, 1985.

Philips, G. *L'union personnelle avec le Dieu vivant: Essai sur l'origine et le sens de la grâce créée*. 2nd ed. Leuven: Leuven University Press, 1989.

Rahner, K. *Foundations of Christian Faith: An Introduction to the Idea of Christianity*. London: Darton, Longman and Todd, 1978.

Ratzinger, J. *The God of Jesus Christ: Meditations on God in the Trinity*. Chicago: Franciscan Herald Press, 1979.

Rondet, H. *Gratia Christi: Essai d'histoire du dogme et de théologie dogmatique*. Paris: Beauchesne, 1948. Translated into English as *The Grace of Christ: A Brief History of the Theology of Grace*. Westminster, Md.: Newman Press, 1967.

Ruiz de la Peña, J. L. *El don de Dios: Antropología teológica especial*. Salamanca: Sal Terrae, 1991.

Russell, N. *The Doctrine of Deification in the Greek Patristic Tradition*. Oxford: Oxford University Press, 2004.

Scheeben, M.-J. *The Mysteries of Christianity*. St. Louis, Mo.: Herder, 1946.

Scheffczyk, L., ed. *Der Mensch als Bild Gottes*. Darmstadt: Wissenschaftliche Buchgesellschaft, 1969.

Scola, A., G. Marengo, and J. Prades López. *La persona umana: Antropologia teologica*. Milan: Jaca Book, 2000.

Trapè, A., *S. Agostino: Introduzione alla dottrina della grazia*. 2nd ed. 2 vols. Rome: Città Nuova, 1987–90.

Van der Meersch, J. "Grâce." In *DTC*, 6:1554–1687.

Von Balthasar, H. U. *Theo-Drama*, vol. 2: *Dramatis Personae: Man in God*. San Francisco: Ignatius, 1990.

Williams, A. N. *The Ground of Union: Deification in Aquinas and Palamas*. Oxford: Clarendon Press, 1999.

Wolff, H. W. *Anthropology of the Old Testament*. 6th ed. Philadelphia: Fortress, 1974.

Zizioulas, J. D. *Being as Communion: Studies in Personhood and the Church*. Crestwood, N.Y.: St. Vladimir's Seminary Press, 1997.

INDEX OF NAMES

GENERAL INDEX

Acceptatio divina (acceptance by God), 181–82, 185–86, 193, 348

Acquired virtue, 302, 305–7, 334, 376. *See also* Infused theological virtues

Alienation, 2, 15, 22–24, 60, 120, 270, 430, 439, 452, 454, 481, 496–98, 537, 563

Anonymous Christianity, 135, 153–54, 388, 399

Anthropocentrism, 29, 36, 39–40, 50, 57, 59–60, 70, 175

Anthropology: Christian, 387–568; general, 17; Greek, 17, 40–44; historical, 35–63; philosophical, 17, 13–34, 387–568; religious, 39–40; scientific, 13–34, 318; theological, 17–18, 215–383

Anthropology and adoration, 20, 29, 33, 45, 54, 56, 66, 90, 99, 102–5, 110, 130, 160, 259, 304–5, 330, 443, 466, 490, 544–47, 549

Anthropology and anticipation, 14, 217, 221, 241–2; and gifts of the Holy Spirit, 338–39; and hope, 322. *See also* Grace and divine foreknowledge

Anthropology and artistic expression, 5, 25, 36, 39

Anthropology and aspirations, 2, 13–16, 26, 33, 70, 74, 437, 444, 453–54, 470, 481, 500, 60–61, 186, 434, 438, 478, 497

Anthropology and communion, 8, 32, 39, 49, 68, 71, 75, 78, 81–82, 215–16, 224–26, 233–34, 247–48, 270–72, 280, 286, 289, 321, 371, 386, 395, 404, 494, 498–99, 511, 520, 535–36

Anthropology and divine transcendence, 2–3, 5, 15–17, 19, 25, 40, 72, 79, 139, 147–48, 184, 199, 203–4, 254, 282–83, 282, 281, 371, 387, 399–403, 407, 435–36. *See also* Pelagianism

Anthropology and eccentricity, 4–5, 36. *See also* Methodology

Anthropology and ecology, 3, 17, 29, 58, 100, 500, 551

Anthropology and epistemology, 1–10, 27, 41–46, 67–69, 76–77, 190, 238, 403–4, 477; and Mariology, 242. *See also* Jesus Christ; Mary of Nazareth; Methodology; Science

Anthropology and Eschatology, 4–8, 76–85, 139, 238–42, 283, 320–21, 365, 405, 420–21, 435–38, 478, 487, 492, 518, 545. *See also* Grace and glory

Anthropology and ethics, 389, 5, 41, 59–61, 156, 178–79, 211, 240, 304–5, 389, 405, 450, 461–68, 469–70

Anthropology and faith, 9, 14, 19–25, 29–31, 38, 48–56, 74–84, 119–20, 127–28, 135–39, 153, 171–72, 191–96, 237–38, 240–45, 291–93, 302–4, 307–19, 321, 327–35, 343–44

Anthropology and hope, 24–25, 37–39, 78, 84–85, 241–42, 244–45, 257, 301, 303–4, 319–27, 332, 381, 389

Anthropology and Judaism, 33, 44–48, 104, 414, 524, 544–45, 547

Anthropology, historical perspectives: Christian (Jesus Christ the savior), 48–49; Greek (cosmos and Logos), 40–44; Jewish (God, only Lord of the Covenant), 44–48; Modern (advent of anthropocentrism), 50–63; primitive (power of nature), 39–40; situating, 38–39; various, 17–18

Autonomy, 9, 14, 32–33, 44, 50–51, 54, 58, 61, 80, 119, 176, 186–87, 199, 208, 219, 270, 283, 287, 304, 319, 444–45, 451, 453, 455–56, 466–67, 489–90, 496–97, 523–24. *See also* Freedom

Basar (flesh), 411–15

Basilea, Council of, 505

Behaviorism, 432–33, 453

Biology, 2, 17–18, 58–99, 254–55, 423–24, 430–35, 441, 453, 460, 472, 517, 527, 531, 565. *See also* Science

Body and Soul, 44, 112–14, 406–41; and anthropological pessimism, 426; in antiquity, 42–44, 408–11; and centrality of human subject, 426–30; in Church Fathers, 417–19; in Church teaching, 419–20; and dualism, 425–28; and evolutionism, 430–32; and hominization, 430–32, 435–36; and hylomorphic theory, 43–44, 410–11, 422–25, 427, 440; in Middle Ages, 420–25; and mind-body relationship, 432–35; in modernity, 55–56, 426–30; and science, 430–35; in Scripture, 411–16; origin of, 435–38; soul in Protestantism, 436–38

Braga, Council of, 420

Individualism, 15, 60, 401, 499, 504, 511, 563. *See also* Gregariousness

Infused moral virtues, 334–35; and virtues and passions of Christ, 335

Infused theological virtues, 176, 249, 279, 291, 297–98, 301–33, 348, 351, 380, 489: Church's teaching on theological virtues, 302–4; infused and acquired virtues, 302, 305–7, 376; theological virtues and ethics, 304–5. *See also* Faith; Hope; Charity; Infused Moral Virtues; Gifts of Holy Spirit; Ethics

Inhabitation. *See* Grace and Trinity

Interpretation of history, 35–63. *See also* Historicity, human

Irreplaceability of the human person, 23–24, 30, 49, 63, 228, 435, 438, 492, 538, 561–62

Jansenism, 54, 60, 199, 206–9, 231, 240, 299

Jesus Christ: anthropology, living perspective, 5, 6–9, 64–85; contrast with humans, 67–68; differentiated solidarity, 67–69, 73; discontinuities, 67–69; epistemological and hermeneutical issues, 67–69; manifestation/redemption, 65–66

Jesus Christ: anthropology in light of, 70–85; and eschatology, 76–79; history of, 72–73; and immortality, 74–75; and love of God: 75–76; and myth, 76–77; and philosophy, 77; spiritual experience of, 71–72

Jesus Christ "reveals man to man," 5, 10, 64, 65, 66, 79, 110, 243; communion, 82–83; faith/conversion, 81–83; and martyrdom, 84; priority, 6–9, 48–49, 64–85; resurrection, 83–84

Jesus Christ: and divinization, 145–46; as grace in person, 117, 119–20; and image of God, 105–14; Logos asarkos/ensarkos, 111–12; and perfect communion with the living man, 81–83

Justification, 117–19, 124–29, 163–65, 182, 189–99, 210–12, 217, 234–38, 291–94, 343–45, 355, 381–83, 437; and faith, 237–38; as forgiveness and sanctification, 343; formal cause of, 197–98; instrumental cause of, 196 (faith and Baptism); meritorious cause of, 196; process of, 196, 342–34; and sin, 235–37

Last end. *See* Grace and last end

Lateran Council IV, 420, 488

Lateran Council V, 425–26

Lēb (heart), 45, 412, 415–16, 429

Liberation, 114–15, 112–14, 122–24, 224, 234, 450, 460, 469–71, 543. *See* Freedom

Liberation theology, 71

Lutheran dialogue: divinization, 54, 150; ecclesiology, 192; experience of grace, 363–64; freedom, 324–22, 341–42; good works, 355; grace, 291–94; JDJ (Joint Declaration on the Doctrine of Justification), 211–12; justification, 194–99

Lutheranism, 291–4. *See also* Names Index; Luther; Lutheran dialogue

Magnanimity, divine, 115, 181, 331 351; human: 331–32

Man and Woman, 499–500, 512, 514–36; in Christianity, 527–29; in Church Fathers, 525–26; con-temporary debate, 516–17; equality and difference between, 531–32; and family, 536; and gender, 58, 514–18, 524, 535; inferiority man/woman, 526–27; in Jewish thought, 527; and Mary of Nazareth, 242–46; in Platonic mythology, 523–24; relationship between, 98–99, 529–31; in Scripture, 519–23, 533–36; as "unity of two," 532–56; theological significance of distinction between, 518. *See* Image of God

Martyrdom, 81, 84–85, 326, 334, 337

Mary of Nazareth, 8, 68; God's revelation to humanity, 243–44; as human prototype, 8, 215, 217, 242–46; and mediation, 372; predestined, 223; role in history, 483–44, 492; sinlessness of, 379; solidarity with all of, 245–46; virginity of, 244, 259; as woman, 246, 527. *See* Divine filiation; Father-Son paradigm

Materialism, 429–30; 433–34, 439; Christian, 418; emergentist, 433–34

Memory: and hope, 322–25; Christian memory, 324; purification, 323–24

Merit, 121, 159, 167–68, 182, 196–98, 200–203, 298–300, 340–42, 345–56, 382–83; Biblical basis for, 346–47; elements of meritorious act (divine presupposition, freedom, historicity, state of grace, upright action), 348–50; and eschatological reward, 346, 354–55, 380–81; increase and loss of grace, 352–54; intention to, 350; object of (condign and congruous), 350–52

Metanarratives, 2, 56

Methodology, 13–85; agnosticism, 28–30, 429; Christological priority, 6–9, 48–49, 64–85; circularity, 31–32; dominion, 27–28; eccentricity, 4–5; epistemology, 14; God's fidelity and universal love, 46–48; limits of science, 31–33; phenomenology, 13; "problem and mystery," 24–25; search for immortality, 5–6; search for unity and integrity, 1–4, 16, 20, 41, 80, 141, 155, 305, 339, 388, 547, 554; sin, 4, 30, 60; spiritual experience, 9–10

Milevus, Synod of, 158

Mind-body relationship, 427, 430, 432–35. *See* Body and Soul

Modernity, 2–3, 50–59, 198, 426–30, 451, 487, 490, 504, 563. *See* Pressure

Mystērion, 216, 221. *See also* Grace and divine project/design

Mysticism, 139, 180, 187–90, 198, 218, 245, 360–62, 429, 485

Myth of eternal return, 319, 478–82, 484, 493–94; anthropological critique of, 481; historiographical account of, 479–80; metaphysical account of, 480–81; scientific critique of, 481–82. *See also* Historicity, human

Natura pura (pure nature), 396–401, 403

Natural and supernatural, 17, 146, 149, 166, 175, 205, 216, 271–72, 281, 284, 296, 306–7, 334, 337, 345–48, 356, 380, 387–405: "obediential potency," 394; "pressure" of the supernatural on the natural, 8, 403–5, 485; "pure nature," 396–401, 403;

Children of God in the World: An Introduction to Theological Anthropology was designed in Garibaldi and composed by Kachergis Book Design of Pittsboro, North Carolina. It was printed on 60-pound Tradebook Recycled and bound by Thomson Reuters of Eagan, Minnesota.